ANNALS OF THE NEW YORK ACADEMY OF SCIENCES
Volume 285

ISSUES IN CROSS-CULTURAL RESEARCH

Edited by Leonore Loeb Adler

The New York Academy of Sciences
New York, New York
1977

Library of Congress Cataloging in Publication Data

Main entry under title:

Issues in cross-cultural research.

    (Annals of the New York Academy of Sciences; v. 285)
    "This series of papers is the result of a conference . . . held by the New York Academy of Sciences on October 1, 2, and 3, 1975."
    1. Cross-cultural studies – Congresses. I. Adler, Leonore Loeb. II. New York Academy of Sciences. III. Series: New York Academy of Sciences. Annals; v. 285.
Q11.N5 vol. 285 [GN345.7] 508'.1s [301] 77-1099
ISBN 0-89072-031-2

S/CCP
Printed in the United States of America
ISBN 0-89072-031-2

ANNALS OF THE NEW YORK ACADEMY OF SCIENCES

VOLUME 285

March 18, 1977

ISSUES IN CROSS-CULTURAL RESEARCH*

Editor and Conference Organizer

Leonore Loeb Adler

CONTENTS

A Plea for Interdisciplinary Cross-Cultural Research: Some Introductory
Remarks. *By* Leonore Loeb Adler 1

Part I. Method and Theories in Cross-Cultural Research

Why Cross-Cultural Research? *By* Ronald P. Rohner 3
Psychology and Anthropology: Possible Common Ground in Cross-
Cultural Research. *By* Gustav Jahoda 13
A Dynamic Model of Relationships among Ecology, Culture and Behavior.
By J. W. Berry 19
Some Theoretical and Methodological Problems in the Study of Ethnic
Identity: A Cross-Cultural Perspective. *By* Vijai P. Singh 32
Theory and Method in Biosocial Psychology: A New Approach to
Cross-Cultural Psychology. *By* John L. M. B. Dawson 46
From Correlations to Causes: A New and Simple Method for Causal
Analysis in Cross-Cultural Research. *By* William Tulio Divale 66
Growth and Development of Hologeistic Cross-Cultural Research. *By*
James M. Schaefer 75
Methods and Issues in Cross-Cultural Research. *Discussant:* Charles
Harrington 89
Cross-Cultural Research in the Next Century. *Discussant:* Dorrian Apple
Sweetser 94
Open Discussion: I 99

Part II. General Issues in Cross-Cultural Research

On the Need for Experimentation in Cross-Cultural Research. *By* Lee
Sechrest 104
Culture and Personality Revisited. *By* R. Díaz-Guerrero 119
Problems of Measurement in Cross-Cultural Research. *By* George M.
Guthrie 131
Problems of Language in Cross-Cultural Research. *By* Hiroshi Wagatsuma . 141
The Robustness of Cross-Cultural Findings. *By* Bernard M. Finifter 151
Ethical Issues Influencing the Acceptance and Rejection of Cross-Cultural
Researchers Who Visit Various Countries. *By* Richard W. Brislin 185

* This series of papers is the result of a conference entitled Issues in Cross-Cultural
Research, held by The New York Academy of Sciences on October 1, 2, and 3, 1975.

Issues Relating to the Publication and Dissemination of Cross-Cultural Research Data. *By* Walter J. Lonner 203
On Some Methodological Issues in Cross-Cultural Psychology. *Discussant:* Carol R. Ember 215
How Cross-Cultural Researchers Relate to their Professions. *Discussant:* Melvin Ember 217
Open Discussion: II 219

Part III. Special Aspects of Cross-Cultural Research

An Intensive "Triangular" Study (Japan—USA—Europe) of Socio-Psychological Variables. *By* Helmut Morsbach 221
The "Fruit-Tree Experiment" as a Cross-Cultural Measure of the Variations in Children's Drawings due to Regional Differences. *By* Leonore Loeb Adler and Beverly S. Adler 227
The Legitimacy of Educational Knowledge: A Neglected Theme in Comparative Research. *By* Robert Cowen 282
Studies of Memory in Culture. *By* David F. Lancy 297
The Problem of Establishing Validity in Cross-Cultural Measurements. *By* Marc Irwin, Robert E. Klein, Patricia L. Engle, Charles Yarbrough, and Sara B. Nerlove 308
Why African Children Are So Hard to Test. *By* Sara Harkness and Charles M. Super 326
Cross-Cultural Cognitive Development: The Cultural Aspects of Piaget's Theory. *By* Pierre R. Dasen 332
Person Perception and Social Interaction of Jewish and Druze Kindergarten Children in Israel. *By* Michaela Lifshitz 338
Special Aspects of Cross-Cultural Research. *Discussant:* Roger R. Woock .. 355
Special Aspects of Cross-Cultural Research. *Discussant:* Leanne G. Rivlin . 359
Open Discussion: III 363

Part IV. Cognition and Perception in Cross-Cultural Research

Developmental Theories Applied to Cross-Cultural Cognitive Research. *By* Michael Cole and Sylvia Scribner 366
A Study in Cognitive Development. *By* Jerome Kagan, Robert E. Klein, Gordon E. Finley, and Barbara Rogoff 374
Maternal Kinesic Behavior and Cognitive Development in the Child. *By* Lorraine Kirk and Michael Burton 389
The Ponzo Illusion among the Baganda of Uganda. *By* Philip L. Kilbride and H. W. Leibowitz 408
Subjective Culture and Interpersonal Relations across Cultures. *By* Harry C. Triandis 418
Objective Indicators of Subjective Culture. *By* Charles E. Osgood 435
Students' Formulating Practices and Instructional Strategies. *By* Hugh Mehan 451
Differentiation of Affective and Denotative Semantic Subspaces. *By* Oliver C. S. Tzeng 476
Comments from an Anthropologist. *Discussant:* Margaret Mead 501
Cognition and Perception in Cross-Cultural Research. *Discussant:* F. J. McGuigan 505
Open Discussion: IV 514

Guest Lecture: Subjective Culture and Technology: A Social Psychological Examination of "Nuclear Allergy" in the Japanese. *By* Yasumasa Tanaka 516

Part V. Modernization in Local Environment

Individual Modernity in Different Ethnic and Religious Groups: Data from a Six-Nation Study. *By* Alex Inkeles 539
Orientation to Change in Advanced and Developing Societies: A Cross-National Sample. *By* Robert C. Williamson 565
Modernization-Relevant Values and Achievement of Native and Rural Populations Assessed within Traditional and Modern Environments. *By* Pauline A. Jones 582
Space, Density, and Cultural Conditioning. *By* R. S. Freed 593
Familistic Social Change on the Israeli Kibbutz. *By* Robert Endleman 605
Sex Roles in Cross-Cultural Perspective. *By* Georgene H. Seward 612
Ideologies of Sex: Archetypes and Stereotypes. *By* Eleanor Leacock and June Nash 618
Problems in Defining and Measuring Marital Power Cross-Culturally. *By* Helen Mayer Hacker 646
Culture, Development and Sex: Notes on the State of the Cross-Cultural Art. *Discussant:* Howard R. Stanton 653
Whither Cross-Cultural Research? *Discussant:* Sheridan Phillips 659
Open Discussion: V 662

Part VI. Psychopathology, Ethnopsychiatry, and Psychotherapy in Cross-Cultural Research

Problems of Defining and Comparing Abnormal Behavior across Cultures. *By* Juris G. Draguns 664
The United States–United Kingdom Project on Diagnosis of the Mental Disorders. *By* Joseph Zubin and Barry J. Gurland 676
Psychiatry and the Polity: The Soviet Case and Some General Implications. *By* Mark G. Field 687
A Comparison of Institutional Services and Resources for the Mentally Retarded in India and the United States. *By* Manny Sternlicht and Meer H. Ali 698
Multidisciplinary Collaboration in Fieldwork: Australian Studies. *By* John Cawte 707
Coping with Unwanted Variables in Cross-Cultural Research: Examples from Mental Health and Treatment of the Aging. *By* S. Stansfeld Sargent 712
Societal Morphogenesis and Intrafamily Violence in Cross-Cultural Perspective. *By* Murray A. Straus 717
Oh Would Some Power the Giftie Gie Us, To See Ourselves as Others See Us. *By* John Beatty 731
Remarks on Cross-Cultural Psychotherapy Research. *Discussant:* Gordon F. Derner 737
Perspectives on Psychopathology. *Discussant:* Herbert Krauss 742
Open Discussion: VI 746

Epilogue: An Exaltation of Cross-Cultural Research – The Nature and Habits of the Hyphenated Elephant. *By* Kurt Salzinger 750

Financial assistance was received from:
- The Grant Foundation, Inc.
- The Japan Foundation

A PLEA FOR INTERDISCIPLINARY CROSS-CULTURAL RESEARCH: SOME INTRODUCTORY REMARKS

Leonore Loeb Adler

Department of Psychology
Adelphi University
Garden City, Long Island, New York 11530

It gives me great pleasure to greet such an illustrious assembly of cross-cultural scientists. This conference on issues in cross-cultural research evolved from a need to bring together behavioral scientists from different disciplines. Therefore I have invited psychologists, anthropologists, sociologists, linguists, and educators to participate in this meeting. The proliferation of cross-cultural activity in journals, academic departments, and new areas of specialization has raised questions about the relationship between theories and the practical aspect of cross-cultural research. We hope that a conference such as this will bring about a useful interchange of ideas to advance our understanding of the problems facing cross-cultural scientists.

The theme of the sessions concerns itself with the fact that central issues in cross-cultural research in psychology, anthropolgy, and sociology are similar although they are approached from different points of view. This conference will provide the opportunity to discuss possible common grounds in cross-cultural research among the disciplines. Beyond providing an understanding of the manners and customs of people living outside our own culture, cross-cultural research compares specific cultures and societies as well as the individuals who are living in and reacting to different environments. Generally cross-cultural investigations, and specifically interdisciplinary research, help not only to foster better understanding of people in other societies and cultures, but also to provide a greater insight into individual actions and group behavior both within and across cultures. They provide us with a greater tolerance toward people living in other cultures and nations, and — it is hoped — vice versa.

In psychology, cross-cultural comparison has a long and honorable history, dating back to Wilhelm Wundt's ten-volume *Völkerpsychologie* (1900–1920. Engelmann. Leipzig, Germany); anthropology and sociology have equally illustrious backgrounds, although they used different approaches to examine the same or similar problems. The aim of the present interdisciplinary cross-cultural conference is to explore and discuss current and crucial topics in cross-cultural research. For example, the present scientific literature is much more likely to report differences rather than similarities between nations or cultures studied. On the other hand, cross-cultural research recognizes that while the discovery of differences may be significant, the finding of similarities may provide even more meaningful information. Because of the ever-increasing spread of Western culture, special emphasis should be placed on such aspects.

In these six sessions, recent theoretical issues and experimental findings will be reported and discussed. This conference may inspire scientists to do some theory-testing in their future cross-cultural research; some participants might seek solutions to particular problems, while others might offer some constructive ideas. Important to a successful conference is the cooperative interaction and congeniality of its participants. The opportunity for representatives of the major sciences to meet for a fruitful interchange of ideas on the problems central to

1

cross-cultural research is provided by this conference. I am confident that the outcome of this gathering will be a renewed enthusiasm and vigor that will in turn furnish a springboard for future interdisciplinary cooperation in cross-cultural research.

The six sessions of this conference will be chaired by scientists who worked in the field, although in different areas. All but one are affiliated in some capacity with The New York Academy of Sciences. Since I am chairing the first session of the conference I would like to extend my thanks to the other five chairpersons — Dr. Ethel Tobach, Dr. Florence L. Denmark, Dr. Joshua A. Fishman, Dr. Stanley A. Freed, and Dr. Kurt Salzinger.

I am grateful to The New York Academy of Sciences for sponsoring this conference, and to The Grant Foundation as well as the Japan Foundation for their support of this cross-cultural meeting. This conference brings together behavioral scientists from 12 countries on six continents. More scientists had been invited: from Brazil, Germany, Nigeria, and the USSR, among others, but unfortunately they could not accept my invitation for various reasons. More Third World representatives would have been invited but for a shortage of funds, which curtailed my initial plans for an even greater international representation. But as it turned out, at least 15 other countries, mainly from Europe and Africa, although some from Asia, have contributed data which will be reported here.

It is my hope that this conference on cross-cultural research will demonstrate that scientists from different parts of the world can congregate in harmony and work together with unified effort to develop and achieve interdisciplinary cross-cultural interaction.

PART I: METHOD AND THEORIES IN CROSS-CULTURAL RESEARCH

WHY CROSS-CULTURAL RESEARCH?*

Ronald P. Rohner

Department of Anthropology
The Catholic University of America
Washington, D.C. 20064

Cross-cultural research has both humanistic and scientific interest. Historically, the greatest contribution of cross-cultural research has been squarely on the boundary between the humanistic and the scientific, in helping to edit and extend man's image of the nature of "human nature." Especially within anthropology, this has been a major if often unintended contribution since the days of Franz Boas after the turn of the century. Boas and his students devoted great effort to combating such uninformed, ethnocentric generalizations about the nature of human nature as: "children are more imaginative than adults." The noted anthropologist Herskovits describes anthropology's refutation of these generalities:

> Human nature was that chameleon-like force in man that was variously held to cause him to seek profits, or to be a monogamist or to have polygamous tendencies, or to strive to better his standard of living, or to do any of those things that seemed obviously basic to students of Euroamerican society. The anthropologist, however, beginning, "But, in Kamchatka . . ." – or in Senegal or Ecuador or Pukapuka – would proceed to give instances where men and women, presumably activated by this same "human nature" eschewed profits, or were polygamist or monogamist, or seemed to be content with their lot. It can, indeed, be said that the philosophy of cultural relativism, that has come to dominate most anthropological thought and, indeed, social science in general, had its beginnings in the refutations of "human nature" that mark the literature of cultural anthropology.[1]

Addressing the same point, Margaret Mead has written:

> It was a simple – a very simple – point to which our materials were organized in the 1920s, merely the documentation over and over of the fact that human nature is not rigid and unyielding . . . but that it is extraordinarily adaptable, that cultural rhythms are stronger and more compelling than the physiological rhythms which they overlay and distort . . . .
>
> The battle [against naive theories of human nature] which we once had to fight with the whole battery at our command, with the most fantastic and startling examples that we could muster is now won. [It is true, however, that some people] still believe in their heart of hearts that all men, Samoan, Manus, Mundugumor, Eskimo and Bantu, are really all made in their own image, with a few nonessential trappings of feathers and cowrie shells to obscure the all-important similarities. But nevertheless the trend towards a deeper appreciation of the malleability of the human being is marked enough so that students of primitive societies and their significance can go on to other questions.[2]

In addition to correcting myths and stereotypes about the nature of human nature, cross-cultural research gives us a clearer understanding of the natural

---

* This paper was written while I was Visiting Professor of Anthropology and Human Development at the Boys Town Center for the Study of Youth Development, and in the Department of Anthropology, The Catholic University of America.

range and variability of human behavior. Paradoxically, an understanding of the range and diversity of man's behavior provides information about many species uniformities. For example, world research shows that children everywhere normally walk before they are two years old. The psychologists Kagan and Klein[3] conclude from this that "a three-year-old unable to walk is physically retarded in the absolute sense, for he has failed to attain a natural competence in the normative time." Without the benefit of cross-cultural research, we would not have the factual basis for making such normative statements.

Thus, cross-cultural research contributes indispensably to the humanistic question, "What does it mean to be a human being?" This question does not ask about what it means to be a Kwakiutl Indian, a Turkish peasant, or a white, middle-income American college student, but it asks about the nature of human nature, about the commonalities and significant differences among men throughout our species. A full understanding of the nature of human nature is yet to be achieved, of course, but it will not be achieved by those who are unwilling to immerse themselves in anthropological materials and in personal cross-cultural experiences. Of course, many scholars do cross-cultural research not from an ideal of understanding human behavior across our species, but with a more modest goal in mind, that of understanding the behavior of some specific culturally organized population. In fact, this orientation characterizes the work of most social and cultural anthropologists in the United States. A good deal of anthropology is oriented toward describing a particular form of behavior within a specific population in a geographically defined region, and within a focused time period, or chronologically over a relatively brief time span. For many behavioral scientists, however, anthropology's idiographic orientation does not go deep enough.[4] These other scholars, especially psychologists, want to develop general laws of human behavior and they want to apply these laws to concrete situations.[5] I share the dream of those scholars who aspire to establishing principles or laws of behavior – that is, to formulate scientifically derived generalizations that can be applied across our species wherever relevant conditions occur. The idiographic, *verstehen* approach of much of anthropology is only a beginning, but it is an indispensable beginning.† Beyond this we can strive to explain behavior through adequate theory construction and worldwide theory testing.

Ultimately, when our understanding is deep enough and our theory is powerful enough, we will be able to make adequate predictions about behavior. This aspiration to establish principles of behavior is no sanctimonious yearning for an unreachable future. In fact, a number of significant advances have already been made in explaining and predicting worldwide behavior, especially various

† In all universalist research an adequate anthropological perspective is required. The anthropological perspective comprises several elements. It includes a profound familiarity with "culture," not as an abstract or as an explanatory concept (see Reference 6) but as a pervasive existential-phenomenological experience. True understanding of the effects of culture-learning on behavior and on behavior-potential comes from a deep immersion in ethnographic materials and, for most people, from an extended period of participant-observation fieldwork or from something equivalent to participant-observation research such as having grown up in a cultural system different from the one in which the investigator is now working. In addition, the anthropological perspective implies a worldwide comparative orientation and a personal introjection of the concept cultural relativity (but not radical relativism). Moreover, a respect for the fact of cultural (and personal) holism or functionalism (but not extreme functionalism) is part of the perspective (see Reference 7).

facets of psychological functioning. For example, Piaget[8] and others have contributed a great deal of information about the development and structure of human cognitive processes. Over one hundred studies have supported, for the most part, Piaget's ideas about the postulated stages of cognitive development.‡ Piaget's work shows that the thought processes of young children everywhere are qualitatively different in some respects from cognitive processes of adults, but that the cognitive functioning of children at a certain age seems to be more or less invariant throughout our species. Similarly, cross-cultural data support the conclusion that children the world over respond in the same way to the absence or significant withdrawal of parental warmth and affection.[7]

In all I have identified more than twenty topics on which significant universalist research is being done. A few more illustrations of these include (a) the evolution of hominid social bonds, especially the nature of the infant's attachments to its mother[10]; (b) worldwide sex differences in human aggression[11]; (c) formal and substantive universals in human language[12,13]; (d) universals in affective meaning[14]; (e) universals in the facial expression of emotions[15]; (f) possible universal stages of moral development[16]; and (g) universals in ethnosemantics.[17]

At this point I should add, as argued repeatedly by cross-cultural psychologists,[18-20] that current psychological theories do not necessarily have universal validity. Indeed, Jahoda[21] strongly suspects that "a high proportion of the generalizations contained in textbooks on the topic [of, for example, experimental social psychology] would not stand up to cross-cultural replication." Most serious cross-culturalists seem to agree that it is entirely problematic to what extent one can generalize to *human* behavior from the work of the current and conventional behavioral sciences, certainly within anthropology and psychology. Part of the reason for this is that, overall, anthropology has very little theory, and most anthropologists are methodologically untutored. Psychologists on the other hand have developed some very good theory, and many psychologists are methodologically competent, but most of them are also conspicuously culture-bound or ethnocentric. The vast portion of human research in psychology comes from a tiny and nonrepresentative sample of the American population, namely college students fulfilling their course requirements in introductory psychology.[22] Implicitly, laboratory psychologists seem to assume that "college sophomores provide an adequate base for a general psychology of man."[23] Serious cross-culturalists, however, recognize that no matter how carefully or elegantly relevant variables have been controlled, it is definitely not proper to claim that a universalist principle has been established after successfully testing an hypothesis within the United States, or even comparatively between samples in two different national groups. The generalizations from these tests may in fact form universalist principles, but this presumption cannot be accepted until the propositions have survived some form of worldwide testing. That is, insofar as behavioral scientists are interested in establishing valid species-wide generalizations about man, their research design must then consider relevant variations found throughout our species, or perhaps simply discover if any variation exists with respect to the behavior in question. In either case, the investigator will be led to something like a comparative, worldwide sampling design in his research. The rationale here is that if behavioral scientists want to be confident about the species-wide generalizability of their

‡ But certain other features of Piaget's system have not fared as well (see Reference 9).

principles, they are obligated to show that the principles can be generalized beyond the population or cognate populations from which they were originally derived or discovered. This point has been emphatically repeated in anthropology and cross-cultural psychology.[21,24,25]

There are many reasons why behavioral scientists might get involved in cross-cultural research. I want to devote the remainder of this paper to a discussion of three compelling reasons, which by themselves – even if nothing else were true – would be rationale enough for behavioral scientists interested in generalizing about *man* to engage in cross-cultural research. The first is *to test for the level of generality of a theory or proposition*. Can the theory be generalized to all mankind, or is it valid only for certain kinds of people, for example, people living in certain physical environments, in certain types of cultural systems, or populations sharing certain genetic characteristics, and so forth? Or is the proposition or the theory true only within a unique setting, or for a specific population; that is, is the theory wholly culture-bound? From the perspective of this rationale, cross-cultural research functions to assess and edit theory, and to test for the level of generalizability of a relationship between two or more variables.

Malinowski's debate with Freud about the universality of the Oedipus complex is a classic illustration of this rationale. Freud claimed that between the ages of two-and-a-half and four years, sons universally develop an incestuous desire for their mothers, and they become hostile toward but fearful of retaliation from their fathers, with whom they are in competition. Drawing on his field work in the Trobriand Islands, Malinowski[26,27] challenged Freud's dogma about the inevitability of the Oedipus complex. Malinowski asked if the Oedipus complex is likely to develop in a matrilineal society where the role of fathers is different from the role of fathers known to Freud in nineteenth-century, upper-middle-class, patriarchal Vienna. In the matrilineal Trobriand Islands, fathers are not considered progenitors of their children. Children are placed in the mother's womb by a deceased kinswoman. Moreover, Trobriand fathers are not disciplinarians of their own children, and they have little authority over them. These roles fall to the mother's brother from whom children also inherit social position, wealth, and power. The maternal uncle is the socially recognized source of authority over children. Fathers more often play the role of loving companion. The authority and discipline exercised by the uncle is often irksome to the child, and even though the child usually reveres his uncle he also resents him. But this hostility must be supressed. Signs of hostility toward the father are rare. Thus, Malinowski concluded, Freud was unable to distinguish in patriarchal Vienna the role of father as mother's lover from father's role as disciplinarian of the child. The Oedipus complex as described by Freud is not universal but, according to Malinowski, a product of the patriarchal family structure of the Western world. Trobriand data seem to show that hostility is sometimes directed toward the maternal uncle, not because of his role as mother's lover (which he is not), but because of his conflicting roles as friendly educator and disciplinarian. Authority combined with intimacy is likely at some point to produce hostility because intimacy leads to the expectation of affection and leniency, whereas authority is often necessarily associated with impersonal dealings. This role conflict seems to have characterized the Viennese families known to Freud.

At about the same time that Malinowski was contesting Freud's Oedipus complex, Margaret Mead set out to discover the extent to which adolescence is everywhere a time of storm and stress, of tension and rebellion as postulated by

G. Stanley Hall, the "father" of developmental psychology. Mead[28] worked for nine months in three Samoan communities, studying fifty girls from the ages of eight to twenty. She concluded from her work there that adolescence was not necessarily a time of stress. In fact, for most Samoan girls, adolescence was a time of pleasure and personal adjustment.

Of course, a single exception does not disprove a theory — unless the theory postulates exceptionless worldwide uniformities as do the theories of both Freud and Hall. Mechanical theories such as these can be discredited by a single exception. Nonetheless, it is true that adolescence is stressful in some social systems aside from our own, and the Oedipus complex no doubt does exist in various parts of the world. It is therefore important for future research to answer the questions, "Under what conditions is the Oedipus complex likely to develop?" and "Why is adolescence stressful in some societies and not in other?".[29] In addition to being interesting issues, answers to these questions may have important implications for therapeutic intervention and treatment.

Today developmental psychologists and educators believe almost universally that restricted stimulation during the earliest years of childhood may impair the child's later perceptual and intellectual development. The belief, however, is challenged by Kagan and Klein,[3] who worked in an isolated Indian village in the highlands of northwest Guatemala. Guatemalan Indian children in this village are given little stimulation during infancy. They spend most of their first 10 to 12 months of life within small, dark, windowless huts. Even though they are usually near their mothers, infants are rarely spoken to or played with. In comparison with American infants, these babies are marked by their "extreme motoric passivity, fearfulness, minimal smiling, and, above all, extraordinary quietness. A few with pale cheeks and vacant stares [have] the quality of tiny ghosts and [resemble] the description of the institutionalized infants that Spitz called marasmic."[3] Eleven-year-olds in this village, however, are active, gay, and intellectually competent. And "since there is no reason to believe that living conditions in this village have changed during the last century, it is likely that the alert 11-year-olds were, a decade earlier, listless, vacant-staring infants."[3]

A second major reason or rationale for doing cross-cultural research is *to be able to test for the effects of more extreme behavior than can be found normally within any single society.* That is, within any given society only a limited range of acceptable behavior-alternatives are open to people, and as a result "normal" behavior occurs within restricted ranges of variation. Those persons who exceed these limits are considered deviant or "sick," and negative sanctions are often placed against them. Excessive or deviant behavior in one society, however, may fall within the range of acceptable and sometimes even preferred behavior in another. Studying child-rearing in Kansas City, for example, Sears and Wise[30] found that only five out of eighty children had not been weaned by seven months of age. No child was still being breast fed by the time he was three years old.§ Such late breast feeding for most Americans would be shocking, but in a worldwide sample of thirty-seven societies Whiting and Child[32] discovered that the age of weaning ranges cross-culturally from twelve months to six years. In only two cases in their cross-cultural sample were children weaned as early as

---

§ The weaning behavior of parents in Kansas City is consistent with the weaning behavior of parents in Boston where Sears, Maccoby, and Levin[31] found that only one percent of the mothers had not begun to wean their children by the time the children were two years old.

Americans, before six months. Thus, in worldwide perspective, the weaning habits of Americans — as generalized from Kansas City — are extreme.

Sears and Wise[30] examined the relationship between age of weaning and the amount of emotional disturbance expressed by infants in their Kansas City sample. The authors concluded that the older a baby is when he is weaned the more emotional disturbance he shows. Can this conclusion be incorporated into a general theory of human behavior? Is it universally true that the older a child is when he is weaned, the more likely he is to find it disturbing? Whiting and Child[32] showed that scholars who generalize from the Sears and Wise study will be misled. Since the vast majority of children in Kansas City were weaned by seven months, the authors had a very restricted time perspective on which to make their conclusions. Drawing on the greater variability of normal behavior cross-culturally than we find in the United States or in any other single social system, however, Whiting and Child discovered that up to thirteen to eighteen months, Sears and Wise were correct. Children really are more likely to become disturbed the older they are when they are weaned. Beyond thirteen to eighteen months, however, children show steadily fewer signs of emotional stress the older they are at weaning. Thus, it seems that a curvilinear — not a linear — relationship exists between age of weaning and emotional stress. This curvilinear relationship could not have been discovered had we not had access to the greater variability or extremes in behavior found cross-culturally than within any single society.

I should also point out that our knowledge about the relationship between age of weaning and emotional disturbance would be incomplete without the data provided by Sears and Wise because only two societies in the trans-cultural sample fell in the time range (i.e., weaning from zero to seven months) reported in the Kansas City study. Without intracultural information such as this, we would have no way of knowing what the effects of weaning are at the lower age limits. This fact shows the complementary nature of intracultural and cross-cultural research.

Another illustration of this rationale for cross-cultural research is found in psychiatric nosology. The discovery of significant cross-cultural variations in psychiatric symptomatology has lead to major dissatisfaction with the standard diagnostic categories of the American Psychiatric Association's *Diagnostic and Statistical Manual of Mental Disorders.*[33] Cross-cultural research has shown that portions of this Western classification of psychiatric disorders are ethnocentric.[34]

A third rationale for cross-cultural research is *to be able to systematically vary factors that cannot be varied within a single population or cultural system.* ¶ The problem here is that certain classes of behavior simply do not occur naturally within certain populations, or if present they do not occur normatively or frequently enough to be utilized without risk. For example, one could not test a hypothesis in this country about the relationship between hunting-and-gathering economies and parental behavior because there are no hunters-and-gatherers here, except for several North American Indian tribes,

---

¶ In the language of scientific measurement, this third rationale for cross-cultural research deals primarily with nominal data — i.e., with the presence or absence of certain classes of behavior — whereas rationale two treats mainly ordinal or interval data — i.e., forms of behavior that occur within populations in varying degrees, to different extents, or in varying intensities.

which take the investigator "across cultures." If, on the other hand, one wanted to look at the relationship between mother-child (i.e., father-absent) households and parental behavior, he could do the research in the United States with relative ease. But the investigator would want to recognize that certain risks are involved. Mother-child households in North America are often the product of divorce, desertion, or some other stressful circumstance. Accordingly, one would have difficulty interpreting the results if he observed that women in father-absent households are less warm toward their children than women in nuclear family households where fathers live together with their wives and children. At least two conclusions are possible. The first is that women who live by themselves with their children — by this fact alone — develop a different quality of interaction with their children from women who live with their children and husbands. If this were true, one could conclude that the simple fact that a woman lives alone with her children is a sufficient condition, all other things being equal, to induce her toward rejection. As noted above, however, mother-child households in North America are often "broken homes." It is entirely possible that women in such homes experience external stress that has little to do with child-rearing per se, but which almost certainly affects their relationship with their children. Therefore, one cannot be sure whether it is mother-child households as such or whether it is those other extraneous stressful forces — or whether there is an interaction between these two factors — that contribute to the differences between father-absent and intact nuclear-family households. This problem of interpretation evaporates when one does cross-cultural research because mother-child households are institutionalized in many societies. The stress that is so often present in father-absent American homes does not exist in these other societies.

A more concrete illustration of this third rationale is found in epidemiological studies of mental and organic disorders: for example, the investigator locates populations where an illness is present and other populations where it is absent, or he locates a population where the incidence of illness is high and another where the incidence is low. He then searches for the factors responsible for the differences. This use of the comparative method has had practical application in helping to control numerous diseases such as yellow fever, typhus, tuberculosis, beri-beri, and sickle cell anemia.[35]

Cross-cultural research has also been used as an experimental treatment for individual subjects. That is, the "culture" where an adult grew up is regarded by the investigator as the "experimental treatment." Amplifying on this point, Strodtbeck wrote, "The most easily conceptualized form of transcultural study equates cultural experience with the laboratory treatment administered to an individual subject. Perhaps the investigator has reason to believe that some kind of experience may affect individuals in a particular way; he may then search for a culture which can serve as a natural experiment to test this idea."[35] For example, Rivers's[36,37] work around the turn of the century in the Torres Straits Islands and among the Todas of southern India foreshadowed a significant modern-day controversy about the mechanisms producing optical illusions. Behavioral scientists interested in perception have always been intrigued by cross-cultural differences in perception. About a decade ago, Segall, Campbell, and Herskovits[38,39] reported on a large cross-cultural study of visual illusions. They found from a sample of 1878 subjects in fifteen societies that Europeans are significantly more susceptible to the Müller-Lyer and the Sander parallelogram illusions than non-Europeans. That is Europeans growing up in highly carpentered environments with many rectangular angles are prone to treat oblique angles in drawings as perspective projection of right angles. "When they see such angles in a drawing, they make perceptual inferences about the point of view and viewing distance of parts of the figure which result in illusory size perception. People growing up in noncarpentered environments don't interpret oblique angles as projections of right angles and hence don't make such incorrect inferences."[40] The horizontal-vertical illusion is experienced more by non-Europeans than by Europeans. From these data, Segall *et al.* concluded that the ecological and cultural environment in which a people live influences their learned habits of visual inference. Recently alternative explanations have been suggested regarding the mechanisms producing optical illusions.‖

Most of the issues described up to now have concentrated on the influence of those varying behavioral and cognitive regularities known as "culture" on psychological functioning, and on human growth and development. Equally as important is the cross-cultural study of the maintenance and change of social systems, and the interaction between personality and culture change and stability. All these forms of cross-cultural research produce new insights into psychological and sociocultural processes that can be and are being used to help solve social, medical, educational, and other problems in the developing countries of the world as well as in America and the West. In so doing, cross-cultural research helps us shift from ethnocentrics to anthropocentrics. Inexorably, man is being driven into one world, or no world at all. The anthropocentric view can help us from reaching "no world" too soon.

ACKNOWLEDGMENTS

I thank the Boys Town Center for their services in helping to prepare the manuscript. I also thank Evelyn C. Rohner for her excellent comments on the manuscript while it was in its formative stages.

REFERENCES

1. HERSKOVITS, M. J. 1956. Man and His Works. Knopf. New York, N.Y.
2. MEAD, M. 1939. 1925–1939 [Introduction]. *In* The South Seas: Studies of Adolescence and Sex in Primitive Societies. William Morrow & Co. New York, N.Y.
3. KAGAN, J. & R. E. KLEIN. 1973. Cross-cultural perspectives on early development. Amer. Psychol. November: 947–961.
4. ROHNER, R. P. 1977. Advantages of the comparative method of anthropology. Behavior Science Research. In press.
5. TRIANDIS, H. C., R. S. MALPASS & A. R. DAVIDSON. 1972. Cross-cultural psychology. Biennial Rev. Anthropol. for 1971.: 1–84.
6. MURDOCK, G. P. 1971. Anthropology's mythology. Proceedings of the Royal Anthropological Institute of Great Britain and Ireland for 1971: 17–24.
7. ROHNER, R. P. 1975. They Love Me, They Love Me Not: A Worldwide Study of the Effects of Parental Acceptance and Rejection. HRAF Press. New Haven, Conn.

‖ Pick[40] describes two alternative explanations of susceptibility to visual illusions. The first suggests that differences in susceptibility to the Müller-Lyer illusion might be attributed to population differences in eye pigmentation. The second is the possibility of cultural experiences permanently biasing certain "feature detectors" in man.

8. FURTH, H. G. 1969. Piaget and Knowledge: Theoretical Foundations. Prentice-Hall, Inc. Englewood Cliffs, N.J.
9. DASEN, P. R. 1972. Cross-cultural Piagetian research: A summary. J. Cross-Cultural Psychol. **3**: 23–29.
10. BOWLBY, J. 1969. Attachment. Vol. 1. Attachment and Separation. Basic Books, Inc. New York, N.Y.
11. ROHNER, R. P. 1976. Sex differences in aggression: Phylogenetic and enculturative perspectives. Ethos **4**(1): 57–72.
12. CHOMSKY, N. 1973. Introduction. *In* Language & Cognition: *v–x*. Adam Schaff, Ed. McGraw-Hill Book Company. New York, N.Y.
13. GREENBERG, J. H. 1975. Research on language universals. *In* Annual Review of Anthropology. Vol. 4.: 75–94. Annual Reviews, Inc., Palo Alto, Calif.
14. OSGOOD, C. E., W. H. MAY, & M. S. MIRON. 1975. Cross-Cultural Universals of Affective Meaning. University of Illinois Press. Urbana, Ill.
15. EKMAN, P., Ed. 1973. Darwin and Facial Expression. Academic Press. New York, N.Y.
16. KOHLBERG, L. 1976. Moralization: The Cognitive-Developmental Approach. Holt, Rinehart & Winston. New York, N.Y. In press.
17. BERLIN, B. 1970. A universalistic-evolutionary approach in ethnographic semantics. *In* Current Directions in Anthropology. A. Fischer, Ed. Bulletin of the American Anthropological Association. Vol. 3, No. 3, Pt. 2: 1–18.
18. TRIANDIS, H. C., R. S. MALPASS & A. R. DAVIDSON. 1973. Psychology and culture. Ann. Rev. Psychol. **24**: 355–378.
19. BERRY, J. W. & P. R. DASEN, Eds. 1974. Culture and Cognition: Readings in Cross-Cultural Psychology: 13–14. Methuen and Co., Ltd. London.
20. DEVOS, G. A. & A. HIPPLER. 1969. Comparative studies of human behavior. *In* Handbook of Social Psychology. Vol. IV. G. Lindzey & E. Aronson, Eds. Addison-Wesley. Reading, Mass.
21. JAHODA, G. 1970. A cross-cultural perspective in psychology. Adv. Sci. **27**: 1–14.
22. CARLSON, R. 1971. Where is the person in personality research. Psychol. Bull. **75**: 203–219.
23. CAMPBELL, D. T. & R. NAROLL. 1972. The mutual methodological and relevance of anthropology and psychology. *In* Psychological Anthropology. F. L. K. Hsu, Ed. Schenkman Publishing Co., Inc. Cambridge, Mass.
24. BRISLIN, R. W., W. J. LONNER & R. M. THORNDIKE. 1973. Cross-Cultural Research Methods: 143–144. Wiley-Interscience. New York, N.Y.
25. DAWSON, J. L. M. 1971. Theory and research in cross-cultural psychology. Bull. Brit. Psychol. Soc. **24**: 291–306.
26. MALINOWSKI, B. 1927. Sex and Repression in Savage Society. Harcourt, Brace & Co. New York, N.Y.
27. MALINOWSKI, B. 1929. The Sexual Life of Savages. Halcyon House. New York, N.Y.
28. MEAD, M. 1928. Coming of Age in Samoa. William Morrow & Co., Inc. New York, N.Y.
29. ROHNER, R. P. 1977. Enculturative discontinuity and adolescent stress. Worldwide test of a hypothesis. Ethos. In press.
30. SEARS, R. R. & G. W. WISE. 1950. Relation of cup feeding in infancy to thumb-sucking and the oral drive. Amer. J. Orthopsychiat. **20**: 122–138.
31. SEARS, R. R., E. E. MACCOBY & H. LEVIN. 1957. Patterns of Child Rearing. Harper & Row. New York, N.Y.
32. WHITING, J. W. M. & I. CHILD. 1953. Child Training and Personality. Yale University Press. New Haven, Conn.
33. AMERICAN PSYCHIATRIC ASSOCIATION. 1968. Diagnostic and Statistical Manual of Mental Disorders. 2nd edit. American Psychiatric Association. Washington, D.C.
34. KENNEDY, D. A. 1961. Key issues in the cross-cultural study of mental disorders. *In* Studying Personality Cross-Culturally. B. Kaplan, Ed. Row, Peterson & Co. New York, N.Y.
35. STRODTBECK, F. L. 1964. Considerations of meta-method in cross-cultural studies. Amer. Anthropol. **66** (Pt. 2): 223–229.

36. RIVERS, W. H. R. 1901. Introduction *and* Vision. *In* Reports of the Cambridge
     Anthropological Expedition to the Torres Sts. A. C. Haddon, Ed. Vol. II.
     Cambridge University Press. Cambridge, England.
37. RIVERS, W. H. R. 1905. Observations on the senses of the Todas. Brit. J. Psychol. 1:
     321–96.
38. SEGALL, M. H., D. T. CAMPBELL & M. J. HERSKOVITS. 1963. Cultural differences
     in the perception of geometric illusions. Science 139: 769–771.
39. SEGALL, M. H., D. T. CAMPBELL & M. J. HERSKOVITS. 1966. The Influence of
     Culture on Visual Perception. Bobbs-Merrill. New York, N.Y.
40. PICK, H. L. 1975. Cultural differences in perception. Newsletter of the Society for
     Research in Child Development. Summer.

PSYCHOLOGY AND ANTHROPOLOGY:
POSSIBLE COMMON GROUND IN CROSS-CULTURAL RESEARCH

Gustav Jahoda

Department of Psychology
University of Strathclyde
Glasgow G1 1RD, Scotland

In 1869 Owen Pike wrote that "without psychology there is no anthropology."[1] A century later Lévi-Strauss[2] echoed this: "l'ethnologie est d'abord une psychologie." Yet, with a few conspicuous exceptions, among which the Cambridge Torres Straits Expedition is probably the most famous, there has been relatively little active collaboration between the practitioners of these two disciplines. The aim of this paper is, first, to speculate a little on the reasons for this state of affairs and, second, to put forward some positive suggestions.

The reasons for the lack of collaboration are probably somewhat different on the two sides of the fence. As far as psychologists are concerned, the main one for a long time was probably lack of interest and an inability to appreciate the potential value of the study of behavior of people in other cultures. Academic psychologists striving for scientific status regarded themselves as being engaged in study of the behavior of *homo sapiens*, their objective being that of arriving at universal laws governing such behavior. On this assumption it does not really matter whether one uses college freshmen or members of distant tribes as one's subjects; and since the former are much more readily available, the bulk of work was done with them. Lest it be though that this is an unfair caricature, it is worth mentioning that such a position has quite recently been seriously defended.[3] Even during the interwar period a minority of psychologists did not share this view, for example Klineberg among social and Bartlett among experimental psychologists. Bartlett expressed the alternative forcefully:

> An air of unreality and abstraction hangs over a great many of the experiments
> of the psychological laboratory. I think nothing can correct this more firmly than
> a study of the culture-determined behaviour of distant, or differently developed,
> groups.[4]

It is only about two decades ago that Bartlett's words have come to be seriously heeded. Psychologists have become more aware of the limitations of studies conducted exclusively within Western culture settings. Those who go out into the cross-cultural field are still a rather small minority, but at least they are no longer regarded as eccentrics by their colleagues. Thus the intellectual climate has become much more favorable to collaboration with anthropologists.

When it is a matter of diagnosing the trouble on the other side of the fence, I feel rather less confident. Although I have enjoyed frequent and profitable contact with anthropologists, the fact remains that my prespective is bound to be that of an outsider. Let me start with the article already cited by Bartlett,[4] which was addressed to anthropologists and suggested mutual cooperation. The response by Nadel[5] was rather cool; he indicated that anthropologists had yet to be convinced of the desirability of such cooperation. Now the interesting thing is that Nadel himself, like some other prominent British anthropologists, had himself first been trained as a psychologist; and he later wrote what in my opinion remains one of the most penetrating discussions of the relationship

13

between psychology and anthropology.[6] At first sight it might seem paradoxical that a man with such a background should react negatively. On further reflection I came to the conclusion that it was precisely his thorough knowledge of contemporary psychology that led to his response. There is no time to explain this in any detail. Briefly, academic psychology of the period was concerned either with psychometrics, of which Nadel was (rightly, as it turned out) sceptical concerning its cross-cultural applications, or the experimental study of specific and limited segments of behavior. In his view neither of these was directly relevant to the primary business of the anthropologist, namely the understanding of the behavior of people within particular sociocultural systems. Given the aims and scope of anthropology at the time, this is perfectly understandable.

What anthropologists were looking for was, if I recall the phrase of Kluckhohn correctly, "a theory of raw human nature"; in other words, a theory that would provide a working tool for understanding the functioning of the whole personality (and not just certain bits of it) within a wide range of social settings. Many American anthropologists thought they had found such a theory in psychoanalysis. British anthropologists were overtly resistant to Freudian ideas, which did not prevent their being profoundly influenced by them. The contrast in attitudes is well illustrated in the debate between Kennedy[7] and Gluckman[8] on psychological versus social explanations of witchcraft. This accounts for the fact that so-called "psychological anthropology" is essentially an American movement. It did not in practice lead to much cooperation, except with psychoanalysts; the fieldwork consisted mainly of personality-and-culture studies conducted by anthropologists schooled in Freudian theory and using projective techniques as their major tools. There are widely divergent evaluations of the outcome of the vast effort expended in this direction. Spiro[9] felt that it had been very successful; Bruner[10] expressed the uncharitable opinion that it had failed dismally to yield any solid findings. Whatever the ultimate verdict, the fact remains that most psychologists felt rather lukewarm about this enterprise and sceptical about Freudian theory, although they themselves had nothing better to offer.

There is another area of anthropological interest going a good deal further back, and that is a concern with what used to be called "primitive" mind or thought. There is a long tradition here from men like Frazer, Lévy-Bruhl or Boas right up to Lévi-Strauss. One would have imagined this to be a topic that lends itself admirably to an interdisciplinary approach, but the extent to which it has happened is disappointingly small. Here again I have to be brief and excessively dogmatic. In general, anthropologists have either tended to concentrate on the *content* of thought exclusively or else they drew inferences from content to process. Psychologists, on the other hand, have mostly been concerned with *process* and in the main have confined their studies to Western cultures. This is very apparent in the recent collection, *Modes of Thought*.[11] It contains a single psychological contribution by Colby and Cole, which is of an entirely different character than that of the rest of the volume. Their contribution, incidentally, develops this point in much greater depth. It could be argued that in this sphere anthropologists could profitably have taken more notice of what psychologists were doing, and perhaps enlisted their cooperation. This has been happening to some extent in an emerging speciality named "cognitive anthropology," which studies the manner in which people in different cultures conceptually organize their environment. In a few specific areas, notably that of the perception and categorization of colors, anthropologists and psychologists have worked together on similar problems, using much the same methods (see the work of Heider and Olivier[12] and that of Tournay[13]). However, on the whole this is exceptional.

Summing up this admittedly inadequate sketch, there are probably two main reasons why anthropologists resorted less to psychology than they might have done: one is that they have perhaps not always been fully aware of what psychology has to offer; the other is that on many issues central to their aims psychology appears somewhat sterile to them. I believe the second of these reasons to be largely justified, but at the same time feel that something could be done about it.

The crux of the problem has been characterized both by a psychologist[14] and an anthropologist,[15] discussing some of the difficulties of cooperation. Audrey Richards observed that the psychologist typically goes into the field to *test a hypothesis*, while the anthropologist tries to *describe a system* "whether of social relationships, activities, symbols or world views" (Reference 15, p. 23). There is a twofold contrast implicit here: (1) focus on a small constituent part versus a global view; (2) experiment versus a descriptive approach. By and large this characterization has certainly been valid in the past. However there has arisen in psychology a new and extremely influential movement where this dichotomy no longer fully applies. I am of course referring to Piaget's genetic psychology. It could reasonably be claimed that the Piagetian approach is more akin to the description of a system than to classical hypothesis-testing; and as Brown said in the previously mentioned paper, it is none the worse for that. This is the ground on which I should like to base the positive suggestions. In order to prevent any misunderstanding, let me state at once that I am not proposing a specifically Piagetian theoretical approach. Rather I shall be advocating the potential value of systematic descriptive studies, largely neglected in recent psychology. Moreover, I would hold that these might be most profitable within the developmental sphere; and above all, one could select topics where the interests of psychologists would converge with those of anthropologists.

In exploring this theme I shall select some illustrative examples, beginning with a topic at least distantly related to psychological anthropology. It seems to me that the attempt to characterize the personality type distinctive of particular cultures was and remains excessively ambitious.* The adequate assessment of personality is still a difficult and elusive matter, even if one does not go outside western industrial societies. There are, on the other hand, some more circum-scribed motivational/emotional dispositions that may be more amenable to cross-cultural study. Perhaps the one of greatest potential interest for both psychologists and anthropologists is that of *envy*. This is a concept employed by both anthropologists themselves and their informants for the purpose of explaining behavior. It has received little attention from psychologists, except for Freud, as can be seen from the comprehensive account in a recent work.[17] The reason for this neglect is probably the practical difficulty of objectively establishing the arousal of envy in a person. Yet this presents no obstacle for the "common-sense" psychology of lay people everywhere. There appear to me to be at least two ways of tackling this issue. One would be to study the actual behavioral cues that lead people to infer the presence of envy, and this would of course be easiest with children, where even some appropriate experimental manipulations could be envisaged (e.g., giving a toy or food to one child and not

* This may not be true of the imaginative scheme put forward by LeVine,[16] which has yet to be tested in practice.

another, at least not immediately). The second way, where a joint anthropological/psychological approach would be essential, could consist of a systematic cross-cultural study concerned with the *attribution* of envy; the relevant variables here would be the types of persons and situations. I realize of course that anthropologists have already done this to some extent within various cultures, but am not aware of any systematic cross-cultural comparisons of this kind.

The second and third examples are directly inspired by Richards,[15] beginning with the question she raised about psychologists' views on the principles of thought postulated by Lévi-Strauss, e.g., binary opposition, thesis, antithesis and synthesis. I have myself discussed some of these issues elsewhere[18] and merely add some general remarks. It appears to me that the general, and very difficult, problem here is that of relating content to process. Piaget,[19] in reply to Lévi-Strauss, objected to inferences made from the former to the latter; he argued that "kinship systems are finished systems, already regulated, and of limited scope. What we want to know about is individual inventions" (p. 117). What will have to be done is to forge a link between the knowledge of kinship systems, myths, etc. on the part of particular individuals in various cultures, and their modes of thinking about social (in the widest sense) and physical reality. This has some affinity with the task of cognitive anthropology, but goes well beyond it. I must confess to having no ready answer as to how this problem could be solved; the only certain thing is that it could not be done without close cooperation between both disciplines.

The other pertinent question raised by Richards is concerned with symbols in society. Psychologists have been much preoccupied with various forms of symbolic behavior, but the acquisition of social symbols has been largely ignored. On the other hand anthropologists commonly assume that the symbolic meanings they have elicited from particular informants are held in common with all members of the given community; it is often also believed that certain rituals serve the function of transmitting such symbolic meanings. However, there is seldom any independent evidence to support such views. Hence Richards[15] pertinently asks: "What is the spread of knowledge of symbolic meanings through the community? At what stages of childhood and adolescence are the deeper levels of meaning associated with each symbol passed on?" (p. 12). Richards appears to take it for granted that the denotative sense of a term invariably precedes the deeper symbolic meaning; on the basis of somewhat casual conversations with young children about such things as "the heart" I would be inclined to doubt that this is necessarily the case. At any rate, teasing out the extent to which social symbols have been mastered would be a subtle and challenging task, requiring the anthropologist's understanding of the prevailing set of symbols as well as psychological techniques that would have to be specially elaborated. The admirable survey of symbols by Firth[20] contains a mine of valuable information for an enterprise of this kind.

My last example concerns the issue of social identities, and the plural is deliberate. I think it is widely agreed by anthropologists that the ultimate criterion for the existence of a social unit such as a tribe, and also for the determination of its boundaries, is the extent to which people *perceive themselves* to be members. In addition to cognitive awareness, and usually prior to it, there is a tendency to respond with positive emotion to the name and symbols of the in-group. Moreover, each individual typically belongs to several units and thus builds up a hierarchy of social identities. In long-established and homogeneous nation-states the development of ideas and attitudes in this sphere is relatively straightforward and has been the subject of study (for example, see the work of Jahoda[21] and that of Tajfel *et al.*[22]). The situation in developing countries is often much more complex, rather little being known about the relative salience of tribal and national identities in various situations. For, in spite of the uniform condemnation of the evil of "tribalism" on the part of the rulers, sectional identities are far from extinct and are apt to govern behavior in certain contexts. It would therefore be valuable to trace the development of these social identities during childhood and adolescence, including, if possible, the changes that are occurring over time.

These illustrations are intended to point to areas of interest common to both disciplines, in which each has a contribution to make whose joint product is likely to be far greater than if either worked on his own. There are of course many practical difficulties in such collaboration, which have been discussed by Richards[15]; but there have also been successful collaborative ventures that show that these difficulties can be overcome. A current instance is the study of the effects of literacy made by a psychologist, Michael Cole, and an anthropologist, Jack Goody.

It is probably evident that my message is mainly directed at psychologists, and I have tried to show that challenging problems exist that are at the same time relevant to the interests of anthropologists. In his book on symbols Firth[20] said that anthropologists must come to terms with psychology. My hope is that psychologists will go further along the way to meet them, and I feel confident that psychology itself would benefit from such a move.

REFERENCES

1. HADDON, A. C. 1934. History of Anthropology. Watts. London, England.
2. LÉVI-STRAUSS, C. 1962. La Pensée Sauvage. Plon. Paris, France.
3. GERARD, H. B. & E. S. CONNOLLEY. 1972. Conformity. *In* Experimental Social Psychology. C. G. McClintock, Ed. Holt, Rinehart & Winston. New York, N.Y.
4. BARTLETT, F. C. 1937. Psychological methods and anthropological problems. Africa 10: 410–419.
5. NADEL, S. F. 1937. Experiments on culture psychology. Africa 10: 421–435.
6. NADEL, S. F. 1951. The Foundations of Social Anthropology. Cohen & West. London, England.
7. KENNEDY, J. G. 1967. Psychological and social explanations of witchcraft. Man 2: 216–225.
8. GLUCKMAN, M. 1968. Psychological, sociological and anthropological explanations of witchcraft and gossip; a clarification. Man 3: 20–34.
9. SPIRO, M. E. 1972. An overview and a suggested reorientation. *In* Psychological Anthropology. Francis L. K. Hsu, Ed. Schenkman. Cambridge, Mass.
10. BRUNER, J. 1974. Concluding comments and summary of conference. *In* Readings in Cross-cultural Psychology. J. M. L. Dawson and W. J. Lonner, Eds. University Press. Hong Kong.
11. HORTON, R. & R. FINNIGAN. 1973. Modes of Thought. Faber. London, England.
12. HEIDER, E. R. & D. C. OLIVIER. 1972. The structure of color space in naming and memory for two languages. Cognitive Psychology 3: 337–354.
13. TOURNAY, S. 1973. Language et perception. L'Homme 13: 66–94.
14. BROWN, R. 1964. Discussion of the conference. Am. Anthropologist 66: 243–253.
15. RICHARDS, A. I. 1970. Socialization and contemporary British anthropology. *In* Socialization. Philip Mayer, Ed. Tavistock. London, England.
16. LEVINE, R. A. 1973. Culture, Behavior and Personality. Hutchison. London, England.

17. SCHOECK, H. 1970. Envy. Harcourt Brace and World. New York, N.Y.
18. JAHODA, G. 1970. A psychologist's perspective. *In* Socialization. Philip Mayer, Ed. Tavistock. London, England.
19. PIAGET, J. 1971. Structuralism. Routledge and Kegan Paul. London, England.
20. FIRTH, R. 1973. Symbols: Public and Private. Allen & Unwin. London, England.
21. JAHODA, G. 1963. The development of children's ideas about country and nationality. Brit. J. Educational Psychology 33: 47–60; 143–153.
22. TAJFEL, H., C. NEMETH, G. JAHODA, J. D. CAMPBELL & N. B. JOHNSON. 1970. The development of children's preferences for their own country. Internat. J. Psychology 5: 245–253.

A DYNAMIC MODEL OF RELATIONSHIPS
AMONG ECOLOGY, CULTURE AND BEHAVIOR*

J. W. Berry

Department of Psychology
Queen's University
Kingston, Ontario K7L 3N6, Canada

INTRODUCTION

Over the past few years a model of ecological, cultural and behavioral relationships has been proposed and elaborated.[3,4,6] This model has been operationalized and evaluated by employing data from a series of field studies,[3,4,7] and by general reviews of the literature.[5,24] With substantial empirical material now available, it is possible to pursue an integrated evaluation of the model across the seventeen field samples collected during this period.

This paper will briefly outline the sets of variables indicated in the title, present a short overview of the structure and content of the model, provide some details about the sources and methods of data collection, and then concentrate upon the relationships that emerge when the data and the model are brought together.

Despite the grandiose title, it will become apparent during the presentation that the model is a research model and not a general one, and that each of the three levels of variables are defined rather narrowly. However, it is possible that the model may have some general applicability beyond the cultural or psychological confines of this program of research.

THE VARIABLES

The general approach is one that views the development of individual behavior as a function of membership in a cultural group; and cultural characteristics are viewed as a function of both the ecological setting of the group and the acculturative influences that impinge upon the group. These functions are not necessarily unidirectional, for cultures may be influenced by the growing individuals, and ecological and intergroup relationships may be altered by cultural patterns. Furthermore, the individual's behavior may exist as a direct function of ecological or acculturative factors (not mediated by his culture), and of course these direct relationships may exert influence *from* the developing individual. We are thus dealing with three levels of variables that are all potentially interacting: extracultural input (ecological and acculturational), cultural, and behavioral.

* Fieldwork was supported by the Canada Council, Australian Research Grants Committee, and by Communications Canada. The paper was prepared while the author was a Fellow at the Netherlands Institute for Advanced Study in the Humanities and Social Sciences.

THE MODEL

These variables have been incorporated into a model,[6] which is reviewed briefly here. In FIGURE 1 six components are included within a single interacting framework. The two basic input components are Ecology (interactions between human organisms and their habitat) and Acculturative Influences (influences, mainly via education and urbanization, from outside the culture). In adaptation to these, are two cultural components: the Traditional Cultural (here limited to those aspects that may be conceived of as ecologically adaptive), and the Contact Culture (parallel to traditional culture, but now altered during acculturation). And finally, two behavioral components are illustrated: the Traditional Behavior component is viewed as being in adaptation not only to Traditional Culture but also to Ecology, and the Acculturated Behavior component is considered as a function both of Traditional Behavior and Acculturation (Acculturative Influences and Contact Culture).

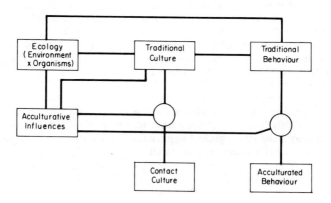

FIGURE 1.   Ecological-cultural-behavioral model.

The content of these six components will become clear during our attempt to operationalize the model. However, in brief, the Ecology component includes the exploitive pattern of a group (e.g., hunting, gathering or agriculture), the settlement pattern (e.g., nomadic or sedentary), and the typical size of the community. The Traditional Culture component includes the level of social and cultural stratification, the family type, and typical emphases during child-rearing. Within the Traditional Behavior component, there is a focus upon those behaviors that may be conceptually related to psychological differentiation,[25] but also included are other perceptual and cognitive behaviors.

At the second (Acculturation) level of the model, the Acculturative Influences component includes such factors as education and urbanization, while the Contact Culture component incorporates changes in traditional features that are a function of these acculturative influences. Finally, the Acculturated Behavior component includes "shifts" in the kinds of behaviors that were considered in the Traditional Behavior component, and "acculturative stress" behaviors that often develop during periods of culture contact and social change.

OPERATING THE MODEL

With the structure and content of the model now outlined, we may proceed to its operationalization. It is apparent, even from this brief glance, that it is not possible to operationalize such a complex model unless some parameters are set. And, of course, by setting these, the generality of the model will be limited. These general limits are three in number: first, the model is intended to apply only to subsistence-level societies (and those that were so until recently), for it is only at this level that ecological adaptation is likely to be meaningfully studied; second, the content of the various components is narrow, being confined to the theoretical and empirical research interests of the present investigator (primarily cultural ecology and psychological differentiation); and third, the model is limited to the kind of a culture-contact situation that typically resulted from the period of European colonial expansion over the past 500 years.

The basic strategy for operationalizing the model was first to select cultural groups (from published ethnographies and archives) that ranged quite widely in terms of their ecological setting. Then, communities within these cultures were selected to represent differing levels of acculturation to European life-style. And finally field work was conducted, during which psychological tests were administered to samples from these various communities. In terms of design, the selection of cultures, communities and samples represents a quasi-manipulation of the "independent" variables, and the testing and interviewing provides the "dependent" behavioral data.

It is not possible to present here many of the details of the cultures, samples and tests employed in the study. However, TABLE 1 provides the essential data needed to operationalize the model. In this Table are listed ten cultural groups, from which seventeen samples were drawn (additionally four European samples were drawn from Scotland and Canada, but they lie outside the model). Also in the Table are the indices which represent various components of the model.

These four indices were derived primarily from the materials prepared by Murdock and others, who have developed the cultural archives,[9,19-23] but are supplemented by other ethnographic sources including material collected during the field work itself. They are presented in standardized form, and are composed of numerous archival ratings and codings, and some self-ratings. These elements are: (1) *Ecological Index:* ratings of exploitive pattern, settlement pattern and mean size of local community (from Murdock[20]). (2) *Cultural Index:* ratings of political stratification, social stratification and family organization (from Murdock,[20] and ratings of socialization compliance-assertion (from Barry, Child and Bacon,[2] supplemented by respondent self-ratings on the same dimension. (3) *Ecocultural Index:* a combination of the first two indices (which in fact intercorrelate +.84) to provide a more general input variable. (4) *Acculturation Index:* ratings of experience of European education, combined with ratings of the degree of urbanization and wage employment in the communities.

It is apparent that the initial selection of cultures and samples for their variation on these dimensions has been moderately successful; there is a fair degree of spread on these indices, which provides the quasi-manipulation that was sought.†

---

† It should be noted, however, that the primary interest during the course of this research was upon the adaptations being made by hunting and gathering peoples; thus they are more common in this sample of cultures than in any random sample of world cultures. This interest stemmed partly from the already heavy concentration of studies on sedentary agricultural peoples; the balance was in need of redressing.

TABLE 1

CULTURES, SAMPLES AND THEIR CHARACTERISTICS

Cultural Group	Location	Sample Name	N	Ecological Index	Cultural Index	Ecocultural Index	Acculturation Index
Temne	West Africa	Mayola	90	−1.98	−1.93	−1.96	−1.68
		Port Loko	32	−1.98	−1.48	−1.66	−0.02
Telefol	New Guinea Highlands	Telefomin	40	−1.53	−1.48	−1.51	−1.47
Tsimshian	Coastal British Columbia	Hartley Bay	56	−0.27	−0.37	−0.34	+0.74
		Port Simpson	59	−0.27	−0.37	−0.30	+1.42
Koonganji	Coastal Australia	Yarrabah	30	−0.27	−0.53	−0.45	−0.38
Motu	Coastal New Guinea	Hanuabada	30	−0.39	−0.53	−0.49	+0.68
Carrier	British Columbia mountain	Tachie	60	+0.18	−0.26	−0.11	+0.47
		Fort St. James	61	+0.18	+0.36	+0.30	+0.95
Arunta	Central Australia	Santa Teresa	30	+0.52	+0.80	+0.72	−1.26
Ojibway	Northern Ontario	Aroland	39	+0.64	+0.64	+0.64	+0.34
		Long Lac	37	+0.64	+0.25	+0.38	+0.80
		Sioux Lookout	31	+0.64	+0.41	+0.49	+1.48
		Wemindji	61	+0.86	+0.75	+0.79	−0.69
Cree	Northern Quebec	Fort George	60	+0.86	+0.64	+0.72	+0.26
Eskimo	Baffin Island	Pond Inlet	91	+1.09	+1.58	+1.43	−1.20
		Frobisher Bay	31	+1.09	+1.57	+1.36	−0.44

Turning to an examination of relationships among these indices and their elements, we may consider them from two points of view: coherence of elements within indices, and independence of the indices from each other. Ideally, of course, we should sample cultures that provide for relative independence between the two levels in the model (the Ecological-Cultural and the Acculturational), but that allow for consistency within levels. In TABLE 2, these relationships are displayed for the samples in this study. It is clear that within the ecological component (cluster A) and within the cultural component, (cluster B) there is a pattern of coherence among the elements that justifies their summation into indices. It is also clear (cluster C) that the two sets of elements are highly related; this pattern is supported by the single correlation of +.84 between the two indices, which led to the decision to incorporate both into a single Ecocultural Index, to represent the first adaptive level of the model.

Similarly, the three elements within the Acculturation Index cohere to a high degree (cluster D). But they do not correlate highly with elements in the Ecological and Cultural Indices (cluster E); this minimal relationship among these elements is supported by the low correlations between the Acculturation Index and the other three indices (+25, +12, and +.16). We may assert that we have met our aim of sampling societies that exhibit a high degree of coherence within components of the model, but that maintain independence between the two major levels of the model.

Although many behavioral tasks and observations were employed, they were not (and, of course, could not be) representative of all behavior in the samples. A selection was made of those behaviors that were theoretically associated with the concepts of psychological differentiation, or were particularly relevant to ecocultural or acculturational adaptation. And of these behaviors, only a sample will be presented here. Differentiation theory is basically a way of conceiving of the degree of structural complexity in an individual's psychological functioning. In the area of perceptual functioning, it is indicated by the ability to disembed item from context, and in cognitive functioning it is indicated by the capacity to analyze and restructure information. In social behavior, it is indicated, for example, by the maintenance of independence of judgment in the face of social influence. These behaviors are considered to develop as a function of specific socialization emphasis: practices that emphasize the achievement of separation and of autonomous functioning tend to foster differentiation, while practices emphasizing obedience and conformity tend to foster lower levels of differentiation.[16]

In addition to the area of differentiation, behavioral measures were made in a number of visual perceptual areas that were considered relevant to subsistence patterns, and estimates were made of stress levels that are often thought to accompany acculturation.[10,11]

To represent these various behavioral measures, six are included in this report: (i) *Discrimination:* a gap-detection task presented in a portable tachistoscope (see Berry[3] for a description), which was employed in eight samples. A high score indicates fine gap-detection. (ii) *Kohs Blocks:* the original 17-design version which is known to load on a disembedding factor; employed in 17 samples. A high score indicates successful analysis and construction of the designs. (iii) *Ravens Matrices:* a test of analytical perceptual and inferential ability, using sets A, Ab and B (colored form); employed in 17 samples. A high score indicates high ability. (iv) *Social Influence*: A task derived from Asch,[1] which estimates the degree to which an individual is able to maintain his own judgment in the face of a suggested group norm. A high score indicates

TABLE 2

INTERCORRELATIONS AMONG ELEMENTS IN THE INDICES ACROSS 17 SAMPLES

Variables	1	2	3	4	5	6	7	8	9	10	11	12	13	14	15
1. Exploitive pattern	—														
2. Settlement pattern	+.85	—													
3. Mean size	+.74	+.90	—												
4. Political stratification	+.91	+.80	+.66	—											
5. Social stratification	+.45	+.64	+.80	+.53	—										
6. Family organization	+.53	+.55	+.56	+.64	+.60	—									
7. Socialization (compliance-assertion)	+.87	+.93	+.89	+.80	+.53	+.46	—								
8. Socialization (self-ratings)	+.91	+.80	+.77	+.75	+.44	+.47	+.89	—							
9. Education	+.42	+.25	-.06	+.32	-.25	+.04	+.11	+.22	—						
10. Wage employment	+.17	-.10	-.35	+.16	-.29	+.03	-.18	+.05	+.79	—					
11. Urbanization	+.24	-.02	-.20	+.18	-.26	+.17	-.08	+.18	+.76	+.87	—				
12. Ecological index	+.70	+.76	—	+.89	+.56	+.56	+.92	+.91	+.33	+.05	+.14	—			
13. Cultural index	—	+.76	+.78	—	—	—	—	—	+.17	-.04	+.09	+.84	—		
14. Eecocultural index	—	—	—	—	—	—	—	—	+.23	-.01	+.10	—	—	—	
15. Acculturation index	+.35	+.12	-.16	+.27	-.29	+.07	+.01	+.19	—	—	—	+.25	+.12	+.16	—

(Groupings labeled A, B, C, D, E are indicated by triangular outlines within the correlation matrix.)

independence of judgment. This was employed in 17 samples. (v) *Stress*: A check-list estimated the degree of psychosomatic stress claimed by the individual. It has 20 items, derived by Cawte[10] from the Cornell Medical Index.[8] It was employed in nine samples. (vi) *Marginality*: A 14-item scale developed by Mann[18] to estimate the feelings of being "poised in psychological uncertainty" during culture-contact and change; it was employed in nine samples.

In TABLE 3, the mean sample results are provided (along with standard deviations). In addition to the 17 samples considered up to this point, data are also provided for the four European samples for general comparative purposes. It is clear that there is wide variation in performance, both between and within samples, on all behavioral measures. This will permit the use of correlational and regression techniques in the evaluation of relationships.

Although any model may be examined be searching for empirical relations among its constituent elements, the theoretical background to the present model permits a statement of expected relationships (essentially a statement of hypotheses). We have, then, two different approaches to the model: in the first, we may evaluate the model by assessing the hypotheses that derive from it; and in the second, we may simply enquire about the arrangement of elements that best fit the observations. Following are analyses of the material from these two different perspectives: in the first, hypotheses are advanced and tested, while in the second a multiple regression analysis is provided.

THE HYPOTHESES

The overall hypothesis was that behavior would not be distributed randomly across these samples, but would vary according to ecological, cultural and acculturational factors. Specifically for those behaviors associated with differentiation theory (Blocks and Influence) it was predicted that behavior would be relatively undifferentiated at the sedentary, stratified end of the ecocultural dimension, and relatively differentiated at the nomadic end. The basis for expectation lies in the theoretical antecedents of psychological differentiation, both in terms of socialization and conformity pressures. In addition, scores on differentiation tasks were expected to increase with acculturation, due both to increased educational experience and the general cultural changes that accompany culture contact.

For the two perceptual-cognitive tests (Discrimination and Matrices) similar hypotheses were advanced. Such visual detection and analysis that are required by these tasks were argued to be present to a high degree for hunters and gatherers, but to a lesser degree for more sedentary peoples; ecological adaptation should lead to appropriate performance. Similarly, experience of education and informal perceptual and analytical training encountered in a technological society were expected to lead to increased performance on these two tasks with acculturation.

For the two measures associated with acculturation (stress and marginality), it was considered that a more complex patterning might emerge. Specifically, it was predicted that greater stress and marginality would be experienced by those peoples whose traditional culture was least consistent with the demands of the society into which they are becoming acculturated; those societies that are loose, minimally-stratified and have low population concentration are clearly most discrepant from the authority and congestion being forced in European towns and areas; while those societies with a traditionally highly-stratified cultural

TABLE 3

MEANS AND SDS ON SIX TASKS FOR TWENTY-ONE SAMPLES

Sample	Discrimination M	Discrimination SD	Blocks M	Blocks SD	Matrices M	Matrices SD	Influence M	Influence SD	Stress M	Stress SD	Marginality M	Marginality SD
Mayola	1.2	6.9	6.4	6.9	13.1	2.4	5.96	3.3	—	—	—	—
Port Loko	3.2	7.1	15.6	14.6	13.9	3.8	6.39	3.2	—	—	—	—
Telefomin	3.5	6.2	9.5	8.6	14.7	4.1	8.10	3.8	—	—	—	—
Hartley Bay	—	—	81.8	27.1	27.7	5.4	11.33	4.6	4.07	3.3	3.25	2.6
Port Simpson	—	—	95.1	28.1	31.1	3.6	11.74	4.6	5.08	3.9	2.88	2.3
Yarrabah	6.2	5.3	50.7	19.6	24.7	5.4	9.64	2.8	—	—	—	—
Hanuabada	9.6	3.9	62.6	21.8	26.1	5.8	10.47	2.8	5.71	4.2	3.86	3.2
Tachie	—	—	115.3	20.1	28.1	6.8	12.04	4.0	5.20	3.5	4.30	3.2
Fort St. James	6.2	5.9	92.4	29.2	26.2	4.8	11.04	4.1	—	—	—	—
Santa Teresa	—	—	39.9	17.3	23.2	4.4	9.78	3.0	3.94	2.3	3.29	2.3
Aroland	—	—	101.1	32.9	27.3	5.4	10.76	3.7	6.00	4.5	5.73	3.4
Long Lac	—	—	99.1	29.0	27.2	5.4	10.78	4.9	5.07	3.3	3.77	2.8
Sioux Lookout	—	—	106.1	28.9	28.7	5.2	9.55	5.5	6.43	4.1	6.30	3.4
Wemindji	—	—	96.6	27.9	24.2	6.9	11.25	4.4	7.03	4.2	5.20	3.0
Fort George	8.5	6.0	96.3	35.6	25.3	7.9	11.07	4.9	—	—	—	—
Pond Inlet	7.7	6.5	78.6	30.6	26.8	3.2	12.25	2.9	—	—	—	—
Frobisher Bay	6.7	5.8	89.9	28.2	28.9	3.1	12.75	2.5	—	—	—	—
Inverkeilor	5.9	6.5	90.2	33.2	29.5	4.9	11.00	3.8	—	—	—	—
Edinburgh	—	—	90.3	31.6	31.0	4.2	11.15	3.0	1.79	2.3	1.89	2.3
Westport	—	—	101.6	24.0	30.5	3.4	12.02	3.6	2.95	2.7	1.83	1.9
Sioux Lookout	—	—	94.1	29.8	29.7	4.9	7.93	5.1	—	—	—	—

TABLE 4

TESTING THE HYPOTHESES: SIMPLE AND MULTIPLE CORRELATIONS AMONG
THE INDICES AND SIX BEHAVIORAL VARIABLES

Statistic	Behaviors					
	Discrimination	Blocks	Matrices	Influence	Stress	Marginality
Simple correlations						
Ecology index	+.82	+.81	+.80	+.84	+.56	+.72
Culture index	+.75	+.68	+.70	+.79	+.38	+.60
Acculturation index	+.53	+.67	+.65	+.38	−.42	−.64
Multiple correlation	.91	.94	.93	.85	.83	.91

system, and higher population concentrations, are clearly more consistent with
the demands being met during acculturation. Turning to the expectations about
the relationships between acculturation level and stress phenomena, it was
considered that a curvilinear relationship might be apparent: that at low levels of
contact, stress levels might be low, but would increase with contact to some
maximal stress level, and then decline as new adaptations are made. With such an
expectation, *where* one samples on the acculturation dimension will determine
whether a positive or negative relationship will emerge. In the present study,
these two tasks were employed primarily in communities that had a fairly long
history of contact, and we thus expected to find a declining (negative)
relationship with acculturation.

These twelve hypotheses (two for each of the six tasks, one pertaining to
ecological and cultural adaptation, and one to acculturation) are all clearly borne
out. Simple and multiple correlations presented in TABLE 4 show that to a large
degree the variation in these behaviors across samples can be comprehended in
terms of long-term ecological and cultural adaptation. And to a lesser extent,
acculturation also contributes. But when all three factors are combined, the
multiple correlations all rise to over +.80. We may conclude that these behaviors
do not vary randomly across cultures in this sample, but are systematically
related to the hypothesized variables. And further, as TABLE 5 indicates, there
is a nonrandom set of relationships among the four traditional behaviors (ranging
from +.83 to +.93), and there is a correlation of +.79 between the two stress

TABLE 5

INTERCORRELATIONS AMONG BEHAVIORS IN THE MODEL

Test	Discrimination	Blocks	Matrices	Influence
Discrimination	—			
Blocks	+.89	—		
Matrices	+.93	+.90	—	
Influence	+.89	+.83	+.89	—
Number of samples	8	17	17	17

behaviors. These latter findings were expected as a corollary of the hypotheses; since the behaviors were expected to vary consistently with the same indices, then they should vary consistently among themselves.

EVALUATION OF THE MODEL

Pushing beyond the hypotheses that derive from the model, we may also evaluate the model itself by considering the strength of some of the modelled relationships, and by carrying out multiple regression analyses between the major input variables and the behavioral variables.

In FIGURE 2, the overall model is presented with Pearson product moment coefficients attached to components and relationships among them. Within components, some of the coefficients are extracted from TABLES 2 and 5; and between components, coefficients are extracted from TABLE 4.‡ It is clear that the within- and between-component relationships are fairly robust.

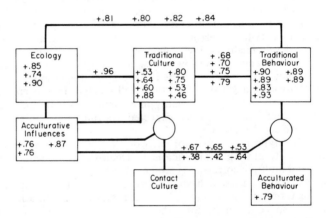

FIGURE 2. Summary of relationships within and between components.

We may also turn our data around for a last look at these ecological, cultural and behavioral interactions. That is, we may approach the data with a question rather than a prediction: what is the optimal arrangement of these data to allow us to achieve maximal predictability with the simplest structure? This question, of course, must be answered within the theoretical and empirical confines of the material available to us. After many analyses and rearrangements of these data, the most elegant solution appears to be a reduction of the model to three components: an Ecocultural component, an Acculturation component, and a general Behavioral component (with different behaviors kept separate within it). The optimal weightings appear to be those indicated in TABLE 6. With these general emphases, the simplest structure and maximal control is attained.

‡ Note that the Contact Culture component was operationalized along with the Acculturative Influences component as part of the Acculturation Index; thus no coefficients are allocated separately to it.

TABLE 6

BETA WEIGHTS FOR ECOCULTURAL AND ACCULTURATION INDICES ON SIX
BEHAVIORAL VARIABLES

Index	Behaviors					
	Discrimination	Blocks	Matrices	Influence	Stress	Marginality
Ecocultural	0.77	0.66	0.67	0.78	0.29	0.40
Acculturation	0.52	0.56	0.54	0.25	−0.29	−0.55

CONCLUSIONS

We may conclude that differences in these behaviors are systematically related to the ecocultural setting and acculturation experience of the groups in the study. These systematic relationships were expected on the basis of theoretical arguments found in the approaches of cultural ecology and psychological differentiation. Although the model that was proposed was not more elaborate than these theoretical bases required, it has become apparent that some features that are theoretically separate are in fact empirically similar. That is, although the proposed model has received a large measure of support, it could have been less complex and still have achieved the same empirical confirmation. Specifically it is probable that future work need only take into account a combined ecocultural variable, a combined acculturation (influences and contact culture) variable, and a single behavioral component. §

We may also conclude that there is an overall emphasis resting upon ecological and cultural variables, and a lesser one upon acculturational ones. Although it was not possible to predict, in precise terms, this relative emphasis, the theoretical approach that was adopted pointed towards the dominant effects of long-term ecocultural adaptation over short-term acculturational adaptation. For how long this will continue, it is not possible to determine from the present data; however, it is clear that many generations of European contact in some of these samples has not markedly altered the behavior which was expected on the basis of their position on the Ecocultural dimension. This, of course, raises some very interesting questions for international programs concerned with education and economic change.

The correlational relations in the model are primarily seen as bidirectional, contributing to a dynamic state of systematic interactions. It is not possible to discover empirically the relative flow in each direction on the basis of the present material. However, it is possible to predict, on theoretical grounds, the balance of flow in some of the relationships; and it may be possible in future longitudinal study to empirically check these predictions. For example, subsistence-level societies are unlikely to be in a position to greatly affect the nature of their ecology (although with acculturation, primarily the introduction of new weapons, some hunters have in the past wiped out their subsistence base). Thus the relationships between ecology, culture and behavior are more

§ For reasons beyond the scope of the paper, the behavioral component would still need to include a wide variety of behavioral measures.

likely to flow in that one direction, than in the opposite direction. In another example, the nature of European technology and education has historically affected traditional cultures more than the other way around. Although, currently some western educational systems are considering other educational forms, and in the past some technology has been developed in response to the needs of other cultures, the predominant flow has been in the one direction.

Finally we may consider the generality of the model and of these findings. We have indicated already some parameters or limits to the model, and these must be observed both in testing it and in generalizing it. But over and above this, we must ask whether the relationships that are found among these cultural samples and these behavioral tests would change if we were to take another set of samples and tests that still observe the parameters of the model. Our expectation is that the general picture would not change very much. On the one hand, similar behavioral measures with other subsistence-level samples are exhibiting, sample by sample, roughly equivalent results.[12,15,17,24] And on the other hand, differing behavioral measures with similar subsistence-level samples are also lending support to the general relationships that have emerged from this study.[13,14] Although in principle the picture could change considerably, in fact it seems to be remarkably consistent. If, as we expect, these relationships among ecological, cultural and behavioral variables continue to emerge through further study, then the value of such an adaptive framework for cross-cultural research may prove to be great indeed, and well beyond the bounds of this single study.

REFERENCES

1. ASCH, S. E. 1956. Studies in independence and conformity 1: a minority of one against a unanimous majority. Psychological Monogr. 70: whole no. 416.
2. BARRY, H., I. CHILD & M. BACON. 1959. Relation of child training to subsistence economy. Am. Anthropol. 61: 31–63.
3. BERRY, J. W. 1966. Temne and Eskimo perceptual skills. Internat. J. Psychology 1: 207–229.
4. BERRY, J. W. 1971. Ecological and cultural factors in spatial perceptual development. Can. J. Behavioural Sci. 3: 324–336.
5. BERRY, J. W. 1971. Psychological research in the North. Anthropologica 13: 143–157.
6. BERRY, J. W. 1975. An ecological approach to cross-cultural psychology. Ned. Tijdschr. Psychologie 30: 51–84.
7. BERRY, J. W. & R. C. ANNIS. 1974. Ecology, culture and psychological differentiation. Internat. J. Psychology 9: 173–193.
8. BRODMAN, K., A. J. ERDMANN, I. LORGE, C. P. GERSHENSON & H. G. WOLFF. 1952. The Cornell Medical Index health questionnaire III. The evaluation of emotional disturbances. J. Clin. Psychology 8: 119.
9. CARNEIRO, R. L. 1970. Scale analyses, evolutionary sequences and the rating of cultures. In A Handbook of Method in Cultural Anthropology. R. Naroll and R. Cohen, Eds.: 834–871. Natural History Press. New York, N.Y.
10. CAWTE, J., G. N. BIANCHI & L. G. KILOH. 1968. Personal discomfort in Australian Aborigines. Austral. New Zealand J. Psychiatry 2: 69–79.
11. CHANCE, N. A. 1965. Acculturation, self-identification and personal adjustment. Am. Anthropologist 67: 372–393.
12. CHANDRA, S. 1975. Cognitive development of Indians and Fijians. In Applied Cross-Cultural Psychology. J. W. Berry and W. J. Lonner, Eds.: 248–253. Swets and Zeitlinger. Amsterdam, The Netherlands.

13. DASEN, P. R. 1974. The influence of ecology, culture and European contact on cognitive development in Australian Aborigines. *In* Culture and Cognition. J. W. Berry and P. R. Dasen, Eds.: 381—408. Methuen. London, England.

14. DASEN, P. R. 1975. Concrete operational development in three cultures. J. Cross-Cultural Psychology 6: 156—172.

15. DAWSON, J. L. M. 1967. Cultural and physiological influences upon spatial perceptual processes in West Africa. Parts 1 and 2. Internat. J. Psychology 2: 115—128; 171—185.

16. DYK, R. & H. A. WITKIN. 1965. Family experiences related to the development of differentiation in children. Child Devel. 36: 21—55.

17. MacARTHUR, R. S. 1973. Some ability patterns: Central Eskimos and Nsenga Africans. Internat. J. Psychol. 8: 239—247.

18. MANN, J. 1958. Group relations and the marginal man. Human Relations 11: 77—92.

19. McNETT, C. W. 1970. A settlement pattern scale of cultural complexity. *In* A Handbook of Method in Cultural Anthropology. R. Naroll and R. Cohen, Eds.: 872—886. Natural History Press. New York, N.Y.

20. MURDOCK, G. P. 1967. Ethnographic atlas: A summary. Ethnology 6: 109—236.

21. MURDOCK, G. P. & C. PROVOST. 1973. Measurement of cultural complexity. Ethnology 12: 379—392.

22. PELTO, P. 1968. The difference between 'tight' and 'loose' societies. Transaction: 37—40 (April).

23. TATJE, T. A. & R. NAROLL. 1970. Two measures of societal complexity: An empirical cross-cultural comparison. *In* A Handbook of Method in Cultural Anthropology. R. Naroll and R. Cohen, Eds.: 766—833. Natural History Press. New York, N.Y.

24. WITKIN, H. A. & J. W. BERRY. 1975. Psychological differentiation in cross-cultural perspective. J. Cross-Cultural Psychology 6: 4—87.

25. WITKIN, H. A., R. B. DYK, H. F. FATERSON, D. R. GOODENOUGH & S. A. KARP. 1962. Psychological Differentiation. Wiley. New York, N.Y.

SOME THEORETICAL AND METHODOLOGICAL PROBLEMS IN THE STUDY OF ETHNIC IDENTITY: A CROSS-CULTURAL PERSPECTIVE

Vijai P. Singh

Department of Sociology; and the
Center for Urban Research
University of Pittsburgh
Pittsburgh, Pennsylvania 15260

Ethnicity has survived the impact of modernizing forces, and in recent years people have deliberately displayed their cultural distinctiveness. Ethnic identity refers to expressions of loyalty, commitment, and belongingness towards an ethnic group. It is essentially ascriptive in nature. The differences based on caste, race, religion, language, and nationality are the bases of ethnic identity. When ethnicity combines cultural identity with economic and political interests, it becomes a powerful mobilizing force.[1,2] Governments have been responsive to the demands made by different groups organized on the bases of caste, race, tribe, religion, language, and nationality. It seems that cultural assimilation of groups is as remote as ever; however, new forms of intergroup adjustments are being evolved. The groups who do not claim a unique cultural heritage are more likely to be absorbed into the dominant culture. But there is no assurance that they will not assert their group identity in the future, even though they have abandoned their traditional rituals and customs temporarily.

Generally, studies of ethnicity have been concerned with the adaptation of ethnic groups in larger social systems. Such studies are essential and useful, but the content of ethnicity or its representation may not be fully ascertained under the "dominant-minority" perspective. The economic and political inequalities are partly the consequences of belonging to a particular group, but these are by no means the "cultural stuff" that define ethnicity. Therefore, our main focus in this paper is the demonstration of a symbolic basis of ethnic identity in the United States and India. We are not concerned with dominant-minority relations or economic and political inequality between ethnic groups except insofar as they help us understand symbolic systems of ethnicity.

The paper is divided into three major sections: first, conceptualization of ethnicity and the symbol system; second, presentation of American data showing the nature of ethnic identification and symbolic reinforcements; and third, application of the symbolic approach to Indian data. The conclusions demonstrate the advantages of studying ethnicity through symbol systems. Whether or not ethnicity is a category of ascription can best be answered by carefully identifying symbols and exploring their meanings in relevant contexts.

THE CONCEPT OF ETHNICITY

Ethnicity is an ascriptive category based on a common cultural heritage,[3-8] but it captures only part of the ascriptive identity of a person. In intergroup contexts ethnic boundaries are clearly delineated. The norms of an ethnic group define proper conduct for its members. The Indian caste system is conceived as an hierarchical ethnic system.[9-11] It is an ascriptive system, and failure to conform does not result in membership in some other group.[12] Ethnicity, however, does not imply an all-or-none property for the members of an ethnic group. It has both aggregate and individual levels. The former is exemplified by affiliation with a caste, race, religion, nationality, language, and region, and the latter involves the degree of loyalty and commitment of the individual to the ethnic group. The two levels are interrelated even though they are analytically distinct. Transmission of ethnic identity across generations is efficient when the ethnic group practices endogamy, as do Indian caste systems.

Sometimes ethnic groups are conceived as preindustrial units, and it is postulated that industrialization, urbanization, and changes in occupational structure and geographic mobility weaken kinship and community ties, facilitating memberships in labor unions, professional and civic organizations, and political parties as viable alternatives.[13] Despite the multiplicity of identifications in modern societies, ethnic identity continues to assert itself because of its roots in primordial ties. When someone is a member of several groups, some identities are more central to his attitudes and behavior than others. When other affiliations reinforce a particular identity, the degree of commitment is strong and ethnic boundaries become clearly marked. In India there are linguistic, regional, religious, and caste identities. These multiple identities need not be in competition or conflict because they are essentially contextual. For instance, when a Tamilian migrates to Bombay, he tries to find people from Tamil Nadu, so that he can speak the Tamil language with them, even though they may be members of different caste or religious groups. But when he is in his state of Tamil Nadu, probably his caste and community identity would be stronger than the linguistic or regional identity. Further, economic and political concerns provide different contexts in which ascriptive identities are organized. The demand for linguistic states in India was intended to forestall political, economic, or cultural domination from the north. Caste and religious identities were subordinated to linguistic and regional identities. Social, economic, and political factors may influence the ways ethnic identities are "played out," but changes in the structural position of an ethnic group need not result in changes in ethnic identity.

ETHNIC SYMBOLISM

Cultural symbols differentiate ethnic identity at various levels. Some symbols such as language or dialect are more central than behavioral or visual types of symbols.[14] Cultural histories of ethnic groups consist of symbols that are passed on from one generation to the next. Each generation learns about its cultural history through events, symbolic outputs, and interdependence of fate.[15] Symbols symbolize objects, events, emotions, and values, and their meaning may be based on objective or subjective realities or both. There are two major types of symbols: referential and condensation.[16] In the former, different individuals assign similar meaning to a particular symbol such as the national flag, speech patterns, racial, ethnic or religious affiliations with a high degree of regularity. Condensation symbols are subjective in that individual feelings and emotions are aroused by certain remote objects, events, and situations. Both types of meanings can be found in a symbol; for instance, the flag of the United States is a national symbol with a high degree of reliability, but it also releases emotional energy on the Fourth of July.[16] Meanings for particular symbols are assigned by people in interaction situations.

Symbols come into play in those situations "where the particular kind of information they contain is lacking, where institutionalized guides for behavior, thought, or feeling are weak or absent. It is in country unfamiliar emotionally or topographically that one needs poems and road maps."[17] This explains the expression of ethnic solidarity among working classes living in large cities and metropolitan areas in the United States. Many of them do not expect much change in their socioeconomic status and have come to recognize the limitations of the great "American dream." They want to have control over what happens to them, especially in the places where they work or live, and many of them are, for instance, against school busing and welfare. It should be noted that various kinds of symbols are invoked in such uncertain situations to promote ethnic solidarity and communal mobilization.

Ethnic identity is expressed through symbols surrounding race, caste, religion, language, food, music, kinship systems, friendship, and residential patterns. An ethnic group in this context can be defined as "a collectivity within a larger society having real or putative common ancestry, memories of a shared historical past, and a cultural focus on one or more symbolic elements defined as the epitome of their peoplehood."[18] This definition of an ethnic group is applicable to both the United States and India. We disagree with Barth, however, who argues that ethnic boundaries can be studied without investigating the cultural elements that each ethnic group encloses.[19] Ethnic boundaries can be forged for immediate economic and political gains without necessarily sharing cultural elements. For instance, in India many people have tried to pass as being of a low-caste status to qualify for preferential treatment reserved only for some traditionally disadvantaged groups by the government. In such disputes, only "cultural stuff" would determine who are the members of the designated groups. Preoccupation with the structural position of ethnic groups has left the cultural aspects of ethnicity somewhat less explored. The primordial loyalty is proudly demonstrated by the people who claim to be rational and quite aware of their self-interest. There are other situations in which commitments to the ethnic group are not publicly expressed, but are nonetheless practiced. It is not uncommon for an educated, self-supporting, and independent Indian who argues emotionally about the "evils" of the caste system to eventually marry within his own caste. Similar examples can be cited from other societies as well.

The conceptualization of the problem of research in this area must precede the concerns surrounding the collection or availability of data. In the study of ethnic identity, the availability of data on economic and political variables has influenced the continuation of the limited theoretical perspective pointed out earlier. Changes in the structural position of a group do create new conditions of intergroup adjustments, but the degree of assimilation in the dominant culture depends on the extent to which members of different groups perceive cultural differences between themselves. Comparative studies of ethnicity would help unravel some of these complexities. Initially, the concepts should be defined and measured in such a way that they are cross-culturally applicable. Both quantitative and qualitative data can be collected as long as they are interpreted within specific cultural contexts. In the next two sections of this paper we will show that the symbolic approach allows the use of quantitative as well as qualitative data and that the two sets of information are complementary in the study of ethnic identity.

DATA FROM THE UNITED STATES

There has been growing interest in the study of ethnic groups in the United States. The United States Bureau of the Census began collecting data on the ethnic origins of Americans in 1969. Its main purpose was to report social, economic, and demographic characteristics of the ethnic groups. This interest has grown as the foreign-born population has been declining. The consistency of reporting ethnic origins in the Current Population Survey of national samples of matched persons 14 years old and over between 1971, 1972, and 1973 was revealing.[20] It was noted that 63.5 percent of the sample reported the same origin in 1972 as in 1971. The corresponding percentage reporting the same ethnic origin in 1973 as in 1972 was 64.3. The data by ethnic groups showed that the Italians and Poles had a higher percentage of consistency than the Germans, Irish and English, Scottish, and Welsh. The consistency of reporting ethnic origins across ethnic groups between 1971–72 and 1972–73 was quite comparable.

In the context of another study we found that people in Pittsburgh had identified themselves with more than 100 different single or multiple ethnic categories. This situation encouraged us to study the bases of ethnic identity using survey research methods. The data reported here are part of the study of ethnic roots in Pittsburgh carried out by the Center for Urban Research, University of Pittsburgh, during 1974–75.

A random sample of 561 respondents was drawn from six communities in Pittsburgh, Pennsylvania. The important criteria for selection of these communities were that they (1) contained a minimal black or Jewish population; (2) differed in their income and occupational composition; and (3) they were predominantly made up of people of a Polish, Italian, German, Irish or White-Anglo-Saxon-Protestant (WASP) ethnic group. Two communities had Polish, two Italian, one German, and one WASP representation. About 16 percent of the respondents identified themselves as Poles, 10 percent as Italians, 10 percent as Germans, 9 percent as Irish, 5 percent as White Anglo-Saxon Protestants, 27 percent as "Americans," and 9 percent indicated that they had no ethnic identity; the remaining 14 percent included Asian, African, and several other European ethnic groups. Selection of the neighborhoods was based on the assumption that their ethnic composition would influence ethnic identity and the sharing of cultural symbols. However, our data revealed that higher numerical representation of one of the ethnic groups and other criteria differentiating communities were insufficient to distinguish them on differential ethnic identifications and participation in the symbol system.

Respondents were asked about the ethnic roots of their families as well as their current ethnic identification. It was noted that 31 percent of the Poles, 35 percent of the Italians, 57 percent of the Irish, 63 percent of the Germans and 70 percent of the WASPs were inconsistent with respect to their objective ethnic background and subjective ethnic identification. The category "American," which constituted only 3 percent of the total sample on objective criteria, swelled to about 27 percent on subjective identification, forming the largest group of all. The "no-identity" group (9 percent in the sample) was also formed subjectively. Germans, Poles, and Italians were heavily represented in the "American" group while primarily Germans, Irish, and WASPs made up the "no-identity" group. Subjective ethnic identification is the focus of our subsequent analysis.

In response to the question whether, as Americans, people should emphasize ethnic, racial, and religious similarities or differences, 58 percent of the respondents favored emphasizing similarities, and 42 percent, differences. Older ethnic groups such as Germans, Irish, and WASPs were slightly more likely to favor emphasizing similarities than were newer groups such as Poles and Italians.

We asked the respondents how their religious, racial, and ethnic backgrounds

TABLE 1

INTERCORRELATIONS AMONG RELIGION, RACE, AND ETHNICITY FOR
THE SELF* AND OTHERS† FOR POLISH RESPONDENTS

	Self			Others		
	Religion	Race	Ethnicity	Religion	Race	Ethnicity
Self						
Religion	–					
Race	.42	–				
Ethnicity	.47	.67	–			
Others						
Religion	.37	.29	.39	–		
Race	.20	.30	.28	.35	–	
Ethnicity	.31	.27	.42	.50	.53	–

* Please tell me which items influence your own thinking and action.
† Now, please tell me which items influence other people's thinking and actions.
NOTE: The responses to these two questions were recorded on a four-point scale: not important; somewhat important; important; and very important.

influenced their thinking and action as well as how these affiliations, in their opinion, affected "others." The responses were recorded on a four-point scale (not important; somewhat important; important; and very important). The correlation matrices for "self" and "others" for the five ethnic groups, "American," and "no identity" groups are presented in TABLES 1 to 7. High correlations among the three variables would indicate that ascription plays an important role in the thinking and actions of the respondents. High correspondence among the patterns of correlations between self and others would exhibit a world view in which rules governing thinking and action are widely shared. High correspondence with high correlations would mean that ascription is a highly

TABLE 2

INTERCORRELATIONS AMONG RELIGION, RACE, AND ETHNICITY FOR
THE SELF AND OTHERS FOR ITALIAN RESPONDENTS

	Self			Others		
	Religion	Race	Ethnicity	Religion	Race	Ethnicity
Self						
Religion	–					
Race	.16	–				
Ethnicity	.44	.75	–			
Others						
Religion	.31	.15	.19	–		
Race	.02	.22	.16	.27	–	
Ethnicity	.09	.32	.40	.30	.55	–

TABLE 3

INTERCORRELATIONS AMONG RELIGION, RACE, AND ETHNICITY FOR
THE SELF AND OTHERS FOR GERMAN RESPONDENTS

	Self			Others		
	Religion	Race	Ethnicity	Religion	Race	Ethnicity
Self						
Religion	—					
Race	.33	—				
Ethnicity	.17	.48	—			
Others						
Religion	.01	.15	.12	—		
Race	−.01	.28	.04	.45	—	
Ethnicity	−.03	.42	.17	.47	.47	—

relevant part of the social system. Low correspondence, on the other hand, would show that beliefs and values of self were different from those of others and that there were variations in the role of ascription in shaping thinking and actions. Unsystematic patterns of correlations would mean that these factors are randomly shared by the respondents and that presumably there were other factors more important than these influencing the thinking and actions of the respondents.

The mean scores for the entire sample indicated that race and ethnicity were more important for the others than for the self in influencing thinking and actions of the respondents. Religion, however, had a slightly higher impact on the self than on the others. This overall pattern was found for Poles, Italians, Irish and "Americans." The differences between the self and the others for race and ethnicity were greater for Irish and "Americans" than for Poles and Italians. For Germans, WASPs and "no-identity" groups, the mean scores on race, ethnicity

TABLE 4

INTERCORRELATIONS AMONG RELIGION, RACE, AND ETHNICITY FOR
THE SELF AND OTHERS FOR IRISH RESPONDENTS

	Self			Others		
	Religion	Race	Ethnicity	Religion	Race	Ethnicity
Self						
Religion	—					
Race	.29	—				
Ethnicity	.32	.51	—			
Others						
Religion	.36	.28	.26	—		
Race	.28	.37	.14	.49	—	
Ethnicity	.40	.14	.34	.48	.43	—

TABLE 5

INTERCORRELATIONS AMONG RELIGION, RACE, AND ETHNICITY FOR
THE SELF AND OTHERS FOR WASP RESPONDENTS

	Self			Others		
	Religion	Race	Ethnicity	Religion	Race	Ethnicity
Self						
Religion	–					
Race	.02	–				
Ethnicity	.43	.45	–			
Others						
Religion	.37	.13	.56	–		
Race	.03	.68	.38	.26	–	
Ethnicity	.18	.26	.43	.47	.39	–

and religion were higher for the self than for the others. The magnitudes of the differences between self and others on race and ethnicity were greater than on the religion. Even though the respondents recognized the influence of race and ethnicity on them, they tended to believe that these have greater impact on the thinking and actions of the others. This feeling is less pronounced among Poles and Italians than in the other groups. The influence of religion on the self was acknowledged by the ethnic groups that seem predominantly non-Protestant (the previous backgrounds of "Americans" were largely Polish, Italian and Irish) but in terms of importance it still ranked lower than race and ethnicity.

The correlation between race and ethnicity for the self was .54, and .48 for the others. The correlations of race and ethnicity with religion for the self were .32 and .36, and the corresponding correlations for the others were .40 and .39, respectively. The three variables are slightly more tightly correlated for the

TABLE 6

INTERCORRELATIONS AMONG RELIGION, RACE, AND ETHNICITY FOR
THE SELF AND OTHERS FOR "AMERICAN" RESPONDENTS

	Self			Others		
	Religion	Race	Ethnicity	Religion	Race	Ethnicity
Self						
Religion	–					
Race	.34	–				
Ethnicity	.39	.39	–			
Others						
Religion	.24	.03	.11	–		
Race	.01	.29	.14	.38	–	
Ethnicity	.11	.14	.31	.33	.45	–

TABLE 7

INTERCORRELATIONS AMONG RELIGION, RACE, AND ETHNICITY FOR
SELF AND OTHERS FOR "NO IDENTITY" RESPONDENTS

	Self			Others		
	Religion	Race	Ethnicity	Religion	Race	Ethnicity
Self						
Religion	—					
Race	.16	—				
Ethnicity	.29	.50	—			
Others						
Religion	.15	.30	.20	—		
Race	−.09	.33	.12	.40	—	
Ethnicity	−.11	.03	−.17	.16	.45	—

others than for the self, indicating that respondents consider themselves less influenced by these factors than the others. Among various ethnic groups, however, correlations for the self are higher for the Poles, followed by the Italians, Irish, "Americans," Germans, WASPs and the group having "no identity." Correlations between race and ethnicity are higher in all groups than any other correlations. Italians have a correlation of .75 between ethnicity and race, followed by the Poles (.67), Irish (.51), Germans (.48), and WASPs (.45). Even though the "American" and "no identity" groups did not subjectively identity with any of the ethnic groups, they show correlations of .39 and .50, respectively, between ethnicity and race. Religion and ethnicity show higher correlations for Poles (.47), Italians (.44) and WASPs (.43) than for Irish (.32) and Germans (.17). The "American" and "no identity" groups have correlations of .39 and .29, respectively. The greatest variation across groups is found in the correlations between religion and race, with a high of .42 among Poles to a low of .02 among WASPs. The patterns of correlations demonstrate that ethnicity is highly associated with both race and religion across these groups.

A comparison across various groups shows that the correlations between ethnicity and race are higher for the self and lower for the others except in the case of "Americans." The discrepancies are larger for Poles and Italians than for other groups. These correlations demonstrate that ethnic, racial, and religious affiliation influence the thinking of both self and others, as perceived by the respondents. Poles and Italians showed a different pattern from the rest in the direction of greater importance of these factors in their world view.

We assumed that the use of a second language, the desire to speak an ethnic language or dialect better, preparation of ethnic foods, listening to ethnic music, having ethnic friends, reading ethnic literature, and the desire to visit places associated with one's ethnic background demonstrated the existence of ethnic identity. English was spoken fluently as their first language by about 91 percent of the respondents, followed by Italian (2 percent) and Polish (2 percent), with the rest of the respondents speaking various other languages. However, the second language, spoken at home with relatives, friends, and neighbors by 67 percent of the respondents, revealed the prevalence of non-English languages.

The Poles were the largest group speaking a second language (85 percent), followed by Italians (79 percent), Germans (49 percent), Irish (44 percent) and WASPs (36 percent). A substantial proportion of the "American" (66 percent) and "no identity" (42 percent) groups also identified themselves with a second language. Most Poles used Polish as their second language. Slightly more than half of the Italians used Italian but some of them also spoke English, French and Spanish as their second language. Most Germans conversed in German, but the Irish and WASPs occasionally conversed in French, German and Spanish. However, the "American" and "no identity" groups were found to use one of the major ethnic languages spoken in the Pittsburgh area.

Our study also explored whether there were any languages or dialects that respondents wished to speak better. About 60 percent of the Germans, 53 percent of the Italians, 52 percent of the Poles, 46 percent of the Irish, and 45 percent of the WASPs expressed the desire to speak a language or dialect better than they did at the time of the interview. Among the "American" and "no identity" groups, the corresponding percentages were 51 and 38, respectively. Of those who wanted to speak a language or dialect better, 61 percent of the Italians wanted to speak Italian better, 43 percent of the Poles selected Polish, and 50 percent of the Germans chose German. The Irish and the WASPs wanted to improve their speaking proficiency in French, German, Italian, and Spanish. The "American" and "no identity" groups had similar preferences to those of the Irish and the WASPs. In the area of language, the ethnic groups showed distinct preferences. With only a few exceptions, the language they spoke at home and in other informal contexts as well as the one in which they wanted to be more proficient was not English. It must be noted, however, that their preferences for non-English languages were not chosen at the expense of English. In fact, for about 91 percent of the respondents English was the first language, but learning and using other languages in their private domains makes them feel closer to a particular cultural tradition.

Preparation of ethnic foods was still another mark of identification with one's ethnic group. It was found that 48 percent of the families of respondents regularly cooked foods associated with their ethnic background, 30 percent occasionally, and only 22 percent never. Italian and Polish families cooked ethnic foods more regularly than did German, Irish, or WASP families. It is interesting to note that "Americans" cooked ethnic foods associated with their ethnic background more regularly than did the Germans, Irish or WASPs, but less regularly than the Poles or Italians. About one-fourth of the "no identity" group claimed that their families still cooked foods associated with their ethnic background.

Slightly more than half of the respondents (52 percent) listened to music associated with their ethnic background. Of those who listened to ethnic music, within each group, the Poles demonstrated the largest proportion (83 percent), followed by the Italians (64 percent), Irish (32 percent), Germans (30 percent), and WASPs (26 percent). The corresponding percentages for the "American" and "no identity" groups were 54 and 33, respectively. Of those who listened to their ethnic music, 61 percent listened to ethnic radio programs.

About two-thirds of the friends for Poles in the sample were other Poles, about half of the friends for Italians were other Italians, but Germans found only slightly more than one-third of their friends from the same ethnic background. Less than one-third of the friends for Irish and WASPs shared the same ethnic backgrounds. "Americans" chose their friends mainly from among the Italians, Germans and Poles. The "no identity" group selected most of its friends from among the Germans, and smaller proportions from among the Irish and the Poles.

About 60 percent of the respondents expressed their desire to visit places associated with their ethnic backgrounds. Slightly more than half of the respondents were aware of the existence of newspapers and magazines associated with their ethnic backgrounds. The three major languages in which this literature was published were Polish (31 percent), English (26 percent), and Italian (19 percent). Of those who were aware of the existence of ethnic publications, 48 percent read them regularly.

These data show that ethnic identity is not empty of cultural content. The patterns of participation in ethnic language, food, friendship, music, and literature are the symbolic expressions of ethnic identity. Individuals recognize these cultural symbols not because they are friendly or antagonistic towards some other ethnic group or because they are seeking some economic or political advantage, but simply to identify with their cultural heritage. Their symbolic participation must make them feel special.

The differences in symbolic participation between ethnic groups are only partly related to the recency of immigration. The more recent immigrant groups (Polish and Italian) are more likely to respond to cultural symbols than the others. However, many of those who identified themselves as WASPs, "Americans" or as having "no identity" could not escape the force of ethnic identity and responded to the symbols that were associated with their families' ethnic backgrounds. Part of the explanation for this finding lies in their desire to participate in a distinctive cultural system in order to attain psychological security and self-fulfillment. These data show that the respondents were not completely assimilated into some dominant cultural system, but they did not necessarily cling to the folkways and customs of the "old country" either. Many of the traditional customs, beliefs, and values were modified through interaction with different institutions and individuals in the United States, but cultural uniqueness was still maintained.

THE INDIAN DATA

Religious and linguistic identities have dominated the South Asian scene for a very long time. Religion was the basis of the division between India and Pakistan in 1947. Linguistic, cultural, and regional identities precipitated the creation of Bangladesh in 1971. Soon after that, language riots broke out in Pakistan over regional autonomy. Even though Punjabi speakers are most numerous in Pakistan, the Urdu language was popularized as the symbol of Muslim nationalism.[21,22] Speakers of other languages occasionally organized to demand greater public recognition for their own languages. These same groups had also rallied in support of the Urdu language when demands for regional autonomy were made in Bangladesh on the basis of linguistic, cultural, and regional differences. In India, writers, poets and novelists formed language societies and promoted the causes of particular languages. One important consequence was the destruction of the historical affinity between the Hindi and Urdu languages because the former became more "Sanskritized" and the latter more "Persianized." Some religious leaders from Hindu and Muslim communities encouraged these divisive efforts.[23] The same processes divided India into linguistic states after independence, and regional sentiments are aroused with little difficulty.

The process of the development of regional consciousness involves the interpretation and communication of symbols to the relevant groups by a handful of elites. For instance, around 1900, Ranade wrote about the Maratha empire, distinguishing it from other Muslim empires, and emphasizing linguistic, religious, and racial solidarity with the desire for political autonomy.[24] A body of literature was produced that interpreted cultural and historical events. Folk songs and plays depicting heroic exploits of the Maratha peoples were popularized. The diffusion of these symbols in rural and urban areas created a regional consciousness among the Marthi-speaking people. After Indian independence they did not accept the bilingual combined state of Gujarat and Maharashtra. Political leaders in favor of a separate Maharashtra state received the political support of the people during the national elections.[25] Finally, in 1960, the Maharashtra state was created. Similar processes can be traced in the creation of other linguistic states in India. What is remarkable is the people's ability to share multiple identities and to invoke one set of symbols, indicating its primacy over the others in a particular context.

The study of caste stratification in India has suffered greatly because insufficient attention has been paid to symbols. There are specific symbols associated with the major caste groups. These symbols define the ritual status of different castes and also serve as the guide for intercaste relations. Such practices as raising pigs, eating beef or pork, drinking alcoholic beverages, worshipping local deities, offering blood sacrifice, working with leather, dressing above one's knees, and widow marriage defined low-caste status. There are other symbols surrounding endogamy, commensality, and deference systems that also govern the interaction between different castes.

The findings of my research reported elsewhere show that patterns of association between caste status, political power, economic status, level of education, and occupational status demonstrate changes in the structural positions of the caste groups, but were insufficient for understanding the beliefs and values that define caste status and the mechanisms through which intercaste boundaries are maintained.[26] Correlations over three generations in three rural communities between these status variables indicated that the caste system was far from rigid and that status inconsistencies pervaded all groups. However, data on kinship and marriage, residential patterns, commensality, worship, friendship, and festivals and other important events clearly showed that the caste system was alive and well despite the low and moderate correlations of caste with other status variables. The caste status of a particular person became clear during a feast attended by people of different castes. For instance, the food had to be prepared by the upper-caste persons, preferably Brahmins, and also served by them. Upper castes had to eat first, while lower-caste persons waited. In addition, the lower-caste person was modestly dressed, took his shoes off before entering the main compound, greeted the higher-caste people first, and then found a place of lower elevation to sit slightly away from the seating arrangements for persons of the upper castes. He generally was a patient listener and spoke only when encouraged by the upper-caste people. This situation prevailed in the same communities in which we had witnessed low and medium correlations among the status variables. Therefore, the status system, caste identities, and relationships between different caste groups were better understood through observations on symbolic participation.

It is not argued that all those who occupied the lower rungs in the stratification system were proud of their caste identity or wanted to preserve it. In fact, just the opposite was true. However, lower-caste persons contemplated changes in their status through acquisition of the very symbols that are the monopoly of the upper castes. This process, in which lower castes emulate the life styles of the upper castes is known as "Sanskritization."[27] In order to raise their caste status through Sanskritization it is necessary for lower-caste persons to become vegetarians, refrain from consuming liquor, practice strict sexual mores, and use Sanskrit concepts and ideas. Emulation must be consistent with the practices of the caste status for which claims are being advanced. Inconsistencies and inadequacies must be explained through the invention of myths. In many cases, the lower-caste person must practice the new life style and wait for some public recognition. In several instances in which members of lower castes attempted to adopt symbols that defined the life styles of the upper castes, the aspirants had only modest success. The legal abolition of the caste system did not give them any new identity. They still lived with their past heritage — in some cases against their will.

The data from urban India showed that caste identities persisted and most people associated with persons of similar caste backgrounds. In his study, Mehta found that the religious and caste segregation in Poona remained largely unchanged over a period of 150 years.[28] Occupational and income differences explained only a little the patterns of residential segregation. Much of the explanation lay in caste and religious differences. Upper castes and Hindus were more residentially centralized than the lower castes and other religious groups. Berreman found that speech, dress, manners, life styles, and physiognomy were important symbols defining group identity. People with similar ethnic backgrounds interacted among themselves more than with the others. Berreman aptly summarized his findings by stating that "those of common ethnic status are likely to live, eat, work, converse, worship and marry together."[29] Many of the symbols that define one's ethnic identity in rural areas operate in urban centers as well. Despite the anonymity of the urban environment, ethnic identities persist and urban residential areas show considerable ethnic segregation.

CONCLUSION

In conclusion, the data from Pittsburgh show that most people identified with specific ethnic groups and responded to a set of symbols in such a way that it made them feel that they belonged to an ethnic subculture. The data from the Current Population Surveys cited earlier demonstrate that such factors as sex, age, education, and family status do not influence the consistency in the reporting of ethnic identity to a very great extent. The consistency depends on the degree of ethnic awareness and the recency of immigration. Our data also support these generalizations. It should be pointed out that there must be other important symbols that were not included in this analysis. What we have demonstrated is that ethnic identity can be studied utilizing quantitative methodology as long as the thrust of investigation is directed toward cultural symbols. The data from rural and urban India showed that demographic profiles of different ethnic groups (caste groups) were inadequate to demonstrate the content of ethnic identity and the nature of interethnic relations. The respondents provided the ritual rankings of the castes, but the meaning of this differentiation and ranking was rooted in the local culture and could not be fully discerned by examining correlations between caste status, political power, economic status, level of education, and occupational status. Caste identities were embedded in the ritual and belief systems. Even those who attempted to change their caste status have done so by emulating the life styles of the upper castes. The process itself involves discarding one set of cultural symbols for the other.

Preferences for food, music, religious rituals, friends, neighborhood, and use of language or dialect defined ethnic identity and were practiced in both the United States and India. There are other symbols that are more commonly shared in the one society than in the other. For instance, widow marriage and the purity-pollution scale are more important in India than in the United States, while color is more salient in the United States than in India. We strongly believe that the conceptualization of ethnicity through cultural symbols is an appropriate approach in cross-cultural research. Participant observation is the most efficient method of identification of symbol systems; however, a representative sample of respondents may be asked to identify symbols that best describe their ethnic identifications. In addition, the contexts in which symbolic participation varies widely should be explored. The comparison of modes of symbolic participation in different contexts provides cultural interpretations of the symbol systems and facilitates the search for functionally equivalent symbols across societies and within a society across time. Through this process an inventory of symbols could be produced that would promote the development of a science of symbols and contribute to the understanding of ethnic identity in particular and interethnic relations in general.

SUMMARY

This paper shows that ethnic identity can best be understood by studying symbol systems across time and space. The data from the United States and India are used to demonstrate the strengths of this approach. The data from six neighborhoods in Pittsburgh confirm that about two-thirds of the respondents identify with an ethnic group. Ethnic consciousness and recency of immigration are strongly associated with consistency in objective and subjective ethnic identifications. Use of a second language (other than English) and the desire to speak an ethnic language or dialect and to visit places associated with one's ethnic background are not strongly associated with recency of immigration. But consumption of ethnic foods, music, and newspapers is slightly higher among recent immigrant groups than the others. They also recognize greater ethnic "differences" than "similarities." The data from India show that associations between caste and other status variables are inadequate to explain caste identifications. Symbols associated with commensality, endogamy, residential patterns, rituals, folk songs and dances, and festivals and other important events better explain the dynamics of the caste system. Emphasis on ascriptive dimensions utilizing a symbolic approach promotes conceptual clarity and methodological sophistication in the comparative study of ethnic identity.

ACKNOWLEDGMENTS

I am thankful to Jiri Nehnevajsa for his encouragement and help during the various phases of the study of ethnicity in Pittsburgh carried out during 1974–75 by the Center for Urban Research, and to Henry Wong for his assistance in the analysis of data reported here for that project. Connie Wicklow's assistance in various capacities throughout and Phillip Windell's help in the earlier phases of the project are also greatly appreciated.

REFERENCES

1. GLAZER, N. & D. P. MOYNIHAN. Eds. 1975. Ethnicity: Theory and Experience. Harvard University Press. Cambridge, Mass.
2. GLAZER, N. & P. MOYNIHAN. 1975. Introduction. *In* Glazer and Moynihan[1]: 15–18.
3. *Ibid.*: 4.
4. BELL, D. 1975. Ethnicity and social change. *In* Glazer and Moynihan[1]: 155–157.
5. PARSONS, T. 1975. Some theoretical considerations on the nature and trends of change of ethnicity. *In* Glazer and Moynihan[1]: 56–57.
6. HOROWITZ, D. L. 1975. Ethnic identity. *In* Glazer and Moynihan[1]: 113.
7. BARTH, F. Ed. 1969. Ethnic Groups and Boundaries. Little, Brown. Boston, Mass.
8. *Ibid.*: 13.
9. BERREMAN, G. D. 1966. Concomitants of caste organization. *In* Japan's Invisible Race: Caste in Culture and Personality. George DeVos and Hiroshi Wagatsuma, Eds.: 308–324. University of California Press. Berkeley, Calif.
10. BERREMAN, G. D. 1960. Caste in India and the United States. Am. J. Sociol. **66**: 120–127.
11. WEBER, M. 1946. Max Weber: Essays in Sociology. H. M. Gerth and C. Wright Mills, Eds.: 188–190. Oxford University Press. New York, N.Y.
12. BARTH, F. *Ibid.*: 27–28.
13. BELL, D. 1975. *In* Glazer and Moynihan[1]: 166–169.
14. HOROWITZ, D. L. 1975. *In* Glazer and Moynihan[1]: 111–140.
15. PARSONS, T. 1975. *In* Glazer and Moynihan[1]: 60–61.
16. SAPIR, E. 1934. Symbolism. *In* Encyclopedia of the Social Sciences, Vol. 14. E. R. A. Seligman and A. Johnson, Eds.: 492–493. Macmillan. New York, N.Y.
17. GEERTZ, C. 1964. Ideology as a Cultural System. *In* Ideology and Discontent. David E. Apter, Ed.: 63. The Free Press, New York, N.Y.
18. SCHERMERHORN, R. A. 1970. Comparative Ethnic Relations: A. Framework for Theory and Research: 12. Random House. New York, N.Y.
19. BARTH, F. *Ibid.*: 15.
20. JOHNSON, C. E. 1974. Consistency of Reporting of Ethnic Origin in the Current Population Survey. U.S. Government Printing Office. Washington, D.C.
21. GUPTA, J. D. 1975. Ethnicity, language demands, and national development in India. *In* Glazer and Moynihan[1]: 471.
22. SINGH, V. P. 1976. Unity in diversity: The dynamics of ethnic relations in South Asia. *In* Ethnic Relations in Asia. T. S. Kang, Ed. Council on International Studies, State University of New York at Buffalo.
23. GUPTA, J. D. *Ibid.*: 476–477.
24. McDONALD, E. E. 1968. The Growth of Regional Consciousness in Maharashtra. Reprint No. 322: 236. Center for South Asian Studies, Institute of International Studies, University of California. Berkeley, Calif.
25. *Ibid.*: 240–243.
26. SINGH, V. P. 1976. Caste, Class and Democracy: Changes in a Stratification System. Schenkman Publishing Co. Cambridge, Mass.
27. SRINIVAS, M. N. 1956. A note on Sanskritization and westernization. Far East. Quart. **15**: 481–496.
28. MEHTA, S. K. 1969. Patterns of Residence in Poona, India, by caste and religion: 1822–1965. Demography **6**: 473–491.
29. BERREMAN, G. D. 1975. Bazar behavior: Social identity and social interaction in urban India. *In* Ethnic Identity: Cultural Continuities and Change. George DeVos and Lola Romanucci-Ross, Eds.: 84. Mayfield Publishing Company. Palo Alto, Calif.

THEORY AND METHOD IN BIOSOCIAL PSYCHOLOGY: A NEW APPROACH TO CROSS-CULTURAL PSYCHOLOGY

John L. M. B. Dawson

Department of Psychology
University of Hong Kong
Hong Kong

INTRODUCTION

The purpose of this paper is to discuss a new approach to cross-cultural psychology that seeks both to minimize and control for a number of problem areas in earlier research. Thus many of these studies have failed to recognize that there are certain other important independent variables involved in cross-cultural studies, in addition to the reported variables. These include the physical and psychological effects of living in different ecologies, differences in climatic adaptation, varying nutritional intake, the effects of living in different types of subsistence societies, the effects of diseases and parasitic infection, differences in population density, living in a "carpentered" versus "noncarpentered" world, and urban-rural and traditional-modern differences. Furthermore, many of these earlier studies have also failed to measure important intervening variables between the independent and dependent variables such as socialization and ecological experience.

Thus the biosocial approach was developed to endeavor to overcome many of these difficulties involved in cross-cultural research. This new approach was presented in my inaugural lecture.[1] A further study of the psychological effects of biosocial change in West Africa has also been completed by me,[2] and a textbook on the subject of human ecology and behavior will be published soon.[3]

THEORETICAL BASES OF BIOSOCIAL PSYCHOLOGY

The biosocial psychological approach has been developed to facilitate the study of biological and social environmental influences on adaptive behavioral responses. The term "biosocial psychology" is preferred to "ecological psychology" or "environmental psychology," since it is better able to emphasize the important interaction between the biological and social independent variables in influencing adaptive psychological behavior.

The biosocial psychological approach is presented as a psychological system. According to Marx and Hillix,[4] a system "is inclusive and organizes theories which themselves possess generality" (p. 66). Thus the biosocial psychological approach is presented as a psychological system that can facilitate and direct the study of the psychological effects of biosocial adaptation to different environments.

The biosocial psychological system would not therefore be expected as a system to generate specific experimental hypotheses, but these would be derived from other psychological theories, applied to biosocial research. Thus a good example of this process is provided in the biosocial studies by Dawson[1,2,5] and

46

Berry.[6] These researches involved a biosocial approach in selected subsistence societies, applying the psychological differentiation theories of Witkin,[7,8] to examine the effects of different ecosystems on the development of adaptive socialization pressures, which further encourage the emergence of the appropriate spatial-perceptual and other behavioral skills that have survival value for these different societies, e.g., hunting, fishing, agricultural or pastoral.

Biosocial psychology as a psychological system therefore seeks to understand the way in which adaptation to different biological environments results in the formation of adaptive social systems, which in turn influence the development of habits of perceptual inference, cognitive processes, behavioral skills, attitudes and values which are thought to have survival value for specific ecosystems. Although biosocial problems arise in modern environments in terms of overcrowding, isolation, territoriality and poverty, these problems are very difficult to analyze because of the diverse nature of such societies.

Brislin et al.[9] in their discussion on biosocial psychology noted "that the above statement abridges a point of view which has generated considerable research. It also summarizes a psychological ecological perspective which seemingly has endless research potential" (p. 180–81). They go on to state that these so-called organismic positions are popular among nearly all behavioral scientists for, as Hall et al.[10] have reminded us, "Who believes that there are isolated events, insulated processes, detached functions? .... We are all organismic psychologists whatever else we may be" (p. 330).

Recent work concerning evolution by Hamburg,[11] Washburn,[12] and Dobzhansky[13] has provided a major link in the biosocial conceptual system since social organization has also been shown to have functioned in evolution as biological adaptation. Hamburg[14] has observed that "group living has conferred a powerful selective advantage," since this includes "protection against predators, the meeting of nutritional requirements, protection against climatic variation, coping with injuries, facilitating reproduction, and preparing the young to meet the requirements and exploit the opportunities of a given environment, whatever its characteristics may be" (p. xii).

Thus social organization has been demonstrated to have functioned as biological adaptation in evolution, which through socialization encouraged the development of those behavioral characteristics that have survival value. Hence those individuals involved in meeting group needs acquire, through the appropriate education and socialization processes, those group skills listed above, which have survival value for specific societies. Furthermore, as these group skills also have considerable social value, as McLearn[15] has stated, such individuals are adapted to the social structure and would therefore have "an enhanced capacity to survive and reproduce" (p. 164), thus selectively ensuring the hereditary bases of these abilities.

This point has also been emphasized by Montagu[16] who has shown "that culture affected not only man's social evolution but also his physical evolution in a process of reciprocating interactive feedback. In this process cultural challenges put a high selective premium on those individuals possessing the necessary abilities to respond successfully — that is to say those possessing the necessary genes" (p. v).

McLearn[15] has also pointed out the need to study the selective pressures that facilitate the development of those behavioral skills needed for survival in industrial and nonindustrial cultures. This, he states, is to better understand the development of those specific behavioral characteristics, such as individual differences in intelligence, aggression, curiosity and emotion, evolved in response to different environments, so that new insights can be gained into those selection pressures that have influenced our present development.

Therefore one of the key links in biosocial psychology concerns the way in which culture has functioned in evolution as biological adaptation, thus permitting the tranmission by socialization and cultural norm enforcement, of these individual behavioral skills needed for survival. Hence Doby[17] argues that "culture is a form of adaptation peculiar to man" (p. 54), and that responses that promote survival, health and reproduction are adaptive responses. Furthermore, Kessler[18] has also observed that the main function of social organization has been to extend the range of behavioral adaptabilities, thereby maximizing the types of relationships that species can make with increasingly diverse types of environments.

Additionally, Dobzhansky[19] in a very important study has argued "that culture is generally a much more rapid and effective method of adaptation to the environment than genetic change" (p. 130). Thus "the more dependent mankind becomes on culture as his chief adaptive instrument, the greater the biological under-pinnings of cultures secure, and thus permit further cultural developments" (p. 131).

Additional evidence that adaptation to different biological environments also results in differences in biosocial adaptation comes from Barry et al.,[20] who studied 104 societies, predicting that those with "hunting and fishing economies" would have "low food accumulation" and that adults should be individualistic and independent, while "agriculturalists" would have "high food accumulation" and should tend to be firm and compliant. They further predicted that socialization in these different societies would reflect the application of the appropriate child-training, with hunters permissive and agriculturalists harsh and conforming. Although this analysis was done through the Yale Human Relations Area Files, the data showed significant relationships between the type of subsistence economy and socialization practices. Their original findings have now been confirmed in cross-cultural research by Dawson[1-3,5] and Berry,[6] thus providing support for biosocial psychological theory and confirming the adaptive link between the biological environment and adaptive social organization.

They concluded that the hunting ecosystem results in pressures to "shape children into venturesome independent adults who can take the initiative in wresting food daily from nature and thus ensure survival in societies with low food accumulation" (p. 63). In direct contrast, the agricultural ecosystem results in higher pressures towards "obedience and responsibility which should tend to make children into obedient and responsible adults who can best ensure the welfare of a society with a high food accumulation economy, whose food supplies must be protected and developed gradually throughout the year" (p. 62).

HISTORICAL ANTECEDENTS OF THE BIOSOCIAL APPROACH

Before discussing the biosocial psychological system, certain early theoretical influences relevant to this system are examined. The roots of biosocial psychology are visible in the work of Darwin and "functional psychology," which was concerned with the function of the organism's behavior in its adaptation to its environment. Darwin[21] and James[22] represented strong early influences in functional psychology, while the formal definition of the theory was due to Angell.[23]

Woodworth,[24] a more recent advocate of functionalism, also noted that Weiss[25] coined the term "biosocial" to characterize human behavior. Thus Weiss, an early behaviorist, was quoted by Woodworth as stating that, "While recognizing the social character of human behavior we must not forget that it is biological at the same time" (p. 96). Murphy[26] has also used the term biosocial to indicate that what is biological is at the same time social. Thus he argues that "The biosocial does not constitute a special class of biological events; practically any biological event can be socially controlled to a visibly recognized degree" (p. 138).

However, while agreeing with Weiss and Murphy that man is a biosocial organism, the main theoretical difference in the present paper is that while man is considered functionally as both a biological and social organism, his biosocial behavior is also studied within a biosocial system (FIGURE 1) involving the study of the interacting effects of the biological and social independent variables on the biosocial psychological dependent variables.

RECENT DEVELOPMENTS IN HUMAN ECOLOGY AND BEHAVIOR

There has recently been a revival of interest in understanding functional relationships between man and environment, resulting in extensive research in both environmental and ecological psychology. Wohwill,[27] in his paper on the emergence of the discipline of environmental psychology, reported that while psychologists have talked about environmental influences, they have rarely, except for the ecological psychologists,[28] been specific about the concept. He emphasized that for the new discipline to succeed it must define and establish conceptual boundaries, while there must also be a receptiveness to interdisciplinary activity.

A collection of readings by Proshansky et al.[29] has been concerned with examining the present status of environmental psychology, while a more recent introduction to environmental psychology has also been published by Ittelson et al.[30] However, it is argued that while the concept of environmental psychology has considerable value in certain contexts, it is in many respects rather limited for it does not emphasize the adaptive relationships that exist between environment, the social system and behavior. Thus it is held that the biosocial approach is better able to analyze these interactions involved in the study of man as a "biosocial organism" within a biosocial ecosystem.

Furthermore, while Barker's[28] concept of "behavior settings" developed within an ecological psychology system is considered to be extremely useful, it is argued that there is insufficient emphasis on the study of the adaptive relationships that exist between behavior settings and related social settings, and the subsequent analysis of these biosocial effects on the individual. So his system only emphasizes the study of the biological environment and behavior, but not the actual biosocial adaptive relationships that are formed between ecology and culture, an analysis of which is crucial for the effective understanding of behavior in specific societies.

In view of these recent theoretical advances concerning the understanding of culture functioning as biological adaptation in evolution, it is again possible to look at the role of environment in eliciting both adaptive social organization and appropriate behavioral skills needed for survival. These new findings have therefore contributed to the formulation of this biosocial psychological system. Moreover, while the functionalists were concerned with adaptive acts in relation to the general concept of environment, they were not concerned with adaptation to specific environments.

Biosocial psychological theory has consequently been developed as a psychological system to facilitate the study of the adaptive biosocial behavior of individuals in different subsistence and modern societies. This approach is not deterministic, but endeavors to achieve flexibility, while the effects of biological and social (biosocial) change are also incorporated into the system. It is also argued that this biosocial system can greatly advance psychological theory in discovering the regularities in the way in which different biosocial ecosystems result in the development of the appropriate behavioral skills needed for survival.

This type of approach is also extremely useful because it brings together a number of disciplines to study more effectively the complex relationships between the organism and the environment. In this regard Glass[31] has commented that "contemporary social scientists no longer adhere to a simplistic environmental determinism, just as contemporary biologists no longer embrace a genetic determinism. In both fields there is an increasing recognition of the importance of an interaction between the organism and the environment" (p. v). Hence the biosocial approach, drawing on the experience of other disciplines, provides an interdisciplinary focal point for studying these complex interacting relationships between the organism and the environment.

ASSESSMENT OF THE BIOLOGICAL AND SOCIAL (BIOSOCIAL) INDEPENDENT VARIABLES

The term "biological environment" includes the physical and living elements, geography, geology, topography, physical features, climate, food resources, altitude, and the relationships of living organisms to that environment. Environment thus represents the totality of the community surroundings. Biological environments are also classified from moderate environments, which carry fewer problems of human adaptation, to extreme environments, where related social organization and other human adaptive responses must also be highly adaptive and closely related to the needs of the extreme environment to ensure survival. The term "biological deficiency" is used to describe those abnormal aspects of the environment such as disease, malnutrition, extreme poverty, overcrowding or isolation, which generally occur in more extreme biological environments.

"Human ecology" is concerned with the dynamic interrelationship of the community and its total environment, which consists of a continuous exchange of materials and energy. Harrison et al.[32] note that adjustments necessary for successful existence in a particular habitat are termed "adaptations." "Adaptability" is a property of each of the individuals making up the group as well as of the group as a whole. The term "ecosystem" is defined as a fundamental biological entity since it is a going concern involving the actual living community satisfying its needs in dynamic relation with the environment.

The scales used to measure those intervening variables between the biological environment (independent variables) and the individual (dependent variable) include the ecological type surveys of Brunswik[33] and Segall et al.,[34] in which experiences of carpentered/noncarpentered and horizontal/closed environments are measured. There is also an ecological index, which can measure physique/somatype, nutritional intake, climatic adaptation, disease and ecological experience.[3]

The most important aspects of social organization to study in biosocial research are those adaptive socialization and educational processes (e.g., *rites de passage*) that tend in subsistence societies to be the key link tetween type of ecology and behavior that reinforce the dominant attitudes and values for that society, whether hunting, fishing, pastoral or agricultural.

It is also important to examine the relevant ethnographic, anthropological and linguistic background of those socieites involved in biosocial research. The Human Relations Area Files and anthropological texts by Kroeber[35] and Beattie[36] are very useful, as is the text by Callan.[37] Also of relevance to biosocial studies are studies of territoriality reported by Johnson,[38] while Klopfer[39] has also noted that territorial behavior had an effect on evolution, as spatial isolation also contributed to the development of small random mutations which eventually led to divisions of populations.

The measures of modernity used in these biosocial research studies are discussed in the concluding sections of this paper. The construction of these scales further allows the assessment and ranging of these different sociocultural ecosystems in terms of traditional, semitraditional, semimodern, and modern aspects of behavior. These traditional-modern (T-M) scales have been constructed for use in West Africa, Australia, Hong Kong, Japan and Alaska.[1-3,40]

THE BIOSOCIAL PSYCHOLOGICAL SYSTEM

The biosocial psychological system is shown diagramatically in FIGURE 1. The examples of the biosocial independent and dependent variables shown are meant to be examples and do not of course represent all possible biosocial research problems.

Biosocial psychology as a psychological system is concerned with the effects of the independent variables, biological and sociocultural (biosocial) stimuli, on the dependent variables, physiological and psychological (biosocial) processes. The initial black arrow at the top of FIGURE 1 going from the biological environment to the sociocultural environment indicates that the biological environment is held to influence the nature of the cultural system evolved in response to the needs of the biological environment. Thus, for individuals to survive in a specific biological environment, an adaptive sociocultural system must be evolved for that environment, which through appropriate socialization encourages the development of the specific behavioral skills needed for survival.

The broken arrow in FIGURE 1 going from sociocultural to biological indicates that as man gains increasing mastery over his environment, he evolves more sophisticated cultural adaptations and new technologies. Such societies further develop more efficient cultural systems, which in turn results in partial mastery over and further changes in the biological environment, such as irrigation, the building of bridges, canals, dams, buildings, cities, planes and ships.

Consequently, by a series of cultural adaptations man gains increasing mastery over his biological environment, becoming at the same time increasingly independent of his biological environment. However, even in the most advanced societies, the cultural system generally still reflects those aspects of culture developed in response to the initial processes of adaptation to the biological environment. A good example of this is in the United States, where values evolved by early settlers in adapting to the North American environment are still very evident, as are also the effects of the Protestant Ethic.

Some of the direct effects of the biological environment on the human organism are listed on the left of FIGURE 1. The first concerns the effects of climate and selective nutrition on physique. Thus Bergmann and Allen's "Ecological Rules" state that with increasing mean annual temperature, body size becomes shorter and limb length longer with the development of thinner, more linear physiques.[32] These processes are also reinforced by selective nutrition: for example, the Eskimo has a traditionally high fat/protein and low carbohydrate diet, while the East African Kikuyu has a high carbohydrate, but low fat/protein diet. Kwashiorkor (protein deficiency disease) also has serious physiological and psychological effects.[41] Moreover, disease and parasitic infection cause physical and psychological disturbances and are selective agents for resistance.[32]

Furthermore, living in different ecologies also results in differences in perceptual inference systems and changes in illusion susceptibility, which can be measured using the "Carpentered-World" and "Horizontal-Vertical" illusions.[34] Individuals living in traditional rural villages are generally less susceptible to the Muller-Lyer and Sander-Parallelogram illusions than those living in carpentered urban environments. Individuals living in open desert and snow develop habits of perceptual inference that allow them to interpret short lines on the retina as long lines extending into space and thus they become more susceptible to the Horizontal-Vertical illusions than those living in closed jungle and urban environments.

The section on the right of FIGURE 1 is concerned with the effects of adaptive sociocultural systems on individual behavior, attitudes and values. Thus adaptive sociocultural systems are held to have evolved from adaptation to specific biological environments, e.g., agricultural, pastoral, hunting, fishing, mountains, or modern. These sociocultural systems in turn, through appropriate educational socialization pressures as well as through indigenous linguistic systems, develop those attitudes, values, perceptual inference systems, personality traits, and other behavioral skills needed to maintain the necessary degree of adaptive control over specific biological environments.

In more extreme environments, such as snow, desert, jungle or high mountains, highly adaptive social systems and psychological skills are found, which are needed to ensure survival in such environments. Thus, Dawson[1-3,5] and Berry,[6] using the Witkin psychological differentiation theories,[7,8] have confirmed that harsh socialization found in stratified agricultural societies results in lower spatial-perceptual skills, while permissive socialization interacts with natural selection processes in hunting and fishing ecosystems to increase field-independence, spatial-perceptual skills, and to improve spatial orientation, which is also reinforced for the Eskimo hunters by a system of linguistic spatial localizers.

The effects of overcrowding and isolation shown in FIGURE 1 are also very complex and again demonstrate many interactions between direct physiological influences and cultural adaptations. Among Hong Kong Chinese these interactions appear to lessen the effects of overcrowding. Hamburg[14] has reported that high population density is associated with increases in adrenal function and aggressive behavior and a decrease in gonadal function. As depicted

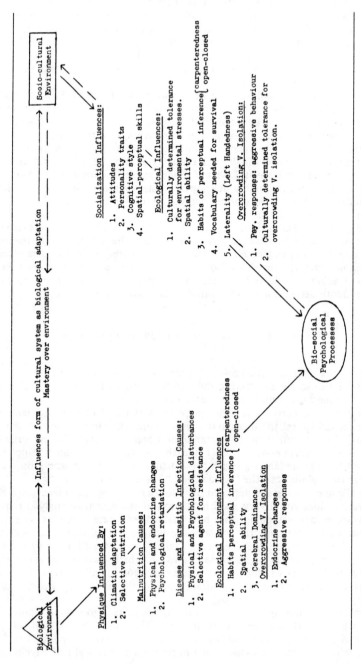

FIGURE 1. The biosocial psychological system. Dependent variables are included under each independent variable shown above.

in FIGURE 1, there is an interaction between physical overcrowding and increased social pressures. Hence it is postulated that people from group-oriented agricultural societies would have a higher culturally determined threshold level to stresses from physical overcrowding than, for example, individuals from isolated snow or hunting environments. Thus the more individually oriented Eskimo and Arunta hunters would be expected to have a lower threshold for the physical effects of overcrowding.

The biosocial psychological system shown in FIGURE 1 is extremely complex and represents the interacting effects of the biological and sociocultural environments as they influence individual biosocial psychological processes. In advanced societies the biosocial environments, often through cultural adaptation, become more technological, but even at that stage some of the cultural influences that originally determined the processes of adaptation to the biological environment are still evident. For example, the present-day Australian Arunta hunters produce highly developed artistic paintings that are completely three-dimensional in representing depth, using the same spatial skills that enabled these Central Australian aborigines to survive in a semidesert locality. Similarly, the Alaskan Eskimo hunters have in transition developed extremely sophisticated three-dimensional art forms, while the art forms of the more conforming field-dependent agriculturalists are invariably more two-dimensional. The Temne agriculturalists' level of pictorial depth perception, even after six months' teaching, could only be improved from 5.6% three-dimensionality on pictorial depth perception to 42.6% three-dimensionality.[2]

A TEMNE VILLAGE AGRICULTURAL ECOSYSTEM

The results of a biosocial research program among the Temne are shown in FIGURE 2 below, demonstrating the complex interactions involved in a West African Temne agricultural village ecosystem.[2]

The Temne, occupying 11,000 square miles and 39% of the total land area, are the second largest tribal group in Sierra Leone. They live in the northern half of Sierra Leone and have 29 Paramount Chiefdoms. The Temne originally migrated to Sierra Leone in the fifteenth century from Guinea. Kup[42] has classified the Temne language with the Northen Atlantic linguistic group, while there are two subdialects, the "Sande" and "Yonni Temne."

The Temne ecosystem depicted in FIGURE 2 is by no means complete. However, it does give a very good indication of the extensive analysis required before some understanding can be obtained of these complex interacting variables that determine the biosocial psychological processes of individual Temne. For example, the Temne socialization and authority systems are controlled by a system of social sanctions, in which "witchcraft accusations" and "swears" ensure the highly conforming and compliant behavior needed for the successful harvesting and accumulation of the basic crop (rice) over the "hungry period."

Furthermore, during weaning, Temne mothers also give their infants "rice pap," which is almost devoid of protein. This, plus the lack of adequate supplementary foods, contributes to the extensive kwashiorkor found in Sierra Leone, which in extreme cases results in permanent physical and psychological damage.[2,32,41]

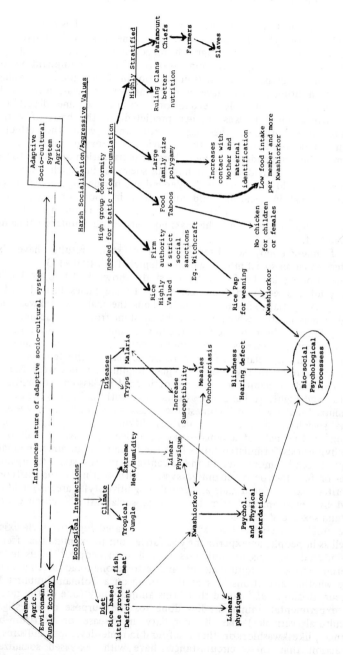

FIGURE 2. A West African Temne agricultural village ecosystem. Dependent variables are listed above.

BIOSOCIAL ADAPTATION AND COGNITIVE STYLE

The Temne/Mende/Eskimo studies and Temne/Arunta studies carried out by Dawson[1,2,5] and Berry[6] involved a theoretical framework partly derived from the findings by Barry et al.[20] that agricultural societies have harsh socialization pressures needed to encourage development of obedient and compliant behavior for effective harvesting and accumulation of crops in static agricultural villages, while nomadic hunting societies have more permissive socialization required to develop the independent attitudes needed for survival in extreme (desert/snow) ecological environments. It was further predicted on the basis of Witkin's psychological differentiation theories,[7,8] concerned with the effect of socialization on field-independence, that individuals from agricultural societies would be more field-dependent, owing to harsher socialization pressures towards conformity, whereas individuals from hunting societies, in which socialization was permissive, would be more field-independent, having higher spatial skills needed for survival in locating food and water in snow or desert. These predictions were confirmed in every case, with the static Temne agriculturalists being more field-dependent and the Eskimo and Arunta hunters being more field-independent.

These Temne-Eskimo socialization/cognitive style results have been incorporated into a biosocial model, which is depicted in FIGURE 3.

A further finding in the Sierra Leone study shown in FIGURE 3 is that kwashiorkor-induced estrogen feminization of Temne males had altered the normally higher spatial skills in the male. Thus the males with kwashiorkor manifested gynecomastia, which is thought to stem from an inability of the kwashiorkor-damaged liver to inactivate the normal amount of estrogen found in the male. The increased estrogen levels are thought to stimulate both the growth of the male mammary gland, so as to resemble that of the female, and the accompanying atrophy of the testicles. These feminized males were found to have, as predicted, a significant reversal of normal sex-associated skills, with lower spatial and higher verbal skills, as contrasted with findings in the controls. These feminized males with gynecomastia were also found to be more vulnerable to maternal socialization processes, which, as Witkin et al.[7,8] note, result in the development in the male of a female-type cognitive style. As a result of this study the hypothesis formulated holds that the brain is programmed neonatally by appropriate sex hormones acting on the central nervous system, to organize it to a male- or female-type of cognitive system, although individual differences from inherited sex-associated male and female cognitive styles are also held to be influenced by environmental stimulation, e.g., socialization,[7] absence of the father,[44] and sex-typed behavior.[45]

Since a number of studies have shown that sex-based cognitive style exists in rats as well as in people, an experiment was carried out to examine the effects of hormone-induced reversals in adult rats as well as in people.[46] This involved administering estrogen to adult male rats and testosterone to adult female rats to determine whether alterations in spatial learning on a Tolman Sunburst Maze would occur. Brislin et al.[9] noted that "this animal study (one of the rare and welcome experimental animal studies done for the purpose of investigating human cultural variables) has its corollary in disease or nutrition-based circumstances, like kwashiorkor, that are found in underdeveloped cultures, and the interaction that these circumstances have with sex-based socialization practices and roles. Dawson's estrogen male rats showed a significant change towards the female spatial learning men after the second try on the Tolman

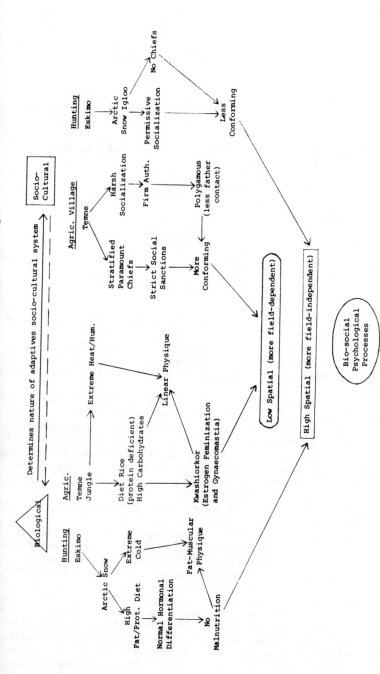

FIGURE 3. Temne-Eskimo biosocial model of sex-hormone differentiation and socialization in the development of cognitive style.

Maze, while no significant changes were found for the testosterone injected females" (p. 185–186). These results supported the hypotheses, while it was also argued that the normal sex difference found on this maze was because females developed a response disposition while males showed a greater degree of place learning.

A more recent developmental study of the effects of these sex-hormone reversals on sex-associated cognitive style in male and female neonate rats showed, as expected, a much greater reversal for both the Activity Wheel, in which normal females are superior, and on the Symmetrical Maze spatial learning, for which normal males are superior. These sex-hormone reversals achieved for both male and female cognitive style were highly significant, thus further confirming the hypotheses.[47]

It was also concluded that "these suggested biological advantages in evolution of higher spatial ability in the human male also help to explain the evolutionary development of a two-way sex hormone relationship with higher male spatial ability and masculine cognitive style, which would have been paralleled by the development of appropriate female perceptual-motor and verbal skills and reproductive activities, also controlled by female hormones in a similar two-way relationship" (p. 39).[46]

THE BIOSOCIAL LATERALITY MODEL

The studies of left-handedness reported in this paper represent an application of the biosocial approach to endeavor to explain cross-cultural differences in left-handedness. This model rejects Annett's purely genetic explanation,[48] and provides biosocial research data from different societies to show that both ecologically determined cultural pressures towards conformity and the genetic model are relevant.

Annett[48] has postulated a model relating to the inheritance of left-handedness and cerebral dominance for which she provided empirical support. It is, however, argued that these hereditary factors cannot adequately explain cross-cultural differences in the incidence of left-handedness, and that these can only be understood in terms of an analysis of ecological pressures to use the right hand. These pressures are held to interact selectively with the genetic model to determine the distribution of handedness in a particular society. This biosocial laterality model is shown in FIGURE 4.

The predominance of the right hand was noted in an analysis of Egyptian artforms 3500–4500 years ago with 9L. to 111R. and 5L. to 100R., respectively. However, going further back, Parello,[49] using the criteria of the Draw-a-Person test, found that from 1,750,000 to 8000 B.C., ancient paleolithic man was either more ambidexterous or that there was a greater proportion of left-handers than there is now. This is an extremely interesting finding that fits in well with the evidence that the main paleolithic economy to 8000 B.C. was hunting, while agriculture began shortly afterwards. Evidence has thus been presented by Dawson[50] to show that among the present-day hunting and fishing peoples left-handedness ranges from 11.3% (the Eskimo), through 10.5% (Arunta), to 9.4% (Hong Kong boat-people), while among the more conforming and compliant agriculturalists, left-handedness ranges from 3.4% (the Temne) through 1.5% (the Chinese Hakka), to 0.59% (the Congo Katanganese). Furthermore, scores on the Asch Conformity Test for these samples has also confirmed that while the Eskimo has extremely independent Asch means, the agriculturalists have extremely conforming means, thus supporting the

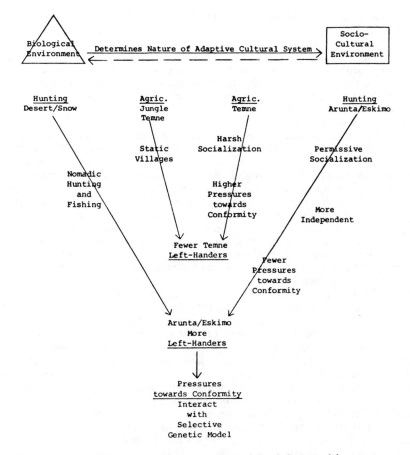

FIGURE 4.   Biosocial psychological left-handedness model.

prediction that these cross-cultural selective pressures towards conformity interact with the genetic model to determine the incidence of left-handedness in a society (FIGURE 4).

It is therefore argued that there has probably been an evolutionary trend from more permissive hunting paleolithic man (more left-handers) to the present majority of the world's population, who have to varying degrees firmer socialization pressures and hence fewer left-handers. Evolutionary evidence has been presented by Levy,[51] who has postulated an evolutionary organizational differentiation of the hemispheres into perceptual and cognitive functions.

A BIOSOCIAL MODEL TO PREDICT SUSCEPTIBILITY TO MODERN CHANGE

It is also important to examine the theoretical implications of biosocial change to see where these variables fit into the biosocial system. Thus, no matter how isolated particular societies may be, e.g., Eskimo, Andean, or Himalayan, all societies at any point in time are undergoing change that on further analysis is biological and social in nature and can therefore be defined as biosocial change.

Furthermore, biosocial change has considerable implications for biosocial psychological theory because an understanding of the effects of biosocial change greatly facilitates the analysis of the precise processes through which psychological skills and attitudes developed through initial biosocial adaptation break down under the impact of rapid biosocial change. This process is selective in nature in subsistence societies, with more important attitudes and values being less susceptible to change.

A biosocial model has been presented which predicts susceptibility to modern change in terms of a traditional-modern (T-M) attitude theory.[2,4] It is then postulated that the potential of a society for modern change can be determined by contrasting agricultural, pastoral, and hunting ecologies, where the traditional subsistence economy can be identified by use of the findings of Barry et al.[20] The model includes the following independent variables: (a) ecology and related subsistence economy, e.g., agricultural, pastoral, hunting and fishing; (b) ecological differences in indigenous authority systems, with agricultural systems stratified and hunting and fishing nonstratified; (c) ecological differences in indigenous socialization pressure with agricultural harsh, mixed pastoral-agricultural severe, pastoral moderate, and hunting-fishing permissive; (d) nature and degree of modern contact.

The effects of these independent variables are then analyzed in relation to the following dependent variables: (a) traditional-modern (T-M) attitude change and attitudinal conflict; (b) achievement motivation; (c) tolerance for cognitive inconsistency in the belief system; (d) potential of a society for economic development. This model is shown in FIGURE 5, and is discussed more fully in the work of Dawson.[2,40] There is extensive evidence to support the model for the agricultural and hunting-fishing societies, in that individuals from agricultural societies have been found to be significantly more susceptible to modern attitude change and have higher motivation and higher potential for economic development than do individuals from hunting and fishing societies.

The T-M attitude change theory states that individuals exposed to conflicting traditional and modern cognitions tend to resolve inconsistency either by the development of adaptive compromise semitraditional or semimodern attitudes; or by such alternate modes of inconsistency reduction as occurs with culturally more important attitudes where peer group support is provided by members of the culture.[52]

Biesheuvel[53] has pointed out how human adaptation to social change "creates stresses of its own which affect man's effectiveness, his physical and mental health, and indirectly on a long-term basis his capacity for survival" (p. 200). Furthermore, it has been confirmed that the resolution of T-M attitudinal conflict (conflicting T-M attitudes) is also involved in this continuing need to adapt to biosocial change. Consequently a failure to achieve compromise T-M attitudes has been found to be related to poorer adjustment under the impact of modern change. This has been confirmed by the Hong Kong G.S.R. (galvanic skin response) experiments, which showed a significant relationship between higher G.S.R. arousal and higher unresolved attitudinal conflict. These studies further confirm the need not only for continuing adjustment under modern pressures, but also for development of more adaptive cognitive styles.

Additionally, in more recent Hong Kong experiments, it has also been demonstrated that successful compromise T-M attitudes are less likely to occur with highly valued traditional attitudes and that these are associated with higher

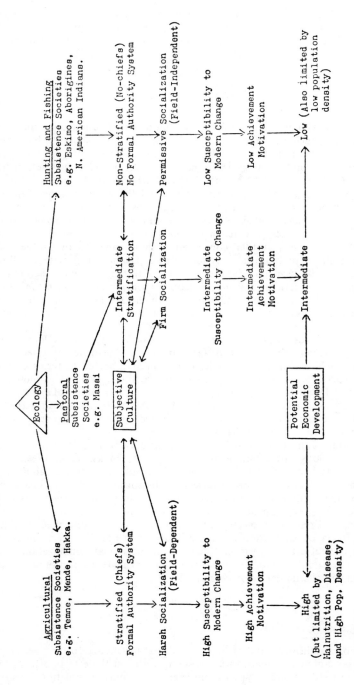

FIGURE 5. A model to predict effects of ecology and subjective culture on motivation for economic development in subsistence societies where modern influences are constant.

T-M attitudinal conflict.[52] Moreover, these more highly valued Chinese attitudes relating to Confucian values were demonstrated under peer group pressure to be less susceptible to modern change, while the less important attitudes were more susceptible.

CONCLUSIONS

Evidence has been presented to show that culture has functioned in evolution as biological adaptation. The validity of this point is fundamental to biosocial psychology as a theoretical system. This evidence has been provided in studies by Hamburg[11,14] and Montagu.[16] It has also been provided in research by Barry et al.,[20] Dawson,[1-3,5] and Berry,[6] who have found significant relationships between biological environments and the emergence of adaptive socialization processes, which in turn encourage those psychological perceptual inference systems, behavioral skills, personality traits, attitudes and values that have survival value for these specific environments.

This paper has been further concerned with an analysis of the general theoretical position of biosocial psychology as a psychological system within which more specific psychological theories can be tested. The early theoretical relationships with functional psychology have been reviewed, as were the more recent studies of human ecology and behavior, which have again confirmed these adaptive links that exist between adaptation to different ecologies, socialization and behavior.

The biosocial research program has also been briefly reviewed, including the analysis of a Temne agricultural village ecosystem. The different effects of Temne-Eskimo biosocial adaptation have also been reported in terms of the effects of socialization and sex hormones on cognitive style. The biosocial laterality model, which attempts to explain conflicting cross-cultural differences in left-handedness, has also been presented. The final section has dealt with the biosocial T-M modernity model, which is designed to predict susceptibility of subsistence societies to modern change.

An important aim of all biosocial research has been to subject these findings obtained in various cross-cultural studies, such as the kwashiorkor-estrogen feminization studies and T-M modernity findings, to intensive laboratory investigations to determine more precisely the biosocial psychological bases of these phenomena, thereby both further extending psychological theory as well as increasing the experimental internal validity of these findings.[46,47,52] Further biosocial research projects currently proceeding are concerned with the biosocial effects of adaptation to high altitudes, cultural differences in color blindness, the effects of varying degrees of hormonal feminization and environmental stimulation on cognitive style, and varying levels of protein intake and environmental stimulation on cognitive style.

SUMMARY

Since more traditional studies of cross-cultural psychology often neglect to control important independent variables stemming from the effects of climate, nutrition, altitude, ecology, type of subsistence economy, population density, etc., which covary with the variables under study, and influence behavior, a new biosocial research approach has therefore been evolved that seeks to analyze the interacting effects of the biological and social (biosocial) independent variables on behavior. Thus biosocial psychology is concerned with the study of adaptation to different biological environments that results in the development of particular habits of perceptual inference, cognitive processes, attitudes, values, and other behavioral skills that have survival value for different ecologies, e.g., desert, snow, jungle, mountains, pastoral plains, rural or modern. The theoretical and research bases of biosocial psychology are presented as well as studies of biosocial adaptation and cognitive style, handedness, and modernity.

REFERENCES

1. DAWSON, J. L. M. 1969. Theoretical and research bases of bio-social psychology. Univ. Hong Kong Gaz. 16 (3): 1–10.
2. DAWSON, J. L. M. 1975. Psychological Effects of Bio-social Change in West Africa. HRAFlex Press. New Haven, Conn.
3. DAWSON, J. L. M. & J. NASH. Human ecology and behavior: A textbook in bio-social psychology. In preparation.
4. MARX, M. H. & W. A. HILLIX, Eds. 1973. Systems and Theories in Psychology, 2nd Ed. McGraw-Hill. New York, N.Y.
5. DAWSON, J. L. M. 1963. Psychological effects of social change in a West African community. Doctoral thesis, University of Oxford.
6. BERRY, J. W. 1966. Temne and Eskimo perceptual skills. Internat J. Psychol. 1 (3): 207–229.
7. WITKIN, H. A. R. B. DYK, H. F. FATERSON, D. E. GOODENOUGH & S. A. KARP. 1962. Psychological differentiation. Wiley. New York, N.Y.
8. WITKIN, H. A. 1967. A cognitive style approach to cross-cultural research. Internat. J. Psychol. 2 (4): 233–250.
9. BRISLIN, R. W., W. J. LONNER, & R. M. THORNDIKE. 1973. Cross-cultural Research Methods. Wiley. New York, N.Y.
10. HALL, C. A. & G. LINDZEY. 1970. Theories of Personality, 2nd Ed. Wiley. New York, N.Y.
11. HAMBURG, D. 1963. Emotions in the perspective of human evolution. In Expression of the Emotions in Man. P. Knapp, Ed.: 300–317. International Universities Press. New York, N.Y.
12. WASHBURN, S. 1963. Classification and Human Evolution. Aldine. Chicago, Ill.
13. DOBZHANSKY, T. 1962. Mankind Evolving. Yale University Press. New Haven, Conn.
14. HAMBURG, D. 1965. Foreword. In Psychobiological Approaches to Social Behavior. P. H. Leiderman and D. Shapiro, Eds.: IX–XV. Tavistock Publications. London, England.
15. McLEARN, G. E. 1968. Social implications of behavioural genetics. In Genetics. D. C. Glass, Ed.: 164–168. Rockefeller University Press. New York, N.Y.
16. MONTAGU, M. F. A. 1968. Culture: Man's Adaptive Dimension. Oxford University Press. New York, N.Y.
17. DOBY, J. T. 1966. Introduction to Social Psychology. Appleton-Century Crofts. New York, N.Y.
18. KESSLER, R. A. 1968. Social behaviour and population dynamics: Evolutionary relationships. In Genetics. D. C. Glass, Ed.: 169–179. Rockefeller University Press. New York, N.Y.
19. DOBZHANSKY, T. 1968. Genetics and the social sciences. In Genetics. D. C. Glass, Ed.: 129–143. Rockefeller University Press. New York, N.Y.
20. BARRY, H., I. CHILD & M. BACON, 1959. Relation of child training to subsistence economy. Am. Anthrop. 6: 51–63.

21. DARWIN, C., 1872. Expressions of Emotions in Man and Animals, 2nd Ed. Collier. London, England.
22. JAMES, W. 1890. The Principles of Psychology. Holt. New York, N.Y.
23. ANGELL, J. R. 1904. Psychology: An Introductory Study of the Structure and Function of Human Consciousness. Holt. New York, N.Y.
24. WOODWORTH, R. S. 1951. Contemporary Schools of Psychology. Methuen. London, England.
25. WEISS, A. P. 1930. The bio-social standpoint in psychology. *In* Psychologies of 1930. G. Murchison, Ed. Clark University Press. Worcester, Mass.
26. MURPHY, G. 1966. Personality: A Bio-social Approach to Origins and Structure. Basic Books. New York, N.Y.
27. WOHWILL, J. F. 1970. The emerging discipline of environmental psychology. Am. Psychol. **25** (4): 303–312.
28. BARKER, R. G. 1968. Ecological Psychology. Stanford University Press. Palo Alto, Calif.
29. PROSHANSKY, H. M., W. H. ITTELSON & L. G. RIVLIN. 1970. Environmental Psychology. Holt, Rinehart & Winston. New York, N.Y.
30. ITTELSON, W. H., H. M. PROSHANSKY, L. G. RIVLIN & G. H. WINKEL. 1974. An Introduction to Environmental Psychology. Holt, Rinehart & Winston. New York. N.Y.
31. GLASS, D. C., Ed. 1968. Genetics. Rockefeller University Press. New York. N.Y.
32. HARRISON, G. A., J. S. WEINER, J. M. TANNER & N. A. BARNICOT. 1964. Human Biology. Clarendon Press. Oxford, England.
33. BRUNSWIK, E. 1955. Representative design and probabilistic theory in a functional psychology. Psychol. Rev. **62**:-193–217.
34. SEGALL, M. H., D. T. CAMPBELL & M. J. HERSKOVITS. 1966. The Influence of Culture in Visual Perception. Bobbs-Merrill. Indianapolis, Ind.
35. KROEBER, A. L. 1957. Anthropology, 2nd Ed. Harcourt, Brace. New York, N.Y.
36. BEATTIE, J. 1964. Other Cultures. Cohen & West. London, England.
37. CALLAN, H. C. 1970. Ethology and Society: Towards an Anthropological View. Clarendon Press. Oxford, England.
38. JOHNSON, R. N. 1972. Aggression in Man and Animals. Saunders. Philadelphia, Pa.
39. KLOPFER, P. H. 1969. Habitats and Territories. Basic Books. New York, N.Y.
40. DAWSON, J. L. M. 1973. Effects of ecology and subjective culture on individual traditional-modern attitude change, achievement motivation, and potential for economic development in the Japanese and Eskimo societies. Internat. J. Psychol. **8** (3): 215–225.
41. SCRIMSHAW, N. S. & J. E. GORDON, Eds. 1968. Malnutrition, Learning and Behavior. M.I.T. Press. Boston, Mass.
42. KUP, P. 1961. A History of Sierra Leone. Cambridge University Press. Cambridge, England.
43. STUART-MASON, A. 1963. Health and Hormones. Pelican. London, England.
44. KUCKENBERG, L. 1953. Effects of early father absence on scholastic aptitude. Harvard University. Unpublished Bachelor's thesis.
45. BANDURA, A. 1969. Social learning theory of identificatory processes. *In* Handbook of Socialization Theory and Research. D. A. Goslin, Ed. Rand McNally. New York, N.Y.
46. DAWSON, J. L. M. 1972. Effects of sex hormones on cognitive style in rats and men. Behav. Genet. **2** (1): 21–42.
47. DAWSON, J. L. M., Y. M. CHEUNG & R. T. S. LAU. 1975. Developmental effects of neonatal sex hormones on spatial and activity skills in the white rat. Biol. Psychol. In press.
48. ANNETT, M. 1964. A model of the inheritance of handedness and cerebral dominance. Nature **204**: 59–60.
49. PARELLO, J. 1970. Digressions on the biological foundations of language. J. Comm. Disord. **3**: 140–149.
50. DAWSON, J. L. M., 1972. Temne-Arunta hand-eye dominance and cognitive style. Internat. J. Psychol. **7** (4): 219–233.

51. LEVY, J. 1969. Possible basis for the evolution of lateral specialization of the human brain. Nature **224**: 614–615.
52. DAWSON, J. L. M., R. E. WHITNEY & R. T. S. LAU. 1972. Attitude conflict, GSR, and traditional-modern attitude change among Hong Kong Chinese. J. Soc. Psychol. **88**: 165–176.
53. BIESHEUVEL, S. 1968. Psychology and the international biological year programme. Internat. J. Psychol. **3** (3): 199–207.

FROM CORRELATIONS TO CAUSES:
A NEW AND SIMPLE METHOD FOR CAUSAL ANALYSIS IN CROSS-CULTURAL RESEARCH*

William Tulio Divale

Department of Anthropology
York College of the City University of New York
Jamaica, New York 11451

INTRODUCTION

Contemporary cross-cultural surveys are more accurate, and their results more believable than earlier ones as a result of many significant methodological advances. Several solutions have been proposed for the problem of diffusion originally raised by Galton.[1,2] Consequently, advancements made in other problem areas; such as, sampling,[3,4] coding reliability,[5] statistical sophistication,[6-8] ethnic unit definition,[9] focusing,[10,11] and data quality control;[12-15] make the criticisms of the cross-cultural method raised years ago by Boas,[16] and more recently by Leach,[17-19] Schapera,[20] Barnes,[21] and many others appear sophomoric. True, there will always be scholars who are opposed to the cross-cultural method because there will always be scholars who are dedicated to the null hypothesis.

Despite these advances, cross-cultural surveys still contain a primary weakness. They are almost without exception, synchronic correlation studies. Although it is impossible to prove beyond any doubt a causal relationship, and that there is an insurmountable gap between the language of theory and the language of research,[22] it is still possible to go beyond simple correlational statements, if in no other area than to be able to show the direction of change. A correlation permits us to say A and B occur together. Even with causal analysis, it may be difficult for the purist to say A causes B, but we will at least be able to say that changes in A precede changes in B.

The literature on causal analysis is quite massive and cannot be reviewed here.[22,23] But there are two methods of causal analysis, which involve making causal inferences from correlations, that have been proposed for cross-cultural studies. They should at least be mentioned in passing. One is known as the Simon-Blalock method, based on a method proposed by Simon.[24,25] The other is known as Influence Analysis and has been proposed and used by Naroll.[26,27] The Simon-Blalock method uses logically deduced "causal directions" between correlations of variables. However, rival theories or hypotheses must be based on the same variables, and no allowances are made for the influences of additional variables (see Tanter[25] for an application). Influence Analysis, which is a special case of Boudon's Dependence Analysis,[28] is said by Naroll to be "that in which one variable is a common effect and all the other variables are independent causal factors."[26] The noncorrelation of the independent variables with each

* An earlier version of this paper was presented at the fourth annual meeting of the Society for Cross-Cultural Research and received the C. S. Ford Cross-Cultural Research Award for 1975.

other and their common correlation with the dependent variable suggests that together they explain the variance in the dependent variable. Influence Analysis makes a very strong case, since it is not composed of one hypothesis but of several; any rival theory must be able to account for all the relationships between the dependent and the several independent variables. This means that a critic must propose a rival process rather than just a rival hypothesis — a much more difficult endeavor.

The traditional approach to causal analysis requires that measurements be made at two points in time on the same variables. Thus, if we wished to test a causal process about social structure; for example, whether a society would pass through a sequence of residence patterns, a traditional causal design would require us to make a series of measurements about residence patterns at different points in time for each society in our sample. With these longitudinal data we could then demonstrate a causal sequence. However, there are only a few societies for which we have ethnographic time-depth coverage of over fifty years, even fewer with a coverage of 200 years, and only a handful with a coverage spanning 2,000 years. It is almost impossible for us, using a traditional causal design, to test theories of process cross-culturally. In most instances, the ethnographic and archeological records are simply insufficient for this type of analysis.

STRATIFIED SAMPLING METHOD

In spite of insufficient archeological and ethnographic data, we can use causal analysis in our research designs. We can do it if we stand the problem on its head. Since we cannot make longitudinal measurements in a sufficient number of particular societies, then we must simulate longitudinal measurements across different societies. The theoretical conception involved is not new; only its application to cross-cultural surveys is new. Simulated longitudinal studies are common in psychology and sociology. For example, in order to study the differences in career development between scholars who rarely publish as opposed to those who frequently publish, it is not necessary to trace the changing careers of a group of scholars for forty years. With a sample of scholars who all share similar backgrounds but are stratified into subgroups at different levels of experience, it would be possible to project the career developments of publishers and nonpublishers and isolate possible factors responsible for the difference.

The epistemic assumption of this method is that for any given sociocultural process, the ethnographic universe contains societies that were at different stages of the process when they were ethnographically described. To set up a causal research design, one has to logically deduce the different stages of the process that a particular society would undergo. But, instead of making a series of diachronic measurements of the variables in each society, the diachronic changes in the variables would be represented by a series of synchronic measurements made in different societies at different stages of the process.

For sampling with this research design the universe of societies must be stratified into clusters using *objective indices* of the different stages of the process. By random sampling from each of the stratified clusters, one has, in effect, a series of diachronic measurements of one of the variables. In other words, the variable has been ranked into an ordinal scale. The remaining variable (which must be at least ordinal level) can then be measured synchronically in each society. If the ranking of the second variable correlates with the ranking of the stratified sampling variable, it is possible to infer cause. Two examples from previous research may help make the use of this method more clear.

TWO PREVIOUS APPLICATIONS

The first example comes from a test of a theory on the causes of matrilocal residence.[29,30] The initial cause of the process is migration of a patrilocal society into a region already inhabited by another patrilocal society. The external warfare that develops will place selective pressure against the internal warfare characteristic of patrilocality. A change to matrilocality is an adaptive response because it disperses the patrilocal fraternal interest groups which are conducive to internal war. This initial change, however, for various reasons, will initiate a series of further changes which eventually, in about 1800 years, will return the society to a patrilocal-patrilineal social structure. Six different stages in social structure can be logically predicted from the process: (1) Matrilocal-Patrilineal, stage occurs soon after the initial migration and patrilineal descent is still present, (2) Matrilocal-Bilateral is a later phase when patrilineal descent has broken down to a bilateral state, (3) Matrilocal-Matrilineal is an even later stage when lineality again develops, only this time it is consistent with matrilocality, (4) Avunculocal-Matrilineal stage marks the first step in the return to patrilocality whereby males of the same descent group are localized, only the kin tie is uncle—nephew rather than father—son, (5) Patrilocal-Double Descent is the next-to-last stage in the process where residence has changed to patrilocal and patrilineal descent has reemerged; matrilineal descent is still present but less important, hence a double-descent system, (6) Patrilocal-Patrilineal is the final stage achieved when matrilineal descent is dropped and the social structure has again returned to one which males are localized into fraternal interest groups.

A traditional causal design would require that I trace these successive changes in residence and descent in a single society through time; a cross-cultural test would require tracing these changes in a sample of societies. Limitations in the literature would not permit a test of this sort. However, using the method proposed here, we can assume that among the world's societies there are some at each stage of the process. If the theory is correct, avunculocal-matrilineal societies were once matrilocal-matrilineal, and before that they were matrilocal-bilateral, and prior to that stage, they were matrilocal-patrilineal. Thus, the dependent variable is the rank ordering of these types of social structure. These types are also objective indices for sampling. I used Murdock and White's 186 society Standard Cross-Cultural Sample as a universe,[4] stratified the universe according to these residence and descent types, and then randomly sampled societies from each cluster. I then had my dependent variable measured.

Matrilocality is supposed to be triggered by a migration; thus migration is my independent variable. I then studied the migration histories of each society in the sample. Had they migrated to their present locales? If so, how long ago? I measured migration on a nine-point ranked scale, from as recent as 37 years before the date of ethnographic focus to as long ago as 4,450 years. If the theory was correct, the antiquity of past migration scale should correlate with the ranked scale of social structures. In other words, matrilocal-patrilineal societies should be the most recent migrants, matrilocal-bilateral societies should be the next most recent migrants, matrilocal-matrilineal societies should be the third most recent migrants, avunculocal-matrilineal societies should be the fourth most recent migrants, patrilocal-double descent should be the fifth most recent migrants; and, finally, patrilocal-patrilineal societies should be the oldest migrants or be indigenous to their locales. If the migration dates correlated with the social structure types, it would be the same as if the sample were composed entirely of patrilocal-patrilineal societies and the sequence of changes had been measured in each society in the sample. Given the limitations of the ethnographic record, it was possible to do the former but not the latter (see TABLE 1).

The second example comes from a test of a theory on the population control functions of female infanticide and warfare in prestate level societies.[31-33] The theory holds that female infanticide regulated excess females before they were able to reproduce. When the young generation reached adulthood, a consequence of infanticide was a shortage of adult women. This shortage was further aggravated by the practice of polygyny, which concentrated many of the females among the older and more influential males. The shortage of marriageable women, especially among the younger males, led to adultry, wife-stealing, and many disputes over women. A war would begin if a man was killed in a dispute, or if his wife was stolen. The principal of blood-revenge would maintain the conflict; and in this manner, the excess male population would be regulated. The constant warfare would place a value on adult males, and this would lead to the preference that the first child be a male. This preference would result in higher rates of female infanticide, and the process would be undergone for the next generation. The constant and circular chain of events would make the system selfperpetuating.

The theory could be tested by demographic analysis of different age groups. If female infanticide were eliminating the excess female population, then there would be a significant excess of boys among the young age group. If warfare were eliminating the excess males, then the excess of males would not exist among the adult age group. Instead, the proportion of adult males to females should be about equal. Thus, it would be possible to examine the sex ratios among societies where infanticide and warfare were practiced, and they would provide supportive evidence if they conformed to the theory. However, the evidence would provide synchronic but not diachronic support; we would have correlational but not causal evidence. This is because there could be an unknown "lurking variable," that was actually causing the generational changes in sex ratios.

With a traditional research design, causal analysis could be applied by measuring the sex ratios in a society when infanticide and warfare were present, and then measuring the sex ratios when warfare was stopped and infanticide no longer practiced. This, of course, would be impossible. We are lucky to find any census data in most societies, much less censuses taken at two points in time, along with measurements on warfare and infanticide for two points in time. However, using this method, it was possible to apply a causal test of this theory. Only this time, sampling was based on changes in the independent variable. If infanticide and warfare were causing the changes in sex ratios, then it could be logically deduced that predictably different sex ratios should exist given certain variations in warfare and infanticide. Three stages in a process were postulated: The first stage was when warfare and infanticide were present; here boys should outnumber girls among the young generation due to infanticide, but the sex ratio should be about equal among the adults owing to warfare; the second

TABLE 1

RECENCY OF PAST MIGRATION AND RESIDENCE-DESCENT PROGRESSION

Recency of Past Migration before Date of Ethnographic Focus	Residence-Descent Progression						Totals
	Matrilocal Patrilineal	Matrilocal Bilateral	Matrilocal Matrilineal	Avunculocal Matrilineal	Patrilocal Double Descent	Patrilocal Patrilineal	
37 to 50 years	Mundurucu	Tupinamba					2
108 to 185 years	Shavante	Warrau	Timbira			Gros Ventre	4
221 to 278 years		Yukaghir Callinago	Hidatsa	Saramacca			4
315 to 336 years	Omaha	Cuna Lengua	Luguru				4
375 to 547 years		Chircahua			Wolof	Kikuyu	3
1000 years		Toradja	Lesu	Trobriand Goajiro	Aranda	Amahuaca	6
1175 to 1970 years		Nicobar Ingalik	Kaska	Palau	Toda	Natchez Papago	7
2000 years				Haida	Manus Tiwi	Banen Otoro Nuba Maria Gond Semang	7
2403 to 4450 years			Veddas			Mbuti Tanala	3
Totals	3	10	6	5	5	11	40

Gamma = .56   Tau-b = .48   p = .00006, one tail, by Naroll's Exact Test

stage would be the period immediately following the cessation of warfare, usually by colonial authorities or missionaries. If a census had been taken within a generation after the cessation of warfare (from 5 to 25 years), I would assume that infanticide is still being practiced, although perhaps not as extensively as before, and boys would still outnumber girls. However, if infanticide is still being practiced but warfare has been stopped, the excess of boys in the young generation should be carried over to the adult generation. Thus, for these societies there should be an excess of males among the young and adult generations. The third stage would be when warfare had been stopped for two or more generations (over 26 years) before a census was taken. Societies that prohibited warfare for over 26 years should have also undergone a fair amount of acculturation to Western values. If a census had been taken this long after warfare had been stopped, I would except that infanticide would also no longer be practiced. Thus the proportion of males and females should be about equal in both the young and adult generations.

The sample was then stratified into the three clusters based on the presence of warfare, or how long ago it had been stopped. Measurements were also made on ethnographer's reports of the frequency of infanticide. If infanticide and warfare were actually causing the variations in sex ratios, then the three clusters of societies should exhibit average sex ratios consistent with the logically deduced fluctuations of the independent variables (see TABLE 2).

DISCUSSION

This method of causal analysjs was developed as a by-product of these two research projects. In both cases, my purpose was to operationalize and test a causal theory, given limitations in the ethnographic record. However, the approach that developed from both tests perhaps would also be useful in testing other theories. The epistemic assumption appears to be sound: that for any sociocultural process or causal sequence, the ethnographic universe contains societies at different stages of that process or sequence. The method can be summarized by its three basic steps: (1) The researcher must be able to postulate beforehand different stages in the process; these could be based on predicted changes in either the dependent or the independent variable. (2) Objective indices of the stages must be operationalized in order to stratify the sample into representative stages of the process: stratification could be based on either the dependent or independent variable. (3) At least one of the variables must be ordinal or interval scale and have a time dimension to it. This latter requirement is not as difficult as it seems since it only needs a reference to the date of ethnographic coverage.

In conclusion, I would like to cite an example of how the method could be used to test a causal theory that has received wide discussion in the literature but still remains untested. I am speaking of Anthony Wallace's theory of Revitalization Movements.[34] Wallace contends that under conditions of extreme cultural stress, a process of revitalization will occur if the culture is to survive. Extreme cultural stress can be brought on by various factors but is usually due to military defeat, political subordination, and/or extreme pressures toward acculturation. Wallace outlines five stages of the revitalization process through which a society should pass: (1) steady stage, (2) period of individual stress, (3) period of cultural distortion, (4) period of revitalization, (5) new steady state.

TABLE 2

VARIATIONS IN SEX RATIOS OF YOUNG AND ADULTS AS A FUNCTION OF VARIATIONS IN WARFARE AND INFANTICIDE

Stratified Sample Clusters Based on Variations in Warfare and Infanticide	Sex Ratio of Age Group 14 Years or Younger (Males per 100 Females)	Sex Ratio of Age Group 15 Years or Older	Number of Populations Censused
1. Warfare: present at time of census Infanticide: commonly or occasionally practiced	133 : 100	96 : 100	110
2. Warfare: stopped 5 to 25 years before census	113 : 100	113* : 100	236
3. Warfare: stopped 26 or more years before census Infanticide: not common or not practiced	104 : 100	92 : 100	102
Totals			448

* Excess of males carried from the young to the adult generation is probably due to survival of males who previously would have been killed in warfare.

T tests for significance of difference between average percent of males for each cluster:
Young Age Group: 1 vs. 2, p = .0005; 2 vs. 3, p = .025; 1 vs. 3, p = .0005
Adult Age Group: 1 vs. 2, p = .0005; 2 vs. 3, p = .0005; 1 vs. 3, p = n.s.

For some of these stages Wallace gives objective indices; such as, alcoholism, or disregard of kinship, but, it would be possible to develop objective indicators for each of the stages. The independent variable of Wallace's theory is political subordination and pressure toward acculturation. The theory could be tested in the following manner. First, a random sample should be drawn from an appropriate universe. Next the societies should be examined for the presence of the indicator variables. Depending on the indicator variables found, the society would be grouped in one of the five stages; a society would be put in the "steady state" cluster if none of the stress indicator variables were found. Finally, the independent variable would be measured. This would be the length of time measured in years, if possible, before the date of ethnographic coverage, when political and military subordination occurred and acculturation pressure began.

If Wallace's theory of revitalization is correct, then we would assume that societies in the stage of "individual stress" have recently undergone political domination; societies in the stage of "cultural distortion" should be the second most recent group to undergo political domination, societies in the "period of revitalization" should be the third most recent group to undergo political domination, and societies in the "new steady state" should be the fourth most recent group. Finally, societies who are in their original "steady state," i.e., those without the stress indicator variables, should have not undergone political and military domination. With this research design we would be able to apply a causal test of the revitalization process. It would probably not be possible to test the theory in the traditional manner; that is, to find evidence of a sequence of changes in these stages for each society in a sample. But such a test is possible with the Stratified Sampling Method.

REFERENCES

1. NAROLL, R. 1970. Galton's Problem. *In* A Handbook of Method in Cultural Anthropology. R. Naroll & R. Cohen, Eds.: 974–989. Natural History Press. New York, N.Y.
2. NAROLL, R. 1964. A fifth solution to Galton's problem. Am. Anthropol. **66**: 863–867.
3. OTTERBEIN, K. F. 1975. Samples and sampling in cross-cultural research. Paper read at the 4th annual meeting of the Society for Cross-Cultural Research. Chicago, Ill.
4. MURDOCK, G. P. & D. R. WHITE. 1969. Standard cross-cultural sample. Ethnology. **9**: 302–330.
5. ROHNER, R. P. & L. KATZ. 1970. Testing for validity and reliability in cross-cultural research. Am. Anthropol. 72: 1068–1073.
6. DRIVER, H. E. 1961. Introduction to statistics for comparative research. *In* Readings in Cross-Cultural Methodology. F. Moore, Ed.: 310–338. HRAF Press. New Haven, Conn.
7. NAROLL, R. 1974. An exact test of significance for Goodman and Kruskal's gamma. Behavior Sci. Res. **9**: 27–40.
8. NAROLL, R. 1974. The use of ordinal statistics in causal analysis of correlations. Social Forces. **53**: 251–253.
9. NAROLL, R. 1971. The double language boundry in cross-cultural surveys. Behavior Sci. Notes. **6**: 95–102.
10. DIVALE, W. T. 1975. Temporal focus and random error in cross-cultural hypothesis tests. Behavior Sci. Res. **10**: 19–36.
11. MICHIK, G. 1974. Multiple coding and ethnic unit focus. Paper read at the 3rd annual meeting of the Society for Cross-Cultural Research. Boston, Mass.
12. NAROLL, R. 1962. Data Quality Control. Free Press, New York, N.Y.

13. NAROLL, R. 1970. Data quality control in cross-cultural surveys. *In* A Handbook of Method in Cultural Anthropology. R. Naroll & R. Cohen, Eds. Natural History Press.: 927–940. New York, N.Y.
14. ROHNER, R. P., B. R. DEWALT, & R. C. NESS. 1973. Ethnographer bias in cross-cultural research: An empirical study. Behavior Sci. Notes. 8: 275–317.
15. DIVALE, W. T. 1975. Female status in cultural evolution: A study in ethnographer bias. Behavior Sci. Res. In press.
16. BOAS, R. 1927. Anthropology and statistics. *In* The Social Sciences and Their Interrelations. W. F. Ogburn & A. Goldenweiser, Eds.: 114–121. Houghton Mifflin Co. Boston, Mass.
17. LEACH, E. R. 1950. Review of G. P. Murdock, Social Structure. Man. 50: 107–108.
18. LEACH, E. R. 1960. Review of S. H. Udy, Organization of Work. Am. Sociol. Rev. 25: 136–138.
19. LEACH, E. R. 1964. Comment on R. Naroll, On ethnic unit classification. Current Anthropol. 5: 299.
20. SCHAPERA, I. 1953. Some comments on the comparative method in social anthropology. Am. Anthropol. 55: 353–362.
21. BARNES, J. A. 1971. Three Styles in the Study of Kinship. University of California Press. Berkeley, Ca.
22. BLALOCK, H. M. 1961. Causal Inferences in Nonexperimental Research. W. W. Norton & Co., Inc. New York, N.Y.
23. BLALOCK, H. M., Ed. 1971. Causal Models in the Social Sciences. Aldine. Chicago, Ill.
24. SIMON, H. A. 1954. Spurious correlation: A causal interpretation. J. Am. Statistical Association 49: 467–479.
25. TANTER, R. 1970. Toward a theory of political development. *In* A Handbook of Method in Cultural Anthropology. R. Naroll & R. Cohen, Eds.: 111–127. Natural History Press. New York, N.Y.
26. NAROLL, R. 1970. Influence analysis – an appendix. *In* A Handbook of Method in Cultural Anthropology. R. Naroll & R. Cohen, Eds.: 108–110. Natural History Press. New York, N.Y.
27. NAROLL, R. 1969. Cultural determinants and the concept of the sick society. *In* Changing Perspectives in Mental Illness. R. F. Edgerton & S. C. Plog, Eds.: 128–155. Holt, Rinehart & Winston, Inc. New York, N.Y.
28. BOUDON, R. 1970. A method of linear causal analysis – dependence analysis. *In* A Handbook of Method in Cultural Anthropology. R. Naroll & R. Cohen, Eds. 99–108. Natural History Press. New York, N.Y.
29. DIVALE, W. T. 1974. Migration, external warfare, and matrilocal residence. Behavior Sci. Res. 9: 75–133.
30. DIVALE, W. T. 1974. The Causes of Matrilocal Residence: A Cross-Ethnohistorical Survey. University Microfilms No. 75–7742. Ann Arbor, Mich.
31. DIVALE, W. T. & M. HARRIS. 1976. Population, warfare, and the male supremacist complex. Am. Anthropol. 78: 521–538.
32. DIVALE, W. T. 1972. Systemic population control in the Middle and Upper Paleolithic: inferences based on contemporary hunter-gatherers. World Archaeol. 4: 222–243.
33. DIVALE, W. T. 1970. An explanation for primitive warfare: Population control and the significance of primitive sex ratios. New Scholar. 2: 172–193.
34. WALLACE, A. F. 1956. Revitalization movements. Am. Anthropol. 58: 264–281.

GROWTH AND DEVELOPMENT OF
HOLOGEISTIC CROSS-CULTURAL RESEARCH

James M. Schaefer

Department of Anthropology
University of Montana
Missoula, Montana 59801

There are cross-cultural studies, and then there are cross-cultural studies. Most of the studies presented in this symposium are studies of a few cultures or nations and are thus considered to be cross-cultural. I want to focus on the other type of cross-cultural study; namely, those studies based on the popular cross-cultural sample survey research design. These studies are in a category all by themselves. They formally test theories by confronting theory with data collected from random samples of societies and by mathematical statistical tests that allow decisions to be made between or among rivaling theories.

A term used by some practitioners of this latter type of cross-cultural research is hologeistic. Hologeistic studies are "holos" – whole, "ge" – earth studies.[1,2] Such studies attempt to test theories about human behavior regardless of space and time. The term helps distinguish our cross-cultural activities from our cross-culturally oriented behavioral science colleagues, and it provides a conveninet referent for the variety of study styles that hologeistic studies encompass.

As a group, hologeistic studies have recently been engrossed in an extremely productive period. The growth curve is currently exponential (see FIGURE 1). It conforms to growth characteristics for scientific activity in general, although social science growth is a fairly recent phenomenon.[3]

Let me turn to a brief characterization of each of the different types of hologeistic study. I will attempt to give a background of each type, show or indicate the growth of each type, and comment on the status of theory and method in each.

The unheralded roots of global comparative study in the social sciences are truly the debates carried out by America's Founding Fathers documented in the Federalist Papers.[4] Hamilton, Jay, and Madison in the middle 1700's were comparing institutional forms of governments in Europe and America in an effort to determine the growth of the United States Government.

A century later we had Bachofen,[5] Tylor,[6] Frazer,[7] and Westermarck[8] assembling masses of comparative data selected to support their ideas about descent, religion, magic, and marriage. The lack of scientific rigor in theory construction, operational categorization, sampling, quality control analysis by these scholars was outweighed by the sheer volume of evidence they brought forth to support their arguments. Their works remain as classics. They stand as a point of departure for the first generation of systematic scientific hologeistic study. Sir Edward B. Tylor perfomed the first hologeistic study in his 1889 paper entitled "On a Method of Investigating the Development of Institutions" applied to laws of marriage and descent.[9] This first holocultural study, or cross-cultural survey, was the model for comparative global studies popularized

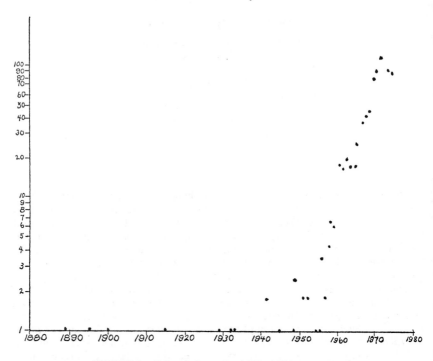

FIGURE 1.   Hologeistic studies 1889–1973 (N = 759).

in the 1940s by George Peter Murdock, Quincy Wright, John Whiting, and others.

Let me review reach of the hologeistic study types at this juncture.

Cross-Cultural Surveys: Holocultural Studies

Holocultural studies are typically conducted by anthropologists and social psychologists. In practice, holocultural studies sample, rather than two whole cultures, typically dozens of whole cultures throughout the world. Usually only the universe of primitive cultures are sampled; that is, societies having no cities and no writing system. The classic holocultural study is George P. Murdock's *Social Structure,*[10] which examines the correlates of kinship patterns. Perhaps the most significant and enduring contribution to hologeistic studies as a whole is Murdock's pioneer work in organizing the plethora of ethnographic data from which holocultural studies emerge. In *Outline of World Cultures* he lists all the known societies geographically.[11] His *Outline of Cultural Materials* additionally lists some 888 cultural categories of general interest to anthropologists and other behavioral scientists.[12] Murdock's role in organizing the Human Relations Area Files (HRAF), a massive system of coding ethnographic data topically, storing, microfilming, and updating information, is well known.[13] Data banking and computer programs are currently HRAF activities as well.

More recently, a major revamping of holocultural research methodology and a major assessment of what we have learned from holocultural studies has been led by Raoul Naroll et al. in Anthropology,[14–31] Marsh in Sociology,[32] and Brislin et al. in Psychology.[33]

Anthropologists have been in the lead regarding methodological criticisms of hologeistic study in general.[1,34–38] Here are some of their questions and some of the current "solutions" for holocultural studies in particular.

1. Sampling. What were the sample size, sample universe, sampling methods?[19,24,25,39,40]
2. Units of study. What was being counted in order to compute tests of association and significance?[19,23,31,40,41]
3. Galton's Problem. Was diffusion a plausible factor in explaining my theoretical finding?[27,40,42–44]
4. Statistics, group probability and significance tests. What statistics were used?[21,30,45–53]
5. Data quality controls. How did I get trustworthy data from untrustworthy sources like ethnographic monographs?[17,28,54–58]
6. Categorization. How do indicators used relate to theories or how were theories operationalized? Coding reliability, validity and documentation. How can the critic be assured that the data used for evidence is reliable?[23,59–64]
7. Deviant cases. Why were there exceptions?[34,39,65–67,69]

The debates have not ended, however at this time, holocultural studies are enjoying a period of steady growth. Since 1889, there have been 300 holocultural studies published (see FIGURE 2). The most productive period

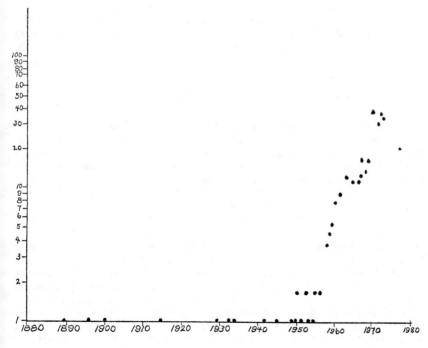

FIGURE 2.   Holocultural studies 1889–1973 (N = 308).

appears to be from 1956 to the present. Jack Roberts in a conversation pointed out that this rapid growth period may well have been stimulated by the publication of coded sets of data like George P. Murdock's World Ethnographic Sample.[69] Later we have his Ethnographic Atlas 1963–1967. It is also possible, that with the coming of the computer, holocultural studies have become simpler to produce. Whatever the stimuli, we see a continued growth in holocultural studies as methodological problems become ironed out and as theoretical perspectives broaden into an interdisciplinary atmosphere in the 1970's.

Cross-Polity Surveys: Holonational Studies

Holonational studies are typically conducted by political scientists and sociologists. In practice holonational studies involve samples of dozens of whole nations or whole societies since 1800. Usually only the universe of diplomatically recognized nations such as those who are fully recognized members of the United Nations are sampled.[69]

Quincy Wright introduced the first holonational study in 1942.[10] The classic holocultural study is David C. McClelland's *The Achieving Society*[70] which examines motivations and the development of society.

The development of holonational research has been largely a function of the availability of huge volumes of governmental statistics in various parts of the world. Considerable work on collecting and systematizing these data has been fostered by Arthur S. Banks.[71,72] Theoretical and methodological reviews of holonational studies have yet to be completed, however basic issues in this field have been addressed by Przeworski and Teune[73] and by Holt and Turner.[74]

Over 450 holonational studies have been conducted since Wright's in 1942. The most productive period has been from 1955 to the present (see FIGURE 3). Here we strongly suspect that the data banks created by Banks *et al.* figure in the continued growth of this field.

Cross-Historical Surveys: Holohistorical Studies

This group of hologeistic studies is the most recently developed variant of the general global correlational study-type: Holohistorical, Holoethnohistorical, Holoarchaeological (cross-historical, cross-ethnohistorical, cross-archaeological). The holohistorical study samples time periods in the great civilizations prior to 1800 A.D. The data base for holohistorical studies are history books written by both global comparative historians or by regional civilization experts. Only two such studies have been completed, the first in 1971.[75,76]

A major problem with holohistorical studies is that the primary historical documents in China, India, the Middle East, and to some extent, Western Eurasia are not in English. As a consequence, secondary works are consulted rather than the potentially richer primary documents. It is too early to assess the harm done to theory tests in holohistorical studies when using secondary sources. However, a recent study comparing holohistorical codings made using strictly secondary historical materials in English[75] on the same topics using regional language histories in India indicate that quantitative measurements although not precise were relative in magnitude. Thus, holohistorically tested theories were found to be supported regionally (India). And the relevant measurements were reasonably accurate.[77]

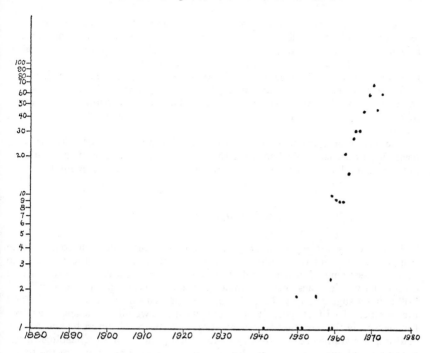

FIGURE 3. Holonational studies 1942–1973 (N = 450).

The holoethnohistorical survey is a special type of holohistorical study. Holoethnohistorical studies sample periods of time from the universe of colonial phases of the great civilizations. The data base for such studies are documents kept by colonial administrators and their staffs, by missionaries, explorers, colonial entrepreneurs, and travellers. These individuals, by habit or by requirement of their organization, wrote about various aspects of the lives of native peoples in assorted places around the world. The richest ethnohistorical documents appear to be those written in the last 250 years, although earlier materials exist. Of course, the types of material required for these studies vary tremendously in terms of time period. For example one research design might require documents twenty-five or so years *after* the termination of colonial rule, or less than fifty years *prior* to colonial rule. Thus, searching for materials on Samoa would be quite different from the search for materials on the Iroquois.

To date, only one holoethnohistorical study has been completed.[78] However, as Divale points out elsewhere in this symposium, this study style holds a great potential in terms of causal analysis of correlations. If nothing else, time series data allow consideration of what psychologists like Donald T. Campbell call panel analysis or cross-lagging of correlations. Essentially, the argument is that if factor A causes or is a strong influence on factor B in a behavioral situation studied over time, then the correlation between factor A at time 1 with respect to factor B at time 2 should be greater than factor A at time 2 with respect to factor B at time 1 (simply $ra_1 b_2 > ra_2 b_1$).

Holoarchaeological studies are yet another modification of the holohistorical technique. Holoarchaeological studies sample archaeological site components following McKern's[79] notion of a space-time specific area of an archaeological site. Time periods involved in these studies range backwards in time from the most recent prehistoric remains in archaeological sites throughout the world.

There has been one holoarchaeological study by Henke[80] but it was not a correlational study. Henke studied the general cultural evolutionary phenomena of site size increase from early stone age to later stone age in the Old and New World.

The major problem in holoarchaeological research is sampling. There is no masterlist of archaeological sites for the world; in fact, regions of the world do not have complete lists of sites. So sampling has to be expert judgmental.

A New Holoarchaeological Study

In a recent study my research group examined thirty-one archaeological site components around the world. We were interested in testing the relationship between settlement growth and technological specialization. This cultural evolutionary idea has been studied for many years by others.[32,81-84] Following a suggestion by Raoul Naroll, we focused on the size of the site and the number of artifact types. We thought that these would be reasonable analogs for measuring the variation in urbanization and specialization in technology. In addition, we studied several quality related factors since some archaeological site reports are of apparent high quality, whereas others are not. Some of the things we looked at included the length of the report (longer reports probably have better information), length-of-stay of field crews (longer excavations probably have better information about the site), and quality and composition of photographs and graphic illustrations (neat, well-labeled and clear illustrations probably indicate greater care in other phases of the archaeological research).

We plotted site size, and number of artifact types on logarithmic paper, and a sloping trend was indicated; however, there were enough deviant cases to wash out any statistically significant correlation. By grouping the data into an ordinal scale, the correlation was a gamma of .40 with $P < .02$. Quality control factor tests with ordinal scale data are reported in TABLE 1.

TABLE 1

PARTIAL CORRELATIONS FOR HOLOARCHAEOLOGICAL STUDY OF
OCCUPATION SIZE, ARTIFACT TYPES AND QUALITY CONTROL FACTORS*

Variable 1	Variable 2	Variable 3	TAU 12.3	Kendall's S
Occup size	Artifact typ	Report length	.23	.05
Occup size	Artifact typ	Stay length	.37	.004
Occup size	Artifact typ	Crew size	.34	.008
Occup size	Artifact typ	Illustration no.	.29	.02
Occup size	Artifact typ	Photo composition	.34	.008

* Program Partau Naroll 1971c.[85]

The quality of archaeological site reports as measured by our group does not significantly diminish the ordinal scale correlation found between occupation size and the number of artifact types. In comparing different artifact type counts from one site to another, (i.e. from one archaeologist to another) a question might be raised as to the intercomparability of their types. At the outset we recognized this difficulty and reasoned that the archaeologists themselves had a better grasp of the function of the different artifacts he found. So at the beginning, we used the raw counts from the reports. Upon closer examination, however, there appeared to be an extensive overlap of certain tool types. Consequently, an etic-level judgment was made on artifact types and a masterlist for this study was constructed. The types reported here originate from this adjusted list. Presently more data are being collected with the hope that a Guttman scale of artifact types might be constructed. At this time, the artifact-type counts are the least satisfactory aspect of this new study technique.

However, these problems may not face others who adapt the technique of studying anthropological and other behavior science theories by using the rich data in archaeological, ethnohistorical, and historical reports.

In conclusion, let me suggest that hologeistic studies allow a researcher to investigate a wide variety of important theoretical problems that confront us presently. It is through the use of the global sample survey design and the use of ethnographic literature, governmental statistics, histories, etc. that enable us to study many problems that societal ethics will not allow us to work on. The ongoing experiments in living should become enlightened by what we can learn from studies of the well-documented experiments in living found in the literature cited above. We have been ignoring these opportunities too long. With the computer age upon us, it should not be difficult to organize these materials in such a way that pressing problems can be solved. All we have to do is make a commitment; and perhaps, new insights into urban problems, pollution, food crises, quality of life, and overpopulation will be made.

SUMMARY

Cross-cultural research has many forms. In this paper I review the growth and development of hologeistic cross-cultural research; by which I mean the global sample survey style, theory-testing by mathematical statistic, type of study. I probe the origins of systematic comparative work and summarize the characteristics of each subfield. I illustrate a new type of cross-cultural study, holoarchaeology with some recently completed research. I conclude that a wealth of theoretically rich material has yet to be used by comparative behavioral scientists (i.e., histories, colonial administrators, and travelers' notes, archaeological site reports). Moreover, I indicate that many contemporary problems in society that cannot be evaluated *in vivo* may well be studied hologeistically, that is, *in vitro*.

ACKNOWLEDGMENTS

In unsponsored research one is constantly prodded by a variety of persons who from time to time take interest in the project. I have been so prodded and here acknowledge my indebtedness to some of the many people who at one phase of this study or another were helpful: Raoul Naroll, George P. Murdock, John M. Roberts, Stewart Gilmor, Dee Taylor, Floyd Sharrock, D. P. Mukherjee, William Divale, Sharron Griffin, Susan Boyd, Michael Beckes and James Keyser. Any errors of omission or commission are my own responsibility.

REFERENCES

1. KOBBEN, A. 1952. New ways of presenting an old idea: The statistical method in social anthropology. J. Roy. Anthropol. Inst. G. Britain Ireland. **82**: 129–146.
2. MOORE, F. W., Ed. 1961. Readings in cross-cultural methodology. Human Relations Area Files Press. New Haven, Ct.
3. DE SOLLA PRICE, D. J. 1963. Little Science, Big Science. Columbia University Press. New York, N.Y.
4. HAMILTON, A., et al. 1975. The Federalist Papers. Modern Library. New York, N.Y.
5. BACHOFEN, J. J. 1861. Das Multerrecht. Basel: Benno Schawabe.
6. TYLOR, E. B. 1871. Primitive culture: Researches into the development of mythology, philosophy, religion, language, art and custom. J. Murray. London.
7. FRAZER, J. G. 1890. The Golden Bough. Macmillan Co. London.
8. WESTERMARCK, E. 1891. The History of Human Marriage. Macmillan Co. New York, N.Y.
9. TYLOR, E. B. 1889. On a method of investigating the development of institutions: Applied to laws of marriage and descent. J. Roy. Anthropol. Inst. **18**: 245–269.
10. WRIGHT, Q. 1942. A study of war. University of Chicago Press. Chicago, Il.
11. MURDOCK, G. P. et al. 1969a. Outline of World Cultures. Human Relations Area Files Press. New Haven, Ct.
12. MURDOCK, G. P. et al. 1969b. Outline of Cultural Materials. Human Relations Area Files Press. New Haven, Ct.
13. FORD, C. S. 1967. Cross-Cultural Approaches: Readings in Comparative Research. Human Relations Area Files Press. New Haven, Ct.
14. NAROLL, R., & R. COHEN, Eds. 1970. A Handbook of Method in Cultural Anthropology. The Natural History Press. New York, N.Y.
15. NAROLL, R., G. L. MICHIK, & F. NAROLL. 1974. Treating Hologeistic theory. In Comparative studies by Harold E. Driver and essays in his honor. Joseph G. Jorgensen, Ed. Human Relations Area Files Press. New Haven, Ct.
16. NAROLL, R. 1961. Two solutions to Galton's Problem. Philosophy of Science. **28**: 16–39.
17. NAROLL, R. 1962. Data Quality Control. Free Press. New York, N.Y.
18. NAROLL, R. 1964a. A fifth solution to Galton's Problem. Am. Anthropol. **66**: 853–867.
19. NAROLL, R. 1964b. On ethnic unit classification. Current Anthropol. **5**: 283–312.
20. NAROLL, R. 1967. The proposed HRAF probability sample. Behavior Sci. Notes. **2**: 70–80.
21. NAROLL, R. 1968. Some Thoughts on Comparative Method in Cultural Anthropology. In Methodology in Social Research. H. M. Blalock & A. Blalock, Eds. McGraw-Hill Book Co. Inc. New York, N.Y.
22. NAROLL, R. 1970a. What have we learned from cross-cultural surveys? Am. Anthropol. **72**: 1227–1228.
23. NAROLL, R. 1970b. The Culture-Bearing Unit in Cross-Cultural Surveys. In A Handbook of Method in Cultural Anthropology. R. Naroll & R. Cohen, Eds. 721–765. The Natural History Press. New York, N.Y.
24. NAROLL, R. 1970c. The Logic of Generalization: Part I: Epistemology. In A Handbook of Method in Cultural Anthropology. R. Naroll & R. Cohen, Eds. The Natural History Press, New York, N.Y.
25. NAROLL, R. 1970d. Chaney & Ruiz Revilla: A comment. Am. Anthropol. **72**: 1450–1453.

26. NAROLL, R. 1970e. "Cross-cultural Sampling" *In* A Handbook of Method in Cultural Anthropology. R. Naroll & R. Cohen, Eds. 889–989. The Natural History Press. New York, N.Y.

27. NAROLL, R. 1970f. Galton's Problem. *In* A Handbook of Method in Cultural Anthropology. R. Naroll & R. Cohen, Eds. 974–989. Natural History Press. New York, N.Y.

28. NAROLL, R. 1970g. Data Quality Control in Cross-Cultural Surveys. *In* A Handbook of Method in Cultural Anthropology. R. Naroll & R. Cohen, Eds. 927–945. Natural History Press. New York, N.Y.

29. NAROLL, R. 1970h. Stratified sampling and Galton's Problem (A comment on "Evaluation of a stratified versus an unstratified universe of cultures in comparative research" By Lenora Greenbaum). Behavior Sci. Notes. 4: 282–283.

30. NAROLL, R. 1971a. Review of the significance test controversy. A reader. Am. Anthropol. 73: 1437–1439.

31. NAROLL, R. 1971b. The double language boundary. Behavior Sci. Notes. 6: 95–102.

32. MARSH, R. M. 1967. Comparative sociology. Harcourt, Brace, & World, Inc. New York, N.Y.

33. BRISLIN, R. W., W. J. LONNER, & R. M. THORNDIKE. 1973. Cross-Cultural Research Methods. John Wiley & Sons. New York, N.Y.

34. KOBBEN, A. 1967. Why Expectations? The logic of cross-cultural comparison. Current Anthropol. 8: 3–34.

35. KOBBEN, A. 1970a. Cause and Intention. *In* A Handbook of Method in Cultural Anthropology. R. Naroll & R. Cohen, Eds. Natural History Press. New York, N.Y.

36. KOBBEN. A. 1970b. Comparativists and Noncomparativists. *In* A Handbook of Method in Cultural Anthropology. R. Naroll & R. Cohen, Eds. Natural History Press. New York, N.Y.

37. SCHAPERA, I. 1953. Some comments on comparative method in social anthropology. Am. Anthropol. 55: 353–361.

38. LEWIS, O. 1956. Comparisons in Cultural Anthropology. *In* Readings in Cross-Cultural Methodology. F. Moore, Ed. Human Relations Area File Press. New Haven Ct.

39. CHANEY, R. P. & ROGELIO RUIZ REVILLA. 1969. Sampling Methods and Interpretations of correlation: A Comparative Analysis of Seven Cross-Cultural Samples. Am. Anthropol. 71: 597–633.

40. MURDOCK, G. P. & D. R. WHITE. 1969c. Standard Cross-Cultural Sample. Ethnology. 8: 329–369.

41. HELM, J., Ed. 1968. Essays on the problem of tribe, Proc. 1967 Annual Meeting Am. Ethnol. Soc. University of Washington Press. Seattle, Wa.

42. SCHAEFER, J. M. 1969. Linked pair alignments for the HRAF Quality Control Sample Universe. Behavior Sci. Notes. 4: 299–320.

43. SCHAEFER, J. M. 1974. Studies in Cultural Diffusion: Galton's Problem, Ed. Human Relations Area Files Press. New Haven, Ct.

44. DRIVER, H. E. & R. P. CHANEY. 1970. Cross-Cultural Sampling and Galton's Problem. *In* A Handbook of Method in Cultural Anthropology. R. Naroll & R. Cohen, Eds. Natural History Press. New York, N.Y. 990–1003.

45. BLALOCK, H. M. Jr. 1960. Correlational Analysis and Causal Inferences. Am. Anthropol. 62: 624–653.

46. BLALOCK, H. M., Jr. 1964. Causal Inferences In Nonexperimental Research. University of North Carolina Press. Chapel Hill, N.C.

47. BOUDON, R. 1967. L'Analyse Mathematique des Faits Sociaux. Plon. Paris, France.

48. BOUDON, R. 1970. A Method of Linear Causal Analysis-Dependence Analysis. *In* A Handbook of Method in Cultural Anthropology. 99: 108. Natural History Press. New York.

49. ROZELLE, R. M. & D. T. CAMPBELL. 1969. More Plausible Rival Hypotheses in the Cross-Lagged Panel Correlation. Psychol. Bull. 72: 74–80.

50. TANTER, R. 1970. Toward a Theory of Political Development. *In* A Handbook of Method in Cultural Anthropology. R. Naroll & R. Cohen, Eds. 111–127. Natural History Press. New York.

51. TATJE, T. J., RAOUL NAROLL, & ROBERT B. TEXTOR. Methodological findings of the cross-cultural summary. *In* A Handbook of Method in Cultural Anthropology. R. Naroll & R. Cohen, Eds. Columbia University Press. New York, N.Y.

52. TEXTOR, R. B. 1967. A Cross-Cultural Summary. Human Relations Area Files Press. New Haven, Ct.

53. WINCH, R. F. & D. T. CAMPBELL. 1969. Proof? No. Evidence? Yes. The significance of tests of significance. The American Sociologist. 4: 140–143.

54. ROSENTHAL, R. 1966. Experimenter effects in behavioral research. Appleton-Century Crofts. New York, N.Y.

55. JANDA, K. 1970. Data Quality Control and Library Research on Political Parties. *In* A Handbook of Method in Cultural Anthropology. R. Naroll & R. Cohen, Eds. Columbia University Press. New York, N.Y.

56. O'LEARY, T. J. 1970. Ethnographic Bibliographies. *In* A Handbook of Method in Cultural Anthropology. R. Naroll & R. Cohen, Eds. Natural History Press. 128–146. New York.

57. RUMMEL, R. J. 1970. Dimensions of Errors in Cross-National Data. *In* A Handbook of Method in Cultural Anthropology. R. Naroll & R. Cohen, Eds. Natural History Press. New York.

58. FORD, C. S. 1967. Cross-Cultural Approaches: Readings in Comparative Research. Human Relations Area Files Press. New Haven, Ct.

59. MOORE, F. W., Ed. 1969. Codes and Coding. Behavior Sci. Notes. 4: 247–266.

60. TATJE, T. 1970. Problems of Concept Definition for Comparative Studies. *In* A Handbook of Method in Cultural Anthropology. R. Naroll & R. Cohen, Eds. Columbia University Press. New York, N.Y.

61. EMBER, M. 1970. Taxonomy in Comparative Studies. *In* A Handbook of Method in Cultural Anthropology. R. Naroll & R. Cohen, Eds. Columbia University Press. New York, N.Y.

62. GOODENOUGH, W. H. 1970. Description and Comparision in Cultural Anthropology. Aldine. Chicago, Il.

63. LeBAR, F. M. 1970. Coding Ethnographic Materials. A Handbook of Method in Cultural Anthropology. R. Naroll & R. Cohen, Eds. Natural History Press. New York.

64. SAWYER, J. & R. LEVINE. 1966. Cultural Dimensions: A Factor Analysis of the World Ethnographic Sample. American Anthropologist. 63: 708–731.

65. DRIVER, H. E. & K. F. SCHUESSLER. 1967. Correlational Analysis of Murdock's 1957 Ethnographic Sample. American Anthropologist 69: 332–352.

66. ERICKSON, E. E. 1972. Other Cultural Dimensions: Selective Ratings of Sawyer and Levine. Factor Analysis of the World Ethnographic. Sample. Behavior Sci. Notes. 7 (2): 95–156.

67. ROSENBLATT, P. C. 1967. Marital residence and the functions of romantic love. Ethnology. 6: 191–203.

68. MURDOCK, G. P. 1957. World Ethnolographic Sample. American Anthropologist. 59: 664–687.

69. O'LEARY, T. J. 1971. Bibliography of Cross-Cultural Studies: Behavior Sci. Notes. Suppl. to 6: 191–203.

70. McCLELLAND, D. C. 1961. The Achieving Society. Van Nostrand Press. Princeton, N.J.

71. BANKS, A. S. 1971. Cross-polity Time Series Data. MIT Press. Cambridge, Ma.

72. BANKS, A. S. & ROBERT B. TEXTOR. 1963. A Cross-Polity Survey. MIT Press. Cambridge, Ma.

73. PRZEWORSKI, A. & H. TEUNE. 1970. Logic of Comparative Social Inquiry. John Wiley & Sons. New York, N.Y.

74. HOLT, R. T. & J. E. TURNER. 1970. The Methodology of Comparative Research. Free Press. New York, N.Y.

75. NAROLL, R., E. C. BENJAMIN, F. K. FOHL, M. J. FRIED, R. E. HILDRETH, & J. M. SCHAEFER. 1971. Creativity: A cross-historical pilot survey. J. Cross-Cultural Psychol. 2 (2): 181–188.

76. NAROLL, R., V. BULLOUGH, & F. NAROLL. 1974. Military deterrence in History. SUNY Press. Albany, N.Y.
77. SCHAEFER, J. M. & M. CHITTI BABU. A regional study of creativity: India 500 BC–1800 AD. Mimeograph Sri Venkateswara. University, Tirupati, India.
78. DIVALE, W. T. 1974. The causes of matrilocal and other matrilineal residence patterns: A cross-ethnohistorical study. PhD thesis. Department of Anthropology, SUNY. Buffalo, N.Y.
79. McKERN, W. C. 1939. The Midwestern Taxonomic Method as an Aid to Archaeological Study. American Antiquity. 4: 301–313.
80. HENKE, R. 1974. Prehistoric settlement size. *In* Main Currents in Cultural Anthropology. R. Naroll & F. Naroll, Eds. Appleton-Century Crofts. New York, N.Y.
81. CARNIERO, R. L. & S. F. TOBIAS. 1963. The Application of Scale Analysis to the Study of Cultural Evolution. Trans. N.Y. Acad. Sci. 26: 196–207.
82. CARNIERO, R. L. 1970. Scale Analysis, Evolutionary sequences and rating of cultures. *In* A Handbook of Method in Cultural Anthropology. R. Naroll & R. Cohen, Eds. Columbia University Press. New York, N.Y.
83. NAROLL, R. 1956. A Preliminary Index of Social Development. American Anthropologist. 58: 687–715.
84. WHITE, L. 1959. The Evolution of Culture. McGraw-Hill Book Co. Inc. New York, N.Y.
85. NAROLL, R. 1971c. Partau. Mimeograph SUNY. Buffalo, N.Y.

                    HOLOARCHAEOLOGICAL BIBLIOGRAPHY

AIKENS, M. C. 1970. Hogup Cave. University of Utah Anthropological Papers 93.
BROYLES, B. J. 1971. The St. Albans site, Kanawha County, West Virginia. Report of Archaeological Investigations 3. West Virginia Geological and Economic Survey.
BULLBROOK, J. A. 1953. On the excavation of shell-mound at Palo Seco, Trinidad, B. W. I. Yale University Publications in Anthropology 50: 1–114.
CARLSON, R. L. 1966. A Neolithic site in the Murshid District, Nubia. Kush, Journal of the Sudan Antiquities Service XIV: 44–68.
COE, M. D. 1961. La Victoria: an early site on the Pacific coast of Guatemala. Papers of the Peabody Museum of Archaeology and Ethnology LIII.
DORTCH, C. E. & D. MERRILEES. 1973. Human occupation of Devil's Lair, Western Australia during the Pleistocene. Archaeology and Physical Anthropology in Oceania VIII.2: 89–114.
DRAGOO, D. W. 1973. Wells Creek – an early man site in Stewart County, Tennessee. Archaeology of Eastern North America I.1: 1–56.
FORBIS, R. G. 1955. The MacHaffie site. Unpublished Ph.D. dissertation. Department of Political Science, Columbia University, New York, N.Y.
GABEL, C. 1965. Stone age hunters of the Kafue. Boston University Press. Boston, Mass.
GIDDINS, J. L. 1964. The Archaeology of Cape Denbigh. Brown University Press. Providence, R.I.
GOULD, R. A. 1968. Preliminary report on excavations at Puntutjarpa rock-shelter – W. Australia. Archaeology and Physical Anthropology in Oceania III.3: 161–18. 161–18.
JOHNSON, F. & H. M. RAUP. 1947. Grassy Island. Papers of the Robert S. Peabody Foundation for Archaeology 1.2.
KING, A. R. 1950. Cattle Point: A stratified site in the southern north-west coast region. Society for American Archaeology, Memoir 7: 1–92.
KLEIN, R. G. 1969. Man and culture in the late Pleistocene. Chandler Publishing Company. San Francisco, Ca.
KOTCH, J. & E. L. STARR. 1968. The Fox Island site. Plains Anthropologist 13.42.1: 310–338.
LAMPERT, R. J. 1966. An excavation at Durras North, New South Wales. Archaeology and Physical Anthropology in Oceania 1.2: 83–118.

LEACH, L. L. 1966. Archaeology of Boundary Village. Department of Anthropology, University of Utah Anthropological Papers 83, Miscellaneous Paper **13**: 87–129.

LEAKEY, M. D. 1971. Olduvai gorge: excavation in beds I and II 1960–1963, 3. Cambridge University Press. Cambridge, England.

LEWIS, T. M. N. & M. K. LEWIS. 1961. Evan, an archaic site. University of Tennessee Study in Anthropology.

LOUW, A. W. 1969. Bushman rock shelter, Ohrigstad, Eastern Transvaal. South African Bulletin **24.94**: 39–51.

MAGGS, T. & E. SPEED. 1967. Bonteberg shelter. South African Archaeology, Bulletin **22.87**: 80–93.

McCOY, P. C. 1973. Excavation of a rectangular house on the east rim of Rano Kau Volcano, Easter Island. Archaeology and Physical Anthropology in Oceania **VIII.1**: 51–67.

PANGBORN, R. E., H. T. WARD & W. R. WOOD. 1971. Flycatcher Village: a non-pottery site in the Stockton Reservoir, Missouri. Plains Anthropologist **16.51**: 60–73.

POWERS, W. R. 1973. Paleolithic man in Northeast Asia. The northeast. Artic Anthropology **X.2**: 74–93.

SHARIF, M. 1969. Excavation at Bhir Mound Taxila. Department of Archaeology and Museums, Pakistan Archaeology 6.

SIMONS, H. A. B. 1968. A late stone age occupation site in the hillside area of Bulawayo. South African Archaeology, Bulletin **23.90**: 45–49.

SPAULDING, A. 1956. The Arzberger site. Occasional Contributions from the Museum of Anthropology of the University of Michigan 16.

TAYLOR, W. E., Jr. 1968. The Arnapik and Tyara sites: an archaeological study of Dorest culture origins. Society for American Archaeology, Memoir 22.

VAILLANT, G. C. 1931. Excavations at Zacatenco. American Museum of Natural History, Anthropological Papers **XXXII**: 1–206.

WEBB, C. H. 1959. The Belcher mound: a stratified Caddoan site in Caddo Parish, Louisiana. Society for American Archaeology, Memoir 16.

WILLEY, G. R. & C. R. McGIMSEY. 1954. The Monagrillo culture of Panama. Papers of the Peabody Museum of Archaeology and Ethnology **XLIX.2**: 8–90.

APPENDIX A

SITE DATA AND BIBLIOGRAPHY FOR HOLOARCHAEOLOGICAL STUDY

by Susan Boyd, Michael Beckes and James Keyser

Key

Component Name & Number: Definition of Component Occupation Area in Square Meters: Page Reference Artifact Type Count: Page References Location: Longitude/Latitude Code String for Traits in following order

1.	Occupation Size	6.	Crew Size
2.	Artifact Type Count	7.	% of Site Dug
3.	Time Period	8.	Illustrations
4.	Report Length	9.	Photos
5.	Length of Stay	10.	Graphics
11.	Three Dimensionals	16.	Photo Labels
12.	Number of Illustrations	17.	Composite Photo Quality
13.	Photo Quality	18.	Research Support
14.	Photo Angles	19.	Research Type
15.	Photo Surfaces	20.	Missing Info Code (Coder Quality)

Bibliographic Reference
All page references for each entry are available upon request from the author.

ALBANS 1. Zone 4
Area: 142 : pg 3
Types: 9 : pp 25–29
Location: 87W/37N
Codes: 52345/39222/27222/28220

ARZBERG 2. Whole Site
Area: 4025 : pp 5–6
Types: 18 : pp 37–61
Location: 95W/45N
Codes: 74152/31222/15222/28220

BELCHER 3. Belcher I
Area: 592 : pp 36–43
Types: 15 : pp 162–178
Location: 93W/32N
Codes: 63253/39222/27222/28--2

BHIR 4. Period III
Area: 248 : pp 10, 18
Types: 17 : pp IX, X, 29–58, 76–88
Location: 72E/33N
Codes: 54244/3-222/27222/28221

BONTBERG 5. (Rockshelter) Level II
Area: 40 : pg 80
Types: 16 : pg 82
Location: 22E/35S
Codes: 34424/-1212/22---/--236

BOUNDARY 6. Fremont Level I
Area: 104 : pp 92–98
Types: 13 : pp 109, 111, 114, 116–118, 121–122
Location: 110W/40N
Codes: 53132/41222/16222/28220

BULAWAYO 7. Wilson Culture
Area: 10 : pg 45
Types: 10 : pg 48
Location: 30W/20S
Codes: 2221-/18212/21---/--226

CATTLE 8. Maritime Component
Area: 11456 : pg 64
Types: 28 : pp 12, 24–25, 29–30, 35–39, 44, 46, 48–50
Location: 123W/48N
Codes: 96–43/38222/25222/28211

DENBIGH 9. Norton Culture
Area: 19 : pg 136
Types: 30 : pp 140–175
Location: 161W/64N
Codes: 26245/32222/27222/-6231

DEVIL 10. (Rockshelter) Trench 2
Area: 340 : pg 90
Types: 6 : pp 99–109
Location: 120E/31S
Codes: 52421/-1212/12---/----8

DURRAS 11. Level III
Area: 100 : pp 87, 89
Types: 4 : pp 93/95
Location: 150E/35S
Codes: 41132/11222/242-2/-4222

EVA 12. Stratum II Three Mile Component
Area: 333 : pg 5
Types: 23 : pp 25–101
Location: 85W/38N
Codes: 5725-/35222/17222/28241

FLY 13. Whole Site
Area: 71 : pp 64–67
Types: 6 : pp 67–70
Location: 94W/38N
Codes: 42122/15222/13111/-3221

FOX 14. Whole Site
Area: 129 : pp 312–314
Types: 14 : pp 314–317, 329, 331
Location: 101W/46N
Codes: 53–3–/-1222/12----/----10

GRASS 15. Whole of Old Surface
Area: 2556 : pg 3
Types: 8 : pg 29
Location: 71W/41N
Codes: 7213-/-1222/14---/----9

GWISHO 16. Level VI
Area: 1061 : pp 24–25
Types: 14 : pp 42–52
Location: 27E/16S
Codes: 73253/1-222/27112/-4222

HOGUP 17. (Rockshelter) Whole Site
Area: 339 : pp 6–7
Types: 32 : pp 32–157
Location: 113W/31N
Codes: 57252/27222/27222/28220

KOSTENKI 18. Tel'manskaya – Horizon I
Area: 45 : pg 113
Types: 12 : pp 22, 116
Location: 35E/50N
Codes: 33455/42212/27----/----225

KUSH 19. Neolithic Component
Area: 11 : pg 54
Types: 8 : pp 56—61
Location: 26E/6N
Codes: 32212/--222/21---/--227

MCHAF 20. Scottsbluff Level
Area: 43 : pg 50
Types: 6 : pp 81, 84, 87, 94—95
Location: 112W/47N
Codes: 42—53/24222/27---/--216

MONA 21. Monagrillo Phase Site HE-5
Area: 18,060 : pg 11
Types: 10 : pp 58—87
Location: 80W/8N
Codes: 92—53/24222/27222/28231

NEASIA 22. Whole Site
Area: 58 : pg 85
Types: 7 : pp 83—85
Location: 161E/56N
Codes: 42425/--212/23---/----9

ORHRIGSTAD   23.   (Rockshelter)
Whole Site
Area: 910 : pg 40
Type: 10 : pp 45—7
Location: 30E/24S
Codes: 62421/11212/22---/--1-6

OLDUV 24. DK Site
Area: 13 : pg 24
Types: 9 : pp 25, 31, 34, 37, 39
Location: 37W/3S
Codes: 3282-/41222/14---2/-2234

PALO 25. Stratum II — Neritina Bed
Area: 40 : pg 18
Types: 7 : pp 30, 41—52
Location: 61W/10N
Codes: 32—42/21212/23---/--236

PUNT 26 (Rockshelter) Whole Site
Area: 66 : pg 164
Types: 8 : pp 166, 175
Location: 128E/28S
Codes: 4232-/1-222/23222/28242

RANO 27. Whole Site
Area: 8 : pg 54
Types: 3 : pp 55—56, 61
Location: 110W/26S
Codes: 21121/-9212/22---/--226

TYARA 28. Level I
Area: 2000 : pg 45 (figure 6)
Types: 19 : pp 49—50
Location: 76W/62N
Codes: 74141/31222/14222/28220

VICTORIA 29. Conchas Phase
Area: 4731 : pg 24
Types: 14 : pp 103—109
Location: 92W/14N
Codes: 73252/31222/27222/-6231

WELLS 30. Whole Site
Area: 82,481 : pg 1
Types: 12 : pp 11, 14, 17, 20, 32,
37, 43
Location: 87W/36N
Codes: 93344/--212/26---/--237

ZACA 31. Middle Period
Area: 13,600 : pg 192
Types: 20 : pp 48—49, 79, 160,
163, 167—168, 172, 175—176
Location: 99W/19N
Codes: 94—52/--221/27111/-3234

METHODS AND ISSUES IN CROSS-CULTURAL RESEARCH

Discussant: Charles Harrington

Anthropology and Education Program
Teachers College
Columbia University
New York, New York 10027

A number of different types of papers were presented in this session. Rohner and Jahoda furnish us with broadly stroked *overviews* of the need for cross-cultural research and collaboration between anthropology and psychology, respectively. Berry and Singh presented us with reports of their own *research*: Berry discussed a fascinating series of studies linking what he calls "ecology, culture, and behavior," Singh enlightened us with a comparison of some data concerning "ethnicity" from Pittsburgh and India. Dawson's was a *review article*, summarizing and synthesizing a number of original research studies in relation to his model of "biosocial" psychology. Divale's paper was essentially an *apologia* for his own approach which, it must be noted, deviates remarkably from accepted anthropological wisdom. Schaefer's paper represented another well known type: the *late* paper, not available beforehand to the discussant, and therefore excluded here.

Rohner's paper offered us a standard set of answers to the question posed in its title: "Why cross cultural research?" The people who seriously ask this question are few in number; but presumably, the number who act as if they have asked it, is considerably larger. I share his vision of anthropology as a theory building and testing science of man. The paper makes some persuasive arguments to support its position but is flawed by some unchecked claims for universals.

We are told that over one hundred studies have supported, for the most part, Piaget's ideas about the postulated stages of cognitive development. Yet, the literature I know casts doubt on the universality of these stages of development outside Western culture; whatever one's perspective about the little data we now have, and I obviously think we have too little to talk to universal stages; there is certainly no data to support Rohner's conclusion that "the cognitive functioning of children at a certain age seems to be more or less invariant throughout our species." The review article of Piagetian research by Dasen[1] cited by Rohner himself concluded that the rate of operational development is affected by cultural factors. The recent work of Cole, Gay, Glick, and Sharp[2] showed the folly of comparing children of the same age across cultures given the age differences in each culture of children's school experiences. The list of so-called universals consistently ignores evidence which counters the universal. In actual fact, every time the word universal is used, the word central tendency (even modal is too strong) would be preferable. I also object to the assertion that anthropologists are methodologically untutored. Surely what the author intended to say was that anthropologists have different methods than psychologists.

Jahoda's article, which in its later pages poses some fascinating problems for future research, takes a stab at the knotty problem of the interface between psychology and anthropology. Jahoda is familiar with students of both anthropology and psychology. He explicitly recognizes the dangers, as a psychologist, of commentary on anthropology. However, in point of fact, the author's descriptions of anthropology are limited to and derived from European (and especially English) anthropology. I agree with his call for more collaboration between anthropology and psychology but I disagree with the premise. His view is England-bound and in no way reflects the collaboration which *does* exist in the United States. American anthropologists from Boas[3] to today have collaborated with psychologists. Nor have we been limited to collaborating with psychoanalysts as Jahoda claims. Whiting and Child[4] (with Hull and Dollard) at Yale in the 40's, Kluckhohn and Murray[5] (and Allport) at Harvard in the 50's, and Cole and his colleagues in the 60's[2] (to mention just three seminal works) can't be simply ignored or brushed aside. It is true that collaboration with *social* psychologists is rare. However, over the last four years of my involvement in such a collaboration, I have discovered not only why such collaborations are rare — the gap between the two traditions is great — but also that there is great potential in such collaborative work.[6]

In addition, there is discussion by Jahoda of the interest in envy as a concept fruitful for future research. This discussion seems unaware of the considerable work in the 50's by Whiting and his psychology collaborators on this topic of status envy,[7-8] which I feel is pertinent, if I understand Jahoda's intent. Similarly the references to ethnic identity seem to ignore much recent American work on the topic not only in anthropology but psychology, political science, and sociology.

I disagree to an extent, with Jahoda's notion that anthropology studies content and psychology process. This is true only to the degree that one is talking about intrapsychic phenomena. In dealing with extrapsychic; e.g., human interactions, it is anthropology that is more concerned with process and setting, while psychology has traditionally been concerned only with measuring outcomes (measurement). Collaboration between anthropologists and psychologists seem most likely when problems that require both sets of skills are under investigation. Thus, Cole, Gay, Glick, and Sharp[2] combine anthropological expertise at delineating setting and process variables external to the child, with psychological skills of measuring their effect. Singh's paper shows a useful combination of participant observation methods with questionnaires and quantitative analysis borrowed from sociology. Psychologists and anthropologists can work together when each recognizes the strengths and limits of his own mode of inquiry and the mutual advantage of combining them for certain critical research questions.

John Berry, a researcher highly regarded and widely cited by psychological anthropologists, presents us with an ambitious and tantalizing paper with new data about the relationships among what he calls ecology, culture, and behavior. This paper and the approach reported are not without problems; the brevity of the paper, however, makes comment difficult since they demand more explicit data than we are given. For example, I think there is a problem with the ecology and socio-cultural indices in that they are composed of such varied components (e.g., European education, urbanization, and wage employment). These are, of course, three aspects relevant only to *Western* acculturation. But we are *not* told how the variables which make these up are scored in relation to the final index. For example, what is the score for "family organization" and what does it signify that psychology is correlated with "political stratification?" These are not apparently ordinal or dichotomous variables. How are they handled?

The basic problem of the indices is deeper: It is the unidimensionality underlying them and the unilinear evolutional assumptions that are implicit in the approach. The indices proceed as if human history, or even the more limited history of the West, were one path on which cultures can be arrayed at some point or other – some more advanced, some more retarded, etc. This is our own cultural chauvinism (projection) and not supported by the anthropology record. All simple societies are not marching inexorably toward our type of complexity. Historically, many cultures "evolved" in reverse order to many of our cherished schema. In anthropology *multi*lineal not *uni*lineal development is the accepted model; and this paper violates it in its indices of social–cultural variables and acculturation patterns.

The way the indices are constructed, with human history on one, two, or three indices, obscures processes of human differentiation. For those who are indeed a part of our own pattern, where the components (e.g., size, complexity, and subsistence patterns) of the index are linked as we think they are, our ideas are likely to work; those who are not, are in effect, statistically eliminated under a value on a correlation matrix, or more important, omitted from the sample. This is especially unfortunate because of the self-validating feature of the enterprise. The cultures are selected to ensure their "variation" along the artifical continua constructed. This biases the sample toward cultures undergoing standard Westernization, thereby homogenizing the results and greatly strengthening correlation coefficients.

Having discussed the ecology and socio-cultural dimensions of Berry's works, let me turn to the "behavior" variable. Of six discrete measures, only two, the Asch experiment and the psycho-stress questionnaire, can be thought of as descriptive or indicative of behavior; the others are all perceptual, cognitive, or psychological tests. Responses to these instruments are not what anthropologists would call behavior. True, this is a problem of disciplinary definition, but it is a problem nevertheless.

The dangers of the faults I have identified are no more apparent than when the author claims that future work need only take into account *one* combined eco-cultural variable, *one* combined acculturation variable, and *one* behavioral component. This is breathtaking conceptual neatness, but so far-removed from the complexity of the ethnographic reality as to leave the author in severe jeopardy of having anthropologists say that he has exceeded what Devons and Gluckman[9] would call his "limits of naivety" as a nonanthropologist. Anthropologists have been wrestling with human diversity and similarities for a long time. They are apt to suspect, with good reason, when they see a Pearson's R of .90 reported for cross-cultural data, that there is either a sample problem (biased toward homogeneity) or that the idea being tested is a tautology. Both factors may be operating here.

I have argued that vestiges of a discredited unilinear evolutionary thought appear in Berry's article. This is one thing in the work of a psychologist, but in the work of an anthropologist it is astonishing, and yet Divale offers us a unilinear evolutionary framework with a vengence unparalleled since the 19th century speculations of Lewis H. Morgan.[10] I'm not against cross-cultural comparisons, I've done cross-cultural research. But to assert, as Divale does, that *all* patrilineal patrilocal societies were once this, then that, and then this, in some grand sequence which he can study on the basis of today's societies is simply unjustifiable, if not incredible. Rohner's analysis of mother–child households, for example, is a refreshing corrective to Divale's unilineal thought.

In addition, the conclusions that Divale draws are not supported by the data. His Table 1 provides statistical justification for arguing that societies which have recent migration are more likely to be matrilocal than patrilocal, but|the data do not attribute a statistical inevitability to the stages that he is describing; i.e. matrilocal-bilateral is not statistically different from matrilocal-matrilineal. Further, the sample shows suspiciously few cases of recent migration given the recent state of anthropological investigations of such societies. Also please note that his second example, the variations in sex ratios of young adults as a function of variations in warfare and infanticide, has nothing to do with the point he's making in the first example of the paper as a whole.

Dawson's article is closely related to Berry's, although with its trappings of "new approaches" and its own jargon, the relationship can be obscured. In fact, Dawson is talking about the same relationship between ecology and socio-cultural factors and perceptual and cognitive style that Berry is, though with more emphasis on bio-chemical influences. Both are applying Witkin's psychologizing to extreme situations where its underlying assumptions can be tested. This literature is well developed and rich; it has recently been reviewed in its entirety by Berry and Witkin[11] in the *Journal of Cross-Cultural Psychology*.

Interesting differences exist between Dawson's model and the anthropologically derived model of John Whiting and his students who investigated many of the variables he says have been largely ignored. Whiting's model is reviewed in his and my chapter in Hsu's *Psychological Anthropology*. This model has even been used to establish fascinating cultural linkages to kwashiorkor raised by Dawson.[12]

Missing from the Dawson article and others here, but present in Whiting and anthropological research, is the effect of psychology on culture, an important concern of anthropologists from Kardiner and Linton *et al.*,[13] to the present day. Psychologists are rarely concerned with the effect of personality on culture, and this represents an important difference between "cross-cultural psychology" and "psychological anthropology" which has not been identified in these papers. Psychologists have tended to view the cross-cultural method as one by which certain assumptions about personality development may be tested. Anthropologists, on the other hand, are more likely to focus on the shared aspects of human behavior within cultures and use such studies as tests of hypotheses concerning the way in which elements of a culture can be integrated by underlying psychological processes. Each field has its own theory. Much can be gained by collaboration, especially in combinations of anthropological and psychological methods as Whiting and Whiting,[14] and Cole *et al.* have shown; but whatever our shared methods, as each discipline pursues its own fundamental concerns, the differences will always remain.

REFERENCES

1. DASEN, P. 1972. Cross-Cultural Piagetian Research: A Summary. *In* Journal of Cross Cultural Psychology. 3: 23.
2. COLE, M., J. GAY, J. GLICK, & D. SHARP. 1971. The Cultural Context of Learning and Thinking. Basic Books. New York, N.Y.
3. BOAS, F. 1911. The Mind of Primitive Man. Macmillan Co., New York, N.Y.
4. WHITING, J. & I. CHILD. 1953. Child Training and Personality. Yale University Press. New Haven, Ct.
5. KLUCKHOHN, C. & H. MURRAY. 1948. Personality in Nature, Society, and Culture. Alfred A. Knopf. New York, N.Y.
6. GUMPERT, P. & C. HARRINGTON. 1973. Intellect and Cultural Deprivation. *In* Teachers College Record. 74 (2).

7. WHITING, J. 1960. Resource Mediation and Learning by Identification. *In* Personality Development in Children. I. Iscoe & H. Stevenson, Eds. University of Texas Press. Austin, Texas.
8. BANDURA, A., D. ROSS, & S. ROSS. 1963. A Comparative Test of the Status Envy Social Power, and Secondary Reinforcement Theories. J. Abnormal Social Psychol. **67:** 527–534.
9. DEVONS, E. & M. GLUCKMAN. 1964. Modes and Consequences of Limiting a Field of Study. *In* Closed Systems and Open Minds. Aldine Publishing Co. Chicago, Ill.
10. MORGAN, L. H. 1877. Ancient Society. New York, N.Y.
11. BERRY, J. & H. WITKIN. Psychological Differential in Cross Cultural Perspective. *In* Journal of Cross Cultural Psychology.
12. HARRINGTON, C. & J. WHITING. 1972. Socialization Process and Personality. *In* Psychological Anthropology. F. L. K. Hsu, Ed. Schenkman Publishing Co., Inc. Cambridge, Mass.
13. KARDINER, A., R. LINTON, C. DUBOIS, & J. WEST. 1945. The Psychological Frontiers of Society. Columbia University Press. New York, N.Y.
14. WHITING, B. & J. WHITING. 1975. Children of Six Cultures. Harvard University Press. Cambridge, Mass.

CROSS-CULTURAL RESEARCH IN THE NEXT CENTURY

Discussant: Dorrian Apple Sweetser

Department of Sociology
Boston University
Boston, Massachusetts 02215

My discussion first presents some reflections on the papers which I had at hand before the conference. Enjoying the chief prerogative of a discussant, I will then point out the need for a paper that nobody wrote. Furthermore, it is a paper that we are presently unable to write. When it is eventually written, this will be a fine paper on a vital topic. It might be called "The shadow society of corporate actors," and it will detail some highly desirable additions to the topics routinely covered in fieldwork so that cross-cultural research can be even more valuable in the next century. First, some reactions to the papers.

I share Rohner's enthusiasm for comparative research, and indeed have made modest contributions of my own, from both cross-cultural data[1-3] and cross-national research carried out abroad.[4-6] From this experience, I endorse wholeheartedly his observations that comparative research allows one to examine the generalizability, the variability, and the correlates of modes of behavior.

Rohner remarks that eventually, when our theory and understanding is deep enough, we will be able to predict behavior. This is part of the conventional wisdom, and we all subscribe to it to some extent; but after some reflection, I now think it conveys an unnecessary reverence. While we revere Science, something has been gaining on us, to paraphrase Satchel Paige. Nonscientists predict behavior all the time, and successfully enough to keep in business: pollsters, people who market new products, actuaries, sincere generals and senior officials who lie to us for our own good. It may be that predicting does not always require profound theory and understanding, only some technical knowledge of the subject matter, plus an audience. For example, if you know that multiple family households are common and preferred in an area, and you know that a company plans to build single family housing for its workers, instantly a prediction should leap to mind. However, unless you can communicate your prediction, it cannot be said to have been made. There are only two routes to an audience; neither of them easy. One is to make a case study of the outcome and try to get it published, thereby adding to the literature on why business (government, medicine, etc.) needs social science. The other route is to set yourself up as a consultant to such businesses, and that is not an easy audience to reach.

Jahoda offers us a cogent and realistic discussion of differences in the assumptions and interests of psychology and anthropology, and of some occasions when these differences have constituted reefs on which hopes for collaboration have been wrecked. I found his distinction between interest in content and interest in process to be particularly illuminating. It is a well known trade secret in anthropology and sociology that one can do perfectly well with most research problems without information about the motives or other psychological processes of individuals. This is due partially to the fact that social life somehow encourages people to want to do what they have to do to sustain social activities; and owing to the fact that in many activities individuals are interchangeable, so if one candidate or incumbent has not the necessary motivation or capacities, a replacement will appear.

Jahoda mentions a one-time search for a theory that would explain the whole personality. This brings to mind a curious phenomenon: periodically, someone from some social science or other will issue a proclamation that this discipline studies "the whole man." I have never seen this occur except as an address to outsiders, when they are told how much the discipline is needed to make mankind's future bright.

I suspect, therefore, that this claim is boundary-marking, an advertising slogan. At any rate, it is a trade secret in sociology that we don't study the whole person, and I trust that this realism is shared by all our colleagues. There is no truly holistic discipline or approach; we all study abstract aspects of behavior in situations. Whether we call what we see "relations of variables," or "patterns," it is never the whole truth.

The originality and scope of Berry's cross-cultural enterprise evoke admiration. The compilation of new cross-cultural measures of acculturative influences alone is a most desirable contribution toward acculturating cross-cultural research to the twentieth century.

Some questions occurred to me about the match between concepts and data. It seems clear that the ecological index is unidimensional; at one end there are hunter—gatherers living in small migrant communities (or descendants of such people), and at the other end there are farmers living in larger, fixed settlements (or their descendants). But what about the culture index? How were the political, stratification, and family variables scored, does a single dimension underlie this index, and if so, what is it? To which sex does the prediction of psychological differentiation from socialization apply, and which sex was tested? Perceptual-cognitive scores were predicted from the traditional means of subsistence. Does this mean that a grandfather's skill in hunting rabbits somehow sharpens the eye of a grandson? How were the psychological test scores correlated with the indexes and their elements; were the sample means used, or the scores of individuals (in other words, what is the sample size for the correlation coefficients)?

Singh gives us a useful and thought-provoking alternative to the demographic conceptualization of ethnicity by his study of the symbols of ethnic identity. The data, and the author's proposals for systematic comparative study of symbolic participation, in particular his proposal that symbols be inventoried, inspire some suggestions. Might we find the following functions of symbols or symbolic behavior everywhere: those which reaffirm for ethnic members their distinctiveness; those which allow the classification of strangers; and those which depict the social distance between ethnic groups?

Dawson briefly refers to several studies, by himself and by others, which have a common feature: explanation of cross-cultural variation in some psychological characteristic, such as handedness, or hormone-related cognitive systems. The interest and promise of these studies contrasts in my mind with the prospectus he offers us on his new-found land of "biosocial psychology."

Dawson's conceptualization of this new field strikes me as imperfectly developed, as lacking in novelty, clarity, and sophistication. For example, why bother to inform us that culture allows faster adaptation to the environment than genetic change? Or that "for individuals to survive in a specific biological environment, an adaptive socio-cultural system must be evolved for that environment, which through appropriate socialization encourages the development of the specific behavioral skills needed for survival." There are tautologies:

"adaptation to different biological environments results in the formation of adaptive social systems . . ." (p. 2). Or, (p. 20) ". . . an understanding of the effects of bio-social change greatly facilitates the analysis of the precise processes, through which psychological skills and attitudes developed through initial bio-social adaptation, break down under the impact of rapid bio-social change."

Divale presents "a new method for causal analysis of cross-cultural surveys . . . The epistemological assumption is that for any given sociocultural process, the ethnographic universe contains societies that were at different stages of the process when they were ethnographically described . . . instead of making a series of diachronic measurements of the variables in each society, the diachronic changes in the variables would be represented by a series of synchronic measurements made in different societies at different stages of the process."

This is not a new method in cross-cultural research; it is a venerable method. Social evolutionists of the nineteenth century used it, and it is still employed. Tyler employed it over eighty years ago in his classic paper, "On a Method of Investigating the Development of Institutions: Applied to Laws of Marriage and Descent."[7] There, for example, he assumes that rules of descent change in a regular way; he reports the relation of the levirate and of couvade to descent, classified as maternal, maternal-paternal, and paternal; and he infers that the results are "only compatible with a tendency of society to pass from the maternal to the paternal systems . . . ." Tyler remarked that "The argument is a geological one." Tyler's metaphor is very like Divale's image of "the universe of human societies as a high-rise apartment building with clusters of societies at different levels . . . ."

Divale specifies that at least one of the variables must have a "time dimension," and his three examples each include the time lapsed since a certain event, such as migration. By comparing societies that differ in the time lapsed since the event, he aims to describe a longitudinal process which began with the event.

As a research design, this is exactly comparable to analyzing data from a "synchronic" (one time only) survey of people of different ages. A variable may be correlated with age because of the process of aging, or because people of different ages belong to different cohorts, or because of a combination of these two reasons. Whatever the reason, the result is a correlation with age.

The author regards his design as an improvement on "synchronic correlation studies." If he means that his design produces something other than correlations of variables that are measured at a single point in time, I disagree. If he means that hypothesis about change or process is better than a hypothesis which is not about change, I share his personal preference. Since history, indeed life, is change, hypotheses about change have a particular interest , in my opinion.

I now take up my second topic, which is the need for systematic collection of new cross-cultural data in the future. In scholarship, new is the name of the game, but I have in mind a novel new area for cross-cultural research, the effect of international politics and international business on daily life in communities. Berry's measures of education, wage employment, and urbanization are moves in this direction. We must go further. To express what I have in mind, I begin by quoting from a recent and most thought-provoking book by James S. Coleman, *Power and the Structure of Society*[8]

> The common-sense way of viewing society is as a vast network or organization of persons. Social scientists as well use that conception, though they

have introduced another, by describing society and social organization as composed of "roles" and "role relations." This depiction of society as consisting of persons occupying roles has, I suspect, been of some value for understanding the functioning of society. But there seems nowhere to exist, neither among social scientists nor among others who discuss these matters, the recognition that the society has changed over the past few centuries, in the very structural elements of which it is composed. (p. 1.)

A sensitive indicator of this change may be found in law, because law (along with politics) is the practicing profession for which social organization is the central field of operations. Thus, legal theory must face problems of social organization as they arise, while academic social theory need not deal with reality, but only with the constructions of it in academic journals. (p. 8.)

Coleman uses the term "natural persons" because corporate actors (corporations, unions, political parties, governments, etc.) are in many respects "juristic persons," according to law. He observes, ". . . there are now two parallel structures of relations coexisting in society — the structure of relations among natural persons, and the structure of relations among those corporate actors that employ the services of persons."[8] Everywhere in the world, no matter how exotic the setting, there are natural resources, and buying and selling. Everywhere in the world, without exception, people have dealings with corporate actors.

A disturbing feature of the difference between persons and corporate actors is that persons are moral; corporate actors, at best, can only be law-abiding. Being moral, a person can see whether there is harm to another person. Being law-abiding, a corporate actor cannot see this. Consider the bloodshed, the devastation, the lies, the waste of the Vietnam war. And all done, for the most part, with perfect legality.

I believe the influence of corporate actors in daily life everywhere is a profoundly different and new feature. This shadow society, invisible until we learn how to see it, affects daily life in a variety of unappreciated ways. For example, purely local markets for labor, crops, or goods are becoming increasingly uncommon around the world. How, precisely, is the economic wellbeing of a community affected by prices and supplies in a national or international market? What are the incentives, and what are the means, for obtaining credit or capital? Should we not describe the banking system of a community in an ethnography, along with the kinship structure? How is the wealth distributed in the community? How do the laws about taxes, including international agreements about taxes, affect the distribution of wealth? Should we not find in the ethnography of a community an account of this dimension of society, along with an account of the indigenous social stratification?

How is the community located with respect to the political, military, and economic zones of influence of great powers, or aspiring powers? Well inside those of one power? At the boundary of zones of competing power? In addition to a description of the climate and rainfall, should we not find a description of the political climate, and of what it brings in the way of foreign investment, foreign aid, and foreign troops? What are the resources and the success of protest movements and the central government in achieving social control? Should not literacy, radio, and television be routinely studied, along with supernatural beliefs?

Corporate actors are creatures of civilization in the technical sense, that is, creatures of cities. As anthropologists turned their backs on cities to go out and find the truth about human nature among peasants and barbarians, it is not surprising to find a lack of the concepts and techniques for the systematic study of this new phenomenon. We sociologists who are specialists in civilization do no better and with less excuse. For comprehension of the economics of corporate actors, particularly corporations, we might reasonably look to the economists. But Galbraith[9] has made a convincing case that economics unwittingly camouflages the activities in this sector of economic life by persisting in interpreting it in terms of neoclassical economic theory — painting over oligopoly with the patriotic colors and homely virtues of free enterprise.

I urge that we develop the concepts and techniques for the systematic reporting of this quiet social revolution going on around the world. It is true that none of us is equipped to do such field work at present; none of us understands the tax laws as they affect business, for example, or the politics of foreign aid, or overseas investments. But once the existence of this new vein of scholarly gold is suspected, the intellectual capital for the mining of it will surely be attracted.

REFERENCES

1. APPLE, D. 1956. The social structure of grandparenthood. Am. Anthropol. 58 (4): 656–663.
2. SWEETSER, D. 1966. Avoidance, social affiliation, and the incest taboo. Ethnology. 5: 304–316.
3. SWEETSER, D. 1966. On the incompatibility of duty and affection: A note on the role of the mother's brother. Am. Anthropol. 68: 1009–1113.
4. SWEETSER, D. 1968. Intergenerational ties in Finnish urban families. Am. Sociol. Rev. 33 (2): 236–246.
5. SWEETSER, D. 1973. Urban Norwegians: Kinship Networks, and Sibling Mobility. Inst. Appl. Social Res. Oslo, Norway.
6. SWEETSER, D. 1975. Education and privilege: An analysis of sibling occupational mobility. Acta Sociologica 18 (1): 23–35.
7. TYLER, E. B. 1889. J. Royal Anthropol. Inst. Great Brit. Ireland. 18: 245–272.
8. COLEMAN, J. S. 1974. Power and the Structure of Society. W. W. Norton Co. New York, N.Y.
9. GALBRAITH, J. K. 1973. Economics and the Public Purpose. Houghton-Mifflin Co. New York, N.Y.

DR. RONALD ROHNER: I will limit my comments to three statements in Harrington's critique. First, his statement that "the people who seriously ask this question [i.e., why cross-cultural research?] are few in number" can be made only by someone who is not seriously involved in cross-cultural comparative research. Those of us who are involved in such research are constantly asked the question — implicitly as well as explicity — by both individuals and by agencies and institutions. One of the important problems of cross-cultural comparative research, in the face of this chronic question, is to demonstrate its value to our colleagues, to funding agencies, and to the various behavioral sciences.

Secondly, Harrington says that my "list of so-called universals. . . consistently ignores evidence which counters the universal." In the context of his surrounding argument this comment points up how an individuals' conceptual predilections are capable of skewing his perceptions. In this case it seems that Harrington's critique is motivated by the idiographic and cultural relativity bias found throughout much of sociocultural anthropology. That is, many anthropologists distrust cross-cultural comparative, generalizing research, especially if the research aims toward establishing psychosocial or cultural universals. Anthropologists are often quick to point out exceptions to these purported universals, and sometimes rightfully so. Here, however, Harrington's conceptual bias seems to have led him to impute something to me that I did not say. My paper does not give a list of universals, as claimed by Harrington. What it *does* do is to cite a few of the more than twenty topics that are now being actively explored for their *possible* universality. Harrington not only misread me, but he overlooked my caution that "most serious cross-culturalists seem to agree that it is entirely problematic to what extent one can generalize to *human* behavior from the work of the current and conventional behavioral sciences, certainly within anthropology and psychology."

Finally, Harrington's objection to my comment that "most anthropologists are methodologically untutored" does not alter the fact that it is the exceptional anthropologist who is well trained in the methodology of behavioral science. Many of us in anthropology are trying to change this, but, as in cross-cultural research, our efforts are often met with resistance.

DR. GUSTAV JAHODA: When one's task is to deal briefly with a large and complex topic it is difficult to avoid oversimplification, and it seems to me that most of Harrington's remarks stem from this flaw, to which I must plead guilty.

Although I probably laid too much stress on the specifically psychoanalytic aspect, two out of the three "seminal" works cited by Harrington as examples of cooperation with psychologists are within the culture-and-personality tradition, and are strongly imbued with psychoanalytic concepts. This is not true of the remaining one, but then I myself cited Cole as an instance of fruitful collaboration. Since I might have given the impression of being unduly negative about both psychoanalytic approaches and culture-and-personality, let me add that I admire LeVine's* attempt to introduce a fresh perspective.

With regard to the suggestions for research that I ventured to put forward, it would appear my purpose was not made sufficiently clear. The operative phrase

---

* LeVine, R. A. 1973. Culture, Behavior and Personality. Hutchinson. London, England.

"systematic descriptive studies ... within the developmental sphere" was intended to refer mainly to work on the development of certain behavioral characteristics within various cultural settings. Hence my concern was not with such high-level abstractions as "status envy," although I am acquainted with the interesting work of Whiting and Bandura *et al.* that Harrington noted. Similarly, I am not entirely unfamiliar with American research on ethnic identity, having done some work in this sphere. If Harrington knows of any such studies in developing countries, to which I particularly referred, he ought to have cited them.

Lastly, one could argue at length about the content-process dichotomy, mentioned only in relation to thought, which is of course an "intra-psychic" phenomenon. I would certainly agree with Harrington that the dichotomy ceases to make sense in relation to wider aspects of human interaction.

DR. J. W. BERRY: Providing detailed criticism and comments on conference papers in a few minutes must be almost as difficult as presenting a conceptually and statistically complex paper in fifteen minutes! My first response, then, is that the major portion of the criticisms can be met by supplying more information, much of which had to be skipped in the interest of time.

A first issue, one raised by both discussants, concerns the nature and assumptions underlying the indices. There are two separate questions, but the theoretical assumptions are perhaps the more basic of the two. Let me state as clearly as possible that the term "evolution" implies two distinctive processes: the first is that organisms *adapt* to changing environments by altering their ecological relationship and adjusting their culture and behavior; the second is that these successive adaptations are deemed to be *progress*, later adaptations are thought to be "better" than earlier ones. I accept the former and reject the latter, and nowhere in my paper do I stray from this position. Thus I do not assume unilinear evolution or development; the only criterion of a better or worse adaptation is its success in a particular adaptive arena. Now when it comes to the second of these two issues, the indices must be constructed according to some quantitative data, and they are, in fact, very simple ones. The first two (the Ecological and Cultural) are based upon the work of such pioneering researchers as Murdock, Naroll and Tatje, and I am pleased to share their "naiveté." Essentially for the Ecological Index, the ratings of variables listed in the paper are summed to provide each sample with a position on a dimension that is anchored at one end by Lee's notion of "nomadic style" and at the other end by its sedentary opposite; there are no implied values, simply an indication of which society has fewer people typically in a community, has a more nomadic settlement pattern, has a greater reliance upon hunting, and so on. For the Cultural Index, a similar operation is made upon cultural variables such as number of political strata, number of social ranks, complexity of family, and so on. It too yields a dimension that implies no value of progress or development. Finally, the Acculturation Index (which is explicitly limited to *western* acculturation) is assembled by quantifying and summing across the number of years of western education, the experience of wage employment and the degree of urbanization of the community. Once again there is no implied "better" or "worse" end of such a dimension. And so the three indices are neither uniquely naive (they have numerous counterparts in anthropological research), nor are there lurking behind them assumptions of unilinear evolution. Most certainly, however, the simplicity of these indices hides much of the underlying cultural complexity of the societies in these studies. On this point, I can only say that my concern is not to model cultures, but to provide a quantification of cultural variables that are predictive of variable behavioral development; in this task, the indices appear to have performed reasonably well.

A second question, one raised by Harrington, pertains essentially to the representativeness of the samples; do the samples included bias the results in favor of the model? Here we must distinguish two quite separate uses of the cultural archives. One (used mainly by anthropologists) strives for cross-cultural generalizations about cultural phenomena; it is a correlational approach that depends greatly upon the independence and the representativeness of samples. The other (being used increasingly by psychologists) is to employ these cultural archives to achieve a quasi-experimental study, in which the background culture variables are "manipulated by selection" and the behavioral variables are studied in the field. In this case, as long as a culture "represents" a particular background condition, it does not also have to "represent" its aspects of cultural variation. Of course, to the extent that a sample is representative in this second sense as well, it provides for greater generalizability; but it is not essential to the design on the study.

A third question, raised by Inkeles as well as by Sweetser, enquired about the use of sample-level analyses, rather than individual-level ones. In fact, individual-level analyses have been carried out† within each sample as this research developed; this paper attempts to put these single studies together at an aggregate level. To mix these two kinds of analyses might be useful, but the interpretation would have to be qualified. That is, if we were to take the 1000 participants in this study, assign each one the Ecocultural and Acculturational Index of his sample, and then correlate his behavioral scores with each Index, we would have a measure, reputedly at the level of individual differences, whose greatest source of variation would actually lie between groups. Such a correlation coefficient would be exceedingly difficult to assess.

Finally a few smaller questions were raised. First, as Harrington points out, the term "behavior" is employed differently in the two disciplines. Given this, I recognize that it remains a problem for interdisciplinary communication, but I fail to see how it remains a problem within the context of a single research model. Second, to comment on a point made by Sweetser, balanced sex samples were employed in all groups, and the question of sex differences has been studied. Essentially, sex differences on behavior were found in those samples at the sedentary and tight end of the Ecocultural dimension, while they tended to be neutralized among the more nomadic and loose samples. Finally, to note another point made by Sweetser, even among relatively acculturated samples, there are numerous cultural features carried over from traditional life; it is essentially an empirical question whether these cultural features are still present, and whether they are still predictive of behavioral development after two or more generations. The data are clear on this point: more acculturated samples from traditionally sedentary and tight populations have mean scores that are closer to their more traditional counterparts than to those of samples who are (or were) more nomadic and loose. To exemplify, the mean performance on Kohs Blocks of PortLoko or Hannabada, do not reach the level in Wemindji or Pond Inlet; the traditional Ecocultural position is a more powerful predictor of behavior than the more recent experience of Western acculturation.

DR. SWEETSER: Might we find everywhere the following functions of symbols or symbolic behavior: those that reaffirm for ethnic members their

---

† See the articles by Berry cited in References 3 and 4 in Berry's paper is this monograph.

distinctiveness; those that allow the classification of strangers; and those that depict the social distance between ethnic groups?

DR. SINGH: I firmly believe that in multiethnic societies, ethnic identities are expressed through participation in the cultural symbols associated with particular ethnic groups. But the intensity of ethnic identification may vary across time and space. In a less differentiated society, it is more likely that a smaller number of symbols would be used for ethnic identification, classification of ethnic "strangers" and ethnic boundary maintenance than would be the case in a more differentiated society: It should be made clear that I do not suggest the replacement of the *demographic approach* by the *symbolic approach*. Both are complementary and reveal different aspects of ethnicity. The symbolic approach is more efficient in the study of ethnic identity, but the changes in the structural positions of ethnic groups can be best explained using the demographic approach. The symbolic approach would enable us to generate inventories of symbols of ethnic identity across time and space and would permit comparative analyses under a functional framework.

MS. GINORIO (*Fordham University, New York, N.Y.*): Using your data, would you say that if acculturation-assimilation were studied using the symbol systems, rather than the demographic data, we would have to conclude that these processes are occurring at a much slower rate than was believed? Do you think these symbols would ever be completely lost by ethnic individuals?

DR. SINGH: The response to the first part of your question is yes. Symbols are part of a cultural system and have considerable staying power. In my sample even those who identified themselves as "Americans" or having "no identity" could not escape from that participation in symbols associated with their objective ethnic backgrounds. Changes in the economic and political position of an ethnic group need not result in cultural assimilation. It is possible that over several generations, some of the old symbols may become less salient or be redefined. However, it is unlikely that an ethnic group in normal circumstances would completely abandon all of its cultural symbols. However, it is possible that new symbols would be created but some form of cultural continuity would still persist. In a differentiated society such as in the United States, one's ethnic identification need not interfere with his participation or performance in various social, economic and political institutions. His abandonment of ethnic identification may not accrue any gains but it may contribute to loss of a pride and psychological security that he may have cherished before.

DR. KRUSZEWSKI (*University of Texas*): In grappling with theoretical and methodological problems in the study of ethnicity in the United States, should not a basic distinction be made between the "immigrant ethnics" and the "territorial minorities" like the Chicano and the Native Americans who found themselves in the United States through shift of borders and, in the case of the Chicanos, who live largely along the United States' southern border and who are in almost daily contact with Mexico?

DR. SINGH: The symbolic approach would not require such distinctions as "immigrant ethnics" and "territorial minorities" in the study of ethnic identities. The cultural symbols associated with ethnic groups need not change in response to economic and political changes. If changes in the symbols occur, the symbolic approach would identify and interpret them in specific cultural and historical contexts. The distinctions suggested by you are relevant mainly in the studies of "dominant-minority" relations.

DR. SARGENT: Do you find any similarity between caste in India and the status of blacks in the United States.

DR. SINGH: In our Pittsburgh study we drew the sample from the communities with minimal Black and Jewish populations. This was deliberately done to maximize ethnic homogeneity within each community and differences among them. However, there are studies in which Blacks in the United States and Untouchables in India have been compared, showing remarkable similarities. It should be pointed out that the Indian caste system is reinforced by religious ideology, while the status of Blacks in the United States has been influenced by their experiences with economic and political institutions since their arrival in America. Both situations can be studied using the symbolic approach. I have already demonstrated that the symbolic approach can be used in the study of ethnic identity both in India and in the United States.

ON THE NEED FOR EXPERIMENTATION
IN CROSS-CULTURAL RESEARCH

Lee Sechrest

Department of Psychology
Florida State University
Tallahassee, Florida 32306

The experimental method is one of several scientific approaches to the attainment of consensus about what we know. However, it is a very important method in psychology, probably the method of choice for a large proportion of researchers particularly for the making of causal inferences. Yet, true experiments are only infrequently encountered in the literature on cross-cultural research. I refer by "true experiments" to investigations in which the level of an important variable of interest is controlled in some manner by the experimenter so that two or more *treatments* result, and in which determination of the level of the treatment to be received by subjects in the investigation is done by random processes. My own surveys of cross-cultural literature indicate that true experiments of that type are very infrequent, probably constituting no more than 5 to 10% of the literature in our best journals.

I also contend that even when experimental procedures are employed, they are often associated with relatively trivial "treatments," and dependent or outcome variables; e.g., two forms of the same questionnaire or different pictorial stimuli, what Brislin, Lonner, and Thorndike call "presentation" experiments.[1] Instances in which investigators have intervened in major ways are few to the point of rarity.

We may assume that the aim of cross-cultural studies as for nearly any other type of research is ultimately to permit the drawing of causal inferences. Specifically, in the case of cross-cultural research we wish to be able to infer with justification that culture or cultural variables are the origin or cause of observed differences in other responses. Again, as with other research, it is necessary to design cross-cultural research in such a way as to weaken those hypotheses which represent plausible rival hypotheses to one of interest; i.e., that observed differences are attributed to culture.[1-3]

The problems of drawing causal inferences in cross-cultural research are the same as in other types of research, particularly that research in which the investigator does not have control of the causal variable. We wish to be able to observe individuals, samples, from two or more cultures and be able to say that differences in their behavior are attributable to the fact that they come from different cultures rather than to any other variable. The problems in making such an inference arise because there is a possibility that individuals from different cultures may differ in so many different ways other than their cultural background e.g., education, social class, understanding of the task, motivation to perform, familiarity with the test situation, etc.[1] Even though such differences arise out of cultural differences, e.g., the general level of education may be lower in one culture than another, they are extraneous in most investigations to the cultural variables of interest.

Theory and Types of Cross-Cultural Research

It is my impression that many of the problems in cross-cultural psychological research stem from failure of researchers to think through in a careful way why they are doing cross-cultural research in the first place. Seemingly a good many published articles are the result of about 40% opportunity and 40% exhuberance, with only the remaining 20% of the impetus stemming from vague ideas about culture and psychological variables.

There are, it seems to me, three distinct types of cross-cultural research which involve different issues and for which different research designs are required.

Type I.   Global Cultural Effects

There is often a phenomenon of general interest in which it is desirable to determine whether there is a cultural influence, because the demonstration of a cultural influence would affect our understanding and interpretation of the phenomenon. Examples are provided by mental disorder, response to alcohol, and differences between sexes in performance on tasks. To show that there are cultural differences in the frequency or patterns of mental disorder,[4] in response to alcohol,[5] or in performances of males and females on common tasks[6] indicates that such phenomena are not to be understood in purely biological terms. It should also be accepted that failure to find cultural differences, whereas perhaps relatively weaker evidence, is suggestive of a fundamental biological cause. The latter point is why the failure to find sex differences in field-independence among Eskimos (Berry, 1966; MacArthur, 1967) is so important.

Type II.   Specific Cultural Variation Effects

There are many phenomena of general interest whose cultural origin is unquestioned, but for which it is desirable to demonstrate the importance of specific cultural influences, usually to pursue some more general theoretical purpose. For example, the well known studies of Whiting and Child,[7] attempting to relate child-rearing practices to adult personality were pursued because of the increased understanding which it was hoped they would provide of the processes of personality development. Another example is the work of Cole and his associates[8,9] on cultural differences in the processes of problem solving. In both cases, the primary interest was in the fundamental psychological processes rather than in the cultural variables *per se*, but in order to improve understanding it was also necessary to focus on particular aspects of the culture. In neither case would the finding of a gross cultural difference have been of much interest or value. In theory Type II, studies could be carried out experimentally, but cross-cultural variations provide an experiment of nature that obviates the practical difficulties that may make controlled experiments impossible. It is my impression that most cross-cultural research is Type II.

Type III

There is a third type of cross-cultural study in which the interest of the investigator is more in the culture itself than in the dependent variable being studied. That is, there is a type of study in which the aim of the investigator is to arrive at a better understanding of the culture, or some feature of it, that he is studying. Thus, for example, Feldman's[10] studies of helping behavior in different cultures are of interest because of their contribution to our understanding of French, Greek, and American cultures. They contributed little to the understanding of helping behavior *per se*.

Plausible Rival Hypotheses in Cross-Cultural Research

Each of the different types of studies described above has associated with it characteristic plausible rival hypotheses which determine in some degree the designs that are desirable for such studies.[2] Type I studies, directed at the determination of cultural influence in a general sort of way, are susceptible to rival hypotheses reflecting genetic, geographic, or ecological factors. Thus, for example, even if cultures differ in frequency or type of mental disorder, we should not leap too readily to the conclusion of cultural causation. Gene pools *may* differ between cultures for factors associated with mental disorder. Climate may be a determinant of some manifestations of mental disorder, and such ecological features as adequacy of nutrition may also be important.[11] Consequently, the design of Type I studies should take such rival hypotheses into account; e.g., by multicultural investigations that eliminate systematic variation associated with rival hypotheses. Better theories that are able to relate specific cultural features to the dependent variables of interest will also help to weaken plausible rival hypotheses, but the more specific the predictions the closer the study will come to being a Type II study.

Studies of the Type II variety are susceptible to rival hypotheses made plausible by the possibility of confounding of theoretically critical variables with other variables of equal, or nearly equal, theoretical standing. For example, general educational level, sophistication in interpersonal settings, competitiveness, and many other variables might be confounded with style or adequacy of problem solving in different cultures and threaten interpretations having to do with specific features of experience provided in the culture. The design of good Type II studies will often require multiculture comparisons so that the proposition that critical variables are systematically confounded with extraneous variables is relatively untenable. One of the strengths of many studies of ethnographic samples[12] is that the sizable number and heterogeneity of cultures available for any given hypothesis makes unlikely the rival explanation that some third and otherwise undetected variable could account for the findings.

In Type III investigations, particular difficulties may stem from inadequate dependent measures or dependent measures inadequately understood, the *emic* vs. *etic* problem.[1,13] If a culture lacked a tradition for or actually had a taboo against giving directions to strangers, an experimental study of helping behavior as reflected in giving directions would be completely misleading. Or if two cultures differ in the extent to which they distinguish between mentally disturbed and mentally retarded individuals, and that difference in distinction is not understood by the investigator of attitudes toward mental disorder, conclusions about cultural differences could be quite erroneous. Adequate Type III studies require careful study and development of dependent measures and may require multiple measures which should produce differential results reflecting the adequacy of the investigator's understanding of the critical variable.

Of course all three types of studies are endangered by sampling differences, inadequacies of communication, and a host of other variables so well described by Brislin, Lonner, and Thorndike.[1] To do good cross-cultural research is at least as difficult as any other kind, and the wise investigator must be far-seeing, imaginative, and quite careful.

Culture as a Quasi-Experimental Variable

One could imagine in some science-fiction way that newborn infants would be systematically collected and shipped randomly all over the world to be reared in whatever societies or cultures they happened to land. Under such circumstances, culture would come close to being a true experimental variable. In fact, the possibilities of different gene pools associated with cultures and differences in prenatal environment and birth practices are the only factors that inhibit us from interpreting the assignment of infants at birth to cultures as a random procedure, and, hence, as experimental. Obvious genetic differences that produce different physical characteristics suggests that it might be hazardous to assume that there are *no* genetic differences between racial, ethnic, and cultural groups with respect to ultimate psychological and behavioral characteristics. That is not to say that such genetic differences do exist; only that it would represent an uncautious position uncharacteristic of science to assume that they do not. However, at least some genetic constancies are assumed, and where such assumptions are acceptable, culture may be thought of as a true experimental variable. One example is ability to learn a language, which is ordinarily *assumed* to be constant across cultures so that children in different cultures seem to learn their languages with equal ease, and children learn the language of the culture in which they are reared without any apparent difficulty attributable to race or ethnicity. A second example is that ability to smile seems a universal human capacity,[14] and any subsequent differences would appear to be attributable to experience, including culture, rather than to race or ethnicity. For both examples the finding of difference between cultures, e.g., in phonemes or in frequency of smiling, is readily attributed to the effects of culture. Other possible factors such as geography or ecology, simply do not seem to be plausible, direct explanations for differences in language or in ease of or occasions for smiling. However, it is unfortunate for purposes of understanding cultural influences on behavior that culture can rarely be taken to be random with respect to genetic potential, and so it cannot be construed as a true experimental variable.

A second difficulty is that there are other variables that are often confounded with culture but cannot be considered to be inherent in culture and are, therefore, threats to the interpretation of cultural influences as causal. Obviously, there are cultural differences in the probable adequacy of the intrauterine environment and of later nutritional status of children, but such differences are not ordinarily themselves a part of the culture, and if children from nutritionally deprived cultures perform inadequately on certain types of problem-solving tasks, inadequate performance usually should not be attributed directly to the culture. Geographical and ecological factors may also have a bearing on some performances without being interpreted as specific cultural effects. There are obviously numerous potential differences between cultural populations which are not directly attributable to the nature of the culture and which, therefore, threaten causal interpretations about cultural influences.

Therefore, culture must be, for most outcomes, considered a quasi-experimental treatment and hence susceptible to all the various threats to internal validity of experiments (Campbell and Stanley, 1966).[2] The task of the cross-cultural researcher is to design investigations in such a way that the plausibility of various threats to internal validity of the cultural experiment is weakened and to plan investigations which overlap and are complementary to each other to such a degree that ultimately the only really viable hypotheses left pertain to the effects of culture on the variables of interest. In general, it can be asserted that the solution to the problems raised, will lie in multiple approaches, multiple methods of attack; a position espoused also by Brislin, Lonner, and Thorndike.[1] It is regrettable that the recommended solution is slowly being implemented and that cross-cultural methodology remains very narrow.

Culture as a Global Treatment

Viewed in an undifferentiated way, culture must be considered to be a global treatment;[2] i.e., it is a treatment with many facets, complex and with diverse potential effects. When a researcher refers to Philippine culture, the reference is to a complex of factors. Is the outcome on some specific measure of Philippine culture, whatever that outcome may be, the result of Catholicism, a peasant outlook, a Spanish heritage, a system of mutual obligations; a combination of two or three or all the factors the characterize Philippine culture? Under many circumstances, the investigator will not be in any position to know.

That culture is a global treatment actually fits the requirements of Type I studies since all that is necessary is to show that culture has an impact on the variable in question; the particular aspects of culture involved makes no difference. Type III studies are also in some degree compatible with the notion of culture as a global treatment, since the purpose of such studies is, in large measure, to further understanding of the nature of that global variable, in effect to permit articulation of some of the distinct aspects. However, Type II studies require a differentiated view of cultures, which permits one to specify just what cultural variable is expected to be operating to produce a particular observed behavior. As a treatment, cultures need to be "deglobalized" for purposes of Type II studies.

The deglobalization of cultures can come about in various ways. In some instances ethnographers or other observers will have done a sufficiently good job of describing cultures which are to be compared that it is possible to specify in some detail just what facets two or more cultures share. In other instances previous research findings will be available. However, for purposes of comparative study and in order to permit the legitimate drawing of causal inferences, the deglobalizing of cultures will ordinarily be possible only by careful and systematic study of three or more cultures which are systematically chosen so as to permit the isolation of the critical cultural features. It is still nearly the rule that cross-cultural studies involve comparisons of only two cultures, one of them usually North American, and it is nearly impossible to know just which of the many differences between two cultures is responsible for observed differences in response variables.

EXPERIMENTS IN CROSS-CULTURAL RESEARCH

Experiments may be thought of as planned, controlled variations in stimuli and/or conditions of responding, and if true experiments are referred to, there is the additional requirement that subjects be allocated randomly to the experimental conditions or treatments. There are, however, various approximations to experiments which have been termed quasi-experiments. Most quasi-experiments come about because for one reason or another subjects are not allocated randomly to conditions. However, there is an additional class of experiments often referred to as experiments of nature in which the variations are neither planned nor controlled. Few experiments of nature involve random allocation of subjects, and so most such experiments must be regarded as quasi-experiments, even though at some level the operation of the experimental variable seems completely unsystematic; e.g., the occurrence of earthquakes within an earthquake belt.

Brislin, Lonner, and Thorndike[1] have made a distinction between "presentation experiments" and "major manipulations," the former referring to variations in stimuli of little inherent importance, e.g., pictures of objects. They perceive quite properly that even questionnaires may be thought of as experiments; in fact, if they are not, then they are trivial. The status of questionnaires as experiments will be discussed later, but at this point, it should simply be noted that the employment of a questionnaire involves planned, controlled variation in stimuli; and when used cross-culturally, the between-subjects treatment variable is simply the quasi-experimental variable of culture. The category of major manipulations refers to experimental treatments in which some major change in stimulus conditions or conditions of responding is effected by the researcher. However, the distinction between mere presentations and major manipulations is not a clear cut one and can only be taken as a general frame of reference. An equally important distinction can be made for response modes, viz.; minor versus major responses. An essential trivial response can be required for a major manipulation, e.g., the verbal response of saying that line A is shorter than line B in a conformity experiment, and a major response can be required in a presentation experiment; e.g., a subject may be asked to commit himself to a protracted social interaction with an individual described in a brief paragraph.

Experimental Designs in Cross-Cultural Research

There are almost no limits on the experimental designs that may be used in cross-cultural experiments, but most research falls into one of only a few fairly discrete types. There is, first of all, and most simply, the single classification design with culture as an independent, subject variable. For example, a straightforward comparison of the responses of samples from two or more cultures on a personality or attitude scale is a common type of research and falls into the single classification category. It should be clear that such a study is rarely interpretable in an unequivocal way and probably only seldom in a way that is really useful. There are too many ways in which samples from cultures may differ other than in cultural background to make a single classification design clearly meaningful. Nonetheless, under some circumstances the single classification design may be useful for Type I and Type III studies. It may be sufficient for some purposes merely to show that two or more cultures differ on some variable, and a difference between cultures may indicate something about the nature of each. There are multivariate versions of the single classification design; i.e., an investigator may have data for two or more dependent measures. Unfortunately, it is still not common for cross-cultural investigators to use multivariate analyses.

A second common research design is a double-classification design with two subject variables, frequently sex of subject in addition to culture. A double classification study does not add anything beyond the contributions of a single classification study unless for some reason the second subject variable is of specific theoretical interest. If, for example, a researcher has a specific prediction about an interaction between culture and sex of subject, a double-classification subject variable design can be informative. The double-classification design is suitable for all three types of cross-cultural studies with the caveat that interpretation of subject variables is as hazardous in cross-cultural as in any other research.[15] Multivariate analyses are appropriate for double-classification studies for which one has multiple dependent variables.

A third type of research design that is relatively common in cross-cultural research is a single-, or sometimes double-, classification on a subject variable, culture at least, with perhaps an additional variable such as sex or age, with two or more stimulus conditions representing different experimental conditions within subjects. In such designs each subject serves as his or her own control. For example, subjects from two cultures might be compared on their ability to solve reasoning problems with and without distracting clues. To the extent that the researcher has a theoretical framework that anticipates culture X experimental condition interactions, the subject variable within subject condition design may be a good one. Many questionnaire studies actually are variations on this design. A typical example would be a study comparing the responses of subjects from two cultures on a personality or attitude questionnaire for which alternate wordings of items would be provided. The subject variable-within subject condition design is often especially useful in ruling out or weakening plausible rival hypotheses by permitting the investigator to predict an interaction involving a cultural difference under one but not the other of two conditions of measurement. The design is adaptable to all three types of studies. Its less obvious application might be to Type I studies, but a conceivable example might be a study in which an investigator predicts a sizable cultural difference on measures of neurotic tendencies but no cultural difference on measures of psychotic tendencies.

One or another of the versions of the within-subjects design is rather frequently encountered in cross-cultural literature, but the employment of the design is often, probably usually, faulty, and the legitimacy of conclusions is suspect. In the within subjects design individuals from two or more cultures are observed under several conditions: usually they are measured on several tests or psychological tasks, and each condition may be thought of as a treatment. The investigator then analyzes the data, more often implicitly than by explicit statistical procedures, for culture X task interactions. However, the interactions are very often not specified in advance, many of them are possible, and what actually results is sheer empirical investigation of the type that if it were used in questionnaire construction, would result in rejection for publication until satisfactorily cross-validated. My own surveys of the literature also suggest that in those instances in which investigators using the within subjects design do specify their predictions in advance, they are correct less than half the time. Another deficiency in the design as it is usually employed is that no attention at all is paid to possible order effects in measurement. Principles of good experimental design in other areas of psychology would call for systematic counterbalancing of the order in which tasks are administered. Cross-cultural researchers rarely specify the order in which tasks are administered and often do not even indicate whether all tasks were given in a single session or in multiple sessions. Now within any one investigation order effects and session effects can be ignored *if*, and the if is critical, the order and session arrangements are the same for every culture studied, although the possibility of culture X task order interactions cannot be excluded out of hand for all types of tasks. However, the problem of order of tasks becomes important when investigators want to make comparisons across experiments as they often do. For example, an investigator may want to compare the magnitude of Rod-and-Frame Test errors obtained in his study with those obtained by other investigators; and if conditions of administration are not comparable, then neither will scores be comparable. If the within subjects design is to continue to be used in cross-cultural psychology, more attention needs to be paid to its specific features and to using it in as strong a form as possible.

A fourth general type of design, one encountered only infrequently in cross-cultural studies, involves the crossing of a subject classification with a between groups experimental design; i.e., a design in which the researcher assigns subjects from each of two or more cultures randomly to different experimental conditions. Such a design results in a true experiment with a condition of critical interest controlled by the experimenter. With such a design the researcher can be confident within reason that differences in the dependent variable that are associated with the experimental conditions are in fact attributable to those conditions. As should be clear from the previous discussion, differences associated with cultural variations cannot quite so confidently be attributed to the cultures themselves, but if the theory underlying the study is well developed, the prediction and confirmation of culture X experimental conditions interaction is grounds for reasonable confidence in one's understanding of the phenomena involved.[15] The subject variable—experimental variable design is especially suitable for Type II and III studies, it being in the nature of Type I studies that they rarely involve genuine experimental manipulations.

Even though with a true experiment an investigator can be confident within limits that his experimental manipulation *and no other variable* was responsible for the findings obtained, it should not be supposed that problems in interpreting an experiment end there. Experimental manipulations in fact very often involve rather global changes in conditions that may extend beyond a researcher's intentions or understanding. Thus, an experimenter may devise a condition intended to enhance competitive motivations, may discover that subjects tested in that condition respond differently from those tested in a control condition, and may be justifiably confident that the difference between conditions was responsible for the difference in performance. Yet, just what features of the experimental manipulation produced the difference in responses, and even whether the critical features are intended by or are known to the experimenter may be uncertain. Current practice in social psychology calls for a manipulation check to determine whether the experimental condition was as intended by the experimenter. Such checks may be difficult in much cross-cultural research, but where at all possible, they should be undertaken.

The subject variable—experimental condition design just described is extendable in the same way as other designs by the addition of other subject variable classifications, by multiple experimental treatments, and by multiple outcome measures. It may even be extended by a within subject treatment if that is desirable. All of the designs mentioned above have their place in the overall strategy of cross-cultural research, but designs incorporating experimental manipulations by the investigator will be the focus of the remainder of this paper.

Cultural Meaning of Stimuli

Essentially an experiment may be thought of as the observation of responses under conditions of controlled stimulus differences. A change in stimuli may be produced by a discrete event, as when an experimenter shifts from one language to another or when an experimenter displays a picture of an outgroup rather than an ingroup member, or by a complex and ongoing series of events such as are involved in producing a "warm" as opposed to a "cold" interpersonal atmosphere. Even so, an experimental condition or treatment had best be thought of as a global stimulus consisting not only of the particular events deliberately manipulated by the experimenter but also of the overall context in which those manipulations occur.

In order, then, to meet the requirement that the meaning of an experimental stimulus be equivalent across cultures[2] it is necessary to take into account the total stimulus context provided by a research project and not simply the experimental stimuli *per se*. Cultural differences in reaction to such experimental arrangements as the presence of a prestigious individual, often an outsider, the necessity to perform while being carefully observed, the use of strange apparatus, etc., must be considered both in the planning and the later interpretation of experiments. When the researcher comes to the conclusion that his experimental group differed from the control group, the entire stimulus situation that distinguished the experimental from the control condition must be regarded as implicated in the results. Perhaps more in some cultures than in others, extra special care must be taken to ensure that the experimental and control groups do not differ in *any* other than the critical and intended ways. Similarly, when the researcher concludes that a sample from one culture differs from a sample from another culture in response to the experimental variable, consideration must be given to the possibility that any differences might be attributable to the greater strangeness of the entire situation to one group as compared to another.

It should not be thought that avoidance of experimental arrangements does away with problems of stimulus meaning. Individuals in various cultures are differentially familiar and comfortable with written documents, answering strange and abstract questions, being interviewed, being observed, trying to excel some standard, etc. On the other hand, some experiments involve arrangements so innocuous, inconspicuous, or routine that problems of differential meaning of stimuli are largely bypassed.

The differential meaning of words as stimuli is apparent to almost everyone, and a good bit of attention has been paid to the need for careful and exact translation.[1,16] It has also been noted quite cogently by the authors cited that the adequacy of a translation is a pragmatic rather than an esthetic, literary, or other concern; what is important is that equivalent responses be produced. It is the *sense* rather than the literal wording of a communication that must be transmitted.

Much the same might be said for nonverbal stimuli. It is important that nonverbal stimuli employed in an experiment produce the same response across cultures or experimental conditions rather than that the stimuli be identical. Thus, for example, a policeman might be chosen as an authority figure in one culture, but if in a comparison culture policemen do not carry an image of authority, then their use in the experiment would be inappropriate despite the equating of occupational roles. Or a researcher might want to vary interpersonal warmth as an experimental condition and might choose in one culture to help establish warmth by maintaining a high level of eye contact, smiling frequently, and making the subject an offer of refreshments. Such behavior might or might not suggest warmth in the same degree in other cultures to be studied. Researchers planning experiments in two or more cultures would do well to study the recommendations made by Brislin, Lonner, and Thorndike[1] concerning translation of verbal material for the light it may cast on the problems involved and the procedures to be followed in developing adequate nonverbal stimulus conditions.

Cultural Meaning of Responses

In most discussions of research methodology for cross-cultural study the problems of equating responses are passed over lightly or even ignored. In fact, however, response equivalence problems are equally as important and as difficult as those involved in stimulus equivalence, a point made well by Berry,[13] whose recommendations deserve adherence. One begins with the fact, usually overlooked, that responses as well as stimuli tend to be global in nature. Researchers are comfortable with the little circles or dots that they get on their answer sheets, but those little pencil squiggles are only a small part, and often a byproduct at that, of the total response of the research subject who may have giggled, squirmed, hurried, sweated, or copied from another person in producing the little squiggles. Or a person adjusting a figure to the upright may have done almost any of the preceding things but may also have made adjustments and readjustments, may have made only a desultory effort, may have been closely observant for cues from the examiner, etc. Clearly, researchers need to be very cautious in abstracting from a total complex performance some little aspect to call the dependent variable in their experiments.

Very often the response variable in a cross-cultural study is a verbal response: sometimes the response is a fairly long string of verbal discourse. Yet problems of translating response variables are infrequently discussed. Investigators will on occasion go to considerable extremes to ensure the equivalence of interview questions, perhaps with decentering and back-translations, and then deal with responses in the most casual way imaginable. More often than not the analysis of responses is scarcely described, and responses are *not* back-translated. Sometimes responses are coded separately in the languages in which they are given, but with no particular attention given to the comparability of the coders or the coding system, and sometimes the responses are translated before coding, without attention to the adequacy of the translation. Admittedly the problems involved in translating responses are formidable since there is often so much more material to be translated than in a single interview form; but the problems will not go away because they are big. At the very least, investigators who plan to use questionnaires should make certain that their response terms, – true of me; strongly agree; false – are equally as carefully constructed and translated as the questions. One suspects that such is not the case, and we do know that achieving equivalence of single words or brief phrases is especially difficult.

Just as nonverbal stimuli may not be equivalent across cultures, so may nonverbal responses. Suppose, for example, that a researcher is interested in some aspects of attitudes of young people toward their fathers and mothers, and suppose that he presents subjects with a picture of either their own mother or father and asks them to punch out the eyes of the picture with a stylus.

Obviously, the response involved may have very different meanings in different cultures. Or, to take another example, the author once wished to compare frequencies across two cultures with which letters "lost" in different locations and with different return addresses would be mailed by finders.[17] Presumably the mailing of a lost letter might be taken as a helping response. However, one of the cultures being studied was characterized by serious poverty, and it was discovered inadvertently that many of the letters that were found were not being mailed because the finder apparently wanted the uncancelled stamps from them. Such variables as eye contact, physical proximity, and touching are obviously potentially different in meaning from one culture to another.

Brislin, Lonner, and Thorndike[1] state that it is necessary to determine whether stimuli are equivalent across cultures and give as an example the determination whether level of aggressive drive is equal in two cultures after exposure to an experimental stimulus. Unfortunately, there is a paradox not easily resolvable, if at all, lying in the fact that the only way to determine whether stimuli are equivalent is to find out whether they produce the same response; but the only way to determine whether responses are the same is to find out whether they are produced by the same stimulus. Thus, since it is possible to assess aggressive drive only by noting some response, the failure to find the same response in two cultures might mean either that the stimulus is not equivalent for the cultures *or* that the response to be observed does not have the same meaning for the two cultures. The problem is not obviated by relying on questionnaires, no matter how carefully translated. The resolution can, in the estimation of this writer, come about only through a *program* of research with multiple methods and with varying stimuli and responses in such a way as to permit an ultimate triangulation upon the best conclusion.

Questionnaires as Experiments

It has already been suggested that the administration of a questionnaire may be regarded as fitting the experimental paradigm; perhaps at this time it would be desirable to explain more fully the sense in which it is true and the types of experimental designs that may result.

To begin with, every experiment must have an "independent" variable; i.e., one which is to vary in such a way that its effects may be observed. Even though culture is not a truly experimental variable in the sense of being manipulable, it is nonetheless *the* independent variable of critical interest in cross-cultural studies. Consequently, when an investigator administers a questionnaire in two cultures with the aim of comparing them, culture is the independent variable, and responses on the questionnaire are the dependent variable. What the investigator will hope to be permitted to conclude is that any differences in the questionnaire responses can be attributed to the cultures of the respondents and not to irrelevant variables such as educational level, age distribution, or the like. The design is quite the same as is involved in administering a Rod-and-Frame Test in two cultures or in counting the number of lost letters that are returned in two cultures. The design can be elaborated by splitting the respondent samples in each culture along lines of sex, age, socio-economic status, urban-rural location, etc. In addition the design might be elaborated by a manipulated variable; e.g., questionnaire administered by male vs. female examiners, under conditions of high or low evaluation apprehension, or in school vs. home settings.

In the devising and analysis of a questionnaire study the individual items can also be treated as an experimental variable within subjects. If there are several items measuring the same response tendency, those items can be treated as replications within subjects in much the same way as would be done with a repeated measure or multivariate design. In addition, however, there are types of studies in which subsets of items can be devised to serve as controls for unwanted sources of variance in the main dependent measures. One example would be the use of items and their reversals to control for an acquiescent response bias. Measures of social desirability or other response biases could also be controlled for by special subsets of items, and the success of the control would be reflected in a significant culture X item subset interaction term in a ANOVA. Subsets of items could even be included to "deglobalize" the cultural variable by measuring and then analyzing for variables that might be confounded with culture, e.g., educational level, in such a way as to obscure the interpretation of a cultural difference. Again, what one would expect to get would be a signicant interaction between culture and the two or more dependent measures. In effect, at least some of what is involved in successful application of questionnaire measures across cultures very much resembles the multitrait-multimethod matrices suggested by Campbell and Fiske[18] for assessing validity of tests. One wants to show that the questionnaire to be employed has convergent validity; i.e., differentiates between cultures in the expected way, but also that it has discriminant validity in not being redundant with other, unwanted sources of variance.

Experiments Within and Across Cultures

Experiments both within and across cultures fit very well the demands of Type II and Type III studies; experimental procedures are probably less relevant to Type I studies. The problems of interpreting experimental studies, particularly those involving subject variables, are primarily the problems of interpreting the main effects, specifically in engendering confidence in the reader that whatever effects are found are attributable to the variable in question and not to some confound. Almost certainly more often than not when a difference is found between cultures, it will not be clear just what aspects of the cultures contributed to the difference or even whether the difference is attributable in a direct way to essential aspects of the culture. Other subject variables such as sex and educational level are similarly difficult to interpret.

It cannot be alleged that there is a straightforward way out of the problem posed here, but the development of manipulated variables for which culture interactions can be predicted will be of great help in facilitating our understanding of the processes of culture. For example, suppose two cultures are found to be different with respect to accuracy of solution of some type of mental problem. That difference could be the result of differences in understanding of the problem, in background information necessary for problem solution, in intelligence level in samples chosen, in motivation, in interfering effects of anxiety, or in any of a myriad of other variables. To the extent that the investigator does not understand the nature of the variable, underlying the difference in performance, he is not in a position to make a clear-cut interpretation of the difference. On the other hand, to the extent that the investigator really understands the variables operating in the situation, he should be able to think of and devise experimental situations in which the cultural difference in performance would be changed markedly, either by being enhanced or by being diminished. If the investigator *can* predict and then produce *interactions* between culture (or other subject variables) and a manipulated variable, he is on much better grounds in making the interpretation of a cultural difference.[15]

What is being proposed here is that cross-cultural investigators should largely abandon the exploratory mode of investigation, the "let's see if there are any cultural differences in *blank*" approach, and begin to try to specify the variables believed to be operating between cultures to produce the effects that should be obtained on outcome measures. Then attempts should be made to show that those variables also produce the same effects within cultures. One way, a reasonably sure way, of testing for such effects is to attempt to manipulate the variable of interest *within* each culture to be studied. To give but one instance, if it is alleged that the difference between Indian and U.S. samples on risk-taking tasks is attributable to achievement motivation[19] then it ought to be possible to show that when achievement motivation is aroused in Indian subjects, they will behave much like their U.S. counterparts, and that the latter will behave like Indians with reduced achievement motivation.

What we are looking for is predictable culture by treatment interactions that reveal within culture sensitivity to the hypothesized between culture variable. Michael Cole and John Gay and their colleagues have shown very convincingly their ability to produce culture X treatment effects experimentally, and in so doing they have left no doubt about the nature of the existing differences between cultures.[9] Most of the other true experiments of a cross-cultural nature known to this writer are in the areas of cognition and perception. Experiments in personality and on social phenomena are rare.

It is, of course, also possible to produce culture X treatment interactions in a quasi-experimental mode, but positive findings are still always open to challenge on the basis of one or more of the threats to internal validity and are not finally so persuasive. One could, for example, show that within *both* Indian and U.S. cultures subjects high in measured achievement motivation differ in risk taking from those low in achievement motivation. However, even if shown, the results may be challenged on grounds of possible correlated differences in other variables. Quasi-experiments can be useful, but in the long run they are more expensive, more tedious, and slower. A good case in point is the linking of smoking in a causal mode to cancer, heart disease, etc., where after the spending of millions upon millions of research dollars and years and years of effort, the causal relationship is still challenged by many persons. One good experiment, admittedly one which could never have been carried out, would very likely have resolved the issue conclusively.

Within-Culture Experiments

There are points in the development of cultural understanding at which experiments carried on completely within a culture may be useful. For one thing, there is nothing quite so telling about our understanding of a complex situation as our ability to anticipate what will happen with changed circumstances. If we really understand a person or a culture, we should be able to predict what will happen if some change, e.g., an experimental manipulation, is introduced.[20] A case in point is the understanding that two of my associates and I thought we had of the separate functions of two languages in a bilingual culture.[21] We had thought from casual interviews and systematic observations, as well as from previous experiments of another investigator, that

English and the local language should produce different responses in a certain type of social situation. We were partially wrong and could only conclude that our understanding of the duality of the languages was faulty. We have never ourselves achieved a better understanding. Even so, this writer continues to believe that the systematic thinking and methodological discipline introduced by the requirements of careful experimentation even carried out within a single culture can be invaluable in enhancing understanding of separate cultures and across cultures and that the nature and level of understanding that will be achieved is not readily achieved by other methodologies, even if they are exemplary of their kind.

CONCLUSION

Despite the potential value of quasi-experimental designs, the writer would like to take a strong position in favor of experimentally controlled or manipulated variables in cross-cultural research. The gain in precision and the consequent increase in confidence about causal inferences clearly justifies a greater effort than has heretofore been made to achieve control over variables in cross-cultural research.

No argument is being made here for doing away with quasi-experimental methodology, correlational analysis, etc. Rather, what is needed is redressing of the methodological balance so that experimental methodology bears a greater share of the burden in cross-cultural research. The power of experimental methodology and the corresponding expansion of our methodological horizons could not but have a salutary effect on cross-cultural research. We need more than a 5% infusion of experimental methodology, and an additional and considerable booster shot of rigor to the alternatives now much in use.

The application of the experimental method in cross-cultural study will not be easy. Not the least of the difficulties will be that there is too little good theory to guide the development of such studies. We badly need some better thinking, more carefully reasoned arguments, and hypotheses. Too much cross-cultural research is done by, more or less, blind uninformed comparison of members of two or more cultures on some variable of interest, with very little thought given to the way in which culture might be linked to that variable. Any two cultures differ in a myriad of ways so that an empirical finding of a difference is not informative. The important problem is to be able to specify the way in which the cultures differ that is responsible for the difference in the dependent variable. Only when we know for sure why we want to do cross-cultural research in the first place will our methodological choices become completely rational and optimal.

REFERENCES

1. BRISLIN, R. W., J. W. LONNER, & R. M. THORNDIKE. 1973. Cross-cultural research methods. John Wiley & Sons. New York, N.Y.
2. CAMPBELL, D. T. & J. C. STANLEY. 1966. Experimental and quasi-experimental designs for research. Rand McNally & Co. Chicago, Ill.
3. WEBB, E., D. T. CAMPBELL, R. D. SCHWARTZ, & L. SECHREST. 1966. Unobtrusive Measures: Nonreactive Measures in the Social Sciences. Rand McNally. Chicago, Ill.

4. SECHREST, L. 1969. Philippine culture, stress, and psychopathology. 306–334. East-West Center Press. Honolulu, Hawaii.
5. MACANDREW, E. & R. B. EDGERTON. 1969. Drunken comportment: A social explanation. Aldine Publishing Co. Chicago, Il.
6. D'ANDRADE, R. G. 1966. Sex differences and cultural institutions. In Development of Sex Differences. E. Maccoby, Ed. 173–204. Stanford University Press. Stanford, Ct.
7. WHITING, J. & I. L. CHILD. 1953. Child training and personality. Yale University Press. New Haven, Ct.
8. COLE, M., J. GAY, J. GLICK. 1968. Some experimental studies of Kpelle quantitative behavior. Psychonomic Monograph Supplements. 2(26).
9. COLE, M., J. GAY, J. GLICK, & D. SHARP. 1971. The cultural context of learning and thinking. Basic Books. New York, N.Y.
10. FELDMAN, R. 1968. Response to compatriot and foreigner who seek assistance. J. Personal. Social Psychol. 10: 202–214.
11. WALLACE, A. F. C. 1972. Mental illness, biology, and culture. F. L. K. Hsu, Ed. In Psychological Anthropology 363–402. Schlenkman. Cambridge, Mass.
12. WORCHEL, P. 1974. Societal restrictiveness and the presence of outlets for the release of aggression. Journal of Cross-Cultural Psychology, 5: 109–123.
13. BERRY, J. W. 1969. On cross-cultural comparability. Internat. J. Psychol. 4: 119–128.
14. EIBLE-EIBESTELDT, I. 1970. Ethology: The biology of behavior. Holt, Rinthart, Winston. New York, N.Y.
15. UNDERWOOD, B. J. & J. SHAUGHNESSY. 1975. Experimentation in Psychology. John Wiley & Sons. New York, N.Y.
16. WERNER, O. & D. T. CAMPBELL. 1970. Translating, working through interpreters, and the problem of decentering. In Handbook of Method in Cultural Anthropology. R. Naroll & R. Cohen, Eds. 398–420. The Natural History Press. Garden City, N.Y.
17. MILGRAM, S. 1969 (June). The lost letter experiment. Psychology Today.
18. CAMPBELL, D. T. & D. W. FISKE. 1959. Convergent and discriminant validation by the multitrait-multimethod matrix. Psychol. Bull. 56: 82–105.
19. CARMENT, D. W. 1974. Risk-taking under conditions of chance and skill in India and Canada. Journal of Cross-Cultural Psychology. 5: 23–35.
20. KELLY, G. A. 1955. The Psychology of Personal Constructs. W. W. Norton. Chicago, Ill.
21. SECHREST, L., L. FLORES, & L. ARELLANO. 1968. Language and social interaction in a bilingual culture. Journal of Social Psychology. 76: 155–161.

CULTURE AND PERSONALITY REVISITED

R. Díaz-Guerrero

Facultad de Psicología
Universidad Nacional Autonoma de México
Ciudad de México
México 18, D.F.

INTRODUCTION

Culture in evolution, as best described by LeVine, can and should certainly be made the crucial concept in an interdisciplinary and necessarily cross-cultural approach for the behavioral sciences.

LeVine[1] describes five theoretical concepts of culture-personality relations. Three of them (personality-is-culture, personality mediation, and the two systems in interaction) are not hermeneutically incompatible and can fundamentally be the conceptual background for the relation between personality and culture. Although the personality-is-culture approach is static, one can certainly think of individuals and occasions where personality and culture are indistinguishable. That culture and personality interact is a truism in a category of occasions. The personality mediation model is the most elegant of the three views.

Formulated first by Abraham Kardiner and Ralph Linton, the personality mediation view was further refined by Whiting and Child. A recent version of the Whiting theory was formulated by Robert A. and Barbara E. LeVine (1966).* Child-rearing practices for socialization of the individual operate within the constraints set by the maintenance system of the culture, which in turn functions for the survival of the society in relation to its external environment. The products or expressive aspects of the culture can be thought of as the projective system. Personality is seen not only as mediating causal influence between two aspects of culture but also as actively integrating them with one another.[3]

Triandis, with his coworkers,[4] fundamentally subscribes to the personality mediation view and provides a nearly exhaustive map of the personality as mediator. He is very careful to point out that there are distal as well as proximal antecedents of subjective culture, and that only research can determine the degree of significance of many of the ordinarily enumerated antecedents. As an exemplar of the psychological approach, he is much concerned with the causation and explanation of behavior. His work with the semantic differential, particularly as utilized for the study of antecedent-consequent relations and to separate cognitive, normative, affective, and other dimensions in the study of attitudes, provides a useful framework to understand and study culture-personality relations.

* Reference 2.

CAUSATION OF HUMAN BEHAVIOR

D'Andrade refers to the four major explanations that are currently endorsed in anthropology:

> The historical (a particular custom exists because it was invented at some previous time, and then transmitted from generation to generation, or from society to society, to its present location in time and space); the structural (a particular custom exists as an expression of some more basic or underlying cultural or social condition, and can only be understood as a manifestation of this more basic condition); the functional (a particular custom exists because it maintains or integrates social life in some beneficial way); and the reductionistic (a particular custom exists because of the operation of some psychological or physiological mechanism).[5]

Melvin Marx speaks of the two major types of scientific explanation in psychology: "1. Reductive, by means of which particular phenomena are functionally related to other phenomena at a different and, in a hierarchical sense, more basic level of description. 2. Constructive, by means of which the phenomena are described in terms of more abstract, or higher order, constructs and hypotheses on the same descriptive level."[6]

In a recent book,[7] I make a radical distinction between the *hows* and the *whys* of human behavior. The hows refer to mental functions or processes such as how we learn, how we perceive, or how we think. These questions in psychology are not different from questions in physiology: how we digest, how we breath, how we excrete, etc. The why of human behavior is something else and necessarily more complex. In one category of occasions it may be that the why is a how: for example, when why is asked when a problem has been solved. In another category of occasions it may be obvious that a reductive explanation is indispensable: for example, when we ask why the leg extends after the knee is tapped. But the whys of human behavior clearly demand explanations beyond the reductive and constructive for many categories of occasions.

FIGURE 1 shows the paradigm with which I describe human behavior to undergraduate students in a course of systems and theories in psychology. The students have no difficulty in grasping the elements of this paradigm. They are only a little startled when they are told that the same human behavior may be the result of different causes or combinations of causes in time and space. My favorite example is found in a book written by R. C. Aukerman,[8] which describes 100 different approaches that have been utilized to teach children to read. My students are somewhat less surprised when I tell them that the same causes or combination of causes in time and/or space may produce different behaviors. Egon Brunswik,[9] discusses similar characteristics of behavior phenomena under the terms of vicarious mediation and vicarious response.

Most behavioral scientists agree that to establish cause and effect relationships we must exercise strict control. There is no doubt that strict control, whether in an experimental or in a statistical sense, is the only avenue open for the serious establishment of cause and effect relationships, that is, between certain antecedent and certain consequent events. But even if I do express allegiance to the use of control in the behavioral sciences, let me add what I told years ago to a group of cross-cultural research experts: We should not deceive ourselves into believing that to label and define operationally a given variable and find it either in an experiment or in a quasi-experimental design associated with some

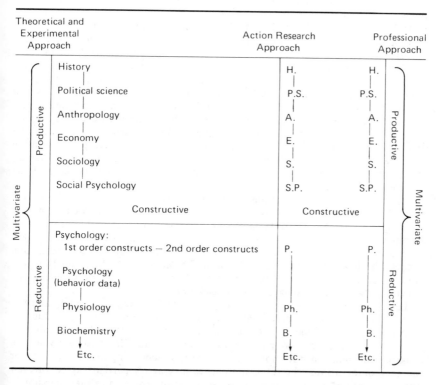

Theoretical and Experimental Approach	Action Research Approach	Professional Approach
History	H.	H.
Political science	P.S.	P.S.
Anthropology	A.	A.
Economy	E.	E.
Sociology	S.	S.
Social Psychology	S.P.	S.P.
Constructive	Constructive	
Psychology: 1st order constructs — 2nd order constructs	P.	P.
Psychology (behavior data)		
Physiology	Ph.	Ph.
Biochemistry	B.	B.
Etc.	Etc.	Etc.

FIGURE 1. Scheme of possible explanations of behavior. Some psychologists accept only constructive and reductive explanations. This scheme does not include all the possible approaches. The three complex approaches illustrated, with their internal variation, are only points of a continuum of possibilities on the time dimension. In the theoretical and experimental approach the scientist wants to know what antecedent "hows, procedures, and environments" (see NOTE below) are "causally" connected with what dependent behavioral events. The time sequence stressed is "past-present." A trial is made to control contemporary and anticipatory events. In the action research approach the scientist wants to know what contemporary "hows, procedures, and environments" produce what objective changes immediately subsequent in dependent behavioral events. The stress is in "present-present" and "present-immediate future." In the professional approach ideally the professional wants to know what specific course or combination of "hows, procedures, and environments" is most efficient to obtain specific objectives. The stress is on the future. To function, he ideally gathers extant knowledge of antecedent-consequent, contemporary, and anticipatory-future relationships.

NOTE: "Hows, procedures, and environments" is an expression that tries to include the many factors intervening. "Hows" in this context refers to the specific reasoning of the scientist or scientists; "procedures" implies the entire translation of the reasoning into experimental actions; "environments" refers to the entire ecology, sociology, and the like where the experiment takes place.

behavioral event means that this is the only, or perhaps even the best, variable to think about, if our goal should be to provoke a change in the associated dependent variable.

Holtzman et al.,[3] report that Mexican school children paired with American schoolchildren in socioeconomic level, age, sex, and school grade, obtained a significantly lower vocabulary score in the Wechsler Intelligence Scale (WISC). Because we had data from an overlapping longitudinal design covering twelve years, it was possible to offer as part of the explanation that programs of education in Mexico are less efficacious than those in the United States. An interview with the mothers and studies of the home environment for the subjects of the study in the two societies made it possible to partially explain the results on the basis that educational elements and intellectual stimuli were not to be found as frequently in the Mexican household. Because we had data indicating that Mexican mothers utilize more authoritarian upbringing techniques than do American mothers, we could have attributed the lower vocabulary score of the children to this cause.

Let us ask the simple questions: Why are Mexican mothers more authoritarian than American mothers? Why is the educational system in Mexico not as effective as the American system? Why is there not as much intellectual stimulation or educational resources in the Mexican household as in the American? The fundamental question could be: Cannot all of these behavioral events (the lower scores in vocabulary of the Mexican children and the more authoritarian mothers) in Mexico be the effects of previous occurrences, the reasons for which we will have to delve back in time?

Let us return to FIGURE 1; the experimental, the action research, and the professional approaches may find only one variable on either the reductive, constructive, or productive ranges, associated to the dependent variable or several variables in various multivariate combinations. The complexity of the causation of behavior does not stop here. Often, depending on the occasion or category of occasions, the three approaches may agree, partially agree, or even disagree regarding the causation of a given behavior. The area of the comparative consequences of intervention on specific human behaviors on the basis of experimental, action research, or professional approaches is important. For instance, is it true that the less I take into account the associated antecedents of a present behavioral pattern when I try to modify it, the less successful I am; and if I should be successful, the more serious the consequences for the individual or group? Do astrological predictions change human behavior? When they do, what are the consequences?

Because the explanation of behavior can be this complex, one must consider the prerequisites that any approach should have to increase the efficacy of explanation in the behavioral sciences.

I believe it is important to start from the only multivariate "given" that exists for all human behavior: culture. Culture should be the baseline for the behavioral sciences. Personality is the psychological "given." Hence, culture and personality are the most important of the relationships for a science of human behavior.

The more complex and significant a behavioral event, the more it is the result of a long and not well understood series of antecedent and concomitant hows and procedures and environments past, present and future (in anticipation), and the greater the need to establish approaches that may link meaningfully at least a few of the various terms.

A HISTORICAL TIME-BINDING VIEW OF CULTURE–PERSONALITY RELATIONS

As in physics, time relationships between behavioral events are crucial. Prediction, the ultimate criterion of truth in the behavioral sciences, has been used to tie the present with future events. The experimental approach does this for the immediate past. Correlations may indicate potential predictions from one to another or among several behavioral phenomena existing contemporaneously. They can be used in an attempt to tie present events with the distant past. Time series, trend analysis, age cohort studies, etc. may try to understand the effects of the passage of historical time. Adequate criteria and methods combined in a meaningful and progressively more complex time-binding approach should be best for the behavioral sciences. In what follows I shall try to illustrate one possibility.

In dealing with present human behavior, the history of the given cultures is the fundamental source. Again we are confronted with the problem of where to stop in history and how to isolate variables from all the antecedents that will be significantly associated with the behavioral events that we are interested in.

In the framework of a historical approach I have arrived at a type of construct that may fulfill a specific technical criterion to adequately measure certain manifestations of culture,† and three time-binding criteria: one, to be related meaningfully to proximal antecedent and to contemporary behavioral events as defined by sociologists and psychologists; two, to connect meaningfully these behavioral events and distant historical antecedents; and three, to meaningfully connect present and future behavioral events. ‡

CONCEPTS AND CONSTRUCTS

For the purpose of the present approach, a socioculture was early defined:

> As a system of interrelated sociocultural premises that norm or govern the feelings, the ideas, the hierarchization of interpersonal relations, the stipulation of the types of roles to be fulfilled, and the rules for the interaction of individuals in such roles: where, when, with whom, and how to play them. All of this is valid for interactions within the family, the collateral family, the groups, the society, and the institutional superstructures, educational, religious, governmental, and for such problems as the main goals of life, the way of facing life, the perception of humanity, the problems of sex, masculinity and femininity, the economy, death, etc.[10]

The empirical construct to deal with culture is the historic-sociocultural premise (HSCP). An HSCP is an affirmation, simple or complex, that seems to provide the basis for the specific logic of the group. We say that when the members of a given group think, their thinking starts from these affirmations, properly called premises; when they feel, their way of feeling is predicated upon these premises; when they act, they will implement these premises or their conclusions, unless a more powerful inner or outer force interferes.

---

† This criterion stands for the characteristics: reliability, validity, etc., of measuring devices.

‡ A greater or a lesser number of points in time may be desirable for different purposes.

For quantitative purposes, an HSCP is: "(a) a statement, a [culturally] significant statement, which is held by an operationally defined majority of the subjects in a given culture; and (b), it is also, preferably, a statement that will be held differentially across cultures."[11]

HISTORIC-SOCIOCULTURAL PREMISES OF MEXICAN FAMILY

Only two areas of human life have been explored thus far using this approach. One has been the Mexican family, which was early perceived as holding explanations for various normal and abnormal behaviors.[12] There were sayings in the indigenous language of Mexico such as "The mother is the dearest being in existence," or "The place for women is in the home." These and others that were inferred appeared in a number of studies and publications, until it was possible to develop a factorial scale of HSCP of the Mexican family.[13] The scale contains 22 items selected from an early questionnaire of 123 on the basis that they had shown the greatest number of statistically significant differences between different groups in prior studies. The highest loading items in this scale are: "A son should always obey his parents," "A person should always obey his parents," and "The word of a father should never be questioned."

Let us see how this factorial scale fulfills the four criteria:

1. Does it measure adequately a manifestation of culture? Test-retest correlations with a three-month interval in children and adolescents, aged 14 to 16 and 17 to 19 years, were found to be .82 and .81, respectively.[14] Additionally, many of the statements of the scale were taken from the indigenous language of the Mexican people.

2. Is it related to proximal antecedent and to contemporary behavioral events as defined by sociologists and psychologists? In TABLE 1, it is clear that the scale holds meaningful relationships with a number of contemporary and reliable personality and cognitive dimensions as defined by psychologists. A few proximal antecedents as defined by social psychologists and sociologists also hold meaningful relationships: a mother's expectation of achievement in the child, socioeconomic level, and the parental attitude of sophisticated acceptance. It also holds a sizable relationship to the two main factors of another measure of HSCPs to be discussed below.

3. Can it serve as a bridge between present and future behavioral events? TABLE 2 illustrates a few of the results of an age cohort study with an 11-year interval for a few simple HSCPs dealing with the role of women in Mexican society.[15] The effects of that historical decade are certainly striking. It can be seen that the same events often affected high school girls attending coeducational high schools in a different way than they did those attending all-girl high schools.

4. No effort has ben made to relate this scale to distant historical antecedents.

For HSCPs and coping style cross-cultural studies, it was universally assumed that people had to deal with problems. An old Mexican proverb says, "There are many ways of killing lice." All people have to grapple with problems, but they have different styles of doing so. The concept of coping style seemed most fitting.[10,16] The Filosofía de Vida questionnaire (FV), originally developed on this basis, was a forced-choice instrument with as many as 75 pairs of statements. It was hypothesized that there were two important coping styles.

The first, representing the traditional way of coping in Mexico, was called a passive coping style. In dealing with problems, Mexicans would tend to actively modify themselves rather than the environment in order to cope with the problem. The second way, the traditional American method of coping with problems, was to actively modify the environment, whether physical, interpersonal, or social. It was realized that the active-passive cross-cultural dichotomy was a complex dimension.[11] Two examples of early items are: (a) it is better to be slow rather than fast; versus (b) it is better to be fast rather than slow.

Even in college students, these statements approximated the J curve of conformity behavior.[1] Obviously the Americans felt it was better to be fast rather than slow, whereas the Mexicans believed the opposite.

TABLE 1

CORRELATIONS BETWEEN THE FACTORIAL SCALE OF HISTORIC-SOCIOCULTURAL PREMISES (HSCPS) OF THE MEXICAN FAMILY AND COGNITIVE, PERCEPTUAL, PERSONALITY, PARENTAL ATTITUDINAL, AND SOCIOECONOMIC LEVEL VARIABLES[19]

Variables	Age I = 12 (N = 37 to 39)	Age II = 15 (N = 42 to 48)	Age III = 18 (N = 34 to 43)
Anxiety (HIT)†			−.35*
Penetration (HIT)	−.34*		
Picture completion (WISC)†		−.40†	
Block design (WISC)		−.38†	
Human figure drawing (Harris)†		−.33*	
Time estimation delay		−.30*	
Picture maturity test	.33*		
Autonomy (PRF)†	−.34*		−.55‡
Harm avoidance (PRF)			.31*
Impulsivity		−.31*	−.34*
Order (PRF)		.36*	.36*
Social recognition (PRF)			.47†
Infrequency (PRF)		.36*	
Mother's expectation of achievement in the child		−.39*	
Socioeconomic level	.33*		
Parental attitude survey			
Factor 2, sophisticated acceptance			−.39*
Reading vocabulary (Manuel)		−.37†	
Reading speed (Manuel)		−.45†	
Reading comprehension (Manuel)		−.38†	
Factor 1, active self-assertion §	−.47†	−.69‡	−.65‡
Factor 2, active internal control §	.46‡		

NOTE: (HIT) = Holtzman Ink Blot test, (WISC) = Wechsler Intelligence Scale, (Harris) = Harris Goodenough Scores, (PRF) = Jackson's Personality Research Form.
* = p < .05.
† = p < .01.
‡ = p ⩽ .001.
§ Factor 1 and Factor 2 are the two main factors of the Filosofia de Vida.

TABLE 2[15]

HISTORIC-SOCIOCULTURAL PREMISES ABOUT THE ROLE OF WOMEN
IN MEXICAN SOCIETY IN COEDUCATIONAL HIGH SCHOOLS AND IN THOSE FOR
WOMEN ONLY IN MEXICO CITY*

		High Schools	
HSCPs	Year	Coeducational	Women-only
100. The place for women is in the home.	1959	90%†	74%†
	1970	79%†	60%†
103. Women should be docile.	1959	63%†	57%
	1970	43%‡	29%†
33. Women suffer more in their lives than men.	1959	63%†	72%
	1970	77%†	61%
47. Most female children would prefer to be	1959	65%	72%
like their mother.	1970	73%‡	57%†
80. Young women should never go out alone	1959	60%	73%
at night with a man.	1970	57%	52%†
96. A good wife should always be faithful to	1959	84%†	94%
her husband.	1970	91%	92%

* The same 18 high schools selected to represent different sections of the city were the units of study. Ninth-grade classrooms were randomly selected within each high school. Total N was 472 in 1959 and 467 in 1970. Close to 200 were women in each occasion.
† Significant beyond .01.
‡ Significant beyond .05.

Another item, (a) life is to be enjoyed, versus (b) life is to be endured, gave a similar curve, with the Americans proclaiming to enjoy life and Mexicans merely enduring it.

The present form of the Filosofía de Vida was "finalized" with several "inputs" from Robert F. Peck and the members of the cross-national study entitled "Style of Coping and Achievement: A Cross-National Study of School Children."[17] It consists of 60 pairs of statements and has gone through several factor analytical studies.

The instrument was applied in the aforementioned cross-national study to 400 14-year-olds in seven nations. A pancultural factor analysis rotated to fit the theoretical structure of the FV permitted interpretation of coping styles across nations from the point of sexual and social class differences.[18] There were 22 factors in this pancultural factor analysis. It was interesting to find out that several of them, particularly in Austin, Texas and in Mexico, but in other nations as well, correlated significantly with criterion measures of mathematic achievement, reading achievement, and grade-point average.[19]

On the basis of the experience and knowledge gained from a large cross-cultural study,[3] the FV was submitted to another factor analysis. A conservative and meaningful four factors were derived.[19] These factors were labeled "active self-assertion (vs. affiliative obedience), active internal control (vs. passive external control), passive cautiousness (vs. boldness), and independence (vs. interdependence). Only results related to the first of the four factors will be illustrated here.

It is convenient to start with the second time-binding criteria. In TABLE 3, taken from Holtzman et al.,[3] we can see the items that turned up to be highest loading of the active self-assertion factor. For all three of the English-speaking groups, the majority of the 14-year-old boys subscribe to active self-assertion as a sociocultural premise; whereas their Mexican counterparts prefer affiliative obedience. Also, the four populations are distributed on a continuum ranging from London, highly active, through Chicago and Austin, moderately active, to Mexico City, which is the least active of the samples.

Now let us turn our attention to TABLE 4. From cross-cultural studies of sociocultural premises of the two countries, as well as a large number of the results from specific psychological tests,[3] it has been possible to selectively reach

TABLE 3

DIFFERENCES AMONG FOURTEEN-YEAR-OLD BOYS FROM FOUR CITIES IN AFFILIATIVE OBEDIENCE VERSUS ACTIVE SELF-ASSERTION[3] *

	Mexico City (%)	Austin (%)	Chicago (%)	London (%)
Affiliative obedience	60	38	26	15
Active self-assertion	40	62	74	85

Item Statement Pairs with Highest Loading:

22a. When a person thinks his (or her) father's orders are unreasonable, he should feel free to question them.

22b. A father's orders should always be obeyed.

40a. A teacher's orders should always be obeyed.

40b. When a person thinks his (or her) teacher's orders are unreasonable, he should feel free to question them.

57a. A person should not question his (or her) mother's word.

57b. Any mother can make mistakes, and one should feel free to question her word when it seems wrong.

NOTE: N = 200 for each percentage.

* Taken from data collected in the Cross-National Study of Coping Styles and Achievement in 1968–1969 by K. Miller (London), R. Havighurst (Chicago), R. Peck (Austin), and R. Díaz-Guerrero (Mexico), using the Filosofía de Vida questionnaire. (See the forthcoming work of Peck et al.)

back in the history of the two nations for evidence regarding the behavior of people in general, in the two ancestral worlds, toward absolute authority, whether religious or state. Perhaps because the Anglo-Saxon and the Spanish-American patterns are as different as possible in both historical antecedents and the present HSCPs, the correlation is perfect.

Criterion 1. Again, many of the HSCPs of the FV are Mexican and American indigenous sayings and inferences from them. María Luisa Morales[14] found for a different type, but also a conservative factor analytical study of the FV, that the first factor, which is fundamentally an active self-assertion factor, had a three-month test-retest reliability in children and adolescents aged 14 to 16 and 17 to 19 of .64 and .81, respectively.

TABLE 4

CRITICAL HISTORICAL INCIDENTS IN THE OVERTHROW OF ABSOLUTE RELIGIOUS AND/OR STATE AUTHORITY

	Mexico (Mexico City)	Austin	Chicago	England (London)
Critical incidents	The Reformation (1860) The Revolution (1910)	Inherits English history (1215–1534) Inherits American history (1649–1779) Inherits Mexican history (1860–1910)	Inherits English history (1215–1534) Religious Freedom (1776) Abolition of tithes (1779)	Magna Carta (1215) English Reformation (1534) Charles I executed by Parliament (1649)
Average historical time	1885	1674	1590	1466

Criterion 2. TABLE 5 shows that again a number of psychological dimensions are to be found significantly correlated with the HSCPs. A social psychological variable, mother's expectation of achievement (taken from an interview), and the sociological variable of socioeconomic level show significant correlations. Since active self-assertion is pretty much the opposite of the affiliative obedience style of coping and the traditionalism featured by the HSCPs of the Mexican family, this test shows substantial to moderately high negative correlations.

Criterion 3. We have no data. The first test in Mexico to a fairly representative sample of ninth-grade high school subjects was given in 1970. We hope to do an age cohort study in 1980.

Above and beyond what has been stated in this paper, there are other theoretical as well as pragmatic reasons for insisting that the critical event in the

TABLE 5

CORRELATIONS OF FACTOR 1 OF THE FV (ACTIVE SELF-ASSERTION) AND COGNITIVE, COGNITIVE PERCEPTUAL, PERSONALITY VARIABLES, AND PARENTAL ATTITUDES[19]

Variables	Age I = 12 (N = 38 to 44)	Age II = 15 (N = 48 to 56)	Age III = 18 (N = 35 to 44)
Reaction time (HIT)†		−.30*	
Rejection (HIT)		−.29*	−.38*
Form appropriateness (HIT)	.44†		
Anxiety (HIT)			.47†
Hostility (HIT)			.44†
Arithmetic (WISC)†		.26*	
Block design (WISC)		.30*	
Defensiveness score (TASC)†	−.34*		
Aggression (PRF)†	.45†		
Autonomy (PRF)	.37*		.44†
Dominance (PRF)	.31*		
Impulsivity (PRF)		.28*	
Order (PRF)		−.32*	
Social recognition (PRF)		−.30*	
Understanding (PRF)		−.27*	
Infrequency (PRF)		−.26*	
Mother's expectation of achievement (Interview)		.31*	
Socioeconomic level	−.40†		
Reading vocabulary (Manuel)		.33*	.49†
Reading speed (Manuel)		.30*	.35*
Reading comprehension (Manuel)		.41†	
Factor 2, active internal control §		−.32*	
Historic SCPs of the Mexican family	−.47†	−.69‡	−.65‡

NOTE: (HIT) = Holtzman's Inkblot Test, (WISC) = Wechsler Intelligence Scale, (TASC) = Saroson's Test Anxiety Score, (PRF) = Jackson's Personality Research Form.
* = p < .05.
† = p < .01.
‡ = p < .001.
§ Factor 2 is the second factor of the Filosofía de Vida.

causation of human behavior is to be found in culture. Several criteria were presented, and a time-binding approach to the study of culture and its relation to personality was illustrated.

REFERENCES

1. LeVINE, R. A. 1973. Culture, Behavior, and Personality. Aldine Publishing Co. Chicago, Ill.
2. LeVINE, R. A. & B. LeVINE. 1966. Nyansongo: A Gusii Community in Kenya. John Wiley & Sons, Inc. New York, N.Y.
3. HOLTZMAN, W. H., R. DÍAZ-GUERRERO, & J. D. SWARTZ (in collaboration with L. LARA TAPIA, L. LAOSA, M. L. MORALES, I. REYES LAGUNES & D. B. WITZKE). 1975. Personality Development in Two Cultures.: 329–330. The University of Texas Press. Austin, Texas.
4. TRIANDIS, H. C. (in association with V. VASSILIOU, G. VASSILIOU, Y. TANAKA & A. V. CHANMUGAM). 1972. The Analysis of Subjective Culture. John Wiley & Sons, Inc. New York, N.Y.
5. D'ANDRADE, R. G. 1974. Sex differences and cultural institutions. In Culture and Personality, Contemporary Readings. R. A. LeVine, Ed.: 16. Aldine Publishing Co. Chicago, Ill.
6. MARX, M. H. 1963. Theories in Contemporary Psychology.: 31. Macmillan Co. New York, N.Y.
7. DÍAZ-GUERRERO, R. 1972. Hacia una Teoria Historico-bio-psico-socio-cultural del Comportamiento Humano. F. Trillas, Editorial. Mexico City, Mexico.
8. AUKERMAN, R. C. 1971. Approaches to Beginning Reading. John Wiley & Sons, Inc. New York, N.Y.
9. BRUNSWIK, E. 1952. The Conceptual Framework of Psychology. The University of Chicago Press. Chicago, Ill.
10. DÍAZ-GUERRERO, R. 1967. Sociocultural premises, attitudes and cross-cultural research. Inter. J. Psychol. 2: 79–87.
11. DÍAZ-GUERRERO, R. 1967. The active and the passive syndromes. Rev. Interam. Psicolog. 1: 263–272.
12. DÍAZ-GUERRERO, R. 1955. Neurosis and the Mexican family structure. Am. J. Psychiat. 112: 401–417.
13. DÍAZ-GUERRERO, R. 1972b. Una escala factorial de premisas histórico-socio-culturales de la familia mexicana. Rev. Interam. Psicolog. 6: 235–244.
14. MORALES, M. L. 1973. Estudio preliminar sobre los factores socio-culturales que influyen en el crecimiento demográfico de México. Unpublished report.
15. DÍAZ-GUERRERO, R. 1974. La mujer y las premisas histórico-socio-culturales de la familia mexicana. Rev. Latinoam. Psicolog. 6 (1): 7–16.
16. DÍAZ-GUERRERO, R. 1965. Sociocultural and psychodynamic processes in adolescent transition and mental health. In Problems in Youth. Sherif and Sherif, Eds. Aldine Publishing Co. Chicago, Ill.
17. PECK, R. F., A. L. ANGELINI, R. DÍAZ-GUERRERO, K. M. MILLER, W. JAIDE, F. WEINERT, R. PIQUARDT, L. ZORMAN, I. TOLICIC, M. CESA-BIANCHI, R. J. HAVIGHURST & S. KUBO. 1972–1974. Coping Styles and Achievement: A Cross-National Study of School Children. (4 vols.) Research and Development Center in Teacher Education. Austin, Texas.
18. DÍAZ-GUERRERO, R. 1973. Interpreting coping styles across nations from sex and social class differences. Inter. J. Psychol. 8: 193–203.
19. DÍAZ-GUERRERO, R. 1976. Hacia una psicologia social del Tercer Mundo. Cuadernos de Humanidades No. 5. Universidad Nacional Autonoma de Mexico.

PROBLEMS OF MEASUREMENT IN CROSS-CULTURAL RESEARCH

George M. Guthrie

Department of Psychology
Pennsylvania State University
University Park, Pennsylvania 16802

In cross-cultural psychological research, we encounter all of the problems of measurement that confront us when we do research at home, plus many other problems that grow out of differences in language and the strangeness of an experimental situation. In both situations, the measurements one makes and the data he collects are determined by the questions he asks or the theories he is testing. Cultural factors are of concern when we ask whether a relationship found in the United States is also present in the Philippines.* Merely collecting data on color vision, or conformity, or memory in another country is not cross-cultural research, unless one attempts to relate differences in vision, conformity, or memory to differences in the cultural patterns between at least two societies. Furthermore, if we simply find differences in conformity between Americans and Filipinos we have no basis to choose among an unlimited number of alternative explanations of the differences. As has been pointed out, a difference between two groups is, by itself, uninterpretable.

In both cross-cultural and domestic research, it is convenient to think of Cronbach's[1] two disciplines of scientific psychology: the descriptive and the experimental. In the former, we are interested in individual differences among people; in the latter, the differences in effects that treatments have on two or more groups whose members have been assigned randomly from a common source. This does not mean we cannot use experiments in cross-cultural research because people are already assigned to societies; it does suggest we inspect the differences between two treatments applied to each of the groups. The minimum, using this line of reasoning, is then a 2 x 2 experiment: a treatment and a control applied in two societies in which the interaction term is of great significance.

In either descriptive or experimental work, measurements of cross-cultural differences need to be derived from our conceptualization of how differences in cultural processes have operated. If we conceive of a cultural process as weakening or strengthening a function such as memory, then we measure the function in question and other functions not subject to differential cultural effects in order to make certain that differences are not due simply to test-taking skills. For instance, Guthrie, Sinaiko and Brislin[2] showed that Vietnamese did very poorly on tests of spatial ability but just as well as Americans on tests of numerical ability and perceptual speed; they interpreted the difference in spatial ability as being due to differences in experience of the members of the two societies.

However, if we are interested in the effects of culture on the patterning of sexual or aggressive behavior, then we must compare patterns. People are not

---

* Because my own experience in cross-cultural research has been in the Philippines, all of my hypothetical examples will involve Americans and Filipinos. This is in contrast to the more abstract Societies A and B that are commonly used. I prefer not to use Society B because I had some unfortunate experiences with them.

more or less aggressive in all of their actions, but rather have different expressions of aggression and different configurations of situations in which they may express aggression. Mischel's[3] emphasis on the situational specificity of an individual's behavior as opposed to general traits is even more applicable in cross-cultural research. Ethnographic accounts, of course, reflect this state of affairs at a verbal, descriptive level, but we often implicitly deny configurational differences when we try to measure aspects of sexuality or aggression in cross-cultural research.

DESCRIPTIVE RESEARCH

The vast majority of cross-cultural studies are descriptive because they ask, "What are the differences between these two groups?" Differences may be sought in intelligence, memory, aggressiveness, or socialization practices.

But our research can become productive only if we go a second step and ask, "How are these differences related to cultural processes?" For example, merely demonstrating that there is less aggression among Filipino children than among American children is only half the job; we need to go further and identify the factors which account for this difference. We found,[4] for instance, that Filipino mothers did everything they could to prevent their children from quarreling with neighbors' children because such a fight would lead to great bitterness among parents. There are alternative explanations of the smaller number of quarrels among Filipino than among American children. It is a weakness of the descriptive approach that it is difficult or impossible to choose among alternative explanations.

There are several other problems in such studies: differences found may be due to the measuring instrument, they may be due to the relationship between the subject and the collector of data, or they may be due to sampling biases. We shall examine these difficulties as they appear with different types of measuring procedures designed for different domains of behavior. Descriptive psychologists have traditionally been interested in such characteristics as intelligence, personality, and attitudes within our own society. It should come as no surprise that they carry these interests with them when they go abroad.

Intelligence

Difficulties in this area have been recognized for many years, and recently they have been rediscovered where intelligence tests are used with cultural subgroups within our own society. No test has been designed which has been accepted as a measure of differences in intelligence between two groups whose previous experience has differed markedly. Within group differences, however, can be measured if we design a new test or reevaluate an established one against the common criteria of test construction. We have, for instance, developed a nonverbal intelligence test for use with Philippine children, the Philippine Nonverbal Intelligence Test (PNIT).[5] With the help of Filipino artists we developed a 100-item test in which the subject points to one of five figures on a card that does not belong with the other four. The test meets many of the criticisms of intelligence tests as applied in and out of the United States: It is untimed, the instructions are simple and do not change, there is no need for words to be exchanged. All of the items present pictures of common objects for Filipino children. Beginning with such simple items as four squares and a circle, the child is asked in his language, "Which one is different, which does not belong with the others?" The instructions may be repeated with the second card. They can even be given in pantomime. The child learns the task with the first three or four items in which five-year-olds show almost 100 percent accuracy. The items are presented in increasing order of difficulty as they go from simple perceptual differences, to differences in function, to differences that require abstract concept formation. Using the total score as a criterion, item analyses can be very simple on programs written to evaluate five-alternative multiple-choice examinations for college students.

These programs provide a comprehensive evaluation of each item including the percentage and mean total score of those who chose each alternative for each item. Carrying out such an analysis separately for age levels and sexes and for different samples enables us to identify items that are culturally biased. The procedure requires hundreds of subjects for each new analysis but it does provide protection against the problems which have beset many attempts at the measurement of intelligence in other societies. Finally, our total scores show a satisfactory rise from one age group to the next and they correlate with school grades as well as IQ tests in American schools.

The PNIT enables us to measure differences within and between groups of Filipinos. The test has also been found by Seymour[6] to be highly satisfactory in Borneo, which has a very similar environment of plant and animal forms. But it would not be satisfactory for comparisons with children from temperate climate areas or the arid tropics because they would not recognize some of the stimuli. In spite of these limitations, it is still useful for cross-cultural studies like those demonstrating that there are no sex differences in the Philippines where the equality of the sexes is emphasized but there are in Borneo where Islamic traditions are more powerful. It has also been used to determine that height and intelligence are positively correlated in areas of severe malnutrition, but intelligence and height are not related to one another in parts of the world where children are more adequately fed.

Most intelligence tests do not translate satisfactorily because many questions deal with experiences that are not worldwide. But the ability to acquire information is a fundamental component of intelligence wherever one lives. The Information subtest of the Wechsler Intelligence Test in its many forms often correlates more highly than other subtests, even Vocabulary, with the total score. Acting on this observation and with the help of Filipino colleagues, we developed an information test of intelligence[7] for use in the rural Philippines. We asked such questions as: A woman puts out some wet clothes on a sunny day. Where does the water go that was in the clothes? If the moon rises at 10 o'clock this evening, when will it rise tomorrow evening? What is soap made from? Where does the water in the coconut come from?

Again, there are computer programs which will carry out in a few seconds the scoring and analysis of the preliminary form of such a test providing item difficulties, item-total score correlations, KR20 estimates of reliability, and many other summary statistics. The merit of this approach is that it enables one to develop tests that are meaningful in the experience of the respondents and that avoid the problems of cultural unfamiliarity which intrude when one uses a test developed elsewhere; translated or original. The absence of time limits, the familiar materials, and the simplicity of instructions are all, in our opinion, assets of efforts of this sort.

There is one problem we have not solved in the Philippines. In the process of training at home and at school, Filipino children learn that any answer, no matter how erroneous, is much better than a failure to answer. Accordingly, on a multiple-choice test of abstract reasoning we found that Filipino college students all finished a difficult test in much less than the 20-minute time limit. Scoring revealed that they solved the first few easy items and then guessed the rest so that they omitted no items in the second-half of the test, they just got chance scores. Even on the PNIT, we encounter the problem that a child will not examine the alternatives carefully when they start to get difficult for him; he continues answering at the same rate and with the same confident gesture in a silent contract with his society that random answers are preferred to a pause that betrays that one does not know.

One may want to assess other cognitive processes, such as reasoning or memory. Cole's work with the Kpelle[8] is a model of the development of measurements that are meaningful within the experience of the subjects.

Personality

Just as is the case with the measurement of cognitive aspects of behavior, personality assessment techniques follow the fashion current at home. A decade ago, the use of projective techniques, especially the Rorschach, declined rapidly both at home and abroad for reasons beyond the scope of this paper.

The inkblots would, at first impression, seem to offer a less culturally biased set of stimuli than do inventories either in their original language or translated. The problem with them was that the system of interpretation developed for the test was based on a theory of inner determinants of behavior which meant that interpretive statements could neither be confirmed or denied. In a broader sense Freudian psychodynamic theory was formulated in a way that could not be confirmed or denied.

Beyond the problems inherent in the way the theory was formulated, was the fact that it left little or no place for cultural factors to operate. The basic stages of psychosexual development, oedipal conflicts, the nature of instinctual strivings, the mechanisms of symptom formation were all assumed, even asserted to be universal. Freudian theory was used to explain behavior, as exemplified in the work of Roheim,[9] Kardiner,[10] Wilbur and Munsterberger,[11] and many others. Data from other cultures were not seen as an opportunity to test the universality of Freud's formulations. Even the so-called cultural school of Sullivan, Erickson, etc., shows no effects of data from other societies.

The Rorschach was a method that produced virtually unverifiable statements that, in turn, were expressed in a theory which left no room for cultural differences. As Hartmann, Kris, and Lowenstein[12] assert with respect to anthropological data:

> It is hardly necessary to emphasize that no data produced and no interpreta-
> tions advanced have been able, or even seriously set out, to modify our views on
> the working of the psychic apparatus. Psychoanalytic assumptions on psychic
> structure and the interrelation of its parts, on the function of psychic energy and
> its working, on the distinction of degrees of neutralization, of mobile and bound
> energies, and hence of primary and secondary processes, supply the best, or more

precisely, the only set of assumptions which at present permits an explanatory approach to mental functioning.

A second projective test, the TAT, was more clearly a product of white, western society; but the strategy that people would reveal themselves in their stories was not tied to one culture pattern. Accordingly, many variations of the TAT were developed including sets for children and blacks in North America. Lagmay[13] developed a set of pictures for use in the Philippines that had Filipino faces and backgrounds. Using the Symonds series in original form with Filipino college students, I found that they told Filipino stories about the figures and seemed unaffected by the fact that the pictures were clearly not of Philippine origin. It is possible that many people have seen so many movies made in America or Western Europe that they are not as influenced by cultural features as one would expect. My experience, at least, led me to doubt that one needs a new set of pictures for each society.

Sentence completion techniques were used productively by Phillips[14] in Thailand. We were able to take the English version of this test and our own Tagalog version and to develop comparisons of Thai and Filipino responses,[15] an analysis that seemed to clarify many of the differences in behavior patterns between members of those two societies. We did encounter some interesting problems of translation of even the sentence stems because Tagalog does not always follow the subject-verb-predicate sequence of English. Putting the subject before the predicate tended to shift the meaning in directions we did not want. Maybe we needed a Sentence Beginning Test.

Still another technique that has proven convenient and productive is the ECHO procedure described by Barthol and deMille.[16] Groups of literate subjects are given 20 cards, 10 of which bear the questions, "What is a good thing to do? and Who would approve?," and 10 cards, each asking "What is a bad thing to do; and Who would disapprove?" Teams of three, drawn from the population who answered the questions on the 20 cards are then asked to sort the responses of the entire sample into piles which say approximately the same thing. In this way piles may be generated which say it is a good thing to respect parents, work hard in school, or love God. "Bad thing" statements may generate piles about stealing, killing, or failing to wash one's hands. Pooling the data from several teams and comparing it with data from other samples and other countries gives one some rather remarkable insights into the moral and social emphases of different social and national groups.

Personality inventories have been used abroad since shortly after their appearance here. The Philippines is an especially convenient setting to evaluate inventories because the majority of potential subjects are literate in both English and a Philippine language, and because the Philippine language and culture is Malayo-Polynesian in its roots rather than Indo-European. Meanings, however, can be lost even without translation, as we found when we used Shafer and Bell's Parental Attitude Research Inventory (PARI)[17] in English with middle class Manila mothers. The factorial structure of the inventory was different from that found with American mothers even though the items tended to remain on the same individual scales as had been found in the original development of the inventory.[18] Dependency, for instance, a sign of the mother's dominance and the child's weakness in the American setting, turned up as a sign of maternal responsibility and the child's respectfulness in the Philippines.

Because personality inventories are basically measures of attitudes toward oneself, problems of scale construction, bias, and meaning will be deferred for a moment and treated with measures of attitudes.

Attitudes

There are formidable problems of assessment of attitudes which parallel those associated with personality measurement. In our opinion the most severe is response acquiescence or the tendency to agree with an item. Closely related and compounding the problem, is the desire on the part of respondent in many societies to give an answer which they believe will please an interviewer. Various measures of alienation, for instance, are almost always written so that agreement counts for alienation. Measures of modernity often suffer the same short-coming.[19] This problem of response-bias has been studied by many psychologists and some techniques have been developed to control these sources of variance. We have surely passed the point where an investigator can make up a set of statements from face validity considerations and use it uncritically as a measure of attitudes toward such socially significant matters as family planning, sanitation practices, or land reform. Unfortunately, in our opinion, the Guttman index of reproducibility, which is often used to evaluate an attitude scale, will be high when response sets are strongest. One solution we suggest is to present the respondent with pairs of statements judged to be equated for social desirability that express pro and con positions on the issue at hand, and ask him to choose the one which best expresses his view.

There are two major problems in the adaptation and use of attitude or personality scales in cross-cultural research. For cross-cultural purposes, one will ordinarily begin with an established scale and translate it. But the statements of an inventory often cannot be translated so that they mean the same thing even if one has the help of a colleague who is a native speaker of the second language. Anyone undertaking such a project should read Werner and Campbell,[20] Brislin,[21] and Sechrest, Fay, and Zaidi.[22] The Sechrest paper is an especially good discussion of the problems one can expect to encounter; it is enriched by clarifying examples of English to Tagalog (Philippines) and English to Urdu (Pakistan).

The translation of personality and attitude items is especially difficult insofar as they emphasize emotions and interpersonal relationships. It is in this domain that members of different societies develop unique behavior patterns so that there are no words in a second language to render adequately an important experience in the first language.

The second problem is the extent to which well translated items belong on the same scales as they were in the original instrument. As we pointed out from our work with the PARI,[18] even without translation the same behavioral reports carried different meanings for Filipino than for American mothers. In light of these considerations, we suggest that translated attitude measures be analyzed by the same methods as were used in the development of the original scale. This would include assessing item intercorrelations, item–total score correlations, and the distribution of responses to the alternatives for each item. The scale should also be examined in a matrix of measures of other attitudes and of such distortions as yea saying, and social desirability, or intent to place oneself in an unduly favorable light. This means, essentially, that as with intelligence tests, we build a new scale; the content would be similar, but the method of construction identical.

Developing new scales in each new society we study would appear to reduce comparability from one society to the next. As I see it, there is a trade-off in which we have to choose between literal accuracy and local validity, between a literally accurate translation of a scale, which may not adequately represent the dimension of behavior under study, and a locally valid measure which reflects the organization of behavior unique to a given society. This is exemplified in the work of Cole on memory[8] and, I believe, in our PNIT.[5]

Beyond these considerations is the larger issue of the relationships between attitudes and behavior.[23,24] Because social desirability is such a strong determiner of responses to attitude questionnaires, we would suggest that researchers explore behavioral measures. Who cares if a mother's attitudes about infant-feeding practices or family planning are favorable? If babies don't gain weight, and if they continue to gain younger brothers and sisters, then attitude measures are pointless. It would seem to be more productive to specify behavioral indications and to measure them. Furthermore, these can often be assessed unobtrusively. If a rural sanitation program is successful, fewer children should be absent from school due to sickness. If a supplementary school feeding program is accomplishing its objectives the results should show up on a set of bathroom scales rather than attitude scales.

EXPERIMENTAL RESEARCH

In this tradition, the investigator is interested in the effects of various conditions he must impose on his subjects, conditions which we call independent variables. In this approach we are not interested primarily in the differences that subjects bring to the experiment; ideally, we would like all of our subjects to come from one litter. Because this is a difficult condition to meet with human beings, an experimenter likes to begin with a relatively homogeneous group of subjects who are then assigned randomly to experimental and control treatments. The less culture the better. But a cultural difference can be studied in this design in a very useful way when it is treated as an independent variable. Of course, the rule of randomization is broken, but randomization remains the rule within societies.

Suppose that we are interested in the effects of cultural differences on the Asch effect. Americans and Filipinos might be assigned randomly in the various conditions of reporting alone, in a pair and in a group of four. We would predict that Filipinos would show a greater effect due to the presence of others than Americans because of the more personalistic qualities of Philippine social patterns. Such a finding is implied by the research of Kubany, Gallimore, and Buell[26] who found that the presence or absence of an experimenter changed the performance of Filipino boys on a test considered an analog of achievement motivation. To be a complete example of an experimental study of cultural differences, however, they should have a sample of American boys tested under similar circumstances.

Hare[25] studied cultural differences in performance in communication networks of Filipino, American, Nigerian, and South African students. In this social psychological experiment, subjects in groups of five could communicate with one another according to specific rules which produced networks that tended either to give each person equal access to information or to give one or more individuals greater access to information from others. Substantial differences in speed of solution and in preference for different networks were interpreted as indicative of cultural trends which emphasized individuality or cooperation and more or less communication in the interests of agreement and understanding.

This design is not used frequently for reasons that we do not fully understand. It seems simple enough to replicate a classical experiment in social psychology in a different society. Experimenters, however, are quite indifferent to cultural factors. With their penchant for sophomores, it is unlikely that many of them will think to inquire whether their results are limited to their own society.

In another sense, the study of behavior in a second culture is referred to as a *natural experiment*. Considerations of ethics, feasibility, and time make it virtually impossible to vary in a controlled way the kinds of events which we believe to be of fundamental significance in personality development. No one has done real life-extended experiments on the effects of early oral, elimination, or sexual training. They have been studied by Mead in Samoa, and Malinowski in the Trobriands, but by few others. But there is no natural laboratory worthy of the name because a host of other factors vary from one society to another in addition to the one we may be interested in, so that we cannot attribute differences in adulthood unequivocally to a childhood socialization practice. Mead's Samoans may show little adolescent stress because of their breadfruit diet or the proximity of the tropical sea. In a formal sense, these are also antecedents of the conditions of adolescence. Malinowski's reasoning has a different status. If he had not backed down in the face of Jones' Freudian pronouncements, he could have argued that his data constituted an exception to the universal resentment of sons toward fathers.

Although he did not state it as a formal experiment, Malinowski also observed that the inhabitants of another island had a different childrearing practice, which, with environmental factors the same, would enable a test of his theory of the origins of tension between fathers and sons. But he reported with regret that he was never able to follow up that idea.

Polynesian fosterage in which more than half of the children in a community move from one family to another and then to a third would, it seems, provide a superb opportunity to test the significance of stability of parents, a matter that our writers deem of profound importance to a child's development. Similarly the apparent permissiveness of Filipino parents toward homosexual behavior in some sons provided an opportunity not available here to study sexual orientation processes in a setting where the matter is not such a source of anxiety and guilt for all concerned. In both cases, we have the potential of obtaining findings that contradict two of the more fundamental premises of our theories of behavior disorders. Maybe stable parental models aren't necessary; maybe sexual orientation is not fixed at an early age but is something one can change back and forth if the society permits.

The measurements one makes in a cross-cultural project depend on his theory and on the measurement that is current at the time. When she was planning her historic research in Samoa, Mead considered using the GSR, which was becoming popular at that time.[26] The Cambridge Expedition used contemporary measuring devices. The Rorschach rose and fell abroad as it has at home. Theory and measurement should go hand in hand, but I am of the opinion that a current measurement technique may dictate too frequently the problem one chooses to study. We study modernity because scales are available. We use the Semantic Differential without asking whether it is precisely what we need. Available instruments probably have the effect of distorting or limiting the problems we tackle when we go abroad. We would suggest that more attention be given to making up a measuring technique that is congruent with our theory and with the language and culture pattern of the host society.

In summary, the purpose of cross-cultural research is to test theories and to investigate relationships under more than one configuration of circumstances. We go to another society for this research because the circumstances which we are interested in are too complex and of too long standing to be manipulated experimentally within our own society. But because the new circumstances vary in many and complex ways, we are left with some ambiguity about what cultural factors are important in the processes with which we are concerned. Accordingly, we need to make multiple measurements and deal with the pattern of results by multivariate methods. Furthermore, because the measures themselves inevitably involve the language and other artifacts of a society, it will be necessary to interpret the measures and configurations of scores within the local cultural context. The measures must be developed within each society; the cross-cultural psychologist's skill lies in his knowledge of measurement strategies and not in his mastery of measurement devices.

REFERENCES

1. CRONBACH, L. J. 1957. The two disciplines of scientific psychology. American Psychologist. 12: 671–684.
2. GUTHRIE, G. M., H. W. SINAIKO & R. BRISLIN. 1971. Nonverbal abilities of Americans and Vietnamese. J. Soc. Psychol. 84: 183–190.
3. MISCHEL, W. 1973. Toward a cognitive social learning reconceptualization of personality. Psychol. Rev. 80: 252–283.
4. GUTHRIE, G. M. & P. J. JACOBS. 1966. Child Rearing and Personality Development in the Philippines. Pennsylvania State University Press. University Park, Pa.
5. GUTHRIE, G. M., A. TAYAG & P. J. JACOBS. 1969. The Philippine Nonverbal Intelligence Test. J. Soc. Psychol. In press.
6. SEYMOUR, J. M. 1974. The rural school as an acculturating institution: The Iban of Malaysia. Hum. Org. 33: 277–290.
7. GUTHRIE, G. M. 1970. A Culture-Fair Test of Intelligence. Tech. Rep. No. 8. The Impact of Modernization in the Philippines. Pennsylvania State University. University Park, Pa.
8. COLE, M., J. GAY, J. GLICK & D. W. SHARP. 1971. The Cultural Context of Learning and Thinking. Basic Books. New York, N.Y.
9. ROHEIM, G. 1950. Psychoanalysis and Anthropology. International Universities Press. New York, N.Y.
10. KARDINER, A. 1945. The Psychological Frontiers of Society. Columbia University Press. New York, N.Y.
11. WILBUR, G. B. & W. MUNSTERBERGER, Eds. 1951. Psychoanalysis and Culture. International Universities Press, New York, N.Y.
12. HARTMAN, H., E. KRIS & R. M. LOWENSTEIN. Some psychoanalytic comments on "Culture and Personality." In Psychoanalysis and Culture. G. B. Wilbur & W. Munsterberger, Eds. International Universities Press. New York, N.Y.
13. LAGMAY, A. 1966. The Philippines Thematic Apperception Test. University of the Philippines Press. Manila, Philippines.
14. PHILIPPS, H. P. 1966. Thai Peasant Personality. University of California Press. Berkeley & Los Angeles, Ca.
15. GUTHRIE, G. M. & F. M. AZORES. 1968. Philippine interpersonal behavior patterns In W. F. Bello & A. de Guzman, Eds. Modernization: Its Impact on the Philippines. Ateneo de Manila University, IPC Papers No. 6. Quezon City, Philippines.
16. BARTHOL, R. & R. DEMILLE. 1969. Project Echo, Final Report. General Research Corp. Santa Barbara, Calif.
17. SHAFER, E. S. & R. Q. BELL. 1958. Development of a parental attitude research inventory. Child Develop. 29: 339–361.

18. GUTHRIE, G. M. 1966. Structure of maternal attitudes in two cultures. J. Psychol. **62**: 155–165.
19. KAHL, J. A. 1968. The Measurement of Modernism. The University of Texas Press. Austin, Texas.
20. WERNER, O. & D. T. CAMPBELL. 1970. Translating, Working through Interpreters, and the Problem of Decentering. *In* R. Naroll & R. Cohen, Eds. A Handbook of Method in Cultural Anthropology. The Natural History Press. New York, N.Y.
21. BRISLIN, R. W. 1970. Back-translation for cross-cultural research. J. Cross-Cult. Psychol. **1**: 185–216.
22. SECHREST, L., T. L. FAY & S. M. H. ZAIDI. 1972. Problems of translation in cross-cultural research. J. Cross-Cult. Psychol. **3**: 41–56.
23. DEUTSCHER, I. 1973. Why do they say one thing, do another? University Programs Modular Studies. General Learning Press. Morristown, N.J.
24. CALDER, B. J. & M. ROSS. 1973. Attitudes and Behavior. General Learning Press. Morristown, N.J.
25. HARE, A. P. 1969. Cultural differences in performance in communication networks in Africa, the United States and the Philippines. Sociol. Soc. Res. **54**: 25–41.
26. KUBANY, E. S., R. GALLIMORE & J. BUELL. 1970. The effects of extrinsic factors on achievement-oriented behavior: A non-Western case. J. Cross-Cult. Psychol. **1**: 77–84.
27. MEAD, M. 1972. Blackberry Winter. Morrow. New York.

PROBLEMS OF LANGUAGE IN CROSS-CULTURAL RESEARCH

Hiroshi Wagatsuma

Department of Anthropology
University of California
Los Angeles, California 90024

Toward the end of the last century in rural Japan, a young man was working as a janitor at an American-run mission school while he was learning English. The youngest son of a bankrupt and broken family, he had an ambition to go to America, although he had never been outside of a few provincial towns. One day, hoping to obtain some useful information, he visited one of the American missionaries and told of his intention to go to America. To his great disappointment, however, the American exclaimed, "What? *you* are intending to go to America?" The missionary's wife was in the same room and the young man felt that both of them "sneered" at him. He felt as if all his blood drained to his feet. He stood silently for a few seconds and then left the room without saying goodbye. The next morning he left the school, determined to get to America. After years of hardship, this man, named Yoshio Markino, became a successful artist, living most of his adult life in the United States and Europe. In 1910 Markino published his autobiography in English and referred to this early painful experience. He wrote that he had always believed that *insincerity* was the greatest crime and that nothing could be more insincere than a sneer. He left the mission school because he understood the sneer of the American missionary as a sign of insincerity, and he felt deeply hurt.

However, Ruth Benedict, who quoted this episode in her renowned book,[1] found it curious that Markino charged the missionary with "insincerity" because the American's exclamation seemed to her quite "sincere" in the American sense of the word. Benedict knew, of course, that Markino was using the word in its Japanese sense, that is, the Japanese deny sincerity to anyone who belittles any person. Benedict pointed out that such a sneer is wanton and proves "insincerity" in the Japanese culture.

The American missionary could have been perceived as a man of sincerity by the young Japanese if, instead of expressing incredulity, he had listened to the young man, sympathized with his ambition, praised his determination, and *then* explained how difficult it would be for a penniless provincial boy to go to the United States to become an artist.

While a young American friend of mine stayed in Tokyo as a Fulbright scholar, his wife taught a young Japanese housewife elementary English conversation and learned some Japanese from her in turn. One day, while practicing her limited English, the Japanese wife asked her American friend, "Is your husband gentle to you?" She meant to ask if the husband of her American friend was *yasashii*. In Japan a husband is often described as *yasashii* if he shows thoughtfulness to his wife by offering to carry the groceries, letting her step into the elevator first, or making tea in the kitchen, instead of being a sheer recipient of her services without any external sign of appreciation. The Japanese housewife wanted to know if the young American Fulbright scholar was such a husband. Perhaps she should have used the English words "considerate" or "affectionate." Instead she translated *yasashii* into "gentle," because that is the first word one finds under *yasashii* in most Japanese-English dictionaries.

141

The American lady did not understand the question. At first it sounded strange, but quickly she interpreted the word "gentle" to be "gentle in love-making." She blushed and could not answer, wondering why her otherwise polite Japanese friend could have asked such an intimate question.

One of the implications of the so-called Whorfian hypothesis is related to the contrasts in codifiability. Language X has a single term for phenomenon x, whereas language Y either has no term at all or it has three terms y_1, y_2 and y_3, all within the same area of reference. As a result, it is much easier to refer to certain phenomena or to certain nuances of meaning in certain languages than in others. There is no handy English equivalent for the German *Gemuetlichkeit* and it has to be explained in a certain phrase. The Japanese verb *amaeru* cannot be translated into a single English or German word, but has to be paraphrased as "to presume upon somebody's love and acceptance."[2] When we, translating one language into another, come across a word not easily translatable we become sensitized to this problem of codifiability and translatability. However, when the equivalent of a word in one language seems readily available in another language, according to a dictionary, one may forget the full implication of the fact that there may not be, and often there is not, an exact semantic (connotative) equivalence between the words x, y, and z, in language X, Y, and Z, although dictionaries say they are the equivalents. This is the case even with the denotative equivalence for certain words. For example, any Japanese who knows some English will translate the word "upper lip" into the Japanese word *uwa-kuchi-biru*. However, the Japanese *uwa-kuchi-biru* (upper-mouth-rim), or the Bengali *uparer toht*, does not denote the part of the face on which one cultivates a mustache, whereas the English word "upper lip" does. For this particular part of the face, the Japanese use a different word, *hana-no-shita* (under-the-nose), and a man spoony on a woman is often called a man with a long "under-the-nose." The Japanese use the same word *hana* for a human nose and an elephant trunk, while the Turkish *buran* and the Russian *HOC* are used for a human nose as well as a bird's beak. Whereas major Western languages describe a human nose as either "big" or "small," or "long" or "short," the Japanese describe it as either "big" or "small," or "high" or "low" (*takai* or *hikui*), but not as long or short. "One's nose is high" in Japanese means either that the nose is actually (physically) "high" or that the person is proud.

When it becomes the matter of abstract concepts what is connoted by a word in one language and what is connoted by another word in another language can be very different from each other. Nobody would disagree that what the word "sincere" in English connotes is not necessarily the same as or similar to what the Japanese word *seijitsu* connotes. Nobody would deny the possibility that a Japanese husband described as *yasashii* and an American husband described as "gentle" may behave differently toward their wives (the former in the kitchen; the latter in bed, perhaps). And yet, this constitutes a serious problem for certain kinds of cross-cultural research; namely, when a questionnaire or a psychological test developed in one language is translated into another languages, and responses to the "same" questionnaire or test in "different" languages are used for a cross-cultural comparison. It is often assumed that the stimulus value of the original questionnaire or test remains the same when translated into other languages, and that the different responses of peoples in different cultures are consequently indicative of differences in culture and/or in psychological characteristics of the peoples. However, the meaning of behavioral characteristics or social phenomena described in a questionnaire or test can be different in different cultural contexts. Also, the sentences or words that describe behavioral characteristics or social phenomena may connote one thing in one language and another in another language. In either case, the stimulus value of the original questionnaire or test certainly becomes lost when translated into another language and used in another culture. And yet, many cross-cultural studies have been carried out precisely in this manner. We do not have to look very hard for such an instance: one might be found in any issue of the *Journal of Cross-Cultural Psychology*.

Let us now be more specific about this problem of language. The Adjective Check List, developed by Dr. Harrison Gough of the Institute for Personality Assessment and Research at Berkeley, is a widely used test and has proven to be highly useful in the United States. It consists of 300 adjectives and the subjects are asked to check those which they consider to be self-descriptive. The test has shown its discriminating ability for various different groups. However, from what has been said above, one can easily see a great danger in using this test in translation for cross-cultural purposes. We have not yet used it in Japan and accordingly we do not yet know how it behaves in Japanese translation. The Adjective Check List does contain both "sincere" and "gentle."

The test has been translated into several Western languages and in the German and French translation we already see some problems. The following are some examples: The English word "appreciative" can mean "capable of understanding music, works of art, or some profound meaning of a philosophical theory," but it can also mean "grateful for somebody's kindness or service." The word was translated into German by *verstaendnisvoll*, which has primarily the former meaning of "appreciative." The French translation is *reconnaisant*, which is closer to the latter meaning of "appreciative." The English word "changeable," when applied to an individual, can refer to his opinions, ideas, moods, emotions, and feelings. The French translation *changeant* may primarily refer to emotional state, whereas the German translation *unbestaendig* definitely implies that somebody has no opinion or principle of his own (which is why his standpoint is "changeable"). The word "civilized" was translated into French as *courtois*, primarily meaning polite or courteous, which is only part of what "civilized" connotes. The English "good-natured" was translated into German *gutmutig* and French *accommodant*, both of which have the "relational connotation," namely, somebody is *gutmutig* or *accommodant* to others; yet the English "good-natured" does not necessarily refer to such an attitude. The English word "hardheaded" can be of negative or positive meaning. A "hardheaded" business-man is practical or analytical, unlike a softheaded individual. However, the German translation of this word, *dickkoepfig* is negative and means that somebody is not only stubborn but stupid. The French translation *rigoureaux* is more positive, but also more limited in its connotations than the English "hardheaded." The English "outgoing" means primarily friendly and responsive to others and the French translation *ouvert* may be fairly close to it. However, the German translation *unternehmend* means primarily enterprising or outgoing in business enterprises, travels, or ventures. The English word "relaxed" was translated into German *entspannt* and French *décontracté* and both words have the connotation that previous to the *entspannt* or *décontracté* state there was a state of tension or hard work, although the word "relaxed" does not necessarily mean the same. The word "self-confident" was translated into German *selbst-bewusst*, which is stronger than "self-confident" and closer to "self-assertive."

A word x in language X may connote a, b, c, and d, whereas a word y in language Y may connote d, e, f, and g. Because both connote d, the word x may very well be translated into y in the translation of a questionnaire or test. If, however, the subjects speaking language X respond mostly to the connotation a, b, or c, rather than d, of the word x, while the subjects speaking language Y mostly respond to the connotation e, f, or g of the word y, the stimulus value of a questionnaire or a test in two languages cannot be the same or equivalent at all. In such a case, the test or questionnaire cannot possibly be used *interculturally*.

The California Psychological Inventory (CPI), also developed by Dr. Gough, has proved very useful in the United States as well as in other countries. Numerous studies using the test in different languages have been published. I was the principal translator of the Japanese CPI and a number of studies using the Japanese CPI have been published.[4-7] A team of Japanese and American psychologists, using their own translation of Femininity Scale items of CPI, compared the degree of masculinity and femininity of the Japanese and American male and female high school students. They found the young American males to be more masculine and the females to be more feminine than the Japanese students![8]

CPI items were gradually developed on the basis of the accumulated empirical data. For example, in order to develop the items for the Dominance Scale, those individuals with a strong tendency to dominate and those lacking such a tendency were empirically selected; those items, the responses to which differentiated between the two groups, were retained, and those that did not were removed. Most of the items in CPI, therefore, were retained because of their ability to differentiate groups empirically identified or defined as different regarding certain characteristics. In order to see what happened to the Japanese translation of CPI, we tried to repeat the procedures in which the items for various scales were originally developed in the United States.

One such scale, made up of 54 items, is called the Socialization Scale. This scale is assumed to measure the degree of social maturity of the subjects. In the United States, the scale differentiates delinquents and nondelinquents. For example, the answers given to these items by 168 male and 178 female nondelinquent high school students and the answers given by 198 male and 105 female inmates of juvenile correctional institutions were different at a significant level.[9-11] We assumed that the Japanese juveniles legally defined as delinquent (as the consequence of their various antisocial behaviors) are the social counterparts of the American delinquents. We collected answers to the Japanese CPI from 113 male and 94 female high school students (age 17 and 18) and from 156 male and 89 female delinquent inmates of a juvenile classification center (age 17 and 18, with more than two records of past delinquent acts) and two correctional institutions and compared their answers. Of the 54 items, only 14 differentiated between the nondelinquent and delinquent males and females at the 0.05% level of significance. (These items are 36, 164, 168, 184, 212, 214, 302, 323, 339, 405, 416, 428, 431, 435). Three other items (182, 386, 398) differentiated only two groups of males, and six other items (245, 257, 336, 393, 429, 457) differentiated only between normal and delinquent females. In their answers to 21 other items, delinquents and nondelinquents did not show any significant differences (see APPENDIX).

Why did so many items fail to differentiate between the two groups? Or perhaps we should ask first why certain items *succeeded* in differentiating between delinquents and nondelinquents. Most of the items that differentiated between two groups refer to some concrete social behavior or situation, and probably their original meaning did not change so drastically when translated, although the connotations of a word like "happy" must be different in Japanese. The following are examples: "When I was going to school I played hooky quite often" (item 36), "My parents have often disapproved of my friends" (164), "My home life was always happy" (168), "I have never been in trouble with the law" (212), "In school I was sometimes sent to the principal for cutting up" (214), "I have often gone against my parents' wishes" (302), "I have never done any heavy drinking" (323), "I have been in trouble one or more times because of my sex behavior" (339), "People often talk about me behind my back" (405), "I don't think I'm quite as happy as others seem to be" (416), "My home as a child was less peaceful and quiet than those of most other people" (428), "As a youngster in school I used to give the teachers lots of trouble" (431), "If the pay was right I would like to travel with a circus or carnival" (435).

Why did the other items not work? There are two possible reasons. First, the kinds of behavior or social phenomena described by each item are not, in Japanese cultural context, related to the kind of social environment in which delinquency is formed, although they are in American society. For example, "It is very important to me to have enough friends and social life" (395) is one of the items to which the delinquents and nondelinquents did not give different answers. It is possible that in a society known for its orientation towards collectivity and its emphasis on social conformity both delinquents and non-delinquents tend to agree to the idea expressed in this item. "I would never play cards (poker) with a stranger" (409) was slightly changed in the translation and reads "I would not like to play for stakes (like Japanese poker) with a stranger." Japanese delinquents do not seem to gamble so much as their American counterparts do. They may bet some money while playing cards or mahjong, but Japanese rarely play with a stranger except at a professional gambling "joint" where the new customers may be admitted with a proper introduction. Generally, the Japanese rarely interact in any way with a "stranger" and the idea expressed in this item may very well have been "strange" for both delinquent and nondelinquent Japanese. The item "It is hard for me to act natural when I am with new people" (284) did not differentiate between the two groups of the Japanese and it is possible that many Japanese − delinquent or nondelinquent − with their strong "in-group" orientation tend to answer affirmatively to this item. The item "I often think about how I look and what impression I am making upon others" (317) did not differentiate between the two groups because most of the subjects agreed to the item, again showing their strong "other-directedness."

The second possibility is that the original stimulus value of the items was somehow lost in translation, although the translator used his knowledge of Japanese and American cultures and did his best in modifying, when necessary, the original sentences, so as to create Japanese sentences that were closer to Japanese social reality than what the direct translation would have described. For example, the item 214, mentioned above, is orginally "In school I was sometimes sent to the principal for cutting up" but in the Japanese translation "sent to the principal" was replaced with "called to the teachers' office" because that is what happens in Japan. This item did differentiate the two groups. More difficult to translate was such an item as "I think Lincoln was greater than Washington" (62) which would have meant little to the Japanese translated directly. "Lincoln" was replaced with "Tokugawa Iyeyasu" and "Washington" with "Toyotomi Hideyoshi." Tokugawa Iyesasu was the founder of the feudal government that ruled Japan for nearly three hundred years until 1868 and is known in Japan as a man of patience, foresight, and careful reflection, whereas Toyotomi Hideyoshi, who ruled Japan before Iyeyasu, is known as a great warrior-strategist with courage and loyalty to the Emperor. A great man of ingenuity and ambition, he, however, is said to have lacked Iyeyasu's careful planning and thinking. It is certain that the stimulus value of the orginal item with Lincoln and Washington was totally lost in this modified translation. In Japanese it did not serve to differentiate between delinquents and nondelinquents. Item 369, "I seem to do things that I regret more often than other people do," was translated very closely to the original and the answers to it did not show any group differences. It is possible that for the Japanese, especially the youth, "regretting" is a sign that shows one has a strong conscience and is capable of development of moral character. In other words, the connotation of this item can be very positive, rather than meaning that one tends to do wrong things often.

Another scale in CPI is called Dominance and there are 46 items. Developing these items, Gough defined what dominating and nondominating persons do, and he asked 100 university students and 124 high school students to name those classmates who they thought had a strong tendency toward dominance and those who lacked it. Gough selected 26 male and 24 female students from the university and high school classes with the strongest dominance tendency and the same number without it. All the items for the Dominance Scale differentiated these 50 males and females with dominance tendency and those 50 without it.[12] We repeated the same procedure, defining dominance and lack of dominance as Gough did, but in Japanese, for 406 boys and 302 girls at six different high schools. We selected 56 boys and 54 girls with a dominance tendency, and 57 boys and 40 girls without it. Of the total of 46 items only three (258, 267, 346) differentiated between the dominance and nondominance groups: "In school I found it very hard to talk before the class" (258), "I am a better talker than a listener" (267), and "I must admit I am a pretty fair talker." It is interesting that these items that "worked" are all related to the capacity for talking. Four other items (207, 385, 412, 452) worked only for boys and other three (34, 179, 359) worked only for girls. Answers to the other 36 items showed no group differences (see APPENDIX).

There are a number of possible reasons for this. First, Gough's definition of dominance became something else when translated into Japanese, and therefore groups thus selected were not "cultural counterparts" of Gough's high school and university students. Second, dominance may be reflected in Japanese cultural context in certain behavioral patterns that are different from those in the American culture, and therefore the Japanese dominance or its lack should have been defined differently. Third, the Japanese with or without dominance do not share with Americans with or without dominance the same thoughts, opinions, or behavior trends that are described by the items for Dominance Scale. For example, the items that worked only for the Japanese males and not for females are: "Sometimes at elections I vote for men about whom I know very little" (207), "It is pretty easy for people to win arguments with me" (385), "I like to give orders and get things moving" (412), "I dislike to talk in front of a group of people" (452). Election may be more of a concern among the young boys than among the young girls. It is possible that in Japanese culture "to have arguments" or "to give orders" is not quite appropriate for young women, even for those with a dominance tendency. It is not clear, however, why the last item, referring to talking in front of a group of people did not work for women like the other three items referring to the capacity to talk. The items that worked only for females are: "There are a few people who just cannot be trusted" (34), "When I work on a committee I like to take charge of things" (179), and "I think I am usually a leader in my group" (359). We cannot explain why they worked only for girls and not for boys. Items like the following may not be relevant to the Japanese social reality: "People should not have to pay taxes for the schools if they do not have children" (315). In Japan public schools are all financed by national and prefectural budget and an individual's payment of tax is not directly associated with the operation of schools. Another item, "We should cut down on our use of oil, if necessary, so that there will be plenty left for the people fifty or a hundred years from now" (303), might be more relevant now for the Japanese after they experienced the "oil crisis" of 1973. It is possible that for the Japanese, with their collective orientation, the following item has a meaning very different from that for the more individualistic Americans: "A person does not need to worry about other people if only he looks after himself" (233). Finally, the stimulus value of many of the original items might have been lost in translation.

Another scale is called the Responsibility Scale and it contains 42 items. Gough defined the sense of responsibility for the class of 100 university and 123 high school students and asked them to name the classmates who they thought had the strong sense of responsibility and those who lacked it. Gough selected 21 male and 20 female students with the strong sense of responsibility and the same number of students without it. He also asked teachers to select from among 282 high school students 20 male and 20 female students who they considered to have the strongest sense of responsibility and the same number of students who lacked it the most. All the 42 items for Responsibility Scale are those that differentiated between the responsible and irresponsible students in Gough's study.[13] We repeated the same procedure, defining the sense of responsibility as Gough did, but in Japanese, with 91 boys and 88 girls at high schools, and we selected 25 boys and 37 girls with a sense of responsibility and 21 boys and 11 girls without it. We also asked teachers at five other schools to select those students with a strong sense of responsibility and those who lacked it. We obtained a group of 37 boys and 20 girls with a sense of responsibility, and 25 boys and 19 girls without it. After testing all these boys and girls with the Japanese CPI, we compared their answers. When the boys and girls were considered together, none of the 42 items differentiated between the responsible and irresponsible groups. Six items (18, 43, 51, 121, 189, 193) worked only for boys. Two others (213, 286) worked only for girls, but at a 0.10% level of significance. Possible reasons for this result with the Responsibility Scale are the same as those we mentioned for the Dominance Scale (see APPENDIX).

We have not yet completed the examination of the results on the Femininity Scale and therefore do not know to what extent it works for the Japanese. The definition of masculinity and femininity or that of masculine and feminine roles is definitely culture-bound. Perhaps this is one of the areas in which a cross-cultural comparison using a single measurement is the most difficult or misleading. What constitutes masculinity or femininity varies with cultures, and accordingly we cannot possibly say the men of culture X are more masculine, or the women more feminine, than those of culture Y, by using one single standard. In translating CPI into Japanese we tried to modify some items in the Femininity Scale to create "Japanese counterparts" rather than translating them directly. For example, "I prefer a shower to a bathtub" (100) would mean nothing for the Japanese because there is no shower in ordinary Japanese homes.

We replaced it with "I mostly don't like sweet things" because in Japan liking sweet cakes and candies is associated with femininity. However, this item did *not* differentiate the men and women in our sample.

For many words it is probably impossible to find a connotative equivalent in other languages, unless a translator is thoroughly bi- or trilingual. The task may remain close to impossible, even for such rare people, because the connotation of words changes with time. It is more difficult to find a social situation or behavior and its cultural equivalent in another society that can be described in a questionnaire or a test. And yet, this basic problem does not seem to have received enough attention from those who are using translated questionnaires and tests for cross-cultural research.

ACKNOWLEDGMENTS

I am grateful to Messrs. Shigeo Kawaguchi and Kenji Shirakura of Toyama and Nagano Family Courts with whom I translated into Japanese the California Psychological Inventory. They kindly allowed me to use the data that I presented in this article regarding the change of stimulus value of CPI when translated into Japanese. I am indebted to Professor Hans Baerwald of the Department of Political Science at UCLA for his valuable advice regarding the German and French translations of the Adjective Check List. I thank Ms. Akemi Kikumura of the Department of Anthropology at UCLA for her capable editorial help.

APPENDIX

Only those CPI items mentioned in the article are listed here to help those readers not familiar with the test.

Socialization Scale

Items that Differentiated between Delinquents and Nondelinquents

36. When I was going to school I played hooky quite often.
164. My parents have often disapproved of my friends.
168. My home life was always happy.
184. I have had more than my share of things to worry about.
212. I have never been in trouble with the law.
214. In school I was sometimes sent to the principal for cutting up.
302. I have often gone against my parents' wishes.
323. I have never done any heavy drinking.
339. I have been in trouble one or more times because of my sex behavior.
405. People often talk about me behind by back.
416. I don't think I'm quite as happy as others seem to be.
428. My home as a child was less peaceful and quiet than those of most other people.
431. As a youngster in school I used to give the teachers lots of trouble.
435. If the pay was right I would like to travel with a circus or carnival.

Items that Worked Only for Males

182.   I would rather go without something than ask for a favor.
386.   I know who is responsible for most of my troubles.
398.   Life usually hands me a pretty raw deal.

Items that Worked Only for Females

245.   Most of the time I feel happy.
257.   I often feel as though I have done something wrong or wicked.
336.   Sometimes I used to feel that I would like to leave home.
393.   I have used alcohol excessively.
429.   Even the idea of giving a talk in public makes me afraid.
457.   A person is better off if he doesn't trust anyone.

Dominance Scale

Items that Worked for Both Males and Females

258.   In school I found it very hard to talk before the class.
267.   I am a better talker than a listener.
346.   I must admit I am a pretty fair talker.

Items that Worked Only for Males

207.   Sometimes at elections I vote for men about whom I know very little.
385.   It is pretty easy for people to win arguments with me.
412.   I like to give orders and get things moving.
452.   I dislike to have to talk in front of a group of people.

Items that Worked Only for Females

 34.   There are a few people who just cannot be trusted.
179.   When I work on a committee I like to take charge of things.
359.   I think I am usually a leader in my group.

Responsibility Scale

Items that Worked Only for Males

 18.   A person who doesn't vote is not a good citizen.
 43.   It's no use worrying my head about public affairs; I can't do anything about them anyhow.
 51.   Every family owes it to the city to keep their sidewalks cleared in the winter and their lawn mowed in the summer.
121.   I was a slow learner in school.
189.   In school my marks in deportment were quite regularly bad.
193.   I would be ashamed not to use my privilege of voting.

Items that Worked Only for Females

213.   It makes me angry when I hear of someone who has been wrongly prevented from voting.
286.   I have never done anything dangerous for the thrill of it.

REFERENCES

1. BENEDICT, RUTH. 1945. The Chrysanthemum and the Sword – Patterns of Japanese Culture. Houghton Mifflin Co. New York, N.Y.
2. DOI, TAKEO. 1962. Amae: A key concept for understanding Japanese personality structure. *In* Japanese Culture: Its Development and Characteristics. R. J. Smith and R. K. Beardsley, Eds. Aldine Publishing Co. Chicago, Ill.
3. SUZUKI, TAKAO. 1973. Kotoba to Bunka (Language and Culture).: 48–49. Iwanami Shoten. Tokyo, Japan.
4. GOUGH, H. G., DeVOS & K. MIZUSHIMA. 1968. Japanese validation of the CPI Social Maturity Index. Psychol. Rep. **22**: 143–146.
5. TOSHIHIKO, NISHIYAMA. 1973. Evaluation of the California Psychological Inventory. Psychologia **16**: 75–84.
6. TOSHIHIKO, NISHIYAMA. 1973. Karihuorunia jinkaku kensa (CPI) no kozo bunseki to sono junka (the structural analysis and purification of CPI). (7): 1–14. Sapientia Eichi University Publications.
7. TOSHIHIKO, NISHIYAMA. 1974. Karihuorunia jinkaku kensa no hyoka (Evaluation of the CPI). (8): 17–23. Sapientia Eichi University Publications.
8. BLANE, HOWARD T. & KANZUO YAMAMOTO. 1970. Sexual role identity among Japanese and Japanese American high school students. J. Cross-Cultural Psychol. **1** (4): 345–354.
9. GOUGH, H. G. 1948. A sociological theory of psychopathy. Am. J. Sociol. **53**: 359–366.
10. GOUGH, H. G. *et al.* 1952. The identification and measurement of predispositional factors in crime and delinquency. J. Consult. Psychol. **16**: 207–212.
11. GOUGH, H. G. 1960. Theory and measurement of socialization. J. Consult. Psychol. **24**: 23–30.
12. GOUGH, H. G. *et al.* 1951. A personality scale for dominance. J. Abnormal Social Psychol. **46**: 360–366.
13. GOUGH, H. G. *et al.* 1952. A personality scale for social responsibility. J. Abnormal Social Psychol. **47**: 73–80.

THE ROBUSTNESS OF CROSS-CULTURAL FINDINGS

Bernard M. Finifter

Department of Sociology
Michigan State University
East Lansing, Michigan 48824

After decades of provincialism and suspected ethnocentrism, the behavioral and social sciences have recently been expanding their horizons by undertaking more and more cross-cultural comparative research. The inventories of theories and empirical findings of Western social sciences are being applied or overhauled with increasing vigor in one or another cross-cultural comparison. Cross-cultural studies are proliferating at an unprecedented rate. While this is certainly a welcome improvement over past trends, there has generally been very little coordination and continuity among these numerous studies. Instead, each has gone off more or less in its own idiosyncratic direction,[80] producing isolated empirical findings usually formulated at very low levels of abstraction and generality.[96] The net result is that little reliable systematic knowledge has been gained at a time when such knowledge is urgently needed.

The findings generated from one-shot cross-cultural comparisons cannot be taken as final products, although tacitly they often are. They are more appropriately to be regarded as highly preliminary and tentative hypotheses that require programmatic follow-up replication tests to ascertain their reliability, validity, generality, and consequences. This paper discusses some of the principles and problems that are involved in constructing and interpreting such tests. The objective is to identify some conditions of research tactics and practice that may adversely affect the robustness of cross-cultural findings. In this context "robustness" means the ability of a cross-cultural finding to retain its essential characteristics when attempts are made to reproduce and extend it under the same and different conditions.

SECOND-ORDER REPLICATIONS AND THE NULL HYPOTHESIS OF CULTURAL DIFFERENCES

The kinds of tests discussed in this paper are of a different order of replications than those that are commonly thought of in relation to cross-cultural comparative research. Initial cross-cultural comparisons do not usually *in themselves* constitute "replications,"* either in the usual sense in which they are used in experimental design[29,99] or in the psychometric sense of stability tests.† This is not as outrageous a statement as it might appear, because when an

---

* Examples of the small number of studies that do incorporate tests for the stability of cross-cultural findings can be found in Alford[2]; Amir, Sharan, and Kovarsky[3]; Bergeron and Zanna[10]; Carment and Hodkin[21]; Kugelmass, Lieblich, and Ben-Shakar[57]; and Lenski.[59]

† Initial, or first-order, cross-cultural comparisons *can* be considered as replications, but in the special sense of tests of scope generalizability (cf. Finifter, p. 135 ff).[28] That is, a phenomenon or relationship that is studied in one culture can be tested in another to see whether the results from the first study still hold up when "culture" (along with all of its known and unknown covariates) is transformed from a fixed parameter into a variable or set

investigator crosses cultural boundaries, a new set of substantive "treatments" potentially has been introduced into his study design in the form of highly complex "cultural" traits and patterns, many of which are not known beforehand. Cross-cultural comparisons can be considered as a version of test-retest reliability only after the analytically important characteristics of the cultures studied (or other cultures that are demonstrably equivalent) have been identified, and shown to be unrelated, or related in specified ways, to the phenomena being explained.

Tests for the *robustness* of initial cross-cultural findings can be called "second-order replications." Second-order replications proceed from the tactical null hypothesis concerning the importance of "culture," namely, that the samples or populations being compared do not differ by their cultures with respect to the phenomenon under study. The dependent variable in such replications is the reliability, validity, and generality of findings and conclusions about cross-cultural differences and similarities. Two cases can be distinguished: (1) replications that test the robustness of findings and conclusions about presumed cross-cultural differences or similarities found in initial studies in which two or more cultures are *directly* compared; and (2) replications that test the robustness of findings and conclusions about presumed cross-cultural differences or similarities based on *indirect* or contrived comparisons; that is, comparisons between results obtained in a single- or multi-culture study and results from a later replication of that study in one or more other cultures. A recent example of this second case is Bergeron and Zanna's test[10] of Byrne's paradigm. Although these replicators studied only Peruvian university students, they constructed a comparison between their data and the results obtained previously in studies by other investigators, and then inferred that cross-cultural differences exist. It is the stability and correctness of Bergeron and Zanna's new finding of an apparent American-Peruvian difference in the effects of belief similarity on interpersonal attraction that is tested in further second-order replications.‡

BASIC POSTURES TOWARD THE CROSS-CULTURAL NULL
HYPOTHESIS AND TYPICAL ERRORS

Cross-cultural studies are vulnerable to the full litany of potential errors that can hamper any research within a single culture.[14,19,20] But studies that compare cultures invite a congeries of additional error-risks that either compound or exacerbate normal risks of single-culture studies, or that are

---

of variables. The point is that because of the existential complexity of "culture" and because of our usual ignorance and uncertainty about other cultures, the question of equivalence between cultures with respect to the phenomenon to be explained is a matter of testing specific empirical hypotheses, not one of *a priori* presumption. This conclusion applies to cultures that are classified as members of a common general cultural family, such as the national cultures of the United States and England (cf. Berkowitz),[11] as well as to cultural groups that appear grossly different, such as the Bantu and the Basques.

‡ Inferences about cross-cultural similarities and differences can be formulated either by the investigator who conducts the later cultural study, or by a reviewer of research conducted in two or more cultures. In either case it is the robustness of these cross-cultural findings and inferences that is at stake in subsequent replications.

unique to cross-cultural research. One unique burden stems from the fact that "culture" is an exceedingly complex and ill-defined amalgam of variance that comes to the researcher prepackaged. Any single component of this variance may act directly or in interactive combination with any other cultural component, and with any noncultural variables (e.g., social structural, ecological), as well as with any methodological factors introduced by the researcher to affect the outcome of a cross-cultural study. All these complexities and uncertainties add up to a near infinity of variously plausible rival hypotheses that challenge the researcher to defend and demonstrate the superiority of his proposed interpretation of cultural differences or similarities. §

Fundamental stylistic differences can be observed among researchers in the way they go about comparing cultures and deciding on the acceptability of the cross-cultural null hypothesis. There are at least three basic postures that researchers adopt in formulating and conducting cross-cultural research. These postures make the researchers especially prone to typical decision errors regarding the null hypothesis.‖ By explicating the nature of these error liabilities and by exploring some of their probable sources, it should be possible to facilitate their early detection and correction through programmatic replications.

For convenience the three postures can be designated as Specifist, Universalist, and Agnostic. These orientations will first be defined briefly for overall comparison; then each will be explicated and illustrated by actual examples from recent cross-cultural studies chosen primarily from the social psychological literature.

The cross-cultural Specifist is oriented toward finding differences among cultures, and toward devising cultural, as opposed to methodological, explanations to account for these apparent differences. Specifists are thereby especially prone to make type I errors¶ with respect to the cross-cultural null hypothesis. In the present context, a type I, or alpha, error is defined as the rejection of the null hypothesis (that there are no cross-cultural differences) when cultures actually do *not* differ, and the null hypothesis is therefore true. That is, the phenomenon under study is universal, or at least it is not affected by the range of cultural variations represented in the data in hand, but the Specifist decides to the contrary.

The cross-cultural Universalist is oriented toward finding similarities among cultures, and toward establishing universal "laws" which are attributed to invariant properties either of the human species or of all human cultures. Parsimony is more highly prized by Universalists than by Specifists as a scientific goal. Universalists are thereby especially prone to make type II errors with

---

§ The adequate interpretation of results has been distinguished in the recent text by Brislin, Lonner, and Thorndike (p. 146)[17] as the single most difficult problem confronting cross-cultural research.

‖ Even though I am applying the logic and language of statistical hypothesis testing to cross-cultural comparisons, researchers do not often in practice arrive at their decisions about cross-cultural differences on the basis of precise stipulations of alpha and beta probabilities. Nonetheless, in effect, this is the decisional process that is being approximated or simulated when researchers arrive at judgments about cross-cultural findings.

¶ Although the present focus is on the standard type I and type II errors of statistical hypothesis testing, there is the additional danger not dealt with here that a cross-cultural study may be making a more serious "error of the third kind," as Mitroff and Featheringham recently pointed out.[66] Type III errors refer to decisions to research the wrong problems.

respect to the cross-cultural null hypothesis. In this context, a type II, or beta, error refers to the acceptance of the null hypothesis of no cross-cultural differences when that hypothesis is false. That is, cultures actually *do* differ, and the phenomenon being explained is conditioned by cultural variables; but the Universalist's orientation may lead him to decide to the contrary.

The cross-cultural Agnostic orientation can be described briefly because it is rare. The Agnostic suspends judgment as to the existence of cross-cultural differences; he shuns drawing conclusions until the weight of evidence makes a particular interpretation virtually self-evident. Although the literature occasionally contains examples of inauthentic pious methodological posturing in support of this scientific ideal, examples of true Agnostics (as in other spheres) are very rarely found. This is undoubtedly due, among other things, to the fact that, ordinarily, abstaining from declarations about "the outcome" of one's investigation requires that the researcher conquer many strong pressures for establishing scientific priority, for enhancing the prestige of his research organization, for personal advancement, ego gratification, etc. A couple of examples can illustrate the Agnostic posture and its consequences in the field of cross-cultural social psychology. Berkowitz[11] conducted a partial replication among teenagers in Oxford, England to test his previous American results. He found that Oxford boys use reciprocity (vs. responsibility) norms in help-giving more than his sample of Wisconsin boys did. Although Berkowitz suggests both a cultural factor and a methodological artifact as possible explanations for this apparent difference, he resisted any decision, and instead called for further research to see first if his findings were reliable before venturing a "cultural" explanation. Another unusual display of suspended judgment about apparent cultural differences is provided in research by Jahoda,[50] who actually withheld publication of results from an earlier study of ethnic preferences among Pakistani immigrant children living in Glasgow, because his findings contradicted previous replicated research. In subsequent research, Jahoda and his colleagues tested a methodological hypothesis that competes with a "cultural" interpretation of their previous findings by changing the ethnicity of the experimenter. Although an experimenter effect was found, their previous finding of differences in ethnic preferences between Pakistani and native Glaswegian children was confirmed, and provided the assurance Jahoda needed to arrive at a clear interpretation of his results and to finally publish them.

SPECIFIST ORIENTATIONS AND THE GENERATION OF TYPE I ERRORS

The Specifist and Universalist orientations can be described succinctly by drawing on some familiar ideas from the field of immunology. This section focuses on Specifist orientations, while the following section describes Universalist orientations. Accordingly, Specifists can be characterized as having heightened sensitivities for expecting, seeking, and finding evidence that can be construed as being consistent with their predilection that cross-cultural differences exist, coupled with an epistemological "allergic" reaction against expecting, seeking, and recognizing evidence to the contrary.

There are probably many different sources of the Specifist's particular sensitivities and allergies and of his or her consequent type I errors. Although the root causes are difficult to ascertain, we may be able to gain a few clues by looking at some of the distinctive signs and symptoms of Specifist orientations. One key indicator is the Specifist's characteristic reaction to finding apparent differences among cultures. His or her first impulse is to proceed directly to the substance of culture in search of an explanation. The possibility of misinterpreting the observed differences is rarely entertained seriously. Yet, immediate recourse to one particular cultural feature to explain an observed cross-cultural difference may be premature in view of the many rival hypotheses that could be formulated concerning differences in the research procedures used in the cultures studied, or differences in the social organization and ecology of these groups, any of which could provide plausible competing explanations.

There is a curious inconsistency in the way researchers interpret results from attempted replications when discrepancies crop up. Failure to reproduce a finding in the *same* culture usually leads the investigator to question the reliability, validity, and comparability of the research procedures used in the two studies for possible method artifacts. But failure to corroborate the same finding in a *different* culture often leads to claims of having discovered "cultural" differences, and substantive interpretations are promptly devised to account for the apparent differences. Most often these "cultural" explanations are highly adventitious, depending more on chance familiarity with a particular ethnographic account, or with current social trends than on systematic analysis of cultural patterns. Moreover, these "cultural" explanations are usually devised after rather than before differences are observed. The abduction of one particular fragment from a total cultural pattern as a preferred explanation for observed differences cannot be convincing when many other cultural features, as well as method artifacts, could just as plausibly be used to account for the same differences.

In TABLE 1, I have extracted observed cross-cultural differences and their proposed "cultural" explanations from over a dozen studies reported in recent literature.** Inclusion of a study in this list does not mean necessarily that the proposed cultural explanation is invalid or that the researcher has already made a type I error, but only that it is far too early to claim any greater scientific status for these findings and interpretations than as highly tentative hypotheses in a teeming field of alternate and rival hypotheses that require testing in programmatic replications. A few of these examples are discussed here to indicate where some of these error liabilities may lie.

When Ancona[4] attempted to test the generalizability of previous Norwegian findings of positive relations between prolonged father absence and a constellation of psychodynamic symptoms in young sons and between sons and their mothers, he was unable to reproduce these findings in an Italian port city. He attributed these apparent differences between the Tonsberg and Genoan samples to a tradition of matriarchal self-sufficiency that is historically rooted in Italian maritime family culture. While this explanation, like so many other proposed cultural explanations, is intriguing and possibly valid, it remains to be demonstrated that it is superior to several other, possibly less interesting but potentially more powerful, explanations. For example, the boys and mothers who provided data in the Norwegian study lived in a town of only 25,000

** Discussion of studies cited throughout this paper is limited to only certain aspects of each study, because it is not possible here to summarize them fully. The interested reader can consult the original references for the complete reports and for references cited in them to previous studies.

TABLE 1

RECENT RESEARCH FINDINGS OF CROSS-CULTURAL DIFFERENCES AND THEIR PROPOSED EXPLANATIONS

Investigators	Cross-Cultural Differences Observed	Proposed "Cultural" Explanations
Ancona[4] (1970)	Studied effects of father's long-term absence from home on sons and wives. Maternal overprotection, pseudo-maturity in child, development of female characteristics, compensatory masculinity, idealization of father figure, hostility toward mother were found in a sample of Norwegian maritime families in the port city of Tonsberg, but were not found in an Italian sample of families in the port city of Genoa.	Differences are attributed to historical tradition of matriarchal self-sufficiency in Italian maritime family culture.
Borke[12] (1973)	Chinese children in Taiwan scored higher than American children on empathic ability to detect "sad" facial expressions.	Differences are attributed to emphasis in Chinese culture on feeling shameful or "losing face."
Botha[13] (1971)	Arab students in a Lebanese university had lower scores than did American undergraduates on achievement imagery.	Low achievement motivation scores are linked to parental authoritarianism and indulgence of dependency presumed to be typical of Lebanese culture.
Chandra[22] (1973)	Indian Fijians showed greater conformity in Asch-type situations than did non-Indian Fijians and previous samples of Brazilians, Lebanese, and Hong Kong subjects.	Indian Fijian conformity is attributed to authoritarian conformity orientation characteristic of their subculture.
England and Lee[25] (1974)	"Loyalty" is more positively associated and "me" is more negatively associated with "success" of Japanese managers, while these two terms are correlated with managerial success in the opposite direction for samples from the United States, Australia, and India.	Japanese departures from other samples are attributed to the influence of rigid hierarchy characteristic of Confucianism.
Fry[31] (1974)	Asian Indians in New Delhi scored lower on self-differentiation and on self-evaluation than did samples of Canadians in Calgary.	Parts of Murphy and Murphy's analysis of Asian psychology is applied to account for the Indian scores: the legacy of rigid social structure in Hindu culture and pessimistic attitudes toward the self are selected as explanations.

Study	Findings	Interpretation
Gonzalez and Davis[34] (1974)	Found no evidence for Heider's balance effects in a sample of 16 high school students from Northern Greece, but did find them for an equal-size sample of students from Southern California.	The Greek cultural value of *philotimos* (love of honor) is invoked.
Gruenfeld, Weissenberg, and Loh[39] (1973)	More than their American counterparts, Peruvian high school students in Lima value personal ability and knowledge over ascription criteria as a means to get ahead.	Cynicism about actual mobility opportunities in American youth culture is used to explain this difference.
Ingham[46] (1974)	Stockholm university students preferred to occupy opposite seating positions more than did a sample of Oxford university students.	The Swedish cultural orientation to avoid failure and loss of face are held responsible.
Iwata[48] (1974)	Japanese-American university students in Hawaii were more sensitive than were their Caucasian-American colleagues to crowding.	Japanese national characteristics of reserve, humility, shyness, introversion, and recessiveness are invoked.
Meade and Barnard[63] (1973)	Chinese students at the University of Hong Kong showed greater conformity than did their counterparts at Western Washington State College.	The characteristic Chinese need to save face is held responsible.
Smith and Grenier[86] (1975)	Whereas French-Canadian children perceive little difference in discipline from mother and father, English-Canadian children clearly differentiate the father as the main disciplinarian.	The rising status of the French in Quebec and the increasing conservatism of Englishmen are held responsible.
Lopreato[61] (1967)	American middle-class upwardly mobile men tend to become politically conservative on their ascent, while their mobile English counterparts do not become more conservative.	A theory of the "cult of gratitude," which new arrivals show their betters in the American stratification system, is offered.

people, while the Italian sample was drawn from a city of over 700,000. There are obviously many covariates of size of place within this span of populations that could account for the observed differences. For example, more use of communication media in the larger city might have contributed to increased family stability in Genoan families, while the Tonsberg families may have been more isolated and without resources for coping with long-term absences of their male heads-of-household. Another possible alternative explanation arises from the differences in age between parents in the two societies. The Tonsberg fathers were between 46 to 50 years old, and their wives were between 41 to 50 years old, as contrasted to ages between 36 to 40 years for both mothers and fathers in the Genoan sample. The younger age of the Italian parents might have reduced the frequency of personality and interpersonal disturbances particularly through the smaller age-gap between mothers and sons, which could have fostered closer communication between them. Although I have not found follow-up studies that test the robustness of Ancona's findings and interpretations, or any rival interpretations, such replications are clearly called for.

In a study that otherwise corroborated her earlier results showing that American children as young as three years old are capable of empathic awareness of others' emotional states, Borke[12] found differences between her samples of American and Taiwanese children in their levels of awareness in recognizing particular kinds of emotional expressions in facial drawings. Chinese children showed greater ability to recognize "sad" expressions than did the American children. Borke attributes this apparent difference to the Chinese cultural emphasis on feeling shameful or "losing face." Although 87 Taiwanese and 96 American children were included in the study, the critical subgroups that produced the American-Chinese difference contained only 24 cases, thus raising the possibility that, in spite of having passed a test for statistical significance, sampling error could account for some or all of these apparent cross-cultural differences, thereby making it unnecessary to invoke a special theory of Chinese character. It is also possible, of course, that Borke has detected real and stable cultural factors. Further replications can tell.

England and Lee[25] studied the relationship between managers' values and managerial success in Australia, India, Japan, and the United States. They were struck by their finding that the relationship between the rating of the value "loyalty" and managerial success is significantly positive for Japanese managers, but is significantly negative for managers in the other three countries. They also observed that the concept "me" is negatively related to success for Japanese managers, but it is positively related to success for managers in the other three countries. England and Lee immediately attributed these apparent cross-national differences to the influence of Confucianism on Japanese behavior and customs, because that philosophy stresses a rigid relationship within a hierarchically arranged society in which members are expected to maintain absolute loyalty and obedience to authority. It is possible that England and Lee have found reliable differences between managers in Japan and those in the other countries studied, and that these differences are indeed reflections of Confucianism. But there are several other less fascinating factors that could compete with these conclusions. One possibility is that the quality of the Japanese data may be lower than the data from the other national samples. Indications of this possible artifact are that the Japanese sample of managers had the lowest response rate (26%) among these nations; also the simple correlation between the managerial success index and the emically-derived scoring key of values was lowest (+.26) for the Japanese sample. Moreover, the probability is fairly large that, among 66 comparisons of value-success correlations, a cross-cultural difference of the size and direction that England and Lee found could have occurred by chance. Whether these researchers have discovered genuine cultural differences or have merely capitalized on error variance is a question requiring further cross-cultural replication studies.

In a test of the universality of Heider's classic theory that individuals align their attitudes to maintain structural balance in their cognitive systems (the P-O-X triads), Gonzalez and Davis[34] claim that no such balance effects appeared in a sample of 16 high school students in a northern Greek city, although balance effects did appear in a similar sample of 16 students from a southern California city. The researchers favor a cultural interpretation of this apparent cross-cultural difference in terms of the Greek value of *philotimos*, meaning love of honor. They reason that this value may have affected the saliency of the cognitions or the strength of the sentiment bond in the minds of these Greek teenagers. The evidence presented by Gonzalez and Davis as a challenge to the generality of Heider's theory is based on such small sample sizes that sampling error alone might account for their findings. If these results are reliably established in further research using larger and more representative samples, it would then be appropriate to test whether *philotimos* (or possibly some other cultural, social, or ecological factor) might affect cognitive structures and processes among Greeks in the ways proposed.

In surveys of high-school seniors in Lima, Peru and in upper New York State, Gruenfeld, Weissenberg, and Loh[39] report finding a statistically significant difference, suggesting that Peruvian students value personal ability and knowledge over ascriptive attributes more than do American students. After showing that this difference persists when socioeconomic status is controlled, these researchers accept this difference as a genuine cultural phenomenon, and proceed to elaborate a theory to account for it. Their theory is based on the premises that Peruvian culture emphasizes the importance of ascription and particularistic criteria for achievement, and Peruvian society is seen to operate according to these values. In contrast, American culture stresses the importance of achievement and universalistic criteria for advancement; but in actual practice, Americans are seen to get ahead by personalistic and ascriptive criteria, such as family connections, race, and ethnicity. American students thus are taught that achievement is the key to success, yet they observe that achievement is not often followed by status rewards, although nonachievement criteria are. This inconsistency between the culturally espoused value of egalitarian opportunity and actual practices in the American social stratification system is seen as causing American youths to become cynical about their own chances for advancement, and consequently about the real value of personal ability and knowledge. This cynicism is suggested as the cause for the apparent tendency of seniors in Lima to value personal ability and knowledge more highly than did their New York counterparts. We have in this study, once again, an interesting line of theory developed after the fact to explain previously unpredicted cross-national differences. The empirical finding appears to be buttressed by the demonstration that it survived a control for socioeconomic status; furthermore, the theoretical arguments devised to explain this finding seem especially compelling, because they are consistent with a large body of fairly well established theory and research about means-ends discrepancies, anomie, and alienation among youths in contemporary American society. However, the empirical difference between Peruvian and American students requires substantiation before it is ready to be linked up with these established lines of theory and research. It is necessary minimally to show not only that this cross-national difference is reproducible by the same and alternate measures of self-reliance, but also that this finding varies with levels of cynicism about the efficacy of personal achievement for upward mobility both within and across cultures.

Iwata[48] reported his finding that Japanese-American student volunteers at the University of Hawaii are more sensitive to variations in objective population density levels than are their Caucasian-American counterparts at the same university. Iwata proceeds to explain this apparent ethnic difference in density-sensitivity by referring to an unpublished study by Meredith that purports to show that male Japanese-Americans of the third generation are more reserved, humble, conscientious, shy, and introverted, and less outgoing, assertive, and venturesome than male Caucasians. Exactly what the causal pathways may be between each of these personality traits and possible differences in density-sensitivities between Japanese and Caucasian students are not specified. But before any theory is elaborated about Japanese character, it would be necessary to corroborate the basic empirical finding through further research. One high priority in such a research program would include demonstrations that the subject recruitment procedures used attracted the same kinds of voluntary responses from the Japanese ethnics as from the Caucasian ethnics: If England and Lee[25] (discussed above) are correct in attributing Confucian authority-responsiveness to Japanese character, it might be possible that Iwata's Japanese sample disproportionately attracted students who were especially responsive to (the experimenter's) authority and eager to behave in a way that they perceived was expected of them; i.e., be sensitive to density. Another high priority should be to demonstrate that the experimental task and measures of density perception have the same meanings for both ethnic groups.

In a recent study of perceived family structure, Smith and Grenier[86] found that their sample of 80 French-Canadian first- and third-grade children perceived no differences between their mothers and fathers in the use of physical disciplinary methods, such as spanking and slapping; but an equal-sized sample of English-Canadian children did see their fathers as the primary disciplinarians. Smith and Grenier attribute this apparent difference to the contemporary rise in egalitarianism and status of French ethnics in Quebec and to a corresponding increase in conservatism among their English counterparts. While such secular trends might accurately describe current events in Quebec society, it may be unnecessary to invoke them as explanations for the differences observed in this study. There are at least two rival hypotheses that need to be considered first. One obvious factor that possibly could account for the observed differences in perceptions of parental participation in discipline is that two different investigators were used to collect data from these children: All of the English children were interviewed by "a young middle-class college student" (presumably the first author, a native English speaker), whereas all of the French children were interviewed by "an older middle class woman" (presumably the second author, a native French speaker). Although the use of same native-language speakers for each ethnic group may have avoided some sources of invalidity in the results, it may have invited others, as Jahoda's work and other extensive research on experimenter effects would suggest.[50,54,81] Specifically, the use of persons who differ in age and possibly authoritativeness may have led students in the two ethnic samples to differentially recall situations of female discipline. The rival hypothesis of investigator bias could have been tested easily had Smith and Grenier exploited a version of *embedded experiments* (discussed in the final section below) by assigning the English-speaking investigator to random half samples of the two ethnic groups and assigning the French-speaking investigator to the remaining halves. A second source of artifact might have arisen from the fact that all of the English children were Protestant, and all of the French children were Catholic. It is possible that because of their social-ization in Catholic Sunday and parochial schools, the French children have had experiences with both men and women in disciplinary roles, whereas the English Protestant children were less likely to have experienced as much discipline from women ("mother figures") as from men ("father figures"). These, as well as other rival hypotheses (e.g., possible differential validity in surrogate reports from children on parental behavior in the two ethnic groups), require testing and rejection if the reported English-French difference is to be accepted as genuine. Once confirmed, this ethnic difference may prove to be a reflection of current social changes in Quebec, or it may be explainable on other grounds. Specific hypotheses on these effects will need to be constructed, tested and corroborated.

With this brief survey of recent examples of some Specifist orientations, we are left with a great number of unanswered questions about the reported differences between cultures and their interpretations. This state of affairs is scientifically necessary for the cumulative growth of reliable knowledge. If the rival hypotheses suggested above (or other alternative hypotheses) are supported by second-order replication studies, the "cultural" explanations proposed by these researchers would be reduced to casualties of alpha errors. However, as Schachter[83] pointed out over two decades ago, demonstrations that cross-cultural findings are mere artifacts are ultimately of trivial import, because they are corrective rather than productive contributions. Yet, there is no real substitute for tests of the robustness of cross-cultural (or any other empirical) findings if we are to know which of the contributions are "productive." The important questions are when and how to test for and eliminate such artifacts so that productive contributions can be expedited.

UNIVERSALIST ORIENTATIONS AND THE GENERATION OF TYPE II ERRORS

The second major style of research, the Universalist, has its own special propensities for error, although they are usually much more difficult to detect, because it is generally easier to raise questions about claims of having discovered cultural differences than it is to question claims of having found cultural similarities. In the first case, something new has to be learned and integrated; in the second case, no new learning is required: What was known appears to be sufficient.

Universalists can be described, according to our immunological analogy, as having acute sensitivities for evidence that can be construed as consistent with their predilection that cross-cultural differences do not exist; or, if they exist, that they are of secondary or trivial importance. These sensitivities are coupled with an epistemological allergic reaction to contrary evidence. For various reasons Universalists are prone to test the cross-cultural null hypothesis by constructing and applying experimental tests of low power,†† and typically

†† In classical statistical theory the technical meaning of "power" is, of course, (1-beta), i.e., the probability of avoiding a type II error. Overall[72] and Tversky and Kahneman[94] show that generally researchers use tests of insufficient power, resulting frequently in wasteful, invalid rejections of the null hypothesis.

apply conceptual schemes, measurement procedures, and analytic instruments that may be insensitive to indigenous cultural features. The results of these decisions often are invalid acceptances of the cross-cultural null hypothesis and consequent spurious conclusions about the generality of behavioral phenomena and "laws."

As was the case with the Specifist's proneness to generate type I errors regarding the cross-cultural null hypothesis, it is also difficult to determine the basic causes of the Universalist's special liability for making type II errors. We are certain to find, however, that these causes are several and diverse. Two possible contributing sources of the Universalist orientation are identified here in the hope of stimulating systematic tests of these metamethodological (or perhaps better stated, researcher-behavior) hypotheses, and the construction of additional ones. Viewed broadly, both of these possible sources are products of professional socialization into certain scientific specialities and their associated intellectual traditions and social networks, which operate to increase the likelihood that a scientist will adopt a Universalist rather than a Specifist orientation to his research practice. One of these specialties includes the areas of developmental theories, particularly those relating to personality and social development. The other is traced to the learning of certain multidimensional analysis models that are precommitted to parsimony and to the discovery of structural invariances.

Jahoda[49] has noted that although many psychologists assert the universality of their theories and findings, they typically ignore cross-cultural testing because of a prior belief that at the level of physiological functioning all members of the human species can be treated as if they are equivalent, cultural variabilities notwithstanding. Many theories of human development are anchored ultimately to some notion of a standard organism that is assumed to be prepotent in causing behavior. But even those developmental theories that avoid such biological determinism are likely to be based on assumptions about fixed ontogenetic sequences through which various kinds of human behavior develop. Culture per se and other environmental factors are presumed to be of little importance in the unfolding of such sequences. Accordingly, our tentative hypotheses are: (1) that socialization into developmental paradigms of behavior will increase the likelihood that a researcher will expect that the developmental processes he studies are generally found among peoples in diverse cultural settings; and (2) that such orientations will increase the probability that these researchers will make type II errors.

It would be convenient, of course, to be able to point to definitive examples from empirical research on human development that could demonstrate the plausibility of these hypotheses. But to ask for such examples presupposes that the state of our knowledge about the cross-cultural applicability of human development theories has advanced far beyond present realities. The problem is precisely that too few cross-cultural tests and corroboration studies have been accomplished to date. What I hope to do here is to suggest additional reasons why such studies ought to be pursued programmatically.

One of the classic developmental schemes is Freud's theory of the Oedipus complex, which is assumed to be characteristic of the entire human species, deriving from universal sexual impulses of young males in all societies. Empirical evidence on the general applicability of Freud's observations is presently inconsistent and controversial. Hall and Domhoff[41] developed procedures of dream analysis to test for some consequences derived from Oedipal theory. They reasoned that if the Oedipal conflict exists, then men should report more male than female characters and more hostile interactions with male characters in their dreams. To dream more about any male figure is taken as symbolic evidence of basic unresolved father-son conflict. Hall and Domhoff collected dream contents from samples of male and female Caucasian Americans, Australian aboriginal Yir Yoront, and Hopi Indians. In all three cultures they found that men dream primarily about male characters, while women dream about male and female characters in about equal proportions. Hall and Domhoff take these findings as evidence of ubiquitous sex differences in all cultures and as support for Oedipal theory.

Later, on the basis of their own clinical experiences, Grey and Kalsched[38] developed a contrary hypothesis that men's and women's dreams are importantly conditioned by their daily interactions in particular sociocultural settings. They tested this rival hypothesis by analyzing dream contents from a sample of 45 female and 51 male students at the University of Allahabad in Uttar Pradesh, a culture in which Grey and Kalsched assume there is greater sexual segregation than in Hall and Domhoff's American sample. (Nothing is said, however, about the comparative sex segregation between their Indian sample and Hall and Domhoff's Yir Yoront and Hopi Indians.) Grey and Kalsched find not only that Indian men exceed Hall and Domhoff's American men in reporting male figures in their dreams (supposedly reflecting the greater sex segregation in Indian vs. American society), but they also find that sex ratios of dream characters vary with the day-to-day social experiences of the dreamers: Indian students who come from very traditional backgrounds have fewer contacts with the opposite sex in daytime interaction, and consequently report fewer opposite sex figures in their nighttime fantasies; less traditional Indian students who have more cross-sex contacts report more opposite sex figures in their dreams. From this evidence, Grey and Kalsched conclude that the sex distribution of dream characters is not determined generically, but instead reflects the dreamer's actual interpersonal interactions. Hall and Domhoff's ubiquity hypothesis is accordingly rejected, and doubt is cast on the universality of Oedipal theory to the extent that Hall and Domhoff's derivation and operationalization is pertinent to that theory. If Grey and Kalsched's results and conclusions are corroborated, then Hall and Domhoff's findings and assertions about the ubiquity of sex differences in dreams may be dismissed as casualties of type II errors. It is also possible, of course, that the empirical findings of *both* Hall and Domhoff's and of Grey and Kalsched's studies are reliable and valid, although, if this turned out to be true, then the importance of the Oedipus complex relative to social interaction would have to be evaluated.

This possibility is suggested by some further research that claims to corroborate Hall and Domhoff's interpretations. Robbins and Kilbride[79] applied the same techniques used by Hall and Domhoff and later by Grey and Kalsched in their own analysis of dreams collected from a sample of 50 male and 44 female Bagandu Bantu secondary-school students in Uganda. Robbins and Kilbride found a tendency (although short of statistical significance) for males to dream more about other males than about females, and for females to dream about both sexes equally. These findings provide only very weak support for Hall and Domhoff's conclusions, thus leaving the question of the universality of sex differences in dreams and of the Oedipus complex still open to more definitive replication tests.

Another well known developmental theory is Kohlberg's theory of moral thinking, based in part on Piaget's work. A central premise of this theory is that there is an invariant trend in the stages of moral development. Kohlberg briefly reported some cross-cultural data in support of his claim that the stages and their sequencing are universal. Recently, Kurtines and Greif[58] evaluated Kohlbergian research. On the basis of available empirical evidence, and particularly Kohlberg's own report of the absence of Stage 6 reasoning among Taiwanese children, Kurtines and Greif conclude that "general cross-cultural age trends in early development provide no support for qualitative differences between stages or their sequential invariance." According to this evaluation, it is possible that other research findings of cross-cultural similarities in the sequential development of moral reasoning are attributable to type II errors, and that cultural variables actually do affect moral development. Kohlberg's theory and research may not be alone, however, in proneness to type II errors.

Rettig and Singh[78] propose an "ethical risk" theory of morality, according to which sociocultural constraints (as opposed to psychological internalization) operate in all human societies to govern moral thinking and behavior. Rettig and Singh present data on moral judgments made by samples of American students and Indian students studying in the United States. They claim that their data confirm the cross-cultural invariance of moral judgments. Although the "ethical risk" hypothesis may be universally applicable, a two-culture comparison provides only the scantiest suggestion. More cross-cultural replications are required to test for the possible sample bias of Rettig and Singh's Indian students, who elected and were selected to study in the United States, and also for the robustness of any resulting invariances across a broader spectrum of the world's cultures.

Recently, Fry[31] reported a study on an hypothesized invariant trend in the development and organization of self-evaluations, which supposedly proceed from global to differentiated. To test for the universality of this ontogenetic hypothesis, Fry collected data from samples of 75 volunteer subjects of different age groups in Calgary, Alberta, and from 75 Asian students of similar different age groups in New Delhi. Comparisons of changes in the age-group self-evaluation scores across these two cultural samples led Fry to conclude that cultural differences do not affect the linear increase in self-differentiation. Because no formal test of the linearity assumption is presented for these data, it is difficult to know whether Fry's finding of no cultural difference is due to a type II error, or whether the trends are actually the same in these samples. But even if we assume that Fry's data successfully pass a test for similarity of linear trends, a great deal more needs to be done before much confidence can be placed in the universality assertion.

The subtle dangers of erroneously concluding that the cross-cultural null hypothesis is true were recognized clearly in these cogent observations by Munnichs[68] in discussing his work on aging: "When one does not find any differences between two countries or two cultures, then this can be due to the research methods employed as well as to the actual situation in those two countries. When for example we hardly find any differences between German and Dutch steelworkers, this does not mean immediately that the situation of old age is the same for steelworkers in these two countries. For it is possible that our research methods did not suffice to discover existing differences." Yet, when researchers have been conditioned to think in terms of certain kinds of human development models, which are predicated in phylogenetic or ontogenetic assumptions of universality, it is at least reasonable, if not natural, that they will construct tests, and collect and interpret their data in ways that predetermine the emergence of cultural differences or that make the investigator insensitive to the significance of such differences when they do appear. Trained insensitivities to cultural differences may also be especially likely to develop when researchers adopt certain kinds of analytic models, as suggested below.

Many of the models that are currently used to determine the structure of conceptual domains or the underlying structure of a set of empirical inter-correlations are predicated on the goal of parsimony and the assumption that invariant structures exist. The most common example of such models is factor analysis,[91] although recent developments in facet analysis[30] and nonmetric scaling techniques are often used for the same purposes. Our tentative hypotheses on the use of these models are: (1) that the learning and use of certain multidimensional analytic models will increase the likelihood that a researcher will expect that the structures he studies are invariant across diverse cultural contexts; and (2) that such orientations will increase the probability that researchers will make type II errors.

Although not all researchers who use factor analysis in cross-cultural comparisons claim that they find invariances,[40,51] most do. Decisions to accept the null hypothesis of no cross-cultural variations are likely to be very complex interactive functions of at least three main sets of variables: (1) the algorithmic properties of ordinary factor analytic techniques and the arbitrary decisions that are required for interpretation of the numerical results; (2) the factor analyst's conscious or unconscious predilection for finding structures that are universal; and (3) the extent to which cultures actually differ in the structuring of the phenomena under study. At present we do not have anything near the amount of information that would be needed to be able to assign even approximate weights to these three sets of variables according to their relative contributions to researchers' decision making. Although we can cite examples where the application of factor analysis has led to conclusions to accept the cross-cultural null hypothesis, the determination that these decisions are valid or erroneous cannot be made until new evidence from certain kinds of replication tests (suggested below) becomes available.

Even in the very few cases where initial findings of cultural similarities in factor structures are repeatedly corroborated across a series of replications, it is not impossible that common biases may exist in the procedures used to collect the data and/or in the factor analysis techniques themselves such that real cultural differences get obscured. Some of our most stalwart findings can be questioned on this basis. The work of Rummel and his colleagues[82,88] for example, which has reproduced similar dimensional structures among samples of nations in at least five separate studies, or the work of Osgood,[70] showing stable structures of connotative meaning across cultures, may be subject to common method biases. To detect such biases requires not a further series of replications that continue the use of the same measurement and analysis techniques, but replications that are faithful in all other aspects to the original studies except in their use of different techniques to collect and analyze the data. If the same results are then obtained across variations in data collection and analysis techniques, we will have a more secure basis for attributing confidence to the decision to accept the null hypothesis of no cultural differences. Such confidence would be augmented to the extent that the techniques used in the new replications have been shown through prior or collateral analyses to be capable of revealing real cultural differences.

In areas where cross-cultural factor analytic studies have been less replicated, additional questions of robustness arise. For example, Tomeh[93] compared the factor structure of moral values obtained from a sample of 150 undergraduate students at Bowling Green State University in Ohio with the structure of moral values obtained from a sample of 136 Arab students (divided about equally between Christians and Moslems) at American University in Beirut. She finds that the structure of moral values is similar in these two cultural samples, and suggests that there may be universal value orientations based on common human problems. Tomeh bases her conclusions about similarities between American and Lebanese students on "invariance coefficients" computed by Ahmavaara's transformation analysis. Because there is no precise sampling theory for these coefficients, any conclusions about the "similarity" between pairs of factors from different cultural samples are necessarily arbitrary. What one analyst (perhaps a Specifist) might take as a "low" coefficient indicating that cultures have different structures, another analyst (perhaps a Universalist) might interpret as a "high" coefficient indicating cultural similarities. Recently, Bechtoldt[9] reported on some advances made by Joreskog in developing more exact statistical procedures for determining factor stabilities. Would Tomeh reach the same conclusions about the cultural invariance of moral values if her data were reanalyzed by these more stringent tests? Would her conclusions also hold up if American and Lebanese peasants were sampled instead of university students, or American students and Lebanese peasants?

Several solutions are available for the problems of constructing probative tests for possible type II errors in cross-cultural factor analyses. Two were mentioned earlier in this section: (1) the use of different data collection and analysis techniques, which are known to be sensitive to real cultural differences; and (2) the application of more exact tests of factor invariance, such as Joreskog's procedures. A further possibility, which has only just recently been suggested, is Buss and Royce's[18] proposal of "intergroup factor analysis." This procedure is based on Tucker's "interbattery factor analysis" model, but the intergroup version is transformed from the original R technique to Q technique. Intergroup factor analysis supposedly is capable of detecting both etic universal structures as well as emic variations, and thus appears for certain purposes to be a very promising tool for avoiding type II errors when cultures are compared.

CONSTRUCTION AND INTERPRETATION OF SECOND-ORDER CROSS-CULTURAL REPLICATIONS

It would seem on the surface that to replicate initial cross-cultural findings is a straightforward matter of repeating the original study, and then seeing whether the same results reappear. Replication research, however, is usually much more problematic and complex. Unless these problems and complexities are identified and dealt with systematically, the prospects for achieving worthwhile advances in cross-cultural (as well as in intracultural) research will be dismal. Some of these difficulties are discussed here to suggest caveats and procedures for testing the robustness of cross-cultural findings.

When a researcher sets out to test the stability, validity, or generality of previous empirical findings, he is confronted with a series of fundamental decisions, each of which can have important consequences for the interpretation of the replication attempt. For example, which particular aspects of a previous study are to be reproduced (e.g., the sampling plan, study populations, subject recruitment policies, investigator personnel, concepts, variables, measuring instruments, analysis techniques, etc.)? What criteria are to be applied in determining when each of the method features of a replication study is sufficiently similar to the reference study to constitute a fair but critical comparison? When is it desirable intentionally to alter or mismatch certain procedural or substantive features of a reference study in a replication? What standards are to be used to determine when a replicated finding is sufficiently similar to or consistent with an original finding to conclude that the initial finding is corroborated; conversely, when is a replication finding sufficiently different from or inconsistent with an initial result to warrant a conclusion of disconfirmation? Such problems are perplexing enough for replications conducted within the *same* culture,‡‡ but they are greatly exacerbated when cultural variability is superimposed on a study design.

TABLE 2 represents a classification of the consequences of second-order replications. The scheme is presented here in a rudimentary and simplified form to facilitate discussion of the logical basis for certifying and extending scientific knowledge through systematic replications. The theory of knowledge adopted here assumes that, with respect to the particular phenomena under study, differences or similarities between cultures actually exist (the "actual states of affairs" in TABLE 2), and that these facts, although not known at present, are ascertainable in principle through replications that are sufficiently numerous, probative, and informative. Each successive study provides a further contribution to a growing network of evidence that is used to generate confidence and to improve knowledge about cultural realities. §§

In TABLE 2 each of the actual-state conditions is divided according to whether an *initial* comparative study finds that cultures differ or that they do not differ in the particular attribute or relationship being studied. Then, each of these logically possible actual-state/initial-outcome combinations is further subdivided according to the results obtained from a second-order *replication* study showing again either that cultures differ or that they are the same. This cross classification yields eight *a priori* logical combinations of results that differ in their implications for the cumulation of valid knowledge. Each type is defined below and is illustrated, where possible, by actual examples of cross-cultural research. Because second-order replications are presently very rare in this field, fully appropriate examples for all eight cases have not yet been found in the literature reviewed.

---

‡‡ Representative examples of *within*-culture studies that illustrate several difficulties encountered in interpreting apparent failures to corroborate previous results can be found in Gorsuch and Smith,[35] Hardyck and Braden,[43] Looft and Baranowski,[60] Oakes,[69] Ostrom et al.,[71] Skolnick,[85] Tognoli and Keisner,[92] Vidmar and Hackman,[97] and Wahrman and Pugh.[98]

§§ This position differs from the logic that scientists in the behavioral and social fields most commonly use to arrive at decisions about the real world, namely, statistical significance tests. Elsewhere[27] I have suggested that these tests are special cases of a general class of hypothetic artificial replications. That is, significance tests are *artificial* because they rely on mathematically derived probabilities rather than on empirical events. That is, they invoke one or another theoretical distribution (e.g., for t, χ^2, F, or other statistic), and assume that the mathematical events contained in them, along with their formal assumptions, apply to the single empirical result being tested. Furthermore, significance tests are *hypothetical* because, even though their statistical inferences are based on an assumption of an extremely large number of trials performed under identical conditions, the trials are only imaginary. Because no one actually carries out the infinity of imagined trials, the only empirical grounds for making decisions about the real world are the data in hand. In contrast, conclusions reached by replication strategies are based on multiple empirical findings obtained over a series of actual trials.

TABLE 2

CONSEQUENCES OF SECOND-ORDER CROSS-CULTURAL REPLICATION STUDIES FOR CUMULATIVE KNOWLEDGE

Original Study Outcome → / Replication Study Outcome ↓	Actual State of Affairs in Populations Studied			
	Cultures Differ (H_1)		Cultures are the Same (H_0)	
	Finds cross-cultural differences	Finds cross-cultural similarities	Finds cross-cultural differences	Finds cross-cultural similarities
Finds cross-cultural differences	(A) Correct corroboration: Original and replication studies agree that cultural differences exist. Phenomena under study depend on cultural variations. Valid consensus builds on H_1.	(C) Original study made type II error: Replication study detected cultural differences original researcher overlooked. If new valid findings are not accepted, previous invalid conclusions may persist. If replicated findings are accepted, new knowledge requires cultural specification of previous conclusions.	(E) Both original and replication studies make type I errors: Cultures really do not differ. Subsequent replication studies may identify common artifacts to correct cumulative misconceptions. Invalid consensus builds.	(G) Replication study makes type I error: Original study is correct: Cultures do not differ. Replication study may be erroneous, noncomparable, or incompetently executed. Unless errors are detected, previous valid consensus to accept H_0 may decrease.
Finds cross-cultural similarities	(B) Replication study made type II error: Original study is correct. Cultures do differ. Replication study may be erroneous, noncomparable, or incompetently executed. Unless replication errors are discovered, previous valid consensus to reject H_0 may decrease.	(D) Both original and replication studies make type II errors: Cultures do differ but neither study was able to detect differences. Further replication is needed to detect common artifacts and correct cumulative misconceptions. Invalid consensus builds.	(F) Original study made type I error: Cultures do not differ. Replication study was correct. Need further replication studies to explore reasons for disparity and seek reconciliation. If error of original study is recognized, valid consensus begins; if not, dissensus increases.	(H) Correct corroboration: Original and replication studies agree that cultures do not differ. Phenomena studied are independent of culture. "Universals" have been found, and valid consensus builds on H_0.

The cases in TABLE 2 have pairwise inverse relationships, depending on the actual state of cultural differences or similarities. The *correct* classification of the findings from a replication study as examples of either member of a given pair constitutes the major problem for scientific verification. For example, case A is the inverse of case E. In both of these cases the results obtained from the initial *and* the replication studies agree with each other. The only difference is that the agreement reached in case E is invalid (both studies have made type I errors), because in reality cultures do not differ. But because that reality is not immediately ascertainable, it is not possible to determine whether an apparent consensus between an initial and a replication study is valid or invalid, until further replication evidence becomes available. Similarly, there is agreement in both cases H and D between the findings obtained from the original and replication studies, but in case D, the consensus is invalid (both studies make type II errors) because cultures really do differ. The problem, of course, is to find ways to distinguish between valid (A and H) and invalid (D and E) consensus, and to learn about the conditions that favor reaching valid consensus and those that predispose to common errors. Consensual errors create scientific myths, and their discovery is the occasion for both embarrassment (the broader and older the consensus) and celebration over the ability of the scientific community eventually to correct its own errors. In the concluding section strategies are suggested to help in the early detection of invalid consensus.

In *case A* the replication study confirms the original study's finding that cultures differ. Both studies *appear* to have correctly rejected the null hypothesis that cultures do not differ, but there is too little information at this stage to be able to draw this conclusion with sufficient confidence. The more that future replications reconfirm this finding, the more robust it will be shown, and the greater will be the consensus around the belief that the null hypothesis is false. Whether this belief is factually warranted or whether it is based on a common misconception will depend on corroborative evidence from future replications, which are designed to be increasingly probative and severe. An example that illustrates either case A or case E (depending on the actual but currently unascertained state of affairs) is Deregowski and Munro's study,[23] which corroborates Wober's earlier finding of "polyphasic pictorial perception" (i.e., the ability to perceive a drawing as portraying a sequence of events) among Ugandan children, as contrasted to the finding of "camera pictorial perception" (i.e., perceiving the same drawing as portraying a single instant in time) among English children. Deregowski and Munro showed that this apparent uniqueness of sub-Saharan African cultures was reproducible when retested on different samples of Rhodesian children and adults, who were compared with Ontario school children. The more that further replications confirm the findings of Wober and of Deregowski and Munro by using different procedures and samples, the firmer will be the basis for inferring that the (African and Western) cultures do differ in this perceptual style. Another likely example of case A is Ramirez, Castaneda, and Herold's[75] further corroboration of findings from Witkin's[100] previous research in Holland, Italy, Mexico, and Norway. These replicators found once again for independent samples of Mexican subcultures that children reared in communities that stress conformity to external authority are more field-dependent than are children reared in communities that have low conformity pressures. Witkin's[100,101] extensive research program on the sources and consequences of psychological differentiation represents one of the very small number of cross-cultural research areas in which a high degree of consensus has been achieved by repeated independent replications in various nations, in this instance showing the effects of subcultural differences in authoritarian conformity. This evidence increases our confidence in the belief that such cultural differences actually do exist in the cultures studied and probably elsewhere.

In *case E* both the original and replication studies agree to reject the cross-cultural null hypothesis even though future replication studies may show that the cultures really do *not* differ with regard to the phenomena studied, and both previous findings have resulted from type I errors. The detection of findings of types D and E requires testing specially formulated hypotheses on the existence of possible constant biases that are shared by an original study and its subsequent replications. If such hypotheses are supported, opposite conclusions would be drawn about the cross-cultural null hypothesis. In areas where a body of research evidence has been generated exclusively by one key researcher and his colleagues and students, the simple change to an unrelated investigator may be sufficient to produce different findings on cultural variations. Although there are sharp differences of opinion as to the wisdom of conducting comparative research with different investigators,[6,53,54] it is a basic requirement of science to demonstrate that findings are not dependent on particular researchers.

Case H (in which the replication study corroborates the original finding of no cultural differences, and both studies *appear* to have correctly accepted the null hypothesis that cultures do not differ) can be illustrated by the series of second-order replications that have shown certain dimensions of nations identified by Rummel to be invariant over differences in national cultures, years, and data sources.[82] The classification of Rummel's research as a possible example of case H instead of case D is not inconsistent with the earlier discussion of this line of research as an example of possible Universalist bias. The apparent consensus resulting from Rummel's and others' series of replications is taken tentatively as a valid description of the "actual state" of national variations in the structure of conflict, pending any subsequent contrary evidence that might require revision of this conclusion. A second example of case H may be Iwao, Child, and Garcia's replication[47] of their earlier study that compared the esthetic judgments of Japanese potters to those of American art students and experts. For the replication study these same researchers collected esthetic preferences from 31 additional Japanese, who were engaged in various traditional arts (e.g., flower-arranging, tea ceremony, etc.), and compared them with the preferences of the original American sample. The finding that there is greater-than-chance agreement between American and Japanese judgments reassured Iwao, Child, and Garcia that different cultural settings do produce similar esthetic evaluations. However, because of possible methodological weaknesses (constant biases due to the use of the same investigators, comparison group, and measuring techniques; the small sample sizes and small between-cultures differences), the classification of this study in case H is highly uncertain. If subsequent replications by different researchers using different and more adequate samples and instruments produce discrepant evidence, then this study, along with its original version, may then be considered to have produced a common type II error, which would reclassify it in case D.

In *case D* both the original and replication studies agree to accept the cross-cultural null hypothesis, even though it is not true. Both of the earlier findings are products of type II errors. As I mentioned above, a potential candidate for case D may be the finding by Iwao, Child, and Garcia. However, the necessary independent replications have yet to be carried out.

The problem of correctly classifying the results of replication studies in the four remaining cases in TABLE 2 involves the explanation of *disagreements* between an initial study and its replicates. For convenience these four cases are paired according to their disagreement rather than by the type of error a study may have made. In the B-C pair the question raised by the divergence of findings is to determine whether a type II error was made by the initial study or by its replicate, because both findings cannot be valid simultaneously. Similarly, in cases F and G the question of disagreement is to determine whether the findings from the original or the replication study resulted from a type I error, because the findings are mutually contradictory.

In *case C* the original study accepted the cross-cultural null hypothesis, while the replication study rejected it. The disagreement between these two findings can be reconciled only by additional replications that take this discrepancy into account either in their design or interpretation. In this case further studies converge on the conclusion that the original findings resulted from type II errors, and that cultures really do differ. When original findings of no cultural differences are validly disconfirmed, something new may be learned about the specific cultural conditions that affect the phenomenon or relationship under study. Presently there are few areas of cross-cultural research that have advanced far enough to provide sufficient replications to allow a determination whether it is the original study or its replicates that produced invalid results. A line of research that probably illustrates case C is provided in Draguns'[24] comprehensive review of the history and status of research on cross-cultural differences in five parameters of psychopathology. While early studies in this area accepted the null hypothesis that cultures do not differ in the frequency and expression of psychopathology, Draguns juxtaposes these findings against a growing body of recent evidence that shows consistent divergences among cultures, and concludes that ". . . cultural differences in psychiatric manifestations have been remarkably refractory to elimination through variations of rationale, perspective, method, instrumentation, setting, and subject pool." A specific example of the series of studies that is generating consensus around the conclusion that the original studies in this area made type II errors is the report by Secrest and colleagues[84] of differences in attitudes toward mental health among Philippine and Pakistani university students. Earlier studies by Thaver and colleagues[89] failed to find such differences among Asian students at the University of Hawaii. Secrest and his colleagues attribute the discrepancy in findings to the small samples used in the original study and to the fact that all of the Asian samples in the Thaver study were students at the same university, suggesting that there may have been some common selection bias that obscured actual cultural differences in mental health attitudes.

In *case B* the original study finds that cultures differ, but the replication researchers decide the contrary. Subsequent replications are also required in this case to determine which study produced invalid results. Although a suitable cross-cultural example of this case was not available, I will describe an intracultural study to illustrate the logic of this type of replication error. In order to use this example, however, I must ask the reader to accept temporarily a shift in the way I have thus far defined the "actual state of affairs" and the null hypothesis being tested. This translation of the specific contents of the null hypothesis should not be troublesome, once it is recognized that the *cross-cultural* null hypothesis is just one extremely important class of null hypotheses among numerous other classes of null hypotheses that happen to be the main focus of this paper. Accordingly, the particular null hypothesis tested in a study conducted solely in the United States by Alexander, Zucker, and Brody[1] is that "the autokinetic effect does not structure experience." The possible "states of affairs" for this study are that autokinetic experiences are not related to need for structure (H_0), and that autokinetic experiences are related to need for structure (H_1). Sherif's and dozens of subsequent studies, of course, had previously agreed to reject the null hypothesis. In contrast, the Alexander team accepted the null hypothesis after demonstrating that the autokinetic effect is subject to situational variations and experimental expectancies. Are Sherif's conclusions now overthrown, or are Alexander's findings invalid? Pollis, Montgomery, and Smith[73] recently addressed this question in a replication designed to incorporate all essential features of the previous studies by Sherif and Alexander's team, and they produced evidence suggesting that the Alexander replication had spawned a type II error, and that Sherif's interpretation remains valid. The net gain of this challenge and response is that there now appears to be an even firmer basis for believing that Sherif and his many corroborating followers have not been perpetuating a highly consensual scientific myth.

In *case F* the original study concludes that cultures differ, but the replication study finds that they do not differ. As more replications are performed, the original study is shown probably to have made a type I error, and consensus builds on this conclusion and on the belief that cultures really do not differ in the feature studied. Studies included in TABLE 1 may provide potential reference studies for examples of case F. One existing example is the original finding by Lopreato[61] of a difference between English and American samples in the relationship between upward social mobility and political conservatism. Thompson[90] later showed that Lopreato's finding was an artifact due to differences in the sex composition of the national samples used. Subsequently, Hopkins[45] and Knoke[55] have provided additional corroboration for Thompson's conclusion that American mobile men are no more conservative than their British counterparts. Another study that is very likely to become an illustration of case F is found in Brehmer's replications[15,16] of earlier findings by Hammond and colleagues[42] from the latter's studies of undergraduate students in Czechoslovakia, Greece, Japan, Sweden, and the United States. The Hammond team studied cognitive conflict patterns, and found that American students decreased conflict at an *even* rate over the series of 20 experimental trials, while students in all of the European samples decreased conflict during the first 10 trials, but then increased it again in the last 10 trials. Brehmer subsequently ascertained that this apparent American-European difference was due to a subtle departure in the presentation order of the stimulus cards used in the United States experiments, and that beyond this there are no cross-national differences in the reduction of cognitive conflict.

Finally, in *case G* the original study accepts the cross-cultural null hypothesis, but the replication study finds that cultures differ. Again further replications are needed in this case that are capable of showing that cultures do not differ, and that the replication study probably made a type I error.

One of the most frequent reasons for erroneous replications (in cases B and G) is their failure to reproduce with sufficient fidelity the conditions and procedures of the original studies whose results they intend to test. Disconfirming evidence from replication studies (when not totally ignored) have sometimes been dismissed by initial researchers as being irrelevant, because of the replicator's intended or unintended departures from some feature of the original study.[76,77] The question of how closely a replication study needs to be to its reference study in order to provide a fair and acceptable test is an exceedingly complex and controversial issue that is discussed briefly below.

The maturity of an area of empirical investigation can be gauged in part by the amount, probativeness, and informativeness of its replication research. It is hoped that in the next few years there will be many more second-order replications in cross-cultural research that can be added to the small number of studies reviewed above and elsewhere. There are many reasons to doubt, however, that replication research will soon be given a very high priority on researchers' agendas. For example, researchers generally place a premium on originality and novelty; so do funding agencies, academic "gatekeepers," and employers; replication research suffers a low prestige reputation; the most eminent scholars have not achieved their prominence by doing replications; there is a reluctance among researchers to adopt and test each other's theories, and a wary reluctance to standardization in this highly entrepreneurial profession; the problems and strategies of replication research are not well taught in professional training programs; there are few institutionalized mechanisms for fostering communication and coordination among researchers in different cultures or even within single cultures.

The list of hindrances to replication research could easily be extended. But now I want to identify only one particular additional factor that is especially important here, although it is not usually thought of as a hindrance, namely, the tendency to assume that statistical significance tests can substitute for actual replications. It appears that researchers often use the results of significance tests as their main or sole source of evidence and confidence in determining the existence of a phenomenon or relationship. But in doing so, they often disregard the fact that alpha and beta error probabilities are necessarily associated with such decisions. Recently, Greenwald[33,36] has presented sobering arguments and evidence showing that many social psychologists court and commit type I errors because they are prejudiced against accepting the null hypothesis, and do not adequately consider the implications of alpha probabilities in designing, conducting, and interpreting their research. Analogous critiques have been cumulating on the high frequency of type II errors in social psychological research,[37,67,72,94] resulting from the use of significance tests with insufficient power and from the researcher's disregard for the consequences that beta probabilities have for his findings and conclusions. It is becoming increasingly apparent that (at least in social psychology, but undoubtedly in other fields as well) the published literature harbors many undetected type I and type II errors currently masquerading as "significant" and "insignificant" findings. These dangers are multiplied, of course, when significance tests are performed on very small sample sizes and crucial cell frequencies. Nearly all of the cross-cultural findings listed earlier in TABLE 1 and elsewhere in this paper have been tested for statistical significance by their authors. But several of these findings are based on such small numbers of cases that their significance test results may well be associated with *effective* alpha and beta probabilities that are considerably higher than the authors of these studies and their readers suspect. This gross uncertainty about the robustness of these and other findings in the cross-cultural literature clearly increases the urgency for conducting second-order replications.

PROCEDURAL FIDELITY VERSUS EXPLORATORY REPLICATION

Because it is obviously impossible to know the weaknesses of a cross-cultural finding before it is replicated, it is difficult to know exactly how to go about designing a critical replication study. That is, empirical findings differ greatly in their fragility and sensitivity to variations in research conditions. Several studies[15,44,71,74] demonstrate that apparently trivial differences in research procedures can drastically alter substantive conclusions. According to this evidence, a researcher would be well advised to design a replication study so that it duplicates exactly a reference study's particular conditions. There are several other reasons, however, that would lead to precisely the opposite advice, that is, to design replications that intentionally alter some or all of the initial conditions. This is a genuine and unavoidable dilemma facing all researchers in designing replication studies. This dilemma is much more severe in cross-cultural comparative research, because of its inherently greater levels of complexity and uncertainty. I will outline very briefly here some of the major advantages and disadvantages of these two opposing positions, and will then conclude by suggesting certain strategies that can be very useful for resolving this dilemma and related problems.

Various replication study designs can be thought of as representing points along a continuum that ranges all the way from very high procedural fidelity to complete absence of procedural fidelity. The "high" extremity of the continuum refers to "exact" (or "literal"[62]) replications, in which there are no procedural mismatches or calibration errors between a reference study and its replicate. The other extremity refers to "exploratory" replications, in which totally different procedures are used. This continuum can be regarded as a scale of "replication distance"[7,32] that encompasses all intermediate degrees of procedural fidelity and departure, including studies that test the robustness of the findings of a reference study, but use only *conceptually* equivalent or even totally *different procedures*. The purpose of designing replication studies that move from the strictest versions of exact replication toward the most unconstrained exploratory designs is to discover the scope conditions that govern the generalizability of original findings. That is, how far can we depart from the particular unique conditions used in an original study before we exceed the domain validity of its findings and disconfirm them?

The unique and considerable advantage of *exact replication* is that it provides a necessary condition for minimizing interpretive uncertainties, when replication studies produce apparently disconfirming results. In this sense, exact replications are indispensable in the knowledge certification process. Sometimes only the strictest reproduction of all reference study conditions will suffice to satisfy the original researcher that a replicate study constitutes a "fair" test of his findings.[76,77] Anything short of complete fidelity would render moot the question of the initial finding's robustness, at least under its original conditions.

As contrasted with this singular advantage, there are several serious limitations of exact replication strategies, not the least of which is that it is often difficult or impossible to duplicate initial procedures exactly. But even when sufficient procedural reproduction has been achieved, exact replications provide the vehicle for perpetuating common biases that may exist in the original study and its replicates.[20] This same danger arises in a more subtle form even when research procedures have been varied, but where the original *investigators* continue to conduct the replicate studies.[6,8,54] A more general limitation, which includes the problem of common biases, is that exact replication studies produce findings that are low in information value. Degree of informativeness,[56] as used here, indicates the amount of new information obtained by a replication study about the robustness of an original finding. In the extreme case of high procedural fidelity, we learn only about the reproducibility and reliability of an initial finding under the same unique conditions of the reference study. But we learn nothing about the existence of possible constant biases, nor about the scope or range of variations in samples, populations, cultures, time points, measuring instruments, investigators, analysis techniques, variables, and other parameters over which the original finding may remain generalizable. Furthermore, because exact replications are low in information value, they represent inefficiencies in the economy of scientific knowledge production. If it is possible to design a replicate study that will yield new information about the applicability of a previous research finding under different conditions, then the cost of that knowledge will be considerably lower than if that replication were first preceded by an exact replication that produced information only about the original finding's reproducibility under the same particular conditions used previously. The choice of which replication strategy to choose in light of these considerations is clearly to prefer the one that produces the most information in the shortest time. And this choice will generally be wise, but only until discrepant findings emerge. Then, the greater the replication distance between studies, the more severe are the problems of interpretation. The converse is also generally true.

Exploratory replication strategies, in contrast, bypass all of the limitations of exact replication, but only until replications fail to confirm previous findings. Replicate study designs that use different samples, measuring devices, variables, investigators, or other parameters of an original study gamble gains in informativeness against interpretive ambiguities. Ostrom, Steele, and Smilansky,[71] for example, accepted this gamble in their exploratory replication of a previous study that found a relationship between perceived discrepancy and attitude change. But the replicators lost their gamble, and had to recourse to an exact replication strategy in order to determine why disconfirmative results were found in their attempted exploratory replication. Yet, the Ostrom team could not have known beforehand just how closely their replication study would have to model the original study in order to yield clearly interpretable results. The same is true of researchers who proceed with more conservative and less informative and potentially more costly exact replication strategies. For example, Carment and Hodkin[21] conducted an exact replication except for using fresh samples of Canadians and Indians to check the reliability of findings from their initial experiment with other samples from these same countries. But a more informative replication could have been attempted, if they had been willing to assume the risk of disconfirming results and their attendant ambiguities, by testing a closely derived hypothesis or by using completely different procedures. Similar dilemmas might have perplexed Iwao, Child, and Garcia[47] in their decision to conduct an exact replicate of their previous finding of esthetic preference similarities between Japanese and Americans by simply adding fresh samples of Japanese artisans. Their replication attempt was successful, but they learned nothing about the possible constant biases that might have run through all their studies because the same investigators, the same measures, and the same American sample were reused. Nor did they learn anything about the generality of esthetic preferences beyond the Japanese-American comparison they began with.

CONCLUSIONS AND RECOMMENDATIONS

Without a strategy that makes it possible to determine the reliability of research findings, little else can be asserted with confidence, especially when discrepant results appear on replication. Yet, the costs of prior commitments to establishing reliability as compared to the costs of testing the scope of generality of findings can often be considerable and unacceptable. The most reasonable available solution of this dilemma is an idea that is at least as old as John Stuart Mill's *System of Logic*.[64] About two decades ago Campbell[19] proposed a name for it, "transition experiments." In the context of Campbell's discussion, a transition experiment involves the use of multiple treatment and multiple measurement experimental designs, at least one segment of which is an exact replication of the original experiment. This proposal has obvious intuitive appeal, and is partially analogous to the use of "marker variables" in interpreting factor analysis results. In both cases the overlap of a few known variables establishes a form of baseline calibration that provides direct comparability and thereby assurance in interpreting the effects of introducing new variables. Although the basic idea of transition experiments has been subsequently rediscovered by others, sometimes using different names (e.g., Aronson and Carlsmith's "balanced designs"[5] and Barker and Gurman's "stepwise departures"[7]), its application in actual research situations has been extremely limited. Part of the reason for its slow adoption may be the reluctance of researchers to design replicate studies that incorporate procedures from earlier studies that are currently considered to be outmoded or even suspected of having produced artifacts. But, as Mills[65] has cogently argued, in order to demonstrate that a finding is due to an artifact it is necessary to design transition replications capable of showing not only that when the procedure suspected of causing the artifact is removed the original finding is altered, but also that when the suspected procedure is faithfully repeated, the original finding is reproduced. The study by Brehmer[15] on Hammond's research on cognitive conflict, discussed above under case F, demonstrates convincingly the strategic utility of this seemingly perverse form of transition replication design.

The more ordinary use of transition designs is illustrated approximately by another study discussed above in describing case A. Deregowski and Munro[23] duplicated the exact stimulus picture used previously by Wober in her study to arrive at the conclusion that Ugandan children (and sub-Saharans in general) have a unique cultural ability, "polyphasic pictorial perception." This strategy allowed Deregowski and Munro to test the stability of Wober's original finding with such fidelity that it would be difficult to disqualify their results as being an "unfair" comparison. But in addition, they introduced several variations in the stimulus picture to test alternative explanations of the corroborated cross-cultural differences in perceptual styles. This study is not a fully "ideal" model of the transition strategy, because two potentially confounding factors were varied, investigators and cultural samples (Rhodesian and Canadian in the replicate study vs. Ugandans and Englishmen in Wober's study). It is not impossible that even after using the identical stimulus picture in the replicate study, Deregowski and Munro's results could have differed from Wober's. Had this happened, residual interpretive ambiguities would then revolve around rival hypotheses as to possible experimenter and cultural sample effects. A completely transitionalized design would maintain *all* parameters of the original study as constant as possible for the crucial exact test for stability under the same conditions as the original study, and would then systematically introduce successive departures, including changes in investigators and cultural samples, and continuing well beyond, perhaps to the point of using entirely different techniques to measure perceptual styles.

In practice, transition designs will usually include "exact" replications that are only pragmatic approximations to a strict point-by-point duplication of initial conditions. But even with such necessary compromises, transition designs can be extremely useful for assessing the reliability, validity, and generality of cross-cultural findings.

Another strategy that would be particularly useful in coping with the added complexities and uncertainties surrounding cross-cultural research can be called embedded or built-in replications. While transition replication studies are undertaken at a later time than an initial study (and usually with different investigators), embedded replications (usually carried out by the same investigators) are built into the overall design of a given study or project, and are integral component sources of the total body of evidence on which the researchers base their conclusions. In implementing this strategy, initial cross-cultural studies are designed to include measures of those variables that will allow explicit testing of highly plausible rival hypotheses in anticipation of the finding that cultural differences either exist or do not exist. These replications can be incorporated into an overall study design in many ways, such as by the use of additional comparison samples, by subgroup analyses, or by using multiple measuring techniques. The purpose of this strategy is to outlaw as early as possible in the broader research process some of the most likely sources of error, so that second-order replications can be designed more efficiently on the basis of greater knowledge. Considerable saving in time, funds, and other resources can be made possible by exploiting embedded replications. Some recent applications of this strategy are briefly described to indicate its utility.

The studies by Alford,[2] the Amir team,[3] Bergeron and Zanna,[10] Carment and Hodkin,[21] and Lenski[59] all illustrate how additional samples can be built into an overall study design to assess the reliability of first-run findings. For example, Alford used many independent survey samples from Australia, Canada, Great Britain, and the United States to assure that his initial findings on the linkages between voting behavior and socioeconomic status were dependable within each country. Using the same data for another purpose, Lenski demonstrated the stability of his initial finding (that status inconsistency increases liberal or leftist political tendencies) by repeating his analysis 25 times in these four countries, and finding that it was supported in 21 of the trials. The Amir team repeated their analysis of cultural differences in the effects of birth-order status on volunteering for military training on samples from two different time periods in order to check the stability of their initial results. When the same relationships reappeared, they were able more confidently to conclude that their complex first results were not artifacts of the particular sample and time period they studied first. Similarly, in Bergeron and Zanna's study of Byrne's theory of the effects of belief similarity on attraction, results from two parallel samples were compared to check on the stability of their single-sample results. Carment and Hodkin ran an initial replicate experiment to ascertain the reliability of their initial finding that Indians are less sensitive than Canadians to the presence of a coactor.

Embedded replications can be used to test many different kinds of rival hypotheses other than sampling stability. For example, Chandra[22] found that Fijians were more likely than Americans, Brazilians, Lebanese, and Hong Kong Chinese to conform in an Asch situation. In order to clarify the nature of this difference, Chandra divided his sample into Indian Fijians and non-Indian Fijians, and found that it is not Fijians in general who have such high conformity tendencies, but that the original difference was limited to the Indian Fijians, presumably because of their authoritarian cultural background that requires high conformity. Another example of this efficient strategy shows how multiple measures can be built into an overall cross-cultural comparison to assure the validity of findings. Feldman[26] studied cultural differences in the treatment of compatriots and foreigners who needed assistance in Athens, Boston, and Paris. He used five separate field experiments — asking for directions, doing a favor for a stranger, falsely claiming money, cashier overpayment, and taxicab charges — and found that Athenians treated foreigners better than compatriots, but that Bostonians and Parisians treated compatriots better than foreigners. Had Feldman used only one of these experiments to measure differential treatment, his findings and conclusions would have been wide open to rival hypotheses about the meaning and validity of his measure in these different cultures. Although Feldman's findings may still be subject to other interpretations, at least the key issue of measurement validity is not as urgent as it would have been without his built-in replications. Further studies of possible cultural differences in guest-host interaction can now be designed around more probing questions to account for these findings.

A final example which clearly illustrates tactical pursuit analysis through built-in replications is a study of cultural differences in galvanic skin responsiveness, GSR. Kugelmass, Lieblich, and Ben-Shakhar[57] were puzzled by their previous findings from a sample of male Israeli Bedouins showing an absence of GSR in a standard experimental task in which the subject is presented with a series of information cards containing a few relevant information items (e.g., subject's name, wife's name) shuffled in with a majority of nonrelevant items. The Kugelmass team returned to the desert and collected comparable data from a different Bedouin tribe, and again found an absence of GSR increases when significant information cards were presented. Because of the possibility that this unusual Bedouin-Western ethnic difference in GSR reactivity may have been due to an artifact of differences in situational variables, Kugelmass and colleagues drew another sample of Bedouins from the same tribe, and retested them not in their customary ecological setting, but under more controlled laboratory conditions in a large city. The researchers were surprised to find that under these conditions the Bedouin GSR levels were very similar to those of Westerners, and were much higher than those previously found for all Bedouin samples. At this point the Kugelmass team could have terminated their research, and concluded that the uncontrolled conditions in the desert testing situation twice produced invalid findings on Bedouin responsiveness. Or, they could have suggested that their new results may be artifacts of the controlled urban laboratory conditions, or possibly that there might have been some inadvertent sampling bias in the particular group of tribesmen who agreed to travel to the urban laboratory, and they could have left all of these different interpretations open to "future research" to answer. But instead, they pressed the analysis a step forward by testing the sampling bias hypothesis, and found a significant positive correlation between the number of years of formal education and reactivity levels of the Bedouin samples. From this refinement of their initial and intermediate evidence, Kugelmass and colleagues were able to conclude (1) that the jump in GSR levels of the Bedouins tested in the urban laboratory was probably due to biases in selecting subjects, and not to environmental or procedural variations; and (2) that there is significant GSR variation within Bedouin culture. Follow-up studies are now able to build on these findings, and explore social structural influences on psychophysiological functioning within Bedouin and other cultures. There is now less urgency for testing whether the desert-city differences in Bedouin reactivity are due to situational variations or to sampling bias.

As these examples show, embedded replications can be used to test highly plausible rival hypotheses, and provide information necessary for evaluating alternative interpretations of initial findings. Such designs thereby reduce the urgency of certain questions, and permit the reordering of priorities for subsequent replications. For example, if an original study has already internally tested the sampling stability of its first results, then follow-up studies can be designed as more adventurous exploratory replications to test the scope generalizability of the original findings.

Transition and embedded replication designs and the related concept of replication distance have differential utilities for solving problems raised in discussing the eight cases in TABLE 2. For example, uncertainties about the validity of consensus reached on decisions to reject the cross-cultural null hypothesis (cases A vs. E) and on decisions to accept that hypothesis (cases D vs. H) may best be resolved by highly adventurous exploratory replications incorporated into a transition design. The dual objectives of such designs are, first, to demonstrate the new study's ability to produce additional evidence consistent with the apparent consensus (on decisions to either reject or accept the null hypothesis), and then to proceed beyond these well rehearsed procedures to introduce different investigators (perhaps those trained in different "schools" of thought), different measuring instruments, different samples, different analytic procedures, different concepts and variables and other departures in search of some common artifact or bias that may account for the previous consensus. The more adventurous and probative these replications are without producing evidence inconsistent with the prior consensus, the more firm the basis for believing that a valid consensus has been reached about cultural realities. But, if adventurous transition replications turn up discrepant evidence, then serious questions are raised about the validity of the prior consensus. For the remaining cases in TABLE 2, transition designs that include high fidelity procedural replications are needed to resolve inconsistencies between original and replication studies. In cases C and F, for example, where it is possible that the original findings resulted, respectively, from type II or type I errors, it will not suffice to design further replications that may be faithful to the *replication* study that first produced the discrepant results while being unfaithful to the particulars of the *original* study, even though the challenging replication study may have used procedures that were far superior to those used in the original study. The study by Brehmer, discussed above, clearly shows the interpretive advantages to be gained from replications designed to include suspected artifacts from an original study, test for their ability to reproduce the same exact results, and then proceed on from that point to more valid and informative tests.

There is obviously a long road to be traveled from the first indications of possible cultural differences or similarities to their eventual confident assertion and valid interpretation. Systematic programs of replication research that exploit the kinds of strategies described here can provide practical vehicles for covering that distance efficiently.

POSTSCRIPT

I am very sorry, Pyrophilus, that to the many (elsewhere enumerated) difficulties which you may meet with, and must therefore surmount, in the serious and effectual prosecution of experimental philosophy I must add one discouragement more, which will perhaps as much surprise as dishearten you; and it is, that besides that you will find (as we elsewhere mention) many of the experiments published by authors, or related to you by the persons you converse with, false and unsuccessful (besides this, I say), you will meet with several observations and experiments which, though communicated for true by candid authors or undistrusted eye-witnesses, or perhaps recommended by your own experience, may, upon further trial, disappoint your expectation, either not at all succeeding constantly, or at least varying much from what you expected.

Robert Boyle, *Concerning the Unsuccessfulness of Experiments* (1673)

The history of social psychology illustrates the importance of the replication of findings in that many of its initial results have not been confirmed by later investigations.

Daniel Katz, *Field Studies* (1953)

ACKNOWLEDGMENT

Useful clarifications were prodded and provided by Ada W. Finifter.

REFERENCES

1. ALEXANDER, C. N., L. G. ZUCKER & C. L. BRODY. 1970. Experimental expectations and autokinetic experiences. Sociometry **33** (1): 108–122.
2. ALFORD, R. R. 1963. Party and Society: The Anglo-American Democracies. Rand McNally. New York, N.Y.
3. AMIR, Y., S. SHARAN & Y. KOVARSKY. 1968. Birth order, family structure, and avoidance behavoir. J. Personal. Social Psychol. **10** (3): 271–278.
4. ANCONA, L. 1970. An experimental contribution to the problem of identification with the father. *In* Readings in Child Socialization. K. Danziger, Ed.: 187–218. Pergamon Press. London, England.
5. ARONSON, E. & J. M. CARLSMITH. 1968. Experimentation in social psychology. *In* Handbook of Social Psychology. G. Lindzey and E. Aronson, Eds. Vol. 2, 2nd ed.: 1–79. Addison-Wesley. Reading, Mass.
6. BAKAN, D. 1968. On Method. Jossey-Bass. San Francisco, Calif.
7. BARKER, H. R. & E. B. GURMAN. 1972. Replication versus tests of equivalence. Perceptual & Motor Skills **35** (3): 807–815.
8. BARNES, L. B. 1967. Organizational change and field experiment methods. *In* Methods of Organizational Research. V. H. Vroom, Ed.: 77–111. University of Pittsburgh Press. Pittsburgh, Pa.
9. BECHTOLDT, H. P. 1974. A confirmatory analysis of the factor stability hypothesis. Psychometrika **39** (3): 319–326.
10. BERGERON, A. P. & M. P. ZANNA. 1973. Group membership and belief similarity as determinants of interpersonal attraction in Peru. J. Cross-Cultural Psychol. **4** (4): 397–411.
11. BERKOWITZ, L. 1968. Responsibility, reciprocity, and social distance in help giving: An experimental investigation of English social class differences. J. Exp. Social Psychol. **4** (1): 46–63.
12. BORKE, H. 1973. The development of empathy in Chinese and American children between three and six years of age: A cross-cultural study. Develop. Psychol. **9** (1): 102–108.
13. BOTHA, E. 1971. The achievement motive in three cultures. J. Social Psychol. **85** (2): 163–170.
14. BRACHT, G. H. & G. V. GLASS. 1968. The external validity of experiments. Am. Ed. Res. J. **5** (4): 437–474.

15. BREHMER, B. 1974. A note on the cross-national differences in cognitive conflict found by Hammond *et al.* Inter. J. Psychol. 9 (1): 51–56.
16. BREHMER, B., H. AZUMA, K. R. HAMMOND, L. KOSTRON & D. D. VARONOS. 1970. A cross-national comparison of cognitive conflict. J. Cross-Cultural Psychol. 1 (1): 5–20.
17. BRISLIN, R. W., W. J. LONNER & R. M. THORNDIKE. 1973. Cross-Cultural Research Methods. John Wiley & Sons, Inc. New York, N.Y.
18. BUSS, A. R. & J. R. ROYCE. 1975. Detecting cross-cultural commonalities and differences: Intergroup factor analysis. Psychol. Bull. 82 (1): 128–136.
19. CAMPBELL, D. T. 1957. Factors relevant to the validity of experiments in social settings. Psychol. Bull. 54: 297–312.
20. CAMPBELL, D. T. 1969. Prospective: Artifact and control. *In* Artifact in Behavioral Research. R. L. Rosnow, Ed.: 351–382. Academic Press. New York, N.Y.
21. CARMENT, D. W. & B. HODKIN. 1973. Coaction and competition in India and Canada. J. Cross-Cultural Psychol. 4 (4): 459–469.
22. CHANDRA, S. 1973. The effects of group pressure in perception: A cross-cultural conformity study in Fiji. Intern. J. Psychol. 8 (1): 37–39.
23. DEREGOWSKI, J. B. & D. MUNRO. 1974. An analysis of "Polyphasic Pictorial Perception." J. Cross-Cultural Psychol. 5 (3): 329–343.
24. DRAGUNS, J. G. 1973. Comparisons of psychopathology across cultures: Issues, findings, directions. J. Cross-Cultural Psychol. 4 (1): 9–47.
25. ENGLAND, G. W. & R. LEE. 1974. The relationship between managerial values and managerial success in the United States, Japan, India, and Australia. J. Appl. Psychol. 59 (4): 411–419.
26. FELDMAN, R. E. 1968. Response to compatriot and foreigner who seek assistance. J. Personal Social Psychol. 10 (3): 202–214.
27. FINIFTER, B. M. 1972. The generation of confidence: Evaluating research findings by random subsample replication. *In* Sociological Methodology 1972. H. Costner, Ed.: 114–177. Jossey-Bass. San Francisco, Calif.
28. FINIFTER, B. M. 1975. Replication and extension of social research through secondary analysis. Social Science Information 14 (2): 119–153.
29. FISHER, R. A. 1942. The Design of Experiments. 3rd Ed. Oliver and Boyd. Edinburgh, Scotland.
30. FOA, U. G., H. C. TRIANDIS & E. W. KATZ. 1966. Cross-cultural invariance in the differentiation and organization of family roles. J. Personal. Social Psychol. 4 (3): 316–327.
31. FRY, P. S. 1974. The development of differentiation in self-evaluations: A cross-cultural study. J. Psychol. 87: 193–202.
32. GALTUNG, J. 1967. Theory and Methods of Social Research. Columbia University Press. New York, N.Y.
33. GILLIG, P. M. & A. G. GREENWALD. 1974. Is it time to lay the sleeper effect to rest? J. Personal Social Psychol. 29 (1): 132–139.
34. GONZALEZ, A. E., J. & W. M. DAVIS. 1974. Sex differences and cognitive consistency: A Greek and North American contrast. J. Cross-Cultural Psychol. 5 (3): 301–311.
35. GORSUCH, R. L. & R. A. SMITH. 1972. Changes in college students' evaluations of moral behavior: 1969 versus 1939, 1949, and 1958. J. Personal. Social Psychol. 24 (3): 381–391.
36. GREENWALD, A. G. 1975. Consequences of prejudice against the null hypothesis. Psychol. Bull. 82 (1): 1–20.
37. GREENWALD, A. G. 1975. Does the Good Samaritan parable increase helping? A comment on Darley and Batson's no-effect conclusion. J. Personal. Social Psychol. 32 (4): 578–583.
38. GREY, A. & D. KALSCHED. 1971. Oedipus east and west: An exploration via manifest dream content. J. Cross-Cultural Psychol. 2 (4): 337–352.
39. GRUENFELD, L., P. WEISSENBERG & W. LOH. 1973. Achievement values, cognitive style and social class: A cross-cultural comparison of Peruvian and U.S. students. Intern. J. Psychol. 8 (1): 41–49.

40. GUTHRIE, G. M. 1966. Structure of maternal attitudes in two cultures. J. Personal. **62**: 155–156.
41. HALL, C. & B. DOMHOFF. 1963. A ubiquitous sex difference in dreams. J. Abnorm. Social Psychol. **66**: 278–280.
42. HAMMOND, K. R., G. B. BONAIUTO, C. FAUCHEUX, S. MOSCOVICI, W. D. FROHLICH, C. R. B. JOYCE & G. DI MAJO. 1968. A comparison of cognitive conflict between persons in western Europe and the United States. Intern. J. Psychol. **3** (1): 1–12.
43. HARDYCK, J. A. & M. BRADEN. 1962. Prophecy fails again: A report on a failure to replicate. J. Abnorm. Social Psychol. **65** (2): 136–141.
44. HAYES, D. P., L. MELTZER & G. WOLF. 1970. Substantive conclusions are dependent upon techniques of measurement. Behavior. Sci. **15** (3): 265–268.
45. HOPKINS, A. 1973. Political overconformity by upwardly mobile American men. Am. Soc. Rev. **38** (1): 143–148.
46. INGHAM, R. 1974. Preferences for seating arrangements in two countries. Intern. J. Psychol. **9** (2): 105–115.
47. IWAO, S., I. L. CHILD & M. GARCIA. 1969. Further evidence of agreement between Japanese and American esthetic evaluations. J. Soc. Psychol. **78**: 11–16.
48. IWAṬA, O. 1974. Empirical examination of the perception of density and crowding. Japanese Psychol. Res. **16** (3): 117–125.
49. JAHODA, G. 1970. A cross-cultural perspective in psychology. Advan. Sci. **27** (131): 57–70.
50. JAHODA, G., S. S. THOMSON & S. BHATT. 1972. Ethnic identity and preferences among Asian immigrant children in Glasgow: A replicated study. European J. Soc. Psychol. **2** (1): 19–32.
51. KAGITCIBASI, C. 1970. Social norms and authoritarianism: A Turkish–American comparison. J. Personal. Social Psychol. **16**: 444–451.
52. KATZ, D. 1953. Field studies. *In* Research Methods in the Behavioral Sciences. L. Festinger and D. Katz, Eds.: 55–97. Dryden Press. New York, N.Y.
53. KELLEY, H. H., *et al.* 1970. A comparative experimental study of negotiation behavior. J. Personal. Social Psychol. **16** (3): 411–438.
54. KINTZ, B. L., D. J. DELPRATO, D. R. METTEE, C. E. PERSONS & R. H. SCHAPPE. 1965. The experimenter effect. Psychol. Bull. **63**: 223–232.
55. KNOKE, D. 1973. Intergenerational occupational mobility and the political party preferences of American men. Am. J. Soc. **78** (6): 1448–1468.
56. KRAUSE, M. S. 1971. Corroborative results and subsequent research commitments. J. Gen. Psych. **84** (2): 219–227.
57. KUGELMASS, S., I. LIEBLICH & G. BEN-SHAKHAR. 1973. Information detection through differential GSRs in Bedouins of the Israeli desert. J. Cross-Cultural Psychol. **4** (4): 481–492.
58. KURTINES, W. & E. B. GREIF. 1974. The development of moral thought: Review and evaluation of Kohlberg's approach. Psychol. Bull. **81** (8): 453–470.
59. LENSKI, G. E. 1967. Status inconsistency and the vote: A four nation test. Am. Soc. Rev. **32** (2): 298–301.
60. LOOFT, W. R. & M. D. BARANOWSKI. 1971. Birth order, sex, and complexity-simplicity: An attempt at replication. Percept. Motor Skills **32** (1): 303–306.
61. LOPREATO, J. 1967. Upward social mobility and political orientation. Am. Soc. Rev. **32**: 586–592.
62. LYKKEN, D. T. 1968. Statistical significance in psychological research. Psychol. Bull. **70** (3): 151–159.
63. MEADE, R. D. & W. F. BARNARD. 1973. Conformity and anti-conformity among Americans and Chinese. J. Soc. Psychol. **89**: 15–24.
64. MILL, J. S. 1950. System of Logic. Hafner. New York, N.Y.
65. MILLS, J. 1969. Experimental Social Psychology. Macmillan. New York, N.Y.
66. MITROFF, I. I. & T. R. FEATHERINGHAM. 1974. On systemic problem solving and the error of the third kind. Behavioral Sci. **19** (6): 383–393.

67. MORRISON, D. E. & R. E. HENKEL., Eds. 1970. The Significance Test Controversy. Aldine Publishing Co. Chicago, Ill.
68. MUNNICHS, J. M. A. 1968. Cross-national psychological studies in aging. *In* Methodological Problems in Cross-National Studies in Aging. E. Shanas and J. Madge, Eds.: 37–40. S. Karger. New York, N.Y.
69. OAKES, W. 1972. External validity and the use of real people as subjects. Am. Psychologist. **27** (10): 959–962.
70. OSGOOD, C. E. 1960. The cross-cultural generality of visual–verbal synesthetic tendencies. Behavioral Sci. **5**: 146–169.
71. OSTROM, T. M., C. M. STEELE & J. SMILANSKY. 1974. Perceived discrepancy and attitude change: An unsubstantiated relationship. Rep. Res. Soc. Psychol. **5** (1): 7–15.
72. OVERALL, J. E. 1969. Classical statistical hypothesis testing within the context of Bayesian theory. Psychol. Bull. **71**: 285–292.
73. POLLIS, N. P., R. L. MONTGOMERY & T. G. SMITH. 1975. Autokinetic paradigms: A reply to Alexander, Zucker, and Brody. Sociometry **38** (2): 358–373.
74. PRICE-WILLIAMS, D. R. & R. A. LEVINE. 1974. Left-right orientation among Hausa children: A methodological note. J. Cross-Cultural Psychol. **5** (3): 356–363.
75. RAMIREZ III, M., A. CASTANEDA & P. L. HEROLD. 1974. The relationship of acculturation to cognitive style among Mexican Americans. J. Cross-Cultural Psychol. **5** (4): 424–433.
76. REISS, I. L. 1969. Response to the Heltsley and Broderick retest of Reiss's proposition one. J. Marr. Family **31** (3): 444–445.
77. REISS, I. L. 1970. Comments on Middendorp's "The determinants of premarital sexual permissiveness." J. Marr. Family **32** (3): 379–380.
78. RETTIG, S. & P. N. SINGH. 1963. The risk hypothesis in judgements of unethical behavior: A cross-cultural replication. Israel Ann. Psychiat. Related Disciplines **1** (3): 225–234.
79. ROBBINS, M. C. & P. L. KILBRIDE. 1971. Sex differences in dreams in Uganda. J. Cross-Cultural Psychol. **2** (4): 406–408.
80. ROBERTS, K. H. 1970. On looking at an elephant: An evaluation of cross-cultural research related to organizations. Psychol. Bull. **74** (5): 327–350.
81. ROSENTHAL, R. 1966. Experimenter Effects in Behavioral Research. Appleton-Century Crofts. New York, N.Y.
82. RUMMEL, R. J. 1972. The Dimensions of Nations. Sage Publications. Beverly Hills, Calif.
83. SCHACHTER, S. 1954. Interpretive and methodological problems of replicated research. J. Social Issues **10** (4): 52–60.
84. SECREST, L., T. FAY, H. ZAIDI & L. FLORES. 1973. Attitudes toward mental disorder among college students in the United States, Pakistan, and the Philippines. J. Cross-Cultural Psychol. **4** (3): 342–360.
85. SKOLNICK, P. 1971. Reactions to personal evaluations: A failure to replicate. J. Personal. Social Psychol. **18** (1): 62–67.
86. SMITH, N. F. & M. K. GRENIER. 1975. English and French-Canadian children's view of parents. Canadian J. Behavioral Sci. **7** (1): 40–53.
87. SUCHMAN, E. A. 1964. The comparative method in social research. Rural Soc. **29** (2): 123–137.
88. TANTER, R. 1964. Dimensions of conflict within and between nations, 1958–1960. J. Conflict Resolution. **10** (1): 41–64.
89. THAVER, F., A. ARKOFF & L. ELKIND. 1964. Conceptions of mental health in several Asian and American groups. J. Soc. Psychol. **62**: 21–27.
90. THOMPSON, K. H. 1971. Upward social mobility and political orientation: A re-evaluation of the evidence. Am. Soc. Rev. **36** (2): 223–235.
91. THURSTONE, L. 1947. Multiple Factor Analysis. University of Chicago Press. Chicago, Ill.

92. TOGNOLI, J. & R. KEISNER. 1972. Gain and loss of esteem as determinants of interpersonal attraction: A replication and extension. J. Personal. Social Psychol. **23** (2): 201–204.
93. TOMEH, A. K. 1970. Cross-cultural differences in the structure of moral values: A factorial analysis. Intern. J. Comp. Sociol. **11** (1): 18–33.
94. TVERSKY, A. & D. KAHNEMAN. 1971. Belief in the law of small numbers. Psychol. Bull. **76** (2): 105–110.
95. VERBA, S., N. H. NIE, A. BARBIC, G. IRWIN, H. MOLLEMAN & G. SHABAD. 1973. The modes of participation: Continuities in research. Comp. Politic. Studies **6** (2): 235–250.
96. VERMEULEN, C. J. J. & A. DE RUIJTER. 1975. Dominant epistemological presuppositions in the use of the cross-cultural survey method. Curr. Anthropol. **16** (1): 29–37.
97. VIDMAR, N. & J. R. HACKMAN. 1971. Interlaboratory generalizability of small group research: An experimental study. J. Soc. Psychol. **83** (1): 129–139.
98. WAHRMAN, R. & M. D. PUGH. 1972. Competence and conformity: Another look at Hollander's study. Sociometry **3**: 376–386.
99. WINER, B. J. 1971. Statistical Principles in Experimental Design. 2nd edit. McGraw-Hill. New York, N.Y.
100. WITKIN, H. A., D. P. WILLIAMS, M. BERTINI, B. CHRISTIANSEN, P. K. OLTMAN, M. RAMIREZ & J. VAN MEEL. 1973 (Oct.). Social conformity and psychological differentiation. Res. Bull. 73–63. Educational Testing Service. Princeton, N.J.
101. WITKIN, H. A. 1975. Psychological differentiation in cross-cultural perpective. J. Cross-Cultural Psychol. **6** (1): 4–87.

ETHICAL ISSUES INFLUENCING THE ACCEPTANCE AND REJECTION OF CROSS-CULTURAL RESEARCHERS WHO VISIT VARIOUS COUNTRIES

Richard W. Brislin

Culture Learning Institute
East-West Center
Honolulu, Hawaii 96822

The major thrust of psychologists' concerns with ethics in recent years[1,12,13] centers around their relation with subjects in their research studies. Stimulated by reports of studies involving intense stimuli that could easily cause severe stress in subjects, and reacting negatively to the seeming routine use of deception in research studies, psychologists have formulated codes of ethics to guide researchers in their relations with subjects. The guidelines include helpful advice on obtaining informed consent from subjects and obtaining colleagues' constructive advice on proposed studies, among many other features. Cross-cultural psychologists (led by June Tapp) have been active in formulating guidelines designed to help researchers meet the special demands of working in cultures other than their own. One of these problems is the feeling on the part of local researchers, in the countries visited by cross-cultural researchers, that the visitors are interested only in adding to their publication list and not doing anything useful to the country. The charge is often made that visiting researchers have "ripped off" and have exploited the country. This issue has been effectively addressed by Tagumpay-Castillo,[20] working from her experiences as a social scientist in the Philippines who has been on the receiving end of visits by researchers from other countries. She has created a character-typology of such visiting researchers as these: (1) The "data-exporter," who does research "safari-style." He takes everything he can by way of data and leaves nothing of value to the country of study. Sometimes he is called the "hit and run" researcher, with more "runs" than "hits." (2) The "greenhorn." The newcomer [can easily be distinguished] from the "old-timer." The former has the explanation, the latter has only a hunch. (3) The "penny-collaborator." He happens to have access to some money, not too much, but some. "How about a cooperative project?", he says. I'll provide the money and you do the study." (4) The "professional overseas researcher." To him, overseas research is a way of life. He lives from research grant to research grant. "Tough life," he says, "I can't stand the winters in New York anymore."[20] (pp. 30–32.)

These labels and descriptions should draw a responsive chord from the most insensitive, hardened hearts. Three cross-cultural psychologists[4] built upon this typology and attempted to suggest guidelines for collaborative efforts with in-country researchers for the mutual benefit of both visitors and residents. They took a practical viewpoint: cross-cultural research is entirely dependent upon the good-will of people in the cultures where research is done. Without their tolerance of researchers and their seemingly endless questions, experiments, and general nosiness, cross-cultural research will die. Attention must be given toward doing something of benefit to cultures visited so that researchers will be welcomed back and (perhaps) even be invited to do a certain piece of research.

Yet, in reading these analyses of cross-cultural ethical concerns it is easy to feel that more should be done than writing essays and suggesting guidelines. My feeling is that more substantive work is necessary, based on empirical data, to provide a prominent spot in cross-cultural psychology for ethical concerns. I would like to see ethical concerns established to the degree that areas such as subjective culture,[21] perception (e.g., see references 18 and 23), and culture-cognition (e.g., reference 8) are accepted, and, like these areas, to have active researchers involved in them.

An operational way of saying this is that empirical methods are needed so that researchers can investigate ethical concerns as a substantive area, and in doing so gain such rewards as tenure, job promotion, salary increases, and so forth, (as do their colleagues working in the three substantive areas mentioned), depending upon the exact nature of their employment. It is fine to appeal to altruistic motives when talking about ethics, but I believe it is unrealistic to appeal only to these motives without also addressing such motives as researchers' need for job security, which often is linked to research-oriented publications. I also think it is unrealistic to expect that ethical concerns will become established within cross-cultural psychology without an empirical base (again, like the three substantive areas mentioned).

The major "ethical concern" I will address in this paper is the necessity for doing research and engaging in scholarly activity of benefit to the host countries that cross-cultural researchers visit. I am assuming that if such research and scholarly activity of this type are done, then countries will be more likely to welcome cross-cultural researchers in the future. Another essay could be written, but I would rather review two efforts in which my colleagues and I have been engaged at the East-West Center. A problem in reviewing research on ethics with which one has been involved is that the writer can come across as a "holier than thou" character. I would like to minimize this attribution by insisting that I am not any more spotless than the mean, and by admitting that my interest in ethics is derived partly from an examination of my own past indifference to host-culture people in my own cross-cultural research. Further, most of the ideas and developments recorded below come out of close collaboration with others at the East-West Center, to whom I am greatly indebted.*

PROJECTS FOR THE DEVELOPMENT OF EDUCATORS AND CROSS-CULTURAL RESEARCHERS

The first activity to be reviewed consists of programs designed to provide advanced training to mid-career professionals. People come to the East-West Center from the United States and from countries in Asia and the Pacific to participate in projects under what we call "cost-sharing" provisions. This means that we pay for 90% of the project costs, which includes housing, a monthly stipend, books, and so forth, and that participants pay 10% of the project cost as well as round trip transportation from their home institutions. People from other countries (e.g., Great Britain, African nations) can and have participated, but unfortunately they have not been eligible for the East-West Center grants because of the Center's administrative policy established by an Act of the United States Congress. There is no "brain-drain" problem since people have good jobs in their home countries, obtain approved leave from their jobs, come to the Center to participate in the project, and then return to their jobs.

* People at the East-West Center to whom I am indebted for the ideas, and support in the work described, include: Verner Bickley, Gregory Trifonovitch, Mark Lester, and Michael Hamnett.

I have been involved (1974–1975) as director of a 5-month project for mid-career professional educators involved in school systems that have adopted or are considering bilingual education programs. The participants were 12 high-level people (district directors of education; high school principals; professors in departments of education; designated bilingual education specialists) from these countries: Philippines, Truk, Palau, Ponape, and the Marshalls in Micronesia; Japan; Taiwan; Indonesia; Thailand; and the United States. That there were over 70 applicants for the program attests to the project's popularity. Please remember that the project is not a "free ride" and that there has to be a real investment from the participants or their sponsoring institutions: 10% of the project cost and round-trip plane fare. To meet these costs, an individual participant's investment can easily be $2500. We feel that the content of the program must be meeting some needs of these countries when there are so many applicants willing to pay the costs, arrange for their work load to be covered during their absence, and so forth. Empirical studies can follow directly from this project, based on the expressed needs for certain research by these educators. The educators have indeed indicated certain areas that they would like to see researched (for instance, tests and measurements, such as reading readiness tests, and tests to measure progress in the languages that are part of the bilingual education program within a given country). Other research can be done with the educators themselves, for instance, their adoption of certain ideas (covered in the project at the East-West Center) back in their home countries. This would be a study of obvious relevance to people interested in educational psychology, social change, diffusion of innovation, and so forth.

I am currently involved (1975 through 1976) as co-director (with Stephen Bochner) of a project designed to provide advanced training in cross-cultural research. I assume that this project will be of interest to readers of this volume, and so I will review it in some detail. We described the project in a brochure and circulated it as widely as possible. In that brochure we indicated that

> the objectives of the project are to provide opportunities for 15 behavioral and social scientists from Asia, the Pacific, and the United States to share ideas about cross-cultural research relevant to:
>
> a. the design of research projects involving empirical data that are gathered in two or more cultures;
> b. the teaching of topics in the behavioral and social sciences based on cross-cultural findings;
> c. the integration and dissemination of findings in cross-cultural research;
> d. ethical concerns in cross-cultural research.

> Cross-cultural research has been described as follows. Accepting the general definition of "culture" as the knowledge and symbols that man acquires as a member of a society, then cross-cultural research refers to the empirical study of members of various culture groups who have had different experiences that lead to predictable and significant differences in behavior. In the majority of such studies, the groups investigated speak different languages and have different political, family, and social structures. The program is most likely to appeal to behavioral and social scientists who have already earned an MA, MS, or PhD degree (or equivalent), and who want to expand their capabilities into cross-cultural studies. Participants will most likely have a background in psychology, sociology, or anthropology; or perhaps political science or linguistics. An interdisciplinary group of participants will be welcome, but applicants should realize that the content and methods of cross-cultural research to be presented by the coordinators have been developed mainly by psychologists and anthropologists.

Further, we described the content of the program as follows:

a. During November and December of 1975, participants will review the basic literature in cross-cultural studies and will share ideas relevant to research needed for the field's development. Books and materials will be provided by the coordinators, and participants will be invited to bring materials from their own countries to share with the others. Early drafts of chapters for the *Handbook of Cross-Cultural Psychology* (see below) will also be used, and participants will have the opportunity to point out materials from their own countries that can be integrated into *Handbook* chapters. Participants will interact in seminars led by the coordinators and by other staff members of the Culture Learning Institute, East-West Center. Participants will also have the responsibility of preparing approximately three presentations that they will share with the rest of the group.

b. During January of 1976, participants will be actively involved with another group, namely the behavioral and social scientists writing chapters for the *Handbook of Cross-Cultural Psychology*. The *Handbook of Cross-Cultural Psychology* is now being developed under the direction of Dr. Harry Triandis of the University of Illinois. To be published in 1977, it will comprise three volumes and 38 chapters, written by 49 scholars from such fields as psychology, sociology, anthropology, linguistics, and psychiatry. . . .
In January, 1976, plans call for a conference consisting of the contributors to the *Handbook*. The purpose will be to have the authors present their chapters to others at the conference and obtain feedback on their efforts, especially from the participants in the project described here. Further, participants will use the chapters as source materials for their own work.

c. In February of 1976, participants will design a research project that they can carry out after returning home. A desirable goal is that various participants design their projects cooperatively so that the findings of one can be integrated with others. After returning home in late February or early March, participants will keep in communication with the coordinators, reporting on progress in carrying out their research projects.
As a final note, we point out for clarification that participants in the project described here are not expected to write a chapter for the *Handbook of Cross-Cultural Psychology*. The participants in this project and the authors of chapters for the *Handbook* are two separate groups. The groups will meet in January, 1976.

We then discussed the cost-sharing provisions, which are the same as with the educators project already reviewed. Again, we had far more applicants than the 15 spots that were available. We take this fact as evidence that we have designed a program that meets a certain set of needs in the countries with which the East-West Center deals. The participants have been selected (letters of acceptance were sent from the Center on August 15, 1975), and they come from these countries: Japan, Thailand, India, Pakistan, Philippines, Fiji, Indonesia, Australia, and the United States.

We consciously designed the project so that there would be three months of solid, intense exposure to the literature in cross-cultural studies, followed by a month in which participants design their own projects. We foresee that, during this last month, each participant will bounce his or her ideas off the others associated with the project. Since the participants themselves are designing studies, it is hoped that most of the research generated by the project will have potential practical benefit to their home countries. Judging from their applications, this is the goal of the participants. This type of project, then, involves teaching and research guidance for a would-be coordinator interested in starting such a project elsewhere. In addition, there would be obvious opportunities for research collaboration between coordinators and participants.

Anthropological Commentary Project

The second activity to be reviewed consists of a research project, now ongoing, which we hope will have some practical applications. The review here consists of a progress report and focuses on some of the core aspects of the project that we feel will always be prominent no matter what exact direction the research takes in the future. It is called the "anthropological commentary" project, and the purpose of it is to obtain reactions to ethnographies from people in the cultures described in the ethnographies. In other words, the project involves having people from various cultures in Asia and the Pacific read and evaluate the work of anthropologists who have written about these various cultures. Thus people from Samoa read the anthropological writings about Samoa, people from Palau read the writings about Palau, and so forth.

The indigenous respondents tell what they feel is right, what is wrong, what parts of the writings have helped the culture, which parts have hurt, and so forth. They also give their impressions about the writer — was he or she competent, sensitive to the intricacies of the culture, and so forth? The respondents do not know the name of the anthropologist as this is erased from the writings, thus partially eliminating biases that the respondents might bring to the task. When the responses from the approximately 100 respondents with whom we will work are summarized, then, we will be able to say with some assurance that certain anthropologists are evaluated highly. This could lead to a recommendation that they be studied carefully by all anthropologists and their students. We will also be able to say what aspects of a culture seem especially hard to document accurately, according to members of that culture. The results from this one criterion of indigenous judgment (which is only one criterion) can then be compared with other quality criteria suggested by anthropologists.

More specifically on this latter point, criteria suggested by antropologists regarding good ethnography have been developed as part of the hologeistic methodology associated with the Human Relations Area Files (introductions available in references 6 and 22). These data quality control criteria are used in a procedure designed to determine whether or not data quality could have affected a hypothesis relating two or more variables. Ethnographies rated "high" and "low" in quality are checked to see if the hypothesis is supported by both types. The quality control index is based on such measures as these:[15,17] ethnographer's knowledge of the language, amount of time in the field, use of case-incident reports rather than reliance solely on the informant's verbal descriptions, number of informants; professional training, verification efforts, and type of participation in the society. These are reasonable criteria, but the commentary project adds another: quality of the ethnography as judged by educated members of the culture (our commentators). It will be important to determine whether or not the same ethnographies rated "high" on the quality control index are also rated high by indigenous commentators. Incidentally, I want to point out that the comments of indigenous respondents will not be considered as final or as the ultimate judgment. For instance, a given commentator may not have had wide experience in all phases of his or her culture and thus may make mistakes in commenting on a certain section of an ethnography. But if there are points and issues in an ethnography that are again and again challenged by commentators, then further examination is called for by behavioral scientists.

An even more practical outcome would occur if certain ethnographies are again and again praised by commentators as being accurate, sympathetic, and so forth. These would be ethnographies that we could then recommend be read by students in cross-cultural studies or by researchers about to enter the field. I assume that if such "models" could be identified and if visiting researchers could learn from the models, then acceptance of the researchers by indigenous people would be likely. It would also be important to determine whether or not ethnographies traditionally considered excellent by the anthropological profession (e.g., those by Raymond Firth, Felix Keesing) are considered excellent by commentators.

Finally, another practical benefit would be specific information about the commentators' culture that could be used in cross-cultural orientation programs[7] designed to instruct people from one culture in methods of nonstressful interaction with people of another culture. The goal of one such type of training, which uses culture assimilators,[9] is isomorphic attribution, or understanding by outsiders of the reasons behind seemingly odd behavior in a culture. In preparing culture assimilators people from a given culture indicate aspects of behavior that might cause misunderstanding by others. Well over 100 critical incidents are generated with four plausible explanations of the incident, only one of which is correct as seen by members of the culture. I have found, however, that it is difficult for people to generate incidents about their own culture when asked to indicate behaviors that might be misunderstood by others. It is rather like our asking each other, "Tell me some funny jokes!" It is hard to respond to such a direct request. But if people have something to which they can react, such as sections of an ethnography, then this motivates them to both write about the ethnography and to expand upon it. Often, the content appropriate for culture assimilator incidents will be the product.

The material gathered from 105 people, from various cultures, who have participated in the "anthropological commentary" project is presented in Appendix I.

CONCLUSION

It is possible, I feel, for cross-cultural psychologists to orient their teaching and research activities so that there will be a greater chance of practical benefit to people from cultures in which the psychologists work. With the growth of colleges of continuing education at many universities (and crises that encourage the involvement of people not traditionally served in universities), there is now an administrative structure for such activities. Obviously, programs designed around the needs of other cultures will also be of benefit to traditional students if, for instance, new programs and standard graduate programs are designed so that they overlap. I do not want to be more specific because, following the dictum of Leonard Doob, people may shun any suggestion put forth here because it will then not be original, and there are strong pressures in academia to engage only in original ventures. But in general, such activities can only help the field of cross-cultural psychology. Generalizing from the common observation that people from other cultures appreciate visitors who take the trouble to learn their language, it seems to me that they will also appreciate any projects which we design to meet their needs.

APPENDIX I

The Anthropological Commentary Project: The Insiders' View†

People from various cultures gave us their reactions to writings by behavioral/social scientists. Since the people commented on writings about their own culture, we refer to them as "insiders." At the time we asked the people to participate in the project, they were studying at the East-West Center in Honolulu, Hawaii. People from Asia, the Pacific, and the United States come to the Center to engage in degree study at the University of Hawaii or to engage in various post-baccalaureate programs related to their professional development. Over a period of four years (1973–1976) we asked 105 insiders to read some material about their cultures and to then comment on it. The insiders came from all areas of the Pacific (Micronesia, Melanesia, and Polynesia) and Asia. The bibliography gives the specific countries from which the insiders come, the numbers from each country, and the published writings on which we asked them to comment.

The specific writings were chosen for several reasons. One was that they were considered to be representative of the better work (by authors' reputation) by social scientists. A good source for such writings was the Human Relation Area Files, which is a carefully organized compilation of ethnographic writings on all parts of the world in which social scientists (especially anthropologists) have worked. For cultures not given extensive coverage in the Files, we chose writings that had seemed to achieve status as shown by frequent citation of them. We also asked specialists on a given country for their recommendations. For certain countries, we knew that we would have a large number of insiders who could comment (Japan, Philippines, and Samoa, especially) and so we made a point of choosing a wide range of materials: some new, some old, some written by indigenous people, some by outsiders, etc. Our purpose was to maximize the range of opinion so that we could identify which writings are considered good, and which are considered bad. With this range, we could then search for possible reasons that would explain the differences in opinion.

A second basis for choosing certain writings was that they deal with topic areas likely to be familiar to the insiders. Highly technical materials on such topics as navigation and complex kinship systems were thus not used. Rather, material on the family, child-rearing, day-to-day subsistence activities, modal personality, folktales, education, and so forth, were chosen. In other words, we hope that we chose material that would be understandable and relevant to any insider who had achieved a university-based education no matter what the specific area of specialization chosen within the university. We removed the names of authors from the writings in case insiders had prior feelings about the authors.

---

† The material on the "anthropological commentary" project has been coauthored by Fahy Holwill. For this reason, the pronoun "we" is sometimes used.

After some pretesting, we found that the following questions yielded a wide range of opinions about the various writings. We decided to use the term "ethnography" since the word best described the vast majority of the writings. Each insider read approximately 10–15 pages of material (from one of the writings: see bibliography) and then provided written answers to the questions. We should note that the formulation of the questions followed our own specific research interests (especially the question on "helping" and "hurting" the culture). Other questions might have yielded quite a different set of responses than those that we summarize in the "results" section, below.‡ The questions we asked of the insiders, after they read about their culture, were:

1. What is right or correct in the ethnography?
2. What is wrong or incorrect in the ethnography?
3. Do you feel the author was sensitive to the intricacies of your culture?
4. Do you feel the ethnography was biased to make your people look inferior and/or silly?
5. What in the ethnography could help your culture?
6. What in the ethnography could hurt your culture?
7. Do you have any feelings about the person who wrote this material? Please elaborate.
8. How could you use such writings as this?
9. Please feel free to expand on any point or clarify a point.

RESULTS

The extensive set of written responses (called protocols) gathered from the 105 insiders were analyzed according to 15 categories. Each separate idea, concept, or opinion that an insider raised was called a unit. These were placed into one of the 15 categories. In most cases, the basic unit was a sentence or phrase within a sentence. Ratings were done independently by two people (the two authors). As a reliability check, they both rated a random sample of 20 protocols (of the 105) and the overlap in their assignment of units to categories was 85%. This figure showed that the system of categories was adequate for the task of summarizing the results.

For the total output of the 105 insiders, there were 1457 separate opinions (units) about various aspects of the ethnographies they read, an average of 13.9 units per insider. The categories are presented below together with the number (and percentages) of units that were placed into each. For each category a number of the best examples are given (verbatim) from the protocols. This should give more insight into the nature of the categories, and it should demonstrate what sorts of statements are made by the insiders. The examples

---

‡ We found that the insiders gave answers that closely followed our questions. This is certainly reasonable and it may seem fatuous that we point it out. Yet in studies with native speakers of English, respondents often go far beyond the questions asked, partly because they are so skillful in the language. But non-native speakers, such as the insiders, are naturally not quite so skillful with the English language and thus do not write about any and all thoughts that come to their minds. Rather, they are more likely to stick to the questions. Thus, the exact set of questions chosen determines the response far more with insiders than with a group of native speakers of English.

chosen for each category are what we judged to be very good, clear, helpful comments. Thus these examples typify how the technique of gathering insiders' opinions works at its best. Material in parentheses is for clarification and was written by us. The categories were:

1. Explicit statement that the author of the ethnography is correct about a certain point (237, or 16.3% of the units).

The emphasis on the group-istic nature of Japanese society and the hierarchy within the group is right indeed. The members of the group are loyal to the group and tend to identify themselves with the group. There is little or no sense of individuality. I agree with the author on these basic points.

(Regarding treatment of skilled artisans and apprentices) I agree with the basic facts – apprentices acted as assistants to the master craftsmen, and so forth. But for the present life of our people this is no longer true in our community. Because of modern skills and Western affiliations anybody with the training can and does build houses and boats. (also would be placed into category 10).

2. Explicit statement that the author of the ethnography is incorrect about a certain point (138, or 9.5% of the units).

(Regarding the self-deprecatory remarks often heard in one culture) The self-deprecatory remarks are a defense mechanism of sorts and need not necessarily mean what it says. It is undue humility of a kind, but this does not mean the individual is not aiming to achieve.

I think the person in our culture who the anthropologist worked with only wanted money from the anthropologist. This is why the interpretation is not accurate. People who really know should not give secrets to a stranger, only to members of their family. The person who worked with the anthropologist really didn't know the secrets.

3. Suggested correction made by the insider; these are likely to follow units placed in category 2 (91, or 6.3% of the units).

(In an article on kinship system of the Singapore Malays): the word "Bomor," described as a person who came to help a sick person. Correct spelling is "Bomoh".

It's true that we learn things by watching our elders but the term "in their own good time" is somewhat misleading: children of poor families are usually forced to pick up the tasks early in their age so that they can help the parents.

4. Statements made by the insider regarding applicability to the exact area within a culture with which insider is most familiar (e.g., exact city within a country or exact atoll within a group of islands: 41, or 2.8% of the units).

I feel that the author does not know what he is talking about because the author, in talking about Samoa, mentioned . . . work which was done in Manua. Western Samoa is very different from Manua and American Samoa.

5. Expansion on a point in the ethnography. Usually the basic point made by the writer is accepted, and the insider provides more detail, more examples, ramifications of point, etc. (460, or 31.6% of the units).

I agree that Western observers complain about our indirect response to things. We consider it polite, Westerners consider it not frank but you have to bear in mind that among Laotians these are not problems. Being in that kind of society with these values, we have learned to understand the message that other people are sending without it being stated in words. (It is not so much what you say, but the way you say it that counts).

(After writer's discussion on innovative technology): So far as Chinese culture is concerned, technology has been the weakest aspect and that explains why Chinese are more ready to accept Western technology than other areas, e.g., philosophy, literature, religion, etc.

(After a description of a situation in which two women, who previously used first names to address each other, entered into marriages which put them into a more formal relationship vis-a-vis each other): The formality is factual but "appeared ill at ease when in each other's company" is too general a statement. It would vary from individual to individual rather than a rule.

6. Statements made about the writer that are positive in tone (94, or 6.4%).

I seem to feel very close to the author when I think of the amount of work and depth gone into.

The author has been quite painstaking, thorough, and unbiased in the preparation of this ethnography on Nepal. This ethnography has been most objectively written and nothing is over-stated or under-stated.

7. Statements made about the writer that are negative in tone (54, or 3.7%).

The author must be an American, writing from an American's point of view and from the grandiose heights of the material culture of the Americans. I wish he would be kinder, though, to those who do not have the material things that they have. Culture is not only material, and besides, each one has his own — which writers from another country should do well not to downgrade. (would also be placed into category 11).

The author is more concerned about presenting the astonishing facts than beginning to be sensitive to the intricacies of our culture.

8. Indications of ways in which writings could help the culture (63, or 4.3%).

It appears that the book as a whole could help the natives to understand the value of their culture in the phase of a fast changing period they are now facing. Furthermore, it could be used as a base in the preparation of a curriculum for the teaching of custom in the Junior Secondary School. It is good reading material for people in my culture; better still for the older people if the book is translated into Fijian.

The author seems to have well-diagnosed our economic problems and the invaluable suggestions which he gives under the head, "Proposals for New Development" will help Nepal preserve not only her culture, but also help develop into a viable economy.

9. Indications of ways in which writings could hurt the culture (22, or 1.5%).

The author makes many general statements about my culture without giving concrete statistics to back up the statements. The reader may become biased in the direction of these unsupported general statements, especially a reader with an ethnocentric viewpoint of Western culture.

10. Bringing material up-to-date; indications of change since ethnography was written (141, or 9.7%).

(In reference to a treatment of the verbal behavior pattern *fääjiro*, spoken as a greeting to people of very high status such as district chiefs or specialists (jitag)): Long ago the word *fääiro* (sic) was true from the young generation to the older but now only the older people use the word *fääiro*. This is due to the parents and the older people never teaching or passing on to the young generation.

Many of the practices described have changed drastically since this was written (1956). There is a contrast between the old and new, especially the bygone superstitions and the present-day modernization.

11. Specific indications that ethnographer had a particular, preconceived point of view in writing about the culture, e.g., judging from Western standpoint; not looking at culture from insiders' point of view (14, or .8%).

The class structure as shown by the author represents an example of imposing Western concepts to the Thai social structure. Other, more careful observers have documented that Thai social structure can be best described in terms of a superior-subordinate society, rather than in terms of Western categories of class structure.

My experience in the past has been that the scholars on Indian culture, or should I call them "intellectuals," having studied the cultural patterns of Indians in India go down to the colonies and try to relate all their hypotheses upon the people of ethnic Indian background. They go there with some preconceived notions and try to search for these elements or they come across some similar notions or gestures get highly excited and jump to sweeping generalizations such as those put forth by the author in this article.

12. Recommendations for more or better ethnography; includes specific how-to-do-it suggestions as well as statements that more is needed, both in general ethnographic work and on specific topic areas (14, or .8%).

Since this piece was written the culture has undergone a considerable change. It is high time for somebody to do more research to bring the information up to date. The culture patterns change due to environmental change so that the survival of mankind will be assured. Culture is a living thing. It must change to adopt to new situations or the environment.

The author got all these ideas from books, instead of really going and seeking information from local sources. I think that is the most important thing if you are trying to write something about somebody, especially a civilization or society, really stay with that environment and part of it then you can come out with the best information.

13. Statements on limitations of self as commentator on the ethnography (10, or .7%).

Today we're losing our culture because the generation today that grew up, such as me for example, didn't bother to learn the culture. Our people think that we have changed our culture to American ways. It's true nowadays – it's very common. Our culture will be lost in the next few years. The culture changes because our people didn't document their culture – it was done orally. The old people teach their children about their culture through oral ways (but the elders are dying off) so the culture is getting weaker and weaker. If a person can't learn the culture from his father or relatives, the culture will die off. Reading this has given me help to know that I must study my culture some more. (would also be placed into category 10).

14. Personal statements stimulated by, but tangential to, the content of the ethnography; thus little to do with the ethnography itself, except as a stimulus (74, or 5.1%).

The author outlines the functioning of the government, which is true, but my point is that I don't accept the functioning of the government in the old fashioned way. It should be changed. Many changes have taken place. There are common people working for the government though they may not be allowed to hold any key position, but gradually this too will be possible. (would also be placed into category 1).

15. Uninterpretable statement – meaning or point unclear (4, or .3%). (By definition, anything we cite verbatim would be uninterpretable, and so we do not provide an example. Most content analyses of written material have such a category, and we were gratified that we could interpret all but 4 of the 1457 units provided by the insiders.)

DISCUSSION OF RESULTS

With such a large amount of material provided to us by the insiders, choices have to be made in deciding what to discuss. We will deal with those aspects that might help social scientists who want to do research which is looked upon favorably by insiders. We assume that such research will be more helpful in increasing intercultural communication and understanding than research which is viewed as acceptable only by outsiders.

The most common types of comments made by the insiders were expansions of points made by the writers (31.6% of all comments). These were often very helpful, cogent, and precise additions to the writers' arguments. We feel that in many cases writers would like to have seen these comments before completing the final draft of their work. These expansions are often the sort of feedback social scientists obtain when they ask colleagues to comment on drafts of their work. For instance, one insider expanded on the complex issue of "face" in oriental cultures.

He pointed out the importance of "face" in Chinese culture but he did no more than other writers he quoted in digging into the intricate nature of the concept. Again he *asserted* that there's a difference between the fear of loss of face of a Westerner and a Chinese but gives no more analysis except the very *vague* sentence "In the east there are matters of face, which is status plus something else like dignity." Even if I buy his assertion, I still don't know *how* they are actually different. Maybe it's not the concept that's so very different — maybe it's the socio-cultural approach to the concept that's so different.

Since more and more insiders are attending college and have attained the skills necessary for reading and criticizing complex ethnographic writings, they can be asked to participate in the original writing of such work. Our general recommendation is that social scientists search out and involve insiders who can make the type of comments that we have presented. In many cases such a procedure will improve writings by making them more accurate, more understandable, more sensitive to the range of variability within a culture, and so forth. Of course, insiders can also be involved at the very beginnings of research projects, an approach for which its proponents argue strongly.[4]

Since we are recommending that insiders be asked to participate in research projects, we should give the reactions of insiders to *our* study. In general, insiders felt flattered to participate. In many cases, our photocopies of the writings were the first published material that insiders had seen on their culture; or this study provided the insiders' first exposure to the exact piece of material that we chose. We helped a number of insiders with various term papers since we were able to give bibliographic references to materials on their cultures. For over half of the insiders, we interacted with them in seminars in which ethnographic field work was discussed, commentaries-on-writings completed, and the general results discussed. We assume that since 105 insiders participated over a 4-year period, and since many insiders brought their friends to participate, their satisfaction led to a word-of-mouth opinion that the project was "O.K." We feel that other social scientists can generate such support for the benefit of their research projects.

Emics and Etics

In recent years, a number of social scientists have dealt with the concepts of "emics and etics" in culture/behavior studies.[2,5,16] "Emics" refer to explanations of behavior according to the insider's point of view or framework. "Etics" refer to theoretical concepts used to make generalizations about more than one culture. Both approaches are important, but there has been an overemphasis on etics. This overemphasis has led to the development of "false etics" such as the intelligence quotient (IQ), which some social scientists have used to compare people from different cultures. Inevitably, some groups do not measure as highly as others (usually, those people in cultures where the tests were *not* designed) and ugly, harmful conclusions are drawn. Critics of this approach (e.g., Berry,[3] Cole and Scribner[8]) argue that the emics of complex construct like "intelligence" must be determined before any attempts at formulating etics can be started. Intelligence has different connotations in different cultures: in one African society, it connotes (among other concepts) "getting along with kin."[19] This is not the major connotation in other societies, such as the United States, where the main connotation is individuals' problem solving activities associated with formal schooling. This or any other US viewpoint should not be imposed as an etic in other cultures.

In its simplest (but perhaps most important) form, the emic-etic distinction is concerned with the imposition of an alien point of view in attempts to understand behavior in a culture other than the researcher's own. If etics are imposed, they are being used unwisely. The emics, or point of view of the insiders, must be understood. There were only 14 insiders' comments in this category (our number 11), but each was made by a separate person. In addition, they were very incisive, pointing out a real problem that a large number of insiders were able to verbalize. Two such comments have already been presented. Another (which, incidentally, was written with no other books or notes on which to draw) was:

The author has managed very successfully to paint only the darkest side of the picture. He looks at everything with dark-tinted glasses and thus finds everything as dark as his glasses and his thoughts and ideas. May I quote one of A. Pope's witticisms (epigrams) to illustrate this article:

All looks evil that the evil espy.
As all looks yellow to the jaundiced eye

Our recommendation here is obvious. Social scientists must continue in their efforts to become more sensitive to the frameworks of insiders and must be careful not to impose their own value system, pet theory, and so forth. The articles suggested earlier by social scientists who have recently grappled with the emic-etic distinction may help. It may also help to remember that there are insiders who can make very penetrating comments if social scientists become careless.

Model Studies §

Some insiders who were from the same culture read and commented on the same material. This allowed us to determine if any writings were frequently considered as good, accurate, perceptive, and so forth. There were three authors whose writings were judged in this light by at least three insiders. We would like to suggest these as examples of what other social scientists might emulate should they be interested in the criterion of insiders' opinions. However, we have to preface the citation of the three examples (and each of them individually) with a

§ The exception, as already reviewed when discussing writings about Samoa, is for cultures which have no written tradition. Thus the ethnographer provides a valuable service in documenting the culture since, years later, it is the only existing record. The advice presented in this paragraph is for research in societies currently undergoing fast change due to pressures of modernization, Westernization, and so forth.

number of caveats. First, we could determine if there were multiple insiders who looked favorably on a given ethnography only if there were a large number of ethnographies for a given culture. For some of the ethnographies listed in the appendix, there were not multiple insiders to comment and so these writings could not be considered for this "model" analysis. Thus some of these writings may be every bit as good as the three we cite below, but the small number of insiders for certain cultures (and small number who read a given ethnography) prevented any documentation of this fact. Second, there were some writings that were viewed quite negatively by at least three insiders, but we do not cite these in this section. We feel that citation of such work will cause the same sort of trouble and hard feelings that we discussed in the early pages of this paper. In addition, we feel as much (or more) can be learned from emulating positive models as from attempting to change, somehow, the factors that led to a negative model.

Given this prelude, (1) insiders from Nepal reacted very favorable to the work of Hasken.[10] The exact material they were asked to read consisted of chapters three and six of this book. (2) Keeping in mind that the field work was done in Manua (in present day American Samoa) in the late 1920s, Samoans reacted favorably to the work of Mead.[14] Insiders who read her work suggested updatings of certain points and mentioned that not all practices in Manua can be generalized to all of Samoa. (3) Keeping in mind that the work was written many years ago and that urban areas especially have changed, insiders from the Philippines reacted favorably to the work of Keesing.[11] For Samoa and the Philippines, insiders suggested that these writings would be excellent source materials for history courses. Ethnographies (especially for Samoa) are sometimes the only written materials available that describe cultures as they were years ago.

Advice For Doing Better Research

At various points in the commentaries, insiders gave specific pieces of advice for doing better research and reporting the results. Combining these into one set of guidelines, insiders advised the following.

(1) Learn the language spoken in the culture being studied. People in the culture will be grateful that outsiders have taken the trouble. More information will be accessible to an ethnographer who has learned the language.

(2) Talk to a wide variety of people, not to just those at the top of the status hierarchy, and not to just one informant.

(3) Specify the exact place within a culture where the data was gathered. Do not generalize beyond this place unless there is evidence that such generalization is justified. Include this specificity in the title of the ethnography, e.g., *Kin and culture in Majuro, Marshall Islands*, rather than *Kin and culture in the Marshalls*.

(4) Provide good evidence for generalizations. Gather data using such techniques as surveys. Avoid generalizations based only on impressions. One such comment was previously reprinted under our category 9.

(5) Avoid the journalistic-like technique of describing specific situations when these can be misinterpreted as being *typical* of the culture. Such descriptions may catch the reader's interest, but there are dangers involved. A specific example is a description like, "A sad-looking young child was walking down the street, crying, but nearby adults paid no attention." Such statements lead to careless generalizations, such as "adult lack of concern," from readers.

(6) Be careful in interpreting motives from behavior. Many times ethnographers are accurate in describing behavior, but are inaccurate in diagnosing the motives or reasons for the behavior. To describe motives, ethnographers must learn the point of view of people in the culture. One insider was explicit on this point:

> The author was sensitive, but he has not researched deeply enough to understand the causes for some of the behavior he observed.

(7) For those cultures that are changing, and whose people have to learn new ways, the ethnographer can help by reading and studying the same sorts of materials (newspapers, technical reports, production figures, projections) that insiders must read. If an outsider just talks to insiders and writes up the conversations, the insiders are not helped because the product is only what the insiders already knew.[8] But if outsiders study the same material as insiders, then the outsider's independent opinion may be very helpful. A specific comment: "We ourselves value those writings whose authors have read the same material that we have to know to make decisions."

It is important to note that many of these points have been recently discussed by social scientists themselves in efforts to improve research.

Use of Writings in Cross-Cultural Orientation Programs

Another use of these writings and subsequent commentary might be possible in cross-cultural orientation programs. In such programs, people from one culture learn about other cultures, and they learn how to interact with a minimum amount of stress in other cultures.[7] Such programs often take place just after people have arrived in a culture other than their own. In such programs, people are often asked to talk about themselves and their culture, but they find it hard to do since they rarely think about their own culture. Certain aspects of people's lives, such as culture and the air they breathe, are accepted and not pondered. But if they are asked to read and then react to *someone else's* thoughts about their culture, the task of self-expression is much easier. They then have a great deal to say, as the verbatim comments presented throughout this paper show.

Concluding Comments

We have attempted to show the wide variety of benefits that are possible if the opinions of insiders are gathered in the process of doing research in various cultures. Writings that reflect the views of insiders will undoubtedly lead to better understanding among people from different cultures since the research procedure, by definition, includes a step in which the outsider makes every attempt to reflect and to understand insiders' opinions. Both the process and outcome of research should thus improve intercultural communication.

REFERENCES

1. AMERICAN PSYCHOLOGICAL ASSOCIATION. 1973. Ethical principles in the conduct of research with human participants. American Psychological Assn. Washington, D.C.
2. BERRY, J. 1969. On cross-cultural comparability. Int. J. Psych. 4: 119–128.

3. BERRY, J. 1973. Radical cultural relativism and the concept of intelligence. *In* Culture and cognition: readings in cross-cultural psychology. J. Berry & P. Dasen, Eds. Methuen. London.
4. BOCHNER, S., R. BRISLIN, & W. LONNER. 1975. Introduction. *In* Cross-cultural perspectives on learning. R. Brislin, S. Bochner & W. Lonner, Eds.: 3–36. Wiley/Halsted. New York.
5. BRISLIN, R. 1976. Comparative research methodology: cross-cultural studies. Int. J. Psych. **11** (3): in press.
6. BRISLIN, R., W. LONNER & R. THORNDIKE. 1973. Cross-cultural research methods. John Wiley. New York.
7. BRISLIN, R. & P. PEDERSEN. 1976. Cross-cultural orientation programs. Wiley/Halsted. New York.
8. COLE, M. & S. SCRIBNER. 1974. Culture and thought: a psychological introduction. John Wiley. New York.
9. FIEDLER, F., T. MITCHELL & H. TRIANDIS. 1971. The culture assimilator: an approach to cross-cultural training. J. App. Psych. **55**: 95–102.
10. HASKEN, F. 1974. The Kathmandu valley towns. Weatherhill. New York.
11. KEESING, F. 1937. The Philippines: a nation in the making. Kelly and Walsh, Ltd. Hong Kong.
12. KELMAN, H. 1968. A time to speak. Jossey-Base. San Francisco.
13. KELMAN, H. 1972. The rights of the subject in social research: an analysis in terms of relative power and legitimacy. Amer. Psych. **27**: 989–1016.
14. MEAD, M. 1937. The Samoans. *In* Cooperation and competition among primitive peoples. M. Mead, Ed., Beacon Press, Inc. Boston.
15. NAROLL, R. 1962. Data quality control. Macmillan. New York.
16. PRICE-WILLIAMS, D. 1974. Psychological experiment and anthropology: the problem of categories. Ethos **2**: 95–114.
17. ROHNER, R., B. DeWALT & R. NESS. 1973. Ethnographer bias in cross-cultural research: an empirical study. Behav. Sci. Notes, 8 (4): 275–317.
18. SEGALL, M., D. CAMPBELL & M. HERSKOVITS. 1966. The influence of culture on visual perception. Bobbs-Merrill. Indianapolis, Indiana.
19. SERPELL, R. 1976. Culture's influence on behavior. Methuen, London.
20. TAGUMPAY-CASTILLO, G. 1968. A view from Southeast Asia. *In* SEADAG, American Research on Southeast Asia Development: Asian and American Views.: 20–49. The Asia Society. New York.
21. TRIANDIS, H. 1972. The analysis of subjective culture. John Wiley. New York.
22. WHITING, J. 1968. Methods and problems in cross-cultural research. *In* Handbook of Social Psychology. G. Lindzey & E. Aronson, Eds. 2nd edit. Vol. 2: 693–728. Addison-Wesley. Reading, Mass.
23. WITKIN, H. & J. BERRY. 1975. Psychological differentiation in cross-cultural perspective. J. Cross-Cult. Psych. **6**: 4–87.

BIBLIOGRAPHY

ETHNOGRAPHIC WRITINGS USED IN "ANTHROPOLOGICAL COMMENTARY" PROJECT

Countries from which insiders came; numbers of insiders from each country (total number = 105); and writings that were used in this project.

Cook Islands: number of insiders participating in project = 1.
  SYME, R. 1955. The Cook Islands. I. Pitman and Sons, Ltd. London.

Fiji: number of insiders = 4.
  HOWARD, A. 1972. Learning to be a Rotuman. Columbia University. New York.
  MAYER, A. 1973. Peasants in the Pacific: a study of Fiji Indian rural society. University of California Press. Berkeley.

SAHLINS, M. 1962. Moala: culture and nature on a Fijian Island. University of Michigan Press. Ann Arbor.
THOMPSON, L. M. 1940. Fijian frontier. American Council, Institute of Pacific relations. New York.

Hong Kong: number of insiders = 3.
HOPKINS, K. 1971. Hong Kong: The industrial colony. Oxford University Press. Hong Kong.
AGASSI, J. & I. JARVIE. 1968. A Study in Westernization. *In* Hong Kong: A society in Transition. I. Jarvie & J. Agassi, Eds., Frederick A. Praeger. New York.

India: number of insiders = 3.
HUTTON, G. H. 1961. Caste in India: Its nature, function, and origins. Oxford University Press. London.

Indonesia: number of insiders = 3.
GRANT, B. 1966. Indonesia. Melbourne University Press. Melbourne.
SOEDJATMOKO. 1970. Problems and prospects for development in Indonesia. *In* Indonesia; plans and prospects. Vol. 19 (Autumn issue), Asia.

Japan: number of insiders = 8.
CAUDILL, W. 1973. The influence of social structure and culture on human behavior in modern Japan. Ethos 1 (3), 343–382.
DOE, T. 1973. The anatomy of dependence. Kondansha International. Tokyo, New York.
EMBREE, J. 1945. The Japanese Nation: a social survey. Farrar and Rinehart, Inc. New York.
HASEGAWA, N. 1965. The Japanese Character: A cultural profile. (translated by John Bester) Kondansha International, Ltd. Tokyo.
NAKANE, C. 1970. Japanese society. University of California Press. Berkeley.

Korea: number of insiders = 4.
HEWES, G. W. & C. H. KIM. 1950. Korean kinship behavior and structure. HRAF. New Haven.
McCUNE, S. 1956. Korea's heritage, a regional and social geography. C. E. Tuttle Co. Tokyo; Rutland, Vt.
OLIVER, ROBERT. 1944. Korea: Forgotten nation. Public Affairs Press. Washington, D.C.

Laos: number of insiders = 3.
LeBAR, F. M. & SUDDARD, A., Eds. 1967. Laos: Its people, its society, its culture. HRAF Press. New Haven.

Malaysia: number of insiders = 5.
DJAMOUR, J. 1959. Malay kinship and marriage in Singapore. Athlone Press. London.

Marshalls: number of insiders = 1.
TOBIN, J. A. 1956. Land tenure in the Marshall Islands. National Research Council, Pacific Science Board. Washington, D.C.

Micronesia (people for whom appropriate writings were not available for their specific islands): number of insiders = 7.
MASON, L. 1968. The ethnology of Micronesia. *In* Peoples and cultures of the Pacific. A. Vayda, Ed.: 275–298. Natural History Press. New York.

Nepal: number of insiders = 4.
HOSKEN, F. P. 1974. The Kathmandu valley towns. Weatherhill. New York.

New Zealand: number of insiders = 1.
BEAGLEHOLE, E. & P. BEAGLEHOLE. 1946. Some modern Maoris. Council for Educational Research. Wellington, N.Z.

Pakistan: number of insiders = 3.
WILBER, D. N. 1964. Pakistan: Its people, its society, its culture. HRAF Press. New Haven.

Palau: number of insiders = 5.

BARNETT, H. 1949. Palauan society. University of Oregon Publications. Eugene, Oregon.

BARNETT, H. G. 1960. Being a Palauan. Holt. New York.

FORCE, R. & M. FORCE. 1972. Just one house. B.P. Bishop Museum Publication No. 235. Honolulu, Hawaii.

Philippines: number of insiders = 10.

GUTHRIE, G. 1967. Cultural preparation for the Philippines. *In* Cultural Frontiers of the Peace Corps. R. Textor, Ed. MIT Press. Cambridge, Mass.

HORN, R. 1941. Orphans of the Pacific. Reynal and Hitchcock. New York.

KEESING, F. 1937. The Philippines: A nation in the making. Kelly and Walsh, Ltd. Hong Kong.

PSYCHOLOGICAL ASSOCIATION OF THE PHILIPPINES. 1965. Symposium on the Filipino Personality. Psychological Association of the Philippines, Manila. (Also in the Philippine Sociological Review, July-October, 1963).

Ponape: number of insiders = 2.

FISHER, J. 1958. Contemporary Ponape Land Tenure. *In* Land Tenure Patterns, TTPI. J. de Young, Ed. Trust Territory Government, Guam.

FISHER, J. 1970. Adoption on Ponape. *In* Adoption in Eastern Oceania. V. Caroll, Ed. ASAO Monograph No. 1.

Samoa: number of insiders = 9.

HIRSH, S. 1958. The Social organization of an urban village in Samoa. J. Poly. Soc. **67**: 266–303.

KEESING, F., & M. KEESING. 1973. Elite communication in Samoa: a study of leadership. Stanford University Press. Stanford, Ca. (also Octagon Books. New York, 1973).

LOCKWOOD, B. 1971. Samoan village economy. Oxford University Press. Oxford.

MEAD, M. 1937. The Samoans. *In* Cooperation and Competition Among Primitive Peoples. M. Mead, Ed. Beacon Press, Inc. Boston. (Reprinted in Peoples and cultures of the Pacific. A. Vayda, Ed. Natural History Press. New York, 1968, pp. 244–273).

Solomons: number of insiders = 2.

IVENS, W. 1930. The Island Builders of the Pacific. Seeley, Service, and Co., Ltd. London.

OGAN, E. 1972. Business and cargo: socio-economic change among the Nasioi of Bougainville. ANU, New Guinea Research Unit Bulletin 44. Canberra, Australia.

Taiwan: number of insiders = 8.

HANG, LI-Wu. 1951. Taiwan Today. Hwa Kuo Publishing Co., Taipeh. Stanford University, 1956. Taiwan handbook. HRAF. New Haven.

Thailand: number of insiders = 13.

BLANCHARD, W. 1958. Thailand: Its people, its society, its culture. HRAF Press, New Haven.

Tibet: number of insiders = 1.

NORBU, T., & C. TURNBULL. 1968. Tibet. Simon and Schuster. New York.

Tonga: number of insiders = 1.

BEAGLEHOLE, E. & P. BEAGLEHOLE. 1941. Pangai, village in Tonga. The Polynesian Society. Wellington, N.Z.

Truk: number of insiders = 4.

FISCHER, F. 1956. The position of men and women in Truk and Ponape. J. Amer. Folk. **69**: 55–62.

GOODENOUGH, W. H. 1951. Property, kin, and community on Truk. Yale University Press. New Haven.

ISSUES RELATING TO THE PUBLICATION AND DISSEMINATION OF CROSS-CULTURAL RESEARCH DATA

Walter J. Lonner

Department of Psychology
Western Washington State College
Bellingham, Washington 98225

In 1968 and 1969 I busied myself with the development of the *Journal of Cross-Cultural Psychology* (*JCCP*), helping to formulate a publication plan prior to the appearance of the first issue in March of 1970. I had assumed that *JCCP* would not only be interdisciplinary and international (which was noted by its somewhat redundant and now defunct subtitle) but also that it would fairly represent human psychology, through the cross-cultural method, on a global scale. Gardner Murphy's phrase, ". . . to consult all that is human," was chosen as our verbal logo, primarily because of its timely appearance in 1969 in an article dealing with psychology in the year 2000.[1] This egalitarian slogan signaled our intent to equilibrate all human behavior, eventually, through the medium of scientific expression and analysis. The editorial advisory board, the keystone in the plan, reflected this grand scheme; some thirty-five scholars from twenty-two geographically dispersed areas and from seven or eight disciplines agreed to serve as consultants. I was pleased and relieved that they all enthusiastically agreed to participate in this venture.

Perhaps I expected that contributions via submitted manuscripts would reflect these strata, and that in time the published articles would indeed cover all that is human. I further assumed that manuscripts would naturally come from all corners of the world, in proportion to the number of researchers who study the various cultures of the world.

Now, nearly six years later, after more than 700 manuscripts, 2,500 pieces of consultant-related correspondence and about 550 painful (usually) letters of rejection, a better image of reality is coming into focus. Helping to sharpen this image has been my involvement in various publications, a few research projects, and participation in quite a number of cross-cultural conferences, where I have met many dedicated colleagues. If I have learned anything at all during this period of rapid ascent of cross-cultural psychology, it certainly encompasses an assortment of issues and problems that are and will be of continuing concern to cross-cultural psychology, and how it is "packaged" and "marketed." In this paper I will try to cover the topic by touching upon several academic disciplines, at least by implication. But my psychological background and my nearly total immersion in cross-cultural psychology may tend to distort the "reality" of publication issues and problems as seen from the offices of editors of anthropology or sociology journals.

There are six issues, or problem areas, with regard to the topic that I will cover in the remaining pages:

(1) The number and nature of cross-cultural publications; (2) the treatment of cross-cultural research in the media and in introductory psychology texts; (3) writing style and jargon differences across both disciplines and cultures; (4) representativeness of cultures investigated; (5) manuscript reviewing procedures; (6) the problems posed by increasing publication expenses.

THE NUMBER AND NATURE OF CROSS-CULTURAL PUBLICATIONS

The uninitiated cross-cultural researcher and most cross-cultural adherents can be overwhelmed by the sheer number of journals that more or less predictably publish cross-cultural research. In addition to all anthropology journals that are obvious sources of cultural data and information, we have *JCCP*, the *International Journal of Psychology*, *Ethos*, and *Topics in Culture Learning*, all chiefly devoted to cross-cultural research. There is the *Journal of Social Psychology*, which traditionally gives priority to the publication of cross-cultural research, as well as many "regional" or "specialty" journals. In 1973 we listed 29 journals[2] that are predictable sources of cross-cultural research reports, and this list could easily be expanded, for any journal in psychology that has a human focus has published cross-cultural research – the *American Psychologist* and the *Journal of Personality and Social Psychology* are just two of the more prominent ones.

Does this proliferation of cross-cultural research present a problem, or is it a boon? Should cross-cultural reports be published in so many periodicals? Some have argued that this brand of psychological research should appear *only* in journals with a particular secular focus. Thus, a developmental article might appear in *Developmental Psychology*, a learning-related paper in *Cognition*, and so forth. One answer to this problem would be to concentrate the publication of the best cross-cultural research in a small number of journals. Unless such a policy of concentration becomes recognized internationally, it will be increasingly difficult to track down cross-cultural research in order to help integrate findings in various domains. We will also continue to see much of the best cross-cultural research appear in journals with five-digit circulation figures, for this is the proven and traditional path to prestige and promotion. The counter-argument is that it would be better to have cross-cultural psychology articles appear in as many publications as possible. I believe that this is wasteful, however, and runs counter to certain objectives.

Harrison Gough made an interesting suggestion with regard to this issue. Since the world is so big, he wonders if our goal should be five to ten "regional" cross-cultural jounals, each stressing some natural geographical/cultural unit that may very well parallel the six-region global partitioning scheme outlined by Murdock.[3] Then, Gough offered, there might be a sort of "coordinating" journal publishing papers on worldwide topics, theory, and so forth. In addition, this inter-regional digest could refer the reader to appropriate regional journals (via abstracts or an annual index) for particular studies. This is utopian thinking: Gough admits that such an operation would be enormously expensive and would, in fact, irritate those who suppose that they already have regional journals.

So many interrelated journals coming from dozens of countries and written in many languages naturally foster another problem – one related to economics and perhaps to ethics. That problem involves the multiple publication of the same data. Nothing prevents a researcher from publishing an article in an Indian journal, for example, and then giving the same data a slightly different twist three months later and submitting it to a journal 6,000 miles away. Of course, a counter-argument is that duplication in publication of the same data would be good, for this would increase the number of people around the world who are exposed to such data. In any case, multiple publication probably happens infrequently, and I am not suggesting that an international watchdog committee on publication ethics be created to guard against this wasteful and inefficient practice. I am suggesting that this practice would be headed off if fewer journals were to be recognized internationally as principal sources of cross-cultural data.

A final recommendation on this topic is merited. More review monographs that focus on specific domains of research are needed. Among several that have lately appeared, Miller[4] prepared one on the perception of pictorial materials, Dasen[5] covered Piagetian work, Draguns[6] reviewed culture and psychopathology, and Witkin and Berry[7] integrated cross-cultural data on psychological differentiation. The forthcoming *Handbook of Cross-Cultural Psychology*[8] has a similar, much broader intent. More people should be involved in such integrated scholarship, for efforts of this kind allow better advances in methodology and a more up-to-date cross-fertilization of ideas. If enough of these monographs were to be done annually, appearing predominantly in three or four journals, they would reduce the need for the creation of regional outlets and coordinating journals. I invite suggestions on the areas of research that need an integrated review, and on who may write them. Alternatively, two or three journals could devote an issue each year to a particular region of the world, if enough manuscripts on hand permitted this. A modest but important step in this direction is a pending review of the "state-of-the-art" in psychology, with a special cross-cultural focus, among Spanish-speaking countries of the Western hemisphere. Being prepared by Gordon Finley, Luiz F. S. Natalicio, and Ruben Ardila, this commentary will also provide a long-overdue link between cross-cultural researchers in North America (generally served through *JCCP*) and their colleagues in Mexico and further south, who have historically been served through the *Interamerican Journal of Psychology*.

TREATMENT OF CROSS-CULTURAL RESEARCH IN THE MEDIA AND IN INTRODUCTORY TEXTS

Behavioral scientists like to see their work cited. When it is cited in publications of a particular guild such as psychology, enough context, shared knowledge and background reduce the possibility of distorted interpretation. But when the best research labor is full of invective or when findings are misinterpreted, hackles will be raised.

For instance, it is common for austerity-minded public figures, such as Senator William Proxmire of Wisconsin, to demean research projects that have been funded by the taxpayer and to treat them as trivial, wasteful efforts. Hypothetical examples of the type of grant title so trivialized would be "The effect of teacher attitudes on self-concept formation of American minorities" and "Factors contributing to dental fears of preschool children." And in *Strictly Speaking*;[9] a best-seller in 1974, Edwin Newman noted that two political researchers, using the Fishbein model of attitude organization and change, came up with an "astonishing" finding during the Nixon-McGovern contest. "The finding," wrote Newman pejoratively, "that an effective message wins over more voters $[p(a_i b_i C(t) < a_i b_i C(t + 1))]$ than it loses $[p(a_i b_i C(t) > a_i b_i C(t + 1))]$ must have stirred politicians all over the country" (p. 75). This is the type of out-of-context citation that is unfortunate. Newman apparently does not understand — at least he failed to note — that the Fishbein model, like other energetic models in psychology, attempts to deal with masses of data with the aim of developing beneficial predictive power.

Many cross-cultural researchers I know are compelled to see that their research becomes recognized through the citation process as a step toward its integration into the general psychological literature. Their compulsiveness is compounded by their second concern: that the reporting and citation are not pulled too much out of context. And if the accurate reportage would hold its own, often it is so brief that the reader is not alerted to the full scope and background of the research and possible alternative explanations.

Introductory psychology texts are increasingly making, at last, more than a few token references to cross-cultural research. It is even becoming stylish to include a chapter on cross-cultural psychology in basic texts. But still the typical introductory text, or personality text, gives narrow accounts of only three or four topics that the authors and publishers assume will be sufficient coverage. Typically mentioned are possible cultural variations in abilities and intelligence (through Piaget), factors affecting susceptibility to visual illusions, and treatment of exotic mental illnesses like latah and pibloktoq. In many of these instances, scant treatment of rather complex phenomena is analogous to giving the reader a brief summary of the best chapter in *War and Peace*.

It would be an exciting and worthwhile project to write an introductory psychology textbook that had an explicit worldwide focus. Perhaps 10 or 15 people could be involved in such an effort. The standard subject matter would be provided, of course; but against such a basic background could be a universalistic approach to psychology.

WRITING STYLE AND JARGON DIFFERENCES ACROSS BOTH DISCIPLINES AND CULTURES

Across Disciplines

Most cross-cultural researchers are either psychologists or anthropologists. If they are from other disciplines (psychiatry or linguistics, for instance), they will likely align themselves with the general methodological tactics taken by exemplars of one or the other major focuses. That is, an anthropological approach in cultural analysis has relied historically upon description, after "total cultural immersion," whereas psychology has its own tradition of explanation via experimentation. Although the line between the two approaches has been fading in recent years (e.g., the formation of new alliances such as psychological anthropology or experimental anthropology), there remains a chasm between the two approaches when it is considered how cultural analysis takes place and how results are reported in various publications. This problem parallels the rough but generally accurate characterization of anthropological research as ambiguous and psychological research as artificial.[10]

The flowing prose of many early anthropologists (Kroeber, Linton, and Kluckhohn, for instance) about human variation stands in sharp contrast to the terse and literarily lean tradition of psychology. Anthropologists more often than not try to emulate the eloquence of their early leaders. Their writing is often highly descriptive and they tend to provide a greater context for the understanding of their work; they often use footnotes and there is an incredible amount of fine-grained documentation in nearly everything they write. Nothing seems to elude these scholarly efforts, even if small print has to be used.

Descriptions of cultures can be endless, although interesting. Characteristically, the ratio of words to numbers, graphs, and tables is high.

By contrast, the "scientific" style of psychological report fostered by the experimental method and demanded by journal editors is spartan, sometimes boringly detailed, but often elegant in its austerity. The verbal content of these reports seems to be like plastic flowers lending a little color to drab fields of data and statistics. Twenty years ago, if Jack Sprat were a cross-cultural researcher, he would have been a psychologist, for he could eat no fat; his wife would have been the anthropologist, for she could eat no lean. Today there is a movement toward a more balanced diet.

These playfully exaggerated characterizations are not meant to imply that one writing style is "better" than the other, or that one research tradition is less "scientific" than the other. This discrepancy between styles, however, causes problems time and again in publication. In my experience, anthropologists more often than psychologists, are requested to give more information about method, sample selection, and data analysis prior to publishing their reports in cross-cultural publications. Psychologists, on the other hand, are frequently urged to sacrifice *some* of the space devoted to method, hypotheses, data analysis, and tables in favor of a deeper ethnographic analysis and a psychological/anthropological rationale for conducting the research being reported. Combining the best of both is obviously one of the nice characteristics of the "experimental anthropology" generation just arising.

A cross-cultural article should have elements of both these traditions. A manuscript simply reads better if it includes the best that both approaches can offer. While I have no privileged information to support the following assertion, my guess is that a major reason why *Ethos* recently joined the ranks of cross-cultural publications was to print articles high in literary, ethnographic, and "culture and personality" appeal, while not losing sight of the kind of solid empirical evidence that the psychologist is trained to expect and demand.

Across Cultures

A large proportion of psychological research is being done by Westerners, i.e., English-speaking psychologists from the United States, Canada, and all countries which are now or once were part of the British Commonwealth of Nations. The same is true of cross-cultural researchers. Not only are they fecund with ideas, grants, and various other means of support, but they are generally also skilled scientific report writers and are well-practiced in applying the formula that leads to publication. Cross-cultural research in psychology and its subsequent publication is largely controlled, albeit magnanimously and with a good deal of concern, by a rather small number of Euro-Americans who would be fully equipped to exercise this control indefinitely if they so desired.

It is an error of both diplomacy and interpretation of the facts to suppose that there is an equality between Western versus non-Western publication rates and publication opportunities. This inequality works against non-Westerners at the English writing level and at the level of technical supports (e.g., high-speed computers) that help Westerners turn out publications at a relatively phenomenal rate. For example, an acquaintance of mine, an American psychologist, at one point in 1973 claims to have had either published, in press, or under editorial review over thirty manuscripts. Most of these were cross-cultural articles based largely upon factor analysis.

A lack of technical supports and the unfortunate inequities imposed by competition with Western counterparts most often penalize psychologists from developing countries and so-called third world countries. Researchers from the latter countries, which account for more than half the world's population, submit articles that are awkwardly written, because they do not have the necessary practice in English composition. Moreover, their data analyses often do not go beyond a simple comparison of means or a chi-square table, because their support facilities preclude anything more elaborate. Their manuscripts are received by editors in tattered shape and typed on poor paper, and they frequently arrive late; the airmail expense incurred by many would be a pittance to a Westerner (whose department absorbs the cost in any case), but to many Asians and Africans it could be a significant drain on their own or their institution's budget.

What can be done about this problem? Often, many sensitive Western researchers coauthor papers with their less practiced colleagues. This gives others practice and assigns credit where it is due, and it should continue. But what of papers authored solely by less practiced researchers from the less advanced, less affluent countries? At least once before I advanced the idea, for discussion purposes, that perhaps standards could be relaxed a bit if it seemed proper to do so in certain situations. This "double standard" (a term that irritates people) could relax rigorous demands for style of expression, clarity of research design, and subsequent analyses so as to decrease even slightly the seriously high rejection rates that so evidently affect most of the non-Western population of researchers, who are virtually forced into attempts to publish their work in Western publications. Obviously, a *minimum* standard should not be compromised. Articles published in less-than-perfect English which explain an "emic" conceptualization and presentation of the research would provide the added benefit of allowing Western researchers and journal readers to understand and perhaps appreciate the "uneticized" modes that are employed by these bilingual natives of distant places.

Without yielding completely on this general argument that there are the "haves" and the "have nots" in getting words into print, a suggestion of Richard Brislin may be more widely accepted by those who insist that a single standard for any science cannot be compromised. Researchers from less developed countries have an advantage over others in one important respect. They have greater and more genuine access to populations that are more fruitful for "pure" cross-cultural research. If these researchers are penalized by not having access to computers, to conventions, and to theory-construction mills known as the Big American University, they can certainly compete in the realm of good ideas. They may not be compelled to put their data through the gauntlet of multivariate statistics, or to explain why their data provide the link between Latest Study X and Next-to-Latest Study Y. They are in a good position to list ideas and to explain why these ideas are good. From their perspective, they are also in an excellent position to condemn what they may believe to be hollow cultural analyses by Westerners, and thus help keep cross-cultural research oriented in the right direction.

Harry Triandis suggested an interesting alternative to this problem. His partial solution would be to "certify publishable" those papers that are good, but not good enough to compete for publication space, and to publish abstracts of them. Interested researchers could then write the authors for copies. The "certified publishable" endorsement would indicate to the academic community that these papers are worthy contributions to the cross-cultural effort, and thus should count when it comes to matters of promotion.

REPRESENTATIVENESS OF CULTURES INVESTIGATED

Students and others often ask, "What is cross-cultural psychology? What do cross-cultural psychologists do?" The stock answer is that cross-cultural psychology attempts to explain how cultural and ecological factors affect human behavior. If the seriously interested inquisitor probes deeper, the discussion will eventually center upon the universality or generalizability of psychological theory. Although the above simply-stated view is essentially correct in principle, the sad fact is that cross-cultural psychology in practice is not nearly so "universalistic" as we might imply.

Who does cross-cultural research, and why? Consider some evidence. According to my tabulations, some 367 researchers (of which many have published more than once in the. *Journal*) from about 40 countries have published research articles in *JCCP* during its six years of existence. These researchers have studied groups of people from at least 36 countries. Considering subgroups studied within these countries, perhaps as many as 75 clearly distinguishable cultural groups have been the focus of the research (very frequently different samples from the same groups). If we tabulated no further, this may look impressive, and in a sense it is. However, approximately 70 percent of research published in *JCCP* concerned cultural groups from the United States, India, Japan, Canada, Australia, and ten widely scattered African countries. More telling is the citizenship of the researchers themselves. The United States has accounted for 53 percent of all 367 authors. An additional 20 percent come from Israel, Canada, Australia, Hong Kong, India, England, and Switzerland. With the exception of India and perhaps of Israel, cross-cultural psychology is dominated by English-speaking psychologists from the affluent West. While this may not represent such a great inequity if Westerners are doing this research out of guilt for long-standing affluence or because they are fed up with an homogenized world-view of psychology, it is nevertheless a fact that should not go unheeded or unanalyzed. Much of the research is still being done during sabbatical leaves, in spite of the pungent and popular indictment of "sabbatical opportunism;" this springboard for research careers has bothered many people during the past few years.

Apparently little can be done about this "inequitable" state of affairs. The centers of research activity are where the money is, where the greatest number of psychologists are, and where seats of higher education are located. The latter are magnets for researchers and for that universal laboratory animal, the "college student." Nor is this rather bleak portrait of the universality problem necessarily an accurate reflection of its entire scope. We do have dozens of other journals, and surely the number of separate culture groups that have been studied would far exceed the figures given here. Nevertheless, it is doubtful that the figures given above for country-of-origin of cross-cultural researchers would significantly alter the imbalance caused by the predominance of researchers from the United States, Canada, and United Kingdom that has been evident for many years in cross-cultural psychology.

MANUSCRIPT-REVIEWING PROCEDURES

Most, if not all periodicals that publish cross-cultural material are refereed. That is, the skills of boards of consultants, or outside reviewers in many cases, are employed to evaluate submitted manuscripts and to make judgments as to their acceptability. *JCCP* makes every effort to send manuscripts to reviewers in the various disciplines covered who are familiar with both the cultures studied and the methods used in the offered paper. Other journals doubtlessly use variations of the same policy. If this tall order of triangulating discipline, culture and method can be met in the selection of reviewers, and often it cannot be, other obstacles can be encountered that can lead to equivocal and painful decisions.

For example, most cross-cultural researchers (a sizable pool of scholars from which reviewers are drawn) have research biases. Some are blinded by a methodological obsession. Many have such a high, and others such a low, opinion of factor analysis that, for instance, on this basis alone a study is either praised or punctured. Others are adamant in their willingness to accept only studies that clearly demonstrate actual behavioral manifestations of test, interview, or contrived laboratory data. It has been documented for at least a brief, recent two-year period that there is a strong tendency for reviewers to favor experimental cross-cultural research over the correlational variety.[11] There is a similar tendency to favor research dealing with "basic processes" such as learning, perception, or cognition, over studies that are within the broad province of personality. Indeed, three of the most potent recent books in cross-cultural psychology[10,12,13] are read more enthusiastically by more cross-cultural psychologists for *research reviews and ideas* than is read, for example, the important new and major treatment of culture and personality research.[14]

A general distrust exists in psychology of correlational research because of its alleged impotence in establishing cause-effect relationships. Ethnoscience studies dealing with personality variables have a history of being long on correlation and speculation and short on experimentation and empiricism. Thus, currently in cross-cultural psychology, any study that attempts to deal with "culture and personality," "national character," or "modal personality" without giving a liberal dose of empiricism will not receive very high priority in competition with those studies that have actually manipulated variables. Any one- or two-culture study in the domain of personality whose sole basis of comparison is the responses to one or two personality tests currently has a slim chance of being recommended for publication. There is no indication that this order of priorities will change, and maybe this is good.

If cross-cultural periodicals accepted for publication only those manuscripts that have been uncritically reviewed without allowing for revisions of any sort, what slim and sparse journals we would have. Psychological studies emanating from just one cultural setting (the usual type of report in psychology that implies nothing about comparisons across cultures) can be criticized on various levels. The three most vulnerable levels are theory and how it is interpreted, method as it relates to theory, and interpretation. In studies that include these levels plus the critical one dealing with culture, a veritable Pandora's box of criticism is opened. A geometric expansion of criticizable elements is evident, and this is where the referees go to work.

It is within this context that it may be beneficial to newcomers to the field of cross-cultural research to present a brief sketch of the "evaluation set" that top-level cross-cultural manuscript referees invoke in reading manuscripts. They let nothing escape their well trained eyes, nor should they. Time and again these people note the following and many other recurring flaws in manuscripts that are rejected (see References 11 and 15 for a broader treatment):

1. Samples are inadequate and generally unrepresentative of the populations investigated;
2. The study is too unicultural (e.g., United States minorities, with extrapolations to other cultures); if not too unicultural then it is viewed as too trivial;

3. Post hoc analyses and armchair speculations are rampant and unchecked, and little support for them is offered;
4. Ethnographic analysis and psychological/anthropological rationale are severely lacking;
5. Scant attention is given to previous work;
6. Tests or instruments used have little proven relevance, reliability, or validity within the context of the cultures examined;
7. Translation problems and general problems of equivalence of tasks have not been attended to.

From this *partial* list of possible criticisms, one could imagine how easy it might be for a well practiced cross-culturalist to cut and slash at any study submitted. However, lest the impression be unfortunately created that reviewers only offer scathing critiques, it must be stated in firm terms that this is not the case. *JCCP* consultants generally supplement their criticisms with ample suggestions concerning how subsequent research can be bettered, using the criticized research as a likely starting point. Indeed, the backbone of *JCCP* is the unselfishness of the Editorial Advisory Board and the unfaltering sound advice that they give to authors.

Are Journals for Researchers or Readers?

At the recent American Psychological Association convention in Chicago, a symposium designed for journal editors addressed the above question among others. Since this paper was prepared before that symposium took place, no comments can be made regarding how the question was answered. Certainly, however, the question begs the problem: Are journals designed so that researchers will have a medium through which to communicate among themselves? If they are also for the public benefit, which is the obvious compromise and diplomatic answer, how can a balance be reached so that respectably high scientific quality is not totally sacrificed in favor or readability by the general public?

Publications in the cross-cultural enterprise face this problem in spades. The problem here is compounded, paradoxically, by two general factors: First, the public's interest in cultural behavioral variations is high, and thus it seems possible to exploit this interest and aid in the reduction of cultural biases. This would generally be an educational function, informing large numbers of people about cultural matters as investigated by behavioral scientists. Many would hold that this is the only valid reason for cross-cultural research. The second factor is on the opposite end of the scale. That is, the tight cross-cultural inner circle (who are at once researchers and reviewers, in a sort of circular reification) is so anxious about sampling procedures, stimulus equivalence, literature review, levels of significance, and alternative hypotheses that the typical well-reviewed and revised study, when published, would draw yawns or bewilderment from those outside the guild. Methodological grandiosity and the study of serious, deep issues excite most of the cross-cultural in-group. This, of course, should and will continue. However, much of what is published in the name of "scientific building blocks" has very little immediate generalizability and understandability to the out-group. This out-group includes not only laypersons, but also academics and even many non-cross-culturalists within psychology if not in some quarters within anthropology.

It will take more efforts like Cole and Scribner's[10] and Witkin and Berry's[7] recently applauded works to transform a lot of esoteric complexity into some major, understandable issues susceptible to resolution. The scope of journals, we know, is correctly aligned with high-level professionalism. I am not suggesting that professional journals emulate *Psychology Today* (although that might not be a bad idea), but that they need not all be written in a code, as they often are, that the public cannot decipher. Again, I exhort readers to nominate areas of research in need of integrated review.

PROBLEMS POSED BY INCREASING PUBLICATION EXPENSES

The soaring price of paper and constantly escalating postal rates pose yet another problem that is easily overlooked by researchers. Running the risk once more of simple overgeneralization, the problem hits hardest those countries with less financial muscle. The more interesting groups to study, both theoretically and practically, are those in which are found those "naturally occurring behaviors and conditions" that are at a premium in cross-cultural work. This means, by and large, the study of individuals in countries that are still unfettered by creeping technology, which confounds clear interpretations. Technology means money, and journals cost money. It is thus a simple but deep problem: many individuals and libraries that should have the full range of journals, cross-cultural and otherwise, cannot afford them. There is a related problem. Since fewer manuscripts can be published from among the increasing numbers being submitted, the likely candidates to be rejected first are those sent in by psychologists in developing countries. This is so because, as mentioned earlier, most of our colleagues from these countries cannot compete with the finesse, and writing skills, and research supports of Euro-Americans.

JCCP has an ongoing modest policy to help correct this imbalance. Every one of the 23 issues published to date have been sent gratis to 75 institutional libraries. These libraries are all in developing countries, and exact locations have been published.[16] As one would quickly guess, these recipient libraries are predominantly in Africa, Asia, and South America. We may be financially able to increase this number in the near future. However, there have been few acknowledgments that these quarterly issues have even been received (and we all know of the strange tricks that the international mail system can play), and so we have no evidence that they all reach their destinations. More importantly, we have not one iota of evidence that they are put to their intended use. It would be of some interest, for a number of reasons, to know whether these journals are read avidly, as hoped, stimulating whatever it is that published cross-cultural research is supposed to stimulate. If they are merely collecting dust in the bush and barrio, we might suspect that it is pretentious, rather than magnanimous, of us to regard these gifts as marks of salvation. If services such as this work, more and similar efforts by various agencies should be made.

This is by no means a totally unique service, however. An assortment of publications are sent around the world gratis, and some in much larger numbers. Three organizations are so involved: The Educational Testing Service distributes its *Newsletter*, and has been doing so for some time. *Communique* is sent free of charge by the Intercultural Communications Network, University of Pittsburgh; and the East-West Center's Culture Learning Institute makes available to more than 3,000 interested persons and institutions its *Topics in Culture Learning*.

North American and Western European psychologists and journals could be of great help to colleagues in the less affluent countries. With little expense unused journals and books can be sent abroad. I recently mailed about 250 books to the University of Yucatan for less than $50.00, thanks to the help of a few colleagues. George Guthrie told me that in the past couple of years he has mailed 500 books at a cost of less than $200.00. On the shelves of every academic psychologist in the United States are dozens of valuable books that they will never use. These books could be put to immediate use in other countries. Journal publishers, at relatively little expense and maybe even as a tax write-off, could send journals to institutions in financially depressed areas. It is of special importance that researchers or their sponsors make certain that when research is done in, for example, the Philippines, abundant copies be sent to these countries so as to benefit their colleagues and their colleagues' countries.

Through an organization that is hard-core cross-cultural, like the International Association for Cross-Cultural Psychology or the Society for Cross-Cultural Research, perhaps enough ingenuity can be mustered to create an abstracting service. For massive free distribution, abstracts could be prepared with care and clarity, covering all current cross-cultural research reports. More than the 100-word, appetite-whetting abstracts that are typically available through assorted abstracting services, these synopses could be miniature versions of all the significant aspects of the study and could include sources where the full report could be found. Better yet, the abstracting organizations could provide copies of the full report upon request. In addition, continually updated bibliographies of research in substantive areas could be maintained for distribution upon request.

This is admittedly utopian thinking, for the price tag for such a clearinghouse service would be high, but not out of sight if several associations, foundations, and institutions would see the merit of such a plan. This miniature, primarily psychological, version of some of the functions of the Human Relations Area Files could be a major advance in the cross-cultural arena. Its successful implementation would greatly ease a major problem in the dissemination of cross-cultural research data, and could be an important way to enhance and improve research efforts. The growing family of cross-cultural researchers may now be large enough to reduce such heretofore utopian thinking to the level of practicality and need.

ACKNOWLEDGMENTS

I wish to thank several colleagues, all associated with the *Journal of Cross-Cultural Psychology* as well as other publications, for their helpful comments and mutual concern about the problems raised in this paper. They are: J. W. Berry, R. W. Brislin, L. W. Doob, J. G. Draguns, H. G. Gough, G. M. Guthrie, and H. C. Triandis. Many of their suggestions are incorporated in this paper; however, several are not, owing to space limitations. I, of course, assume full responsibility for its content.

REFERENCES

1. MURPHY, G. 1969. Psychology in the year 2000. Am. Psychol. 24(5): 523–530.
2. BERRY, J. W., W. J. LONNER, & J. LEROUX. 1973. Directory of Cross-Cultural Research and Researchers. Department of Psychology, Western Washington State College, Bellingham, Wash.

3. MURDOCK, G. P. 1969. Outline of World Cultures, 3rd ed. (revised). HRAF Press. New Haven, Conn.
4. MILLER, R. J. 1973. Cross-cultural research in the perception of pictorial materials. Psychol. Bull. 80(2): 135–150.
5. DASEN, P. R. 1972. Cross-cultural Piagetian research: A summary. J. Cross-Cultural Psychol. 3(1): 23–39.
6. DRAGUNS, J. G. 1973. Comparisons of psychopathology across cultures: Issues, findings, directions. J. Cross-Cultural Psychol. 4(1): 9–47.
7. WITKIN, H. A. & J. W. BERRY. 1975. Psychological differentiation in cross-cultural perspective. J. Cross-Cultural Psychol. 6(1): 4–87.
8. TRIANDIS, H. C., Ed. Handbook of Cross-Cultural Psychology. Allyn and Bacon. Boston, Mass. In press.
9. NEWMAN, E. 1974. Strictly Speaking. Bobbs-Merrill. Indianapolis, Ind.
10. COLE, M. & S. SCRIBNER. 1974. Culture and Thought: A Psychological Introduction. John Wiley & Sons, Inc. New York, N.Y.
11. LONNER, W. J. 1975. An analysis of the prepublication evaluation of cross-cultural manuscripts: Implications for future research. In Cross-Cultural Perspectives on Learning. R. Brislin, S. Bochner, & W. Lonner, Eds. Sage/Halsted. Beverly Hills, Calif.
12. BERRY, J. W. & P. R. DASEN, Eds. 1974. Culture and Cognition: Readings in Cross-Cultural Psychology. Methuen. London, England.
13. LLOYD, B. B. 1972. Perception and Cognition: A Cross-Cultural Perspective. Penguin Books. Baltimore, Md.
14. LeVINE, R. A. 1973. Culture, Behavior and Personality. Aldine Publishing Co. Chicago, Ill.
15. BRISLIN, R. W. & W. J. LONNER. 1974. Methodological Approaches to Cross-Cultural Research. In Readings in Cross-Cultural Psychology: Proceedings of the Inaugural Meeting of the International Association for Cross-Cultural Psychology. J. Dawson and W. Lonner, Eds. Libra Press. Hong Kong, China.
16. Editor's note. 1973. J. Cross-Cultural Psychol. 4 (4): 394–396.

ON SOME METHODOLOGICAL ISSUES
IN CROSS-CULTURAL PSYCHOLOGY

Discussant: Carol R. Ember

Department of Anthropology
Hunter College of the City University of New York
New York, New York 10021

The papers in this section raised a number of methodological issues that should be considered in designing a cross-cultural field study. Wagatsuma and Guthrie have called attention to the need to adapt measuring instruments, particularly psychological ones, to the particular cultural context of the study. In particular, Wagatsuma reminds us that semantic differences between languages require more than simple translations to ensure comparability. And Guthrie suggests that a measuring instrument should not be simply transferred to a new cultural context, but should be redesigned to fit the new context in much the same manner the instrument was designed in the first place. If at all possible, I suggest that such redesigning should involve the help of not simply a translator, but a local person who is interested in social science research. In many countries this procedure is quite possible. Brislin has raised the question of what research does for the people studied. I think that Brislin suggests a good way to meet this ethical problem when he urges collaboration with local researchers. The researcher from outside would undoubtedly benefit by adapting his measuring instruments to the new cultural context, and the local researcher might learn about new kinds of research. An example of such a collaborative effort is the research done under the auspices of the Child Development Research Unit at University College of Nairobi, where Americans have worked with Kenyans.

The suggestions just discussed relate to how we can improve a field study in a new cultural context. However, even if such a study is designed as suggested, there is still the major problem that such a study, no matter how well designed, is only a study of one cultural case. The main purpose of a study in a new cultural context is often to see if principles which work in our cultural context work in others. But, in fact, what can one legitimately conclude from one new case? If the results are different from what obtained in this country, it could be because the new case happens to be a rare exception. Or, as Finifter has pointed out, methodological differences may falsely produce differences. If the results are similar to what obtained in this country, there is still the possibility that many if not most societies would provide different results. While it is easy to say that this is a serious methodological problem for researchers who work in other cultural contexts, it is not so easy to think of practical solutions to this problem. Field studies cost a lot of time and effort; and they have to be undertaken if no one has previously measured the variables of interest, which is often the case with psychological or attitudinal variables. The question then is: Can anything be done to increase the number of cases under consideration in order to enable a statistical test of a hypothesis and, at the same time, save on field expenses and time?

Guthrie and Sechrest suggest that we build culture into the research design. So, for example, in a comparison of Filipinos and Americans, one could test for the main effect of cultural difference and also for the interaction between culture and some experimental manipulation. But perhaps more can be done than that. Cross-cultural anthropologists do not treat culture as an independent variable, as psychologists may. We try to ask what particular aspect of life might account for a particular phenomenon. Díaz-Guerrero in a sense asked such a question. If a researcher has an idea of exactly what about the culture, or what about the physical or social environment, might be the critical factor in accounting for a difference in perception, cognition, or some aspect of performance, then it is possible to use individual variation within a society to help explain cultural differences, as Sechrest also suggests. For example, in an analysis of data from the Six Cultures Project, Beatrice and John Whiting found that children in three of those cultures were on the average more nurturant in their social behavior than children in the other three cultures (Beatrice B. and John W. M. Whiting, *Children of Six Cultures*, 1975). They thought that the difference might be due to the differential time children spent on chores in the two clusters of cultures — the more chores, the more likely nurturant behavior would be exhibited. The two clusters of cultures did seem to differ on the assignment of chores to children, and in fact the rank-order of the cultures on chores assigned to children corresponded exactly to the rank-order of the cultures on degree of nurturant behavior exhibited by children. But the Whitings were able to say more than that, because they also had individual data on each child for both chores and social behavior. So they then looked to see if the two sets of data were positively correlated across individuals in each of the six cultures. The results were consistent with the cross-cultural differences. Although one cannot always infer from individual to group differences, the fact that, in this case, the individual and cultural analyses parallel each other supports the notion that it may be the differences in chore-assignment between cultures that account for the differences in social behavior between children of those cultures. Almost any field study could similarly build in an analysis of individual differences which would parallel the hypothesized cultural differences without a great deal more expenditure of time and effort.

There is another way to increase the number of cases employed in a cross-cultural psychological study, and that is to use the strategy more often employed by cross-cultural researchers in anthropology. The usual kind of cross-cultural study in anthropology utilizes a world-wide sample of societies. In a way we are fortunate, because we rely on ethnographic data already collected and so we can have a large enough sample to test our hypotheses statistically with a minimum of time spent on data-collection. Psychologists probably feel that, because the data they would ideally like have not previously been collected, they must collect the data themselves. But I wonder if ethnographic data couldn't be used more often by psychologists. For example, one could measure psychological variables on the basis of projective cultural materials such as folktales, myths, religious beliefs, art, and music. This strategy was often used in the recent past and maybe it is appropriate to revive it. If such cultural materials can be used to measure motives, preoccupations, and cognitive interests of a group of people, then they might be used in at least preliminary tests of hypotheses relating cultural variation to psychological variables.

In summary, the methodological problems of cross-cultural psychology seem to involve the competing demands of trying to ensure validity by "seeing the people" in a field study, and trying to establish the generalizability of results across cultures. A field study may maximize the former, but severely limits the latter. A cross-cultural study of the anthropological variety suffers in some eyes from the validity problem, but it does offer the greatest potential for generalizability. This paradox is likely to plague us all forever. Perhaps the only solution for us is to acknowledge that paradox, and then do the best we can.

HOW CROSS-CULTURAL RESEARCHERS RELATE
TO THEIR PROFESSIONS

Discussant: Melvin Ember

Department of Anthropology
Hunter College of the City University of New York
New York, New York 10021

In my comments here, I should like to address myself to how cross-cultural researchers relate to their respective professions. Although I focus here on cross-cultural psychology as compared with cross-cultural anthropology, my remarks may also be relevant to how cross-cultural sociologists and political scientists relate to their respective professions.

As a cross-cultural anthropologist, what strikes me most about research in cross-cultural psychology is that the battles within that discipline seem to be different from the battles in anthropology. Most members of my discipline still do not believe that it is possible to arrive at general explanations of cultural variation, and so we, who do believe it is possible, encounter incredulity and even rejection. Most cultural anthropologists are still preoccupied with the description and clinical analysis of a particular community, culture, or (at most) local region. Those who wish to do more, to test explanations or discover relationships that are generalizable to all societies, are often accused of distorting ethnographic reality, wrenching cultural data out of their contexts, ignoring supposedly critical variables, and invoking a system of magical principles called inferential statistics to claim a false true-value for general explanations. In short, the battles in anthropology have to do with the legitimacy of doing science in cultural anthropology. It seems that the battles of cross-cultural psychologists are entirely different. For them, and I envy them for it, science is legitimate. But their battles are with those in psychology who think on the basis of their own research (proverbially on sophomores and rats) that they already have general explanations of behavior. That is, cross-cultural psychologists are suggesting that psychology may not know that much about human behavior, that the psychological principles and laws often taken for granted may not work in other cultural contexts or may work only under certain cultural conditions. For cross-cultural anthropologists, the concern is to discover which particular explanations (ethnographically derived or not) work generally; for cross-cultural psychologists the concern is to discover which presumably general explanations work particularly.

Even though our battles seem to be different, we do share a similar preoccupation, namely, with methodology. Every meeting we have had of the Society for Cross-Cultural Research, and this conference too, has devoted at least one session to issues of methodology. Why is this so? No doubt some of this preoccupation is appropriate. Every new field of research confronts new problems requiring new techniques of data-collection and analysis. But I wonder if some of our preoccupation with methodology is a defensive response to our insecurity as a minority in our respective professions. That insecurity may be understandable, but I doubt that it is very productive. Aside from agreement about certain very general methodological principles (for example, the need for culturally appropriate measuring instruments), we don't have to agree on all methodological issues. Indeed, it doesn't seem to be very productive to talk about methodology in the abstract, independent of particular research problems.

217

As Guthrie has suggested, the particular problem we investigate should mostly influence exactly how we collect our data.

Perhaps then we are so preoccupied with methodology because we hope that our concern will somehow legitimize our results in the eyes of our skeptics. However, the people who are skeptical probably are so because what we do or hope to achieve threatens their own majority status and security. In anthropology, for example, the ethnographer (who functions very much like a clinician except that he or she hardly ever makes the people studied any better) may feel threatened by the possibility that his or her life's work could find its way into an exceptional cell of a contingency table. Even if a person's life-work should turn out to fit some general relationship, it becomes just another sample case. In psychology, the researcher who has spent years documenting a particular relationship in his "territory" may be similarly threatened by a cross-cultural psychologist who finds that the relationship does not obtain elsewhere. Will our colleagues be convinced of our legitimacy if we try to assure them that we are careful methodologists? I think not, and it may be that such a methodological display makes things even worse for us. After all, a more careful methodology is more likely to yield reliable and valid results, and such results may more convincingly contradict the conventional wisdom.

Would anything convince the skeptic? Perhaps nothing in the short run. But in the long run I think we would all agree that evidence cannot be put down forever. Thus, I guess the moral of my story here is that if we stop worrying and keep doing our research, the skeptics will have more and more to contend with, so that eventually they will not find it so easy to deny the legitimacy and even desirability of cross-cultural research.

OPEN DISCUSSION: II

DR. TOBACH: I find implicit in this session the following assumption: Cross-cultural research, by describing universals, gives us information about genetic processes and behavior. Am I correct in understanding that the panel supports that assumption?

I must disagree with this assumption. The similarities of behavior in different cultures are the products of species-typical developmental experiences. Genes function on the biochemical level within a biochemical milieu. Developmental geneticists have expressed this concept clearly, both in their experimental work and in their conceptualization of genetic processes. The many levels of organization intervening between such biochemical phenomena and behavioral phenomena make it impossible to pose scientifically valid and answerable questions about *genetic* function by comparative studies of *behavior* in different cultures. The emphasis placed by Díaz-Guerrero and Wagatsuma on language as an important aspect of cultural differences is sound, particularly if one accepts the concept that human behavior cannot be studied without involving those characteristics that are particularly human.

DR. LEE SECHREST: Dr. Tobach's comments on the possibility of discovering something about genetic processes by cross-cultural research is interesting and provocative. My answer is not particularly definitive; I just want to call something to the attention of the audience. However, I have a slight disagreement with Dr. Tobach; it seems improbable to me that we will get detailed information on the relationship between genetics and specific behaviors from cross-cultural studies. But I do think that cross-cultural studies may help at a more molar level to determine that the two assess the probability that various behaviors and social patterns have a genetic basis. Discovering the nature of that basis and pinning down the answer is something else again.

DR. TOBACH: Dr. Finifter, given the continuous changes in society, would you suggest any special caveats for replication, in terms of design and instrumentation rather than in terms of statistical treatment of data? Should research proposals always include replication provisions?

DR. BERNARD FINIFTER: To respond briefly to your first question, let me suggest the general proposition that the faster the rate of social and cultural change, the greater are potential threats to the robustness of past empirical findings and conclusions, and the more urgent is the need for updating replication studies. What is needed is a set of criteria for deciding on which previous research is to be given priority in systematic replication programs. Preliminary proposals along these lines have been suggested by Duncan* and Krause† ‡ and several "classic" studies have been recently updated. The interpretation of results obtained from such studies can be greatly facilitated when the follow-up researcher faithfully reconstructs and reapplies the same instruments that were used to collect and analyze data in the earlier study, even

---

* DUNCAN, O. D. 1969. Toward Social Reporting: Next Steps. Russell Sage Foundation. New York, N.Y.

† KRAUSE, M. S. 1967. Proving causal propositions: The foundations of program and experiment design. *In* Multivariate Behavioral Research. **2**: 349–376.

‡ KRAUSE, M. S. 1971. Corroborative results and subsequent research commitments. J. Gen. Psychol. **84**(2): 219–277.

though other, perhaps superior, instruments are currently available and are used collaterally. Furthermore, collaborative efforts to develop standardized measures and instruments will increase opportunities for meaningful comparisons across studies. Elsewhere § I have argued that statistical significance tests are often poor substitutes for the evidence we need as a basis for placing confidence in research results and conclusions, and that programmatic replications can provide more satisfactory information for such purposes.

I find it difficult to argue with the implication of your second question: I strongly urge that replication studies be incorporated into research proposals in order to anticipate and respond to as many plausible rival hypotheses as possible. Research funding agencies should encourage applicants to budget for a wide range of relevant-replication studies in the form of "embedded experiment" designs, as discussed in the present paper, and "random subsample replications" § as well as independent follow-up studies. Periodically over the past few years various writers have expressed their discontent over the shoddy condition of most behavioral and social research by proposing that journal editors reject manuscripts that do not provide results of replication tests of their initial findings.‖ I suspect that a major reason why more research is not replicated is that reviewers of proposals are inadequately sensitized to the importance of designing replication tests into research plans from the beginning. Perhaps the emphasis placed on incorporating and exploiting replication tests can serve as one indicator of the maturity of our science.

DR. TOBACH: I think that such replication should be required. I also think that some of Dr. Brislin's and Dr. Lonner's suggestions should be incorporated in all applications so that scientists who use humans as subjects can fulfill their ethical and social responsibilities to their human sources of knowledge.

---

§ FINIFTER, B. M. 1972. The generation of confidence: Evaluating research findings by random subsample replication. In Sociological Methodology 1972. H. Costner, Ed.: 114–177. Jossey-Bass. San Francisco; Calif.

‖ WALSTER, G. W. & T. A. CLEARLY. 1970. A proposal for a new editorial policy in the social sciences. Am. Statistician 24(2): 16–19.

PART III. SPECIAL ASPECTS OF CROSS-CULTURAL RESEARCH

AN INTENSIVE "TRIANGULAR" STUDY (JAPAN – USA – EUROPE) OF SOCIO-PSYCHOLOGICAL VARIABLES

Helmut Morsbach

Department of Psychology
University of Glasgow
Glasgow, Scotland

All Conference participants are likely to agree that cross-cultural research in social psychology is of intrinsic value. I think that it is especially interesting and important to study Japan in this way. In my paper I would therefore like to discuss the following points: First of all, what the German author Krusche[1] calls the "fundamental otherness" (*konkrete Fremde*) of Japan. Secondly, attempts to get a little closer to a comprehension of Japanese socio-psychological variables by a "triangular" approach; i.e. by also looking at Continental (especially German) writings on the topic of Japan. In this context I will suggest the usefulness of the concept "dialectic hermeneutics," as described by the German sociologist Juergen Habermas,[2] and finally, I will propose that research methods adopted from Human Ethology may be of help in obtaining a better understanding, since these might more easily facilitate a true dialogue between members of the various cultures who will be able to critically assess the results from their respective viewpoints.

Unlike the overwhelming majority of Oriental countries, Japan has never been a Western colony, and until 1945, was never defeated once in its long history. Furthermore, it is to date the first (and only) non-Western country to have achieved a very high degree of industrialization. Western values never had to be taken over *en bloc*, but entered the country selectively, so that one could speak of an "osmotic process."

Because of its industrialized state, Japan is being increasingly lumped together with "the West" in writings dealing, e.g. with world economics, and this "block" is then contrasted with the rest of the world. Unfortunately, it is implicitly assumed that, in parallel with this economic similarity, the attitudes, motives, behavior etc. of "the Japanese" are basically the same as those of Westerners; or, if not, will converge in time. However, Bennett[3] points out that over the last century, Japan has worked toward rapid technological and institutional change, but was able to control or deliberately retard social change. Change in Japan has largely been carried out from above, by the Samurai and their leaders during the Meiji period (1868–1912) and by the American Occupation forces following World War II. There has been a tendency to consider the Japanese system of social relations as a vehicle for action toward change, but *not* as the object of change itself. Japan has thus been able to modernize by making use of traditional, non-Western social and psychological factors. Caudill[4] remarked,

> I believe that ... position in modern social structure and continuity of historical culture exerts a relatively independent influence on human behavior, and that *both* dimensions need to be considered simultaneously in the investigation of the psychological characteristics of a people.
> There is a tendency in scientific writing to blur the distinction between social

221

and cultural dimensions of behavior by such terms as "sociocultural", or by subsuming one dimension under the other or by simply ignoring one dimension. My position is to stress the relative separateness of these two dimensions of human life: considerable change can take place in the social dimension with the result that several countries do come to be alike in important ways; yet in the cultural dimension, characteristics persist which keep each country quite distinctive.

In spite of the relative ease with which an affluent person can visit Japan since 1945, and in spite of the daily contact which every one of us has with one or another product of Japanese industry, the socio-psychological variables underlying Japanese behavior are frequently seen as "mysterious" and are largely misunderstood. Why should this be so? Krusche[5] has argued that Europe's relationship, and that of the U.S. (hereafter called "the West") with non-Western cultures is still determined by the colonialist epoch which evaluates the strange cultures not on their own terms, but in comparison with unquestioned Western standards. Inevitably, this leads in many aspects to the devaluation of the other cultures as being "less than" one's own.

Most Westerners (including many social scientists) believe themselves to be in possession of the true knowledge of what constitutes "general human nature." The suspicion is repressed that "general human nature" might be nothing but the idealized projection by the West of itself. This tendency to see the world in Western terms could mainly be due to the efficient way in which the West conquered nature (and other nations) by scientific and technological means. Industrialization and Westernization are seen as closely linked, and a non-Western alternative to rapid industrialization cannot be conceived of. Technology applied in Japan is thus "obviously" seen as leading to a type of social interaction resembling that of the West.

Krusche maintains that there is yet another, more subtle form in which the need to "assimilate" that which is foreign manifests itself: The typical Western urge to go to the remotest regions of the world in order to find oneself! If metaphysical needs dominate, one embarks on a pilgrimage to one's Guru in the Himalayas or to seek Zen, not only as a form of self-training, but as a way of salvation.

Japan has always been a goal of Western yearning for strangeness, or "otherness." But in the Western-centered worldview this "otherness" was not left alone, was not seen as a historical alternative to the West, but attempts were made to incorporate it into a kind a Western "province." Such an engagement with Japan was therefore a comparison, with "the West" as a baseline, and with Western values as the indubitably "correct" ones.

It is only recently that Westerners have been forced to admit that a new center of the world is emerging in Japan, one which is relatively independent of the "natural" center Europe/United States. (The same realization happens to be coming about in the case of China, but here the argument can still be used that it is "not yet fully industrialized"). We are confronted here with a "historical otherness" which is "resistant" to the West. It is thus becoming increasingly necessary to aim at a *new* understanding of this cultural-historical distance and *new* attempts to bridge it if fundamental misunderstanding is not to remain the dominant result of meetings with Japan.

Could it be that the paradox of social "uniqueness" and technological "sameness" is possibly due to the special forms of human interaction developed in Japan? These are based on a highly consistent set of rules, developed over more than a thousand years, and largely uninfluenced by the West. The writings of Nakane[6] have highlighted certain unique aspects of Japanese society, and some major factors are the following:

1. From early times onwards, Japan has developed a *unitary* social structure, based on homogeneity of food production (rice), religion (a symbiosis of Shinto and Buddhism), language, ethics (Confucianism), and government.

2. There is an extraordinary *continuity* in the history of the Japanese cultural tradition, symbolized by the Emperor system.[7] In Japanese popular mythology (and in its official history until 1945), the ruling Emperor is regarded as being the direct descendent of the first Emperor, Jimmu Tenno, who is said to have ascended the throne in 660 B.C.; i.e., representing an *unbroken* line of rulers for over 1600 years.

3. Life on the Japanese islands has necessarily been one of great density, enforcing a high degree of *standardization* and *ritualization* concerning interpersonal relations, expressed, e.g., in special forms of nonverbal communication.[8]

4. *Isolation* of the islands and the successful exclusion of foreign powers allowed for all potentially harmful foreign powers to be kept at bay, which led to a consciousness of being *unique* and *incomparable*; even a mysterious feeling of being a *"chosen people."*

This isolation of Japan is the reason why its "fundamental otherness" was (and is) experienced so drastically by the rest of the world. There is no other example in world history where such a complex culture could keep itself so utterly apart from the rest of the world for such a long time (i.e. between about 1600 and 1860). This "fundamental otherness" is troublesome to the Westerners who think in ethnocentric terms, who are unwilling or unable to engage in a true dialogue with Japanese as equal partners. In any case, attempts at such a dialogue can rarely be carried out by using the Japanese language in equal parts with English.

Since the "otherness" is seen as relative to one's own cultural baseline, some travellers easily and uncritically romanticize certain aspects of Japan (e.g., Zen), while others show acute embarrassment when they interpret Japanese society in terms of their own and find it horrifying.[9]

From our Western vantage point we are often unaware of fundamental aspects influencing Japanese behavior. This could be so for several reasons: Apart from plain indifference or ignorance, it could be our inability to investigate certain aspects of the other culture because a certain constellation of problems does not exist in our own, or it has a different meaning. Excellent examples are provided in the paper by Wagatsuma[10] on "Problems of language in cross-cultural research," where he found that several US questionnaires (e.g. the Adjective Check List and the California Personality Inventory) lost their validity when given in Japan. For these, and other Western tests "culturally equivalent" translations seem impossible (a) because of fundamental problems of translation, and (b) because the test itself is based on Western presuppositions.

To complicate matters, social scientists interested in cross-cultural research have to additionally consider the rather strictly defined role of "the foreign professor" while working in Japan. Anyone who has been in Japan as a high-status visitor (e.g., as conference delegate) can testify that his/her treatment as "special person" or "honorable visitor" has been qualitatively different from that in other countries. This will naturally color the response by Japanese subjects to interrogations and questionnaire studies carried out by foreigners.

Because of many historical factors the ambivalence that most Japanese feel towards Westerners – feelings of inferiority alternating (or interwined with) those of superiority – make it difficult to establish a true dialogue in a spirit of equality and partnership.

This different behavior of Japanese in, e.g. the testing situation, often leads to results with low validity. In the West (especially the US) it is usually taken for granted that behavior in the testing situation is more or less the same as in "real life." However, Harré and Secord[11] warn that it is a myth to think that there must be a one-to-one correspondence between social and biological selves. This assumption, they argue, is not based on observation, but on our conceptions of moral responsibility and our religious theory of the soul. However, one should not presuppose that there will be only one consistent set of rules in use all the time by each biological individual.

Naturally, this discrepancy can be (and usually is) far more striking in Japan, where religious beliefs do not insist on a "unified self" as ideal, and where Confucian ethics demand far greater subjugation to the hierarchically structured norms and goals of reference groups – groups which can change according to circumstances. What this basically amounts to is a Western tendency to think in terms of the dichotomy "either A *or* B" (mutually exclusive), although there might be a tendency in Japan to think more in terms of "*both* A *and* B" (depending on circumstances, e.g. the role one is forced to play at a given moment).

If this role-specific self-presentation is noticed by Westerners, the Japanese are quickly labeled as "inconsistent," or, at its most derogatory, as "schizophrenic" or "suffering from a split personality." An example is the "incomprehensible" behavior shown by the relatively small number of Japanese soldiers who were captured alive by the Allies during World War II. Since they had not been specifically instructed to behave in a certain way in the role of POW (their only inculcated aim having been to win or to die fighting), they were frequently willing to cooperate fully with the Allies, divulging everything they knew about their own units. Some even flew along with Allied spotter planes to point out their old units' positions.

Such deep-rooted personality differences have far-reaching implications concerning the study of socio-psychological variables in Japan. One striking example concerns the outcome of Asch-type conformity experiments, conducted in Japan by Frager,[12] who found an unexpectedly high degree of *anti*-conformity among his subjects. This is contrary to "reasonable" expectations which would predict that the Japanese Ss., on the whole, would be more conformist than Western Ss. It may be that the experimental laboratory setting and the Western idea of what constitutes a "reference group" was so unusual for the Japanese Ss. that many purposely gave a *hantai* (i.e. obstinate) response. Further research as to why their behavior should be so is urgently needed.

Most studies concerning socio-psychological variables of Japan in a cross-cultural setting have been done by social scientists in the U.S., who hold their own unquestioned beliefs[13] concerning what is important to look for and what isn't. It may therefore be profitable to look at the European Continent for fresh ideas. This might lead to "triangular" studies which allow one's own blind spots to be perceived more easily. In strong contrast to Japan, Anglo-American culture is in many ways similar to Continental culture (e.g., both share basic Christian unquestioned beliefs, which the Japanese do not), but there is still sufficient divergency to make for an interesting reciprocal comparison. For example,

Japanese surface politeness in face-to-face interaction may be somewhat closer to the British ideal of "gentlemanly" behavior (e.g., talking about the weather to avoid getting too personal), while the strong emphasis on hierarchy in the Japanese might to some extent find a parallel in behavior between German superiors and subordinates.

In this difficult field of cross-cultural comparison, the concept of *hermeneutics* might be useful, of which the German philosopher Dilthey[14] remarked, "Interpretation would be impossible if the expressions of life were totally alien. It would be unnecessary if there were nothing alien in them. Hermeneutics thus lies between these two extreme opposites. It is required when ever there is something alien that the art of understanding has to assimilate."

The use of hermeneutics in a dialectic way has been proposed by Habermas[2] who wrote,

> ... objectivity of understanding is possible only within the role of the reflected partner in a communication structure.
>
> Whether dealing with contemporary objectivations or historical traditions, the interpreter cannot abstractly free himself from his hermeneutic point of departure. He cannot simply jump over the open horizon of his own life activity and just suspend the context of tradition in which his own subjectivity has been formed in order to submerge himself in a subhistorical stream of life that allows the pleasurable identification of everyone with everyone else. Nevertheless, hermeneutic understanding can arrive at objectivity to the extent that the understanding subject learns, through the communicative appropriation of alien objectivations, to comprehend itself in its own self-formative process. An interpretation can only grasp its object and penetrate it in a relation in which the interpreter reflects on the object and himself *at the same time* as moments of objective structure that likewise encompasses both and makes them possible.

The major problem therefore seems not to be a lack of research money or zeal in cross-cultural testing, but a Western disinterestedness in one's own subjectivity plus the failure to seek for real cooperation with an equal partner in the other culture (in this case Japan), so as to get deeper than the misleading questionnaire-type approach.

Harré and Secord[11] remind us that socio-psychological studies are usually on what people *say* they will do in a hypothetical situation; but urge that instead, more emphasis be placed on the *rules* governing their behavior. Apart from open-minded listening to one's partner(s) in the other culture, a promising approach seems possible through application of human ethological study methods. Here, filming of culturally comparable social interaction settings over a long period of time (e.g., filming of free play sessions in Japanese and in Western playschools) may allow social scientists of the relevant cultures (plus others) to give their own interpretation of the perceived events and their interpretation of the underlying factors. The film material could be viewed (a) completely independently, and (b) as often as one desires. With such a method, a better understanding of the other culture, as well as a realization of one's own previously unquestioned presuppositions might be facilitated.

As Krusche[15] pointed out, such an involvement with Japan (more than with most other non-Western countries) can help us to become aware of the difficulties in experiencing a "fundamentally other" culture, to reduce our blinkered "know-it-all" attitude and to work towards greater partnership in cross-cultural research.

REFERENCES

1. KRUSCHE, D. 1973. Japan – konkrete Fremde. Eine Kritik der Modalitaeten europaeischer Erfahrung von Fremde. Meta Verlag. Munich, Germany.
2. HABERMAS, J. 1972. Knowledge and Human Interests. Heinemann. London, England.
3. BENNETT, J. 1968. Tradition, modernity, and communalism in Japan's modernization. *In* Tradition and Modernity: Conflict of Congruence. J. Gusfield, Ed. Entire issue of Journal of Social Issues, 24: 25–64.
4. CAUDILL, W. 1973. The influence of social structure and culture on human behavior in modern Japan. Ethos, 1: 343–382.
5. KRUSCHE, D. 1974. Formen japanischer Mitmenschlichkeit – Erster Teil. Wirklichkeit und Wahrheit. Heft 4: 257–267.
6. NAKANE, C. 1970. Japanese Society. Weidenfeld and Nicholson. London, England.
7. HALL, J. W. 1965. The historical dimension. *In* Twelve Doors to Japan. J. W. Hall & R. K. Beardsley, Eds. McGraw-Hill. New York, N.Y. Chap. 3: 122–184.
8. MORSBACH, H. 1973. Aspects of nonverbal communication in Japan. J. Nervous Mental Disease. 157 (4): 262–277.
9. KOESTLER, A. 1960. The Lotus and the Robot. Hutchinson. London, England.
10. WAGATSUMA, H. 1975. Problems of language in cross-cultural research. This monograph.
11. HARRÉ, R. & P. F. SECORD. 1972. The Explanation of Social Behaviour. Basil Blackwell. Oxford, England.
12. FRAGER, R. 1970. Conformity and anticonformity in Japan. J. Personal. Soc. Psychol. 15: 203–210.
13. HOFSTAETTER, P. R. 1973. Einfuehrung in die Sozialpsychologie. Kroener Verlag. Stuttgart, Germany.
14. DILTHEY, W. 1913. Gesammelte Schriften. Vol. 1. *In* Knowledge and Human Interests. J. Habermas. Heinemann. London. 1972.
15. KRUSCHE, D. 1975. Erfahrung von Fremde als Erfahrung von Geschichte. Unpublished typescript.

THE "FRUIT-TREE EXPERIMENT" AS A CROSS-CULTURAL MEASURE OF THE VARIATIONS IN CHILDREN'S DRAWINGS DUE TO REGIONAL DIFFERENCES

Leonore Loeb Adler*

Department of Psychology
Adelphi University
Garden City, New York, N.Y. 11530

Beverly S. Adler†

Department of Psychology
Queens College of the City University of New York
Flushing, New York, N.Y. 11367

INTRODUCTION

The study of children's drawings has been a standard technique not only with "primitive children,"[1] but also in the practice of clinical psychology, when it was desirable to eliminate the language barrier and gain access to nonverbal patterns of behavior. Dennis found that children's drawings were useful for the investigations of group values,[2] intellectual functioning and degrees of Westernization.[3] However, no specific information was available about the process that prompted children to respond with a specific picture.

In previous cross-cultural "fruit-tree experiments,"[4-6] Adler found that when children were asked to "Draw a picture – any scene – with a fruit tree in it," the majority of the children responded with a graphical representation of an apple tree. This was so, even in tropical countries where no apple trees grow, such as Zaïre (formerly known as the Congo) in Africa, and the Netherland Antilles in the Carribean. And it was also true for such arctic locations as Greenland where no fruit trees grow at all.

The results of the children's drawings gave rise to such suggested explanations as the effect of: one, the alphabet; and two, the Bible. In the English and German languages the first letter of the alphabet, "A", is usually introduced to schoolchildren with a picture of an apple. In Latin languages, however, such as in Zaïre, where French is spoken, the apple is translated as *pomme*; and "P" comes in the middle of the alphabet. While it was also proposed that the Bible story of Adam and Eve, traditionally pictured with an apple, exerted an influence on the children, the Pidgin English editions of the Bible circulated in Zaïre featured the native mango or orange as the forbidden fruit.[5]

In a test–retest procedure, the reliability of the results was studied.[6] Seven countries (Argentina, Australia [Fullabo Tribe], Chile, Germany, Greenland, Peru, and the USA) participated in this study and the same children were retested either one month or after three to four months' intervals. While the

---

* Currently also affiliated with The College of Staten Island of the City University of New York.
† Currently an undergraduate student in the Department of Psychology.

highest ranking response of apple trees remained stable, regardless of length of time interval, more than one third of the subjects – 178 out of 465 children – repeated the same fruit-tree variety. Of these, more than half ($n = 103$) pictured apple trees both times.

It had been suggested previously by some teachers that the time of the year, such as harvest time, would influence the responses. However, the results of the retest, especially those with three or four months delay, did not bear out this assumption.

In order to attain a simple measure of the importance of language on the perception of bilingual Aboriginal children in Central Australia, Cawte and Kiloh[7] and Cawte[8] used the fruit-tree study. On hand of the children's drawings, they compared the effects of the introduced Western cultural environment with that of the native environment. They used a counterbalanced procedure, where the sequence of the instructions in the vernacular and in the English language was alternated after a three-day interval. The results showed that when the children were asked in English they drew pictures with "introduced fruit trees," the highest ranking variety being apple trees. However, when the children were instructed in their native language their first preference was the bush banana, an indigenous shrub-like tree which has edible leaves and green, somewhat banana-shaped fruits.

A similar "fruit-tree study" in New Britain by Veness and Hoskin[9] tested the effect of language on the association processes. The results showed that *pineapples* were consistently associated with *apples* in the drawings by the children, that they were similar to those obtained in Central Australia. The investigators concluded that: "English and Tolar or Walbiri are languages that subserve vastly different and contrasting realities. In such transcultural circumstances it might be reasonable to conclude, on the basis of the fruit-tree experiment, that trains of association set in motion by a stimulus in one language will differ from those set in motion by a stimulus in the other . . . The 'fruit-tree experiment' appears to provide a convenient practical measure of this effect in a given transcultural situation."

These studies with bilingual children gave rise to the question: Can a new stimulus in a monolingual situation also set a new train of association in motion? Two successive fruit-tree experiments in the USA were undertaken to find an answer to this query. The first study dealt with normal public school children[10,11] and in the second investigation emotionally disturbed children, whose IQs were from dull normal to borderline, were tested. They resided in a private residential treatment center; the school they attended was part of the city's educational system.[12] In both experiments the effects of a brief, one-time exposure to a short unfamiliar story were analyzed. The same two stories of historical facts were read to the classes by the teachers immediately before the second fruit-tree drawing session (out of three, spaced one week apart). The Experimental Groups heard a story about a fig-tree harvest with the help of monkeys (baboons) in ancient Egypt. This story was selected because in the native region of these school children, no child had ever pictured such a tree in previous experiments. The Control Groups were told about some aspect of the domestication of the dog by stone-age man. This story was considered "neutral," because it did not mention any trees. Each story had about 150 words; the focal words *fig* and *dog* were mentioned twelve times each, and *monkey* and *man* six and five times, respectively, in the stories. Of course the instructions for the fruit-tree drawing sessions were always the same as in previous studies. The results showed strong responses to the unfamiliar stories in both, the experimental and control conditions. In other words, this brief one-time exposure gave a new direction to the thought association and imagery to a significant number of children. A comparison between the normal children and the emotionally disturbed children showed that the children in both experiments responded in similar ways.

These studies demonstrated that children could be indirectly influenced to draw a new and different variety of fruit tree than previously pictured. It was probable that other conditions could direct children's imagery into drawing different varieties of fruit trees as well. For instance, color might influence the children's choice of a tree, thus the idea of limiting the children to specific colors appeared important. It was therefore decided to analyze the fruit-tree preferences of children who had only a limited range of colors or no colors available.

Another two successive fruit-tree experiments[13,14] were carried out in the USA. The first study was with normal children from three elementary schools in different geographical locations. And the second study was with mentally retarded children with an IQ range from 31 to 77, who resided in a state institution. The chronological ages corresponded to those of previous subjects, which included children from five to twelve years old. In both experiments the children were divided into four groups: Group A had all colors available; Group B could only use red, blue and yellow; Group C was restricted to green, brown and orange; and Group D had no colors available and was limited to either a blue pen or a black pencil. (No mixing of colors was permitted for Groups B and C.) The results of the normal children showed that apple-tree preferences ranked highest in Groups A, B, and D. However, apples were in second place in Group C, and orange trees ranked in first place; though in Group B no child had pictured an orange tree. Comparing these results with those of the retarded children, a striking similarity in trends was found. The highest percentage of apple-tree pictures occurred also in Group D and the lowest in Group C, whereas Group A had more apple-tree responses than Group B. However, orange-tree pictures in Group C tied with apple-tree representations for first rank.

These two experiments showed that the availability of certain colors such as orange – and the unavailability of other colors, such as red – gave new directions of thought associations and imagery for a significant number of normal and of retarded children, even though the latter's responses were not as strong as those of the normal children. Adler[14] proposed that, "while it could be possible that the lessened effects with the retarded children might reside in the lack of attentiveness alone, one might wonder whether it is not appropriate to advance, in addition, a parallel to Zeaman and House's[15] 'attention deficiency theory of retardate discrimination learning,' namely, to expand it to include an 'association deficiency theory of retardate imagination.' This (broadened theory) would also involve a two-stage process: First, the child has to attend to or be aware of the relevant stimulus dimension (let us say the orange color); and second, the child has to make an appropriate association with the relevant stimulus cue (for instance, think of/imagine an orange tree, when asked to draw a fruit tree). Perhaps the retarded child is defective (slow), not only in the attentional phase, but in the associational phase of the process as well." In this way, the data of the two fruit-tree experiments could explain the greater change in responses of the normal children when compared to the retardates under the same conditions.

The ranking of fruit-tree varieties (18 for the normal children and 13 for the retardates) corresponded very closely not only between these two groups of children, but also when compared to the world-wide survey of a previous cross-cultural study[6] with apple in first, orange (tangerine) in second, and cherry in third place.

One other aspect was important to follow through, namely, the effects of the different age levels. Adler[5] reported in an earlier cross-cultural study, where children could use all colors, that the "younger" age group (5 to 8 years) had significantly more responses of apple trees than did the "older" age group (9 to 12 years). It was suggested that this might be a sign of more stereotyped thinking of the "younger" group, since a significant number of "older" children were more readily influenced by the new and unfamiliar story than the "younger" age group.[11] However, under varied conditions of color availability, children in the USA responded in the same manner, regardless of age. "It appeared that color exerted the same influence regardless of age group, to effect a change in content of fruit-tree drawings."[13]

Yet two additional studies with older age groups reported interesting results. Cawte and Kiloh[7] and Cawte[8] describe a fruit-tree experiment with subteen and teenage (12 to 15 years) Australian Aboriginals. The students were divided randomly into halves, each receiving either English or Walbiri instructions. The results were analyzed as "introduced" or "native" fruit trees. When instructed in English, 78% drew introduced trees, which was similar to the results of the younger age groups tested in a counterbalanced design. Analyzing the data given by Cawte and Kiloh[7] showed that of the Walbiri children — younger and older age groups combined — who were instructed in English 64.5% drew introduced trees; of these, 43.8% were apple trees. (In comparison, 83% of all children instructed in the vernacular drew native fruit trees, and 42% of these pictured the bush banana as their first preference.)

The other study was conducted by Thomas and Osgood[16] and was designed to examine college students' (ages 18 to 22 years) preferences of fruit trees under the same conditions of varied color availability, using the same procedure, and, in addition, to compare these findings with those reported by Adler.[13] These investigators also extended their fruit-tree experiment and examined the apple-tree responses in a word association test with "fruit tree" as one of the stimulus words. The results showed that, although the trends remained stable, the degree of the fruit-tree preferences was significantly stronger with college students. For example, apple-tree responses; in Group I, college students: 75%, schoolchildren: 53%; Group II, college students: 83%, schoolchildren: 53%; Group III, college students: 21%, schoolchildren: 16%; Group IV, college students: 68%, schoolchildren: 60%. Orange-tree responses for Group III were for the college students 74% and for the schoolchildren, 67%. Apple trees in the word association test represented 71% of the responses. Thomas and Osgood offered no explanation for these results for the present: "although in view of the current collegiate emphasis on 'doing your own thing,' it was surprising to find the college student's preferences so homogeneous and conforming. This conformity (or uniformity) was again reflected in the number of different trees selected: Ten varieties for the college students compared to 18 varieties for the schoolchildren."

Since these experiments, under varied conditions of color availability, were undertaken in different parts of the USA, it remained to do a cross-cultural study and to see whether children in other geographical locations would respond in the same manner. It was hypothesized that children in various parts of the world would respond with different fruit-tree preferences, depending on the colors associated with the type of fruit tree represented.

The present cross-cultural fruit-tree experiment was designed to compare responses from children from three continents: North America, Central Europe, and East Asia. In this way, the authors hoped to be able to investigate regional differences in children's drawings of fruit trees, as well as the effects, if any, exerted on their fruit-tree preferences as a consequence of access or limitations to specific colors. In other words, the current study sought to find out whether the results of investigations in the USA would be replicated cross-culturally.

METHOD

Subjects

All 2,675 participants (subjects) were normal schoolchildren attending regular classes and were between the ages of five and twelve years. The ages of the children, 9 to 12 years for the "older" and 5 to 8 years for the "younger" groups, were tabulated as was the sex distribution for each geographical region (TABLE 1).

Each child contributed one graphic representation of a fruit tree to this study. The children lived in seven countries on three continents. In order to measure the environmental effects, the children were grouped by geographical areas on different continents. Schoolchildren from Canada ($n = 83$) and the United States of America ($n = 494$) made up the "North American Group" ($N = 577$). Contact in four countries in Europe was established, where different languages (other than English) were spoken. The children constituting the "Central European Group" ($N = 396$) resided in Denmark ($n = 38$), France ($n = 121$), Germany ($n = 209$), and Switzerland ($n = 28$). Children in three of these countries had drawn apple trees as their first preference in a previous study[6] while the fourth country was added for this experiment. It seemed, however, more meaningful and conclusive to test children from a country where

TABLE 1

SUBJECTS' DISTRIBUTION BY AGE AND SEX AND GEOGRAPHICAL AREAS
FOR THE FOUR COLOR CONDITIONS COMBINED

a.	Continent	Younger	Older	Total
	North America	238	339	577
	Central Europe	138	258	396
	East Asia	525	1,177	1,702
	Totals	901	1,774	2,675
b.	Continent	Boys	Girls	Total
	North America	318	259	577
	Central Europe	179	217	396
	East Asia	829	873	1,702
	Totals	1,332	1,343	2,675

the first preference was any other than an apple tree. Looking at the same fruit-tree experiments in which children from 24 countries participated, it was found that in 17 of these, apple-tree preferences ranked highest. Of the seven countries where apple trees were either in second or third place, four were bordering the Mediterranean Sea, and the other three countries were in the Orient touching the Western Pacific Ocean. In all these countries, indigenous trees were in first place. In the Orient, Japanese children had predominantly pictured persimmon trees (34%) compared to South Korea where persimmon trees (28%) almost tied with apple trees (25%) for first place; and in the Philippines the coconut palm was in first place. While Group C's participants were allowed to use only green, brown, and orange, it was the orange color which exerted the greatest influence on students in the USA. Therefore, it was deemed best to test Japanese children's fruit-tree responses for this study, and test the Philippine children at a future time. The Japanese children in the present experiment ($N = 1,702$) were designated the "East Asian Group."

Procedure and Material

The same procedure was used that had been adopted previously. In order not to disrupt the general classroom routine by outside visitors, each teacher administered the fruit-tree test to the class as a group during regular class period.

Duplicating the procedure of Adler's[13,14] previous "varied color availability studies," each teacher gave each child in her class one sheet of drawing paper, the size and quality of which was unimportant to this study. Next, the teacher divided the class at random into four groups of different color conditions: Group A, which served as a Control Group, had no restrictions and could use all colors; Group B was only allowed to use red, blue, and yellow; and Group C was permitted only to paint or draw with orange, green and brown; (neither of these two last groups could mix colors to make up for missing colors; such as mixing blue and yellow to make green;) Group D could not use any colors and therefore could draw only with a black pencil or a blue (ballpoint) pen. Then the teacher told the class: "Draw or paint a picture – any scene – with a fruit tree in it." Since the term "fruit tree" did not exist in the Japanese language, the teachers were asked to explain: "A tree that bears fruits we can eat." This terminology was chosen so that the children could differentiate between fruit-bearing trees, like oak or pine, and trees bearing edible fruits for human consumption.[5]

There was no time limit set for drawing the picture and each child had ample time to finish. Upon completion, the teacher asked the older children to record the following information on the back of the picture: (1) The type of fruit tree the child had represented. (It was immaterial if the child's drawing was not a true representation. Artistic ability was not considered important for an objective analysis that was based entirely on content.) (2) The child's first and last name. (3) The sex of the subject. (4) The chronological age of the child – and special attention was given to the Oriental manner of counting age. (5) The class by grade. (6) The group by letter. Since the younger children could not write well, the teachers filled in the same information, which the children provided verbally.

Before sending the Japanese pictures to the investigators, the collaborator translated the children's responses into English and recorded the items on the back of each picture. The responses on the pictures from Central Europe were translated by the investigators.

RESULTS

The evaluation of the drawings was done entirely objectively, based on content only. Fruit-tree varieties for each of the four groups in the three geographical areas were tabulated and then analyzed. Whenever there were multiple types of trees in one picture, they were recorded but not added to the total of the different tree varieties, since it was impossible to say which was the first preference. The designation of orange–tangerine was retained in keeping with previous studies[4–6] but only for the Japanese children, since no Central European nor any North American child drew a tangerine tree. Since the hypothesis tested concerned the effects of access to and limitations of colors on children's drawings of fruit trees in different geographical areas, the first group of chi square (χ^2) tests were made to analyze apple-tree responses for the three different geographical locations (TABLE 2).

As anticipated, the results of the North American children's drawings showed that the apple-tree responses in the four conditions were significantly differentiated (df = 3; $\chi^2 = 79.22$; p $<$ .001). In Groups A, B, and D (with 55, 55, and 60%, respectively for each group total) the apple tree ranked in first place. However, in Group C, orange trees predominated with 68% of all fruit-tree pictures in this condition; apple trees were in second place with 14% of the group total.

For comparison, the apple-tree responses of the Central European children were analyzed. This time there were no significant differences (df = 3; $\chi^2 = 6.60$) between the four color conditions (Gr. A = 63%; Gr. B = 54%, Gr. C = 49%, and Gr. D = 64%) with apple-tree responses ranking in first place in all the groups.

The East Asian schoolchildren's drawings were analyzed next. Here apple-tree responses resulted in a highly significant $\chi^2 = 101.52$, df = 3, p $<$ .001, showing that the apple-tree responses of the four color conditions were highly differentiated. Looking at TABLE 2, it appeared that apple-tree preferences were only once in first place in Group B with 33%. In Groups A and D (24 and 16% respectively) apple trees ranked in second place; and in Group C (6%), they were in third place.

However, a total of the persimmon-tree responses of all four groups made up 637 pictures or 37% of the overall total of 1,702 East Asian pictures (see TABLE 3).

Persimmon trees were in first place in Groups A with 38%, Group C with 51%, and Group D with 37%. In Group B, persimmon trees ranked second (24%). It was thought advisable to analyze the persimmon-tree responses, which resulted in a significant χ^2 of 62.0, df = 3, p $<$ .001. It appeared that the "red" in Group B exerted an effect that caused apple-tree responses to replace persimmons in first place. And the "orange" in Group C was probably the stimulus for the children to draw more orange trees (27%) in this group than in any other. However, the fact that persimmon preferences ranked in top place in three groups is probably due to the popularity of the fruit in Japan. Not one North American nor any Central European child had pictured this fruit.

In the overall tabulation, apple trees were in the second highest rank of the East Asian Group with 20% of the grand total of 1,702 pictures; orange-tangerine trees were in third highest place with 11%, followed by grapevines in fourth rank with 5% of the total.

But with the North American Group, by combining all color conditions, apple trees were the top preference with 46% of the 577 children's drawings. Then orange trees (20%) were followed by cherry trees (12%) and pear trees (6%) for second, third, and fourth rank. The 396 Central European school-

TABLE 2

UNDER VARIED CONDITIONS OF COLOR AVAILABILITY, 2,675 SCHOOLCHILDREN'S 1st, 2nd, AND 3rd PREFERENCES IN FRUIT-TREE DRAWINGS

Geographical Areas (Countries)	Group A			Group B			Group C			Group D		
	Tree	f	%	Tree	f	%	Tree	f	%	Tree	f	%
North America	(n = 153)			(n = 134)			(n = 141)			(n = 149)		
(USA & Canada)	Apple	84	55	Apple	74	55	Orange	96	68	Apple	90	60
(n = 577)	Cherry	21	14	Cherry	28	21	Apple	20	14	Cherry	15	10
	Orange	15	10	Pear	10	8	Pear	6	4	Pear	10	7
Central Europe	(n = 109)			(n = 94)			(n = 92)			(n = 101)		
(Denmark, France,	Apple	69	63	Apple	51	54	Apple	45	49	Apple	65	64
Germany & Switzerland)	Cherry	11	10	Plum/			Orange	23	25	Cherry	10	10
(n = 396)	Plum	9	8	Cherry	12	13	Cherry	6	7	Pear	8	8
East Asia	(n = 413)			(n = 405)			(n = 386)			(n = 498)		
(Japan)	Persim.	157	38	Apple	135	33	Persim.	197	51	Persim.	186	37
(n = 1,702)	Apple	101	24	Persim.	97	24	Or/Tang.	103	27	Apple	82	16
	Or/Tang.	31	8	Grape/ Or/Tang.	23	6	Apple	23	6	Grape	46	9

children placed apple trees in first rank with 58% of the overall total of all the drawings. The cherry tree was in second place with 10% of the total; and orange trees and plum trees tied with 7% each for third and fourth rank.

The question occurred: why did the European children respond with apple-tree preferences in first place in Group C? Perhaps the answer can be found in the popularity of different types of apples throughout Central Europe. For example, "greenings," which as the name implies, are green (sour) apples, or "leather apples," which have a brown skin and have a refreshing flavor. On the other hand, it is not that the children are unfamiliar with oranges. Even though the orange is a southern fruit, which is mainly grown around the areas of the Mediterranean Sea, oranges are plentiful in fruit stores in the cities all over Europe. Yet the distribution of orange trees pictured differed significantly from that of plum trees (df = 3; χ^2 = 25.33; p < .001) as seen TABLE 2. The percentage distributions were as follows: for orange-tree pictures, Gr. A = 2; Gr. B = 1; Gr. C = 25; and Gr. D = 3; for plum-tree representations, Gr. A = 8; Gr. B = 13 (which tied with cherry trees for second place in this Group); Gr. C = 5; Gr. D = 3 (which tied with orange-tree pictures for fourth and fifth place in this Group). That one child drew an orange tree in Group B was somewhat surprising, since no North American child in this study contributed an orange-tree picture in this Group. Still, the effect of the availability of the "orange" color was probably the reason why 25% of the schoolchildren drew orange trees in Group C. And most likely, because of the effect of the "blue" color, the plum-tree responses increased slightly to 13% in Group B.

In order to test the similarity or dissimilarity between the geographical regions, apple-tree responses of North American and Central European children were compared in a 2 x 4 design and the results found significant differences (df = 3; χ^2 = 16.60; p < .001). Since this difference was thought to be due to the responses of Groups C, a 2 x 3 analysis was performed, omitting both

TABLE 3

FOUR HIGHEST RANKS OF FRUIT-TREE PICTURES IN EACH
GEOGRAPHICAL AREA

North America, N = 577:	Tree	f	%
	Apple	268	46
	Orange	116	20
	Cherry	68	12
	Pear	36	6
Central Europe, N = 396:	Tree	f	%
	Apple	230	58
	Cherry	39	10
	Orange/Plum	29	7
East Asia, N = 1,702	Tree	f	%
	Persimmon	637	37
	Apple	341	20
	Orange-Tangerine	187	11
	Grape	91	5

Groups C. The results confirmed this assumption, when no significant differences were found between Groups A, B, and D (df = 2; χ^2 = 0.45; n.s.).

Another 2 x 4 comparison was performed between the top ranking apple trees of the North American groups and with the first preferences persimmon trees of the East Asian groups. This test resulted in a significant difference between the groups (df = 3; χ^2 = 38.73; p < .001). A further analysis indicated that Group C for North American and Group B for Japanese children exerted the greatest experimental effects. The outcome of a 2 x 2 test (American Groups A and B, and East Asian Groups A and C) confirmed that the children in these groups responded equally to the color availability of "red" and "orange," respectively (df = 1; χ^2 = 0.002; n.s.).

In an earlier cross-cultural study,[5] which sampled children's pictures from 13 countries on six continents, the "younger" children (5–8 years) preferred apple trees significantly more frequently than did the "older" age group (9–12 years). However, in the previous US study on children's preferences of fruit trees under four conditions of color availability or limitations, no differences between age groups were found. In other words, the influence of access to, or restrictions of colors was the same for both age groups. TABLE 4 shows the distribution of fruit-tree preferences of each age group for each of the three geographical locations.

Four χ^2 tests were performed: the first one with North American children repeated the nondifferentiated results of the previous experiment when comparing apple-tree preferences of Groups A, B, and D, in a 2 x 3 test (df = 2; χ^2 = 3.17; n.s.) (Since Groups C each had ten apple-tree pictures there was no contest between the two age groups.) The results of the apple-tree responses of Central European fruit-tree pictures in a 2 x 4 χ^2 test of the four color conditions and the two age groups showed no significant differentiation (df = 3; χ^2 = 2; n.s.). The next analysis concerned the East Asian children's apple-tree pictures. Leaving out Group C, which contained a very small percentage of apple trees in both age levels (see TABLE 4), the resulting χ^2 was not significant (df = 2; χ^2 = 1; n.s.), showing that there were no differences between the two age groups with respect to apple-tree responses. Since the persimmon was the overall preference, another 2 x 4 χ^2 test was calculated with these fruit-tree responses. A significant difference between the "older" and "younger" children's responses of persimmon trees resulted (df = 3; χ^2 = 11.81; p < .01). Inspection of TABLE 4 showed that the "younger" children reacted more strongly with persimmon-tree preferences to the nonavailability of "red" in Group C than the "older" children. And in Group A, with all colors available, the apple-tree- and persimmon-tree responses were reversed for first and second highest ranks in the two age groups.

To complete the statistical analyses, the percentage distributions of the responses of boys were compared to those of girls for each of the three geographical regions. Three 2 x 3 χ^2 test for apple-tree preferences were performed. In order not to confound the results, Groups C for the North American and for the Central European analyses, and Group B for the East Asian analysis were omitted. The results were respectively χ^2 = .42; χ^2 = 1.35; and χ^2 = 2.87, all with df = 2; none reached a significant level. And because the persimmon-tree preferences were in first place with East Asian schoolchildren, another statistical comparison was done of the same three color conditions, leaving out Group C, since both boys and girls responded with 51%, which was higher than in any other group. The resulting χ^2 = .42, df = 2, was not significant. In other words, in none of the apple-tree- or persimmon-tree preferences tested in this experiment were there any differences found between the responses of boys and girls.

In keeping with previous studies, it may be of interest here to report on the number of fruit-tree varieties pictured for each geographical group: the greatest versatility was apparent in the East Asian Group's ($N = 1,702$) pictures where the children drew 27 different varieties; the North American children ($N = 577$) represented 19 varieties of fruit trees, and the Central European schoolchildren ($N = 396$) contributed 12 fruit-tree varieties to this study.

DISCUSSION

The results of the present study confirmed the hypothesis that children in various parts of the world would respond with different fruit-tree preferences, depending on the colors associated with the type of fruit trees represented. This effect prevailed even though the children responded with different varieties of fruit trees as their first preference. As seen in TABLE 3, in the North American continent children responded overall with more apple trees than with any other variety when asked to "draw a scene with a fruit tree in it." The apple tree was also the first-ranking fruit tree in Central European pictures. But in Eastern Asia the representations of persimmon trees were in overall first place. While a previous US study established that children respond with different fruit trees depending on the availability of colors, the present cross-cultural research showed that the children on the three continents responded in similar ways to the unavailability, as well as to the accessability of specific colors. Furthermore, it was shown that local fruits, specific to the geographical areas, seemed to exert an influence on the preferences of fruit trees in children's drawings.

For example, in the East Asian Group the effects of color on the imagery and associative thinking in schoolchildren were very significant. While the color of the top preference in Groups A, C, and D, the persimmon, was a shade between red and orange, the present study revealed that the availability of the "red" color without "orange" (Group B) increased the apple-tree responses, and the "orange" color when "red" was not available (Group C) did the same for the orange-tangerine tree preferences (see TABLE 2). In the Central European Group, apple trees were in first place in all four groups, though there were fewer apple-tree responses in Group C than in the other three conditions, although the difference was not significant. Yet there was a significant increase in plum trees due to the access to "blue" in Group B; and in Group C there was a significant increase in orange-tree responses, influenced by the "orange" color, though apple-tree drawings decreased insignificantly. The North American children also responded to the unavailability of the "orange" color by omitting orange trees altogether in Group B; but in Group C with the "orange" color − but not the "red" − available to the children, increases in orange-tree preferences reached the highest level for any variety of fruit trees; whereas apple-tree drawings ranked highest in Groups A, B, and C.

One can only speculate at present, why the "younger" (5 to 8 years) East Asian children pictured the large number of apple trees. In the present study the only significant differences between the "younger" and the "older" (9 to 12 years) age groups tested were found with the East Asian children in their persimmon-tree responses. The "older" age group drew significantly more persimmon trees than did the "younger" age group. The Japanese children were the only group in the present study to represent this variety of fruit tree. No

TABLE 4
2,675 SCHOOLCHILDREN'S 1st, 2nd, AND 3rd PREFERENCES IN FRUIT-TREE DRAWINGS
(Divided by two age groups)

Geographical Area (Countries)	Group A			Group B			Group C			Group D		
	Tree	f	%	Tree	f	%	Tree	f	%	Tree	f	%
							Younger Children (5–8 years)					
North America	(n = 61)			(n = 60)			(n = 59)			(n = 58)		
(USA & Canada) (n = 238)	Apple	30	49	Apple	30	50	Orange	37	63	Apple	40	69
	Orange	8	13	Cherry	16	26	Apple	10	17	Pear	5	9
	Cherry	7	11	Pear	5	8	Pear/Cherry	3	5	Cherry	3	5
				(no Orange)								
Central Europe	(n = 35)			(n = 34)			(n = 32)			(n = 37)		
(Denmark, France, Germany & Switzerland) (n = 138)	Apple	20	57	Apple	21	62	Apple	16	50	Apple	24	65
	Cherry	5	14	Cherry	5	15	Orange	9	28	Pear/Cherry	3	8
	Plum/Coconut	3	9	Plum	3	9	Banana	2	6			
				(no Orange)								
East Asia	(n = 139)			(n = 138)			(n = 111)			(n = 137)		
(Japan) (n = 525)	Apple	50	36	Apple	65	47	Persim.	66	59	Persim.	36	26
	Persim.	30	22	Persim.	20	15	Or./Tang.	31	28	Apple	35	26
	Or./Tang.	14	10	Banana	12	9	Apple	8	7	Or./Tang.	13	9
				(Or./Tang. 9)								

Older Children (9–12 years)

Region				
North America (USA & Canada) (n = 339)	(n = 92) Apple 54 59 Cherry 14 15 Orange 7 8	(n = 74) Apple 44 59 Cherry 12 16 Pear 5 7 (no Orange)-	(n = 82) Orange 59 72 Apple 10 12 Pear 3 4	(n = 91) Apple 50 55 Cherry 12 13 Pear 5 6
Central Europe (Denmark, France, Germany & Switzerland) (n = 258)	(n = 74) Apple 49 66 Pear 8 11 Plum/ Cherry 6 8	(n = 60) Apple 30 50 Plum 9 15 Cherry 7 12 (Orange 1)	(n = 60) Apple 29 48 Orange 14 23 Cherry 5 8	(n = 64) Apple 41 69 Cherry 7 11 Pear 5 8
East Asia (Japan) (n = 1,177)	(n = 274) Persim. 127 46 Apple 51 15 Or./Tang. 17 6 (Grape 16)	(n = 267) Persim. 77 29 Apple 70 26 Grape 21 8 (Or./Tang. 14)	(n = 275) Persim. 131 48 Or./Tang. 72 26 Apple 15 5	(n = 361) Persim. 150 42 Apple 47 13 Grape 41 11

significant differences between the two age groups were found with apple-tree preferences in any of the three geographical areas tested in this experiment. Inspection of TABLE 4 revealed some differences between the "younger" and "older" age groups. Perhaps individual analyses would have revealed some significant differences, but these would have been meaningless and even more difficult to interpret. Therefore, the overall comparisons were reported here.

If a specific color is associated with a specific fruit tree, how can one explain the distributions of fruit-tree preferences in Group D in which no colors were available to the children? The answer must lie with the associative thinking of the schoolchildren. The instructions to "draw any scene with a fruit tree in it" must have had the same effect on the children participating in the present study, as the word-association test had on the college students in the Thomas and Osgood[16] fruit-tree experiment. These investigators found that no significant differences between the highest ranking apple-tree responses existed when Groups I and V were compared. In Group V the written items that first came to the students' mind in response to the orally presented stimulus word "fruit tree" were apple trees to a large degree. (It appeared, when comparing the means, that there was no difference between the apple-tree responses of Groups IV and V.)

Thomas and Osgood[16] felt that "this conformity (or uniformity) was again reflected in the number of different fruit trees selected: Ten varieties for college students ($N = 178$) compared to 18 varieties for children (p. 255)." The present group of 577 North American children drew 19 different fruit-tree varieties, while in the 396 Central European pictures 12 different fruit-tree varieties were represented, and 27 varieties were drawn by the East Asian schoolchildren. Compared to the results of a previous study[5] where Japanese children ($n = 367$) contributed 18 different types of fruit trees and US schoolchildren ($n = 884$) pictured 24 varieties. (No comparative data were available for Central European countries.) While it may not always be so, it is likely that, the larger the groups of children, the greater the number of different fruit-tree varieties that may be pictured.

The distribution of the top-ranking fruit-tree responses, in the three geographical areas tested, always included apple trees and to a lesser degree orange-tangerine trees. Perhaps this is a clue to the similarities in the schoolchildren's expressions of their experiences. Even though they had enormously different environments and backgrounds, the overall effects of colors on their imagery were similar. The flexibility with which they responded to the controlled stimuli differed, but only to a degree.

The present cross-cultural study showed that availability of particular colors in the absence of specific other colors was an important factor influencing the fruit-tree preferences, as it interacted with the social and cultural background of the children in determining the varieties of fruit trees represented.

SUMMARY

A total of 2,675 schoolchildren from three continents participated in this cross-cultural fruit-tree experiment: 577 lived in North America, 396 were from Central Europe and 1,702 had their home in Eastern Asia. Of these, 901 were designated the "younger" (5–8 years) and 1,774 formed the "older" (9–12 years) age groups. 1,332 were boys and 1,343 were girls.

The children were tested in their classes after they were randomly divided into four groups of different color availability or limitation. Then the teachers told the children: "Draw a picture — any scene — with a fruit-tree in it."

The present cross-cultural fruit-tree experiment showed that children living on different continents, belonging to various cultural backgrounds, growing up under manifold environmental conditions, and speaking different languages, all responded in a similar way to the limitations or availability of specific colors when told by their teachers to "draw a picture — any scene — with a fruit tree in it." It is not only the differences that are of importance in cross-cultural studies, but almost more important are the similarities. And such were the results of the children's drawings in the present study. While casual inspection of the accompanying tables revealed great differences among the responses by the children from the three geographical areas, careful analyses showed that the same trends, with the same fruit trees, occurred simply because the children had either colors available or unavailable, which were associated with specific fruit trees. The effects of "red" when "orange" was not given, was noticeable in the apple-tree responses of children from all three continents — though to a greater or lesser degree. The same was true for "orange" leading to orange-tangerine tree responses, when "red" was unavailable to the children. In other words, schoolchildren, who pictured local fruit trees under conditions when either all or no colors were available, were influenced to respond with different fruit trees when they were limited to the use of only a few specified colors. The present cross-cultural fruit-tree experiment showed that different associations and imagery resulted due to the relevant stimulus of the available colors, regardless of the social or cultural background of the children.

ACKNOWLEDGMENT

The authors wish to express their thanks and appreciation to Mrs. Mashiko Fukae for her help and effort with this research.

[NOTE: FIGURES 1—48, illustrating some of the subjects' fruit-tree drawings, appear on the following pages.]

FIGURE 1. USA. Group A. F, 8 years, Apple tree

FIGURE 2. USA. Group B. M, 9 years, Apple tree

FIGURE 3.   USA. Group C. F, 7 years, Orange tree

FIGURE 4.   USA. Group D. M, 12 years, Apple tree

FIGURE 5.   Canada Group A. F, 8 years, Apple tree

FIGURE 6.   Canada Group B. M, 10 years, Apple tree

FIGURE 7. Canada Group C. F, 9 years, Orange tree

FIGURE 9.   Denmark Group A. M, 12 years, Apple tree

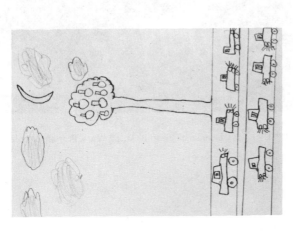

FIGURE 8.   Canada Group D. M, 7 years, Apple tree

FIGURE 10.   Denmark Group B. M, 12 years, Pear and Apple trees

FIGURE 11. Denmark Group C. M, 10 years, Apple tree

FIGURE 12. Denmark Group D. M, 12 years, two Plum trees

FIGURE 13. France Group A. M, 10 years, Apple tree

FIGURE 14.   France Group B. M, 11 years, Coconut palm

FIGURE 15.   France Group C. M, 12 years, Orange tree

FIGURE 16.   France Group D. M, 12 years, Apple tree

FIGURE 17.   Germany Group A. F, 10 years, Apple trees

FIGURE 18.   Germany Group B. F, 10 years, Apple tree

FIGURE 20.   Germany Group D. F., 12 years, Apple tree

FIGURE 21.   Switzerland Group A. F, 7 years, Apple trees

FIGURE 22.   Switzerland Group B. F, 8 years, Plum tree

FIGURE 23. Switzerland Group C. M, 8 years, Apple tree

FIGURE 24. Switzerland Group D. M, 8 years, Apple tree

FIGURE 25.   Japan Group A. F, 8 years, Persimmon tree

FIGURE 26.   Japan Group B. F, 10 years, Apple and Banana trees

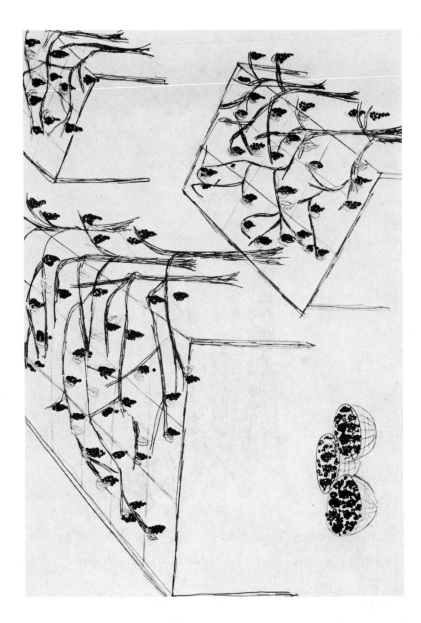

FIGURE 27. Japan Group C. F, 12 years, Green Grapevine

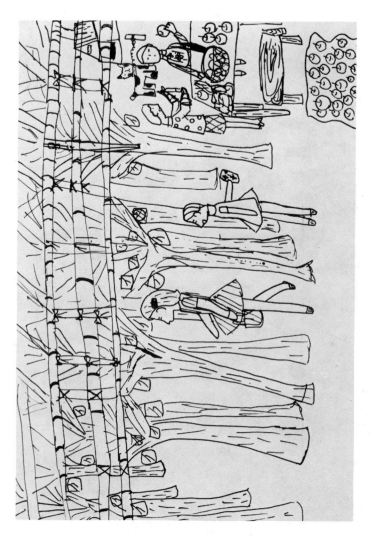

FIGURE 28.   Japan Group D. F, 10 years, Pear trees

FIGURE 29.   Japan Group A. F., 8 years Apple trees

FIGURE 30. Japan Group B. F, 12 years, "blond" Persimmon tree

FIGURE 31. Japan Group A. F, 10 years, Orange trees

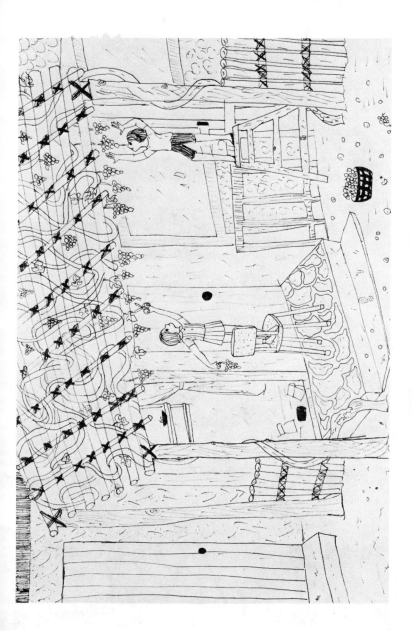

FIGURE 32. Japan Group D. F, 10 years, Grapevines

FIGURE 33. USA. Group A. F, 7 years, Apple tree

FIGURE 34. USA. Group B. F, 8 years, Cherry tree

FIGURE 35.   USA. Group C. F, 11 years, Coconut palms

FIGURE 36.   USA. Group D. M, 6 years, Apple tree

FIGURE 37. Canada Group A. F, 10 years, Apple tree

FIGURE 38.   Canada Group A. F, 11 years, Apple tree

FIGURE 39.   Canada Group B. F, 10 years, Pear tree

FIGURE 40.   Canada Group C. F, 8 years, Orange tree

FIGURE 41. Canada Group D. F., 9 years, Apple trees

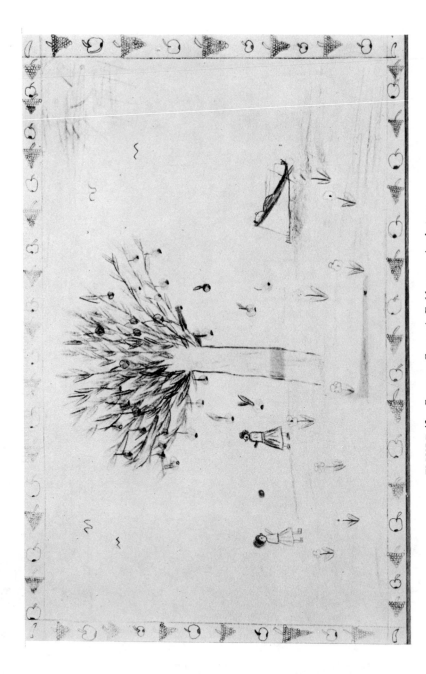

FIGURE 42.   Germany Group A. F, 11 years, Apple tree

FIGURE 43.   Japan Group A. F, 9 years, Apple tree

FIGURE 44.   Japan Group A. F, 9 years, Grapevine

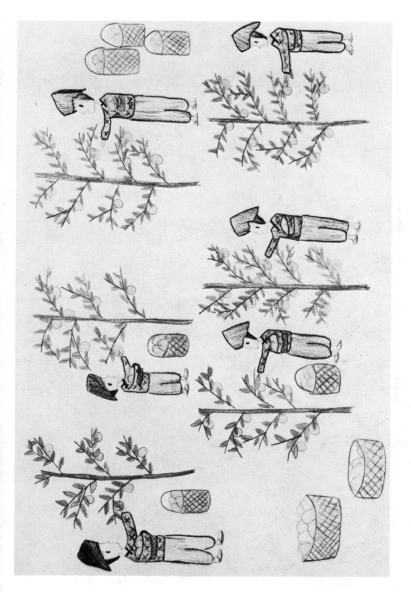

FIGURE 45.   Japan Group A. F, 9 years, Orange trees

FIGURE 46. Japan Group D. M, 10 years, Persimmon tree

FIGURE 47. Japan Group A. F, 7 years, Watermelon vine

FIGURE 48. Japan Group A. F, 10 years, Apple tree

REFERENCES

1. MEAD, M. 1946 & 1954. Research on primitive children. *In* Manual of Child Psychology, 2nd ed. L. Carmichael, Ed. John Wiley & Sons. New York, N.Y. 735–780.
2. DENNIS, W. 1966. Group values through children's drawings. John Wiley & Sons, New York, N.Y.
3. DENNIS, W. 1970. Goodenough scores, art experience, and modernization. *In* Cross-cultural Studies of Behavior. I. Al-Issa & W. Dennis, Eds. Holt, Rinehart & Winston, New York, N.Y. 134–152.
4. ADLER, L. L. 1965. Cross-cultural study of children's drawings of fruit-trees. Paper presented at The First New York City Psi Chi Psychological Convention. New York, N.Y.
5. ADLER, L. L. 1967. A note on cross-cultural preferences: Fruit-tree preferences in children's drawings. J. Psychol. **65**: 15–22.
6. ADLER, L. L. 1968. A note on the cross-cultural fruit-tree study: A test-retest procedure. J. Psychol. **69**: 53–61.
7. CAWTE, J. E. & L. G. KILOH. 1967. Language and pictorial representations in Aboriginal children. Soc. Sci. Med. **1**: 67–76.
8. CAWTE, J. 1974. Medicine is the law. The University Press of Hawaii. Honolulu, Hawaii.
9. VENESS, H. & J. O. HOSKIN. 1968. Psychiatry in New Britain: A note on the "Fruit-Tree Experiment" as a measure of the effect of language on association processes. Soc. Sci. & Med. **1**: 419–424.
10. ADLER, L. L. 1969. The fruit-tree study as a measure of associative thinking and imagery in children of different ages. Develop. Psychol. **1**: 444.
11. ADLER, L. L. 1970. Influencing associative thinking and imagery as measured by the "Fruit-Tree Experiment" in children's drawings. Soc. Sci. Med. **4**: 527–534.
12. ADLER, L. L. & P. H. BERKOWITZ. 1976. Influencing associative thinking and imagery in emotionally disturbed children. Psychol. Rep. **39**: 183–188.
13. ADLER, L. L. 1970. The "Fruit-Tree Experiment" as a measure of children's preferences of fruit trees under varied conditions of color availability. J. Genet. Psychol. **116**: 191–195.
14. ADLER, L. L. 1970. The "Fruit-Tree Experiment" as a measure of retarded children's preferences of fruit trees under varied conditions of color availability. J. Psychol. **76**: 217–222.
15. ZEAMAN, D. & B. J. HOUSE. 1963. The role of attention in retardate discrimination learning. *In* Handbook of Mental Deficiency. N. R. Ellis, Ed. McGraw-Hill, New York, N.Y. 159–223.
16. THOMAS, G. & S. W. OSGOOD. 1971. College students' performance on the "Fruit-Tree Experiment" under varied conditions of color availability. J. Psychol. **77**: 253–256.

THE LEGITIMACY OF EDUCATIONAL KNOWLEDGE:
A NEGLECTED THEME IN COMPARATIVE RESEARCH

Robert Cowen*

*Department of Social Foundations
State University of New York at Buffalo
Buffalo, New York 14261*

I want to ask how we come to accept certain arrangements of educational knowledge in schooling systems as legitimate and how these legitimated curricula are sustained through time in selected nations; in what circumstances and for which groups in such nations fresh arrangements of the stock of knowledge are most likely to occur, and how such educational changes are related to the broader social context.

The general issue of the legitimacy of educational systems, or parts thereof, has been raised by such writers as Illich, Freire, Reimer, Friedenberg and Goodman, Holt, Herndon, and Kozol for contemporary audiences. And the broad theme of the socialization functions of formal schooling systems has been of concern to sociologists at least since the writings of Marx, Weber, and Durkheim. However, this particular theme – the role of educational knowledge in the socially based construction of consciousness and the relation of this educational knowledge to different social systems – has been (despite the earlier work of Karl Mannheim) rather recently raised as problematic. University-based academics, drawing mainly from European traditions of thought, especially in the sociology of knowledge, phenomenology and varieties of Marxism, have regenerated the topic as central to the problem of cultural transmission.[1] Philosophers and social critics, such as Jurgens Habermas and Raymond Williams; sociologists such as B. Bernstein, P. Bourdieu, Ioan Davies, P. W. Musgrave, and Michael F. D. Young; anthropologists such as R. Horton and Mary Douglas; and some comparativists such as J. A. Lauwerys, Martin Carnoy, and especially M. Scotford-Archer, Michalina Vaughan, and Richard D. Heyman have all participated in this shift in perspective.

Inside this perspective, the particular question asked here focuses upon educational knowledge – the kinds of knowledge selected from the general knowledge stock to be institutionalized in schooling systems. How does it, in particular forms, become valued and sustained; in what circumstances does it become changed; and what does a cross-national comparison of such processes and contents suggest about the reciprocal relationships between educational knowledge, social change, social consensus, mobilization and the division of labor?

In many instances, the data requisite for such an analysis are not available. Even when data are available, the problems of a multidisciplinary analysis for one country are considerable; as a comparative exercise in a short paper the task is of severe difficulty. And until a more thorough theoretical and documentary analysis has been done on an initial basis, the value of detailed empirical surveys seems doubtful. As a consequence, the analysis that follows is speculative, from

* Present address: University of London Institute of Education, Bedford Way, London WC1H 0AL, England.

secondary sources, eclectically multidisciplinary, and occasionally quite abstracted. The alternative seems to be to allow the availability of measurement techniques and data collected for other purposes to determine the questions that may be raised in public.

Fortunately, it is possible to begin answers from the existing literature. J. A. Lauwerys provided a brilliant early sketch of what is now one of the conventions of comparative education — that different national educational systems tend to celebrate, in their knowledge patterns and pedagogic practices, nation-specific models of man through their traditional conceptions of general education.[2] He describes such models of man for England, France, Germany, the USA, and the USSR, and the way in which such educational identities are confirmed by curriculum provision.

Broadly speaking, a similar line of analysis will be followed in this paper. Models of man and the "cultural histories" from which such models are abstracted will remain a starting point. But two nuances will be added. More attention will be given to the educational, institutional provisions by which such legitimations are sustained through time. Secondly, "cultural histories," and the "ideologies of legitimization" abstracted from them to justify educational knowledge, will be interpreted as socially constructed and sustained. Men, in particular times, places, social positions, and in particular socioeconomic, religious, and political contexts — and always in revolutionary situations — debate such legitimations, confirm them institutionally, and gradually or suddenly renegotiate them. But if such ideologies of legitimization for educational knowledge are products of social action, what "knowledge-constitutive interests" are being defended by such legitimations; how are such interests institutionalized and sustained in education; and what "lag-phenomena" emerge between relatively stable normative justifications for educational knowledge and changes in the economic, political, and social structures?

Some effort will be made to treat of these issues in a series of comparative sketches. Firstly, the selfconsciously class-based societies of England and France will be examined in parts of the nineteenth century as they renegotiated or reaffirmed their legitimations of educational knowledge under the impact of a political revolution and an industrial revolution. For contrast, the other paradigm case(s) of mechanisms and styles of legitimation of educational knowledge—the self-declared classless and revolutionary situations of Cuba and China—will be reviewed. The analysis, despite its compression, indicates the way in which educational knowledge is, crudely speaking, a politicized phenomenon, perceived by social actors as crucial in the process of cultural transmission, and considerably constrained by the sociotemporal circumstances in which cultural transmission is proceeding. In other words, the legitimations and forms of educational knowledge stand in reciprocal relationship to the society in which the educational knowledge is located: such legitimations reflect certain major characteristics of the society and the educational knowledge creates nationally differentiated, and in certain circumstances, subnationally differentiated, reality-definitions among educands.

If we look at nineteenth century educational history in England, a minor paradox seems clear. On the one hand, Oxford and Cambridge, somewhat indifferent as teaching institutions and removed from some of the major trends in creative thinking in the period 1750 to 1850, had by the end of the century, reestablished themselves as the apex institutions of English education. On the other hand, by the end of the century, the English chose to establish the institutional frame of a state school system and, for the first time since the medieval period, established new universities. At the same time as Oxbridge in conjunction with the "public" schools was reaffirming the virtues of "one principal branch of study," especially classics or mathematics in the education of Christian gentlemen for professional, clerical and political leadership, so were new arrangements of educational knowledge being generated and legitimated for the working and middle classes. What are the characteristics of both the stability and the change?

By midcentury, the Royal Commissioners reported that in Oxford, largely through internal reforms of the tutorial and examination systems "the grosser exhibitions of vice, such as drunkenness and riot have . . . as in the higher classes generally, become rare."[3] (p. 65) The curriculum, which now allows "special studies of law and history, or mathematical science or natural science . . ."[3] (p. 68) still has a base in classics. The rationale (on the nature of "liberal education") is clear:

> It has been held to be the sole business of the University to train the powers of the mind, not to give much positive or any professional knowledge; and the study of the classical books is regarded as the best means of refining and invigorating the mind. The education given has hitherto been the same for all, whether clergymen or barristers, medical men or private gentlemen. . . .[3] (p. 68)

The rationale itself is clear; the debate had been considerable. What was on offer was a debate on the new classical humanism, which saw the restructuring of a somewhat pedantic, linguistic study of Greek and Latin into a broader study of civilizations that produced their own moral, political, and intellectual messages interpreted as directly relevant to Victorian England. The particular version of the rationale took different forms in the hands of particular individuals — Thomas Arnold, Newman or Pattison, Mill, Matthew Arnold, or Sidgwick — but the problems of establishing social order, high morale, and cultural standards, often with the assistance of the church, and the need for providing leadership by those who were best educated were a constant theme in the debates.

Thus, the institutional matrix, of the "public" schools and Oxbridge, ensured that the members of the religious and political elites of England in the nineteenth century received their symbolic education within particular institutions valuing certain curriculum forms. Social mobility in this period was not a function of the schooling system, confirmation of social status was. Despite pressure from nonconformists and entrepreneurial groups, Victorian certitudes were clear both on the moral content of an appropriate education and on the institutions in which such an education could be gained.

The debate about the education of leaders took place within a broader debate on the purposes of the schooling system. As Raymond Williams has succinctly pointed out, nineteenth century England was characterized by a debate between "the public educators, the industrial trainers, and the old humanists."[4] (p. 142) Over this debate:

> The shadow of class thinking lies . . . as over so much other nineteenth-century educational thinking. The continued relegation of trade and industry to lower social classes, and the desire of successful industrialists that their sons should move into the now largely irrelevant class of gentry, were alike extremely damaging to English education and English life. As at the Reformation, a period of major reconstruction of institutions was undertaken largely without reference to the best learning of the age, and without any successful redefinition of the purposes of education and of the content of a contemporary liberal culture.[4] (p. 143)

The preempting of the curricula of elite education by the languages of ancient Greece and Rome and mathematics also involved exclusion, specifically the exclusion of knowledge of the natural sciences and technology: ". . . the decisive educational interpretation of this new knowledge was not in terms of its essential contribution to liberal studies, but in terms of technical training for a particular class of men."[4] (p. 142) Thus, in secondary and tertiary educational institutions, class-specific curricula were developing at various times in the nineteenth century.

The slowly developing elementary system was hindered by both religious and financial difficulties (and little of the Newcastle Report was adopted by the government of the day). But curriculum provision was not seen as a major difficulty. Evidence presented by the Rev. James Fraser, an assistant commissioner with whom the Commission agreed, outlined the following philosophy:

> I venture to maintain that it is quite possible to teach a child soundly and thoroughly . . . by the time that he is 10 years old. If he has been properly looked after in the lower classes, he shall be able to spell correctly the words that he will ordinarily have to use; he shall read a common narrative – the paragraph in the newspaper that he cares to read . . . he knows enough of ciphering to make out, or test the correctness of, a common shop bill . . .; and underlying all . . . has . . . a sufficient recollection of the truths taught him in his catechism, to know what are the duties required of him towards his Maker and his fellow man. I have no brighter view of the future or the possibilities of an English elementary education, floating before my eyes than this.[3] (pp. 75–76)

Similarly, an explicitly class-based analysis of the education of middle class children was provided by the Taunton Commission. Within the middle classes, the Commission discerned three main groups. For the "first grade" group, remaining in the educational system until 18 years, the provision was to be essentially classics and mathematics. For those who intended their children to leave school at 16 for the army and other professions, a different curriculum was offered by the Commission:

> It may be said, that in education of this grade a certain amount of thorough knowledge of those subjcts which can be turned to practical use in business, English, arithmetic, the rudiments of mathematics beyond arithmetic, in some cases natural science, in some cases a modern language, is considered by the parents absolutely indispensable, and that they will not allow any culture, however valuable otherwise, to take the place of these.[3] (p. 94)

For the lower middle classes, "the smaller tenant farmers, the small tradesmen, the superior artisans" the prescription was "very good reading, very good writing, very good arithmetic."[3] (p. 95)

Few of the Taunton Commission's recommendations passed into legislation, but of course what is noteworthy about them here is the degree to which they further differentiate what was already class-based curriculum provision. Gradations of occupational status and probable future are punctiliously marked.

The English debate on the educational system, including appropriate curricula, in the nineteenth century was, of course, in part a debate about social stability and integration. But this political debate also included reference to the industrial system as this affected both tertiary and elementary education toward the end of the century. The rationale for the establishment of the "civic universities" in London and the big industrial towns of the North, including Manchester, Birmingham, Leeds, and Liverpool, was partly related to religious dissent; but it was also heavily economic, being concerned with countering the industrial competition that was developing in Europe. Thus, these new higher education institutions stressed in their curricula both management and the application of technology to industrial processes.

The twin arguments – the economic, and the political argument stressing social stability – were in fact presented together in W. E. Forster's speech in favor of his 1870 Elementary Education Bill:

> Upon the speedy provision of elementary education depends our industrial prosperity. It is of no use trying to give technical teaching to our artizans without elementary education ... and if we leave our work-folk any longer unskilled, notwithstanding their strong sinews and determined energy, they will become over-matched in the competition of the world. Upon this speedy provision depends also, I fully believe, the good, the safe working of our constitutional system. ... I am one of those who would not wait until the people were educated before I would trust them with political power ... but now that we have given them political power we must not wait any longer to give them education.[3] (p. 104)

Thus, toward the end of the nineteenth century the developing schooling system can be seen in reciprocal relationship with both the political and industrial systems. Extensions in political franchise are correlated with extensions in the educational franchise. Changes in the industrial system very gradually produce provision of new curricula forms in new tertiary institutions of education. For most of the century, education for nonelite groups was self-generated and on a voluntarist basis. As gradually the State moved to specify educational provision, through commissions and then legislation, and subsequent schooling structures, class-based definitions of curricula emerged that linked skills and consciousness to probable adult occupation. Throughout the nineteenth century, there was a continual concern, however, for the formation of elite consciousness through classical and mathematical curricula, taught in particular institutions. These institutions, essentially the public schools and the apex institutions of Oxbridge, and their teaching staffs were associated with the Church of England, and their curriculum provision saw to the production of cultivated Christian gentlemen. This training remained largely unproblematic and remained undisturbed by many features of industrial and political change.

This situation was in many respects dissimilar from that prevailing in France in approximately the same period.[5] The central fact about French educational history in the first half of the nineteenth century was that France had experienced a political revolution at the end of the eighteenth century. There were three particular correlates of the revolution that are especially relevant here: firstly, the role of the Catholic Church in the general provision of education and in the formation of curricula was severely diminished; secondly, a new political class, the bourgeoisie, came to power and proceeded to create an educational system appropriate to its interests; and thirdly, under the stress of the revolution, the two principles of egalitarianism and national unity were invoked. We shall look in a moment, at the decline of egalitarianism; but the principle of national unity led to a considerably different provision of educational structures. The French created a nationally administered educational system, which soon after the Revolution was construed as a State organized meritocracy to provide skilled talent for the national administration. The curriculum fairly rapidly bifurcated to support this system – basic literacy for all and special skills for some.

Thus, in terms of the English parameters of the nineteenth century schooling situation – religion, markedly differentiated class curricula in a piecemeal administrative provision for education, and adjustments made for both extensions of suffrage and extensions of industrialization – the French parameters appear in different importance and weights. Religion as a constraining factor was severely muted; such class-oriented discussions as there were over curricula were debates between sections of the bourgeoisie; and industrialization did not generally alter curricula until the end of the century.

One of the major similarities, however, between English and French education in the nineteenth century is that the French, too, made careful and serious provision for elite education; and this of course is the paradox of French education in the nineteenth century: a revolution that made explicit the principles of egalitarianism is followed within two decades by an educational system that stressed elitist meritocracy.

Condorcet's writing is conventionally taken as the touchstone of republican aims in education. He offered a plan for a national system of education that would be universal and offer primary instruction to all. Such institutions would both develop rationality and provide a base on which, by a secondary system, further training could be offered to the talented. Thus, both equality of opportunity and the free development of individual potentialities would be developed by the same structural system.

However, under the Empire, the balance between (a) education as a right of citizens and (b) as a necessity for the administration of the State shifted. Napoleon's reforms concentrated upon the provision of trained talent and new elites to fill the gap left by the destruction of the aristocratic elites:

> Whereas the early republicans sought to embody in the educational system the duty of the State towards the citizen, the imperial heirs of the revolutionary tradition founded educational institutions on citizens' obligations to the state. This definition of citizenship as a commitment rather than a right was in no way alien to the spirit of republican France, since it could be traced to Jacobin policy, dictated by considerations of national necessity rather than enlightened idealism. Liberty may have provided a source of inspiration, but as a subject of instruction it soon appeared aimless.[6] (p. 78)

The institutional structure that Napoleon established was the Imperial University, which essentially centralized and supervized the system of *lycées*, a reorganized École Polytechnique, and a recreated École Normale. Entrance to these institutions was by competitive examination, the *concours*, and thus could be justified on meritocratic criteria.

Of more immediate importance here, is curriculum provision. As Vaughan has translated and quoted Napoleon, curriculum provided both an intellectual *and* conservative training:

> Above all, let us give some sound and strong reading material to the youth of the regime. Corneille, Boussuet, those are the masters it needs. That is great, sublime, and at the same time regular, peaceful, subordinated. Those do not make revolutions; they do not inspire any. On the sails of obedience, they enter into the established order of their time; they strengthen it, they embellish it.[6] (pp. 87–88)

In the *lycées* themselves, at that time numbering about thirty, and boarding schools, classics and mathematics were at the center of the curriculum. In the *colleges*, the curriculum ". . . included French, Latin, the elements of geography and history, and mathematics."[7] (p. 220) To the primary schools – under Napoleon essentially handed back to Catholic teachers – went very little attention. On this development, Scotford-Archer and Vaughan are severe:

> Under the successful revolutionary regimes, the church had been debarred from dispensing primary education, while the state had proved incapable of doing so. Napoleon's decision to restore the teaching orders to their former position

reflected a realistic assessment of educational priorities in relation to state needs and resources. The overt endorsement of a policy of social control for the lower orders made it possible to dispense with the lip-service which revolutionary Assemblies had paid to egalitarianism and to concentrate on secondary instruction for an elite. Leaving primary schooling to the clergy implied the official endorsement of a double standard – reason being the preserve of the bourgeoisie and faith the guarantee of popular passivity.[5] (p. 118)

Although elementary education became compulsory in 1816, without sanctions to enforce attendance, it is perhaps of more importance to note here that curriculum provision was limited to the three Rs and that ". . . under the decree of 1811, inspectors were to verify that, apart from religious knowledge, no other subjects were taught."[5] (p. 125) This division between primary education – for the undefined Fourth Estate – and secondary education, continued during the nineteenth century and had still not been removed by the 1880s. Even by 1886 there had been no joining of ". . . primary education and its various prolongations (Complementary Courses, Upper Primary Schools) to the older forms of secondary education. Parallel to the education given in *lycées* and *colleges*, the establishments set up by the law of 1886 were organized into a separate system tending to satisfy different needs and a different clientele."[8] (pp. 1–2) By 1887 the elementary school curriculum had altered, and the curriculum included:

> . . . ethics and civic education; reading and writing; arithmetic and the metric system; history and geography, with particular reference to France; elements of natural science; drawing and singing; and manual work, principally as applied to agriculture . . . physical education.[9] (p. 63)

Technical education, like industrialization, came late to France. Essentially dating from 1892, it was added to earlier forms of education. The result was that "Each one of these successive establishments, necessary and fruitful in itself contributed by its practical character to the organization of the different schools [i.e., the *lycées*, the *colleges*, the elementary schools] as separate closed systems with recruitment from distinct social classes and with different aims."[8] (p. 2)

The French, then, like the English were providing status specific curricula: in the elementary school, a form of political education appropriate to social quiescence, and in the elementary school and in the technical system, toward the end of the century, an education that more readily supported the needs of a growing industrial system. The elite forms of education were not merely supplied in different institutions – the *lycées* and the *colleges* – but were defined by different curricula. The curricula are essentially examples of "lag phenomena," in this case definitions of ways of training men's mind embodied in Jesuit traditions that passed into the Napoleonic definition of the situation. These traditions included ". . . reasoned exegesis of texts, frequent repetition of what has been learned, learning by heart, frequent translations, imitation and disputation."[8] (p. 24) Compare this with a statement made in the 1950s:

> . . . there are periods in the intellectual development of man which we must use exclusively for the training and not for the filling of the mind. At these times we must learn those methods of work which impart a taste for free thought, sound judgment and criticism. And nothing is better fitted to that purpose than the exercise of translating the ancient languages. Because it teaches nothing. It trains.[8] (p. 46)

These apparent criticisms are not of course to deny that the curriculum of the *lycées* was a subject of nineteenth century debate. But there are two things that help place this debate in perspective: firstly, it was a debate among the bourgeoisie about the nature of a bourgeois education, i.e., the specific definition of *culture générale*; and secondly, despite changes in industrial and agricultural techniques that had produced pressure for curriculum reform at the ministerial level by the 1860s, the debate — a three-way debate among classicists and modern language and natural science advocates — was not resolved until the decade 1892–1902.

One adaptation made in curricula, to deal with changes in the agricultural and industrial base, was made in the new *Ecoles Primaires Supérieures* created in 1876. Provision was made for the treatment, in this extended form of elementary education, for topics of an agricultural, industrial, commercial, and maritime nature. Thus, these schools provided both for a practical training and an appropriate avenue for working-class ambition. But even here these schools were a separate educational channel — they did not give direct access to the *lycées*. As Talbot points out in his monograph on French education ". . . over the course of the nineteenth century, the design of men in power had made of primary and secondary education two separate worlds, unlike in purpose, spirit, methods, and in the social origins of their clientele."[10] (p. 30)

Thus, France, like England, shows considerable tendencies toward the construction of class-specific consciousness through differentiated curricula in the schooling system. Like England, there was considerable consensus upon the institutional routes and the substantive areas through which elite consciousness would be trained. Like England, the elite secondary and higher institutions were strongly articulated — though in the case of France, and in accord with French meritocratic principles, the articulation mechanism was competitive examination. Like England, the elite form of education proved inappropriate in value-stance for close involvement in technology or the details of industrial technique. And like England, France gradually created a set of technical institutions with their own carefully separated curricula at a time of increased industrialization. Like England, and despite a much more egalitarian political philosophy and a far greater concern for meritocratic principle, France made little provision for elementary education until late in the nineteenth century. The curriculum definition of the situation stressed the rudiments of a practical education toward the end of the century and careful political socialization throughout the century.

Both countries arrived at a definition of social integration through differentiated class-specific consciousness. Both countries developed a fairly consensual definition of the form, substance and purpose of elite education; both stressed in practice the freeing effects of what were taken to be nonutilitarian, disinterested curricula, and both used the education for functional purposes. Both made reluctant adjustment to the claims of science and technology for places in the schooling curriculum; and both ensured that such forms of education were, for a long time, nonelite forms of education in substance in England and in substance, and in pedagogic method in France. The example of both countries suggests that if there are certainties about elite education, what becomes problematic is the provision of mass education. Let us now look at two countries where there are relative certainties about the provision of mass education.

At first glance, the concrete situations of Cuba and China — the differences in population size, geographic area, agricultural and industrial base — seem sufficient to invalidate comparisons between them and, of course, between them and nineteenth century England and France. But in terms of the theme of this paper, the comparison is highly germane. Firstly, the stated perspectives of the actors in the nineteenth and twentieth century situations, the attitudes to socioeconomic groupings to the distribution of educational knowledge and to a definition of societal future, are diametrically oppositional. A comparison between such dissimilar positions throws into sharp perspective that which otherwise may seem a matter of nuance in the educational knowledge arrangements of many Western societies. Secondly, Cuba and China share the fact of their revolutionary situation and the attempt to operationalize in the twentieth century the fundamentally nineteenth century solution to the problems of social organization propounded theoretically by Marx. This has significant consequences for a similar definition of educational knowledge and informs the principles by which it is legitimated and distributed.

In this perspective, even the literacy campaigns and the adult education movements of Cuba and China become not simply efforts toward "modernization" and the eradication of a past influenced by colonialism, but exercises in the distribution of educational knowledge in accord with revolutionary political principles. In Cuba, 1961 was decreed the "Year of Education" and a major effort was made to eliminate illiteracy. Through a varied set of techniques including adult volunteers (*alphabetizadores*) and mobile student volunteer brigades (*brigadistas*) working in both town and country, the national average illiteracy rate was brought down below five percent. In China, estimates of illiteracy at the time of liberation approached 80 or 90 percent; and the illiteracy problem was of course compounded by the issue of what constituted a basic vocabulary (of characters) whether or not *hanyn pinyin* was initially used. Furthermore, China too was affected by both the regional problem, complete with minorities and the rural—urban difficulties that Cuba also experienced. In China, it was not until 1956 that efforts to eliminate illiteracy in rural areas became strenuous. Nevertheless, there is some consensus among China experts that currently illiteracy is no longer a major problem.[11]

In both China and Cuba, the literacy campaigns were followed by or associated with major efforts at adult education. In Cuba, the initial effort was to provide education for half a million adults up to third-grade level, and this was followed by efforts to provide the equivalent of education up to the sixth grade.[13] In China, the history of the adult education movement goes as far back as the Yenan period when adult education was given precedence over the education of children. Political night schools, classes in communes and in factories, and special study sessions continue the process contemporariously. The adult education movement in China, as in Cuba, has three aims: to confirm literacy, to advance specific occupational skills, and to continue and reaffirm political education and awareness.[12]

Two things are noticeable in this context. Firstly, while China and Cuba share with a large number of other third world countries a desire to eradicate illiteracy and raise the educational level of adults, their stance toward literacy and adult education is informed by mass mobilization, revolutionary principle, and considerable success. Literacy campaigns and adult education are also a continuous process for both revolutionary political and economic reasons. As well as providing an increase in the skills of the adult population, literacy and continuous adult education provide access to political writings and political thought. In this sense the more or less equal distribution of educational knowledge is both a revolutionary right and duty. The analogue is perhaps less to a technically sound campaign to reduce illiteracy than to a religious movement that needs literacy in its initiates so that they can follow holy texts.

The second characteristic of both countries is that literacy and adult education is "exported," in the sense that if conventional schooling institutions are not available, educational provision – in the form of paraprofessionals, youth half-way through their own education, army groups, and organizations of workers – is taken to the recipients. In Cuba, for example, three different educational calendars exist (for rural, mountain, and urban areas) that are a function of argicultural exigencies; in China, industrial and other production units and local communities have established their own schools.[13] Thus, the principle of the revolutionary distribution of educational knowledge is matched by the development of fresh mechanisms to carry out the task.

The conception of a schooling system is also broader than the Western conventions in this area. There is an extremely explicit articulation of the wider society and the conventional schooling system that *school-age pupils* attend. In China there is considerable emphasis upon pupils learning from "the workers, soldiers, and peasants"; to implement this, pupils will often visit factories, communes, and other places of work during their schooling, as well as experiencing further attachment to a production unit at the end of their school careers as a *sine qua non* for admittance to tertiary education. In both China and Cuba, productive labor classes will find a place within the school curriculum even for very young children.

A similar nonwestern broadening of the schooling situation occurs through the efforts made to avoid, among the teaching group, a sense of separateness and "academic bourgeois professionalism." For example, in China, not only are efforts made to disturb (since the Cultural Revolution) what was interpreted as the incipient authoritarianism of teachers, but the schooling system is also penetrated by adults (and thus role models) who are not formally trained as teachers. Thus, most schools have both Mao Tse Tung Thought Propaganda Teams and also experienced workers who act as teachers (in lessons of, say, elementary engineering principles or rice-planting techniques). These general characteristics of "permeability" are referred to as making an "open door school."

The principle involved here is fascinating and important: it is the wider society itself, and especially the proletarian work situation, that is properly educative. The schooling system and the educational knowledge defined therein focuses on "real-world" and especially work-knowledge. The schooling system becomes a convenient institutional location for the organization of the age-cohort in that transmission.

The broad legitimation through which this redefinition of educational knowledge (and of course the significance of literacy, adult education, and the enlarged conception of the schooling system) is made appropriate is the particular reinterpretations of Marxism worked out in Cuba and China. In general, these reinterpretations and the new models of man they espouse are well known and will not be presented here. The "curriculum theory" (in Western terms) is conventionally called "polytechnical," but in this case the confusions grow myriad enough for the term to be avoided and the specific situations of Cuba and China in terms of curriculum provision to be described briefly.

In Cuba, within a frame of socially useful work such as care of the school premises, the elementary school curriculum includes language, spelling, drawing, music, and manual arts, mathematics, social studies, various natural sciences and ". . . health and safety (elementary anatomy, physiology, hygiene, first aid, camping, physical education)."[13] (p. 433)

The secondary provision, in which student enrollment is low, sees ". . . courses in history, Spanish, geography, biology, chemistry, mathematics, physics, polytechnical instruction, and agricultural-livestock production. The humanities play a very minor role."[13] (p. 435) (Students of course in addition, participate in organized productive labor.) After basic secondary schooling, vocational and technical education is provided.

In higher education, major revisions have occurred. The major stress has been upon the technological and natural sciences. The proportion of students in humanities has dropped sharply from about one-third to around one-twentieth.

To repeat, the frame of this formal curriculum is a stress upon productive labor. Elementary school pupils work for two hours daily; secondary school pupils may do as much as four hours productive labor per day, and universities, as indicated, both by shifts in curriculum and occasionally by physical relocation of individual faculties (e.g., engineering to civil construction projects) have become technologized and involved with the work situation.

The role of the curriculum and its relationship with work is moral rather than economic:

> Through productive labour, students and teachers learn that in the society we are constructing, a society of workers, work constitutes the most precious value of man. Also, students and teachers realise the worth of production. Work in agriculture modifies the consumer mentality which characterizes capitalist society, because in a socialist society the men that are formed have a mentality geared to the production of wealth. Moreover, students and teachers acquire a strong agricultural orientation with scientific and technical foundations, which is very important for the economic development of our country . . . Although this plan was not conceived for economic reasons, but as a pedagogical tool, it has also helped to solve our production problems.[13] (pp. 448–449)

In China within the new, shortened 5-2-2 schooling structure, "the primary school subjects are politics and language, arithmetic, revolutionary literature and art, military training and physical culture, and productive labor."[12] (p. 53)

In the middle school, the curriculum core is Mao Thought and Politics. Productive labor, physical culture and military training also have a place in the curriculum. And the conventional academic subjects of the Western world, mathematics and the sciences, are often taught in applied form being firmly linked with production problems in the agricultural and industrial spheres. Similarly in higher education, especially since the Cultural Revolution, the curriculum has been simplified. The study of humanities now occupies a small role and the stress has moved further toward the study of politics and the applied sciences, where the practicalities of production and immediacy of contribution to the problems of China are stressed. Thus, "the university exists for service and for the revolution; its mission is to produce a proletarian intelligensia, not an intellectual elite. It is no place for academic research on topics of no immediate practical use. The dominance of the triad of 'teachers, classrooms, textbooks' has been shattered."[12] (p. 154) This interpretation of the role of the university is, of course, reinforced both by the curriculum core (agriculture, industry, military affairs, and politics stressed in the May 7 Directive) and by the productive labor experience of students before and during their studies, and by the regular involvement of college teachers in productive labor away from the institutions of higher education.

The consequences and correlates of these forms of curriculum provision within the broader value frame of legitimation are of some importance. Crucially, it seems as if an effort has been made to break the linkage between educational certification and occupational placement. Occupational placement remains partly a function of the (formal) educational history and level attained by an individual; but especially in China, attainment within the educational system is seen as a function of a high level of revolutionary consciousness. This is measured primarily by peer evaluation in a work situation. The steps for gaining admittance to higher education in China include individual application, assessment by the "masses" (i.e., work-peers) and approval by the Party leadership at the local level. Formal conventional academic examinations have in China, unlike Cuba, been abolished. Thus, educational knowledge successfully mastered and (in Western terms) conventionally measured is not the sole or major criterion for admission to the next level of the educational system or to the occupational structure. It is worth repeating here that Cuba, without a "cultural revolution," has not yet broken this nexus in the fundamental fashion of the Chinese effort. Indeed, Cuba possesses a comprehensive system of examinations organized at the national level.

Secondly, changes in educational knowledge are fundamentally legitimated at the national level, from the center, in both countries, though in China such changes may be operationalized in text books, etc., in the concrete circumstances of a locality. Thus, the question of "for which groups is educational knowledge most easily changed" is an inappropriate one; educational knowledge is changed for all, from the center and in this facet is standardized and nondivisable because of the centrality of a *Weltanschauung* and the importance of its universal distribution.

The centrality of a *Weltanschauung* and the importance of its universal distribution is related in part to the problem of "lag phenomena," the persistence through time of older value patterns while the institutional framework of society has undergone rapid transformation. Thus, in Cuba there is explicit consciousness about the crucial role of education in revolutionizing consciousness, and in China, the cultural revolution itself and the current campaign against Lin Piao and Confucius (merging currently into a fresh campaign on the "dictatorship of the proletariat") is in heavy measure *past* oriented. Although the structural-objective conditions for the creation of class consciousness have in the Chinese interpretation been removed, persistence of "old ideologies" is explicitly recognized by the Chinese as possible. The role of a universally distributed educational knowledge is crucial in this battle. The evidence from the Cuban situation is slight, but there are some indications that this struggle is proceeding less well than the Chinese effort since the Cultural Revolution.

The dispersion of social, economic, and political power in the two countries is construed as potentially socialist, and the impact of this on the way educational knowledge is legitimated and distributed is of course, obvious; a classless society involves classless knowledge distribution. In Western bourgeois terms there is an *inversion* of Western status patterns. The dominant social groupings, in principle, are the workers, soldiers and poor and lower middle peasants; intellectuals are to be proletarianized and workers intellectualized. The referent for appropriate educational knowledge becomes that which is appropriate for use in the concrete life-situations of workers, soldiers and peasants.

The thrust of legitimation is thus, firmly toward the definition of "mass knowledge." What becomes problematic is the legitimation and distribution of "elite" knowledge. In specific context, the general proposition is well illustrated in the Chinese debate about "red and expert." Partly, of course, the answer to the problem was reworked during the Cultural Revolution: redness was to guarantee expertise. But the problem remains at a number of levels. How, theoretically, is "elite knowledge," more appropriately termed "expert" knowledge, to be justified, transmitted, and utilized without the growth of bourgeois consciousness? The development of "expert" knowledge implies the nonequal distribution of educational knowledge, and the differentiation of educational knowledge among subgroups in the population. The institutional solutions, in the socialization of students in the May 7 Cadre Schools or, for example, in the Peking Peoples University, pay a great deal of practical attention to the solution of the problem. But the problem is not simply a theoretical one, nor one for which particular solutions are being worked out institutionally. It is a national problem, both because of Chinese aspirations for an independent world role, and for economic growth. The early industrial revolutions of the Western world – including those of the two Western countries analyzed here – were essentially pragmatic, practical piecemeal revolutions. The organization of science to affect the industrial sector, the structured generation of applied science in specialist research institutions was a late nineteenth century German phenomenon, and one to which France and England reacted belatedly, and for which their elite forms of knowledge, conferring status and honor, ill-prepared them. But the "institutionalization of innovation" affects subsequent industrializers, and is an economic fact that makes the generation of expert knowledge in China necessary (if her self-defined economic goals are to be attained) and problematic at the level of legitimation and social control.

The implications of the comparative sketches presented above are numerous. Obviously, one area open for further exploration is whether the educational knowledge forms available in French and English schools have continued their status-specific characteristics. Major national reports such as for England the Newsom Report and the Plowden Report might be examined in such terms to see how detailed and innovative knowledge-specifications are, and how such specifications are legitimated. Similarly the analysis would be well extended to such countries as the USSR, Nazi Germany, Tanzania, and Spain; or to countries like Sweden, Canada, and the USA, which have made major efforts to "democratize" their educational systems. In the USA itself a series of case studies might be carried through to analyze how particular groups, especially blacks and women, were able to legitimate and institutionalize their specialized versions of educational knowledge.

Substantively, it is clear that what was legitimated in France and England in the nineteenth century was not educational knowledge, but a series of educational knowledges. Distribution of educational knowledges to other than elite groups was slow, at times a little reluctant, and tended toward a stress on social control ("our future masters . . . should at least learn their letters"). Considerable certainties were generated over elite knowledge and what became problematic were the terms on which knowledge might be distributed to other groups. The basic parameters of the situation seem to have been political rather than economic. The elite forms of knowledge in England were for the definition of moral and political certainties, and in France even the *grandes écoles* became affected by traditions that predated the Empire. For most of the nineteenth century the links of educational knowledge with the economic system were not pronounced. Technological knowledge could remain low status; industrial progress did not depend primarily upon an applied science "service elite." In contrast, of course, in contemporary China (though to a much lesser extent in Cuba because of its different economic base and its world situation) expert, technological knowledge is needed and must be generated within a world context of the "institutionalization of innovation." As a consequence it is suggested that although the certainties about mass knowledge, its type and the generality of its distribution, are relatively high, how to legitimate and institutionalize expert ("elite") knowledge in China and Cuba is problematic.

The roles of the educational institutions in the two sets of countries in institutionalizing (and thus sustaining the legitimations of educational knowledge) are interestingly different. On the one hand, in France and England the *lycées and grandes écoles*, and the public schools and Oxbridge sustained and preempted the most prestigious forms of knowledge. (In England the public schools influenced the state-developed sector at the levels of both formal and hidden curriculum; and Oxbridge tended to be extremely influential in status terms over other English universities.) On the other hand, China and Cuba have tended to avoid the creation of "apex institutions" and have introduced institutional innovations both because of their perception of the social role of knowledge and the intention of generally diffusing that knowledge. The institutional and normative orders show, logically enough and also in the intentions of the social actors, strains toward consistency.

At a more general level, the analysis implies questions about the basic sociological perspectives through which we carry out analyses of educational systems. Following Scotford-Archer and Vaughan's analysis, it can be suggested that traditional Marxist theory becomes a poor predictor of educational events in England and France in the nineteenth century. In England the economically most powerful new middle class of entrepreneurs failed significantly to affect the provision of educational knowledge until the late 1880s. Similarly, a conventional Marxist analysis fails to explain changes in French education before industrialization in the 1860s and 1870s. Agriculture remained the basic mode of production and yet the definition of the educational situation changes. As Scotford-Archer and Vaughan suggest, changes in education were a consequence of the new political role of bourgeoisie. The central problem is, of course, a theoretical one: until Marxist theory develops a more complex and delicate statement of the determined linkages between material base and superstructure, it will remain illuminating as a perspective but a weakened guide to comparative analysis.

At first glance, Weber's general theory of "rationalization" and his more education-specific construct of the "cultivated" and the "expert" seems to help with the explanation of developments in all societies. But the expert-cultivated dichotomy is problematic. The difficulty here is not with nineteenth century Europe, which Weber was in part concerned to analyze. The problem is with China and Cuba. The universally distributed knowledge possessed by the masses hardly fits Weber's definition of "cultivated." Such knowledge possesses none of the charisma-conferring characteristics of the educational knowledge preferred for the English gentleman or the Chinese mandarin. Nor yet, despite certain of its specialized, secular characteristics is it "expert." It fails to differentiate the population of educands. In fact, the suggested problematic theme for Chinese and Cuban education was the creation and justification of such (differentiating) expertise.

This is not, of course, to suggest that the short comparative sketch provided in the paper offers a direct critique of some of the major sociologists of the Western world. It is to suggest that the very recent debate of a hitherto neglected topic could, if it were sustained, be illuminating at the practical level of educational policy formulation and possibly stimulating for a reconceptualization of the relationships between schooling systems and the societies in which they are located.

REFERENCES

1. YOUNG, F. D. M., Ed. 1971. Knowledge and Control: New Directions in the Sociology of Education. Collier-Macmillan Publishers. London, England.
2. LAUWERYS, J. A. 1967. Opening address. *In* General Education in a Changing World: Containing the Papers Read Before the Society at the Second General Meeting Berlin 1965. The Comparative Education Society in Europe. Martinus Nijhoff. The Hague, Netherlands.
3. MACLURE, J. STUART. 1965. Educational Documents: England and Wales 1816–1967. Chapman and Hall Ltd. London, England.
4. WILLIAMS, R. 1961. The Long Revolution. Columbia University Press. New York, N.Y.
5. VAUGHAN, M. & M. SCOTFORD-ARCHER. 1971. Social conflict and educational change in England and France 1789–1848. Cambridge at the University Press, England.
6. WILKINSON, R., Ed. 1969. Governing Elites: Studies in Training and Selection. Oxford University Press. New York, N.Y.
7. BARNARD, A. C. 1969. Education and the French Revolution. Cambridge at the University Press, England.
8. FRASER, W. R. 1963. Education and Society in Modern France. Routledge and Kegan Paul. London, England.
9. MALE, G. A. 1963. Education in France. U.S. Department of Health, Education, and Welfare. Washington, D.C.
10. TALBOTT, J. E. 1969. The Politics of Educational Reform in France, 1918–1940. Princeton University Press. Princeton, New Jersey.
11. PRICE, R. F. 1970. Education in Communist China. Praeger Publishers. New York, N.Y.
12. CHEN, T. H. 1974. The Maoist Educational Revolution. Praeger Publishers. New York, N.Y.
13. BONACHEA, R. E. & N. P. VALDES. 1972. Cuba in Revolution. Anchor Books. Doubleday and Company, Inc. Garden City, N.Y.

STUDIES OF MEMORY IN CULTURE

David F. Lancy

Learning Research and Development Center
University of Pittsburgh
Pittsburgh, Pennsylvania 15260

INTRODUCTION

The studies reported here grew out of a sense of frustration for what might be called the "standard" procedure in cross-cultural research. In a series of studies conducted over a three-year period this investigator and colleagues[1] compared the word-recall performance of American and Kpelle subjects.[2] Reliable differences between these two groups were consistently found. Specifically, it was found that Americans when confronted with a task that required the recall of randomly presented words, tended to cluster those words into taxonomic categories and showed, thereby, improved recall. Kpelle subjects, except those that had at least a sixth-grade education, did not show such clustering effects and consequently showed a marked deficit in recall as compared to their American counterparts.

This appeared to be a relatively straightforward finding of an overall absence in one culture of the use of the taxonomic properties inherent in words to aid recall. Several further findings, however, made the results appear less straightforward. First, through a variety of techniques it was established that the Kpelle do indeed categorize common objects (the stimuli used in the free-recall experiments) and that there was good agreement across informants on the nature and content of these categories. Second, in one study by Cole, et al.,[1] the twenty stimuli used in several of the experiments were held for a few seconds over one of four chairs. Even though the objects were presented randomly, all five objects from any one of the four categories represented in the stimuli list were held over one of the chairs. Thus, each chair cued for one and only one category. This procedure greatly enhanced both taxonomic clustering and recall for Kpelle subjects. On the other hand, several replications of this study done by this investigator (previously unreported) failed to show such effects. These replications used smaller objects placed in a matrixlike grid and tested the assumption that something like "cueing by spatial location" accounted for the "chairs" results. No such assumption was supported by the results.

What we had then was a culture—memory interaction but we knew too little about the culture variable to account for either the absence or presence of taxonomic clustering in general; nor did we know enough about Kpelle culture to account for why chairs should be an effective cueing device. In fact, chairs are a Western introduction, they are absent in traditional Kpelle culture. It was the aim of the present series of studies then to describe memory in the context of Kpelle culture. I wanted to discover, if possible, the extent of taxonomic clustering or any other memory process in the naturally occurring tasks which members of the Kpelle tribe habitually encounter and require the recall of verbal stimuli.

I would also argue, incidentally, that the problem we encountered is not unique. All too frequently, cross-cultural studies show differences in performance for some test by people from two or more cultures without being able to satisfactorily account for these differences. For this reason no theory of the relationship between culture and thought has emerged with any credibility. The remedy appears to be to redo, wherever possible, the ethnographies of primitive or traditional societies with an eye for the kinds of situations that will have an impact on cognition. We must have the kind of cultural accounts which will allow us to predict with some confidence the presence or absence of particular cognitive traits on the part of all members or some specified subgroup of the society under investigation. In other words, cross-cultural psychology must be preceded by within-culture psychology.

The research to be reported here addresses questions of memory variations within a single cultural setting in the belief that such studies, buttressed by an extensive ethnographic account, will ultimately lead to the discovery of those features of culture which are most likely to affect human memory. Four such questions are raised here and a piece of research that was designed to provide some answers is described.

These questions are:

1. What are the tasks in a particular culture that require the exercise of memory?
2. Do individuals vary in their involvement with these tasks?
3. What memory processes are implicated in these tasks?
4. Are these memory processes employed in novel situations?

What are the Tasks in a Particular Culture that Require the Exercise of Memory?

Virtually all tasks one could name involve memory, but in this study the question is constrained in several ways. First, tasks are here taken to mean well-defined and bounded activities that are stable within a society over time. Second, the tasks are limited to those that demand verbal memory, or memory for spoken words, phrases, narratives, etc., as against memory for pictoral, written, kinaesthetic, or sensori-motor images. Basically, I was looking for clear task-verbal memory relationships such as the Iatmul custom of totem-naming which Bateson[3] saw as making very specific demands on memory. Third, in selecting a traditional, nonliterate West African society for the research, the number of possible tasks that met the first two criteria was lessened considerably.

This society was set in a Liberian hinterland town (population ≈ 800) inhabited principally by members of the Kpelle tribe. The principle tasks that demand an exercise of verbal memory by residents of the town of Gbarngasuakwelle (GSK) are storytelling, singing, a game called *KɔIɔη* and leaf-naming. There are four types of stories (*PɔIɔ*). *Meni-pele* are relatively simple in structure and have themes that stress clear-cut values. They always include a 2–3 line song that acts as refrain at intervals in the story. Even the nonsong portion is refrainlike in that a basic theme is changed as it is repeated only by the insertion of differing characters or activities. *PɔIɔ-γee* are parables; phrased as morality tales with a predictable ending or as creation myths. They are often quite long and involved (the telling may last 20 minutes) and are structurally more complex than *meni-pele*. *Sia-pɔIɔ* are riddles. These vary in length but most can be told in less than five minutes. Each riddle ends with a question which is then debated by the participants, with the teller having a final voice on the outcome. In debating, participants expand on the basic premises of the story to support their own interpretations. In *wei-meni-pele* a single-storyteller will entertain a crowd of people for hours, often all night. Here stories are strung together, interspersed with songs and gestures (often ribald). The stories are partly improvised and partly recalled, with the central theme being the natural and supernatural exploits and characteristics of various animals. The animals "stand for" humans and their traits and foibles.

Leaving aside for the moment the improvisation in *wei-meni-pele*, it seemed obvious that storytellers were recalling stories and not making them up on the spot. This impression is based on nearly a dozen storytelling sessions I set up where groups of children and of adults gathered in the evening and took turns telling stories, which I observed and simultaneously tape recorded. As a check on this, I asked one young boy to retell two of his *meni-pele* after a ten-day interval. I tape-recorded both the initial and retold versions of this boy's stories, and although the second versions were not identical with the first, they were clearly the same stories. If the boy had in fact been improvising, one would expect considerable variation from one telling to the next, which was not the case.

There appears to be three types of songs. These types, unlike stories, are not distinguished in Kpelle. The first type is short and the phraseology doesn't vary much from one occasion to the next. These songs as well as the other two types are mostly "call and response." A lead singer sings a line of verse, then a chorus sings a short (5 words or so) refrain. The second type of song tends to the other extreme. In this song there is total improvisation. The words appear only to serve the purpose of sustaining a melody. The third type lies midway between the first two. It is fairly long (20–40 lines) and it is not completely improvised, some elements may be retained from one occasion to the next. I collected songs in a manner similar to the story-collection procedure. Here I had two adults (one male, one female) each resing two of their songs after a ten-day interval. The extent of overlap for these four songs ranged from 10 to 50 percent. Thus, it may be true that being a good storyteller requires the exercise of verbal-recall abilities, other skills such as the ability to sing well and to keep up harmony and rhythm are clearly more salient in singing.

KƆlƆŋ is essentially a verbal memory game. Like some stories and songs, doing *KƆlƆŋ* requires the learning and production of linked phrases. This game is played by two teams composed of one to eight players each. These are two parts to the *KƆlƆŋ*. The first part, a stimulus phrase is called "*kƆlƆŋ*" the second or response part is called the "answer." One team begins by having one of its members tell a *kƆlƆŋ* or stimulus phrase. Members of the opposing team confer and try to supply the correct answer to match the offered *kƆlƆŋ*. If they succeed, they may now offer a *kƆlƆŋ*; if they fail the first team gives the answer then offers another *kƆlƆŋ*. An example of *kƆlƆŋ* and answer pair:

K: I fall this way and I fall that way.
A: A calabash can't say it won't sit under the palm-wine.

An interesting feature of *KƆlƆŋ* is that the answers are proverbs. The one in the example means, in effect, children can't refuse to obey their parents. Children who play the game are, however, not aware of this connection until late adolescence, when they begin to be aware of and use proverbs.

I asked 32 male and female informants of varying ages to tell me all the *KƆlƆŋ* they remembered. The total number of *KƆlƆŋ* pairs collected was 87. For all informants, the average number remembered was eight pairs. *KƆlƆŋ*, then appear to be learned and remembered by virtually all residents of GSK.

Leaf-naming as a task was quite difficult to elucidate. Leaves are the principle components of medicines, and medicine-making is a secret activity in GSK. Medicine-men are called *Zo* by the Kpelle, and young men and women undergo a lengthy apprenticeship before achieving *Zo* status. One part of this process is the learning of leaf names. An apprentice goes into the forest with a *Zo* master and is tutored in leaf names. Later, he or she will be sent into the bush to bring back a "shopping list" of leaves. If the wrong leaves are brought, he or she is severely castigated and made to go again. The memory requirement, then, is the pairing of a leaf as object with the name for that particular leaf. Flora are elaborately taxonomized by the Kpelle, so the leaf-namer has class and taxa names to aid in discriminating the leaves. Stories, songs, the *KɔlɔN* game, and leaf-naming exhaust the verbal-memory tasks posed by this society. No other realm of activity whether work, play, or ritual appears to pose this kind of demand on memory. We turn now to a complementary question.

Do Individuals Vary in Their Involvement with these Tasks?

There is no Kpelle noun corresponding to "memory" and "being able to remember things" is not a prominent virtue. Adults are sometimes critical of children who forget things, but there is no praise for someone who remembers well. Nevertheless, from a performance standpoint, individuals are bound to vary in their verbal memory ability, and in this section, I hope to question whether differential involvement with the types of tasks described earlier might affect memory. Among the Tswana, for example, certain individuals are assigned the role of "rememberancer" in ward courts.[4] Here, there is a clear correlation between a memory-related task and a specific set of individuals.

In GSK these relationships are less obvious. Stories, in general, are told only by males and *meni-pele* by young boys exclusively. When I solicited *meni-pele* from children, some could tell as many as 10–14 such stories, others, of the same age could tell none. More systematically, I took a random sample of 20 from all boys aged 9–13 in the town. The 20 boys were divided into two groups and on several consecutive evenings, these boys were asked (one at a time, in random order) to tell a riddle (*sia-pɔlɔ*) they knew. The nine-year-olds could tell none and among the 10–15-year-olds the range of total riddles told was from 0–3, with a mean of 1.4. In a second study on riddle production, 10–13-year-old girls were asked to tell any stories they knew including riddles. None from this group could recall any stories. Finally in a third riddle study, seven adults (five male and two female) were asked to tell riddles. The women told no riddles and participated minimally in the debates that ensued. The men told from 2–4 riddles each of generally greater length and complexity than those told by the 10–13-year-old boys.

Coupled with participant observation of naturally-occurring storytelling sessions, these studies permit a few generalizations. First, although females listen to stories being told, they do not themselves tell stories, and they cannot *recall* stories when asked to do so. This finding might indicate only shyness with me and my (male) assistant as we attempted to collect stories from women, except that they willingly recalled *KɔlɔN* for us under similar conditions. Second, *meni-pele* are told and remembered by young boys (under age 10), older boys don't tell them nor recall them. There is, however, considerable variation here. Some young boys could recall many *meni-pele* others could recall few or none. I can't account for this finding other than to say that the high recall individuals obviously relished storytelling and would do so for their friends at the slightest urging. These boys demonstrated no other singular abilities or qualities. Third, *pɔlɔ-ɣɛɛ* and *sia-pɔlɔ* are told by older boys and men, but here the size of the repertory is less variable across individuals. Most males can tell at least one such story, few apparently can tell more than six.

The *wei-meni-pele* storyteller is indeed a specialist, I located only one individual in the town who has a reputation for *wei-meni-pele*. The ability to perform *wei-meni-pele*, doesn't, however, imply any special recall facility because, the stories are, to a large extent, improvisations. He must be rather clever, witty, socially perceptive, erudite, etc. Similarly, there are noted singers who are much sought after in ceremonies, but the performance is, again, largely improvisatory. The first of the song-types identified does require the exercise of memory. These songs remain intact from one occasion to the next. Knowledge of them peaks in late adolescence, with some males and females able to recall as many as eight such songs. An interesting point is that my informants had great difficulty recalling the songs unless they were singing *and* dancing. They could not reproduce them in a monotone or while stationary. Children from the age of four participate in circle-dances for which these songs are sung. These young children perform as part of the chorus which sings the response part of the song. By the age of nine, children occasionally take the lead in singing the call parts, but, this role is most often filled by adolescents. Hence, one can safely conclude that the learning of the songs requires no striking specialization in the use of verbal memory.

A similar pattern prevails with *Kɔlɔƞ*. Younger children are included on a team even though they may know few *Kɔlɔƞ*. As players, they are exposed to new *Kɔlɔƞ*, and a reasonable hypothesis would seem to be that children gradually acquire *Kɔlɔƞ* as they grow older. In the study mentioned earlier, young informants (8–13 years old, N = 16) produced two fewer *Kɔlɔƞ* pairs on the average than older informants (14-plus years old, N = 16). Another finding was that females play the game less frequently than males and recalled only half as many *Kɔlɔƞ* in the study.

All Kpelle make some medicines and all, therefore, learn the names of some leaves. *Zos* are specialists in medicine-making and, by inference, in the knowledge of leaf names. The secrecy shrouding medicine-making prevents an accurate assessment of the number of such specialists, but the number can't exceed ten in a town the size of GSK. Of this number the great majority are men. These specialists must indeed exercise extraordinary (relative to the population as a whole) memory abilities, not only with respect to leaf-naming, but in regard to the learning of medicine-making in general.[5] Again, however, secrecy prevents a more thorough analysis of the memory abilities of *Zos*; in fact, I was able to find only one such person who willingly announced his *Zo* status.

To summarize this section, it's clear there is differential involvement with tasks that require verbal memory. Leaf-naming is truly mastered only by specialists. Greater involvement by males in storytelling and *Kɔlɔƞ* is reflected in higher increased recall of stories and *Kɔlɔƞ* by males over females. Recall of songs appears to be a function of age with adolescents most involved in singing and, therefore, recalling more songs than any other age groups.

What Memory Processes are Implicated in These Tasks?

That societies create mnemonic devices to aid in storing and recalling information is well known.[6] The Kpelle employ nothing as obvious as a knotted cord, but a pattern does emerge in considering several of the tasks described above. I'm referring to the persistent tendency for verbal materials to be "paired." Virtually all songs are of the call and response type, where phrases are paired in song. *Meni-pele* stories also contain such songs. *Kɔlɔŋ* is a paired-phrase game, and leaf-naming is done through the pairing of a leaf with its name. Under the fourth question, a study designed to assess the strength of this "pair-associating" tendency is presented. This pronounced pairing tendency may not be a coincidence, but may represent a convergence of culture (the tasks) and memory, where it's true that "structured" material is more easily remembered than unstructured material.

Stories, on the other hand, seem to require what Bartlett[7] called "reconstruction." A story may be recalled in a series of context-bound premises which are then filled-in in an appropriate fashion. The powerful influence of context on the interpretation of *sia-pɔlɔ* (riddles) was demonstrated in an earlier paper.[8] The manner in which stories are learned was probed by an experiment. With the aid of informants, I wrote a *pɔlɔ-yee* creation myth about how the duck got its beak. This story was completely novel in content, but in structure closely paralleled other such stories that I'd collected. This story is henceforth called the duck story. In the experiment, samples of ten were drawn from the populations of boys aged 6–9 and 10–13. My (Kpelle) assistant read the story to these boys on three consecutive Sundays. Then on the following three consecutive Fridays, the boys were asked simply to recall the story. I was interested in answering three questions with this experiment. First, I expected older boys to recall the story better than younger boys, from the earlier evidence I'd collected that stories of this type are told by older boys and adults and in fact this was true in most cases. Second, I wanted to know whether recall would improve over trials; whether boys' grasp of the story would increase with repeated exposure to it. This also was true in most cases and contrary to earlier free-recall experiments on the Kpelle where there was little improvement over trials.[1] Third, a more complex question was just how the recall would occur. There seemed to be three alternatives. A boy might recall only isolated bits of the story, with little thematic continuity; he might reall only a central theme and add contextually appropriate, but improvised elements to flesh out the theme, or he might truly recall the story including the theme and the content as given. The latter alternative was true for all subjects. Even when recall was very poor (only 10% of the best performance) the theme was intact and original elements were used in the appropriate places. Novel elements were rare in the recalled stories. Hence, with each new trial, subjects told a longer story which was also a more complete copy of the original.

The same samples of children were also given two further tests. They had to recall a randomly ordered 16-word list (also for three trials) and were asked to recall as many *pɔlɔ-yee* and *sia-pɔlɔ* as they knew. These tests were added to see whether any "general memory-ability" could account for the differences in recall performance on the duck story. And whether their recall performance might have been influenced by a learning set, or what Bateson[9] has called deutero-learning. If there is such a thing as general memory ability, the free-recall paradigm used with the 16-word list should tap it; there was, however, no correlation between performance on this test and recall of the duck story.

Individuals who know many stories may have formed a story-learning set; they may have internalized a strategy for learning stories that gives them an advantage over similar individuals who haven't previously learned any stories. There was, however, no evidence of a learning set at work. There was only a very low correlation between the number of stories a boy could remember and his recall of the duck story.

Boys then, appear to learn a new story quite easily, and improve their recall with repeated exposure to it. The structure or theme of the story is remembered along with specific elements of content. Older boys perform better than younger ones and this is consistent with the results of all studies of Kpelle memory. The difference can't be accounted for by older boys knowing more stories and thereby having formed a learning set for stories. What seems more likely is that a universal and, as yet unclear, developmental effect is at work. Subjects may use thematic elements as cues in "reconstructing" a story, and the experiment described in the next section will shed some light on this issue.

Are These Memory Processes Employed In Novel Situation?

Bartlett (1932)[7] first pointed out that memory can be an active process, something he called reconstruction. In Miller's[10] review, reconstruction becomes recoding. In order to remember isolated "bits" of information humans recode these into chunks containing more than one "bit." The more bits that can be successfully recoded and "chunked" together, the more efficiently they are remembered. The number of ways that this recoding can be accomplished is very large indeed, however, there is a suggestion that the number of possible recoding processes or memory-strategies that people actually use is quite small. There is considerable evidence,[6] for example, that individuals the world over who have had at least some secondary education will use a taxonomic recoding procedure when asked to remember a string of words. There is also evidence that the Kpelle, at least, who have not had such education do not use the taxonomic procedure. Attempts to discover what recoding procedure they might use have been unsuccessful.[1]

I felt that if one wanted to know how the Kpelle recode novel verbal material, a reasonable place to begin would be to find out how nonnovel material is coded. In preceding sections, I have sought to describe examples of traditional verbal materials and how these are coded. Songs, $K\supset l\supset\eta$, and leaf-naming seem to involve a pairing or paired-associate code. After the "bits" of information have been chunked into phrases or names, these isolated chunks are coded into a large chunk with two elements.

The coding that underlies the recall of stories must be part of the same process that makes humans universally use sentences to communicate with one another. Sentences chunk together isolated words and stories chunk together sentences. As mentioned earlier, the notion of context is important in this process. Words as symbols place things in some functional relationship to each other. Taken together these relationships form the context of a sentence, a story, or an epic narrative.

An analysis of the tasks residents of GSK engage in that require verbal memory would seem to indicate that two coding strategies are employed: pairing and chunking bits together on the basis of contextual (meaningful) relationships. The question to be answered here is whether individuals use either of these strategies when confronted with a novel task which requires the use of verbal memory.

The novel task in question was a free-recall experiment, which has been extensively used in studies of memory in the U.S. and among the Kpelle as described in the introduction to this paper. Subjects are taken individually and read aloud a list of words, then asked to recall them in any order they choose.

> The subject is told: "You and I will do a play. This play which we will do is about things. I will call the thing's names first before you call their names. Listen to me carefully." The experimenter then reads the list of sixteen items (a random order was used) and says: "I am finished, you call the thing's names now." The experimenter notes down the child's responses as he gives them. If the child can't remember any more items and says so, or after a pause of 20 seconds, the experimenter returns to the beginning of the instructions. This procedure is repeated three times for a total of four trials. The measure of performance used is the number out of sixteen that the child correctly recalls.

The principle advantage of the free-recall technique, is that a variety of recall strategies can be employed by the subject. Rote-memorization, for example, would be indicated by a recall order that closely matched the presentation order. Since the words are presented randomly, the order of recall reveals whether the subject has recoded items and chunked them together in any way. This chunking in free-recall studies has been called "clustering." If clustering occurs, the expectation is that, over trials, recall will improve as the recoding makes memory more efficient. The absence of clusters indicates that no recoding has taken place. In this experiment, five different word lists were used to test whether subjects would: (a) recode taxonomically, (b) recode contextually, (c) recode by pairing, or (d) not recode at all.

The lists (in Kpelle) were constructed in the following manner. Ten adults; five females and five males, were read a list comprised of seven exemplars each from the classes of trees, tools, traps, and carrying things. The ten informants were asked to name at least four words that come to mind as they heard the stimulus word. These response words were recorded and all those words and their associates which gave evidence of a contextual relationship were isolated. For example, "soap" was a frequent response to *goá* the name of a tree. Potash is extracted from the ashes of the *goá* to make soap, and hence the two are contextually related. *Fali-kolii* is a fence trap and its frequent associate was "ground-hog." Ground-hogs are, of course, caught in fence traps. Hence, words can be related contextually (*goá* and soap) or taxonomically (*faan* and *gbale* – both traps).

The five lists were as follows: List I was a random list, the 16 words were taxonomically discreet and no two of them had been associated in the free-association study. This list presumably offered minimal chances for recoding; List II had four exemplars from each of four categories, no two of these words had been associated in free-association; List III had two exemplars from each of eight categories, no pair of words had been associated; List IV contained no two words from the same taxonomic categories, but pairs of words on this list were highly associated; List V contained no two words from the same taxonomic categories but there were four groups of four highly associated words (example: *bunuŋ*, bamboo, fish, palm nut: *bunuŋ* is a *fish* trap made of *bamboo* that is baited with a *palm nut*).

It was expected that if subjects recoded taxonomically, Lists II and III should produce better recall; if by pairs, Lists II and IV should produce better recall and overall lists recall should be clustered in pairs; if recoding was by contextual relationship then lists IV and V should produce better recall.

In addition to the five lists, the study also varied age and sex. Random samples of 20 from the populations of boys age 8−10, girls aged 8−10, boys aged 11−13, and girls aged 11−13 were tested. The expectation here was that girls would recall fewer words than boys given their overall lower level of involvement in tasks that require verbal memory and that older children would recall more words than younger children as had been found in the previous study described above.

The results demonstrated that none of the three possible strategies were employed by these children. Recall was uniformly low for all five lists, with a small but consistent increment over trials. The complete absence of clusters indicated that no recoding had taken place. Furthermore, recall orders were sufficiently different from presentation orders as to rule out rote memorization.* If the tasks which require verbal memory in GSK do indeed incorporate a recoding strategy as discussed under the third question above, then it is not the case that these strategies transfer to novel situations.

Boys did indeed recall more than girls; the difference was smaller than might have been expected, but consistent with the finding that strategies don't transfer. Older children also performed slightly better than younger children.

Summary and Conclusion

The fine-grained research that seems required if we are to advance to a theory of culture and memory, must proceed in several directions. The steps taken here were to study memory intraculturally as a prerequisite to cross-cultural studies. Working within a single cultural setting, one can ascertain the nature and range of recurring tasks that require the exercise of memory. Using a traditional Kpelle town as the cultural setting, this investigation turned up four tasks: storytelling, singing, the $K\Im I\Im\eta$ game, and leaf-naming as making demands on memory.

It is further true that involvement in memory-related tasks is not always uniform over a single, homogeneous population. In studying memory intraculturally it is necessary not only to isolate and describe memory-related tasks, but, where possible, to specify the characteristics of subsets of the population that habitually perform these tasks. In GSK, males are more heavily involved than females in storytelling and the $k\Im I\Im\eta$ game than females. Females can recall no stories and they recall fewer $K\Im I\Im\eta$ than males. Older males are more likely to tell the $sia\text{-}p\Im I\Im$ and $p\Im I\Im\text{-}\gamma e\epsilon$ type stories than younger (under age nine) males and they both recall more of these stories and learn a novel $p\Im I\Im\text{-}\gamma e\epsilon$ story more easily. There was also a high degree of specialization in the performance of the tasks of leaf-naming and *wei-meni-pele* storytelling. Finally, of three song-types, one appeared to require verbal memory and this type is most often sung by adolescents of both sexes.

The four tasks appear to employ one of two types of code. The presence of such codes allows individuals to employ a recoding strategy in learning or remembering new material for the same task. Leaf-naming, songs, and $k\Im I\Im\eta$ are arranged in pairs, while stories maximize contextual relationships. These codes

---

* Far from being a simple and mechanical form of memory, rote-memorization may be one of the most difficult ways to remember verbal material. One must *work at* remembering things in rote order. One of the reasons that "primitive" peoples give frequent evidence of using rote-memorization is that the tasks they must perform, require it. That is, the tasks require recall that has an invariant order.

might be applied in a novel task which also involves remembering verbal materials. In an experimental test of this proposition, it was found that subjects did not recode words using a pairing, a contextual, or a taxonomic strategy.

It's clear now why the Kpelle do not use a taxonomic recoding strategy in free-recall. There is no task in their society that requires such behavior. On the other hand, we have some evidence, based in an analysis of naturally occurring tasks, that two other processes are used in remembering. Neither of these processes is evident, however, in the free-recall results.

A related question, not addressed in this study has been the focus of several previous studies. This question is whether Kpelle subjects *can* use a recoding procedure in the free-recall task. The evidence indicates that they do not do so spontaneously, except when chairs are used as cues. Yet no explanation was found for this phenomenon. Cole[1] found that Kpelle children could be *taught* to use a taxonomic code and they then successfully applied this recoding strategy in the free-recall experiment. In a recent study, Scribner[11] had Kpelle subjects sort objects into piles repeatedly until they achieved a stable sort (i.e., same objects grouped together on two adjacent trials). She then asked them to recall the names of the items. Subjects in fact did use their own code as manifested in the sorting task to recode the randomly presented words. However, these codes were highly idiosyncratic. The results of these several studies inform us that the Kpelle are capable of learning and applying a taxonomic code or inventing their own code. Unfortunately these results tell us nothing about culture and memory, except that culture provides at most a disposition to respond in certain ways rather than a determination.

To return to the central problem, in order to establish the links between culture and memory, we must first describe memory-related tasks in culture. Relying entirely on novel tasks like the free-recall experiment always leaves open the trap of cultural bias. We must, however, go further and specify just what kind of memory process is required in these tasks. This process can't be inferred from an examination of the task alone, but must be verified by showing that individuals who habitually perform the task or tasks are more fluent in the process than those who don't.

The final step would appear to be to compare the performance of groups from different cultures on some test which displays the process. The feasibility of this last step is called into doubt by the experiments reported here and in Cole *et al.*[1] Goodnow[12] has reviewed a variety of cross-cultural findings focusing on inconsistencies in the results. She finds that the experiment whether free-recall or otherwise, is not culture-free. Built into all experiments are assumptions like "speed is a reflection of ability," or "everyone should do his or her best in experiments or tests," and so forth. Experiments work in western societies because people indeed share the assumptions on which they are built; they don't work (aren't valid) in societies where these assumptions fail.

The problem will only be solved through the use of "representative experiments"[13] and these respresentative experiments can only be designed from a thorough knowledge of the recurring tasks in the societies we wish to compare.

REFERENCES

1. COLE, M., *et al.* 1971. The cultural context of learning and thinking. Basic Books. New York, N.Y.
2. GIBBS, J. L. 1965. The Kpelle of Liberia. *In* Peoples of Africa. Holt, Rinehart, & Winston. New York, N.Y.

3. BATESON, G. 1958. Naven. Stanford University Press, Palo Alto, Ca.
4. SCHAPERA. 1955. Tswana Law and Custom. 2nd ed. Oxford University Press. London, England.
5. LANCY, D. F. 1974. Work, play, and learning in a Kpelle town. Doctoral dissertation, University of Pittsburgh. Pittsburgh, Pa.
6. COLE, M. & S. SCRIBNER. 1975. Cross-cultural studies of memory and cognition. Rockefeller University, New York, N.Y.
7. BARTLETT, F. C. 1932. Remembering. Cambridge University Press. London, England.
8. LANCY, D. F. 1972. An experimental analysis of riddles and rule-based problem-solving. Paper presented at the Society for Applied Anthropology. Montreal, Canada.
9. BATESON, G. 1972. Steps to an Ecology of mind. Chandler Publishing Co. San Francisco, Ca.
10. MILLER, G. A. 1967. The psychology of communication. Basic Books. New York, N.Y.
11. SCRIBNER, S. 1974. Developmental aspects of categorized recall in a West African Society. Cognitive Psychology. 6: 475–494.
12. GOODNOW, J. 1975. The nature of intelligent behavior: Questions raised by cross-cultural studies. L. Resnick, Ed. *In* The Nature of Intelligence. Lawrence Erlbaum Associates. Hillsdale, N.J. (In press.)
13. BRUNSWIK, E. 1956. Perception and the representative design of psychological experiments. University of California Press. Berkeley, Ca.

THE PROBLEM OF ESTABLISHING VALIDITY IN CROSS-CULTURAL MEASUREMENTS*

Marc Irwin, Robert E. Klein, Patricia L. Engle, and Charles Yarbrough

Division of Human Development
Institute of Nutrition of Central America and Panama (INCAP)
Guatemala City, Guatemala

Sara B. Nerlove

State University of New York
Binghamton, New York 13901

Understanding the causes of behavior requires going beyond the behaviors observed. It requires operating in the realm of constructs, like intelligence and need for achievement, which cannot be measured directly. To be useful, such constructs must be operationalized or linked to behaviors that can be measured. Whether a set of operations can be described as measuring the construct it purports to measure is generally assessed through the process of construct validation.[11] This process involves working backwards from the behaviors measured, through conceptual networks, to predictions about other behaviors which constitute operationalizations of related constructs. Constructs and the operationalizations by which they are measured are together validated to the extent that predictions are successful and the logical structure through which they are generated is persuasive.

Understanding the causes of behavior in a strange culture also requires the use of inference, constructs, and operationalizations. Construct validity of behavioral measurements under these circumstances can have at least three distinct meanings. The three types of validity appropriate to measurement in a culture other than that of the researcher correspond to three approaches to cross-cultural research identified by Berry:[3] the imposed etic, emic, and derived etic. Berry's use of these terms to construct a typology of cross-cultural research techniques contributed a good deal to understanding of the dangers inherent in cross-cultural comparisons. The fact that Berry's typology has not generated a great deal of research can probably be traced to his failure to suggest adequate operational definitions for his terms. In the present paper, an attempt is made to operationally define imposed etic, emic, and derived etic validity. Efforts to establish each of these forms of validity in a cross-cultural investigation in progress in rural Eastern Guatemala are also described.

One of the approaches to cross-cultural research described by Berry is the imposed etic investigation. Imposed etic investigations employ (or impose) imported constructs in attempting to describe behavior in the host culture. Correctly noting the abuses that such an approach has generated in past comparative cross-cultural studies (particularly studies of intellectual ability), Berry dismisses the imposed etic approach as unable to produce more than anecdotal data of the "in culture X, they score Y on test Z" variety.[3] Yet, an

* This research was supported by Contract No. N01-HD-5-0640 from the National Institute of Child Health and Human Development, National Institutes of Health, Bethesda.

308

imposed etic approach is not inherently fatal to attempts to understand behavior; for example, in child, rather than cross-cultural psychology, Piaget has employed it extensively to explain developmental phenomena among children, who are not likely to possess the concept of groupings.[13]

Imposed etic constructs may have within the setting where they are employed a species of validity which is independent of the host culture conceptual system. Establishing imposed etic validity involves the same procedure an investigator would use in his own culture; by reference to a conceptual network (probably, but not necessarily, imported from his own culture), the investigator attempts to predict various behaviors implied by that network, on the basis of his behavioral measurements. To the extent that this enterprise is successful, a case is made that the imposed etic constructs measured represent meaningful ways of describing the structure of behavior, that these constructs are related in the way the investigator has supposed, and that they have been adequately operationalized in that particular research setting. An example of successful imposed etic validation was Angelini's[1] demonstration of increased n ach test scores among Brazilian Ss, following experimentally manipulated failure experiences, a behavioral outcome predicted from research among Ss in the USA.

As noted, the establishing of imposed etic validity is independent of host-culture world view or categories of experience; Angelini's Brazilian Ss, for example, may or may not have possessed concepts equivalent to his notions of failure or need for achievement. However, successfully establishing imposed etic validity does imply that measurement techniques employed are relatively free of the measurement error introduced by unfamiliar stimulus materials, failure to understand instructions, and poor motivation to respond accurately or honestly.

Though ignoring the conceptual system of the host culture, valid imposed etic measurement is useful in explaining the causes of behavior in that culture. It may also yield important information concerning the universality of behavioral causality. In addition, imposed etic measurement is appropriate where the investigator is interested in predicting behavior on a specific criterion measure, such as performance in a Western-type school,[4] exported from his own culture.

Where an investigator wishes to understand the structure of behavior from the point of view of the host culture, a second approach to measurement, the emic approach, is appropriate. Berry described emic investigations as ones in which the investigator progressively modifies his imposed etic entry categories to the point where they accurately reflect indigenous categories of experience. Thus, the researcher's task in such an investigation involves not only transcending empirical observation but also one's conceptual networks as well. In a sense, the researcher in a strange culture must move like a child through the conceptual realm of the host culture, always doubting his own conceptions and heavily dependent upon the guidance of local informants.

The process of emic validation of behavioral measurements is in its general outlines similar to that of construct validation in one's own culture, and to that of imposed etic measurement validation. It consists of making predictions about behaviors on the basis of other measured behaviors, by reference to the investigator's understanding of the host culture's conceptual system. However, establishing emic measurement validity requires that the behaviors predicted be of a particular type: They must be judgments which are assumed to employ the construct dimensions that the investigator is attempting to measure. If in fact the investigator is validly measuring constructs that correspond to indigenous units of organizing the world, he should be able to predict the outcomes of these judgments on the basis of his behavioral measurements. Normally, these judgments will not be made by the S whose behavior is being measured but will be judgments of S by peers, family members, etc. In the study to be described in this paper, an attempt is made to establish emic validity of psychometric measurements of child Ss by examination of correspondence between these measurements and judgments of the children by their parents and other village adults. We know of no previous attempt to objectively establish emic validity in the cross-cultural literature.

The third class of cross-cultural measurement described by Berry, derived etic measurement, is appropriate where an investigator wishes to make cross-cultural comparisons that take into account the conceptual system of each culture compared. Though derived etic validity can theoretically be established for any number of cultures, this discussion will be confined to the prototypical case of two culture comparisons between the investigator's culture and the host culture.

According to Berry, comparisons are only meaningful for those constructs that constitute a derived etic, or lie in the intersection of the conceptual systems of the two cultures being compared. In fact, it is also meaningful to compare two cultures by employing constructs that have proven to have imposed etic validity when exported from the first culture to the second; the special contribution of derived etic validation is in uncovering cultural commonalities in how the world is viewed.

Establishing derived etic validity is, as its name suggests, a derivative procedure that cannot be undertaken until imposed etic and emic validity have been established. One method of identifying derived etics consists of identifying those aspects of measured constructs that have proven to possess both imposed etic and emic validity. These conceptual units represent an empirical convergence of home and host culture ways of organizing the world.

Establishing emic and imposed etic measurement validity of constructs involves the prediction of behaviors that operationalize related constructs. These related constructs may also possess derived etic validity. Those constructs employed in establishing emic validity originate in the investigator's understanding of the host-culture conceptual system; those constructs employed in establishing imposed etic validity are usually representative of the investigator's home culture conceptual system. The requirement of prior validation of each of these sets of constructs, necessary before derived etics can be sought in their intersection set, is satisfied where they have been involved in successful predictions of behavior. This is the case since construct validation is a reciprocal process in which measurement validity is established simultaneously for predictor and predicted constructs.

Identifying derived etics among constructs that have been predicted by emic measurements and those that have been predicted by imposed etic measurements proceeds by an examination of the interrelationships among operationalizations of the two. Where such interrelationships are found to exist, a derived etic convergence of constructs is empirically established.

The above description of establishing validity in cross-cultural measurement has been drawn in somewhat cleaner strokes than it could have been; for example, the distinction between predictor and predicted measures is in practice a rather arbitrary one. In practice too, the apparently separate activities of establishing imposed etic, emic, and derived etic validity of measurements tend to coalesce into a general exploration of the structure of behavior in the host culture. They do so because the testing of a construct's emic validity implies the exploration of the local conceptual realm, and that exploration is almost invariably guided, at least at first, by the conceptual system which the researcher brings with him to the host culture. These activities also tend toward simultaneity because of the nature of all human efforts to understand; as Donald Campbell, who has probably contributed more to our understanding of the epistemology of social science and cross-cultural research than any other individual[6-8] has noted, it is virtually impossible to understand a cultural element without simultaneously understanding its larger cultural context.[7]

An important methodological implication of Campbell's statement is the advisability of testing many rather than few hypotheses about the nature of a target construct in the host culture's conceptual system. Both Campbell[6] in his statement about the need to generate many data points in cross-cultural research, and more recently Cole and his coworkers[9,10] have made this argument. By probing many dimensions of a construct, the researcher may be able to construct an interpretable picture of that construct's validity and meaning in the host culture, and its overlap with constructs emic to his own culture. The researcher's dilemma is analogous to that of a blind man with blind friends who wishes to describe an elephant; his best chance of doing so accurately lies in delegating as large a committee of his blind friends as possible to each explore one part of the elephant and to then assemble all of their information into a single description.

Unlike Berry, whose 1969 paper emphasized the epistemological importance of cultural overlaps, Campbell[7] has argued that it is possible to understand cultural differences, when these differences are viewed against a background of shared similarities. This view suggests that nonintersecting portions of the conceptual systems of the researcher's culture and the host culture can provide comparative information as valuable as that provided by the derived etic, or matching portions. The cross-cultural researcher with a pattern of derived etic conceptual similarities as well as conceptual differences characterizing his own and the host culture in hand is like a paleontologist (the former blind man, whose sight has been restored, and who, inspired by his success in describing the elephant, has gone on to study paleontology) attempting to reconstruct the skeleton of an unknown prehistoric beast; faced with sufficient similarity to a known culture or creature, the cross-cultural psychologist or paleontologist can each reconstruct the unique portion, and then venture comparisons of the old and the new.

We have thus far defined three forms of measurement validity that may characterize behavioral measurements made in a strange culture, and discussed rather generally their use in the field. The remainder of this paper will consist of a concrete example of the efforts of one research group to establish the emic, imposed etic, and derived etic validity of a set of psychometric measurements.

The study to be described is the Institute of Nutrition of Central America and Panama's (INCAP) longitudinal study of the relationship between moderate malnutrition and mental development, being carried out in rural eastern Guatemala. The existence of the study was occasioned by a problem of great importance; the need of third world policy makers for data concerning the effects of moderate malnutrition that would permit scarce resources to be allocated in a rational way. Though only preliminary results are yet available,[18] these results (not discussed in the present paper) suggest the first causal link yet established between malnutrition and deficient mental development, pinpoint gestation as a crucial period during which poor nutrition exerts its negative effect on later mental test performances, and identify children of the lowest socioeconomic level of a population that is almost uniformly poor to begin with, as particularly vulnerable to nutritional insult to mental test performances.

In our attempt to measure the INCAP study dependent variable of mental development, establishing the validity of measurements of intellectual ability in children of various ages has been a continuing concern. Berry has argued that concepts of intelligence "can have no use in a study carried out within the imposed etic—emic-derived etic comparative framework".[3] His argument of why this should be the case is that behaviors assumed intelligent in culture X would probably not be considered so in culture Y, that only fragments of derived etic similarity would remain, and that these "scraps" of the emic wouldn't tell the researcher anything about the global term intelligence. Whether or not Berry is correct can, of course, only be determined empirically. We shall be arguing, through the data we present, that once the necessity of approaching intelligence as if it were a global entity is dispensed with, and the possibility of interpreting cultural differences as well as similarities is acknowledged, that Berry was unduly pessimistic.

THE INCAP STUDY

In 1969, a longitudinal study of the relationship between malnutrition and mental development was begun in rural Eastern Guatemala by INCAP. Though a number of studies had previously examined the question, none had been sufficiently well designed to yield more than suggestive evidence of an association between nutritional history and mental test performance, rather than compelling evidence of a causal link between the two. In addition, the INCAP study was unique in focusing on moderate malnutrition, which probably afflicts three-fourths of all children growing up in the world's developing countries,[2] rather than severe malnutrition, which is a relatively rare condition.

The design of the INCAP study is quasiexperimental. Dietary supplement beverages are made voluntarily available to all residents of four villages. In two of these villages, the beverage is a warm gruel, high in proteins and high in calories, and similar to an indigenous drink known as *atole*. In the remaining two villages, the beverage is a cold drink containing no protein and only one-third the calories of the first beverage. It is similar to a local cold drink called *fresco*. Both beverages contain the vitamins and minerals known to be limiting in the local diet. In addition to dietary supplementation, residents of all four villages have been provided with free outpatient medical care since the inception of the study. This care has had a substantial impact on villager health, eradicated some endemic diseases from the communities, and helped to cut infant mortality rates to one third what they were before INCAP's arrival.

The four communities participating in the study are Ladino, or Spanish-speaking and of mixed Spanish and Indian blood. Virtually all community families are engaged in subsistence agriculture. The main crops grown are corn and beans, and these crops are almost entirely consumed within the community in which they are grown. There is little permanent migration to or from the communities. Contact with the world outside the village is primarily limited to trips to nearby markets. Seasonal migration of some community men does occur once a year when these men travel to the coastal zone to harvest cash crops.

The pervasive poverty of these study communities is conveyed by the median family income, approximately $200 per year. Families live in houses constructed of materials obtained locally, mainly adobe. These houses generally contain two rooms, one of which serves as sleeping quarters for the whole family. Houses nearly all lack sanitary facilities. Both infectious diseases and moderate malnutrition are endemic. A brief ethnography of life in the villages can be found in Nerlove, *et al.*[20] A full ethnography is provided by Mejía Pivaral.[19]

The research team conducting the INCAP study is interdisciplinary. Epidemiology, pediatrics, developmental and cross-cultural psychology, physical and cultural anthropology, sociology, and mathematical statistics are all represented by one or more professionals and a number of paraprofessionals. In addition to data on nutritional status and mental development, a large number of anthropometric, morbidity, and social-environmental variables are also being measured longitudinally.

The basic sample of children for whom data are presented in the present paper consists of a subsample of 64 children (though, as will be noted, data are missing for three children for one of our measures, and for five others for another measure) drawn from the several hundred sample children residing in two of the four villages involved in the longitudinal study. These children participated in special studies of free behavior observation, in 1971, and of adult rankings of intelligence, in 1973. The special sample was constructed by persons having no knowledge of previous measurements of members of the longitudinal sample, employing as criteria for inclusion that both parents be living and residing in the same household, and age, sex, and family variables; a reasonably successful attempt was made to match same-sex children from one participating village with same-sex children from the other village for these variables. No more than one child in the sample came from the same family.

At the time of the free behavior and ranking of intelligence studies, sample children ranged in age from five to eight. TABLE 1 presents a breakdown of the sample by age, sex, and village.

TABLE 1*

SAMPLE DISTRIBUTION BY AGE, SEX, AND VILLAGE†

Age in Years	Boys			Girls		
	Village 1	Village 2	Total	Village 1	Village 2	Total
5	3	3	6	6	5	11
6	9	9	18	6	5	11
7	4	4	8	3	5	8
8	0	0	0	1	1	2
Total	16	16	32	16	16	32

* After Nerlove, *et al.* (1974), p. 279.

† As of October, 1971.

PSYCHOMETRIC MEASUREMENT OF CHILDREN'S INTELLECTUAL ABILITY

Mental testing in the INCAP study begins within a few days after birth, with the administration of the Brazelton Neonatal Scale.[5] At 5-1/2, 7-1/2, 9-1/2, 11-1/2, and 13-1/2 months, an infant cognitive battery designed by Jerome Kagan to measure reactions to stimulus events, their repetitions, and discrepancies from expected stimuli[21] has been administered to infants in the sample.

Each infant has also been administered the Composite Infant Scale, composed of items selected from the Bayley, Cattell, Merrill-Palmer, and Gesell infant scales at 6, 15, and 24 months. Since the problem of cross-cultural validity is of a somewhat different nature, and probably much reduced, with infant tests, these tests will not be discussed in the present paper.

Beginning at 36 months of age, study children are annually administered the Preschool Battery, consisting of 24 tests[21] This battery was designed to tap a variety of cognitive skills, and to represent diverse psychological orientations (e.g., learning, psychometric, Piagetian). The multifactor approach to measurement of intellectual ability employed has been dictated both by INCAP's desire to identify as specifically as possible the effects of malnutrition on mental development, and by the research team's view that intelligence is best conceived of in terms of a number of discrete, though related, abilities.

Tests in the Preschool Battery were adapted to the research setting by a team consisting of American and Guatemalan psychologists, a Guatemalan cultural anthropologist, and Guatemalan testers and cultural informants.[15] Two years of pretesting, during which some tests went through as many as ten revisions, were devoted to developing test materials and instructions that both the intuitions of testers as well as the performances of local (pilot sample) children of various ages suggested were appropriate and meaningful.

Tests are administered in Spanish by Guatemalan female testers. Testing takes place in adobe testing-houses equivalent to village houses, but equipped with one-way viewing mirrors and battery-operated intercoms. Testers are extensively trained and highly competent; nevertheless, they are checked monthly for inter-tester reliability, and all data protocols are routinely doublechecked for irregularities.

Ten of the 24 tests in the Preschool Battery were instituted after the special studies described in this paper were completed. For the purposes of the present paper, data for five tests determined by earlier factor and content analysis to be representative of the 14 tests administered to the special study sample children will be presented and discussed. These five tests of vocabulary, verbal reasoning, discrimination learning, short-term memory, and perceptual analysis are the following:

Vocabulary. A picture recognition task similar to the Peabody Picture Vocabulary test. The child is shown a page of pictures and asked to point to the "horse," etc.

Verbal Reasoning. A sentence completion task in which E reads an analogy, omitting the last word in the sentence, which the child must supply (e.g. "the skin of the pineapple is rough, the skin of the banana is _____").

Discrimination Learning. A series of four discrimination learning problems. Each employs two pairs of stimuli differing along one dimension. In the first two problems, one value on the dimension (e.g. "big") is reinforced. In the second two problems, the opposite value is reinforced.

Short-Term Memory. A digit-span task in which the child repeats strings of digits of increasing length until three strings in a row are failed.

Perceptual Analysis. An embedded figures test adapted from one developed by Karp & Konstadt[14] in which the stimuli consist of 12 pictures with a triangle hidden in each. The child's task is to locate each embedded triangle.

Interobserver and test-retest (one-week interval) reliability have been computed for each of these tests. Interobserver reliability is above .99 for each of them. Test-retest reliabilities were .91 for Vocabulary, .87 for Verbal Reasoning,

.46 for Discrimination Learning, .65 for Short-Term Memory, and .69 for Perceptual Analysis.

As previously noted, Preschool Battery tests are administered to each child yearly. The scores used in the analyses for the present paper were those for the testing closest to the time of the behavior observation study. Thus, Preschool Battery scores used here represent five-year-old performances for some children, and six-, seven-, or eight-year-old performances for others.

ESTABLISHING EMIC VALIDITY OF PSYCHOMETRIC MEASURES: MEASURES OF VILLAGE ADULTS' PERCEPTIONS OF CHILDREN'S INTELLECTUAL ABILITY

Listura Rankings

The most direct way of determining how local adults view a child is to ask them. We wished first to learn what place, if any, the notion of intelligence has in the conceptual universe of our study villages. Through systematic ethnographic interviews with rural Ladino adults probing indigenous conceptions of intelligence,[17,16] it was determined that the most descriptive indigenous term for intelligence is *listura*, which is most often translated back to English as "smartness." The concept of listura appeared to coincide closely with what is commonly referred to as "brightness" or "quickness" in the United States; the behavioral characteristics used by adults in the villages when describing children who are *listo* are "verbal facility," "good memory," "alertness," "independence," and a high level of physical activity.

Listura rankings for this study were generated in each village by photographing each child in a standing position against the same neutral background, and having a sample of women judges who were near childbearing age and did not have a close relative among the sample, use the photographs to make a series of random pairwise same-sex comparisons.[20,21] Each child was assigned a listura score on the basis of the rankings of all the judges who knew him or her. The score consists of the percentage of times the child was ranked as more listo divided by the total number of times ranked. (See Nerlove and Walters[21] for a method of composite rank-ordering based on a least squares solution used on this same body of data and resulting in different scores.)

Chores

A second measure of how village adults (in this case parents) perceive the intellectual ability of their children consisted of an index of the chores the children were assigned. Life is difficult in our study villages, and with few exceptions, families must struggle to survive. Under these circumstances, children are expected to contribute what labor they can to the family. Assuming that an important determinant of the extent to which parents assign tasks to their 5–8-year-old is their perception of the child's intellectual maturity, measures of children's chore participation have been correlated with psychological test performances and other indices of intellectual ability. The chore measure consists of the number of observations out of a random sample of 20 observations per child[20] in which the child was performing a chore. The average number of observations in which boys were performing chores was 6.78 (SD = 3.68). The average number for girls was also 6.78 (SD = 3.26).

As will be noted in the results section, this measure was highly correlated with test performance and other indices of intellectual ability for girls. It was not related to other measures for boys. However, the number of intellectually demanding chores performed by the child was related to test performances among boys, and this latter chore measure is used for boys. The classification of chores into intellectually demanding or not was done by the Guatemalan cultural anthropologist, Victor Mejía Pivaral, author of the definitive ethnography of the four villages,[19] who has worked in the villages continuously for the last six years. The average number of intellectually demanding chores engaged in by boys was 1.66 (SD = 1.77).

School Attendance

Still another measure of parental judgments of their child's intellectual ability employed was the number of years of schooling completed by the child, as of January 1975. Since children do not normally begin school before eight years of age in the study villages, school attendance took place long after all of the other behaviors measured in the present study; our analyses involving this variable included predictions of events up to three years in the future.

Though each of the study villages has an elementary school, school attendance is sporadic and not universal among village children. Given the important economic contribution that the children increasingly come to make to their families at this time, we have hypothesized that an important determinant of the extent to which parents permit their child to attend school is their perception of the child's intellectual ability; where all resources including energy are in short supply, it would appear to make little sense to send a potentially productive family member to school if that individual were unlikely to benefit from the experience. The average number of years of schooling completed, as of January 1975, was 1.00 (SD = 1.11) for boys, and .88 (SD = 1.01) for girls, and 31 children had not completed a year of school by that date.

ESTABLISHING IMPOSED ETIC VALIDITY OF PSYCHOMETRIC MEASURES: MEASURES OF INTELLECTUAL ABILITY BASED ON CHILDREN'S BEHAVIOR

Self-Managed Sequences

One of the investigators' (imposed etic) assumptions about intellectually able children everywhere was that they are more likely than less able children to engage, without supervision, in complicated activities. To index the tendency to do so, a variable developed by Nerlove[20] in the observational study described previously is employed in the present analyses. This is the number of self-managed sequences in which each child was engaged out of 20 random observations. For this variable, the activities indexed are ones in which the child was at least to some degree in control of the situation, and thus giving indication of his or her level of cognitive development.

The self-managed sequence measure is an index that includes both work and play activities. Work activities included were those not easily supervised and involving transformations of objects and systematic movement through space, and those performed alone and requiring going outside the community or gathering, transforming, and relocating objects. Play activities included were those involving rule games, interactive role play, joint or systematic construction, or play that involved going outside the community. The average number of self-managed sequences engaged in out of 20 observations was 3.60 for boys (SD = 2.46) and 2.13 for girls (SD = 1.41). For a more complete description of this variable and observed behavioral examples, the reader is referred to Nerlove *et al.*[20]

School Performance

School performance is commonly associated with the concept of intelligence in Western culture. This association may be explainable by the fact that the first intelligence test, developed by Binet in 1905,[22] was designed to predict school success, and school grades have continued to correlate with IQ test-scores ever since. In the present study, the measure of school performance employed was the ratio (for those 33 children who had completed a year or more of school), of the number of years passed to the number of years attended. Though teacher grades for the years 1972–1974 were not available, records of passing and failing are kept by the Guatemalan Ministry of Education, who made these data available to us. The mean ratio of years of school passed to years of school attended was .86 for boys in the sample (SD = .33), and .78 for girls (SD = .36).

RESULTS

CORRELATIONS BETWEEN PSYCHOMETRIC, ADULTS' PERCEPTIONS, AND CHILDRENS' BEHAVIOR MEASURES OF INTELLECTUAL ABILITY

The following section will present correlations obtained between psychometric measures of intellectual ability, measures of village adult's perceptions of children's intellectual ability, and measures of intellectual ability based on children's behavior. The issue of validity will be taken up in the discussion section to follow, since establishing emic and imposed etic validity involves interpreting the patterns of correlations found between measures, whereas establishing derived etic validity is a kind of third-order operation involving examining the interrelationships of operationalizations of constructs which have had emic and imposed etic validity established. Also, since scores on the Preschool Battery tests have easily communicable meaning only relative to other scores on the same tests, summary information for these scores will not be presented in the present paper. TABLE 2 presents the intercorrelations for the five Preschool Battery tests employed. It will be noted that Vocabulary correlates most strongly with the other tests included, and particularly with scores on the Perceptual Analysis test. Intercorrelations are generally higher for girls than for boys, though the differences must be taken only as suggestive, due to small *n*s. However, a consistent finding of the longitudinal study has been that of differential interrelationships by sex, and all results reported in the present paper will be presented separately by sex.

TABLE 2

INTERCORRELATIONS AMONG PRESCHOOL BATTERY TESTS*
FOR BOYS AND GIRLS

	Vocabulary	Verbal reasoning	Discrimination learning	Short-term memory	Perceptual analysis
Vocabulary		.53†	.35‡	.31	.62§
Verbal reasoning	.57§		.08	.35‡	.40‡
Discrimination learning	.47§	.10		.37‡	.15
Short-term memory	.59§	.42‡	.26		.24
Perceptual analysis	.79§	.49§	.29	.50§	

(Boys above the diagonal; Girls below the diagonal)

* For testing closest to time of behavior observation study performed in 1971, when sample children ranged in age from 5–8 (See Table 1).

† N = 32 for all correlations, excepting those involving girl's Verbal Reasoning, where n = 31.

‡ P < .05.

§ P < .01.

Correlations between Preschool Battery scores, perceived intellectual competence scores, and measures of intellectual competence based on children's behavior are shown in TABLES 3 and 4. As TABLE 3 indicates, for boys, various perceived competence and children's behavior measures correlated significantly with tests in the Preschool Battery. Of these, listura rankings and years of schooling correlated most highly with Preschool Battery test scores. Listura rankings correlated .60 (p ∠ .01) with Vocabulary, and .59 (p ∠ .01) with Perceptual Analysis. Number of years in which the child was kept in school, correlated .63 (p ∠ .01) with Verbal Reasoning, .45 (p ∠ .01) with Vocabulary, and .36 (p ∠ .05) with Perceptual Analysis. No measure of intellectual ability correlated consistently well with all of the psychological tests, and significant correlations between measures of intellectual ability and test scores were spread evenly across the five Preschool Battery Tests; in addition to the significant correlations seen between listura and Vocabulary and Perceptual Analysis and between number of years a child was kept in school and Verbal Reasoning, Vocabulary, and Perceptual Analysis, significant correlations were found between number of intellectually demanding chores assigned and Discrimination Learning and Short-Term Memory (r learning = .35, p ∠ .05; r memory = .35, p ∠ .05) and between self-managed sequences and Discrimination Learning (r = .40, p∠ .05) and Perceptual Analysis (r = .39, p ∠ .05). Of all the nonpsychometric measures of intellectual ability, only school passing ratio failed to correlate significantly with any test. The highest correlation between school passing ratio and Preschool Battery tests was that with Perceptual Analysis (r = .25, n.s.).

Among the nonpsychometric measures, a fair amount of agreement was observed. Listura scores correlated significantly with years of schooling (r = .39, p ∠ .05) and self-managed sequences (r = .41, p ∠ .05). Number of intellectually

TABLE 3

CORRELATIONS BETWEEN PRESCHOOL BATTERY SCORES, MEASURES OF VILLAGE ADULTS' PERCEPTION OF CHILDREN'S INTELLECTUAL ABILITY, AND MEASURES OF INTELLECTUAL ABILITY BASED ON CHILDREN'S BEHAVIOR: BOYS

(n) =	Preschool Battery					Perceived Intelligence			Behavioral Intelligence	
	Vocabulary	Verbal reasoning	Disc. learning	Short-term memory	Perceptual analysis	Listura	Demanding chores	Years schooling	Self-managed sequence	School passing ratio (n = 17)
Perceived intelligence:										
Listura (29)	.60†	.36	.20	.09	.59†		.18	.39*	.41*	.26
Demanding chores (32)	.12	.12	.35*	.35*	.18			.39*	.64†	.10
Years of schooling (32)	.45†	.63†	.02	.25	.36*				.51†	.33
Behavioral intelligence:										
Self-managed sequences (30)	.37	.17	.40*	.20	.39*					.34
School passing ratio (17)	.00	−.11	−.08	.13	.25					

* p < .05
† p < .01

TABLE 4

CORRELATIONS BETWEEN PRESCHOOL BATTERY SCORES, MEASURES OF VILLAGE ADULTS' PERCEPTION OF CHILDREN'S INTELLECTUAL ABILITY, AND MEASURES OF INTELLECTUAL ABILITY BASED ON CHILDREN'S BEHAVIOR: GIRLS

(n) =	Preschool Battery					Perceived Intelligence			Behavioral Intelligence	
	Vocabulary	Verbal reasoning (n = 31)	Disc. learning	Short-term memory	Perceptual Analysis	Listura	Chores (all)	Years Schooling	Self-Managed Sequence	School Passing Ratio (n = 16)
Perceived intelligence:										
Listura (30)	.75†	.39*	.61†	.38*	.55†		.51*	.53†	.23	.17
Chores (all) (32)	.53†	.40*	.44*	.38*	.33			.57†	.36	.09
Years of Schooling (32)	.56†	.22	.38*	.40*	.37*				.37*	.30
Behavioral intelligence:										
Self-Managed Sequences (31)	.44*	.19	.26	.18	.26					.18
School Passing Ratio (16)	.52*	.34	-.22	.14	.02					

* p < .05
† p < .01

demanding chores also correlated significantly with both years of schooling ($r = .39$, p $\angle$ .05) and self-managed sequences ($r = .64$, p $\angle$ .01). It should be noted that the substantial relationship between Demanding Chores and Self-Managed Sequences is partially explainable by the fact that approximately a third of the behaviors scored as Self-Managed Sequences were also scored as Intellectually Demanding Chores. Years of schooling also correlated significantly with self-managed sequences ($r = .51$, p $\angle$ .01). Interestingly, the number of years a child was allowed to remain in school was not significantly related to school-passing ratio ($r = .33$, n.s.).

As TABLE 4 indicates, a somewhat different picture emerged for girls. As compared to those for boys, Preschool Battery test correlations with adult perception and children's behavior were more often significant. Furthermore, all three measures of adults' perceptions of children's intellectual ability correlated roughly consistently with all five tests. Correlations with Listura rankings were particularly high, ranging from $r = .38$ (p $\angle$ .05) for Short-Term Memory to $r = .75$ (p $\angle$ .01) for Vocabulary. In further contradistinction to the pattern observed among boys, one Preschool Battery Test, Vocabulary, emerged as most consistently correlated with nonpsychometric measures of intellectual ability, correlating significantly with all five of these, with correlations ranging from $r = .44$ (p $\angle$ .05) for self-managed sequences to $r = .75$ (p $\angle$ .01) for Listura. In addition, a correlation of .52 (p $\angle$ .05) was obtained between Vocabulary and School Passing Ratio.

In general, the picture that emerges for girls suggests that Preschool Battery tests are measuring a more unitary intellectual ability trait, of which Vocabulary is most representative, for girls than for boys. Though again, it must be noted that sex differences in intercorrelational patterns must be viewed only as suggestive in the present study, due to small *n*s, both the pattern of inter-test correlations seen in TABLE 1 and previous factor analyses (which technique was not feasible in the present analyses because of small sample sizes) support this contention.[16]

As was true for boys, some agreement was seen among measures of adults' perceptions of intellectual ability. Listura correlated significantly with chores assigned ($r = .51$, p $\angle$ .05) and with years of schooling ($r = .53$, p $\angle$ .01). Years of schooling also correlated significantly with chores assigned ($r = .57$, p $\angle$ .01), and with self-managed sequence ($r = .37$, p $\angle$ .05). As was also the case for boys, years of schooling was not significantly related to school passing ratio for girls ($r = .30$, n.s.), though this variable was significantly related to one children's behavior measure of intellectual ability, self-managed sequences ($r = .37$, p $\angle$ .05).

DISCUSSION

With the empirical evidence of presence or absence of interrelationships between our psychometric measures (five Preschool Battery tests) and measurements of village adults' perceptions and children's behavior presented in the previous section, we are now in a position to assess the emic, imposed etic, and derived etic validity of our psychometric measurements of sample children's intellectual ability. Since the five Preschool Battery scores obtained by each child yield a pattern of intercorrelations with each adult's perceptions and children's behavior measure, it is also possible for us to define each of our nonpsychometric measures in terms of its psychometric test intercorrelation profile. These explorations of the empirical meaning of listura or self-managed sequences, for example, must be viewed as suggestive rather than definitive; *ns* for the present study are small, and a certain amount of subjectivity was necessarily involved in selection of Preschool Battery tests employed here. Finally, we will attempt to assess the derived etic validity of our measures, thus defining the shared meaning of intellectual ability for rural Guatemalan Ladinos and ourselves.

Emic Validation of Psychometric Measurements

Our attempt to test the emic validity of our measurements of intellectual ability began with asking villagers about the ways children could be categorized. Out of that probing emerged our knowledge of the local concept of *listura*, which appeared to coincide closely with what is commonly referred in the U.S. as "brightness" or "quickness." Our first test of whether our measurements of intellectual ability had emic validity in the host culture was to correlate listura rankings with five Preschool Battery tests. The match between listura and all tests was relatively good for girls, and it was good for two tests, Vocabulary and Perceptual Analysis, for boys.

We further explored the local emic validity of the concept of intellectual ability by postulating that if such a concept were part of the local world view, then logically it would be employed as a judgmental dimension in making the economically important decisions concerning the assignment of chores to children at an early age, and later sacrificing or not sacrificing an important labor source by sending and keeping a child in school. As we have reported, the match between the proportion of observations in which 5–8-year-old girls were engaged in chores, and tests scores was relatively good. For boys, the proportion of observations in which a child was engaged in intellectually demanding chores was significantly related to Learning and Memory scores. Furthermore, the number of years a child was allowed to remain in school was significantly related to four out of five test scores for girls, and to scores on three of the tests, Verbal Reasoning, Vocabulary, and Perceptual Analysis, for boys.

In summary, we believe that the evidence is substantial that the concept of intellectual ability, as operationalized in the five tests of our Preschool Battery, is emic to the rural Guatemalan Ladino villages where we are conducting our longitudinal study. As the culture of these villages incorporates rigid sex-typing it is not surprising that our data suggest that local concepts of intellectual ability differ for girls and boys. As it applies to girls, the concept of intellectual ability seems to be a relatively unitary one which is best reflected by the skills measured by our Vocabulary test. *Lista* girls tended to do well on all five of our tests and especially on Vocabulary. They were assigned many chores at a young age, and allowed to remain in school for a relatively long time, though they did not particularly excel in their schoolwork.

Our data suggest that the concept of intellectual ability as it applies to village boys may be a less unitary one. Being *listo* related significantly only to some of the tests in our battery (Vocabulary and Perceptual Analysis). Listura for boys was related to the ability to engage precociously in self-managed sequences, and it appears to connote a different kind of intelligence than that required to do intellectually demanding chores. Not surprisingly, village parents tend to assign such chores to boys who score well on tests of simple learning and memory, and who are able to engage in self-managed sequences. As was true for *lista* girls, *listo* boys were likely to be allowed to remain in school for a relatively long time, though they did not tend to excel in their schoolwork.

Imposed Etic Validation of Psychometric Measurements

In addition to assessing the emic validity of our psychometric measurements, we also wished to know whether our Preschool Battery measurements of village children possessed construct validity with reference to our own Western conceptions of intellectual ability. To assess the imposed etic validity of our psychometric measurements, two predictions were tested. The first was that high scorers on the Preschool Battery would be more likely to engage in self-managed complicated behavior sequences during random free-behavior observations. The use of this outcome measure was dictated by our imposed etic assumption that intellectual ability of children in any society will be reflected in the complexity of their activities. Although Preschool Battery scores showed less agreement with these behavioral predictions than had been found for villager judgments of intellectual ability, significant relationships were found between these psychometric measures and self-managed sequences. For boys, both Discrimination Learning and Perceptual Analysis scores were significantly related to the tendency to engage in self-managed complicated behavior sequences; for girls Vocabulary scores were significantly related to the tendency to engage in such sequences.

The second prediction employed to assess the imposed etic validity of our psychometric measurements concerned school performances. As previously noted, school performance is closely identified with intelligence in Western culture. Our measure of school performance predicted by Preschool Battery scores was ratio of years passed to years of school attended, and only those (33) children who had finished a year or more of schooling were involved in these analyses.

School performances were found to correlate relatively poorly with Preschool Battery scores. For boys, no test was significantly related to passing ratio; for girls, only Vocabulary was significantly related. Though the sample of school attenders in these analyses was very small, and the pass/fail measure from which the passing ratios were constructed was obviously incapable of very precise discriminations between children, we are inclined to accept the probability that school success is less related to intellectual ability in rural Guatemala than in the USA, for example. A study of antecedents and consequences of school attendance currently in progress in our study villages,[12] which employs much larger *n*s, has yielded Preschool Battery : school passing ratio correlations similar to those in the present study. It appears not unlikely that school success among our sample children is as much dependent upon nonintellectual factors, such as family modernity, or press for success, as upon intellectual ones. We are presently exploring this proposition in our study communities.

Derived Etic Validity of Psychometric and Nonpsychometric Measurements

We have presented empirical evidence that our psychometric measurements of intellectual ability have both emic and imposed etic validity within our rural Guatemalan research setting. Thus, the concept of intellectual ability, as operationalized in our five Preschool Battery tests, constitutes a derived etic; by the logic of construct validation, the concept of intellectual ability has meaning both with reference to our own and our host culture's conceptual systems and we have measured the relative amounts of it possessed by sample children.

Defining the shared meaning of intellectual ability for rural Guatemalans and ourselves is more difficult to do than establishing that the global concept is shared. We have had only the limited data of this exploratory study to assist us in defining the indigenous concept, and despite decades of research, there exists no commonly accepted definition of intelligence for Western society. However, it is possible to assess the derived etic validity of our psychometric measurements of intellectual ability not only as a whole, as we have done, but also for each of our five component tests, and it is through an assessment of derived etic validity of these measures and of our nonpsychometric measures that we will seek shared meanings.

For boys, perceptual analysis skill constituted a derived etic component of intellectual ability; our measurements of this skill achieved both emic and imposed etic validity. Perceptual analysis tasks have frequently been employed as an operational measure of field independence-dependence.[2 3] Our findings support Berry's contention[3] that measures of perceptual analysis skill represent a promising cross-cultural comparative tool.

In addition to perceptual analysis skill, our data suggest that discrimination learning may also constitute a derived etic component of intellectual ability, for boys. However, the evidence supporting derived etic status of this component of intellectual ability is less strong.

For girls in our study sample, our measurement of vocabulary knowledge demonstrated both emic and imposed etic validity, correlating significantly with all of our adult perception and child behavior measures. Thus, vocabulary knowledge constituted a derived etic component of intellectual ability, for girls.

As we have earlier noted, our measures of adults' perceptions of children's intellectual ability and our measures of intellectual ability revealed in children's behavior represent an additional source of possible derived etics. These measures originated in our understanding of the host culture conceptual system and our own culturally conditioned preconceptions about behavioral causality, respectively. The emic validity of the notion that children differ in intelligence and can be evaluated with respect to it was demonstrated by the significant associations seen between adults' perceptions measures and Preschool Battery scores; as noted, construct validation is a reciprocal process. The imposed etic validity of our self-managed sequences measure was also established by its significant associations with Preschool Battery scores.

Both the emic notion that children's intelligence can be evaluated and the imposed etic one that intellectually able children are likely to demonstrate that ability in their ordinary behavior, proved to constitute derived etics; self-managed sequences was significantly related to the number of years girls were allowed to remain in school. It was significantly related to all three of the adults' perceptions of children's intelligence measures for boys. These correlations signal a final derived etic convergence of the way in which we and the rural Guatemalan villagers who have suffered us to study them, view the world.

REFERENCES

1. ANGELINI, A. L. 1966. Measuring the achievement motive in Brazil. J. Soc. Psychol. 68: 35–40.
2. BEHAR, M. 1968. Prevalence of malnutrition among preschool children of developing countries. *In* Malnutrition, Learning and Behavior. N. S. Scrimshaw & J. E. Gordon, Eds. M.I.T. Press. Cambridge, Mass.
3. BERRY, J. W. 1969. On cross-cultural comparability. Inter. J. Psychol. 4: 119–128.

4. BIESHEUVEL, S. 1969. Psychological tests and their application to non-European peoples. *In* Cross-Cultural Studies. D. R. Price-Williams, Ed. Penguin. Middlesex, England.

5. BRAZELTON, T. B. 1973. Neonatal Behavioral Assessment. William Heineman Medical Books. London, England.

6. CAMPBELL, D. T. 1961. The mutual methodological relevance of anthropology and psychology. *In* Psychological Anthropology. F. L. K. Hsu, Ed. Dorsey Press. Homewood, Ill.

7. CAMPBELL, D. T. 1964. Distinguishing differences of perception from failures of communication in cross-cultural studies. *In* Cross-Cultural Understanding: Epistemology in Anthropology. F. C. S. Northrop & H. H. Livingston, Eds. Harper & Row. New York, N.Y.

8. CAMPBELL, D. T. & D. W. FISKE. 1959. Convergent and discriminant validation by a multitrait-multimethod matrix. Psychol. Bull. **56**: 81–105.

9. COLE, M., J. GAY, J. W. GLICK, & D. W. SHARP. 1971. The Cultural Context of Learning and Thinking. Basic Books. New York, N.Y.

10. COLE, M. & S. SCRIBNER. 1974. Culture and Thought: A Psychological Introduction. John Wiley & Sons, Inc. New York, N.Y.

11. CRONBACH, L. J. & P. E. MEEHL. 1955. Construct validity in psychological tests. Psychol. Bull. **52**: 281–302.

12. IRWIN, M., P. L. ENGLE, R. E. KLEIN, C. YARBROUGH, & S. ROSENHOUSE. 1975. Ability, sex, and schooling in rural Eastern Guatemala. Manuscript in preparation. DHD/INCAP. Guatemala.

13. KAGAN, J. 1975. Personal communication.

14. KARP, S. A. & N. L. KONSTADT. 1963. Children's Embedded Figures Tests. Cognitive Tests. New York, N.Y.

15. KLEIN, R. E., O. GILBERT, C. A. CANOSA & R. DE LEON. 1969. Performance of malnourished in comparison with adequately nourished children on selected cognitive tasks (Guatemala). Annual Meeting of the Association for the Advancement of Science. Boston, Mass.

16. KLEIN, R. E. & H. E. FREEMAN. 1975. Indigenous conceptions of intelligence. A cross-cultural replication. Manuscript in preparation. DHD/INCAP. Guatemala.

17. KLEIN, R. E., H. E. FREEMAN, & R. MILLET. 1973. Psychological test performance and indigenous conceptions of intelligence. J. Psychol. **84**: 219–222.

18. KLEIN, R. E., M. IRWIN, P. L. ENGLE & C. YARBROUGH. 1975. Malnutrition and mental development in rural Guatemala: An applied cross-cultural research study. *In* Advances in Cross-Cultural Psychology. N. Warren, Ed. Academic Press. New York. N.Y. (In press).

19. MEJÍA PIVARAL, V. 1972. Características económicas y socio-culturales de cuatro aldeas Ladinas de Guatemala. Guatemala Indígena (Monografía), Vol. **VIII**(3).

20. NERLOVE, S. B., J. M. ROBERTS, & R. E. KLEIN. 1974. The smart child: Women's judgments of *listura* in two Guatemalan communities. American Anthropological Association Meetings, Symposium on Comparative Field Studies in Child Socialization. Mexico City, Mexico.

21. NERLOVE, S. B. & A. S. WALTERS. 1975. Pooling intracultural variation: A composite rank-ordering of community judgments. Mathematical Social Science Board Conference on Standardization and Measurement in Social and Cultural Anthropology. Coloma, California.

22. NERLOVE, S. B., J. M. ROBERTS, R. E. KLEIN, C. YARBROUGH, & J-P. HABICHT. 1974. Natural indicators of cognitive development: An observational study of rural Guatemalan children. Ethos **2**: 265–295.

23. DHD-INCAP. 1975. Progress Report 1974/75. Contract PH-43-65-640. Division of Human Development, Institute of Nutrition of Central America and Panamá. Guatemala.

24. TUDDENHAM, R. D. 1963. The nature and measurement of intelligence. *In* Psychology in the Making. L. Postman, Ed. Knopf. New York, N.Y.

25. WITKIN, H. A., R. B. DYK, H. F. FATERSON, D. R. GOONEOUGH, & S. A. KARP. 1962. Psychological Differentiation. John Wiley & Sons, Inc. New York. (Republished in 1974. Lawrence Erlbaum Associates. Potomac, Md.)

WHY AFRICAN CHILDREN ARE SO HARD TO TEST*

Sara Harkness and Charles M. Super

*Department of Psychology and Social Relations
Harvard University
Cambridge, Massachusetts 02138*

When child psychologists explore the generality of their theories in other cultures, they frequently turn to Africa. An examination of LeVine's bibliography[1] in the Mussen handbook, for example, suggests that Africa has been the locus for nearly half of the existing cross-cultural research on children. A substantial portion of this research reports the performance of relatively nonwesternized children on psychological tests. In addition to issues of adapting test content to the local culture, authors often report problems that seem to relate to the test situation itself.[2,3] Consider, for example, our experience in testing children in Kokwet, a rural farming community of Kipsigis people in western Kenya. Several children – siblings or neighborhood peers – are brought to a traditional hut, where a familiar local woman adminsters several tests in a friendly and relaxed context. Children waiting to be tested play nearby, and because the house is used by our project staff, there is often someone making tea or doing other familiar chores. As part of the test battery the child is told a story of ten sentences about a boy who was given a special stick to help him herd the family's cows. He is then asked to tell the story back to the experimenter. The chances that the child will repeat any portion of the story, no matter how short or garbled, are not great: only 10% of the three-year-olds say anything in this situation, and the proportion of children answering does not reach 50% until six or seven years. Even by age ten, a full third of the children do not give a scorable reply.

These children are generally healthy and well nourished. In everyday circumstances they can be as active and vocal as children anywhere, swinging from the rafters of a maize storehouse, boisterously roughhousing, or gleefully teasing a goat. What needs to be explained, then, is why the children of Kokwet – and apparently much of the rest of Africa – are so hard to test. Why does the testing situation, even the most friendly and familiarized version of it, produce such inhibition of thoughful response?

Researchers commenting on this problem have suggested that the testing situation conflicts with behavior required of children in traditional settings. "Only when the authority figure withdraws," writes Greenfield of her work in rural Senegal, "does the child turn fully to the logically essential parts of the action."[3] Cole and Gay, similarly, look to traditional life for an explanation of problems in eliciting responses from their Liberian subjects. "If [the Kpelle child] asks 'Why' or acts in a manner unsanctioned by tradition," they write, "he is likely to be beaten."[2] To our knowledge, however, there has not yet been any investigation of the ontogeny of test-related behavior in African children. Thus our purpose here is to present some observations on early childhood social-

* This work was supported by the Carnegie Corporation of New York through the Bureau of Educational Research (formerly Child Development Research Unit) of the University of Nairobi, and by the Grant Foundation of New York.

ization that should contribute to a fuller, more differentiated understanding of this problem.

Our observations are drawn from a study of child language socialization[4] that included 20 children in the community of Kokwet whose ages ranged from two to three-and-a-half years. The children were tape-recorded and observed at home in naturally occurring situations, and their mothers were interviewed about beliefs and values related to child language development. The study of child language socialization is pertinent to our present concerns for two reasons: first, the structure of verbal interactions between the young child and others should indicate how much practice the child receives in the type of talking that is necessary for responding to psychological tests; and second, the acquisition of communicative competence reflects the child's learning of more general norms of social behavior with different classes of people.

Recent research indicates that American middle-class mothers typically adapt their speech to young children in several ways.[5,6] In addition to simplifying their speech, these mothers seem consciously oriented toward teaching their children to talk. Teaching techniques observed include, for example, eliciting practice through questions[7] and conversation based on picture books.[8] Gleason[9] has described verbal interaction between American middle-class mothers and their preschool children as an extension of this teaching situation in which the focus is now the acquisition of sociolinguistic rather than linguistic skills. It seems likely that this kind of verbal interaction lays a favorable groundwork for the child's subsequent reaction to testing situations. His experiences in learning to talk have taught him, as well, that conversation with adults is apt to be framed as teaching and learning, and that his own role is to perform well as a pupil.

In contrast, the Kipsigis mothers of Kokwet take a much less active role in teaching their children to talk. Only 25% of the mothers, for example, mentioned language teaching as a reason that one should talk to babies, and the majority of the mothers judged that children learn to talk primarily from other children. The Kokwet mothers' most frequently mentioned language teaching technique (mentioned by 55% of the mothers) was giving commands, such as "Bring the kettle" or "Watch the fire, it's hot!" Only 40% of the mothers reported that they had explicitly taught their children the names of objects. In the mothers' recorded speech to their children, imperatives were the most common form of utterance (47%). An obvious feature of imperatives is that they generally demand a response in action, not words. Questions, which do require a verbal response, were a poor second in frequency (27%), while statements, which constitute the bulk of dialogue, were third (19%).[10] The Kokwet mothers' reported language teaching techniques and observed speech behavior thus indicate that the most important language skill for the Kokwet children is comprehension, not production. In this context, it is noteworthy that mothers' attempts to elicit speech from their children in the recordings generally met with minimal success. The normal mode of Kokwet mothers' speech to their young children seemed to be sporadic utterances whose purpose was to direct or control, to comfort, or to scold. It is therefore not surprising that the total amount of mothers' speech to their children was small: only 67 utterances, on the average, during a two-hour recording.[11]

Relationships between the children's language environment and their age and sibling status indicate clearly the thrust of child language socialization in Kokwet. These trends reflect Kipsigis norms of communicative competence, regardless of their relationship to the acquisition of purely linguistic competence. You will recall that the children we studied ranged in age from two to three-and-a-half years, a period that spans the transition from late infancy to early childhood. During this period, most children in Kokwet move from the favored status of youngest member of the family to the peripheral position of second to youngest, no longer the object of the playful attention character-istically bestowed upon babies, but not yet old enough to contribute to the maintenance of the household. The Kokwet mothers issued many more commands and prohibitions to the children who were older or who were not the youngest member of the family. More strikingly, the mothers also increased reprimands and insults[12] to these children. (TABLE 1). Reprimands and insults included such remarks as "What's that you're doing?" (delivered in a threatening tone of voice), "Sit properly, damn you," and the inevitable "I'll beat you." While the younger children were hardly ever reprimanded or insulted by their mothers, remarks of this type comprised up to 20% of mothers' utterances to the older children (TABLE 1). At the same time, our behavior observations indicate that the older children spent less time interacting with adults in general and more time with children. Concomitant with this trend, the older children were talked to less and also talked less themselves. In short, the Kokwet mothers' verbal interactions with their toddlers tended to become more directive and more negative as the children grew older or acquired a younger sibling, and the total amount of attention the children received from adults decreased.

All these trends point to the socialization of an important aspect of communicative competence in Kipsigis society: silence when in the presence of older or higher status people. This behavior carries over to adulthood and is difficult to alter, as we have found to our discomfort with various research assistants. The trends in language socialization that we have described relate negatively, in general, to the rate of acquisition of syntax and vocabulary; but at the same time it is clear that young children in Kokwet learn a great deal about *not* talking.

Thus, we suggest two aspects of socialization that are important in the ontogeny of test-related behavior in the children of Kokwet. First, by comparison with mother-child verbal interaction in middle-class America the Kipsigis norms of verbal interaction offer little practice in the kind of talking

TABLE 1

CORRELATIONS BETWEEN SUBJECTS' AGE AND SIBLING STATUS,
AND LANGUAGE ENVIRONMENT VARIABLES*

	S's age	S's sibling status
Mothers' commands and prohibitions ($n = 13$)	.51†	−.31
Mothers' reprimands ($n = 13$)	.42	−.20
Mothers' insults ($n = 13$)	.77§	−.49†
Subjects' time with adults ($n = 19$)	−.45‡	.56§
Others talk to subjects ($n = 19$)	−.56‡	.72§
Subjects talk ($n = 19$)	−.38†	.52‡

* Youngest sibling is coded as positive, nonyoungest as negative.
† $p < .10$ (two-tailed)
‡ $p < .05$ (two-tailed)
§ $p < .01$ (two-tailed)

required in psychological tests. Second, the relationship between the Kipsigis child and important adult figures undergoes a profound change during the second and third years of life, which has the effect of creating social distance between himself and adults and of discouraging verbal expressiveness.

Explaining the African child's test behavior in terms of his early socialization, however, only begs an explanation at the next theoretical level: namely, why should the mothers of Kokwet neglect their children's speech development, and why should the social and emotional relations between the toddler and important adults undergo the change we have described? The relative absence of language teaching by the Kipsigis mothers is somewhat reminiscent of reports on class differences in speech to young children.[13,14] It has been suggested that styles of verbal interaction between American working-class mothers and their infants reflect the mothers' fatalistic attitude toward the future.[14] Without reviewing the complexities of the literature on class differences, we may note that in comparison to American middle-class mothers, the Kokwet mothers give *more* training to their infants in some areas, specifically, motor development.[15] Any theory of general cultural impoverishment or maternal fatalism, therefore, is clearly not applicable to the Kipsigis case. We have already suggested a more positive reason for the Kipsigis approach to child language socialization: comprehension, not production, is the important linguistic skill by traditional criteria. The traditional attitude may well be that children will learn to talk on their own soon enough, but that they must be taught to understand requests and commands, and to respond appropriately to them. It is interesting, in this context, that the more modern mothers in Kokwet were somewhat less dominant ($r = -.37$, n.s.) and more sociable ($r = .35$, n.s.) in verbal interactions with their children, and they tended strongly to favor a more active teaching role in their children's language development. ($r = .68$, $p < .05$)

The traditional emphasis on language comprehension rather than production fits within the larger cultural values of obedience and respect as they are realized in many African societies.[16,17] Obedience and respect are required in many relationships between people of differing status in sub-Saharan Africa: children and parents, women and men, younger people and older people, apprentices and masters, clients and patrons. The expression of obedience and respect characteristically entails a quiet, even impassive demeanor and may actually be socially encoded as an avoidance requirement between certain categories of people.[18] LeVine has attributed the emphasis on obedience characteristic of traditional African societies to economic insecurity, while the Whitings look to the African extended family structure for an explanation.[18,19] They suggest that the greater disciplinary harshness of mothers in societies similar to Kipsigis is due to the necessity of raising children who will quickly take their place as responsible and contributing members of a large household, to be entrusted with child care and other chores essential to the well-being of the family. The Whitings demonstrate that such societies are characterized by greater social distance between the father and other members of the family than is true in societies with nuclear family arrangements. The social distancing between mothers (and other adults) and their children that is evident in our observations of child language socialization seems to reflect a similar norm. The period corresponding to the early stages of child language learning is precisely that time when the child must learn to take his place as a contributing member of the family group. For the traditional Kipsigis mother, the most important aspect of her child's development at this stage is not self-expression but rather the acquisition of obedient and respectful responsibility.

Now let us return to the testing problems that we described at the beginning of this paper. You will recall that in a simple task of retelling a story, a substantial proportion of the Kokwet children aged three to ten failed to respond at all. Clearly, the primary skill required in this task was verbal production. If the child could not produce anything verbally, no other skill such as memory or cognitive organization could be measured. What of the children's performance on tasks that did not require verbal production? In Kagan's Matching Familiar Figures Test[20] the child is required to understand verbal instructions and to follow them by pointing to the figure that exactly matches a standard. Of the 185 children tested, only two failed to respond to this test. This pattern is repeated in other tests in the battery — frustrating reticence to tasks demanding verbal responses, a high rate of response to those that do not.

The use of psychological tests with nonwesternized African children is obviously a difficult endeavor. First, the test materials and the test situation are culturally strange, a problem that most of us have now learned to deal with in one way or another. Second, the status differential between the adult tester and the child subject interferes with free responses through the norms of obedience and respect. One answer to this problem, we suggest only half in jest, is that the best psychological testers for traditional African children might be other children.[21] Finally, better results with psychological tests will be obtained from African children if we consider the modes of response that children receive practice in at home. Only when all these problems are minimized will we be able to test the development of nonwesternized children as we originally intended.

ACKNOWLEDGMENT

We are grateful to Robert LeVine for his helpful and encouraging comments on an earlier draft of this paper.

NOTES AND REFERENCES

1. LeVINE, R. A. 1970. Cross-Cultural Study in Child Psychology. *In* Manual of Child Psychology. P. Mussen, Ed. Vol 2: 559—611. John Wiley & Sons. New York, N.Y.
2. GAY, J. & M. COLE. 1967. The New Mathematics in an Old Culture. Holt, Rinehart & Winston. New York, N.Y.
3. GREENFIELD, P. On Culture and Conservation. *In* Bruner, J. S., R. R. Olver & P. Greenfield. 1966. Studies in Cognitive Growth. John Wiley & Sons. New York, N.Y.
4. HARKNESS, S. 1975. Child Language Socialization in a Kipsigis Community of Kenya. Unpublished Ph.D. thesis. Harvard University. Cambridge, Mass.
5. BROEN, P. 1972. The Verbal Environment of the Language-Learning Child. Monogr. Am. Speech Hearing Assoc. 17.
6. SNOW, C. E. 1972. Mothers' speech to children learning language. Child Devel. 43: 549—565.
7. REMICK, H. 1975. Maternal speech to children during language acquisition. *In* Infant Speech and Baby Talk. Neurolinguistics, Vol. IV. W. von Raffler-Engel and Y. Lebrun, Eds. University of Brussels Press.
8. MOERK, E. 1974. Changes in verbal child-mother interactions with increasing language skills of the child. J. Psycholinguistic Res. 3 (2): 101—116.
9. GLEASON, J. B. 1973. Code switching in children's language. *In* Cognitive Development and The Acquisition of Language.: 159—167. T. Moore, Ed. Academic Press. New York, N.Y.

10. The remaining 7 percent of mothers' utterances are accounted for by simply calling the child's name.
11. In contrast, Nelson (NELSON, K. 1973. Structure and Strategy in Learning to Talk. Monogr. Soc. Res. Child Develop. **38** (1–2)) was able to use "the first 200 utterances" for analysis in a comparable study with American middle-class mothers. Mothers' presence was not strictly controlled in the Kipsigis study, but the recordings were made when the mothers were most likely to be present, and all mothers were present for at least part of the recording.
12. These categories are derived from the Whitings' system of coding social behavior (see note 19).
13. SNOW, C. E., A. ARLMAN-RUPP, Y. HASSING, J. JOBSE, J. JOOSTEN, & J. VOORSTER. 1974. Mothers' speech in three social classes. Mimeo, Institute for General Linguistics, U. of Amsterdam.
14. KAGAN, J. & S. TULKIN. 1972. Mother-child interaction in the first year of life. Child Develop. **43**: 31–41.
15. SUPER, C. M. 1975. Environmental influences on motor development: the case of "African infant precocity." Developmental Medicine and Child Neurology. In press.
16. LeVINE, R. A. 1974. Parental goals: A cross-cultural view. Teachers College Record. **76** (2): 226–239.
17. MONROE, R. L. & R. H. MONROE. 1972. Obedience among children in an East African society. J. Cross-cultural Psychol. **3** (4): 395–399.
18. LeVINE, R. A. 1973. Patterns of personality in Africa. Ethos. **1** (2): 123–152.
19. WHITING, B. B., & J. W. M. WHITING. 1974. Children of Six Cultures. Harvard University Press. Cambridge, Mass.
20. KAGAN, J. 1965. Individual differences in the resolution of response uncertainty. J. Pers. Soc. Psychol. **2**: 154–160.
21. As an illustration of this point, we know at least one case in which a 5-year-old gave no response to the story memory test, but then went home and told the story to his brother.

CROSS-CULTURAL COGNITIVE DEVELOPMENT: THE CULTURAL
ASPECTS OF PIAGET'S THEORY*

Pierre R. Dasen†

*Faculté de Psychologie et
des Sciences de l'Education
Université de Genève
Switzerland*

When discussing Piaget's theory in the context of cross-cultural psychology, we first of all have to make a distinction between Piaget's own major goal and the way in which his theory has been used by developmental psychologists. Piaget is an epistemologist rather than a psychologist, studying the ontogenetic and philogenetic development of scientific knowledge; developmental psychologists (including those interested in cultural aspects) have used Piaget's epistemology as a theoretical framework to study cognitive development in individuals. Under their influence, Piaget's structural theory, and especially his concepts of "stage" and *structures d'ensemble* have gradually been expanded to encompass more contextual aspects.

Flavell and Wohlwill,[17] for example, have suggested a model that introduces a distinction between competence and performance, patterned on Chomsky's theory of psycho-linguistics. In their views:

> . . . a psychological theory that accounts for complex behavior will have two principal components: a *competence* model, which is a formal, logical representation of the structure of some domain (. . .); an *automaton* model (. . .), which represents the psychological processes by which the information embodied in competence actually gets accessed and utilized in real situations. The competence model gives an abstract, purely logical representation of what the organism knows or could do in a timeless, ideal environment, whereas the automaton model has the job of describing a real device that could plausibly instance that knowledge or skill, and instance it within the constraints (memory limitations, rapid performance, etc.) under which human beings actually operate. (p. 71)

The probability that a given child will solve a given task can be formulated in the following equation:

$$P(+) = P_a \times P_b^{1-k}$$

where P_a reflects the degree to which a given operation has become established in a particular child, or in other words, the presence or absence of the operational structure (competence). P_b is an attribute of the task. It represents the likelihood for any given task that the operation will in fact be called into play, and its end product be translated into the desired output. The parameter k has to be introduced because these task-related variables vary with age. The values of all three factors are expected to vary between 0 and 1, which gives rise to a four-phase process of cognitive development. In the initial phase, $P_a = 0$, i.e.

* The preparation of this paper was assisted by a grant from the Fonds National Suisse de la Recherche Scientifique (grant no. 1.7640.72 to Prof. B. Inhelder).
† Present address: Bureau of Educational Research, University of Nairobi, P.O. Box 30197, Nairobi, Kenya.

the child lacks the given operation. In a transitional phase, P_a changes from 0 to 1, while k is assumed to remain equal to 0. In a period of stabilization, the contribution of the task-related variables gradually decreases ($1 - k$ tends towards 0), and during the terminal phase the child "is able to bring the operation to bear on the problem successfully, regardless of the situational and task variables involved." (p. 101) The model is able to handle many empirical results on horizontal décalages and lack of inter-task consistency.

However P_b, in Flavell and Wohlwill's model, is an attribute of the task, whereas what is needed to explain the competence/performance distinction in some cross-cultural situations is a variable that is an attribute of the culture. Thus I propose to introduce the variable P_c, representing the likelihood for any given task that the operation will in fact be called into play in a given cultural milieu. P_c is likely to change with age, and its effects will probably increase with age; this is why it has to be raised to the power k. The complete equation now becomes:

$$P(+) = P_a \times P_b{}^{1-k} \times P_c{}^k$$

One of the tasks of cross-cultural Piagetian psychology is to define more precisely how cultural factors influence the different components of the equation, particularly whether they influence competence (P_a) or performance ($P_b{}^{1-k}$ or $P_c{}^k$).[‡]

According to the competence/performance model, an initial answer a child gives to a Piagetian task may not necessarily reflect his "true" cognitive level, i.e. the underlying structure or competence. This situation seems to occur particularly frequently in cross-cultural situations. Generally speaking the rate of development of concrete operations in rural nonwestern children is reported to lag behind western norms,[8] and the development curves are often asymptotic.[9,13] Does this mean that the rate of development of P_a is affected?

There are indications that, in some cases at least, very little "help" is needed, in the form of further questioning, additional task situations or exposure to other operational tasks and training procedures, in order to "actualize" the latent structure.

De Lemos,[16] for example, discussing the effects of familiarity with the testing situation in Australian Aborigines, states that

> because the Aboriginal society does not appear to recognize or encourage the development of concepts of conservation, these may not be clearly formulated even when the operational capacity is present. In this case it is likely that a little experience with the test situation would be sufficient to develop the concepts. (p. 264-5)

Examples of such rapid *Aktualgenese* are provided by Bovet[4] in Algerian illiterate adults, when testing for conservation of weight, and to some extent for conservation of length. During the interview, some of Bovet's subjects went through the complete sequence from pseudoconservation to nonconservation to end up with operational conservation, and others changed from nonconservation to operational conservation after weighing the two pieces of clay once. On other concepts, such as speed and time, which were thought to be less culturally relevant, no such actualization occurred.

---

‡ I am using this formula as a heuristic device. It is not essential to this discussion, and I do not wish to suggest that we may be able to attach real probabilities to its components.

The illiterate children, in Bovet's study, also gave more advanced answers after being exposed to some training situations. There are other examples of rapid learning of operational concepts. For example, Pinard, Morin, and Lefebvre[23] report on the average similar rates of learning conservation of quantity (liquids) in French Canadian, unschooled Rwandan and schooled Rwandan children aged 7 years. One difference however was found between the three groups: there were 7 (of 16) subjects in the unschooled Rwandan group who were successful on the training exercises after one single session, whereas there were only 3 in the schooled group and none in the French Canadian group. Dasen[12,15] reports very rapid learning of conservation of quantity in Eskimo children aged 12 to 14; some children moved from nonconservation to full conservation after a mere exposure to other operational tasks and some moved from nonconservation to the intermediate stage in the same way, and then acquired full conservation very rapidly during the training phase. On the other hand, the subjects aged 10 and 11 remained at stage 1 despite exposure to other operational tasks, but then started to aquire the necessary operational structures during the training phase.

This is not to say that learning is always as fast as illustrated in these examples; I have picked out only those occasions in which the competence/performance distinction seems to be applicable. My interpretation of rapid learning in these examples is that the children already had a latent competence for conservation of quantity, but, for some reason, were not able to demonstrate it on the pretest; it was then activated by a minimum of operational training. In other words, these children were probably at Flavell and Wohlwill's phase 3, where P_a is equal or close to 1, but k still equals 0. The immediate effect of the training procedure is not to change P_a but to change the value of P_b^{1-k}; this is what probably occurred with the Eskimo children in our example who were 12 to 14 years old. In the subjects aged 10 to 11 years, the training probably started to build up P_a.

Flavell and Wohlwill's competence/performance distinction was first introduced to cross-cultural Piagetian psychology by Heron[20] to explain the discrepancy in performance on tasks that ought to be characteristic of the same stage.[19,21,22] Heron[20] concludes: "I find myself increasingly inclined to the view that the apparent unity of (the concrete operational) stage has been generated by the cognitively-relevant cultural homogeneity in development of the children serving as subjects in most European and North American studies" (p. 100). Consistency in performance across tasks is only an ideal end-product of the stage; this seems to be rarely attained in "nonwestern" or "nontechnological" milieux, where a sort of "stretching of Piaget's transitional period"[20] (p. 97) seems to occur. Heron suggests that, over and above such factors as "schooling" or "European contact" or urban/rural residence or social class, which have often been shown to influence the rate of development of concrete operations,[8,10] one should consider the cognitive "ambience" in which the children develop. By this term, he means the "values with cognitive relevance that are *implicit* in the total pattern of adult and older sibling behavior within which (early) development takes place"[20] (p. 97).

One should not assume that this cognitive ambience is generally favorable or unfavorable to the development of all concrete operational concepts. A recently published study[11] has demonstrated that "rates of development are not uniform across different areas of concrete operations, and that these rates may reflect the adaptive values of the concepts concerned." Extending Berry's[2,3] model of ecological functionalism to Piagetian developmental psychology, it was predicted that nomadic, hunting, subsistence-economy populations would develop spatial concepts more rapidly than sedentary, agriculturalist groups, whereas the latter would attain concepts of conservation of quantity, weight and volume more rapidly than the former. The model was largely supported by the results of a study involving 190 children aged 6 to 14 from three cultural groups: Canadian Eskimos, Australian Aborigines and Ebrié Africans.

Such a quasi-experimental study is a modest step towards specifying the variable P_c, which is seen to vary according to the ecocultural demands placed on a population (or, in other words, to the ecocultural relevance of the particular concrete operational concepts). If we hypothesize these ecocultural factors to determine P_c to a greater extent than P_a, this distinction is not trivial. It implies that the competence for concrete operational structures is likely to be universal, but that the way in which this competence is translated into spontaneous behavior is culturally determined.

This interpretation comes very close to Cole and Bruner's[5] position on intra-cultural, social-class differences, namely that the "deficit" interpretation ought to be replaced by a "difference" interpretation:

> The crux of the argument, when applied to the problem of "cultural deprivation", is that those groups ordinarily diagnosed as culturally deprived have the same underlying competence as those in the mainstream of the dominant culture, *the differences in performance being accounted for by the situations and contexts in* which the competence *is expressed.* (p. 238)

Similarly Cole et al.[6] concluded from a large-scale study in Liberia that "cultural differences in cognition reside more in the situations to which particular cognitive processes are applied than in the existence of a process in one cultural group and its absence in another." (p. 233) Cultural factors however influence the way basic processes get organized into "functional systems" and how these are applied in any given situation.[7] This functional systems approach could certainly be highly beneficial to future research in cross-cultural developmental psychology.

However, Cole's formulation applies to processes, whereas we have been discussing so far only the structural aspects of Piaget's theory. The qualitatively different structures that characterize each successive stage are the products of the same basic processes of adaptation (assimilation and accommodation) and equilibration, which have their roots in basic biological processes. These processes are no doubt universal, but little attention has been given to this aspect of Piaget's theory in the cross-cultural literature.

The various cognitive structures are not biologically predetermined: they result from the constant interaction between the acting subject and his environment, and they tend towards an adaptive state of equilibrium. Thus, even "competence" (P_a) is a product of epigenesis, and is not determined only by genetic (i.e. hereditary) factors. Depending on the characteristics of the environment (physical and social), this competence could take different adaptive forms. This possibility has been discussed by Greenfield,[18] at least as far as the end-state of development is concerned: Piaget's end-state is a western scientist, which does not necessarily represent the forms of thought valued in other cultures. The functional divergence of structures is likely to be most noticeable in the end-state of development, but is not necessarily limited to it.

Thus, according to a first hypothesis, cultural factors influence P_c as well as the rate of development of P_a; techniques to distinguish competence from performance should be used systematically to distinguish the two. Whenever P_a

is present, it takes the same structural form, and we may consider it to be a so-called "weak"§ universal.[14]

On the other hand, according to a second hypothesis, P_a itself may take different forms in different cultures, although the basic processes of development may still be universal. In the formula, we may replace P_a by $P_a C_i^k$: C indicates the cultural relativity of P_a, i is the indice of the particular culture, and k is used to suggest that the cultural differences are likely to increase with development.

Little is yet known about the forms $P_a C_i^k$ could take, but the hypothesis implies that they would be more adaptive than P_a. The testing of this second hypothesis will require an enormous program of research: a Piagetian psychology to each culture, now on an emic rather than etic basis.[1] As Greenfield[18] has suggested, such a program would be based on Piaget's theory rather than on the tasks derived from it, and would ideally be carried out by a member of his own culture (with or without a multicultural team). Universals in processes and structures would then be derived from the common aspects of these developmental psychologies.

In summary, I am suggesting that future cross-cultural Piagetian psychology should become more emic, and more process-oriented. Until that is possible, the interpretation of etic studies should take into account more contextual aspects, such as the competence/performance distinction and ecological functionalism.

REFERENCES

1. BERRY, J. W. 1969. On cross-cultural comparability. Int. J. Psychol. 4: 119–128.
2. BERRY, J. W. 1971. Ecological and cultural factors in spatial skill development. Canadian J. Behav. Sci. 3: 324–336. (Reprinted in Culture and Cognition. J. W. Berry & P. R. Dasen, Eds.: 129–140. 1974. Methuen. London.)
3. BERRY, J. W. 1975. An ecological approach to cross-cultural psychology. Nederlands Tijdschrift voor de Psychologie 30: 51–84.
4. BOVET, M. C. 1974. Cognitive processes among illiterate children and adults. In Culture and Cognition. J. W. Berry & P. R. Dasen, Eds.: 311–334. 1974. Methuen. London.
5. COLE, M. & J. S. BRUNER. 1971. Cultural differences and inferences about psychological processes. American Psychologist 26: 867-876. (Reprinted in Culture and Cognition. J. W. Berry & P. R. Dasen, Eds. 231–246. 1974. Methuen, London.)
6. COLE, M., J. GAY & D. W. SHARP. 1971. The Cultural Context of Learning and Thinking. Basic Books. New York, N.Y.
7. COLE, M. & S. SCRIBNER. 1974. Culture and Thought: a Psychological Introduction. John Wiley. New York.
8. DASEN, P. R. 1972. Cross-Cultural Piagetian research: a summary. J. Cross-cultural Psychol. 3: 23–39. (Reprinted in Culture and Cognition. J. W. Berry & P. R. Dasen, Eds., pp. 409–423. Methuen. London.)
9. DASEN, P. R. 1973. Biologie ou culture? La psychologie inter-ethnique d'un point de vue Piagétien. Canadian Psychologist 14: 149–166.

§ The definition of a "weak" universal follows Flavell and Wohlwill's[17] distinction between "strong" and "weak" sequential invariance: "A sequence is weakly invariant if, when present, it is universally fixed. One may be able to find children who do attain A, or B, or both; but for all children who do attain both, the order of attainment is the same." (17, p. 84 fn)

10. DASEN, P. R. 1974. The influence of ecology, culture and European contact on cognitive development in Australian Aborigines. *In* Culture and Cognition. J. W. Berry & P. R. Dasen, Eds., pp. 381–408. Methuen. London.
11. DASEN, P. R. 1975a. Concrete operational development in three cultures. J. Cross-cultural Psychol. **6**: 156–172.
12. DASEN, P. R. 1975b. Le développement des opérations concrètes chez les Esquimaux Canadiens. Int. J. Psychol. **10**: 165–180.
13. DASEN, P. R. 1975c. Cross-cultural data on operational development: asymptotic development curves. Paper presented at the C.E.R.I.-C.N.R.S. conference on Dips in Learning and Development Curves, St. Paul de Vence, March 1975.
14. DASEN, P. R. 1975d. "Strong" and "weak" universals: sensori-motor intelligence and concrete operations. Paper presented at the conference on Universals of Human Thought: Some African evidence. Centre for African Studies, Cambridge, April 1975.
15. DASEN, P. R. Are cognitive processes universal? A contribution to cross-cultural Piagetian psychology. *In* Studies in Cross-cultural Psychology, Vol. 1. N. Warren, Ed. Academic Press. London. In press.
16. deLEMOS, M. M. 1969. The development of conservation in Aboriginal children. Int. J. Psychol. **4**: 255–269.
17. FLAVELL, J. H. & J. F. WOHLWILL. 1969. Formal and functional aspects of cognitive development. *In* Studies in cognitive development. D. Elkind & J. H. Flavell, Eds., pp. 67–120. Oxford Univ. Press. New York.
18. GREENFIELD, P. 1975. Cross-cultural research and Piagetian theory: paradox and progress. *In* The developing individual in a changing world. K. Riegel & J. Meacham, Eds., Mouton. The Hague.
19. HERON, A. 1971. Concrete operations, 'g' and achievement in Zambian children. J. Cross-cultural Psychol. **2**: 325–336.
20. HERON, A. 1974. Cultural determinants of concrete operational behavior. *In* Readings in cross-cultural psychology. J. L. M. Dawson & W. J. Lonner, Eds. pp. 94–101. Hong Kong Univ. Press.
21. HERON, A. & W. DOWEL. 1973. Weight conservation and matrix-solving ability in Papuan children. J. Cross-cultural Psychol. **4**: 207–219.
22. HERON, A. & W. DOWEL. 1974. The questionable unity of the concrete operational stage. Int. J. Psychol. **9**: 1–9.
23. PINARD, A., C. MORIN & M. LEFEBVRE. 1973. Apprentissage de la conservation des quantités liquides chez des enfants rwandais et canadiens-français. Int. J. Psychol. **8**: 15–24.

PERSON PERCEPTION AND SOCIAL INTERACTION OF JEWISH AND DRUZE KINDERGARTEN CHILDREN IN ISRAEL*

Michaela Lifshitz

Department of Psychology
University of Haifa
Haifa, Israel

The aim of this study is to assess (1) the general effect of socialization practices upon kindergarten children's sensorimotor and conceptual development on both neutral and interpersonal levels; (2) the possible differential effect of the socialization milieu upon boys' and girls' perception; and (3) the figure (person) in the child's life who can be perceived as instrumental in this perceptual development.

Kindergarten age was chosen for two reasons: it is the first year of formal education, the beginning of the institutionalized implementation of social values and practices; and it is a stage of perceptual development[46] where sensorimotor and conceptual processes interact closely.

Special place is given during the kindergarten age to the concept of differentiation,[15] i.e. ability to perceive objects as having unique qualities distinct from other objects, in contrast to the concept of sameness. The progressive perceptual differentiation is counteracted, to forestall feelings of confusion and insecurity, by the process of integration, in which irrelevant or superfluous information is eliminated.[47] Studies[37] suggest that people consistently use a small number of categories to describe others and themselves; these can be regarded as a set of implicit rules or assumptions about people in general and about some persons in particular.

That which we see, or otherwise sense (i.e. felt qualities) is not necessarily describable in words[1,47] although all human perceptions are partly directed by verbal references learned through acculturation. Prelinguistic mastery in the functions of concept formation and communication is available through sensorimotor skills. Such skills are geared to visual spatial information,[7] which is strongly related to overt activity.[8]

Cognitive processes can be inferred only from evidence relating to cognitive products. At preschool levels, these products are mainly sensorimotor, as assessed through copying of diverse forms,[49] the Bender Gestalt Test,[24] and drawings.[14,25,28,29]

The body image as expressed in the child's drawing of a person is considered[11,14,38,54] to be a concrete representation of the self and hence, the self-concept. When describing the self or important people in their lives, young children tend to lean heavily on items of appearance.[37] Perception of the self and of other meaningful people in the child's life can be assessed from differentiation within and among drawn figures on qualities of line and color.[26,30,41] Color represents also affective values.[51]

* The study was supported by a grant from the Faculty of Social Sciences and Mathematics at the University of Haifa. The author is indebted to the following who collaborated in the study: Smadar Eshel, Rivka Chason, Dalia Ladkani, Channa Ram, Zulia Zeidan, Sara Zidulkin and Naomi Shor. Special thanks go to the children and teachers who participated and the Israel Education Ministry.

338

If words are attached to the cognitive sets, we get verbal concepts that are an abstraction from actuality.[47] Since preschool children's perception is considered to be predominantly concrete, studies tend to refrain from assessing their conceptual interpersonal organization (i.e., how children label and verbalize principles underlying categories) before the age of eight.[37] However, Steinberg[56] found that three-year-olds were already able to code the conceptual characteristics of presented stimuli, and Bigner[6] found that children aged two to eight could already describe liked and disliked siblings, though the number and quality of constructs changed with age.

Within these considerations of general developmental trends, which can be perceived as biological (i.e. maturational) and universal,[25] differences between the sexes are discussed. Almost uniformly, girls as young as age three and up were found to have a more differentiated visuomotor and person perception than did boys, as shown both by drawings[14,16,21,22] and concepts.[37] Explanations for these results vary from physiological maturity[16] to characteristics inherent in sex differences, such as girls' greater interest in people.[37] The latter could be a by-product of girls' greater dependency needs,[36] which may be culturally determined.

Actually, as "no man is an island unto himself,"[11] the context of the social or ethnic culture into which a person is born and within which he is raised could have bearings upon his freedom to perceive and act.[17,25,37,38,43,48,52] Pepper[47] contrasts a functional authoritarian society with an individualistic democratic society. It can be assumed that children raised within a stable society that espouses values of duty, loyalty and discipline would develop a much lower perceptual differentiation than would children raised within a more mobile culture that supports individual enterprise, initiative and tolerance.

Researchers seem to agree that as children grow older, their perceptual performance represents their group norms more and more; this representation of group norms may still be lacking at the age of five to six, prior to school experience.[10,29] Ethnic influences were reported only from the first grade in visuomotor performance[22] and conceptual differentiation.[10]

Who can be considered to be the figure that symbolizes the sought-for cultural norms for the child?[31] An assumption implicit in several studies[6,25,37,50] is that the figure with whom the child identifies, i.e. toward whom he is drawn and like whom he would like to be, is perceived as more differentiated than other figures, and is usually the first figure to be drawn by the child.

Bigner[6] found that children used more constructs in describing liked persons than disliked ones. In contrast, Livesley and Bromley[37] suggested that the important factor in the complexity of description was the sex of the described person in reference to the child's age at that time: before adolescence, children tend to describe females in more detailed and differentiated forms, while in adolescence a shift occurs toward the male figure. This shift seems to depend on frequency and affective value of the child's interactions with female and male figures at different stages of his life. Drawings of seven-to-nine-year-old children and high school and college students, across cultures and ethnic groups,[4,13] where the father figure was either drawn first or separated from the rest of the family, were interpreted to indicate that the "masculine god" is still considered the higher goal in our society for both sexes.

Researchers[25,43,50] also looked at the spatial organization[46] of the drawing of family members: near whom does the child place himself? Whom does he perceive as giving him support? Evans' and Howard's[13] observation that persons who are more friendly with each other exhibit smaller personal zones than those who are not viewed as friends, can be applied to drawings.

Since in the kindergarten age the child's focus of interest begins to shift from family members to peers, studies dealt with children's approach either toward family members only[6,43,50] or toward peers only, but not toward same and opposite-sex parents and peers at the same time. The latter approach would enable an assessment of the child's perception of the relative value of peers and parents.

The following hypotheses are based on the ideas and findings presented above: (1) within each sociocultural group girls will show a higher level of perceptual and conceptual development than boys; (2) the more the socialization practices of the socio-cultural group promote and support individuality and active manipulation of surroundings, the more differentiated and integrated will be the perceptual and conceptual level of the children raised within it, both in neutral areas and in person perception; and (3) female figures (e.g., mother, peer-girl) with whom kindergarten age children have more direct interactions than with males, will be perceived by the children as more differentiated than will be the male figures.

METHODS

Subjects

The sample consisted of 120 Israeli kindergarten children (compulsory education), age five to six, out of whom 80 were Jews (42 boys and 38 girls) and 40 were Druze (20 boys and 20 girls). Excluded from the study were children who were considered by the teacher to be problematic or who had an organic impairment (e.g., blindness, deafness, paralysis, etc.) Jewish children were randomly selected from five secular city kindergartens; the Druze children from five mixed (boys and girls) kindergartens in their villages.

All subjects came from intact families with middle class incomes and lived in the same geographical region (Mount Carmel). The Hebrew-speaking Jewish children lived mainly in the city, mainly in apartments, and there was an average of 2.5 children per family. The Arabic-speaking Druze sample were from 2 villages, lived mainly in small buildings, and had an average of 4.9 children per family.

Socialization practices of the two groups vary considerably and represent the two extremes of the social system described above. The Druze[3] represent the authoritative ethnoreligious society that adheres strongly to certain traditional values that members must obey; the Jews represent the democratic society that permits the individual to exercise ample freedom within his surroundings.

Experimenters

The study was conducted by six female social work students in an advanced research seminar in psychology at the University of Haifa. The experimenters were intensively trained in the use of the measures and in scoring procedures, but were naive as far as the hypotheses of the study were concerned.

Each pair of experimenters was assigned to observe and test 40 children. Four Jewish experimenters tested the Jewish population. Two Arabic speaking experimenters (one, herself a Druze) tested the Druze population. In order to ensure optimal level of achievement,[22] all individual testing of Druze children was conducted by the Druze experimenter. Observations and the Cognitive Complexity Test results were scored by experimenters different from those who recorded the responses. Interscorer reliability during the training period reached 90%. All protocols of the Bender Test and Human Figures drawings were analyzed blindly by the author.

Measures

In order to encompass the complex nature of human-environment variables in cognitive skills,[13] a combination of different techniques was called for. Each child was then seen individually, and a test of Cognitive (conceptual) Complexity (specifically adapted and modified for kindergarten children), a Human Figures Drawing test and a Bender Motor test were administered in that order. At the end of the study, teachers were asked to rate each subject on a questionnaire on the dimensions of popularity, social involvement, cooperation, leadership, and success in coping with school tasks.

Observation of Behavior

All behavior carried out by the subject toward others and by others toward him, all mutual activities with others, and activities with no direct social contact were recorded during relatively unstructured periods. Data were later transferred into behavioral categories, which were subsequently analyzed by multidimensional scales.[35]

Cognitive (Conceptual) Complexity

In accordance with prior suggestions[5,23] and experience with children,[34] constructs (dimensions for assessment) as well as persons were specified. The ten bipolar constructs were chosen on the basis of their commonality,[1,37] in a pilot study that encompassed Israeli middle-class kindergarten children from six different kindergartens, each of whom was asked to describe himself, his father, his mother, his best friend, and his teacher. The constructs were: beautiful—ugly; big—small; working—not working; glad—angry; good—bad; fat—thin; tall—short; strong—weak; smart—stupid; nice—not nice. The five meaningful figures, who were assumed to be manageable for subjects and not resistance-arousing[39] and whom the child was asked to rate on the ten constructs, were: himself, same-sex friend, mother, opposite-sex friend, and father. Since children's thinking at this age is still concrete and they tend to rely on immediate visual stimuli and appearance in their person perception,[9,37] the following procedure was finally selected as providing a more or less neutral visual point of reference to which the mental image of the person to be rated[47] can be anchored.

The child was presented with five same-sized, different-colored wooden blocks out of which he was asked to choose one block to represent each of the five figures. Then the child was presented with a white 50 x 10 cm cardboard divided into six equal parts; in each part a number was drawn from 1 to 6. This cardboard was to be used as a rating scale. For each of the ten bipolar constructs the child was told which end represented one pole and which the other. In order to avoid the child's tendency to equate the square of number 6 with the favored pole, the poles of the constructs were randomly assigned, and were only inverted later for the scoring. For each of the 10 constructs the experimenter explained to the child which end of the cardboard was considered to be the extreme of the construct, while the other squares were intermediate levels directed more to one pole or the other.

Explanations were given for each construct independently of the others. For each construct the child was asked to place each of the five blocks — "*figures*" — on the square that he considered to be the "true" description of the figure. Each block/figure was removed before the next one was placed. Subjects' placements were recorded by the experimenter into a 5 x 10 grid form[23] where constructs were placed on the rows and the columns represented the figures.

Scoring

The following scores were derived from each subject's responses:[5,32,34] (1) degree of diversity in describing each of the five figures. Each grid was scanned for (a) the most differentiated figure (i.e., the figure that received the highest diversity score); (b) the most undifferentiated figure (i.e. the figure whose diversity score was the lowest; (2) total number of differences in ratings within the entire grid (vertical comparisons); and (3) quantity of differences in ratings (horizontal comparisons) among the five figures,[44] between two each time, totalling 10 comparisons.

Human Figures Drawing

Subject was presented with a 28 x 22 cm piece of white drawing paper, placed in front of him horizontally, a pencil and an eraser, and several open boxes of crayons of various kinds and colors. The subject was asked to draw the five figures dealt with in the previous task, i.e., himself, his father, his mother, same-sex friend, and opposite-sex friend. The child was free to draw in any way he liked and to choose his medium of drawing, i.e., a pencil, different colors, to use more than one sheet of paper, etc.[20,55]

Scoring

The data were analyzed for (1) diversity and differentiation within the most differentiated figure drawn[14,21] (if all figures looked the same, the figure that was drawn first was analyzed); (2) differences among the figures in structure and colors[21,26,30,41,57,50] when each is compared with all others; (3) degree of integration of the most differentiated figure (how parts are put together) and the spatial arrangement of the five figures in relationship to each other in the allocated or secured space (i.e. arrangement on page or pages); and (4) indicators of emotional difficulties.[12,19,25]

A note was taken of the figure, out of the five drawn, that seemed to be the most diversified or that was drawn first.[4] Differentiation scores as applied to this figure referred to: (1) indices of structure (form) — number of details of face and body parts, clothing, etc.; and (2) color – number of colors used; differential use of color, i.e. parts of body are covered with color, other parts are left empty, in contrast to uniformal (sameness) approach. Then number of expected and expectional items in the most differentiated, or first drawn, figure were used to get an estimation of the child's intellectual level.[20],[25] In order to avoid negative scores, the value of 7 (compared to 5 in Koppitz[25]) was added to the sum of all negative (if a child omitted an expected item) and positive scoring points. Scores of faulty integration of the most differentiated figures referred to number of unrealistic assemblies of parts, distortion of the human figure, and an exaggerated disproportion.

The five drawn figures were compared with each other. Each pair of figures was compared for: (1) number of differences in form and structure. References were made to differences in line (e.g., one figure has curly hair, the other straight hair) and size of each part of the body, to addition or elimination of details, to change in position of figure (e.g., father sitting, mother standing) and spatial location (e.g., girlfriend is located on the margin of the page, mother appears in the middle of the page); and (2) number of differences in coloring of the same parts and differential uses of color in the drawing of the figures. Each difference was given one point. No special concern was given here to differential stereotyped sex typing.[4],[21],[29],[57] Differences in form for the 10 comparisons were summed up to yield one differentiation score, as were differences in color.

Spatial arrangement (integration) of the figures, i.e. segment–whole relationships, was analyzed for the following indices:[58] (1) expansiveness, e.g., every figure on a different paper; one figure covers the entire page; (2) constriction, e.g., all figures drawn very close to each other on a small part of the page; and (3) figures drawn on same page but seem to be unrelated to each other. Relationship was judged by proximity (e.g., mother and father stand close to each other) vs. remoteness[3] and by function (e.g., one looks at the other, father stands before the child as if protecting him, holding hands, etc.). If the figures seemed to relate to each other, a further analysis was carried out for the existence of specific kinds of relationships.

Analysis for emotional indicators[26] was carried out only on the drawing of self. One point was given in case of the existence of each of the following indices: (1) dark colors; (2) filling in areas with color; (3) strong and emphasized lines; (4) total number of missing sensory parts, e.g., no eyes, no mouth, no nose; (5) total number of missing motor (movement) parts, e.g., no hands, no legs, no body; (6) a very small figure;[38],[48],[57] and (7) faint lines.

Bender Motor Gestalt Test.

This test which, being neutral, was given as a control for the children's general level of perceptual development, was presented last in the battery. The test was presented and analyzed in the standard way.[2],[13],[24],[40],[45],[46]

Results

Results of each task were analyzed in a 2 x 2 (sex x ethnicity) factorial design.[42] Results will be presented according to the order of the hypotheses and the hierarchical cognitive development (i.e., observed behavior, perception, and conception).

1. *Effect of sex.* Sex by itself was not found to be a significant factor in any of the dependent measures. However, significant sex differences were found within each ethnocultural group (an interaction of sex x ethnicity).

2. *Ethnocultural effect.* Jewish children were found to be significantly different from Druze children in many of the dependent measures. However, since in nearly all cases of significant ethnocultural effect, a significant interaction of sex x ethnicity was also found, presentation of results would focus on interaction findings.

3. *Effect of ethnicity and sex.*

(a) Observed behavior. Significant F values, means and standard deviations of main dimensions of observed behavior within the kindergarten setting and teachers' evaluations of Jewish boys (n = 42), Jewish girls (n = 38), Druze boys (n = 20) and Druze girls (n = 20) are presented in TABLE 1.

Generally, compared to the Druze children, the Jewish children were found to be significantly more involved in direct and forceful social interactions as manifested in leadership interactions with boys (T_1), leadership interactions with girls (T_2), aggression with girls (T_3), aggression with boys (T_9), seeking adults' help (T_4), obedience to boys and adults (T_7) and active involvement with girls (T_8). Within each ethnic group boys differed significantly from girls, and interaction was mainly with same-sex peers: boys had more leadership interactions with boys (T_1) than did girls with boys ($F_{3/116} = 14.68$, p $<$ .005); girls had more leadership interactions with girls (T_2) than did boys with girls ($F_{3/116} = 13.40$, p $<$ .005); boys showed more aggression toward girls (T_3) than did girls toward other girls ($F_{3/116} = 8.13$, p $<$ .005); boys also showed more aggressive interactions with other boys (T_9) than did girls with boys ($F_{3/116} = 8.62$, p $<$ .005). Girls sought adult help (T_4) significantly more often than did boys ($F_{3/116} = 7.25$, p $<$ .005), and girls also had more active involvement with same-sex peers (T_8) than did boys with girls ($F_{3/116} = 14.13$, p $<$ .005). Boys showed more obedience to other boys and adults (T_7) than did girls ($F_{3/116} = 4.15$, p $<$ .01).

Teacher's evaluation yielded a significant interaction effect of sex x ethnicity in two items: degree of social involvement within the kindergarten ($F_{3/116} = 3.12$, p $<$ .05) and ability to cope with task demands ($F_{3/116} = 3.81$, p $<$ .05). For both items, Jewish boys were rated as higher than girls, whereas the Druze teachers rated Druze girls as higher than Druze boys.

(b) Bender-Gestalt Test. Though specific results of the Bender Test will not be discussed in this paper, suffice it to say that Jewish children executed the forms significantly more accurately (i.e., differentially) than did Druze children ($F_{3/116} = 27.68$, p $<$ .005) and thus their corresponding mental age was significantly higher. Druze children more often than Jewish children showed the phenomena of perseveration and sameness in executing the forms ($F_{3/116} = 6.23$, p $<$ .005). Girls performed better than boys within each ethnocultural group.

(c) Figures Drawing. Significant F values, means and standard deviations of the four groups are presented in TABLE 2. Results show that within each ethnocultural group, girls' perception was much more differentiated than that of boys, but that the perceptual level was, almost consistently, significantly higher in the Jewish group, compared to the Druze. It appeared in the number of details in most differentiated figure (item 6, $F_{3/116} = 17.48$, p $<$ .005), in the number of colors in most differentiated figure (item 7, $F_{3/116} = 16.07$, p $<$ .005), estimation of intelligence (item 9, $F_{3/116} = 21.06$, p $<$ .005), in the number of differences in colors between self and father (item 21, $F_{3/116} = 9.73$,

TABLE 1

SOCIAL INTERACTION WITHIN THE KINDERGARTEN

Mean Scores and Standard Deviations (SD) for Teacher's and Observer's Behavioral Categories with Significant Interaction Effects (F values) for Sex × Ethnicity

Code	Variable	F Value		Jewish Boys n = 42	Jewish Girls n = 38	Druze Boys n = 20	Druze Girls n = 20
T_1	Leadership interactions with boys	14.68‡		35.17	13.24	16.10	7.05
			SD	25.96	13.24	14.78	8.41
T_2	Leadership interactions with girls	13.40‡		3.86	11.58	2.95	6.05
			SD	4.87	8.52	3.22	5.42
T_3	Aggression with girls	8.13‡		4.02	3.61	1.80	1.00
			SD	2.78	3.23	1.77	1.26
T_4	Vicarious strength seeking through adults' help	7.25‡		1.83	4.40	.55	1.90
			SD	3.41	4.36	.89	1.99
T_7	Obedience to boys and adults	4.15†		24.19	19.89	19.75	14.80
			SD	10.25	10.22	11.02	7.68
T_8	Active involvement with girls	14.13‡		9.05	26.79	4.55	10.75
			SD	13.35	20.53	5.84	9.55
T_9	Aggressive interactions with boys	8.62‡		9.59	4.18	3.85	2.20
			SD	8.83	5.37	3.12	3.32
49	Teacher's evaluation of degree of social involvement within the kindergarten	3.12*		3.59	3.45	2.95	3.45
			SD	.70	.86	.95	.61
52	Teacher's evaluation of ability to cope with task demands	3.81*		3.52	3.29	2.90	3.45
			SD	.67	.69	.85	.61

The degrees of freedom (df) for the sex × ethnicity effects are 3/116.

* $p < .05$.
† $p < .01$.
‡ $p < .005$.

TABLE 2

HUMAN FIGURES DRAWING

Mean Scores and Standard Deviations (SD) for Categories with Significant (F values) Interactions for Sex × ethnicity

Code	Variable		F Value	Jewish Boys n = 42	Jewish Girls n = 38	Druze Boys n = 20	Druze Girls n = 20
6	No. of details in most differentiated figure		17.48‡	8.88	9.63	3.45	6.00
		SD		2.35	2.96	4.43	4.85
7	No. of colors in most differentiated figure		16.07‡	2.52	4.18	1.00	1.20
		SD		1.94	2.78	1.00	.62
8	Variability in the use of color (e.g. certain parts of body filled in)		7.65‡	.29	.50	.05	.05
		SD		.46	.51	.22	.22
9	Estimation of intelligence (after Koppitz)		21.06‡	15.00	15.58	5.90	10.00
		SD		2.64	3.79	7.25	7.71
20	No. of differences in structure between boyfriend and girlfriend		3.04*	3.02	1.97	2.40	2.10
		SD		1.94	1.39	1.67	1.41
22	No. of differences in colors between self and mother		9.74‡	2.29	3.50	.15	.65
		SD		2.82	3.38	.36	.93
23	No. of differences in colors between self and boyfriend		10.20‡	2.14	3.55	.15	.85
		SD		2.54	3.39	.36	.88
24	No. of differences in colors between self and girlfriend		10.16‡	2.24	3.47	.15	.60
		SD		2.56	3.50	.37	.59
25	No. of differences in colors between father and mother		10.47‡	2.05	3.68	.10	.70
		SD		2.69	3.57	.31	1.08
26	No. of differences in colors between father and boyfriend		8.92‡	2.21	3.13	.10	.70
		SD		2.64	3.13	.31	1.08
27	No. of differences in colors between father and girlfriend		10.33‡	2.07	3.53	.10	.65
		SD		2.54	3.52	.31	.81
28	No. of differences in colors between mother and boyfriend		8.64‡	2.19	3.05	.10	.65
		SD		2.72	3.08	.31	.93
29	No. of differences in colors between mother and girlfriend		9.23‡	2.05	3.26	.10	.70
		SD		2.37	3.25	.31	1.06

No.		F (ethnicity, df 1/118)			Jews, n = 80	Druzes, n = 40
30	No. of differences in colors between boyfriend and girlfriend	9.33‡	SD	2.05 / 2.37	.10 / .31	.80 / 1.06
32	Sum of no. of differences in color among all figures	11.55‡	SD	21.50 / 24.33	1.20 / 3.14	7.15 / 8.54
34	Existence of constriction within the page	6.42‡	SD	.17 / .38	.45 / .61	.65 / .59
35	Existence of relationship between parents, apart from others	4.11†	SD	.31 / .47	.00 / .00	.05 / .22
37	Child is drawn apart from others	36.8*	SD	.19 / .39	.00 / .00	.00 / .00
38	Child appears closer to peers than to parents	3.12*	SD	.52 / .51	.15 / .37	.35 / .49
39	Child is between peers and parents	2.93*	SD	.14 / .35	.10 / .31	.05 / .22
42	Child is near mother, not extreme in the page	2.74*	SD	.10 / .29	.00 / .00	.00 / .00
44	Figures emphasized by dark colors, strong lines, filling in structure with color	5.11‡	SD	.79 / .89	.10 / .31	.25 / .64
45	Sum no. of missing sensory parts of face in drawing of self (i.e. no eyes, no nose, no mouth)	17.74‡	SD	.38 / .73	2.15 / 1.22	1.30 / 1.49
46	Sum no. of missing movement (motor) body parts, in drawing of self (i.e.: no hands, no legs, no body)	9.13‡	SD	.64 / .66	1.40 / .94	1.20 / 1.00
43	Child is near father, not extreme in the page	ethnicity df 1/118 4.37*	SD		.10 / .30	.00 / .00

The degrees of freedom (df) for the sex x ethnicity effects are 3/116.

* p < .05
† p < .01
‡ p < .005

$p < .005$), in the number of differences in colors between self and mother (item 22, $F_{3/116} = 9.74$, $p < .005$), and likewise, in the number of differences in color between all other pairs (items 23–30; see details in TABLE 2), and in the total number of differences in color among all figures (item 32, $F_{3/116} = 11.55$, $p < .005$). Jewish children, especially girls, also showed significantly more variability in the use of color than did both Druze boys and girls (item 8, $F_{3/116} = 7.65$, $p < .005$). The total number of missing sensory parts of face was significantly higher among Druze children, especially the boys, compared to Jewish children (item 45, $F_{3/116} = 17.74$, $p < .005$). Druze children, especially boys, also tended to omit body parts more often that did Jewish children (item 46, $F_{3/116} = 9.13$, $p < .005$). The number of differences in structure between boyfriend and girlfriend, was significantly more noticeable in boys' drawings than girls' drawings in both ethnic groups (item 20, $F_{3/116} = 3.04$, $p < .05$). Jewish children, especially boys, tended to emphasize figures by dark colors, by strong lines, by filling in structures with color, significantly more than did Druze children (item 44, $F = 5.11$, $p < .005$). Among the Druze, girls tended to emphasize figures significantly more than boys.

In organizing the figures in relationship to each other, it was found that Druze children tended to group all figures together, where no specific relationships could be discerned, while Jewish children tended to form specific and differentiated alliances with parents and peers (see items 34, 35, 37, 38, 39, and 42 in TABLE 2).

(d) Cognitive (Conceptual) Complexity Test. No significant sex x ethnicity effects were found in the overall score of differential assignment of concepts to self and meaningful figures (i.e., father, mother, boyfriend, girlfriend), nor in specific differential scores between self-father, self-mother, self-boyfriend, etc. Significant interactions were only found in the frequency in which "self" appeared as the most conceptually differentiated figure in the grid ($F_{3/116} = 6.20$, $p < .005$): within each ethnic group boys perceived themselves as significantly more differentiated than did girls, and Druze children did so significantly more frequently than did Jewish children (see means and standard deviations in TABLE 3).

4. *The most differentiated figure in child's perception.* Information about this topic was secured from two sources: (a) Figure drawings; and (b) Cognitive Complexity Test.

In the drawings, significant effect of ethnicity was found in the frequency with which boyfriend was the most differentiated figure ($F_{3/116} = 11.14$, $p < .005$). The boyfriend was more often the most differentiated figure for the Druze children than he was for the Jewish children. Means and standard deviations of frequency of usage of each of the five figures, as most differentiated, are given in TABLE 3.

As can be seen from TABLE 3, in drawing, self was the most differentiated figure for all children (disregarding their level of differentiation) followed by the father, and for the Druze children also by the boyfriend.

In conceptual differentiation, own self was least differentiated for Jewish boys and girls whereas the girlfriend was perceived to be the most differentiated. The second most differentiated was the father figure. Self was most differentiated for Druze boys, followed by the girlfriend, while Druze girls perceived the girlfriend as the most differentiated figure, a little more often than they perceived themselves as the most differentiated.

The mother figure, contrary to expectation, was more often undifferentiated (i.e., perceived globally) than differentiated.

TABLE 3

FREQUENCIES OF MOST DIFFERENTIATED FIGURE, IN DRAWINGS AND COGNITIVE (CONCEPTUAL) COMPLEXITY TEST

Drawings	Self	Father	Mother	Girlfriend	Boyfriend	
	n = 120	n = 120	n = 120	n = 120	Jews n = 80	Druze n = 40
Mean	0.38	0.25	0.14	0.12	0.05	0.25
SD	0.49	0.44	0.35	0.32	0.22	0.44

Cognitive (Conceptual) Complexity	JB*	JG	DB	DG	Father	Mother	Girlfriend	Boyfriend
	n = 42	n = 38	n = 20	n = 20	n = 120	n = 120	n = 120	n = 120
Mean	0.10	0.03	0.34	0.29	0.20	0.15	0.31	0.16
SD	0.27	0.16	0.43	0.43	0.38	0.32	0.43	0.32

*JB = Jewish boys; JG = Jewish girls; DB = Druze boys; DG = Druze girls.

DISCUSSION

The results support the hypotheses regarding the effects of sex and ethnocultural group upon the child's perceptual level. Significant sex x ethnicity effects show that socialization practices intervene to depress or accelerate maturational processes: (1) girls performed better than boys within each ethnic group[14,16,21,25] in the visuomotor differentiation-integration tasks, but the Druze children performed on a much lower level than the Jewish children, and (2) the conceptual level, generally considered to be based on sensorimotor development,[15,46] was not lower among the Druze children than the Jewish children.

Several studies found ethnicity to be an important factor in perceptual development.[17,18,22,28,29] Differences were attributed to differential cultural rewards and punishments for various skills or achievements from an early age.[52] However, those studies dealt with school-age children, assuming that cultural norms are not yet established before at least age six.[10] Here, cultural effects were already found by kindergarten age.

Specific socialization practices within each ethnic group may explain findings in this study:

1. *Freedom of movement.* The Druze is a religious minority group[3] that has to resort to authoritative disciplinary methods in order to ensure group integrity and continuity. Physical activity is not encouraged. Until very recently (about four years ago), the traditional custom, exercised by most mothers, was to tie the child completely until the age of three months. When the child grows older, because the large number of children at home does not allow the mother to give much individual attention to each child,[25] and because of her concern for maintaining a neat house, the child's physical activity is further curbed. Breaches of the group norms are often punished physically; this could have an additional inhibiting effect on the use of the body in sensing and manipulating objects.

Within the kindergarten, as at home, the atmosphere is mainly formal and austere. Children are discouraged from moving freely around; they have to sit around tables and follow the teacher's uniform instructions. Individual and physical achievements (e.g., in drawing) are far less rewarded than answering in unison with a certain established norm of right and wrong. Facilities in the kindergarten are limited. Children have no classes for physical education. Thus, the educational emphasis is on listening and obeying, simplicity and sameness, not on experimenting individually. In contrast, the middle-class Jewish children are encouraged and stimulated to engage in bodily experimentation both at home (where the average number of children in the family is 2–3) and in the kindergarten setting. Children can freely interact with each other and find their own place in the social hierarchy much more freely than Druze children can or are allowed to.

2. *Appearance.* Kindergarten children's sensorimotor development is considered to depend to a large extent on concrete qualities of appearance.[37] Nevertheless, the Druze stress uniformity in traditional (male vs. female) dressing and simplicity in appearance. Women cover their heads and use no makeup. They stay mainly at home, segregated from men, and the child has almost no opportunity to see how women appear or act in various situations.

3. *Male vs. female position.* In contrast to the relative equal status of females and males in the secular Jewish middle-class, there is a sharp traditional distinction between female and male status in the Druze society. Women are brought up to be wives and mothers, and barely interact with the male society

outside the home. The company of the Druze boy of preschool age, before traditional and formal initiation into the Druze ethnic and religious values, is mainly with the women at home, where he may already feel an outsider, whereas the girl is among her own kind and is more physically active helping the mother with household tasks or with the female teacher at the kindergarten, preparing herself for her future role.

All these factors, inherent in the social system, depress the Druze children's development of differentiation (except for the sharp distinction between boy and girl) and eventually their individualized integration of the body image. Both in the Bender Test, which deals with neutral stimuli, and the Figure Drawing, which deals with meaningful social stimuli, the results were the same: Druze children, compared to the Jewish children showed inferior differentiation within and among the diverse objects and tended to repeat the same response; the Druze children drew figures with fewer details, fewer sensory parts and motor parts, with fewer colors, projecting many fewer differences in structure and color among the various meaningful figures. They were also inclined to cluster all the figures together on a small part of the page in an undifferentiated mass, as if clinging to each other (in a circular insulated shape) and guarding against possible external influence.[13] Youngleson[61] found in socially deprived institutionalized children an increase in affiliation motivation, mediated by fear of rejection. This finding could perhaps apply to the young Druze children, who, because of lack of sufficient development of own differentiated body image, may feel too much anxiety when they are apart from the group.

All children showed in their drawing a greater concern about self body image than about other figures. For all of them, self was the most differentiated figure. Though the greater "self" differentiation could perhaps attest to the child's egocentricity, a different interpretation is also possible. The frequent and relatively uninhibited exercises with own body may be prerequisite for constructing the concrete representation of the body image,[60] and integrating the differentiated units into one structure, i.e., the self.[11] The drawing of self is an externalization of a structure.

Self identity, as described in concepts, is a further abstraction, which to a larger extent than the body image, is mediated by responses of others toward self.[27] Self-identity (my view of myself) is a theoretical construct, not a concrete reality. It is generally accepted,[15,23] and supported by studies,[31] that the younger the person, the more concrete his thinking, and the more he looks for external models around whom to shape or integrate his behavior; the older and more experienced in life the person is, the more abstract his thinking, the more able he appears in extracting the essence of concrete elements; he is also more capable of internalizing the values, thus becoming himself a model for others to emulate. In this respect the Druze children's level of abstraction, especially that of boys, was more advanced than that of the Jewish children. For the Jewish children the most conceptually differentiated figure was the girlfriend, who, being far more perceptually developed than the boy, was the concrete figure whom the children could observe directly and like whom they aspired to perform. On the other hand, the Druze viewed themselves as most conceptually differentiated. Druze girls only differentiated themselves a little less than their girlfriend.

What can be seen here, in the case of the Druze children, is an internalization and abstraction of qualities. This could occur when physical freedom is curbed, and one thus has to resort more to self-reflection, which is mainly based on listening, since the activation and use of other senses is limited. This self-reflective quality that seems to have produced a more differentiate perception of self is less developed in the Druze girls who are more physicall active than the boys. The self percept of the more active Jewish kindergarte children was the least differentiated as compared to other figures.

Blank[7] observed that in the absence of visual spatial information, or in th presence of other forms of information, the child begins to employ his verba system. Visual-spatial cues are probably not suited for the study of perceptua development of the Druze children where this function is not emphasized in their culture.[49]

In line with Piagetian theorizing and findings,[8,41] where the sensori-moto level of development is the substratum for the later development of th abstract-conceptual level, several studies[33,59] pointed to a proneness t emotional disturbances in cases with a large gap between a develope abstract-verbal level and an undeveloped or poor visuomotor performance. Thi gap was present in the Druze children, but no higher proportion of emotiona difficulties were reported for them compared to the Jewish children. It could b that the very cohesive and stable Druze social system and its traditional values act as an external, security-providing framework[53] on which members can lea for guidance in everyday conduct and performance. On the other hand, th Jewish children, raised, like in many other Western cultures, in a mobile an rapidly changing society, where moral values may be ambiguous, contradictory or even completely lacking, need to resort much more to own self identit (which is an integration of own bodily experiences and differentiated percep tions and conceptions) as an internal guide in the world.

REFERENCES

1. BANNISTER, D. & J. M. M. MAIR. 1968. The Evaluation of Personal Constructs Academic Press. London.
2. BENDER, L. 1938. A Visual Motor Gestalt Test and its Clinical Use. The America Orthopsychiatric Association. New York.
3. BEN-DOR, G. 1971. The Druzes in Israel. University of Haifa Press. Haifa, Israel.
4. BIELIAUSKAS, V. J. 1974. J. Ind. Psychol. 30: 92–97.
5. BIERI, J., A. L. ATKINS, S. BRIAR, R. L. LEAMAN, H. MILLER & T. TRIPODI 1966. Clinical and Social Judgment. Wiley. New York.
6. BIGNER, J. J. 1974. Child Dev. 45: 317–323.
7. BLANK, M. 1974. Dev. Psychol. 10: 229–245.
8. BRAINERD, C. J. 1973. Psychol. Bull. 79: 172–179.
9. CANTOR, G. N. & C. E. PATERNITE. 1973. Child Dev. 44 (4): 859–861.
10. CAVIOR, N. & D. A. LOMBARDI. 1973. Dev. Psychol. 8: 67–71.
11. CHEIN, I. 1972. The Science of Behavior and the Image of Man. Tavistock Pub London.
12. ENGLE, P. L. & J. S. SUPPES. 1970. J. Proj. Tech. Pers. Assess. 34: 223–231.
13. EVANS, G. W. & R. B. HOWARD. 1973. Psychol. Bull. 80: 334–344.
14. FATERSON, H. F. & H. WITKIN. 1970. Dev. Psychol. 2: 429–438.
15. FLAVELL, J. H. 1963. The Developmental Psychology of Jean Piaget. Van Nostran Co. New Jersey.
16. FORD, M. A., D. N. STERN & D. J. DILLON. 1974. Perc. Mot. Skills. 38: 1188.
17. GARDINER, H. W. 1974. J. Cross Cult. Psychol. 5: 124–130.
18. GILMORE, G., J. CHANDY & T. ANDERSON. 1975. Psychol. in Schools 12 172–175.

19. HARE, P. A. & R. T. HARE. 1956. J. Gen. Psychol. **89**: 51–59.
20. HARRIS, D. B. 1963. Children's Drawings as Measures of Intellectual Maturity. Harcourt, Brace and World, Inc. New York.
21. HAWORTH, M. R. & C. J. NORINGTON. 1961. J. Proj. Tech. **25**: 441–448.
22. ISAAC, B. K. 1973. J. School Psychol. **11**: 47–56.
23. KELLY, G. A. 1955. The Psychology of Personal Constructs. Norton. New York.
24. KOPPITZ, E. M. 1964. The Bender Gestalt Test for Young Children. Grune & Stratton. New York.
25. KOPPITZ, E. M. 1968. Psychological Evaluation of Children's Human Figure Drawings. Grune & Stratton. New York.
26. KUGELMASS, S. & E. DONCHIN. 1960. Magamot **10**: 271–281 (Hebrew).
27. LAING, R. D., H. PHILLIPSON & A. R. LEE. 1966. Interpersonal Perception. Tavistock. London.
28. LAOSA, L. M., J. D. SWARTZ & W. H. HOLTZMAN. 1973. Dev. Psychol. **8**: 350–356.
29. LAOSA, L. M., J. D. SWARTZ & R. D. GUERRER. 1974. Dev. Psychol. **10**: 131–139.
30. LIBBY, W. C. 1974. Color and the Structural sense. Prentice-Hall. Englewood Cliffs. New Jersey.
31. LIFSHITZ, M. 1974. Brit. J. Soc. Clin. Psychol. **13**: 183–189.
32. LIFSHITZ, M. 1975. J. Clin. Psychol. **31**: 126–130.
33. LIFSHITZ, M. 1975. (accepted for publication) Psychological and psychomotor tests. *In* Follow-up of High Risk Children for Schizophrenia. D. Rosenthal, Ed. National Institute of Mental Health. Bethesda, Maryland.
34. LIFSHITZ, M. 1975. (accepted for publication) Brit. J. Med. Psychol.
35. LIFSHITZ, M. 1975. Early sex-linked social differentiation: A multi-dimensional scaling analysis of the social behavior of kindergarten children. Paper presented to the Annual Scientific Convention of the Israeli Psychological Association. Haifa, Israel.
36. LIFSHITZ, M., R. REZNIKOV & M. ARAN. 1975. Child Psychol. Hum. Dev. **5**: 150–160.
37. LIVESLEY, W. J. & D. B. BROMLEY. 1973. Person Perception in Childhood and Adolescence. Wiley. New York.
38. LUDWIG, D. J. 1969. J. Proj. Tech. Pers. Assess. **33**: 257–261.
39. MAIR, J. M. M. 1967. Brit. J. Psy. **58** (3): 271–282.
40. MARATSOS, M. P. 1973. Child Dev. **44**: 747–752.
41. NELSON, K. 1973. Merril-Palmer Q. **19**: 21–39.
42. NIE, N. H., BENT, D. H. & C. H. HULL. 1970. Statistical Package for the Social Sciences. McGraw-Hill. New York.
43. OLIVERIO, A. F. 1973. Int. J. Psychol. **8**: 153–158.
44. OSGOOD, C. E., G. J. SUCI & P. H. TANNENBAUM. 1957. The Measurement of Meaning. University of Illinois Press. Urbana, Illinois.
45. OSTROIL-WOLFSON, T. 1967. Standardization of the Bender Motor Test. Israel Government, Education and Labor Ministry, Jerusalem.
46. PIAGET, J. & B. INHELDER. 1967. The Child's Conception of Space. Norton. New York.
47. PEPPER, S. C. 1966. Concept and Quality: A World Hypothesis. Open Court. La Salle, Illinois.
48. PRYTULA, R. E. & G. G. LEIGHT. 1972. J. Clin. Psychol. **28**: 377–379.
49. RAND, C. W. 1973. Child Dev. **44**: 47–53.
50. REZNIKOFF, N. A. & H. R. REZNIKOFF. 1956. J. Clin. Psychol. **12**: 167–169.
51. RORSCHACH, H. 1942. Psychodiagnostics: A Diagnostic Test Based on Perception. Hans Huber. Bern.
52. ROSENFELD, H. M. & P. GUNNEL. 1973. Merrill-Palmer Q. **19**: 81–94.
53. SCARFE, N. V. 1972/3. Int. J. Early Childhood. **4**: 27–30.
54. SCHILDER, P. 1950. The Image and Appearance of the Human Body. International Universities Press. New York.

55. SCHWARTZ, J. 1972. Psychological Expression in Children's Drawings. (in Hebrew). Lastudent. Haifa, Israel.
56. STEINBERG, B. M. 1974. Child Dev. **45**: 503–507.
57. VINEY, L. L., M. AITKIN & J. FLOYD. 1974. J. Clin. Psy. **30**: 581–586.
58. WALLACH, M. A., L. R. GREEN, P. D. LIPSITT & J. B. MINEHART. 1962. Psy. Monogr. **76** (1).
59. WECHSLER, D. 1969. The Range of Human Capabilities. Hafner, New York.
60. WOLFF, P., J. R. LEVIN & E. T. LONGOBARDI. 1974. Child Dev. **45**: 221–223.
61. YOUNGLESON, M. L. 1973. J. Pers. Soc. Psychol. **26**: 280–86.

SPECIAL ASPECTS OF CROSS-CULTURAL RESEARCH

Discussant: Roger R. Woock

State University of New York
Buffalo, New York 14214

The papers to which this response is addressed range from an examination of the relationship between culture and memory to the legitimation of educational knowledge and from the problems of testing African children to the cultural aspects of Piaget's theory. This diversity has in fact forced me to do what I wished to avoid, to make a few comments about each of the papers individually and hope that others will come up with more universal questions that might be appropriate for all Special Aspects of Cross-Cultural Research.

Let me begin with Dr. Lancy's "Studies of Memory in Culture." The topic Dr. Lancy chooses is certainly an important one, which in and of itself seems to be cross-disciplinary; memory is an important psychological concept and culture the fundamental meta concept of anthropological research. Dr. Lancy is very clear and straightforward in describing the operations of his research, the selection of the four activities and the selection of the population, to participate in that part of his research involving memory strategies in novel situations. Dr. Lancy says, and I quote, "The fine grained research that seems required if we are to advance to a theory of culture and memory must proceed in several directions." I am not at all clear what those directions are. Indeed, the author prefaces his selection of the tasks that he uses in his paper by saying virtually all tasks one could name involve memory. This strikes me as something of a problem. Even if one limits tasks in the way that he does, saying that these tasks are well defined and bounded activities stable in a society over time and are tasks that demand verbal memory or memory for spoken words, the selection must be in some sense arbitrary. If it is arbitrary, then how does one ultimately go about developing cross-cultural indices? Certainly, all cultures would have some form of story telling and probably singing, although the singing itself would vary considerably. Whether other cultures would have a game called *collon* would seem to me highly questionable, and leaf-naming seems quite idiosyncratic. Depending upon the kind of cross-cultural research that would eventuate, the tasks themselves may not need to be constant. Yet if the tasks are not, I can see serious problems developing for the comparison of different cultures. Dr. Lancy seems to have a concern about this himself since he says on the last page of his paper "Relying entirely on novel tasks like the free recall experiment always leaves open the trap of cultural bias." I am afraid that I see the dangers of cultural bias creeping into at least two and probably three of the four tasks that he selected. In his concluding paragraph, the author suggests that this sort of research done in a variety of cultures would ultimately lead to a theory that has developed a taxonomy of tasks, taxonomy of memory strategies, taxonomy of individuals and the interrelationships of these three. I only wish that Dr. Lancy had been able to give us a hint of what such a theory would look like. Certainly, to be a theory of relationship between memory and culture it must contain considerably more elements than taxonomies and relationships between them. In fact some branches of social science have developed very complex taxonomies with virtually no theory at all.

"Why African Children are So Hard to Test" by Drs. Harkness and Super presents quite different problems, at least partly because the question the authors set out to answer is at least as straightforward as questions in social science can be, and I suppose would be perceived by most of us to be a question of practical importance. Why is it that African children are hard to test? The answer to this question also seems to be straightforward. They are hard to test because certain patterns of behavior in early childhood, patterns of interaction between parents and children emphasize larger cultural values like obedience and respect, which, when translated into language, emphasize comprehension, rather than production. The authors warn the reader of the superficial resemblance of their findings to some research on social class differences in language performance in the United States, especially the work of Jerome Kagan. They emphasize that there appears to be no general cultural impoverishment or maternal fatalism, something that Kagan emphasizes. To put the results another way, it seems clear that the use value of children verbally responding to adults in a "testing" situation is very low in the Kipsigas culture.

My questions about this paper are questions about its framing, if you will. The authors say towards the end of the paper that using psychological tests with unwesternized African children is obviously a difficult endeavor. I would ask another question. If it is a difficult endeavor, then why do it at all? That is, what is the purpose of developing tests for African children? This is obviously a question that falls outside of the scope of the paper itself but nevertheless is important. I note that the work was supported by the Carnegie Corporation of New York through the Bureau of Educational Research, the University of Nairobi and the Grant Foundation in New York. I would be interested in knowing how this work fits into the educational programs at Nairobi and also if they have studied the impact of testing, however carefully designed, on African culture. On page 329, the authors say that it is interesting in this context "that the more modern mothers in Kokwet were somewhat less dominant and more sociable in verbal interactions with their children and they tended strongly to favor a more active teaching role in their children's language development." Would one of the objectives of the kind of research described by Drs. Harkness and Super be to develop more modern mothers in Kokwet and to develop a more active teaching role in the children's language development? If this in fact is one of the goals, then I think it opens up for discussion a whole series of questions and problems related to intellectual imperialism that have not been dealt with in the paper.

In a very concise way Dr. Dasen in "Cross-Cultural Cognitive Development: The Cultural Aspects of Piaget's Theory" isolates an important problem of Piaget's theory, namely, that in some cross-cultural research the rate of development of concrete operations in rural, nonwestern children is generally reported to lag behind Western norms. If this lag is in fact real, it is quite clear that considerable doubt is thrown on the universality of Piaget's theoretical constructs. His brief summaries of other research suggest quite clearly that this lag may well not be real in the sense that it reflects true intellectual or cognitive differences across cultures but rather experience and exposure to certain operations. I am somewhat disturbed by his favorable adoption of Harens concept of "cognitive ambiance," since I am not sure that it advances our knowledge any more than did cultural deprivation, a concept that Dr. Dasen quite accurately interprets his whole paper as disparaging. Dr. Dasen paraphrases Haren approvingly saying that over and above such factors as schooling or European contact or urban, rural residence or social class one should consider the "cognitive ambiance" in which the children develop. In his own very interesting research Dr. Dasen predicted that nomadic hunting populations would develop spatial concepts more rapidly than sedentary agriculturalist groups, whereas the latter would attain concepts related to quantity weight and volume more rapidly than the former. This difference does not require the concept of cognitive ambiance. I question whether any cross cultural research does.

As I said initially, the paper and its arguments are clear, perhaps almost too clear. If it is true that with very little practice groups that formerly scored considerably below western norms were able to raise their performance on certain operational tasks, why have we not been able to accomplish any kind of significant task improvement among our urban, nonwhite school populations? As a sociologist I must insist that the formidable power of our institutions and the class structure of our society cannot be overlooked as factors producing the considerable difference in performance that we see. Dr. Dasen and Piaget may be quite right in their contentions that Piaget's theories may be ultimately vindicated cross culturally, but will this vindication help us very much in attempting to explain differences that we see within our own society?

Professor Cowen in "The Legitimacy of Educational Knowledge: A Neglected Theme in Comparative Research" attempts what can only be described as an ambitious and far reaching undertaking. The second half of his title is I believe completely accurate, certainly the legitimation of educational knowledge has been a neglected theme not only in comparative research but in all social science research. Partly I suppose this neglect has come from the unwillingness of social scientists in North America to take the educational enterprise seriously, at least that part of it which doesn't affect them directly. The historical reasons for this neglect are clearly beyond the limits of Professor Cowen's paper and my comments as well. But this neglect has resulted in a strange situation. We have at this conference, I am sure, people from the disciplines of psychology, anthropology, sociology, and social psychology. I wonder how many of them have any idea of how their discipline is organized, simplified, included or excluded from the curriculum of elementary and secondary schools. Even stranger than not knowing this is the assumption that curriculum at the primary or secondary level is something a scholar should not be expected to know anything about. After all, more psychology teaching is done by elementary school teachers than by professors of psychology.

To study the legitimation of educational knowledge one of course must have a theory of the process of legitimation. One must have some knowledge of how the process of legitimation operates in other areas; how political, religious and economic institutions are legitimated. One must have a theory of the sociology of knowledge, that is, the relationship between knowledge and the social milieu in which it develops. All of this must undergird the development of a theory of the legitimation of educational knowledge. While Professor Cowen is certainly aware of this requirement, his paper makes almost no reference to it.

Another concern that I have is the degree of investment that Professor Cowen has in the nation-state. Obviously, nations are extraordinarily important in shaping educational institutions and educational knowledge, and data available for educational comparison are organized by nations. As someone who has taught in Canada and the USA extensively and Great Britain for a short period of time, I am not convinced that the differences between Canada and the USA in terms of the legitimation of their educational knowledge are differences that make a difference.

I believe it would be interesting and important to ask about the relationship between a society's definition of educational knowledge and its socioeconomic system directly without filtering it through culture or politics. While interesting, this would clearly be a different kind of analysis and hence a different paper.

SPECIAL ASPECTS OF CROSS-CULTURAL RESEARCH

Discussant: Leanne G. Rivlin

Graduate School and University Center
City University of New York
New York, New York 10036

Four papers form the basis of these reflections, Dr. Morsbach's "An Intensive 'Triangular' Study (Japan-US-Europe) of Socio-Psychological Variables," the Adlers', "The 'Fruit-Tree Experiment' as a Cross-Cultural Measure of the Variations in Children's Drawings Due to Regional Differences," Dr. Irwin's, "The Problem of Establishing Validity in Cross-Cultural Measurements" and that of Dr. Lifshitz, "Person Perception and Social Interaction of Jewish and Druze Kindergarten Children in Israel." Three of these papers deal directly with a double problem – comparisons across cultures (the theme of the conference) and the equally difficult assessment of developmental differences. In a real sense, this represents two cultural comparisons, if we view children as a subculture within a specific group. We might even add cross-sex and cross-age comparisons as additional factors since these are included in the papers. It seems critical to mention these intracultural factors, for they further complicate an already difficult problem and remind us that specific cultural groups under study are not monolithic. In order to pursue the meaning of these internal and external comparisons, let us first consider the two "empirical" studies, and then examine the other papers for some methodological considerations.

Dr. Lifshitz' paper provides some stimulating material and some questions as well. In considering the social base of person perception among Druze kindergarten boys and girls in comparison with Jewish children, a variety of information is gathered. In a sense, the work represents a study of social spatial factors in two different social groups; one is very traditional, a minority within the Israeli setting, and a minority among Muslim sects, secretive in its ritual, but from current accounts, slowly changing as well.[1] The other group is the majority within Israel, but except for the information that the children came from middle class backgrounds, we do not have details on length of residence in Israel or the family's country of origin. The study addresses a series of questions regarding perceptual and conceptual development, with particular concern for sex differences within the groups.

In bringing a personal set of concerns to my reading, a number of issues come to mind. First, the measures used certainly do point up differences, pinpointing the consequences of background on the tests and measures involved. Yet there is a gnawing question regarding the meaning of measured differences for the two groups under study. Kindergarten children were selected with the reasonable assumption that they were: (1) at the beginning of their formal education and at the onset of "institutionalized implementation of social values and practices" and (2) they were at "a stage of perceptual development where sensori-motor and conceptual processes interact closely." Presumably, this placed each group at the same point in their development history. Although one can only speculate from the limited information on the two groups, the details that are available (and, I might add, that are used to explain some of the results) suggest that, in fact, the initial experiences of the two groups differed greatly, despite similarities in age and school history. There is a strong possibility that the Jewish group not only entered school with greater "social maturity" (as defined within a school context) but that they were more familiar with this institutional form. It is important to consider social maturity when looking at test results of young children for the simple fact that it may affect the ease with which they take tests.

Perhaps more significant for the present study is the issue of prior drawing experiences. If the two groups in question differ in this respect, some of the results may need to be reviewed. The Jewish group, more "modern" in its viewpoint and urban in its life style, might be expected to provide both drawing materials and drawing experiences to its preschool children. In contrast, in some Muslim sects there is a prohibition against representations of human figures and a consequent discouragement of drawing in children. If such is the case among the Druze, there is an additional explanation to the differences in perceptual differentiation based on drawing skills and experience. It also raises some questions concerning the potential effects of schooling on the differences that were demonstrated. The school experiences of the two groups could reinforce original differences or provide similar social and educational programs that would bring the two groups closer. The author suggests that the Druze kindergarten, much as the Druze home, discouraged physical movement and exploration. The facilities were described as limited and drawing, as a skill, was not emphasized. Although the effect of the school was not the focus of the study, it is a direction of interest, not merely from the view of enrichment programs alone, but in terms of the stability of the cognitive and perceptual processes that were examined. The cognitive (conceptual) complexity tasks also raise some questions. Developed out of pilot work with Israeli children, one wonders if the meaning was the same for the Druze children.

Although cross-group and cross-sex comparisons are interesting, what seems critical is information across the developmental continuum. The nagging question is not only what the next year would reveal, but what the adults are like in these groups. If, in fact, Druze appearances are more homogeneous, less detailed, with less emphasis on individual decoration and variety of dress, the undifferentiated drawings of the children must be viewed in another light, and consequently this also raises questions about adults as well.

The paper by Leonore and Beverly Adler presents another set of data based on children's drawings. It also points up the powerful effects of varying the test materials, in this case the colors, on the final products. As an environmental psychologist, I was intrigued by the variations in the fluency of responses across cultures. The 27 different varieties of trees drawn by East Asian children stand in marked contrast to 19 for North Americans and 12 for Central Europeans. There appears to be a rather powerful environmental message in these differences and the nature of the landscapes that produced them. Yet there is another problem in identifying the origins of the fluency difference, since the authors cite earlier data, with somewhat different results. Clearly, the size of the group and the point in time that they are studied are crucial ingredients. Some of the countries grouped together may not, in fact, represent unitary geographic or cultural areas, and this may obscure some potentially interesting differences.

In their discussion of results the authors raise an interesting question. Why did European children give apple tree preferences at all in Group C, that is, where the colors orange, green and brown were presented? Although apples come in a fair range of colors in Europe, and are familiar to children, why avoid drawing the "logical" orange form? We really do not know. This kind of dilemma highlights the problem of interpreting children's drawings. We can see much, as Dr. Lifshitz did in her analyses, but many puzzles remain. Some of them I think can be avoided. This simple drawing technique, easy to use, could gain with supplementary information in the form of explanations from the children themselves, especially in cases where simple logic does not seem to guide the selections.

In the closing section of their paper, the Adlers mention that "It is not only the differences that are of importance in cross-cultural studies, but almost more important are the similarities." The other side of the coin is seen in Dr. Irwin's paper. This methodological and empirical presentation echoes the importance, cited by others, of probing many dimensions of a construct – that the overlap between two cultures is important, but so too is the area of divergence. Dr. Irwin offers a particular strategy for establishing validity of a construct, i.e., whether the researcher can use the construct to predict behaviors in the host culture on the basis of other measured behaviors. It is not an unfamiliar procedure, but it is too often omitted in the haste to work with a concept of validity anchored in the researchers own value system. Irwin's study of Guatemalan villages proceeds without the conception of intelligence as a universal and singular dimension. Rather, the tests that are used have been examined against (1) competence rankings of adults and (2) children's behavior.

Dr. Morsbach's paper presents a critically vital caution, but also a research suggestion that strikes a most sympathetic note. His case for rethinking both the specific construct we are examining across cultures, and the base line against which we are checking it, really seems most important. The question of base line or criteria is one central to the approach in Irwin, as well. Dr. Morsbach makes the suggestion of a multi-dimensional approach in cross-cultural comparisons. He takes the position of the "fundamental otherness" of Japanese society. He contends that traditional Western-oriented research such as attitude studies may have very different meanings in Japan. This point, although recognized by others, cannot be underlined too often. I really do not know what the drawings we have discussed mean to Druze, American, Israeli Jewish or other children, but unless we understand their meaning, not the internal content alone, the degree to which we can generalize about the content is limited. Dr. Morsbach describes the use of multi-angular studies, research proceeding from the specific views of professionals both native to the culture and visitors, with each professional using the perspective they hold. I think there is a difficulty here, common to interdisciplinary work as well, of the integration of final results. This is not insurmountable, and may yield to the task that Dr. Morsbach cites, "continuous reciprocal exploration and interpretation."

In emphasizing the rich and varied information essential for understanding Japanese at any level, Morsbach draws me back to many of the questions raised by the empirical studies in this section, and suggests a number of directions (none of them new) for cross-cultural work. These include (1) greater reliance on the study of naturally occurring events, such as spacing behaviors; (2) use of measures that are neither intrusive nor reactive; (3) use of converging information with members of each cultural group under study participating in the design of the study, collection of data and the interpretation of results (Obviously the level of participation may vary under particular conditions, but an effort should be made toward exploration of the meaning of issues under study from the view of those *being* studied. Clearly, children too are to be included in this category, and they can be involved to a greater extent than has been done in the past.); (4) study of constructs and issues over *time* – an effort toward longitudinal data, if necessary repeated testing seems essential; and (5) recognition that some issues may not be appropriate or meaningful for cross-cultural study.

As Dr. Irwin suggests, cross-cultural researchers must move like a child in the host cultures' conceptual realm, doubting their own conceptions, questioning, and learning as much detail as possible about the overall context.

REFERENCES

1.   MAYER, E. Becoming modern in Bayt Al-Shabab. The Middle East Journal. 29 (No. 3): 279–294.

OPEN DISCUSSION: III

DR. PIERRE DASEN: In his discussion of the papers in this session, Dr. Woock mentioned that the phrase "cognitive ambience" to him had a strong connotation of "cultural deprivation," and he wondered whether it was necessary or useful in the context of the ecocultural hypothesis.

The possibility of such a connotation had not occurred to me, and I definitely would not want to use it, if it carries with it any value judgment. I have found Heron's suggestion useful, insofar as he points to cultural factors that are very general and pervasive in the child's environment, and at the same time are likely to lead to the specification of the mechanisms of cultural influences. For example a nomadic, hunting and gathering ecology, say of the Eskimo, seems to lead to a high level of spatial concept development: to demonstrate this relationship says little of the mechanisms involved. What are the day-to-day activities and experiences of the Eskimo child — in other words, what are the aspects of the "cognitive ambience" in Eskimo culture — that favor spatial skills? We do have some general ideas about the frequency of spatial terms in the language, the precision with which localizers are used, the possible influence of socialization toward independence, or the actual training in hunting and orientation skills, but we need to be able to specify these in more detail. These aspects of cognitive ambience are likely to be quite different in a sedentary, agricultural, culture, such as an African culture, but of course it would be meaningless to speak of cultural deprivation in this context.

DR. WOOCK: So many intracultural studies are being carried out — will we ever get to cross-cultural studies?

DR. DAVID LANCY: In many areas of cross-cultural inquiry, such as kinship, economics, and child-rearing, we have excellent ethnographic data from which to work. In an area of cognitive psychology, especially memory and problem-solving, basic ethnographic data are lacking, hence the need for intracultural research.

MICHAEL GREENE: (*Columbia University, N.Y., N.Y.*) How do you account for the differences in what you call the "general process effect" within and between cultures?

DR. LANCY: Where general process effects are found, they will be accounted for by differential involvement culture-specific tasks.

A. IBERALL: Dr. Cowen, if it were possible — and I believe it is coming — to develop a rather general knowledge base that could serve both elite and populace, would this be useful and could it be usefully propagated?

DR. R. COWEN: The analysis in my paper suggests that in two societies with monolithic central value systems and characterized by "revitalization movements," in the technical sense, there is a wide diffusion and standardization of educational knowledge of a particular kind. The styles of this educational knowledge, its legitimatization, its distribution and its content, are comprehensible mainly in terms of the societies in which it is located. The creation, in the vocabulary of the question, of a "general knowledge base" was a consequence of societal revolutions, not of an educational "revolution" within relatively stable social parameters.

It follows, in my view, that the creation of a "general knowledge base" is unlikely in the countries of Northwestern Europe, and in Canada and the United States. It is not clear to me who would develop such a general knowledge base, nor how it would be socially propagated, nor what functions it would usefully serve. In other words, it is unclear how a general knowledge base would be socially rooted in Western societies.

I would, in fact, prefer to follow and test the opposite hypothesis in comparative perspective for the countries of Northwestern Europe and North America: That educational knowledge will become increasingly psychologized at the elementary levels of educational systems (i.e., selected and learned in accordance with the putative interests of the individual educand), elective at the secondary levels, and differentiated by the occupational structure at important points of educational selection and in tertiary education.

DR. DÍAZ-GUERRERO: The procedure for idiosyncratic validation is optimal. Why do you think that in spite of the fact that "listura" can be well identified by adults, this is not the criterion used by teachers when grading children?

DR. MARC IRWIN: Children's school grades reflect both teacher judgments and actual performances in our study villages. That portion of a child's grade dependent upon teacher judgments probably does not agree very closely with villager "listura" rankings because the schoolteachers are quite unlike village residents in many respects. They tend to be from lower-middle class rather than subsistence farming backgrounds, and to identify much more than do the villagers with modern urban values.

School grades reflect objective performance level somewhat more than teacher judgments; grading is supposed to be guided (though not totally dictated) by performances on national multiple choice exams given annually to all students. The failure of "listura" rankings to agree with school passing ratios thus suggests that "listura" is simply not the same thing as "school intelligence."

ANGELA B. GINORIO (*Fordham University, New York, N.Y.*): Do you attribute the greater consistency of results in the attributions of "listura" to girls to cultural definitions of sex roles? Namely, to be "lista" a girl has to excel in everything, while a boy has only to excel in some areas.

DR. IRWIN: Sex-typing is quite rigid within these rural Ladino communities, and it is likely that the differential patterns of correlations between "listura" rankings and test performances for boys and for girls is a product of well-differentiated sex-roles. In addition to the greater number of significant correlations between "listura" and test scores for girls than for boys, "listo" boys tended to engage in many self-managed complicated behavior sequences, but to not necessarily be assigned many chores, while "lista" girls tended to be assigned many chores but not necessarily to engage in many self-managed sequences. Though the rs in question did not differ significantly by sex, probably owing to small ns, these data suggest that definitions of intelligence for boys and for girls differ in our study village.

MELANIE SCHNEIDER (*Bloomingdale Head Start, New York, N.Y.*): Can you generalize the difference in emphasis (verbal comprehension vs. verbal production) to mothers of various ethnic groups in the United States and, if so, what implications do you see for preschool education?

DR. SUPER: Although we have little research experience ourselves with American ethnic groups, there is certainly reason enough in the literature to think that related differences exist. We have recently learned, for example, that such a contrast in language socialization patterns may exist among Chinese-American groups; middle-class Chinese-American mothers probably encourage their children's verbal expressions more than do lower-class Chinese-American mothers.

If so, this would help to explain observed differences in the verbal behavior of lower- and middle-class Chinese-American children in day-care centers. Whether such differences persist in later test performances – usually a highly verbal behavior – is an open question. Chinese-Americans, on an average, score well on such tests in school, so maybe one cannot assume that such early differences are immutable. It is presumed, or rather hoped, that preschool teachers are responding more to each child's present behavior and needs than to his or her ethnic and class background, but this kind of research should help educators understand some of the factors that lie behind group differences in children's verbal performance.

S. S. SARGENT (*Oxnard, California*): In Riesman's terminology, are the Japanese more "other-directed" or "tradition-directed"? And to what extent are they "inner-directed"?

DR. MORSBACH: In my opinion, Riesman's thinking is largely based on the "either–or" (i.e., mutually exclusive) thinking typical of Western culture. It is my feeling that the average Japanese is able to be inner-, tradition- and other-directed, depending on the social situation he/she is in and the role which is being played at that time. Two examples might aid in explaining what I mean:

1. In the typical life cycle, mother–infant interaction is largely "tradition-directed," as has been shown by Caudill.* While growing up, the child and adolescent is instilled with "inner-directed" behavior (e.g., strong achievement motivation in sons) by the mother, as shown by DeVos.† "Other-directed" behavior is strongly evident in group activities, as described by Nakane.‡ It is also evident in many Japanese novels where a common theme is something like, "He was trying to guess what she thought concerning what he was thinking," etc.

2. In the process of mate selection and marriage, the professed ideal by most youngsters is a love match ("outer-directed"), since this is considered "Western" and therefore modern. However, Blood§ has shown that in spite of this, many Japanese accepted the traditional selection of bride or groom by their parents and a go-between ("tradition-directed"). Finally, strong "inner-directed" desires were evident when adolescents were asked to write about their future as realistically as possible.¶

*   CAUDILL, W. A. & C. SCHOOLER. Child Behavior and child rearing in Japan and the United States: an interim report. J. Nervous Mental Diseases. **157** (5): 323–338.
†   DE VOS, G. A. (Ed.) 1973. Socialization for Achievement – Essays on the Cultural Psychology of the Japanese. U. California Press. Berkeley, Ca.
‡   NAKANE, C. 1970. Japanese Society. Weidenfeld and Nicholson. London, England.
§   BLOOD, R. O. 1967. Love Match and Arranged Marriage: A Tokyo–Detroit Comparison. The Free Press. New York, N.Y.
¶   MORSBACH, H. 1969. A cross-cultural study of future expectations and aspirations among adolescent girls. Japan. J. Ethnol.: Proceedings of the 8th International Congress of Anthropological and Ethnological Sciences. Tokyo: 381–385.

DEVELOPMENTAL THEORIES APPLIED TO
CROSS-CULTURAL COGNITIVE RESEARCH*

Michael Cole and Sylvia Scribner

Laboratory of Comparative Human Cognition
Rockefeller University
New York, New York 10021

Almost from the outset, psychologists engaged in cross-cultural research seemed to realize that their work posed methodological problems different from, and probably in addition to, those that faced their colleagues in other branches of their science. It has been generally understood that it is one thing to observe a difference in behavior across cultural groups and quite another to interpret it.

This realization is reflected in the continuous concern of cross-cultural psychologists with problems of methodology, dating from Rivers[19] and Titchener[22] to contemporary investigators such as Campbell,[3] Berry,[1] Goodnow,[12] Glick,[11] and others. We, too, have been concerned with questions of method and the special difficulties of inference from observation to psychological process that are endemic to the cross-cultural enterprise. Some of our work has been concerned with the problems of specifying the culturally determined independent variables that relate to the dependent variables we study (Cole, Gay, Glick and Sharp[5]). Following the lead of Campbell and many others, we have sought to use the opportunities offered by different cultural settings to deconfound theoretically promising causal factors that are ordinarily "packaged" in modern, technological societies (Whiting[26]). This work has engaged us in a companion issue that has been of great concern to us: what significance can we attach to our dependent variables? Here we enter the perennial debate between anthropologists and psychologists as to the proper methods for studying cognitive behavior, a debate that has centered around deciding what inferences about psychological processes of individuals are warranted on the basis of experimental and naturalistic observations (c.f. Cole and Scribner[7] and Scribner.[21])

Like most anthropologists, we are committed to the view that observations of intelligent behavior in everyday life are an important source of information about culture and cognitive processes. But we also believe experiments to be important and probably necessary tools for disentangling the complex relationships among culturally determined experiences and specific intellectual skills. To use Scribner's[21] term, this position requires us to "situate" the psychological experiment as one of many contexts in which to sample behavior. This approach to "behavior-in-context" leads us to question the generality of inferences from experiments that are not corroborated by nonexperimental data. At the same

* Support for the preparation of this paper was provided by the Carnegie Corporation and the Ford Foundation.

time, it leads us to attempt a more precise characterization of the cognitive demands of nonexperimental situations.[7]

The distinctions that we have in mind can be briefly illustrated by our research on free recall. In several of these studies (see reference 6 for a summary) our concern was with specifying population characteristics correlated with performance differences in multi-trial free recall of categorizable nouns. Age, educational status, and exposure to a modern cash economy were some of the variables found to be associated with improved recall performance in some of these studies. But finding such differences held no magic key to explaining them in terms of the variations in memory processes that underlay the performances we were observing. To approach an explanation at that level required a program of experimentation during which aspects of the task were systematically varied – the items to be recalled, the contexts in which the items were presented, the incentives for good performance, and others. Even when much of that work was done, we were left with the question of how we could generalize from performance in our experiments to memory tasks that our subjects faced daily, but that we were not observing. This question was particularly pertinent in the case of memory, because the lore of anthropology had led us to expect fine performance in our experimental task, but such outcomes were rare and restricted to special task formats.

In this entire line of work, our range of inference and interpretation was restricted to generalizations about one particular set of skills – memory skills. We were not attempting to make inferences about intellectual performance or cognitive status *in general.* When cross-cultural research attempts such global assessment within the framework of some general developmental theory, a host of new conceptual and methodological problems are superimposed on those we encountered. The enterprise is broadened. The investigator not only has the task of interpreting the relationship between particular performances and the operations accounting for them, but of characterizing those operations according to some hypothesized developmental sequence. An entirely new chain of inference is involved in moving from an analysis of performance to an assessment of what that performance represents in developmental terms.

It is our impression that cross-cultural cognitive research would profit from a better understanding of the conditions under which it is legitimate to draw developmental conclusions on the basis of differences in cognitive performance. As our contribution towards this goal, we would like to examine the requirements that developmental theories themselves prescribe for making inferences about "developmental status," and consider whether these have been satisfied in cross-cultural research.

At the risk of inviting misunderstanding through oversimplification, we will try to characterize the main features of the two developmental theories that have been applied most widely in cross-cultural research: the theories of Piaget and those of Witkin. Setting aside for the moment the radically different approaches they take to cognition, we believe they share certain common characteristics:

1. Both theories characterize development in terms of an orderly progression in the organization of systems composing the individual's psychological structure. They postulate, so to speak, "one developmental process," in terms of which psychological changes occurring from infancy to adulthood are to be understood.

2. This developmental progression is conceived as characterizing the person as a whole – the individual's entire intellectual and social functioning. Within

both theories, therefore, it is possible to speak of a "level of development" that a given individual has attained (although it is acknowledged that individuals may not always operate at the highest level they have attained). These levels of development are generally ordered with reference to age.

3. Within this conceptual framework, tasks in various domains of performance are often used in the manner of diagnostic instruments to assess where the person stands in the developmental sequence.

Although this line of theorizing has been dominant for some time, it has encountered increasingly strong challenges in recent years. Without taking sides, we would like to suggest that some of the debates that appear in the cross-cultural literature are similar to (and we would argue, might be formally identical to) debates that are currently emerging around the proper interpretation of age-related differences in performance on various cognitive tasks investigated within *one* culture. Controversies surrounding the general set of propositions characterized as Piagetian theory can serve as a case in point.

Investigators have found, in a whole host of instances, that changes in performance related to modifications in experimental procedures[2,10,15,23] and contexts[20] suggest a characterization of young children's competence different from that originally proposed by Piaget. The thrust of this work is to make problematic the interpretation of performance on tasks that have been usually assumed to be diagnostic of developmental level. Neither *presence* of a particular performance nor *absence* of that performance is clearly interpretable with respect to a child's development level — a general point clearly stated by Werner[25] nearly 40 years ago. Although we still find differences that are generally correlated with age, evidence of variability related to task modifications suggests a line of theorizing about development that emphasizes not only basic competencies but the operational skills that children acquire and employ in different ways, depending upon specific features of the task and situation. This point of view is exemplified in the seminal paper by Flavell and Wohlwill,[9] which distinguishes between formal and functional subcomponents in the developing competence of the child, and in the current work of Pascual-Leone[17] and Case.[4]

The import of this line of work is that characterization of a person's developmental status on the basis of experimental performance is debatable even when the research is entirely intracultural.

Nonetheless, the problems raised by this evidence do not have to be interpreted as fundamentally damaging to Piaget's theoretical position. Although it is possible to find variability on almost every Piagetian task and it is also possible to provide alternative interpretations of performance on any single task, the general theory is bolstered in the face of local difficulties by the enormous range of correlated phenomena that it accounts for. Essentially, it is the interweaving of evidence from performance in many different domains of children's activities that gives credence to Piaget's interpretation of performance in localized contexts. Piaget himself is quite explicit on this point:

> We have just described the cognitive aspects of the developmental process which connect the structure of the initial sensori-motor level with those of the level of concrete operations . . . The affective and social development of the child follows the same general process, since the affective, social and cognitive aspects of behavior are in fact inseparable.[18] (p. 114)

His general point is illustrated in Goodnow's particularly lucid discussion of cross-cultural Piagetian research, in which she emphasizes that the transfer of the same underlying operations across the range of tasks that presumably require them is the necessary condition for making judgments about the child's developmental level (reference 12, pp. 443f).

The importance of this general point of "domain consistency" to the support of general developmental theory is also made explicit by Witkin and Berry:[27]

> Progress toward greater differentiation during development involves the organism as a whole, rather than proceeding discretely in separate domains. Hence, a tendency toward more differentiated or less differentiated functioning in one domain should 'go with' a similar tendency in other domains, making for self-consistency. (p. 6)

What happens when this debate is moved to the cross-cultural arena? All the specifications of the theory that apply *intra*culturally should also apply *inter*culturally, respecting the added methodological difficulties of cross-cultural research that we talked about in our introduction.

Does the cross-cultural research evidence meet the criteria of adequacy that the theories themselves prescribe for *intracultural* validation? When we examine the evidence from this perspective, we are led to conclude that in spite of the many sound developmental studies that have been carried out, neither Piaget's nor Witkin's theories has ever actually been tested in cross-cultural research. Since so much has been written on culture and cognitive development, and the impression seems so widespread that developmental theories have been tested extensively, we must take some space to justify this conclusion.

We are led to this position not because of methodological problems with individual studies but because it is our reading of the literature that: 1. there has not been a single nonwestern culture in which investigators have made the wide range of observations necessary to demonstrate that behaviors across tasks and domains go together in the way required by the theory; and 2. in the few instances where more than one task and one domain have been investigated simultaneously, the evidence is ambiguous, if not negative, with respect to such consistency.

We will try to support this position by an examination of cross-cultural research on Witkin's theory of psychological differentiation. We select Witkin rather than Piaget because Witkin and Berry[27] have stated the theory and its testing requirements so clearly, and have reviewed the research evidence so thoroughly that we can best illustrate our position with respect to this work.

As we have already stated, Witkin and Berry[27] (p. 5) characterize psychological development in terms of a "differentiation theory," which maintains that "the typical progression in psychological development is from less to more differentiation." More differentiation implies greater specialization and separation of individual functions; perception is differentiated from feeling, thinking from action. It implies as well "specificity in the manner of functioning *within* an area." While differentiation thus proceeds in many psychological subsystems, Witkin and Berry maintain that it is an organismic, and not a subsystem, process. Research requirements are relatively clear. It is necessary to find precise and valid indicators of differentiation appropriate to the various psychological domains; to demonstrate that these indicators are highly interrelated *within* any one domain; and then to demonstrate that they are highly interrelated *across* domains.

The first issue, and a critical one, concerns the "indicators" of psychological differentiation. Witkin and Berry review these with heavy emphasis on the perceptual domain. The most widely used perceptual tests have been the rod and frame test, the embedded figures test, and the body adjustment test. Consistency in the degree of "differentiation" measured by these tests, at least by adolescence, has been widely reported for studies in the United States. Once we move beyond the perceptual domain, both the question of indicators and the problem of consistency become much more problematic. Witkin and Berry conclude that self-consistency has been demonstrated within the United States in such additional domains as cognition, body concept, and the nature of the self. There are two problems here. To begin with, it is not clear that the indicators in these hypothetically separate domains are separate in the way claimed. The tests in the cognitive domain that correlate with perceptual tests consist mainly of such tasks as block design, picture completion, and the like, for which we can assume heavy perceptual involvement. Similarly, the indicator of a developed body concept is often some form of a draw-a-man test in which perceptual skills related to pictorial representation clearly must play a part. (This problem has been discussed by Vernon.[24])

If we go further afield to indicators of differentiation in the social sphere, the problem is somewhat different. To take an example: Witkin and Berry[27] (p. 9) tell us that reliance on external sources of information for self-definition is a good indicator of lack of differentiation in the social domain; field-dependent people (as measured in the perceptual domain) are more sensitive to the social content of their surrounding. But in the social domain, who is to say what is figure and what is embedding context? If problem solution depends upon the adequacy of manipulating other people it may not be adequate to treat others as "context," distinguished from the "self" as figure. The central problem in these important extensions of the differentiation notion is the difficulty of assessing the adequacy of the metaphors that suggest the connection between social and physical events.

None of these problems is inherently insurmountable, and we do not intend to denigrate the serious efforts that have been made to come to grips with these issues in the work of Witkin and many others. We only want to suggest that real problems exist *intraculturally* in establishing the main tenets discussed so far.

When we move from the intracultural to the intercultural arena, even the problematic canvas that we have been discussing is not adequately represented. With only a few exceptions, research is centered squarely in the perceptual domain and even here some significant problems are evident in the uneven levels of differentiation or field independence that have been found in some studies between sensory modalities. We can do no better than to quote Witkin and Berry's careful summary evaluation of their review of cross-cultural research on self-consistency:

> ... we find that many studies have investigated and found evidence of self-consistency within the perceptual domain and between the perceptual and body-concept domains. Relatively little has yet been done in non-Western settings to extend the study of self-consistency, as a function of level of differentation, to the domains of separate identity and defenses. The few studies on record hardly provide substantial evidence of the self-consistency to be expected from differentiation theory and from results of many Western studies on record.[27] (pp. 29–30)

When the authors turn, however, to a consideration of studies testing hypotheses about the role of ecological-cultural factors and socialization practices in differentiation, they no longer confine their theorizing to the limited domains to which their test batteries apply. Rather, they revert to the use of the general concept of over-all psychological differentiation, and come to con-clusions about the developmental status of the individuals studied. Not only individuals within cultures but entire populations and ways of life are assessed in terms of the global characteristic of field independence or dependence. For example, the authors speak of social arrangements in different types of society that "influence development toward greater or more limited differentiation (p. 57)" and reach the conclusion that agricultural and hunting-and-gathering societies foster different modes of functioning, which can be characterized in terms of the unitary psychological dimension of "field dependence."

It is our contention that this kind of speculation cannot be warranted in the absence of prior demonstrations of domain consistency.

The status of cross-cultural Piagetian research is not dissimilar. While there have been extensive studies covering a small set of tasks (c.f. Dasen[8]) there have been none meeting Piaget's own requirements for the range of observations, tasks and spheres of activity necessary to support generalizations about developmental levels. Again, important inconsistencies within psychological domains crop up in the cross-cultural literature, such as those reported recently by Otaala,[16] Heron and Dowel,[13] and Holos.[14]

We believe, although we cannot document the statement here, that the same problems exist for other general developmental formulations as well. Although it is unpalatable, we have been led to conclude that we simply cannot assess the general significance of a great deal of cross-cultural research that is nominally in the developmental mode. The problem is that deprived of the consistencies in performance across tasks, psychological functions, and behavioral domains which carry the interpretive power of the theory, we do not know how to generalize beyond the performances reported in individual studies. When the studies do not hang together in the theoretically prescribed way, each individual study is of very limited value in serving either as a test of the general theory or as a measure of the developmental status of people in different cultures. This is not to say that such studies can be of no theoretical or practical interest in and of themselves. If they are designed to discover variations in performance associated with features of the task (nature of the material used or response mode analyzed, for example) or with the specialized experiences of different groups (occupation, schooling and the like) such studies can move us toward a more precise characterization of both the independent and dependent variables related to performance in cognitive investigations.

Nor do we mean to imply that researchers must abandon the effort to generate and test general developmental hypotheses cross-culturally. Several strategies are available.

One is to follow the path so clearly outlined by Witkin and Berry.[27] This involves investigation of the systems or structures defined by the theory in many areas of cognitive activity and many domains of behavior. The great value of the research inspired by Witkin is that it does demonstrate culture-cognition relations, even if the generality of the results is in dispute.

With respect to this approach, we would like to suggest that an extremely useful course to follow might be the involvement of anthropologists in helping to gather data from behavioral situations which are typically inaccessible to psychologists. We have in mind here not only getting anthropological advice on making psychological test instruments culture-sensitive, but in obtaining observational data of the sort that psychologists usually eschew.

While recognizing the legitimacy of this course, we find ourselves uncomfort-able with its central thesis: that people can be characterized in terms of a single (or even a small set) of processes that organize their thinking in all aspects of their lives.

It seems at least an interesting possibility that the consistency observed in Euro-American studies of development is in fact a characteristic of the cultures studied rather than a universal characteristic. If so, a cross-cultural strategy based on the assumption of consistency in performance among various cognitive operations and in various behavioral domains may be going at the task of identifying culture-cognition relations in exactly the wrong way. If cognitive performance is often and importantly specific to a given domain, we ought to be *looking* for variability and its cultural sources rather than explaining it away when we find it. Paradoxically, we may find that, just as the pursuit of consistency has made an important contribution in exposing unexpected variability, the search for variation may lead us to consider the uniformities of cognitive development from a fresh perspective.

In either event, if we are correct in our analysis, there should be an explicit admission on the part of cross-cultural psychologists that their data are silent with respect to the developmental status of various Third World peoples. The ascription of childlike status to adults is too serious a conclusion to rest upon the evidence at hand.

REFERENCES

1. BERRY, J. W. 1969. On cross-cultural comparability. Intern. J. Psychol. **4**: 119–128.
2. BRYANT, P. 1974. Perception and understanding in young children. Basic Books. New York.
3. CAMPBELL, D. T. 1961. The mutual methodological relevance of anthropology and psychology. *In* Psychological Anthropology. F. L. K. Hsu, (Ed.) Dorsey Press. Homewood, Ill. pp. 333–352.
4. CASE, R. 1974. Structures and strictures: some functional limitations on the course of cognitive growth. Cognitive Psychol. **6**: 544–573.
5. COLE, M., J. GAY, J. GLICK, & D. SHARP, Eds. 1971. The Cultural Context of Learning and Thinking. Basic Books. New York, N.Y.
6. COLE, M. & S. SCRIBNER. 1974. Culture and Thought. Wiley. New York.
7. COLE, M. & S. SCRIBNER. Theorizing about socialization of cognition. Ethos **3**: 250–268.
8. DASEN, P. R. 1974. The influence of ecology, culture and European contact on cognitive development in Australian aborigines. *In* Culture and Cognition. J. W. Barry & P. R. Dasen, Eds. Methuen. London. pp. 381–408.
9. FLAVELL, J. H. & J. F. WOHLWILL. 1969. Formal and functional aspects of cognitive development. *In* Studies in Cognitive Development. D. Elkind and J. H. Flavell, Eds. Oxford University Press. New York, N.Y.
10. GELMAN, R. 1972. The nature and development of number concepts. *In* Advances in Child Development and Behavior, Vol. 7. H. W. Reese, Ed. Academic Press. New York.
11. GLICK, J. 1974. Cognitive development in cross-cultural perspective. *In* Review of Child Development Research, Vol. 4. J. Horowitz, Ed. Russell Sage. New York.
12. GOODNOW, J. J. 1969. Problems in research on culture and thought. *In* Studies in cognitive development. D. Eckind & J. H. Flavell, Eds. Oxford University Press. New York.
13. HERON, A. & W. DOWEL. 1974. The questionable unity of the concrete operations stage. Intern. J. Psychol. **9**: 1–10.
14. HOLOS, M. 1975. Logical operations and role-taking abilities in two cultures: Norway and Hungary. Child Develop. **46**: 638–649.

15. MARASTSOS, M. 1973. Nonegocentric communication abilities in preschool children. Child Develop. **44**: 697–700.

16. OTAALA, B. 1973. The development of operational thinking in primary school children: An examination of some aspects of Piaget's theory among the Itseo children of Uganda. Teachers College Press. New York.

17. PASCUAL-LEONE, J. 1975. A view of cognition from a formulist's perspective. *In* Current Issues in Developmental Psychology. K. Riegel, Ed. S. Kazgu, Basil. New York.

18. PIAGET, J. & B. INHELDER. 1969. The psychology of the child. Basic Books. New York.

19. RIVERS, W. H. R. 1901. Introduction and vision. *In* Reports of the Cambridge anthropological expedition to the Torres Straits. Vol. II, Pt. 1. A. C. Haddon, Ed. The University Press. Cambridge, England.

20. SHATZ, M. & R. GELMAN. 1973. The development of communication skills: modifications in the speech of young children as a function of the listener. Monographs of the Society for Research in Child Development **38**: 1–38.

21. SCRIBNER, S. 1975. Situating the experiment in cross-cultural research. *In* The Developing Individual in a Changing World. Vol. I. K. F. Riegel & A. Meacham, Eds. Aldine. Chicago, Ill.

22. TITCHENER, E. B. 1916. On ethnological tests of sensation and perception. Proc. Am. Phil. Soc. **55**: 204–236.

23. TURIEL, E. 1974. Conflict and transition in adolescent moral development. Child Develop. **45**: 14–29.

24. VERNON, P. E. 1969. Intelligence and cultural environment. Methuen & Co. London.

25. WERNER, H. 1937. Process and achievement — a basic problem of education and development psychology. Harvard Educational Review 1937, 7: 353–360.

26. WHITING, B. 1973. Comparative studies of social and cognitive development. Paper delivered at the biennial meetings of the international society for the study of behavioral development. Ann. Arbor, 1973.

27. WITKIN, H. A. & J. W. BERRY. 1975. Psychological differentiation in cross-cultural perspective. J. Cross-cultural Psychol. **6**: 4–87.

A STUDY IN COGNITIVE DEVELOPMENT*

Jerome Kagan, Robert E. Klein,† Gordon E. Finley,‡ and Barbara Rogoff

*Department of Psychology and Social Relations
Harvard University
Cambridge, Massachusetts 02138*

The purpose of this research is to inquire into the differential growth of selected cognitive processes during the period 6 through 13 years of life, in cultural settings differing in isolation, modernization, and child-rearing practices.

A basic presupposition behind this work is that one can differentiate between fundamental cognitive processes and culturally specific ones through study of their growth functions. It is assumed that performance on tests of basic cognitive processes generally will show a linear increase with age in all cultural settings, although rate of improvement and the age at which asymptotic functioning is reached will be a function of local cultural characteristics. Performance on tests of culturally specific functions will differ markedly in both their growth functions and asymptotes across different societies.

Tests of recall memory and conservation were administered to children 6 to 13 years of age living in two neighboring rural villages in northwest Guatemala – one modernizing and one less modern – and to a sample of children from the Boston area in order to determine the differential growth functions for these two competences.

SAMPLES

The Boston children (n = 59) came from relatively well-educated, self-selected families. The children from the modernizing village of San Pedro (n = 126) were a representative random sample from the village (stratified by occupation and land-holdings). The children from the more isolated village of San Marcos (n = 141) essentially represented all children of those ages in the village. The battery of tests was administered in 6 to 12 sessions of 20 or 30 minutes each. In the two Guatemalan villages, instructions were given in the local Indian dialect by a person from the town while a psychologist supervised the testing. It will be useful to give a brief ethnographic sketch of the two Indian towns before describing the tests and the results.

The inhabitants of San Pedro and San Marcos are both of Mayan origin. They speak differing but mutually intelligible dialects. Although the two towns are but a few miles from each other, their language and customs are distinct because of the relative isolation resulting from steep terrain and a large lake.

Both towns are primarily agricultural, raising the staple crops of corn and beans. However, the inhabitants of San Pedro also raise a large amount of cash crops: coffee, avocados, and onions. In addition, San Pedro has a growing number of people who depend on nonagricultural occupations, either as a

* This research was supported by a grant from The Grant Foundation, New York City.
† INCAP, Guatemala City, Guatemala.
‡ Florida International University.

374

secondary source of income, or as the only source. Approximately 40% of the Pedranos depend, to some extent, on a nontraditional occupation such as owning a store or performing a service (e.g., transporting vegetables, teaching, or carpentry). In San Marcos, agriculture is primarily on a subsistence level and very few men work outside of agriculture. In both towns, the women weave clothing, sew, make tortillas, care for the house, and tend children. San Pedro women can often make a little money for themselves with their weaving and sewing.

These variations in economic structure are influenced by the differential contact the two towns have with the outside world. San Pedro has a dirt road passable by trucks, leading toward larger towns, whereas San Marcos has no road. San Pedro has motor boat and canoe service to other towns on the lake; San Marcos has neither. This difference in accessibility results in many more goods being available in San Pedro – more radios, more tourists, more news of the outside world.

Both towns have recently acquired 24-hour electricity, which has begun to make changes in the lives of the Pedranos, who now own a number of TV sets, refrigerators, and are beginning to think of electric appliances. The inhabitants of San Marcos are slower to push for these changes, primarily for economic reasons.

Until a half century ago, both towns were entirely Catholic, with *cofradias* and religious roles and obligations closely meshed with secular and political life. This tradition still persists to a large extent in San Marcos. But in San Pedro, many community members have converted to various fundamentalist Protestant religions. About a third of the people are Protestant, and the Catholic Church in San Pedro has abandoned the traditional *cofradia* system.

Both towns have schools, which give instruction in Spanish, the official language of the country. The children begin school at about age seven. In San Marcos the school continues through the sixth grade, in San Pedro through the ninth grade. Pedranos place a much higher importance on education than do Marqueños. Many children from San Pedro have continued their education after the ninth grade in other towns, studying to be teachers, pastors, accountants, doctors. This has not happened in San Marcos.

There are also child-rearing differences between the two villages. Infants in San Marcos are kept inside their own house for the first 6 to 8 months of life. They are protected from contact with strangers and the variety of stimulation inherent in the outside world. San Pedro infants, after the two or three months, may be carried in mother's arms as she goes on an errand. Preschool children in San Pedro have greater independence of movement and freedom from direct supervision than those in San Marcos. Older children in San Pedro play more complicated games and attend school more regularly than children in San Marcos, who are more likely to be involved with economically important chores. Both villages are traditional insofar as there is early differentiation of the sexes with respect to child-rearing techniques, chores, dress, and play.

PROCEDURES

Memory Span for the Order of a Series of Familiar Pictures

In this task, the child must recall a series of colored line drawings of familiar objects, beginning with two pictures and proceeding to twelve. First, the child is shown the pictures and told to remember their order. The pictures are then turned over, the child is given a duplicate set of pictures and asked to match them to the examiner's pictures. The examiner's pictures are turned face up again and if the child was correct a third picture is added. This procedure is continued – adding a picture each time – until the child fails twice or until he completes the test at the final, twelfth item.

Memory Span for Orientation of Dolls

The child must remember the orientation of a series of dolls placed either upside down or right side up. After he studies the array, the dolls are covered with small boxes. The child is given some dolls and is asked to reproduce the orientation of the covered dolls. The first item involves two dolls, and the number of dolls is increased until the child reaches twelve dolls or until he fails a particular item twice.

Memory Span for Words

The procedure for words is similar to that for pictures and dolls. The child must remember a series of nouns in his mother tongue, beginning with two and increasing to twelve, with a new word added each time he is successful.

Operations on Memory: Pictures

This test uses the same set of pictures in the same order as the "picture span" test. This time the child must not only remember the original order of the pictures, but also subsequent changes in that order. After the examiner turns the pictures face down, he alters the position of one or more of them and asks the child to match the new order. The number of pictures in the series and the number of alterations is increased gradually. The test is continued until the child solves the last item (12 pictures and 11 alterations) or until he is unable to handle even one alteration with a given number of pictures.

Operations on Memory: Dolls

This test uses the same dolls and orientations as used in "memory span for orientation." The child is taught that when a dot is placed in front of the box that covers a particular doll, he must mentally invert the orientation of that doll when he places his dolls. After he studies the dots, the dots are covered, and therefore, neither dolls nor dots are available to him. For example, if the original order of the dolls were up-down-down-up, and a dot were placed in front of doll 1 and doll 4, the child must invert those dolls. His correct response would be down-down-down-down. The number of dolls and dots are increased gradually, until the child fails twice or until he solves the last item (12 dolls and 11 dots).

Conservation

The child is given tests of conservation of matter and conservation of liquid administered in standard procedures.

Since the three settings differed along many dimensions – modernization, isolation, resources, child-rearing practices, education, and stimulation – analyses of differences within each setting are important. In addition to the test battery, we have census data on the children and are currently gathering spot observations on the activities and responsibilities of daily life for the best and poorest performing children in the two less modern communities. We expect these data to aid explanation of patterns of performance within and between towns, since Nerlove[2] found this approach to be useful.

RESULTS

The Cambridge children showed their greatest improvement in performance on the span tests between 6 and 9 years of age with most children reaching the ceiling of the test by age 10. The performance of the children in the more modern of the two Guatemalan villages (San Pedro) was generally two years behind the Cambridge children, with the most rapid improvement between 8 and 10 years of age, and stabilized performance at about age 12 to 13. The children in the more isolated village were several years behind those in the modernizing village, and even at age 13, many had not reached the limits of the tests.

FIGURES 1, 2, and 3 present the growth functions for the three span tests for the children from the three settings. For the two Guatemalan groups, recall was best for pictures and words, which revealed similar levels of performance, but much poorer for orientation of dolls. The test using dolls involves events that are not familiar to the Indian children — noticing whether a doll is upside down or right side up is not a salient unit of information, while words and pictures of real objects are a more familiar aspect of the daily environment. Additionally, the cognitive units to be recalled are more distinctive for the

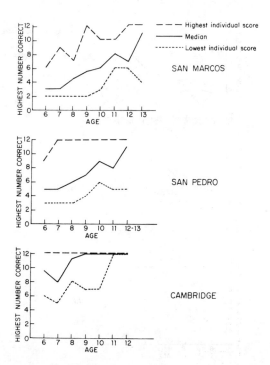

FIGURE 1. Median, highest, and lowest span attained for pictures.

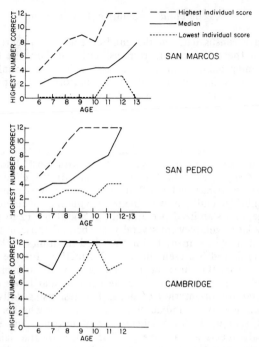

FIGURE 2. Median, highest, and lowest span for orientations of dolls.

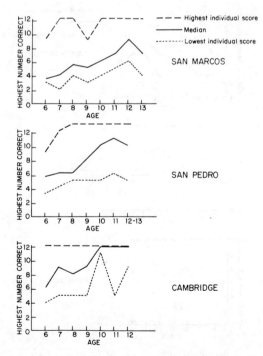

FIGURE 3. Median, highest and lowest span for words.

pictures and words, because each is different, while there are only two orientations for the dolls. The Cambridge children fared better with pictures and orientations than with words. This pattern implies that the Cambridge children were more successful in inventing efficient strategies for coding pictures and orientations than they were for words (which lend themselves less easily to efficient organization).

It should be noted that in spite of the poor average performance of the San Marcos children, by 10 years of age there were several children in each age group whose performance matched that of the best performing children in the other two groups. This implies that maturation of the cognitive processes that mediate performance on these tests is not *necessarily* impeded by the cultural isolation, inadequate schooling and lack of variety in the village.

The variability in childrens' performances was greater in the villages, which appear to be relatively homogeneous, than it was in the Cambridge-Boston area, where, on the surface, the environment appears to be so diverse. We believe that the greater variability among the village children is a function of greater variability in motivation. In the villages, the children were selected randomly from census listings, while in Boston the children were volunteers recruited from a newspaper advertisement. Thus the Boston children and their parents had chosen to participate in the tests, and their parents went to some effort to bring the child to be tested. In the villages we made a strong attempt to test every child who had been randomly selected and had very few refusals. But not all children were interested in being tested. These differences in sample selection should be kept in mind as comparisons of the three settings are made.

FIGURE 4 shows the average number of pictures at which any operation

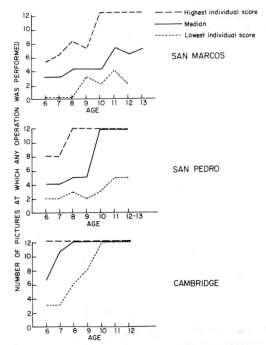

FIGURE 4. Median, highest, and lowest number of pictures at which any operation was performed successfully.

(alteration of a position of a picture) was performed successfully. The San Marcos children were more impaired than those from San Pedro or Cambridge, FIGURES 5, 6, and 7 illustrate the age curves for (a) the average number of operations for a given number of pictures, for all children in an age group, and (b) the average number of operations for a given number of pictures, only for those children who reached that level of pictures. In Cambridge, but not in the

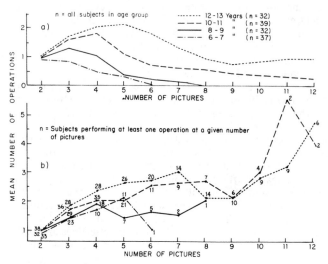

FIGURE 5. Average number of operations performed on each level of pictures by the different age groups in San Marcos.

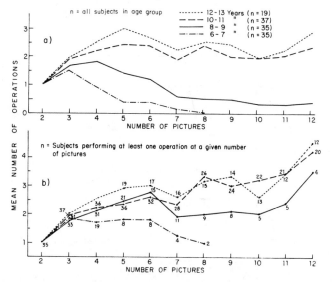

FIGURE 6. Average number of operations performed on each level of pictures by the different age groups in San Pedro.

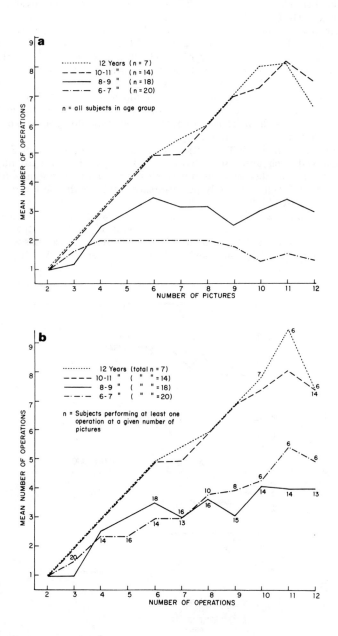

FIGURE 7. Average number of operations performed on each level of pictures by the different age groups in Cambridge.

two villages, there were major age differences in the number of operations that could be handled successfully, with many more operations possible for the children age 10 and older. The average performance for the older children in both San Marcos and San Pedro involved 12 pictures and 4 operations. But in San Marcos only 6 of 32 children were able to do any operation with 12 pictures, while in San Pedro, 12 of 19 children were able to remember some operations with 12 pictures. In Boston, the average performance among the older children was 12 pictures, 8 operations (6 of 7 children were able to do at least one operation with 12 pictures). It should be noted that difficulty did not increase linearly with number of operations. But generally a child who handled more operations with the same number of pictures was doing more mental work than one who did fewer operations.

Performance on the doll operations test was much poorer among San Marcos than San Pedro children (see FIGURES 8 through 11), both for number of operations and number of dolls on which they could perform any operations. Most of the children could only perform successfully with one inversion of the dolls. The oldest children averaged 4 inversions, for the 5 (out of 32) children who got as far as 12 dolls. The San Pedro children were much better at this task. The oldest children averaged 6 operations with 12 dolls, for the 10 of 19 children who progressed to 12 dolls. All of the Boston 12 year olds were able to do operations on 12 dolls, and averaged 9 inversions. We interpret the

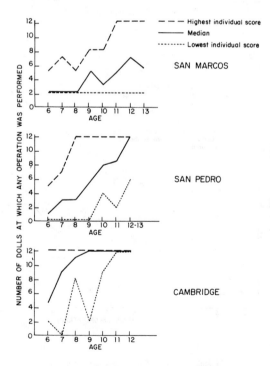

FIGURE 8. Median, highest, and lowest number of doll orientations at which any operation was performed successfully.

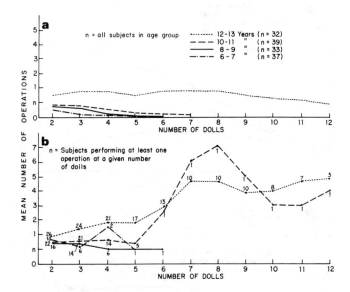

FIGURE 9. Average number of operations performed for increasing numbers of dolls by the different age groups in San Marcos.

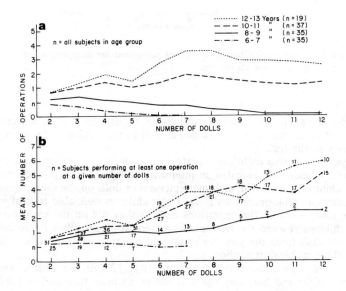

FIGURE 10. Average number of operations performed for increasing numbers of dolls by the different age groups in San Pedro.

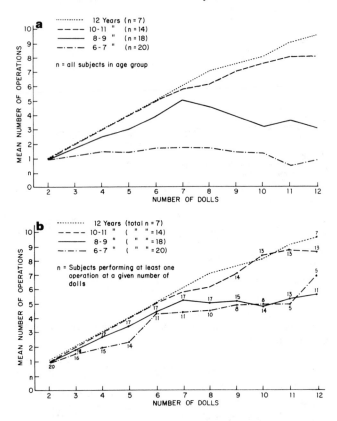

FIGURE 11. Average number of operations performed for increasing numbers of dolls by the different age groups in Cambridge.

differences between the cultural settings to be due to the effectiveness of strategies of organization and rehearsal, as well as motivation and systematicity of approach to the test.

Comparison of each child's best performance on each operations task and the corresponding span task revealed an interesting developmental progression. The younger children could deal with more pictures or dolls on the simple span than on the corresponding operations tasks. Older children were able to deal with as many or more units on the operations tasks as they did on the span tests. San Marcos children showed the less mature pattern at all ages; San Pedro children showed the shift from the younger to the older pattern at about age 9; Boston children showed this shift at about age 7.

With respect to conservation (see FIGURE 12) all the Boston children conserved matter and liquid by age 9. However, no more than 80% of the oldest Guatemalan children were able to conserve matter and liquid, suggesting a culturally significant component to this task.

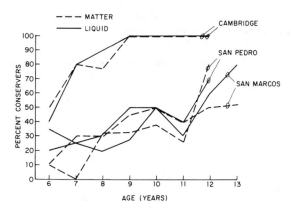

FIGURE 12.   Percentage of conservers of matter and liquid by age group.

Within-village Differences in San Pedro

We have performed a preliminary analysis of the relation of family status variables to child performance within San Pedro. Categorization of families in San Pedro can involve several variables, including occupation, land holdings, religion, education, dress, and house type. These are not independent. One useful breakdown appears to involve two independent dimensions — traditional versus nontraditional occupation (typically agriculture versus commerce), and amount of land holdings. Families with a nontraditional occupation (they may do agriculture in addition) are better educated, speak more Spanish, have larger houses, are more likely to have given up the traditional costume, and are more likely to have converted to Protestantism, but they have about the same amount of land as those in traditional occupations. The families with a nontraditional occupation and a large amount of land are the wealthiest in town; those who rely on agriculture but have very little land (they often hire themselves out to work for others) are the poorest. The other two groups are intermediate in wealth, but quite different in other terms. Families with a nontraditional occupation and little land are similar in religion, education, house size, and dress to the wealthy group with nontraditional occupation and much land. Those who are purely agricultural with a large amount of land appear to hold the most "traditional" values — they dress traditionally, speak Spanish less well, tend not to send their children to school, depend on time-honored methods in making a living, and are more likely to refuse to allow children to participate in the tests because "they work here in the house; if we allow them to wander in the streets like other children they will learn to be lazy."

The performances of the children from the four groups were different. We devised a scheme that pooled each child's performance on four of the memory tests (picture span, doll span, picture operations and doll operations), in order to select the very best and very poorest performers from each age-sex group. This procedure typically selected the three best and three poorest from each group.

TABLE 1

RELATION OF FAMILY OCCUPATION AND LAND HOLDINGS
TO TEST PERFORMANCE

(Numbers refer to the number of children from each family category who displayed
the best or poorest performance)

	Best	Poorest	Total number of children in group
Nontraditional occupation much land	14	9	27
Nontraditional occupation little land	11	6	23
Traditional occupation much land	3	14	28
Traditional occupation little land	10	11	41

TABLE 1 summarizes the relation between family status and test performance. The San Pedro children with the poorest performance came from the most traditional homes — those with much land and engaged in agriculture. Indeed, the performance of these children was similar, in many respects, to the average child from the more isolated, totally agricultural village of San Marcos.

DISCUSSION

Although the memory functions tapped by our procedures improved regularly with age, the most isolated children lagged behind those in the other settings at all ages, especially on the more difficult operations tests. Although there is undoubtedly a small effect due to the more isolated children being less familiar with the requirements of a testing situation, we view the differences in performance as primarily reflecting the failure to activate appropriate strategies of organization and rehearsal. In order to recall the longer series of pictures or orientations the child must actively impose an organization on the information. In the orientations test one might group the dolls into pairs or trios. On the doll operations test when greater than half the number of dolls are to be inverted, it is useful to focus on the number of dolls that are *not* to be inverted, rather than on those that have to be reversed. On the basis of observation during testing and some preliminary error analyses, most Cambridge children and many of the San Pedro children seemed to use these effective strategies, whereas the San Marcos children did not. We believe that the activation of these strategies is one of the functions of an executive cognitive process that matures during the period 5 through 12 years of age.

Some of the functions of the executive include:

1. Recognition of the nature of the problem and its requirements. Study of recall memory suggests that young children do not appreciate what is being asked of them. Flavell[3,4] has suggested that such a general factor has a large influence on young children's performance in tests of memory and

communicative skills. In the doll operations tasks, for example, the young child may not appreciate the fact that he is only to invert the doll that has a dot in front of it rather than all the dolls.

2. Appreciation of the difficulty of the problem and adjusting effort in accord with task difficulty. Rogoff, Newcombe, and Kagan[5] found that 4 and 6 year olds did not adjust their study time of pictures in a recognition test in accord with the length of time that they had to remember the pictures, while 8 year olds did show this form of planfulness.

3. Increased flexibility coupled with systematicity — the ability to discard an inefficient solution hypothesis and search systematically for better alternatives.

4. Activation of strategies of organization and rehearsal. The older child searches for organization of a problem in an attempt to aid in its solution. Many young children know rules, but they often fail to use those rules in appropriate problems. Gibson, Poag, and Rader[6] describe a lovely example that points up the young child's resistance or inability to see a pattern in a task, which would facilitate task mastery. Subjects were second and fifth graders who were given a reinforcement in a standard discrimination learning task if they pressed one of the keys designated as correct when a given word was projected on a small screen. One group (the pattern group) saw pairs of words that had a similar spelling pattern and sound. Hence *king* and *ring* might have been the negative pair, while *yarn* and *barn* the positive pair. The two similar spelling and rhyming patterns were designated as either both positive or both negative. The control group saw words that were spelled and sounded differently (rose, king, bell, and dog). After they had mastered the discrimination all children were given a transfer task with two pairs of new words that were spelled similarly and rhymed (boat and coat vs. cake and rake). The fifth graders were significantly better than the second graders in both stages of the experiment when the pattern words were used, but were not better than the younger children when there was no organizational principle. If the fifth graders did not detect the organization pattern in the first stage, they did not use it in the second stage.

5. Speed of information processing. Some believe that the speed with which cognitive units can be retrieved from memory improves with age, making it possible for the child to integrate more information in the short interval known as short term memory store.

6. Control of distraction and anxiety. The sixth function of the executive is to keep attention focused on the problem and resist being distracted by extraneous stimulation, as well as the ability to control anxiety that mounts when a problem is difficult.

7. Faith in the power of thought. The belief that when one is having difficulty it is useful to suspend action and think, in the hope that one might generat the useful idea as well as avoid absent-minded errors.

Even though the two Guatemalan villages are only a few kilometers apart and share many of the same cultural traditions, the growth of these executive functions is markedly different in the two settings. Since the two villages differ in their practices toward infants and young children, quality of and attitude toward schooling, exposure to daily variety, and many other factors, it is not possible at this time to assign differential explanatory power to the various factors in our attempt to understand the differential rate of growth of these executive functions. It is our hope that the ongoing observations of the children and interviews of their parents will clarify this issue. That fact that the performance of the San Pedro children from families with traditional occupation and much land resembled closely the performance of the isolated San Marcos children, despite the better nourishment and less isolated setting of the former group, implies that intrafamilial experiences play a major role in producing the pattern of cognitive performances described.

ACKNOWLEDGMENTS

We wish to thank Herman Mendes, Elizabeth Nolan, Mark Szpak, Michael Richards, Julie Becker, Elena Hurtado, Lucas Perez Puzol and Pablo Cox Bixcul for their assistance in collecting and analyzing the data upon which this paper is based.

REFERENCES

1. KAGAN, J. & R. E. KLEIN. 1973. Crosscultural perspectives on early development. American Psychologist 28: 947–961.
2. NERLOVE, S. B., J. M. ROBERTS, R. E. KLEIN, C. YARBROUGH & J. P. HABICHT. 1974. Natural indicators of cognitive development: an observational study of rural Guatemalan children. Ethos Vol. 2, No. 3.
3. FLAVELL, J. H. et al. 1968. The Development of Role-taking and Communication Skills in Children. John Wiley. New York.
4. FLAVELL, J. H. 1970. Developmental studies of mediated memory. In Advances in Child Development and Behavior. Vol. 5. Academic Press. New York.
5. ROGOFF, B., N. NEWCOMBE & J. KAGAN. 1974. Planfulness and recognition memory. Child Develop. 45: 972–977.
6. GIBSON, E. J., M. K. POAG & R. RADER. 1972. The effect of redundant rhyme and spelling patterns as a verbal discrimination task. Appendix to Final Report in Project 90046, Grant OEG 2-9-42044601071: Cornell University, U.S. Office of Education.

MATERNAL KINESIC BEHAVIOR AND COGNITIVE DEVELOPMENT IN THE CHILD*

Lorraine Kirk

*Department of Sociology and Anthropology
University of Missouri
St. Louis, Missouri 63121*

Michael Burton

*School of Social Sciences
University of California, Irvine
Irvine, California 92717*

INTRODUCTION

This paper addresses itself to an old question: we know that children differ in the rates at which they achieve cognitive skills; to the extent that such differences are due to nongenetic influences, what environmental factors can account for the differences? This problem has been approached in the United States and Ghana through isolation of both subcultural and maternal behavior variables. These studies focus on the mother-child dyad as a potential source of cognitive differences in children. In the United States, Hess and his colleagues[2-7] tape and observe mother and child in teaching interaction under laboratory conditions, demonstrating relationships among maternal behavior, socioeconomic status, and the child's test performance. In Ghana, Kirk[8-10] examines relationships between the Piaget test performance of Ga children of three subcultures and the verbal behavior of their mothers in teaching them a mechanical task. It is found in Ghana that subculture has minimal effect on Piaget test performance, while maternal verbal behavior is useful in predicting the test scores of the children.

The present study takes a closer look at maternal behavior, focusing on the mother's nonverbal behavior, while examining the mother-child dyad among another people: the Kikuyu of Kenya. In the Kikuyu study we analyze a motion film record of mother-child teaching interaction. Relationships are demonstrated between the mother's nonverbal communicative behavier and the child's rate of cognitive development.

PROCEDURE

To examine the effects on child cognition of nonverbal behavior in the mother, we gather three kinds of data. The child's rate of cognitive development is measured with a battery of ten cognitive tests; the mother's nonverbal behavior is measured in terms of five body motion variables derived from

* The research on which this study is based was supported by a grant from the Carnegie Foundation to the Bureau of Educational Research of the University of Nairobi.

389

analysis of a motion film record of mother-child interaction. Several demographic and educational variables of the child and nuclear family are also included as controls. These data are subjected to a multivariate analysis using (a) zero order correlations and (b) multiple linear regressions to validate the inferences from the zero order correlations.

The Cognitive Tests

In 1973 a battery of cognitive tests was administered by Streeter, Landauer, and Whiting to approximately 500 children in Ngecha, a Kikuyu community in the Central Province of Kenya. For our purposes we are concerned with ten of these tests† :

(1) *Conservation of Area.* In this test the child was presented with small-scale representations of two pastures, eight houses, and two cows. One cow was located on each pasture. Transformations were made in the amount and distribution of surface area left exposed on each pasture when the numbers and positions of houses were manipulated by the examiner. Following each transformation, the child was asked whether the cows had the same amount of grass to eat, or whether the cow on one pasture had more to eat than the cow on the other. Two scores were computed for this test, based on (a) the number of correct choices made by the child and (b) the reasons given by the child for his choices.

(2) *Bender Gestalt.* In this test the child was asked to copy a drawing of a circle and a parallelogram, with the vertex of the parallelogram contiguous with the left side of the circle.

(3) *Embedded Figures.* Here the child was shown a series of drawings, each containing a hidden equilateral triangle. The child had been given a cardboard triangle identical in size and shape to those in the drawings, and was instructed to identify the triangles in the drawings by covering them with the cardboard triangle.

(4) *Rank Order Recall.* In this test the child listened to a series of lists of three words each. In one subtest the child was asked to repeat the three-word list; in a second subtest, the child was asked to identify the sequential position of a word in the list.

(5) *Checker Diagonal.* This test required the child to replicate a model pattern of checkers prearranged in a diagonal line on a checkerboard.

(6) *Body Parts.* In a first subtest (A), the examiner pointed to parts of the child's body and asked for appropriate labels from the child. In a second subtest (B), the examiner named body parts and asked the child to locate them on his own body.

(7) *Auditory Integration.* In this test common words were presented with delays of one and three seconds between syllables. The child was asked to identify the words presented.

(8) *Serial Pointing.* Here the child was asked to touch sets of checkers, ranging in number from one to seven, in sequences demonstrated by the examiner.

---

† A complete description of the tests can be found in a forthcoming publication by Streeter *et al.* (Bell Laboratories).

(9) *Animal Listing.* In this test the child was asked to name all the animals he could think of within a one-minute period.

(10) *Tactual Perception on Face and Hands.* The blindfolded child was touched on the cheek and/or hand, sometimes in two places at once, sometimes in one place only. The child was asked to indicate where he had been touched. The authors of this test were particularly interested in children's ability to perceive two simultaneous touches occurring in contralateral positions (one hand and the opposite cheek).

Sampling

From the sample of children tested by Streeter, Landauer and Whiting, a subsample was selected in which the children's ages were estimated to be between 5½ and 6½ years. Age was estimated using a technique outlined in Kirk,[11,12] which involves observation of the total dental eruption pattern. The resulting subsample of 42 children and their mothers was observed in teaching interaction.

The Mother's Nonverbal Behavior

In order to analyze the mother's nonverbal behavior within the mother-child teaching interaction, mothers were taught to construct a puzzle in the absence of their children; subsequently the mothers were asked to teach their children to construct the puzzle. While each mother was teaching her child, the interactional behavior of the pair was recorded on motion film and sound tape.

The puzzle utilized in this experiment was a small car built from "Lego" blocks and wheels. The mother was taught to construct the car according to an initial model with which she was presented. Errors of orientation were corrected, while errors of sequence were ignored. In teaching the mother, a standard verbal protocol was followed, in which specific descriptive terms were avoided. The task was analyzed into steps. Mistakes of position made by the mother in learning the task were corrected through repetition of the problematic step together with the appropriate section of restricted verbal protocol.

Two sessions of teaching were distinguished. In the first session, the mother was instructed to teach the child in any way she liked. This session was terminated when five minutes had elapsed or when the child had completed construction of the puzzle, whichever occurred first. In the second session, the mother was instructed to teach the child again, but this time without touching the puzzle. This was intended to encourage (a) an increase in the mother's body motion and (b) an increase in the mother's specificity of verbal reference. It was anticipated that much of the increase in body motion from the first to the second session would occur as abstractions to one degree or another of the motions involved in the mother's actual construction of the puzzle. The second session was terminated when ten minutes had elapsed or when the child had completed the puzzle, whichever occurred first.

Twenty-four seconds of silent motion film were taken of each interacting pair. The filmed sample began two minutes into the second session of mother-child teaching interaction, in which the mother had been asked to refrain from touching the puzzle.

A series of indices of maternal kinesic behavior were constructed. From observation of the mother's behavior on silent film, each mother was given a score on each kinesic index:

(1) *Proportion of Single-Finger Movement.* This index is a ratio of the number of frames in which an isolated finger is in motion to the total number of usable‡ frames in the sample. Finger movement is defined as a change in angle at the knuckles of the finger or thumb. This index is intended as a measure of the mother's nonverbal specificity in communicating with her child. §

(2) *Predominance of Single-Hand Movement.* This is a binary variable that contrasts mothers who predominantly use one hand only (coded 2) to mothers who predominantly use both hands (coded 1). This index is another measure of the mother's nonverbal specificity. §

(3) *Task Relatedness.* This is an index of the proportion of time in which the mother is focused on the construction or teaching process rather than on other stimuli in the room. It is computed as the number of frames in which the mother is relating to the task divided by the number of usable frames in the interaction.

(4) *Amount of Construction of the Puzzle by the Mother.* This is a measure of the degree to which the mother fails to follow the instruction to refrain from touching or assembling the puzzle during the second (filmed) session of teaching interaction. It is computed as the number of frames of the mother's body motion that are involved in or necessary to touching the puzzle, divided by the total number of frames of teaching interaction.

(5) *Interactional Synchrony.* This index, unlike the preceding four indices, does not involve systematic counts of objective physical events. It is based, rather, on judgements on a five-point scale of the degree to which the mother and child are in interactional synchrony; that is, the degree to which they parallel each other in body positioning (positional isomorphism) and/or rhythm (rhythmic synchrony). This index is in part a test of the intuitive faculty as a yardstick in the measurement of microinteractional events.

Characteristics of the Child and Nuclear Family

For all 42 mother-child pairs, information was recorded on several demographic and educational variables. These are defined:

(1) *Age of the child* was estimated in months by observation of the exact stages of tooth eruption at each position in the child's mouth.[11,12] Ages ranged from 66 to 78 months, with a mean of 72.78 months.

---

‡ Usable frames are defined here as the number of frames in which the mother is not involved in assembling the puzzle herself, timed from the beginning of the film to either completion of the teaching session or the end of the film, whichever occurs first.

§ Nonverbal specificity in the communication of the mother with her child can be seen in a number of body parts, but is easiest to perceive and count in the fingers and hand, where motions such as pointing, pinching, grasping, pressing firmly, rotating, and pushing convey specific information from mother to child about manipulations or the spatial organization of the puzzle. When the mother is being specific, she is usually referring to a single part of a structure; this is generally more easily done with a single hand. Addition of the second hand would often make the referent more ambiguous. We predict a positive association between maternal specificity and the child's cognitive test performance, as mothers who are more specific will provide the child with more information about contrasts in the environment.

(2) *Age of the mother.* Since few mothers knew their exact ages, estimates of age were made by local research assistants in ranked categories by ten year intervals.

(3) *Mother's education* was recorded as the total number of years the mother attended school. It ranged from 0 to 8 years, with a mean of 3.03.

(4) *Father's education* ranged from 0 to 12 years, with a mean of 5.62.

(5) *Position of the child in the birth sequence of the mother.* Since some families are polygynous, this is not identical to the position of the child in the birth sequence of the family unit. Position in the birth sequence of the mother ranged from 1 (eldest child) to 11, with a mean of 4.08.

(6) *Sex of the child.* There were 24 boys and 18 girls in the final sample of 42 children.

DATA ANALYSIS

A statistical model for prediction of the children's cognitive test performance was formulated. Using correlational analysis and multiple regression analysis,|| the model was tested on two samples: (a) the sample of 41 mother-child pairs (the full sample less one spastic and/or retarded child) and (b) the sample of 41 less all mothers who did any touching or constructing of the puzzle themselves during the film segment. The reduced sample contains 33 mother-child pairs. The model was tested on the reduced sample as a cross-check on the full sample, to eliminate the possibility that counts of the motor activity of the mother in the full sample could have been altered by the mother's preparation for or recovery from her own touching or construction of the puzzle.

The model was designed to explain each of the cognitive variables taken separately, and to explain a composite cognitive variable that was constructed by dividing each cognitive test score by its maximum value and summing the results. We treat each of the cognitive tests separately since we do not assume that there is any single factor that is measured by the several tests. Rather, we allow for the possibility that the tests measure disparate achievements, and that some of the tests may not be appropriate for the age range of the present sample, with the consequence that variability in those tests would tend to be random. Independent variables for the regression analysis consist of the kinesic indices plus the demographic and educational variables.

In this section we discuss correlations (a) between the cognitive and independent variables, (b) among the independent variables, and (c) among the cognitive variables. We then use regression analysis to validate the inter-relationships between the cognitive and independent variables that are found among the zero order correlations.

Correlations between Cognitive and Independent Variables

TABLE 1 presents correlations between the cognitive and independent variables. Among the kinesic variables, task relatedness stands out as the best predictor of cognitive performance, having a number of strong positive

---

|| This analysis used the Jaguar program for multiple regression and congruencies written by Charles Lave.

TABLE 1

CORRELATIONS BETWEEN COGNITIVE AND INDEPENDENT VARIABLES (N = 41)

	Proportion of Single-Finger Movement	Predominance of Single-Hand Movement	Mother's Task Relatedness	Amount of Construction by Mother	Interactional Synchrony	Age of Child	Age of Mother	Education of Mother	Education of Father	Birth Sequence	Sex of Child
Auditory integration	−.03	.13	.15	−.32	.09	.35	.19	−.09	−.01	.03	−.12
Conservation (correct choices)	.16	.19	.07	−.15	−.26	.21	.24	−.21	−.08	.13	−.04
Conservation (reasons)	.43	−.04	.06	−.18	.14	.32	.12	−.21	−.25	.04	−.10
Checker diagonal	−.03	−.04	.11	−.14	−.16	.10	.44	−.05	−.05	.28	.07
Serial pointing	.13	.43	.17	−.33	.07	.12	.29	−.25	.00	.11	.05
Bank order recall (positions)	−.01	.18	.23	−.26	.05	−.02	.00	.06	.10	−.10	.15
Rank order recall (lists)	.11	.07	.14	−.34	−.11	.20	.06	−.07	−.16	.12	.11
Bender gestalt	.12	.49	.45	−.06	.40	.16	.01	.07	.01	.02	.11
Face and hands	−.10	−.09	−.05	−.26	−.04	.00	−.01	.18	.20	.02	.05
Body parts (subtest A)	.08	.32	.43	−.12	.04	.13	.26	−.18	−.18	.08	−.09
Body parts (subtest B)	−.03	.03	.00	−.08	−.26	.28	.37	−.23	.05	.04	−.06
Embedded figures	.36	.42	.36	−.04	.07	.19	.28	−.08	−.03	.26	.10
Animal listing	.28	.13	.16	−.14	.32	.15	.11	−.14	−.12	−.08	−.06
Composite index	.22	.30	.30	−.30	.09	.30	.39	−.15	.00	.18	.02

NOTE: Significance levels are as follows (one tailed t test): $p \leqslant .001$, $r \geqslant .44$; $p \leqslant .005$, $r \geqslant .33$; $p \leqslant .01$, $r \geqslant .27$; $p \leqslant .05$, $r \geqslant .20$.

correlations (maximum r = .45, p < .001) with scores on the individual cognitive tests. There are, further, no substantial negative correlations between task relatedness and any of the individual cognitive tests. Task relatedness shows a correlation of .30 (p < .01) with the composite cognitive test score.

Predominance of single-hand movement is also a good predictor of cognitive test performance, having a number of high positive correlations (maximum r = .49, p < .001), but also having some weak negative correlations. Predominance of single-hand movement has a correlation of .30 (p < .01) with the composite cognitive test score.

Amount of construction of the puzzle by the mother is useful in predicting performance on Rank Order Recall (lists), Serial Pointing, Auditory Integration, and Tactual Perception on Face and Hands, with correlations ranging from −.34 to −.26 (p < .005 to p < .05). All but one of the cognitive tests (r = .14) correlate negatively with amount of construction by the mother. Construction has a correlation of −.30 (p < .01) with the composite cognitive test score.

Proportion of single-finger movement is useful in predicting scores on Conservation of Area (reasons), Embedded Figures, and Animal Listing, with correlations of .43, .36, and .28, respectively (significance levels ranging from .005 to .01). This kinesic index shows some weak negative correlations (r = −.10), but all substantial correlations are positive.

Interactional synchrony is an unreliable predictor of cognitive test performance. There are four correlations between synchrony and individual cognitive test scores that are significant between the .005 and .05 levels, but there is an inconsistency in the direction of the correlations (synchrony correlates negatively with Conservation (correct choices) and Body Parts subtest B, but positively with the Bender Gestalt and Animal Listing). The correlation of synchrony with the composite cognitive test score approaches zero. Synchrony also, however, has positive associations with predominance of single-hand movement and with task relatedness. Given that each of these two kinesic variables has a much stronger relationship with cognitive performance than does synchrony, it seems probable that much of the effect of synchrony on cognitive performance is indirect, mediated through the other kinesic variables. On the other hand, systematic counts of objective events (similar to those used for the other four kinesic variables), rather than partial reliance on intuitive judgement, might produce more consistent results for this index.

Of the cognitive tests considered, five have strong associations with the nonverbal teaching behavior of the mother. Performance of the child on the Bender Gestalt test shows high correlations with the task relatedness of the mother's movement, predominance of single-hand movement, and synchrony. Embedded Figures is highly correlated with task relatedness, predominance of single-hand movement, and proportion of single-finger movement. Body Parts, subtest A, is highly correlated with task relatedness and predominance of single-hand movement. Serial pointing has high correlations with predominance of single-hand movement and amount of construction by the mother. Conservation (reasons) is highly correlated with proportion of single-finger movement.

Among the demographic and educational variables, child's age and mother's age both have all positive correlations to the cognitive variables, with one nonsignificant exception. Mother's and father's education parallel each other in their patterns of correlation, but father's education shows consistently lower correlations. The child's sex and position in the birth sequence have low correlations with the cognitive variables.

TABLE 2
CORRELATIONS AMONG INDEPENDENT VARIABLES (N = 41)

	Proportion of Single-Finger Movement	Predominance of Single-Hand Movement	Mother's Task Relatedness	Amount of Construction by Mother	Interactional Synchrony	Age of Child	Age of Mother	Education of Mother	Education of Father	Position in Birth Sequence	Sex of Child
Proportion of single-finger movement	X	.45	.05	-.19	.32	.12	-.02	-.08	-.36	.00	-.10
Predominance of single-hand movement		X	.32	-.38	.59	.13	-.15	.25	.04	-.23	.13
Mother's task relatedness			X	-.20	.22	-.08	.02	.10	-.09	.15	.24
Amount of construction by mother				X	-.24	-.05	.01	-.14	-.24	-.05	-.14
Interactional synchrony					X	-.11	-.30	.21	.11	-.36	-.07
Age of child						X	.15	.05	-.18	-.07	-.03
Age of mother							X	-.71	-.26	.69	-.33
Education of mother								X	.46	-.51	.43
Education of father									X	-.22	.43
Position in birth sequence										X	-.09
Sex of child											X

NOTE: Significance levels are as follows (one tailed t test): $p \leq .001$, $r \geq .44$; $p \leq .005$, $r \geq .33$; $p \leq .01$, $r \geq .27$; $p \leq .05$, $r \geq .20$.

Correlations among Independent Variables

TABLE 2 lists correlations among the independent variables (kinesic, demographic and educational). Several strong patterns can be seen from the correlations:

(1) *Kinesic Variables.* Among the kinesic variables, the predominance of single-hand movement correlates .45 with the proportion of single-finger movement. These two kinesic indices are both measures of the mother's nonverbal specificity. Both measures of specificity are highly associated with our judgement of interactional synchrony ($r = .59$ and $r = .32$, respectively).

Amount of construction by the mother is negatively correlated with all of the other four kinesic indices. Thus, mothers who construct part or all of the time for their children tend to exhibit less single-hand movement, less single-finger movement, less synchrony, and less task relatedness.

Task relatedness is positively associated with predominance of single-hand movement and synchrony, but the association between task relatedness and single-finger movement is close to zero.

(2) *Demographic and Educational Variables.* In Ngeca, educational opportunities have been increasing rapidly for many years. Consequently, older people have less education than younger people, and the correlation between mother's age and mother's education is $-.71$. There is a negative correlation between mother's age and father's education, and a positive correlation between mother's education and father's education. We assume that age is a mediating factor in the latter correlation. In addition to having less education, older women have more children. Consequently, children of older mothers in our sample have more older siblings: there is a correlation of .69 between mother's age and the position of the child in the birth sequence.

Correlations among the Cognitive Variables

TABLE 3 presents intercorrelations among the cognitive variables. The correlations do not support the notion that a single underlying factor can account for the various tests: there are many low positive correlations and some negative correlations between tests. The highest correlations are between Rank Order Recall (subtest A) and Tactual Perception on Face and Hands (.55), between body Parts A and Body Parts B (.59), and between Bender Gestalt and Embedded Figures (.54).

Model for Regression Analysis

In the previous section we have discussed the correlations of several independent variables with cognitive test performance. Many of these independent variables have high correlations with each other. Consequently, any single correlation may be due to the influence of some third variable that is highly correlated with both the independent and the dependent variables. In order to control for the effects of third variables, we construct multiple linear regression models of the interrelationships between the independent and dependent variables. Regression analysis treats the dependent variable as a function of

TABLE 3
CORRELATIONS AMONG COGNITIVE VARIABLES (N = 41)

	Auditory Integration	Conservation (correct choices)	Conservation (reasons)	Checker Diagonal	Serial Pointing	Rank Order Recall (A)	Rank Order Recall (B)	Bender Gestalt	Face and Hands	Body Parts (A)	Body Parts (B)	Embedded Figures	Animal Listing	Composite Index
Auditory integration	X													.53
Conservation (correct choices)	.26	X												.54
Conservation (reasons)	.41	.42	X											.59
Checker diagonal	-.08	.09	.07	X										.33
Serial pointing	.39	.47	.19	.06	X									.56
Rank order recall A (positions)	.12	.11	.17	.21	.17	X								.51
Rank order recall B (lists)	.35	.33	.19	.08	.50	-.07	X							.33
Bender gestalt	.44	.21	.21	.06	.44	.14	.34	X						.57
Face and hands	.05	-.03	.05	.00	-.18	.55	-.31	-.12	X					.30
Body parts (A)	.50	.34	.24	.07	.45	.42	.23	.36	.10	X				.62
Body parts (B)	.43	.54	.39	.03	.29	.29	.21	.23	.12	.59	X			.62
Embedded figures	.10	.17	.09	.13	.41	.12	.17	.54	-.14	.36	.30	X		.42
Animal Listing	.30	.17	.47	-.05	.13	.27	.15	.40	.19	.34	.38	.14	X	.62
Composite index	.53	.54	.59	.33	.56	.51	.33	.57	.30	.62	.62	.42	.62	X

NOTE: Significance levels are as follows (one tailed t test): $p \leqslant .001$, $r \geqslant .44$; $p \leqslant .005$, $r \geqslant .33$; $p \leqslant .01$, $r \geqslant .27$; $p \leqslant .05$, $r \geqslant .20$.

several independent variables. It computes a regression coefficient for each of the independent variables, which estimates the effect of that independent variable on the dependent variable, controlling for the effects of all other independent variables included in the equation.

The model used to guide the regression analysis appears in FIGURE 1. In this model we predict the effects of the independent on the dependent variables (the interrelationships among the independent variables in the model are consistent with those found through simple correlational analysis). We organize the following discussion of the predictions by tracing a path through the independent variables of FIGURE 1.

The first prediction of FIGURE 1 is that the mother's education will be positively associated with the child's cognitive test performance. We anticipate that educated mothers will provide training that is relevant to some, but not all, of the cognitive tests. For instance, educated mothers are more likely to expose their children to printed matter (magazines, newspapers), which contains abstract visual representations. This exposure has often been hypothesized as an important process by which education produces cognitive changes in children.[1] Mother's education should have particularly strong effects on tests requiring geometric skills, such as the Checker Diagonal, Bender Gestalt, and Embedded Figures.

We assume that older mothers will be more experienced than younger mothers in teaching their children, and hence that the mother's age will have a positive effect on the child's test performance, were all other variables to be held constant. Since, however, mother's age has a negative relationship with mother's education, we shall control for education in order to test this proposition.

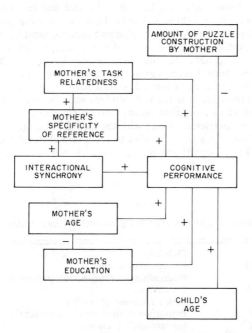

FIGURE 1. Model of interrelationships among independent and cognitive variables.

We predict a direct positive link between the mother's specificity in communication with her child and the cognitive performance of the child. Specificity has direct links to interactional synchrony and to the mother's task relatedness. Thus, it is in a central position among the kinesic variables.

We would expect a positive link between interactional synchrony and cognitive performance. However, there is also a strong relationship between synchrony and specificity. Thus, an observed correlation between synchrony and one of the cognitive tests will be a partial consequence of the relationship between synchrony and specificity. In order to assess the effect of synchrony on cognitive performance, we shall control for specificity.

We predict that mothers who pay less attention to the task will also tend to pay less attention to the child's other learning activities, with a resulting depressant effect on the child's cognitive development. Thus, in FIGURE 1 we have indicated a direct positive link between task relatedness and cognitive performance.

In constructing the car for the child, the mother denies the child opportunities to deal with the new problem. This kind of behavior, occurring habitually over time, should tend to limit the child's opportunities to learn. Thus, we predict a negative link between the amount of construction by the mother and the cognitive performance of the child.

Regressions for Individual Cognitive Tests

For each of the cognitive tests, the model of FIGURE 1 was tested using multiple linear regression analysis, for both the full and reduced samples (the latter with constructing mothers deleted). In no cases were there substantial differences between regressions for the full and reduced samples, indicating that the inclusion of partial constructors in the full sample did not appreciably distort the behavior counts. In this section we discuss the best regression equations for those tests having significant associations with the explanatory variables. In all regression equations, Y stands for the cognitive variable under consideration. Abbreviations for the independent variables are listed in TABLE 4. For each independent variable that enters into an equation, the t-score is listed under the regression coefficient, along with the associated significance level.

Embedded Figures. This test of ability to recognize abstract geometric figures in a complex field has a significant association with mother's age, as well as with

TABLE 4

ABBREVIATIONS FOR INDEPENDENT VARIABLES

A	Child's age
EM	Education of mother
H	Predominance of single-hand movement
MA	Mother's age
R	Task relatedness of mother
SF	Proportion of single-finger movement
SY	Interactional synchrony

three kinesic indices: predominance of single-hand movement, task relatedness, and proportion of single-finger movement. As can be seen in the regression equation below, each kinesic index has an independent relationship with Embedded Figures. Embedded Figures is the only cognitive test that is related to both measures of specificity (predominance of single-hand movement and proportion of single-finger movement).

$$Y = 2.83(MA) + 83.7(R) + 4.38(H) + 13.1(SF) + 15.8 \qquad r = .556$$
$$t = 2.4 \qquad t = 1.7 \qquad t = 1.7 \qquad t = 1.4 \qquad\qquad N = 31$$
$$p < .05 \qquad p < .05 \qquad p < .05 \qquad p < .10$$

Body Parts A (encoding). This version of the Body Parts test shows patterns of association similar to those of the Embedded Figures test: both have positive associations with mother's age, task relatedness, and predominance of single-hand movement, as predicted by the model. Unlike the Embedded Figures test, however, Body Parts A has no relationship with single-finger movement.

$$Y = .613(MA) + .855(H) + 25.5(R) + 6.53 \qquad r = .493$$
$$t = 2.1 \qquad t = 1.5 \qquad t = 2.1 \qquad\qquad N = 31$$
$$p < .05 \qquad p < .10 \qquad p < .05$$

Body Parts B (decoding). The regression equations for this subtest have very little explanatory power. As with Body Parts A, there is a significant association with mother's age, but the relationship with proportion of single-hand movement has become very weak, and task relatedness has dropped entirely out of the picture.

$$Y = .751(MA) + .297(H) + 2.76 \qquad r = .316$$
$$t = 2.5 \qquad t = .5 \qquad\qquad N = 31$$
$$p < .01 \qquad \text{n.s.}$$

Serial Pointing. Serial pointing is positively associated with predominance of single-hand movement and with the age of the mother. Serial pointing and Body Parts A have similar regression equations, and are highly correlated. These two tests are at the same time similar in their patterns of association with the kinesic variables, and kinesically similar: in both tests the examiner uses pointing to elicit a response from the child.

$$Y = .903(H) + .415(MA) + 3.16 \qquad r = .520$$
$$t = 3.1 \qquad t = 2.7 \qquad\qquad N = 31$$
$$p < .005 \qquad p < .01$$

Bender Gestalt. Two kinesic indices (predominance of single-hand movement and task relatedness) have strong relationships with this test.

$$Y = .796(H) + 15.8(R) + 3.75 \qquad r = .550$$
$$t = 2.4 \qquad t = 2.3 \qquad\qquad N = 31$$
$$p < .05 \qquad p < .05$$

Synchrony also has a high correlation with the Bender Gestalt test. The following regression shows that this association remains strong under controls for task relatedness:

$$Y = 20.9(R) + .279(SY) + 2.07 \qquad r = .593$$
$$t = 3.2 \qquad t = 2.0 \qquad\qquad N = 32$$
$$p < .005 \qquad p < .05$$

However, due to the high association of synchrony with predominance of single-hand movement, these two variables cannot be used together to predict the test: once predominance of single-hand movement is used to explain the test, the partial correlation with synchrony is no longer statistically significant.

Conservation (reasons). The adequacy of the reasons given by children for their choices on the conservation test is associated with the age of the child and with the mother's specificity (as measured by the proportion of single-finger movement).

$$Y = .066(A) + 1.89(SF) - 4.72$$

		$r = .458$
$t = 1.5$	$t = 1.9$	$N = 32$
$p < .10$	$p < .05$	

Note, however, that the relationships in the regression equation are in the direction predicted by the model.

Checker Diagonal. Performance on this test is related to mother's education. This can be seen in the regression equation, but not in the zero order correlations since the regression equation controls for mother's age in order to be able to assess the effect of mother's education. It is evident from the difference in t-scores that the effect of the mother's age is stronger than the effect of the mother's education.

$$Y = .830(MA) + .144(EM) - 2.61$$

		$r = .539$
$t = 4.3$	$t = 2.7$	$N = 41$
$p < .001$	$p < .005$	

The Checker Diagonal test is the only test that has the predicted association with mother's education.

Animal Listing. This is the only test having a strong relationship to synchrony. It also has a positive relationship to mother's age.

$$Y = .689(MA) + .811(SY) + 1.24$$

		$r = .327$
$t = 1.5$	$t = 2.2$	$N = 37$
$p < .10$	$p < .025$	

Auditory Integration. The more the mother constructs, the lower the child's score on Auditory Integration. Scores on this test are also related to the task relatedness of the mother and the age of the child.

$$Y = .529(A) + 44.0(R) - 5.01(C) - 30.0$$

			$r = .459$
$t = 2.5$	$t = 1.6$	$t = 2.5$	$N = 37$
$p < .01$	$p < .10$	$p < .01$	

Rank Order Recall. Like Auditory Integration, the Rank Order Recall tests are tests of verbal ability. All three tests show very similar patterns of relationships to the independent variables. Rank order lists are related to child's age, task relatedness and amount of construction:

$$Y = .118(A) + 14.9(R) - 2.13(C) - 3.17$$

			$r = .366$
$t = 1.3$	$t = 1.3$	$t = 2.5$	$N = 37$
$p < .10$	$p < .10$	$p < .01$	

Rank Order positions are related only to amount of construction and to mother's task relatedness:

$$Y = 48.5(R) - 4.16(C) + 8.90$$

		$r = .324$
$t = 1.8$	$t = 2.1$	$N = 37$
$p < .05$	$p < .025$	

Regressions on the Composite Index

The strongest predictive variable for the composite index is mother's age. This can be seen in the following equation:

$$Y = 1.58(MA) + 10.0 \qquad\qquad r = .359$$
$$t = 2.6 \qquad\qquad\qquad\qquad\qquad N = 40$$
$$p < .01$$

If we control for mother's age, we see that child's age also has a significant positive association with the composite index, even though child's age is restricted in our sample to 12 months of variation.

$$Y = 1.43(MA) + .291(A) - 10.7 \qquad\qquad r = .401$$
$$t = 2.4 \qquad t = 1.6 \qquad\qquad\qquad N = 40$$
$$p < .01 \qquad p < .05$$

Task relatedness and predominance of single-hand movement have approximately equally strong relationships with the composite index. Both relationships are in the direction predicted by the model. This can be seen in the next two regression equations, which measure the effects of each of the two kinesic variables while controlling for the two age variables.

$$Y = 1.38(MA) + .335(A) + 45.7(R) - 13.2 \qquad\qquad r = .494$$
$$t = 2.4 \qquad t = 1.9 \qquad t = 2.1 \qquad\qquad N = 36$$
$$p < .05 \qquad p < .05 \qquad p < .05$$

$$Y = 1.67(MA) + .224(A) + 2.32(H) - 2.99 \qquad\qquad r = .505$$
$$t = 2.9 \qquad t = 1.3 \qquad t = 2.2 \qquad\qquad N = 30$$
$$p < .005 \qquad p < .10 \qquad p < .05$$

The best regression equation for the composite index involves mother's age, child's age, task relatedness, and construction:

$$Y = 1.40(MA) + .313(A) + 56.1(R) - 4.28(C) - 11.0 \qquad\qquad r = .614$$
$$t = 2.7 \qquad t = 2.0 \qquad t = 2.8 \qquad t = 2.9 \qquad\qquad N = 37$$
$$p < .01 \qquad p < .05 \qquad p < .005 \qquad p < .005$$

The best equation for predicting the composite index from kinesic variables alone (excluding demographic and educational variables) uses only task relatedness and construction. The multiple correlation for this regression (.430) is higher than the multiple correlation when the composite index was regressed on mother's age and child's age alone (excluding kinesic variables):

$$Y = 54.2(R) - 4.35(C) + 16.0 \qquad\qquad r = .430$$
$$t = 2.4 \qquad t = 2.6 \qquad\qquad\qquad N = 37$$
$$p < .025 \qquad p < .01$$

CONCLUSIONS

This study evaluates the usefulness of nonverbal maternal behavior in predicting the cognitive development of 5½- to 6½-year-old Kikuyu children. For this purpose, ten cognitive tests were used as measures of the children's cognitive performance, and five body motion variables were used as indices of nonverbal behavior in analysis of a motion film record of 42 mothers in teaching interaction with their children.

Zero Order Correlational Analysis

The present indices of maternal kinesic behavior are found useful in predicting the cognitive test performance of the children. The indices play an important role in predicting scores on eight of the cognitive tests, and contribute to prediction of a composite cognitive test score.

The two kinesic indices of maternal interactive behavior that show consistently strong correlations with cognitive test performance are task relatedness and predominance of single-hand movement. Proportion of single-finger movement and amount of construction by the mother are also good predictors of cognitive performance. Mother-child interactional synchrony is a less adequate predictor, having inconsistent and indirect correlations with cognitive performance.

Among the battery of cognitive tests, the Bender Gestalt, Embedded Figures, Body Parts, and Serial Pointing tests are the most accessible to prediction using the nonverbal indices of maternal interactive behavior. A compositive index of cognitive test performance is also amenable to prediction using the kinesic indices.

The age of the mother shows strong and uniformly positive correlations with the child's cognitive performance. Other demographic and educational variables, such as child's age and parental education, have much weaker correlations with cognitive performance.

Verification of Correlational Analysis with Regression Models

Since there are high correlations among some of the independent variables, zero order correlational analysis must be supplemented. In order to disentangle the web of interrelationships among the cognitive, kinesic, demographic and educational variables, we cross-check the results of the correlational analysis using multiple linear regression analysis. This style of analysis is similar in many ways to some common forms of causal analysis, such as path analysis.¶ We

¶ The results of this study raise the question of causal inference. For the background variables such as mother's age, this question is easily resolved. There is no plausible way to argue that mothers become older because their children are more proficient on cognitive tests. We must conclude that mother's age is either a direct cause of said proficiency, or an indirect cause through some intermediate variables that we have not measured. In the case of the kinesic variables, however, we find it more difficult to make such secure causal inferences. The kinesic indices are intended to measure the mother's proficiency as a teacher. A more proficient teacher should produce a higher rate of cognitive development in the child. One might argue, however, that successful children elicit from their mothers the kinesic behaviors that we have measured in this study: that mothers with receptive children are motivated to be more specific in their reference to the task; that mothers who are low on task relatedness have lost interest in the task because their children are doing poorly; and that mothers construct the car for their children because they feel that the children are unlikely to be able to do it by themselves. This counter hypothesis, however, would imply that mothers adapt to the children's behavior more than the children adapt to the mothers' behavior. This would dubiously attribute disproportionately high control and low adaptation to the least powerful and most rapidly developing figure in this small group interaction. Be this as it may, the process of mother-child interaction might also be seen as a feedback system in which mothers influence children and children influence mothers (not necessarily with equal strength). In this ecological model the two actors are interdependent; a circular system of causation holds. An exogenous infusion (deliberate or coincidental) of a new set of habitual behaviors into the cycle by the mother should alter the dynamics of the interaction. If we assume this ecological model to be accurate, a change in the mother's behavior should lead to a change in the child's behavior.

control for the effects of third variables, and attempt to ascertain whether each independent variable has a direct effect on cognitive performance, or an indirect effect, mediated through other independent variables. In general, the regression analysis demonstrates the same patterns of association between independent and dependent variables that can be seen by examining the zero order correlation tables: individual kinesic variables have the relationships with cognitive performance that are predicted by the model, even when we control for mother's age and the other kinesic variables. An exception to this pattern is interactional synchrony, which appears to have only an indirect association with cognitive performance.

DISCUSSION

Four measures of nonverbal maternal behavior have emerged as good predictors of the child's cognitive performance. These are task relatedness, predominance of single-hand movement, proportion of single-finger movement, and amount of construction of the puzzle by the mother. Task relatedness accounts for the greatest amount of the variance within the total set of cognitive tests. Specificity of communication, however, as measured by the predominance of single-hand movement and by proportion of single-finger movement, is of greatest theoretical interest. In a previous study across three Ga subcultures in Ghana,[8-10] where verbal specificity was measured, and in the present study, where nonverbal specificity was measured, strong positive associations have been found between the specificity of the mother's communication with the child in the teaching interaction and the prior cognitive test performance of the child.

Both the Kenya and Ghana experiments focus on the mother's behavior in teaching a spatial task: the construction of a three-dimensional toy car from "Lego" blocks and wheels. In the Kenya experiment, two nonverbal variables are used to measure specificity of reference to the manipulations or spatial organization of the puzzle. The cognitive tests that are best predicted by the two nonverbal indices of maternal specificity in the Kenya study are all spatial tests: they require the child to perform operations on a spatial structure [Embedded Figures, Bender Gestalt, Body Parts Naming, Serial Pointing, and Conservation of Area (reasons for correct choices)]. Similarly in the Ghana experiment the mother's verbal specificity in teaching her child the same spatial task ("Lego") can be used to predict the child's performance on spatial tests of conservation. These facts can be interpreted in terms of the shared spatial features of the variables: the child's level of spatial awareness is measured by his performance on spatial cognitive tests; the quality of the mother's communication with her child on spatial matters is measured by the specificity of her communication with the child in the context of a cooperative solution of a geometric problem. The mother's behavior as a teacher in this context predicts the child's performance on cognitive tests of spatial ability. It would appear, then, that mothers who habitually convey a great deal of specific information about topological matters tend to produce children who excel on tests of spatial ability. However, the spatial problem used in the teaching interaction may elicit from the mothers behaviors that are most relevant to solutions of strictly spatial problems. Hence, the relationships observed here between maternal specificity and rate of cognitive development in the child might be very different if the study were to use a nonspatial task as a focus for the mother-child teaching interaction.

In this and previous studies, the mother's behavior has been observed in experimental settings in which the mother is teaching the child. Parallel results have been obtained measuring (a) the mother's verbal behavior and (b) the mother's kinesic behavior. An important question for future research is whether or not the observed behavior can be generalized to less rigidly structured interactional frameworks. Can we conclude that mothers who score high on specificity in the spatial/geometric teaching interaction experiment would also score high on specificity if observed at home in natural interaction with their children? Can we assume that mothers who score high on task relatedness in our experiments also pay more attention to their children's activities in other situations? The cross-cultural experiments on teaching interaction are based on the hope that such generalizations can be made; that mothers are consistent in their behavior from setting to setting, so that behavior in our experimental situation is a representative sample of the mother's overall teaching behavior. We suggest, then, that the next step in cross-cultural research on teaching interaction should combine the approach of Whiting and Whiting,[13] using systematic observations of mother-child teaching interaction at home in naturally occurring situations, with the present experimental approach. Since the present study uses a spatially oriented task (construction of a "Lego" car), while many naturally occurring interactions between mothers and children will have a nonspatial focus, it would at the same time be desirable to modify the present experiment by incorporating nonspatial tasks, such as verbal and motor learning problems, into the teaching interactions. With these two modifications of the present experimental design, it would be possible to compare maternal behavior at home with maternal behavior in the experimental teaching interaction, and to couple the two sets of observations in predicting the child's cognitive performance.

SUMMARY

The Kenya study has established that the rate of cognitive development in the child can be predicted from three nonverbally measured features of the mother's behavior: (a) her specificity in communication, (b) her attention to the experimental problem, and (c) her tendency to allow the child to perform operations for himself.

The Ghana and Kenya studies have together established (a) that both the verbal and nonverbal teaching styles of the mother can be used independently to predict the child's rate of cognitive development and (b) that verbal and nonverbal communicative specificity of the mother have parallel relationships with the child's cognitive growth rate.

The specificity of the mother's communication with her child seems to be a relevant variable in the development of cognitive ability. This variable may be both cross-cultural and cross-channel in its association with cognitive growth: it has appeared associated with the child's rate of cognitive growth in both cultures, and in both verbal and nonverbal channels of communication.

REFERENCES

1. COLE, M., J. GAY, J. GLICK & D. SHARP. 1971. The Cultural Context of Learning and Thinking. Basic Books. New York, N.Y.
2. HESS, R. D. & V. C. SHIPMAN. 1965. Early experience and the socialization of cognitive modes in children. Child Devel. 36: 869–886.

3. HESS, R. D. & V. C. SHIPMAN. 1968. Maternal influences upon early learning: the cognitive environments of urban preschool children. *In* Early Education. R. D. Hess and R. M. Bear, Eds. Aldine Publishing Company. Chicago, Ill.

4. HESS, R. D. & V. C. SHIPMAN. 1967a. Cognitive elements in maternal behavior. *In* Minnesota Symposia on Child Psychology. J. P. Hill, Ed. Vol. 1. University of Minnesota Press. Minneapolis, Minn.

5. HESS, R. D. & V. C. SHIPMAN. 1967b. Maternal attitude toward the school and the role of the pupil: Some social class comparisons. *In* Teaching and Learning in Depressed Areas. A. H. Passow, Ed. Columbia University Teacher's College. New York, N.Y.

6. HESS, R. D., V. SHIPMAN, J. BROPHY & R. BEAR. 1968. The Cognitive Environments of Urban Preschool Children. Graduate School of Education, University of Chicago. Chicago, Ill.

7. OLIM, E. G., R. D. HESS & V. C. SHIPMAN. 1967. Role of mother's language style in mediating the preschool children's cognitive development. *In* The School Review. 75(4). University of Chicago Press. Chicago, Ill.

8. FITZGERALD (KIRK), L. 1970. Cognitive Development among Ga Children: Environmental Correlates of Cognitive Growth Rate within the Ga Tribe. Doctoral dissertation. University Microfilms, University of California, Berkeley.

9. KIRK, L. 1977. Maternal and subcultural influence on cognitive growth rate: the Ga case. *In* Piagetian Psychology: Cross-Cultural Contributions. P. R. Dasen, Ed. Gardner Press. New York. In press.

10. KIRK, L. 1976. Cross-cultural measurement of maternal behavior in mother-child teaching interaction. *In* Quality and Quantity: European-American Journal of Methodology. **10**: 127–143.

11. KIRK, L. 1975. Estimating the ages of children in non-literate populations: a field method. Journal of Cross-Cultural Psychology 6(2): 238–249.

12. KIRK, L. & M. BURTON. 1976. Age estimation of children in the field: a follow-up study with attention to sex differences. Journal of Cross-Cultural Psychology. 7(3): 315–324.

13. WHITING, B. B. & J. M. WHITING. 1975. Children of Six Cultures. Harvard University Press. Cambridge, Mass.

THE PONZO ILLUSION AMONG THE BAGANDA OF UGANDA*

Philip L. Kilbride

*Department of Anthropology
Bryn Mawr College
Bryn Mawr, Pennsylvania 19010*

H. W. Leibowitz

*Department of Psychology
The Pennsylvania State University
University Park, Pennsylvania 16802*

Many cross-cultural studies have demonstrated that individuals from various cultural groups differ in their susceptibility to visual illusions. Such studies date back to that of Rivers in 1901.[1] The most recent comprehensive study is by Segall, Campbell, and Herskovits, who showed a marked effect of culture on illusion magnitude.[2] Some of the better researched illusions, all of which are seemingly affected by cultural factors, include the trapezoidal illusion,[3] the Muller-Lyer and horizontal-vertical illusions,[2,4,5] and the Ponzo perspective illusion.[6-9] To date, however, no satisfactory explanation for group differences in illusion susceptibility enjoys universal support among contemporary researchers in this field. The most commonly discussed theory is the "ecological hypothesis," which assumes that the influence of cues involved in producing an illusion depends ultimately upon an individual's history of exposure to the particular cues in question.[2] For example, exposure to such "carpentered" stimuli as street corners, square rooms, or other angular material artifacts is thought to be responsible for the effect seen with the Muller-Lyer figure. Environments rich in perspective (e.g., roads, railway tracks) or those that contain a broad open vista are hypothesized to produce an illusion response to the Ponzo and the horizontal-vertical illusions, respectively. Unfortunately, empirical findings do not always lend support to a simple causal relationship between environmental experience and perception. Such factors as mode of presentation, cognitive style, child-rearing patterns, retinal pigmentation, and sex are correlated with susceptibility to visual illusions.[10]

Of particular interest to the present paper are the many studies that show that cross-cultural differences also exist in the perception of pictorial depth cues such as perspective, object-size, and superimposition.[11-13] That is, individuals in cultures where exposure to reading materials, photographs, and representational art is limited or nonexistent are not generally cognizant of the symbolic cues that in our culture serve to indicate depth or distance on a two-dimensional pictorial surface. Growing up in a "pictureless environment" typically results in a cognitive disposition to view pictures in only two dimensions (perception of the "real world," of course, is three-dimensional, as in our own culture). The implications of these data for cross-cultural research involving visual illusions are profound for the following reasons: (1) the *spatial*

* The field research and analysis for this study were supported by Grants MH22538 and MH08061 from the National Institute of Mental Health.

cue of perspective, or, more broadly, cues to "distance," is theoretically thought to activate an illusory response for several illusions (e.g., Ponzo illusion, Muller-Lyer); (2) visual illusions are often presented in a pictorial mode; (3) pictorial depth perception is not a cultural universal. It follows therefore that individuals who are not cognizant of symbolic depth cues in pictures would *not* be expected to demonstrate an illusion even though their history of exposure to the relevant cues may be extensive. Many writers have, in fact, pointed out that pictorial depth perception "should be" an experiential factor of importance in illusion research.[2,4] Rarely, however, is research presented in which empirical data are provided that would establish the precise relationship between pictorial depth perception and performance on a given optical illusion. The purpose of the present paper is to provide such evidence for the Ponzo perspective illusion.

One of the oldest explanations offered for the Ponzo illusion (FIGURE 1) is that it represents the misapplication of depth cues that normally operate in three-dimensional space.[14] According to this theory, the perspective cue represented by depth cues such as railway tracks is usually associated with depth in three-dimensional space, and is inappropriately activated while viewing the two-dimensional Ponzo figure. Since in our normal interaction with space we "correct" for distant objects in the interest of size constancy, this same correction mechanism is misapplied in a two-dimensional presentation, thereby producing an illusory enlargement of the object located "far away" near the

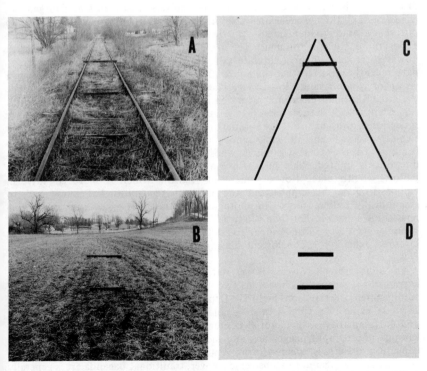

FIGURE 1.   The stimuli used in the main experiment. The extent of the horizontal lines in these examples is the same. (After Leibowitz *et al.*[6])

point of convergence of the figure. This "misplaced constancy" hypothesis is, in general, supported by both developmental and cross-cultural research. It has been determined that both the Ponzo illusion[15] and size constancy for distant objects[16,17] increase as a function of chronological but not of mental age. If one assumes that one of the monocular cues involved in size constancy is perspective, then it would follow that development of the strength of this cue, through developmentally acquired perceptual learning resulting from exposure to the environment, is responsible for the similar age trends reported for the Ponzo and size constancy data.

Cross-cultural research attempts to investigate populations of human subjects whose history of exposure to perspective cues is different from those found among American college populations. It should theoretically follow that individuals reared in an environment with fewer converging lines would exhibit a reduced Ponzo illusion as compared with those whose environment required many occasions to associate converging lines with distance. To date, one long-term cross-cultural project in Guam and Uganda has produced promising results in support of an ecological hypothesis.[6-8] Guam has no railroads; vistas on land are comparatively short due to hilly terrain; and roads are winding rather than straight. Guamanian University students produced significantly lower illusion magnitudes than did Pennsylvanian and Ugandan college students. The latter, like their American counterparts, have experienced exposure to straight roads, railway tracks, and comparatively "open" vistas. Although no data are provided, it is reasonable to assume that university students are, in general, cognizant of three-dimensional pictorial cues so that reported cross-group differences among Guamanians, Americans and Ugandans may very likely reflect exposure to the environment. The problem of pictorial depth perception is, however, crucial when nonliterate samples are included. Leibowitz and Pick[7] have recently reported that the Ponzo illusion is essentially nonexistent among a group of rural Baganda in Uganda. These data were particularly puzzling since the rural Ugandan environment is rich in perspective cues. Leibowitz and Pick suggested that "flatness cues" (e.g., absence of binocular disparity, surface reflections, presence of the border of the photograph, etc.) inherent in two-dimensional line drawings and photographs might have dominated the response of the rural Ugandans whose exposure to two-dimensional reproductions is limited. This line of reasoning is technically different from the pictorial depth perception argument of Hudson, which is more cognitive in emphasis since he emphasized the lack of recognition of cues used to symbolically indicate depth in photograph portrayals (e.g., overlap, converging lines, object size) rather than "flatness" cues. In any case, both interpretations would suggest a two-dimensional bias in the rural Ugandan sample, which would, in turn, explain the nonexistent illusion response reported by Leibowitz and Pick.

Previous research in Uganda does, in fact, show that rural, traditional Baganda overall do perceive pictures in two dimensions. Kilbride and Robbins[18] administered the Hudson Pictorial Depth Perception Test[11,12] to 104 adult Baganda living in a rural area of Uganda. These individuals had experienced a limited familiarity with pictorial content and three-dimensional representation through photographs, magazines, and motion pictures. Their exposure to formal education in schools, where the conventions of western pictorial representation are learned, was also not extensive. Moreover, traditional Baganda art is generally nonrepresentational. Baskets and woven mats containing two-dimensional geometric designs are widely used by these rural Baganda. When asked to identify a road (linear perspective cue) appearing in Hudson's test, 87% of the Baganda reported a two-dimensional object (e.g., hill, ladder, house, camera tripod, pitchfork). In the same study 118 urban-living Baganda were also shown the Hudson pictures. The mean of 7.47 years of schooling per urban subject, although not high, is nevertheless double that of the rural sample. Whereas most rural Baganda are farmers, 29% of the urban sample are teachers, engineers, nurses, clerks, and secretaries. These modern occupations include considerable exposure to printed matter. The higher educational level and comparatively greater participation in modern occupations of the urban group are reflected in their response to the Hudson "road." A significantly greater proportion (35%) of the urban sample responded "road," whereas only 13% of the rural sample were cognizant of the linear perspective cue. These data show that (1) most Baganda perceive pictures in the second dimension and (2) pictorial depth perception is acquired with exposure to western conventions of pictorial representation (for example, in schools and modern jobs).

Recent Ugandan data[9] demonstrate (1) the importance of pictorial perception as a factor in the magnitude of Ponzo illusion and (2) that cognitive factors may be more salient than flatness cues. This study utilized the same stimuli and procedures as in the previous experiments, and was carried out in the same geographical area of Uganda. The illusion was evaluated by means of a series of stimuli with increasing amounts of context, including a plain background, a background consisting of two converging lines (classical Ponzo figure), a photograph of a plowed field, and a photograph of railroad tracks (FIGURE 1). A progressively larger illusion effect is predicted as the richness of the background depth cues is increased.

EXPERIMENT I

Method

The original sample consisted of 105 Baganda. For reasons to be mentioned later, only 82 Baganda, 53 males and 29 females, are included in the present analysis. These subjects ranged in age from 16 to 80 years, with a mean of 31 years. Formal education varied from none to 12 years, with a mean of 5.5 years. The subjects were selected from the same rural Ugandan population as in the previous study. However, an effort was made to include subjects who varied in the amount of their formal education as well as two-dimensional reproductions in their homes. Most of these subjects were full or part-time cultivators, with some working in clerical or commercial occupations. Therefore, the sample varied in both education and in terms of exposure to mass media. Many homes, for example, contain photographs, printed materials, and in a few cases television sets. Their visual environment typically consists of small hills of no more than 500 feet in height, separated by valleys. Human settlement is usually confined to the higher elevations, with the homes dispersed and embedded among plantain gardens. Numerous roads and paths transverse the area, offering vistas with perspective, sometimes for several miles. The Baganda tend to reside on or near roads, which are important in their daily commerce and communication.

Before administration of the Ponzo figures, each subject was shown the track

FIGURE 2. Photographs of a rural road in Uganda. This photograph, along with that shown in FIGURE 1A, was utilized in the preliminary experiment to classify the subjects as "two-" or "three-" dimensional perceivers. (After Kilbride and Leibowitz[9].)

stimulus and a photograph of a local road (FIGURE 2) and asked, "What do you see?" While asking the question, the experimenter traced his finger over the railroad tracks or the borders of the road. The purpose of this procedure was to classify subjects as "two"- or "three"-dimensional perceivers, following the distinction made by Kilbride and Robbins.[18] The subjects were classified as three-dimensional if responses to both photographs corresponded to three-dimensional objects, i.e., road, track, river, or bridge. Two-dimensional perceivers were so classified if their responses corresponded to two-dimensional objects in both cases, i.e., house, ladder (most frequent), hill, roof, hill with ladder. Those subjects who gave a two-dimensional response to one stimulus and a three-dimensional one to the other were classified as "mixed." A description of the three groups by age, sex, and education is given in TABLE 1. TABLE 2 shows the range of object identifications considered to be "two-dimensional."

TABLE 1

SEX, AGE AND EDUCATIONAL DATA FOR EACH SUBGROUP

Subgroup	Male	Female	Mean Age (yr)	Mean Educational Level (yr)
2-D	11	8	36.2	4.4
Mixed	8	3	39.2	4.1
3-D	34	18	27.4	6.2

TABLE 2

TWO-DIMENSIONAL OBJECT IDENTIFICATIONS

Road Stimulus	N	Railtrack Stimulus	N
House	14	Ladder	15
Hill	3	House	4
Roof	1	Roof	2
		Hill	2
		Hill w/ladder	1
		Poles	1

Administration and scoring methods of the Ponzo test were identical to those followed in the previous studies.† Twenty-three subjects were eliminated because they failed to produce correct judgments for both extreme conditions in one or more series of stimuli.

Results

The principal datum, the magnitude of the Ponzo illusion expressed as the percentage overestimation of the upper line for the four backgrounds, is presented for the various background conditions in FIGURE 3, with the data for

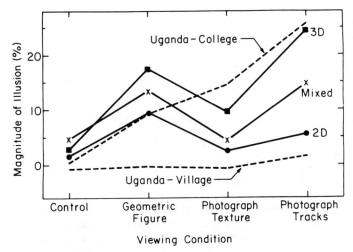

FIGURE 3. The magnitude of the Ponzo illusion for the principal stimuli reproduced in FIGURE 1. The subjects have been separated into groups based on their responses to the preliminary test. For comparison, the data from the previous study are indicated by the dotted lines. (After Kilbride and Leibowitz[9].)

the subjects separated, depending upon whether they were classified in the "two-," "three-," or "mixed-" dimensional categories. For comparison, the data from the previous study for the villagers and for the college students are also reproduced. It will be noted that the data for the three-dimensional perceivers are similar to those of the college students in the previous Ugandan (as well as Pennsylvanian) study. The general trend of the data is the same for the mixed

† Test administration was in Luganda. Instructions were translated into Luganda through the technique of back translation. Each subject was asked (for 10 cards on each of the four series): "On each of these pictures there are two horizontal lines." "I want you to tell me which of the two lines is longer than the other. If it is the top, say 'top.' If it is the bottom, say 'bottom.' " ("*Ku buli bifaananyi bino, kuliko ennyiriri biri ez'obukiika. Njagala ombulire kunyiriri ezo ebiri luluwa olusinga lunalwo obuwanvu. Bweruba nga lwawaggulu 'gamba nti lwawagullu' bweruba nga lwawansi 'gamba nit lwawansi.' "*) In all stimulus cards, the upper line was constant in length while the length of the lower lines was presented in random order. For all observation conditions, the equality value was determined by interpolation as the midpoint of the region at which the subject's responses changed. The magnitude of the overestimation, or illusion, is the percentage overestimation of the upper line.

and for the two-dimensional perceivers, but the absolute values are systematically lower.

A two-way analysis of variance with repeated measures was performed for the illusion scores for the "2-D," "mixed," and "3-D" groups.[19] This analysis indicated that there was a significant effect of groups (F = 11.05, df = 2,79, p < .01), a significant series effect (F = 43.64, df = 3,237, p < .01), and a significant interaction (F = 4.64, df = 6,237, p < .05).

An analysis of the simple main effects for the series factor was performed. This analysis showed that for both the "3-D" group and the "mixed" group there was a significant series effect (F = 47.60, df = 3,237, p < .01, and F = 47.60, df = 3,237, p < .05, respectively), whereas the "2-D" group showed no significant effect of series (F = 2.31, df = 3,237, p > .05). These findings are interpreted to support the expectation that Baganda who perceive depth (e.g., perspective) in pictures are responsive to the Ponzo illusion, whereas those who perceive no depth are not responsive.

An analysis of the simple main effects for the group factor was also performed. This analysis showed that for both the control and geometric viewing conditions there was no significant group effect (F = .41, df = 2,316, p > .05, and F = .90, df = 2,316, p > .05, respectively). For both the phototexture and the phototrack series, there was a significant group effect (F = 3.94, df = 2,316, p < .05, and F = 21.92, df = 2,316, p < .01, respectively). These data indicate that there is a significant difference among "2-D," "mixed," and "3-D" groups in the photographic viewing contexts only.

In effect, the classification of the subjects, based on the results of the preliminary tests, reveals that the results for the rural Ugandans classified as three-dimensional perceivers are strikingly similar to those of the college-educated groups previously tested. The two-dimensional perceivers show no illusion magnitude for any of the background conditions, as reported previously for a group of rural Ugandans. The mixed group produced intermediate illusion values.

EXPERIMENT II

Experiment II was designed as a direct test of the hypothesis that flatness cues may have been responsible for the lack of illusion magnitude in the previous study as well as accounting for the similar results for the two-dimensional perceivers in Experiment I of the present investigation. To this end, the same stimuli were presented in a viewing box specially designed to minimize flatness cues. The stimuli were mounted vertically at a distance of 63 cm and viewed against an opaque background. This viewing distance was chosen because it represented the "ortho" viewing position, i.e., the distance at which the absolute angular dimensions of the stimuli are identical to those in the original scene from the camera position. This distance has been shown to maximize the "reality" or "plastic" depth in photographs.[20,21] This arrangement also minimizes cues to flatness, such as the familiar background against which the stimuli are ordinarily viewed, borders, and reflections from the surface.

Twenty-six additional rural Baganda subjects, selected and tested in the same manner as those in Experiment I, were utilized. The data, separated into two-dimensional and three-dimensional perceivers (there were no mixed responses among this group), are plotted in FIGURE 4. The three-dimensional group is similar to the previous three-dimensional perceivers as well as to the college students, whereas the two-dimensional group, as was true for the previous subjects, demonstrated no increase in illusion magnitude with increasing background complexity.

A two-way analysis of variance with repeated measures on one factor for the illusion magnitudes for the "two-dimensional" and "three-dimensional" groups indicated that there was a significant effect of groups (F = 28.80, df = 1,24, p < .01), a significant series effect (F = 4.10, df = 3,72, p < .01), and a significant interaction (F = 5.10, df = 3,72, p < .01).

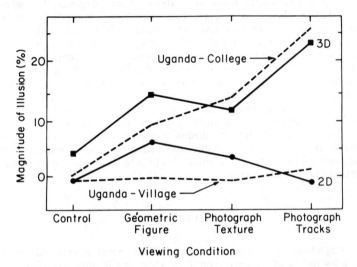

FIGURE 4. The magnitude of the Ponzo illusion under presentation conditions designed to eliminate or minimize cues to flatness. Classification as 2D or 3D is based on the preliminary test. For comparison, the data from the previous study are indicated by the dotted lines. (After Kilbride and Leibowitz[9].)

An analysis of the simple main effects for the series factor showed that for the "three-dimensional" group there was a significant series effect (F = 6.90, df = 3,72, p < .01). whereas the "two-dimensional" group showed no significant effect of series (F = 2.47, df = 3,72, p > .05). These findings are interpreted to support the cognitive style interpretation, since Baganda who perceive no depth (e.g., perspective) in pictures are not responsive to Ponzo stimuli in a viewing situation where flatness cues have been markedly reduced, whereas "three-dimensional" perceivers are responsive.

An analysis of the simple main effects for the group factor was also performed. This analysis showed that for both the control and geometric viewing conditions there was no significant group effect (F = 1.69, df = 1,24, p > .05, and F = 4.01, df = 1,24, p > .05, respectively). For both the phototexture and the phototrack series, there was a significant group effect (F = 4.27, df = 1,24, p < .05, and F = 31.66, df = 1,24, p < .01, respectively). These data indicate that there is a significant difference between "2-D" and "3-D" groups in photographic viewing contexts only.

DISCUSSION

The present study provides empirical support for the hypothesis that a cognitive factor is responsible for the previously observed differences in illusion magnitude between populations of college students as compared with rural Ugandan villagers. Contrariwise, the hypothesis that the group differences are a result of the ability to disregard flatness cues must be rejected. The critical factor is whether the subjects are sensitive to symbolic depth cues as evidenced by their responses to the pretest photographs. This finding is in agreement with the ecological hypothesis mentioned above. Rural Baganda, for whom the pictorial Ponzo illusion is relevant (e.g., the "3-D" group), do produce an illusion. This is not surprising given the visual ecology of rural Baganda. The present data have methodological implications for future cross-cultural research involving the Ponzo, and perhaps other illusions. Unless attention is paid to the intervening variable of pictorial perception, there is a danger of falsely interpreting a lack of responsiveness as due to a reduced strength of the space cues in question. To avoid this problem, three-dimensional stimuli should be used whenever possible, thus bypassing the question of whether the subjects are responsive to cues presented in the two-dimensional mode. With this precaution being borne in mind, future illusion research should be directed toward nonliterate populations who inhabit contrasting visual environments. Developmental studies in such societies would also help to fill the void present currently in this important research area.

SUMMARY

The magnitude of the Ponzo perspective illusion was determined among rural Baganda by means of pictorial stimuli in which the illusion was embedded in a series with increasing depth cue complexity. For some Baganda, there was a systematic increase in the illusion magnitude and the trend of the background cue complexity was similar to that found among American and urban Ugandan college students. However, for other rural subjects, essentially no illusion was found. The difference between these groups is based on a cognitive factor in pictorial depth perception. Those subjects who gave three-dimensional responses to photographic stimuli are classified as "3-D perceivers," whereas those for whom the same stimuli elicited two-dimensional responses are classified as "2-D perceivers." The trends for the 3-D perceivers among the rural population were similar to those of the college students, while the 2-D perceivers were relatively insensitive to the depth cues inherent in these stimuli. Implications for cross-cultural research with pictorial stimuli as well as for perceptual methodology and theory are discussed.

ACKNOWLEDGMENTS

The senior author would like to express his gratitude to those at the Makerere Institute of Social Research, Makerere University College, Kampala, Uganda, for their assistance during his tenure there as a senior research associate from June

1972 to May 1973. Professors Clive Davis and Michael C. Robbins offered invaluable assistance during various phases of the field research and Mr. Joseph Busuulwa served as our Muganda colleague throughout various phases of the field work.

REFERENCES

1. RIVERS, W. H. R. 1901. Introduction and Vision. *In* Reports of the Cambridge Anthropological Expeditions to the Torres Straits (2). A. C. Hadden, Ed. The University Press. Cambridge, England.
2. SEGALL, N. H., D. T. CAMBELL & M. J. HERSKOVITS. 1966. The Influence of Culture on Visual Perception. Bobbs-Merrill Co. New York, N.Y.
3. ALLPORT, G. W. & T. F. PETTIGREW. 1957. Cultural influence on the perception of movement: The trapezoidal illusion among Zulus. J. Abnormal Social Psychol. **55**: 104–113.
4. JAHODA, G. 1966. Geometric illusions and environment: A study in Ghana. Brit. J. Psychol. **57**: 193–199.
5. DAVIS, C. M. & M. H. SEGALL. 1971. Effect of relative positions of segments on strength of the Mueller-Lyer illusion. Perceptual and Motor Skills **33**: 1051–1058.
6. LEIBOWITZ, H. W., R. BRISLIN, L. PERLMUTTER & R. HENNESSY. 1969. Ponzo perspective illusion as a manifestation of space perception. Science **166**: 1174–1176.
7. LEIBOWITZ, H. W. & H. PICK. 1972. Cross-cultural and educational aspects of the Ponzo illusion. Perception and Psychophysics **12**: 403–432.
8. BRISLIN, R. W. 1974. The Ponzo illusion, additional cues, age, orientation, and culture. J. Cross-Cultural Psychol. **5**(2): 139–161.
9. KILBRIDE, P. L. & H. W. LEIBOWITZ. 1975. Factors affecting the magnitude of the Ponzo perspective illusion among the Baganda. Perception and Psychophysics **17**(6): 543–548.
10. STEWART, V. M. 1971. A Cross-cultural Test of the "Carpentered Environment" Hypothesis Using Three Geometric Illusions in Zambia. Unpublished doctoral dissertation. Northwestern University, Chicago, Ill.
11. HUDSON, W. 1960. Pictorial depth perception in sub-cultural groups in Africa. J. Social Psychol. **52**: 209–219.
12. HUDSON, W. 1967. The study of the problem of pictorial perception among unacculturated groups. Internat. J. Psychol. **2**: 90–107.
13. MILLER, R. J. 1973. Cross-cultural research in the perception of pictorial materials. Psychol. Bull. **80**: 135–150.
14. GREGORY, R. L. 1963. Distortion of visual space as inappropriate constancy scaling. Nature **199**: 678–680.
15. LEIBOWITZ, H. W. & J. JUDISCH. 1967. The relation between age and the magnitude of the Ponzo illusion. Am. J. Psychol. **80**: 105–109.
16. ZEIGLER, H. P. & H. W. LEIBOWITZ. 1957. Apparent visual size as a function of distance for children and adults. Am. J. Psychol. **70**: 106–109.
17. LEIBOWITZ, H. W., S. W. POLLARD & D. DICKSON. 1967. Monocular and binocular size-matching as a function of distance at various age levels. Am. J. Psychol. **80**: 263–268.
18. KILBRIDE, P. L. & M. C. ROBBINS. 1969. Pictorial depth perception and acculturation among Baganda. Am. Anthropol. **71**(2): 293–302.
19. WINER, B. J. 1962. Statistical Principles in Experimental Design. McGraw-Hill. New York, N.Y.
20. HARDY, A. C. & F. H. PERRIN. 1932. The Principles of Optics: 465–469. McGraw-Hill. New York, N.Y.
21. SCHLOSBERG, H. 1941. Stereoscopic depth from single pictures. Am. J. Psychol. **54**: 601–605.

SUBJECTIVE CULTURE AND INTERPERSONAL RELATIONS
ACROSS CULTURES

Harry C. Triandis

Department of Psychology
University of Illinois at Urbana-Champaign
Champaign, Illinois 61820

It seems appropriate for a conference on cross-cultural research to focus to some extent on the future directions of such research. My particular area of interest is social behavior, with a special concern for the cultural determinants of social behavior. This paper will examine directions for research on the relationship between ecology and social behavior.

The topic is, of course, central to social psychology. Social psychology is now in a state of crisis. There are many reasons for this crisis, which I have discussed elsewhere.[42] I will here only summarize some of the arguments.

(1) The variables of social psychological theories account for too little variance. Most social phenomena are outcomes of many and complex influences. Any process summarized or modeled by a theory is like a drop in the bucket when it comes to accounting for a phenomenon. The drop may be real (valid) enough, yet it makes very little difference. To use an analogy, imagine Newton's problem, when he was working on mechanics, if the forces of *friction* had been immense, relative to the force of gravity and the other forces he was considering. The laws he developed would still be valid, but they would have almost no social relevance.

(2) The variables of social psychological theories are operating as the theory specifies in only a limited range of samples of people and in limited time periods. Interactions between variables across samples and across time are so important that main effects are often of little social significance. Cronbach[8] has summarized the argument for the importance of interactions, and has even challenged time-honored laws, such as Weber's Law, which states that a person's difference limen is smaller for stimuli of smaller magnitude. Gergen[13] has presented the case for interactions involving time.

(3) Our theories do not make point predictions. Meehl[30] observed that when we predict a difference (as most experiments that involve an experimental and a control group do) rather than a particular value – or at least a region within which the values of observations are likely to be found – the more observations we make, the more likely we are to reject the null hypothesis and accept our theory. If we use very large samples to test our theories, any theory, no matter how idiotic, has a .5 probability of being confirmed.[27]

The crisis in social psychology has been discussed by many. McGuire[29] has offered prescriptions for new directions, suggesting that we must (a) develop more complicated theories, (b) train our students to be creative, (c) reject linear models in favor of interactive and feedback models, (d) obtain much broader data bases by making more observations without theory, (e) use more social data archives, (f) collect data at different points in time and use path analysis or related procedures to determine the direction of causation, and so on. Harré and Secord[16] presented an approach that is a radical departure from present social psychological theorizing. Israel and Tajfel[19] offered much criticism and some suggestions for new directions.

But the crisis seems even deeper. It seems to be a fundamental crisis for all the social sciences that has to do with the impossibility of applying theories, in the sense that the term "theory" is used in the physical sciences.

Perhaps the most fundamental challenge comes from those who are steeped in epistemology and the philosophy of science, such as Meehl.[31,32] Meehl[31] goes so far as to say that he is forced to the "conclusion that a large portion of current research in the behavioral sciences, while meeting the conventionally accepted standards of adequate design, must be viewed as methodologically unsound." (pp. 401–402)

My conclusion from reading this literature is as follows: Theory that might account for reasonably broad social phenomena, as opposed to a limited phenomenon, is an illusory goal. But we can do two things: (1) We can describe particular populations, at particular points in time. (2) We can develop loose theoretical frameworks that include the explanatory concepts likely to deal with particular social phenomena, and learn which frameworks to use for what purposes. The frameworks will help us think about broad social phenomena, but they will not be either predictive systems or systems that account tightly for the complexity of these phenomena.

This conclusion is not too different from the conclusion that Cronbach[8] reaches in his recent paper: "Though enduring systematic theories about man in society are not likely to be achieved, systematic inquiry can realistically hope to make two contributions. One reasonable aspiration is to assess local events accurately, to improve short-run control (Glass, 1972). The other reasonable aspiration is to develop explanatory concepts, concepts that will help people use their heads." (p. 126) Cronbach ends his paper with the following point: "The special task of the social scientist in each generation is to pin down the contemporary facts. Beyond that, he shares with the humanistic scholar and the artist in the effort to gain insight into contemporary relationships, and to realign the culture's view of man with present realities. To know man as he is no mean aspiration." (p. 126)

The genius of the social scientists, in my opinion, lies in the development of methodology. We are also good at developing loose theoretical frameworks that suggest *what* we must look for in any particular social situation. However, our real contribution is in demonstrating *how* to look — how to check the reliability of observations, and how to combine the myriads of observations into meaningful patterns that can be communicated to other people. If what we can do best is describe, we had better produce superb descriptions. But the second task, the development of theoretical frameworks that hold from one time and place to another, is no less important. We must make sure that the framework will consist of *concepts* and *dimensions* that are universal across time and space. In the present paper I will attempt to explore concepts that might become part of such a framework.

The specific focus of this paper is on interpersonal behavior. First, it will be argued that interpersonal behavior has some universal (etic) attributes that can become the standards of investigations in all cultures. Second, the etic determinants of these attributes will be discussed. Among these determinants is the way different groups of humans perceive their social environment, which is defined as their "subjective culture." Third, the relationship between subjective culture and behavior will be discussed. In the fourth section of the paper, it will be argued that we need to learn about varieties of subjective culture and interpersonal behavior in different kinds of ecologies. A model of such relationships will be presented. Finally, the overall research strategy for establishing evidence of such relationships will be outlined and some early experiments will be reviewed.

The study of interpersonal behavior across cultures is not only central to social psychology, but it has also important applied aspects, since the increase in international travel has changed enormously the opportunities for interaction across cultures. While the central focus here will be on dyads, where one member has been socialized in one culture and another member has been socialized in a different culture, the argument applies generally to dyads consisting of individuals who differ in their social experiences. For instance, when two people differ in age, sex, social class, race, or other such attributes, they often develop points of view about social behavior that are sufficiently different to lead to difficulties in inter-personal communication and behavior.

The next two sections of the paper are attempts to develop an etic theory of social behavior. Such a theory by its very nature is a challenge to anthropologists, who will want to discover instances where the theory does not apply. Attempts to disconfirm this theory should improve our understanding of social behavior in different ecologies.

ETIC DIMENSIONS OF INTERPERSONAL BEHAVIOR

There is considerable evidence now available that four etic dimensions characterize social behavior. These dimensions are reflected in discussions of (a) the behavior of primates,[28] (b) observations of the behavior of children in different cultures,[25,49] (c) observations of undergraduates in laboratory settings,[3] (d) peer ratings,[34] (e) observations of mother behavior,[52] (f) observations of leader behavior,[39] (g) self-reports both within a culture[26,4] and across cultures,[47,11] (h) proxemic behavior,[33] (i) descriptions of personality,[23] and (j) the perception of emotion,[38,44,50,35] and have much in common with Osgood's dimensions of affective meaning.[36] The fact that the same dimensions emerge in different cultures across different kinds of observations, research methods, and topics suggests that they reflect some fundamental, etic characteristic of human social behavior. In TABLE 1 the studies mentioned earlier are listed together with the four dimensions. All dimensions do not emerge in all studies, because when there is no variance in a given dimension it does not have a chance to emerge.

The four dimensions are as follows:

I.   *Association* (including helping, supporting, agreeing) versus *dissociation* (including avoiding, aggressing against, hurting, blocking).

II. *Superordination* (including criticizing, supervising, checking) versus *subordination* (including obeying, asking for help, asking for advice).

III. *Intimacy* (including kissing, petting, touching) versus *formality* (including writing a "thank-you" note, greeting in formal manner).

IV. *Overtness* (including visible behavior like hitting, kissing) versus *covertness* (including thinking, feeling, planning behavior with another).

TABLE 1

EMPIRICAL SUPPORT FOR TYPOLOGY OF SOCIAL BEHAVIOR

	Dimension			
Study	Association-Dissociation	Superordination-Subordination	Intimacy-Formality	Overt Covert
Triandis et al[4][7] (1972)	*	*	*	*
Bales[3] (1950)	*	*		
Norman[3][4] (1969)	*	*		
Mason[2][8] (1964)	*	*		
Foa[1][0] (1971)	*	*	*	
Schaefer[5][2] (1965)	*	*		
Benjamin[4] (1974)	*	*		
Mehrabian[3][3] (1970)	*	*	*	
Lorr and McNair[2][6] (1965)	*	*		
LaForge and Suczek[2][0] (1955)	*	*		
Stogdill and Coons[3][9] (1957)	*	*		
Longabaugh[2][5] (1966)	*	*		
Whiting and Whiting[4][9] (1975)	*		*	
Leary[2][3] (1957)	*	*		
Schlosberg[3][8] (1954)	*	*		*
Triandis and Lambert[4][4] (1958)	*	*		*
Lambert and Lambert-Wolf[5][0] (1973)	*	*		*
Osgood[3][5],[3][6] (1966, 1971)	*	*		*
Brown[6] (1965)	*		*	

ETIC DETERMINANTS OF THE ETIC DIMENSIONS

Different researchers have, of course, given different names to the four basic dimensions of social behavior. This should not confuse us. Upon reflection it is perfectly clear why variations in social behavior along these four dimensions are likely to emerge.

The first dimension, association-dissociation, reflects the nature of interdependence among humans. If two persons, or two groups, have many common goals they will tend to behave associatively; if they have goals that preclude the other person or group from reaching its own goals, behavior will be dissociative. Humans are organized in groups involving cooperation and competition to exploit the resources of their environment. Cooperative groups include family, tribe, nation, or other units that humans use as *ingroups*. For particular individuals the scope of such an ingroup can be very narrow (say, the nuclear family) or very wide (say, mankind). One can see that in certain cultures the ingroup is narrow. For example, Foster's discussion[12] of limited good, a point of view that supposedly is found among peasants, describes it as characteristic of societies with narrow ingroups. Triandis and Vassiliou[46] have discussed the functions of the ingroup in traditional Greek society.

Superordination-subordination, the second dimension, is usually a reflection of resource distribution. While the first dimension is concerned with who is going to cooperate/compete in exploiting resources, the second is concerned with who is going to control others. Of course, this is usually done by controlling resources. Resources are of many kinds — love, status, information, goods, services.[11] A person who is in a position to give a resource can act superordinately; one who must seek a resource usually acts subordinately.

It is a common observation that as people interact, their interpersonal relationship changes. First-encounter associative interaction is characterized by formality and by little amplitude (it rarely includes screams, a great deal of physical contact, or an intensive experience). Such formal behavior is likely to be under the control of norms, to a much greater extent than intimate behavior. Old and well-established relationships permit intimacy. As people interact they establish "credit" with each other. One is willing to tolerate behavior that is adverse to himself, if it comes from an old friend or relative, which one would not tolerate from a new acquaintance. Credit is created when the rewards received from the interaction exceed the costs of the interaction. As credit builds up, more intimacy is possible, since behavior that is not in accordance with norms (and hence unexpected) can be tolerated.

Intimate behavior has a larger impact in changing a relationship, within a given unit of time, than does formal behavior. Kissing or hitting is a more significant event for a social relationship than is a polite greeting. When much credit is established, an intimate behavior that has negative consequences for the relationship usually does not destroy it, while such a behavior can terminate the relationship when there is no credit.

Rewards are behaviors that give a resource, such as love, information, or money, to another. However, it is not so much the behavior itself, but the *meaning* to the recipient of the behavior, that determines if it is rewarding. For example, if A gives money to B, B will react in one way if he attributes to A's behavior the cause "he is trying to help me," and in a different way if he attributes to A's behavior the cause "he is trying to bribe me." In short, it is not the objective but the subjective aspect of the interpersonal event that determines whether an interpersonal behavior is rewarding.

In addition, behavior that is expected is rewarding, while behavior that is very unexpected is often disorienting and can create a problem for the relationship. For example, if A was expected to give a $20 Christmas present and instead gives a $2000 present, this action is likely to create a problem in spite of the greater value of the exchanged resource. It is, in part, the unexpected and inappropriate character of the exchange that creates the problem.

Finally, the consequences of the behavior may determine part of the reaction to it. For example, if A gives a compliment to B, but B realizes that this creates many problems in his relationships with his peers, he will not appreciate A's compliment nearly as much as if such consequences were not perceived. Again it is to be noted that subjective factors, such as the perceived consequences of a behavior, are important in understanding the behavior's reward value. Similar analyses lead to the argument that costs are behaviors that remove or deny resources, that are unexpected, and that appear to have negative consequences.

It is clear that some behaviors are covert because the consequences of overt behavior are perceived to be negative. For example, one might criticize his supervisor's behavior, but not in front of the supervisor. Many kinds of inter-personal behavior, such as those involving fantasies, plans, or problem-solving, are much easier when covert than when carried out overtly.

Other *probably* universal interpersonal relationships are those that involve reciprocity and equity. The norm of reciprocity — e.g., if someone does something good for you, you must at least not harm him, and if possible you must return the favor — appears to be universal.[15] Similarly, the norm of equity appears in many societies, though its universality is not as yet established. According to one version of this norm, a rich person should spend more money for the the common good than should a poor person. Gregory,[14] basing his findings on work he did among the Mopan Maya Indians, uses a cumbersome term, *expectation of circumstantially balanced reciprocity*, to describe equity. Several anthropologists in responding to his description found this process present in many societies with which they were familiar, suggesting that equity may be a general human cognitive mechanism for dealing with resources and their allocation among people.

To summarize this section, then, we have argued that there are four universal dimensions that characterize interpersonal behavior. These dimensions are a function of the way humans exchange resources, change their relationships through time, and give meaning to interpersonal behavior. The meaning of interpersonal exchanges helps to determine the course of the interaction, as do subjective reactions to overt social behavior. The argument is that the dimensions described above are universals of interpersonal behavior.

If subjective reactions to interpersonal behavior are important, we need to examine them. The study of subjective culture does just that.

SUBJECTIVE CULTURE

Culture can be defined as the man-made part of the human environment.[17] Subjective culture is the subjective response to the man-made part of the environment, or a group's characteristic way of perceiving its social environment. Certain aspects of subjective culture are particularly important in determining social behavior. These include *norms, roles, perceived consequences of behavior*, the *values* of different interpersonal exchanges, the *expectations* of behavior and the *attributions* made concerning the causes of this behavior. This last determination often utilizes the other factors. For example, a person might attribute the behavior of another to norms or roles.

In studies of subjective culture[36,47] individuals from different communities are asked to make judgments concerning the extent to which social stimuli are associated with particular attributes. FIGURE 1 shows some typical judgments have been asked of subjects. The social stimuli can be generated following a factorial design, thus allowing for an analysis of variance of the relative importance and significance of the attributes related to each stimulus. Samples of scales, reflecting the behaviors of interest, can be included. Both the social stimuli and the attributes are usually derived from an elicitation procedure that has much in common with ethnographic interviewing.[45] Tucker's[48] three-mode factors analysis is often most conveniently used. This procedure yields (a) the factors that characterize the stimulus persons, (b) the factors that characterize the attributes, and (c) the patterns of consistency among the responses of the subjects, as well as the relationships among these three sets of factors. Thus one is able to make statements of the general form: "People of type X judge stimuli of type Y as high on attribute type Z." Consistencies among such statements, derived from different methods of data collection, can avoid artifacts that are due to method variance having determined the particular factor structures. A study by Triandis and Vassiliou[46] is an example of the use of this approach in comparisons of Greek and American subjective cultures; a study by Triandis[43] is an example of its use in analyzing varieties of subjective culture among blacks and whites in the Midwest.

While the multidimensional structures so extracted give the differences in point of view that characterize particular populations, they do not necessarily help in the *prediction* of social behavior. However, a specific subset of subjective culture measures, placed in a model presented by Triandis,[41,42] does predict behavior. For example, Adamopoulos and Brinberg[1] predicted the behavior of university students in volunteering for an experiment with a multiple correlation of .6 (p < .001). Pomazal[51] predicted volunteering to give blood at a blood clinic (an associative behavior) with a multiple correlation of .51 (p < .01). Landis, Triandis, and Adamopoulos[21] predicted classroom behavior of teachers towards their pupils with multiple correlations ranging from zero to .45 (p < .001). In the last study it was not possible to predict the frequency of physical contact, or the frequency of affective clarification (giving explanations to a student that clarify the bases of his feelings, e.g., fear, happiness). However, accuracy of prediction of the frequency of corrective feedback and of making requests and commands (superordinate behaviors) was good. This model is a step in the direction of considering interactions of behavior and situation.

Habits: Observations of the frequency of the behavior under similar conditions

or   Asking subject: e.g., "How many times have you given blood to a

          blood clinic?"

Behavioral Intentions

A 25-year old, black, medical student, whose father is an unskilled laborer

    would ____:____:____:____:____:____:____:____:____ would not
                              date

Role Perceptions

    Medical Student--Medical Student
        (male)   (female)

    would ____:____:____:____:____:____:____:____:____ would
                              date

    black male--white female

    would ____:____:____:____:____:____:____:____:____ would not
                              date

Norms

Do you believe that your parents would approve or disapprove of your dating a

25-year old, black, male, medical student, whose father is an unskilled laborer?

Would strongly approve ____:____:____:____:____:____:____:____:____ Would strongly
                                                                     disapprove

Do you believe that your friends would approve or disapprove of your dating...

Self-Concept

Are you the kind of person who would date a 25-year old, black, medical student, whose father is an unskilled laborer?

Definitely yes ___:___:___:___:___:___:___:___:___ Definitely no

Do you feel that you have a moral obligation to date a 25-year old, black, medical...

Affect toward the Act

Dating a 25-year old, black, medical student, whose father is an unskilled laborer would be

delightful ___:___:___:___:___:___:___:___:___ disgusting

dull   ___:___:___:___:___:___:___:___:___ exciting

enjoyable ___:___:___:___:___:___:___:___:___ nauseating

Perceived Consequences

If I date a 25-year old, black, medical student, whose father is an unskilled laborer, the chances are that I will be invited to dinner at his father's house.

Chances: ___:___:___:___:___:___:___:___:___:___
          0   1   2   3   4   5   6   7   8   9   10

out of 10

Value of Consequences

Being invited to dinner at the house of the father of a 25-year old, black, medical student, whose father is an unskilled laborer

good   ___:___:___:___:___:___:___:___:___ bad

pleasant   ___:___:___:___:___:___:___:___:___ unpleasant

disagreeable ___:___:___:___:___:___:___:___:___ agreeable

Layout for Analysis

Three-mode factor analysis is particularly appropriate for this situation, and the layout is shown below. See Tucker (1966) for details.

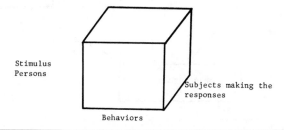

FIGURE 1. Typical operationalizations of the variables of the model.

In summary, there is evidence that certain subjective culture measures do relate to observed social behavior. A model we have used to make predictions of such relations appears to be satisfactory, at least for some behaviors. Limitations of space preclude a presentation of the conditions under which the model is appropriate; these are discussed in Triandis.[53]

Given that some subjective culture variables do predict behavior, there are a number of interesting questions that can be asked. The most important is: "What is the relationship between ecology and subjective culture on the one hand, and subjective culture and interpersonal behavior on the other hand? To assist in the speculations that follow, a broader and more schematic model of behavior is needed.

A BROAD MODEL OF SOCIAL BEHAVIOR

FIGURE 2 presents a broad model of social behavior. The *ecology* includes the flora and fauna, climate, terrain, resources, and so on, that are characteristic of a given geographical location. The *individual system* includes modes of perception, thinking, and behaving of individuals in the particular environment. An important aspect of this system, *subjective culture*, takes into account consistencies across individuals in perceiving the social environment (Durkheim's collective representations). *Interpersonal behavior* includes attributions that people assign to others, such as stereotypes, their perceptions of the causes of the behavior of others, interpersonal attraction, and interpersonal responses characterized by differences in association, superordination, intimacy, and overtness, as discussed earlier.

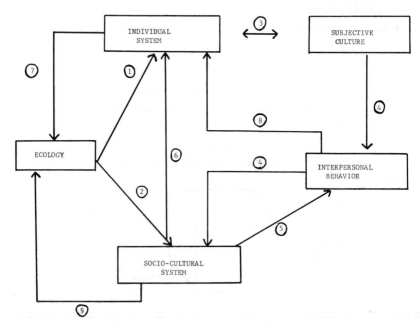

FIGURE 2. Schematic determinants of social behavior.

Child-rearing patterns are among the most studied interpersonal behaviors. These can be characterized as warm (associative) or cold (dissociative), controlled (superordinate) or autonomous (minimally superordination), with intimacy (much touching, kissing, hitting) or formality (distance), and are typically overt. In most cases the warm-cold dimension is closely related to the intimacy-formality dimension, so that both dimensions are not needed to characterize the child-rearing pattern. Severe socialization usually involves cold-controlling behaviors; lenient socialization often involves warm-autonomous behaviors. Cold-controlling/warm-autonomous seems to be an important axis in characterizing parental behavior in different cultures, because agricultural, food-accumulating societies tend to show severe, and hunting and fishing societies lenient, socialization patterns.

The *sociocultural system* includes the typical activities of members of a culture in the economic, religious, social, and political domains, including settlement patterns, social structure, laws, division of labor, and behavioral patterns that correspond to (define, implement, enforce) the norms, roles, and values of the group.

It is possible to find studies that connect each aspect of the diagram with every other aspect. Just to sketch this, without taking the space to elaborate, Relationship 1 is exemplified by studies relating ecology to perception, such as the studies of the relationship of carpenteredness to susceptibility to visual illusions. Relationship 2 is exemplified by studies relating ecology to forms of economic exploitation of the environment, such as fishing versus agriculture. Relationship 3 is exemplified by studies showing that attitudes and beliefs change to conform to behavior (e.g., the forced compliance literature). Relationship 4 concerns the relationships we reviewed in the first part of this paper. Relationship 5 concerns links between the sociocultural system and interpersonal behavior, such as the influence of "objective" norms on behavior, even if these norms are not reflected in subjective culture. (Since norms change reinforcement patterns, a person may be influenced by new norms even when he lacks the ability to describe the norm to others.) Relationship 6 can be exemplified by the relationship between (a) the extent to which schooling is available in a given society and (b) the modernity of people in that society.[18] Relationship 7 might be exemplified by the extent to which modern people, in Inkeles' sense, modify their environment, by building bridges, dams, and irrigation systems, or by increasing pollution and nuclear explosions. Relationship 8 is exemplified by McClelland's argument that emphasis on early independence leads to high need for achievement. Relationship 9 can be exemplified by the extent to which high levels of economic development are associated with changes in the physical environment.

The attributes of the sociocultural system are numerous, but among the most important are its degree of complexity[24] and the extent to which norms are enforced rigidly or loosely (Pelto's[37] discussion of tight versus loose societies).

A STRATEGY FOR THE INVESTIGATION OF THE RELATIONSHIPS
WITHIN THE BROAD MODEL

The sketchy presentation above suggests that cross-cultural scientists have already started studying the various links shown in the model. The model can be made more realistic — but, alas, also more complicated — by thinking of the states shown in the boxes across *time* as well as across *cultures*. Another way to extend it is to follow Berry,[5] who has considered the effects of acculturation, which takes into account the interaction among cultures. It is probable that each of these approaches will prove valuable.

A multimethod measurement of the key attributes of the entities in the boxes is indicated. Observations, interviews, questionnaires, and other methods should be used simultaneously to cross-check the validity of the data. A number of interesting questions are suggested by this model that need to be investigated by cross-cultural psychologists. Only those of direct relevance to interpersonal behavior will be mentioned here.

1. What kinds of ecology promote (or inhibit) what kinds of social behavior? Some wild speculations: frontier-type ecologies are associated with a smaller frequency of adoption of a "limited good" point of view, and with more associative interpersonal relationships with strangers, than are agricultural, stable, nonfrontier ecologies. Helping behavior is more probable in frontier ecologies than in settled agricultural ecologies, as suggested by the study of L'Armand and Pepitone.[22]

2. What kinds of sociocultural systems promote (or inhibit) what kinds of social behavior? Speculation: in relatively stable, simple social systems, where people are likely to interact with people with whom they have already interacted many times in the past, communication depends on *context* much more than in fluid, complex social systems where people often communicate with strangers, and frequently through the printed page. It seems probable that many of Cole's observations[7] can be understood within this framework. Cole tells us that some Kpelle farmers had trouble communicating in an experiment involving the identification of sticks. Instead of specifying a stick by means of unambiguous language, such as, "the one that is thick and flat, and is crooked after the halfway point," they said instead, "one of the sticks." If communication typically depends largely on context, then "one of the sticks" communicates perfectly, since it might be accompanied by the person's pointing to one of the sticks. One really needs no more details if he can point. The problem is different when we communicate without common context. Those of us who do a lot of writing develop tendencies to define out terms, etc., which is not typical of folk societies.

3. What are the relationships between different ecologies and different subjective cultures? Speculation: in ecologies where change is very frequent, people do not value planning behaviors. Triandis and Vassiliou[46] explained the disinterest of traditional Greeks in planning by noting the frequency of social change (coups, revolutions, wars). Of course, other factors might also acount for such devaluation of planning, and it is necessary to test this speculation by examining the proposed relationship in many more contexts.

These three examples suggest, in a very sketchy way, the kinds of studies that are being proposed. As an illustration of how the various links of the model of FIGURE 2 might be investigated, I will focus on the relationship between subjective culture and interpersonal behavior.

SUBJECTIVE CULTURE AND INTERPERSONAL BEHAVIOR

There is much evidence that when two persons, P and O (other), have different subjective cultures, their interpersonal relationship suffers. Negative stereotypes, the wrong attributions, low levels of interpersonal attraction, and avoidance or even aggression are likely outcomes of sharp differences in subjective culture. Given the fact that people with different subjective cultures often do have to work and live together, and in some cases are even married to each other, it is a problem of considerable practical significance. We need to know how to change interpersonal relationships, taking differences in subjective culture into account.

We do have methodologies that can give us a very good description of the subjective culture of samples of individuals. As mentioned earlier, our procedures can tell us what type of person responds to what type of social stimulus with what type of response. When the types of persons that make different responses correspond to the individuals in a particular social relationship that we wish to improve, we know at once that the differences in subjective culture require that we train one or both of these individuals.

MODIFYING INTERPERSONAL RELATIONSHIPS

There are three broad categories of procedures that can be used to change interpersonal relationships. They will be labeled *attribution training, affective training,* and *behavior modification.*

In *attribution training,* a person is asked to learn the attributions that are commonly made by people from another culture. This can be accomplished by a procedure known as the culture assimilator.[9] Culture assimilators consist of from 100 to 200 episodes involving interpersonal behavior between people who belong to different cultures. Each episode is described in less than a page, followed by several attributions that might plausibly explain the events. The central question is, "Why did so and so behave the way he did in that episode?" Attributions are usually obtained from the two cultural groups mentioned in the episode. For example, if an American is to be trained to understand the attributions made by Thais concerning social behavior, he will be presented with an episode together with three attributions commonly made by Americans and one attribution commonly made by Thais. He will be asked to explain the behavior of the Thai in the episode. The assumption is that Thais make more accurate attributions concerning the causes of their own behavior than do Americans. Therefore when the subject selects an attribution frequently made by Americans, he is told that this is not the best choice; he should read the episode once more and select a different attribution. When he finally selects the Thai attribution, he is told that this is indeed the correct way of thinking about the problem. He is also given about a page of cultural information reflecting enthographic material and studies of subjective culture in which differences in perception of the social environment between Thais and Americans have been detected.

The steps for the actual development of assimilators are now quite clear:

1. A sample of about 500 episodes should be developed through interviews with members of the two cultures that are in frequent contact. For example, fifty Thais who frequently interact with Americans and fifty Americans who frequently interact with Thais might be interviewed informally. Each of them might describe incidents that changed his mind about interaction with the other cultural group. The episodes are then edited to construct a smaller set of episodes that apparently have some sort of cultural basis. (Many of the episodes obtained in interviews are trivial, reflect personal idiosyncracies, or have no apparent relationship to cultural differences and must be discarded.)

2. The smaller set of episodes is edited and presented to new samples of individuals from the two relevant cultures. In this case, the subjects are asked to make an attribution and to answer the general question, "Why did so and so act that way?"

3. The attributions are then categorized and their frequencies noted. Attributions that are frequently made by one cultural group but not the other are used in the next step.

4. The edited episodes together with the attributions obtained in step 3 are assembled to form the culture assimilator items.

5. The effectiveness of the culture assimilator is tested in situations involving interaction among people from different cultures. In different studies, we determined that cultural assimilators (a) increase the accuracy of the attributions that people make concerning the behavior of members of another culture,[54] (b) reduce culture shock and dissatisfaction with members of another culture, and (c) increase the feeling of "adjustment" to another culture.[9] However, there is no evidence of changes in interpersonal behavior. One possible explanation for this negative finding is that time is required for the changes in attributions to modify the extent to which interaction with members from another culture is rewarding; when such changes do take place, interpersonal attitudes and behavior will be changed. More research is needed to check this possibility.

In *affective training*, the individual experiences pleasant events in the presence of members of another culture. The attempt is to develop, through classical conditioning, positive attitudes toward members of the other culture. If the presence of a member of the other culture elicits positive affect because it has been frequently associated with positive events such as good food, sexual relations, an enjoyable party, etc., it is assumed that the attitudes towards other members of the other cultural group will be changed. Such attitude change may also be obtained, under some conditions, in sensitivity groups or other laboratory training groups, such as those described by Back.[2]

In *behavior modification*, a therapist focuses on some specific behaviors that are objectionable and associates unambiguously these behaviors with negative events. At the same time, the environment is arranged in such a way that desirable behaviors, particularly if they are incompatible with behaviors that are undesirable, are followed by positive events.

At the interpersonal level, it is possible for members of the two cultural groups to discuss particular behaviors that annoy them and to learn to reward the other when such behaviors are absent or when the other emits behaviors that are incompatible with the annoying behaviors. Such an approach leads to changes in behavior that can make the dyad relationship more rewarding and less costly than would be the case without training.

It is obvious from the above discussion that each form of training has rather specific consequences, and that the optimal training strategy will be the *combined application of the three training approaches*. In this way the individual will learn to make culturally appropriate attributions concerning the behavior of the other, will change his behavior so that it is less annoying to the other, and will learn to like the other. There are, as yet, no studies in which this combination of changes has been accomplished, so the effectiveness of the combined approach has not yet been determined.

USE OF INTERCULTURAL TRAINING TO TEST THE BROADER MODEL

It is clear from the discussion of training presented above that we are able to manipulate experimentally a number of variables of interpersonal experiences that may have effects on interpersonal behavior. Such studies tell us whether the changes we introduce, such as through training, have enduring consequences for the social relationship. As we do more and more such studies we will be able to map more precisely the relationship between changes in subjective culture on the one hand and changes in interpersonal relationships on the other. Thus, we will gradually understand the links between subjective culture and interpersonal behavior.

In principle, it is possible to develop similar procedures to test the other links of the model of FIGURE 2. Thus, we might investigate why different ecologies result in different sociocultural systems, why different ecologies result in different subjective cultures, and so on.

For example, we might investigate the relationship between food accumulation and severe socialization. What are the links between food accumulation and subjective culture, and between subjective culture and severe socialization? My speculation here is that food accumulation is found in agricultural societies that require more cooperation among large groups of people than is typical in gathering, fishing, or hunting societies. Cooperation requires coordination, which requires that the young learn to obey a leader. Severe socialization is functional because children learn to obey and to conform to group norms.

As an example of investigation of the relationship of ecology and subjective culture, consider a study which examined why people differ in their meaning of *work*. The data came from a large project that will be described by Osgood in this volume. This is a large data set that concerns the affective meaning of some 600 concepts in about thirty cultures. After looking at the Human Relations Area Files, Triandis[40] noted variations in ecology and variations in the meaning of work that seem to fall into a pattern. The Osgood data were used to confirm the hunch that was thereby developed. Triandis noted three kinds of ecologies: (1) very easy ecologies where work situations are characterized by a person's having enough resources to satisfy his basic needs with very little effort; (2) very difficult ecologies where a person would have to work very had to survive; and (3) intermediate conditions. Work was seen as a necessary evil in the first and second of these three kinds of ecologies, while it was seen as relatively challenging, exciting, and a method to validate the self-image in the ecologies of intermediate difficulty. Looking at Osgood's data on the meaning of work and related concepts, it became possible to check if this pattern is really there. In Osgood's data, the societies that had the most positive view of work were societies that could be classified as intermediate in difficulty. They were Yugoslavia, Greece, and Iran. By contrast, the postindustrial societies, such as the United States and Sweden, have an environment that is very easy (with welfare and minimum wage laws guaranteeing survival), and the less developed countries, such as Thailand, have an environment that is rather difficult. So it was not surprising that the image of work and work-related concepts in Osgood's data was most positive in societies that are "up and coming," and less positive or somewhat negative in societies where making a living requires a considerable struggle *or* is quite easy.

Looking to the future, then, we need to move in the direction of operationalizing dimensions of the ecology in the same way that we have operationalized dimensions of subjective culture and dimensions of interpersonal behavior, and to carry out similar sorts of studies. Then we will be in a position to study objectively the relationships between ecology and subjective culture and interpersonal behavior. Similarly, we should operationalize the major attributes of the sociocultural system. For example, we should be able to measure directly the complexity or looseness of social systems so that we can tie existing data about subjective culture to the indices that characterize the sociocultural system.

CONCLUDING COMMENT

It is my impression that in the study of the relationships between ecology, subjective culture, and interpersonal behavior we have only scratched the surface; we need thirty years of intensive studies before we begin to make sense of the most important relationships. While we have some methodologies for the study of the relationship between subjective culture and interpersonal behavior that are applicable to any culture, we have done too little on the measurement of the important dimensions of ecology and of the sociocultural system. We urgently need to know what are the important dimensions that contrast different ecologies and different social systems, and how to measure these dimensions. In this respect, we are probably at the point where zoologists were in the late eighteenth century. We have not yet collected most of our specimens, we are not yet near taking the voyage of the "Beagle," and we have not yet found our Darwin to put the whole thing together.

Much of the work that needs to be done requires the development of methodologies for the measurement of key variables of the ecology and the sociocultural system, and of concepts that will tie these variables to subjective culture and interpersonal behavior variables. This effort should, at the end, tell us what concepts are likely to prove of enduring value in understanding social behavior. Armed with good methodologies for the measurement of these concepts at different points in time and in different cultures, we should be able to do the best that is possible: to provide a superb description of social phenomena across time and place. When all this is done and our Darwin has appeared, the theory that will emerge will not be specific, in the sense that Darwin's theory is not specific. Note that his theory cannot predict which forms of animal life will emerge in the year 2000; it is only a framework for understanding evolution. In the same sense, social science theories of the future will be frameworks for understanding why certain kinds of social relationships emerge in certain kinds of ecologies. But such frameworks, together with effective descriptions of contemporary social events, are no mean aspirations.

REFERENCES

1. ADAMOPOULOS, I. & D. BRINBERG. 1975. An examination of the determinants of social behavior. Submitted for publication.
2. BACK, K. 1973. Beyond Words. Penguin Books. Baltimore, Md.
3. BALES, R. F. 1950. Interaction Process Analysis. Addison-Wesley. Cambridge, Mass.
4. BENJAMIN, L. S. 1974. Structural analysis of social behavior. Psychol. Rev. 81: 392–425.
5. BERRY, J. W. 1975. Ecology, cultural adaptation and psychological differentiation: Traditional patterning and acculturative stress. In Cross-Cultural Perspectives on Learning. R. W. Brislin, S. Bochner and W. J. Lonner, Eds.: 207–230. Halsted/Wiley. New York, N.Y.
6. BROWN, R. 1965. Social Psychology. Free Press. New York, N.Y.
7. COLE, M. 1975. An ethnographic psychology of cognition. In Cross-Cultural Perspectives on Learning. R. W. Brislin, S. Bochner, and W. J. Lonner, Eds.: 157–176. Halsted/Wiley. New York, N.Y.
8. CRONBACH, L. J. 1975. Beyond the two disciplines of scientific psychology. Am. Psychol. 30: 116–127.
9. FIEDLER, F. E., T. MITCHELL & H. C. TRIANDIS. 1971. The culture assimilator: An approach to cross-cultural training. J. Appl. Psychol. 55: 95–102.

10. FOA, U. G. 1971. Interpersonal and economic resources. Science 171: 345–351.
11. FOA, U. G. & E. B. FOA. 1974. Societal Structures of the Mind. C. C. Thomas. Springfield, Ill.
12. FOSTER, G. M. 1965. Peasant society and the image of limited good. Am. Anthropol. 67: 293–315.
13. GERGEN, K. J. 1973. Social psychology as history. J. Personality Social Psychol. 26: 309–320.
14. GREGORY, J. R. 1975. Image of limited good, or expectation of reciprocity. Curr. Anthropol. 16: 73–92.
15. GOULDNER, A W. 1960. The norm of reciprocity: A preliminary statement. Am. Sociol. Rev. 25: 161–178.
16. HARRÉ, R. & P. F. SECORD. 1972. The Explanation of Social Behavior. Rowan and Littlefield. Totowa, N.J.
17. HERSKOVITS, M. J. 1955. Cultural Anthropology. Knopf. New York, N.Y.
18. INKELES, A. & D. H. SMITH. 1974. Becoming Modern. Harvard Press. Cambridge, Mass.
19. ISRAEL, J. & H. TAJFEL. 1972. The Context of Social Psychology: A Critical Assessment. Academic Press. New York, N.Y.
20. LaFORGE, R. & R. SUCZEK. 1955. The interpersonal dimension of personality, III. An inerpersonal checklist. J. Personality 24: 94–112.
21. LANDIS, D., H. C. TRIANDIS & ADAMOPOULOS. 1975. The prediction of teacher classroom behavior. Submitted for publication.
22. L'ARMAND, K. L. & A. PEPITONE. 1975. Helping to reward another person: A cross-cultural analysis. J. Personality Social Psychol. 31: 189–198.
23. LEARY, T. 1957. Interpersonal Diagnosis of Personality. Ronald Press. New York, N.Y.
24. LOMAX, A. & N. BERKOWITZ. 1972. The evolutionary taxonomy of culture. Science 177: 228–239.
25. LONGABAUGH, R. 1966. The structure of interpersonal behavior. Sociometry 29: 441–460.
26. LORR, N. & D. M. McNAIR. 1965. Expansion of the interpersonal behavior circle. J. Personality Social Psychol. 2: 823–830.
27. LYKKEN, D. 1968. Statistical significance in psychological research. Psychological Bull. 70: 151–159.
28. MASON, W. A. 1964. Sociability and social organization in monkeys and apes. In Advances in Experimental Social Psychology. L. Berkowitz, Ed.: 277–305. Academic Press. New York, N.Y.
29. McGUIRE, W. J. 1973. The yin and yang of progress in social psychology: Seven koans. J. Personality Social Psychol. 26: 446–456.
30. MEEHL, P. E. 1967. Theory testing in psychology and physics: A methodological paradox. Philosophy of Science 34: 103–115.
31. MEEHL, P. E. 1970. Nuisance variables and the ex post facto design. In Minnesota Studies in the Philosophy of Science. M. Radner and S. Winokur, Eds. Vol. 4: 373–402.
32. MEEHL, P. E. 1970. Some methodological reflections on the difficulties of psychoanalytic research. In Minnesota Studies in the Philosophy of Science. M. Radner and S. Winokur, Eds. Vol. 4: 403–416.
33. MEHRABIAN, A. 1970. A semantic space for nonverbal behavior. J. Consulting and Clin. Psychol. 35: 248–257.
34. NORMAN, W. T. 1969. To see ourselves as others see us! Relations among self-perceptions, peer perceptions and expected peer-perceptions of personality attributes. Multivariate Behavior Res. 4: 417–443.
35. OSGOOD, C. E. 1966, Dimension of semantic space for communication via facial expressions. Scandinav. J. Psychol. 7: 1–30.
36. OSGOOD, C. E. 1971. Explorations in semantic space: A personal diary. J. Social Issues 27: 5–64.
37. PELTO, P. J. 1968. The differences between "tight" and "loose" societies. Transaction (April): 37–40.

38. SCHLOSBERG, H. 1954. Three dimensions of emotion. Psychological Rev. **61**: 81–88.
39. STOGDILL, R. M. & A. E. COONS. 1957. Leader Behavior: Its Description and Measurement. Research Monograph No. 88. Ohio State University. Columbus, Ohio.
40. TRIANDIS, H. C. 1973. Work and nonwork: Intercultural perspectives. *In* Work and Nonwork in the Year 2001. M. Dunnette, Ed. Brooks/Cole. Monterey, Calif.
41. TRIANDIS, H. C. 1975. Culture training, cognitive complexity and interpersonal attitudes. *In* Cross-Cultural Perspectives on Learning. R. Brislin, S. Bochner and W. Lonner, Eds.: 39–77. Sage and Wiley/Halsted. New York, N.Y.
42. TRIANDIS, H. C. 1975. Social psychology and cultural analysis. J. Theory Social Behavior **5**: 81–106.
43. TRIANDIS, H. C., Ed. 1976. Variations in Black and White Perceptions of the Social Environment. University of Illinois Press. Champaign, Illinois.
44. TRIANDIS, H. C. & W. W. LAMBERT. 1958. A restatement and test of Schlosberg's theory of emotion with two kinds of subjects from Greece. J. Abnormal and Social Psychol. **56**: 321–332.
45. TRIANDIS, H. C. & R. S. MALPASS. 1970. Field guide for the study of aspects of subjective culture. Technical Report No. 4. Psychology Department, University of Illinois, Champaign, Illinois.
46. TRIANDIS, H. C. & V. VASSILIOU. 1972. A comparative analysis of subjective culture. *In* The Analysis of Subjective Culture. H. C. Triandis, Ed.: 299–335. Wiley. New York, N.Y.
47. TRIANDIS, H. C., V. VASSILIOU, G. VASSILIOU, Y. TANAKA & A. V. SHANMUGAM. 1972. The Analysis of Subjective Culture. Wiley. New York, N.Y.
48. TUCKER, L. R. 1966. Some mathematical notes on three-mode factor analysis. Psychometrika **31**: 279–311.
49. WHITING, J. W. M. & B. B. WHITING. 1975. Children of Six Cultures: A Psychocultural Analysis. Harvard University Press. Cambridge, Mass.
50. WOLF, A. Quoted in W. W. Lambert and W. E. Lambert. 1973. Social Psychology, 2nd ed. Prentice Hall. Englewood Cliffs, N.J.
51. POMAZAL, R. J. 1974. Attitudes, normative beliefs and altruism: Help for helping behavior, Unpublished doctoral dissertation. University of Illinois.
52. SCHAEFER, E. S. 1965. A configurational analysis of children's reports of parental behavior. J. Consulting Psychol. **29**: 552–557.
53. TRIANDIS, H. C. 1977. Interpersonal Behavior. Brooks/Cole. Monterey, Calif.
54. WELDON, D. E., D. E. CARLSTON, A. K. RISSMAN, L. SLOBODIN & H. C. TRIANDIS. 1975. A laboratory test of effects of culture assimilator training. J. Personality and Social Psychol. **32**: 300–310.

OBJECTIVE INDICATORS OF SUBJECTIVE CULTURE

Charles E. Osgood

Center for Comparative Psycholinguistics
University of Illinois
Champaign, Illinois 61820

Concern about the development, collection and validation of social indicators has been developing rapidly over the past few years. But this concern has been mainly with indicators of objective culture and with national rather than international indicators, leaving mostly lip-service to be paid to the nature and measurement of change in subjective culture. As far as the methodology of generating subjective social indicators is concerned, at least three major orthogonal dichotomies can be distinguished.

(1) *Objective versus subjective*: Although the intuitions of astute historians like Alexis de Tocqueville, trained cultural anthropologists, and sophisticated observers and reporters of the mass media are most useful for hypothesis-forming, they are useless for hypothesis-testing — and they obviously do not lend themselves to correlational analyses with objective social indicators. Objective subjective indicators transform the mental states of members of a culture into quantitative forms capable of statistical manipulation.

(2) *Differential versus global*: Whereas global subjective indicators reflect an overall estimation of some state of affairs (e.g., satisfaction with life) and may be objectively assessed — Hadley Cantril's self-anchoring "ladder" technique is an example — differential subjective indicators apply a constant methodology across a *sample* of subjective states (e.g., attitudes toward diverse issues, meanings of diverse concepts), the sample being representative in terms of social concerns and investigator interests.

(3) *Systematic versus topical*: Whereas in topicality a kind of "newsworthiness" criterion determines the questions asked and the concepts tapped (public opinion polling is a good example in the objective form), systematicity requires that one tap concepts that are reasonably stable over times and places (e.g., physical and mental health, interpersonal relations, attitudes toward work and play), even though feelings and beliefs *about* the things referred to may be quite labile.

In this paper I propose that the semantic differential technique, particularly in its cross-cultural applications, has potential as a means of providing objective indicators of subjective culture. Methodologically, it represents the "positive" poles of these three dichotomies: it yields objective, quantifiable data, it applies the same procedures differentially over indefinitely large samples of concepts, and it is clearly systematic rather than topical with respect to times and places.

SEMANTIC DIFFERENTIAL TECHNIQUE

I assume reasonable familiarity with the SD technique and can therefore be appropriately brief: In ordinary language, humans use substantives (nouns) to refer to entities, qualifiers (adjectives) to differentiate among entities in the same conceptual classes, and quantifiers (adverbs) to indicate degrees of qualifier-substantive relationship. These appear to be universals in human languages. When a native speaker rates a CONCEPT on a +3 to −3, 7-step scale in the SD technique, e.g.

$$\text{COWARD}\quad \underline{\text{kind}\quad \underset{+3}{:}\ \underset{+2}{:}\ \underset{+1}{:}\ \underset{0}{:}\ \underset{-1}{X}:\ \underset{-2}{:}\ \underset{-3}{:}\quad \text{cruel}}$$

where 3 means *very*, 2 means *quite*, 1 means *slightly* as quantifiers, and 0 means *either* or *neither*, he is creating a kind of "sentence" (N (is) Qt Q1) — in this case, say, (*a*) *COWARD* (*is*) *slightly cruel*.

The factor analytic measurement model assumes that the meanings of concepts can be represented as points in an n-dimensional space, where the dimensions are defined by the factors, or underlying semantic features of bipolar qualifiers (e.g., *good-bad, strong-weak, quick-slow*, etc.). Both concept-points (as factor scores) and scales (as factor loadings) can be represented in the same hypothetical space and are characterizable in terms of their *distances* (degrees of meaningfulness) and *directions* (qualities of meaning) from the meaningless central origin of the space. FIGURE 1 provides an illustration. The solid black lines represent the E-P-A factors and the fine dashed lines represent the projections of a concept point (COWARD) and the termini of a scale (*kind* and *cruel*) on these three factors. All scales are assumed to be straight lines through the origin, here shown as a bamboo-type line, and we get the locations of the

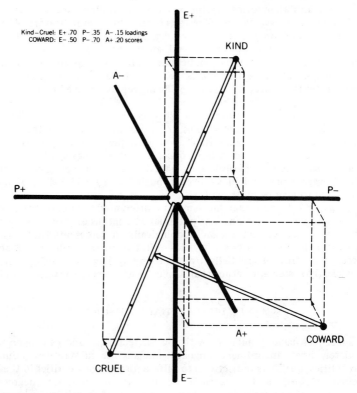

FIGURE 1. Geometric representation of the rating of a concept on a scale in the semantic differential technique.

termini from the loadings of scales on the same factors. Thus *kind* is very Good, quite Weak and slightly Passive, and *cruel* (reciprocally) is very Bad, quite Strong and slightly Active. What happens when a subject rates COWARD on the *kind-cruel* scale? Geometrically, the answer is very simple: we just project the COWARD point at right angles onto the *kind-cruel* line (the arrow) and we find that this speaker said, "COWARDS are slightly cruel"!

When a sample of speakers rates a sample of concepts against a sample of scales, a cube of "sentences" of this form is generated, with concepts X scales X speakers as sources of variance, as shown in FIGURE 2. Correlational and

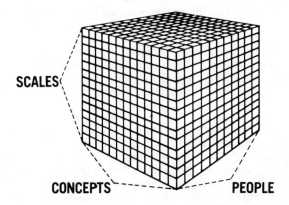

FIGURE 2. The three-mode cube of semantic differential data.

factorial analyses are based on the assumption — as are all linguistic and philosophical conceptions of meaning with which we are familiar — *that semantic similarity is indexed by similarity in distribution of usage in the language.* Thus concepts, qualifier scales, and even speakers are semantically similar to other members of their sets to the extent that they produce similar kinds of "sentences" as the other two sets are varied systematically. During the 1950s we collected many such cubes of SD data from widely diversified samples of speakers of American English, and, as far as the factor analyses of qualifier-scale relations were concerned, we kept getting the same basic factor system: a dominant Evaluation (E) factor, a Potency (P) factor, and an Activity (A) factor.

We refer to this E-P-A subsystem as *affective meaning.* It appeared to be based on the way humans universally attribute primitive emotional *feelings* to signs representing persons and things in their environment. However, up until 1960 our research had been focussed on humans sharing a common (American) culture and speaking a common (English) language. It was a least *conceivable* that the dominance of Goodness, Strength and Activity was attributable to something peculiar about the American culture or the English language or both.

CROSS-CULTURAL SD RESEARCH

Our sampling among the world's communities began with six highly diverse languages and cultures: Finnish, Arabic in Lebanon, Farsi in Iran, Kannada in Mysore, Chinese in Hong Kong, and Japanese (see APPENDIX). During the

15-year life of this project we have gradually extended our research to 30 human communities. Since we were interested in gross differences in culture and language, we decided to maximize sociometric *equivalences* across communities, in all cases using teenage male students in average high schools in urban settings. The research falls naturally into two phases, "tool-making" and "tool-using."

Tool-making

The first step was *to obtain a sample of productive qualifiers* in each community. A set of 100 nouns was used as stimuli in a modified word-association test to elicit 100 adjectives from each of 100 teenage boys. The nouns were selected to be culture-common, being drawn mainly from lists developed by glottochronologists who study changes in word forms and meanings over long periods of time in families of related languages. The 100 concepts shown in TABLE 1 are those that remained after careful translation checks of some 200 candidates. There are many abstract (TRUST, CHOICE, WEALTH) as well as concrete (HOUSE, CAT, MAN) concepts among the 100, and all are very familiar notions.

When the 10,000 qualifier tokens had been collected in each community (100 boys giving their responses to the 100 nouns), they were shipped to Illinois and computer-analyzed *in the native language* (that is, blindly, untouched by Western minds!). The qualifier types were first ordered in terms of their overall frequencies and diversities of usage across the 100 nouns and then were pruned in terms of their correlations in usage with all higher-ordered types — this last to maximize diversity of the semantic dimensions tapped.

The second step in "tool-making" was *collection of data for concept-on-scale factorizations.* Another group of teenage male subjects in each community rated the same 100 culture-common concepts against the 50 most productive bipolar

TABLE 1

THE 100 CULTURE-COMMON CONCEPTS USED IN QUALIFIER ELICITATIONS

1. House	21. Bird	41. Cat	61. Success	81. Man
2. Girl	22. Hope	42. Poison	62. Snake	82. Wednesday
3. Picture	23. Heat	43. Tree	63. Hand	83. Chair
4. Meat	24. Map	44. Hunger	64. Mother	84. Guilt
5. Trust	25. Husband	45. Choice	65. Knot	85. River
6. Tooth	26. Rain	46. Noise	66. Life	86. Peace
7. Defeat	27. Truth	47. Need	67. Head	87. Hair
8. Book	28. Stone	48. Doctor	68. Thunder	88. Food
9. Lake	29. Pain	49. Anger	69. Luck	89. Danger
10. Star	30. Ear	50. Tongue	70. Author	90. Policeman
11. Battle	31. Respect	51. Horse	71. Music	91. Father
12. Seed	32. Laughter	52. Marriage	72. Sleep	92. Fear
13. Sympathy	33. Moon	53. Game	73. Future	93. Root
14. Progress	34. Courage	54. Color	74. Egg	94. Purpose
15. Cup	35. Work	55. Heart	75. Crime	95. Fire
16. Wind	36. Story	56. Friend	76. Sun	96. Rope
17. Thief	37. Punishment	57. Death	77. Belief	97. Power
18. Bread	38. Wealth	58. Smoke	78. Money	98. Window
19. Love	39. Woman	59. Freedom	79. Knowledge	99. Pleasure
20. Fruit	40. Cloud	60. Dog	80. Fish	100. Water

scales. So imagine, if you will, 30 data cubes like that I described earlier for American English. To determine the functional equivalence in usage (meaning) of scales in different languages *independent of translation*, we must put these 30 cubes into a single mathematical space for analysis, and this requires that at least one of the three sources of variance (subjects, scales, or concepts) be shared. Although subjects are obviously different and the scales are quite varied, the 100 concepts are carefully *translation-equivalent* and the data can be ordered in their terms. FIGURE 3 illustrates the design of our monstrous *pancultural factorization* of the scale mode.

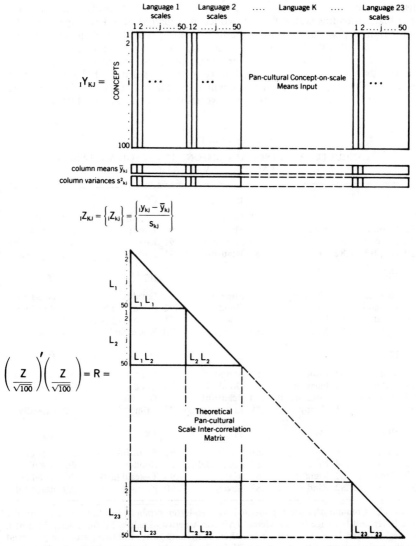

FIGURE 3. Design of pancultural factor analysis of scales for 23 language/culture communities.

The logic of this procedure is as follows: Suppose that there is a very high correlation between scale #21 for AE (American English), *good-bad*, and scale #37 for JP (Japanese), *iwa-matsu* — meaning what, we deliberately have no idea. This means that, regardless of the translation, we can conclude that the Japanese use their *iwa-matsu* to differentiate among the 100 translation-equivalent concepts in a way that is *functionally equivalent* to the way Americans use their *good-bad* scale. We are thus applying the psycholinguistic definition of similarity of meaning — similarity in distribution of usage — but now *across* languages.

The proof of this particular pudding, however, lies in the *results* of the factorization. The results for E, P and A, respectively, for 20 communities are displayed in TABLES 2, 3, and 4, but only giving the "positive" terms of the four highest-loading scales. We use two-letter (usually Locus/Language) codes for our communities: thus AE for American English, AD for Afghan Dari, and BF for Belgian Flemish, but not where language and locus coincide, e.g., FF for Finnish, FR for French, and GK for Greek. Of course, in order to communicate the results here, we have translated all terms into English, but this had nothing to do with which scales appeared on which pancultural factors. A mere scanning of TABLE 2 is convincing as to the universality of the Evaluative factor, and the

TABLE 2

PANCULTURAL PRINCIPAL COMPONENT FACTOR ANALYSIS —
FACTOR 1: EVALUATION

AE		AD		BF		CB		DH	
.94	Nice	.88	Good	.91	Good	.93	Beautiful	.83	Glad
.92	Good	.85	Well	.89	Magnificent	.93	Lovely	.83	Good
.90	Sweet	.84	Safe	.88	Agreeable	.91	Kind	.81	Ambrosial
.89	Helpful	.82	Lovely	.88	Beautiful	.91	Finest	.80	Superior
FF		**FR**		**GK**		**HC**		**IF**	
.88	Nice	.90	Pleasant	.93	Superb	.92	Lovable	.92	Good
.87	Pleasant	.89	Good	.91	Good	.92	Good (not bad)	.89	Worthwhile
.86	Good	.88	Nice	.88	Friendly	.91	Good (not poor)	.88	Best
.81	Light	.86	Magnificent	.85	Useful	.90	Respectable	.88	Auspicious
IT		**JP**		**LA**		**MK**		**MS**	
.93	Valuable	.93	Good	.90	Sound	.78	Merciful	.93	Admirable
.92	Beautiful	.92	Pleasant	.90	Good	.76	Good	.93	Agreeable
.92	Desirable	.91	Comfortable	.90	Beautiful	.75	Delicate	.92	Good
.92	Good	.91	Happy	.89	Enlivening	.74	Calm	.92	Friendly
ND		**SW**		**TH**		**TK**		**YS**	
.91	Pleasant	.86	Good	.88	Useful	.91	Beautiful	.93	Pleasant
.91	Happy	.84	Nice	.87	Comfortable	.90	Good	.92	Good
.90	Good	.82	Right	.87	Right	.90	Tasteful (art)	.91	Lovable
.87	Nice	.82	Kind	.87	Loving	.90	Pleasant	.89	Beautiful

NOTE: Communities are represented by two-letter symbols, location indicated by the first letter and language by the second (AE for American English, BF for Belgian Flemish); where locus and language coincide and there is no ambiguity, the two letters simply stand for the language (thus FR for French, GK for Greek, and so forth).

loadings are nearly all in the .80's and .90's. Scales translating as *good, beautiful, pleasant* and *nice* appear repeatedly.

While the scale loadings for the Potency factor, shown in TABLE 3, are somewhat lower (ranging from the .40's into the .70's), common strength and magnitude flavors are evident in scales translating as *big, strong, heavy* and *tall*. But note also some generalizations of Potency into scales like *military, difficult* and *brave*. As is always the case, even for American English, the Activity scales shown in TABLE 4 have somewhat lower loadings (ranging from the .30's into the low .70's), but, with the possible exceptions of DH (Delhi Hindi), LA (Lebanese Arabic), and MK (Mysore Kannada), the Activity flavor is clear and is evident in the most common scales, *fast, quick, alive* (and *lively*), and *active* itself. Again you will note some common generalizations — to *young*, to *noisy*, and to *red* and *bloody*.

This is rather convincing evidence for the universality of the E-P-A affective meaning system and, although procedures were standardized at all critical points, our young subjects were free to produce *any* kinds of qualifiers and use them in *any* ways in rating concepts to create *any* kind of semantic space.

The final step in the tool-making phase is the production of short-form semantic differentials based upon the pancultural factorization. For each community we select those four indigenous scales that have the highest and purest loadings. The pancultural SDs thus consist of 12 scales, four representing each of the E-P-A factors. To the extent that we have identified truly universal

TABLE 3

PANCULTURAL PRINCIPAL COMPONENT FACTOR ANALYSIS —
FACTOR 2: POTENCY

AE		AD		BF		CB		DH	
.68	Big	.55	Great	.57	Strong	.62	Huge	.47	Strong-of-its-kind
.68	Powerful	.45	Military	.57	Big	.60	Powerful	.47	Brave
.57	Strong	.40	Absolute	.54	Heavy	.55	Big	.46	Heavy
.57	Deep	.37	High, loud	.50	Deep	.54	Strong	.44	Difficult
FF		FR		GK		HC		IF	
.60	Large	.68	Large	.60	Big	.76	Tall, big	.62	Heavy
.59	Sturdy	.59	Strong	.59	Strong	.75	Big	.50	Severe
.51	Heavy	.57	Huge	.46	Brave	.72	Strong	.47	Thick
.40	Rough	.52	Heavy	.39	Difficult	.68	Significant	.42	Stout
IT		JP		LA		MK		MS	
.68	Big	.66	Heavy	.51	Large	.44	Wonderful	.60	Giant
.55	Strong	.63	Big	.42	Strong	.41	Huge	.58	Big
.54	Wide	.59	Difficult	.41	Long	.41	Big	.55	Major
.49	High, tall	.56	Brave	.38	Heavy	.34	Great	.54	Strong
ND		SW		TH		TK		YS	
.57	Big	.50	Difficult	.50	Heavy	.67	Big	.72	Big
.55	Heavy	.50	High	.49	Deep	.58	Heavy	.67	Bulky
.54	Strong	.46	Strong	.43	Old	.53	Large	.67	Strong
.48	Special	.45	Long	.42	Big	.51	High	.55	High, tall

TABLE 4

PANCULTURAL PRINCIPAL COMPONENT FACTOR ANALYSIS. –
FACTOR 3: ACTIVITY

AE		AD		BF		CB		DH	
.61	Fast	.51	Fast, rapid	.69	Quick	.47	Alive	.47	Gay
.55	Alive	.41	Sharp	.65	Active	.43	Fast	.36	Thin (slim)
.44	Young	.40	Tender, soft	.42	Bloody	.43	Active	.34	Soft
.42	Noisy	.36	Narrow	.40	Impetuous	.38	Light	.30	Loquacious

FF		FR		GK		HC		IF	
.67	Fast	.61	Lively	.55	Quick	.68	Agile	.53	Active
.66	Flexible	.57	Fast	.52	Young	.54	Fast	.52	Exciting
.64	Agile	.56	Living	.39	Active	.49	Alive	.41	Fast, sharp
.52	Lively	.42	Young	.39	Thin	.46	Red	.31	Warm

IT		JP		LA		MK		MS	
.66	Fast	.48	Noisy	.35	Fast	.35	Loose	.56	Active
.47	Mortal	.45	Active	.31	Infirm	.34	Unstable	.46	Young
.47	Young	.44	Soft	.30	Thin	.33	Fast	.44	Fast
.40	Sensitive	.42	Fast	.29	Alive	.27	Few	.37	Soft

ND		SW		TH		TK		YS	
.72	Active	.66	Bloody	.56	Agile	.50	Fast	.63	Lively
.71	Fast	.63	Swift	.44	Fast	.47	Living	.54	Fast
.51	Fascinating	.62	Lively	.39	Thin	.43	Soft (flexible)	.45	Young
.48	Warm	.54	Sensitive	.28	Naughty	.42	Young	.41	Soft

dimensions of meaning, these pancultural SDs are reasonably comparable "yardsticks" for measuring the affective aspects of subjective culture, and we have thus succeeded in piercing at least a hole in the language barrier.

Tool-using

The major use of these pancultural SDs so far has been in the compilation of what we rather grandiosely call an *Atlas of Affective Meanings*. I say "grandiosely" because it only includes 620 concepts as sampled in only 30 language-culture communities, but it is at least a beginning in the exploration of subjective culture. The *Atlas* contains a tremendous amount of quantitative information. We estimate about 7,800,000 "bits" of raw data. Obviously this mass of numbers has to be organized into chunks and analyzed in revealing formats if it is to be comprehended. A way of "chunking" the data was to assign the 620 concepts, with considerable overlapping, to approximately 50 categories of manageable size for analysis. TABLE 5 lists these categories, organizing them under 12 "Super-categories". Thus Super-Cat TIME includes The Age Continuum (from BIRTH to DEATH with stops in between), Months and Seasons, Time Units (from MOMENT to ETERNITY), and the trichotomous category Future-Present-Past (which includes contrasting sets of concepts like

TABLE 5

FORTY-SEVEN CATEGORIES OF ATLAS CONCEPTS (BY 12 SUPERCATEGORIES)

1–Time
  A. Age continuum
  B. Months, seasons
  C. Time units
  D. Future-present-past
2–Ego identification
  A. Kinship
  B. Races, religions, continents
     directions, -isms
  C. Male-female
  D. Ingroup, alters, outgroup
  E. Intimacy-remoteness
3–Abstract symbolisms
  A. Emotions
  B. Numbers
  C. Colors
  D. Geometricals
  E. Days
4–Concrete symbolisms
  A. Natural and potentially aesthetic
  B. See-hear-touch-smell-taste-(ables)
  C. Means-expressive-ends
5–Environmentals
  A. Food objects
  B. Animals
  C. Habitations
6–Carnalities
  A. Body parts
  B. Body characteristics, processes
  C. Sex and sensuality
  D. Health, sickness

7–Human activity
  A. Occupations
  B. Commercial, economic
  C. Work-play
  D. Success-failure
8–Interpersonal relations
  A. Private-public
  B. Social status
  C. Moral-immoral
  D. Inter-group relations
  E. Affiliative-achievement
9–Society
  A. Institutions
  B. Mordern-trans-traditional
     technology
  C. Modern-trans-traditional values
10–Communications
  A. Literacy
  B. Lanuage and literature
  C. Communications
11–Philosophy
  A. Philosophicals
  B. Supernaturals
  C. Idealism-realism
  D. Concrete-abstract
  E. Congnitive-gut
12–Things and stuffs
  A. Static, dynamic nature
  B. Static, dynamic artifacts
  C. Stuffs

TOMORROW/TODAY/YESTERDAY, and PROGRESS/WORK/TRADITION).
Glancing through this table gives some idea of the variety of conceptual
categories included in the *Atlas*.

The other way of making these data manageable was to devise a chain-linked
series of computer programs, designed to highlight the most interesting aspects
of the data for each category. We are looking for *Universals* (nonchance trends
across all societies), *Subuniversals* (clusters of societies sharing certain patterns
of deviation), and *Uniquenesses* (deviations of individual societies from universal
trends) in the attribution of affect to various facets of human culture. I will
review these analysis formats briefly, using the small Color Category for
illustration.

Format 1 pulls the basic data strips for each concept from the Atlases for the
individual communities. TABLE 6 illustrates this for only two concepts
(COLOR and BLACK) and for only a few cultures: E, P and A are the averaged
factor scores; E-Z, P-Z and A-Z are these scores standardized over the 620 *Atlas*
concepts for each culture (note that while COLOR is positive on E and BLACK
is very negative, BLACK is the more Potent by far); F-Z are standardized scores
on a familiarity scale and D-O are distances from the origin, indexing a concept's

TABLE 6

BASIC MEASURES FOR COLOR CATEGORY

	E	P	A	E-Z	P-Z	A-Z	F-Z	D-O	P-I	P-G	CI	CI-Z
Color												
AE	1.5	0.9	−0.2	0.6	−0.1	−0.5	1.1	1.7	1.4	1.0	0.4	−0.6
FR	1.3	−0.1	1.0	0.8	−0.8	0.9	0.7	1.7	1.2	0.9	0.3	−0.9
BF	1.3	0.3	−0.1	0.7	−0.2	−0.5	1.0	1.4	1.2	0.7	0.5	−0.7
ND	1.0	−0.1	0.5	0.5	−0.7	0.2	0.5	1.2	1.2	0.6	0.6	−0.5
GG	2.0	0.2	−0.3	1.0	−0.5	−0.5	0.3	2.1	1.6	1.1	0.6	0.1
.												
.												
MN	1.4	0.2	0.3	0.6	−0.5	0.1	0.8	1.5	1.3	0.8	0.5	−0.5
S	0.4	0.4	0.4	0.3	0.4	0.7	0.9	0.4	0.3	0.2	0.2	0.6
Black												
AE	−0.5	0.4	−0.1	−1.3	−0.7	−0.2	−0.5	0.6	1.5	0.5	1.1	2.7
FR	−1.1	1.3	−1.1	−1.6	1.5	−2.2	−0.8	2.0	2.3	1.2	1.1	1.5
BF	−0.1	1.1	−0.7	−0.6	1.4	−1.4	−2.0	1.3	1.6	0.7	0.9	1.7
ND	−0.7	1.3	−0.6	−1.2	1.2	−1.3	0.4	1.6	1.8	0.9	0.9	0.8
GG	−0.9	0.5	−1.3	−1.4	−0.1	−1.5	0.6	1.7	1.4	0.9	0.5	−0.5
.												
.												
MM	−0.4	0.7	−0.5	−1.1	0.2	−1.2	−0.2	1.2	1.5	0.7	0.8	0.8
S	0.7	0.6	0.6	0.6	1.0	1.0	0.8	0.7	0.4	0.4	0.3	1.2

NOTE: N = 20 communities.

affective intensity; next come Individual (P-I) and Group (P-G, averaging) *polarization* scores, the former absolute values (noncanceling) and the latter algebraic (canceling) in terms of +/− scale directions; CI, *cultural instability*, is simply the subtraction of P-G from P-I, and its standardized values, CI-Z, reflect degrees of *within-culture disagreement* in affect attribution (note that AE [American English] has a "thing" about BLACK − for readily discernible social reasons).

Format 2 gives the *intercultural correlations* on these basic measures. The average correlations on E are significantly positive at the .01 level and nearly so for both P and A, so we can expect many universal trends in the Color Category.

Format 3 transforms the basic measures into *ranks within each culture*. TABLE 7 illustrates such ranks for the Color concepts, but only for E and P factors and only for the 20 communities available at the time. Using a .01 criterion (no more than 4 of 20 deviants), we note that COLOR and BLUE are universally +E and BLACK and GREY −E (as marked by U's); BLACK and RED are universally +P and YELLOW and WHITE −P. And note that SW and FF (the Swedes and Finns, our two most northern communities) display an interesting Subuniversal (marked by a slashed U) − YELLOW (sunlight?) has unusually high Evaluation. And there are Uniquenesses (marked with ?'s), for example, for Delhi-Hindi speakers GREY is unusually Good (term also used for the light skincolor preferred in young girls) and BLACK is unusually Weak (also refers to the skincolor of Southern Indians).

Format 4 is a *componential analysis* of these ranks. After the fashion of cultural anthropologists, for each conceptual domain we try to intuit the possible cognitive bases for differentiating the meanings of concepts and then

TABLE 7
RANKS FOR COLORS

	AE	FR	BF	ND	GG	SW	FF	YC	MS	IT	YS	GK	LA	TK	IF	DH	MK	TH	HC	JP	Mean
												Evaluation									
Color	1	1	1	1	1	3	1	8?	1	1	2	2	4	1	1	4	1	2	1	5	2.1 U+
Black	8	8	8	8	8	8	8	4?	8	8	8	7	8	8	6	8	8	8	8	7	7.6 U−
Grey	7	7	7	7	7	7	7	7	7	7	7	8	5	7	5	3?	7	6	7	8	6.8 U−
Red	2	5	2	6	2	5	4	5	6	6	5	5	7	5	5	5	4	7	5	4	4.8
Yellow	6	6	6	4	6	1	2⫶	6	4	5	6	6	6	6	8?	1?	3	1?	6	6	2.8 U+
Blue	3	2	3	2	3	2	5	1	2	4	1	4	1	4	2	2	6?	4	3	2	3.7
Green	5	3	4	3	5	4	6	2	3	2	3	1	2	3	4	7	5	5	4	3	3.5
White	4	4	5	5	4	6	3	3	5	3	4	3	3	2	3	6	2	3	2	1	
												Potency									
Color	2	6	5	4	4	4	6	6	5	5	1?	4	6	5	3	4	6	5	2	3	4.3
Black	5	1	2	1	3	3	1	1	2	4	5	2	5	1	1	8?	1	1	6	1	2.7 U+
Grey	8	3	7	5	5	7	2?	8	7	8	8	6	7	3	7	5	7	3	8	4	5.9
Red	1	2	1	2	1	2	5?	2	1	2	2	1	4	2	2	2	4	2	1	2	2.0 U+
Yellow	6	8	6	8	7	5	8	7	8	7	7	7?	8	6	8	7	8	7	7	7	7.0 U−
Blue	3	4	3	3	2	1	4	5	3	1	3	7?	3	8	4	1	5	6	4	5	3.8
Green	4	7	4	6	6	6	3	4	4	3	4	3	1?	4	5	3	3	4	5	6	4.3
White	7	5	8	7	8	8	7	3	6	6	6	8	2?	7	6	6	2?	8	3	8	6.0 U−

TABLE 8

COMPONENTIAL ANALYSIS FOR COLORS (3-C)*

Codings	Br	Hue	Sat	Color
Color	00	00	00	+
Black	−	00	00	−
Grey	0	00	00	−
Red	00	+	+	+
Yellow	00	+	−	+
Blue	00	−	+	+
Green	00	−	−	+
White	+	00	00	−

* Components: (1) brightness (bri̇ght/da̅rk); (2) hue (rėd/blu̅e); (3) saturation (ri̇ch/pa̅le); (4) color/noncolor (+/−). Tests: (1) Brightness: Whi̇te/Bla̅ck; Whi̇te/Gre̅y; Gre̅y/Bla̅ck. (2) Hue: Re̅d/Blu̅e; Ye̅llow/Gre̅en. (3) Saturation: Re̅d/Ye̅llow; Blu̇e/Gre̅en. (4) Color: Colȯr/Gre̅y, Colȯr/White-Black.

test to see which components are predictive of the attribution of affect. As shown in TABLE 8, to the three familiar physical components − Brightness, Hue and Saturation − we added a Color/Noncolor feature (BLACK, GREY, and WHITE being Noncolors). Double OO's indicate that a component is irrelevant for a given concept (e.g., the concept COLOR can refer to any Hue, Brightness or Saturation); single O's indicate neutrality on a feature (e.g., GREY is O on Brightness). At the bottom of this table are given the concept-pair tests for each component − ideally minimal pairs (opposed signs on only the component in question) − but we often have to compromise. TABLE 9 gives partial results (for E and P factors) for the Color Category, but I will summarize all of the Universals found: Across our little world, Brightness is more Valued and more Active than Darkness, but Darkness is more Potent; Brightness also is more familiar and has less conflict than Darkness. For an animal that depends dominantly on vision, these universal tendencies are not surprising. As to Hue, Reds are less Good than Blues, but more Active; Reds also tend to have more conflict about them. As to Saturation, Rich colors (RED, BLUE, and we could include BLACK) are more Potent than Pale colors (YELLOW, GREEN, and we could add both WHITE and GREY). Colors (RED, YELLOW, GREEN, BLUE and the word COLOR itself) are more Good, more Active and less conflictual than Noncolors (WHITE, GREY and BLACK).

Format 5 selects two types of subsections of a *pancultural distance matrix.* Each triangular section along the main diagonal of FIGURE 4 is the *interconcept distance matrix for each community* − thus, a picture of the affective structuring of the conceptual domain (here, Colors) for each culture − and all pairs of cultures can be compared for their similarities and differences in structure. From each of the interculture square matrices in the body of the table we extract only the diagonal − thus the *intercultural distances* for all pairs of cultures for all translation-equivalent concepts in the category. Presumably the smaller the distances in affect across the concepts for a pair of cultures, the more easily they should be able to communicate in that conceptual domain. Let me note in passing that Americans could communicate very easily with Iranians about colors, but have one hell of a time with Swedes!

TABLE 9

COMPONENTIAL ANALYSIS RESULTS FOR COLORS

	AE	FR	BF	ND	GG	SW	FF	YC	MS	IT	YS	GK	LA	TK	IF	DH	MK	TH	HC	JP	RATIO
Evaluation:																					
(1) Brightness																					
W/Blk	+	+	+	+	+	+	+	+	+	+	+	+	+	+	+	+	+	+	+	+	20/20 U+
U+ W/Gy	+	+	+	+	+	+	+	+	+	+	+	+	+	+	+	−?	+	+	+	+	19/20 U+
GY/Blk	+	+	+	+	+	+	+	−	+	+	+	−	+	+	−	+	+	+	−	−	16/20
(2) Hue																					
Rd/Bl	+	−	−	−	+	−	+	−	−	−	−	−	−	−	−	−	+	−	−	−	5/20
Yl/Grn	−	−	−	−	−	+	+ⱳ	−	−	−	−	−	−	−	−	+	+	+ⱳ	−	−	5/20
(3) Saturation																					
Rd/Yl	+	+	+	−	+	−	−	+	−	−	+	+	−	+	+	−	−	−	+	+	11/20
Bl/Grn	+	+	+	+	+	+	+	+	+	−	+	−	+	−	+	+	−	+	+	+	16/20
(4) Color																					
U+ Color/Grey	+	+	+	+	+	+	+	−?	+	+	+	+	+	+	+	−?	+	+	+	+	18/20 U+
U+ Color/Bl-W	+	+	+	+	+	+	+	−?	+	+	+	+	0	+	+	+	+	+	+	0	17/18(20) U+
Potency:																					
(1) Brightness																					
U− W/Blk	−	+	−	−	−	−	−	−	−	−	−	−	−	+?	−	+?	−	−	+?	−	3/20 U−
W/Gy	+	−	−	−	−	−	+	+	+	+	+	−	+	−	+	−	+	−	+	−	9/20
Gy/Blk	−	−	−	−	−	−	−	−	−	−	−	−	−	−	−	+?	−	−	−	−	1/20 U−
(2) Hue																					
Rd/Bl	+	+	+	+	+	−	−ⱳ	+	+	−	+	+	−	+	+	−	+	+	+	+	15/20
Yl/Grn	−	−	−	−	−	+?	−	−	−	−	−	−	−	−	−	−	−	−	−	−	1/20 U−
(3) Saturation																					
U+ Rd/Yl	+	+	+	+	+	+	+	+	+	+	+	+	+	+	+	+	+	+	+	+	20/20 U+
U+ Bl/Grn	+	+	+	+	+	+	−	−	+	+	+	−	−	−	+	+	−	−	+	+	13/20
(4) Color																					
Color/Grey	+	−	+	+	+	+	0	+	+	+	+	+	+	0	0	+	+	0	+	+	16/20
Color/Bl-W	+	−	0	0	0	0	0	−	0	0	+	0	−	0	0	+	−	0	+	0	4/8 (20)

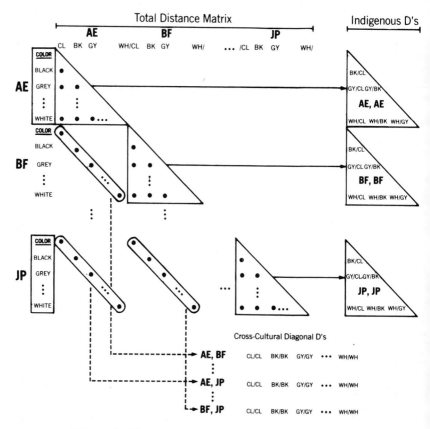

FIGURE 4. Illustrative distance matrix analysis for color category.

CONCLUSION

Let me now return to my title: "Objective Indicators of Subjective Culture". Although our *Atlas of Affective Meanings* is limited in scope at present, its technology is now developed to the point where it could be extended quickly and efficiently both in terms of concepts and human communities sampled. It does get at the affective dimensions of subjective culture in rigorous, quantitative ways, and I would argue that the Good-Bad, Strong-Weak and Active-Passive of culturally significant things are peculiarly important determiners of how we vote, what we buy, what we protest about, how satisfied we are in life and so on through the array of social behaviors.

Our technology is impelling us at an ever-increasing pace into one, interdependent world, where what happens "there" has as much relevance to our own future as what happens "here." If there is anything we should have learned over the past couple of decades about the adoption of technological innovations, whether it be automation, crop rotation or birth control, it is that people's

GENERAL INDICES AND TWO-LETTER KEY FOR 30 LANGUAGE/CULTURE COMMUNITIES TO BE INCLUDED IN *ATLAS CATANS*

Key	Location and Language	Site of Collection	Language Family	Geographic Region
AD	Afghanistan, Dari	Kabul	Indo-European (Iranic)	West Asian
AE	United States, American English	Illinois	Indo-European (Germanic)	North American
AP	Afghanistan, Pashtu	Kabul, Kandahar	Indo-European (Iranic)	West Asian
BE	United States, Black English	Chicago	Indo-European (Germanic)	North American
BF	Belgium, Flemish	Brussels	Indo-European (Germanic)	West European
BP	Brazil, Portuguese	Sao Paulo	Indo-European (Romance)	South American
CB	Calcutta (India), Bengali	Calcutta	Indo-European (Indic)	South Asian
CS	Costa Rica, Spanish	San Jose	Indo-European (Romance)	Central American
DH	Delhi (India), Hindi	Delhi	Indo-European (Indic)	South Asian
FF	Finland, Finnish	Helsinki	Finno-Ugric	North European
FR	France, French	Paris, Strasbourg	Indo-European (Romance)	West European
GG	Germany (West), German	Munster	Indo-European (Germanic)	West European
GK	Greece, Greek	Athens	Indo-European (Greek)	Mediterranean
HC	Hong Kong, Cantonese	Hong Kong	Sino-Tibetan	East Asian
HM	Hungary, Magyar	Budapest	Finno-Ugric	Central European
IF	Iran, Farsi	Tehran	Indo-European (Iranic)	West Asian
IH	Israel, Hebrew	Haifa, Tel Aviv	Afro-Asiatic (Semitic)	Mediterranean
IT	Italy, Italian	Padova	Indo-European (Romance)	Mediterranean
JP	Japan, Japanese	Tokyo	Japanese	East Asian
LA	Lebanon, Arabic	Beirut	Afro-Asiatic (Semitic)	Mediterranean-West Asian
MK	Mysore (India), Kannada	Mysore City, Bangalore	Dravidian	South Asian
MM	Malaysia, Malay	Kuala Lumpur	Malayo-Polynesian	South East Asian
MS	Mexico, Spanish	Mexico City	Indo-European (Romance)	Central American
ND	Netherlands, Dutch	Amsterdam	Indo-European (Germanic)	West European
RR	Rumania, Rumanian	Cluj	Indo-European (Romance)	East European
SW	Sweden, Swedish	Uppsala	Indo-European (Germanic)	North European
TH	Thailand, Thai	Bangkok	Kadai	South East Asian
TK	Turkey, Turkish	Istanbul	Altaic	Mediterranean-West Asian
YC	Yucatan (Mexico), Spanish (Mayan)	Ticul, Chablekal, Kom Chiem	Indo-European (Romance)	Central American
YS	Yugoslavia, Serbo-Croatian	Belgrade	Indo-European (Slavic)	Mediterranean-East European

attitudes, values and customs are prime determiners of social development and change. If our progress toward one interdependent world is to be anything but willy-nilly, then comparable cross-national objective indicators of subjective culture are essential.

STUDENTS' FORMULATING PRACTICES AND
INSTRUCTIONAL STRATEGIES*

Hugh Mehan

Teacher Education Program
University of California, San Diego
La Jolla, California 92093

This paper is a preliminary report on a study that examines instruction formulating practices and instructional strategies that Black and Mexican-American students use to accomplish academic tasks in teacher-student and student-student interactional settings. The materials for the study were gathered in the spring quarter of academic year 1974—75 in a multi-grade, ethnically mixed classroom taught by Courtney B. Cazden and LaDonna Coles in San Diego, California.

This paper describes our research design and presents a preliminary analysis of representative materials. Since our analysis is still in progress, these are only tentative findings, better seen as suggestive rather than as conclusive.

ETHNOGRAPHIC BACKGROUND

Courtney B. Cazden, a noted authority in child language and education,[1-6] took leave from Harvard Graduate School of Education (1974—75) to return to an earlier career as an elementary school teacher. Cazden assumed full teaching responsibilities: she designed curricula, conducted lessons, evaluated students, met with parents, and attended faculty meetings. She taught in a cross-age, ethnically mixed classroom in which there were an equal number of boys and girls, Blacks and Mexican-Americans, and first-, second-, and third-graders.

During the Fall quarter we conducted a "videotape ethnography" of the social organization of Cazden's classroom. Treating the classroom as a social organization implies that there is a normative system of order; classroom participants, both teachers and students, engage in interactional activity that sustains the sense of normative order in the classroom.[7-23]† Studying the classroom as a social organization also implies that there are certain objectives to be met and appropriate means to achieve these ends. We observed in the classroom regularly and videotaped the same hour of classroom activity every day of the first week of school and once every three weeks for the remainder of the Fall quarter. Our videotape materials are enabling us to describe the

* With the assistance of Sue Fisher and Nick Maroules. The materials for this study were gathered by means of the assistance of Ford Foundation Grant No. 740—0420.

† For a general discussion of the social accomplishment of social organization see References 7 through 15; for a discussion of the social accomplishment of social organization in educational settings see References 16 through 23.

interactional activity that teachers and students employ to achieve the organized character of the classroom. We are documenting what students need to know and do in a classroom in order to be successful. We are revealing the educational objectives of the classroom and specifying the often unstated normative rules for appropriate social behavior expected by the teacher. We are describing the often implicit ways in which these educational objectives and rules for socially appropriate behavior are communicated to the students.[24]

During the Fall quarter, Cazden was assigned a "project follow-through" aide. When this aide had to be removed from the classroom for budgetary reasons, arrangements were made for Cazden to be joined by LaDonna Coles in a "team teaching" situation in December. Cazden and Coles organized their classroom in the direction of a "learning centers" approach in the Winter quarter.

When the class was reorganized, the first hour of the day was designated "choosing time." The students were free to choose an academic activity from those the teacher made available. Students could listen to stories on headphones connected to tape-recorders. Educational games, especially of the concrete reasoning variety, were laid out. A "library" was in a quiet corner of the room. Arts and crafts were in a central portion of the room. A more formal learning center included experiments in measurements and metrics. Students could explore on their own and then respond to teacher-initiated questions.

The learning center approach enabled the teachers to build lessons based on the students' interests: pictures of monsters painted in the morning became stories about monsters written later in the day, and vocabulary enrichment lessons later in the week; an interest in baseball led to lessons in probability; a Mexican flag drawn by one student became incorporated into geography and social studies lessons.

Following "choosing time" the teachers and students assembled as a group "on the rug." Here the teachers invited students to display their work and read stories in Spanish and English. Announcements of schedules and news of changes in procedures were made.

After "the rug," the students were divided into small math and reading groups. Some groups started working alone, while the others started with the teachers. At designated times, the groups rotated between self- and teacher-supervised work. Recess and another cycle of directed activities completed the morning.

This classroom arrangement provided students with a diverse range of educational experiences: (1) they worked alone or in small groups on a classroom activity of their own choice; (2) they were involved in whole-class procedural and academic activities; (3) they worked in small groups on a classroom activity of the teachers' choice.

This range of classroom activity also provided us with a vehicle to examine the students in a variety of educational circumstances. We placed a wireless microphone on a different student in the classroom each day in the Spring quarter of the year. The broadcast unit of the microphone was sewn into a pouch on the back of a shirt that the target student wore. The microphone itself was discreetly placed under the collar of the shirt. We videotaped that student during the closing minutes of "choosing time," while the teacher and students were "on the rug," and while the students worked in small groups. This procedure gave us a continuous hour of videotape on each student in a student-centered academic/social activity, a teacher-directed academic/ procedural activity, and a teacher-directed academic activity.

We have 18 hours of tape on individual students. We are examining these "hour in the life" tapes for the language and the interactional practices that the students use in different classroom situations. Our analysis of these tapes will enable us to contrast students' interactional practices and language use when they are with peers and when they are with adults. This contrast will reveal a view of classroom activities, lessons, and organization from the point of view of the students. It will provide a more complete view of students' interactional competence than is presently available.

THE INSTRUCTIONAL PROTOCOL DESIGN

We have devised an "intervention" procedure that fits within the ongoing learning center routine. The intervention procedure enables us to examine the students' formulating and instructional strategies in teacher-student and student-student learning situations under more controlled circumstances.

During the final moments of students' "choosing time," one of the teachers called aside the "target student" (i.e., the student with the wireless microphone for that day). She asked the target student to give instructions to the work group. After the teacher gave the target student instructions and checked the work, all the students were assembled on the rug in the usual manner. The teacher assigned tasks to all but one work group in the usual way. She announced that one student in the remaining group had their instructions. That student was our target student. We videotaped the teacher with the target student, the target student with the work group, and the teacher's evaluation of the students' work after the task was completed.

Thus the basic design of this quasi-experimental procedure takes the form of a communication chain.[25,26] The complete set of steps in the communication chain are:

(1) *Teacher formulation of instructions to target student.* The teacher gives a set of instructions concerning an academic task to the target student.

(2) *Target student formulation of instructions to teacher.* The teacher asks the target student for the instructions (s)he will give to the work group.

(3) *Target student task completion with teacher.* The target student completes the task in the presence of the teacher.

(4) *Target student formulation of instructions to work group.* The target student then instructs the work group, consisting of one to four other students.

(5) *Work group task completion.* The target student and the work group complete the task assigned by the teacher.

(6) *Post-task teacher evaluation.* When the target student and the work group have completed the task, the teacher meets with the target student. She asks the student about the completed task and the work of the group.

The steps in the communication chain are shown in FIGURE 1.

We left the classroom as soon as we had gathered an hour of tape of the target student. As soon as possible after the lesson, we interviewed the teacher regarding the target student's formulation of instructions, their work, and her evaluation of it.

The use of a structured data gathering procedure in a naturally occurring situation is a "controlled ethnography."[27-29] It is an important methodological strategy for a number of reasons.

The studies of learning in naturally occurring situations are generally descriptive ethnographies. While these ethnographies describe learning *in situ*,

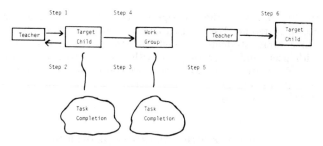

FIGURE 1.   The instruction protocol design.

they have an anecdotal and ad hoc quality. Since the data base of controlled ethnography is audio and videotape, data can be retrieved for reexamination. A controlled ethnography enables observations made in naturally occurring situations to be compared to observations made in structured variations of those naturally occurring situations.

Many studies of children's learning are conducted in the laboratory. Such studies attempt a more rigorous examination of learning by comparing the effects of some variables across time and between control and experimental groups. The problems of generalizing from conclusions drawn in lab conditions to naturally occurring situations are well known and tend to challenge the validity of findings derived from such studies. A controlled ethnography, however, facilitates the comparison of interactional processes across naturally occurring and more contrived situations. A learning task that employs familiar materials can be used in the context of actual, ongoing, classroom routines. The same student working on equivalent tasks in contrasting situations and the teacher's treatment of different students can thus be compared.

This controlled ethnographic procedure enables us to examine the practices by which (1) teachers and students formulate instructions; (2) teachers and students provide instructions; and (3) the teacher evaluates student performance. Instruction formulation is analyzed by comparing the target student's activities with the teacher and with the work groups (steps 1, 2, and 4 in FIGURE 1). Instructional strategies are analyzed by comparing the strategies that the teacher uses to complete the task with the target student to the strategies that the target student uses with the work group (steps 3 and 5 in FIGURE 1). The teacher's evaluative practices are studied by examining the way the teacher evaluates the student's work after the task (step 6 in FIGURE 1) by comparison with interviews made while she was watching the videotape of the day's session.

This paper reports on the formulation of instructions and strategies of instruction in two of the 18 instructional protocol designs. We videotaped the instruction protocol sessions and prepared transcripts of the teacher-student exchanges. We analyze the videotape and transcripts for the instruction-formulating practices and the instructional strategies used by the teacher and students in the two sessions below.

INSTRUCTION FORMULATION

In this section the teacher's formulation of instructions to the target student is compared with (a) the target student's formulation of instructions back to the teacher, and (b) the target student's formulation of instructions to the work group. We are interested in the ways in which information is exchanged in each of these situations and the competencies displayed in the instructional formulations.

We conceive of instructions in the classroom as occurring in at least two modalities: a verbal and an extraverbal modality. The verbal modality includes the grammatical, semantic, and phonological aspects of language. The extraverbal modality includes the kinesic and paralinguistic aspects of communication, including gesturing and ostensive pointing.[30-32]

We will now examine the teacher's instructions and two sets of target student instructions. We are interested in the information that appears in the verbal and extraverbal modalities of the instructions. We are particularly interested in any modification of the teacher's instructions by the target student. These instructions are given for a practical purpose: to accomplish a classroom academic task. We are examining the formulation of instructions to see the function that the verbal and extraverbal materials serve in the accomplishment of the academic task in the respective situations.

The target student for the first instructional protocol was a Black female third-grader. The task was a language exercise. It had two parts. For the first part of the task, the teacher had isolated sentences about two stories that the students were reading. A word was omitted from each sentence. The list of missing words was provided at the bottom of the page. The students were to put the appropriate word from the list in the sentences. For the second part of the task, the students were to sound out the number of syllables in the list of words and enter that number in the blanks provided. A facsimile of the worksheet for this task is reproduced in TABLE 1.

This protocol begins with the teacher (T) giving the target student (C) instructions for the first part of the task:

5   T: I think you've read both of these stories, haven't you? Yeah, so, uh, you find a word, are you listening?
6   C: (*giggles*)
7   T: You find a word down here that fits into each sentence and write it in. Uh, for instance, let's see number, the first one.

She tells the student to complete the sentences associated with the first story. The teacher and student work together to complete the sentences (see lines 8–18, APPENDIX I).‡

When they have finished, the teacher reformulates the instructions for the first part of the task that the student has just accomplished, and gives her instructions for the second part of the task:

19   T: Ok, good, now, after you finish putting the words into these sentences, then here you write the number of syllables, uh, for instance, scary.

Again, the teacher works with the student as she completes the task (see lines 20–27, APPENDIX I).

The teacher-student portion of the design is completed when the teacher obtains the target student's version of the instructions:

27   T: A-no-ther. Three, yeah. Ok. So, now, um, just so I can make sure you're gonna be able to tell the other children, uh, tell me, say back to me what you're gonna do.

---

‡ Symbols used in text and appendices are as follows: . . . = a fading utterance; // = an interruption of one speaker by another; [= two utterances or actions occurring simultaneously; _____ = an unidentified speaker or utterance; " " = a quote of material by a speaker; O-N = a speaker spelling a word.

TABLE 1

TASK FOR INSTRUCTION PROTOCOL 1

Big Brother

Regina is a girl and Cynthia is _____ girl.

The snow was _____ .

Sliding down the hill seemed fun and _____ .

The tray made _____ sled.

One girl said, "How do you _____ me to walk on the slippery hill?"

Monkey in the Middle

One _____ stands in the middle.

You're not _____ to tackle anybody.

But Leslie _____ .

At the end, the dog is in the _____ .

In this game, you need at least _____ people.

scarey	_____	cheats	_____
another	_____	person	_____
expect	_____	middle	_____
slippery	_____	supposed	_____
perfect	_____	three	_____

28	C:	You gonna use these words and put them here and down here you gonna use these words.
29	T:	Ok, and what else?
30	C:	And you gonna do the syllable.
31	T:	Ok. Very good.

The target student then assembles her work group. In this case the assembly of the group is marked as much by sociability as by academic concerns. The target student decides who will play with whom and who will be the recipient of instructions. Initially the instructions are given while the group is assembling. While handing out the work sheets, C says:

36	C:	You choose these words for that one and fill right here at the top, look W, well, then don't listen you wildcat . . .

She then turns her attention to L, a particularly close friend in the work group. She tries to give her special instructions, but L refuses:

36	C:	. . . L, L, see right here? Right here, L, L. Listen, these words
37	L:	I know I know I know

With these exchanges, the students in the work group busy themselves with the task.

The teacher's formulation of the instructions for this task, the target student's formulation of the instructions back to the teacher, and the target student's formulation of the instructions to the work group are recapitulated below:

	Teacher to Student	Student to Teacher	Student to Students
Part 1	You find a word down here that fits into each sentence and write it in	You gonna use these words and put them here and down here you gonna use these words	You choose these words for that one and fill right here at the top
Part 2	write in the number of syllables	and you gonna do the syllables	See, these words you use for here and right here you use this, right here

The target student in the second instruction protocol is a Black female third-grader. The teacher employed a word puzzle for the instruction task. The puzzle asks a question: "Why did you bring a calendar to the dinner party at my diner?" The students are presented a list of words to form an answer to the puzzle question. The task has five steps. The students are to: (1) find a word that is opposite of the one presented; (2) cross out the letters of that word from the scrambled letters of the indicated message word; (3) locate the word made by the remaining letters; (4) enter the letters of the remaining word in the message blank indicated; and (5) read the message created by the words in the blank. The message answers the puzzle question. The answer is in the form of a pun: "You told me to be sure to have a date." A facsimile of the puzzle page is reproduced in FIGURE 2.

The exchange between the teacher and target student begins with the teacher reading the puzzle question. She then goes through the steps of determining the answer words. The teacher first has the target student name the letters in the first scrambled letter list and write them on a portable chalkboard in front of them (see lines 3–5, APPENDIX II). She has the student spell the opposite word (see APPENDIX II, lines 9–11), cross out the letter in that word (lines 11–14, APPENDIX II), identify the word that is left (see lines 15–18, APPENDIX II), and write that word in the space provided (see lines 19–20, APPENDIX II).

This step-by-step procedure is followed for a few puzzle word entries (see lines 21–38, APPENDIX II). The teacher then obtains the target student's version of the instructions:

39   T: ... Now, so I so we can be sure that you'll be able to help them to do it, tell me what you are going to tell them to do.
40   L: Spell these letters, and then put out that letter and have that letter left.

The teacher was not satisfied with that formulation of the instructions, and so elicited further information from the target student (see lines 41–53, APPENDIX II), and went through the entire word list with her (see lines 53–99). At this point, the teacher again asks the target student to formulate the instructions:

99   T: ... Let's go over it once more, what are you going to tell them to do?
100   L: To do the opposite of this. You got to write "old." I'm gonna tell 'em: you gotta write old, cross out old and you have another letter left.

Would You Believe December?

Fargo has a note from Vi.
It says, "Why did you bring
a calendar to the dinner
party at my diner?"

i. new   6. sick—
2. no   7. west east
3. off   8: you
4. out   9. short
5. sell   10. down

Now fill in the blanks
with the letters that are
left. Don't delay!

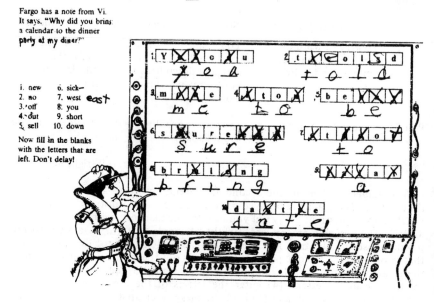

FIGURE 2.   Task for instruction: protocol 2.

The teacher concludes this section of the protocol with her own formulation of the task:

> 101 T: Ok, find, think of the opposite, cross the opposite word out and you have another word left or another letter left.

The target student then assembles the work group. As she passes out worksheets and pencils, she comments on the difficulty of the task and settles disputes between other students (see lines 102–104 and 115–22, APPENDIX II). The target student gives the following instructions to the work group at the outset:

> 105 L: You gotta write what is the opposite of new, is old. So you gotta cross O-L-and-D, and you have a letter left, and you put the letter left in these words.
> 106 E: Oh, that's a _____
> 107 L: I know. See you gotta do the opposite of no. No is yes on number two, no is yes. So you got to write Y-E-S. Then you have a "told" left. So you write T-O-L-D. See, the opposite of "off" is "on," so you gotta cross, in number 3, so you gotta cross "on" off. O-N.

She continues this procedure throughout the remainder of the worksheet (see lines 107–47, APPENDIX II).

The teacher's formulation of the instruction for this task, the target student's formulation of the task to the teacher and the target student's formulation to the work group is recapitulated below:

Teacher–Student	Student–Teacher	Student–Students
think of the opposite, cross the opposite word out and you have another word left or another letter left	(1) Spell these letters and then put out that letter and then you have another letter left	You gotta write what is the opposite of new, is old, so you gotta cross O-L and D and you have a letter left, and you put the letter left in the words
	(2) Do the opposite of this you got to write old. I'm gonna tell 'em: you gotta write old, cross old out and you have another letter left	

The target students' formulation of instructions to the teacher and to the work groups appears to be less elaborate than the teacher's. In the first protocol, while the teacher specifies that *words* are to be *written* in *sentences*, the student says that *words* are to be *used, chosen*, and *put at the top* and *right here*. This represents a considerable reduction of information in the verbal channel.

There appears to be some reduction in information in the second protocol as well. While the teacher says, "*think* of the opposite" word, the target student says, "*do* the opposites." While the teacher employs general categories ("words"), the target student uses specific instances of categories ("letters" and "old," "new," etc.).

One conclusion that has been reached about the child, especially the minority child who uses a reduced or restricted version of an adult's verbal message, is that (s)he has impoverished verbal or cognitive skills.[33–36] Before that conclusion can be accepted, however, it is necessary to determine the manner by which the student fulfills the functions of communicating the requisite information in these tasks.[37–39]

At each step in these tasks, the person passing on information must communicate the operation to be performed, the material to be used, and the location of the material to be used. The steps in the task, and the modality used to accomplish these instructional functions for the first instructional protocol, are displayed in TABLE 2.

The target student encodes information extralinguistically to describe and locate the materials to be used and to communicate the operations to be performed on the materials. As the target student described the operation to be performed to the teacher ("you gonna use these words"), she simultaneously pointed to the two groups of vocabulary words and showed where they were to be placed in the sentences. As the target student initially formulated the materials and their location to the work group verbally ("you choose these words"), she simultaneously showed them the words, their location, and the sentence slots.

This instruction formulation procedure is evident in her instructions to the individual members of the group during the course of their work as well. At one point (line 38), she sees student E looking away from his work. While saying, "listen E, see these words right here, you use this right here," she simultaneously pointed back and forth to the words and where they are to be inserted in the sentences (see line 38).

At another point a student asked for help: "C, where do you get the words to put up here?" (line 39, APPENDIX I). While the target student responded "right

TABLE 2

SUMMARY OF INSTRUCTIONS FORMULATED: FIRST TARGET STUDENT

Instructional Function	Modality	Teacher-Student	Student-Teacher	Student-Students
Part I				
Describe and locate materials	Verbal	find a word down here	gonna use (these words)	you choose these words
	Extraverbal	(points to word list)	(points to word list)	(points to word list)
Indicate operation	Verbal	write it in	put them here	fill right here at the top
	Extraverbal	(points to sentence slot)	(points to sentence slot)	(points to sentence slot)
Part II				
Describe and locate materials	Verbal			see the word you use for here
	Extraverbal			(points to word list and answer blank)
Indicate operation	Verbal	write in the number of syllables	do the syllables	you use this
	Extraverbal	(points to answer blank)	(points to answer blank)	(points to words and answer blank)

there and right there" (line 40) she pointed to the word lists for the stories. She then sounded out the number of syllables in the words for the group to hear:

40 C: ...and then you write the syllables, these are like per-son, lit-tle, sup-pose, three, scar-y, an-no-ther, ex-cept, slippy, and per-feck, pro-tect

A similar relationship is evident in the second protocol. This task has five steps (see p. 9, above). The teacher's formulation of these steps and the two formulations by the target student are summarized in TABLE 3.

To communicate the procedure involved in step one, the teacher employs a cognitive operation 'think' while the target student describes this step in more mechanical terms: 'do' and 'write.' The teacher employs a general category ("word") while the student employ's specific instances of the category ('letters,' 'new') and the highly indexical expression "this" to communicate the materials on which the operation is to be performed.

Both teacher and student describe the procedure to be followed in step 2 in similar terms. The teacher again uses a general category term ('word') while the student employs specific instances of the category (letters, and a particular word, "old," "off," etc.) to communicate the materials on which the procedure is to be performed.

Both the teacher and the student describe the result of the location procedure in a similar way. The teacher describes both possible outcomes (words and letters), while the student describes one possibility or the other in her formulations.

The target student explicitly told the students in the work group that they were to put the remaining letters in the remaining blank (step 4). The teacher did not include this instruction in her summary formulation for the target student; but she did include this step in her earlier instructions to the student (see line 19, APPENDIX II, for example).

FUNCTIONALLY EQUIVALENT FORMULATIONS

The reduction in information in the verbal channel is not critical for the communication of instructions to the work groups. The requisite functions of these exchanges are communicating the operations to be performed and the materials to be used. The teacher used the verbal modality primarily to accomplish these instructional functions. The target students employed both verbal and extraverbal modalities to accomplish these same functions. These students have, in effect, taken information that was coded by the teacher in the verbal modality and coded it in other modalities.

This operation is an instance of cross-modal information transfer.[40,41] It does not represent a loss of information; it is a transformation of information. Although the target students have not duplicated the information that appeared in the verbal modality of the teacher's instructions, they have provided functionally equivalent instructions.

If children do not duplicate adult forms of speaking, it does not necessarily imply that they have limited competence. It may be a display of functional linguistic[42,43] or functional interactional competence.[44-46] Those who conclude that children who do not speak like adults have a limited competence overemphasize the verbal mode of expression and the grammatical aspects of

TABLE 3

SUMMARY OF INSTRUCTIONS FORMULATED: SECOND TARGET STUDENT

Steps in Task	Instructional Function	Modality	Teacher-Student	Student-Teacher	Student-Students
1. Locate opposite word	Describe and locate materials	Verbal	words	letters	"new"
		Extraverbal	(points to list)	(points to list)	
	Indicate operation	Verbal	think of the opposite word	spell; do the opposite	write the opposite
		Extraverbal			
2. Cross out scrambled letters	Describe and locate materials	Verbal	the opposite word	that letter; "old"	"old"
		Extraverbal			
	Indicate operation	Verbal	cross out	cross out	cross out
		Extraverbal			
3. Locate remaining word	Describe and locate materials	Verbal	you have another word or letter left	you have another word left; you have another letter left	you have another word left
		Extraverbal			
4. Enter remaining word in message blank	Describe and locate materials	Verbal			
		Extraverbal			
	Indicate operation	Verbal			put letters in words
		Extraverbal			(points to answer slots)

language. They equate the use of well-formed sentences with intellectual achievement. This view does not recognize that there are alternative ways of accomplishing the same communicative end. The same communicative form can be expressed in many ways, both in the verbal modality and across modalities. People, especially those from culturally different backgrounds, have functionally equivalent procedures for communicating information and accomplishing objectives. Functional equivalence must not be confused with radical subjectivism. Alternative interactional practices do not imply impenetrably separate realities. Variation in expression is only made possible by an invariant interpretive skill.[47-49] We will continue to explore the varieties of expression and structural invariance in our remaining tapes.

The preceding analysis of instruction formulation illustrates functionally equivalent cross-modal information transfer by the target students. The following discussion illustrates functionally equivalent instructional strategies by the target students.

INSTRUCTIONAL STRATEGIES

In this section the teacher's strategies for completing the task are compared with the target students' strategies for completing the assigned tasks with the work group. We want to see if the students employ instructional strategies that are similar to or different from the teacher's to accomplish the assigned task.

The teacher uses the following procedures when instructing the target student in the protocols. From the first instructional protocol:

7	T:	You find a word down here that fits into each sentence and write it in. Uh, for instance, let's see number, the first one.
8	C:	*(reading)*: Regina is a girl and Cynthia is –
9	T:	One of these words will fit in these and make sense. Cynthia is blank girl.
10	C:	*(pause)* Another
11	T:	Another, right. Okay, and then you just write in "another" in here. And the words for these sentences are here. Now, just read over these words, so . . .
12	C:	Scary
13	T:	Scary
14	C:	Another, ⌈expect, slippery, perfect –⌉
	T:	⌊expect, yeah ⌋
15	T:	Yeah, perfect
16	C:	Cheats
17	T:	Cheats
18	C:	Person, middle, suppose, three
19	T:	Ok, good, now, after you finish putting the words into these sentences, then here you write the number of syllables, uh, for instance, scary.
20	C:	Two
21	T:	Another
22	C:	One, one
23	T:	Say it
24	C:	Ano – two
25	T:	Say it again
26	C:	A-no- ther! Three
	J:	another, another, another//

27   T: A-no-ther. Three, yeah. Ok. So, now, um, just so I can make sure you're gonna be able to tell the other children, uh, tell me, say back to me what you're gonna do.

And from the second instructional protocol:

5   T: (*Writes Y, O, L, O, D, U on chalkboard in front of them*) Ok, now number one here says "new." What's the opposite of new?
6   L: Now
7   T: No the opposite like up-down, stop-go, in-out, what's the opposite of new?
8   L: Old
9   T: Old. How would you spell old?
10   L: O-L-D
11   T: Ok, in the letters that are on this paper, that we put on the board, cross out, right here on the board, the letters that you just used for spelling old.
12   L: Make an X?
13   T: Yeah, just put an X on them.
14   L: (*Crosses out letters O, L, D*)
15   T: Good. What word is left?
16   L: Y-O-U
17   T: What does that spell?
18   L: You
19   T: Ok, and down here you write y-o-u.
20   L: (*Writes on worksheet*)
21   T: Ok because that's the first word of the message. Now let's try one more.

The teacher is *demonstrating* the mechanics of the task. The demonstration entails going through the steps of the task, engaging the student in the cooperative completion of the objective. Both the teacher and the student work together to arrive at the answer. At first the teacher guides the student by her words (see lines 5–21, APPENDIX II, and lines 11 and 19, APPENDIX I); then the student begins to guide her own behavior (see lines 53–96, APPENDIX II, and lines 16–19, APPENDIX I).

The target students, on the other hand, instruct the work groups in the following way. From the first protocol:

40   C: Right there, and right down here, and then you write the syllables, these are like per-son, lit-tle, sup-pose, three, scar-y, an-no-ther, ex-cept, slippy, and per-feck, pro-tect (*group works for two minutes*)
41   W: The snow was blank, the snow was —
42   L: (*Shows paper to C; asks indistinguishable question*)
43   C: . . . . copycatter, scare, scary, another, a-no-ther, accept, slip-per-y, per-fect, per-son, mid-dle, suppose, sup-pose, sup-three (*leaves table to put worksheet in file*)

And from the second protocol:

105 L: (*goes to get pencils, then returns to work table*) It is hard. You gotta write what is the opposite of "new," is "old." So you gotta cross O-L and D, and you have a letter left, and you put the letter left in these words.
106 E: Oh that's a_____
107 L: I know. See you gotta do the opposite of "no." "No" is "yes" on number two. No is yes. So you gotta write Y-E-S. Then you have a "told" left. So you write T-O-L-D. See the opposite of off is on so you gotta cross, in number three, so you gotta cross "on" off. O-N.

The target students are instructing the work group by *performing* the activity. They do each step of the task so that the others can see and hear. The target students indicate the material to be used, i.e., the puzzle word list, the scrambled letters, the answer slots, often by pointing. They then *do* the required operations on those materials. In the first protocol, the target student sounds out the number of syllables in the words. In the second protocol, the target student spells the "opposite words," crosses out their letters, and puts the letters left in the answer slots.

DEMONSTRATED AND MODELED INSTRUCTIONS

A demonstration and a modeling procedure for instructing students are revealed in these instructional protocols. The teacher employs the demonstration procedure and the target student employs the modeling procedure.

These students *model* the task to be accomplished. They do the work that their work groups are to do, out loud, in front of them to see and hear. This modeling instructional procedure contrasts with the teacher's procedure of *demonstrating* instructions. Demonstration involves an intentional showing of the work and engaging the learner in the accomplishment of the task. Modeling incorporates the showing of the steps, but does not involve a cooperative completion of the task. Modeling shows *what* to do; it does not show *why* to do it. The learners are left to imitate the work of the teacher.

The modeled instructions are not private, personal acts; they have definite utility for these students, especially those in the second work group. Each student completed the worksheets to the teacher's satisfaction. They also demonstrate their understanding in other ways. Students E, W, and C say the steps to be followed out loud as they complete their tasks:

```
115   E & W:   (write and spell) Y-O-U
126      W:   I got it, "well."
```

They articulate the steps in disputes over correct answers:

```
137   W:   (Tapping L on head) You did this one wrong. The opposite of "out" is
           "in."
      L:   T
138   L:   I know it
               //W: I-N
                  //L: So what?
                     //W: I-N
                        //L: So
                           //W: In
                              //L: You got to
      write it here
      * * *
145   C:   Wait, let me see. That's "date."
```

While we have described the differences between the two instructional strategies, our analysis is not complete enough to comment on the frequency, superiority, or preference of modeled or demonstrated instructional strategies. We are examining the remaining protocols to determine the strategies that students use to instruct their work groups and the utility of the strategies.

There is a parallel to be drawn between these students' teaching strategies and the methods of informal learning in which basic cultural values and traditions are passed on from generation to generation.[50,51] Demonstrations and models are the mechanism of learning in these informal situations. Verbal formulations are seldom relied on. Because they learn by observation and imitation, learners are said not to acquire general principles.

Language is the predominant mode of transferring information in formal school settings. In extreme views, language is said to be sufficient for learning. Learners need only be exposed to meaningful verbal messages to learn.[52] Teaching in schools consists of the verbal formulation of concepts. Students are to link concepts to each other and eventually to empirical counterparts, thereby arriving at general principles or rules.

If we continue to find that students model tasks with each other and are able to apply principles to new situations, then a de-emphasis of purely verbal instruction and an emphasis on activity-based learning will be recommended.[53,54] This shift of emphasis might involve starting instruction with concrete learning experiences in which the reasoning practices and strategies of learners are visible in the task. Students would progress through a learning cycle in which free exploration and concrete learning experiences would be followed by symbolic representation.

Reflexive awareness, application of principles to new situations, and symbolic representation are all necessary components of this conception of a learning cycle. The reflexive awareness would involve developing an ability to formulate, in verbal and extraverbal ways, the procedures by which a task is accomplished. The test of learning would be the application of these procedures to new situations. Symbolic representation would always evolve from concrete experiences, not be a hollow conceptual apparatus removed from experience.

CONCLUSION

This report of research *displays* students' language using and reasoning practices. The potential implications of demonstrated and modeled instructions for classroom instruction have been discussed. The display of practices as compared with an abstracted tabulation of the frequency of their occurrence has a further educational implication for multicultural education. Students from minority backgrounds fail in American schools. The document of their failure is achievement and IQ test results.[55−57] Test results are equated with intellectual ability. The test is a product measure, operating on behavioristic principles. It appears in an S-R format. Students are presented with stimuli items in the form of test questions. Students produce responses in the form of answers to questions. The answers are tabulated and then correlated with social characteristics like ethnicity and SES.

That method does not reveal the practices that students use to make the linkages between the questions and the answers. Because students may have different but functionally equivalent ways of experiencing, expressing, or completing educational tasks, it is necessary to examine the reasoning and communicative practices that students employ, not just correlate student characteristics and educational outcomes to assess competence.[58]

This report of research displays our "controlled ethnographic" research technique. This technique contrasts a naturally occurring situation with a modification of the naturally occurring situation. We start by conducting a conventional ethnography of a naturally occurring situation. We supplement our field observation by videotaping the situation on a regular basis. A phenomenon of interest emerges from the ethnography and repeated examinations of the videotape. In this case, the phenomenon is the students' formulating and instructional practices. We describe the phenomenon's occurrence in the naturally occurring situation in as much detail as possible. We then devised a structured intervention procedure within the context of the naturally occurring situation. We utilize existing materials, classroom arrangements and activities as much as possible. We then compare findings gathered in the naturally occurring situation with those generated in the intervention procedure.

It is important to note how a controlled ethnography differs from a laboratory experiment and a field experiment. Lab experiments study behavior in a situation removed from naturally occurring situations. Classic experimental designs make measurements before and after the application of experimental treatment and between experimental and control groups. Lab results are seldom formally compared to naturally occurring situations; statistical inferences to naturally occurring conditions are made.

Field experiments conduct studies in naturally occurring situations, but do not use naturally occurring procedures or materials. It is a laboratory study that happens to occur in a field setting. The phenomenon studied does not emerge from the observation of naturally occurring behavior. The naturally occurring situation is not modified to obtain the intervention procedure. Comparison of results from intervention procedures are not compared to naturally occurring materials.

The intervention procedure, like the routine classroom activity from which it is derived, has an educational objective: the exchange of educational information between teacher and learner. The participants employ certain formulating and instructional practices to accomplish these educational objectives. Our study reveals the interactional practices that assemble the socially organized character of these classroom activities.

We use videotape as a data-gathering device. We use videotape and transcripts of verbal and extraverbal material between teachers and students derived from the videotape as a data display device. We conduct an intensive analysis of the complete course of interaction across the situations studied. We provide transcripts along with our analysis. The videotape and transcripts provide the grounds of our interpretation as we move up the ladder of abstraction from raw materials to coded data to summarized findings. This practice enables others to follow the logic of our analysis and affords the possibility for alternative interpretations to be made on the same materials.[59,60]

ACKNOWLEDGMENTS

Special thanks are extended to Marjorie Martus for her support of this research, and to Professor Jeffrey Shultz, Harvard Graduate School of Education, for his assistance with the audiovisual equipment. The cooperation of the San Diego Unified School District, especially that of Edward C. Cain, is gratefully acknowledged. In addition to agreeing to have their classroom teaching subject to daily scrutiny, Courtney B. Cazden and LaDonna Coles have made many valuable suggestions about the substance of this paper and its impact on improved classroom instruction.

REFERENCES

1. CAZDEN, C B. 1972. Child Language and Education. Holt, Rinehart and Winston. New York, N.Y.
2. CAZDEN, C. B., V. P. JOHN & D. HYMES, Eds. 1972. Functions of Language in the Classroom. Teachers College Press. New York, N.Y.
3. CAZDEN, C. B., R. BROWN & U. BELLUGI. 1969. The child's grammar from I to III. *In* 1967 Minnesota Symposium on Child Development. J. P. Hill, Ed.: 28—73. University of Minnesota Press. Minneapolis, Minn.
4. CAZDEN, C. B. Approaches to social dialectics in early childhood education. *In* Sociolinguistics: A Cross Disciplinary Perspective. R. Shuy, Ed.: 70—81. Center for Applied Linguistics. Washington, D.C.
5. CAZDEN, C. B. 1968. The acquisition of noun and verb inflections. Child Devel. **39:** 443—48.
6. CAZDEN, C. B. 1966. Subcultural differences in child language. Merrill-Palmer Quart. **12:** 185—219.
7. GARFINKEL, H. 1967. Studies in Ethnomethodology. Prentice-Hall. New York, N.Y.
8. GARFINKEL, H. & H. SACKS. 1970. The formal properties of practical actions. *In* Theoretical Sociology. J. C. McKinney and E. Tiryakian, Eds. Appleton-Century-Crofts. New York, N.Y.
9. CICOUREL, A. V. 1968. The Social Organization of Juvenile Justice. John Wiley. New York, N.Y.
10. CICOUREL, A. V. 1973. Cognitive Sociology. Macmillan. London, England.
11. CICOUREL, A. V. 1974. Theory and Method in a Study of Argentine Fertility. John Wiley. New York, N.Y.
12. MEHAN, H. & H. WOOD. 1975. The Reality of Ethnomethodology. Wiley Interscience. New York, N.Y.
13. POLLNER, M. 1974. Mundane reasoning. *In* Philosophy of Social Sciences **4:** 35—54.
14. POLLNER, M. 1975. The very coinage of your brain. *In* Philosophy of the Social Sciences **5:** 411—430.
15. SACKS, H., E. SCHEGLOFF & G. JEFFERSON. 1974. A simplest systematics for the organization of turn taking in conversation. Language **50:** 696—735.
16. CICOUREL, A. V. *et al.* 1974. Language Use and School Performance. Academic Press. New York, N.Y.
17. CICOUREL, A. V. & J. KITSUSE. 1963. Educational Decision Makers. Bobbs-Merrill. Indianapolis, Ind.
18. ERICKSON, F. 1975. Gatekeeping and the melting pot: Interaction in counseling encounters. Harvard Ed. Rev. **45:** 44—70.
19 ERICKSON, F. & J. SHULTZ. 1975. Developing indicators for interactional quality. Paper presented at AERA. Washington, D.C. April, 1975.
20. McDERMOTT, R. P. 1974. Achieving school failure. *In* Education and Cultural Process. G. D. Spindler, Ed. Holt, Rinehart and Winston. New York, N.Y.
21. MEHAN, H. 1973. Assessing children's language using abilities. *In* Methodological Issues in Comparative Sociological Research. J. M. Armer and A. D. Grimshaw, Eds. John Wiley. New York, N.Y.
22. MEHAN, H. 1974. Ethnomethodology and education. *In* Sociology of the School and Schooling. D. O'Shea, Ed. National Institute of Education. Washington, D.C.
23. SHUMSKY, M. & H. MEHAN. 1974. The comparability practice of description in two evaluative contexts. Paper presented at VIIIth World Congress of Sociology. Toronto, Ontario, Canada. August, 1974.
24. MEHAN, H., C. B. CAZDEN, L. COLES, S. FISHER & N. MAROULES. The Social Organization of Classroom Lessons. CHIP Report. UCSD. La Jolla, Calif.
25. ALLPORT, G. W. & L. J. POSTMAN. 1945. The basic psychology of rumor. Trans. N.Y. Acad. Sci. 8: 61—81.
26. FESTINGER, L., K. BACK, S. SCHACHTER, H. KELLEY & J. THIBAUT. 1950. Theory and Experiment in Social Communications. Institute for Social Research. Ann Arbor, Mich.

27. COLE, M. 1974. Toward an experimental anthropology of education. CAE Journal: 7–11.
28. COLE, M. et al. 1971. The Cultural Context of Learning and Thinking. Basic Books. New York, N.Y.
29. SHUMSKY, M. & H. MEHAN. 1974. The comparability practice of description in two evaluative contexts. Paper presented at VIIIth World Congress of Sociology. Toronto, Ontario, Canada. August, 1974.
30. BIRDWHISTELL, R. L. 1970. Kinesics and Context. University of Pennsylvania Press. Philadelphia, Pa.
31. PITTENGER, R. E., C. F. HOCKETT & J. J. DANEHY. 1960. The First Five Minutes. Paul Martineau. Ithaca, N.Y.
32. JULES-ROSETTE, B. 1974. Reflexive ethnography. Paper presented at Ethnomethodology Colloquium. July, 1974.
33. BEREITER, K., & S. ENGLEMAN. 1972. Teaching the Disadvantaged Child in the Preschool. Prentice-Hall. Englewood Cliffs, N.J.
34. HERRNSTEIN, R. J. 1974. IQ in the Meritocracy. Little Brown and Company. Boston, Mass.
35. HESS, R. D. & V. C. SHIPMAN. 1968. Maternal influences upon early learning: the cognitive environments of urban preschool children. In Early Education. R. D. Hess & R. M. Bear, Eds. Aldine. Chicago.
36. JENSEN, A. R. 1969. How much can we boost IQ and scholastic achievement? Harvard Ed. Rev. 39 (1): 1–123.
37. SEBEOK, T. A. 1962. Coding in the evolution of signalling behavior. Behavioral Science 7 (4): 430–42.
38. HALLIDAY, M. A. K. 1970. Language structure and language function. In New Horizons in Linguistics. J. Lyons, Ed. Penguin. London.
39. HYMES, D. 1971. Competence and performance in linguistic theory. In Language Acquisition: Models and Methods. R. Huxley and E. Ingram, Eds. Academic Press. New York, N.Y.
40. GUMPERZ, J. J. 1971. Language in Social Groups. Stanford University Press. Stanford, California.
41. CICOUREL, A. V. 1973. Cognitive Sociology. Macmillan. London, England.
42. CAZDEN, C. B. et al. 1972. Functions of Language in the Classroom. Teachers College Press. New York, N.Y.
43. SHUY, R. & M. GRIFFIN. 1975. A proposal to study children's functional language and education in the early years. Center for Applied Linguistics. Unpublished material.
44. MEHAN, H. 1972. Language using abilities. Language Sci. 22: 1–10.
45. CICOUREL, A. V. 1973. Cognitive Sociology. Macmillan. London, England.
46. CICOUREL, A. V. et al. 1974. Language Use and School Performance. Academic Press. New York, N.Y.
47. PIAGET, J. 1970. Main Trends in Psychology. Harper and Row. New York, N.Y.
48. CICOUREL, A. V. 1973. Cognitive Sociology. Macmillan. London, England.
49. MEHAN, H. 1972. Language using abilities. Language Sci. 22: 1–10.
50. MEAD, M. 1964. Continuities in Cultural Evolution. Yale University Press. New Haven, Conn.
51. COLE, M. & S. SCRIBNER. 1973. Cognitive consequences of formal and informal learning. Science 182: 553–59.
52. AUSUBEL, D. P. 1967. A cognitive-structure view of school learning. In Instruction: Some Contemporary Viewpoints. L. Siegal, Ed.: 207–57. Chandler. San Francisco, California.
53. BRUNER, J. 1966. Toward a Theory of Instruction. Harvard University Press. Cambridge, Mass.
54. PIAGET, J. 1969. Science of Education and the Psychology of the Child. Viking Press. New York, N.Y.
55. COLEMAN, J. S., et al. 1966. Equality of Educational Opportunity. U.S. Government Printing Office. Washington, D.C.
56. JENCKS, C. et al. 1974. Inequality. Basic Books. New York, N.Y.

57. MAYESKE, G. W. 1973. A Study of Our Nation's Schools. U.S. Department of Health, Education and Welfare. Washington, D.C.

58. MEHAN, H. 1973. Assessing children's language using abilities. *In* Methodological Issues in Comparative Sociological Research. J. M. Armer and A. D. Grimshaw, Eds. John Wiley. New York, N.Y.

59. CICOUREL, A. V. 1968. The Social Organization of Juvenile Justice. John Wiley. New York, N.Y. (especially p. 2).

60. MEHAN, H. 1973. Assessing children's language using abilities. *In* Methodological Issues in Comparative Sociological Research. J. M. Armer and A. D. Grimshaw, Eds. John Wiley. New York, N.Y. (especially p. 328).

APPENDIX I

NOTE: CIS 11, Instructional Protocol, Teacher (T), Target Student (C), Students in Work Group (L, W, E, D)

Teacher with Target Student

1   T: Now, C, um, I want to explain your work to you so you'll know how to do it. Come here.

2   C: Wait, I got to do something (*to L*)

3   T: Um, these are sentences about the first two stories in the Exploring book. Big Brother, and Monkey in the Middle.

4   C: You read those, you read the book. Regina is a girl, Cynthia is too

5   T: I think you've read both of these stories, haven't you? Yeah, so, uh, you find a word, are you listening?

6   C: (*giggles*)

7   T: You find a word down here that fits into each sentence and write it in. Uh, for instance, let's see number, the first one.

8   C: (*reading*): Regina is a girl and Cynthia is —

9   T: One of these words will fit in these and make sense. Cynthia is blank girl.

10   C: (*pause*) Another.

11   T: Another, right. Okay, and then you just write in "another" in here. And the words for these sentences are here. Now, just read over these words, so . . .

12   C: Scary

13   T: Scary

14   C: Another, ⌈ expect, slippery, perfect —
     T: ⌊ expect, yeah

15   T: Yeah, perfect

16   C: Cheats

17   T: Cheats

18   C: Person, middle, suppose, three

19   T: Ok, good, now, after you finish putting the words into these sentences, then here you write the number of syllables, uh, for instance, scary.

20   C: Two

21   T: Another.

22   C: One, one

23   T: Say it

24   C: Ano — two

25   T: Say it again

26   C: A — no — ⌈ ther!   Three
     J: ⌊ another, another, another//

27   T: A-no-ther. Three, yeah. Ok. So, now, um, just so I can make sure you're gonna be able to tell the other children, uh, tell me, say back to me what you're gonna do.

28   C: You gonna use these words and put them here and down here you gonna use these words.

29 T: Ok, and what else?
30 C: And you gonna do the syllable.
31 T: Ok. Very good.

Target Student to Work Group

32 C: Hey, boy, ok, you know what to do, I ain't gonna explain it to you
33 E: You don't even know. I'm doin' my paper
34 C: Well then I ain't showing you how. D! She said she gonna play with R, but not F
35 D: I know, that's what I was gonna tell you
36 C: You choose these words for that one and fill right here at the top, look W, well then don't listen you wildcat. L, L see right here? Right here, L, L, L, listen. These words —
37 L: I know, I know, I know (*group works on papers without talking for three minutes*)
38 C: E, listen, see these words you use for here, and right here you use this, right here. But don't you copy me (*group works silently for two minutes*)
39 D: C! C! Where do you get the words to put up here?
40 C: Right there, and right down here, and then you write the syllables, these are like per-son, lit-tle, sup-pose, three, scar-y, an-no-ther, ex-cept, slippy, and per-feck, pro-tect (*group works for two minutes*)
41 W: (*Shows paper to C; asks indistinguishable question*)
42 L: The snow was blank, the snow was —
43 C: Right here. How many more do she got left? I wanna carry my purse with me (*one minute pause*) You tryin' to copy! (*to W*) (*two minutes of work*) Copycat (*to W*) you mama, you can't even do none of the bottom . . . You ain't shittin' on me, you better go and shit on your momma (*30 seconds of work*) copycatter, scare, scary, another, a-no-ther, accept, slip-per-y, per-fect, per-son, mid-dle, suppose, sup-pose, sup-three (*leaves table to put worksheet in file*).

APPENDIX II

NOTE: CIS 23, Instructional Protocol, Teacher (T), Student (L), Another Student (C)

Teacher with Target Student

1 T: Would you want to come back with me a minute, I want to explain your group's work.
2 C: Oh, I want to, can I do it?
3 T: We'll see, C, we'll see. (*Teacher & L leave circle at rug; go to table*). Now let's see, if you sit down here (*directs L to seat*) now this is a new kind of work. Um, it says, "Fargo has a note from Vi." Like a Fargo, North Dakoter, from Electric Company. It says, "Why did you bring a calendar to the dinner party at my diner?" Now number one says "new," what's, and number one here has all these letters. L read me the letters in those boxes.
4 L: Y, O, L, O, D, U.
5 T: (*Writes Y, O, L, O, D, U on chalkboard in front of them*) Ok, now number one here says "new." What's the opposite of new?
6 L: Now
7 T: No the opposite like up-down, stop-go, in-out, what's the opposite of new?
8 L: Old
9 T: Old. How would you spell old?
10 L: O-L-D
11 T: Ok, in the letters that are on this paper, that we put on the board, cross out, right here on the board, the letters that you just used for spelling old.

12	L:	Make an X?
13	T:	Yeah, just put an X on them.
14	L:	(*Crosses out letters O, L, D*)
15	T:	Good. What word is left?
16	L:	Y-O-U
17	T:	What does that spell?
18	L:	You
19	T:	Ok, and down here you write y-o-u.
20	L:	(*Writes on worksheet*)
21	T:	Ok because that's the first word of the message. Now let's try one more. There's an eraser over there, could you get it. Let's take the second word in the message. Read me the words that are here.
22	L:	T-Y-E-O-L-S-D
23	T:	T-Y-E-O-L . . .
24	L:	D, S-D
25	T:	Ok, now number two here says . . .
26	L:	No, now
27	T:	Number two says . . .
28	L:	No
29	T:	No. What's the opposite of no?
30	L:	Yes
31	T:	Ok. How do you spell yes?
32	L:	Y-e-s
33	T:	Alright, now, what are you going . . .
34	L:	(*Crosses out letters y-e-s on chalkboard*) Told
35	T:	What have you got left?
36	L:	Told
37	T:	Alright so what are you going to write here?
38	L:	Told
39	T:	Ok that's the way you figure out what the message is in this puzzle. Now, your job is to explain that to the other children in your reading group. The second page you won't need to explain, that's an easy one, that's where you just look up at the picture and fill in the letters they'll know how to do that. But this one is going to be tricky. Now so I so we can be sure that you'll be able to help them do it, tell me what you are going to tell them to do.
40	L:	Spell these letters, and then put out that letter and then have another letter left.
41	T:	Well, how are they going to know which ones to cross out here so they'll have some letters left?
42	L:	Gotta cross out the letter right there, now . . . new.
43	T:	No we didn't, now wait a minute what's . . .
44	L:	Y-O-L-O and you gotta cross out
45	T:	We, what, how did you know what letters to cross out here? This, number one these letters say new,
46	L:	Old, you gotta cross out old.
47	T:	Ok, but how did you find out it was old?
48	L:	Because it was new, its old, is that right?
49	T:	Yeah, you want to cross out the opposite of new. You better say that because that's going to be really important. They are going to read "new" and then what are they going to do?
50	L:	Do the opposite of it
51	T:	Do the opposite of it. And the opposite of new is . . .?
52	L:	Old
53	T:	Alright, now we better go through this and see if you sure what the opposites are. Number two says . . .
54	L:	No
55	T:	The opposite would be?
56	L:	Yes
57	T:	Number three?

58	L:	Off
59	T:	The opposite would be?
60	L:	On
61	T:	On
62	L:	Out ⌈in. Sail, ⌈sell
	T:	⌊in ⌊sell
63	T:	Now in a store somebody sells something and somebody, what would be the opposite of sell? It's kinds hard.
64	L:	Don't sell
65	T:	Well yeah, don't sell is one kind of an opposite. Think of two people in a store, the lady behind the cash register is gonna sell something and the other person is gonna . . .
66	L:	Buy
67	T:	Buy. That's what they are looking for. Sell, buy. Ok?
68	L:	Stick
69	T:	Not stick but
70	L:	Sick
71	T:	Sick, the opposite is . . .
72	L:	Sick
73	T:	If you're sick in bed and then the opposite would by you're . . .
74	L:	Sick
75	T:	No now think of something that means the opposite like: sell-buy, out-in, off-on. A person's sick and then he's . . . What would not sick mean? If you're not sick you are . . .
76	L:	Well
77	T:	Well yeah, Ok this is a hard one too.
78	L:	West
79	T:	West. I'll probably have to tell you that one. That's east and maybe I better write that one on your paper because that will give you trouble (*leaves to get pencil*). I'll write that one here because that's really a hard one. So if they have trouble with that you can help them and this will be just your paper. Now what's number eight?
80	L:	Short
81	T:	No, eight, eight
82	L:	Oh, you
83	T:	The opposite of you is . . .
84	L:	Me
85	T:	Yeah!
86	L:	Short
87	T:	Good, short. The opposite of short is . . .
88	L:	Long
89	T:	Ah yeah it could be long, let's see what it looks like, there's another opposite for short, think of a person, a person is short (*raises hand above head*) or . . .
90	L:	Small, long, big
91	T:	What do you call it when, like you are . . .
92	T:	You're not short, you are . . .
93	L:	Tall
94	T:	Tall! That's what they are looking for here, tall. What's
95	L:	Down up
96	T:	Down up, Ok. Now
97	D:	(*Approaches teacher;* _____)
98	L:	I don't know now . . .
99	T:	(*to D*) No you go to the circle now, you go over to the rug now. D please go over there. Thank you. Um, Ok. Let's go over it once more, what are you going to tell them to do?
100	L:	To do the opposite of this. You got to write old, I'm gonna tell 'em: you gotta write old, cross old out and you have another letter left.
101	T:	Ok, find, think of the opposite, cross the opposite word out and you have

another word left or another letter left. //L: You. //T: They will have you left. Ok that's pretty tricky. So you'll have to be a pretty good teacher to help them understand that. And then of course when you finish they put their name on it and put them in their folders. Just like always. Ok, fine, L, thank you.

Target Student to Work Group

102	L:	See C, it is hard (*passes out papers*), it is hard, it's hard
103	W:	This is D's pencil
104	C:	That's mine, and I'm giving it to you
105	L:	(*goes to get pencils then returns to work table*) It is hard. You gotta write what is the opposite of "new," is "old." So you gotta cross O-L and D, and you have a letter left, and you put the letter left in these words.
106	E:	Oh that's a_____
107	L:	I know. See you gotta do the opposite of "no." "No" is "yes" on number two. No is yes. So you got to write Y-E-S. Then you have a "told" left. So you write T-O-L-D. See the opposite of off is on so you gotta cross, in number three, so you gotta cross "on" off. O-N.
108	C:	I know, I already did that. And it's "me."
109	L:	And it's "me" left, M-E.
110	C:	L and M got to do this
111	L:	I got to tell them how to do it. Four: "out" is "in." "Out" is "in."

//W: The

opposite of new is old

//L: and you got "to" left: T-O

112	W:	No. O-N.
113	E:	You
114	L:	You gotta cross um you got to cross the opposite of that out. "New" is "old" You got to cross "old" out. O-L-D. And you got Y-O-U left, and so you put Y-O-U.
115	E & W:	(*write and spell*): Y-O-U
116	L:	(*Leaves table and returns with eraser for E & W*) Here. (*gives eraser to E & W*) Five. Now number five is "sell."
117	F:	That's my red pencil.
118	W:	It's mine
119	F:	It's mine. L
120	L:	"Sell" is "buy."
121	F:	L, ain't that my red pencil?
122	L:	Yeah (*F retains pencil*). Sell is buy. Number five. Sell by B- Buy B-
123	E:	Like that? (*returns to work*) I got it. I only got three more to do.
124	L:	"sick," "sick." That's number 6: I-C-K
125	W:	The opposite of "off" is . . . "on."
126	C:	I got it, "well."
127	W:	L, what's the opposite of "off?"
128	E:	On
129	W:	But they don't got "on" on here
130	L:	C, you got yours wrong. The opposite of sick is well. So you got to call it W-E-L-L. And you have a letter left. See: "sure."
131	C:	Oh (*erases page*)
132	L:	And you spell S-U-R-E. See?
133	C:	Sure!
134	L:	"West." "East." Here goes "east." "East" is right here, seven (*points to C's page*) East. E-A-S-T
135	E:	Oh, you done it ⎡wrong (*to L*) She done it wrong (*to C*)
	L:	⎣E
136	C:	No she didn't
	L:	A – S

137 W: (*Tapping L on* ⌈*head*) You did this one wrong. The opposite of "out" is "in."
     L: ⌊T
138 L: I know it
                 //W: I-N
                      //L: So what?
                           //W: I-N
                                //L: So
                                     //W: In
                                          //L: You got
         to write it here
139 W: See, I told you (*to W*) I told you
140 L: You gotta write "short" is . . .
141 C: I'm stuck on this one
142 L: "Tall." "Tall." "Tall" ain't on here uh uh. Eight, number eight. Eight
143 W: (*to E*) You didn't do this
144 L: Eight. "You" is "me." You, me: M-E. So you write B-R-I-N-G. Bring. ing. Now
         you write nine, "short" and you're "tall," T-A-L-A 9 heh heh. An you got to
         write "down" is "up," U-P. And you write bate. You-all know how to do that
         one.
145 C: Wait, let me see. That's "date."
146 L: I know. You all know how to do this.

DIFFERENTIATION OF AFFECTIVE AND DENOTATIVE SEMANTIC SUBSPACES†

Oliver C. S. Tzeng ‡

Department of Psychology
University of Illinois
Urbana-Champaign, Illinois 61820

According to Tzeng,[9] in ordinary daily lives, human perceiving and judging involves three major variables: (1) unique characteristics of the *individuals* processing the information (individual differences in personality and other demographic variables); (2) characteristics of *objects* of perception and judgment (signs of events, personalities, merchandise, etc.); (3) and characteristics of the *meaning systems* (the underlying psychological frame of reference) these individuals have developed as criteria. The structure of the meaning systems or components is historically dependent (i.e., the experience of the organism) on the other two variables — *interaction* of humans with objects (including other humans) in their environment. Therefore the meanings of signs of the same objects for different individuals will vary to the extent that their behaviors toward the objects have varied. This implies that the meanings of signs will, to varying degrees, reflect the idiosyncrasies of individual learning experiences. In the present article, we are concerned only with reasonably stable indications of human cognition both within and across individuals.

Affective and Denotative Meaning Systems

Because of different processes in formulating psychological dispositions and conceptions, meanings of objects can be dichotomized into two aspects — affective and nonaffective. According to Osgood,[4] for survival in the evolutionary sense, it is crucial for the human as well as other higher organisms to use central representations of the innate emotional (autonomic) reaction systems as a mediating semantic system to distinguish among the *signs* of things as being good or bad, strong or weak, and active or passive with respect to himself when confronting any behavioral decision (or judgment) situation. These representation processes under such circumstances are primarily emotional in nature and thus can be termed an *affective meaning system*. When representational mediation processes are established in terms of the sensorimotor dicrimination systems of the brain and characterize objects or events *referentially*, such meaning components of signs are primarily nonaffective in nature, and thus may be defined as part of a *denotative meaning system*. Typically, these two meaning

† This research was part of the project "Studies in Comparative Psycholinguistics" supported by grants from the National Institute of Mental Health (NIMH 07705) and the National Science Foundation (NSF GS 2012X) to the University of Illinois at Urbana-Champaign during 1968–1973 (Professor Charles E. Osgood, Principal Investigator).

‡ Reprint requests may be sent to Oliver Tzeng at his present address: Department of Psychology, Indiana University — Purdue University at Indianapolis, 1201 E. 38th Street, Indianapolis, Indiana 46205.

systems – affective and denotative – are simultaneously involved in human perceptual and judgmental situations. While affect reflects a person's feelings about (including attitude toward) an object, denotation reflects a person's implicit judgment criterion or semantic "theory" about the categorization of the object.

Measurement of these two aspects of meaning in relation to individual and object variables is basic to the social and behavioral sciences. These meaning systems, as the underlying semantic criteria of differential cognition, render many diverse objects and overt behaviors functionally equivalent within and even across cultures. In order to understand intra- and interpersonal behaviors, the identification of semantic features in any particular conceptual domain and their influence in individual differences becomes a prime goal in the social and behavioral sciences.

Measurement of Affective Meaning: The Semantic Differential

Osgood et al.[6] have developed the semantic differential (SD) technique for measuring certain aspects of the meanings of perceptual and linguistic signs. The SD has been applied to diverse groups of subjects judging diverse sets of concepts (from natural space concepts such as RIVER and ROCK to abstractions such as EDUCATION and PEACE), and compelling evidence for massive and universal affective dimensions of Evaluation, Potency, and Activity (E, P, and A) has been found in both indigenous and cross-cultural studies.[4,5] Given the necessarily metaphorical use of scales in rating 100 or more heterogeneous concepts (e.g., TORNADO: fair-unfair; SYMPATHY: hot-cold; etc.) and their resultant rotations toward their dominant affective features, the three resultant dimensions, E-P-A, have been assumed to represent purely affective components of the human semantic system. Given the diversity of scales used, the E-P-A dimensions would seem to be the maximal number of affective components in the semantic space. They seem essentially identical to Wundt's three dimensions of feeling – pleasantness/unpleasantness, tension/relief, and excitement/quiet.[3]

Tzeng[9] has argued that, in the judgment of a set of more homogeneous concepts (e.g., all relating to personalities) on SD-type scales, the affective meaning space can be separated from the remaining factor structure by using the "markers" of the Osgood pancultural E-P-A dimensions as control traits in each indigenous culture spatial configurations of scale vectors. The structure of the denotative meaning system can then be analyzed independently. The simultaneous influences of affective and denotative meaning components on each scale can also be differentiated. As Osgood[2] pointed out a decade ago, development of a rigorous method for such a simultaneous and differential identification is one of the most important problems for contemporary psychosemantics.

The present paper presents a newly developed methodology by Tzeng[8] for separating the affective and nonaffective (denotative) meaning systems in judgments of representative personality concepts in four language/culture communities – Finland, Finnish (FF); Britain, English (BE); Japan, Japanese (JP); and Belgium, Flemish (BF). On the basis of Ledyard Tucker's three-mode factoring technique,[7] the differential influences of these dichotomous meaning systems on individual (subcultural) differences in human conceptions of personality factors are also illustrated.

METHOD

Material

The data reported in the present study were collected following a standard procedure for our Personality Differential project at the Center for Comparative Psycholinguistics, University of Illinois, as follows:

Selection of Stimulus Personality Concepts. In order to cover personalities most familiar to average individuals in different language/culture communities, a representative sample of personality terms is determined according to the following five categories: (a) five ego-related concepts (e.g., MYSELF, MYSELF AS A FRIEND, and MYSELF AS A FATHER OR MOTHER); (b) six kinship concepts (e.g., MY FATHER, MY SON, and MY GRANDFATHER); (c) two well-known personalities (e.g., EINSTEIN and the president or premier in the country of collection); (d) six professions or trades (e.g., TEACHER, SALES-WOMAN, and MEDICAL DOCTOR); and (e) two animal concepts (e.g., THE DOG and THE CAT). For cross-cultural as well as indigenous subcultural comparisons on solutions, the actual concepts used in each of the four cultures underwent some substitution, omission, and addition – 24 concepts used in BE and FF, 40 in BF and 42 in JP. Detailed information can be found in Tzeng[8,9] and Tzeng and Hogenraad.[10]

Subjects and Scale Elicitation. In each community, adults of both sexes (age 18 to 50), belonging to the middle class and with at least primary school education, were sampled from an urban area (Sheffield, Helsinki, Tokyo, and Brussels), but we excluded the highest academic levels. Using a restricted word-association task, qualifier responses (adjectives in each indigenous language) for each personality concept were elicited in each community. The data obtained in each culture were then submitted to "blind" computer analyses in the native language at The University of Illinois, and a list of about 70 to 80 qualifiers simultaneously ordered in terms of the total *frequency*, *diversity*, and *independence* of usage from other qualifiers was derived and used to generate a set of standard SD bipolar scales. In each final scale pool, indigenous semantic differential "markers" representing the Osgood pancultural common E-P-A affective semantic features were included. Thus the total numbers of scales were 58 for BE, 59 for FF, 60 for JP, and 40 for BF.

Concept-on-Scale Task. The selected personality concepts were rated against seven-step bipolar scales by a new sample of subjects stratified by sex in each of the four communities – 80 in BE, 100 in both FF and BF, and 160 in JP. This resulted in a total of eight data cubes (subjects by concepts by scales) from both sexes of the four language/culture communities.

Treatment of the Data

In order to investigate the structure of the two semantic subspaces and their influences in individual differences on personality conceptions, the following data processing procedure was applied:

(1) *Separating Affective and Denotative Factor Structures.* For each group, the scale mode of the data cube was analyzed by Tzeng's[8] methodology. Given the premises that E-P-A exhaustively represent the affective semantic space in

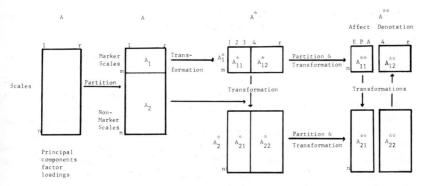

FIGURE 1. Semantic procedure for separation of semantic space to two subspaces.

human judgment, and that the Osgood pancultural E-P-A marker scales represent the affective dimensions in each indigeneous scale configuration, the following procedure, shown in FIGURE 1, was applied to an initial principal components solution for the scale-by-scale cross-product matrix, computed across the concepts and subjects in each three-mode raw data matrix:

(a) Partition the initial scale factor matrix, A (n scales by r factors retained), into two subdomain matrices — A_1, as the marker domain of m E-P-A marker scales by r, and A_2, as the nonmarker domain of (n − m) elicited scales by r.

(b) Rotate A_1 to a simple structure matrix A_1^* (on the theoretical assumption that since the m marker scales are functionally equivalent to the E-P-A affective dimensions in the judgment of homogeneous personality concepts, A_1^* should be three dimensional with null loadings on the remaining (r − 3) dimensions).

(c) Use the transformation matrix T_1 as derived from rotating A_1 to A_1^* in (b) to make a corresponding rotation in the nonmarker scale domain (i.e., $A_2 T_1 = A_2^*$). The above three steps will accomplish the separation of affective and denotative semantic spaces in the initial scale configuration A, with the first three dimensions in the affective space and the remaining dimensions in the "other" (denotative) space.

(d) After isolating A_1^* into a m x 3 matrix with the m marker scale loadings on the first three dimensions in the affective space and isolating A_2^* into a (n − m) x (r − 3) matrix with the nonmarker scale loadings on the remaining dimensions in the denotative space, rotate them separately into two simple structures. From the affective space, one can evaluate the purity of the pancultural marker scales as E-P-A affect markers when used in a homogeneous personality concept domain, and from the denotative space one can identify the character of "other" dimensions when affective "contimination" is eliminated.

(e) The two transformation matrices obtained from the affective and denotative spaces in (d) are then used in their respective spaces to rotate the nonmarker scales on the purified E-P-A dimensions (i.e., (n − m) x 3) and also rotate the m marker scales onto the resultant denotative dimensions, m x (r − 3). From this step, the amount of affective salience for each nonmarker scale (i.e., percentage sum of squares accounted for by E-P-A dimensions) can be determined in the affective space, and the degree of nullity of E-P-A markers on the "other" dimensions (in the denotative space) can also be examined.

(2) *Within-Group Three-Mode Factor Analysis*. The concept and subject modes of each data cube were analyzed by principal components analyses and subjected to rotational schemes (both orthogonal and oblique) for identification of the meaningful simple structures of personality concept factors and subject homogeneous response types. A parsimonious three-mode inner core matrix was finally computed using Tucker's three-mode factor analytic model for integration of the three sources of variance: (a) group personality "theories," with affective and denotative factors separated in the semantic space; (b) patterns of personality concept factors; and (c) homogeneous idealized subject types. The entries in the core matrix would represent "judgments" of subject types on concept dimensions against criteria of dichotomous meaning components. In order to facilitate interpretation, subjects' demographic characteristics such as sex, age, marital status, education, language, and vocation were related to the distribution of subject factor loadings.

(3) *Indigenous Cultural/Sex Comparisons on Factorial Congruences*. For each indigenous culture community, the concept and scale factors matrices of both sexes were evaluated for their agreement by coefficients of congruence. Statistically, this stage of analysis was to provide bases for intracultural comparisons in the core matrices among subgroups of subjects of both sexes. Psychologically this analysis was to provide information about culture/sex differences with respect to personality "theories" and concept clusterings.

(4) *Cross-Cultural Similarities and Differences*. Based on the psychological meanings of salient concepts and scales on their respective dimensions from the four different cultures, the following integration was made: (a) *Cross-cultural concept factors in the personality domain*. This was to summarize all indigenous concept factors into a single cross-cultural personality factor structure for all communities involved. (b) *Cross-cultural semantic components in the personality domain*. This is a summary of scale dimensions for all four language/culture communities as a presentation of cross-cultural personality "theories." (c) *The cross-cultural inner core matrix*. This is an integration of all obtained inner core matrices from different cultures. This matrix in theory can be inferred as a core matrix obtained in a single personality differential study with subjects sampled from different cultural origins. This made possible the identification of intra- and intercultural differences in application of semantic meaning components to concept factors.

RESULTS

Indigenous Culture/Sex Group Factorization

Each cube of scale by concept by subject data was analyzed independently following a standard procedure of data treatment. To illustrate the procedure detailed results for the BF-Male group are presented.

Based on the distributions of eigenroots from the principal components solutions on the three cross-products matrices of 40 scales, 25 concepts and 50 subjects (each computed across the other two modes), significant factors were retained — six for the semantic scale mode (with 71.03% of the total sums of squares accounted for), four for the personality concept mode (with 70.20% of the sums of squares), and three for the individual subject mode, accounting for 57.04% of the total sums of squares.

Scale Factors

The sums of squares accounted for by six eigenvalues of just the *affective marker domain* (A_1) proved to be three dimensional. The roots drop abruptly between the third and fourth, and taper off from the fourth root. The first three roots accounted for 93.84% of the total sum of squares of the 9 (markers) by 6 (dimensions) factor loadings. The final rotated factor loadings of 40 scales, in TABLE 1, indicate that A_{11}** is simple structure with the markers uniquely salient on their respective E-P-A features (with two exceptions, however) and that A_{12}** is null. This confirms the validity of our assumption that E-P-A marker scales also function as Affective components in the homogeneous personality concept domain.

Affect. The most salient factor is the first, which is led by three pancultural Evaluation markers with 25 out of 31 scales having a loading higher than +20.00, as shown in TABLE 1. These represent a generally social evaluative meaning with such dominant traits as *good, nice, pleasant, honest, just, sincere, polite, serviceable, sensible, sympathetic, friendly, generous,* and *trusting.* The second factor in the Affective space has two pancultural Potency markers and one Activity marker salient on it. Such traits as *old, strong, heavy, large, calm, clean, hard-working, courageous, cultured, rich, honest,* and *intelligent* appear to represent the Potency feature of Affective meaning. The salient scales of the third factor are led by three Activity markers along with one Potency marker. The cluster of vectors contains such salient scales as *young, light, living, fast, nervous, beautiful, thin, joyous,* and *amusing* and is obviously closest to the pancultural semantic differential factor of Activity. These three affective dimensions account for 83% of the total retained sum of squared loadings for all 40 scales.

Denotation. The remaining three factors are in a separate semantic space orthogonal to the Affective space represented by E-P-A. These three factors are hypothesized to be representations of Denotative aspects of meaning. The first dimension contains such scales as *optimist, openminded, happy, hot, simple, sympathetic, wholesome, rich,* and *clean* versus their opposites, *pessimist, closeminded, unhappy, cold, complicated, unlikeable, unwholesome, poor,* and *dirty.* This dimension seems to describe a disposition of looking on the more favorable side of events versus looking on the negative side of events, and hence it can be referred to as a *Positivism* (or *Negativism*) dimension. The second factor is dominated by the scales *discreet, trusting, calm, sober, simple, living, sincere,* and *thin* versus their opposites *curious, distrusting, nervous, greedy, complicated, dead, lying,* and *big,* apparently reflecting stable versus unstable patterns of behavior. Therefore, choosing from the left term scales, this factor is called a *Predictability* dimension. The last Denotative dimension seems to characterize people's style or pattern of dealing with personalities, being either *cultured, nervous, complicated, intelligent, hard-working, active,* and *curious* or *uncultured, calm, simple, stupid, lazy, inactive* and *discreet.* This factor might be dubbed an *Involvement* dimension. These three "other" factors, on which

TABLE 1

FACTOR LOADINGS OF SCALES

	Affect			Denotation			Scales
	E	P	A	I	II	III	
				Marker Domain			
1	47.59*	-2.66	8.87	-1.77	4.63	0.68	pleasant/unpleasant
2	61.17*	5.97	-8.22	4.12	-0.68	1.51	good/bad
3	55.46*	1.22	-1.75	3.11	-.24	-1.03	nice/wicked
4	-3.62	17.34*	5.46	-7.59	16.96	-9.07	large/little
5	-4.19	26.58*	-35.38*	6.01	-12.58	-12.16	heavy/light
6	13.65	28.10*	-8.58	-4.20	18.15	14.79	strong/weak
7	-12.42	8.55	32.53*	15.96	5.96	14.28	fast/slow
8	11.90	10.73	33.99*	-7.31	28.48*	15.65	living/dead
9	-2.98	-32.30*	56.17*	0.04	6.16	-3.24	young/old
				Nonmarker Domain			
10	45.22*	12.65	-5.22	15.60	1.65	-9.27	generous/stingy
11	5.20	26.66*	-5.74	22.37*	3.74	31.33*	rich/poor
12	50.61*	10.06	1.40	17.75	-8.02	-16.07	friendly/unfriendly
13	38.84*	36.75*	-13.47	20.37*	2.80	13.69	clean/dirty
14	41.94*	29.51*	-9.42	14.66	2.79	-0.29	courageous/coward
15	27.11*	-9.20	10.13	34.43*	-2.81	-2.46	hot/cold
16	-17.00	-15.49	20.90*	-16.13	-32.71*	-11.60	greedy/sober
17	16.74	6.71	9.90	47.52*	5.79	20.24*	optimist/pessimist
18	7.94	9.01	-25.43*	2.82	-22.31*	-6.53	big/thin
19	-0.87	4.65	1.86	-10.69	69.78*	-22.36*	discreet/curious
20	34.74*	10.39	3.03	38.97*	-1.82	11.87	happy/unhappy
21	16.20	0.81	16.23	16.56	4.54	3.23	loving/indifferent
22	-27.89*	-39.02*	29.10*	-4.19	-34.97*	37.51*	nervous/calm
23	51.10*	8.46	1.62	26.58*	-5.85	-10.54	sympathetic/unlikable
24	61.34*	26.55*	-18.77	18.60	-0.25	-5.97	honest/dishonest
25	37.28*	-9.68	3.91	46.82*	5.69	2.99	openminded/closeminded
26	27.74*	5.21	-1.21	31.20*	28.87*	-34.10*	simple/complicated
27	30.19*	21.73*	6.02	24.92*	-2.33	-2.31	wholesome/unwholesome
28	57.21*	21.39*	-18.48	-1.46	8.62	11.61	polite/impolite
29	38.73*	23.10*	-7.81	-6.13	6.53	33.47*	intelligent/stupid
30	43.68*	28.43*	-18.01	-4.69	13.14	37.96*	cultured/uncultured
31	27.86*	-10.59	-11.69	9.11	4.41	11.25	joyous/sad
32	59.48*	11.60	22.76*	-1.92	7.63	5.12	just/unjust
33	49.33*	33.22*	-25.13*	2.10	12.79	30.22*	hard-working/lazy
34	20.79*	-19.48	27.10*	-3.33	7.17	1.55	beautiful/ugly
35	28.38*	-17.25	22.67*	3.72	10.42	7.46	amusing/boring
36	59.75*	8.58	-17.50	-0.37	23.02*	9.19	sincere/lying
37	55.00*	6.98	-5.38	1.47	12.52	-3.28	serviceable/selfish
38	42.33*	-20.14*	-1.36	13.32	38.75*	16.15	trusting/distrusting
39	32.69*	24.61*	2.15	0.37	0.52	24.95*	active/inactive
40	53.02*	9.55	2.64	-2.16	-5.07	-1.89	sensible/insensible

* Salient loadings.

affective markers have no systematic loadings, clearly reflect "affect-free" nonmetaphorical features of cognition, representing the descriptive character of psychosemantic differentiation among the common personality concepts.

Concept Factors

The salient concepts from the rotated concept factor structure by both varimax (orthogonal) and oblimax (oblique) procedures are given in TABLE 2. The leading concepts for the first factor are: MY SPOUSE, MYSELF AS A PARENT, MY SON OR DAUGHTER, MYSELF, THE AIR HOSTESS, MYSELF AS A MEMBER OF A GROUP, MYSELF AS A FRIEND, MYSELF AS A CHILD, etc. These concepts are highly correlated with ego and family (except the concepts THE AIR HOSTESS and THE JET-PILOT). It seems quite reasonable to define it as a "SELF-INDENTIFICATION" dimension. The salient concepts for the second factor are DE GAULLE, THE POLITICIAN, EINSTEIN, THE BANKER, THE TEACHER, MY GRANDFATHER, THE PARISH PRIEST, THE FAMILY DOCTOR and MY GRANDMOTHER. Except possibly for the concepts of grandparents, all are socially obvious leaders in various aspects of life and, of course, for Belgian French-speaking males grandparents also have such status, according to our colleagues in Belgium. It may be identified as a "POWER" dimension. The salient concepts for the third factor are THE MURDERER, THE THIEF, HITLER, THE BOXER on one side, and MY GRANDMOTHER, MY GRANDFATHER, GOD, THE PARISH PRIEST, and MY MOTHER on the other side. This factor may be termed "IMMORAL (or MORAL) MODELS" since the dominant concepts on one end are considered "immoral." The last dimension has socially dependent concepts – THE CHILD, THE CAT, THE DOG, THE COW, THE MENTAL PATIENT, THE PROSTITUTE, and THE MAIDSERVANT. It may be identified as a "SOCIALLY DEPENDENT" dimension.

Subject Factors

Factor 1, accounting for 52.05% of the total sum of squares, is a representation of the average subject (group mean) with high loadings from all 50 subjects. Subject Factor 2 with 2.84% of the total sum of squares accounted for is dominated by two subgroups of subjects: four subjects from both vocational categories (students in the Royal School of County Police and civilians applying to be an officer during their military duty) at the positive end of the dimension, and three unique students, all from the Royal School, at the negative end. Subject Factor 3 is also dominated by two subgroups of subjects with another four students from the Royal School on the negative pole and four prospective military officers on the positive pole.

The Core Matrix

The raw (unrotated) three-mode (6 x 4 x 3) core matrix was first counter-rotated by the transformation matrices used in the scale mode for the Affect/Denotation separation. Since two different methods of rotation have been applied to the concept principal components solution, two additional

TABLE 2

SALIENT CONCEPTS FROM TWO SOLUTIONS

| | Rotational Scheme | |
Concept	Varimax	Oblimax
Dimension I		
MY SPOUSE	93.53	108.01
MYSELF AS A PARENT	90.15	108.28
MY SON OR DAUGHTER	87.12	108.93
MYSELF	85.75	109.42
THE AIR-HOSTESS	84.35	97.05
MYSELF AS A MEMBER OF A GROUP	83.35	107.02
MYSELF AS A FRIEND	82.98	103.68
MYSELF AS A CHILD	82.87	107.93
THE NURSE	77.13	68.61
MY MOTHER	76.21	55.96
MY SISTER	70.34	61.74
MY FATHER	70.24	56.99
THE JET-PILOT	66.42	76.54
MY BROTHER	65.49	71.98
THE FAMILY DOCTOR	61.23	38.20
THE PARA-COMMANDO	60.62	91.73
Dimension II		
DE GAULLE	55.65	12.19
THE POLITICIAN	50.67	18.85
EINSTEIN	48.26	20.51
THE BANKER	47.22	20.09
THE TEACHER	38.89	14.33
MY GRANDFATHER	38.62	25.86
THE PARISH PRIEST	38.43	34.24
THE FAMILY DOCTOR	38.28	11.69
MY GRANDMOTHER	38.10	39.44
Dimension III		
THE MURDERER	63.85	45.59
THE THIEF	61.76	40.77
HITLER	54.47	66.38
MY GRANDMOTHER	−38.83	−14.79
THE BOXER	32.12	33.59
MY GRANDFATHER	−31.71	−4.71
GOD	−31.65	−8.05
THE PARISH PRIEST	−30.76	−8.33
MY MOTHER	−30.27	−12.93
DE GAULLE	5.75	35.75
Dimension IV		
THE CHILD	49.63	51.57
THE CAT	48.49	57.50
THE DOG	43.27	48.05
THE COW	37.98	41.20
THE MENTAL PATIENT	39.94	41.39
THE PROSTITUTE	35.46	43.22
THE MAIDSERVANT	30.99	28.16
THE THIEF	18.87	20.89

counterrotations on the concept mode of the core matrix were next performed. In general, these counter-rotational procedures resulted in a similar pattern of scale by concept factor interactions in the core. Thus only the resultant core matrix from a varimax rotation would be examined for interpretation. This matrix is strung out to form a Kronecker two-mode matrix, as seen in TABLE 3, with the subject factors as the columns and the concept factors nested in the scale factors as the rows.

For the first idealized subject, the concept factor "SELF-INDENTI-FICATION" is characterized as highly positive on all meaning systems in both spaces. The personalities of Power (Factor II for concepts) are perceived as good (+E), strong (+P), cultured (+Involvement) and somewhat optimistic (+Positivism), but extremely slow or inactive (−A). Concepts related to Immoral Standards (i.e., MURDERER, THIEF, and HITLER) from Concept Factor III are seen as extremely bad (−E), somewhat closeminded (−Positivism), and curious (−Predictability); but they are seen as very active (+A) and cultured (+Involvement). The most interesting result for these subjects might be their

TABLE 3

ROTATED CORE MATRIX*

Scale Factors	ISC	ICO	Subject Factors			Concept Factors
			1	2	3	
I. AFFECTIVE SPACE						
Evaluation	1	1	163	−7	19	SELF-IDENTIFICATION
	1	2	68	−17	−1	POWER
	1	3	−113	0	4	IMMORAL MODELS
	1	4	16	−2	5	SOCIALLY DEPENDENT
Potency	2	1	42	−9	−7	SELF-IDENTIFICATION
	2	2	80	1	−11	POWER
	2	3	−7	−3	1	IMMORAL MODELS
	2	4	−21	−10	4	SOCIALLY DEPENDENT
Activity	3	1	31	13	−2	SELF-IDENTIFICATION
	3	2	−52	−3	6	POWER
	3	3	48	5	−10	IMMORAL MODELS
	3	4	39	10	−9	SOCIALLY DEPENDENT
II. DENOTATIVE SPACE						
Positivism	1	1	51	−22	6	SELF-IDENTIFICATION
	1	2	18	−16	8	POWER
	1	3	−18	−10	−2	IMMORAL MODELS
	1	4	5	−9	−3	SOCIALLY DEPENDENT
Predictability	2	1	27	−8	5	SELF-IDENTIFICATION
	2	2	−7	−10	0	POWER
	2	3	−19	11	−3	IMMORAL MODELS
	2	4	−47	−6	9	SOCIALLY DEPENDENT
Involvement	3	1	22	−6	12	SELF-IDENTIFICATION
	3	2	34	1	0	POWER
	3	3	13	−6	−7	IMMORAL MODELS
	3	4	−32	−7	9	SOCIALLY DEPENDENT

* For better identification of factors, ISC stands for scale factor number and ICO for concept factor number.

loadings for the last concept factor, "SOCIALLY DEPENDENT." Such concepts as CHILD, CAT, DOG, and COW are perceived as very active (+A) and slightly good (+E), but impotent (−P), curious (−Predictability), and uncultured (−Involvement).

Unlike the group mean subjects, the second idealized individual has a rather different pattern of concept by scale interactions. The first concept factor "SELF−IDENTIFICATION," except for being active (+A), is relatively negative on all semantic components: bad (−E), weak (−P), pessimistic (−Positivism), curious (−Predictability), and uncultured (−Involvement). The personality concepts salient on the "POWER" factor are characterized mainly as bad (−E), closeminded (−Positivism), and curious (−Predictability). The "IMMORAL MODELS" concept factor is perceived only as relatively closeminded (−Positivism) and rather discreet (+Predictability); the three affective semantic components are not differentiable in judgment. As to the "SOCIALLY DEPENDENT" factor, Ideal Subject 2 rated it as fast (or active) on A like the "SELF-INDENTI-FICATION" dimension, but negative on all other scale dimensions. It is interesting to note that the four subjects leading the positive pole of this subject factor tended to use the denotation of −Positivism uniformly in judgment of all four kinds of personalities regardless of their constructive or destructive role in society. This might reflect a type of person with melancholy character.

The third idealized subject has also a clearly different pattern of person perception as reflected in its scale and concept factor interactions. The concepts of "SELF-IDENTIFICATION" are notably high on Evaluation and also on all three denotative scale dimensions, but they are negatively rated on Potency and Activity. The personalities salient on the factor "POWER" are, curiously, rated on four dimensions as weak (−P), but active (+A), optimistic (+Positivism) and cultured (+Involvement). As to the "IMMORAL MODELS" dimension, it is, strangely enough, rated as inactive (−A) and uncultured (−Involvement). No other meaning components seem important for their differentiation. In comparison with the first two subject factors, this ideal subject also has a rather unique pattern in perceiving the "SOCIALLY DEPENDENT" concept factor. That is, while both Ideal Subjects 1 and 2 have loadings positive on Activity, but negative on Potency, Predictability and Involvement, Ideal Subject 3, on the contrary, has negative loading on Activity, but positive loadings on Potency, Predictability, and Involvement.

Cross-Cultural Factor Similarities

Indigenous Factorizations of Other Culture/Sex Groups

For each data cube of the other seven culture/sex groups of subjects — males and females from England (BE-M and BE-F), Finland (FF-M, FF-F), and Japan (JP-M, JP-F) as well as the BF-F group, the indigenous three-mode factorizations as applied to the BF-M group resulted in four kinds of solutions, namely, (a) factorial structures of affect and denotation; (b) characteristics of personality concept factors; (c) characteristics of subject homogeneous response types; and (d) the interactions of the three-mode factors. For the JP data, however, only the scale model solutions were obtained because of the inadequacy of the data for the three-mode factor analysis.[8] The retained numbers of scale, concept, and subject factors as reflected by the order of the respective core matrices are 7 x 4 x 3 for BE-M, BE-F and FF-M, 8 x 4 x 2 for FF-F and 6 x 4 x 3 for BF-F.

Scale Factor Similarities

In the scale mode, the results of all seven groups having factor characteristics similar to the BF-Male group indicate that the factor loadings of E-P-A markers are simple in the A_{11}** space and null in the independent A_{12}** space, reflecting high stability and reproducibility (reliability) of factor structures of the Osgood pancultural affective markers. Salient loadings of the nonmarkers in the affective markers-defined space (A_{21}**) also clearly suggest the dominance of underlying psychological connotations in the process of human perceptions of other human beings. That is, the pancultural Evaluation dimension has saliences for such nonmarker scales as *kind-unkind, generous-selfish, honest-dishonest*, and *reputable-disreputable*; the pancultural Potency dimension has saliences on *dominant-submissive, tough-tender, courageous-timid*, and *sturdy-delicate*, etc., and the pancultural Activity dimension has saliences for *capable-incapable, inventive-uninventive, flexible-stubborn* and *active-inactive*, etc. This strongly supports the generality (validity) of the E-P-A constructs. TABLE 4A presents the scales most salient on resultant dimensions of both semantic spaces in all eight indigenous factorizations. Each dimension is also labeled by an appropriate name (in quotes).

For the two indigenous culture/sex groups within each language/culture community in which identical scales and concepts were used, intracultural comparisons on their implicit "theories" of psychosemantics in personality ratings were performed by computing coefficients of congruence between all possible combinations of factors from both resultant factor loading matrices. These coefficients give indices of similarity of factors between the male and female solutions.

For all four culture communities, the one-to-one correspondence of E-P-A factors in the Affective spaces of both sexes is clear. Except for the JP data with .99 for E and relatively low indices for P (.82) and A (.74),§ all E-P-A corresponding factors for the other three cultures have almost perfectly congruent coefficients (.99 for E and at least .95 for P and A). The within-cultural average of three coefficients across E-P-A corresponding factors is therefore extremely high: .98 for BE, .97 for FF, .96 for BF, and .85 for JP.

In the Denotative subspaces, however, the factor configurations of both sexes within each culture are not unanimously agreeable: only two dimensions are congruent for BF, three dimensions for BE and four dimensions for both FF and JP. Compared with the coefficients in the affective spaces these congruent factors have relatively lower indices (between .71 and .95 with median = .82). The remaining noncongruent factors are considered as within-culture sex specific.

TABLE 4B summarizes the factor identifications across all eight culture/sex groups of subjects based on intracultural factor similarities and intercultural

---

§ Examination of the differences of relative importance of P and A dimensions indicates that for JP-Male subjects, scales are much more salient on P than on A (19 vs. 7), while for JP-Female subjects, the number of salient scales on P and A are very close (14 vs. 15).

TABLE 4A

HIGHEST-LOADING SCALES FOR EIGHT CULTURE/SEX GROUPS
IN INDIGENOUS FACTORIZATIONS

BE – Male

AFFECT

Evaluation		Potency		Activity	
nice*	56.45	heavy*	34.26	active*	56.65
pleasant*	55.58	large*	31.51	agile*	49.81
good*	44.65	forceful*	28.10	fast*	45.73
beautiful*	26.79	strong*	24.88	strong*	39.83
kind	49.87	sturdy	31.09	capable	52.09
generous	49.38	demanding	28.95	clever	43.25
honest	47.85	dominant	27.45	bright	42.88
loyal	46.71	dogmatic	25.78	determined	41.41
forgiving	45.41	tough	25.55	ambitious	40.88
necessary	44.71	critical	24.95	dominant	38.55

DENOTATION

I. "Morality"		II. "Rationality"		III. "Extro/Introversion"	
critical	29.33	patient	33.18	sociable	33.80
religious	28.06	rational	31.65	ambitious	23.87
ambitious	25.73	predictable	28.88	immoral	23.24
moral	23.59	unemotional	25.30	noisy	21.25
determined	22.69	reasonable	21.88	companionable	20.27
knowledgeable	21.79			lucky	20.05
careful	20.88				

IV. "Predictability"	
usual	37.77
sociable	26.72
companionable	24.33
moral	18.95
boring	18.77
faithful	17.92

BE – Female

AFFECT

Evaluation		Potency		Activity	
pleasant*	43.93	heavy*	23.84	active*	44.69
nice*	41.48	large*	23.23	agile*	36.32
good*	36.80	strong*	15.06	fast*	29.77
beautiful*	17.84	sturdy	23.92	capable	39.87
honest	42.75	arrogant	18.08	determined	34.78
kind	38.56	dogmatic	17.42	ambitious	32.95
generous	38.36	impatient	17.31	bright	29.96
faithful	37.75	dominant	17.23	dominant	29.74
loyal	37.68	tough	16.17	careful	28.76
necessary	37.02				

DENOTATION

I. *"Rationality"*		II. *"Ambitiousness"*		III. *"Morality"*	
unemotional	27.65	ambitious	29.14	rigid	20.29
predictable	27.56	critical	23.54	dogmatic	20.00
rational	26.11	knowlegeable	23.07	necessary	19.97
patient	23.58	clever	19.29	moral	18.43
reasonable	18.46	unusual	18.96	religious	17.61
good-tempered	17.74			determined	16.00
careful	17.65				
quiet	15.04				

IV. *"Predictability"*	
sociable	30.35
companionable	21.56
usual	19.95
familiar	12.89

FF – Male

AFFECT

Evaluation		Potency		Activity	
pleasant*	57.45	sturdy*	42.99	fast*	42.80
good*	52.44	large*	39.22	agile*	38.11
nice*	49.10	heavy*	32.85	lively*	25.55
light*	47.12	strong*	31.40	flexible*	25.16
honest	62.25	courageous	30.92	inventive	43.36
trustworthy	61.62	self-confident	22.89	attentive	34.97
necessary	56.95	unyielding	22.53	individualistic	33.13
reputable	54.53	old	22.28	courageous	32.75
faithful	54.30			wholesome	28.06
kind	52.45			careful	25.62

DENOTATION

I. *"Morality"*		II. *"Predictability"*		III. *"Humility"*	
usual	36.08	calm	41.00	simple	35.37
reputable	35.51	patient	35.16	poor	29.24
honest	32.46	predictable	26.72	broad-minded	27.49
moral	29.94	yielding	22.91	insecure	25.12
trustworthy	29.64	unselfish	20.44	humble	20.08
faithful	29.40	humble	20.28		

IV. *"Sociability"*	
sociable	35.41
gregarious	32.49
usual	30.58
regular	22.81

Continued

Table 4A—*Continued*

FF — Female

AFFECT

Evaluation		Potency		Activity	
pleasant*	49.37	sturdy*	37.84	fast*	36.73
good*	46.22	large*	34.52	agile*	34.54
light*	43.91	strong*	32.15	flexible*	28.78
nice*	42.72	heavy*	31.94	lively*	21.15
honest	55.70	courageous	27.97	individualistic	36.82
trustworthy	53.69	self-confident	22.73	inventive	31.33
necessary	50.90			courageous	28.29
reputable	49.17			attentive	25.46
straight	46.93			sense of humor	24.36
gentle	46.90			knowing	22.76
kind	46.41				

DENOTATION

I. "Morality"		II. "Integrity"		III. "Predictability"	
careful	29.44	honest	28.71	calm	37.46
narrow-minded	29.01	straight	27.37	patient	29.72
logical	28.96	wholesome	26.93	predictable	23.98
attentive	26.44	faithful	26.85	humble	19.18
clean	24.49	trustworthy	26.17	yielding	18.95
knowing	21.89			usual	18.03

IV. "Humility"		V. "Sociability"	
simple	28.86	sociable	30.47
poor	27.19	gregarious	28.99
tolerant	25.54	selfish	24.99
broad-minded	20.82	wholesome	21.82
sense of humor	20.82	usual	19.57

JP — Male

AFFECT

Evaluation		Potency		Activity	
comfortable*	67.21	brave*	37.85	soft*	52.14
good*	64.53	heavy*	32.98	vivid*	51.54
pleasant*	62.06	big*	31.67	flexible	34.98
happy*	42.66	strong	45.73	sociable	28.73
liked	64.48	energetic	41.94	excitable	24.07
reputable	62.96	high	32.17	smiling	22.69
honest	61.62	extroverted	31.44	extroverted	21.67
rational	60.62				
light	60.56				
obedient	59.17				

DENOTATION

I. *"Energeticness"*		II. *"Uniqueness"*		III. *"Predictability"*	
busy	46.72	individualistic	40.62	tangible	38.93
tense	41.13	unusual	33.50	predictable	35.51
sensitive	33.62	free	27.12	comprehensible	31.69
diligent	30.94	sensitive	26.13	extroverted	28.16
enthusiastic	27.17	candid	24.90	familiar	25.79
serious	21.97	solitary	24.17	usual	24.96

IV. *"Rationality"*		V. *"Sophistication"*	
calm (not excited)	43.30	sophisticated	28.07
logical	42.57	logical	23.89
calm (nonviolent)	26.94	unhappy	22.58
flexible	25.79	clever	22.17
quiet	24.81	obedient	21.42
rational	22.36	proud	21.37

JP – Female

AFFECT

Evaluation		Potency		Activity	
comfortable*	70.47	big*	51.07	vivid*	47.24
good*	69.66	heavy*	41.25	noisy*	42.94
pleasant*	67.57	hard*	38.96	excitable	37.37
happy*	54.40	brave*	33.40	extroverted	35.64
liked	70.13	strong	39.43	proud	35.17
obedient	68.15	energetic	33.33	violent	34.78
light	67.45	busy	27.81	impudent	34.65
reputable	66.68	high	25.88	sociable	32.24
kind	65.02	tense	24.67		
serious	64.20				
wise	61.79				
honest	59.72				
warm	59.25				

DENOTATION

I. *"Cold Rationality"*		II. *"Energeticness"*		III. Uniqueness"	
logical	44.49	tense	41.14	unusual	38.79
calm (not excited)	34.01	sensitive	39.57	individualistic	35.95
sophisticated	27.43	busy	39.29	solitary	25.24
rational	21.52	enthusiastic	28.49	violent	24.42
unhappy	20.91	diligent	20.92	sensitive	23.26
cold	20.66			free	22.55

IV. *"Predictability"*		V. *"Flexibility"*	
tangible	42.99	flexible	30.48
familiar	38.77	calm (not excited)	29.03
predictable	38.39	clever	22.07
comprehensible	35.07	calm (nonviolent)	19.54
usual	21.52		
easy	21.17		

Continued

Table 4A—*Continued*

BF – Male

AFFECT

Evaluation		*Potency*		*Activity*	
good*	61.17	old*	32.30	young*	56.17
nice*	55.46	strong*	28.10	light*	35.38
pleasant*	49.59	heavy*	26.58	living*	33.99
honest	61.34	large*	17.34	fast*	32.53
just	59.48	calm	39.02	nervous	29.10
sincere	59.75	clean	36.75	beautiful	27.10
polite	57.21	hard-working	33.22	thin	25.43
serviceable	55.00	courageous	29.51	lazy	25.13
sensible	53.03	cultured	28.42	joyous	22.76
sympathetic	51.10	rich	26.66	amusing	22.67

DENOTATION

I. *"Positivism"*		II. *"Predictability"*		III. *"Involvement*	
optimist	47.52	discreet	69.73	cultured	37.96
open-minded	46.82	trusting	38.75	nervous	37.51
happy	38.97	calm	34.97	complicated	34.10
hot	34.43	sober	32.71	intelligent	33.47
simple	31.20	simple	28.87	hard-working	30.22
sympathetic	26.56	living	28.48	active	24.95
wholesome	24.92	sincere	23.02	curious	22.36
rich	22.37	thin	22.31	optimist	20.24
clean	20.37				

BF – Female

AFFECT

Evaluation		*Potency*		*Activity*	
good*	62.06	heavy*	49.15	fast*	53.53
nice*	58.41	old*	45.95	living*	41.04
pleasant*	46.98	strong*	30.45	large*	40.18
honest	63.38	big	48.37	wholesome	35.31
sincere	62.42	ugly	28.30	active	35.22
just	62.11	hard-working	25.75	rich	28.06
serviceable	60.96	rich	19.74	distrusting	25.66
sensible	56.42	calm	18.73	courageous	25.58
polite	53.50	courageous	17.92	clean	25.15

DENOTATION

I. *"Cultural-Socialization"*		II. *"Predictability"*		III. *"Positivism"*	
cultured	51.34	calm	69.97	open-minded	47.98
intelligent	45.59	discreet	65.98	optimist	40.17
sober	44.09	simple	44.42	hot	34.72
hard-working	43.44	sober	20.93	trusting	33.69
discreet	38.46	generous	20.90	happy	27.97
clean	35.82				
polite	32.34				
rich	26.47				

* Indigenous Affective markers.

TABLE 4B

CROSS-CULTURAL SEMANTIC COMPONENTS OF MEANING IN PERSONALITY RATINGS

	BE-M	BE-F	FF-M	FF-F	JP-M	JP-F	BF-M	BF-F	*
AFFECT									
Evaluation	E	E	E	E	E	E	E	E	CC
Potency	P	P	P	P	P	P	P	P	CC
Activity	A	A	A	A	A	A	A	A	CC
DENOTATION									
1. "Predictability"	IV†	IV	II	III	III	IV	II	II	CC
2. "Rationality"	II	I	I	I	IV	(I)‡			CC
3. "Morality"	I	III			I	II			CC
4. "Energeticness"			III				(III)§		cultural
5. "Humility"			IV	IV					cultural
6. "Sociability"				V					cultural
7. "Uniqueness"					II	III			cultural
8. "Positivism"							I	III	cul/sex
9. "Extra/Introversion"	III								cul/sex
10. "Ambitiousness"		II							cul/sex
11. "Integrity"				II	V				cul/sex
12. "Sophistication"						V			cul/sex
13. "Flexibility"									cul/sex
14. "Cultural-Socialization"								I	cul/sex

* CC = cross-cultural = common factor; cultural = cultural unique factor; cul/sex = culture/sex unique factor.

† Dimension numbers in respective indigenous factorizations in Table 4A.

‡ But here "Cold Rationality."

§ Defined as "Involvement" here.

common scale items and/or intuitively common factor characteristics. E, P and A are found to be clearly Universals across all indigenous Affective subspaces. In the Denotative spaces, three types of factors emerge: (a) *cross-cultural common*: A factor labeled as "Predictability" appeared in all eight samples, the "Rationality" factor appeared common to BE and JP subjects of both sexes, the "Morality" factor appeared common to two cultures (BE and FF subjects of both sexes), and the "Energeticness" appeared common to both JP groups as well as BF males (but identified as "Involvement"). (b) *Culture specific*: "Humility" and "Sociability" are unique for the Finns, "Uniqueness" for the Japanese, and "Positivism" for the Belgians. (c) *Culture/sex specific*: Each of the four cultures displays at least one factor difference between sexes: British males (but not females) have an "Extro/Introversion" factor, and conversely for "Ambitiousness"; Finnish females differ from Finnish males only in having an additional "Integrity" factor, Japanese males have a unique "Sophistication" factor; Japanese females have a unique "Flexibility" factor; and Belgian females have an additional "Cultural-Socialization" factor (not shared with the males).

Concept Factor Similarities

After the rotated concept factor loadings matrices were obtained through principal components analyses and the varimax criterion on the concept mode for all six culture/sex groups (except for JP subjects), within-cultural concept factor similarities were computed. For the British males and females, the four one-to-one corresponding factors, each with coefficient of congruence over .85, were identified by their salient concepts as (a) "ADMIRATION-AFFECTION," characterized by leading concepts SOMEONE I ADMIRE, A CLOSE FRIEND, MY BROTHER, and MY PARENTS; (b) "POPULARITY", characterized by THE BEATLES, ELIZABETH TAYLOR, and HAROLD WILSON; (c) "AUTHORITARIANISM" defined by ENA SHARPLES (a TV character), SOMEONE I DISLIKE, WINSTON CHURCHILL, HAROLD WILSON, POLITICIAN, and TEACHER; and (d) "REMOTENESS", characterized by SPIDER, TIGER, THIEF, ATHLETES, and DOGS.

For the Finnish males and females, three of the four pairs of factors are highly congruent in terms of their salient concepts. The characteristics of the first two congruent dimensions, labeled as "ADMIRATION-AFFECTION" and "POPULARITY" are similar to these of the British structures under the same names. The third congruent dimension dubbed as "SOCIALLY UNDESIRABLE" is defined by the person terms THIEF, MURDERER, ALCOHOLIC, and ARTIST. The unique factor for Finnish males was characterized by socially respected male personalities (e.g., MEDICAL DOCTOR, MY UNCLE, MY COLLEAGUE, MY IDEAL SELF, MY FOREMAN, and POLITICIAN) and was labeled as a "MALE IDENTIFICATION" dimension. On the other hand, the Finnish females have a unique "SELF-IDENTIFICATION" factor which was represented by the concepts directly related to ego, including MYSELF AS A CHILD, MYSELF, MYSELF AS A FRIEND, MY BROTHER, MYSELF AS A MOTHER, MY MOTHER, and MY SISTER.

For the Belgian subjects, the total picture between two factor structures of males and females is strikingly high (with congruent indices of at least .85). The four one-to-one corresponding factors are identified as (a) "SELF-IDENTIFICATION," dominated by such ego-related concepts as MY SPOUSE, MYSELF

AS A PARENT, MY SON OR DAUGHTER, and MYSELF AS A FRIEND; (b) "POWER" or "AUTHORITARIANISM," characterized by DE GAULLE, THE POLITICIAN, EINSTEIN, THE BANKER, THE TEACHER, and THE PARISH PRIEST; (c) "SOCIALLY UNDESIRABLE" or "IMMORAL MODELS," characterized by THE MURDERER, THE THIEF, HITLER, THE BOXER, and THE PROSTITUTE; and (d) "SOCIALLY DEPENDENT," characterized by THE CHILD, THE CAT, THE DOG, THE MENTAL PATIENT, THE PROSTITUTE, and THE MAIDSERVANT.

Based on simultaneous evaluation of the characteristics of all six culture/sex group factor configurations, a cross-cultural concept factor structure is summarized in TABLE 5 with salient concepts on each indigenous culture/sex dimension listed at the bottom. Among the eight resultant factors, the first five are cross-cultural in nature, including "ADMIRATION-AFFECTION" and "POPULARITY" common to BE and FF of both sexes, "AUTHORITARIANISM" (or "POWER") common to BE and BF, "SOCIALLY-UNDESIRABLE" (or "IMMORAL MODELS") common to FF and BF, and "SELF-IDENTIFICATION" common to FF females and BF subjects of both sexes. As to the remaining three factors, the "REMOTENESS" and "SOCIALLY DEPENDENT" factors are culturally unique for BE and BF, respectively, and the "MALE IDENTIFICATION" dimension is specific to the Finnish males only.

Cross-Cultural Comparisons of Group Mean Ratings

Given the fact that there are within-cultural similarities as well as differences with respect to both underlying psychological semantic structures and personality concept factors and that the differences between cultures are greater than within, a question pertinent to ask is to what extent average individuals in various culture/sex groups as a whole are similar or different in "perceptions" or "judgments" of concept types with respect to the psychosemantics of personality. Based on the summaries of cross-cultural semantic components and concept factors (TABLES 4B and 5) a "cross-cultural" inner core matrix was constructed, given in TABLE 6, with rows consisting of all eight resultant concept factors and columns consisting of all scale dimensions in both semantic subspaces. Cell values in the first columns of all six (except for JP) indigenous inner core matrices were accordingly transformed into this matrix. However, in order to overcome nonstandardizational properties of these core matrices (i.e., sums of squares are different), the entries are coded schematically into seven-step categories, ranging from extremely positive (+++), to extremely negative (−−−) through neutrality (0). A blank entry indicates that the corresponding meaning feature was not found for the given group of subjects.

Major intra- and intercultural similarities and differences in personality judgments with respect to cross-cultural "theories" of psychosemantics can be observed: (a) The three Affective E-P-A features appear to be cross-culturally ubiquitous and most dominant with consistently high saliences on all concept factors. However, as far as the cross-cultural comparison is concerned, denotative dimensions are also differentiable. (b) Despite the fact that various culture/sex groups may share identical structures of personality perceptions in the concept mode and similar semantic configurations in the scale mode, their interactions of concept and scale factors are not automatically and/or proportionally the same.

TABLE 5

CROSS-CULTURAL CONCEPT FACTORS IN PERSONALITY RATINGS*

	BE		FF		BF	
Concept Factors	M	F	M	F	M	F
1. "ADMIRATION-AFFECTION"	I	I	I	IV		
2. "POPULARITY"	II	III	II	II		
3. "AUTHORITARIANISM"	III	II			II†	II†
4. "SOCIALLY UNDESIRABLE"			IV	III	III‡	III‡
5. "SELF-IDENTIFICATION"				I	I	I
6. "REMOTENESS"	IV	IV				
7. "SOCIALLY DEPENDENT"					IV	IV
8. "MALE IDENTIFICATION"			III			

* Salient concepts on each factor for all culture/sex groups are as follows:

1. "ADMIRATION-AFFECTION"
   BE (M and F) – SOMEONE I ADMIRE, A CLOSE FRIEND, MY BROTHER, MY FATHER, MY MOTHER, MYSELF
   FF (M and F) – MY IDEAL SELF, MY BROTHER, MY MOTHER, MYSELF AS A FRIEND, MY SISTER, MYSELF AS A PARENT.
2. "POPULARITY"
   BE (M and F) – THE BEATLES, ELIZABETH TAYLOR, HAROLD WILSON, ATHLETES.
   FF (M and F) – POLITICIAN, TEACHER, POLICEMAN, MY FOREMAN, SALESWOMAN.
3. "AUTHORITARIANISM" ("POWER")
   BE (M and F) – ENA SHARPLES, SOMEONE I DISLIKE, WINSTON CHURCHILL, HAROLD WILSON, POLITICIAN, TEACHER.
   BF (M and F) – DE GAULLE, THE POLITICIAN, EINSTEIN, THE BANKER, THE TEACHER, THE PARISH PRIEST.
4. "SOCIALLY UNDESIRABLE" ("IMMORAL MODELS")
   FF (M and F) – THIEF, MURDERER, ALCOHOLIC, ARTIST, POLITICIAN.
   BF (M and F) – THE MURDERER, THE THIEF, HITLER, THE BOXER, THE PROSTITUTE.
5. "SELF-IDENTIFICATION"
   FF-F – MYSELF AS A CHILD, MYSELF, MYSELF AS A FRIEND, MY BROTHER, MYSELF AS A MOTHER, MY MOTHER, MY SISTER.
   BF (M and F) – MY SPOUSE, MYSELF AS A PARENT, MY SON OR DAUGHTER, MYSELF, MYSELF AS A FRIEND, MYSELF AS A CHILD, MY MOTHER, MY SISTER, MY FATHER.
6. "REMOTENESS"
   BE (M and F) – SPIDER, TIGER, THIEF, ATHLETES, DOGS.
7. "SOCIALLY DEPENDENT"
   BF (M and F) – THE CHILD, THE CAT, THE DOG, THE MENTAL PATIENT, THE PROSTITUTE, THE MAIDSERVANT.
8. "MALE IDENTIFICATION"
   FF-M – MEDICAL DOCTOR, MY UNCLE, MY COLLEAGUE, MYSELF AS A FATHER, MY IDEAL SELF, MY FOREMAN, POLITICIAN.

† Defined as "POWER."
‡ Defined as "IMMORAL MODELS."

TABLE 6

SCHEMATIC REPRESENTATION OF GROUP MEAN DIFFERENCES IN THE CROSS-CULTURAL INNER CORE MATRIX*

| | | Scale Factors | | | | | | | | | | | | | | | |
| | | Affect | | | Denotation | | | | | | | | | | | | |
Concept Factors	Culture Sex Group Means	E	P	A	1 Pred	2 Rati	3 Mora	4 Ener (Invo)	5 Humi	6 Soci	7 Uniq	8 Posi	9 Ex/In	10 Ambi	11 Inte	12 Soph	13 Flex	14 Cult
I. "ADMIRATION-AFFECTION"	BE-M	++	-	0	-	++	+		-	0			++					
	BE-F	++	0	++	+	+	0							+				
	FF-M	+++	+	++	0		++		0	+					++			
	FF-F	+++	++	++	+		++		-						+			
II. "POPULARITY"	BE-M	++	0	0	0	++	+						++					
	BE-F	++	0	++	0	0	0							+				
	FF-M	++	++	++	0		++		+	+					+			
	FF-F	0	++	-	0		++		-	+								
III. "AUTHORI-TARIANISM" ("POWER")	BE-M	++	0	0	0	+	+						++					
	BE-F	++	0	++	0	0	0							0				
	BF-M	++	+++	--	0			++				+						
	BF-F	++	++	++	-							0						++
IV. "SOCIALLY UNDESIRABLE" ("IMMORAL MODELS")	FF-M	0	0	++	-	0	0			0								
	FF-F	--	0	++	-	0	0		+	0					-			
	BF-M	---	0	++	-			+	+			-						
	BF-F	---	--	++	-							-						-
V. "SELF-IDENTIFICATION"	FF-F	++	0	+	-		-		++	0								
	BF-M	+++	++	++	+			+				++			+			
	BF-F	+++	0	++	+							++	+					++
VI. "REMOTENESS"	BE-M	++	0	0	0	0	0						+					
	BE-F	++	0	++	0	0	0							+				
VII. "SOCIALLY DEPENDENT"	BF-M	+	-	++	-				+			0						
	BF-F	++	+	-	0							-						-
VIII. "MALE IDENTIFICATION"	FF-M	0	++	+	0	0	0		+	0								

* No inner core matrices for JP males and females are available.

NOTE: Entries in table indicate that the concept factor and scale factor were obtained for the subject group. The sign combinations (the seven steps from +++ through 0 to ———) signify the direction and relative magnitude of the three-factor interaction. For example, for BE-M, the concept factor ADMIRATION-AFFECTION is *highly* positive (++) on Evaluation but *slightly* negative (-) on Potency.

For example, the concept factor VII "SOCIALLY DEPENDENT" was "viewed" by average BF males as very active (+A) and slightly good (+E), but impotent (−P), curious (−Predictability) and simple (−Involvement). On the other hand, for average BF females, the socially dependent concepts THE CHILD, THE CAT, THE DOG, etc. were "viewed" as very good (+E) and potent (+P), but passive (−A), uncultured (−Cultural Socialization) and closed-minded (−Positivism). (c) Between cultures, various differentiating patterns of concept dimensions can be identified. For example, in the affective space, while the two most ego-related personality factors (i.e., "ADMIRATION-AFFECTION" and "SELF-IDENTIFICATION") are cross-culturally good (+E) and active (+A) (and also tended to be potent [+P]), the ego-dissociated "IMMORAL MODELS" dimension is cross-culturally bad (−E) (and also tends to be impotent [−P]), but very active (+A). In the denotative space, however, the two ego-related concept factors are generally considered with few exceptions on the YANG (positive) side of various bipolar semantic features and the ego-dissociated factor is towards the Yin side of the continuums.

SUMMARY AND DISCUSSION

In the present study, the theoretical foundation of affective and denotative meaning systems has been formulated according to Osgood's representational mediation theory of human cognition and behavior. It is important to note that the differentiation of these two meaning subsystems is based on the nature of responses (R_T's in Osgood's terms) from which mediator components (r_m's) are derived.[8] In order to illustrate empirically this dichotomy and its influence on human judgments, a representative group of homogeneous personality names that are familiar to average individuals was used as stimuli of ratings. The semantic differential scales used were from two sources: (a) the functionally equivalent E-P-A markers derived from the Osgood et al.[5] pancultural factorizations with respect to 100 heterogeneous concepts; and (b) the nonmarkers − a set of concept dominant relevant traits − elicited from subjects of the same population in naturalistic responses to the same stimulus personality terms. Under such circumstances, the content validity of traits (scales) for investigation of human psychosemantics used in indigenous cultural personality judgments was guaranteed and the construct validity of the resultant solutions was therefore expected to be maximal.

Methodologically, the newly developed quantitative technique for differentiating these two meaning subsystems possesses both the exploratory and confirmatory properties of general factor analytic techniques. First, the assumption was confirmed that when the indigenous E-P-A markers were used as controlled traits in the respective personality descriptor vector spaces of the eight culture/sex groups, they functioned well in recapturing the simple structure of the affective semantic subspace. This indicates the high generality (external validity) and convergent (internal) validity of the E-P-A psychological constructs. These marker scales had also been confirmed to be extremely reliable for scalings in the concept domains of natural (i.e., concepts like VALLEY, WOODS, and POND) and built (e.g., BRIDGE, CHAPEL, and ELEVATOR) spaces based on data collected in Belgium.[1]

The present research also provided an exploration of other nonaffective semantic components that were usually hidden in the undifferentiated, affectively dominant semantic factor space, particularly as assessed by the semantic differential technique. In supporting the premise of this study that E-P-A exhaust the *Affective* subspace, all 15 orthogonal scale dimensions identified in the "other" (denotative) indigenous subspaces of the eight culture/sex groups appeared clearly to be interpretable "affect-free" semantic features in distinguishing meanings of common personalities.

However, it should be noted that due to the ubiquitous dominance of E-P-A dimensions in human judgments, scales characterizing a given denotative dimension frequently have saturations on one or more affective dimensions, signifying a high *congruence relationship* between the affective and denotative dimensions (e.g., in TABLE 1, Denotation I Positivism goes with Evaluation). In ordinary factor analysis of semantic differential data, these "other" dimensions following E, P and A would usually be identified as "secondary" *affective* dimensions. Therefore, given this more powerful mathematical model, the semantic differential technique becomes more capable of identifying *psychological* denotative semantic features used in judgments of other concept domains with varying degrees of homogeneity, without, however, disturbing (or excluding) the ubiquitous E-P-A saturations in the special configurations of semantic vectors. It is possible, thereby, to determine the simultaneous but differential contribution of these two semantic subsystems to the meaning of each pair of scale terms. For example, the scale *clever/stupid* has about 90% Affect for BE and FF subjects, but has only 32% Affect for JP subjects. This kind of information reflects the implicit characterization of cultural meaning of each scale, which has practical significance for intra- and intercultural communications.

The present research strategies emphasize direct and simultaneous solutions of the concept factors, two semantic meaning subsystems and their interactions for each homogeneous subject group with similar response patterns. Although interpretation of the dynamics of the intra- and intercultural differences would require more socio- and culturological knowledge of each indigenous community, the comparisons of average individuals' "judgments" in the cross-cultural inner core matrix in TABLE 6 clearly provided evidence for different influences of subjective cultural implicit "theories of personality" on perceptions of other human beings in society.

As indicated earlier, human judgment is a function of subjects, objects (or concepts), and psychosemantic components. The individual differences in the relationship of concept factors and different meaning components in any homogeneous concept domain are extremely important in social psychology today. The methodology developed in the present study by the conjoint application of the SD technique and the three-mode factor analysis can be applied to other subject and/or concept domains. By testing specifically on psychosemantic systems of different age groups, for example, one might reveal unique patterns of cultural changes on a given concept domain (such as moral standards). Cross-cultural comparisons on such information could be of considerable importance for international understanding.

ACKNOWLEDGMENTS

I wish to express my gratitude to our foreign colleagues, Drs. P. B. Warr, J. Kuusinen, Y. Tanaka, and R. Hogenraad for their cooperation in data collection in Britain, Finland, Japan and Belgium, respectively. I am indebted to Professor Charles E. Osgood for his continuous encouragement in this research.

REFERENCES

1. HOGENRAAD, R. & O. C. S. TZENG. 1975. Affective and denotative meaning systems in natural and built space conceptions. In preparation.
2. OSGOOD, C. E. 1964. Semantic differential technique in the comparative study of culture. Am. Anthropologist 66(3): 171–200.
3. OSGOOD, C. E. 1969. On the whys and wherefores of E, P, and A. J. Personality Social Psychol. 12(3): 194–199.
4. OSGOOD, C. E. 1971. Exploration in semantic space: a personal diary. J. Social Issues 27(4): 5–64.
5. OSGOOD, C. E., W. H. MAY & M. S. MIRON. 1975. Cross-cultural Universals of Affective Meaning. University of Illinois Press. Urbana, Illinois.
6. OSGOOD, C. E., G. J. SUCI & P. H. TANNENBAUM. 1957. The measurement of meaning. University of Illinois Press. Urbana, Illinois.
7. TUCKER, L. R. 1966. Some mathematical notes on three-mode factor analysis. Psychometrika 31: 279–311.
8. TZENG, O. C. S. 1972. Differentiation of affective and denotative meaning systems in personality ratings via three-mode factor analysis. Unpublished Ph.D. dissertation Urbana: University of Illinois, 1972. (University Microfilms No. 73-17, 454, 278.)
9. TZENG, O. C. S. 1975. Differentiation of affective and denotative meaning systems and their influence in personality ratings. J. Personality Social Psychol. 32(6): 978–988.
10. TZENG, O. C. S. & R. HOGENRAAD. 1975. Implicit personality theories and their influence in person perceptions. In preparation.

COMMENTS FROM AN ANTHROPOLOGIST

Discussant: Margaret Mead

American Museum of Natural History
New York, New York 10024

I would like to give my commentary on this session from an anthropological standpoint; but first I would also like to emphasize that I think it is deplorable that we have three (and sometimes even four or five) human science disciplines, each studying the same problems from different points of view, using different assumptions, incomparable units and methodologies that are imperfectly understood by the other disciplines. There is no other field of science where we have disciplines working parallel to one another and yet refusing to pay attention to each other's work. In a conference where there has been so much talk about understanding, I think this should be emphasized.

I have not only heard the papers actually presented here, but I have also read a variety of other papers sent me by the participants in lieu of or supplementary to the papers that they planned to present. My comments, therefore, will inevitably include these background materials as well.

I would like to deal first with those things that anthropologists would like to learn from psychologists and about testing techniques that have been well developed and experimentally validated. For example, we may need to know the distribution of some measurable trait within the population that we are studying, like hand-eye coordination, a certain kind of rote memory, facility in identifying illusions, ability to deal with opposites, speed of color naming, or acuity of vision. If it is a society into which the Euro-American style of schooling has been introduced, we may want some measure of what we presently call "intelligence" – that is, the developed capability to meet the requirements of a Euro-American type schooling. Even among people who have not yet been introduced to schooling, we may want some way of communicating an estimate of some aspect of "intelligence." For example, I have used the Ball and Field Test in this way, among a people to whom even the use of a pencil and paper was unfamiliar. The very brightest children – judged by my experience of their abilities in their own culture – can do the superior plan. This parallels the findings of Kilbride and Leibowitz that in a culture that has been test-characterized as two-dimensional, there will be found an occasional three-dimensional individual. The extent to which individual capabilities are cultivated, neglected or stunted is one that can only be well explored if there are tests that are cross-culturally valid. The extreme difficulty of adapting even very simple psychological tests – like the recognition of an illusion – to different cultures is well illustrated.[1]

Parenthetically I might add that Professor Cole's little anecdote about the interchange between Dr. Kagan and myself is less relevant than he seemed to think, as I am fully familiar with what psychologists are trying to do. I started working with psychological testing in 1923, and I have been au courant with such developments as exist ever since.[2]

Anthropologists would also like to work with psychologists in systematically exploring particular characteristics of the members of societies in which the culture has been studied intensively. This can be done in a variety of ways: by an anthropologist who has psychological training in the use of intelligence, projective or objective tests, as Theodore Schwartz and his students have done in Manus in the last few years;[3] by an anthropologist and psychologist working together, of which an outstanding example is the cooperation of Rhoda Metraux and Theodora M. Abel;[4] by an anthropologist working in a team in studying several cultures;[5] or in the kind of large scale research that we conducted for the Columbia University Research in Contemporary Cultures.[6]

I am fully in agreement with Professor Cole in that work in primitive cultures should be hypothesis-generating, and that testing the hypotheses so generated should be reserved for more controlled conditions. It is wasteful to undertake such validating work in areas where the investigator's exposure to mosquitoes and dysentery can be better justified by a study of the vanishing culture itself. Many primitive cultures cannot provide adequate samples: ages are not known, the societies are too small, distances are too great, et cetera. A small amount of psychological investigation is sufficient to raise the kind of questions for which we need extreme culture contrasts.

A second use for testing is to provide for communication between psychologists and anthropologists. This communication is valuable even though no new knowledge comes from it. For example, students who know something about Chinese culture, but have little psychodynamic background can learn from Muensterberger's study of the Chinese,[7] and specialists in psychodynamic studies can profit from this study as well. Performance on tests provides a common media of exchange and multidisciplinary studies can be very much facilitated by such forms of communication. The kind of test that Margaret Lowenfeld called *objective* because it does not need to be mediated by words,[8] the Draw a Man Test, and children's drawings are all particularly useful as the independent analyst does not need a delicate knowledge of the language; a large number of "products" can be placed side by side for demonstration and analysis. All such materials can be very useful to both experimentalists and clinicians.

I very much doubt the usefulness of fractionating cultural data by imposing test materials constructed for Euro-American culture without a primary study of the cultures involved. Studies like that of Professor Osgood, which include so many items and such a vast amount of data, might make it possible to put together some coherent picture of the individual cultures, very much as an environmental impact statement puts together the knowledge of some ecological whole that has been fractionated and distributed to different government agencies. I say it might, but I doubt it. It is true that we can make translations between the Islamic week, the Hebrew week, and the Christian week when children who have been exposed to schooling are asked about "Wednesday," but to make generalizations from such data about the nature of the perception of time, without including cultures in which there are no weeks, and cultures in which there are half a dozen kinds of weeks, is premature and likely to produce not general laws, but obfuscation. However we do not know whether the use of massive amounts of such computerized data may yield something about whole cultures. If it does not, it is most unlikely that it will provide a firm basis for any general laws of human nature.

Alan Lomax's work on Choreometrics and Cantometrics is a brilliant example of the use of cross-cultural material, originally collected as wholes (as tapes of music, films of dance, et cetera) and then subjected to trait analysis using trained human observers to produce profiles that can then be correlated with large scale technological and ecological differences.[9] A principle difference here is in the nature of the original sample of behavior, whether it is holistic and complex, and tightly coupled,[10] or fractionated by the way in which the test is constructed.

The Gleser and Gottschalk schedules provide a sophisticated combination of such methods for use in ethnic groups within American culture, but when translations of tests using non-European languages are used, the problem becomes much more complicated.[11]

I am in tremendous sympathy with what Professor Cole has been doing to discriminate between "informal teaching and learning" and the effects of schooling. As we have imposed our type of school system all over the world, this has had a homogenizing effect on the performance of children on our kind of tests. Standardization of age of school entry obscures the differences due to different rates of maturation. As Erik Erikson once remarked: "Latency in the United States begins at six," e.g., the decreed age of school entry. But I believe a great deal of time would have been saved if Professor Cole and his collaborators had been working with anthropologists from the start. It is terribly expensive for human scientists to keep on making the same discoveries over and over.

I do not believe that we can make much further progress without collecting our materials in a form that can be computerized. But preparing materials for ultimate computerization or premature fractionization is a terrible temptation, one to which psychologists, so many of whom skipped the natural history phase in the development of their science, are especially subject, and to which many anthropologists have succumbed during the last 25 years.[12]

REFERENCES

1. SEGALL, M. H., D. T. CAMPBELL & M. J. HERSKOVITS. 1966. The Influence of Culture on Visual Perception. Bobbs-Merrill. Indianapolis and New York.
2. MEAD, M. 1927. Group Intelligence Tests and Linguistic Disability among Italian Children, School and Society **25**, (No. 642): 465–468.

 MEAD, M. 1928. Coming of Age in Samoa, Appendix V. Morrow. New York.

 MEAD, M. 1931. The Primitive Child. *In* A Handbook of Child Psychology. Carl Murchison, Ed. Clark University Press. Worcester, Mass. pp. 669–686.

 MEAD, M. 1932. An Investigation of the Thought of Primitive Children, with Special Reference to Animism, Journal of the Royal Anthropological Institute **62** (January–June): 173–190.

 MEAD, M. 1932. Research on Primitive Children. *In* Manual of Child Psychology, Second Revised Edition. Leonard Carmichael, Ed. John Wiley & Sons. New York. pp. 735–780.

 MEAD, M. 1946. Research on Primitive Children. *In* Manual of Child Psychology. Leonard Carmichael, Ed. John Wiley & Sons. New York. pp. 667–706.

 MEAD, M. 1974. Margaret Mead. *In* A History of Psychology in Autobiography, Vol. VI, Gardner Lindzey, Ed. Prentice Hall. Englewood Cliffs, N.J. pp. 293-326.

 MEAD, M., R. METRAUX & T. ABEL. Exhibit of comparative use of various psychological tests, at the American Psychological Association, 1954, and the American Anthropological Association, 1960.

 MEAD. M. The Evocation of Psychologically Relevant Responses in Ethnological Field Work, *In* The Making of Psychological Anthropology. George and Louise Spindler, Eds. (in press).

3. SCHWARTZ, T. Cognitive Acculturation in the Admiralty Islands. Paper presented at the meeting of the American Anthropological Association, Mexico City, 1974. (unpublished).

 SCHWARTZ, T. A Study of Cultural Heuristics. National Institute of Education grant application, 1976.

4. METRAUX, R. & T. ABEL. 1957. Normal and Deviant Behavior in a Peasant Community. American Journal of Orthopsychiatry **27** (No. 1): 167–184.

METRAUX, R. & T. ABEL. Universals and Cultural Regularities: Aspects of Performance in the Lowenfeld Mosaic Test. Presented at the Annual Meeting of the American Anthropological Association, Mexico City, 1974.

METRAUX, R. & T. ABEL. 1975. Culture and Psychotherapy. College and University Press. New Haven, Conn.

5. EDGERTON, R. 1971. The Individual in Cultural Adaptation. University of California Press. Berkeley.

6. MEAD, M. & R. METRAUX, Eds. 1953. The Study of Culture at a Distance. The University of Chicago Press. Chicago.

MEAD, M. 1974. A Note on the Evocative Character of the Rorschach Test, *In* Toward a Discovery of the Person: The First Bruno Klopfer Memorial Symposium, and Carl G. Jung Centennial Symposium. Robert Davis, Ed. Monograph of the Society for Personality Assessment. Burbank, California. pp. 62–67.

7. MUENSTERBERGER, W. 1951. Orality and Dependence: Characteristics of Southern Chinese. *In* Psychoanalysis and the Social Sciences, III. Geza Roheim et al., Eds. International Universities Press. New York. pp. 37–69.

8. LOWENFELD, M. 1950. The Nature and Use of the Lowenfeld Method Technique in Work with Children and Adults. Journal of Psychology 30: 325–331.

LOWENFELD, M. 1954. The Lowenfeld Mosaic Test. Newman Neame. London.

9. LOMAX, A., Ed. 1968. Folksong Style and Culture. American Association for the Advancement of Science, Symp. Vol. No. 88. Washington, D.C.

LOMAX, A. 1972. The Evolutionary Taxonomy of Culture. Science 117: 228–239.

10. WEAVER, W. 1955. Science and People, Science 122 (No. 3183): 1255–1259.

11. GOTTSCHALK, L. & G. GLESER. 1969. The Measurement of Psychological States Through the Content Analysis of Verbal Behavior. University of California Press. Berkeley.

12. SHAKOW, D. 1959. Research in Child Development: A Case Illustration of the Psychologist's Dilemma, The American Journal of Orthopsychiatry 21 (No. 1): 45–59.

COGNITION AND PERCEPTION IN CROSS-CULTURAL RESEARCH*

Discussant: F. J. McGuigan

Performance Research Laboratory
University of Louisville
Louisville, Kentucky 40208

The announced purpose of this Conference is to consider relationships between theories and practical aspects of cross-cultural research. The approaches include those of not only psychologists, but also of sociologists and anthropologists. To assess the progress of this panel toward the accomplishment of this admirable goal, I propose to consider our general theme and the individual presentations within the framework of four more specialized topics: (1) theory, (2) research methodology, (3) processes of generalization, and (4) technological implications.

THEORY

The most impressive representation of a theoretical orientation is made by the three "Illinois" papers by Triandis, Osgood, and Tzeng, all of course stemming from Osgood's work on meaning (although Triandis also developed his own theory). To summarize Osgood's theoretical framework, he starts with the common linguistic and philosophical conception of meaning to the effect that semantic similarities can be indexed by similarity in the distribution of language usage — speakers are semantically similar to the extent to which they produce similar kinds of linguistic responses. This kind of assumption then led to his subsystem of affective meaning, the type of meaning in which humans (apparently universally) attribute emotional feelings to signs that represent persons and things. The E, P, and A representational processes are crucial in our struggle for existence in that representation of emotional reactions constitutes a mediating semantic system that allows us to make critical discriminative responses. We thus behave toward aspects of our environment on dimensions of good versus bad (E); of strong versus weak (P); and of active versus passive (A). However, as Tzeng emphasized, both affective *and* denotative meanings are simultaneously involved in one's interaction with his environment. Affective meanings reflect how a person feels about a sign, while denotative meaning reflects one's semantic theory about the categorization of signs. This makes Tzeng's development of scales for denotative meaning most impressive, and perhaps the most important new development reported at this symposium.

In considering Osgood's theory, it is especially interesting to note the far reaching (in a cross-cultural context one might even say "global") applications of behaviorism to the arena of international behavior. With regard to cross-cultural phenomena, the three Illinois papers are based on the semantic differential that derives from Osgood's representational meaning reaction (r_M) — and r_M in turn derives in part, I suspect, from Hullian theory and especially Hull's $r_G - s_G$

---

* This paper was based on the manuscripts furnished to me in sufficient time for study prior to the oral presentations.

mechanism. Elsewhere Osgood's behaviorism has been applied to graduated and reciprocated initiatives in international tension reduction.[1]†

While thus calling attention to the widespread applicability of behavioristic theories, and of the theoretical formulations of Hull and Osgood in particular, we should emphasize that the word "theory" is used in its own special sense in psychology and related biosocial sciences. Triandis provided us with a realistic, if somewhat humbling, statement to this effect. After his valuable examination of reasons for what he holds a crisis in social psychology, he concluded that theory as the term is used in the physical sciences is an illusory goal for the social sciences. The most that we can do, he suggests, is to develop loose theoretical frameworks that will help us to "think about" social phenomena. Such theoretical frameworks, which should consist of concepts and dimensions that are universal across space and time, can guide our empirical research by suggesting what we should look for, namely, accurate descriptions of particular populations at particular points of time. Triandis then offered us four such possible concepts in the form of universal dimensions that "characterize interpersonal behavior." I am very favorably impressed by Triandis' analysis of his four universal dimensions, especially his discussion of dyadic relationships in terms of credit, and the like. These four dimensions, he holds, are a function of the way humans exchange resources, change relationships through time, and give the meaning to interpersonal exchanges that determines the course of social interactions. Because "subjective" reactions to overt behavior are critical in social interaction, he was led to the study of "subjective culture." Triandis then related subjective culture to interpersonal behavior as a function of kinds of ecologies. Whereas culture is defined as the man-made part of the human environment, subjective culture is a characteristic group way of perceiving its social environment.

I wonder about the theoretical status of the concept of "subjective culture," as well as possible methodological difficulties in studying such a concept. To study subjective culture Triandis has individuals make judgments about the extent to which social stimuli are associated with particular attributes. He then arrives at statements of the class: "People of type X judge stimuli of type Y as high on attribute type Z." However, the common definition of "subjective" is in reference to one's private experience, which is unobserved by others. But Triandis measured "subjective culture" in terms of a person's overt, objectively observable reaction to certain items. Perhaps what is at issue here is the classical distinction between introspection of one's private experience versus the concept of the "verbal report." If so, Triandis' use of "subjective culture" may be a misnomer in that Triandis studied what the individuals *said* their judgments were, which is not necessarily what they really were (if it *had* even been possible to determine what the individual's perceptions "really' were). Perhaps his approach is not so much the use of a direct measure of subjective culture to predict behavior, but the use of empirical relationships between overt test-taking behavior to predict observed social behavior. From the point of view of a psychology of overt behavior we have, then, verbal reports of *presumed* perceptions. Osgood, perhaps sensing the same kind of difficulty that I am expressing here, used the term *objective indicators* of subjective culture, a view with which I would totally agree. The implication of this discussion, then, is that

---

† Because my very similar operant-based foreign policy publication in the *Revista Latino Americana De Psicologia* has been such a well-kept secret, I might take the liberty of mentioning *it* here as a similar international application of behaviorism.[2]

"subjective culture" may have the status of a logical construct that can be indirectly studied in terms of antecedent external stimuli and consequent overt behavior. This, of course, is the classical model which, *I* think, can be improved on by the *direct* study of the logical construct, if it is of the hypothetical construct variety.[3] Triandis astutely recognizes the importance of covert behavior in responding in social situations, such as when a person covertly evaluates a disliked action of his boss (it would be socially unwise for the person to make such covert responses overt). To neglect covert behavior in a complex social chain would leave out a critical component in the communication network. It is through the direct psychophysiological study of covert behavior that I think we can make "subjective experiences," such as perceptions, public, at least in principle. The strategy here is to have an individual's psychophysiological signals enter a computer with a readout that displays and interprets the perception (and other private experiences) for the observer.[4,5]

Tzeng emphasized the origin of meaning and the differentiation of two meaning subsystems, based on Osgood's assumption that mediator components (r_m's) are derived from overt responses (R_T's in Osgood's terms). As the language user matures, the assumption continues that r_M becomes "centralized," so that representational mediation processes are "established in terms of the sensory-motor discrimination systems of the *brain*." I would suggest that the underlying theory about affective and denotative meaning systems is *not* affected by the bodily locus of the various information-processing systems, so that it is unnecessary for Tzeng (and perhaps Osgood too) to take the position that sensory-motor discrimination systems occur solely in the brain. This point is part of my friendly "quarrel" with Osgood,[6] in which I argue that we have enough evidence to assert with a reasonable degree of probability that mediational processes involve neuromuscular circuits throughout the entire body, using informational feedback from the activation of critical, localized muscle responses.[7]

I have concentrated on Osgood's theory because of its highly sophisticated development and its extensive application throughout psychology. Among the other interesting theoretical aspects of the presentations is Kagan and his colleagues' use of growth functions as criteria for differentiating between fundamental cognitive processes and culturally specific ones. Kagan *et al.* assumed that fundamental cognitive processes grow with age in all cultural settings, but that local cultural characteristics are a function of growth rate and age at which asymptotes are reached. Test performance of culturally specific functions thus should not show regular improvement with age and rates of growth, and asymptotes should differ among cultures. "Culture" of course is an exceedingly complex variable that can be fractionated to learning variables, performance variables, etc. One might then ask which fractionated cultural variables are the ones that affect growth parameters, and one might even wonder whether noncultural variables such as genetic factors might affect the growth parameters too.

METHODOLOGY

The papers present a variety of methodologies and well illustrate the difficulty that we face in conducting cross-cultural research. Our difficulties probably arise when it is not feasible to conduct true experiments. And lacking true experiments, it is difficult, if not impossible, to establish causal relationships between cultural variables and classes of behavior. I will use the work of Kagan *et al.* to illustrate this kind of problem, although other research could as easily have been selected for this purpose. They studied three samples of children from three different locations in an effort to establish three points on a scale of modernization (their "independent variable"). They found a number of interesting differences among their three groups, but a conclusion that the differences were due to different degrees of modernization would be a tenuous one at best. While the groups certainly differed in degree of modernization, they also differed in so many other respects that the confounds are sufficiently serious as to greatly limit what we might say about the effects of the independent variable. Differences in research techniques also can account for group differences: in this instance, different researchers confronted various groups (for example, in the Guatemalan villages, the battery of tests were administered by local individuals using the appropriate Indian dialect, which certainly represents a different method than the data collection procedures used in Cambridge, Massachusetts). And we know that certain characteristics of the research situation, especially with respect to the person who is collecting the data, can greatly influence the dependent variable values.[8]

Similarly, the finding of Kagan *et al.* that variability in performance was greater in the Guatemalan villages than in Cambridge suggested to them "that the greater variability among the village children is the function of greater variability in motivation." This is certainly a possibility, but one might just as well reason in the opposite direction, and there are no data apparent for invoking a motivation variable as an explanation. The greater variability in performance might have been a function of so many other variables, such as genetic differences, testing conditions, form of test item, unique language characteristics, etc.

Among the very interesting findings of Kagan *et al.* was that all the American children conserved matter and liquid by age 10, but no more than 80% of the oldest Guatemalan children were able to conserve matter and liquid. But again, there are so many differences in characteristics among the groups and in testing procedures that it is difficult to select any specific variable or variables that determine this group difference. Perhaps the best that can be done with this type of design is to speculate that a difference is a function of a global, nonfractionated variable, which is what the authors do here: their finding suggests "a culturally significant component to this task." But even this tentative "explanation" doesn't tell us very much and it too prematurely excludes noncultural variables (genetic factors, etc.). Similarly, interesting differences in memory functions are viewed as "reflecting the activation, or the failure to activate, strategies of organization and rehearsal." The speculation continues that the use of effective strategies by American children, and by some of the San Pedro children, is one of the functions of an executive cognitive process that matures during the period between five and twelve years of age. While their interpretation is not at all unreasonable, it certainly far departs from their data. The most that can be ascertained by this type of research design is that there are certain differences, very interesting ones in this case, among the groups, and that these differences may be a function of a large number of variables, the number depending on how globally one defines the variables. With such enormous confounds in nonexperimental research, one can only speculate about functional relationships. While the results reported by Kagan *et al.* and their interpretations are interesting, the connection between the two is weak. In their conclusion the authors seem to recognize these difficulties by stating that "it is not possible at this time to assign differential explanatory power to these or other factors in our attempt to understand the differential rate of growth of these executive functions." (The factors they cited are differences in the two Guatemalan villages of practices toward infants and young children, quality of schooling, and exposure to daily variety and parental attitudes.) These are some of the possibilities, but even here the authors don't seem to recognize the great (impossible?) difficulty of explaining differences among groups with this type of design, for they conclude that they are "in the process of collecting observations on the children and interviewing their parents in the hopes that this additional information will clarify this issue." I think that if they do not employ a more powerful research design, they will have to place special emphasis on the "hope" variable.

A correlational class of design for cross-cultural research is exemplified by the work of Kirk and Burton. Their correlational analysis was verified using multiple linear regression analysis, which the authors state is "similar in many ways to some common forms of causal analysis." In this way they attempt to "control" for the effects of extraneous variables. One must admire their painstaking methods and applaud their conclusions while, at the same time, recognizing that correlational analysis of whatever form and extent cannot lead to such high probability statements as result from true experimental designs in which independent variables are purposively manipulated. That is, with an infinite (or at least indefinitely large) number of variables in the world, one can never remove the effects of all extraneous variables through correlational analysis, *even* if he uses analysis of covariance. At least at this stage of our methodological development, only the (true) experiment can do that, and then only 95% of the time (at the .05 level of alpha).

One interesting methodological question arises in the Kirk study of nonverbal maternal behavior as a possible source of variation in *cognitive* growth rate among Kikuyu children. Their findings that maternal kinesic behavior plays an important role in predicting scores on seven of the cognitive tests and contributes to prediction of a composite cognitive test score are very impressive. In measuring "cognitive growth" perhaps they might also independently consider verbal and nonverbal cognitive growth, with the possibility that the nonverbal "independent variable" would relate more strongly to a nonverbal cognitive measure. This procedure might result in even more verbal cognitive factors being predicted.

When a problem is simply not amenable to true experimentation, the next best thing that we can do is to employ a modified experimental design in the form of a quasi-experimental design. Quasi-experimental designs, especially some of the more sophisticated and powerful ones, *should* be widely applicable in cross-cultural research. We see an instance of the use of a quasi-experimental design in Mehan's work. Mehan's application was to include the child as a component in the instructional chain, "observing" the child by means of a microphone and videotaping. The same child thus worked on the same task in contrasting learning situations, allowing the researcher to achieve some control over the learning task under classroom conditions. In this way various conditions were related to differences in the child's behavior. Even so, confounding necessarily results from such quasi-experimental designs. Perhaps this is the major methodological problem in cross-cultural research, and it occurs when we are unable to employ true experimental designs.

With regard to the formation of hypotheses and the methodological question of testing them, I especially liked Osgood's emphasis on the distinction between hypothesis formation and hypothesis confirmation, viz., that while intuitions of historians and other professionals (competent though they are) are useful for hypothesis formation, such notions are useless for hypothesis testing and for quantitative analyses. Failure to make this distinction is widespread in our society so that individuals often confuse what they read, as in novels, with what is true. While insights of great writers are potentially valuable, such "insights" by themselves do not solve problems. They might be useful guides for data collection.

The rationale for the three Illinois papers was to correlate scales and to find concepts that are functionally equivalent, thus applying the psycholinguistic definition of similarity of meaning — similarity in the distribution of usage — across languages. In this way the semantic differential technique was used as a means of providing objective indicators of "subjective culture." This is an approach that presumably: (1) yields quantifiable data; (2) applies the same procedures differentially over concepts; and (3) is systematic rather than topical with respect to times and places. These are admirable efforts to obtain valuable data of a generalizable nature and lead us to the topic of generalization.

GENERALIZATION

A critical issue, conceivably the most important one for all of the behavioral sciences, concerns the degree to which one may generalize results obtained by means of research designs such as those employed by members of this symposium. If the cross-cultural researcher is interested in specifying universal characteristics of behavior, then he should employ our classical generalization model, in which the researcher specifies a well-defined population from which he draws a random sample of subjects; the findings for the sample are then inferred to be characteristic of the parent population. Ideally, this model calls for a representative sample from all cultures throughout the world, a task that is made even more difficult if one introduces a time variable so that the generalization is made for all humans living, dead, and yet to be born. In the face of such overwhelming demands, what does the cross-cultural researcher do? Triandis' introduction of a temporal variable gives an admirable recognition of the scope of the problem that we face.

First, the cross-cultural researcher may not be interested in arriving at universal characteristics of behavior, but merely in describing unique characteristics of only some members of a given culture. In this instance, he might well achieve his limited goal by sufficiently well describing a very limited sample. However, cross-cultural researchers seem, at least implicitly, to seek universal characteristics of behavior, but the samples that have been specified in these papers are extremely limited. Even Osgood, in his massive cross-cultural work across some 30 communities throughout the world, felt it necessary to maximize sociometric equivalences across communities by studying teenage male students in average high schools and urban settings. The samples of subjects studied are limited indeed. Perhaps the status of cross-cultural research with regard to generalization is not far from Beach's[9] assessment of the status of comparative psychology in his "The Snark was a Boojum." There he held that the comparative psychologist, instead of sampling along the entire phylogenetic scale, had succeeded only in developing a psychology of the white rat. The similar point is often made that those of us who study humans have only developed a psychology of the American college sophomore.

In the hope of arriving at universal characteristics of behavior, and of being able to specify cultural differences too, we indeed should be able to obtain representative samples of people throughout the world. Osgood's work represents a strong effort to obtain such a representative sample. His systematic approach assumes that he is tapping concepts that are reasonably stable over time and place, although he recognizes that "feelings and beliefs" about things may be quite labile. The implication is that the concepts he is studying do not interact with cultures and a temporable variable, which certainly seems to be the case *so far* for his E, P and A scales – with few exceptions, E-P-A show amazingly similar loadings across many cultures. Still, the young subjects that he studied might (and probably do) behave differently with regard to E, P and A than do older individuals: e.g., what is good for the young is not necessarily good for the old (E); the young might perceive activity and potency differently than do elderly individuals (P); and one might suspect that the elderly are slower and less active (A). Values for E, P, and A as a function of age would conceivably provide some very interesting insights.

Tzeng studied results from adults of both sexes of ages 18 to 50 from urban areas, but excluded those of the highest academic levels. This would appear to form a *relatively* sound data base for generalizing to universal characteristics. Since one of the long-range goals of cross-cultural research is to be able to understand interpersonal behavior among the world's political leaders, one might wonder about the confidence to be placed in such a set of generalizations gained from data on high school students (Osgood) or on individuals who did not advance to the higher academic levels (as in Tzeng's sample).

Given that we seek to generalize as widely as possible, in any given research the question is how widely is it reasonable to generalize from samples that are not representative of the world's population? Basically, the answer is that we can generalize to the degree to which our independent variables do not interact among cultures. The implication is that we should employ factorial designs that allow us to study such interactions. There would be three cases of special interest: (1) The case in which the same results are obtained among different cultures so that there is no interaction; this allows unrestricted generalization to be made. We could illustrate this instance by citing the interesting Ponzo illusion (along with controlled treatments) studied by Kilbride and Leibowitz. (2) The case in which performance variables differ as a function of the culture studied, but the independent variables do not interact with the culture variable. In this case we can make statements to the effect that members of one culture behave differently than members of another, but we can generalize our treatment effects over cultures. (3) The case in which a given independent variable does interact with a cultural variable; here we must sharply limit the degree to which we generalize about behavior among cultures.

But if the researcher has no knowledge about interactions between the independent variable and cultures, he still might tentatively offer a generalization. When other cross-cultural researchers replicate the study, the various extraneous variables will assume different values from those that occurred in the original study (either as the result of intentional control or because they were allowed to randomly vary). If, then, in the replication of the study the original results are confirmed in other cultures, it is likely that the independent variable does not interact with the cultural variable. On the other hand if replications of the study by others under different conditions do not confirm the original findings, then there is probably at least one interaction that needs to be discovered. At this point both thorough and piecemeal analysis of the differences between the two cultures needs to be made in order to discover the reason for the interaction.

TECHNOLOGICAL IMPLICATIONS

To now consider the practical aspects of cross-cultural research, we may note a major goal that the present researchers emphasized, namely, increasing ease of communication among cultures. By understanding thought processes in different cultures, we can perhaps increase the ability to communicate our thoughts and perceptions of the world, perhaps making our interpersonal communications more efficient. It remains as an empirical question, however, as to whether or not increased effectiveness of communication among cultures actually does decrease the degree of intercultural hostility. On this point Osgood concluded that progress toward one interdependent world requires comparable cross-national measures of subjective culture. Triandis asserts that there is considerable evidence that if two individuals have different subjective cultures, their interpersonal relationships suffer, including wrong attributions, avoidance, and even aggression. Osgood belives that he has succeeded in piercing a hole in the language barrier to thus facilitate communication by identifying universal dimensions of meaning in his pancultural application of the semantic differential. Osgood's suggestion is to plot interconcept distances for all pairs of cultures. Presumably, the smaller the distances in affect across concepts for a pair of cultures, the easier should be communication in that conceptual domain. The members of the State Department could use this procedure for affective meanings so that in communicating with members of other cultures on a given topic, they can recognize where they would or would not have special difficulties and plan accordingly. As Osgood so effectively put it: "Americans could communicate very easily with Iranians about color, but have one hell of a time with Swedes."

Still, the problem of generalization crops up again in that this approach at increasing communication effectiveness rests on the generalization from limited samples to political leaders. We may not be at all sure that loadings for high school students, for example, would be sufficiently similar to those of the world's political leaders to justify such a generalization. Cole and Scribner's emphasis of the lack of data on the developmental status of various third world people further points out our need for a firm data base in order to arrive at beneficial intercultural exchanges.

REFERENCES

1. OSGOOD, C. E. 1962. An Alternative to War or Surrender. University of Illinois Press. Urbana, Ill.
2. MCGUIGAN, F. J. 1970. Reducción de la tension international. Rev. Latino Americana Psicologia 2: 327–341.
3. MACCORQUODALE, K. & P. E. MEEHL. 1948. On a distinction between hypothetical constructs and intervening variables. Psychol. Rev. 55: 95–107.
4. MCGUIGAN, F. J. 1973. Electrical measurement of covert processes as an explication

of "higher mental events." *In* The Psychophysiology of Thinking. F. J. McGuigan and R. A. Schoonover, Eds.: 343–385. Academic Press. New York, N.Y.

5. MCGUIGAN, F. J. Principles of Covert Behavior. A Study in the Psychophysiology of Thinking. Prentice-Hall. Englewood Cliffs, N.J. In Press.

6. OSGOOD, C. E. & F. J. MCGUIGAN. 1973. Psychophysiological correlates of meaning: Essences or tracers? *In* The Psychophysiology of Thinking. F. J. McGuigan & R. A. Schoonover, Eds.: 449–492. Academic Press. New York, N.Y.

7. MCGUIGAN, F. J., V. I. CULVER, & T. S. KENDLER. 1971. Covert behavior as a direct electromyographic measure of mediating responses. Cond. Reflex 6: 145–152.

8. MCGUIGAN, F. J. 1963. The experimenter – a neglected stimulus object. Psych. Bull. 60: 421–428.

9. BEACH, F. A. 1950. The snark was a boojum. Am. Psychologist 5: 115–124.

OPEN DISCUSSION: IV

DR. HARRY TRIANDIS: Dr. Mead has raised an important epistemological question that has been central to the disagreement between anthropology and psychology for a long time. Namely, is it our job to be as exact as possible in describing human behavior, or should we try to discover generalities and patterns that approximate the laws underlying behavior? Dr. Mead stresses the accuracy of the description, and that certainly has its place. But we must not get carried away by this effort and miss the discovery of basic laws. We have in Dr. Mead's statement an emphasis on cultural differences. Well, there are lots of differences among the chairs in this room, but we do not find it useful to focus on such differences. If we make the description of differences the only concern of our scientific activities, we will have so much to do that we will not be able to discover any generalities. Her criticism of Osgood's studies overemphasizes differences. Sure there are human groups that do not have the concept "Wednesday," but we must not let that stop us from studying how other groups react to the names of the days of the week. Osgood's findings about variations in the meaning of the names of the days of the week show some universal patterns, as well as cultural differences, and throw much light on the question of how time is perceived by different humans. If we focus only on those humans who do not use time-related concepts, we will simply know less rather than more about the way humans deal with time.

DR. BERNARD FINIFTER: Dr. Osgood, to what extent do you think that the cross-cultural similarities you found may have been preconditioned by the semantic differential and factor analytic techniques used to collect and analyze the data? Have other independent techniques been used to check the possibility that method dependencies are at work?

DR. CHARLES OSGOOD: There is *no way* that either SD technique or factor analysis could force the Evaluation, Potency and Activity dimensions of affective meaning to appear if they did not exist as universals in the minds of humans in the diverse cultures using diverse languages: in the "tool-making" stage, the young subjects in the various locations were completely free (a) to produce *any* types of qualifiers that occurred to them for the 100 culture-common substantives, (b) to use the 50 most productive qualifier scales resulting in *any* ways they wished to differentiate the meanings of the same 100 concepts, and thereby (c) to come up with *any* set of correlations among the scales, and hence *any* type of factor structure — but in fact they come out with highly similar factor structures. There have been independent techniques used to check the validity of these factors — e.g., sorting techniques, global similarity judgments (or both concepts and scales), and nonverbal "graphic" differentials, to name a few.

DR. YRAN BORDELEAU (*Université de Montréal, Montréal, Québec*): You talked about the multiple meanings of words between cultures, Dr. Osgood. What do you think about the possibility of having different meanings of words within the same culture (possibly caused by regional and individual differences)? In that context, what do you think about the use of psychological questionnaires?

DR. OSGOOD: There are two basic ways in which words may have "different meanings" for individuals (and groups) within the same general culture: (1) There may be *different senses* of the same word forms (homonyms are the extreme case), and the full range and availabilities of the different senses may differ for individuals within the same culture — these often being shifts in reference, e.g., he told me a story (*lie*) about the story (*report*) the man on the third story (*level*) of the building gave the police; (2) there certainly will be *different affective* meanings (as well as associations, etc.) for the same word forms, when the referents stay the same — and this may be within cultures (e.g., the affective meanings old vs. young, male vs. female, Republican vs. Democrat speakers have for the same concepts) as well as between cultures (e.g., the obvious example of COW for Indians in Delhi vs. Americans in New York City), and it is *these* differences in "meaning" that the semantic differential technique is designed to get at, of course. I am at a loss to answer the second question — about what I think about "psychological questionnaires."

SUSAN SPIELBERG (*Columbia University, New York, N.Y.*): Dr. Kirk, what do you see as the *nature* of the relationship between the mother's movements and the child's cognitive development? Do you see the specificity of the mother's movements as *facilitating* cognitive performance, and/or could it be that the mother's movement is merely a *manifestation* of a cognitive style that is passed on to the child?

DR. KIRK: It would seem that in being more specific, the mother helps facilitate cognitive growth in the child by focusing more of the child's attention on differences, similarities, and other relationships in the environment; but in so doing, the mother also serves as a model in cognitive style.

BIG-QU CHIN: (*Harvard Graduate School of Education, Harvard University, Cambridge, Mass.*): If your studies were done with teachers in classroom or small group situations, what do you think the findings would be?

DR. KIRK: In larger groups we might have to focus more on verbal than nonverbal specificity, but I would expect that teachers who are more specific in their communication with students will, by alerting the children to more detailed contrasts and congruencies in the environment, help the children to learn. This would have to be tested over a long period of time, holding constant either the teacher or the program. The mothers in our sample had had six years in which to influence their children. We do not know how long specificity of input takes to affect the child: whether it is a matter of months or of years. Nor do we know the ages at which children are most susceptible to this influence.

ROD MARDEN (*Department of Psychology, Adelphi University, Garden City, L.I., N.Y.*): Would you comment on the tabled negative correlations between educational level and some of the measures, especially the conservation (reasons) measure. Are there any data on the relation between educational level of the mother and predominance of nonverbal interactions between mother and child?

DR. KIRK: Mother's education has a negative correlation with age in our sample, and age of the mother has a positive relationship with many of the cognitive test items; hence it is understandable that mother's education has a negative relationship with cognitive performance. Our results suggest, moreover, that the mother's education has little *direct* effect on cognitive performance. We found a negligible correlation (.088) between the education of the mother and the amount of nonverbal activity by the mother in the Kenya teaching interactions.

SUBJECTIVE CULTURE AND TECHNOLOGY:
A SOCIAL PSYCHOLOGICAL EXAMINATION OF
"NUCLEAR ALLERGY" IN THE JAPANESE*

Yasumasa Tanaka

Department of Political Science
Gakushuin University
Tokyo, Japan

THE DAWN OF A NUCLEAR AGE

Our century is characterized by two great achievements of science and technology: nuclear and space explorations. Science and technology are mankind's hope in time and space, and a real power has been attained in the shaping of twentieth century civilization – a power by which man makes the hitherto unknown known, the hitherto impossible possible.

On the other hand, we must recognize the note of apathy and uncertainty about the future that exists in every community in the world. In the developed countries, this attitude is mingled with the fear of nuclear war, the population explosion, environmental crisis, and bewilderment caused by rapidly changing societal norms and mores. In the developing countries, these attitudes are compounded by the frustrations associated with unfulfilled desires for rapid development of economy and industry and the suspicion that these countries are prey for exploitation by the more developed. One wonders if science and technology can help reduce the fear, bewilderment, and suspicion concomitant to the rapid growth of science and technology in the same manner as they have managed to send men to the moon.

This year we have been celebrating the thirtieth anniversary of the end of World War II. A period of 30 years is long enough to bury previous hostile memories in oblivion, and it has passed without a recurrence of total war, which would have inevitably been a nuclear war. In the wake of new hostilities, however, there have been several threatening moments in recent memory when the world stood on the brink of nuclear war.

Nuclear arms control is a reasonable means by which we can approach world peace, even if it does not prevent an occurrence of conventional warfare. It would certainly enable us to live in a less fearful world. It is hoped that nuclear arms control negotiations, such as the Strategic Arms Limitations Talks (SALT) and the Nuclear Non-Proliferation Treaty (NPT) will be successful. Even here, we have some discouraging signs. While these talks continue, so too do nuclear

* The studies reported in this paper were carried out from 1961 through 1972 and were supported in part by grants from the National Institute of Mental Health (MH 07705) and the National Science Foundation (NSF GS 160) to Charles E. Osgood and the Center for Comparative Psycholinguistics, University of Illinois, from the Office of Naval Research (NR 177-472, Nonr 1836 [36]) to Harry C. Triandis, and from the Japanese Ministry of Education (ME No. 72-745032) to Yasumasa Tanaka.

testings – both atmospheric and underground. Thus, since the dawn of the nuclear age in the summer of 1945, there have been more than 900 confirmed nuclear blasts: nearly 550 by the United States, more than 250 by the Soviet Union, about 60 by France, 26 by Britain, 16 by China, and one by India. Nations might agree in theory upon the sublime principle of world peace, but at the same time widely disagree upon the means by which it should and can be implemented, for what is at stake is their national security as well as world peace. The international system of nuclear arms control exists, but it is still a fragile system, incapable of very effective limitation of the nuclear arms race.

Reflecting upon the world milieu since 1945, we note that there have been some significant changes in the structure of the world community. These changes are particularly worthy of close examination.

First, with respect to the international system, we now live in a polycentric world where no one nation can possess or exercise its absolute dominance over the rest of the world. The Cold War divided the world into two major contesting blocs, the East and the West. At present, however, we find more diversified centers of political gravity, and more complicated nets of relations and influences among and within these large blocs and small sub-blocs.

Second, and not unrelated to the first, is the emergence of what has been called the "Nuclear Club," consisting of those nations that possess nuclear arms. Since the Soviet Union had its first successful nuclear test in August 1949, breaking the monopoly of nuclear power that the United States had enjoyed since 1945, membership in this "Nuclear Club" has steadily increased. In 1957, Britain emerged as the third member of the Club, followed by France in 1960, China in 1964, and India in 1974. So the Club has six exclusive members now. The term, "nuclear proliferation," which is in common use today, means an increase in the number of nations that own nuclear weapons, as well as an increase in the nuclear arsenal of a particular nation. The purpose of the Non-Proliferation Treaty (NPT) is to curb such nuclear proliferation.

Third, nationalism is increasing in importance in the nuclear-space age. Nationalism has always been an important factor in the conduct of national behavior. In this connection, it seems pertinent to call our age an age of *nuclear-space nationalism*. Nuclear-space nationalism is a special kind of nationalism maintained by relatively wealthy, advanced "have" nations, who have demonstrated their capability in nuclear-space science and technology, their economic and industrial capacity, and their pool of brain-power and know-how. Note, for example, how a name like "Nuclear Club" conveys a flavor of exclusiveness, status, prestige, and power, mixed with an obvious feeling of nationalistic pride. Only a few elite nations can join the Club. Furthermore, it is assumed that the nuclear-space weapon, whether for offensive or defensive use, tends to nullify the "superiority gap" by serving as an "equalizer" between greater powers and lesser nations. The nuclear weapon can be used as one of the most tangible and quick means to upset the hitherto maintained balanced of power, and hence contributes to achievement of the national goal. Admission to the Nuclear Club has thus become a sign of advanced development of national potential, and is generally accepted as an international status symbol in the nuclear-space age. France under the late General de Gaulle and China under Chairman Mao were the first, in the real sense of the term, to successfully achieve nuclear-space nationalism, by using their bombs not in war but in diplomacy, as an equalizer to upset their relative inferiority to the United States and the Soviet Union. They were able to demonstrate that lesser nations that seek to own the bomb to equalize their position in the international community do so, not to increase their military security, but to achieve greater independence from, and greater self-assertion to, the superior powers.

In this connection Japan also seems to be changing the "undercurrent" of her policy on nuclear matters after three decades of peace and recovery from the shock of Hiroshima and Nagasaki in August 1945. While Japan maintains the official stance of the "three-no" policy, which means "no manufacture, no possession, and no placing of nuclear weapons on Japanese soil," there are a number of factors operating in the international environment that push Japan towards nuclearization. Some of the factors center on the increase in prestige that come with super-economic power status and that can also be used in the form of influence to promote Japan's political as well as economic interests abroad. Other factors include the Chinese threat and the lack of American credibility as a protective and deterrent force.[1]

In February 1970, Japan signed the NPT two years after it received it. But by the summer of 1975, it appeared quite unlikely that the NPT will be ratified in the Japanese Diet in the near future. This strange behavior of the Japanese caused one of the American specialists on nuclear diplomacy to comment as follows:

> Almost no one in Japan is at all enthusiastic about the NPT. All opposition parties have taken stands criticizing the treaty. A significant part of the governing Liberal Democratic Party (LDP) is more quietly unhappy about the treaty. Public opinion, to the extent that the public is aware of the issue, is negative. So also is business, so also are Japan's major newspapers. Wherefrom springs so much reluctance and opposition when Japan, being either protected by the American nuclear umbrella or unprotected by any means, has no imminent need for nuclear weapons? Given Japan's "nuclear allergy" in the aftermath of Hiroshima and Nagasaki, why is the NPT not made-to-order for Japan? The Japanese response is interesting, in part because it illustrates feelings that may show up in other nations as they reach advanced stages of economic development.[2]

In this quotation, "nuclear allergy" is a generic term that means "hypersensitivity toward nuclear matters" and it often connotes for the Japanese deep "anti-nuclear-weapon sentiments." The genesis of this term is not without reason. On August 6, 1945, in the bright morning sun of that day, there was a sudden blinding flash and a deafening sound as the atom bomb burst over the city of Hiroshima, accompanied by the rapidly growing mushroom of the fireball. Although they did not realize it at the moment, in the midst of the mushroom cloud, whose shape has since symbolized the nuclear blast, the Japanese were crossing the threshold of a new age unprecedented in human history, which was later named the Nuclear Age. The Japanese felt, and still feel, angry, because they, and they alone, were the victims of this unconventional weaponry. They also fear that the same or a far more devastating disaster will strike them again in the event of a total war. And so they cling to the "three-no" policy with the hope that it may earn them immunity from a nuclear attack. These are the emotional tones that underlie the Japanese nuclear allergy.

In the rest of this paper, I will examine the Japanese nuclear allergy as a social psychological process. The basic approach in the present study is provided by a multilingual, multidimensional model for attitude measurement, namely, the semantic and behavioral differential methods. Using these methods, we have carried out several cross-cultural studies to test the consistency in Japanese attitudes toward nuclear matters.

In the analysis of the Japanese nuclear allergy, it is postulated that what is called nuclear allergy is actually a heavily emotion-laden negative attitude toward any attitude object related to nuclear matters. As such it is susceptible to what is termed by Osgood "assign learning",[3] a process by which meanings of signs are literally "assigned" to the signs via association with other signs rather than via direct association with the object signified. For example, Japanese (or American) high-school boys understand the concept of ATOMIC BOMB, but none of them have encountered ATOMIC BOMB objects themselves. They have seen pictures of them or pictures of the mushroom cloud; they have been told that it was dropped over Hiroshima and Nagasaki a long time ago; or they have read about NUCLEAR ARMS RACE, whereby nations seek to increase and improve their ATOMIC BOMBS. Almost all the nuclear-related signs that will be dealt with in the subsequent sections of this report as "assigns" in this sense.

With these basic postulates in mind, let us examine the structure and dynamics of the nuclear allergy in the Japanese in some detail.

"ATLAS" MEANINGS OF ATOMIC BOMB

It will be recalled that Osgood and his associates have been conducting extensive cross-cultural research in more than 23 language/culture communities since the later 1950s, with the aid of what they call "multilingual semantic differentials." In their recently published *Cross-Cultural Universals of Affective Meaning*, they report portions of their tool-making studies and the results of very sophisticated cross-cultural comparisons.[4] Among these studies are what they call the "Atlas testings", involving some 500 male teenage subjects (Ss) in each community, with at least 40 Ss rating sets of 50 out of a total of 620 concepts against a 13-scale "pancultural semantic differential" developed in the tool-making stage. Fortunately for the purpose of the present paper, the concept ATOMIC BOMB was included in the Atlas ratings in the 23 communities, thus making it possible to compare its meaning across the 23 subject groups. The Atlas, or more precisely the "Atlas of Affective Meanings," employs eight basic measures to probe the affective meaning of various concepts across different cultures. We will next examine the meanings of meaning of ATOMIC BOMB. TABLE 1 shows the entry of the concept ATOMIC BOMB in the same manner as it is actually shown in the Atlas.

Raw E-P-A Composite Scores

The first three columns in TABLE 1 give the mean Evaluation (E), Potency (P), and Activity (A) scores across 40 Ss for the four scales assigned to each of these factors. These scores indicate the directions and intensity of affecting meanings along each of the three (E, P, and A) orthogonal dimensions obtained from factor analysis. This composite is expressed as a deviation (+ or − to a maximum of 3.0) from the origin of what is called a semantic space, the + being arbitrarily assigned to the *Good* (E), *Strong* (P), and *Active* (A) poles of the factors. Of the three kinds of the composite, the E-composite is considered most important, for plus or minus values on E is a function of learning the meaning of signs and is hence highly susceptible to cultural influence. Looking at TABLE 1, we note that ATOMIC BOMB is intensely −E (*quite to very bad*) and +P (*quite to very strong*), and similarly so across all the 23 communities, although it varies markedly in A (from *very active* to *quite inactive*). Here we have some empirical

TABLE 1

"ATLAS" MEANINGS OF ATOMIC BOMB ACROSS 23 LANGUAGE-CULTURE COMMUNITIES

	E	P	A	E-Z	P-Z	A-Z	F-Z	D-O	P-I	P-G	CI	CI-Z
America	-1.3	2.5	1.5	-2.0	2.0	2.3	-1.8	3.2	2.3	1.8	0.5	-0.3
France	-2.2	1.7	1.4	-2.8	2.0	1.4	-1.0	3.1	2.2	1.8	0.3	-0.7
Belgium	-2.4	1.7	1.9	-2.7	2.6	3.0	0.5	3.5	2.3	2.0	0.3	-1.8
Netherlands	-2.2	2.3	2.2	-2.7	2.5	2.3	-0.6	3.8	2.3	2.2	0.1	-2.8
Germany	-2.5	2.6	2.5	-2.6	2.3	2.2	-0.1	4.4	2.8	2.5	0.2	-1.7
Sweden	-2.2	0.7	1.7	-3.4	1.0	2.6	0.6	2.8	1.9	1.6	0.3	-1.8
Finland	-2.6	2.5	0.4	-2.5	2.4	0.1	-0.5	3.6	2.5	2.0	0.4	-1.1
Yucatan	-0.7	1.6	0.1	-1.8	1.8	-0.1	-2.1	1.8	2.4	1.2	1.2	0.6
Costa Rica	-1.3	1.9	1.6	-2.0	1.7	1.2	0.0	2.8	2.2	1.6	0.6	0.5
Mexico	-1.3	1.6	0.3	-2.2	1.8	0.0	-2.1	2.1	2.0	1.4	0.6	0.4
Italy	-1.5	1.4	1.6	-1.9	1.3	2.5	-1.6	2.6	2.1	1.5	0.6	-0.0
Yugoslavia	-1.9	1.5	1.2	-2.3	1.2	2.1	-0.0	2.7	2.0	1.6	0.5	-0.4
Greece	-0.9	1.4	0.3	-1.6	1.7	-0.4	0.5	1.7	1.8	1.1	0.7	1.8
Turkey	-0.7	2.0	-0.2	-1.9	2.3	-0.8	-3.3	2.1	2.2	1.7	0.4	-0.6
Lebanon	-2.0	0.9	-1.4	-2.5	0.4	-2.0	-0.6	2.6	2.1	1.5	0.6	0.0
Iran	-1.2	1.9	1.8	-1.9	3.2	1.0	-2.0	2.9	2.5	1.7	0.9	0.8
Afghanistan	-2.2	0.9	0.4	-2.5	1.5	0.0	-0.1	2.4	1.6	1.3	0.3	-0.1
Delhi	-1.1	1.7	-0.4	-2.5	2.3	-0.4	-1.3	2.1	2.2	1.5	0.7	0.6
Calcutta	-2.0	1.6	1.5	-2.5	1.3	1.5	-1.2	2.9	2.3	1.7	0.6	-0.5
Mysore	-1.2	1.1	0.4	-2.6	1.9	0.7	0.1	1.7	1.9	1.2	0.7	-0.9
Thailand	-1.8	1.9	0.2	-2.6	2.5	0.3	-2.6	2.6	2.4	2.0	0.4	-2.0
Hong Kong	-1.5	1.6	0.7	-2.2	1.8	0.5	0.8	2.3	1.8	1.4	0.4	-0.8
Japan	-2.2	1.4	0.4	-2.7	1.8	0.4	-1.1	2.6	2.2	1.6	0.6	-0.4
MN	-1.7	1.7	0.9	-2.4	1.9	0.9	-0.9	2.7	2.2	1.7	0.5	-0.5
S	0.6	0.5	0.9	0.4	0.6	1.3	1.1	0.7	0.3	0.3	0.2	1.1

evidence that ATOMIC BOMB is an absolutely negatively valued object, irrespective of differences in the linguistic and cultural origin of the communities investigated.

Standardized E-P-A Composite Scores

The next three columns in TABLE 1 show the standardized E-P-A composite scores (E-Z, P-Z, A-Z), standardization being done by using the means and standard deviations of all 620 concepts for each factor dimension. In short, this standardization has the effect of transforming the origin of the semantic space for each culture to the centroid of its own concept points and it establishes directly comparable standard units of measurement along the three factor axes. Inspecting the E-Z, P-Z, and A-Z scores for ATOMIC BOMB in TABLE 1, we may note a few interesting differences across the communities. Although the Japanese teenage boys rate it as highly −E (−2.7), as might have been expected, they are not alone in the negative judgment of ATOMIC BOMB. Almost all the West European (French, Belgian, Dutch, German), Scandinavian (Swedish and Finnish), West and East Asian (Afganistan, Thai, Hong Kong), and Indian Subcontinent (Delhi, Calcutta, Mysore) groups hold an extremely negative (below −2.5) evaluation of ATOMIC BOMB. American, Latin American (Yucatan, Costa Rican, Mexican), and Mediterranean (Italian and Yugoslavian) groups seem to view ATOMIC BOMB as less negatively valued (above −2.0), which might reflect their somewhat more optimistic inclinations toward the object. A difference greater than 0.5 scale unit between the composites has been proved statistically significant at the .05 level. If we use this criterion, the difference between −2.7 and −2.0 may well be indicative of a real difference between the Japanese and American groups in their attitudes toward ATOMIC BOMB, the Japanese more intensely rejecting it than the Americans.

Standardized Familiarity Scores

In the semantic differential test form for each community, a *familiar—unfamiliar* scale was included in addition to 12 E, P, A scales in order to get a reading on the familiarity of concepts to the teenage Ss. Although such a scale is liable to confusion between "familiar as a term" and "familiar as a referent," in case of ATOMIC BOMB such confusion would be minimal because no one has seen the object in his real life. Inspection of the standardized familiarity scores (F-Z) in TABLE 1 suggests that ATOMIC BOMB is *unfamiliar* in 14 out of the 23 communities, where the familiarity scores are found to be significantly negative in direction, that is, equal to or below −0.5. We speculate that male high-school Ss in these 14 communities may have rated the concept with its dominant "referent" meaning, for ATOMIC BOMB may be familiar as a word but be very remote from the subjects' experience. On the other hand, in the Netherlands, Sweden, Greece, and Hong Kong, the F-Z scores are clearly positive, being equal to or above 0.5, indicating that Ss may have rated the familiarity of the word, rather than that of the referent. It can also be seen that the F-Z scores are near zero in Germany, Costa Rica, Yugoslavia, Afganistan, and Mysore. It is quite likely that the scale tapped both "familiarity as a word" and "unfamiliarity as a referent" in these groups, cancelling out the "word familiarity" with the "referent unfamiliarity," thus causing the F-Z scores to approach to the neutral zero point. We also note that ATOMIC BOMB (probably more dominantly as a referent in this case) is more familiar to the Japanese teenage boys (−1.1) than to the American (−1.8), as might be expected from the knowledge of the Japanese "nuclear allergy." It must be recalled that the Japanese and American Ss were born after World War II and had no experience with war. A formidable object like ATOMIC BOMB is certainly not in the everyday experience of the Japanese and Americans, even though they may hear about nuclear-related matters from time to time. That fact that the Japanese seem to have a more intense cognitive experience with ATOMIC BOMB suggests that they are susceptible to more intense and frequent assign learning processes, probably because their primary and secondary school education included ample textbook documentation of the dropping of atomic bombs over Hiroshima and Nagasaki and because of their exposure to postwar victims of lethal nuclear hazards. There is also extensive mass media coverage of events related to nuclear matters, such as the SALT and the NPT.

Distance from the Origin

Distance of a concept from the neutral origin of the E-P-A semantic space is considered as an index of the intensity of affective meaning. This distance measure (D-O) is computed from the following formula:

$$D\text{-}O = (E^2 + P^2 + A^2)^{1/2}$$

In theory, the distance may vary from a maximum of 5.196 (when E, P, A are all + or −3) to a minimum of zero (when E, P, A are all zero). It was found in the present analysis that ATOMIC BOMB is among those concepts that generate the most intense feeling for teenagers throughout the 23 communities, as might have been expected. Other most "most" meaningful concepts cross-culturally are MOTHER, FREEDOM and GOD. On the other hand, notions like KNOT and YESTERDAY were found nearly meaningless affectively.

Individual and Group Polarization Measures

For each Atlas concept, there are N Ss rating a concept on n scales, and so the investigator can deal with either group mean scores or individual subject scores on scales. In computing the *group measure* (P-G), individual deviations in one direction from the neutral midpoints of scales are scored as positive, and deviations in the other are scored as negative. If Ss give intense (that is, near 3) ratings on the scale but disagree among themselves as to direction, there will be a cancellation, and the group polarization score will approach toward zero. In computing the *individual measure* (P-I), the deviations from the midpoints are transformed into absolute values and summed over individuals, and so there will be no cancellation. In short, the group measure (P-G) reflects the *cultural meaningfulness* of a concept, taking into consideration within-culture disagreements on its meaning, whereas the individual measure (P-I) reflects the *individual meaningfulness* of a concept, disregarding within-culture disagreements and reflecting pure intensity of affect. For ATOMIC BOMB shown in TABLE 1, the concept is associated with a very high P-I and P-G scores in each community. In fact, as given at the bottom of the table, the mean P-I and P-G values (symbolically, MN) computed over the 23 communities are 2.2 and 1.7, respectively, with a standard deviation (symbolically, S) of only 0.3 in both cases. From these figures we conclude that ATOMIC BOMB does indeed have an intense affective meaning with very few disagreements among individuals within each culture, and so similarly across all the 23 communities.

Cultural Instability Index

For any concept the value of P-G must be equal to or less than the value of P-I. The value of their difference is termed an index of "cultural instability" (CI). To make the index more comparable across communities, the values are standardized across all concepts for each community to a mean of zero and a standard deviation of 1.0. The standardized scores thus derived (CI-Z) are given in the last columns of TABLE 1. They vary from high plus values (high within-culture disagreement) through zero to high minus values (high within-culture agreement). It is interesting to note that in many Western European and Scandinavian communities, the concept seems to have *stereotyped meaningfulness*, their Ss agreeing on both its semantic direction and its affective intensity, while in the Mediterranean and West Asian communities, the concept shows varying degrees of cultural instability, indicating that the concept would be highly conflictual semantically, because of either its cognitive unfamiliarity or its socially controversial nature in the respective cultures. Surprisingly enough, in both Japan and the United States, cultural stability is about average, ATOMIC BOMB's affective meaning being only modestly stereotyped within each culture.

Thus, the meanings of meaning of ATOMIC BOMB have been tested by the eight basic measures used in the Atlas of Affective Meanings, and compared across the 23 communities. These tests show, however, that there is no obvious symptom of nuclear allergy with respect to the Japanese teenagers. Certainly, the Japanese hold a highly negative evaluative view of ATOMIC BOMB, but so do the teenagers in the other communities. The concept is highly meaningful affectively, not only for the Japanese but also for the rest of the 23 communities. As for cultural conflict, which could have been very intense if the meanings of ATOM BOMB had been socially controversial and Ss had disagreed among themselves, the Japanese are only average, not too distant from the other cultures. The result of these cross-checks suggests that the Japanese teenagers are by no means *deviant* in their affective attitudes toward ATOMIC BOMB. This may bring about some suspicion that a notion of the Japanese nuclear allergy would be only hypothetical, unwarranted by clear scientific evidence.

SOME CONSIDERATIONS ON PSYCHOLOGIC OPERATING IN THE THINKING ABOUT NUCLEAR MATTERS

It has been said that the Japanese are incapable of a "rational" and "realistic" approach to the nuclear problem, mainly because of their nuclear allergy. Whether this is true or not, it is quite appropriate that we should continue to probe the dynamic process of human thinking about nuclear matters. And so our next interest lies in a cross-cultural examination of what is termed "cognitive interaction," that is, interactions among concepts.

The Congruity Model

Using the semantic differential measuring system, Osgood, Suci and Tannenbaum formulated the general theoretical approach to the problems of semantic interaction between two or more cognitive events.[3] Cognitive interaction is approached in the following way: that is, cognitive elements in the congruity model are equated with the affective meaning of concepts. In the measuring system provided by the semantic differential method the factorial meaning (i.e., in terms of composite factor scores) of a concept is given by its location along factor dimensions. It follows that if "two or more signs associated with different meanings occur near-simultaneously, only one cognitive reaction can occur in the system, and this must be a compromise."[5] Such a compromise, which Osgood calls "congruity resolution," between the interacting concepts reflects itself both in the change in the meaning of input concepts (i.e., the meaning of the cognitive elements originally put into interaction) and in the locus of resolution between the interacting concepts (i.e., the meaning of the complex concept). This theoretical approach, which Osgood, Suci and Tannenbaum called the *congruity hypothesis,* is given in the following general statement:

> Whenever the two concepts are related in an assertion, the affective meaning reaction characteristic of each concept shifts toward congruence with that characteristic of the other, the magnitude of the shift being inversely proportional to the intensities of the interacting reactions.[5]

The two cross-cultural studies that will be dealt with in the following sections are an extension of the work of Osgood and Ferguson (Reference 5, pp. 275–284), in which combination of qualifiers and nouns, or word mixtures, were used as interacting concepts for English-speaking American subjects. Using eight qualifiers and eight nouns, Osgood and Ferguson predicted the meanings of the 64 possible word mixtures (i.e., compound concepts such as SINCERE PROSTITUTE) from the meanings of the component qualifiers and nouns (i.e., component concepts such as SINCERE and PROSTITUTE). In the present studies, somewhat more restricted classes of qualifiers (or qualifying phrases) and nouns (or noun phrases) are used — for example, nationality concepts such as JAPANESE or AMERICAN as qualifiers and political concepts such as NUCLEAR TESTINGS or FOREIGN POLICY as nouns.

Japanese-Finnish Political Stereotype Study

To test the congruity hypothesis cross-culturally, three semantic differential experiments were performed, two in Japan in 1961 and 1966 and one in Finland in 1961.[8] Totals of 40 and 47 college students served as Ss in the 1961 and 1966 Japanese experiments, while a total of 50 college students served as Ss in Finland. All these Ss belonged to a postwar generation, having little or no experience with war. The second Japanese experiment was carried out in November 1966, shortly after China's successful test of a nuclear missile.

The concepts used as stimuli consisted of five nationality concepts (i.e., AMERICA, CHINA, JAPAN, ?????????, and SOVIET UNION), five nouns denotating political phenomena (i.e., NUCLEAR TESTINGS, FOREIGN POLICY, MILITARY STRENGTH, GOVERNMENT and PEOPLE), and their 25 compounds (e.g., AMERICAN NUCLEAR TESTINGS, or CHINESE PEOPLE). To index the affective meaning of concepts, a 26-scale semantic differential was constructed in Japanese and Finnish. The same set of 26 translation-equivalent scales was used throughout, after they had been randomized in order and direction uniformly in both the Japanese and Finnish groups.

Subsequently, scale-by-scale factor analysis was carried out, so as to determine the structure of the affective dimensions of attitudes and to obtain evidence that the same attitudinal criteria had been used across the Japanese and the Finish groups and over time by the Japanese. Principal axis solutions and varimax rotations were used throughout.

In connection with the Japanese data, each of the 1961 and 1966 subject groups was divided into two subgroups (A and B) in order to test the overall generality of affective meaning system both through time and across subjects. The data thus obtained was tabulated separately for each subgroup and submitted to factor analysis. The same factor analytic procedure was repeated for the Finnish data as a whole. The results are shown in TABLE 2.

The three most salient factors extracted in all groups are clearly identifiable as *evaluation, dynamism*, and *familiarity*. The first factor in every case accounts for more variance and is identified by scales such as *bad-good, unpleasant-pleasant*, and *ugly-beautiful*; the second factor is defined by scales such as *strong-weak, large-small, sturdy-fragile*; and the third, which accounts for less variance than the other two, is defined by scales such as *near-far, familiar-unfamiliar*, and *common-rare*.

It is evident in the table that the coefficients of these factors overlap in magnitudes to such an extent that both the subgroups (A and B) in the 1961 and 1966 Japanese studies and the 1961 Finnish group contribute similarly to each of the factors. For example, the first factor is composed of the scales of the two subgroups in the 1961 Japanese data, and of the scales of the two subgroups in the 1966 Japanese data, and of the scales of the 1961 Finnish data. Identical meanings and nearly identical factor loadings can be noted despite their different origins. The dimensions, in other words, are culture-common and almost equally defined by all samples; no separate factors for the three separate experiments or for four Japanese subgroups are found, as might have been expected if there had been great cultural differences and diachronic inconsistencies in the affective use of scales. We thus have clear overall evidence of the cross-cultural generality of affective system across the Japanese and Finns and for its intracultural, diachronic stability among the Japanese.

Next the prediction of subject judgments of complex concepts from a knowledge of subject judgments of components was attempted with the congruity formula.† The purpose of this analysis was to determine the extent to which cognitive interaction is consistent in judging complex international political events and to discover under what condition such consistency in cognitive interaction fails to be found in culturally heterogeneous groups. By

† The congruity formula is given as follows:

$$p_R = \frac{/p_1/(p_1)}{/p_1/ + /p_2/} + \frac{/p_2/(p_2)}{/p_1/ + /p_2/},$$

where $/p_1/$ and $/p_2/$ are the absolute values of polarization of the components (i.e., the qualifiers and nouns), and (p_1) (p_2) are the signed algebraic values corresponding to the polarization of the components.

TABLE 2

VARIMAX-ROTATED FACTORS AND HIGH-LOADING SCALES IN THE 1961 and 1966 GROUPS

	Factor I (E)					Factor II (D)					Factor III (F)				
	1961-F	1961-J A	1961-J B	1966-J A	1966-J B	1961-F	1961-J A	1961-J B	1966-J A	1966-J B	1961-F	1961-J A	1961-J B	1966-J A	1966-J B
Bad-good	.90	.95	.94	.96	.96										
Unpleasant-pleasant	.98	.97	.97	.95	.95										
Ugly-beautiful	.94	.93	.94	.95	.95										
Dark-light	.80	.97	.97	.86	.90						(.39)			(−.40)	(−.37)
Unwholesome-wholesome	.88	.96	.96	.89	.95										
Undemocratic-democratic	.89	.95	.93	.76	.80						(.35)			(−.51)	(−.42)
Strong-weak						.85	.94	.94	.97	.98	(.36)				
Large-small						.72	.92	.94	.95	.94					
Sturdy-fragile						.91	.92	.88	.89	.92					
Thick-thin						.91	.82	.82	.85	.89					
Fast-slow						.74	.80	.85	.78	.77		(.37)		(.46)	(.53)
Near-far											.90	.92	.91	.92	.91
Familiar-unfamiliar	(.61)	(−.49)		(−.42)	(−.44)						.75	.81	.90	.84	.85
Common-rare											(.50)	.81	.84	.61	.70
% TV	41.5	37.2		34.2		21.3	26.4		28.7		12.8	19.8		17.1	

NOTES: 1961-F, 1961-J, and 1966-J represent 1961-Finnish group, 1961-Japanese group, and 1966-Japanese group, respectively; A and B subgroups. E, D, and F represent evaluation, dynamism, and familiarity, respectively. Parenthesized figures indicate secondary factor loadings greater than .33.

applying the congruity formula, an appropriate predicted value was computed from the composite factor score of a nationality component (e.g., AMERICA) and the composite factor score of a noun component (e.g., NUCLEAR TESTINGS). It will be recalled that the composite factor score is an average of several scale values representative of each of the major semantic dimensions, ranging from −3 to +3. The *predicted* values were then compared with the corresponding *obtained* meanings of the compound (e.g., AMERICAN NUCLEAR TESTINGS) within each subject group. To generalize the predict-ability of the congruity method, correlations between corresponding *predicted* and *obtained* values were computed for 20 meanings separately in each semantic dimension for the two Japanese (1961 and 1966) groups and for 25 meanings in each semantic dimension for the Finnish group. All correlations are significant (p < .05), although the predictability of the model for *dynamism* and *familiarity* are somewhat poorer than for *evaluation* in all three groups.

Despite this overall evidence of the cross-cultural consistency in cognitive interaction, some unique errors found in predictions are of considerable interest. Before we enter into the problem, however, let us present graphically some patterns of cognitive interaction from our data.

FIGURE 1 displays two-dimensional (i.e., *evaluative* and *dynamism*) factor spaces. In each space the locations of the *obtained* meaning of NUCLEAR-TESTINGS-related concepts are shown separately for the 1961 Japanese

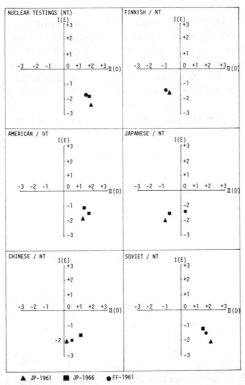

FIGURE 1. Affective meanings of various "NUCLEAR TESTINGS."

(indicated by triangles), the 1966 Japanese (squares), and the 1961 Finnish (circles) groups. From the left to the right columns the two-dimensional meanings of NUCLEAR TESTINGS as the noun component, and of the 5-compound concepts containing NUCLEAR TESTINGS as a component, are graphically presented. You will note that the meaning of NUCLEAR TESTINGS as the noun component is *bad* and *strong* in all three groups. This is consistent to the Atlas ratings of ATOMIC BOMB as *bad* and *strong* in the 23 language/culture communities, including Japan and Finland. It is also interesting to inspect how the meaning of NUCLEAR TESTINGS interacts with the meaning of qualifying nationality component. For example, when NUCLEAR TESTINGS is put into interaction with CHINESE, FINNISH and JAPANESE as the qualifying component, the obtained meaning of their corresponding compound is considerably changed. Note how NUCLEAR TESTINGS interacting with CHINESE, FINNISH and JAPANESE is "pulled" toward the negative (i.e., *weak*) pole of the *dynamism* dimension, although the changes along the *evaluative* dimension look less obvious in FIGURE 1.

FIGURE 2 "magnifies" somewhat different patterns of interaction found in the two Japanese groups for the three-compound concepts having NUCLEAR TESTINGS in common. In (A) the location of the *obtained* meaning of two components (i.e., a nationality concept and a noun), which are subject to interaction, are shown in a two-dimensional space for 1961 and 1966. This space, like that shown in FIGURE 1, is defined by the two most salient factors of *evaluation* and *dynamism*. It can be seen that the location of NUCLEAR TESTINGS is fixed throughout, whereas the location of the interacting qualifying component varies. In (B) the relative locations of the *obtained* meaning (o) of the compound concepts are given against those of the *predicted* meaning (p) of the corresponding compound. In the diagram the subscript o indicates an *obtained* meaning, and, p, a congruity prediction. It should be remembered at this point that the congruity formula requires that the *predicted* meaning always

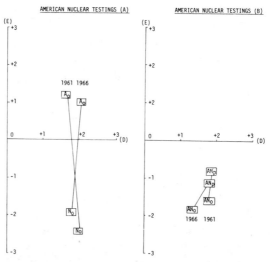

FIGURE 2A. Patterns of cognitive interaction for the NUCLEAR-TESTINGS-related compound concepts in the Japanese (AMERICAN NUCLEAR TESTINGS).

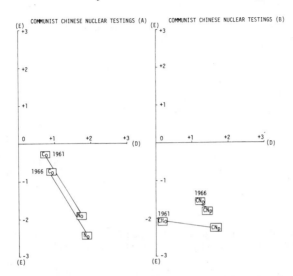

FIGURE 2B. Patterns of cognitive interaction for the NUCLEAR-TESTINGS-related compound concepts in the Japanese (COMMUNIST CHINESE NUCLEAR TESTINGS).

fall between those of the interacting components, whereas the position of the *obtained* meaning of the compound, reflecting either the actual effect of cognitive interaction or a constant error, may fall anywhere on the composite scale. In order to index whether the *predicted* meaning is significantly different from the *obtained* meaning, the half-a-composite-scale-unit criterion may be used as rough estimation.

First in the AMERICAN (*good-strong*) versus NUCLEAR TESTINGS (*bad-strong*) interactions, predictions appear to be reasonably accurate, each prediction falling between the interacting components. Although not shown in FIGURE 2, predictions of SOVIET NUCLEAR TESTINGS are also found to be reasonably precise, from SOVIET UNION (*bad-strong*) and NUCLEAR TESTINGS (*bad-strong*) put into interaction.

Secondly, in predicting CHINESE NUCLEAR TESTINGS from CHINA (*bad-strong*) and NUCLEAR TESTINGS (*bad-strong*), a unique type of error appears in our 1961 Japanese data; that is, predictions along the *dynamism* dimension do not fall between the interacting components but are "pulled" toward the less *dynamic* end of the composite scale by more than a full scale unit. This is what we have roughly seen in FIGURE 1, comparing NUCLEAR TESTINGS with CHINESE NUCLEAR TESTINGS. In any case, this suggests that with regard to *dynamism* CHINESE NUCLEAR TESTINGS may have been an incongruent complex concept for the Japanese in 1961; hence a factor of "incredulity" interfered with actual interaction. It should be recalled that China had not had a nuclear weapon until 1964. Note, on the other hand, that near-perfect congruity is achieved in 1966 both on *evaluation* and *dynamism*, after China in fact completed its own nuclear experiments and incredulity was removed.

Finally, the interaction between JAPANESE (*good-weak*) and NUCLEAR TESTINGS (*bad-strong*) presents a unique extreme case of the same type of

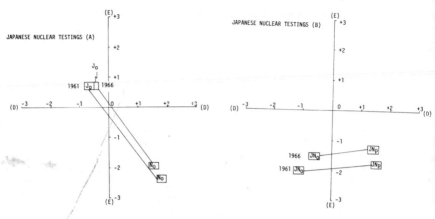

FIGURE 2C. Patterns of cognitive interaction for the NUCLEAR-TESTINGS-related compound concepts in the Japanese (JAPANESE NUCLEAR TESTINGS).

error. Both in 1961 and in 1966 predictions are a complete failure. Theoretically, it should be *bad* and *strong*, but the "pulling power" of the noise factor is so strong along the *dynamism* factor that not only does the actual resolution occur far outside the interacting components in each case, but also it is "pulled" from the theoretical point of resolution by as much as one and half scale units and enters into the semantically opposite *negative dynamism* domain! For both the 1961 and the 1966 Japanese, a notion of JAPANESE NUCLEAR TESTINGS may have been more incredulous and incongruent than that of CHINESE NUCLEAR TESTINGS in 1961.

For the Finnish data the same type of error is also found with respect to CHINESE NUCLEAR TESTINGS, JAPANESE NUCLEAR TESTINGS, and FINNISH NUCLEAR TESTINGS, none of which appeared "thinkable" in 1961. FIGURE 3 illustrates the predictions of FINNISH NUCLEAR TESTINGS from FINNISH (*good-strong*) and NUCLEAR TESTINGS (*bad-strong*). In theory, it should be *slightly bad* and *quite strong*, but again the interference of the noise factor is so strong both along *evaluation* and *dynamism* that the actual point of resolution falls far off the interacting components. Along *evaluation the actual point of resolution is "pulled" from the theoretical point by more than a full scale unit (quite bad)*, whereas along the *dynamism* factor it is "pulled" toward the negative end of the composite scale by more than two scale units (*fairly weak*)!

We speculate that the failure in these cases might be attributable to incredibility as a psychological noise that causes disturbance in cognitive interaction. As shown above, CHINESE NUCLEAR TESTINGS in 1961 for both the Japanese and Finns, JAPANESE NUCLEAR TESTINGS in 1961 and in 1966 for the Japanese, and FINNISH NUCLEAR TESTINGS in 1961 for the Finns all seem to illustrate an unpredictable abnormal interaction pattern. Such disturbance appears to occur most frequently when there is a small probability that the interacting concepts would co-occur in real life — CHINESE NUCLEAR TESTINGS in 1961, for example. In the previous study by Osgood and Ferguson, SINCERE PROSTITUTE might have been a similar case. It also appears worth nothing that the interfering noise would "oscillate" and com-

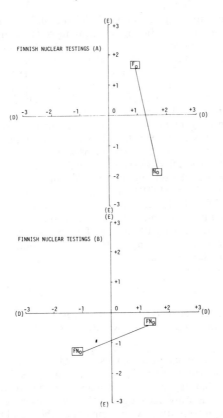

FIGURE 3. Patterns of cognitive interaction for the NUCLEAR-TESTINGS-related compound concepts in the Finnish.

pletely block normal cognitive interaction, especially when both Japanese and Finnish Ss judge at the same time highly "hypothetical" and very "unthinkable" cognitive events related to their own countries.

It would be appropriate at this point to ask which of the two components, adjectival or nominal, would be the better predictor of the compound. *Multiple regression*, a method of using scores on two or more variables to predict scores on another variable called criterion can be applied in the analysis of semantic interaction in question. The same data described above were analyzed by the multiple regression method to answer the preceding question. To put it more precisely, the purpose of this specific analysis was to determine the extent to which the meaning of complex compounds can be linearly predicted from the meaning of the nationality and the political concepts put into interaction and to arrive at the relative *weights* of the components in that linear prediction. In the present case, we are particularly interested in examining whether the meaning of the NUCLEAR-TESTINGS-related compounds can be linearly predicted from the meaning of its adjectival nationality concepts and the meaning of NUCLEAR

TESTINGS by the multiple regression method, and discovering which component can contribute more to predicting the meaning of the compound.

To examine this problem multiple correlations and regression weights were computed for the NUCLEAR-TESTINGS-related complex concepts. Multiple correlations thus obtained for the Finnish and for the 1961 and the 1966 Japanese are .64, .80, and .85, all correlations being significant beyond the .05 level. These high correlations indicate that all predictions are reasonably successful, although those in the Finns are somewhat poorer. As for regression weights, they are obviously higher for the fixed nominal concept, NUCLEAR TESTINGS, than for the adjectival nationality concepts in all three, and even more so in the two Japanese groups. This happens with regard to the compounds related to NUCLEAR TESTINGS, despite the fact that nationality concepts clearly appear to be the better predictors for those concepts related to GOVERNMENT, PEOPLE and FOREIGN POLICY, again in all three. When dealing with NUCLEAR TESTINGS, the Japanese seem to discount, more obviously than do the Finns, the meanings of nationality concepts in semantic interaction. The meaning of NUCLEAR TESTINGS thus becomes the major determinant in predicting the meaning of the related complex concepts. This might indicate that the Japanese preoccupation with nuclear matters is subtle but real in their thinking.

THE PREDICTED TIMING OF JAPAN'S "GOING" NUCLEAR: A JAPANESE-AMERICAN COMPARISON

In previous studies on Japanese attitudes toward nuclear arms,[7,8] Tanaka found during the period from 1965–1966 that as many as 75% of some 400 college Ss "anticipate" that Japan will "go" nuclear in the "foreseeable" future (within 20 years), whereas only 25% believe that will never occur. It was also found in the semantic differential experiments that the "evaluative" cultural meaning of nuclear-related concepts had shifted significantly in a *"less undesirable"* direction in a 5-year period between 1961 and 1966.

These studies were subsequently extended in 1967 to a construction of a combined semantic and behavioral differential for the Japanese and in 1969 to a cross-cultural study using the above-mentioned new method.[9] Two major purposes of these studies were (1) to examine the predicted timing of Japan's going nuclear, and (2) to probe the subjects' attitudes toward various complex concepts related to nuclear and space science and technology in multidimensional affective-conative spaces. In the sections that follow, we will look more closely at the results obtained from these studies.

First, a three-item questionnaire was prepared in which Ss were asked (1) to give the names of five nations that already own some kind of nuclear weapons (to test the subject's knowledge of the current state of affairs in nuclear proliferation); and to predict (2) the three nations that are most likely to go nuclear as a sixth, seventh, and eighth nuclear nation after China (to test the subject's judgments of the future of nuclear proliferation), and (3) the number of years (i.e., within 5, 10, 15, or 20 years from now, or never) in which Japan would be most likely to go nuclear (to test the anticipation concerning Japan's possible involvement in nuclear proliferation). A translation-equivalent questionnaire form was prepared in English and used in the American experiment.

TABLE 3 shows the results of the 1969 questionnaire survey for both

TABLE 3

PREDICTIONS AS TO WHEN JAPAN GOES NUCLEAR

	Within 10 years	Within 20 years	Never	N.A.
Japanese college Ss (1967, N = 169)	34(%)	19(%)	36(%)	11(%)
Japanese college Ss (1969, N = 86)	34	34	33	0
American college Ss (1969, N = 90)	79	9	8	4

Japanese and Americans. We note that as many as 80% of American Ss hold that Japan will go nuclear within 10 years in contrast to 10% who believe Japan will never go nuclear. Chi-square test results indicate that American Ss are significantly different from the 1967 Japanese ($\chi^2 = 42.1590$, df = 2, p < .001) and from the 1969 Japanese ($\chi^2 = 44.0812$, df = 2, p < .001). The relative proportion of those who believe Japan will *never* go nuclear appears far greater in the Japanese than in the American sample, as might have been expected. The Japanese, however, are more sharply divided among themselves than are the Americans concerning the future state of affairs in nuclear Japan.

PROBE IN AFFECTIVE-CONATIVE SPACES:
A JAPANESE-AMERICAN COMPARISON

"Concepts" that were used in the experiments were constructed by means of facet design. Three facets were used for this purpose: (1) technoscientific cognitive events (NUCLEAR TESTINGS, MISSILE TESTINGS, COOPERATION AMONG SCIENTISTS); (2) conditions under which such events would occur (IRRESPECTIVE OF PURPOSE AND KIND, ASSOCIATED WITH ARMS DEVELOPMENT, INTENDED FOR PEACEFUL USE); and (3) spatial specification as to where they would occur (IN ALL NATIONS, IN DEVELOPED NUCLEAR NATIONS, IN DEVELOPING NUCLEAR NATIONS). Each of these facets defines a three-dimensional realization of technoscientific events. Thus, by combining subfacet (i) of *event*, (i) of *condition*, and (i) of *spatial specification*, we obtain a complex concept: NUCLEAR TESTINGS IN ALL NATIONS IRRESPECTIVE OF PURPOSE AND KIND. A total of 27 (3 x 3 x 3) complex concepts were thus generated.

As to the measuring instruments, in order to index the affective and conative meaning of concepts, a 22-scale form of combined semantic and behavioral differential was constructed. A total of ten SD scales (four *evaluative*, three *dynamism* and three *familiarity*) were selected and used on the basis of the factor analytic results obtained from the 1961 Japanese and Finnish studies on political stereotypes. As to BD scales, two *negative* (or prohibiting) and one *positive* (or encouraging) verbs were combined with four auxiliary verbs, generating a total of 12 compound predicate types. The two negative verbs are *ban* and *limit* and the positive verb is *encourage*, a lexical antonym of the foregoing two. The four auxiliary verbs combined with verbs are: *will* (futurity), *can* (possibility), *should* (valuation), and *would better* (preferability). The passive mode was used in constructing a bipolar BD scale, such as *should be banned-should not be banned*, throughout the testings.

TABLE 4 displays the factor analytic results of the Japanese and American data. The three factors in the table can readily be identified as *desirability, dynamism-familiarity,* and *pure potency* factors. We note that nearly all BD scales load highly on Factor I, and on this factor alone, in both groups. It is evident in *TABLE* 4 that coefficients of the first factor overlap in magnitude to such an extent that each group nearly equally contributes to the factor. On the other hand, we also have evidence of the culturally unique use of scales for Factors II and III. Japanese scales loading high on Factor II are pure *familiarity* scales, whereas American scales loading high on the same are a coalescence of both *familiarity* and *dynamism* scales. On Factor III only Japanese scales load significantly high. It must be noted that nearly all the BD scales are found to load highly on the *desirability* factor. This can be taken as an indication that both the Japanese and Americans in this study did not discriminate among the

TABLE 4

VARIMAX-ROTATED PANCULTURAL FACTORS AND HIGH-LOADING SD AND BD
SCALES IN THE JAPANESE-AMERICAN 1969 STUDY

	Factor I (Desirability)		Factor II (Dynamism-Familiarity)		Factor III (Potency)	
	JP	AE	JP	AE	JP	AE
Beautiful	.95	.96				
Bright	.96	.96				
Slow		(.61)		.74		
Pleasant	.95	.97				
Democratic	.95	.96				
Rare	(.47)	.80	.70			
Weak				.95	(.56)	
Fragile				.94	.72	
Far			.79	.71		
Unfamiliar			.78	.76		
Should [be encouraged]	.96	.94				
Would better [be encouraged]	.95	.96				
Can [be encouraged]	.73	.96				
Will [be encouraged]	(.50)	.95			−.61	
Should not [be banned]	.94	.97				
Would not better [be banned]	.95	.96				
Can not [be banned]	.68	.96				
Will not [be banned]	.80	.94				
Should not [be limited]	.94	.96				
Would not better [be limited]	.96	.96				
Can not [be limited]	.51	.95				
Will not [be limited]	.57	.94	(.50)			

NOTES: JP indicates Japanese; AE, American. Figures in parentheses are secondary factor loadings. Percent total variance for Factor I, II, & III are 64%, 13%, & 7%, respectively.

connotative meaning of the auxiliary verbs at all. On the other hand, directions of both SD and BD scales seem quite consistent and logically reasonable.

Next, we assume that the Japanese and Americans not only belong to different language/culture communities but also that they differ in their perception of the real world. The purpose of the following analyses is to examine the ways in which the Japanese and Americans perceive the concepts related to the proliferating nuclear-space science and technology and to find the extent to which their ways of seeing is consistent across the two culturally heterogenous groups.

In order to answer these questions two composite factor scores, each representing one of the most salient factors of *desirability* and *dynamism-familiarity*, were computed in each group. Our first interest lies in finding whether the cultural meanings of the concepts are similar or different across the two subject groups. To get at this problem we correlated the corresponding composite factor scores between the Japanese and American groups over the concepts separately for each factor dimension. A correlation coefficient of .91 and .67 was, obtained for *desirability* and for *dynamism-familiarity*, respectively. The correlation is extremely high for *desirability*, accounting for more than 80% of the variance, while it is somewhat poorer for *dynamism*. In other words, the cultural meanings of the concepts are found to be reasonably stable across the two groups in both factor dimensions. It is particularly noteworthy that in the judging of a variety of cognitive events related to nuclear-space science and technology, the *evaluative* criteria both for the Japanese and for the Americans thus prove to overlap in significant magnitude, despite all the other differences in their cultural, linguistic, and political backgrounds.

Our second interest lies in finding the extent to which the corresponding concepts are similarly or differently located in multidimensional affective-conative spaces. To get at this question the "relative" distance between the Japanese and American cultural meanings for the corresponding concepts was examined by t-tests. The t-test results showed that the cultural meanings do significantly ($p < .01$) differ between the Japanese and American groups in the *desirability* dimension, and in this dimension alone; no significant difference was found in *dynamism-familiarity*. By inspection it is clear that the Japanese tend to rate *undesirable* concepts as *more undesirable* than do the Americans. In other words, although both groups basically agree in the direction of evaluation as to whether an object of judgment is *desirable* or *undesirable*, they differ significantly in the "intensities" of evaluative meaning. For example, the mean *desirability* composite score computed over all the concepts was as large as −.86 scale unit for the Japanese whereas it was only −.04 for the Americans.

The foregoing argument may further be illustrated by FIGURE 4, where for both subject groups a total of seven concepts related to NUCLEAR TESTINGS but varied in *condition* and *location* are assigned to each of the four "quadrants" in a two-dimensional affective-conative space. In addition a PEACE-related concept, COOPERATION AMONG SCIENTISTS IN ALL THE NATIONS FOR PEACEFUL USE OF SCIENTIFIC RESEARCH, is also displayed in the Figure so that we can compare different classes of concepts in the same semantic space across the two groups.

First, we note that nearly all the cross-cultural differences in the location of the corresponding concepts are along the *desirability* factor dimension. It is evident that the meanings of concepts interact with culture more in *desirability* (vertically) than in *dynamism-familiarity* (horizontally). The only exceptions are NUCLEAR TESTINGS IN DEVELOPING NUCLEAR NATIONS ASSOCIATED

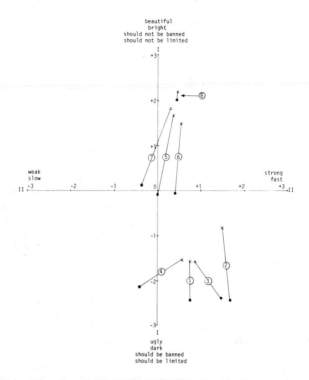

FIGURE 4. Allocation of NUCLEAR-TESTING-related concepts in a two-dimensional semantic space: a Japanese-American comparison. The circled numbers have the following meanings: ① = NUCLEAR TESTINGS IN ALL THE NATIONS ASSOCIATED WITH ARMS DEVELOPMENT; ② = NUCLEAR TESTINGS; ③ = NUCLEAR TESTINGS IN DEVELOPED NUCLEAR NATIONS ASSOCIATED WITH ARMS DEVELOPMENT; ④ = NUCLEAR TESTINGS IN DEVELOPING NUCLEAR NATIONS ASSOCIATED WITH ARMS DEVELOPMENT; ⑤ = NUCLEAR TESTINGS IN ALL THE NATIONS FOR A PEACEFUL USE OF SCIENTIFIC RESEARCH; ⑥ = NUCLEAR TESTINGS IN DEVELOPED NUCLEAR NATIONS FOR A PEACEFUL USE OF SCIENTIFIC RE-SEARCH; ⑦ = NUCLEAR TESTINGS IN DEVELOPING NUCLEAR NATIONS FOR A PEACEFUL USE OF SCIENTIFIC RESEARCH; ⑧ = COOPERATION AMONG SCIENTISTS IN ALL THE NATIONS FOR A PEACEFUL USE OF SCIENTIFIC RESEARCH. (● and x indicate Japanese and American, respectively.)

WITH ARMS DEVELOPMENT (3) and NUCLEAR TESTINGS IN DEVELOP-ING NUCLEAR NATIONS ASSOCIATED WITH ARMS DEVELOPMENT (4) in which there is as much difference in meaning between both groups in *dynamism-familiarity* as in *desirability*. The Japanese seem to discriminate in this case between *developed nuclear nations* and *developing nuclear nations* more sensitively (*dynamic* versus *static*) than do the Americans to whom three concepts differing in *location*, NUCLEAR TESTINGS *IN ALL THE NATIONS* ASSOCIATED WITH ARMS DEVELOPMENT, NUCLEAR TESTINGS *IN DEVELOPED NUCLEAR NATIONS* ASSOCIATED WITH ARMS DEVELOP-MENT, and NUCLEAR TESTINGS *IN DEVELOPING NUCLEAR NATIONS* (1, 3, 4 in FIGURE 4), mean almost the same thing connotatively.

Secondly, there is clear evidence of semantic interaction. For example, NUCLEAR TESTINGS, which by itself is viewed as highly *undesirable* in both subject groups, is made *more desirable* when associated with *PEACEFUL* USE (5, 6, 7), but *equally undesirable* for the Japanese and *more undesirable* when combined with *ARMS* DEVELOPMENT (1, 3, 4). The pattern is quite consistent across the two groups. However, in most cases, the concept related to *location* seem to exert only a little influence on such semantic interaction.

Thirdly, we note a near-perfect agreement in the meaning of COOPERATION AMONG SCIENTISTS IN ALL THE NATIONS FOR PEACEFUL USE OF SCIENTIFIC KNOWLEDGE (8) between the Japanese and Americans. In other words, the concept has universal meaning for the both cultures. Hence, it may be assumed that the cross-cultural differences we find in the meanings of all the nuclear-related concepts between the Japanese and Americans are not mere statistical artifacts but are real, reflecting true differences in sensitivity, knowledge, and learning experience unique to each culture.

In the last analysis, some Japanese absolutely reject all the NUCLEAR-TESTINGS-related concepts even when they are associated with PEACEFUL USE. We recall that a similar phenomenon has been found in the Japanese-Finnish political stereotype study, in which NUCLEAR TESTINGS as the nominal component proved to be the better predictor of the meaning of NUCLEAR-TESTINGS-related complex concepts. Normal semantic interaction and congruity resolution did not occur under this condition.

This consistent affective "rejection reaction" might well be identified with "nuclear allergy," the term now in common use. It is obvious in FIGURE 4 that such a "traumatic" nuclear allergy is not present in the Americans who discriminate between *acceptable* NUCLEAR TESTINGS and *unacceptable* NUCLEAR TESTINGS. In contrast, no such discrimination is made by the Japanese. Once touched by the powerfully negative emotional overtones associated with NUCLEAR TESTINGS, the evaluative meaning of the complex concepts is always "pulled" toward the negative end of the composite scales as if it was contaminated by a "kiss of death"!

CONCLUSIONS

On the basis of these cross-cultural studies it may be concluded that the Japanese nuclear allergy is not very salient in the postwar Japanese youth tested. The Japanese do not exceedingly differ from the youth in the other language/culture communities in their attitudes toward the atomic bomb and other nuclear-related concepts. Furthermore, a majority of the Japanese youth are found to believe that Japan will go nuclear within a limited length of time. Even so, all the concepts related to the nuclear testings are seen as being *undesirable*, even when they are associated with peace, which represents a positive value for the Japanese.

These results may have important implications for the future of nuclear-space science and technology and their applications to industry, as well as for Japan's ultimate policy toward nuclear armament. Note also that the problem is not limited to Japan, but may be extended to developing nations which are capable of producing the nuclear device. Many nations in this category face the same "incongruent" situations, with social, economic, and political considerations for the future need for nuclear arms balanced against the costs of having nuclear weapons (e.g., the high cost of production and the risk of nuclear retaliation by the opponent in the event of war). While statesmen, administrators, business-men, and political and economic scientists may deal with this critical question from a pragmatic point of view, the same question might also be the concern of social and cross-cultural psychologists, sociologists, and anthropologists, for their primary interest lies in the analysis of universals and specifics of human thinking and behaviors. These behavioral scientists, and they alone, can answer the questions as to whether, how, and when a congruence is achieved to reduce the psychological *incongruity*. We are not so certain about the direction in which such incongruity is reduced. It may be toward greater limitation of nuclear proliferation, or conversely it may be toward joining the Nuclear Club. The critical decision-making of a nation is dealt with not only by historians and political scientists, but also by psychologists.

As George Quester put it in *The Politics of Nuclear Proliferation*, which was quoted earlier in this paper, "The Japanese response is interesting, in part because it illustrates feelings that may show up in other nations as they reach advanced stages of economic development." The subject matter reported and discussed in this brief paper is quite relevant to the question presented by Quester, and suggests an urgent need for more systematic, interdisciplinary, cross-cultural research ventures in this area with respect to the conduct of human as well as international behavior.

ACKNOWLEDGMENTS

I am indebted to Steve Schwarts for carrying out the American portion of the study, Dr. Marti Takala of the University of Jyväskilä for arranging data collection in Finland, and Yoko Iwamatsu for taking part in the Japanese studies.

REFERENCES

1. BULLARD, M. R. 1974. Japan's nuclear choice. Asian Survey. 15(9): 845–853.
2. QUESTER, G. 1973. The Politics of Nuclear Proliferation.: 104. The Johns Hopkins University Press. Baltimore, Md.
3. OSGOOD, C. E., G. J. SUCI & P. H. TANNENBAUM. 1957. The Measurement of Meaning.: 7. University of Illinois Press. Urbana, Ill.
4. OSGOOD, C. E., W. H. MAY & M. S. MIRON. 1975. Cross-Cultural Universals of Affecting Meaning. University of Illinois Press. Urbana, Ill.
5. OSGOOD, C. E. 1960. Cognitive dynamics in the conduct of human affairs. Public Opinion Quart. 34: 347.
6. TANAKA, Y. 1972. A study of national stereotypes. *In* The Analysis of Subjective Culture. H. C. Triandis, Ed.: 117–179. John Wiley. New York, N.Y.
7. TANAKA, Y. & Y. IWAMATSU. 1968. An exploratory semantic differential study of the affective and the cognitive components of the attitudes held by Japanese college Ss toward nuclear testings and proliferation. Peace Research in Japan, 1968.: 25–70.
8. TANAKA, Y. 1970. Japanese attitudes toward nuclear arms. Public Opinion Quart. Spring: 26–42.
9. TANAKA, Y. 1973. A cross-cultural psycholinguistic study of attitudes toward nuclear-space development: A case-study of learning in subjective culture. Japan. Psychol. Res. 15(2): 65–81.

INDIVIDUAL MODERNITY IN DIFFERENT ETHNIC AND RELIGIOUS GROUPS: DATA FROM A SIX-NATION STUDY

Alex Inkeles

Department of Sociology
Stanford University
Stanford, California 94305

From the classic studies of Max Weber[1] to the more nearly contemporary research of Everett Hagen[2] comes a continuous line of research that identified certain religious and/or ethnic groups as manifesting special psychosocial traits, which, in turn, induced and facilitated the group's members to become entrepreneurs or otherwise to play a distinctive role in economic development.[2] The interpretation of some of the key cases has been vigorously challenged and as energetically defended.[3,4] But whatever the merit of those challenges, the proponents of the Weber-Schumpeter type of theory must admit that they have so far mainly picked dramatic cases to illustrate the basic relationship in which they are interested. The *generality* of the theory across large numbers of cases has not been tested. The research reported here seeks to make such a test, at least with regard to one facet of the larger theory.

In Weber's[1] work, and also in the later work of McClelland[5] and Hagen,[2] the critical link was that between the psychocultural characteristics of a set of individuals and their later performance as economic actors. In the research to be reported here we have no data, at least none really adequate, on the differential economic performance of the individuals selected as presumably embodying different psychocultural characteristics.[6] Rather we focus mainly on an issue that may be defined as logically prior to that with which Weber *et al.* were concerned. The question we ask is this: Is it generally true that sociocultural subgroups typically produce individuals with personality characteristics of the sort likely to lead them to perform quite differently once they enter the economic realm?

To represent the psychosocial side, we used a measure of individual modernity, the OM scale, which delineates a set or syndrome of qualities including dimensions similar to those emphasized in the work of Weber[1] and McClelland.[5] These qualities include a sense of personal efficacy, autonomy in dealing with authority, and openness to new experience. The ethnic and religious groups studied were drawn from six developing countries – Argentina, Chile, East Pakistan (now Bangladesh), Nigeria, India, and Israel. All comparisons were made on a within-country basis, and therefore on different sets of religions and ethnic groups as we moved from country to country. Thus, the Indian study compared so-called "tribal" and "nontribal" groups, and within the tribal we distinguished "Hindu" from "Christian." In Israel, all were Jewish immigrants to that country, but they differed in having come from the Near East, North Africa, or Asia. And so on, as further explained below.

Our theoretical orientation and our actual experience had indicated that individual modernity was strongly influenced by the amount of education, the degree of mass-media exposure, and the amount of factory experience people had had.[7] But in the phase of our project reported in this communication, our concern was with the extent to which "culture," broadly conceived, contributed to individual modernity above and beyond the "objective" facts of education or mass-media exposure. In this research specific cultural differences in values, child-rearing practices, interpersonal relations patterns, and the like were not explicitly measured, but were represented by the global characteristic of "religion" and/or "ethnic" membership. In a statistical perspective, this actually put the culture variable in a strong position, because it meant, in effect, that a lot of the inevitably unexplained variance in individual modernity scores might be assigned to the credit of the global "culture" measure.

Our basic method for testing the contribution of "culture," as measured by membership in an ethnic or religious group, was to create sets of individuals who were matched on all major characteristics, such as age, sex, and education, but still differed in culture-group membership. The matches were then used to test the association of individual modernity with culture group, in order to yield a correlation coefficient. As a standard, one might keep in mind that when individuals were so matched in groups divided into the more and the less educated, the match correlations were consistent across six countries, and in the median case, the figure was .35, significant at better than .01 (Reference 7). As will be seen, the case to be made for the importance of religious and ethnic differences in explaining individual modernity is much weaker and far less consistent. Changing the method of analysis to utilize a dummy variable in a regression analysis somewhat improved the performance of ethnic-religious variables as predictors of individual modernity, but did not raise them to anything approaching the power of education, occupation, or the mass media in accounting for individual modernity.

THE PROJECT ON SOCIAL AND CULTURAL ASPECTS OF ECONOMIC DEVELOPMENT

The specific objectives of this communication will be better understood if they are seen in the context of the larger research program of which this report is a part, namely the Project on the Social and Cultural Aspects of Economic Development, previously at Harvard but now located at Stanford University.[8] The project is an investigation of the forms and sources of modernization in individuals. Its focus is on the person rather than the society or the institution, and its emphasis is sociopsychological rather than purely sociological or structural.

The study is based on an extensive interview, of up to four hours' duration, administered to a highly purposive sample, including subgroups of cultivators, migrants to the city newly arrived, urban workers earning their living outside large-scale productive enterprises, and workers in industry. Industrial workers were the largest group in each country, some 600 to 700, whereas the other subgroups were to be 100 each. These targets, while not always reached exactly, were well approximated. The selection of cases was on the basis of the respondent's meeting certain common characteristics as to sex (all male), age (18–32), education (usually 0–8 years), religion, ethnicity, rural or urban origin, residence, and, of course, the occupational characteristics already mentioned.

Respondents were chosen within "sites," the most important being the factory. Up to 100 factories were included in each country. In practice, virtually everyone meeting the sample criteria was selected from each factory, except the very largest. In the latter, up to twenty men were selected at random from among the pool of eligible subjects. Factories were selected on the basis of differentiation by size (five categories), product (seven categories), and relative "modernity" (two categories). Villages were chosen on the basis of either being the same as those from which the migrant industrial workers had come originally, or being precisely equivalent in region, culture, crop, and the like. Urban nonindustrials (UNI's) had to work outside large-scale production organizations in the same cities as the workers, and otherwise meet the general sampling criteria. Since we are not making generalizations about the national populations, we emphasized more keeping the subsamples broadly similar in most respects (except occupation), rather than selecting them to be representative of any "parent" population. Nevertheless, our industrial samples proved to be very similar to their defined parent populations, although more so in some countries than in others.

The main objective of the larger research program was to test a theory concerning psychosocial modernity. Individual modernity is here conceived of as a complex set of interrelated attitudes, values, and behaviors fitting a theoretically derived model of the modern man, at least as he may appear among the common men in developing countries. Whether this syndrome actually exists in nature, and is the same from country to country, is one of the prime questions to which the project addressed itself. We already have an answer to this first question: the syndrome does indeed exist in nature. Furthermore, the psychological "structure" of individual modernity is now known to be basically very much the same in all six of the very different countries we studied.

We believe our evidence, presented in some detail in *Becoming Modern*,[7] shows unmistakably that there is a set of personal qualities that reliably cohere as a syndrome and that identify a type of man who may validly be described as fitting a reasonable theoretical conception of the modern man. Central to this syndrome are: (1) openness to new experience, both with people and with new ways of doing things, such as attempting to control births; (2) the assertion of increasing independence from the authority of traditional figures, such as parents and priests, and a shift of allegiance to leaders of government, public affairs, trade unions, cooperatives, and the like; (3) belief in the efficacy of science and medicine, and a general abandonment of passivity and fatalism in the face of life's difficulties; and (4) ambition for oneself and one's children to achieve high occupational and educational goals. Men who manifest these characteristics (5) like people to be on time, and show an interest in carefully planning their affairs in advance. It is also part of this syndrome (6) to show strong interest and take an active part in civic and community affairs and local politics; and (7) to strive energetically to keep up with the news, and within this effort to prefer news of national and international import over items dealing with sports, religion, or purely local affairs.

This syndrome of modernity coheres empirically to meet the generally accepted standards for scale construction, with reliabilities ranging from .72 to .91 in the six countries.[9] Looking at the range of items that enter into the scale, one can see that it has a compelling face validity. In addition, the empirical outcome accords well with our original theoretical model and, indeed, with those of numerous other students of the problem. Evidently the modern man is not just a construct in the mind of sociological theorists. He exists and he can be identified with fair reliability within any population that can take our test.

The second major objective of the Project is to assess the determinants of individual modernity. We are asking: What makes a man modern? Part of the story bearing on this issue has also now appeared in print.[7] In this article we plan to supplement the available answers to that question by testing an additional personal attribute often assumed to be important in shaping the modern man, namely, his origin in one or another religious and/or ethnic group within his given national population.

RELIGION AND ETHNICITY AS DETERMINANTS OF MODERNITY

One of the most common forms of either advantage or handicap that men experience stems from their origin and membership in one or another ethnic and religious group. Not only may such ethnic membership place a person at a disadvantage by denying him legal rights and economic opportunities, but also the traditional culture of his group may inculcate in him attitudes, values, and action tendencies that impede his ability to function effectively in the modern world.

It was clear, therefore, that in developing a general model to account for individual OM scores, we had to allow for the possibility that a man's modernity might in good part stem from his membership in an ethnic or religious group whose culture patterns made its members decidedly more modern than other groups. Despite the many criticisms directed at them, Max Weber's[1] classic thesis about the role of Protestantism in the rise of modern capitalism in Europe, and David McClelland's[5] later research on "the need for achievement" as a force accounting for national economic development, had obvious implications for our work.[10] Consequently, we felt it incumbent on us to take careful note of the religious and ethnic characteristics of those who entered our samples.

As it turned out, there were indeed marked differences in the average modernity scores of the major ethnic and religious subgroups in our samples. For example, in Israel the percentage scoring in the upper third of the distribution on OM ranged from 16% among those Jews who had originated in Tunisia to 56% among those who came from Turkey. And in Nigeria only 26% of the Ekiti scored as modern, whereas 82% of the Ife so qualified.[11] Clearly, some ethnic and religious subgroups in our samples were decidedly more modern than others. But how far was this truly a *cultural difference*, and how far the product of differential opportunity? Since education and factory experience are highly effective in modernizing individuals, the men from certain ethnic and religious groups might have scored as they did mainly because they had had more contact with modernizing institutions. Indeed, we knew from government statistics that groups such as the lower-caste Hindus of India suffer marked disadvantages in education. Therefore, before we could conclude that cultural differences were an independent factor contributing to the standing of men as more modern or traditional, we had to control such factors as education, factory experience, urbanization, and contact with the mass media.

Some might argue that the act of "bringing under control" the influence of such variables as education and industrial experience is to beg the very question under investigation. In this view it is precisely through their differential readiness to stay in school, or move to town, or enter industry that tribal, religious, and ethnic groups express their cultural differences. Those who take this view will want to give particular weight to the straightforward zero-order correlations which we present, and will grant less validity to matching, partial correlations, and regression analysis. Others, however, will accept a different model.

One such alternative model assumes that the typical education or occupation of religious and ethnic groups is largely a result of their physical location, or of social forces external to any subgroup culture, such as a climate of prejudice and discrimination. In such cases, to obtain a fair picture of the residual contribution that group culture makes to individual modernity, one must adjust the individual scores to take into account the differences in the objective life chances common to a whole group.

A second alternative approach is to accept the assumption that cultural differences *per se* influence the pursuit of education or the choice of occupation, yet to insist on knowing whether or not there is any further residual effect of culture *after* differences in education and the like are taken into account.

These two alternative models might be tested either by a natural experiment or by a longitudinal study. Neither resource is available to us here. We must, therefore, fall back on other methods, meaning essentially statistical manipulations, in our effort to isolate the effects of some cultural residue which may exert its influence even after group differences in education, occupation, and the like have been taken into account. In this report we have relied mainly on two such statistical devices, one quite familiar, the other relatively little known.

Our less well-known method we call "matching." Matching is done by a special computer program which generates two (or more) sets of individuals differentiated on the match variable, but otherwise more or less exactly alike on other critical variables. Thus, to facilitate comparing Protestants and Catholics in Chile, the matching program pairs each Protestant to a Catholic who is like his "match" in education, occupation, age, mass-media exposure, residence, rural origin, and urban residence. The resultant matched groups permit us to examine the influence of any single variable while the other main variables are simultaneously controlled.[7] Otherwise, the results we obtained in any comparison might reflect not so much the influence of the experience we intended to assess, but rather that of some other variable that happened, in our sample, to be closely associated with the one in which we are interested. Under the condition of matching, any differences we observe between two matched groups may be relatively unambiguously assumed to reflect the influences of the match variable, rather than being spuriously produced by one or more of the "uncontrolled" variables.

As a method of bringing "extraneous" variables under control, matching has the great advantage that one always knows concretely which people one is comparing, and one compares actual scores and not artificial scores generated by a process of statistical weighting. Nevertheless, we must acknowledge two attributes of matching that lead some to question its suitability.

First, the nature of the matching process may extract from the larger sample as representatives of the parent group those individuals who, in fact, are in the statistical sense most unrepresentative of that parent population. To match cultivators and industrial workers on education in a given country, for example, one may be obliged to rely on only those farmers with more than eight years of schooling, despite the fact that farmers with that much education are one in a hundred and are special in other ways, such as owning much land. Perhaps even more important is the fact that the matching process inevitably greatly reduces the total number of cases with which the analysis is conducted. The smaller the N, the greater the size of the mean difference required to qualify at any given level of statistical significance.

To meet these objections, we sought a method that permitted working with the total sample, yet somehow approximated the flexibility and specificity of the matching method. The technique we hit on, well known in economic research, is called dummy variable analysis. For this purpose a set of nominal categories, as is the case with ethnic or religious groups, is organized as an ordinal variable by pitting everyone in one group against those in other groups, and assigning arbitrary values, such as 1 and 2 to those on either side of the line. By this method we could create a variable that would pit each Nigerian subgroup, such as Egba or Ekiti, successively against the others. Once such a variable is created, correlation coefficients indicating the strength of each dummy variable may be obtained. To control for the influence of other factors, one may resort to either partialling the correlation or including it in a linear multiple regression analysis. Still other procedures might have been used, but our experience with these data leaves us quite confident that alternative methods would not have substantially altered the impression one is led to draw from these materials.[12]

ETHNICITY IN INDIA

We begin our exploration of ethnic and religious influence with our Indian sample because it included the most striking subgroup differences. We selected our Indian sample to include more-or-less equal numbers of four major groups: high-caste Hindus, low-caste Hindus, tribal Hindus, and tribal Christians.[13] The two caste groups require no special explanation, except perhaps for the observation that we made the distinction between "high" and "low" caste in accord with Indian law and on the basis of local expert opinion.[14] As to the tribal groups, they were part of what the Indian Constitution calls "the scheduled tribes,"[15] which probably need a fuller introduction.

The State of Bihar, locus of our work in India, was home to 4.2 million members of the scheduled tribes, 94% of them concentrated in the Chotanagpur Division, which was the main center of our field work in the province. It was therefore particularly appropriate that in doing his sampling, Dr. Singh, our project field director for India, decided that about half of his 1300 cases should be tribal, with strong representation in each of our standard occupational subsamples. On the recommendation of our local advisors, these so-called tribal men were further subdivided on grounds of religion, to separate those who had adopted Christianity from those who followed a Hinduized version of their tribal religion.[16,17]

Our local advisors considered these divisions to be culturally very meaningful. Yet we could not go directly to comparing their relative modernity without the risk of confusing cultural distinctiveness and social advantage. These groups were not merely culturally different; they also enjoyed very different opportunities in life. For example, the Bihar census for 1961 revealed that the percent literate among the higher-caste males was more than three times that for the lowest castes and twice the proportion prevailing among tribals.[18] Despite the narrow educational range over which we selected the cases, our sample sub-groups also displayed marked differences in educational attainment, reflecting the sharp differentiation within the parent population.[19] We therefore had great need of our matching procedure to permit us to compare any one of the four ethnic-religious groups with any other under such conditions that those compared would be almost exactly alike in education, occupation, and other important variables.

We looked first at a series of "two-way" matches, which pitted the groups against each other, one pair at a time. This method permitted us to obtain quite a large number of cases for each pair. The striking fact about the series of matches, as shown in TABLE 1, was that all of them revealed only very modest differences between the pairs of ethnic-religious groups, so modest, indeed, that in no case was the difference statistically significant, despite the ample number of cases in almost all the matches. Even in those instances in which we had expected the greatest contrast, for example, between high-caste Hindus and either tribal Christians or tribal Hindus, the high caste showed very little advantage over the others. We must conclude that in our Indian sample neither religion, caste, nor ethnic group had any significant independent effect in determining men's modernity when the individuals compared were otherwise alike in the degree of their contact with modernizing institutions.

We should not be understood as asserting that these four groups, as one encounters them in all walks of life, are basically alike. We have already seen that they differ greatly in their life conditions, and we can affirm that because of those differences in life condition *on the average* they do differ in modernity. What we are suggesting, rather, is that individuals from these groups, however different they may be at the start, become increasingly more alike to the extent that they are equally exposed to the influence of modernizing institutions. The point may be dramatically illustrated by comparing the OM scores of representatives of the four Indian ethnic-religious groups in a simulation of a "before-and-after" experiment. This could be done by using sets of "four-way" matches, i.e., with each subset of men matched exactly to those in the other three sets.

TABLE 1

MEAN MODERNITY SCORES AND CORRELATIONS WITH INDIVIDUAL MODERNITY (OM) FOR MATCHED INDIAN GROUPS FROM DIFFERENT RELIGIOUS AND ETHNIC BACKGROUNDS

Match No.	No. of Pairs in Match	Matching Groups Coded:		Correlation of Groups with OM†	Mean OM Scores*	
		Group 1	Group 2		Group 1	Group 2
19	110	Tribal Hindu	Nontribal Hindu	.04	48	49
19B	84	Low-caste Hindu	High-caste Hindu	.06	57	58
19C	95	Tribal Hindu	Low-caste Hindu	.06	47	48
19D	26	Tribal Hindu	High-caste Hindu	.07	55	56
18	104	Tribal Hindu	Tribal Christian	.07	52	54
18C	79	Low-caste Hindu	Tribal Christian	.08	53	54
18D	27	High-caste Hindu	Tribal Christian	−.03	57	57

* Positive correlation signs indicate that the group coded 2 had higher OM scores; negative correlations indicate the group coded 1 had higher scores. The correlation coefficients reflect the association of the codes 1 or 2 with the OM score of each individual in the match.

† Significance: Using a two-tailed t test, none of the correlations or mean differences were significant at the .05 level.

First, consider the OM scores of men from the four groups under the condition that all are cultivators and have little schooling. At this stage of development, despite their being exactly matched on education, occupation, and several other variables, the four groups show marked differences in OM-score, as indicated in the first line of TABLE 2. Indeed, the gap of ten points separating the low-ranking tribal Christians and the top ranking high-caste Hindus was significant at the .01 level, despite the small number of twenty cases involved in the match comparison. The tribal Hindu also fared badly in comparison with the high-caste Hindu. Ethnicity, caste, and religion evidently made quite a bit of difference in determining a man's modernity score when we tested the power of these identities in a group of cultivators with little education.

We next asked whether the differences persisted in the case of men more exposed to modernizing experiences. To get the answer, we re-did the matches with each of the four ethnic-religious groups now represented by men drawn exclusively from among the better-educated factory workers. The situation these matches revealed was quite different, as may be seen in TABLE 2. The gap separating the high-caste Hindus from the tribal Christians shrank from ten points to two points and the gap separating them from the tribal Hindus shrank from eight points to one. When the comparison is at the level of well-educated industrial workers, there are no longer statistically significant differences between the high-caste Hindus and either of the two tribal groups.

We may conclude that in our Indian samples tribal, religious, and caste differences cease to have an independent effect on individual modernity scores, once men have attained equality in the advantages provided by education, factory experience, and exposure to the mass media. Being born a high-caste Hindu evidently increased a man's chances of ending up among the more modern, but caste in itself did not confer a unique advantage secure against competition. Evidently the lowliest tribal member, Christian or Hindu, can be brought to almost the same level of modernity as any high-caste person merely by being given equal access to modernizing institutions.

TABLE 2

MEAN OM SCORES FOR MATCHED ETHNIC-RELIGIOUS GROUPS AT DIFFERENT
EDUCATIONAL-OCCUPATIONAL LEVELS IN BIHAR, INDIA

Match Identification	No. of Individuals in Each Group	Educational- Occupational Level	Ethnic-Religious Groups			
			I Tribal Christian	II Tribal Hindu	III Low-caste Hindu	IV High-caste Hindu
19XC	20	Cultivators averaging 5 years schooling	45	47	51	55*
19X	19	Workers averaging 10 years schooling	61	62	62	63*

* Significance: Using a two-tailed t test, in Match 19XC differences in mean OM score were as follows: I vs. III .05, I vs. IV .01. In Match 19X none of the differences was significant.

RELIGION AND ETHNICITY IN NIGERIA[20]

The "Yoruba people" are overwhelmingly predominant in the Western Region, to which we largely limited our work in Nigeria. There is no way of defining a Yoruba other than that he will acknowledge himself to be so when asked, and will be able to speak the "standard" Yoruba language. However, virtually all Yoruba-speaking people also identify themselves as members of one of the more-or-less distinctive tribes that share the Yoruba language. In some cases a man will actually respond to the question, "Are you a Yoruba?" by asserting, "No, I am Ijebu," even though as an Ijebu he will be speaking the Yoruba language. Moreover, the members of each tribe within the language family still know something of their separate history, and each tribe sees itself as descended from a particular tribal ancestor, even though a new ideology emphasizing the common descent of all the Yoruba has been gaining some currency.

Dr. Edward Ryan, field director for the Nigerian phase of our research, had hoped to keep his sample as homogeneous as possible in terms of tribal membership. Various available tribal groups were, therefore, considered ineligible on the grounds that they were not distinctly part of the Yoruba group, or, in any event, did not contribute substantially to the industrial labor force.[22] Nevertheless, the necessity to broaden the base from which he drew his cases obliged Dr. Ryan to include in his sample a reasonable diversity of cultural backgrounds. Consequently, we could make at least two important distinctions within our Nigerian sample, one on grounds of religion, the other a tribal classification on the basis of "degree of Europeanization."

In Western Nigeria, and particularly among the groups we studied, the old tribal religions are no longer the basis on which men habitually identify themselves.[23] Among the men in our sample, 43% considered themselves Muslim, 57% Christian.[24] Despite the vigor with which most men affirmed their religious identity, some of our advisors doubted that such religious distinctions are culturally as fundamental in Nigeria as they often are elsewhere. Nevertheless, the issue seemed important enough to warrant the expenditure of effort required to develop a match.

The match, putting the Christians and the Moslems in competition, failed to show either group to have any significant advantage over the other. These results were confirmed by the regression analysis, which yielded partial correlations with OM so low as to indicate that once we controlled other variables, religion played an absolutely negligible role in predicting individual modernity in Nigeria.[25]

To assess the effect of subtribal differences in Nigeria proved a bit more complex. We had taken into our sample representatives of four main tribes: Ijebu, Egba, Ekiti-Ondo, and Ijesha. In addition, small numbers from other subtribes were included.[26] Over the last hundred years, some of these groups had evidently shown greater interest than others in adopting the institutions and practices brought to Nigeria in the colonial era. These differences did not, so far as we know, result mainly from the initiative of the colonial authorities and the differential application of their policies. Rather, they stemmed in good part from propensities rooted in the different tribal cultures. For example, the Egba and Ijebu were reputed to have shown interest in education much earlier than did other Yoruba groups. The Ijebu also were widely credited as being outstanding traders and as having been quicker than most to see the advantages their children might gain from professional training.[27]

These impressionistic observations were supported by objective census reports that revealed the differences between the groups to be often quite marked. The Egba, for example, were only about 8% of the population in the Western Region, but contributed 31% of its industrial labor force, whereas, the Ondo were 21% of the population, but made up only 14% of those working in industry. As many as a third of the Egbado followed the native religion, whereas this was true for only 6% of the Ijebu and 11% of the Egba, who had much more uniformly become followers of either Islam or Christianity.[28]

Taking into consideration such evidence of tribal differences, Dr. Olatunde Oloko, our Nigerian collaborator, ranked the subtribal groups, placing at the top those "that had and still have the longest and most varied contacts with the agents of European commerce, industry, education, administration, and religion." Dr. Oloko concluded that the Ijebu and the Egba shared the first rank, but should be maintained as separate groups. He recommended that all the others, in descending order on the scale — Ijeshas, Ondos, Ekitis, Ifes, and Egbados — could be grouped together as a set of tribes generally less exposed to outside contact.

We followed Dr. Oloko's ranking in constructing our ethnic matched groups in Nigeria, keeping the Egba and the Ijebu separate, and creating an "other" category in which we placed all the remaining subtribes. By means of such a "three-way" match, the two leading groups could be compared with each other and be paired in turn with the "others" in a separate comparison, all the while holding other relevant variables constant.[29]

It occasioned no great surprise that in their match the Ijebu and the Egba did not show significant differences in modernity.[30] These groups live in a contiguous area, they have similar histories, they both have the reputation of having been quick to take up the advantages offered by contact with the colonial administration, and their standing on an array of objective indicators of modernization led our Nigerian collaborator to rank them equally as most advanced.

It was more notable, however, that the group of "other" tribesmen, which had been collectively rated "low" in relative cultural modernity on the basis of both reputation and historical evidence was not significantly more traditional when our match placed them in competition with either of the two more highly rated subtribes. If anything, the residual group came out ahead of the other two, although not at a statistically significant level.[31]

Since this outcome was so far contrary to the expectation established by our local expert, it seemed particularly important to check the findings by another method.

The "dummy variable" analysis tested seven combinations, each successively evaluated in the context of a regression analysis which, in effect, brought under control the same variables taken account of in the matching. The result confirmed the findings obtained by matching. Groups other than the Egbado, Egba, and Ijebu were the more modern, but none of the Beta weights were significant. No single subtribal group was at all distinctive, or even outstanding, in the modernity manifested by its members when the comparison rested on statistical procedures designed to take account of differences in life chances. Details are given in TABLE 3.

In sum, the data seemed to warrant the conclusion that within the larger Yoruba-speaking Nigerian community, knowing a man's subtribe is of very little value in predicting his modernity, at least once account is taken of his education, occupation, and other "life chance" factors.

ETHNICITY IN ISRAEL

Israel is simultaneously one of the most homogeneous and heterogeneous nations in the world. The Hebrew population, to which our study was restricted, came from many different countries. In each period of its recent history Israel experienced new waves of immigration. Between 1948 and 1953 alone, some 375,000 entered Israel from North Africa, the Near East, and Asia Minor, greatly

TABLE 3

RELATION BETWEEN INDIVIDUAL MODERNITY AND DUMMY VARIABLES FOR RELIGION-ETHNICITY EXPRESSED AS ZERO-ORDER CORRELATIONS†
AND BETA WEIGHTS‡

Argentina			*India*		
All others vs. Parent's Birthplace	r	Beta	All others vs.	r	Beta
Both Argentina	−.27***	−.10**	Tribal Hindu	−.28***	−.03
Both Italy	.04	−.01	Low-caste Hindu	−.16***	−.03
Both Spain	.03	−.01	Tribal Christian	.08**	−.02
Argentina and Italy	.10**	.04	High-caste Hindu	.35***	.10
Other Europeans	.14***	.06*			
Argentina and Spain	.17***	.07*			

East Pakistan			*Israel*		
All others vs. District:	r	Beta	All others vs. Origin in:	r	Beta
Dacca	.02	−.08	Asia	−.02	−.03
Comilla	−.08*	−.05	North Africa	−.10**	.00
Barisal	−.05	−.03	Near East	.12**	.02
Chittagong	.15***	.01			
Mymensingh	−.12***	.02	*Nigeria*		
Khulna	.07*	.03	All others vs. Tribe:	r	Beta
Faridpur	−.00	.03	Ijebu	−.03	−.04
Noakali	.07*	.06	Egba	−.06	−.04
			Egbado	−.02	−.00
			Ondo	.08*	.05
			Ife	.08*	.05
			Ekiti	.02	.06
			Ijesha	.08*	.06

NOTE: Significance levels indicated as follow: * = .05, ** = .01, *** = .001. All others not significant. The significance of the Betas was established by the rule that a Beta should be twice the standard error to be treated as significant at .05.

† In the dummy variables "all others" were coded 1, the named group was coded 2. The zero order correlation expresses the association between the variable so coded and individual modernity (OM) scores. Positive correlations indicate the named groups generally had higher OM scores, negative correlations indicate the named groups had lower scores than the "others."

‡ The Beta weights are from a linear regression of OM on eight variables. In addition to the ethnicity-religion dummy variable, the other variables in the regression were those listed in TABLE 4.

augmenting the 650,000 Jews who were there in 1948. These immigrants from Africa and Asia Minor were mainly Sephardic, as contrasted with the Ashkenazi, who made up the bulk of the population in the earlier waves of immigration, which had come predominantly from Europe. Collectively, the Mediterranean immigrants came to be called the "Oriental" Jews.

Their lack of educational attainment limited the Oriental Jews to positions in the rank and file of the working class. Indeed, as we studied the composition of the industrial labor force, it quickly became apparent that among those under the age of 32, the great majority were men who had come to Israel from Asia and Africa as young immigrants.[32] This seemed to us no great disadvantage, however, because it meant that the Israeli sample would be more broadly comparable to those from the other countries than would have been the case had the Israeli workers been predominantly of European origin and culture.

Because men of European origin were so scarce among the younger Israeli industrial workers, we restricted our sample to the Oriental Jews, and thus precluded a comparison of the relative modernity of the two groups. Those who were classified as Oriental, however, listed thirteen different nations as "country of origin." It was not feasible to pursue the influence of such origins for all these groups, especially since several had very few representatives. Yet there was no obvious and compelling principle to guide us in deciding how to combine the thirteen national origin groups into more manageable sets. We therefore followed our standard practice of taking the advice of our local collaborator.

Dr. Uzi Peled, who ran the project in Israel, recommended that we define three broad categories of origin: the Near East, North Africa, and Asia.[33] This division was not merely geographical, but also cultural. The Near East division, for example, brought together the Arab countries, and the North African division consisted mainly of men who had lived in an area that had experienced colonization and other cultural influences from France.

By our matching procedure we succeeded in locating three sets of men alike in education and other important respects, but different in their national origins. Essentially the same groupings were the basis for constructing dummy variables for use in a regression analysis, presented in TABLE 3. Both methods yielded findings basically in accord with each other.

The group we have designated as Asian, generally called "Eastern" Jews by the Israelis, was consistently the least modern, even when we adjusted their OM scores to account for group differences in education and other life chances. Those from the Near East were most consistently ahead in comparison with the other two. Those from North Africa fell in a middling position. We should note, however, that the observed correlations and Betas were generally not significant, and the absolute magnitudes, mostly below .10, very modest.[34] The conclusion seems warranted, therefore, that Israeli groups having different ethnic origins are not, on those grounds, reliably distinguishable as to the psychological modernity characterizing their representatives within our samples.

Our conclusion, that the culture areas in which Israelis were born and in which their forebears had lived for generations played only a very modest role in determining the scores they eventually earned on our modernity scales, should be hedged round by a number of reservations. First, we must emphasize that our stated conclusion applied only within the limits of variation encompassed by our sample. We studied only Oriental Jews and searched for differences by country of origin within that realm alone. It might well be that had we compared Jews of European origin with those of Oriental background, we would have found evidence that one's region of geographical-cultural origin did play a more substantial role in accounting for the modernity of individuals.

Second, we must acknowledge that our way of grouping the national cohorts may have obscured differences by moving all three origin sets toward some arbitrary meaningless common denominator. As noted earlier, inspection of the average OM score for each origin group did reveal some high- and some low-scoring national contingents within each set.[35] However, with thirteen countries of origin to deal with, we felt that a comparison pair by pair across the set of all possible pairs presented a task too complex for our resources and too methodologically risky, given the size of our samples.

Third, we must recognize that three-fourths of the men in our sample had spent ten or more years in Israel before we interviewed them. Half of them had been 14 or under when they had come to the country. Most spent some time in Israeli schools, virtually all had served a spell in the Israeli army, and all worked in Israeli factories and farms. This common experience could have exerted so powerful a homogenizing influence, especially during their formative years, as to overshadow most cultural differences in relative modernization that might have been manifested in their parents' generation.

This last interpretation, which we favor, again underlines our main point. Men having different social origins will differ in their individual modernity only so long as their life situation, and especially their adult experience, exposes them to highly differentiated life conditions. If men of diverse social origins get the same amount of schooling, and then as adults work at similar jobs and are exposed to the same mass media, they may be expected to become increasingly alike in the degree of their modernity, despite the countervailing influence of the contrasting social milieux in which they had their personal origins.

RELIGION IN CHILE

Although Chile, like all of Latin America, has always been overwhelmingly Catholic, Protestantism has been well established there since the mid-nineteenth century. The early Chilean Protestantism had a decidedly middle- and upper-class character, and was identified with the more "established" sects brought to Chile by immigrants from Europe. In the last few decades, however, Chile has experienced the rapid spread of a different kind of Protestantism. The sources of influence have been the Pentecostal and Evangelical sects, among them the Iglesia Metodista Pentecostal and the Iglesia Evangelica Pentecosta. So rapid was their expansion that the number of Protestants doubled between 1940 and 1952. By 1960, 5.6% of the population was classified as Protestant, as against 1.4% in 1920. Of the total Protestant population, some 85% was by 1960 Pentecostal. The sects have recruited chiefly in the Chilean lower classes, and more particularly the industrial working class. The main concentrations are in the industrialized areas, and the prime source of converts is believed to be among those newly migrated to the city.

Looking to the values that figure prominently in our project's conception of the modern man, the Chilean Pentecostals seemed likely to gain points for their reported tendency to grant equality to women, their emphasis on the independent conjugal family rather than the extended family, their concern with being on time and frugal, and their strong aspirations for decent housing and some reasonable level of comfort through use of the gadgetry of modern living.

Against these tendencies we must, however, balance the fact that the Pentecostal Protestants in Chile evidently do not value education highly. Even though they consider simple literacy highly desirable, they are not noted for founding schools, and may even be characterized as anti-intellectual. Although they have a strong sense of group membership, they do not extend their concern to the rest of the community in which they live. For example, they are not inclined to join organizations other than their church. Among them political activity is at best tolerated and is often discouraged. The dominance of their lay preachers, and their fundamentalist emphasis on the infallibility of Scripture, introduce elements of authoritarianism into these groups and a tendency toward dogmatic and sometimes rigid thinking. They are not necessarily open to new ideas or ways of doing things. Finally, their spiritualism is not very compatible with scientific explanations of natural events.

We were, of course, aware of the theories that assign the Protestants in Catholic countries a special role in the economic development of nations. In the light of what we had learned about the ideas and manners of the Chilean Pentecostals, however, it seemed to us unlikely that they would be markedly more modern than the Catholics.[36,37] But the issue could be settled only by the data.

Some 6% of our Chilean sample, fifty-seven men in all, acknowledged themselves to be Protestant.[38] By our matching procedures we were able to find thirty-four men among the Catholics who were otherwise almost exactly like the Protestants in education, age, occupation, income, and the like.

Comparison of the Catholic and Protestant groups indicated that the Protestants were somewhat more modern men, even when we controlled for differences in background and experience other than religion. Protestants had an OM score of 54 against 53 for the Catholics. Expressed as a correlation between religion and modernity, the figure was .10. However, these differences failed to reach the .05 level of significance in a match with only thirty-four cases.[39]

Partial correlation analysis with the total sample led to the same conclusion. With other differences controlled by partialling, Catholics and Protestants were very much alike. The partial r was only .06, again favoring the Protestants, but not at a statistically significant level.[40] Thus, the theory that Protestant minorities may be expected to play a relatively more modernizing role in Catholic countries got no support from our Chilean sample.

RELIGION AND ETHNIC ORIGIN IN ARGENTINA

The pattern of settlement in Argentina has not been too different from that in the United States. In 1850 the country had not more than 1.5 million people. Massive waves of immigration between 1857 and 1937 brought some 6.5 million people, although this was balanced by an outflow of some 3 million who returned to their homelands or went elsewhere. Of the net immigration, 43.5 percent was Italian and 27 percent Spanish, the rest being distributed among much smaller groups from all over Europe. In Argentina, as in the United States, the official language was rapidly adopted by almost everyone. Assimilation in other respects was profound, and there emerged a new and distincitve cultural amalgam fairly uniformly spread across the country.

Under the circumstances, it did not seem especially urgent to attempt any division of our Argentinian sample according to ethnic origin. We assumed that for most people those origins came too far back in time, and had been followed by too much intermarriage, to be very meaningful. There were, however, enough individuals in the labor force who were more recent migrants from Italy and Spain to warrant establishing a special category of the "foreign born" in our Argentinian sample. There also were a small number of Protestants in our Argentinian sample, sufficient to support a match similar to the one made in Chile.

When the Catholics and Protestants in our sample were compared under matched conditions, the Protestants proved to be the more modern. The match correlation was .16, the OM score of the Catholics being 52 against 55 for the Protestants. Given the small N of eighteen cases in the match, however, the differences were not statistically significant. The partial correlation using the total sample did not challenge this finding.[41]

Turning next to the native- vs. foreign-born distinction, we found that some forty-eight foreign-born had entered our Argentinian samples, all of them industrial workers. In matching, we found twenty-nine of the native-born who were in all important respects exactly like an opposite number among the foreign-born.

In making a comparison of these groups, we took no position as to which should be more modern. If Spain and Italy were considered more advanced countries than Argentina, the immigrants might turn in a superior performance. But we thought it would be difficult to make this case forcefully, especially for Spain, which is one of the least-developed countries of Europe. On the other hand, many social scientists, and not a few others, are firmly convinced that immigrants are self-selected to be more independent and open to new experience. If that were true, the immigrants could be expected to outperform the native-born on the OM scale. The native-born, however, had the advantage of greater familiarity with the language and the style in which the interview was conducted. So we made no prediction.

The outcome of the comparison of native- and foreign-born gave neither a significant edge over the other, but on the whole tended to favor the native-born. The OM score of the latter was 56, against 54 for the foreign-born. The correlation of the match on origin with the overall modernity score was .18, favoring the native-born, but not with statistical significance.[42] The partial-correlation procedure used with the larger group from which the matches were drawn also favored the native-born, but this advantage was far below any acceptable level of statistical significance.

Although the foreign-born/native-born distinction was not very productive, our local advisor felt there might be differences, within the set of native Argentinians, varying in accord with the national origins of their forebears, even though there was no obvious basis for asserting which groups should be in the lead. Therefore, we added an extensive dummy variable analysis to see if any combination of background was associated with noticeably more modernity among those having particular ethnic and religious origins. By this procedure we did indeed find three combinations that were associated with greater modernity at a statistically significant level, even when other major variables were controlled in a regression analysis. When they were placed in competition with all others, the groups that emerged were those with: both parents Argentinian; one parent Argentinian, the other Spanish; or both parents from "other" parts of Europe. The details are given in TABLE 3.

These differences were not predicted on the basis of any theory. They arose from a simple empirical exercise, and may be freely interpreted by one and all. We do note, however, that all of the observed differences are of very modest magnitude.

RELIGION AND REGION IN EAST PAKISTAN

Our Pakistani sample was the most homogeneous, and therefore did not lend itself readily to further study of the role of ethnic and religious factors in accounting for individual modernity. We did make some effort to get a sample of Hindus still living in East Pakistan. They were a hard-pressed minority, however, and not easy to reach. Nevertheless, before we gave up searching for eligible Hindus we had interviewed twenty-eight men. Fortunately we succeeded in matching all but seven of these to Moslems who were like them in education, occupation, and other characteristics.

The correlation of the match with OM was .09, indicating the Moslems were slightly ahead. This was also reflected in the mean OM scores for the two matched groups, which were 55 for the Hindus and 57 for the Moslems. However, these differences were not statistically significant. They indicate some advantage for the Moslems, but hardly permit one to argue that religious background was a truly independent factor in determining individual modernity in East Bengal.

Since the Hindu-Moslem comparison rested on such a small number of cases, we were eager to find some related source of contrast within the Pakistan sample. Other than religion, the chief basis for such distinctions was a man's district of origin. Regional differences *within* a country are likely to be less fundamental than those between separate countries. Regional cleavages also generally mean less than religious or tribal divisions. Nevertheless, what we know of the contrast between the northern and southern regions in countries as different as the United States and Italy indicates that one can hardly rule out regional factors as a source of cultural influence on individual modernity.

The several districts of East Pakistan seemed to have a rather definite character. The men we interviewed were not only quick to identify themselves with their districts of origin, but they also knew about and took an interest in that sort of information as it applied to people they worked with or met in other contexts. Moreover, each of the districts had a fairly well-defined image in the popular mind, a kind of collective reputation. For example, men from Barisal were seen as aggressive and hot-tempered, whereas the image of men from Noakhli stressed their qualities as pious men who were nevertheless shrewd and concerned with money.[43]

To assess the modernity of the men from the different districts of East Pakistan, we again relied on dummy variable analysis. In the regression analysis that tested the eight districts, none showed a statistically significant advantage over the others in the proportion of its men who scored as modern.[44] The results (TABLE 3) do not argue for an important and distinctive contribution of the local cultures of different districts as sources of more modern men.

SUMMARY

By matching we were able to test the effect of religion in five countries. Once our matching procedure equated men so that their education, occupation, and other salient characteristics were more or less identical, the residual differences in OM score were generally two points or less, yielding correlations of .10 or less, none of which was statistically significant. This outcome could be challenged on the grounds that the matches were limited to only a few select cases. However, regression analysis using dummy variables and partial correlations, both drawing on the total sample, confirmed the match findings. Indeed, they gave a possibly starker picture. The Beta weights available for four comparisons in as many countries were in the very narrow range of .00 to .04, none of them significant, as may be seen in TABLE 4. Across the range of groups we studied, religion decidedly failed to prove itself an important independent characteristic for identifying groups of individuals who were more modern than their countrymen from other denominations.

Ethnic and regional bases of cultural and social differentiation showed themselves somewhat more effective as distinctive indicators of modernity. For example, Argentinians whose parents were both native-born were significantly less modern than those whose parents had come from Europe. However, it was only in a few scattered comparisons that such differences were statistically significant, and in magnitude the association between ethnic status and modernity, as expressed by Beta weights, never was greater than .10 when the influence of other variables was controlled in a regression analysis. The details are given in TABLE 3.

What then can we say to those who assume that the subcultures of religious and ethnic groups are fundamentally important in imbuing their members with qualities that will qualify them as more or less modern? Our results provide, at best, only very weak support for their assumption, and at worst may be interpreted as disproving the hypothesis. Since our findings rather challenge more sanguine estimates, we should both elaborate and clarify our position.

First, we acknowledge that our cases were certainly not selected with the purpose of *highlighting* the independent role of religious and ethnic factors as a determinant of individual modernity. Admittedly, differences in district of origin in Pakistan are not ordinarily assumed to be very dramatic. It might well be that if in Israel we had compared Arabs and Jews, or in Nigeria had put the Ibo in competition with the Hausa, then the striking differences that the culturological perspective anticipates would have been evident in our data as well. Nevertheless, we feel that the contrasts between low-caste and high-caste Hindus in India, Hindu and Moslem in Pakistan, and Catholic and Protestant in Chile would generally be accepted as being quite fundamental. The fact that they did not prove to be so does not deny that in other places and times comparable distinctions may have produced dramatic differences. Our findings do, however, cast serious doubt on the *generality* of the proposition that such differences are absolutely key factors in accounting for individual modernity.

Second, we recognize that our method of combining sets of ethnic groups under collective headings such as "Jews from North Africa" or "Yoruba tribes *other than* Egba and Ijebu" might cover up the distinctiveness of precisely that one group that could prove the point about the importance of ethnic and religious differences. In most cases, however, the matches did pit one discrete group against an "other." And while the dummy variables almost always used an "other" category as criterion, each separate group in turn got to pit its strength against that "other." Nevertheless, it is true that we did not test all possible pairs, and so may have missed the one case that might have produced an outstanding performance. Even in the unlikely event that that had happened, however, we would still feel constrained to state that those who insist that powerful effects on modernity are most everywhere associated with religion and ethnicity have exaggerated the distinctive contribution of such characteristics.

Third, we are aware that by applying multiple controls through matching, partialling, and regression, we may have been following an inappropriate model.

TABLE 4

BETA WEIGHTS OF A SET OF INDEPENDENT VARIABLES AS PREDICTORS OF INDIVIDUAL MODERNITY

Variables Entering Regression§	Beta Weights for Regression including Variable for:								
	Religion†				Ethnicity‡				
	Argentina	Chile	East Pakistan	Nigeria	Argentina	East Pakistan	India	Israel	Nigeria
Education	.39***	.34***	.30***	.23***	.39***	.30***	.50***	.34***	.22***
Mass-media exposure	.20***	.22***	.20***	.24***	.20***	.20***	.20***	.24***	.24***
Occupation	.17***	.21***	.16***	.11*	.17***	.17***	.12***	.16***	.11*
Living standard	.00	.11***	.16***	.13***	.00	.16***	.09***	.10**	.13***
Father's education	.07*	.08*	.01	.04	.08*	.01	.06*	.05	.04
Urbanity	.05	.06*	.05	.16***	.05	.05	.18***	.16***	.16***
Life-cycle stage	.10***	.09**	.04	-.01	.10***	.04	.00	.03	-.01
Religion/ethnicity	.03	.04	.03	-.00	.12***	.05	.04	.06	.10*
Zero-order correlation for ethnicity/religion	.03	.04	.07*	.08*	.30***	.13***	.43***	.17***	.10**
N =	817¶	931	654	721	817	1001	1300	739	721

NOTE: Significance: * = .05, ** = .01, *** = .001.

† For the religion variables, the order of punching, by country was: Argentina — (1) Catholic, (2) Protestant. Chile — (1) Catholic, (2) Protestant. East Pakistan — (1) Muslim, (2) Hindu, applying to factory workers only. Nigeria — (1) Muslin, (2) Christian.

‡ For the ethnicity variables, the order of punching, by country was: Argentina — parents were (1) both Argentinian; (2) both Italian or Spanish; (3) Argentinian and Italian; (4) Argentinian and other, both other Latin American, both other; (5) other European; (6) Argentinian and Spanish. East Pakistan — (1) Mymensingh, (2) Barisal, (3) Comilla, (4) Faridpur, (5) Noakali, (6) Khulna, (7) Chittagong, (8) Dacca. India — (1) Hindu low-caste or tribal non-Christian, (2) tribal Christian, (3) Hindu high-caste. Israel — (1) Iran, India, Afghanistan; (2) Morocco, Tunis, Algeria, Libya; (3) Syria, Lebanon, Egypt, Iraq, Yemen, Turkey. Nigeria — (1) Ijebu, (2) Egba, (3) Egbado, (4) Ekiti, (5) Ondo, (6) Ijesha, (7) Ife.

§ For a description of each of the variables making up this set, see Appendix C of Inkeles and Smith.[7]

¶ N's are approximate because of cases missing on some variables.

What is distinctive about certain cultures may express itself most clearly in the differential propensity to obtain more schooling, more industrial work, or more exposure to the mass media. To control statistically for such propensities may, therefore, be to expunge the critical antecedent indicators of which the adult modernity score is only the final expression. From this point of view, a relevant test of whether subgroups differentially socialize their members to greater modernity would require us to test children before they go to school, or to follow a long-term longitudinal design, or perhaps to do a path analysis. In the absence of such data, the argument continues, one should give serious attention to the zero-order correlations.[45] Since we have no interest in sweeping this argument under the rug, we presented the relevant zero-order correlations in TABLES 3 and 4.

In the case of religion, there were no difficult measurement problems, because only two sets of individuals entered into each comparison. As may be seen in the first part of TABLE 4, the religious differences are very modest in size, although in two of four cases they reached statistical significance.

The correct procedure to use in the case of multiple ethnic groups is more problematic; but the dummy variables, as presented in TABLE 3, seem to be appropriate measures. In this case a more diversified picture emerged. In Nigeria, two subtribes were noticeably more modern. In Argentina, those men whose parents had both been born in that country were decidedly more traditional, and in India, the high-caste Hindus were markedly more modern. Indeed, in the list in TABLE 3, one can find up to a dozen groups whose sociocultural background seems to identify them as noticeably and, in the statistical sense, "significantly" more modern or traditional as judged by zero-order correlations. But whether this is a large or a small number of cases depends on one's expectation, which, in turn, rests on one's theoretical orientation and one's comparative experience. We know of no objective standard for making that judgment. We prefer, instead, to note that after obtaining these figures we are, in effect, "back in square one." After all, at the very outset of this article we showed that some groups in our sample clearly had a high proportion of modern men. The zero-order correlations merely restate that fact in a different form. The basic issue, however, is what meaning or weight to assign to zero-order correlations, especially in the context of the investigation here undertaken.

Our inclination is not to give them great weight for two reasons. Perhaps the most serious consideration is that our samples are not representative, and hence are not suited to intergroup comparison except insofar as some process of standardization on key variables is undertaken. In addition, there is the fact that in applying statistical controls to the religious/ethnicity variable, we are doing to that variable nothing more nor less than we did to the measures of other social factors, such as education, occupation, and mass-media exposure when those variables were evaluated as part of the larger research program.[7] This observation may serve as introduction to our fourth point, concerning the competition among explanatory variables.

As our fourth point, then, we note the importance of distinguishing between an analysis designed to identify particular groups that are distinctively modern, and one oriented toward assessing the relative importance of religion and ethnicity as variables entering into competition with other dimensions of social structure. For example, we can assess the importance of education by comparing the mean modernity score of high-school graduates otherwise matched to primary-school graduates. But we also can, and do, treat education as a continuous variable forming an ordinal scale on which we place all individuals according to the years each spent in school. In that form, the variable "education" yields correlations and can be entered into regressions to assess its contribution in competition with other variables as predictors of modernity. Ethnicity and religion are prototypically nominal variables, which leads to their being used more as we have used them here in the matching, in order to compare one completely discrete group with another. But if a set of ethnic groups is assigned values according to the presumed degree of modernity inherent in their respective cultures, the resultant ordinal scale can be used in operations just like those used with the measure of education.

On the basis of our dummy variable analysis, we arranged the ethnic and religious groups within each country on a scale from least to most modern, and then, through a linear regression analysis, placed those scales in competition with measures such as education, mass-media exposure, and other important dimensions.[46] Under these conditions, the *relative* importance of some forms of religious/ethnic membership was enhanced, at least in some countries. The summary of the results is given in TABLE 4.

In this new arrangement, no surprises are given us by the four available measures of religion. In the linear regression analysis, the Beta weights for religion are consistently the lowest in the set of eight. Moreover, the Beta weights are all well below .05 in magnitude, and none is statistically significant.

However, when the ethnicity measure was rearranged to give it as much influence as possible in its competition with other variables, it did not fare so badly. We do see here again the extent to which the ethnic groups that were outstanding in modernity depended for that advantage on their superior education and occupational placement. This is most dramatically illustrated in the case of India, where a strong zero-order correlation of .43 for the ethnicity variable was reduced to a trivial Beta weight of .04 in the regression. But this should be contrasted with the cases of Argentina and Nigeria, where the characteristic onslaught of the regression analysis nevertheless could neither reduce the Beta weights below .10 nor impugn their claim to be statistically significant.

Returning to the issue of the importance of ethnicity *relative* to other variables, we may note the following: overall, the ethnicity measure was substantially less important than education, mass-media exposure, or occupation in accounting for individual modernity, in competition with the set of seven other variables entering into the regression. The Beta weights for education, occupation, and mass-media exposure were always at least .10, and with one exception, significant at .01 or better. By contrast, three of the five Beta weights for ethnicity were below .10 in magnitude and were not statistically significant. This makes a less than compelling case for the variable. But on the positive side one should note that the ethnicity variable, in the median case, was more important than father's education or the age-life-cycle measure, and was about as important as urban experience in accounting for individual modernity.[47]

CONCLUSION

In this research in six developing countries, we explored the role which the religious, ethnic, and regional origins and identity of workers and peasants played in determining how far they were "modern" or "traditional" men. Religion consistently failed to prove itself a significant indicator of modernity.

Some ethnic and regional groups did, however, seem typically to turn out men who were appreciably more modern or traditional than were their countrymen from other sociocultural milieus.

Such differences could readily result from differential access to education, factory work, and mass-media exposure, which we know to be powerful forces in making men modern. We therefore needed to test whether there was a distinctive cultural residue effective in making men modern above and beyond the "objective" advantages granted to certain groups by virtue of local public policy, prejudice, or historical accident. An outstanding example of the operation of such factors was found in India, where the high-caste Hindus scored as much more modern than did either low-caste Hindus or tribal Christians, both objectively disadvantaged groups. When we controlled statistically for other factors such as education, however, the edge of modernity earlier displayed by certain groups was largely erased.

These results have important bearing on our assessment of the Weberian model of economic development. Our data in no way disprove the cases cited in research in that tradition. But our results do suggest that the cases often used to support the Weberian hypothesis were probably special cases. Our data indicate that, *in general*, religious and ethnic groups are not markedly differentiated on a dimension such as modernity, at least once one takes into account their differential access to education, factory work, and the mass media.

We must acknowledge, however, that the application of statistical controls, in effect equalizing the life chances of different groups, may obscure the basic process by which groups that actually *are* culturally distinctive manage to bring their members to a state of greater modernity. It may be precisely by keeping children in school, or directing them to industrial employment, that certain cultural groups express their greater modernity. The issue can probably be settled definitely only by carefully controlled longitudinal studies. As a substitute for that, path analysis was used in our research, and it did indicate that in some groups, at least, the path to the relative modernity of their members is in good part due to heavy reliance on schooling, which in turn leads to greater individual modernity.

Thus, we can see that some cultures and subcultures may produce a greater proportion of modern men because they more encourage their youngsters to follow life paths which, in turn, inculcate in them modern attitudes and values. From this fact one can move back into the cultural group to probe more deeply the qualities that lead them so to guide their young and the processes that in turn generate those tendencies. Alternatively, one can, as we prefer to do, focus attention on the noncultural life chances that produce the observed individual modernity. In particular, we choose to stress the permeability of the barriers to individual modernity. Even where ethnic and religious traditions typically operate to produce men who are less modern, individual change is possible. Our analysis leads us to affirm that men from very traditional groups become as modern as those from communities more modern in outlook if the men concerned can gain more contact with modernizing institutions. Given the right opportunity by their larger society, most men may become more modern.

ACKNOWLEDGMENT

The analysis on which this paper is based was done in collaboration with David Smith, and I am indebted to him for his substantial contribution.

NOTES AND REFERENCES

1. WEBER, M. 1969. Protestantism and the Rise of Capitalism. Translated by T. Parsons. Charles Scribner's Sons. New York, N.Y.
2. HAGEN, E. 1962. On the Theory of Social Change. Dorsey Press. Homewood, Ill.
3. SAMUELSSON, K. 1961. Religion and Economic Action: A Critique of Max Weber. Basic Books. New York, N.Y.
4. EISENSTADT, S. N., Ed. 1968. The Protestant Ethnic and Modernization. Basic Books. New York, N.Y.
5. McCLELLAND, D. C. 1961. The Achieving Society. D. Van Nostrand Co. Princeton, N.J.
6. Our project did make an estimate of the "productivity" of each industrial worker in our samples. In general, the more "modern" the individual proved to be, as judged by our test of individual modernity, the greater was his productivity. This relationship held with education and skill controlled. The correlations were, however, of modest magnitude, even though statistically significanct.
7. INKELES, A. & D. H. SMITH. 1974. Becoming Modern. Harvard University Press. Cambridge, Mass.
8. My chief collaborators from the early days of the project were Howard Schuman and Edward Ryan, who served respectively as field directors for Pakistan and Nigeria, and David H. Smith, who was my assistant in Chile and later was assistant director of the project in Cambridge. The field work and later analysis were greatly facilitated by the work of our local collaborators in all six of our countries. We owe particular debt to Juan César and Carlotta Garcia, Perla Gibaja, and Amar Singh, who were field directors for Chile, Argentina, and India, respectively, and to Olatunde Oloko, who was assistant field director in Nigeria. In its different aspects, stages, and settings, the research had been supported by the Rockefeller Foundation, The Ford Foundation, the National Science Foundation, and the National Institutes of Mental Health. The Cultural Affairs Division of the Department of State provided local currencies to support our field work in India, Israel, and Pakistan, and the office of Scientific Research of the U.S. Air Force supported technical exploration in problems of translation and computer analysis undertaken in Cambridge. All of these organizations gave their support through the Center for International Affairs of Harvard University, which was the initial sponsor and the institutional home of our project, and later through Stanford University, to which the project was moved in 1971.
9. The figures given result from application of the Kuder-Richardson formula to OM-3, as described in Inkeles and Smith.[7]
10. Some of my reservations about this work were expressed in: INKELES, A. 1971. Continuity and change in the interaction of the personal and sociocultural systems. *In* Stability and Social Change. B. Barber and A. Inkeles, Eds. Little, Brown & Co. Boston, Mass.
11. Except where otherwise noted, all the individual modernity (OM) scores reported in this article are for OM-3, as described in Inkeles and Smith.[7] In some instances, where the appropriate computer run for OM-3 was not available, we substituted OM 500, a virtually identical scale. The figures on the percentage modern for different groups are for OM 500. The samples were divided into thirds in each country, and all those in the upper third on the distribution of OM scores were classified as "modern." Subgroups with less than ten cases were excluded from consideration. If they had not been excluded, the contrast between the percentage modern in the different subgroups would have been even greater.
    We cannot urge too strongly the importance of not jumping to conclusions about these striking differences. It should especially be remembered that our research design made no provision for insuring that any subset of men entering our sample was in any way representative of a defined "parent population" having the same ethnic or religious identity, affiliation, or origin. People entered our sample because they happened to be in the factories we studied and fit the broad

categorical sampling criteria, of age, education, and occupation, used in the larger study, as fully described in *Becoming Modern*.[7] We have no way of knowing the relation between the characteristics of the 39 people from Turkey included in our samples on the one hand, and, on the other, the set of *all* Jews in Israel who had emigrated from Turkey.

12. Analysis of covariance would have yielded modernity scores for each ethnic group, adjusted for the differences in exposure to modernizing influence. Path analysis would make clearer the degree to which initial cultural orientations work through differential educational and occupational paths to influence eventual modernity. Such analysis will be undertaken in time, but it seems quite clear that these methods, while supplementing the information available, will not challenge the main conclusions reached in this paper.

13. Their numbers were, respectively, 314, 431, 284, and 271.

14. Those classified as "high" caste were Brahmin, Kshatriya (Rajput), Bhumihar, and Vaishya (Bania). All others, such as Kurmi, Kahar, Hazam, etc., were treated as "low" caste.

15. The Indian Constitution, Article 46, grants special privileges to both the "scheduled castes," which we call "low caste," and the "scheduled tribes." However, the distinction between what we have called "low-caste" Hindu and tribal groups, also known as Adivasi, is also one which can be maintained only very imprecisely. Tribal groups often move up in the status hierarchy, and pass over into the lower rungs of the Hindu caste system.

16. According to 1961 Indian Census[17] figures, of each 1,000 tribals, 720 were Hindus, 175 Sarna, and 105 Christians. Those who are Hindu, however, often retain many elements of their tribal-religious beliefs, and those who remain Sarna practice a religion much infused with Hinduism. We therefore decided to treat them as a single group under the designation "tribal Hindu." In making these distinctions within the tribal group, we disregarded the fact that they are also divided into four well-recognized tribes: Mundas, Oraon, Ho, and Santal. Widespread intermarriage and cultural diffusion among the members of these groups led Dr. Singh to consider the tribal differentiation less important than the religious.

17. THE CENSUS OF INDIA. 1961. Vol. 4:23. Bihar.

18. The original figures were given as the number literate per 1,000 males, and ran: low caste 111, tribals 152, residual 349.[17] These residuals were, presumably, the equivalent of our high caste Hindus.

19. This was especially true in the range commonly defined as "low" in education. Among the farmers in that range, high-caste Hindus had an average of more than five years of education; tribal Sarnas had only one year; whereas tribal Christians had attained a rather better average of 3.6 years of schooling presumably because they had had missionary schools to attend. Similarly, among workers, the average number of years in school varied markedly as one moved from one to another ethnic-religious group. Under the circumstances, any usual "control" that divided the sample into groups "low" and "high" on education would be prejudicial to the tribals, especially the Sarna. One ethnic group "low" in education might actually have five times as many years in school, on the average, as a second ethnic group also classified as "low" in education.

20. *In* preparing this section we have drawn on two unpublished documents: Dr. Edward Ryan's unpublished "Field Director's Report for Nigeria," and Dr. Olatunde Oloko's dissertation.[21]

21. OLOKO, O 1970. Some social and psychological factors affecting commitment to industrial employment in Nigeria. Ph.D. thesis submitted to Department of Social Relations, Harvard University, Cambridge, Mass.

22. These included, notably, the more north-western Yoruba – Oyo, Ibadan, and Oshun. Also excluded were people from the Okitipupa division; the Owo division on the extreme eastern border of the Yoruba territory; the Eko of Lagos; the far northern Yoruba of Ilorin and Kabba; the Egun, living west of Lagos, and the Aworri.

23. We asked our question about religion in this form: "Which *orisha* do you worship?"

The *orisha* is the focus of ritual and the object of veneration in traditional Yoruba religion. Dr. Ryan asked the question in this form because he felt that using the Yoruba word for religion (*esin*) might lead the respondents to answer in terms of more formal religions. Nevertheless, only 6 in some 700 men responded by naming a tribal deity. Virtually everyone countered by saying, "Well, I am Christian (or Moslem)." We do not mean to assert, however, that elements of the traditional religions do not infuse these later acquisitions.

24. The 1952 census of Nigeria's Western Region showed the people of Egba Division to be 55% Moslem and 34% Christian.[21] In the Ijebu division the proportions were, respectively, 49 and 46. Together, the Egba and Ijebu made up three-fourths of our sample. It is evident, therefore, that in religious composition our sampled groups were similar to the census population.

25. The match on religion in Nigeria (#18) yielded a correlation of −.03, indicating the Moslems were slightly, but far from significantly, more modern. Using the total sample rather than the match group, we obtained zero-order correlation of religion with OM of .08, significant at .05 in favoring the Christians. But the standard partialling process reduced that figure to −.00. For the comparable Beta weight see TABLE 3.

26. These subtribes in our sample numbered: Ijebu 245, Egba 313, Ekiti-Ondo 63, and Ijesha 52. The Ijebu include the Ijebu-Remo, and the Ekiti-Ondo group include 13 who were classified Akure and Idanre. There were also 37 who defined themselves as Egbado, and 11 who were Ife, Modakeke, or Origbo. The bases for deciding which of the Yoruba subgroups to include were established by Dr. Ryan, as field director. First, he felt it important to include a set which was culturally homogeneous, so that cultural proclivities to enter select occupations would not confound our study of the relative modernity of the incumbents of those occupations. Second, he ruled, on grounds of efficiency in locating cases, not to include groups who were known to contribute very few men, in absolute numbers, to industrial employment.

27. The unpublished doctoral dissertation of Olatunde Oloko[21] includes numerous citations from historical sources to support these statements.

28. Quoted from an appendix to the official 1952 census of the Western Region of Nigeria (in Oloko[21]).

29. The resultant match (19X) produced a comfortable N of 69. The match was of good quality, except that the three groups differed markedly in mass-media exposure. To effect equalization on this variable required reducing the N (in Match 19XM) to only 23 cases. The results with this stricter match were in accord with those from the larger match.

30. In the match with N = 69 (19X) the correlation of OM with ethnicity in the match groups was .04, favoring the Ijebu over the Egba. In mean score, the Ijebu earned about one point more on OM than did the Egba. However, none of these differences was statistically significant.

31. In Match 19X, N = 69, the correlation in the match "Others-Ijebu" was −.11, and in the match "Others-Egba", −.14, thus both times favoring the "Others", who were ahead by two OM points. in Match 19XM, controlling more strictly for mass-media exposure, but with N = 23, the respective figures were −.10 and −.09. None of the correlations was statistically significant.

32. EISENSTADT, S. N. 1967. Israeli Society. Basic Books. New York, N.Y.

33. The countries making up these groups and the size of the respective cohorts were: Near East – Iraq 154; Yemen/Aden 104; Egypt 33; Syria 7; Lebanon 2. North Africa – Morocco 209; Tunisia 49; Algeria 21; Libya 18. Asia – Iran 43; Turkey 39; Afghanistan 5; and India 7. There were 48 cases whose country of origin was not recorded. Of course, these placements are subject to debate. For example, some would challenge including the Turks with the Asian group. Indeed, in TABLE 4 they were regrouped with the Near East.

34. The Beta weights from the regression analysis will be found in TABLE 3. In the three-way match 19X, with N = 19, we obtained the following pattern of correlations: North Africa/Asia −.12; Asia/Near East .10; Africa/Near East −.01.

Mean OM scores were: Asia 57, Africa 59, Near East 59. In both the matches and the regression the countries were grouped as described in the preceding footnote.

35. Among the African Jews, for example, the Libyan contingent had 44% scoring high on OM, whereas only 16% of the Tunisians were so outstanding. In Asia Minor the figures were 23% for Iran and 56% for Turkey. These differences were manifested on OM 500, trichotomized, in groups not controlled for education or the other variables taken into account in the matches.

36. In this review of the characteristics of the Pentecostal Protestants in Chile, we relied heavily on Emilio Willems.[37] Willems did not, however, take a stand on the probability that they would or would not score as more modern than Catholics. That judgment is our responsibility.

37. WILLEMS, E. 1967. Followers of the New Faith. Vanderbilt University Press. Nashville, Tenn.

38. Our Chilean sample came predominantly from the province of Santiago, in which Protestants made up 5.2% of the industrial labor force. We drew smaller groups of men from Concepcion and Valdivia, in whose industrial labor force Protestants made up more than 9%. The average of 6.1 in our total sample, therefore, seems very close to the standard in the parent population.

39. Results reported are for match #18.

40. In the total sample the religion variable, entered in the order Catholic/Protestant, yielded the very small zero-order correlation of .04, favoring the Protestants. When seven other main variables were controlled, the correlation was .06, providing one of those rare instances in which a partial was higher than a zero-order correlation. Even with the aid of the clarification provided by the partial, however, the correlation of religion and OM was far below statistical significance.

Since the Protestants were so small a segment of the total sample, we decided to check this relationship within the factory-worker group alone. We now obtained a zero-order correlation of .02 and a partial of .03. Thus, these results support the conclusion that differences in the modernity of working-class Catholics and Protestants do not persist once one takes account of education, mass-media contact, and occupation.

41. For the total sample the zero-order correlation, favoring the Protestants, was .03, and the partial, .04, neither significant.

42. The N for the match was only 29, which made it less likely that the observed differences would attain statistical significance.

43. SCHUMAN, H. 1966. Social change and the validity of regional stereotypes in East Pakistan. Sociometry 29 (4): 428–440.

44. This was the result when the analysis was applied to the total sample.

45. A path analysis of the influence of religion/ethnicity on individual modernity has been completed and will be reported separately. However, we should note here the main results. Like father's education, one's ethnicity/religion did not seem to confer *directly* any very great advantage or disadvantage with regard to OM scores. Most of the impact of such ethnic or religious background was *indirect*, mediated through intervening variables. We did find some significant *true* indirect effects of ethnicity/religion upon OM scores, mediated through significant relationships with the intervening variables of education-literacy and occupational type. This suggests that men from ethnic-religious groupings that we ranked as more modern tend to achieve a higher education-literacy level and a higher occupational-type level than men from less modern ethnic-religious groups. Thus, it seems that it is not the ethnic-religious group experience *per se* that is a modernizing experience. Instead, being a member of a given ethnic-religious grouping tends to make more probable a man's exposure to greater or lesser amounts of directly modernizing experiences, such as formal education or experience in factory work. The supply of education and factory experience can, of course, be more readily increased and diffused than could some more distinctive cultural value scheme.

46. The ordering of groups within each variable was determined by the outcome of the more detailed dummy variable analysis presented in TABLE 3. Thus, in Argentina, those whose parents were both Argentinian were punched 1, and so on through the

category "Argentinian plus Spanish," which was punched 6 because that group had shown itself most modern. It should be recognized that constructing the ethnicity measure in this way, based on the criterion itself, gave the variable a decided advantage in competition with other variables in the regression that had been constructed in more conventional ways.

47.   In assessing these results, one must keep in mind that in linear regression analysis the outcome for any variable depends not only on its association with other variables in the set, but also on the initial strength of association with the dependent variable. Ours were special samples limited to the working class, and so the range on many variables, such as own education and father's education, was much more truncated than would have been the case if we had had fuller national samples across the whole available range.

ORIENTATION TO CHANGE IN ADVANCED AND DEVELOPING SOCIETIES: A CROSS-NATIONAL SAMPLE

Robert C. Williamson

Department of Social Relations
Lehigh University
Bethlehem, Pennsylvania 18015

A fundamental question in the twentieth century is the determination of factors surrounding the process of modernization in underdeveloped or transitional societies. What conditions promote change and how do these differ among nations? What attitudes and values accompany industrialization and urbanization? How do these factors vary among nations and social classes, and between the generations?

Clearly, the present study is a tentative inquiry into a complex set of questions. Although more a pilot study than an exhaustive analysis of the subcultural variables underlying the process of modernization, it illustrates some psychological correlates accompanying social change. The study, which was carried out between 1965 and 1968, includes adult and student samples from Colombia, Western Germany, Japan, and the United States, together with adult samples from Chile and Spain.* I have reported in other publications the findings regarding class differences in Colombia[1] and Chile,[2] along with a cross-national comparison among student samples.[3] This paper presents the national and generational comparison in a broader focus and arrives at some general conclusions. To a certain extent, the study may be regarded more as a comparison of given cities than of countries since the samples were drawn from Bogotá and Santiago among the transitional countries, from Munich, Barcelona, Tokyo, and a middle-sized city (Allentown, Pennsylvania), among the industrialized ones. Basically, we are comparing four samples of industrialized Western cultures with two samples from Latin American nations in different stages of development. The comparison will focus on the Colombian, German, Japanese, and American samples since they included both adults and students. Despite the emphasis on cross-generational and cross-national comparisons, the effect of social class will not be ignored.

THE CONCEPTUAL FRAMEWORK

Since the study deals with several social psychological factors associated with modernization, a statement about my conceptual outlook is in order. Without elaborating a theory of social change from either a "macro" or a "micro" viewpoint, I must make clear my functionalist viewpoint. That is, the study

---

* A university strike and vacation schedules prevented the inclusion of Chilean and Spanish student samples. There was also an Indian (New Delhi) student and adult sample; however, the responses were of questionable validity and are therefore omitted from the present analysis.

accepts the characterization of Van de Berghe that a structural-functional approach is based on several assumptions:[4]

1. Societies are to be analyzed as Gestalts of "systems of interrelated parts."
2. Cause and effect relationships are "multiple and reciprocal." A "dynamic equilibrium" prevails in social systems in that adjustment to forces within the system is usually made with as little change as possible.
3. Integration between the old and new is usually partial and imperfect; that is, change is more often a slow, adaptive development than a revolutionary process.
4. Change is the end result of adaptation to forces more often outside the system, with differentiation, innovations, and an integration of the system through emergent and shared values.

The above model is oriented to attitudes surrounding modernization. The emphasis in the present research is directed not only to the social system, but also to the constellation of attitudes that precede and accompany social change. The present analysis proceeds on the basis that urbanization and modernization are, among other things, a drift from Gemeinschaft to Gesellschaft, from sacred to secular norms, and from primary to secondary group affiliations. In other words, institutional shifts, notably in the family, imply that the universalistic aspects take precedence over the particularistic. Despite the differences implied by urbanism and modernism in various areas of the underdeveloped and advanced worlds, an index of the traits involved in modernization includes: flexibility, rationality, role segmentation, and a sense of mobility, both horizontal and vertical. The differentiation of the social system as it moves from primary to secondary and tertiary production leads to cleavages within the society that are relatively unknown in the feudalistic universe characterizing much of Latin America and other underdeveloped regions. Too, there is a tendency for "modernizing stimuli" to produce higher levels of aspiration. Usually the society's ability to satisfy the aspirations tends to rise at a slower rate than do the aspirations.[5]

There is no agreement, for instance, as to whether a person experiences alienation when a relatively static social system undergoes industrialization and urbanization. Urbanization itself has been variously viewed as an enriching of the individual's social, economic, and cultural life to one of considerable mental strain, with Oscar Lewis and Robert Redfield, respectively, representing the two viewpoints. My research suggests that the migrant to the Latin American city, despite his initial shock at adjustment, views his opportunities as considerably expanded. As with its counterpart in Africa and the Near East, the Latin American city often grows more as an escape from an overpopulated rural landscape than as an industrial mecca.

In this process of urbanization, it is assumed that the individual participates in the mass media and the various social institutions of the city. As he moves from the rural habitat into the urban milieu, his outlook becomes more secular and assumes rationalistic values, as my research in Central America bears out.[6] Not only does his range of communication and social participation broaden, but if he is fortunate enough to find employment, he is increasingly likely to aspire to a better position in life. The acquisition of rationalistic values, however, is a slow process. Moreover, it is my contention that modernization begins primarily in the middle class. If anything, the recent migrant who joins the urban lower class retains more of the traditionalistic outlook of the rural population rather than adopting the outlook of the urban middle class.[7]

The study of the factors underlying modernization has occupied social scientists for some time. The pioneering work of Daniel Lerner on the effect of the mass media and other modernizing agencies in the Near East is an example.[8] I am also indebted to Joseph Kahl for his modernism scale employed in Brazil, Mexico, and the United States.[9] The most far-reaching study of modernization was made by Alex Inkeles in six nations (Argentina, Chile, India, Israel, Nigeria, and East Pakistan). It stressed the factors of industrial employment, urbanization, the mass media, and particularly education.[10,11]

Cross-National Comparisons

Any analysis of development and underdevelopment must be viewed in the context of varying national cultures. Of the four developed nations, three have experienced an overwhelming dislocation in the middle of the century. Both Germany and Japan were defeated in war, with far-reaching changes in public policy and governmental operation. These events predisposed individuals, especially the younger generation, to view the national value structure more critically than if there had not been this break in the social system. Japan underwent a transformation from its pattern of "conformity and competition" as it moved from the imperial order to the status of an occupied state, and later to a mélange of Eastern and Western social institutions.[12] The redefinition of statuses and roles became even more intense with the rampant industrialization and urbanization in the 1950's. The feeling of insecurity after a shattering war and the impact of Westernization made for a serious questioning of the present and past.[13]

Germany, too, experienced a strong generational conflict as the country assessed the legacy of the Third Reich and its subsequent role in the Western alliance at a time of world crisis. Spain continued in a dictatorship while evolving from a quasifeudalistic to an industrialized order. The United States differs as much from the other three industrialized nations as they differ from each other. Notably it has had relative continuity in its sociopolitical development over the last half century. But even so, the degree of social change has intensified the personal search for upward mobility as well as the individual's defining his role in society. Even though the theory of Riesman regarding the "other directed" man has been partially discarded, the national culture has leaned more toward conformity and traditionalism than have nations that have known political disruptions and until recently had a lower standard of living.[14]

In the underdeveloped nations even more discontinuities would seem to be apparent than is the case with the advanced economies. Yet the underdeveloped world, particularly with reference to Latin America, has a number of common problems: for example, a relatively unstable democracy or an authoritarian regime superimposed on a monocultural economy, a feudalistic land tenure system, a growing population without adequate increase in capital, industrial bases, or an educational system that might promote usable skills or literacy levels sufficient either for employment or for participation in the democratic process. In addition to the vested interests within the national power structure that discourage social change, the various nations still have a semicolonial status vis-a-vis the developed world, which in the case of Latin America is inevitably the United States. Consequently the individual is likely to be influenced by this sense of inferiority. He may also feel victimized, not only by the foreign imperialists, but also by his own elites, whether landowners, a political-military oligarchy, or, in the most backward regions, the Church hierarchy.

Inevitably, an easy generalization can gloss over the realities of the social systems, which differ for three score of nations in the underdeveloped world. And within the Latin American orbit, any two nations, for example Colombia and Chile, can differ considerably. Colombia presents a more archaic social order, but its industrialization has passed the incipient stage, and its political process remains in the democratic ledger, even though racked by *violencia* from the late 1940s to the early 1960s. In a 1950 study of the class structure, Lynn Smith questioned whether the Colombian middle class could be considered more than a marginal segment of the upper class,[15] but few would question today that in Bogotá at least a fourth of the population could be identified as middle class, even though this class represents two or three readily recognizable levels.

During the late days of the Frei regime, when the present study was carried out, Chile was committed to the values of the Western world and to an educational system that permitted segments of its urban population to realize their aspirations toward upward mobility. Despite the remnants of an oligarchy that based its power on a medieval land system and the copper economy, there was little expectation by most observers that the country would drift into the unhappy Allende regime and its even more tragic aftermath.

The Generational Chasm

Since the focus of this analysis is on generational as well as national differences, it is pertinent to examine the position of university students within the four nations (Colombia, Germany, Japan, and the United States). The research was conducted before the student revolts of the late 1960s in the United States and certain European countries, and so it was hardly anticipated that there would be complete discontinuity between the two generations. At the same time, student activism has a lengthy history in Latin America, dating from the Córdoba manifesto of 1918. In Colombia, as in a number of other developing areas, students have long been agents of social change; the fall of Rojas Pinilla in 1957 was precipitated, or at least preceded, by a student revolt. Japanese students have been no less militant ever since the initiation of the Zengakuren in 1948, and they were successful in preventing the visit of President Eisenhower to their country in 1960. By the 1960s, German students were already showing a keen interest in politics. Indeed, only American students could be described as bystanders to political events. Again, because of the continuity in its institutions, Americans felt more secure toward their past, present, and future.

It is in the underdeveloped countries that awareness of the need for change would be expected to be the greatest. As they are exposed more to the achievements of the developed world, students become more conscious of the inferiority of their nation.[16] In Latin America, student strikes have long been the means of articulating discontent and redressing grievances. However, these characteristically aimed at specific university-related inadequacies as perceived by the students — the appointment of a rector, the failure of a dean, the lack of student scholarships, or a rise in the bus fare. More typically, in the last decade strikes have been directed toward a social issue.

Students, who are primarily of middle-class origin, are caught in a conflict, in that while they constitute tomorrow's elite, they are, notably in developing nations, aware of the somber realities of the career market. For instance, in the author's 1961 study of 610 students of the National University of Colombia, only 46 percent of the sample thought it likely that three-fifths of their classmates would find employment in their respective fields within the first year after graduation.[17] In reality, a follow-up of graduates demonstrated that this estimate erred in its optimism. Economic strain during the years of university study, along with the inadequacies of the university regime, only add to the frustration students feel in the national scene. These problems surface in the advanced countries, too, but not to the same degree. Among the exceptions are, in Europe, the polarization since the late 1960s and, in the United States, the national convulsion over the Viet Nam war, which had its own kind of battleground on many campuses.

RESEARCH DESIGN

The investigation was based on a number of working *hypotheses* oriented to the concept of modernism. Since a number of items involved subhypotheses, it would be more accurate to describe the design as clusters of hypotheses. Among the central hypotheses were:

1. Social participation, as measured by the number of intimate friendships and the preference of friends over relatives, is positively related to membership in an urban-industrial culture as opposed to a traditional culture, to middle class more than lower class, and among younger more than older respondents.
2. Positive attitudes toward the future (anticipating a better economic position, personal success, and a "happier world," as well as perception of the present as preferable to the past) are positively related to urban-industrial cultures, middle class, and youth.
3. Rationalism, as indicated by higher scores in selected items of the modernism-traditionalism scale, is positively related to advanced culture, middle class, and youth.

Subsidiary hypotheses were also implicit. For instance, respondents in a nation that has undergone frustrating crises, as defeat in war for Germany and Japan (or the civil war in Spain), or deep-seated political and economic unrest, as in Colombia, will tend to be more critical towards their social institutions than will respondents in a nation having greater continuity in its social structure, as the United States. Still other hypotheses dealt with questions like, for example, universalistic as opposed to particularistic role prescriptions, as reported in the analysis of the students' responses.[3]

Research Methods

The samples for each nation were representative, but not random, for the urban cultures selected. The adult samples were selected among the lower and middle class in Allentown, Pennsylvania; Munich, Germany; Tokyo, Japan; Bogotá, Colombia; Santiago, Chile; and Barcelona, Spain. Similarly, the student samples were more representative than random. For the United States, 321 were selected from five institutions: Cedar Crest College (32), Kutztown State College (58), Lehigh University (52), Moravian College (73), and Temple University (105), providing for both small and large public and private institutions. The 96 German students were from five *Fakultäten* (Law, Medicine, Natural Sciences,

Philosophy, and Theology) of the University of Munich. Three-fourths of the Japanese sample were from Tokyo Metropolitan University, and one-fourth from International Christian University. The Colombian sample of 82 was randomly chosen from the schools of Economics, Education, Engineering, Medicine, and Psychology of the National University of Colombia in Bogotá.

The samples may be summarized as follows:

United States
95 Adults (48 lower class, 47 middle class)
321 Students
Western Germany
102 Adults (54 lower class, 48 middle class)
96 Students
Japan
139 Adults (64 lower class, 75 middle class)
112 Students
Colombia
229 Adults (98 lower class, 131 middle class)
82 Students
Chile
329 Adults (155 lower class, 174 middle class)
Spain
98 Adults (54 lower class, 44 middle class)

The adult samples were drawn from representative neighborhoods of the lower and middle classes in the respective metropolitan area, with roughly every fifth to seventh house selected. The interviews were conducted in both the day and the evening, and in most of the countries slightly over half of the interviewees were women. The interviews, which lasted 55 minutes on the average, were conducted by advanced students of sociology, who were given special training for interviewing techniques by the investigator. The refusal rate was approximately 30% in all countries except Spain and Chile, for which the rate approached 35%, and in Germany nearly 50% rejected the interview. For Colombia and Chile, middle- more than lower-class residents rejected the interview, but the reverse was true of Germany. On the whole, younger middle-class professionals were the most eager to be interviewed, but time considerations were often a negative factor.

All the student samples were selected from undergraduate populations, with representative basic courses being the means of administering the 13-page questionnaire. However, in Germany the questionnaire was administered in small groups of a randomized sample from the five *Fakultäten*.

DESCRIPTION OF THE SAMPLE

The samples, as would be expected, represented primarily manual workers for the lower class, and white collar and a small number of skilled workers for the middle class. The age was in the upper 40s in the advanced nations, but dropped to 45 for Chile and 38 in Colombia, reflecting the age distribution for those countries. The lower class tended to be, on the average, a year or two younger, since entry into the middle class depends on achieving a given occupational or economic base over time. The mean educational level was nearly 15 years for the

United States, 12 for Germany and Japan, 8 for Spain and Chile, and 7 for Colombia. The greatest education differential was found in Chile, with the average educational level being 5 years for the lower class and 11 years for the middle class. However, the greatest income differential was in Colombia, with a gap of nearly four to one between the two classes. The Latin American samples had a higher percentage of immigrants, roughly half of the interviewees or their spouses having been reared outside Bogotá or Santiago.

The student samples were disproportionately of middle-class origin, particularly in the German and Colombian samples. The United States had the largest portion of lower-class students, with Germany and Japan intermediate between the United States and Colombia. The German sample was 78% male, the Japanese and Colombian 59%, and the American 46%. It may be added that sex appeared to be less a determinant of responses than was nationality. The average age of the sample was 20.7 years, with relatively little cross-national variation. The average duration of university study, at the time of the interview, was 1.9 years for the four samples. Over 95% of the students were single. Approximately three-fourths of the students were dependent on their parents, except for the German sample, for which the ratio was three-fifths. The German sample also had the highest number of students on scholarship.

FINDINGS

The items were analyzed by a t test and the X^2 test. The following analysis is primarily based on the responses to the several clusters of hypotheses concerning both national and generational differences. Since the effects of social class have been reported in previous articles, only partial reference is given to that variable in the analysis.

Patterns of Social Participation

Among the assumptions underlying the investigation is that modernism is associated with a relatively high level of communication and social participation. For one thing, the samples in advanced nations had a wider exposure to the mass media, including newspapers, television, and motion pictures. Only radio-listening failed to show a difference between the samples in developed and underdeveloped countries. Also, membership in voluntary associations, as well as participation in social gatherings, was higher in the advanced societies.

As indicated in TABLE 1, preference for friends over relatives was generally demonstrated both for the advanced nations and for students, over that of the older generation. However, some qualification is in order. Although the European and United States samples surpassed the Colombian respondents in the extent of "close friendships" (No. 1), the lowest number of close friendships was reported by the Japanese, the latter being the only instance of the adults surpassing the students. At the same time, the Japanese apparently preferred to have additional intimate friends (No. 2), whereas the Germans were seemingly satisfied with the number of their attachments. The tendency for advanced countries and for student samples (with the exception of Germany) was to enjoy friends over relatives (No. 3). Notably, Colombia and Spain lean to kinship rather than friendship in their social interaction. Not surprisingly, the middle

TABLE 1

SOCIAL PARTICIPATION PATTERNS

	American		German		Japanese		Colombian		Chilean Adults* (329)	Spanish Adults (98)	Level of Significance†	
	Adults (95)	Students (321)	Adults (102)	Students (96)	Adults (139)	Students (112)	Adults (229)	Students (82)			Adults	Students
1. Average number of "close friends"	3.9	4.2	3.2	4.1	2.7	2.6	3.7	4.7	2.2	3.4	N.S.	<.05
2. Wish for more friends with whom "you could confide"	26%	19%	11%	15%	47%	40%	34%	45%	33%	35%	<.02	<.01
3. Enjoyment of friends over relatives	67%	84%	68%	59%	63%	82%	4%	23%		15%	<.001	<.001
4. Prefer to consult in solving personal problems:												
Friend	23%	63%	36%	69%	22%	55%	19%	35%		37%		
Relative	39%	25%	32%	22%	60%	28%	62%	20%		47%		
Other	38%	13%	32%	10%	17%	16%	19%	45%		16%	<.01	<.01

* Certain items were not included in the Chilean questionnaires.

† In this and the following tables, the χ^2 test compares separately the adult and student samples. The presence of statistical significance does not necessarily indicate that it is in the direction of the hypothesis.

class had wider social contacts than did the lower class. In Colombia, with its strong affiliation with kinship, the middle class was more kin-oriented than was the lower class, for whom finances and distance made for little interaction with either relatives or friends.

The tendency to go to someone outside the family in resolving personal problems characterized the advanced nation and student samples (No. 4). However, the Japanese adults were nearly as kinship-oriented as were the Colombians. In a previous study, the investigator found adult samples in El Salvador and Costa Rica to exhibit this preference for kin even more dramatically.[6] It is conspicuous that the Colombian students were especially prone to choose neither kin nor friends for discussing their personal problems. Among the resources most mentioned were "resolving the problem myself," talking over the question with a professor, the university chaplain, or some other professional. The American sample showed no less a difference between the generations in the turning to friends as opposed to resolving the problem oneself. Even though the tendency to seek out friends was higher for students than for adults, the difference is less acute when one compares nations. On the whole, one mark of advanced nations may be the movement away from kinship moorings; however, the explanation for the findings lies in the strong kinship ties among most Latin nations as compared to, say, northwest Europe and the United States. Parenthetically, the stongest preference for kin was found for India, even if the lack of validity did not warrant inclusion of these data in the tables.

Mobility, Satisfaction, and Future Aspirations

As another measure of modernism, a number of items centered on the respondent's perception of the status quo and on his sense of mobility for the future (TABLE 2). It was hypothesized that optimism about the present and the future would be correlated with orientation toward change.

The tendency of the respondent to see a brighter economic future for himself (No. 1) followed no orderly relation either to the level of the society or to the generational differential, even though the difference in response between the samples was statistically significant. The optimism of Americans and Colombians stands in contrast to the pessimism of the Germans, with Japanese, Chileans, and Spanish occupying an intermediate position. Possibly the optimism of the Colombians was because they had the farthest to move, but it is questionable whether in a decade after this investigation one would find their economic situation markedly improved. Yet the pessimism of the Germans, especially the students, is hardly justified in view of their continued economic advance over the last several years. Possibly the projections toward the future are more a measure of the restrained outlook within the national culture than of the events the respondents are judging.

Too, the assignment of success to life chances or "fate" (No. 2) would seem to be more a product of given cultures, as in the case of Latin and Japanese cultures, than of the level of development of the society or the respondent's stage of the life cycle. At least, fate was rejected in the German and United States samples. Self-accomplishment was especially stressed by students in these two countries.

In regard to the "world of 20 or 30 years in the future" (No. 3), the

TABLE 2
MOBILITY, SATISFACTION, AND FUTURE ORIENTATIONS*

	American Adults (95)	American Students (321)	German Adults (102)	German Students (96)	Japanese Adults (139)	Japanese Students (112)	Colombian Adults (229)	Colombian Students (82)	Chilean Adults (329)	Spanish Adults (98)	Level of Significance Adults	Level of Significance Students
					Percent of Responses							
1. What kind of an economic situation do you foresee in ten years:												
Better	74	72	41	15	68	48	69	90	51	61		
Same	24	26	46	53	29	36	13	0	28	35		
Worse	3	3	13	32	4	11	18	10	21	5		
2. To what degree does success in life depend on:												
Your own accomplishments	70	83	57	77	57	45	38	52	44	45		
Uncertain	12	6	31	4	2	8	16	13	17	10	<.05	<.02
Life chances	19	11	12	19	41	41	46	34	39	45		
3. Do you think the world in 20–30 years will be:												
Happier	40	32	31	8	41	38	24	24	19	30		
The same or uncertain	37	53	63	76	38	8	30	59	33	37	<.05	N.S
Less happy	20	15	34	16	21	40	46	17	48	33		
4. Do you think the people of 100 years ago were:												
Happier	42	18	31	9	28	8	57	29	14	38		
The same or uncertain	49	75	63	77	30	36	24	51	36	30	N.S.	<.05
Less happy	9	7	6	9	42	53	19	20	50	32		
5. Percent of individuals you perceive as happy:												
0–40	18	28	65	86	38	41	62	73	56	58		
41–60	26	32	21	8	25	18	29	24	13	34	<.05	<.05
61–100	55	42	13	3	38	28	15	4	30	15		
6. Percent of marriages you perceive as happy:												
0–40	12	25	46	69	32	35	82	70	58	36		
41–60	30	32	23	16	29	23	13	19	18	27	<.02	<.05
61–100	68	42	31	16	39	32	15	11	25	36		

* In items for which the percentages do not total 100, the remaining percent represents nonresponses.

developing countries (Colombia and Chile) were the least sanguine. Except for the Americans, no significant difference was found between the two generations. Possibly all the samples would see a more foreboding future if the question were asked today. In any event, the adults were markedly more nostalgic about the past (No. 4), and the students were more cautious about making any judgment — only the Japanese students were willing to think of the people of a hundred years ago as distinctly happier or unhappier than those of the present.

Another indicator of satisfaction were the two projective items asking the respondent to estimate the percentage of individuals (No. 5) and marriages (No. 6) they perceived as "happy" or "unhappy". The estimates in part indicated the degree of satisfaction the interviewees perceived in the world about them, and were likely a reflection of their own level of happiness or unhappiness. No association was found with the stage of industrial development, since the most negative outlook appeared for Germans and Colombians, and the most positive estimates were by Americans, particularly adults. In fact, for all countries with student samples, the happiest projections for both individuals and marriages were those of the adults. This finding is somewhat the reverse of the data on psychological well-being in a large-scale United States sample, for which happiness decreased with age (even though health and economic status were more powerful factors).[18]

On the whole, the projections of mobility and satisfaction, for whatever implications they might have in regard to modernism and acceptance of social change, did not give clear support to the hypothesis. The Colombians showed some negative affect in regard to the question of self-initiative and projected happiness, yet along with the Americans they were optimistic about their personal economic future. Also, it would be difficult to assert that students in the four cultures were necessarily more positive than adults on these indices of satisfaction.

The Rationalism-Traditionalism Continuum

Members of culture in the process of modernization are expected to prefer rationalistic over traditionalistic values. As a measure of modernism, rationality is expressed by low kinship-orientation, preference for an urban rather than agrarian life style, belief in the mutability of "human nature," low stratification of life chances, universalistic criteria for mobility and related aspects of the Gesellschaft value structure.[9] In other words, one would anticipate that urban samples from Japan, the Unites States, Western Germany, and, likely, Spain, are more rationalistic than those from Chile and, especially, Colombia.

Generally, as shown in TABLE 3, the hypothesis was supported; however, the two United States' samples proved to be fairly traditionalistic in contrast to the Germans and the Japanese. The most traditionalistic scores were for Chile, followed by Colombia and Spain, the latter being not far from the United States profile. As in previous areas of the questionnaire, but to a lesser extent, the responses appear to reflect national culture values as well as differences between advanced and developing nations. For instance, one encounters the Latin tendency to perceive the family as sacred (No. 1) and the stereotype of an insistence on personal detachment (No. 8) associated with Chileans and certain Western Europeans (in this instance, Germans). Still, the hypothesized difference between advanced and developing societies generally held — that is, if we

TABLE 3

AGREEMENT WITH SELECTED TRADITIONALISM-RATIONALITY STATEMENTS

	American		German		Japanese		Colombian		Chilean Adults (329)	Spanish Adults (98)	Level of Significance	
	Adults (95)	Students (321)	Adults (102)	Students (96)	Adults (139)	Students (112)	Adults (229)	Students (82)			Adults	Students
	Percent of Responses*											
1. The family is a sacred institution divinely established	49	45	51	37	33	9	93	70	89	82	<.02	<.001
2. A child should not be permitted to talk back to his parents	71	50	39	11	22	9	77	46	73	66	<.02	<.001
3. The city is not an agreeable place; one can only have friends among his own people	14	19	17	5	22	12	46	27	47	42	<.05	<.05
4. Human nature being what it is, there will always be wars and conflict	84	74	65	55	44	39	74	65	71	71	<.02	<.02
5. The most important thing a child can learn is to obey his parents	70	54	56	18	37	20	50	15	87	47	<.05	<.01

Item												
6. The best way of understanding what is going on in the world today is to listen today and give attention to our national leaders	34	24	23	3	19	8	49	15	50	31	<.05	<.001
7. Most politicians are primarily devoted to the public good, and only secondarily are concerned with getting elected	23	8	42	27	10	3	16	6	28	30	<.02	<.01
8. We can only have confidence in those we know well	38	37	55	68	48	46	68	60	82	59	<.05	N.S.
†9. The incomes of certain occupations and professions are too high	33	13	42	29	72	36	55	44	70	72	<.05	<.02
10. The son of a worker has little likelihood of entering of the professions	7	7	17	24	11	10	54	40	64	80	<.01	<.001
11. The family with several children is happier than with none, or one at most	53	42	58	49	26	67	31	19	38	31	<.02	<.01

* Percents are based on first two of a five-point scale: "strongly agree," "agree," "disagree," "undecided" and "strongly disagree."
† With the exception of No. 9, agreement with the item represents a traditional attitude.

disregard the conservative responses of the Americans, notably in the integrity of the family (No. 1), subservience of children (No. 2), deference to authority (No. 6), and inflexibility of human nature (No. 4 — the citizens of a nation that has been involved in three major conflicts during the quarter of a century preceding the interviews might well think of wars as inevitable!). In fact, in most items the United States sample was closer to the traditionalistic stance of the Latins, as compared to the rationalistic values of the Germans and the Japanese.

The difference between the two generations was striking. In only four items (Nos. 1, 4, 8, 10) was the difference between students and adults not significant statistically, and then for at most only two of the four countries. (Ambiguity of these items may be the explanation for their inability to yield significant difference.) The explanation for the generational difference lies in the gap in educational level, differential receptivity to change, peer reinforcement of scepticism toward the status quo, and the cultivated awareness of the need for altering the society. Yet these factors seemed to have less impact for the American student sample.

In summary, the data supported the hypothesized relationship between nationalism and socioeconomic development. The strongest expression of rationalism was in connection with political leadership. With the exception of the Chilean and Colombian adults there was a rejection of national leaders (Nos. 6 and 7). However, with regard to the honesty of politicians (No. 7), the Germans were the most traditionalistic, possibly because corruption was less evident in that country than in others. In respect to stratification of life chances (Nos. 9 and 10), Chile and Spain were less rationalistic than was Colombia, but in these two items the American sample joined the others in assuming a rationalistic attitude.

CONCLUSIONS

The present article is focused on three aspects of orientation to change (social participation, indices of mobility and satisfaction, and given items in the rationality-traditionalism scale), as indicated in three industrial democracies (Japan, United States, and Western Germany) and three countries in various stages of development (Colombia, Chile, and as the most developed, Spain). In fact, since the Spanish sample was from Barcelona, the investigator has placed the country with the developed ledger. Besides offering cross-national comparisons, the data also reflect generational differences except for Chile and Spain, for which only adult samples were surveyed.

In regard to the central hypotheses, the following conclusions can be drawn:

1. Respondents in the advanced societies tended to prefer friends to kin and had wider social involvements. Various items also showed a more interpersonal communication and greater exposure to mass media.
2. The hypothesis regarding mobility aspirations and satisfaction with the status quo was only minimally supported. Even though there were statistically significant differences between the national samples, there was no consistent relation between socioeconomic development of the nation and the respondent's tendency to feel optimistic about the present or the future.
3. The clearest differentiation between advanced and developing societies was shown in the responses to the modernism or rationality items, but there was some discrepancy between cultural needs and the degree of social development. As illustration of this, the American stood close to the Latin samples in traditionalism scores.

Concerning the adult and student samples, the students displayed considerably more social participation, but they did not exhibit a clear difference from the adults in the measures of mobility. However, with very few exceptions the students were more rationalistic than the adults on the modernism scale. Again, the German and Japanese students assumed less traditionalism than did the Americans, not surprising in view of the more militant outlook of students in Europe and Asia. Moreover, the American students were partly from private institutions representing fairly conservative student bodies. The traditionalism of the Colombian students, although as in all samples more rationalistic than their adult counterparts, seems surprising, but it must be recalled that only a minority of students has been directly involved in the sociopolitical movements at most Latin American universities.

The factor of social class has largely been ignored in the discussion since I have analyzed it in previous publications.[1,2] However, class differences generally supported the hypotheses concerning friendship, mobility aspirations, and in the rationality-traditionalism scale in all six nations. Only a minority of the items proved to be statistically significant between the middle and lower class as for Americans and Germans. For instance, in only three of the eleven items of the modernism scale did the difference fail to reach the .05 level in the Colombian sample.

A few qualifications should be made in interpreting the findings. First of all, it may be asked why, for instance, the Germans were so pessimistic in their responses as compared to the optimistic or positive approach of the Americans. This negative outlook seems all the more surprising in view of the selectivity in the German sample — nearly 50% having rejected the interview. In reality, neither the German nor the American sample was demographically typical of its nation, and certainly each was different from the other. The Germans were from a city of over a million population, the third largest city in Germany. On the other hand, the American sample was from an urban area of a half million on the edge of a megalapolis. Nearly a third of the American respondents were migrants from smaller and quite traditional towns. (Both the German and the American samples represented the smallest cities tapped in the survey.) Also, the American student sample had a lower sex ratio than did the German. More important, the Americans, both student and adult, had a much higher rate of religious attendance — actually comparable to that of the Spanish women — whereas the Germans reported very infrequent religious attendance.

Another factor to be considered in interpreting the German and the Japanese responses is the critical questioning of their institutions as a result of the national upheaval following their defeat in World War II. Presumably in the German sample the consent to be interviewed may be interpreted as a willingness to assess social problems critically. Consequently, it would be idle to pretend that the responses are necessarily representative of the people as a whole.

Where are the implications of these findings? With only partial confirmation for the first hypothesis regarding socialization, at most a marginal tenability for the hypothesis on future goals, and strong support for the hypothesis on rationalism-traditionalism, what conclusions are to be drawn? In answering this question, it is appropriate to note that we have worked with only small samples from three heavily industrialized nations, and with three quite differently developed Latin nations. In other words, only a fraction of the cultural complex in the third world has been examined. Despite these difficulties, the data are in agreement with the viewpoint that social settings and institutions have functional value for the individual, namely, changing his or her outlook from rigid traditionalist notions to a more sophisticated perspective. Interaction with a wider portion of fellow citizens, exposure to the mass media, the experience of complex organizations like the factory, and most important, the channel of communication and mobility offered by the school, are critical variables.

In the broad theme of modernization, there remain several problems, mostly beyond the scope of this analysis. Yet central among these is whether exposing the individual to the industrial and urban social order may be a means of focusing and crystallizing discontent to the point of almost complete negativism toward the future. The rural person is not confronted with the same degree of anxiety-provoking stimuli. The end result may be that the city dweller reacts to the prospect of change with more fear than desire. (This factor may well have complicated our second cluster of hypotheses.)

We are not asking whether, as Inkeles puts it, modernism is necessarily good or bad. Rather, in a modest way the inquiry has posed the question as to what factors may be associated with the process of modernization. However limited our findings, they would be in harmony with the following characterization of modern man:

> He is an informed participant citizen; he has a marked sense of personal efficacy; he is highly independent and autonomous in his relations to traditional sources of influence, especially when he is making basic decisions about how to conduct his personal affairs; and he is ready for new experiences and ideas, that is, he is relatively open-minded and cognitively flexible.[11]

ACKNOWLEDGMENTS

I wish to thank the Research Institute of Lehigh University for its assistance in this project. Similarly I am grateful to the Fulbright Commission and the staff of sociology institutes of the Catholic University of Chile, the National University of Colombia, the University of Barcelona, the University of Munich, and the University of Tokyo. Among the many individuals to whom I am indebted are Salustino del Campo, Gabriel Gyarmati, Horst Holzer, William Newman, and Takoko Sodei.

REFERENCES

1. WILLIAMSON, R. C. 1968. Social class and orientation to changes: Some relevant variables in a Bogotá sample. Soc. Forces. 46: 317–328.
2. WILLIAMSON, R. C. 1972. Social class, mobility, and modernism: Chileans and social change. Sociol. Soc. Res. 56: 149–163.
3. WILLIAMSON, R. C. 1970. Modernism and related attitudes: An international comparison among university students. Intern. J. Comp. Sociol. 11: 130–145.
4. VAN DEN BERGHE, P. 1973. A structural-functional approach to modernization. In Perspectives on social change. R. H. Lauer, Ed.: 65. Allyn and Bacon. Boston, Mass.
5. KELMAN, H. C. & D. P. WARWICK. 1973. Bridging micro and macro approaches to social change: A social-psychological perspective. In Processes and Phenomena of Social Change. G. Zaltman, Ed.: 13–60. John Wiley. New York, N.Y.
6. WILLIAMSON, R. C. 1962. Some variables of middle and lower class in two central American cities. Soc. Forces. 41: 196–207.
7. WILLIAMSON, R. C 1963. Some factors in urbanism in a quasi-rural setting: San Salvador and San José. Sociol. Soc. Res. 47: 187–200.

8. LERNER, D. 1958. The Passing of Traditional Society. Free Press. New York, N.Y.
9. KAHL, J. A. 1968. The Measurement of Modernism. University of Texas Press. Austin, Texas.
10. INKELES, A. 1969. Making men modern: On the causes and consequences of individual change in six developing countries. Am. J. Sociol. 75: 208–225.
11. INKELES, A. & D. H. SMITH, 1974. Becoming Modern: Individual Change in Six Developing Countries. Harvard University Press. Cambridge, Mass.
12. ISHIDA, T. 1971. Japanese Society. Random House, New York, N.Y.
13. TSURUMI, K. 1970. Social Change and the Individual: Japan Before and After Defeat in World War II. Princeton University Press. Princeton, N.J.
14. WILLIAMS, R. M. 1970. American Society: A Sociological Interpretation. 3rd ed. Alfred A. Knopf. New York, N.Y.
15. SMITH, T. L. 1950. Observations on the middle classes in Colombia. *In* Materiales para el Estudio de la Clase Media en la América Latina. T. R. Crevanna, Ed. Panamerican Union. Washington, D.C.
16. LIPSET, S. M. 1967. University students and politics in underdeveloped countries. *In* Student Politics. S. M. Lipset, Ed. Basic Books. New York. N.Y.
17. WILLIAMSON, R. C. 1962. El Estudiante Colombiano y Sus Actitudes. Monografías Sociológicas, No. 13. Facultad de Sociología, Universidad Nacional de Colombia, Bogotá.
18. BRADBURN, N. M. 1969. The Structure of Psychological Well-Being: 41–54. Aldine Publishing Co., Chicago, Ill.

MODERNIZATION-RELEVANT VALUES AND ACHIEVEMENT OF NATIVE AND RURAL POPULATIONS ASSESSED WITHIN TRADITIONAL AND MODERN ENVIRONMENTS*

Pauline A. Jones

Institute for Research in Human Abilities
Memorial University of Newfoundland
St. John's, Newfoundland, Canada

The analysis of "economic development," or modernization, has become an important concern for contemporary social and behavioral scientists. Most researchers investigating the effects of psychological variables involved in modernization have been primarily concerned with the role of attitudes and values. Inkeles and Smith[1] endeavored to examine whether the transition in developing countries (Argentina, Chile, Israel, East Pakistan, India, and Nigeria) from village to city or from farm to factory and the subsequent modernizing experiences are harmful to mental health. They concluded that failure to become integrated in an urban industrial setting may generate "psychic strain." Kahl,[2] in studies in Brazil and Mexico and limited studies in the United States, found that education and socioeconomic status are the best predictors of modernism, and that modernism in values can be used as a predictor of educational aspirations and accomplishments. While, as Kahl and Inkeles and Smith suggest, variables such as amount of education or urban factory experience modernize an individual's attitudes and values, a wider range of independent variables were found to be relevant in Dawson's studies.

Dawson[3] proposes a traditional-modern (T-M) consistency theory of attitude change, where conflicting traditional-modern cognitions are seen as tension arousing. His model includes the following independent variables: (a) ecology and related subsistence economy, (b) nature of traditional socialization, (c) the degree of stratification of traditional authority systems, and (d) nature and extent of modern contact. The effects of these independent variables are then considered in terms of the following psychological dependent variables: (a) traditional-modern attitude change, (b) tolerance for cognitive inconsistency in the belief system, and (c) achievement motivation. Following Barry, Child, and Bacon,[4] Dawson notes that ecological systems have adaptive socialization processes, and also vary according to the type of formal authority system. These two variables interact to give certain cultural groups more tolerance for cognitive inconsistency and thus less susceptibility to modern attitude change. Thus in hunting and fishing societies where formal authority systems have been traditionally absent (as with the Eskimo), individuals will experience difficulty in internalizing the values of unfamiliar, modern authority systems and related attitudes. Individuals socialized in such relatively permissive societies, where independence is encouraged, would be more tolerant of immediate inconsistencies between conflicting traditional and modern cognitive elements in their belief system, and would therefore not be as vulnerable to pressures to change in a modern direction. By contrast, individuals exposed to severe socialization tend to develop more rigid conforming values; they may be

* This research was supported by Canada Council Research Grant S74-1101.

intolerant of ambiguity and therefore less able to accept inconsistencies between conflicting traditional and modern cognitions in their belief system. These individuals would be motivated to reduce the ambiguity by developing semitraditional-semimodern compromise attitudes.

It is noted, somewhat parenthetically, that Dawson includes the field dependence-independence variable in his consistency theory of attitude change, with field dependency being linked, as expected, to stress for conformity or harsh socialization, as is the case for greater susceptibility to attitude change and potential for economic development. It appears to the present writer that if potential for economic development is viewed in a broad sense as including not only motivational adaptability but also aptitude for educational achievement, field dependency will not necessarily be a positive predictor. On the contrary, field independence, relating as it does to overall analytical and spatial ability, would appear to positively predict greater achievement in several educational fields. One of the aims of the reported research, consequently, was a clarification of the interrelationships among field dependency, achievement motivation, and susceptibility to traditional-modern attitude change as predictor variables of potential for achievement under modernizing conditions.

In terms of assessing the significance of the reported research, it might be stressed that studies of modernization have in general operated at the level of assessing the dependent variables of susceptibility to modern attitude change and modernization-relevant values, without then using such variables as direct predictors of achievement for individuals acting under conditions of modernization. Nevertheless, the overriding postulate of most modernization theories is that modernism in values or modernization-relevant values are, as Dawson points out, indicators of potential for economic development, and as such should be predictive of achievement under conditions of increasing modernization. It is true that evidence from studies reviewed can be taken as indirect validation of this assumption. Thus Tanaka[5] computed an index of familiarity with modernization-relevant values and made comparisons across communities varying in level of economic development. Similarly Dawson's model has been confirmed in terms of achievement motivation studies — for example, in Australia[6] and in Japan[3] — to the effect that Ss with more susceptibility to modern attitude change had higher achievement motivation.

The reported research at one level aimed to test the validity of Dawson's T-M model for potential attitude change by assessing the traditional and modern values as compared between high school students who have been exposed to contrasting socialization practices. Communities sampled included small, rather homogeneous fishing communities with more formal authority systems, such that the effect of the ecological system could be related first of all to socialization practices, and both to susceptibility to attitude change. Modernism in values would be related to achievement motivation, to field dependency, and also to educational achievement. In addition to measuring T-M attitudes within rural communities, high school students from selected towns and cities of the Province of Newfoundland and Labrador were also sampled. The inclusion of these students permitted a comparison of modernism in values across urban and rural, or more versus less developed, communities, as has been the object of studies by Kahl[2] and Tanaka.[5]

A second phase of the reported research examines modern attitude change and traditional-modern attitude conflict experienced by students from rural communities when they move to larger, more urban centers to attend vocational schools, trade colleges, or universities. The amount of attitude change and attitude conflict is in turn related to the measure of susceptibility to attitude change as determined for students at this first stage, and also to the independent variables, socialization, and ecological system. Modern attitude change and T-M attitude conflict are also related to achievement level attained in vocational school. Few, if any, modernization studies have involved high school students undergoing moves to other learning situations involving increased modern contact. It is worth stressing, therefore, the potential value of the second phase of the reported research, not only in providing direct validation data for existing theories of modernization, but for studying the mobility process at a point that is undoubtedly basic to industrialization.

RESEARCH DESIGN

Communities within the Province of Newfoundland and Labrador offer considerable ecological and cultural contrast. Communities on the Labrador south coast and, to a lesser extent, on the Newfoundland south coast are extremely isolated. These communities are small, homogeneous, and rather self-sufficient. Cut off except by sea from all but the nearest coves, the community revolves around fishing. The smaller of these fishing communities, particularly on the Labrador coast, have no medical services and few of the amenities of modern municipal life. Schools often have only two or three rooms; most of the communities on the Labrador coast have no broadcast television, and newspapers, when available, are usually several days late. Areas of Newfoundland have been classified on a 10-point peasant-urban continuum, with assessment being based on seven variables, including degree of industrialization, strength of transportation link, and TV coverage. The southern Newfoundland and coastal Labrador fishing communities occupy the most extreme position at the peasant end, and stand in sharp contrast with the city of St. John's (population 120,000), which occupies the extreme urban, industrialized position.

Besides sampling from fishing communities of Newfoundland and Labrador, students from other small, isolated communities were studied. It was expected that in general these communities would stress social conformity, primarily in regard to family and religious authority. Many of these communities are highly homogeneous with respect to religion, with schools in certain of them being operated by either the Roman Catholic or the Pentecostal Religious Board. In many of these rural communities the merchants, clergy, and teachers are the local power structure, each in their own sphere generally supreme.

The sampling procedure followed in the reported study was determined mainly by the overall objective: namely, to study, during a second phase of the research, the T-M attitude conflict and related achievement of students who move from small, traditional communities to attend vocational or trade schools or universities in larger centers. Thus students from small, traditional communities were sampled, both those who indicated that they would be moving to a larger center to attend a postsecondary educational institution during the current year and, for control purposes, students who would not be moving. Similarly Grade XI students from larger towns and urban areas having postsecondary educational institutions were sampled. The academic achievement and modernism in values of incoming students are compared with those of students attending postsecondary school in their home towns. By comparing the attitude change of incoming students against that of resident students, sources of the change may more clearly be traced to increase in modern contact and not to other variables. One of the questions under investigation in a second phase of the reported research is whether or not students with more susceptibility to attitude change will, subsequent to increased modern contact, show greater modernism in values and less T-M attitude conflict.

During the second half of the 1974–75 academic year the first phase of the present research was completed, and preliminary findings from this phase will be discussed in this paper. The second phase of the research has just commenced, as students who completed Grade XI during 1974–75 have now either entered various postsecondary institutions elsewhere or have remained in their home towns to work or gain further schooling. The second phase of the research will address parameters of Dawson's model relating to traditional-modern attitude change and the validity of categories of susceptibility to attitude change based on socialization and ecological variation. Data collected during the first year of this research are of value, as this paper will suggest, in drawing tentative conclusions concerning relationships between the independent variables of Dawson's model. They permit as well an assessment of the interrelationships of various operational definitions of modernism and provide an indication of the predictive validity of these measures.

During the first phase of the reported research approximately 1100 Grade XI students were tested. Data entering into this report were derived from a subsample of this number – the 641 students for whom we had complete data across the large number of measures administered. (The process of obtaining further or missing data from other students was in progress at the time when analyses for this paper were begun.) The present report should be viewed as preliminary also in the sense that all available measures have not entered into the analysis simply because the time since completion of data collection has been too short to permit complete coding and tabulation of the data. It will be obvious, therefore, that subsequent reports of findings relative to questions raised in this paper may modify or extend any tentative conclusions now drawn. This will be particularly true of reports to be made at the end of the second phase of this research, now in progress.

The 641 students of the present sample during 1974–75 attended Grade XI in one of 43 communities in the Province of Newfoundland and Labrador. Of these, 20 were small, traditional communities of population less than 500. An additional 11 communities had populations less than 1000. The majority of these 31 communities were isolated either in having no road links with other communities, as in coastal Labrador or parts of southern Newfoundland, or in being separated from the nearest community by a number of miles of gravel road. In 25 percent of all communities, students attended an all-grades school. Students of the remaining 12 communities lived in small towns, ranging in size from 1000 to 10,000, or in the university cities of Corner Brook and St. John's, with populations of 25,000 and 120,000 respectively. Certain of the small, isolated communities, such as Conche on the northern Newfoundland coast and Forteau on the southern Labrador coast, were homogeneous fishing communities. Others, such as Roddickton and Campbellton, were primarily logging communities.

INSTRUMENTATION

Several measures of traditional-modern attitudes were administered. Following the method used by Dawson,[6] a questionnaire was developed which consisted of four items for each of 14 concepts, ranging from traditional through semitraditional and semimodern to modern. The items of the scale were modifications of certain items from Dawson's T-M scales and others from an attitudinal modernity scale developed by Smith and Inkeles.[7] Subjects responded to concept items using one of the following: Agree strongly, Agree, Not sure, Disagree, and Disagree strongly. The T-M questionnaire was scored across the 14 traditional items, across the 14 semitraditional items, the 14 semimodern, and the 14 modern items. An additional score was obtained for each subject by subtracting the traditional subscale score from the modern subscale score, to give a Range of Variation score (RV). T-M unresolved attitudinal conflict was measured by classifying the individual's responses according to the four item groups. A subject was considered to be in attitudinal conflict when his responses to the attitude statements were internally inconsistent (e.g., agreeing with both the traditional and modern statements for the same concept).

A second scale consisting of 22 T-M item pairs was developed from modifications of items used in a scale of modernism constructed by Kahl.[2] In addition, 20 T-M item pairs from Guthrie's[8] Traditional-Modern Schedule I were administered and referred to as T-M scale three. Both the scale constructed from Kahl and the Guthrie 40-item scale utilized the same response format as that used in the Dawson-type scale. Each of the former two T-M questionnaires was scored across the traditional items and across the modern items. In each case an RV score and a T-M attitudinal conflict score were derived in the manner used with the first, Dawson-type questionnaire.

Guthrie's 28-item Traditional-Modern Schedule II was also administered. The test battery also included two of the 10-item scales used by Doob[9] in measuring modernism. These scales are: (1) Temporal orientation — a future rather than a past or present emphasis; (2) Confidence and optimism — a feeling that life is pleasant and that people control their own destinies. In addition, cultural attitudes held toward modernization-relevant values — Work, Leisure, and Education — as assessed by Tanaka[5] through use of the semantic differential, were measured.

Two measures of socialization practices were used. Each student was asked to rate both mother and father on a three-point scale of strictness of disciplining. Additionally, the mother of each student was given items from a questionnaire developed by Witkin and colleagues to classify mother-child interactions as fostering or interfering with the development of field independence.

The Group Embedded Figures Test was used as a measure of field dependence-independence. The grades that the Grade XI students received on the Newfoundland and Labrador Department of Education Provincial Examinations are available as achievement measures. As part of the preliminary findings reported in this paper, only two measures are included. These are the score received on the Provincial English Examination and the score assigned by the school in the area of English achievement.

RESULTS AND DISCUSSION

While it is the author's intention to perform item and factor analysis on the items of the various T-M scales used in this research, for the present report several points can be made from an examination of the intercorrelations of these scales, as presented in TABLE 1. As may be seen from an examination of the small boxes along the diagonal, similar measures derived across different scales tend to interrelate more significantly with each other than they do with other T-M indices. Admittedly the correlation coefficients, although significant, are not large. Thus the three traditional scales interrelate at approximately the .45 level. It might also be noted that both the Guthrie and Doob modernism scores correlate significantly and negatively with each of the three traditional scores. Similarly the three modern scores from the T-M scales are significantly intercorrelated, as are the three RV scores. It is of interest to point out that while the Guthrie and Doob modernism scales are not related with the T-M modernism scores, they are related to T-M range of variation. Thus the distance of a modernism score from a traditional score is more predictive of modernism on the Guthrie and Doob scales. T-M attitudinal conflict scores are significantly interrelated.

It can also be noted that persons with more traditional scores tended to have more unresolved T-M attitudinal conflict, as suggested by the correlations of .19 and .28 between traditional and conflict scores on the first two T-M scales respectively. Similarly a higher modern score on the third T-M scale was inversely related to T-M conflict as measured by this scale ($r = -.26$). Both the Guthrie and Doob scales tended to relate significantly with the modernization-relevant values of Work and Education. It might also be noted that the students' evaluations of the three concepts Work, Leisure, and Education were significantly interrelated. (The score used in this analysis was then given on a seven-point Good-Bad evaluation dimension.) One also notes a tendency for those with higher traditional scores on each of the three T-M scales to evaluate Education less highly.

It is the author's intention prior to the further assessment of T-M attitudes during the current phase of this research to thoroughly examine the intercorrelations of the items of the various T-M scales administered during phase I. It is hoped that from the large number of items available a more valid measure of modernism, judged by the criterion of its ability to predict achievement in modern educational settings, will be constructed. Further analysis of scores available for the 20 concepts of the two T-M scales constructed by the author will be carried out.

The concepts of these scales and those assessed by scales of Guthrie, Doob, and Tanaka require analysis for an assay of their potency as exemplars of modernization-relevant values. There perhaps needs to be a distinction between concepts that are important in reflecting traditional culture versus, perhaps, Western culture, and those concepts that can be said to be modernization-relevant in the sense of promoting economic development and the further advancement of industrialization. The holding traditional as against Western values may be more or less conducive to the adoption of modernization-relevant values; nevertheless, conceptually the distinction would appear to be useful.

In order to assess parameters of Dawson's model relating ecological and authority systems to T-M attitude change, a subsample (N = 239) of the total 641 students was selected so as to permit comparisons across groups varying in occupation and religion. Students were placed in one of four groups by occupation of the father. Accordingly one group (N = 80) consisted of students whose fathers were fishermen; another, carpenters (N = 37); a third, loggers or pasture workers (N = 20); and a fourth, of students whose fathers were engaged in an occupation other than the above three, but one that could be equated with

TABLE 1
INTERCORRELATIONS OF TRADITIONAL-MODERN SCALES (SAMPLE SIZE = 641)

	1. T_1	2. T_2	3. T_3	4. M_1	5. M_2	6. M_3	7. RV_1	8. RV_2	9. RV_3	10. c_1	11. c_2	12. c_3	13. Guthrie	14. Doob	15. T-W	16. T-L
1. Trad$_1$																
2. Trad$_2$	.48															
3. Trad$_3$ (Guthrie)	.47	.46														
4. Mod$_1$	-.11	.03	.01													
5. Mod$_2$	.24	.01	.22	.28												
6. Mod$_3$ (Guthrie)	.08	.04	.16	.30	.36											
7. RV$_1$	-.76	-.31	-.32	.72	.01	.14										
8. RV$_2$	-.17	-.67	-.18	.17	.67	.21	.22									
9. RV$_3$ (Guthrie)	-.31	-.33	-.69	.20	.08	.59	.34	.29								
10. T-M c_1	.19	.10	.04	.16	.15	.10	-.02	.02	.04							
11. T-M c_2	.16	.28	.13	-.01	.04	.01	-.12	-.19	-.08	.27						
12. T-M c_3	-.07	.00	-.07	.05	-.02	-.26	.08	-.01	-.12	.16	.29					
13. Guthrie	-.24	-.26	-.27	.20	.05	.11	.30	.22	.29	.01	-.06	.01				
14. Doob	-.24	-.38	-.26	.05	-.06	.02	.20	.20	.21	.00	-.14	-.04	.18			
15. T-W	-.07	-.06	-.07	.06	.05	.09	.09	.07	.12	.02	.04	-.03	.13	.17		
16. T-L	-.13	-.05	-.04	-.01	-.05	.01	.09	.00	.03	-.05	.01	.07	.08	.12	.31	
17. T-E	-.13	-.11	-.12	.07	.05	.13	.14	.09	.18	-.04	.00	.03	.21	.19	.49	.37

them in terms of socioeconomic level. Occupations represented in this fourth group (N = 102) included truck driver, laborer, cook, clerk, and janitor. The total of 239 students came from communities of less than 2500, and in most cases less than 1000. It would therefore be accurate to say that the four occupational groupings were at an equivalent and very low socioeconomic level and that cultural stimulus of the community was equivalent for the groups.

Main interest lay in comparing the fishing group with the "other occupation" category, the categories of carpenter and logger being placed in the middle. While speculative, it was postulated that carpenters are somewhat like fishermen in that they are thought to have developed carpentry skills through boat building, and perhaps earlier had been fishermen themselves. It was further speculated that the forestry occupation of logging should be considered as somewhat to the right on a fishing-agricultural continuum.

The F ratios obtained by applying one-way analyses of variance across these four groups are shown in TABLE 2. Interest lay in determining whether the sons of fishermen were in fact more tolerant of T-M attitudinal conflict, as Dawson's model would suggest, and therefore not as vulnerable to change in a modern direction. As shown by the F ratios, there were no significant differences in either RV scores or conflict scores on any of the three T-M attitudinal scales, nor in modernism scores derived from the Guthrie and Doob scales. The significant F ratio on the evaluative rating for education showed that sons of carpenters rated education as of somewhat less value. This, however, would seem to be of no particular theoretical relevance.

The fact that in all T-M and modernism measures the sons of fishermen were no different than other occupational groupings would seem to bring into question the validity of a hypothesis stating that pressures of the fishing ecology have differential value in making individuals less susceptible to change. Dawson's model states that ecological systems such as found in fishing societies produce adaptive socialization processes, when such systems are at the level of subsistence economy. While the groups studied in the present research were

TABLE 2

INDEPENDENCE OF MODERNISM MEASURES FROM
OCCUPATIONAL AND RELIGIOUS CATEGORIES
(SAMPLE SIZE = 239)

Modernism Index	F Value (Occupation)	t Value (Religion)
RV_1	1.62	−.39
T-M c_1	.76	.37
RV_2	.69	−.26
T-M c_2	.49	.43
RV_3 (Guthrie)	.22	−.38
T-M c_3 (Guthrie)	.38	1.70
Guthrie	.14	.30
Doob	.32	−3.13*
T-W	1.37	−.65
T-E	3.07*	.47
T-L	1.66	.10

* $p < .01$.

undoubtedly not at the extremely low economic level of groups such as Dawson's Aboriginal samples, they nevertheless were very far down. The psychological significance of the fishing way of life may be reflected in the fact that the fathers had been fishermen all their lives, and in most if not all cases were the descendants of families who adopted fishing in the early 1500's, when Newfoundland was first settled. Research previously reported by the author[10] failed as well to find any support for the claim that pressures of the fishing ecology lead to adaptive socialization processes. In fact it was reported that the sample (of three groups of Grade VI boys who were the sons of fishermen) most characteristic of the traditional fishing society had socialization practices less conducive to the development of independence. The combined results of these two studies, then, offer convincing evidence against which to assess the generalizability of the ecological pressure hypothesis.

The same 239 students whose scores were examined in the above analysis were also dichotomized by religion of the school they attended. Thus one group (N = 64) consisted of students who attended schools operated by either the Roman Catholic or Pentecostal Religious Board. This meant as well that in most cases the communities in which they lived would be homogeneously of the same religion, and the family also of that religion. Adherence to the authority of the church would be strong in these communities. On the assumption that exposure to such an authority system would make them more susceptible to modern attitude change, these students were compared with students who attended an integrated school (N = 175). Across these two groups occupational level and size of community were held constant. The t values of TABLE 2 are, again, essentially nonsignificant – giving little support to a hypothesis linking exposure to formal authority systems with susceptibility to attitude change (as realized in higher RV scores and lower conflict scores). The one scale showing a significant t ratio did support the prediction that the Roman Catholic and Pentecostal students would show higher modernism scores, and the near-significant t ratio for the Guthrie T-M conflict scale showed these students as having less conflict. It might be noted that the students of the Roman Catholic and Pentecostal schools tended to rate both their mother and father as being more strict in disciplining (t = 1.42 and 0.92, respectively).

Coefficients of both TABLES 1 and 2 have addressed the question of the construct validity of the various traditional-modern indices used in this research. While the combined information available has not been very supportive, it is not possible to draw any firm conclusions concerning whether these data suggest revision of instrumentation or revision of theory. It is likely that both would be of value, and both will certainly be ongoing processes. To add independent and more positive support for the validity of certain of the traditional-modern attitude measures, TABLE 3 presents their individual correlation coefficients with two measures of academic achievement. (Scores for English achievement are reported simply because this was the one subject all students were required to take.) The data were subjected to a stepwise regression analysis so that it is possible to determine to what extent the T-M measures in combination increase predictability of achievement.

This analysis shows that students' traditional scores on the Dawson-type T-M scale are the most predictive of English achievement as assessed by the school examination. This measure accounts for 9 percent of the variance. By adding the student's evaluation of the Work concept, his modernism score on the Doob scale, and his level of field independence, the predictability rises to 19 percent. Similarly the student's achievement in the Department of Education Provincial English Examination is best predicted by the modernism score on the Doob

TABLE 3

CORRELATIONS OF SELECTED TRADITIONAL-MODERN SCALES
WITH ACHIEVEMENT
(SAMPLE SIZE = 641)

Dependent Variables					
English Ach. A			English Ach. B		
Beta Weight	r		Beta Weight	r	
Trad$_1$	−.21	−.30	Doob	.22	.32
T-W	.18	.22	Trad$_1$	−.20	−.31
EFT	.15	.23	EFT	.18	.27
Doob	.15	.27	Sex	.13	.13
School size	.14	.20	School size	.12	.19
Sex	.13	.12	T-L	.11	.17
R^2	.22			.24	

scale, which accounts for 10 percent of the achievement variance. Taking account of the student's Embedded Figures Test (EFT) score, and his traditional score on the Dawson-type T-M scale, increases this predictability to 16 and 20 percent, respectively.

It might be noted that the other traditional scores also significantly predict achievement. They are not entered in TABLE 3 because they do not add significantly in the presence of T_1. Thus T_2 correlates −.28 and −.27 respectively with the two achievement measures, and T_3 correlates −.19 with each achievement measure. Similarly the evaluation of the Education concept correlates significantly with achievement (.26 and .17, respectively), but is not entered in the regression analysis because of the presence already of the Work concept.

In view of the consistent and significant correlations of traditionalism and achievement, a continuing and exciting phase of this research will be an identification of factors defining students with high traditional values. They apparently are not the students we predicted they would be, namely those from specific ecological and authority systems. Nor were students from small, one- and two-room schools any more traditional in their values than were students from large urban high schools. However, the more traditional students would appear to be ones with, for example, low field independence (T_1, T_2, and T_3 correlated −.13, −.19, and −.11 with the EFT respectively). By working backward in this way we should be able to meaningfully redefine theory − suggesting new dimensions for ecological pressure that may be more relevant in societies at more acculturated levels than the fishing-agriculture dimension would appear to be.

REFERENCES

1. INKELES, A. & D. H. SMITH. 1970. The fate of personal adjustment in moderniz- ation. Int. J. Compar. Sociol. 11: 81−114.
2. KAHL, J. A. 1968. The Measurement of Modernism: A Study of Values in Brazil and Mexico. University of Texas Press. Austin, Texas.

3. DAWSON, J. L. M. 1973. Adjustment problems encountered by individuals in the process of modernization in the resolution of traditional-modern attitudinal conflict. Paper presented at the East-West Culture Learning Institute, University of Hawaii. Honolulu, Hawaii.

4. BARRY, H., I. CHILD & M. BACON. 1959. Relation of child training to subsistence economy. Am. Anthropol. 61: 51–63.

5. TANAKA, Y. 1973. Toward a multi-level, multi-stage model of modernization. Int. J. Psychol. 8 (3): 205–214.

6. DAWSON, J. L. M. 1969. Attitude change and conflict among Australian Aborigines. Aust. J. Psychol. 21 (2): 101–116.

7. SMITH, D. H. & A. INKELES. 1966. The OM scale: A comparative sociopsychological measure of individual modernity. Sociometry 29: 353–377.

8. GUTHRIE, G. M. et al. 1970. The Psychology of Modernization in the Philippines. Manila University Press. Quezon City, Philippines.

9. DOOB, L. W. 1967. Scales for assessing psychological modernization in Africa. Public Opinion Quart. 31: 414–421.

10. JONES, P. A. 1975. Maternal socialization practices and spatial-perceptual abilities in Newfoundland and Labrador. In The Developing Individual in a Changing World. Historical and Cultural Issues. K. F. Riegel and J. A. Meacham, Eds. Vol. 1: 345–352. Mouton. The Hague, The Netherlands.

SPACE, DENSITY, AND CULTURAL CONDITIONING

R. S. Freed

Department of Sociology and Anthropology
Seton Hall University
South Orange, New Jersey 07079

This paper explores two related facets of human behavior: cultural conditioning to space, i.e., the way in which members of a society learn their culture's way of using or accommodating to space; and the relationship of this process to the density and space that specific human populations occupy. Since culture is the continuing adaptive device by which humans accommodate to their environment,[1] this paper raises the question as to whether cultural conditioning regarding the use of space is an adaptive device relative to the density of a population based on change and indirectly controlling the growth of human populations. The micro basis of this question derives from demonstrable data that the human animal selects distance ranges for particular types of interaction.[2] The macro basis of the same question derives from cultural data from prehistory, history, and the present regarding types of human societies, their use of space, and their cultural controls of population density in such space. Related to the micro basis of the use of space is the possibility that these learnings of spatial behavior are patterned, may persist through time, and may or may not be adaptive when change occurs.

The human animal differs from all other animals through the learning process called cultural conditioning. The potential for this learning process is biological, but the process itself is cultural and goes on throughout life, beginning with the socialization and enculturation of the individual, and encompassing any learning brought about through cultural change. These cultural learning processes result in conditioning, which provides a human being with a set of rules and norms for behavior that is context-dependent and almost uniquely human.[3] This learned cultural behavior is, in effect, a cognitive map for a great variety of situations. The map is learned early and well so that the individual considers much of this behavior to be natural; but it is not. It is culturally conditioned.

This cultural map provides the individual with ways to carry out all aspects of the culture, including the use of space. Habits of using space are learned so early that individuals do not realize they have them unless they come in conflict with people who use space otherwise. A well known example of this kind of conflict occurs when a person from the United States works in a Latin American society and finds that the spatial distances in conversations with Latins as compared with Americans differ. The Latin places himself considerably closer to the American than the American finds comfortable, so the American backs up; the Latin then moves closer and eventually the American may find himself backed against a wall.[4]

An example of the changing use of space within our society can be seen in any New York subway. Men customarily sit with their knees spread apart and women until recently, and even now through habit or when wearing skirts, may hold them together. With the advent of pants as an almost universal costume among females, many a male on the subway now looks considerably irritated when a female in pants takes up more than "her allotted room," with her knees spread apart so that the male cannot sit with his knees spread apart. He may feel that she is infringing on his space. In this case, the female has adapted to a change in culture; the male has not. Examples such as these illustrate the minutiae of space usage.

Density implies a number of people within a bounded area. Associated with the concept of density is the concept of crowding, which implies that the population within a specific area has become so dense that the people are in closer proximity than they normally can tolerate. In cases of nonhuman animals, such crowding may result in fights to the death, migration out, or if the animals are confined, the emergence of a despot and pariahs.[5] When crowding occurs or population density is high in animal society, violence may break out, which will tend to decrease the population. Does this apply to human populations? The evidence is not clear.

Alland suggests that irritability, a trait that all animals, including humans, have in common, results in adaptation to environmental problems. The inference is that irritability due to crowding may result in such cultural adaptation as migration, war, restructuring of social and political systems, and the like. Crowding due to density is here defined as infringement on previously learned cultural usages of space. The crowding may result in learning new usages of space. A *caveat* to remember is that what might have been crowding to people who learned an earlier usage of space may not be crowding to people who never experienced the old ways of handling or living in their space.[1]

In the prehistory and history of mankind, population size has gradually escalated, but at the same time human beings have spread over the face of the earth. In so doing, they have learned cultural ways of dealing with the space in which they live. The question, then, is whether they can continue to learn or adapt, despite the increases in population through time. This poses the further question of whether there are or will be absolute limits to population increase for humans.

Demographic evidence from prehistory and history indicates that hominids have exercised cultural controls on natality and mortality to curb fecundity and length of life as adaptations to the space within which they live, and as adaptations to the subsistence techniques that are a part of their cultural heritage. As these subsistence techniques have changed, so too have the cultural controls on natality and mortality and presumably on cultural conditioning with regard to the use of space. Although there are numerous divisions and subdivisions of subsistence techniques, basically three major types are useful in this analysis: nomadic gathering, sedentary agricultural, and modern industrial societies, listed in order of development. Correlated with these three types are different patterns of adaptation to the use of space, which depend on the cultural controls of natality and mortality.

The gathering type consists of hominids who maintain themselves through hunting, fishing, and collecting in small bands over a fairly large space relative to the density of the population. It existed as a sole type for millions of years until the beginnings of sedentism, at which time there were approximately 3 to 5 million people in the world. It still persists in marginal regions of the world today. Certain cultural features are essential to its survival: small bands move through space regularly to find food and other essentials for survival. Mating and/or marriage occurs early, with females usually at or around nubility, and females are impeded from functioning and possibly even surviving in this system if they have more than one child in arms at a time. Thus, births are spaced and on the average a female has no more than one child every 3.5 to 4 years.[6] Control of natality and mortality is through customs such as abortion, infanticide, postpartum sexual taboos for extended periods of time, and abandonment of the aged and disabled under specific circumstances. In this type of society the nuclear family acts as an economic, social, and affective unit, in which parents are responsible for progeny. Chapple provides an example from the Eskimo where "the home ranges needed to provide the caloric intake may be extremely great," but the food supply, which is scarce, must be balanced by restrictions on population growth. These restrictions are abortion, infanticide, and abandonment of the aged and disabled in bad times.[2]

With the advent of agriculture, the second type of society worked out new cultural adjustments to space and especially to the sedentary occupation of space. Great increases in population are correlated with agriculture and sedentism. From the end of the Pleistocene the population increased approximately 160 times to some 800 million people by 1750 A.D. Correlated with sedentism, there were increases in natality because of the value put on children as a potential work force on the land and in mortality because of the greater incidence of diseases in sedentary societies. In some societies, if not all, curbs were probably put on birth that were a part of the culture, but by and large agriculturists have a greater rate of natality and of population increase than do gatherers, this despite the association of land scarcity in due time with all agricultural, settled populations. Correlated with agricultural sedentary societies was an attendant migration across the globe to find further lands to farm. By 1750 A.D. these migrations were contributing to the industrial age and modern urbanization.[6]

The third type of society is correlated with the industrial and medical revolutions and tends in the long run to reduce and curb both natality and mortality. This type of society is similar to the gatherer society with its nuclear family, as compared to joint and extended families among agriculturists. In it the care and raising of each child depends on the parents, who are the major economic and affective unit. The cost of raising a child becomes sufficiently great to cause the overall population in such a type society to aim at barely reproducing itself.[6]

The balance of this paper will apply the micro and macro concepts of cultural conditioning to the use of space by contrasting examples from India and the United States.

Settled agricultural communities have existed in India since at least 4000 B.C. in a region of the subcontinent that today belongs to Pakistan. These communities became urbanized and are known as the Harappan civilization. This civilization worked out an accommodation to the increasing density of population within its urban centers that appears to have persisted to some degree to the present day. Archaeological reconstructions indicate that this accommodation took a pattern of spatial hierarchy, segregation, and centralized authority. It is possible that this mode of life was the adaptive means by which previously rural people were able to space themselves, i.e., live together in an increasingly dense population and at the same time live apart in privacy as they had in smaller communities. In this sense it is possible to compare this adaptation to the animal adaptations to crowding where despots and pariahs arise.

This Harappan civilization dates from approximately 2500 to 1500 B.C. It covered a territory of nearly half a million square miles. The major cities of the area show uniform and similar planned use of space. Each city was laid out on a grid plan with the main streets oriented to the cardinal points of the compass. Side streets or lanes intersected them. Dwellings had blank walls facing the street with a single door opening inward to a courtyard where family members might be in the open air, but with privacy, and where cattle were kept. This arrangement of courtyard and living quarters behind a blank wall allowed for secusion of the family from the city. A staircase usually led to the roof, where the inhabitants perhaps slept in hot weather. Some houses had a second storey. Houses of the same type and size were arranged in sections of the city and were similar to modern row houses in their standardization. The smaller row houses were arranged around sources of livelihood such as a granary or pottery kiln. Merchants and possibly persons of importance had larger residences in wealthier quarters. The sections and sizes of the residences reflected compartmentalization by rank, wealth, and occupation. This settlement pattern may reflect the accommodation of an earlier way of life to an urban way of life that permitted the perpetuation of separate communities related through ties of real or fictive kinship.

The Harappan civilization expanded in its approximately one thousand years of existence. The major cities built and rebuilt within the city walls. The cities were built on major rivers that seasonally flooded, and the remains reflect this flooding. The floods became progressively severe. All building was of clay bricks with the same dimensions, which were fired with wood. No doubt the expanding population, the need for more food, and the depletion of the forests contributed to exhaustion of the resources. Today a part of this region is desert country, where once it was heavily forested, and most of the agriculture depends on irrigation.

Throughout the thousand years of its existence, the Harappan culture clung to its form of settlement pattern even though at the end the cities showed crowding. Houses were eventually subdivided into apartments, a fate similar to that of old brownstones and apartments in the New York City of today. The demise of the Harappan civilization has variously been attributed to invading Indo Aryans, flooding, depletion of resources, and disease, but more probably it was due to a combination of factors brought on by overcrowding and overuse of resources. When the people migrated southward, they carried what they had learned of their culture, including the use of living space in hierarichal and segregated fashion.[7,8]

A modern, small-scale example of this persistent pattern of spatial accommodation is the village of Shanti Nagar, located about eleven miles to the northwest of the City of Delhi. It is an agricultural village about 600 years old, had a population of 799 people at the time of study, and is in the process of becoming urbanized since about half of its adult males have had urban experience. The village land reserved for housing is densely inhabited. House sites are crowded against each other so that they share walls both at the side and back of houses. The agricultural land lies around the village and is fragmented by centuries of joint patrilineal inheritance.

In Shanti Nagar, there are thirteen castes, of which two are of the lowest, and three border between upper and lower castes. Position in the caste hierarchy is based on a complex of beliefs and custom, but traditional occupation, whether practiced or not, has served as a fulcrum for divisions. The village settlement pattern reflects the hierarchy of castes. Those castes that are lowest form a compact settlement on the low-status side of the village; the rest fit in between or are on the high-status side of the village. Similarly, those of the castes that have the most land and highest status live on the high-status side and have the best houses and houses sites. Thus, the spatial arrangements reflect the social structure, while enforcing it by segregating caste community from caste community, so that the activities of families and lineages of each caste can be carried out in considerable privacy from the observation and interference of members of other castes.

This patterning of segregated social and spatial relationships reaches into the family in that the activities of males and females are separate and so are their living quarters. Females in India rank lower than males so this segregation is consistent with other hierarchical separations in space. For those who can afford it, one building may be for the women and children; another for the men; and a third for the cattle. Sometimes men, women, and cattle are housed in one building, or there may be different combinations such as men with cattle or women with cattle. No matter what the combinations within a building or in separate buildings, males and females are segregated. When men and women are housed in one building, specific areas are for female activities and others for male. Sections of the dwelling may be partitioned. Males learn that they must give signals by coughing or calling out when they approach the women's section.

This separation of the sexes is carried out to such a degree that the only time that husband and wife regularly sleep together is when they are first married. As soon as a young wife has had a child, she thereafter sleeps in the women's section with her child. This arrangement continues in perpetuity with the wife and husband having coitus only when he calls her and at a time and place when they may have privacy. The smaller the household and the larger the number of people within it, the greater the problems of sexual cohabitation; but then the couple may resort to using another kind of space — the fields.

These two features of the use of space — hierarchical and segregative — influence numerous activities and pervade the very manner in which a male or female walks, talks, sits, and lies down. The one word which is most descriptive of these patterned activities is "containment." A child is contained in movement by age ten. Girls by age ten are little women who sit quietly, do not romp or run around, and are careful with whom they play, talk, and walk. Boys show containment in their behavior, but have more freedom to move around and beyond the village.

This system of spatial behavior is upheld by male heads of families and lineages who are authoritarian. Families live side by side with members of their immediate patrilineage, and the adults in this kin group can and do admonish, punish, and report children who do not behave. There is no anonymity. The eyes and ears of the small community, particularly, one's family, lineage, and clan members, are upon one all of the time. The household space which families inhabit is not large. Some houses have one or two rooms; a few of the wealthy houses may have a larger number, perhaps from ten to fifteen, but they may have from ten to twenty members or more. All of the houses on the high-status side of the village have courtyard space, which provides some degree of privacy. Among the low castes, there are no courtyards, but there are compounds that are used jointly with other caste members.

Within each household, there is ranking by sex and age so that the oldest man in the family has the highest position and the best accommodations; the oldest woman has a similar position, but only vis á vis the females in the house. The children rank low by virtue of age, and the females by virtue of sex.[9]

Present-day India has had a steadily increasing population over the centuries, but it was checked by diseases, famines, infanticides, wars, and other cultural customs. The British outlawed infanticide and since the medical revolution, one of the major population controls — disease — has been reduced. Although India is industrializing, there is some question as to whether the population as a whole can or will make the "demographic transition," i.e., change their cultural adaptations to the type of family and use of space correlated with western industrialized countries. By the standards of the west, the population of India might be considered to have gone beyond its limits in exhaustion of resources or ratio of resources to people. But the same might be said about the Harappan civilization and its pattern of spatial relationships, which still appear to exist in Shanti Nagar, and in somewhat modified form in the modern city of Chandigarh, the capital of the Punjab.

The city of Chandigarh was planned by a number of experts, including the American, Albert Mayer, and the famous French architect, LeCorbusier. The only people who were not consulted on these spatial living arrangements were the inhabitants, primarily educated and somewhat modern government workers.

The city is designed on a grid plan with sectors devoted to specific functions: The government buildings are one sector; there are special sectors for industry, and for the university; but the most typical sectors are for housing, schools, and a shopping center. Each sector was to serve a different purpose, but to the people who live in this city this kind of division means separation from kin and friends. It also means that there are long distances between sections and that the planners did not take into consideration the fact that the inhabitants and workers might have preferred planning for other activities. For example, in the government section, there was no allowance, perhaps intentionally, for coffee shops for the workers.

It is in the housing that the conflict between western and Indian ideas of household space is most apparent. On first sight, it would seem that the living rooms are used for bedrooms and the stoves, for storing food; and the cooking is carried out on the floor. Why are these spaces so occupied?

In the house of a civil servant, there are four rooms — a combined living-dining room, two bedrooms, and a kitchen. In addition, there is a bathroom, front yard, rear courtyard, and rear veranda. When this house is occupied by the middle-class, educated family — a man, his wife, three children, and the man's grandfather — how do they use this space? In the rear bedroom, the man, wife, and six year old daughter sleep in one bed. A son, age nine, sleeps beside them on the floor. The grandfather and oldest son, age 13, sleep together in one double bed in the living-dining room.

The living-dining room is divided into two parts by a curtain hanging down the middle of the room. The second bedroom is used as a formal entertaining area. When the husband invites friends to the house, they use this room so that they do not trespass in the family areas: kitchen, sleeping space, rear veranda, courtyard, or bath. These areas are restricted as the part of the household in which women tend to circulate. Even so, the guests must enter through the partitioned part of the living-dining room. Once they have gone into the formal entertaining area the family members can move about freely.

In former days, women never came into rooms where men were entertaining. Today in this modern city they only enter if their husbands ask them to do so. This segregation of male and female activities is now symbolized by the curtain dividing the family area from the reception-formal entertaining area. It represents the same principle observed in Shanti Nagar — the segregation and seclusion of women. It also maintains family privacy.

No one eats in the living-dining room. The family eats in the kitchen. In cities as well as villages, cooking and preparation are done both inside and outside. Many tasks are performed on either the floor or ground in the deep-squat position or on a low stool. The family members eat sitting cross-legged on the floor, and they eat in shifts according to age and sex. At breakfast, the children are fed first, then the men eat, and the woman or women eat last. Even at dinner they eat in shifts. These shifts occur in villages as well as in Chandigarh and represent segregation of activities by sex and age. Cooking is on a portable kerosene stove placed on the floor; preparations are made on the veranda. A dining table and six chairs provided in the living-dining room are used only if the man of the house entertains Westerners.

Other differences in the use of space can be seen. In hot weather, Indians prefer to sleep outdoors on the rooftops, which catch more breeze than the ground and are better protected, so the families do not sleep in the rear courtyard. Some of the living and bedroom windows face outward on the street in accordance with the western custom of exposure to the street and sunlight (of which there is too much in India). The Indian family invariably pastes paper over these windows so that the family preserves its accustomed privacy and segregation from an anonymous urban community, as in the Harappan civilization and in Shanti Nagar.

The rear courtyard is used by the family to illegally quarter cattle. Since there is no rear entrance or exit to the courtyard, the cattle quite openly are brought through the front door and house to the courtyard, another persistence through the centuries.

Both cattle and street vendors are illegal in Chandigarh because this was to be a modern city. In all cities in India one sees and bumps into cattle on every street; and there are numerous hawkers and vendors of all sorts. So too in Chandigarh, despite the planning and the laws banning them.

The plan of the shopping sections was to have shops representing the various items people would need in each housing section so that they could get everything they needed on one street and in their residential area. This does not suit the people for two reasons: they like to go into a string of shops in a row all having one kind of merchandise so that they can bargain for the lowest prices; they would prefer to shop all around the city and to visit friends and kin at the same time from whom they are now separated in space. In other words, the kind of segregation provided by the planners for Chandigarh is not the kind of segregation to which they are accustomed where members of a lineage, clan or caste abide together.

There are other facets of the use or misuse of Chandigarh's planned space, but the lesson to learn is that the way people visualize and use space is culturally conditioned and cannot be changed by the world's finest planners. The resilience or resistance of the population in taking over this beautifully planned city and adapting it to their own culturally conditioned ways raises the question of how long it takes to change such ways — whether they are to be changed because of city planners or because of population density, or whether cultural conditioning in patterned ways is tenacious, despite change and density. It also raises the question of whether segregation and hierarchical arrangements may be necessary for harmonious living in very densely inhabited space.

After twenty years of living in this city, the citizens like to boast of their modern amenities — flush toilets, running water, and electricity — but they say that they are not as close together as in the old cities and that they do not share one another's joys and sorrows: in other words they do not inhabit space in the way in which they have been accustomed. They prefer their form of segregation into close communities where kin live side by side, and where males and females perform their separate activities.[10]

In addition and in contrast to Chandigarh and its experts, the headquarters of

Deere & Co., producers of farm machinery in Moline, Illinois, provide another example of planning by experts. The building is described as "a breathtaking structure in Cor-Ten steel and glass that looks as though some genie has transported it intact from the hidden valley of a Japanese emperor . . ."[11] It is a direct reflection of the company's William A. Hewitt, and the famed architect Eero Saarinen, although other executives and architects had additional influence. The building is beautiful, but it is a building where the aesthetic point of view of the architect and "the preferences of top management have been taken into consideration."[2] The Halls[11] conducted interviews before the employees moved into this building in April 1964, after they had moved in October 1964, and finally in April 1969. In the earlier interviews there was little criticism, but the criticisms in the last interviews may be pertinent to the design. The Halls provide a different interpretation in their study than do I.

First, the design allows for little privacy. Except for executive offices, many desks are either arranged together in a large space, such as for the secretaries, or they are arranged in private offices with glass walls. The sizes of offices depend on rank in the business hierarchy; and correlated with the size of office or working spaces are desks designed by Saarinen to fit the space. There are three basic sizes with the exception of the executive offices on the second floor and the nonpartitioned room for secretaries. Even employees from the executive floor lack acoustical privacy since sound travels in a way that indicates some defect in planning. The floor levels are designed to accommodate different levels of work, and the work is an indication of prestige and status in the company. All floors but two have great expanses of glass windows from which to view the beautifully landscaped grounds surrounding the building. Those employees working underground and on the ground floor have no views and say they feel oppressed, confined, and cut off from the world. The secretaries, although located on higher floors, are contained between the executive offices and have little or no view. They are in the center of the floor and the executive offices have the windows. The secretaries complain of the cold and drafts, and are displeased because their work space was not partitioned from that of other secretaries, which they find distracting. This long work tunnel for secretaries may be related to the lack of auditory privacy. The Halls attribute complaints about temperature control to women's feeling chillier than men. No one appears to have investigated the relationship of the rather drab coloring and the lack of windows to this complaint.

Although the employees often state that they are proud of the new building and boast about it to their friends and acquaintances, they note that the new building is tiring to them, perhaps because they are exposed to watchful eyes. They now dress more carefully than they did in their previous quarters, indicating that the eyes of their work world are upon them.

Because the plant is located outside of Moline, the employees now eat in the company cafeteria; previously they had a choice of places to eat. In addition, their lunch hour has been cut from one hour to a half hour, so that this too bothers them. There are no places where the employees, except for top executives and their guests, can congregate in friendly interaction. Possibly the building was planned to militate against long lunch hours, gathering, and wasting time, but friendliness within a corporation can be useful.

The Halls write glowingly of the building's design, the compartmentalization of which projected the organization of the company, and the uncluttered look of the desks and offices, for individuals cannot put up their own pictures or clutter their desks. The effect on the reader, however, is not only one of hierarchical compartmentalization, but also of militant planning against individualistic touches.

Three main criticisms emerge from the data: the coloring of the interior, which was drab, cold, and impersonal; the temperature-humidity control; and the parking facilities, which were at a distance from the main building so that in winter or wet weather it was difficult to get to the plant. There were additional complaints about privacy, always being on display, and about overcrowding in departments that had grown, especially for the secretaries whose desks were in close proximity, contributing to lessened efficiency. Some mentioned that the new building was not as cozy or friendly as the older buildings. Since the study occurred in the midwest from 1964 to 1969, one wonders how the employees at Deere at present might react to questioning about the building if they were interviewed away from it. The overall effect of the Halls' study is one of a strong management imposing its ideas upon its employees, giving them a place of which they could boast and in which they could perform their work well, but of imposing values and demands on them by spacing them within this building according to their and the architect's views.[11]

Since Moline, Illinois, is sufficiently in the midwest to reflect a central position in American culture and its use of space, let us switch back in time and review the use of space in Yankee City, a town in Massachusetts near Boston, which was established in 1635. In 1935, this city observed its tercentenary, at which time plaques were placed on places of historic interest, of which half were all occupied houses, and the rest were public buildings, churches, graveyards, etc. The houses and graveyards reflect social structure by their occupation of space. Almost all of the houses are on Hill Street or very close to it. This was the most desirable and apparently the highest position spatially and socially in the past and present. The homes reflect the positions of those founding fathers, who came from England, received the best land grants, and were merchant princes in the heyday of Yankee City. Many of these houses are still occupied by their descendants, who represent the elite of Yankee City, despite the influx through three centuries of diverse populations. Most of them represent the upper class and old family aristocracy.

The cemetery in which the ancestors of these families were and are buried is Elm Highlands, which is also the most modern cemetery in Yankee City, although it was consecrated early in the last century. The primary organizing principle in this cemetery is around family, lineage and religion. Segregation by religion exists; Protestants are buried in Protestant cemeteries; and Jews and Catholics in their cemeteries. In the family plots of Elm Highlands cemetery, reflecting the upper-class generally, the family of orientation is more important than the family of procreation, although occasionally there may be competition between the two. The father and mother occupy a central position, with the father's place more important than the mother's. Male children and their wives are placed on each side of them, and grandchildren are placed on the periphery. If there is dissension between the family of procreation and orientation, then the male head, his wife, and unmarried children are buried together. In surveying the cemeteries, these two patterns are most characteristic of the upper class, with lineage or extended family type in most evidence. If the patronym of married women is significant among this upper class group, it is included on the headstone of the female. Thus, these graves affirm the status of the elite and of their families. Other classes do not tend to have the lineage, or extended family type. Instead they have nuclear family grave plots. The cemetery in which the graves are, the arrangement of the families in the plot, and the use of significant patronyms affirm the wealth and prestige of these upper classes as do their houses and locations. This pattern was present in colonial times, was brought from England, and existed at the time of the study.[12]

The occupancy of space in America so far presents a picture of hierarchy and compartmentalization. The data on Deere & Co. suggests hierarchy, authority, and impersonality. The data from Yankee City suggests an elite or aristocracy, whereas Deere suggests powerful executive management. These traits exist in American culture. But the examples may exist in areas that today are not the most densely populated.

It we contrast these examples to micro uses of space in New York City, perhaps we may see some differences. New York City and its related hinterland today is the conurbation with the largest population in the world:[13] 14,114,927 people live in the New York-New Jersey area.

In this area, there are numerous apartment buildings rising many stories; city blocks may have 10,000 or more people; the so-called suburbia consists of condominiums, apartment buildings, and single family dwellings. Highways within this area are consistently jammed at peak traffic hours. Transportation consists of planes, cars, trains, buses, subways, bicycles, and feet; and individuals have become accustomed to being spaced and sometimes crowded through many of these means of transportation. Where the Yankee City ancestors moved west when they were crowded, today a number of generations in New York conurbation have expanded upward and condensed their available space. Many have never known a time when they did not live in a densely populated environment. Here are some of the changed kinds of spatial behavior that may be a result of crowded, urban living.

The invention of the cocktail party sometime during this century has contributed to a kind of social crowding and culturally learned behavior that is both fashionable and acceptable. This social institution allows a host or hostess to serve thirty to a hundred or more guests in a relatively small space. In the process of such a party, guests stand closer to each other than may formerly have been customary, crowd back-to-back, cram five or six onto a couch designed for three or four, sit on the floor, lean against walls, sit on window sills, and in some cases, a cocktail party being what it is, lie or fall down. In this bleary and blurred atmosphere as physical contacts are intimate so too are the conversations, although they may be with strangers.

Housing has had adjustments in kinds of space and size, with a relative reduction downward in total space, but some adjustment upward in bathrooms. The dining room has virtually been eliminated as a result of ranch house and modern apartment planning. The lessening of complete walls, possibly to reduce the expenses of building, has contributed to a reduction in privacy and supposedly to "togetherness." In a society accustomed to privacy, togetherness may be a new accommodation to crowding.

For those under thirty-five, new accommodations to space are sitting on floors, pavements, the ground, steps or curbs — behavior that twenty-five years ago would have been for the homeless. The current generations of young and even middle-aged adults do not require the same amount or kind of furniture when they sit. A number live together in "pads," with little or no privacy. They cook, study, work, and sleep together. They also drink and eat when walking along the street or driving in cars or public vehicles. These changes from the past must have begun in their early years in ways that have yet to be verified. Perhaps some of the factors that contributed to these changes are the differences that have occurred in domestic architecture since the 1940s, the increasing density of the population, and the placing of children in schools ever earlier.

Some of these changes in culturally conditioned use of space may have occurred in the educational process. In the present school era informality is encouraged and children may not have regularly assigned desks or seats, at least not in nursery school, kindergarten, or the first grade. These youngsters often sit on the floor, move about, play in a house, or do whatever they fancy. The overt motivation behind this training is to develop creativity, but it may be an accommodation to density and crowding.

Along with these changes, individuals living in apartment buildings get together where formerly they did not even nod to their next door neighbor. Block parties joining total strangers in social activities are the order of the warm summer months in New York City. Do these accommodations reflect a new cultural conditioning of the use of space? Are the hierarchical and segregative patterns of India, and the hierarchical and compartmentalized patterns of Deere and Yankee City being torn down?

This paper is aimed at raising questions about the culturally conditioned use of space both on a micro and macro level, in a culturally patterned sense, and as the use of space is related to the prehistory, history, and present of hominids. It has suggested possibilities that existed in the past and present regarding human accommodation to space, but it provides no answers for the future. This study only asks questions.

REFERENCES

1. ALLAND, A., JR. 1972. The Human Imperative: 150, 157–158, 168–169. Columbia University Press. New York, N.Y.
2. CHAPPLE, E. D. 1970. Culture and Biological Man: 153, 178–9, 197. Holt, Rinehart & Winston, New York, N.Y.
3. PILBEAM, D. 1975. The fashionable view of man as a naked ape. In The Human Way: Readings in Anthropology. H. R. Bernard, Ed.: 216–218. Macmillan. New York, N.Y.
4. HALL, E. T. 1975. How different cultures use space. In The Human Way: Readings in Anthropology. H. R. Bernard, Ed.: 110–121. Macmillan. New York, N.Y.
5. RUSSELL, C. & W. M. S. RUSSELL. The natural history of violence. In Aggression and Evolution. C. M. Otten, Ed.: 240–241. Xerox College Publishing. Lexington, Mass.
6. DUMOND, D. E. 1975. The limitation of human population: A natural history. Science 187(4178): 713–721.
7. TYLER, S. A. 1973. India: An Anthropological Perspective: 30–40. Goodyear Regional Anthropology Series. Pacific Palisades, Calif.
8. WHEELER, SIR M. 1966. Civilizations of the Indus Valley and Beyond: 11–36, 61–91. McGraw-Hill. New York, N.Y.
9. FREED, S. A. & R. S. FREED. 1976. Shanti Nagar: The Effects of Urbanization in a Village in North India, Vol. 1: Social Organization. AP-AMNH. Vol. 53 (1): 32–36, 63–78. New York, N.Y.
10. BROLIN, B. C. 1975. Chandigarh was planned by experts but something has gone wrong. In The Human Way: Readings in Anthropology, H. R. Bernard, Ed.: 376–383. Macmillan. New York, N.Y.
11. HALL, M. & E. HALL. 1975. The Fourth Dimension in Architecture: The Impact of Building on Man's Behavior: 7–12, 14–16, 20–30, 37–45. The Sunstone Press. Santa Fe, New Mexico.

12. WARNER, W. L. 1959. The Living and the Dead: A Study of the Symbolic Life of Americans: 282, 287–288, 295, 297. Yale University Press. New Haven, Conn.
13. DAVIS, K. 1972. The urbanization of the human population. *In* Biology and Culture in Modern Perspective: Readings from Scientific American.: 375. W. H. Freeman & Co. San Francisco, Calif.

FAMILISTIC SOCIAL CHANGE ON THE ISRAELI KIBBUTZ

Robert Endleman

Department of Sociology
Adelphi University
Garden City, Long Island 11530

This paper deals with an aspect of social change going on in some of the Israeli kibbutzim. This change is regarded by the participants as being in a more "modern" direction, as opposed to the now-traditional (though once strongly radical) patterns of the early kibbutz, and in that sense this discussion falls into the purview of "modernization in the local environment." It also fits into "modernization" in an additional sense: the changes here discussed are associated with one feature of "modernization," namely industrialization, which has been proceeding apace in the kibbutzim in the past 25 to 30 years.

The familistic social change is a shift from entirely communal housing for infants and children, to a familial, or a combination of communal and familial, sleeping arrangement, for children of certain ages.

This change is taking place against a backdrop of basic patterns of social and ecological organization of the Israeli kibbutz that have become familiar since the founding of the first kibbutz in 1909. Since these patterns are already well documented in the social science literature,[1-8] I will here sketch only the essentials of that background.

The kibbutz, a collectively organized small agricultural community, was formed to put the ideals of Zionist socialism into practice: it is a homeland on the soil for previously nationless and perennially wandering and very urban Jews. It transcends industrialized capitalism by a totally collective organization of the local socialist community, living the motto "from each according to his abilities, to each according to his needs." Although not initially a cornerstone of the kibbutz system, the pattern of communally housing and socializing the infants and children of the kibbutz — improvised at first from expendiency, and later rationalized and perpetuated in terms of collectivist ideology — became before long one of the essential features of any kibbutz. This feature distinguishes the kibbutz not only (and quite radically) from standard nuclear-family patterns of most modern communities, but also from such variant forms of agricultural settlement as the *moshav*, which attempts to combine collectivized production with private consumption in nuclear-family-based households. Collective child-rearing on the Kibbutz means the newborn infant is placed in the infants' house as soon as the mother returns with him to the kibbutz from the hospital (usually in a nearby city or town), and put in the regular care of a functionary called a *metapelet* (plural, *metaplot*; roughly, "caretaker.") The regular residence of all infants and children through to the end of high school is a communal house either for infants and toddlers, prepubertal children, or adolescents. Mothers come to the infants' house to visit and (usually) nurse the infants in the first year, and fathers visit too. After about six months the child has regular visits to the parents' apartment, once a day plus Sabbath and special holidays. The time of the daily visit is late afternoon to early evening. It is called the "children's hour," and is usually looked forward to with enthusiasm by both parents and children. Adolescents, in high school, visit the parents less frequently.

Correspondingly, the major part of the socialization of infants and children is carried out, not by the parents, but by the functionaries, *metaplot* only at first, later a combination of *metaplot* and teachers, and male counselors for boys — plus the peer group of the children themselves. Alongside these, the parents play a quantitatively minor role as pleasuring people who might provide some slight indulgences to the child during the children's hour visits, but have no formal role in educating, training, or disciplining the child.

Kibbutz ideology defends and extols this system as not only practical, but eminently desirable ideologically. For thereby, the argument runs, the children learn collectivism from the very beginning, experience it in practically all aspects of their daily lives, and thus become the kind of "new men" and "new women" needed to carry kibbutz collectivism into the succeeding generations. Accounts in the standard social science literature on the now-"traditional" kibbutzim indicate that the children growing up in this communal housing and child-rearing pattern do in fact think and feel in group terms far more intensely than do any comparable modern rural youngsters raised in nuclear-family settings.[1,2,4,5]

The intensity of this collectivist experience, however, is partially muted by the role of the parents during the visiting-time periods. These periods amount to an island of privatism in the sea of collectivism that is the kibbutz child's normal life.[2] They provide an intense and positively toned emotional connection between child and parents that is devoid of any parental authority or disciplinary functions and is free of performance demands. As one consequence, oedipal involvements have by no means disappeared on the kibbutz (as might be expected if the socialization were exclusively collective), but rather are in part intensified and given a particular quality by the special circumstances of the child's relationship to the parents.[2]

CHANGE

The change discussed here refers to the housing arrangements for the children. A number of kibbutzim have now shifted over, or are in process of shifting, from the purely communal residence of all infants and children to familial residence, or a combination of communal and familial residence, at different ages of the child. Specifically, prepubertal children of certain ages now sleep in the apartment of the parents, a residence pattern not much different from that of a nuclear family. Sleeping in the parental residence, the child also spends the late afternoon and evening there, although eating is still mostly done in the various communal dining rooms, adults separately and children with their age-peers.

As of 1971, about 30 kibbutzim of the approximately 280 total kibbutzim of all federations have, or are changing to, some form of familial housing for at least some of the children. The qualified phrasing is necessary because the exact nature of the pattern varies from one kibbutz to another, and has changed in some of these kibbutzim over a period of 20 years or more. A number of kibbutzim were visited in the summers of 1970 and 1971, in some of which some form of the "new" familial housing of children existed or was being started; and in some of which the "traditional" kibbutz system of infants and children living in children's houses throughout was still being practised. Data on current practice on a number of other kibbutzim were also acquired from informants on the kibbutzim that were visited or from federation offices.

The precise pattern of the familial sleeping arrangement varied considerably among the kibbutzim that were directly observed or were learned about from members of other kibbutzim. Some have children sleeping in the parental house for only a few years of childhood, and sleeping for the rest of the time in traditional children's houses or in youth houses. Some have them sleeping in the parental house all through childhood and adolescence, to the end of high school and departure for army service. This appears to be a minority of the familial housing cases. One has infants and children only up to the age of seven in familial sleeping arrangement, while all children over seven sleep in children's houses. But the greater likelihood appears to be the reverse: infants and very young children in the chidldren's houses, older children, from the age of four or five to puberty in familial housing, then teenagers again in separate children's houses. Some informants say that in the kibbutz movement as a whole one could find every imaginable combination of children's house and familial sleeping arrangements. There is even a reported case of a kibbutz where (as of 1970–71) the option was left to each parental couple, and apparently varied from one month to another for each family so that no one knew exactly how many and which children were living in children's houses and which with their parents, at any time. The informant admitted that this was a chaotic and necesarily transitory situation, and that the kibbutz in question would have to make a definite choice one way or the other before long.

Some have had children sleeping "at home" right from the time of the founding of the kibbutz. Some of these go back to the 1920s, and some to the late 1940s. Some informants report that the original kibbutz, Degania, never had children's houses at all. Others have shifted to familial housing in the 1960s, and still others were just in the process of instituting this kind of change at the time of these field observations (1970–71). Since such matters are the local decision of each particular kibbutz (i.e., where the federation allows such a change at all), one could expect such considerable local variation. However, all of the cases observed or heard about were kibbutzim of one particular federation only, Ichud Hakvutzoth VeHakibbutzim, which could be described as the most moderate or least ideologically dogmatic of the three nonreligious federations. At the opposite pole is the federation of Kibbutz Ha'artzi, or Hashomer Hatzair, which remains today the most ideologically rigid, or fundamentalist, of these three federations. Between these two on such ideological questions is the smaller federation called Hameuchad, a splinter from Ichud.

As of 1971, to the best of my knowledge, no Shomer Hatzair kibbutz had shifted from children's house residence to any version of familial housing. In fact, until that year, federation-wide meetings of Shomer kibbutzim representatives would not even allow the question of any possible change in children's housing to be introduced into the assembly; and certainly no Shomer kibbutz could introduce such a change on its own. The Ichud federation, by contrast, is a much less centralized structure, and has left matters such as these to local option. People of this federation also generally pride themselves on being more "flexible, pragmatic, modern, open to change," and definitely less ideological than those of Hashomer Hatzair. Shomer kibbutzniks wanting a change to familial housing for their children have been reported in several instances as making a move themselves (i.e., as separate couples) to Ichud kibbutzim that have made this shift.

Kibbutzniks of any federation make a special point to tell any visitor or observer that kibbutzim are all so different one from another — on any matter you might be interested in — that it is simply impossible to make any generalizations about "*the* kibbutz." In defiance of the folk wisdom of the participants, however, I shall attempt to make a few generalizations.

The context of the shift to familial housing in a minority of kibbutzim is that regardless of the housing pattern for children, *all* kibbutzim are still firmly dedicated to the basic socialist kibbutz principles of collective production, equitable allocation of work among the adult population, and equitable distribution of all the product and resources of the kibbutz among all of the members according to need, with the basic assurance that no one starves or lives in squalor while others feast and live in luxury. All informants agreed that these principles prevailed as a matter of course. Further, where familial sleeping arrangements for children do exist, despite variations in pattern, the dominant emergent pattern seems to be this: Infants up to and perhaps including toddlers, to the age of somewhere between three and five, continue to sleep at night in children's houses, attended by caretakers; children older than that, and up to pubertal age, sleep in the parent's apartment, which now has one additional bedroom for one to three children and two additional bedrooms for four or more; then, at puberty the adolescents move to the youth dormitories, where they live, increasingly separated from the parents, until the completion of high school and entrance into the army. On some kibbutzim the people will tell you that "of course the children sleep at home" – implying those of all ages – and then you discover them taking their infants and toddlers to the children's houses, to be put to bed, while their adolescent offspring are away at the high school youth dormitories. Moreover, all children, of all ages, are in children's groups, all day, every day except on the Sabbath and holidays; and children's houses, even in kibbutzim where children sleep "at home," all have sleeping facilities set up just like those on totally-collective-residence kibbutzim, just as though the children slept there regularly at night, as well as for afternoon naps. More recently built children's houses are also likely to have underground bomb shelters, where all the children will sleep during times of heightened danger of enemy attack on the kibbutz. Evidently at these times familial housing is discarded in favor of greater protection of the children. (This recalls what many accounts and present-day informants claim was the original purpose of children's houses, located originally in the most protected, central part of the kibbutz.)

Members of kibbutzim that have made this change in recent years (e.g., since 1960) view themselves as more "modern," "up-to-date," "in tune with changing times," and as less ideologically hidebound, than the kibbutzim that have not changed in this way, and especially than the whole federation of Hashomer Hatzair. Some claim that the ideological justifications that were developed for the communal children's-house system were built upon misguided notions of human psychology; and that the womanpower-conserving arguments advanced under the spartan conditions of the early kibbutzim are not apposite under the relatively affluent conditions of the kibbutzim of today. Many young mothers who favor having the children at home at night say simply, "It's more natural, that's all," and dismiss the question at that point. Some claimed it was too burdensome to go to three or four different-aged children in three or four different children's houses to put them to bed at night, and dismissed as pointless any argument that mothers had more work with children sleeping at home. Where the change was recent, the pressure for the change had come primarily from young mothers, many or most of them sabras (i.e., native kibbutzniks) who had grown up in the children's-house system. Nearly all informants on kibbutzim where this kind of change had been made denied that this change in itself had any major significance, and denied that having children *housed* communally was in any way ideologically essential to the kibbutz way of Zionist socialism. A few older informants (on such kibbutzim) did see the change as a part of a whole complex of changes, all in the direction of greater privatization and less collectivism of life. (Staunch Shomer ideologists, of course, saw such change as yet another chink in the armor of collectivist purity, a further demonstration of the error of allowing that first private steam-kettle in a parental couple's room.)

Approvers of this new arrangement are also likely to claim that the change will soon be widespread on the kibbutzim, many claiming to know other kibbutzniks on other, traditional kibbutzim who are ready to push for this kind of change on their own kibbutz, threatening, if necessary as a political tactic, to move elsewhere in large numbers.

All informants agree that the drive for this change comes primarily from the women, with the husbands offering little or no opposition to the idea.

THE REASONS FOR CHANGE

One may speculate on the reasons for the changes toward more nuclear-family type sleeping arrangements. Since the push for this change has come primarily from the women, one may first relate the change to the common observation that any dissatisfaction that exists on the kibbutz is more likely to come from the women than the men. After the first flush of sexual-egalitarian zeal of the early pioneering days of the kibbutz, where women participated side by side with men in nearly all kinds of tasks, including those that required heavy labor, the kibbutz soon evolved a division of labor by gender not much different from that of contemporary modern countries. Men were therefore primarily engaged in the "productive" sector, women primarily in the "service" sector. The latter includes communalized versions of all of the standard household tasks traditionally done by women in noncollectivist societies: cooking, taking care of the kitchen and dining room, sewing, laundry, and care of infants and young children, as well as such traditionally "feminine" jobs as teaching in the early grades, nursing, and dealing with children's distress. Women are rarely in the position of political executive (*maskir*, usually translated as "secretary") of the kibbutz or the even more crucial one of economic manager, although they are theoretically equally eligible for such an office. (Most women interviewed on this point said they wouldn't want such a job in any case, because its intense demands would cut into cherished private time with children and husband.) Many older women have come to the realization that collectivization of household and child-rearing tasks has only resulted in women doing the same kind of work they would have been doing otherwise, but now as functionaries and for the whole kibbutz, rather than for their own family. Thus tasks that might have been tedious, but personally meaningful because devoted to one's immediate family, have been transformed into simply tedious chores for the whole collective. The dissatisfaction of kibbutz women is therefore not so much focused on the paucity of opportunities for more "fulfilling" or "creative" work (although that complaint does appear), as on the absence or loss of domestic satisfactions attendant upon collectivization of household tasks. This is not necessarily articulated in quite this form, but does seem to be one of the meanings behind their saying that having children sleep at home is simply "more natural," although in fact it does mean more work for the wife-mother who still has to get up early in the morning to go to her kibbutz work. (It is still true on all these kibbutzim that all nonincapacitated adults of both sexes do work at a job for the kibbutz; there are still no women who are "only housewives" on the kibbutz.)

But why should some women want this change to familial sleeping for their children, if these women are themselves sabras of the kibbutz and who were therefore raised in communal housing and child-rearing arrangements? One would expect that if the product of such child-rearing experiences were in fact the "collective personality" intended by the ideology of the communal system, she would happily hand over her own children to such communal child-rearing. But that is not the case for the women considered here. We may hypothesize the following: Since career opportunities for females are very limited on the kibbutz, and since sabras generally lack the ideological intensity of the *vattikim* ("veterans," i.e., first-generation settlers of a particular kibbutz), and therefore do not have such a strong ideological stake in the maintenance of the collectivized institutions, some of these women may try to increase the satisfactions of the "private sphere"[2] against those of work. These may well be women who have as infants and children experienced a special satisfaction in that "island of privatism" and emotional vitality that marked the periods spent with the parents, in contrast to the affective restraint of the collectivized part of life spent with the peer group under the aegis of *metaplot* and teachers.

It is also possible that there is a selective factor at work: that those women who are *not* so close to having what has been described in the literature as typical personality characteristics of sabras of Kibbutz are those more likely to favor institutional changes in the direction of greater familism, and this change specifically to familial housing of the children. The "typical" characteristics referred to are *Sachlichkeit* (a cool fact-mindedness), flatness of affect, a cool hard-headedness, lack of intensity of emotional expression.[1-3] Since it is most unlikely that a whole second generation of kibbutzniks fits these personality characteristics closely, it may well be that those who least approximate these characteristics are in the forefront of the shift to greater familism. And it may also be that these are women who have experienced greater emotional depth and intensity in the relationship with their parents when they were infants and children, and that this affectivity has not been entirely countered by the opposite pressures that come from the collective sphere of the children's group life.

Besides the personal selective factors influencing the women more likely to be predisposed to favor changes of this kind, we can point to general socio-cultural trends of the kibbutzim of recent years.

Generally the change toward familial housing, in some form, does appear to be part of a larger syndrome of changes, all in the direction of greater familism, greater feminine interest in domesticity and strengthening of nuclear-family bonds. Women have demanded and received shorter working hours than men (typically, a six-hour day, compared to the men's eight- or nine-hour one; and much less during pregnancy and the immediate postpartum period). In almost reverse pattern to the feminist militancy of western countries, kibbutz women tend to want less of work and more of family. By an apparent paradox, however, many of the same want the very young infants to continue sleeping in infants' houses at night, but older children (i.e., from three or four years of age) sleeping at home.

A related change is the trend toward parents eating the (usually cold) evening meal, sometimes along with their children, in the parental apartment, a significant departure from the totally communal eating of the "traditional" kibbutz. And even where the children still sleep in children's houses, the "children's hour" period appears to be lengthening significantly, from a former one-to-two-hour period, to one of at least three and up to four hours. Another related change is the progressive decrease in the number of children per group under the care of one *metapelet*: On more affluent kibbutzim, it is now not unusual to have five toddlers or preschoolers under the care of three *metaplot* (or two *metaplot* plus a teenage girl helper). (When the interviewer suggested to women on that kibbutz that such an arrangement meant no economy of womanpower at all — compared to mothers caring for their own babies — they scoffed at this as totally irrelevant, arguing, or at least implying, that such economy was not at all the point of the *metapelet* system.)

There are also indications that family size is increasing — many kibbutzim report five children per couple as becoming the usual number in their community — along with the women's increased domestic interest.

Correspondingly, the once-intense collectivism of the early kibbutz is considerably muted today — on all kibbutzim evidently, but more particularly on those of this reformist, self-styled "progressive" and "modern" federation, the Ichud.

All of these changes would appear to be consonant with the other major drift of change on the kibbutz — the growing industrialization. Now most kibbutzim have an economic base divided, in some proportion, between agriculture and animal husbandry, on one side, and light industrial manufacturing (e.g., plastics or electronics components) on the other. The agriculture itself, except for orchards, is now also predominantly mechanized as well, as are animal and poultry husbandry. Production for market, rather than for subsistence by the kibbutzniks themselves, is now the prevailing pattern.

In the industrialized countries, preschool children are increasingly in a variety of day-care facilities outside the nuclear-family home; and older children are in schools or other directed activities outside the home throughout most of the day and most of the week. Accordingly, the differences between the kibbutz children's experiences and those of most of the population of industrial countries like the United States, are tending to decline. Likewise, the current changes in the kibbutz toward greater emphasis on the nuclear family are shifting the kibbutz to greater similarity to the family and socialization patterns of the industrial West.

REFERENCES

1. BETTELHEIM, B. 1969. The Children of the Dream. The Macmillan Company. New York, N.Y.
2. ENDLEMAN, R. 1967. Personality and Social Life.: 127–178. Random House. New York, N.Y.
3. NEUBAUER, P. Ed. 1965. Children in Collectives: Child Rearing Aims and Methods in the Kibbutz. Charles C. Thomas. Springfield, Ill.
4. RABIN, A. I. 1965. Growing Up in the Kibbutz. Springer. New York, N.Y.
5. SPIRO, M. 1958. Children of the Kibbutz. Harvard University Press. Cambridge, Mass.
6. SPIRO, M. 1956. Kibbutz: Venture in Utopia. Harvard University Press. Cambridge, Mass.
7. TALMON, Y. 1964. Mate selection in collective settlements. Am. Sociol. Rev. 29: 491–508.
8. TALMON, Y. 1952. Social differentiation in cooperative communities. Brit. J. Sociol. 3: 339–357.

SEX ROLES IN CROSS-CULTURAL PERSPECTIVE

Georgene H. Seward

Department of Psychology
University of Southern California
Los Angeles, California 90007

In line with the theme of this Conference, my main emphasis will be on certain modernizing trends that have affected social sex roles. We shall then look at the contemporary scene in terms of cross-cultural attitudes toward these roles. To demonstrate modernizing influences, I have reviewed radical agricultural, industrial, and social innovations throughout our cultural history.

MODERNIZING TRENDS

Agricultural Revolution

Modernization may be said to go back to the last Ice Age, about 10,000 years ago, with the Agricultural Revolution.[1] During this period man began to take advantage of the new vegetation that sprang up after the glaciers retreated. In some places he even started to cultivate plants and to domesticate animals. For at least a million years previously he had lived exclusively by hunting, following the migratory herds for food, and like them, keeping continuously on the move.

Once man gave up the nomadic life and settled down on his own land, the possibilities for cultural diversity became manifold. Since the shift from hunting to agriculture was not an all-or-none process, many societies, though no longer nomadic, still derived much of their subsistence from hunting. Here power was vested in the male because of his great strength, endurance, and the special skills he acquired to insure the food supply. The family in such cases became institutionalized around the men. In cultures where subsistence was derived mainly from gathering and accumulating grain, the men did not enjoy the especially high status they had in those depending on hunting large animals. A smaller, nuclear family made up of parents and their children was typical, with power more evenly divided between husband and wife.[2] But even in these rarer societies, the men who still had the advantage of being able to perform the more hazardous tasks dominated the women and controlled the group's resources.[3]

As cultures evolved from tribe to kingdom, where control was centralized through political and military organization, the male's highly prized skills in weaponry and the hunt enabled him to maintain his priority of status.[4] The tight feudal structure built on this model gradually gave way as new possibilities for individual enterprise appeared in the wake of establishing trade routes around the world. Now the family as a unit became a production center for making articles to be sold on the new international market, which ushered in the Industrial Revolution, the second major modernizing influence I should like to consider.

Industrial Revolution

As long as the focus of life was in the home, the struggle for existence demanded cooperation among all members, resulting in a rough and ready equality between man and wife. Women, no less than men, were trained in skills with economic value, and men, no less than women, participated in domestic affairs. When technological advances made mass production possible, much of the manufacturing had to be moved from the home to newly established factories in urban centers at a distance. The heavy machinery, like the large animals of a former era, required male strength to handle, a situation that prevented the women from following their men to the cities to take part in production as they had in the home industries. Exceptions were the very poor women who were forced by necessity into sweatshops, where they were exploited as cheap labor for the profit of wealthy owners.[5]

With the advent of automation, brawn was eliminated as an issue since it took no greater muscular energy for a woman than for a man to push the necessary buttons. Nevertheless, jobs continued to be unevenly distributed between the sexes, even in white-collar industry. As at the factory level, offices were concentrated in cities, on the outskirts of which "bedroom" communities gradually grew. "Suburbia" became the new design for living, representing a kinship system that segregates the nuclear mother-child unit from the father-commuter group as effectively as any primitive society that dichotomizes the sexes so that the two halves live in different worlds. This way of life restricts women to family and local affairs, but it is just as restricting for men, who are banished to the more remote community of impersonal business matters. To communicate across this artifical subcultural barrier is as difficult as to cross the barriers of language and custom. Both men and women are seriously deprived of each other's companionship, and of mutual sharing in the lives and interests of their growing children.

Social Change

A third modernizing influence basically altering the roles of men and women may be attributed to the radical social changes of war and peace during the current century. We shall try to evaluate some of these effects by comparing the revolutionary Soviet system in Russia with the more gradually evolving Swedish models, as "societal experiments."

Dialectic in Soviet Sex Roles

Nowhere were changes in masculine and feminine roles more conspicuous than in the USSR immediately after the Revolution. According to the early ideologists, women were to share equally with men in all the privileges and responsibilities of the "New Society." This model, however, proved so unrealistic that the radical changes were soon radically revised. Under Stalin, the new mores were reversed, with the glorification of parenthood, stricter regulation of marriage and divorce, and the illegalization of abortion.[6] Following Stalin, the dialectic pendulum again swung to the liberal side. Marriage and divorce procedures were simplified, abortion relegalized, and birth control information freely disseminated.

Recently career orientation of both parents has been abetted by a boom in child-care facilities, which have taken over many functions previously performed within the home. Statistics show that women make up half of the wage-earning labor force,[7] and that employed women represent nearly all those below retirement age.[8] Behind the cold figures lies the continuing manpower shortage that lends added thrust to the socialist ideal of sex equality. Theoretically, women are accepted on a par with men and although there are no vocational fields barred to them except the military underground and the command of small fishing boats, sexist attitudes have not disappeared. Nor have the women freed themselves from deep-rooted traditions about occupations. A survey within the past five years of high-school seniors in various Soviet cities, showed a cleavage in vocational interests — girls still preferring educational and cultural areas; boys, engineering.[9]

The "new freedom" for women has not meant the substitution of a single standard for the old double standard. It has actually introduced a new form of double standard, involving the dubious privilege of carrying the burden of two worlds. While enjoying equality with men outside the home, woman's chief responsibility is still considered to lie within it by Soviet husbands, who have shown great reluctance to take up dishpan and diaper. The puzzling line separating the private from the public domain in Soviet life, however, is not merely a patriarchal vestige; it gives the family an anonymity desperately needed to protect the individual of both sexes from totalitarian encroachments.

Feminine roles in the USSR are far from the utopian dream of the early idealists. Conflict and confusion are characteristic of women's attitudes and contribute to a soaring divorce rate.[7] Basing their conclusions on evidence from both fact and fiction, Field and Flynn[10] have suggested a four-fold typology, distinguishing "comrade positive," the patriotic and dedicated activist, "comrade willing, but," "comrade reluctant," and the socially regressive and disgraced "comrade parasitic."

Swedish Models

Because of the various dislocations and disruptions in the economy resulting from political convulsion, the USSR has failed to present a clear picture of what might be expected under conditions of more gradual change. Clearer models are provided by Sweden with its long history of progressive social attitudes. Here the traditional family has given way to an egalitarian form implemented by liberalized marriage and divorce laws in which family planning is central.

Emancipation of women. According to Liljeström,[11] Eva Moberg's daring challenge to the prevalent idea of women's two roles — in the home and on the job — initiated a decade-long debate that culminated in the *Report to the United Nations*, which urged absolute emancipation of women and unqualified equality between the sexes.[12] The basic argument is that sex differences concern only reproductive functions and do not justify putting people into separate social roles. The goal of this thinking is to create new, flexible, *human* roles in which the same possibilities are open to members of both sexes within the family, in the labor market, and also in all other social situations.[13]

Emancipation of men. Freeing women from role stereotypes that prevented their developing individual talents led to an analogous "emancipation" of men.[14,15] The Industrial Revolution, which had taken the man out of the formerly self-sufficient production unit of the home, was viewed as a threat to family cohesion that should be counteracted by restoring him to his proper function within as well as outside the home. Both parents were seen as sharing equally in the domestic and vocational fields according to personal preference rather than biological accident. At one extreme, a man would be free to choose the role of "househusband," just as his wife might still choose that of "housewife," although the entire gamut of jobs would be open to members of both sexes.

Training for the new roles. To implement the new equality between men and women requires support at all levels of society. New school curricula with updated textbooks giving both boys and girls the same opportunities to learn cooking, sewing, child-care, shop, and manual work are prerequisites to such a program.[13] Moreover, this basic change in educational policy needs reinforcement by parental and public opinion or it cannot take firm root. Powerful blocks, however, to full acceptance of the new look in gender roles lurk below the level of conscious awareness. A number of studies bearing on "the debate," show discrepancies between verbal and behavioral attitudes on the part of parents.[16] Interviews indicated that parents who expressed their intention in good faith to rear their boys and girls alike, actually applied sanctions reflecting their own deeply ingrained social sex-role concepts and biases.

THE CONTEMPORARY SCENE

Cross-National Attitudes Toward Social Sex Roles

American and German Intercomparisons

To gauge the way today's youth views social sex roles in socialist as compared with typical capitalist countries, I planned to survey student groups in the USSR, the two Germanies, and the United States. Refused permission to conduct the research in the Soviet Union on the ground that the subject was "too sensitive," I had to restrict my program to samples from the other groups.[17] Intercomparisons on semantic-differential adjective scales revealed not the anticipated cross-national differences, but for the most part, similarities. Modern youth, as sampled in this research, were looking to their peers for new role models rather than to their parents, whose life-styles were seen as outmoded and inappropriate. In other words, the postwar generation of boys and girls, whether from the United States or the Germanies, expressed their willingness to share responsibility for rebuilding the remnants of their society. In general, a flattening of sex differences suggested a trend away from the former duality.

Transcultural Comparisons

More light is thrown on cross-national sex role concepts by a series of studies ranging over a wider transcultural radius and focusing specifically on self- versus family-orientation. During the past decade Anne Steinmann and her collaborators have carried out an extensive research program on gender-role perceptions. They gathered data on thousands of men and women of all ages, from many nations of Europe, from North and South America, and from the Near and Far East, as well as from various subcultures within the major ones.[18-25]

On the basis of inventories of male and female values, they determined for each sex, concepts held of the self, the ideal self and of the opposite sex's ideal.

What stood out most clearly and consistently in the results was the distortion with which each sex perceived the other sex's ideal. While women saw themselves and their own ideal as well-balanced between self- and family-orientations, they believed that men idealized a much more traditional woman for whom the role as wife and mother took precedence over any self-achieving ambition. This stereotyped feminine ideal was attributed to men by females the world over.

The parallel male data revealed the same kind of failure in communication:

the men's self-perceptions, as well as their closely related masculine ideals, showed a good balance between self-achievement motivation and family devotion, but their concepts of women's ideal man was tilted toward family-centeredness. Paradoxically, although both sexes hold very similar ideals for their own sex, neither seemed to have an accurate image of what the other wants.

If the results can be taken at face value they should go far toward dispelling the mistrust between the sexes, replacing it with understanding and the joy of working together for common social objectives.

DISCUSSION

In the accelerated space-time perspective of this brief paper a few points stand out with special clarity:

1. The biological bedrock of sex differences remains: Male hormones underlie the greater muscular strength that predisposes men toward aggressive and dominant behavior. Female reproductive functions, involving childbearing and nursing, have kept women closer to hearth and home. Thus the groundplans as originally laid down in nature prepared the way for what Steven Goldberg[26] has called "the inevitability of patriarchy."

2. Changes in the course of technological development made biological sex differences less relevant to social role: Machine operation, replacing crude brawn, has opened many fields to women that were previously dependent on male muscle strength. At the same time, female biological functions have become less handicapping with the move toward sex equality in education, and toward family planning. Today we are in an era of open choices for both sexes. Indeed, as we have noted, men and women actually have the same ideals for themselves. It might seem as though we were on the brink of a gender, if not a sexual utopia. But we dare not leap to that attractive conclusion without a final caveat:

3. The crucial question that has not been answered is: to what extent do each of the sexes feel comfortable with the new balance between the sexes? Throughout our review, there have been disquieting indications that beneath the conscious level there was conflict: Soviet women holding back, Swedish parents inadvertently sex-typing their children, and women of all nations sampled, erroneously thinking that men wanted women to continue the traditional pattern – all such tendencies suggest an undertow in "the wave of the future."

What is needed to clinch the issue as to whether or not males and females differ in ways unrelated to biological function is research aimed at discovering the degree of inner satisfaction each sex derives from sex-"appropriate" versus sex-"inappropriate" social activities. But regardless of the outcome, as long as free choices are possible, there can be no argument for not keeping those choices equally open to both sexes.

REFERENCES

1. BRONOWSKI, J. 1973. The Ascent of Man. Little, Brown. Boston, Mass.
2. D'ANDRADE, R. G. 1966. Sex differences and cultural institutions. *In* The Development of Sex Differences. E. E. Maccoby, Ed.: 174–204. Stanford University Press. Stanford, Calif.

3. HARRIS, M. 1971. Culture, Man, and Nature. Thomas Y. Crowell. New York.
4. STEPHENS, W. N. 1963. The Family in Cross-cultural Perspective. Holt, Rinehart & Winston. New York, N.Y.
5. STERN, B. J. 1939. The family and cultural change. Amer. Sociol. Rev. 4: 199–208.
6. BRONFENBRENNER, U. 1968. The changing Soviet family. *In* The Role and Status of Women in the Soviet Union. D. R. Brown, Ed.: 98–124. Teachers College Press. New York, N.Y.
7. MANDEL, W. M. 1971. Soviet women and their self image. Sci. & Soc. **35** (3): 286–310.
8. MANDEL, W. M. 1971. Soviet women in the work force and professions. Amer. Behav. Sci. **15** (2): 255–280.
9. YANOWITCH, M. & N. T. DODGE. 1969. The social evaluation of occupations in the Soviet Union. Slav. Rev. 28 (4): 619–641.
10. FIELD, M. G. & K. I. FLYNN. 1970. Worker, mother, housewife: Soviet women today. *In* Sex Roles in Changing Society. G. H. Seward and R. C. Williamson, Eds.: 257–284. Random House. New York, N.Y.
11. LILJESTRÖM, R. 1970. The Swedish model. *In* Sex Roles in Changing Society. G. H. Seward and R. C. Williamson, Eds.: 200–219. Random House. New York, N.Y.
12. DAHLSTRÖM, E. 1971. Analysis of the debate on sex roles. *In* The Changing Roles of Men and Women. E. Dahlström, Ed.: 170–205. Beacon Press. Boston, Mass.
13. LINNÉR, B. 1971. What does equality between the sexes imply? Amer. J. Orthopsychiat. **41** (5): 747–756.
14. DAHLSTRÖM, E. & R. LILJESTRÖM. 1971. The family and married women at work. *In* The Changing Roles of Men and Women. E. Dahlström, Ed.: 19–58. Beacon Press. Boston, Mass.
15. PALME, O. 1972. The emancipation of men. J. Soc. Issues **28** (2): 237–246.
16. BRUN-GULBRANDSEN, S. 1971. Sex roles and socialization process. *In* The Changing Roles of Men and Women. E. Dahlström, Ed.: 59–78. Beacon Press. Boston, Mass.
17. SEWARD, G. H. & W. R. LARSON. 1968. Adolescent concepts of social sex roles in the United States and the two Germanies. Human Devel. **11**: 217–248.
18. STEINMANN, A., J. LEVI & D. J. FOX. 1965. A cross-cultural study of women's attitudes towards career and family roles. J. Health Educ. 8 (4): 188–195.
19. STEINMANN, A. & D. J. FOX. 1966. Male-female perceptions of the female role in the United States. J. Psychol. **64** (2): 265–276.
20. STEINMANN, A. & D. J. FOX. 1968. Male-female perceptions of the female role in England, France, Greece, Japan, Turkey, and the United States – A cross-cultural study. Mental Health Res. Newsletter 7: 13–16.
21. STEINMANN, A., D. J. FOX & R. FARKAS. 1968. Male and female perceptions of male sex roles. Proc. Amer. Psychol. Assoc.: 421–422.
22. STEINMANN, A. & D. J. FOX. 1969. Specific areas of agreement and conflict in women's self-perception and their perception of man's ideal woman in two South American urban communities and an urban community in the United States. J. Marr. Fam. **31** (2): 281-287.
23. RAPPAPORT, A. F., D. PAYNE & A. STEINMANN. 1970. Perceptual differences between married and single college women for the concepts of self, ideal woman, and man's ideal woman. J. Marr. Fam. **32** (3): 441–442.
24. STEINMANN, A. 1971. Cross-cultural perceptions of women's role in men and women as of 1970. Unpublished Paper. Eastern Psychol. Assoc.
25. STEINMANN, A. & D. J. FOX. 1974. The Male Dilemma. Jason Aronson. New York, N.Y.
26. GOLDBERG, S. 1973. The Inevitability of Patriarchy. Morrow. New York, N.Y.

IDEOLOGIES OF SEX: ARCHETYPES AND STEREOTYPES

Eleanor Leacock and June Nash

Department of Anthropology
The City College
City University of New York
New York, New York 10031

The cross-cultural understanding of sex roles prior to the period of European-colonialism is confused by an emphasis on supposed universals of sex-related behavior and attitudes that disregards profound changes that have taken place. In order to assess the effects of contemporary modernization on the roles of women and men, therefore, it is necessary to redefine baselines for change. Accordingly, we address ourselves to an earlier period of "modernization," when we can trace the transformation of egalitarian social forms into hierarchical ones. Using material from several culture areas in as much historical depth as possible, we intend to clarify the ethnocentric errors contained in a formulation of female/male roles that has recently gained wide currency. This is the view that femaleness has always and everywhere been devalued by contrast with maleness, and that such devaluation is linked to a universal association of women with inferior "nature" in contrast to men as superior "culture." Such a view not only distorts perceptions of female/male relations that are independent of European and Euro-American tradition, but also, as we shall show, it ignores the historical relation between ideological and structural change.

At a time when research is documenting the practical importance of women in economic, social, and political decision-making in egalitarian societies, and when the historical sources of women's relegation to an inferior status are being examined, the argument for female subordination has shifted to the ideological sphere. It is argued that even if women were autonomous in a practical sense in such societies, they were ideologically and socially devalued. This devaluation is said to follow from their participation in the "natural" functions of birth and suckling, and their involvement in what is defined in terms of European family organization as the private and restricted "domestic" sphere, downgraded by contrast with the important public world of men. Some measure of practical subordination, ill-defined, is then said to follow from this symbolic subordination.

Our intention here is not to demonstrate the falsity of the assumption that women have always been socially subordinated to men. We shall only note that for some cultures there is full documentation of the autonomous and public roles women played before their land rights were abrogated, their economic contribution and independence undercut, and their administrative responsibilities abolished by the economic conditions and administrative strictures imposed by European colonization; while for many other cultures a skimming of the ethnohistorical and archaeological evidence indicates that women's participation and standing in group affairs was in times past of no less importance than that of men.[1-11] Our immediate purpose, however, is to present data that contradict the ideological aspect of what has become a largely tautological argument for female subordination, and to disclose the superficiality of cross-cultural generalizations that are filtered uncritically through European categories of thought.

STATEMENTS OF THE NATURE/CULTURE THESIS

Lévi-Strauss, to whom "human society is primarily a masculine society" built an assumed devaluation of women and nature into his thesis of culture origins,[12,13] and de Beauvoir elaborated upon it in her exposition of the masculine ideology in which women are entrapped today.[14] Drawing on the writings of Lévi-Strauss and de Beauvoir, Ortner has recently reasserted a female/male dichotomy as universally linked with a nature/culture polarity, as a response to "the most generalized situation in which all human beings, in whatever culture, find themselves," and as underlying what she sees as the subordination of women to men "in every known society," past and present.[15] Rosaldo, writing in the same vein as Ortner, concurs with her in accepting de Beauvoir's formulation that "it is not in giving life but in risking life that man is raised above the animal;" hence "superiority has been accorded in humanity not to the sex that brings forth but to that which kills."[16,17]

Lévi-Strauss does not address himself to female subordination as such; he simply takes it for granted. In fact, he could well argue that women are valued highly, for they are, he writes, "the group's most important assets," "the supreme gift." It is through the exchange of this "most precious possession" that men set up the network of intergroup ties that supersedes the family, in Lévi-Strauss' view, and "ensures the dominance of the social over the biological." Women are even central to the emergence of symbolic thought, Lévi-Strauss states, for this development "must have required that women, like words, should be things that were exchanged."[18]

De Beauvoir's aim was to challenge the prevailing ideology of our culture with regard to sex, and to demonstrate the ramifications of men's definition of women as the "other," as deviants from a norm, as the inessential object by contrast with the essential subject. Her contribution to the understanding of women's present position, particularly its psychological aspects, was considerable, and we do not wish to discount it. Our argument with de Beauvoir lies with her implicit acceptance of Hegel's formulation that man is the active principle, in consequence of his differentiation, while woman is the passive principle, because in her unity she remains undeveloped,[19] and with de Beauvoir's projection of the existential phrasing of women as "immanent" and man as "transcendent" beyond patriarchal society onto the totality of human experience.

"This has always been a man's world," de Beauvoir states, by way of introduction to early society, and she quotes Lévi-Strauss that "the reciprocal bond basic to marriage is not set up between men and women, but between men and men by means of women, who are only the principal occasion for it." She pictures women, in "the age of the club and the wild beast," as suffering under "the bondage of reproduction," "a terrible handicap in the struggle against a hostile world." Women produced more children than they could care for; their "extravagant fertility" prevented them from increasing group resources while they "created new needs to an indefinite extent." Hence men "had to assure equilibrium between reproduction and production." Women knew no pride of creating; engaged in "natural functions," not "activities," they were trapped in repetitive tasks that "produced nothing new," while men were the inventors, furnishing support through "acts that transcended . . . animal nature," "prevailed over the confused forces of life," and "subdued Nature and Woman."[20] What is noteworthy about this formulation is not the lack of awareness it shows about the economic contribution and myriad technological activities of women in hunting/gathering societies or the practice in various ways of population limitation. It is surprising, instead, how readily borrowed it has been by those who should be familiar with the ethnographic record.

As for horticultural society, however, de Beauvoir herself contradicts the information she presents. She describes women as farming and manufacturing, as engaged in barter and commerce, and as "the prosperity of the group," the "soul of the community," and often priestesses, sometimes sole rulers. However, quoting Lévi-Strauss to the effect that "public or simply social authority always belongs to men," she writes:

> In spite of the fecund powers that pervade her, man remains woman's master as he is the master of the fertile earth; she is fated to be subjected, owned, exploited like the Nature whose magical fertility she embodies. . . Her role was only nourishing, never creative. In no domain whatever did she create; she maintained the life of the tribe by giving it children and bread, nothing more.

In woman, de Beauvoir writes, "was to be summed up the whole of alien Nature."[21]

In developing her recent formulation of "is female to male as nature is to culture," Ortner necessarily pays respects to women's role as substantial creators of culture. Her position is that women's procreative functions and "domestic" activities overrule their other cultural contributions. Women are seen as *closer* to nature than men, she argues, as "something intermediate between culture and nature, lower on the scale of transcendence than men." Ortner parenthetically relegates the whole association of men with culture and women with nature to the realm of the unconscious, an area less subject to falsification by contradictory data.[22]

To be sure, the processes whereby symbolic equations are made and concepts linked are largely unconscious. However, the linkages themselves, if they exist, must reveal themselves in art, literature, religious belief, and/or social injunction. If the propositions cited above are to stand up, they must be reflected in symbolic clusterings associated with female and male terms in world-wide ideological materials over recorded time. Yet artistic, mythological, and religious materials from contrasting societies in different world areas negate the proposition that male as culture is universally conceived as superior to female as nature. Instead, cross-cultural historically oriented survey of ideological data indicates (1) that the linked derogation of women and nature is not a characteristic of egalitarian societies; (2) that male assertiveness does not automatically flow from some psychologically conceived archetypical source, but is related to a developing competition over social and economic prerogatives among men and between men and women in advanced horticultural societies; (3) that ideological trends foreshadowing the European ethos accompany the emergence of full scale hierarchical organization in both eastern and western hemispheres; and (4) that the formulae regarding female nature as opposed to and inferior to culture, as stated above, are suspiciously European, and in some respects of recent vintage.

Lévi-Strauss himself makes no direct attempt to justify a nature-culture dichotomy. As with the subordination of women, he simply takes such a dichotomy for granted, and establishes it by applying it as an unquestioned principle of analysis.* Yet, as his own work demonstrates, it is the earth, the

---

* One way Lévi-Strauss deals with the lack of sharp dichotomy between nature and culture in mythic materials is to raise as a special case, in relation to fish poisons, the "reciprocal transparency" between them, their "mutual impermeability." (Reference 13, pp. 275–281.)

sky, the heavenly bodies, the weather, and plants, animals and minerals that are individually symbolized as variously female and male, never nature as the sum total of existing things counterposed to human society and manufactures. He does not ask what the general lack of terms for a dichotomized "nature" and "culture" might signify in societies structured differently from our own, nor does he inquire into the import of wholly different conceptions of nature.

The classical Ionian philosophers used the term for "nature" to refer to the essential character or essence of a phenomenon. This remained the normal sense of the term in Greek writings, according to the philosopher Collingwood, although the alternate sense of the term as an aggregate appeared in the late fifth century.[23]† Yet it was a nature still endowed with purposive intelligence of a human order, the Greek philosophical concomitant to the once universal conception of the nonhuman world as alive with spirits that had to be variously honored, respected, or feared. The historian, Lynn White, suggests that the idea of an intelligent humanity, standing apart from nature and rightfully exercising a kind of authority over it, accompanied a heightened and conscious exploitation. By destroying "pagan animism," he writes, "Christianity made it possible to exploit nature in a mood of indifference to the feelings of natural objects."[24]

The contemporary concept of mastering nature through science in the interest of social benefit is a product of the seventeenth century. It received its full expression in the hands of Bacon in the period when commercial and technological expansion, linked with colonial exploitation, was laying the foundations for the industrial revolution. In a book on the concept of dominating nature, Williams Leiss writes of the seventeenth century as absolutely obsessed with the idea of achieving mastery over "her" secrets; nature "was said to require the superintendence of man in order to function well." Leiss writes that this idea

> ... was used to justify the conquest and resettlement of the so-called backward areas, such as the New World of the Americas, where it was claimed the native populations were not improving sufficiently the regime of nature.[25]

Descartes' concern was with the formulation of mind as distinct from matter, and not with nature as such. However, borrowing the phrasing of his time, he wrote of the new practical knowledge that if we know the movements of natural forces "as we know the different crafts of our artisans," we can "render ourselves the masters and possessors of nature."[26] Such mastery was expressed at the time in male/female terms. Bacon's phrasing, Leiss notes, "displays strong overtones of aggression, ... including the sexual aggression connected with ... the use of 'her' as the pronoun ... 'hounding,' 'vexing,' and 'subduing' nature,"[27]

This, then, is the European view. It stands in direct contradiction to the so-called primitive view that human society should be at peace so as not to offend the gods of the animals and the weather and upset — in our terms — the balance of nature. Let us now consider, in their own terms, alternatives to the European view.

DICHOTOMY AS UNITY IN THE SEX SYMBOLISM OF THE ARAPAHO

The Arapaho, like a number of Plains peoples, were agricultural villagers who became highly mobile buffalo hunters when the horse became available, trade in buffalo hides profitable, and settled life difficult. The principal Arapaho

† For the development of the concept itself see pp. 29–30.

ceremony was the Sun Dance that developed on the Plains during the late eighteenth century. George Dorsey witnessed the ceremony twice, and published an extremely rich and detailed account of it in 1903.[28] He and Alfred Kroeber also collected a fine body of Arapaho myths.[29] Suggestions of a European deity seem discernable in this material, but little else of direct foreign identity. Given the military and economic conditions of the Plains in the nineteenth century, and their adverse effects on the status of women,[30] one might expect to find elaboration on themes concerning men as warriors and a corresponding devaluation of female attributes along European lines. Such themes are not found in the mythology or the ritual symbolism of the Sun Dance. Their absence attests to the strength of Arapaho resistance and their commitment to contrasting goals and ethics, based in interpersonal relations and a world view with roots in an egalitarian society of the Eastern Woodlands type, where the full public participation of women in early times is documented for the Cherokee and Iroquois, and evidenced archaeologically for the Late Archaic period.[31-33]

We have pointed out that in his formal analysis of mythic structures, Lévi-Strauss takes for granted, as universal, western themes of male as culture dominating female as nature, and projects these onto his data. However, when the entire body of Arapaho ritual and mythic materials collected by Dorsey and Kroeber is systematically examined for overt symbolic linkages with the concepts, female and male, plus explicit and implied attitudes towards natural phenomena, the following associations emerge:

1. Generative force and nurturance as central concerns link and subsume maleness and femaleness, which are ritually expressed as principles in beneficial union, not as apposite qualities. In symbolic objects, ritual acts, and certain deities, interpenetration and occasionally interchangibility of male and female symbols recur.[34] (Lévi-Strauss' treatment of differing associations with male or female in similar cultures affords an interesting comment both on his unquestioning assumption of polarization, and his gratuitous interjection of a hierarchical principle into this polarity. Justifiably pointing out that one cannot suppose an invariant "simple correlation between mythological imagery and social structure," he goes to some length to explain how it can be that the sky, which he refers to without comment as the "high category," can be female in one matrilineal culture, the Iroquois, while it is the earth, or "low category" in his terms, that is female in another, the Mandan.[35] Thus, in the course of a characteristically fascinating elaboration of mythic ideas — and the ensuing discussion includes an important digression into his method — he quietly imposes on his material a mechanical and psychologically loaded classificatory assumption derived from our own cultural tradition.)

2. "Natural" physiological attributes, such as human blood and urine, buffalo feces, and the "spitting" of a skunk, are not treated as disgusting or alienating, as the writings of Lévi-Strauss, de Beauvoir, and others might suggest, but figure in myth and ritual in positive ways. For instance, Skunk wins a dispute with Bear over a road by spitting in Bear's eyes. The rite of spitting imitates the skunk (the healer) when charging a bear (sickness and evil) and is a cleansing rite that also symbolizes breath, life, and knowledge.[36,37]

3. Women emerge in the mythic materials as commonly associated with artistic skills and technical knowledge of a practical order as well as with important ritual information. Stress is laid on women's skill in descriptions of material comforts that were obviously important to the Arapaho, and in one set of myths, the beautiful and intricate workmanship of a young woman figures in the plot, for a pursuer must stop and work out the symbolism before moving

on.[38]‡ Women are often the mythic givers of knowledge; a woman showed the Arapaho how to dance the war and scalp dances, saying, "I come to show you how to be happy while you live on earth, and to love each other."[39] (The comment on associations with war is interesting; prior to the development of war on the Plains as a tribal fight for survival, war parties of young men produced wealth, mostly in horses, to be given to kin, and there was little loss of life.)

As another contradiction of the nature/culture as female/male hypothesis, the common mythic occurrence of males giving birth turns up in Arapaho mythology also. (Lévi-Strauss disposes of the pregnant man of mythology summarily as "human antinature.")[40]

4. Anxiety associated with the lack of control over necessities of life is expressed in mythic ambivalence of the particular feature, particularly in the buffalo, but also to an extent water. These closely associated concerns figure importantly in benign symbolic forms in the Sun Dance ceremony and appear mythically in the form of potentially dangerous monsters or demigods. An important myth, common in Plains cultures, relates that Blue Feather married the daughter of Lone Bull, leader of the man-eating buffalo, and defeated him, thereby making the buffalo useful to human beings. Lévi-Strauss writes of this myth, "The marriage exchange thus functions as a mechanism serving to mediate between nature and culture, which were originally regarded as separate," thus confirming his suggestion that "the 'system of women' is, as it were, a middle term between the system of (natural) living creatures and the system of (manufactured) objects."[41]

Such a conclusion, if I may be forgiven for saying so, is typical of Lévi-Strauss' nineteenth century style of picking out the particular aspect of a totality that suits his thesis, while ignoring the rest. Using as examples social structures of eastern Asia, he has defined marriage as the exchange of women whereby man — and not in the generic sense — originally overcame and continues to overcome nature. Blue Feather's victory over the buffalo is drawn in as one small piece of the elaborate mosaic Lévi-Strauss has created in his definition of this supposed universal of social structure as an expression of the universally determinant cognitive constructs through which he seeks to bring both ideology and society into a frame that is coordinate with European "terministic screens."§ However, if one follows through a body of mythology in its own terms, in this case that of the Arapaho, a far richer dialectic emerges than that to which Lévi-Strauss' analysis would reduce the material, a dialectic interplay between humanity and natural features that unites symbolically the "social" and "natural" problems faced by the people.

In one myth, Crow scares the buffalo away, and is said to be "in a sense a murderer, because it starved the people."[43] It is in this sense that the buffalo are potential murderers who must be subdued. The full role of the buffalo in Plains material life is conveyed when following the mythic defeat of Lone Bull, his body is made up of different everyday articles — articles made from buffalo hide. Thus, the myth ends, "a life was reversed."[44] These themes of conflict are elaborated in a positive form in the symbolism that surrounds the buffalo skull and other central ritual objects in the Sun dance, through which the fight against

‡ Allusions to women as craftsworkers are found throughout the myths, but see especially pp. 75, 114, 169, 205, 207, 209, 240–246.

§ The concept is borrowed from Burke.[42]

hunger is equated with the fight against disease and with the fight against human competitors for the buffalo, and linked with the goals of health, old age, and increase of the tribe.[45]

In addition to illustrating themes of human unity with and respect for — rather than separation from and superiority over — nature, Blue Feather also illustrates the generative function of sexuality as encompassing and superseding specific maleness and femaleness. Blue Feather is also Moon, brother of Sun. He married a human woman and their original intercourse cased the "first flow of blood, meaning the child," seen on the moon's face. (Blood, far from polluting, is associated with the people, with ritual paint, life, fire, earth, the female form, old age as a valued goal, and meekness as a central virtue for both sexes.) The moon's marks are also Water Woman, Sun's wife, and in this form also represent the pregnancy of women and the growth of humanity. Moon thus links male/female associations, and is also spoken of as female and paired with the Sun as male. She is "our Mother," whose intercourse with the Sun created the people. Indeed, Moon may be spoken of as both male and female by the same informant in the same statement. Such usage is also true of Lone Star, or Morning Star, variously the son of the Sun and the Moon, or of the Moon and the human woman, whose rising tells of the first intercourse and origin of humanity. Though male in the myths, the Morning Star is ceremonially called both "the father of humanity" and "our Mother."[46,47] The rite of intercourse in the Sun Dance, that symbolizes the birth and increase of the tribe, therefore represents either the intercourse of Sun and Moon, or of Moon or Buffalo and the mother of the tribe, transformations that arise not merely in Lévi-Strauss' terms, from the tendency "to exhaust all the possible codings of a single message,"[48] but also from the meaningful interlinking of symbolic associations in response to actual social relations.

Historically, Arapaho society was linked with the southeast where the autonomous cooperation of the sexes in economic and political life is documented for the Cherokee. Arapaho stories of female/male relations, with their interplay of desire, jealousy, anger, and other emotions, express some fear of overly aggressive sexuality by either sex, but nothing like the ritualized sex hostility of lowlands South America or Melanesia. In parts of Melanesia, a highly productive sweet potato horticulture had developed, with trade, some specialization of labor, and the importance of the domesticated pig in intergroup alliances and exchanges. Women are not involved in this trade; instead, control over their farm produce has been passing into the hands of men via pigs, and enabling "big men" to assert themselves and comandeer the work both of wives and "rubbish men." Thus the basis for sex hostility is real enough. In any case, themes concerning sex are of conflict, not archetypically given female inferiority. Read writes for the Gahuku-Gama of the New Guinea central highlands:

> . . . men recognize . . . that in physical endowment men are inferior to women; and, characteristically, they have recourse to elaborate and artificial means to redress the contradiction and to demonstrate its opposite.[49]

IDEOLOGY OF DOMINANCE IN THE TROPICAL FOREST

Evidence that the ideological assertion of male dominance over the female is a culturally imposed standard, not a universal primordial sentiment is best recorded, paradoxically, in the myths of those Amazonian tribes where men are described as the clearly dominant sex.[50] Better historical understanding is needed of the chiefdoms and towns that existed prior to the colonial period, of the impact decimation by disease had on the people, and of the slave hunting for plantation workers that involved some groups as middlemen. There is evidence of the very early origins of manioc cultivation,[51] which in contemporary populations is done by women, and women participated along with men in intertribal warfare.[52] Roughly parallel experiences probably existed for the many ideological similarities with Melanesian populations. Just as Read[53] says of the New Guinea highlanders that the put-down of women was never cast in terms of natural weakness, so the phrasing of subordination of the women, as Bamberger[54] summarizes the myths of South America, is clearly stated as a culturally contrived defeat wherein the men seized the symbols of supernatural intermediacy with the gods.

The myth of the sacred trumpets of the Mundurucu related in the Murphy's study[55] is one of the most clear-cut statements relating the story of the transfer of power from women to men through the theft of the trumpets. The role reversal that ensued is said to have changed the whole division of labor as well as the initiation of sexual advances. Similarly the Witoto of the Northern Amazon, the Mojo, the Achagua, the Sáliva and Tacana kept the sacred instruments away from the women to ensure male power.[56,57] The Arawakan people of the upper Ucayale River, Eastern Peru and Bolivia held taboo to women the sacred flutes and bark trumpets in a feast dedicated to nature spirits. The most explicit ritualization of a past conquest of males over females is found among the Sherente, who have a women's society functioning in the naming ceremony for boys during which men enact a sham killing of women.[58] As the Murphys suggest, "The very fact that the women were believed to have once been dominant bespeaks a latent fear that they can become dominant again."[59]

The contradiction in these societies, where male dominance is flaunted at the same time that women's contribution in gardening and food preparation is an overwhelming part of the subsistence base, is revealed in myths, some of which credit women with much of the creativity of the universe along with other myths that assert a male creator. Even within a single myth there is often a switch from a male creator to female inventors and originators of particular culture traits and complexes.

For example, in the myths of the Desana[60] there is a complementarity of male and female creative power that was superseded when acculturation to Christian myths denied the dual source of generative and creative force. The Desana credit the Daughter of the Sun with cultivating the first field of manioc, with inventing the woven tube for preparing the manioc, with teaching pottery, basket weaving and the use of wild berries to the people. Furthermore, she is said to have invented fire and the stone axe.[61]

In the story of creation,[62] the morality fable unfolds much like that of the Bible, asserting that the Sun created the Universe, and, as the father of all the Desana, is called the Sun Father. The phrasing "The Sun planned his creation very well and it was perfect" reveals the influence of biblical style and meaning, although Reichel-Dolmatoff does not indicate the level of acculturation of his informant. In a sequel that tells of how Daughter of the Sun buried her sons when they died and taught the people the rites of death, the final statement contradicts the assertion of a single male creator with the words, "Thus it was that the earth was created. It was the Sun, the Daughter of the Sun and the Daughter of Aracu who created things and taught people how to live well."[63]

The story takes on even more of the biblical plot in a sequence in which the

Father Sun, after making love to his daughter, causes her blood to flow "and since then, women must lose blood every month in remembrance of the incest of the Sun and so this great wickedness will not be forgotten."[64] Just as Eve must bear children in pain to atone for Adam's sin of eating of the forbidden fruit, so Daughter of the Sun must pay for the sins of her father. The story follows with Daughter of the Sun becoming sickly and pale because she likes sex too much, and when she nearly died after her second menstruation, the Sun brought her back to life with tobacco, an act which is incorporated in the puberty ritual for girls.

In a sequel to the creation myth, after Daughter of the Sun had shown everything she had taught the people to Vího-mahse, she was cooking a meal and the contents boiled over, almost putting out the fire. In anger she urinated on the embers, which burned her pubic hairs, spreading an odor everywhere. The story concludes that, "Vího-mahse was looking and became distracted. Then instead of observing the world from the Milky Way, he began to think of the vagina of the Daughter of the Sun."[65]

At an overt level in the myths, the male principle is dominant over the female, but at a deeper level there is the sense of the overpowering force of women, which has to be controlled by male intervention with the supernatural. The contradiction between the need to foster the fertility of the creatures of the forest and rivers, and at the same time limit it in human species, which preys on them, seems to cultivate the tensions revealed in the myths. Thus the myths blame women for all the trouble at one level, while they recognize their contribution toward maintaining an equilibrium of forces. At the manifest level, the Desana have fashioned an ideology to preserve the privileges of men, while at a covert level they recognize the dual principles of male and female power that are projected in sexual metaphors.

Lévi-Strauss, as a European who has learned to be turned off by odors of burning pubic hair and whose schema of wife-giving and wife-taking enables him to transcend the themes of cannibalism, eroticism, and zoomorphism, has no problem in analyzing the myths of the Bororo and Sherente. When men cannot compete with women in fishing, when men are threatened with being eaten by their wives, or when they kill all the women save one, Lévi-Strauss sees all of these problems as part of the "meta-system [that] relates to the condition of wife-givers. . . ."[13] This ignores the dramatic leitmotif of unequal exchange between men and women without the intermediacy of brother-in-law that recurs repeatedly in the corpus of myths he covers. This theme and how it is dealt with at a conscious and subconscious level requires a far more extensive treatment. [66]

IDEOLOGICAL TRANSFORMATIONS IN THE CENTRAL PLATEAU OF MEXICO

In the tropical forest we lack the historical depth to analyze the process of change and the effects of acculturation on the people's expression of their world view. In the Central Plateau of Mexico, however, we have evidence in the archeological record and codices to show the transformations first from worship of the natural forces through the intermediacy of females to propitiation of those forces through androgynous representations, which was later followed by paired bisexual deities who were supplanted by male deities at the apex of a supernatural hierarchy. This emergent tendency visible in the late Aztec period was reinforced by the arrival of the Spanish conquerors, who projected their own image of the world on the Aztec cosmology.

The clear break in the populations occupying the Central Plateau when Teotihuacan was abandoned is followed by an ideological transformation, even after the development of a distinctly Aztec culture. The gods of these mythic dramas often remained the same, absorbing new figures along with the old, but their relative powers shifted with the changing cultural emphasis as the society moved from an undifferentiated horticultural and hunting complex to that of settled agriculturalists with an expanding military force. In the latter periods, the pictographs and Spanish chronicles recorded from the information supplied by the Aztec sages provide a knowledge of the culture, but always filtered through the European categories of thought. We shall examine these changes as they influenced the attitudes toward nature and culture in the ideological elaboration of roles based on rank and sex.

In the early farming villages of the plateau, there was no social differentiation beyond that of sex and age. Female figurines were the most frequently found in the early sites. The usual designation of such figurines as "fertility representations" is far from what one can infer from the representations themselves, especially from the El Arbolillo early Zacatenco figurines, where interest is centered on the head and not the procreative parts.‖ At a later period, these figurines were found along with male representations, which Vaillant interprets as meaning that a "theology was becoming more complex." With the emergence of status differences, as indicated by grave goods in the early preclassic period, there is indication of a high valuation of women (FIGURES 1 and 2).

FIGURE 2.   Feminine figure Dicha Tuerte, Veracruz.

FIGURE 1.   Pregnant woman.

‖ George Vaillant emphasizes the fertility features[6 7]; Philip Phillips points to those features mentioned in the text. The figurines, shown in a wide variety of contexts, reveal the complexity and variety of female functions.[6 8]

The history of the late Teotihuacan is reinterpreted by Spanish priests and indigenous intellectuals such as Ixtlilxochitl,[69] Tezozmoc and Chimalpain, who received their training in Christian missions and who drew upon the earliest historians, Quetzalcoatl and later Nezahualcoyotzin and the sons of Huitzil-huitzin, as those who declared that "the universal God of all things, creator of them and by whose will all creatures lived, Señor of heaven and earth who had created all things visible and invisible, created the first fathers of men, from whom the rest proceeded; and the habitation he gave them was the earth."

The temples of the Sun and the Moon, of the Rain God and the Frog Goddess, as well as that of Quetzalcoatl in Teotihuacan give silent evidence of the great diversity and range in the forces that recognize both male and female principles. The divergence between text and architecture indicates not only the elimination of female personifications, but also the obliteration of the diversity and the equilibrium achieved by the balance of dual forces as the principle of a single ruler at the apex of a dominance hierarchy was laid like a grid on the past

FIGURE 3. Coatlicue.

in conformity with the Spanish view of society and the gods current at the time Ixtlilxochitl wrote. Given the sex-segregated cosmology, the Spaniards eliminated the ambiguity inherent in the dual and often androgynous representations.

There is a tendency throughout the literature on Tula and Aztec divinities to ignore or play down the female personification of natural forces. Coatlicue, as represented in the monumental stone image found in the central plaza of Tenochtitlan, is a prime example of the simplification by the Spaniards, who called it Lady of the Snaky Skirt, and treated it as a mother-earth symbol. Justino Fernandez, an art historian who has the courage to believe in what he sees, has done an extensive analysis in which he convincingly demonstrates that Coatlicue is an amalgam of various deities, both male and female, which contains all of the basic components of the Aztec cosmology. In the base is a representation of Mictlantecuhtli, god of death. The skull over the umbilicus, or place where Xiuhtecuhtli, god of fire, rests, may refer to that deity, and paired with the skull in the rear, they may well represent Mictlantecuhtli and Mictecacihuatl, lord and lady of the world of the dead, of night and day. The talons and the feathers that appear below the skirt of snakes relates the image to Huitzilopochtli, god of war, and to Tonatiuh, god of sun or fertility (FIGURES 3 and 4). Fernandez[70] summarizes the iconography as follows:

> The Sun and the Earth are warriors, as unified elements in a dual principle: feminine and masculine, as lighters and fertilizers, as forces or fundamental principles with their own dynamic activities and their fertile complement: the rain; and all as a necessary process to the maintenance of life. One treats then, of the Earth and of the Sun, of rain and fertility, of the astral movement and of the maintenance of life, more mythic and with the warrior principle as the fundamental explanation of the movement moreover reaffirming fully its meaning.

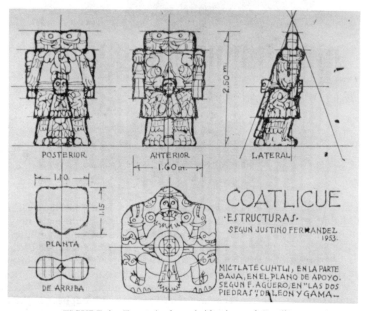

FIGURE 4.   Front, back, and side views of Coatlicue.

As the mediator between dry and wet regions, the link between sky and earth, Coatlicue loomed as an important figure encompassing the entire cosmology. A later representation (FIGURE 5) shows the separation out of a distinctly female figure.

FIGURE 5.   Coatlicue.

Recent investigations of the Tepantitla murals in Teotihuacan reveal that the central figure of the *tablero*, the deity Tlaloc, has neither male nor female characteristics. Pasztory[71] describes the figure as bisexual and combines all the destructive and constructive potential of the universe. She adds that, of the three possible interpretations as to whether the deity is male, female, or ambisexual, it is more probable that it is either female or ambisexual since the priests are shown wearing female dress, as they did when attending to female deities, and the connotations of the tree, the cave, and the spider that appear in the *tablero* are feminine. The significance of this interpretation is not so much that one of the principal gods of the Aztec was either female or bisexual, but that there was a transition in forms responding to ideological orientations that reflected the changing social outlook of the nation. Pasztory links this figure to the Lord and Lady of Duality, Ometecuhtli and Omecihuatl, who were superseded by Quetzalcoatl.

The European notion of the earth as female and the sky as male made it difficult for the European scholars to recognize the dual representations of the earth in Tlazolteotl, the female power, and Tlatecuhtli, the male power[72] or of the sky in Ilancueye and Iztec Mucatle. Similarly, there was a god and goddess of fire and earthquake, of pulque, and of voluptuousness, and these paired opposites are often lost in secondary accounts.[67] Similarly, the divine pair, Ometecuhtli and Omecihuatl, to whom the creation of the world and the other gods is attributed,[73] were often reduced to Ometecuhtli, or the "Lord of Duality" as Vaillant and Fehrenbach[74] refer to him. The Sun, Tonatiuh, and the Moon, Metztli, both of whom are treated as male, have a feminine and possibly androgenous correspondent, Coyolxauhqui and Tezcatlipoca, the night sky, who is referred to as the father and mother of the people.[76,77] ¶ Recognition of the fact that the moon was both masculine and feminine would have helped Anderson and Dibble in the confusion they encountered in their translation into English of the Florentine Codex.[80] They point out that, although the codex refers to the moon as feminine, they have chosen to refer to it as male in order to bring about compatibility with the fable of the rabbit and the moon in which the moon is referred to as male. Thus with one pronoun they negate the androgynous thought that was the essence of Aztec cosmology.

The written record of the preconquest cosmogeny was more subject to the distortions caused by filtering myth and history through the Spanish chroniclers than were the pictographs of the Aztec codices. The twenty divine couples of the Codex Borgia bear witness to the equality of male and female representations, shown at an equal level, eye to eye, which is a clear sign of equality with the status-conscious Aztec (FIGURE 6). Vaillant[81] comments that the appearance of the goddesses seemed "as if the idea of reproduction of male and female principles were dawning in Aztec theology." It is more likely that it was the final stage in the segmentation of androgynous forces.

The notion of hierarchy and the dominance of a single male god in the supernatural pantheon did not occur immediately with the arrival of the Aztecs in the Central Plateau. The Codex Ramirez indicates that Huitzilopochtli was a talking god who led the Chichimecs into the Central Plateau. He was brother of a female sorceress who held authority over the Chichimecs at the time of their drive into the Central Plateau, which was formerly occupied by the Toltecs. Her power derived from her ability to tame wild beasts, which she afterwards used against men. Huitzilopochtli advised his people to abandon her as they approached Teotihuacan since "he did not want the people whom they engaged in combat to be subjugated by the incantations of this woman, but that they must conquer by their courage, the alliance of their hearts and the force of arms."[82] In the conflict between Huitzilopochtli and his sister in the advance of the Chichimecs we have a clue to the historical context in which the separation of male and female spheres of dominance in relation to control over culture (arms and combat) and control over nature (incantations to animals) may have

---

¶ While Sahagun[78] refers to Tezcatlipoca as "the true and invisible God," Soustelle[79] uses the full translation of "father and mother of the people," suggesting an androgenous or dual source.

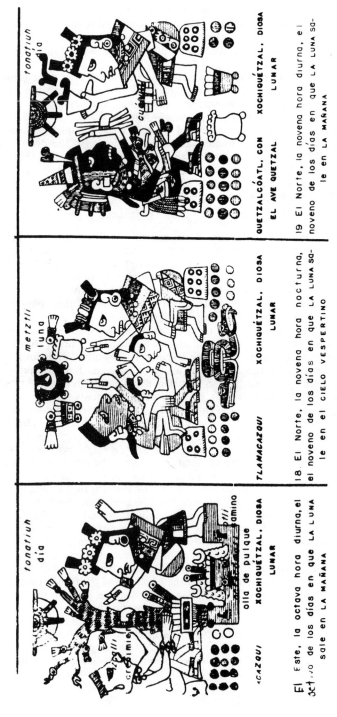

FIGURE 6. The twenty divine pairs. Representations of the moon. (From *Codex Borgia*.)

occurred. This is proof not of the universality of the dichotomy, but of its co-occurance in the historically specific context of predatory expansion.

In the early fifteenth century major changes[83] occurred in the warring city-states of the Central Plateau that gave rise to a new ideology. Nezahual-coyotl, the king of the Texcoco city-state, initiated a trend toward worship of a single god. The Aztecs at the same time, during the reign of their king, Itzcoatl, elevated the rule of Huitzilopochtli to a high status as a god of war. The importance of the conception, according to Fehrenbach, was to provide the Aztecs with the ideology for predatory conquest. Huitzilopochtli was said to have chosen the Mexica for a great mission to bring together all the nations into the service of the Sun. By rationalizing the conquests in the interests of feeding the Sun with the hearts of slain captives, he succeeded in institutionalizing the militaristic nobility. There is some evidence of the resistance of the *ilamatinimi* the intellectuals of their day who served as astronomers and engineers, to this transformation, and they continued to believe in the "Lord of Duality", Ometotl in Nahuaque, Lord of the Near Vicinity, and Ipalnemouhuan, Lord of the giver of Life.[84] Sahagun[85] treats the god "Vitcilupuchtli" [sic] as an interloper, saying that he was "another Hercules", killer of people who "posed as the chief god," so it was clear that his informants did not accord respect to the so-called master god. He preferred to think of Tezcatlipoca as "the true and invisible God," drawing a parallel with the Christian God. Even Seler,[87] who had less commitment than the priest, Sahagun, to have his theology rediscovered in the New World, makes it clear that he considered the identification of Quetzalcoatl as the "Creator God" an achievement, "purifying the chaotic and savage polytheism of the past." It is therefore clear that the European scholars underwrote cosmological conceptions of a single male creator/destroyer God that were compatible with their own conceptions of the supernatural, even though these had not been fully crystalized in Aztec thought.

Along with this upgrading of a single male deity by European scholars, there was an opposite tendency to downgrade female deities. One of the striking examples of this is the transmogrification of the goddess "Civacoatl", the goddess of Earth[88] and birth[89] (FIGURE 7). Sahagun[90] calls her "the goddess who granted adverse things." She had indeed become "a presage of war and other disasters" as the goddess of the souls of women who died in childbirth and of those who protested the loss of their children and husbands in the mounting death tolls of the late Aztec wars.[91] but not, as Sahagun suggests, the cause of them. She was often called "our mother" as her name signifies, "she who plants root crops."[92] In a late representation of her, she is shown putting the sacrificial knife in the crib of a newborn baby.

This simplistic equation — women = life-givers/men = life-takers[93] — is denied in the complexity of Aztec dialectics. To die in childbirth was the equivalent for women of men dying in battlefield; however, the man who took a captive in war[94] was the equivalent of a woman who gives birth to a live child. Men and women are both givers and takers of life, as the Aztec ideologues were asserting the claim the military held over the citizens and denying the life-giving principle of the goddesses themselves.

An even more subtle transmogrification occurs with the goddess Chantico, the goddess of fire and water, whose name means "inside the house" or "peace where the fire is." It also signifies the firey chile plant which is eaten with every meal and immediately after a fast. As a synechdoche for food, since it accompanies every meal, the chile draws the faster back over the threshold to human existence when one is in a liminal state. However, Seler[94] interprets this

FIGURE 7. Civacoatl.

as the sign of the eternal Eve, tempting man to depart from holy ways as she delivered him over to temptation.

What seems to be happening in the European interpretations of New World cosmology is an attempt to limit and codify a pantheon, the essence of which was diversity and transformation, the linked duality of male and female principles, and to exaggerate or acclaim those tendencies toward hierarchy and male dominance in the cosmology that coincided with the Christian-Judaic traditions. In the course of translating the supernatural conceptions into Spanish, German and English versions, there was a consistent downgrading and/or neglect of female duality and androgynous conceptions. If we take just a few examples of this, we can see how the whole dynamic of Aztec philosophy was obscured in the Spanish rendition. In the duality of dark and light, represented by Tezcatlipoca and Huitzilopochtli, the energy that made the movement of the sun, the moon, and the celestial bodies was engendered. Similarly in the duality of fire and water, sun and rain, we see the combined force of nature that produced crops, an understanding projected in the equal and opposite forces that sustained the dynamic dialectic of life and motion. For the Spaniards, who kept the world going through hierarchy and dominance, it was a difficult if not repugnant conception, and they treated it either by funneling the binary concept into a unitary deity or by forcing the constantly transforming deities into a static mold.

The transformations in the Aztec cosmology that occurred before the arrival of the Spaniards were inspired by changes in the social relations in the developing Aztec state, and they in turn provided a rationalization for the concentration of power and consolidation of control. In the early archeological record of the horticultural and hunting societies, there is no evidence of class distinctions.[96] It is more than likely that matrilineal descent characterized the Tula and possibly early Aztec society. In the Codex Florentine and the script recorded by Sahagun, Soustelle, drawing information from Ixtlilxochitl, states that "in former times, women had the supreme power in Tula" and in the beginning of the Aztec dynasties, the royal blood ran through the female side, that of Ilancueitl, a woman who was the origin of royal power in Mexico. The emperor was known as the "father and the mother of the people"[97] and the vice emperor, though a man, was called "Woman Serpent" as the representation of Coatlicue. In the Florentine codex[98] father is referred to as "the source of the lineage, who is sincere, diligent, solicitous, compassionate, sympathetic, a careful administrator," who "rears and teaches others, leads a model life, stores up for others and cares for his assets." Mother "has children and suckles them"; she too is sincere and diligent, but also "vigilant, agile, energetic in work, watchful, solicitous and full of anxiety." She teaches people, but also "serves others" and is "apprehensive for their welfare, careful, thrifty, and constantly at work." However, when we look at the ideal great-grandmother, she is said to be "the founder, the beginner of her lineage," while there is no such designation for great-grandfather.[99]

The emphasis on egalitarian relationships between the sexes in the early empire seemed to be eroded in later days as concessions were made to the warriors, allowing them to take pleasure in the brothels provided by the army. The change in human moral standards is shown in the god figures; FIGURE 8 from the Codex Borgia shows Xochipilli-tlamacazqui fighting with Xochiquetzal, representing conjugal love and the patroness of the *ahuiani*, or companions of the warriors.

FIGURE 8. Xochipilli-tlamacazqui and the goddesses of love: Xochiquetzal and *ahuiani* of the warriors.

The structural shift from matrilineal to patrilineal in the Central Plateau had behavioral correlates. A story from the eleventh century of the "Princessa Guerrillera" tells of a woman who entered into combat for her father's realm. Counseled by the priests to defend her rights to the throne, she went to the town of her fiancée and was wed. As the priest carried her in the wedding march, she was insulted by the enemies of her father. Indignant, she returned to the town and another priest urged her to revenge herself. She fared forth and led a party of warriors that took the men prisoners and had the sweet revenge of watching the sacrifice of the victims as their hearts were torn from their breasts. After that she and the prince were able to live happily ever after (FIGURES 9, 10, and 11).[100]

Ixtlilxochitl's narration** of the battle of the armies of Topiltzin in 1008 tells of how "Almost all of the people were killed in this battle. Many Tultec women fought violently, helping their husbands, dying and ... finally all were killed, old people and servants, women and children, not losing any because all were joined together, women and children." In the later Aztec chronicles, when military exploits were an exercise of professional soldiers recruited from among the male members of the calpules, there is no match for these early Toltec women.

The division of labor by sex was well established in the late Aztec period. The codices show men teaching boys to fish, cultivate and work metal, while women show the girls how to weave, tend babies and cook (FIGURES 12 and 13). But what is often left out of summary accounts, both in the modern period as well as in colonial times, is the fact that women were not only destined to domestic roles as Vaillant claims, but were also professional doctors, priestesses, and merchants in local trade; among the *macehuali*, or commoners, women were horticulturalists and they hunted small animals (FIGURE 14). Hellbom,[102] who compared the text and pictures of the codices, points out that there is a consistent tendency in the script of Sahagun to gloss over the sex distinctions in occupations or to refer only to men, especially in the merchant group. This provides at least one case of the superiority of pictographic over phonetic writing for overcoming the bias of the interpreter.

We must recall that in the domestic mode of production characteristic of Aztec society, the women were not as deprived of their productive role as were the Spanish women who were the models of the chroniclers. Weaving, cooking, cloth-dyeing and dressmaking were professional activities entering into exchange. The three goddesses who supported and in turn were generated by the common people — Chalchihuitlicue, goddess of water; Chicumecoatl, goddess of food; and Vixtocivatel, goddess of salt — were all female.[103] The codices reveal the sense of pride in work, the love of material splendor created by both male and female crafts, who had both male and female deities in charge of the guilds. In the Anderson and Dibble translations of the Florentine Codex[104] the script mentions that there were four grandfathers and fathers of lapidaries in times of old, devils whom they regarded as gods. The name of the first was Chiconani itzcuintli; and "*her* names were also Papaloxanal and Tlappopalo" — in other words, the grandfathers were both male and female.

There is some evidence that women protested the increasing wars and the loss of their husbands and male children. They deplored the festivities for the deadly

---

** Vaillant[101] talks of priests, but not priestesses, male trades and crafts, but not female, male merchants but not female, although all such occupations were filled by women as well.

FIGURE 9. *Left:* Advised by the priest, "6 Zopilote," the princess decides to defend her rights to the throne and goes on a trip. *Right:* She arrives at the town of Craneo, where, with her betrothed, she listens to the priest, "9 Herbs." After taking a ritual bath, she becomes the wife of the prince, "11 Winds."

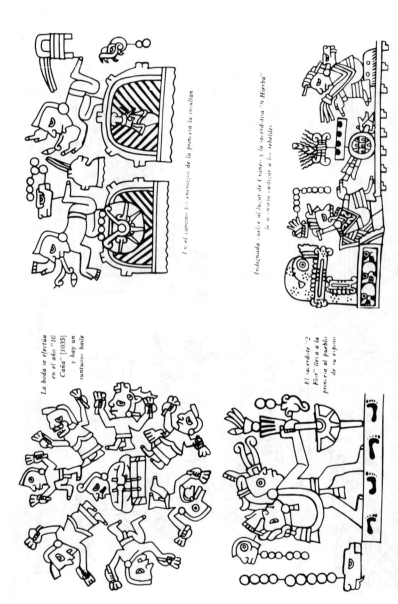

La boda se efectúa en el año "16 Caña" [1035] y hay un suntuoso baile

En el camino los enemigos de la princesa la insultan

Indignada sube al lugar de Craneo y la sacerdotisa "9 Hierba" le aconseja castigar a los rebeldes

El sacerdote "2 Flor" lleva a la princesa al pueblo de su esposo

FIGURE 10. *Left:* (top) The wedding was made in the year 1035 and there was a sumptuous ball. (bottom) The Priest "2 Flowers" carried the princess to the town of her husband. *Right:* (top) On the way the enemies of the princess insulted her. (bottom) Indignant, she returned to Craneo and the priest "9 Herbs," who advised her to attack the rebels.

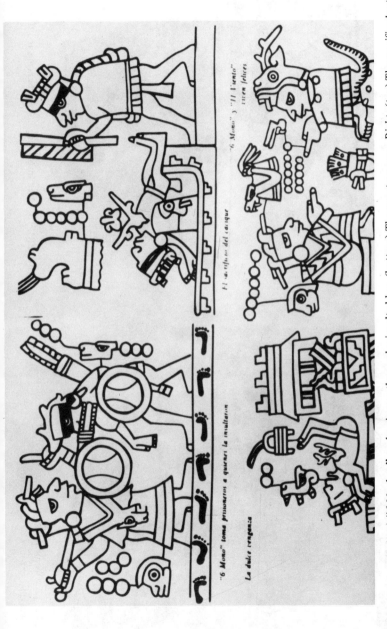

FIGURE 11. *Left:* (top) "6 Monkey" took prisoner those who insulted her. (bottom) The sweet revenge. *Right:* (top) The sacrifice by the *cacique.* (bottom) "6 Monkey" and "11 Winds" live happily ever after.

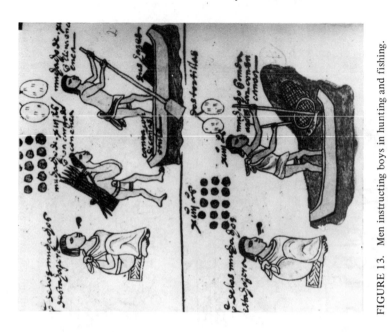

FIGURE 13. Men instructing boys in hunting and fishing.

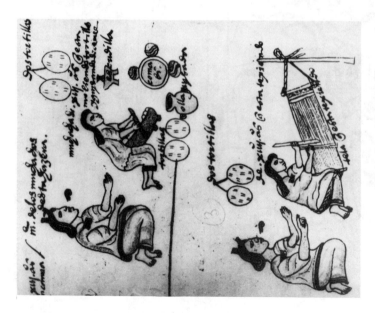

FIGURE 12. Women instructing girls in food preparation and weaving. (From *Codex Florentine*.)

FIGURE 14. Women depicted in dance, marketing, etc. (From *Codex Florentine*.)

destiny of the young warriors, although often they did not dare do much more than cry for the many sacrificial victims.[105] The alliance between the rival city of Tlatelolco was broken when the Tlatelolcan women "flaunted their backsides at the enraged Tenocha visitors," according to Bancroft.[106]

The consolidation of the state under military rule was never assured, and the attempt of the ruling elite to exercise control over the women, who provided sons for combat as well as some of the basic necessities, had to be supported by ideological persuasion backed by force.

Within a few decades after the Spanish conquest, the Christian ideology had become impressed upon the relations between the sexes, reinforcing those tendencies that were emerging in the theocratic state. Zorita[107] quotes a speech of an Indian *Principal*, or headman, which shows the use of the Christian precepts to enforce the subservience of women:

> Remember that you who are a woman, as you sit at your spinning or other labor, as you nurse your children, and do not reject the good that is offered you, do not reject the advice of one who tells you of God, placing the words in your heart as if he were placing precious jewels around your neck. You who are a peasant, think about God as you go ascending or descending with your staff and burden covered with sweat, exhausted, filled with anguish, longing for a journey's end that you may find repose. The teaching of God must bring you strength and consolation.

The suffering Virgin Mary replaced the powerful fecund image of Coatlicue as the Indians were brought under the control and domination of the Spaniards.

CONCLUSIONS

Throughout the twentieth century, anthropologists of the western world have aimed at replacing their own concepts with the conscious representations of people from diverse cultures. Lévi-Strauss and others have tried to go beyond such relativistic constructs. However, in going underground, into the subconscious, they project their intuitive understanding, based on Judeo-Christian precepts, onto a presumed universal structural framework of human thought. Through this ahistorical method, cross-cultural comparisons are being made about universals and particulars of sex-role definition that serve to crystallize the ethnocentric categories already imposed on the ethnographic data in the process of fieldwork and subsequent interpretation. We have reviewed material that is available in the ethnographic literature. The paper is by no means a voyage of discovery, but a cruise through familiar territory. We have demonstrated some of the selective biases and distortions of indigenous beliefs in the New World as they were cast into the stereotypes and archetypes of European iconography. This brief exercise points to the need for a thorough analysis of the processes by which aboriginal thought has been distorted in terms of European assumptions.

REFERENCES

1. BROWN, J. K. 1975. Iroquois women: An ethnohistoric note. *In* Toward an Anthropology of Women. R. R. Reiter, Ed. Monthly Review Press. New York.
2. HOFFER, C. P. 1974. Madam Yoko: Ruler of the Kpa Mende Confederacy. *In*

Women, Culture & Society. M. Z. Rosaldo and L. Lamphere, Eds. Stanford University Press. Stanford, Calif.

3. LEACOCK, E. 1974. The structure of band society. Rev. Anthropol. I (1): 212–221.
4. LEACOCK, E. 1976. Class, commodity, and the status of women. In Women Cross-Culturally: Change and Challenge. R. Rohrlich-Leavitt, Ed. Mouton. The Hague, The Netherlands.
5. LEACOCK, E. 1976. Women in egalitarian society. In Becoming Visible: Women in European History. R. Bridenthal and C. Koonz, Eds. Houghton Mifflin. Boston, Mass.
6. LEBEUF, A. M. D. 1971. The role of women in the political organization of African societies. In Women of Tropical Africa. D. Paulme, Ed. University of California Press. Berkeley, Calif.
7. MEEK, C. K. 1937. Law and authority in a Nigerian tribe. Oxford University Press. London, England.
8. REID, J. P. 1970. A Law of Blood, the Primitive Law of the Cherokee Nation. New York University Press. New York, N.Y.
9. ROHRLICH-LEAVITT, R. 1976. Women in transition: Crete and Sumer. In Women Cross-Culturally: Change and Challenge, op. cit.
10. ROHRLICH-LEAVITT, R., B. SYKES & E. WEATHERFORD. 1975. Aboriginal woman: Male and female anthropological perspectives. In Toward an Anthropology of Women, op. cit.
11. SUTTON, C. R. The power to define: Women, culture, and consciousness. In Contemporary Perspectives on Alienation. R. S. Bryce-Laporte and C. R. Thomas, Eds. Praeger. New York, N.Y. In press.
12. LÉVI-STRAUSS, C. 1969. The Elementary Structures of Kinship. Beacon Press. Boston, Mass.
13. LÉVI-STRAUSS, C. 1970. The Raw and the Cooked.: 276. Harper & Row. New York, N.Y.
14. DE BEAUVOIR, S. 1952. The Second Sex. Alfred A. Knopf. New York, N.Y.
15. ORTNER, S. B. 1974. Is female to male as nature is to culture? In Woman, Culture & Society, op. cit.
16. ROSALDO, M. Z. & J. M. ATKINSON. 1975. Man the hunter, and woman: Metaphors for the sexes in Ilongot magical spells. In The Interpretation of Symbolism. Roy Willis, Ed. Association for Social Anthropology Studies. Malaby Press.
17. DE BEAUVOIR, S., op. cit.: 58.
18. LÉVI-STRAUSS, C. 1969, op. cit.: 62, 65, 479, 496.
19. HEGEL, G. W. F. 1952. Philosophy of Nature.: 31. Humanities Press. Hillary House. Atlantic, New Jersey.
20. DE BEAUVOIR, S., op. cit.: 57–58, 60.
21. Ibid.: 63, 65, 66–67.
22. ORTNER, S. B., op. cit.: 75–76.
23. COLLINGWOOD, R. G. 1960. The Idea of Nature.: 43–46. Oxford University Press. New York, N.Y.
24. WHITE, L., Jr. 1968. Machina ex Deo: Essays in the Dynamism of Western Culture.: 86. Massachusetts Institute of Technology Press. Cambridge, Mass. Quoted in LEISS, W. 1972. The Domination of Nature.: 30. George Braziller. New York, N.Y.
25. LEISS, W., op. cit.: 74.
26. Ibid.: 81.
27. Ibid.: 60.
28. DORSEY, G. A. 1903. The Arapaho Sun Dance. Field Columbian Museum Publication 75. Anthropological Series, Vol. 4. Chicago, Ill.
29. DORSEY, G. A. & A. L. KROEBER. 1903. Traditions of the Arapaho. Field Columbian Museum Publication 81. Anthropological Series, Vol. 5. Chicago, Ill.
30. LEWIS, O. 1942. The Effects of White Contact upon Blackfoot Culture, with Special Reference to the Role of the Fur Trade. American Ethnological Society Monograph No. 6. New York.

31. BROWN, J. K., *op. cit.*
32. REID, J. P., *op. cit.*
33. WINTER, H. D. Value systems and trade cycles of the late Archaic in the midwest. *In* L. Binford and S. Binford, Eds. New Perspectives in Archaeology. Aldine. New York, N.Y.
34. LEACOCK, E. 1946. Some Aspects of the Philosophy of the Cheyenne and Arapaho Indians. Unpublished Master's Essay. Columbia University.
35. LÉVI-STRAUSS, C. 1970b. The Savage Mind.: 331–334. University of Chicago Press. Chicago, Ill.
36. DORSEY, G., *op. cit.* .: 17, 43.
37. DORSEY, G. & A. L. KROEBER, *op. cit.*: 288–289.
38. DORSEY, G. & A. L. KROEBER., *op. cit.*
39. *Ibid.*: 50.
40. LÉVI-STRAUSS, C. 1970b, *op. cit.*: 127.
41. *Ibid.*: 128.
42. BURKE, K. 1966. Terministic screens. *In* Language as Symbolic Action. University of California Press. Berkeley, Calif.
43. DORSEY, G. & A. L. KROEBER., op. cit.: 320.
44. *Ibid.*: 418.
45. DORSEY, G., *op. cit.*: 39, 94, 97, 117.
46. DORSEY, G., *op. cit.*: 64, 75, 106, 99, 119, 176–177, 219–221, 228.
47. DORSEY, G. & A. L. KROEBER., *op. cit.*: 149, 233, 368, 388ff.
48. LÉVI-STRAUSS. 1970a, *op. cit.*: 332.
49. READ, K. E. 1971. Nama Cult of the Central Highlands, New Guinea. *In* Melanesia, Readings on a Culture Area. L. L. Langness and J. C. Weschler, Eds. Chandler Publishing Co. Scranton, Pa.
50. MURPHY, Y. & R. F. MURPHY. 1974. Women of the Forest. Columbia University Press. New York, N.Y.
51. LATHRAP, D. 1970. The Upper Amazon.: 57. Praeger, New York, N.Y.
52. LEONARD, I. A., Ed. Colonial Travellers in Latin America. Knopf. New York, N.Y. Reprinted from The Discovery of the Amazon According to the Account of Fr. Gaspar de Caravel and Other Documents. Special Publication No. 17. 1934. American Geographic Society. New York, N.Y.
53. READ, K., *op. cit.*
54. BAMBERGER, J. 1974. The myth of matriarchy: Why men rule in primitive society. *In* Woman, Culture and Society. M. Z. Rosaldo and L. Lamphere, Eds.: 263–281. Stanford University Press. Stanford, Calif.
55. MURPHY, Y. & R. F. MURPHY, *op. cit.*: 88–89.
56. STEWARD, J. H. & L. C. FARON. 1959. Native Peoples of South America.: 256–7, 301, 305–7. McGraw-Hill. New York, N.Y.
57. GOLDMAN, I. 1963. The Cubeo Indians of the Northwest Amazon.: 191. The University of Illinois Press. Urbana, Ill.
58. STEWARD, J. H. & L. C. FARON, *op. cit.*: 367.
59. MURPHY, Y. & R. F. MURPHY, *op. cit.*: 90.
60. REICHEL-DOLMATOFF, G. 1971. Amazonian Cosmos: The Sexual and Religious Symbolism of the Tukano Indians. University of Chicago Press. Chicago, Ill.
61. *Ibid.*: 36.
62. *Ibid.*: 24.
63. *Ibid.*: 37.
64. *Ibid.*: 28.
65. *Ibid.*: 36.
66. SISKIND, J. Kinship, the division of labor and the mode of production. Unpublished paper read at the New School, 1975.
67. VAILLANT, G. 1947. The Aztecs of Mexico, Origin, Rise and Fall of the Aztec Empire. Doubleday. Garden City, N.Y.
68. PHILLIPS, P. 1966. The role of transpacific contacts in the development of New

World Columbian civilization. *In* Handbook of Middle American Indians, Vol. 4. R. Wauchope, Ed.: 296–315. University of Texas Press.

69. IXTLILXOCHITL, F. DE ALVA. 1801. Obras Historicas. Vol. 1.: 20. Oficina Tip. de la Secretaria de Fomento. Mexico.
70. FERNANDEZ, J. 1959. Coatlicue.: 230. Mexico: Instituto de Investigaciones Esteticas, Universidad Nacional Autonoma de Mexico. Mexico City, Mexico.
71. PASZTORY, E. 1976. The Murals of Tepantla, Teotihuacan. Garland Publishers. New York, N.Y.
72. SELER, E. 1963. Comentarios al Codice Borgia.: 124. Fondo de Cultura Economica. Mexico.
73. SOUSTELLE, J. 1962. The Daily Life of the Aztecs on the Eve of the Spanish Conquest.: 91. Macmillan. New York, N.Y.
74. VAILLANT, G., *op. cit.*: 72.
75. FEHRENBACH, T. R. 1973. Fire and Blood: A History of Mexico. Macmillan. New York, N.Y.
76. SELER, E., *op. cit.*: 47–54.
77. HELLBOM, A. 1967. La Participación Cultural de las Mujares Indias y Mestizas en el México Precortesiano y Postrevolucionaria.: 248. The Ethnographical Museum Monograph Series, No. 10. Stockholm, Sweden.
78. SAHAGUN, B. 1938. Historia General de las Cosas de Nueva España.: 25. Mexico.
79. SOUSTELLE, J., *op. cit.*: 139.
80. ANDERSON, A. J. O. & C. E. DIBBLE. 1961. General History of the Things of New Spain, Florentine Codex, Book 10, Part 11, Translated from the Aztec into English. School of American Research, Santa Fé.
81. VAILLANT, G., *op. cit.*: 175.
82. SÉJOURNÉ, L. 1956. Burning Water: Thought and Religion in Ancient Mexico.: 21. The Vanguard Press. New York, N.Y.
83. *Ibid.*: 110.
84. FEHRENBACH, T. R., *op. cit.*: 69, 94.
85. SAHAGUN, B., *op. cit.*: 25.
86. FEHRENBACH, T. R., *op. cit.*: 94.
87. SELER, E., *op. cit.*: 22, 69.
88. SAHAGUN, B., *op. cit.*: 26.
89. HELLBOM, *op. cit.*: 38.
90. SAHAGUN, B., *op. cit.*: 26.
91. HELLBOM, *op. cit.*: 23, 38.
92. *Ibid.*: 38.
93. ROSALDO, M. Z. & J. M. ATKINSON. 1975. Man the hunter and woman; metaphors for the sexes in Ilongot magical spells. *In* The Interpretation of Symbolism. Roy Willis, Ed. Malaby Press.
94. SELER, E., *op. cit.*: 25.
95. *Ibid.*: 224.
96. VAILLANT, G., *op. cit.*
97. SOUSTELLE, J., *op. cit.*: 88, 182–3.
98. ANDERSON, A. J. O. & C. E. DIBBLE, *op. cit.* Book 14, Part 13.: 45, 51, 55.
99. *Ibid.*: 2.
100. STEN, M. 1972. Las Extraordinarias Historias de los Codices Mexicanos. Editorial Joaquin Mortiz. Mexico.
101. VAILLANT, G., *op. cit.*: 122–3.
102. HELLBOM, *op. cit.*: 130.
103. *Ibid.*: 28.
104. ANDERSON, A. J. O. & C. E. DIBBLE, *op. cit.* Book 14, Part 10: 79.
105. HELLBOM, *op. cit.*: 264.
106. Quoted in Vaillant, G., *op. cit.*: 114.
107. DE ZORITA, A. 1963. Life and Labor in Ancient Mexico.: 166 Translated by Benjamin Keen. Rutgers University Press. New Brunswick, N.J.

PROBLEMS IN DEFINING AND MEASURING MARITAL POWER CROSS-CULTURALLY

Helen Mayer Hacker

Department of Sociology
Adelphi University
Garden City, Long Island, New York 11530

Much research effort has been invested in measuring the relative power of husbands and wives and in seeking the determinants of marital power without coming to grips with the concept of power itself. Interest in this problem may result from the wish simply to gain enhanced understanding of what is culturally defined by these investigators as an important aspect of family structure and process or, more pointedly, to evaluate the conditions that facilitate or militate against sex equality in both the familial and extrafamilial domains.

The first difficulty in defining the concept of power is to decide whether it should be considered from the actor's or the observer's point of view – a question that becomes especially pressing in cross-cultural research. Power in the Weberian[1] tradition has been defined as the ability to achieve goals that run counter to the goals of other actors in the situation. This model implies the overcoming of resistance in getting one's own way and makes power a zero-sum concept. In the absence of opposition can the question of power be raised? And how can this view of power be reconciled with the familiar proposition that that power is greatest which is most invisible? Sociologists who have been socialized in a society that places a high premium on equality, individuality, nonexploitation, and the provision of a wide range of choices may well adjudge persons or groups as relatively powerless who themselves are quite accommodated to their subordinate status and limited options. The sociologist may see them as victims of false consciousness.

Conversely, more privileged persons or groups may lack any awareness of power. A homely example of this reciprocal situation is provided in the case of the wife of an American career diplomat who automatically discarded her own plans for graduate education to accompany her husband to a foreign capital. It is possible, of course, that if she had not acquiesced so willingly, her husband might have resorted to persuasion or even coercion. It is also possible that the young husband might have preferred to decline the opportunity, but was constrained by the requirements of the masculine role to accept it. Or he may have acceded to the wishes of his wife, who deemed her husband's career a more profitable investment than her own. Clearly, the dyadic model cannot stand alone. Both spouses are helped or hindered, according to their outlook, by dominant value orientations and social structures.

Thus, the Weberian model, which focuses on the actors' perception of the situation and the degree of legitimacy they accord to cultural definitions of appropriate actions, may appear inadequate to the researcher who seeks to transcend cultural relativity. Other frequently cited concepts of power are similarly deficient in bridging the gap between the subjective awareness and the objective manifestation of power. Bierstedt,[2] for example, defines power as latent force or the ability to employ force. But how can a latent force be measured? Bierstedt states further that "authority is institutionalized power." Authority appears more amenable to investigation. Informants can report who is invested by cultural norms and/or legal sanctions with the authority to make decisions in certain situations or relationships. They may not, however, be able to ascertain the wishes of the persons involved or to specify the circumstances when authority is whittled down by manipulation or influence. In short, although authority may be a source of power, it does not automatically confer power in the face of opposition. Power, as distinct from authority, is noncultural. It exists in the interstices of culture. The dilemma remains. The researcher who wants to compare relative spousal power cross-culturally must decide whether to look through the eyes of participants in assessing familial processes, such as decision-making or conflict resolution, or to compare husbands and wives in terms of such objective indicators as education, health, leisure time, sexual freedom, control of reproduction, freedom of movement, possibility of divorce, marketable skills, possibilities for remarriage, alternatives to marriage and so on.

In a sense, most investigators of marital power have resolved the dilemma either by using marital power as an indicator of the general relative power of men and women in a society or by making certain assumptions in regard to the structural and cultural support given to either sex and then examining individual differences in spouses' ability to capitalize upon the advantages or to surmount the difficulties presented by the larger social context.

In regard to the former approach, Strodtbeck,[3] in his 1949 comparison of conjugal power among Navaho Indians, Mormons, and Texans, deliberately selected these groups because they "presumably differed in terms of the degree to which the wife was favored by the cultural phrasing of power." Blood and Wolfe,[4] on the other hand, have been criticized, most notably by Gillespie,[5] for erroneously assuming that American husbands and wives embark on their marriages against an equalitarian background so that subsequent power differentials may be attributed to disparities in their competence as marital partners. Gillespie argues that the resources that bolster competence and power are not randomly distributed among individuals but "structurally predetermined in favor of the male." (Further methodological objections will be considered subsequently.)

In addition to the dilemmas and difficulties in the conceptualization of marital power are the problems of the validity of the measuring instruments employed that confront the investigator of any social phenomenon or relationship. Historically, researchers in this area have not utilized the objective indicator approach discussed above, but have chosen direct observation of individual couples and families. Roughly their strategies fall into two chief categories: (1) the investigation of real-life processes of marital interaction and (2) simulated situations that involve laboratory methods or some kind of game-playing. Both methods encounter methodological hazards when used cross-culturally.

Although participant-observation might be considered a good example of the first strategy, it is impractical on several counts, including time and nonaccess to the husband-wife exchanges that take place behind closed doors. Investigators in this category have typically settled for some kind of self-report measure. Thus Blood and Wolfe identified eight areas which they considered important and typical for the average American family, and the wives in their Detroit sample were asked who usually made the final decision in regard to such matters as what job the husband should take, what car to get, whether or not to buy life insurance, where to go on vacation, what house or apartment to take, whether or not the wife should go to work or quit work, what doctor to have when someone is sick, and how much money the family can afford to spend per week on food.

Obviously, many of these decisions would be quite irrelevant in another society. The substitution of relevant questions in terms of the cultural context might permit the cross-cultural comparison of power scores were it not for the fact that the method itself leaves much to be desired: (1) Safilios-Rothschild[6] has dubbed it "wives' family sociology" since husbands may have a different view of the decision-making process; (2) self-reports are subject both to the distortions of recall and to the tendency to give socially approved responses; (3) the "scope" of the eight areas varies widely; and (4) the salience of the problem for the couple queried is conjectured on the basis of a general knowledge of the society rather than constructed empirically from reports of the respondents concerning the importance and frequency of various decisions according to their particular life circumstances. This last difficulty theoretically could be overcome, but would require considerable methodological sophistication in weighting and standardizing the actual conflicts reported so as to facilitate comparative studies.

More crucial to cross-cultural comparisons, however, is the validity of decision-making itself as a criterion of power. Here one must ask whether a decision made by one spouse runs contrary to the wishes of the other, and over what time period. It may happen that a spouse who "lost" a decision may later discover that the actual decision made did indeed conduce to his or her greater satisfaction in the long run and retroactively change his mind.* Or trade-offs may occur over the family life cycle which nullify the appraisal of the balance of power made at only one point in time. The more fundamental objection, though, lies in the equating of decision-making with power. Couples may agree on the independent domain of each or gladly abdicate responsibility even in what they view as their shared domain — indeed the struggle may be over who decides who is to decide. On the whole it would seem that Blood and Wolfe are really concerned with relative authority more than power.

Does the second main strategy of games or laboratory experiments hold more promise for cross-cultural research? These approaches have the merit of building conflict into the situation so as to provoke disagreement and consequent power struggle between spouses. Even more than decision-making, however, they pose the problem of validity or the resemblance of outcomes in these simulated situations to outcomes in everyday life. They depend upon the involvement of the couple in the game or test, as well as upon cultural norms which do not differentiate between the kinds of means that are appropriate for winning in the situation set up by the game as compared to disagreements in family matters. For example, Strodtbeck's Revealed Differences method, previously alluded to, requests subjects who have shared experiences to make individual evaluations of them and then jointly to reconcile any differences they may have in their interpretations. More specifically, they are asked to decide which one of three families they know well best fulfilled some twenty-six conditions presented by the experimenter. The initial responses given separately by the husband and wife are compared with the single, joint decision which emerges from their subsequent discussion of each question in order to determine which spouse won the decision. It is interesting to note that talking was positively correlated with winning. The question arises, though, of whether talking more is cause or

---

* An operational definition of power that included A's ability to change either the goals or the perceptions of B would require longitudinal studies.

consequence of power, and whether this relationship would obtain in "real life" conflicts of presumed greater importance to the "silent sex."

Since Strodtbeck's pioneering work, several variants of the Revealed Differences technique, such as color-matching, have been employed. One that to some extent overcomes the problem of validity and appears adaptable to cross-cultural research is the Inventory of Marital Conflict (IMC) developed by David Olson and Robert Ryder.[7] This inventory consists of eighteen case descriptions of problems likely to arise in the early years of married life of the prototypical white American middle class. Although the same essential facts concerning each case are presented in the forms administered separately to the husband and to the wife, in six cases the language is identical and in the remaining twelve the language is emotionally slanted to favor the wife's point of view on the wife's form and the husband's point of view on the husband's form. Regardless of language, half the stories appear to represent the wife, and the other half the husband, as the instigator of the problem. After registering their opinions separately as to who is primarily responsible for the problem and which spouse should modify his or her behavior to solve the problem, the couple is asked to engage in a discussion and arrive at a single joint opinion. For research that I am currently conducting I have added a question concerning the strength of their feeling about the case which will be used to weight the scores and thus help surmount the problem of saliency.† A query whether the husband or wife has had a similar problem, coupled with a conscious attempt to make the case descriptions culturally relevant, may heighten the validity of this technique in comparison to revelation of differences that may not matter very much to spouses, especially in societies in which competitive norms are not fostered, and to games, such as the SIMFAM technique employed by Straus[8] in three societies, and the "two-person bargaining game" in which each operates a vehicle that must travel from separate starting points to separate destinations in the least possible time, as described by Ravich.[9] (Although Straus has persuasively argued the case for "experimental isomorphism," he admits the need for "constant interplay between laboratory studies and field studies.")[10] Practical considerations, however, often make interview methods more feasible than laboratory experimentation.

So far this discussion has centered on problems in the conceptualization and measurement of power with scant attention to the sources of power. I should like now to describe a unique structural and cultural setting to which the inventories of marital conflict and family values might be adapted for the purpose of investigating the relationship between the private or dyadic or domestic power of women as individuals to the social power of women as a collectivity or their status as a group. This project ties in with the normative-resources theory of power propounded by Blood and Wolfe. An interesting contrast with the United States is provided by the *moshav shitufi*, a cooperative form in Israel which combines equality of income with traditional family patterns. This type of social organization represents a compromise between a *kibbutz* and a regular *moshav*. Productive work is carried out on a communal basis as in the *kibbutz*, but each family lives in its own home, as in the *moshav*, and draws up its own budget. The collective income in distributed to families according to the number of persons in the household. Men and women alike are expected to work an eight-hour day, but married women are given "credit"

---

† I am indebted to Dr. Lenora Greenbaum for the insight that winning decisions about which one does not fill strongly indicates greater power than if one did care.

towards their required hours for the performance of household tasks in amounts varying with the number of children in the family. In effect, then, women are paid by the community to perform homemaking and childrearing functions. Since women are economically independent of their husbands, and *kibbutz*-type collectivized services are lacking, it might appear that wives have the potentiality of greater power than their husbands in the marital relationship. The very fact, however, of women's partial or total release from collective work serves to separate them from prestigeful and policy-making positions, leaving them dependent upon a male-dominated community. This situation challenges the Marxist view of economic dependence on the husband as the chief cause of women's inferior social position. In this type of structure husbands do not mediate any economic rewards to wives, although rewards from differential standing in the community are not to be excluded. Furthermore, there is no place for a single man without a woman to take care of him. Women, it is assumed, can cook and clean for themselves. In regard to the determinants of marital power the question arises as to which factor carries greater weight — women's monopoly of housework and domestic services or the superior representation of men in prestigeful work and in political and economic decision-making positions in the community?

Field work relating to work satisfaction has already been conducted in two of the *moshavei shitufiyim*.[11] Planning is now in progress to measure relative spousal power against a background of the comparative resources of husband and wife and the cultural expectations about the distribution of marital power. In adapting the inventories of marital conflict and family values to the special case of the *moshav shitufi* the issue of the cultural equivalence of the vignettes must be faced. In the following examples I have retained the format of the Olson and Ryder approach, but have concocted stories based on my observations and experiences during a ten day sojourn in one of these communities in 1974.

Inventory of Marital Conflicts

Original Case Description (Nonconflict)

Bob and Frank are good friends. Janis, Bob's wife, likes Frank but is increasingly annoyed with his unannounced and excessively long visits to their apartment, especially at mealtimes. She has suggested to Bob that he ask Frank to please phone before visiting, but her husband feels this would be insulting to his friend. Janis suggests that she might ask Frank to please phone before visiting, but this only makes her husband angry. After accusing his wife of interfering with his friendship, he refuses to discuss the matter further.

Substitute Israeli Case Description (Nonconflict)

A childless couple, Aaron and Devora, frequently visit another family, the Yaari's, who do have children, often around afternoon coffee time. The husbands like each other, but Haggit Yaari is annoyed by the constant complaints of Devora about other women's lack of responsibility in their work assignments. She would like to tell Aaron and Devora not to come so often, but Shmuel, her husband, objects.

Original Case Description (Conflict)

Husband's version: It is Friday evening and the Carter family has a dinner engagement, which had been made the previous week. Frank comes home a half hour early so he can be sure to be ready on time. He showers, shaves and is dressed and ready to leave on time. But when it is time to go, Mary is still in the bathroom combing her hair and putting on makeup. Since Mary almost always makes them late this way, Frank becomes upset. Mary retorts that she isn't very concerned about being late since they always get where they are going sooner or later.

Wife's version: It's Friday evening and the Carter family has a dinner engagement, which had been made the previous week. Frank surprises his wife by getting home from work a half hour early and uses the bathroom continuously until it is almost time to leave. Since it takes Mary more than the few minutes Frank has left her to wash, comb her hair, and put on her makeup, it becomes obvious that they will be late for their appointment. Frank raises his voice and accuses her of always making them late. Mary tries to calm Frank down by saying that being a little late is not all that serious, but Frank just becomes more enraged and an argument develops.

Substitute Israeli Case Description (Conflict)

Husband's version: Yosef wants his wife Rachel to accompany him to a meeting and in general to take a more active part in community affairs so as to set an example for the other women. Rachel, however, thinks the meeting will be boring and prefers to stay home and watch television. When his attempts to persuade her fail, Yosef leaves the house before he says anything he may regret later.

Wife's version: Yosef wants his wife Rachel to accompany him to a meeting. Since Rachel has no experience in the branch that is presenting a problem that night, she does not feel she can make any contribution and therefore prefers to stay home and watch television. When she tries to explain her reasons to Yosef, he refuses to listen and leaves the house without saying goodbye.

An additional seven stories of the eighteen in the IMC have been recast in the spirit of cooperative communities in Israel. Obviously this adapted form will require pretesting for relevancy and degree of involvement. It will also be interesting to find out whether *moshav shitufi* members believe the discussions in which they jointly resolved their differences to be as therapeutic as Olson and Ryder report their American subjects did.

Concluding Remarks

In conclusion, this brief paper has attempted only to indicate rather than to resolve some of the problems in defining and measuring marital power, both within the confines of one society and cross-culturally. Indeed, efforts to carry out such research in social and cultural contexts that differ markedly from our own force attention to the theoretical and methodological difficulties besetting investigators whose work is confined to the American scene. A cross-cultural perspective, however, can be helpful in identifying the conditions that account for variations in power, that is, the sources of power. Although some may consider the measurement of marital power an ethnocentric enterprise, characteristic of a competitive society in which individuals are socialized to be power-seekers and to convert all relationships into a power struggle, others would justify it as one indicator of the extent to which equality of the sexes has been achieved.

Postscript: Many of the problems raised here are treated in depth in an excellent volume published after this paper was written: Cromwell, R. E. and D. H. Olson. 1975. Power in Families. Halsted Press (a division of John Wiley & Sons). New York, N.Y.

REFERENCES

1. WEBER, M. 1964. The Theory of Social and Economic Organization. Translated by A. M. Henderson and T. Parsons.: 152. The Free Press. New York, N.Y.
2. BIERSTEDT, R. 1950. An analysis of social power. Am. Sociol. Rev. 15 (6): 730–738.
3. STRODTBECK, F. L. 1951. Husband-wife interaction over revealed differences. Am. Sociol. Rev. 16 (8): 468–473.
4. BLOOD, R. O., Jr. & D. M. WOLFE. 1960. Husbands & Wives: The Dynamics of Married Living. The Free Press. New York, N.Y.
5. GILLESPIE, D. L. 1971. Who has the power? The marital struggle. J. Marr. Family 33 (3): 445–458.
6. SAFILIOS-ROTHSCHILD, C. 1969. Family sociology or wives' family sociology? A cross-cultural examination of decision making. J. Marr. Family 31 (2): 290–301.
7. OLSON, D. H. & R. G. RYDER. 1970. Inventory of marital conflicts (IMC): An experimental interaction procedure. J. Marr. Family 32 (3): 443–448.
8. STRAUS, M. A. & I. TALLMAN. 1971. SIMFAM: A technique for observational measurement and experimental study of families. *In* Family Problem Solving: A Symposium on Theoretical, Methodological, and Substantive Concerns. J. Aldous, T. Condon, R. Hill, M. Straus and I. Tallman, Eds.: 381–438. The Dryden Press Inc. Hinsdale, Ill.
9. STRAUS, M. A. 1970. Methodology of a laboratory experimental study of families in three societies. *In* Families in East and West: Socialization Process and Kinship Ties. R. Hill and R. König, Eds.: 552–577 (esp. 556–557). Mouton. The Hague.
10. RAVICH, R. A. 1969. The use of an interpersonal game-test in conjoint marital psychotherapy. Am. J. Psychotherapy 23 (2): 217–229.
11. RODMAN, H. 1972. Marital power and the theory of resources in cultural context. J. Comparative Family Stud. 3 (1): 50–69.
12. PADAN-EISENSTARK, D. & H. M. HACKER. 1974. Ideological factors in the selection of a reference group: Women in a cooperative community in Israel (the Moshav Shitufi) Eighth World Congress of Sociology, Toronto, Canada. To be published.

CULTURE, DEVELOPMENT AND SEX:
NOTES ON THE STATE OF THE CROSS-CULTURAL ART

Discussant: Howard R. Stanton

Department of Psychology, Sociology and Anthropology
The College of Staten Island of the City University of New York
Staten Island, New York 10301

Cross-cultural research implies a design in which the "same" phenomenon is observed in "different cultures." If the phenomenon does not vary from culture to culture, we may presume it is not culturally determined.

Two classic examples are:

(1) Margaret Mead's conclusion that sex roles may be culturally determined (as opposed, say, to biologically determined) since they vary from one culture to another.

(2) Max Weber's conclusion that economic roles may be culturally determined (as opposed to being, say, an historical-material evolution) since he found Protestant areas more capitalist than Catholic areas.

Neither of these examples was accepted without dispute. One form taken by the dispute was that of increasingly careful research design. We are considering here some of the most recent work on economic and sex roles, following the lines of which Mead and Weber were a part. Weber is an example of one approach: collecting comparable data from a number of different cultures. Mead is an example of another: a "case study" of a single culture compared with known data from others. What is the state of this art today? What kinds of design are in use and what sorts of theoretical subtleties are they meant to detect?

One objective of cross-cultural research is to discover whether particular phenomena are or are not culturally determined. Another objective is to understand more concretely how the process of cultural determination works. For both of these objectives, the definition of "culture" is a central issue. Should the definition be broad or narrow? A broad definition of culture helped anthropology to take an inclusive view of man. This has been such a profitable position that it can only be narrowed with reluctance. But if we are to contrast the culturally determined with phenomena determined in other ways, we need to base the research design on a narrower construction of the cultural process.

The operational definition for this kind of design has become one that sees culture as "those common understandings that are both arbitrary and conventional," or, more technically, as "symbolic systems." When "different cultures" are compared, different religious or ethnic groups are most often meant, an even narrower construction than the definition above.

To what extent are economic roles shaped by cultural processes? The established view of economic development has (1) identified development with individual roles, such as the entrepreneurial, (2) has explained those roles as an outcome of certain social attitudes and/or motivations (sometimes called "modern" as contrasted with "traditional"), and (3) finds these to be an aspect of different cultural values.

The established view has at least one advantage. It helps answer a persistent question: why are a few particular cultures (especially the Northwest European) prominent in developed economies? The suggested answer is that they are the ones that happened to have cultural values consistent with modern economic roles. If these hypotheses are confirmed they carry with them some implications for action: specifically, that economic development might be speeded up by programs of cultural change, for example, by Europeanization.

How does the established view fare in recent research? In the studies of Inkeles, Jones and Williamson, modern design designates sets of interrelated variables which are analyzed elaborately to see whether a generally consistent picture emerges. This is a substantial advance over the simple two-variable correlations with which some cross-cultural research began and which necessarily limited us to relatively simple theory.

Inkeles, whose research, in quality as well as in quantity, makes him an acknowledged leader in this field, enhances the precision of his analysis with careful control and matching of other (especially functional and structural) variables to isolate the cultural — generally religious or ethnic — background. In this analysis he is contrasting different cultural groups within the same national background, repeating this comparison in each of six different nations. The work of Jones and Williamson is similarly careful in the specificity of the hypotheses and the control of contrasting variables. Each has some theoretical elaboration and corresponding design features going beyond those of Inkeles in certain areas.

All three authors are beginning to introduce at least a hint of components usually limited to the "case study" type of approach. These are the "emic" and "diachronic" components. Emic elements (respondent's categorization of his own situation) include Inkeles' use of local consultants to identify the cultural groups most likely to differ in relevant social attitudes, Jones' use of a single, small nation of her own culture with presumably less variation in cultural cognition, and Williamson's introduction of political and economic considerations that might affect the respondents' point of view. Diachronic elements (data from different time points in the process) include Inkeles' use of stages in the migratory sequence, Jones' forthcoming analysis of before-and-after migration data, and Williamson's use of major historical circumstances affecting each nation.

As design becomes more sophisticated, the findings appear more discouraging to the established view. Attitudes (modern or traditional) do not appear to vary greatly from one cultural group to another — *if variables such as income, education and occupation are controlled.* On the other hand, those variables that are clearly correlated to "modernity" are the same variables that we use as indicators of social class in industrial economies. This lends further support to the "functional" hypothesis — as opposed to the established cultural view — that (1) industrialization opens new kinds of roles, (2) the occupants of which develop attitudes and values congruent with their positions. Hence "modern" social attitudes are a consequence, not a precondition, of economic development. This has important implications for programs of development — in particular it suggests that failures in development may be due to something other than traditional cultures of unwilling groups.

The design of this line of research may profit from further tightening, especially as we begin to assume that the economic and social processes involved are in all likelihood considerably more complex than either of the above relatively simple alternatives. All three of the authors cited above are already moving toward greater complexity. We may look at a further example of potential theoretical complexities and congruent design complexity: between the "traditional" peasant cultivator and the "modern" urban factory or office worker lie other role complexes, one of which at least (the agricultural wage laborer or plantation worker) has been the subject of considerable study. If we examine some of the role elements and attitudes of this group, will it not shed some light on the transition to economic development?

The social attitudes and motivations of plantation workers differ markedly from those of peasants. This difference is enhanced when other factors, especially cultural background, are controlled. Furthermore, the attitudes and motivations of plantation workers are similar in some respects to more modern groups such as urban industrial workers. For example, in many cultures, plantation families are more receptive than peasant families to women working, fewer children, equal authority, and easy divorce.

As more phases are added to the presumed sequence, the design needs to be more diachronic — to provide more careful collection of data at different time points. What is the order of the changes? For changes that take place within a period of a few years, longitudinal studies are feasible and desirable. For processes that require decades for completion, a few longitudinal studies can be planned, but mostly data must come through situations which, though contemporaneous, represent populations at different points in the sequence. A further improvement is to follow each situation long enough to overlap with preceeding and following phases.

As theoretical approaches begin to presume more specific varieties of situations, design needs to be more "emic" — to describe the situation within the categories of experience used by the participants themselves. For example, the plantation worker case referred to above appears emically somewhat as follows: As peasants are drawn into plantation labor, they lose direct contact with subsistence — that is, their efforts do not have manifest survival consequences, but rather are monetarized. The connection with survival is not only indirect, but also intermittent. A plantation worker cannot guarantee continuous support to his family. Therefore, women form coalitions (usually within the consanguine family) of mutual support whereby, if at least one man — or in times of severe emergency, one woman — has earnings, the coalition of related households will get by. The changing attitudes are described by the participants themselves as supportive of this kind of functional arrangement.

Cross-cultural research design focused on the development of economic roles will need to enhance significantly the diachronic and emic components if it is to deal with theories of more complexity or subtlety. For example, cross-national surveys can use very large clusters so that interviewers can double as participant observers and the "panel" of clusters can be revisited for longitudinal data.

To what extent are sex roles shaped by cultural processes? With respect to changing sex roles, the principal established view is strongly "functional," similar to that which is now emerging from cross-cultural research on economic development. Seward provides a good summary of one (there are many other) variant of this general view: male/female roles are less differentiated (more egalitarian?) when gathering — such as fruits and roots — is a major survival economy, and again in recent years when the light white-collar economy has become dominant in some industrial countries. On the other hand, in economies dependent for survival on hunting, especially of larger mammals, on warfare, or on heavy machine work — in all of these — women's roles would be subordinated. Sex roles, then, are defined functionally (by what "works best") and eventually absorbed into the cultural matrix. Another interesting variation on this is Freed's suggestion that domiciliary segregation of males and females in the Indian subcontinent may have had a population-control function.

Some sex-role-change theory relates to shorter time periods — for example, that dealing with sex-role changes during industrialization. But some theory deals with time periods of long historical depth. For these, the diachronic component may be especially difficult. How do we get data from different points in historic time? Leacock and Nash point up some of the problems involved. Ethnographic records, even those dating from first contact, may report behavior distorted by the reverberating consequences of indirect contact, and the reports themselves may be distorted by the preconceptions of the early observers. (With respect to sex roles this may be especially significant since the early observers were nearly all male.)

Content analysis of mythic and artistic materials preserved relatively unaltered up to our time adds diachronic and emic components to cross-cultural research, even for very long time-depth changes. The analysis shows that the European deprecation of female roles is not found in all cultures (hence it may be culturally determined) but the conclusions of the study appear largely functional (relating historically to the development of horticulture, and recently to the development of science, for example).

Some recent research poses problems for this approach, challenging the accepted functional view. These include: (1) Seward's report of trends in Russia and Sweden where politicolegal regulation consistent with ideological positions of equality and democracy have been less than completely implemented, due, perhaps, to cultural resistance; and (2) the reports of Endleman and Hacker that recent changes in Israel have sometimes meant *less* equality, *greater* differentiation in sex roles and *greater* emphasis on home/child tasks for women. Further, both authors report that these changes have often been urged by women themselves even when (as sabras) they have been raised in more equalitarian subcultures, or (as in the *moshav*) they have been given almost total economic independence.

Why would women, given political, economic and ideological support for equality choose more differentiated, more home-bound, less egalitarian roles? A tempting answer with some emic support ("comfortable," "natural") is that sex roles are cultural, and therefore would resist structural and functional pressures for change. A modification, still giving primacy to the functional, would be the classic cultural-lag approach, assuming that recent functional changes take one or more generations before cultural values will be brought in line.

Again, more sophisticated design may force us into more complex theoretical positions which may require still more elaborate design to unravel. These studies reflect an increasing emphasis on representational and quasi-experimental components in the research design. Hacker, especially, considers at length the prospects for simulated situations in the assessment of power, Both she and Endleman treat recent trends in Israel as natural experiments, as does Seward with respect to changing family law in Russia and Sweden. All of the authors are careful to place their data in its broader context, as contrasted with the simpler approach sometimes found of treating each case as an independent world.

If this line of research continues, what implications might it have for strategies of social change? It might, for example, de-emphasize legal-structural efforts and reinforce consciousness-raising and other more culture-oriented approaches.

The functional explanation of shifts in women's roles assumes that activities are rewarded with prestige and power in proportion to their manifest importance for survival. Logical as this may appear to be, the data here seem to support an opposite interpretation. Survival activities have minimal prestige. Expressive activities with no manifest survival implications have the highest prestige, and prestige is associated with power and privilege. Hence, women's roles may be more egalitarian when they are less "functional." Child and home activities are survival activities. To the extent that they are assigned to women, women's roles will carry little power or privilege. To this extent, if sex roles are seen as analogous to organizational positions, they may be said to be determined more by structural type processes than by functional.

The ordinary daily useful tasks are not the source of prestige and power. In fact, what is most prestigious can only be indirectly useful if at all. It is not *work* that brings prestige in a society but *money*. Prestige items are useless items. Women's roles earn less prestige because they are usually useful. Are not the most inequitable situations precisely those where men's roles are largely expressive, while women are directly responsible for day to day survival.

Functional processes, we should note, often are characterized by protection against fluctuations which might threaten survival. In other words, the most dramatic functional roles are not those that sustain the society under average conditions, but those that anticipate negative conditions and hedge against them. A woman whose children are being cared for by someone else may nevertheless define her situation according to the possibility of an emergency alternative. If her personal intervention is the only alternative, then she can not be considered free to define her time as expressive, hence her prestige is low.

If we were to design cross-cultural research to test an approach of this kind, what would we look for? In peasant communities, are men often free for a good part of their time to participate in expressive tasks? If so, and if women are more totally committed to survival tasks, we may expect unequal role definitions. In plantation communities, men's tasks are not directly and manifestly productive of survival. Does the intermittent and uncertain nature of the wages focus attention on survival alternatives that provide protection in case of negative fluctuations? If so, men may be less involved in expressive competition than their peasant brothers. On the other hand, the women's (consanguine) coalition could provide some release from survival obligations, bringing about some access to prestige and more egalitarian sex roles than those of peasant communities. Urban industrial households may be somewhat less egalitarian than those of plantation workers if their circumstances are a bit less uncertain, and/or if the women cannot as easily form effective consanguine coalitions.

The urban white-collar class in industrialized economies is totally separated, occupationally, from survival tasks and is substantially protected against fluctuation by governmental guarantees. This allows men to commit themselves totally to expressive tasks. Women's roles may still be survival-oriented, either directly or in terms of emergencies. In that case, sex roles may be sharply differentiated and unequal. On the other hand, alternate child- and home-care arrangements (if effectively guaranteed against emergencies) make more egalitarian relationships possible.

We may assume that survival tasks generate conservative, traditional, low-risk attitudes, while expressive tasks permit the luxury of "modern" mobility-aspiration, flexible-rational attitudes. This would be in agreement with the correlation between social attitudes and social-class variables, as well as the scarcity of significant correlations between these attitudes and cultural groupings.

We may also assume that survival tasks must be rewarded more or less proportional to effort, accomplishment, or need. Expressive tasks, however, have no such limitation: they may even be recompensed on a winner-take-all basis, since survival is not directly or manifestly involved. Thus, expressive task situations should show much greater inequality.

To what extent can this type of analysis suggest strategy for economic development?

1. Developed economies must organize the exchange of expressive services, but must also guarantee survival needs even in bad times. Can the world's economy be so organized that most of us are in such a favored position at the same time? The less favored have lower status and less "modern" attitudes.

2. For now, these favored economic roles in any number can be guaranteed stability only by government action. The effect of economic fluctuations can be softened for some, but are these cycles passed on with increased amplitude to others? Favoring some may directly disfavor others.

3. The protected class can afford modern attitudes and nuclear families, but they may be accused of doing so at the expense of others. If all the world cannot be favored, can survival tasks be shared more equally so that expressive activities are also more equally available? Can we who write these prestigious pieces also plant an occasional potato? Why not?

The issues are urgent, the research is serious, but the answers are not forthcoming. How are culture, development and sex interconnected? Perhaps the state of the cross-cultural art can not answer. Yet, even if not, we may see glimpses of the next generation of cross-cultural research in the touches of emic, diachronic, representative and quasi-experimental design.

In summary, sex roles as well as economic roles can plausibly be regarded as determined by cultural process, functional process, structural process, or, more likely, some combination of the above. If cross-cultural research has any effect on government policy (and increasingly, it does) then the kind of explanation accepted for these phenomena can have major consequences for world economic and political planning.

Cross-cultural research, as in the examples of Mead's and Weber's conclusions, once used rather simple design to examine rather simply stated theoretical alternatives. The research that has followed along those lines has become increasingly sophisticated in design, and generates increasingly more complex theroretical approaches. The most recent research seems to continue that trend. To fit the accumulated data, interrelated cultural, functional and structural processes may be posited. But these will require even more careful design. The next generation of cross-cultural research may have to be emic, diachronic, representative and quasi-experimental, all at the same time in order to catch the nuances of the hypothesized processes. Difficult as this may appear to be, a combination of existing survey and case-study methods may offer a solution. Large clusters, randomly selected from relevant strata, studied by resident interviewer-observers, revisited as a continuing panel, and used for testing experimental programs: would not a design of this kind bring us data as challenging as that which we see in the studies discussed here, but with the added value of allowing us to analyze the interrelationships between the processes?

WHITHER CROSS-CULTURAL RESEARCH?

Discussant: Sheridan Phillips

Institute of Advanced Psychological Studies
Adelphi University
Garden City, Long Island, New York 11530

Most of the papers presented have emphasized the *process* of change that occurs during modernization. As a keynote, consider the following remarks by Williamson:

> We are not asking whether, as Inkeles puts it, modernism is necessarily good or bad. Rather, in a modest way the inquiry has posed the question as to what factors may be associated with the process of modernization.[1]

Clearly, human beings are malleable and continually changing, both as individuals and collectively. The kind of change that occurs in modernization involves a continual interaction between the environment and the individual, entailing reciprocal influence. Different aspects of the environment, including the purely physical, social/cultural structure, and economic forces, clearly affect the individual living within that environment. In addition, however, individuals act upon their environment so as to modify it: changes in attitude can alter social institutions and even the physical environment. Such environmental changes will then in turn exert an effect on individuals. This continued reciprocal influence reflects the dynamic nature of social systems.[2]

Studying the process of change during modernization thus entails assessing the respective contributions of each factor, and their joint influence on the course of development. Inkeles' paper addresses such questions most directly, investigating the specific role of attitudinal mediators. His paper evaluates the validity of a model that assumes that different subgroups in the population possess different attitudes (homogeneous within the group) which directly influence the actions of individuals (having an effect on the environment) such that different individual actions are mediated by individual attitudes that merely reflect their subgroup membership. His results indicate that it is exposure to education, factory work, and the mass media that influences individual attitudes regarding modernization. Thus, it appears likely that the individual mediating attitudes are influenced more directly by environmental forces other than ethnic/religious subgroup membership.

Inkeles admits the limitations of his matching procedures, and thus is unable definitively to identify the causal agent; for example, it is possible that different subgroups have differential access to the relevant environmental influences that lead to different individual attitudes. However, the study does engender a more sophisticated view of the complexities involved in the reciprocal-influence process of societal change. Clearly, the causal agent at any given point in time could be attitudes, or aspects of the environment to which individuals are exposed, or an interaction of the two which is probably cyclical.

Thus, all the papers presented were concerned with further understanding the process of change during modernization. In addition to Inkeles, Williamson, Freed, Endleman, Seward, and Nash have approached the question directly. Hacker's paper involved an indirect approach, validating measures to locate and accurately tap change. Jones utilized a combination of approaches, both validating measures and gathering information directly.

What is the purpose of further understanding the change process? Presumably, it is to enable us to predict likely developments and thus to provide information as to how to facilitate the change process. For example, Freed's paper suggests that inducing change in cultural patterns of space utilization may promote better adaptation to social reorganization prompted by industrialization. Jones' paper also attempted to identify factors that facilitate the modernization transition for individuals. Again, the implication is that we could learn how to structure aspects of the environment so as to foster integration as quickly and painlessly as possible.

This approach is directly related to the further questions of what state of affairs will be facilitated, and what the effects of this will be on the individual. For example, Inkeles and Smith[3] have suggested that failure to become integrated in an urban industrial setting may generate "psychic strain." Such questions invoke both philosophical issues regarding Utopia, and empirical issues regarding the nature of man.

Americans have traditionally emphasized the environment, and view man as totally malleable. Skinner, for example, personifies this *tabula rasa* approach. More recently, however, several noted ethologists (e.g., Tinbergen and Lorenz) have generated evidence that questions the assumption of complete malleability of organisms, and they have begun to exert an influence on American psychology.[4]

Fortunately, these are empirical questions, and it is at least theoretically possible to study the effects of changing environments on the individual. Cross-cultural research has already provided useful information, for example, in the area of sex roles/sex differences, allowing exploration of alternative family structures naturally occurring in different cultures, and examining corollary psychological factors for males and females.[5] Parallel explorations might aid societal decisions regarding the best way to proceed in social adaptation to modernization.

One final question concerns the use to which such information is put. Given that we accumulate knowledge that allows us to predict, control, and influence the process of change during modernization, who will decide how to employ such information? This philosophical/ethical concern has become increasingly widespread with regard to the control exerted on individuals. It seems appropriate to extend the same question to the broader arena of societal/cultural control.

SUMMARY

Discussion has covered several different issues raised by the papers presented on modernization. These issues fall into two general classes, one largely empirical and one largely philosophical or ethical. The questions that have been raised are:

(1a) How can we best increase our knowledge regarding the process of change during modernization?

(1b) How will such information allow facilitation of the change process?

(1c) What effect will different routes of development have on individuals in the changing culture?

(2a) What do we see as the ideal end product of change?

(2b) Who will control and utilize the information that allows for planned facilitation of change?

REFERENCES

1. WILLIAMSON, R. This monograph.
2. KRASNER, L. & L. ULLMANN. 1973. Behavior Influence and Personality: The Social Matrix of Human Action. Holt, Rinehart & Winston. New York, N.Y.
3. INKELES, A. & D. H. SMITH. 1970. The fate of personal adjustment in modernization. Intern. J. Comp. Soc. 11: 81–114.
4. GARCIA, J., B. McGOWAN & K. F. GREEN. 1971. Biological constraints on conditioning. In Classical Conditioning II. A. H. Black and W. R. Prokasy, Eds. Appleton-Century-Crofts. New York, N.Y.
5. MACCOBY, E. & C. JACKLIN. 1974. The Psychology of Sex Differences. Stanford University Press. Stanford, Calif.

OPEN DISCUSSION: V

ANGELA GINORIO: Dr. Inkeles, since you keep referring to your subjects as "men," I assume you did not include women in your sample. Why did you exclude women? Do you think your results would be significantly different if you included women?

DR. INKELES: The inference that we studied only men, at least in the first wave of our study, is correct. In several of the countries in which we conducted our research women were very rarely employed in industry, and industrial workers were to be the largest component of our sample. In addition, in a number of these countries interviewing women posed special problems, which would have been a considerable burden for already heavily burdened field directors. For these and other reasons we regretfully decided to focus initially on men exclusively.

Subsequently, associates of our modernization project did apply the modernity (OM) scale in a way that permitted us to learn something of the role played by gender in influencing individual modernity. The scale was used with children of both sexes in the third to fifth grade in Brasilia, with boys and girls in high school in Puerto Rico, with a sample of Black women in Roxbury, Massachusetts, and with a representative sample of adult men and women registered voters of the Third Congressional District of Massachusetts.

On the basis of these efforts we may note the following:

(1) The component attitudes and behavior that constitute the OM syndrome in female subjects are basically the same as those we had earlier observed to constitute the modernity syndrome in males.

(2) The factors that explain or "predict" modernity in women (and younger females) are basically the same as those that earlier accounted for modernity in males. Most important as predictors are education, employment, and occupation.

PROF. JAMES SCHAEFER (*Department of Anthropology, University of Montana*): My concern, Dr. Inkeles, is with your research design. The issue is diffusion. Don't you think that Argentina/Chile and Bihar/Bangladesh tend to merge developmentally? Is the N = 2 or 4? In other words, what about Galton's problem? (Israel and Nigeria seem fine.) I would argue that with an N of 6, unless you are matching societies for some reason, the units should be far apart.

DR. INKELES: Our societies were, in fact, matched to provide certain contrasts. For example, at the time the fieldwork was conducted, East Pakistan was governed by an authoritarian government with military origins, whereas India was a multiparty democratic polity. But the more basic point is that our analysis does not involve comparing groups *across* countries, but rather *within* countries. Variations attributable to the qualities of a national setting were thereby brought under relative control. In addition, by making comparisons only *within* countries, as in comparing Catholics and Protestants in Chile, we rendered our data more appropriate for Weberian hypothesis, which also relied mainly on contrasts within the same broad civilization.

Viewed in these terms, our N is not 6, but rather larger. Each time any one religious, ethnic, or regional group was compared with the rest, that pairing constituted one test case of the hypothesis. Considering only the pairs in TABLE 3, the comparisons there presented total 30, which may then be taken as the N for the study as a whole.

As to the second issue of contrast, that is a matter partly of preference, partly

662

of purpose. If one wished only to *illustrate* the role of religion and ethnicity in accounting for differences in modern orientation and behavior, then, obviously, the greater the contrast the more striking the illustration. But if one's purpose is to test the generality of an observed association, the cases should be taken as they are found "in nature," without being purposely selected in advance for the sake of contrast.

DR. S. STANSFELD SARGENT: Dr. Hacker, how about de-emphasizing power-seeking in favor of empathy, giving and compromise?

DR. HELEN HACKER: As I said in my opening remarks, "Measuring marital power might be considered an ethnocentric enterprise. Scientific interest in this question is often felt to be characteristic of a competitive, capitalistic society in which individuals are socialized to be power-seekers and to convert all relationships into a power struggle." However, family sociologists have devoted considerable attention to communication, empathy, and the development of interpersonal skills in marriage, but we do need to distinguish between those situations in which power is operating and those in which it has no appreciable effect on other aspects of marital and familial interaction. Further, in the light of utilizing wives' marital power as a rough indicator of the general status of women in society, emphasis must equally be concentrated on husbands' accommodation, empathy, and moral support.

PROBLEMS OF DEFINING AND COMPARING ABNORMAL
BEHAVIOR ACROSS CULTURES

Juris G. Draguns

Department of Psychology
Pennsylvania State University
University Park, Pennsylvania 16802

Twenty years ago, Devereux[1] identified distinguishing between normal and abnormal behavior as the key problem in the application of psychiatric knowledge beyond our own cultural frontiers. In the ensuing two decades, interest, investigation, and speculation pertaining to psychopathology across cultures have experienced tremendous expansion. Surprisingly, this growth of empirical effort and theoretical concern has not been accompanied by a proportionate concentration of attention upon the problem of delimiting that segment of the population in cultures outside of our accustomed one that is disturbed and that is to be cross-culturally compared. Implicitly, three solutions have been applied to the problem of operationally defining abnormality within a given cultural setting.

The first of these is typical of comparative investigations of psychopathology across cultural lines. Characteristically these studies are conducted with relatively small subject pools and emphasis is placed, at least in the modern versions of this type of research, upon maximally equating its participants from two or more cultures by matching on several relevant social and diagnostic parameters,[2-4] restricting the comparison to a homogeneous diagnostic category,[5,6] or finding the exact counterparts, in social and demographic terms, of the pool of subjects studied in another culture.[7] In all of these cases, the need for defining that which is normal or abnormal in a given cultural setting is bypassed and left in the hands of the patients' own peers, the members of their communities and families who have labeled their behavior aberrant and in need of expert intervention. To put it differently, this kind of study proceeds from the definition of abnormality that has already been applied in a given setting. Thus we arrive at what has elsewhere been called "a cross-cultural comparison proceeding from the culture's most disturbed members."[2] Less charitably, such a research strategy might also be called the path of least resistance. From the practical, if not the conceptual and methodological standpoints, this type of study is tempting to undertake and relatively easy to execute. After all, the subjects are already there as hospitalized psychiatric patients or members of an identified clinic population, often, although not always, living in a psychiatric fishbowl, subject to continuous observation and copious recording of their behavior as a matter of routine of the institutions in question. Moreover, my own experience suggests that subjects for a cross-cultural comparison of psychopathology are a lot easier to obtain than their normal counterparts. In more ways than one, the investigations are dealing with a captive population whose behavior comes close to constituting raw material for unobtrusive measures, in the sense of Webb et al.[8] i.e., behaviors that spontaneously occur without being elicited by the experimenter. The various kinds of currently available sophisticated symptom scales[9] need only be applied and the gap between the symptomatic observations and diagnostic judgments can be objectively and publicly bridged by means of a variety of recently developed computerized procedures.[10-12]

These advantages are outweighed, however, by the methodological and conceptual complexities of interpreting the results of such comparisons. It is widely recognized that cross-cultural symptom differences, which commonly constitute the dependent variables of such study, are traceable to a variety of sources: prominent among these are: the patient, the expert, the setting in which the observations were obtained, and the wider community.[13] There are ample data, summarized elsewhere,[13,14] that point to the influence of each of these four variables both upon discrete symptom manifestations and on patterns thereof. What is not known is the relative weight, or the mode or degree of interaction, of these several variables, both intraculturally and cross-culturally. The time is not yet at hand for writing a mathematical formula that would specify and delimit the contribution of each of these factors to the final product of symptom manifestation. In any case, comparative studies of this type rest on a minimal definition of abnormality or psychopathology, predetermined as they are by the considerations that led to the voluntary or involuntary psychiatric hospitalization in the first place, or to the decision, made by client or others, to seek psychiatric or psychological help. It is a truism well documented in the literature (e.g., reference 15) that only a portion of the total population of disturbed individuals – however defined – is under the care of mental health professionals. Whatever results then emerge from the kind of comparisons described are restricted to this portion of the total range of psychological disturbance. What further augments the ambiguity of interpreting these kinds of cross-cultural findings is the fact that the lines between normal and abnormal, as well between publicly disturbed and individually maladjusted, patterns of behavior are themselves inescapably subject to cultural shifting and shaping. Moreover, the application of this minimal standard of abnormality rests on the existence of comparable psychiatric institutions and services at both points of the cross-cultural comparison, a criterion that is not likely to be met at sites of marked or extreme cultural contrast. In many of the traditional non-Western cultures such institutions may not exist at all, even though the consensus of the cross-cultural psychology literature (see references 16–18) is that all, or nearly all, human societies make some explicit provision for segregating, socially influencing, and attempting to change the most incapacitatingly deviant of their members. In many other cultures with different social and historical traditions, custodial and therapeutic institutions may exist, but they are more limited in scope, function, and meaning than are their Western prototypes.[13,14] Often, the psychiatric hospital functions as the institution of last resort, reserved for those instances of disturbance with which the culturally indigenous modes of treatment have failed. Thus, the comparison of hospitalized and psychiatrically identified individuals only remains a practical option at degrees of moderate or mild cultural contrast and, even at such points, the results obtained are more useful for the questions they raise than for the answers they provide.

The second solution to the problem of operationally defining abnormality in cross-cultural research is best exemplified by the epidemiological or psychiatric census studies in this country (e.g., reference 19) or abroad.[20,21] While the studies of the preceding type were predicated upon the implicit acceptance of a limited and stringent standard of abnormality, epidemiological research in psychiatry is undertaken with the basic objective of bringing to light the cases of psychological disorder that have not yet been identified. The question, once again, is where to draw the line. In practice, epidemiological investigators usually have cast their nets rather widely, with the result that disturbance has come to be equated with symptom presence, or with a derivative judgment of severity of disturbance based upon the symptoms recorded. It is on the basis of these procedures that we have learned that only 18 percent of the population of midtown Manhattan are free of psychological disturbance.[19] Such data, and their counterparts in many other parts of the world, may provide useful or even unique information; however, this information pertains to something that is qualitatively distinct from "psychological disorder," "mental illness," and their semantic equivalents as they are socially applied and understood. Not only are the operational definitions of abnormality broad and inclusive in such studies, but they also vary from one project to another and are exceedingly difficult to interpret in some sort of a universal, comparative framework. Dohrenwend and Dohrenwend[22] have reviewed this body of research and have highlighted the difficulties of synthesizing any general principles from its accumulated store of findings. Mariategui *et al.*[23] have arrived at similarly cautious and tentative conclusions upon surveying the yield of investigations that pertain to a more limited and homogeneous part of the world, the several republics of Latin America. A cross-culturally acceptable, universal standard of abnormality is clearly lacking at this time; yet the various epidemiological investigations appear to proceed from the implicit assumption that the concepts of psychiatric impairment and of the various diagnostic syndromes have substantive reality and cross-cultural constancy. This assumption is repudiated, or at least challenged, by the very wide discrepancies in the results obtained; no one is at this point inclined to refer all of these differences to the populations studied. The only remaining question concerns the proportions of these differences that are traceable to the subjects and to the investigator, as well as to the interactions of the two. Thus, epidemiological studies exemplify the use of maximal, overinclusive, standards of psychopathology and show high potential for overestimates of psychological disorder.

A third type of standard of abnormality needs to be mentioned, even though, conceptually and methodologically, it is not parallel to the two foregoing ones. It deserves, however, to be included because of its historical prominence in the overall enterprise of cross-cultural investigation of psychopathology. This approach involves the description, clinical analysis and, in some recent studies,[24] even epidemiological investigation, of culturally distinct patterns of maladaptation of culture-bound syndromes.[25,26] Under this heading come the strange psychopathologies of remote and exotic lands: Amok and Latah of South East Asia, Wiitiko of the Ojibwa Indians, Susto of the South American Andes, and many more. In settings geographically closer and culturally more related, there are instances of the evil eye or *mal ojo*;[27] Yap,[28] one of the most thorough and persistent investigators of this subject, goes so far as to suggest that more than a few of the disorders in the current Diagnostic and Statistical Manual (DSM-II) may turn out upon cross-cultural analysis to be widely diffused Western culture-bound syndromes. None of the investigators of these culturally patterned manifestations of psychopathology alleges that they constitute the sole variants of psychopathology of their cultural milieus. Nonetheless, the prominent place that these syndromes have occupied in the literature may have inadvertently (if inescapably) biased the view of psychopathology of their respective sites of occurrence in the direction of exoticism. Thus, in contrast to the biases of the preceding two approaches, the investigation of culture-bound syndromes slants the standards of abnormality toward the unfamiliar and strange.

Taken together, the three approaches summarized minimize, maximize, and dramatize the standards of psychopathology in other cultures. Historically, each of these approaches has had an important and valuable role to play in enriching our knowledge of psychopathology in relation to culture. Yet, the relativity and ambiguity of these standards does not permit us to answer the question that is basic to comparative psychopathological research: Do cultures differ in the incidence and prevalence of psychiatric disorders and in the representation of specific categories within these disorders? To be sure, there are wide discrepancies in hospitalization rates and in the proportions of various prominent diagnostic categories represented even among countries that are culturally and historically related.[28] On searching investigation, however, some of these differences have recently been proven to be more dependent on the operations of the psychiatrists than the behavior of the patients.[29,30]

Thus, the three approaches described provide only a partial view of the cultural vicissitudes of maladaption. They urgently need to be supplemented by types of investigation designed to transcend their limitations. The remainder of this paper is devoted to the attempt to outline some of the features and requirements of such investigations.

What we need is: (1) a clear, unambiguous standard of disturbance that is cross-culturally acceptable, at least for purposes of comparative research; (2) operational measures that embody this concept in a manner applicable across cultures; and (3) demonstrations of equivalence of these measures in different cultural locales. The first requirement is easier to state than it is to fulfill. Even in a culturally unitary milieu, abnormality is a flexible and elusive concept, riddled with exceptions, given to multiple explanations, productive of intractable disagreements. The difficulties are compounded cross-culturally. Jahoda's[31] well known criteria of mental health involve self-acceptance, ability for growth, development, and self-actualization, capacity for integration, sense of autonomy, perception of reality, and environmental mastery. All of these standards appear cogent and applicable in our own Western cultural milieu, but how many of them would survive scrutiny on a worldwide basis? In fact, in a somewhat different context, an Indian psychiatrist, Chakroborty,[32] has criticized some similar criteria of mental health or illness for their covert dependence upon the implicit acceptance of Western, culturally limited, views of human nature and condition.

There are two possible reactions to this state of affairs. One of them is exemplified by Misra's[33] proposal to shift emphasis from the criteria of mental health and illness for purposes of cross-cultural research in order to concentrate instead on the comparison of culturally mediated satisfaction and frustration inducers, both actual and perceived. The other approach, represented by the recent contributions by Fabrega[34,35] and Yap,[36] is to search for the cross-culturally constant features in the concepts of illness. These analyses have independently led their authors to the upset of equilibrium between the individual and his social and physical environment as the core element in the experience and conceptualization of illness. This basic element remains to be embodied in concrete and individually applicable measures.

The application of this standard, however, requires coming to grips with two subsidiary yet important distinctions that so far have greatly complicated the delimitation of normality and disturbance on a cross-cultural basis. Reference here is to the demarcation of personal disturbance from social maladaptation, a distinction that looms large in Kluckhohn's[36] and DeVos's[37] writings, and to the exact location of the line between the physical and psychological disorders. In relation to the former distinction, judgments of adequacy or inadequacy of personal adjustment are based on absolutes and ideals, the assessment of the quality of social adaptation is relative and inextricably dependent on the considerations of time, place, and circumstance. According to DeVos,[37] there is overlap, but no correspondence between these two standards. If this distinction is accepted, four groups of individuals are to be distinguished: (1) those free of both social and personal maladjustment; (2) those socially, but not personally madadjusted; (3) those personally, but not socially maladjusted; and (4) those both personally and socially maladjusted. The grey area of ambiguity and controversy would pertain to the classification of individuals in categories 2 and 3. Conceptual and definitional issues would need to be resolved to establish practical distinctions between individuals merely in a state of dissatisfaction with their society and those personally disturbed. The issue that is faced is that of plasticity of social roles in relation to psychopathology. Are one society's madmen another society's prophets? This question, of historical importance in relation to the broad problem of cultural relativism,[1,38] has recently been clarified by the careful empirical studies of shamans in relation to the adequacy of their adjustment.[39,40] The results of these studies roughly suggest that, in the light of direct and indirect indicators of their adjustment, these individuals are not the counterparts of the psychotics on the back wards of our public psychiatric institutions. The idea of infinite plasticity of social roles and of unbounded cultural relativism has been dealt a blow by these findings, even though negatives are notoriously difficult to prove conclusively. Thus, there may yet be a group in which chronic schizophrenics perform a healing function, but such a group remains to be found.

The distinction between psychological and physical dysfunction appears, at first glance, to be both less important and less obtrusive; consequently, it has received less attention in the cross-cultural literature. The complication that one encounters, however, is that in many non-Western cultures the dichotomization of mental and physical does not exist.[41] Thus, there is but one category of illness dealt with by physical, psychological, or social means, as expedient. Conversely, Western investigations have recently been criticized for their "psychiatric bias" in readily assimilating any unknown culture-bound manifestation of distress to psychological factors[35] and for falsely dichotomizing cultural versus biological influences.[42] Culture can influence biology and be in turn influenced by it, as Leighton and Hughes[43] have indicated in their early, but still valid, review of the mechanisms by means of which psychopathology and culture interact. The same point is made at greater length in Wallace's[42] careful analysis of the biological and cultural aspects of the culture-bound psychological disorder of the Eskimo, pibloktoq. The recent theoretical formulations by Dawson,[44] Diaz-Guerrero,[45] and Berry[46] have potential for disentangling these interactions and converting them into universal step-by-step sequences. At this point, what needs to be reiterated is that different societies draw the lines between physical and psychological disorder at different points and with different degrees of sharpness. Even in societies as comparable as Japan and the United States, this issue creates problems. In our own research,[2] my coauthors and I were surprised to discover a considerable number of individuals with psychophysiological diagnoses in a large pool of patients in four psychiatric hospitals in the Tokyo area. Committed as we were to the methodological requirements of diagnostic and biographical matching across culture lines, we were more irritated than fascinated by this adventitious discovery. Now, with the benefit of hindsight as well as greater methodological flexibility, I am more impressed with the possible significance of this observation, especially since not a single instance of psychophysiological diagnosis was found in the available cohort of American psychiatric patients.

The cross-cultural investigators of psychopathology should both take note of and analyze these distinctions of categorization before they attempt the development of universally acceptable standards of abnormal behavior that could be used to distinguish it from psychologically normal behavior as well as from social maladjustment and those aspects of physical disorder that are assumed to bear little or no relevance to psychological stress and conflict. Once these issues are resolved on the conceptual plane, they could be tackled in reference to the development of measures. The discussion of these issues in the cross-cultural literature in psychopathology is remarkably sparse.[47,48] A leaf could be taken from a variety of recent methodological writings in the "mainstream" areas of cross-cultural psychology, those pertinent to the variation of human behavior across cultures in their normal range.[49-51] Without recapitulating this literature, the measures developed should be high in meaningfulness, acceptability, and equivalence, three standards that have a way of exercising a pull in different, or even opposite directions. That a high degree of these characteristics can be simultaneously achieved is attested by the World Health Organization pilot study of schizophrenia in nine countries[52,67] and the United States-United Kingdom project on the diagnosis of affective and schizophrenic psychosis in some of the major psychiatric centers of the two countries.[29] What is sought is a pancultural or etic standard of abnormality. Yet, whatever its details might be, it would be open to the charge of being conditional and relative. Such is the fate of any attempt to break up a continuum into qualitatively distinct segments. While at first glance the conditionality of such distinctions appears to be a drawback, it can be turned into an advantage.

The etic standard of psychopathology could be used with the full awareness of its conditional nature and could be juxtaposed to the culture's own accustomed standard of abnormality. Thus the future course of research on psychopathology could be charted in reference to the distinctions between the emic, culture-bound, and the etic, universally acceptable, criteria of abnormality. The yardsticks of both social maladaptation and personal maladjustment would be incorporated into this scheme and the discrepancies between them would be explicity noted. The gaps between these two indices would become not only additional sources of information, but would provide potentially worthwhile means of characterizing culture.

In an early article, Arsenian and Arsenian[52] proposed classifying cultures on the continuum from tough to easy, referring by these terms to the degree of stringency of demands imposed by the society upon the individual. Both the degree of social stress imposed and the rigidity of social response permitted or tolerated characterize a tough culture; its opposite is marked by a low degree of stress and a wide latitude of socially tolerated behavior. Within this scheme one would expect a high degree of contrast between emic and etic criteria of abnormality in tough cultures, with the former being much broader than the latter. To reverse the relationship, such a contrast would be an indicator of the culture's toughness, in the sense in which Arsenian and Arsenian formulated the concept.

Another problem that might be clarifed by the application of this dual standard is that of the "sick society." This term and its various equivalents have been in use for a long time to characterize cultures. Benedict[38] inaugurated the tradition of applying diagnostic labels to actual cultural groups, although she was well aware of the limitations and pitfalls of this practice. Others, (see e.g., references 53–55) less cautiously, bandied about group and cultural diagnoses in the emotional heat of World War II and its aftermath, often forgetting the difference between descriptive and metaphorical use of diagnostic concepts. These abuses brought the concept of sick society into ill repute, and the view gained wide acceptance in the cultural and behavioral sciences that a society composed of neurotics is an impossibility (see e.g., reference 16). Jacoby[56] has attempted to rescue the concept of a sick society by proposing concrete criteria for the specification of both individual and social dysfunction in cross-cultural perspective. Within this scheme, abnormality of a social group is diagnosed when the total social grouping exhibits aberration in reference to universal standards of mental health and adaptation. Jacoby hastened to admit that such standards had not been developed by the time of his writing and the situation has not markedly changed since then. Going beyond Jacoby's proposal, there are four usages of the term "sick society" that can be distinguished.

(1) The society in question exhibits insoluble conflicts and contradictions, engages in elaborate mechanisms of self-deception, and generally, deals with its existing problems in an unrealistic and irrational manner reminiscent of the operations of psychotic, neurotic, or otherwise psychologically disturbed individuals. Used in this sense, the concept is controversial and its usefulness is questionable. As is well known, the medical model has been forcefully challenged even in its application to psychological disturbance; its extension from individuals to social units brings more problems in its wake. Not the least of these dilemmas is the specification of objective criteria for such social sickness. Moreover, the evaluator has to place himself outside or above the society he is evaluating, a stance becoming to a social polemicist, but one experienced as distinctly uncomfortable by empirically oriented social scientists. On the individual plane, psychiatric name-calling is one of the abuses of the legitimate enterprise of psychiatric diagnosis; its occurrence becomes virtually inevitable when diagnostic labels are pinned to supraindividual social entities. Perhaps the recourse to the metaphor of sick society is justifiable as a rhetorical device in social criticism, but it is too subjective and value-laden a characterization to serve any useful purpose in empirical social science.

(2) The society consists of individuals who, subject to the criteria of our own Western diagnostic categorization would be properly diagnosed as suffering from a psychological disorder, even though in their own cultural domain they adequately fill their respective social niches and do so, apparently, without an undue degree of functional impairment and personal distress. Benedict's[38] application of the terms megalomaniac and paranoid to the Kwakiutl is a case in point. Two recent ethnographic and psychological descriptions of cultural groups grossly deviant from our concepts of adequate interpersonal relations and a "good life" in general may serve to illustrate the potentials and limitations of this use of the concept. One of these accounts is Turnbull's[57] description of the social fabric of the Ik of Uganda, a society with a minimum of empathy, trust, or social solidarity, where hostility and suspicion are the common coin of social intercourse. The other report is by the Swiss psychoanalytic-anthropological team of Parin, Morgenthaler and Parin-Mathey[58] on the Agni of the Ivory Coast. It emphasizes the ubiquity of social fear, the anticipation of harm, and the pervasiveness of distrust. It would be tempting to characterize the typical members of these societies as exemplars of antisocial or paranoid personality

disturbance, but, to the credit of the authors of these accounts, they have resisted this temptation. Turnbull's report is free of psychopathological reference or interpretation, although it includes a detailed and specific description of the Iks' characteristic subjective frames of reference, their ways of viewing the world. Parin et al. include in their monograph a number of case studies of individuals who, on the basis of intracultural standards, were found to be psychologically disturbed. Unfortunately, they do not go as far as they might in articulating the distinctions between this minority of individuals and the cultural mode of the Agni. In terms of the scheme proposed, it is moot whether the typical member of these societies could be legitimately diagnosed as being personally maladjusted or abnormal; the authors of both monographs stress that the modal personality of the Agni and Ik is very much in balance with the social setting in which it must function.

(3) The sick society concept can also be used in reference to the phenomenon of a social group or a section thereof consisting of individuals who clearly exhibit behaviors normally recognized as symptomatic by the wider society, but accepted as reasonable by the members of the subgroup. One of the two cases in point[59] was the refusal to believe by a considerable section of the linguistically and socially isolated Japanese immigrant community in Sao Paulo, Brazil the news of Japan's surrender at the end of World War II, a conviction that survived for a decade or more, bolstered by the equally unshakable belief that the Japanese had, in fact, emerged victorious from that conflict. Here would seem to be a case of a collective delusion and, indeed, it is presented by the authors of the article as such. Yet, unlike most noncollectively delusional individuals, persons who harbored this belief continued to go about earning their livelihood and maintaining their social relations, focusing them admittedly upon the community of their compatriots committed to their shared conviction. It is unfortunate that this report, which freely employs psychiatric nomenclature and concepts, stops short of the specific characterization of the psychiatric state of the members of this socially aberrant group. By inference, a sense of the encapsulation of the socially shared delusional belief is conveyed, in the context of otherwise normal and adequate social and individual functioning. The other example is better known;[60] it pertains to the interesting participant-observer study of the disproof of a prophecy of imminent destruction of the world on which the common bond of the members of an emerging religious sect was based. This study was conducted in the context of testing some of the tenets of the cognitive dissonance theory. For this reason, any individual descriptive detail in this study is sparse and sheds little light on the characteristics of these people, so unusually inclined to accept or expect unrealistic experience. Another report from France,[61] however, suggests that, in the light of personality inventories and psychiatric interview data, the members of a similar sect, committed to socially deviant and apparently bizarre beliefs, are utterly unremarkable and nonpathological in their psychological functioning. The findings in these three reports, moreover, are pertinent to two considerations. For one, the fact that the members of these deviant groups were not automatically classified as crazy, sick, legally insane, or psychologically disturbed testifies to the breadth of the limits of permissible deviance of the three cultures in question and to their tolerance for various expressions of social eccentricity. For another, these phenomena can also be brought in relation to the assessment of the areas of concern or vulnerability. Traditionally, religion in the modern West has been a domain in which a wide range of disagreement has been tolerated and in which the threshold for the bizarre and unacceptable has been kept high. Somewhat more

surprising is the tolerance of deviant socially unshared belief in the area of mass communication; for are the media of mass communication not the purveyors and arbiters of reality beyond the individual's limited range of immediate experience? Observations on this subject have come from Brazil, and one is left to wonder whether the results would have been identical in an even more highly media-saturated society such as that of the United States.

(4) Finally, the sick society refers in a concrete sense to an aggregate of individuals with an unusually high proportion of actual psychological disturbance. It is in this operational sense that this term has been used by Cawte[62,63] whose interdisciplinary field teams have located several groups with a disproportionate percentage of psychiatrically impaired and incapacitated individuals among the Australian aborigines. One such group was located on one of the islands off Northern Australia.[63] Geographically displaced, socially marginal in relation to its neighbors, the Kaiadlit of Mornington Island do exhibit an unusually high rate of moderate or more severe disturbance, reaching about a 20 percent of their total very meager number. To guard against the possible criticism of Western, extraneous norms being imposed, it is well worth noting that, in this case, judgments of disturbance were made on the basis of a consensus of external and indigenous assessments, a safeguard also adopted in some other modern epidemiological studies (see e.g., reference 64). The question that these findings raise concerns the upper limit of psychological disturbance that a society, large-scale or miniature, can tolerate without disintegrating. In Cawte's view, which is consonant with Leighton's[65] well known position, psychopathology both thrives on social disintegration and breeds it; social disintegration begets psychopathology, which begets more disintegration. It is this sense of sick society that appears to be most defensible and real and that might profit from the application of the two standards of abnormality proposed, in isolation.

The formulations as well as the application of these two standards of abnormal behavior would then appear the proper vehicle for transcending the limitations of the minimal, maximal, and exotic perspectives of psychopathology that have so far characterized most of the research on cross-cultural psychopathology. Elsewhere[66] it has been pointed out that, while great strides have been made in our knowledge of pathoplasticity, the mode and manner in which cultural factors shape psychopathological expression, information at our disposal remains fragmentary concerning pathogenesis, the contribution of culture to the causation of psychological disorder. The establishment of conceptually solid operational standards of what is normal and what is not constitutes a prerequisite for filling this major lacuna in our understanding of the interplay of culture and psychopathology.

REFERENCES

1. DEVEREUX, G. 1956. Normal and abnormal. *In* Some Uses of Anthropology: Theoretical and Applied. Anthropological Society of Washington, Washington, D.C.
2. DRAGUNS, J. G., L. PHILLIPS, I. K. BROVERMAN, W. CAUDILL & S. NISHIMAE. 1971. The symptomatology of hospitalized psychiatric patients in Japan and in the United States: A study of cultural difference. J. Nerv. Ment. Dis. 152: 3–16.

3. FABREGA, H. J., J. D. SWARTZ & C. A. WALLACE. 1968. Ethnic differences in psychopathology: Clinical correlates under varying conditions. Arch. Gen. Psychiat. 19: 218–226.
4. FUNDIA, T. A. de, J. G. DRAGUNS & L. PHILLIPS. 1971. Culture and psychiatric symptomatology: A comparison of Argentine and United States patients. Soc. Psychiat. 6: 11–20.
5. SCHOOLER, C. & W. CAUDILL. 1964. Symptomatology in Japanese and American schizophrenics. Ethnology 3: 172–178.
6. MURPHY, H. B. M., E. W. WITTKOWER & N. A. CHANCE. 1967. A cross-cultural inquiry into the symptomatology of depression: A preliminary report. Internat. J. Psychiat. 3: 6–15.
7. BRITTON, R. S. & C. K. CORDES. 1970. A comparison of child psychiatric morbidity in American and British military families overseas. J. Roy. Army Med. Corps 116: 11–16.
8. WEBB, E. J., D. T. CAMPBELL, R. D. SCHWARTZ & L. SECHREST. 1966. Unobtrusive measures: Nonreactive Research in the Social Sciences. Rand-McNally. Chicago, Ill.
9. WITTENBORN, J. R. 1972. Reliability, validity, and objectivity of symptom-rating scales. J. Nerv. Ment. Dis. 154: 79–82.
10. SPITZER, R. & J. ENDICOTT. 1969. Diagno II: Further developments in a computer program for psychiatric diagnosis. Am. J. Psychiat. 125: 12–20.
11. FISCHER, M. 1974. Development and validity of a computerized method for diagnosis of functional psychosis. Acta. Psychiat. Scand. 50: 243–288.
12. SCHARFETTER, C. 1971. AMP-Manual. Springer. Berlin, Germany.
13. DRAGUNS, J. G. 1973. Comparisons of psychopathology across cultures. J. Crosscult. Psychol. 4: 9–47.
14. DRAGUNS, J. G. & L. PHILLIPS. 1972. Culture and Psychopathology: The Quest for a Relationship. General Learning Press. Morristown, N.J.
15. DOHRENWEND, B. P. & B. S. DOHRENWEND. 1969. Social Status and Psychological Disorder. Wiley. New York, N.Y.
16. KENNEDY, J. G. 1973. Cultural psychiatry. In Handbook of Social and Cultural Anthropology. J. H. Honigmann, Ed.: 1119–1198. Rand McNally. Chicago, Ill.
17. KIEV, A. 1972. Transcultural Psychiatry. Free Press. New York, N.Y.
18. PFEIFFER, W. M. 1970. Transkulturelle Psychiatrie: Ergebnisse und Probleme. Thieme. Stuttgart, Germany.
19. SROLE, L., R. S. LANGNER, S. T. MICHAEL, M. K. OPLER, & T. A. RENNIE. 1962. Mental Health in the Metropolis: The Midtown Manhattan Study. McGraw-Hill. New York, N.Y.
20. LEIGHTON, A. H., T. A. LAMBO, C. C. HUGHES, D. C. LEIGHTON, J. M. MURPHY & D. B. MACKLIN. 1963. Psychiatric Disorders among the Yoruba. Cornell University Press. Ithaca, N.Y.
21. LIN, T. 1953. A study of the incidence of mental disorder in Chinese and other cultures. Psychiatry 16: 313–336.
22. DOHRENWEND, B. P. & B. S. DOHRENWEND. 1974. Social and cultural influences on psychopathology. Ann. Rev. Psychol. 25: 419–452.
23. MARIATEGUI, J., V. ALVA & O. DeLEÓN. 1969. Epidemiologia psiquiatrica de un distrito urbano de Lima: Un estudio de prevalencia en Lince. Rev. Neuropsiquiat. 32, Suppl.
24. RUBEL, A. J. 1964. The epidemiology of a folk illness: Susto in Hispanic America. Ethnology 3: 268–283.
25. MURPHY, H. B. M. 1972. History and the evolution of syndromes: the striking case of Latah and Amok. In Psychopathology: Contributions from the Biological, Behavioral, and Social Sciences. M. Hammer, K. Salzinger & S. Sutton, Eds.: 33–55. Wiley. New York, N.Y.
26. YAP, P. M. 1974. Comparative Psychiatry: A Theoretical Framework. University of Toronto Press. Toronto, Ont.
27. RUBEL, A. J. 1966. Across the Tracks: Mexican-Americans in a Texas City. University of Texas Press. Austin, Texas.

28. KRAMER, M. 1969. Application of Mental Health Statistics. World Health Organization. Geneva, Switzerland.
29. COOPER, J. E., R. E. KENDELL, B. J. GURLAND, L. SHARPE, J. R. M. COPELAND & R. SIMON. 1972. Psychiatric Diagnosis in New York and London. Oxford University Press. London, England.
30. COPELAND, J. R. M., M. J. KELLEHER, J. M. KELLETT, A. J. GOURLAY, G. BARRON, D. W. COWAN, J. DeGRUCHY, B. J. GURLAND, L. SHARPE, R. SIMON, J. KURIANSKY & P. STILLER. 1974. Diagnostic differences in psychogeriatric patients in London and New York: United Kingdom-United States diagnostic project. Canad. Psychiat. Assoc. J. **19**: 267–271.
31. JAHODA, M. 1958. Current Concepts of Positive Mental Health. Basic Books. New York, N.Y.
32. CHAKROBORTY, A. 1974. Whither transcultural psychiatry? Transcult. Psychiat. Res. Rev. **11**: 102–107.
33. MISRA, R. K. 1975. Mental health: A cross-cultural approach. *In* Applied Cross-Cultural Psychology. Papers from the Second International Conference of I.A.C.C.P. J. W. Berry & W. J. Lonner, Eds. Swets & Zeitlinger. Amsterdam, The Netherlands.
34. FABREGA, H. 1972. The study of disease in relation to culture. Behav. Sci. **17**: 183–203.
35. FABREGA, H. 1974. Disease and Social Behavior: An Interdisciplinary Perspective. M.I.T. Press. Cambridge, Mass.
36. KLUCKHOHN, C. 1962. Navajo Witchcraft. Beacon Press. Boston, Mass.
37. De VOS, G. 1965. Transcultural diagnosis of mental health by means of psychological tests. *In* Transcultural Psychiatry. A. V. S. DeReuck & B. Porter, Eds.: 84–108. Little Brown. Boston, Mass.
38. BENEDICT, R. 1934. Culture and the abnormal. J. Genet. Psychol. **1**: 60–64.
39. BOYER, L. B. et al. 1964. Comparison of the shamans and pseudo-shamans of the Apaches of the Mescalero Indian Reservation: A Rorschach study. J. Proj. Tech. Pers. Assm. **28**: 173–180.
40. FABREGA, H. & SILVER, D. B. 1973. Illness and Shamanistic Curing in Zinacantan. Stanford University Press. Stanford, Calif.
41. DRAGUNS, J. G. 1975. Resocialization into culture: The complexities of taking a worldwide view of psychotherapy. *In* Cross-Cultural Perspectives of Learning. R. W. Brislin, S. Bochner & W. J. Lonner, Ed.: 273–289. Halsted Press. New York, N.Y.
42. WALLACE, A. F. C. 1972. Mental illness, biology, and culture. *In* Psychological Anthropology, New Edition. F. L. K. Hsu, Ed.: 363–402. Schenkman. Cambridge, Mass.
43. LEIGHTON, A. H. & J. M. HUGHES. 1961. Cultures as causative of mental disorder. Millbank Memor. Fund Bull. **39**: 441–472.
44. DAWSON, J. L. M. 1969. Research and theoretical bases of biosocial psychology (cited in Cross-Cultural Research Methods. Wiley. New York, N.Y. 1973.) R. W. Brislin, W. J. Lonner & R. M. Thorndike, Eds.
45. DIAZ GUERRERO, R. 1972. Hacia una teoria histórico-bio-psico-socio-cultural del comportomiento humano. Trillas. Mexico City, Mexico.
46. BERRY, J. W. 1975. Ecology, cultural adaptation, and psychological differentiation: Traditional patterning and acculturative stress. *In* Cross-Cultural Perspectives on Learning. R. W. Brislin, S. Bochner & W. J. Lonner, Eds. Halsted Press. New York, N.Y.
47. MURPHY, H. B. M. 1969. Handling the cultural dimension in psychiatric research. Soc. Psychiat. **4**: 11–15.
48. BRODY, E. B. 1966. Recording cross-culturally useful psychiatric interview data: Experience from Brazil. Am. J. Psychiat. **123**: 446–456.
49. BRISLIN, R. W., W. J. LONNER, & R. M. THORNDIKE, Eds. 1973. Cross-Cultural Research Methods. Wiley. New York, N.Y.
50. BOESCH, E. E. & L. H. ECKENSBERGER. 1969. Methodische Probleme des interkulturellen Vergleichs. *In* Handbuch der Psychologie. Band 7/1 C. F. Graumann, L. Kruse & B. Kroner, Eds. Verlag für Psychologie. Göttingen, Germany.

51. TRIANDIS, H. C., R. S. MALPASS & A. H. DAVIDSON. 1973. Psychology and culture. Ann. Rev. Psychol. **24**: 355–378.
52. ARSENIAN, J. & J. ARSENIAN. 1948. Tough and easy cultures: A conceptual analysis. Psychiatry **11**: 377–385.
53. BRICKNER, R. M. 1943. Is Germany Incurable? Lippincott. Philadelphia, Pa.
54. LaBARRE, W. 1945. Some observations on character structure in the Orient: The Japanese. Psychiatry **8**: 319–342.
55. MONTAGUE, A. 1961. Culture and mental illness. Am. J. Psychiat. **118**: 15–23.
56. JACOBY, J. 1967. The construct of abnormality: Some cross-cultural considerations. J. Exp. Res. Person. **2**: 1–15.
57. TURNBULL, C. 1972. The Mountain People. Simon & Schuster. New York, N.Y.
58. PARIN, P., MORGENTHALER, F. & PARIN-MATTHEY, G. 1971. Fürchte deinen Nächsten wie dich selbst. Suhrkamp. Frankfurt/Main, Germany.
59. KUMASAKA, Y. & H. SAITO. 1970. Kachigumi: A collective delusion among the Japanese and their descendents in Brazil. Canad. Psychiat. Assn. J. **15**: 167–175.
60. FESTINGER, L., RIECKEN, H. W. & SCHACHTER, S. 1956. When Prophency Fails. University of Minnesota Press. Minneapolis, Minn.
61. DELAY, J., P. PICHOT, J. F. BUISSON & R. SADOUN. 1955. Etude d'un groupe d'adeptes d'une secte religieuse. Encéphale **53**: 138–154.
62. CAWTE, J. 1972. Cruel, Poor, and Brutal Nations: The Assessment of Mental Health of an Australian Aboriginal Community by Short-Stay Psychiatric Field Team Methods. University Press of Hawaii. Honolulu, Hawaii.
63. CAWTE, J. 1974. Medicine Is the Law. Studies in Psychiatric Anthropology of Australian Tribal Societies. University Press of Hawaii. Honolulu, Hawaii.
64. BASH, K. W. & J. BASH-LIECHTI. 1969. Studies of the epidemiology of neuro-psychiatric disorders among the rural population of the province of Khuzestan. Iran. Soc. Psychiat. **4**: 137–143.
65. LEIGHTON, A. H. 1971. The other side of the coin. Am. J. Psychiat. **127**: 123–125.
66. DRAGUNS, J. G. (in preparation.) Psychopathology. In Handbook of Cross-Cultural Psychology. H. C. Triandis et al., Eds. Allyn-Bacon. Boston, Mass.
67. WORLD HEALTH ORGANIZATION. 1973. Report of the International Pilot Study of Schizophrenia. World Health Organization. Geneva, Switzerland.

THE UNITED STATES–UNITED KINGDOM PROJECT ON DIAGNOSIS
OF THE MENTAL DISORDERS

Joseph Zubin and Barry J. Gurland

Biometrics Research Unit
New York State Psychiatric Institute
New York, New York 10032
and Columbia University
New York, New York

INTRODUCTION

No one can really understand his own culture, the anthropologists tell us, until he develops an understanding of a contrasting culture. This holds true especially of the culture of psychopathology. As long as American diagnostic procedures and treatment remained isolated and self-enclosed it was difficult for us to conceive of any other system.

The United Kingdom was chosen as the contrasting culture because, although the total admission rates for mental disorder in the two countries were nearly identical, the relative admission rates for the two functional psychoses — schizophrenia and affective disorders — were strikingly different. There were relatively only half as many admissions for schizophrenia as for the affective psychoses in the UK but twice as many in the USA, so that relatively speaking there was a fourfold difference in the ratio of first admissions for the two functional psychoses in the two countries.

Similarly, the ratio of first admissions for functional psychoses to chronic organic brain syndromes was approximately ten in the US and approximately one in the UK, or a tenfold difference. Whether these discrepancies were due to cultural, biological or classification differences, or to differences in hospital utilization in the two countries was the focus of the inquiry of the USA–UK Project.

The choice of the UK was also based on the fact that despite differences in culture, the English language was common to both countries and a deep and abiding interest in psychopathology and its classification permeated the teaching and practice of psychopathology in both.

The first need that had to be met was the provision of a common system of interviewing that could be used in both countries. Fortunately, in the USA as well as in the UK considerable work was already in progress in transforming the free-wheeling psychiatric interviews into systematic structured instruments that could be used in a standard fashion. A combination of the items from the Present State Examination[14] prepared in London by the Social Psychiatry Research Unit under Dr. John Wing and his associates and from the Psychiatric Status Schedule[12] prepared by our own Biometrics Research Unit under the guidance of Dr. Spitzer and his associates was hammered out into a joint instrument, and additional forms for obtaining history information and social data were developed.

The project staffs in the two countries were trained in the use of the prepared interview schedules until a high degree of reliability was obtained in the precoded ratings of psychopathology based on the responses of the patients to the specific items of the interview schedules. The eighth edition of the ICD (International Classification of Diseases) and the accompanying Glossary of Mental Disorders compiled in the UK by the General Register Office, which is quite similar to the American Psychiatric Association's Diagnostic and Statistical Manual, were utilized to yield operational definitions and categories.

There were three types of studies undertaken: (1) examination of admissions to mental hospitals, (2) showing of videotapes of the same patients to audiences of clinicians in many parts of the UK and USA and Canada and (3) analysis of case records of earlier cases for historical analysis of trends.

HOSPITAL STUDIES

In order to compare the data on admissions in the two countries, the individual items in the interview schedule were clustered according to clinical judgment on the standard dimensions of psychopathology — viz., anxiety, depression, depersonalization, etc. These item clusters were then subjected to a factor analysis in order to attain greater internal consistency for each dimension and better differentiation between the dimensions, and the resulting factors standardized with a mean of 50 and a standard deviation of 10. Profiles of the standard scores for each patient were then drawn up and the average profiles for the patients in the two contrasting categories of schizophrenia and affective disorders based on project diagnosis are shown in FIGURE 1 and FIGURE 2. It will

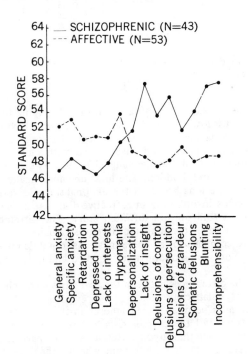

FIGURE 1. Mean section score profiles for Brooklyn patients diagnosed by the project team as schizophrenic or affective.

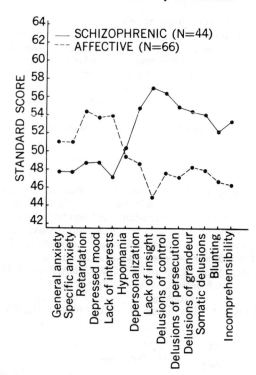

FIGURE 2. Mean section score profiles for Netherne patients diagnosed by the hospital staff as schizophrenic or affective.

be noted that the dimensions reflecting mood disorder, lying to the left, show the schizophrenics with low scores and the affectives with high scores, whereas the dimensions reflecting behavioral and conceptual disorganization show the schizophrenics with a high profile and the affectives with a low profile.

The initial studies covered the age range 20–59 in two large public mental hospitals in New York and London. The local diagnoses made by the hospital staff lived up to expectations based on the national statistics revealing the great discrepancies between schizophrenic and affective disorders in the two countries. The project diagnoses told quite a different story. The differences practically disappeared though a small residue of differences remained. In order to get a more representative comparison, all the admissions to public mental hospitals in metropolitan New York and London were sampled and the results are shown in FIGURE 3.

It is clear that the differences between the two cities were inherent not in the patients but in the psychiatric culture.

Since the differences between the diagnoses in the two cities seemed to be based upon the attitudes of the psychiatrists towards the utilization of the two diagnostic categories rather than upon differences in the patients, an appeal was made to signal detection theory to determine whether the differences inhered in the criterion for judgment of the presence or absence of the disorders or in the sensitivity to the presence of the two disorders.

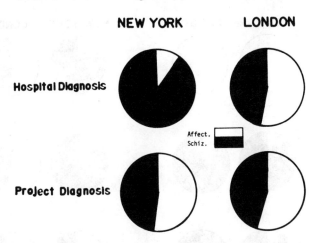

FIGURE 3. The ratio of schizophrenia and affective disorders among admissions to public mental hospitals, as judged by hospital and project diagnosis.

There was little or no difference in the sensitivity of the two groups of psychiatrists to the presence of psychopathology of the affective disorders or of the schizophrenic disorders, but there were significant differences in the criterion. The American psychiatrists were reluctant to use the label of affective disorders but were free in their use of the schizophrenic label whereas the reverse held true of the British psychiatrists.*

VIDEO TAPE STUDIES

In order to replicate the finding that the differences inhered in the psychiatric culture rather than in the patients, the same video tapes of patient interviews were shown to groups of psychiatrists in the various parts of the USA, UK and Canada. The results of this study are shown in FIGURE 4.

The predilection for the diagnosis of schizophrenia on the part of the American psychiatrists and the corresponding preference for the diagnosis of affective disorders on the part of the British is quite clearly borne out.

Those patients who inspired transatlantic diagnostic disagreement were generally diagnosed as schizophrenic by the American psychiatrists; they received a wide range of British diagnoses, however. Diagnoses of the manic-depressive disorders were common, but also neuroses and personality disorders were diagnosed. There was no group of patients whom the British tended to call schizophrenic more often than did the Americans.

* This analysis is reported by Dr. W. Crawford Clark in an unpublished study. Although the two circles for London representing the hospital and project diagnoses seem quite similar, there was a considerable change between these two diagnoses for many patients, but the proportions remained quite similar.

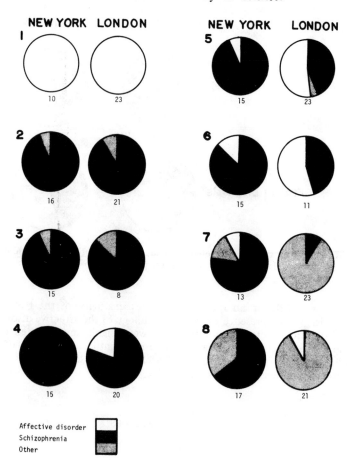

FIGURE 4. Eight videotaped interviews as diagnosed by psychiatrists at The New York State Psychiatric Institute and at The Maudsley Hospital, London.

Some biases† toward the diagnosis of schizophrenia were about equally powerful in the two countries, and therefore did not alter the level of transatlantic diagnostic disagreement. For example, in both countries younger patients were more likely to be called schizophrenic than were older patients with similar psychopathology.[3] Surprisingly there was no evidence of bias associated with the social class of the patient in either country; the significance of this result is questionable, however, since there was only a very narrow spread of social classes within the patient population under examination.[3]

In both countries, there was a strong association between race and the hospital diagnosis of schizophrenia.[11] In London, this association was con-

---

† Here and elsewhere, a reference to diagnostic bias means that there was an association between diagnosis and a demographic variable (e.g., age, race, sex) even when psychopathology was held constant.[6]

founded by the fact that all of the black patients were also recent immigrants, but the symptomatology of this group was consistent with the hospital diagnosis. In New York, it became clear that there was a bias on the part of the hospital psychiatrists toward diagnosing schizophrenia in black patients. Project psychiatrists in New York, on the other hand, showed no such bias and found no increased frequency of schizophrenia in the black patients; nor were the symptoms shown by the patients diagnosed schizophrenic by the project team any different in the black than in the white patients.

FOLLOW-UP STUDY

A two-year documentary unpublished follow-up of duration of hospital stay showed about the same predictive power for project and hospital diagnoses in London, but the hospital diagnoses in New York more sharply discriminated the prognosis of affective and schizophrenic groups than did the project diagnoses (although both the hospital and project diagnoses showed a worse prognosis for the schizophrenic than for the affective groups of patients). However, whereas the project diagnosis was made without foreknowledge of the patient's progress, the hospital diagnosis may have reflected an awareness of the patient's response to treatment. It is possible, for example, that in those few cases that the New York hospital diagnosed as affective disorder, the diagnosis was predicated on the patient's rapid recovery. There are additional reasons for a cautious interpretation of follow-up data based on routine hospital records. Apart from the usual errors in documentary information and the omission of data on the progress of symptoms, the duration of hospital stay may be altered by administrative events such as a strike of staff members, availability of beds, or fiduciary considerations, and rehospitalization rates may depend more on the family structure than the patient's symptoms, as shown in another study undertaken by project members.[1] These follow-up data, consequently, may be of limited value as a test of the predictive validity of the diagnosis.

Insofar as the operational definition of schizophrenia in the ICD of DSM II is based on descriptive psychopathology, there appears to be greater internal consistency in the British than in the American concepts of the disorder. The British hospital diagnoses show a stronger relationship to psychopathology (independently measured by the project) than the American hospital diagnoses.[4,10]‡

CASE RECORD STUDY

Whatever the relative utility of the narrow and the broad concepts of schizophrenia, held respectively by psychiatrists in the UK and USA, it is

‡ For more incisive testing of the usefulness of the different concepts of schizophrenia, one must turn to studies in the field of genetics by other workers,[7] to studies on the relationship between diagnosis and treatment response, or between diagnosis and physiological variables. Recent studies by the Cross-National Project, in collaboration with the Biometrics Laboratories under the direction of Dr. Samuel Sutton, have used an "iterative technique"[13] to reduce inconsistencies between neurophysiological and clinical classifications. In this way, data have been collected on the concurrent validity of the two modes of classification.[2]

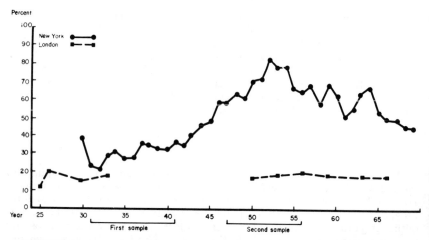

FIGURE 5. Total admissions, including first and readmissions. Profiles of proportion schizophrenic for first admissions and readmissions separately are only available for 1934–1957, and are nearly identical.

interesting to explore the development of these concepts in the two countries. For this purpose, a case record was carried out at two institutes of psychiatry (New York State Psychiatric Institute and the corresponding Institute of Psychiatry at Maudsley Hospital). These two institutes were chosen because they have wielded considerable influence in shaping the concepts of schizophrenia. The proportion of admissions annually diagnosed by the hospital psychiatrists as schizophrenic between 1930 and 1970 was found to be fairly constant in London, but to have increased dramatically in New York across the years 1942–1952. A sample of the New York case records was drawn from the years 1932–1941 and 1947–1956, censored to remove references to diagnosis and year of admission, and then presented to 16 American-trained psychiatrists and one British-trained project psychiatrist for diagnosis. The rediagnoses showed no change in the proportion of schizophrenics admitted annually across the decades (see FIGURE 5). The conclusion was that the concepts of schizophrenia had been much the same in London as in New York in the decade 1930–1940, but that the concept of schizophrenia held by New York psychiatrists had greatly broadened after the second World War.§

§ The psychiatric traditions emanating from Pinel in France, Kraepelin in Germany, and Freud in Austria-Hungary, which so largely determined the trends in psychiatry today, underwent a confluence in both the United States and the United Kingdom, even though each tradition was weighted differently. Furthermore, Adolf Meyer, who was such an important influence in the United States, also had disciples in the United Kingdom, especially in Scotland, so that the two countries were exposed to similar influences that had differential impacts. By comparing the United States and the United Kingdom in the 1970s, we are examining the influence of the same traditions and the way they were incorporated in the two countries. A discussion of some of the factors that led to a broadening of the concept of schizophrenia in the United States in the 1940s, and later, has been broached elsewhere.[5] Certainly, the growth of psychoanalytic therapy in the United States brought with it a heightened interest in the detection of milder or borderline forms of schizophrenia, and possibly an increased tendency to infer the presence of this disorder from subtle or intuitive signs.

DISCUSSION

In the absence of clear evidence in favor of one or the other concept of schizophrenia, one might ask which concept, if wrong, is likely to do the least harm to the patient. If wrong, the broad concept of schizophrenia would include patients suffering from depressive and manic disorders, and there would be a theoretical danger that the patient's depression or mania would not receive specific treatment and that the relatively poor prognosis expected in schizophrenia would lead to a delay in discharging the patient from the hospital. An analysis of the data from the hospital studies showed that patients with mainly depressive symptoms were less likely to receive antidepressive treatment in the New York than in the London hospitals and that this was at least partly due to the fact that many of the New York patients received a hospital diagnosis of schizophrenia.[5] The New York—London contrast in therapy, however, might have been more serious had the New York psychiatrists not paid attention to symptoms rather than diagnosis in selecting treatment (i.e., a large proportion of New York patients with depressive symptoms received antidepressive treatment despite a hospital diagnosis of schizophrenia). Furthermore, there was no evidence of a self-fulfilling prophecy, since the patients with mainly depressive symptoms had a relatively short duration of hospitalization, whether or not they were called schizophrenic by the hospital psychiatrists. Nevertheless, it seems that the narrow concept of schizophrenia has an edge over the broad concept until further evidence accrues.

The major thrust of this paper has been in the direction of demonstrating the reliability of psychopathological ratings and of diagnoses. The only validity aspects dealt with was the demonstration that schizophrenics tended to require longer hospitalization than affectives. But there is more to validity than outcome. If we appeal to the six scientific models of etiology: genetic, internal environment and neurophysiology on the one hand and ecological, developmental and learning, on the other hand,[15] we can demonstrate that depending upon the model one adopts, certain diagnostic approaches seem to be more valid than others. Thus, accepting the genetic model, Essen-Möller's more middle-of-the-road concept of schizophrenia, neither as wide as the American nor as narrow as that of the British, shows the highest rate of genetic transmission of the disorder in relatives.[9] Accepting the neurophysiological model, it can be demonstrated that with processing of information as our touchstone, certain groups of schizophrenics, e.g., those with thought disorder, differ in their central nervous system functioning from other schizophrenics, depressives and normals insofar as they have a shorter critical duration for sensory integration. Similarly, manic-depressives tend to differ from schizophrenics and normals in their auditory threshold as well as in their capacity to benefit from an additional energy input that follows 15 msec after the initial input, than do the other groups. There are several other findings of this type indicating that the information processing is different in certain types of psychopathology, and in all of these findings, the patient group in question excels the normals, thus eliminating the explanation that patients do worse because they are unmotivated.[13] These laboratory findings can provide indicators that would fortify the diagnostic category of the patients who exhibit the indicators.

Similar findings could be based on the application of the learning theory model, which would indicate that those who are more responsive to immediate rather than nonimmediate stimulation by the environment are more likely to be schizophrenic.[8] Similar indications can be found for the developmental model, the internal environment model, and the ecological model, but these would take us too far afield from our topic. Perhaps the best summary one can make of the approach suggested here is to indicate the need for culture-free and culture-fair indicators of psychopathology. We must distinguish between two cultures: the culture of the patient and the psychiatric culture of the psychiatrist. Armed with such transcultural measures, it would become possible to make comparisons cross-culturally despite the occluding influences of disparate patient cultures. The neurophysiological indicators mentioned above might well serve this purpose.

The work reported here identifies at least one of the factors that confound cross-cultural comparisons of psychopathology, namely, the effect on perception and labeling of psychopathology of variation in *psychiatric* culture. The methods used by the USA–UK project staff were designed to control the effects of variation in psychiatric culture by such means as structured interview techniques, a glossary of psychiatric labels, and classification based on statistical analysis of discrete ratings. We have presented evidence of the success of these methods in reducing spurious findings of cross-national differences in the distribution of types of mental disorder.

Unfortunately, methods of assessing and defining mental disorders that are based on phenomenology (as are the methods reported here) are vulnerable to cultural biases other than those operating through the psychiatrist. Most importantly, the *patient's* culture may influence the way in which a given mental disorder is manifested. It is taken for granted that the content of abnormal behavior is culture-bound and little is yet known of the extent, if any, to which the form of psychopathology is also culture-bound. Thus, the degree to which a given culture elicits, contains, suppresses or occludes manifestations of psychopathology is still unknown. It would clearly be of value to cross-cultural research to have available indicators (of mental disorders) that are not affected by the culture of the milieu nor of the psychiatrists. Tests of neurophysiological function offer promise in this respect.

The Venn diagram (FIGURE 6) can be used to illustrate some conceptual problems in developing objective indicators of mental disorders for cross-cultural research. Three subpopulations of patients with mental disorders are shown: (1) those who actually have mental disorder X; (2) those so diagnosed by psychiatrist A and (3) by psychiatrist B. It will be noted that both psychiatrists include in their diagnoses individuals who do not belong to category X of mental disorder. Both the diagnoses of psychiatrist A or of psychiatrist B can be objectified by use of reliable methods for assessing phenomenology or by finding, for example, physiological correlates of one or other set of diagnoses. Yet these objective methods might indicate subpopulations that overlapped but did not coincide with the actual cases of mental disorder X. Thus it is necessary to be clear about what we wish to objectify and what we wish to indicate.

Ideally, an objective indicator of mental disorder should be positive only with actual cases of a given mental disorder, with all such cases and with no other cases. It is more likely, however, that objective indicators available now or in the near future will be positive with a substantial but unknown proportion of actual cases of a given mental disorder and with some cases of other mental disorder. It might therefore seem reasonable in the interim to attempt a study of the pathoplastic effects of culture by the following expedient: (1) select two or more defined populations, each representing contrasting cultures, and screen them for cases of putative mental disorder X by use of a method that is free of variation due to psychiatric culture; and (2) test the two resulting subsamples

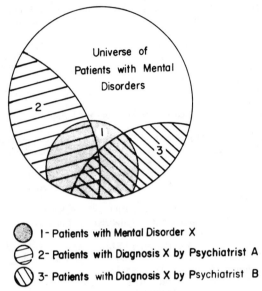

Universe of
Patients with Mental
Disorders

2

1

3

1- Patients with Mental Disorder X
2- Patients with Diagnosis X by Psychiatrist A
3- Patients with Diagnosis X by Psychiatrist B

FIGURE 6.

with the most relevant of the available neurophysiological indicators. If the proportions of each subsample found to be positive on the neurophysiological indicator are essentially equal then it is likely that the patients' culture has only a weak effect, if any, on the form of mental disorder X. In that event we will be in a position to proceed to examine the effects of the patients' culture on the incidence, and course of that mental disorder. For this purpose, and under the circumstances outlined above, indicators of mental disorder X could be chosen either from objectified phenomenological assessments (keeping psychiatric culture constant) or from the neurophysiological or other biological fields.

REFERENCES

1. BARRETT, J. E., Jr., J. B. KURIANSKY & B. J. GURLAND. 1972. Community tenure following emergency discharge. Am. J. Psychiat. 128: 958–964.
2. BRUDER, G., S. SUTTON, H. BABKOFF, B. J. GURLAND, A. YOZAWITZ & J. L. FLEISS. 1975. Auditory signal detectability and facilitation of simple reaction time in psychiatric patients and non-patients. Psychiat. Med. 5: 260–272.
3. FLEISS, J. L., B. J. GURLAND, R. J. SIMON & L. SHARPE. 1973. Cross-national study of diagnosis of the mental disorders: Some demographic correlates of hospital diagnosis in New York and London. Int. J. Soc. Psychiat. 19: 180–186.
4. GURLAND, B. J., J. L. FLEISS, J. E. COOPER, L. SHARPE, R. E. KENDELL & P. ROBERTS. 1970. Cross-national study of the diagnosis of mental disorders: Hospital diagnoses and hospital patients in New York and London. Compr. Psychiat. 11: 18–25.

5. GURLAND, B. J., J. L. FLEISS, J. E. BARRETT, Jr., L. SHARPE & R. J. SIMON (U.S.) with COPELAND, J. R. M., J. E. COOPER & R. E. KENDELL (U.K.). 1972. The mislabeling of depressed patients in New York State hospitals. *In* Disorders of Mood. J. Zubin & F. Freyhan, Eds.: 17–31. Johns Hopkins Press. Baltimore, Md.

6. PROFESSIONAL STAFF OF THE U.S.–U.K. CROSS-NATIONAL PROJECT. 1974. The diagnosis and psychopathology of schizophrenia in New York and London. Schiz. Bull. No. 11 (Winter): 80–102.

7. ROSENTHAL, D. & S. KETY. 1968. The Transmission of Schizophrenia. Pergamon Press. New York, N.Y.

8. SALZINGER, K. 1973. Schizophrenia: Behavioral Aspects. John Wiley. New York, N.Y.

9. SHIELDS, J. & I. GOTTESMAN. 1972. Cross-national diagnosis of schizophrenia in twins. The heritability and specificity of schizophrenia. Arch. Gen. Psychiat. **27**: 725–730.

10. SIMON, R. J., B. FISHER, J. L. FLEISS, B. J. GURLAND & L. SHARPE. 1971. Relationship between psychopathology and British or American-oriented diagnosis. J. Abn. Psychol. **78**: 26–29.

11. SIMON, R. J., J. L. FLEISS, B. J. GURLAND, P. STILLER & L. SHARPE. 1973. Depression and schizophrenia in hospitalized black and white mental patients. Arch. Gen. Psychiat. **28**: 509–512.

12. SPITZER, R. L., J. ENDICOTT, J. L. FLEISS & J. COHEN. 1970. The Psychiatric Status Schedule: A technique for evaluating psychopathology and impairment in role functioning. Arch. Gen. Psychiat. **23**: 41–55.

13. SUTTON, S. 1973. Fact and artifact in the psychology of schizophrenia. *In* Psychopathology: Contributions from the Social, Behavioral and Biological Sciences. M. Hammer, K. Salzinger & S. Sutton, Eds.: 197–213. Wiley. New York, N.Y.

14. WING, J., J. E. COOPER & N. SARTORIUS. 1974. The Measurement and Classification of Psychiatric Symptoms. Cambridge Univ. Press. New York, N.Y.

15. ZUBIN, J. 1972. Scientific models for psychopathology in the 1970's. Seminars in Psychiatry. **4**: 283–296.

PSYCHIATRY AND THE POLITY: THE SOVIET CASE AND SOME GENERAL IMPLICATIONS*

Mark G. Field

Department of Sociology
Boston University
Boston, Massachusetts 02215; and
Russian Research Center
Harvard University
Cambridge, Massachusetts 02138

A psychiatric evaluation of behavior requires references to socially accepted behavior standards, and therefore an objective and value-free psychiatric opinion is difficult to imagine.

David L. Bazelon, Chief Judge,
U.S. Court of Appeals for the
District of Columbia Circuit

The purpose of this communication is to discuss some problems inherent in the comparative examination of psychiatric practice in two or more cultural settings. I have chosen to focus on psychiatry in the Soviet Union because I am familiar with it, and because it represents certain interesting issues having to do with the general setting of psychiatric practice and with the importance of the polity to that setting. The implied comparative focus is with the United States. The basic point of departure is that psychiatry, unlike most other medical specialties, is primarily concerned with a symptomatology that consists of behavior. As such, this specialty is heavily involved in the evaluation of the ways in which people act, think, express affect, and interact with others. It is concerned with socially expected role performance and with the critical question of conformity/nonconformity. What we label "mental illness" is qualitatively different from, let us say, cardiovascular disease, a broken leg, or a ruptured appendix. The psychiatrist is called in primarily because someone behaves in a bizarre, unexpected, inappropriate, or abnormal manner.

SOVIET SOCIETY AND MENTAL ILLNESS

It is a claim often made by Soviet writers on the subject that the nature of the Soviet sociopolitical order, with its public ownership of all the means of production, the lack of antagonistic classes, and the absence of the exploitation of man by man, and indeed of "socialism" itself, is such that mental illness is bound to decline from year to year, that it is indeed declining, and that it will

* This paper has benefited in part from the support of Grant No. R 01 HS 00272 National Center for Health Services Research, Health Resources Administration, Department of Health, Education and Welfare.

disappear altogether once the perfect and harmonious society of communism finally emerges. Soviet society is described officially as being in a state of transition from socialism to communism. On the other hand, the same writers claim that under the conditions of "decadent capitalism" (as in the United States), the increasing contradictions and class conflicts, the widening spread between the very rich and the very poor, and the insecurity tied to unemployment and economic cycles of boom and bust, racial and other tensions, and the ever-present fears of war, are such that mental illness and serious psychiatric disturbances are bound to be constantly on the rise, and that indeed they are.[1-4]

It is extremely difficult to carry out cross-national and cross-cultural comparative studies in the field of mental illness and emotional disturbances. The lack of common terms, the absence of standardized, cross-nationally valid definitions, differences in basic conceptualizations and approaches to mental illness and in therapeutic orientations, may indicate differences (or similarities) that do not exist in reality. Cultural differences add to the complexity of the task. At the same time, the assumption of a direct, causal etiological link between social structure and mental illness is far from firmly established, particularly for the psychoses. A great deal of the so-called "increase" in mental illness observed over the last hundred years is due to better case finding, better diagnostic facilities, and an improved reporting system. I must report that I tried, a few years ago, to verify the Soviet claim of a major difference in the incidence and the prevalence of mental illness between the United States and the USSR. Accepting the major diagnostic categories utilized in the two societies at their face value (a probably dangerous assumption), and trying to reconcile the differences in terms and practices, I came to the conclusion that the general (i.e., not only the treated) incidence and prevalence of the psychoses and the neuroses in the two societies were strikingly similar. I have not been able to carry out the same analysis for the decade 1964–1974, although it is my impression, from a cursory examination of the evidence, that the same conclusion (of the lack of an important difference) would be reached at the present time. There is thus little justification for the claim of a major difference, at least on this score, between the two societies. Such an assertion, it seems to me, may be more an implication of an ideologically determined belief that there *should* be less mental illness in one case, and more in another. By the same token there *should* be less alcoholism, juvenile delinquency and adult crime, family disorganization, divorce, and illegitimacy in the Soviet Union than in the West, and these social problems *should* be on the decline.[5] And yet they appear to be on the increase, as is generally the case in societies undergoing a fairly rapid process of modernization and urbanization. I believe this applies to the neuroses.

Insofar as the psychoses are concerned, the regularity with which they are found at about the same incidence and prevalence rates in a variety of cultural settings, in developed as well as in underdeveloped societies, seems to suggest the etiological importance of a genetic or somatic factor. This does not deny the fact, of course, that the expressions of psychotic disturbances are shaped by cultural images and symbols.

Thus the nature and the magnitude of the mental illness problem in Soviet society is not substantially different from that in the United States. In previous work I have described, in some detail, the differences in the responses the two societies make to that problem.[2] I have pointed out that in both cases the availability of psychiatric personnel per constant units of population was pretty much the same (although slightly better in the USSR) and was rising at about the same rate. I indicated that Soviet psychiatry tended to give more weight (for a variety of reasons) to the outpatient treatment of mental illness than American psychiatry did; and that the supply of psychiatric beds in the United States to the population was much larger than in the Soviet Union; indeed, about a decade ago or so, there were four times as many psychiatric beds for the population in the United States as in the USSR.[2] In the last few years, a concerted program for the deinstitutionalization of psychiatric patients in the United States has substantially reduced the number of such beds; the Soviets, on the other hand, have moved in the direction of increasing their psychiatric bed capacity. At present, the supply of American psychiatric beds per constant units of the population is only about 1.6 times as large as the Soviet (data for 1972).[6] It is thus interesting to note that the two societies, independently of each other, seem to be converging toward an index of about one psychiatric bed per 500 members of the population.

THE SOVIET POLITY AND PSYCHIATRY

There is, on the other hand, an aspect of Soviet society and Soviet psychiatry that represents a major departure from practices in the West and that has received a fair amount of international attention: the utilization, in the post-Stalin years, of the psychiatric diagnosis and psychiatric hospitalization to isolate and silence and possibly "reform" those who do not see eye-to-eye with the regime.[7-26]

I might begin by relating a Soviet story of the Stalin days. In a situation where the ability to express one's opinions is severely curtailed (and often harshly punished), humor plays an important function. As the story goes, Stalin made a speech on the radio on December 17, 1935 in which he said, having reviewed the events of the past and the difficulties inherent in forced-draft industrialization and forcible collectivization, that "life has become better, life has become more joyful." Given the nature of the cult of personality, where every utterance of the personality becomes holy writ (as in Mao's China), that sentence became the leitmotiv of the system of propaganda and agitation. The story has it that a high party official, in the course of an inspection tour of institutions and facilities, visited a provincial psychiatric hospital. And as he entered the ward, all the patients rose as one and sang out, "Life has become better, life is more joyful!" The inspector, of course, was gratified that the slogan had penetrated even the confines of a mental hospital, but his satisfaction was marred when he observed that one person had remained silent in a corner. He went up to the man and asked: "How come you did not shout, 'Life has become better'?" "Excuse me," the silent one replied, "I am not crazy. I work here."[27] The import of the story is that the "sane" population says to the regime (in that instance to the dictator) that one must be "insane" to accept at its face value the statement that life is better when in fact it is as bad as ever, and probably getting worse. The Emperor has no clothes. And the regime's answer is that anyone foolish enough not to accept and repeat the proclaimed slogans, i.e., the official or state truth, must, almost by definition, be considered a deviant, possibly a subversive or, as the case might be, not quite normal. What we have seen unfold in the last two decades in the Soviet Union is the application of the psychiatric-medical labels of "insanity", "abnormality", and so on to individuals whose pronouncements, interpretations, writings, and other acts have not been consonant with those of the regime, and whose silence could not be secured through either intimidation or court trials. Thus, doctors at a psychiatric hospital told one dissident (Viktor Feinberg):

> Your release depends on your behavior, and your behavior, to us, means your political views. In all other respects, your behavior is perfectly normal. Your illness consists of your dissenting opinions. As soon as you renounce them and adopt a correct point of view, we will let you go.[28]

It is tempting, of course, to go back into history to find antecedents for the use of the "insanity" label to discredit or silence those who do not agree with the regime. The most famous case is that of Chadaev, who in the nineteenth century had made some rather unflattering remarks about Russia and whom Tsar Nicholas I had had officially declared mad in 1836. Interestingly enough, the use or misuse of psychiatry under tsarist conditions is strongly condemned by contemporary Soviet writers. For example, Drs. G. V. Morozov, Ia. M. Kalashnik, and D. R. Lunts, whose names have been associated on many occasions with the psychiatric examinations of dissidents, write in a book on forensic psychiatry published in 1967:

> Under conditions of class terror and brutal reprisal against revolutionaries, especially during the intense reaction after 1905, the courts of Tsarist Russia sometimes prescribed an expert examination in order to create at least the external appearance of impartiality of their actions, while at the same time they attempted to use such examinations in their class interests.[29]

Although there is some indication that psychiatric hospitalization was used for political purposes under Stalin,[10,18] given the nature of that regime, there really was little need for psychiatric silencing because the legal system was completely subverted to the needs of the polity. Ironically, the present practice arose precisely because of certain liberalizing changes following Stalin's death and the attempt by his successors to introduce a certain degree of socialist legality, i.e., to dismantle the apparatus of arbitrary terror and arrest that had reigned during the heydays of the Stalin era. The Medvedevs have described this process as follows:

> [Stalin's] successors affirmed the principle of strict legality, but they soon came up against numerous difficulties created by the contrast between the relatively democratic Constitution of USSR and the by no means democratic system of government. It was frequently necessary to punish people who had not in fact gone beyond the bounds of what was permitted by law. "Mild" repression such as dismissal from work was not always very effective. And then someone had the simple idea that the increasing number of political trials and prisoners made a very poor public impression, while an increase in the number of patients under treatment in hospitals would be a very good indication of social progress. From this moment on, the psychiatric hospitals began to expand.[30]

In the early sixties (1961) a little-publicized set of instructions was issued (with revisions in 1967)† which coated the whole process with some legality and made it considerably easier than it had been in the past. There is enough evidence from the Soviet Union, as indicated earlier, to consider the practice well established, although, as might well be expected, it has been denied officially[31,32] as "... Malicious concoctions alleging that in the Soviet Union mentally healthy people are being placed in mental hospitals for their 'dis-

---

† Reproduced in Morozov and Kalashnik[29] pp. 1v–1vii.

senting' political views. . ."[33] In spite of these disclaimers the practice does not seem to have ceased. Perhaps the best known and documented case is that of Zhores Medvedev. It was this case that prompted Solzhenitsyn to write in a letter dated June 15, 1970:

> Without any arrest warrant or any medical justification four policemen and two doctors arrive at the home of a healthy man. The doctors declare he is mad, the police major shouts: "We are the agency of enforcement. Get to your feet!" They twist his arm behind his back and take him off to the madhouse. . . . Because of the very diversity of his talents, he is charged with being abnormal, a "split personality." His very sensitivity to injustice, to stupidity, is presented as a "morbid deviation," "poor adaptation to the social environment." Apparently to harbour thoughts other than those which are prescribed means that you are abnormal. Well-adjusted people all think alike. . . . If only this were the first case. . . . Some of the victims are well known, others remain obscure. Servile psychiatrists, who break their Hippocratic oath and are able to describe concern for social problems as "mental illness" can declare a man insane for being too passionate, or being too calm, for the brightness of his talents or the lack of them.[34]

DISCUSSION AND IMPLICATIONS

The utilization of psychiatry as an instrument of ideological control and political repression in the Soviet Union fits rather well with the hypothesis often expressed in the sociological literature of medicine as an instrument for the social control of deviance.[35-37] And indeed, if deviance can be defined in medical terms (alcoholism, for example), then medical intervention is indicated. The whole argument, of course, rests on that "if." Without espousing Thomas Szasz's extreme view that there is no such thing as "mental illness,"[38] one must recognize the temptation, in almost all social situations, to attribute non-conforming, eccentric, different behavior to external factors, whether it be possession by witches or demons in an earlier age, or invasion by noxious agents, i.e., by a "disease" over which the afflicted individual has no control and for which he should not be blamed. After all, we are told in the United States, mental disease is like any other disease.

Because of space limitations I will limit my discussion to a few brief implications raised by Soviet practices which bear on the importance of culture in a cross-cultural perspective.

Normative Aspects of Psychiatry

Psychiatry as a "medical" specialty has, as one of its mandates, the evaluation of behavior and the determination whether such behavior is the result of pathological conditions, i.e., of an "illness" over which the individual has no conscious control and for which he should not be held accountable (socially, morally, legally). Thus, in a historical perspective, the placing of the erratic or "abnormal" behavior of the insane under a medical umbrella (as happened about two centuries ago) was a progressive and humane step as compared to the treatment meted to "lunatics" until then. To determine whether a person was "responsible" at the time he committed a crime, or at the time he is put on trial, has become an accepted principle of jurisprudence. But the very exculpation of the individual's responsibility is a two-edged sword, because it can so easily be abused even with the best of intentions and because the "diagnosis" can be so subjective and culture-bound. Here the critical issue has to do with differentiating behavior that does not conform to certain socially and culturally established standards from behavior that can be attributed to illness. And the line differentiating them is a very thin one. Of course, one might say that in the Soviet case, it is more humane to place a dissident into a psychiatric hospital than into a concentration camp. Yesenin-Volpin has stated that "this kind of treatment has at times saved people from even greater calamities"[39] although Solzhenitsyn has not hesitated to describe that practice as ". . . *spiritual murder*, a variation on the *gas chamber* and even more cruel. . ."[40]

The Psychiatrist as a State Functionary

Although Solzhenitsyn refers to servile psychiatrists who break their Hippocratic oath, it should be pointed out that Soviet physicians do not take this oath. For many years after the Revolution no such oath was required of physicians. Recently a new one has been introduced that is apparently not entirely inconsistent with what we see being done in psychiatry. But the fact of the matter is that the Soviet physician, whoever he or she is, is a state employee‡ and has little recourse but to obey when ordered to do so by his superiors. The Soviet physician is not unique in being a state employee. But he lacks what physicians (and other professionals in the West) have, and that is a sense of professional autonomy *and* of a corresponding professional association or society that would insure some independence in professional judgment and would aid the individual physician to resist state-originated pressures.

The Issue of the "Compliant" Psychiatrist

It is at least conceivable that the average Soviet psychiatrist, brought up within the context of Soviet culture and values, will assess the very idea of opposition to the regime, of developing ideas independently of Party direction, or of interpreting or indeed applying a strict interpretation of the ideology to Soviet reality, as *prima facie* evidence of some kind of deep disturbance or maladjustment, and this without prompting from higher official sources. Some of the diagnostic labels themselves are revealing (if not, at least to Western observers, ludicrous): "counter-revolutionary delusion,"[10] "schizoheterodoxy or obsessive reformist delusions."[14] Other symptoms of mental illness have been reported as: "persistent mania for truth-seeking," "wears a beard," "meticulousness of thought and insufficient insight with regard to the actual situation," "considers the entry of Soviet troops in Czechoslovakia as an act of aggression," "considers that he should devote his life to the ideals of communism." Former General Pyotr Grigorenko was diagnosed as follows in 1964:

> Paranoid development of the personality, with reformist ideas arising in the personality, with psychopathic features of the character and the presence of symptoms of arteriosclerosis of the vessels of the brain.[43]

‡ For a description of the manner in which the regime silenced the medical profession after the Revolution see Reference 41.

David Bazelon, in his introduction to a text on Soviet forensic psychiatry, has pointed out that in this country (the United States):

> Our experience . . . strongly suggests that a forensic psychiatrist's testimony and recommendations may be influenced both by his professional orientation in psychiatric theory and by his personal and political preferences. . . . It would be absurd to expect psychiatrists to remain aloof from the political currents that sweep people into this process.

And Bazelon adduces some instances in which American psychiatrists have apparently cooperated with the courts.[38] But the number of cases in which psychiatry has been involved with political cases in the United States seems very limited. Beyond the Ezra Pound commitment and the attempt (unsuccessful) to commit General Edwin A. Walker, it is difficult to find more.[45]

I think that the question of the "compliant" psychiatrist has to remain moot, at least for the time being. Undoubtedly some Soviet psychiatrists, particularly those who have close ties with the whole process of certifying dissidents for the Serbskii Institute in Moscow, are fully conscious of the fact that they are performing a political task rather than a medical one. This is, in essence, the charge made in a letter by T. Velikanova and V. Lashkova on behalf of Natasha Gorbanevskaya: "What has happened to Natasha unfortunately convinces us not that our psychiatrists are insufficiently qualified doctors, but that they can make the wrong diagnosis *on purpose*."[46] For others, it is quite possible that they think they are performing a legitimate medical task. Indeed, some are probably convinced that they are providing a medical umbrella to protect the dissidents and nonconformists from the harsher aspects of the criminal process and punishment. General Grigorenko reports that one of the psychiatrists who supervised him in 1964, Margarita Feliksovna, asked the question: "Pyotr Grigorevich, at the Academy you received about 800 rubles. What then incited you to your anti-State activities?" And Grigorenko adds that to that psychiatrist: ". . . a person who risks material comforts is insane, no matter what high ideals had prompted him to act."[47]

Having said this, we must be careful not to fall into the trap of exaggerated cultural relativism. Since it is patently impossible for non-Soviet psychiatrists to examine the dissidents who have been hospitalized into mental hospitals, the next best thing would be to send their medical records to foreign psychiatrists. This is what Vladimir Bukovsky did when he managed to send abroad the histories of Grigorenko, Yakhimovich, Gorbanevskaya, Feinberg, Borisov, and Kuznetsov to a group of Western European psychiatrists. The forty-three who signed a letter to the London *Times* felt "impelled to express grave doubts about the legitimacy of compulsory treatment for the six people concerned, and indefinite detention in prison mental hospital conditions."[48] They added that it seemed to them that the diagnoses established for the six were the results of their exercising fundamental freedoms. And the Medvedevs themselves come to the crux of the problem by stating that:

> . . . psychiatrists make a clear-cut distinction between real mental illness, which means that a man is not responsible for his actions and must hence be placed in a mental hospital, and the various neurotic conditions which are regarded as anomalous features of a person's volitional and emotional make-up, but which do not prevent him from being fully conscious of his actions and fully accountable for them in legal and moral terms.[49]

The "Self-fulfillment Prophecy", Punishment and Brainwashing

If the mental "illness" for which dissidents and other nonconformists are hospitalized in psychiatric institutions is the holding of unorthodox views, the hospitalization process, according to the testimony that has filtered to the West, may itself lead to mental and other illness as a result of the "treatment" process meted out to the inmates. Incarceration into cells with highly disturbed mental patients (often with violent tendencies), the injection of powerful drugs (Aminazin, Triptazin-dihydrochloride, Haloparidol, Tizertsin, Melipramin, Cyclodol, Sulfrazin),§ the placing of the individual in a wet canvas (the "roll-up") that shrinks as it dries up, and physical punishment by "warders" rather than "orderlies"[50] may indeed produce mental disturbances and somatic changes that were not present at the time of hospitalization. Andrei Amalrik, referring to such persons as General Grigorenko, Ivan Yakhimovich, and Natasha Gorbanevskaya, states: ". . . they are completely normal and clear-thinking people, and they have been meted out a terrible fate — to have to live among genuinely deranged people, and moreover for an utterly undefined period, since the period of detention . . . is not laid down [by] the court."[51] In essence, it is difficult to draw a line between what is described as "treatment" and what is "punishment" for the holding of allegedly anti-Soviet or subversive thoughts. And there is little doubt, furthermore, that these hospitals partake of the characteristics of total institutions so graphically described by Goffman in *Asylums*. Natasha Gorbanevskaya eloquently described that feeling of humiliation and degradation in the hospital where she was held:

> [The doctor] a tall, rather beautiful woman of about my age . . . clearly considered me a creature of a lower order, a small, dishevelled shortsighted woman, dressed in the preposterous hospital smock and slippers . . . not only the physical inequality, but also the attitude so common among our doctors that the patient is completely in their power and that he must be treated like a silly baby with neither mind nor will of his own.

Gorbanevskaya, however, admits that "even among psychiatrists I have met some humane people who neither hunger after power nor wish to repress others."[52] Apparently "cure" consists of the ability *and* the willingness on the patient's part to articulate orthodox thoughts, as seen earlier in the case of Viktor Feinberg.[28] In this context, psychiatry has become part of a brainwashing or thought-reform process. Testifying in greater detail on this specific point of "release" from the psychiatric hospital, Yesenin-Volpin specifies that it usually depends "on the readiness of the patient to give the desired answers to certain questions . . . recognition of the correctness of . . . confinement, admission that his views are wrong, and the promise to conform with the established ideology in the future." Dr. Yesenin-Volpin then adds that such admissions are often impossible on a moral basis, and that in such cases compulsory treatment may continue indefinitely.[53] And indeed it is the indefiniteness of the sentence (as compared to legal sentences) that is perhaps the worst punishment imposed on those dissenters who are confined in mental hospitals.

---

§ For the chemical composition of these compounds, see Reference 21 (p. 241).

Psychiatry and the Social Control of Deviance

The issues raised here apply not only to Soviet psychiatric practice, but are inherent in psychiatry the world over. The phenomena described above are perhaps most clearly etched in the Soviet case, but the dangers exist everywhere that a benevolent occupation might easily turn into a malevolent instrument of repression. It is thus sad that, as Tarsis recounts, in the psychiatric wards where he was being held there were neither patients nor doctors, but only jailers in charge of inconvenient citizens. The doctors came to be known as the enemies (a play on the Russian words for doctors, *vrachi*, and enemies, *vragi*), and in *Ward 7* the day began with a parody of the "Internationale":

> Arise ye starvelings from your slumbers,
> Arise ye psychic slaves of woe,
> For reason in revolt now thunders
> Against the psychiatric foe . . .[54]

I might end on an ironic or dialectical note, in this following once more the Medvedevs' analysis. They state that the totalitarian centralization of the medical service, while introducing the principle of free health care for all, has also made it possible to use medicine as a means of government control and regulation. The availability of medical dossiers makes the role of physicians, and particularly psychiatrists, critical in many peoples' lives and careers.[55] I think that the use and abuse of these dossiers and the increasing lack of confidentiality with which they are kept and utilized is an issue that cuts across national borders and cultures, and deserves greater comparative analysis.

And finally, as abusive as the treatment of the mentally ill in a "punitive" way is the imposition of the label of mental illness upon those who happen to disagree with the prevailing ideology or culture, but are otherwise free of pathology.

REFERENCES

1. FIELD, M. G 1960. Approaches to mental illness in Soviet society: Some comparisons and conjectures. Social Problems 7 (4): 277–297.
2. FIELD, M. G. 1964. Soviet and American approaches to mental illness: A comparative perspective. Rev. Soviet Medicine 1 (4): 1–36.
3. FIELD, M. G. 1967. Soviet psychiatry and social structure, culture and ideology: A preliminary assessment. Am. J. Psychother. 21 (2): 230–243.
4. FIELD, M. G. 1968. Psychiatry and ideology: The official Soviet view of Western theories and practices. Am. J. Psychother. 22 (4): 602–605.
5. CONNOR, W. D. 1972. Deviance in Soviet Society: Crime, Delinquency and Alcoholism. Columbia University Press. New York, N.Y.
6. FIELD, M. G. Unpublished data.
7. TARSIS, V. 1966. Ward Seven. W. W. Norton. New York, N.Y.
8. NEW YORK TIMES. 1966. Soviets reported tightening surveillance over nonconformist intellectuals. February 17: 33.
9. MARCHENKO, A. 1969. My Testimony. Translated by Michael Scannel. E. P. Dutton and Co. New York, N.Y.
10. AN OBSERVER. 1970. Political "patients" in the Soviet Union. Letters to the editor. Am. J. Psychiatry 126 (9): 161.

11. EXECUTIVE COMMITTEE OF THE SECTION ON PSYCHIATRY, BRITISH COLUMBIA MEDICAL ASSOCIATION. 1970. Resolution endorsed by the Board of Directors, Canadian Psychiatric Association (mimeo).
12. ASCHERSON, N. 1970. Asylums await Soviet rebels. Washington Post January 5: A9.
13. TIME. 1970. Notes from a Soviet asylum. April 6: 40.
14. BRUMBERG, A. 1970. How Russia uses asylums to kill dissent. Washington Post October 18: B2.
15. CHALIDZE, V. 1970. Sovietskie dokumenti o prinuditel'noi gospitalizatsii v psikhiatricheskie bol'nitsi. Novoe Russkoe Slovo (New York). 60 (23009): 2, December 25.
16. MEDVEDEV, ZH. & R. A. MEDVEDEV. 1971. A Question of Madness. Knopf. New York.
17. SHABAD, T. 1971. Two dissidents in Soviet prison hospital charge drugs are used to change beliefs of political prisoners. New York Times March 19: 17.
18. PISAREV, S. P. 1971. From the Russian underground. New York Times July 6: 31.
19. SHABAD, T. 1971. Dissident poet in Turkmenia is reported sent to a hospital. New York Times September 28: 13.
20. SHABAD, T. 1971. Soviet denies charges on dissidents. New York Times October 24: 3.
21. U.S. SENATE JUDICIARY COMMITTEE. 1972. Abuse of Psychiatry for Political Repression in the Soviet Union. United States Government Printing Office. Washington, D.C. (Also available from Arno Press. New York, N.Y.)
22. STONE, I. F. 1972. Radicals and asylums in the Soviet Union. New York Times February 2: 31.
23. TIME. 1972. Asylums or prisons. February 7: 33.
24. VOLPIN, A. 1972. The medical police. New York Times December 9: 33.
25. TIME. 1972. Crackdown on dissent. December 18: 31–34.
26. Chronicle of Human Rights in the USSR. 1: 9, 17, 20. 1973. Khronika Press. New York, N.Y.
27. ANDREEVICH, E. 1951. Kremlin and the People-Political Anecdotes. Munich, Germany.
28. U.S. SENATE JUDICIARY COMMITTEE, op. cit.: 136.
29. MOROZOV, G. V. & IA. M. KALASHNIK. 1970. Forensic Psychiatry: A Translation of a text approved by the R.S.F.S.R. Ministry of Higher and Secondary Education. :9. Introduction by David L. Bazelon. Interaction Arts and Sciences Press, White Plains, N.Y.
30. MEDVEDEV, ZH. & R. A. MEDVEDEV, op. cit.: 199.
31. PETROV, G. 1971. Falsifikatori. Izvestiia March 18:4.
32. BRIANTSEV, K. 1971. Lzheradeteli v triasnie kleveti. Izvestiia October 24: 4.
33. Soviet psychiatry: The doctors reply. 1973. The Guardian September 29.
34. MEDVEDEV, ZH. & R. A. MEDVEDEV, op. cit.: 135–136.
35. ZOLA, I. K. 1975. In the name of health and illness: On some socio-political consequences of medical influence. Soc. Sci. & Med. 9 (2): 83–87.
36. PARSONS, T. 1951. The Social System. Free Press. Glencoe, Ill.
37. TWADDLE, A. C. 1973. Illness and deviance. Soc. Sci. & Med. 7 (10): 751–762.
38. SZASZ, T. S. 1961. The Myth of Mental Illness. Hoeber-Harper. New York, N.Y.
39. U.S. SENATE JUDICIARY COMMITTEE, op. cit.: 7.
40. MEDVEDEV, ZH. & R. A. MEDVEDEV, op. cit.: 136 (emphasis in the text).
41. FIELD, M. G. 1972. Taming a profession: Early phases of Soviet medicine. Bull. New York Acad. Med. (second series) 48: 83–92.
42. U.S. SENATE JUDICIARY COMMITTEE, op. cit.: 26.
43. Ibid.: 97.
44. MOROZOV, G. V. & IA. M. KALASHNIK, op. cit.: xiii.
45. Ibid.: xxxv–xxxvi.
46. U.S. SENATE JUDICIARY COMMITTEE, op. cit.: 114.
47. Ibid.: 79.
48. JENNER, F. A. et al. 1971. Dissenters in Soviet mental hospitals. Letter to the Times, London, September 16.

49. MEDVEDEV, ZH. & R. A. MEDVEDEV, *op. cit.*: 19.
50. BUKOVSKY, V. 1970. Three voices of dissent. Survey 77: 142.
51. AMALRIK, A. 1970. Three voices of dissent. Survey 77: 131.
52. U.S. SENATE JUDICIARY COMMITTEE, *op. cit.*: 130.
53. *Ibid.*: 6.
54. TARSIS, V., *op. cit.*: 25.
55. MEDVEDEV, ZH. & R. A. MEDVEDEV, *op. cit.*: 194–195.
56. U.S. SENATE JUDICIARY COMMITTEE, *op. cit.*: 226.

A COMPARISON OF INSTITUTIONAL SERVICES AND RESOURCES FOR THE MENTALLY RETARDED IN INDIA AND THE UNITED STATES

Manny Sternlicht and Meer H. Ali*

Department of Psychology
Yeshiva University
New York, New York 10033; and
Willowbrook Developmental Center
Staten Island, New York 10314

India is one-third the area of the U.S., but it has almost three times the population, more than 560,000,000 people. After having been exploited by colonial powers for more than a century, India, which was wealthier than England 150 years ago, is now suffering from poverty and its insufficient (or untapped) resources cannot meet the needs of its teeming millions.

Although India gained its independence from the Britisn just about 30 years ago, the developmental pace of this "democratic" nation has been much slower than that of its neighboring communist country to the North. Notwithstanding the great deal of progress that has been made since independence, much remains to be done: the basic needs of all of its people have yet to be met, the masses are uneducated, and the country lacks agricultural and industrial self-sufficiency. In view of this general underdevelopment, it is not particularly surprising that the needs of the mentally retarded are at the bottom of the totem pole of human priorities. Nagaraja[4] has stated that "Until recently there has been no organized movement for the retarded in our country". What is surprising, perhaps, is that this same ordering of priorities exists in the affluent United States, where an average of but $6.71 per day is spent per institutionalized retarded resident!

DEMOGRAPHIC CONSIDERATIONS

Although no precise figures are known, the prevalence of mental retardation in the United States is estimated at approximately 3%, and it is believed that there are about 5–6,000,000 retarded individuals here. Of this total, according to Baumeister and Butterfield,[1] nearly 200,000 reside in 400 facilities for the retarded. In 1970, according to Conley,[2] $4.6 billion was spent for the residential care of the retarded. In India, although no large-scale surveys have been conducted, a leaflet announcing the 1968 Conference on Mental Retardation in India estimated that there were between 3,000,000 and 4,000,000 retarded persons in India. (This lesser number of retarded individuals in India as against the United States may be due to the lesser number of facilities servicing this segment of the population, as well as the fact that mildly retarded persons may more easily be fitted into an agricultural environment as contrasted with a heavily industrialized one.) However, Kaur and Sen,[3] estimated in 1974 that there were between 5–19 million retarded individuals in India, i.e., that 3–4% of the population was mentally retarded. In 1968 there were only 73 institutions serving the retarded in India, according to a report compiled by the

---

* Counselor at City College of the City University of New York.

India Conference of Child Welfare. (In 1947, there were only three such facilities.) Of these 73 institutions, 30 were residential facilities, while the rest provided only educational and/or vocational and medical services.

A little over 2100 mentally retarded individuals are currently receiving some sort of institutional care in India (as contrasted to nearly 200,000 in the United States). A breakdown of the services provided is shown in TABLE 1.

According to a 1970 report of the Department of Social Welfare (Government of India), there were only five schools in all of India that offered training programs for teachers of the mentally retarded: one each at Ahmedebad, Chandigash, New Delhi, and two in Bombay. In contrast, there are more than twice this number of training programs in New York City alone. In 1970,[2] $1.5 billion was spent on special education in the United States.

We will now follow with a reasonably detailed representation of a kind of typical institution for the mentally retarded in one of the states of India.

Rehabilitation Center for the Mentally Retarded
(Somajiguda, Hyderabad, India)

This facility is the only institution for the training and education of the mentally retarded in the entire city of Hyderabad and one of the two in the entire state of Andhra Pradesh. Hyderabad is the fifth largest city in India, with a population close to two million. It is the capital of the State of Andhra Pradesh, a populous, industrial, and agricultural state in South India. There are hundreds of schools for normal children in the city, both public and private, for elementary and secondary education. There are two medical colleges in the city and one university, but only exceedingly limited facilities for the handicapped in general. Thus, there is only one public school for the deaf and dumb, and these children must be of at least average intelligence. No public facility whatsoever is available for the mentally retarded. In addition, public schools only provide education for those "normal" children who are fortunate enough to be able to attend. Although education is free on the elementary level, thousands of poverty stricken families in this city, as anywhere else in the country, cannot afford to send their children to school. In general, mental retardation does not seem to be an overwhelming problem, although statistics are lacking. Retarded children are generally taken care of by their families, regardless of the degree of retardation, because of lack of alternatives. The Rehabilitation Center for the Mentally Handicapped Children is a private facility organized by the Andhra Pradesh State Council for Child Welfare, a voluntary nonprofit organization. The center was established in September 1968 through private contributions. In 1970–71 the State government made nominal grants to the center. In 1972–73, the budget for the Center was (Rupees) Rs. 110 000 ($14,666.00), of which the State government granted a sum of Rs. 55 000, or 50% of the total budget. The rest was raised by the A. P. State Council for Child Welfare, the parent organization, through contributions by charitable institutions and some industries.

Nature of Student Population

The center's goal is to help mentally retarded children to develop self-sufficiency and better social relationships so that they may return the

TABLE 1

INSTITUTIONS AND SERVICES FOR MENTALLY RETARDED INDIVIDUALS IN INDIA*

States	Total Pop. (as of 1971)	Clinical Services	Inst. for MR Persons	Vocational Services	Educational Services	Medical Services	Residential Services	Total Persons
Andhra Pradesh	45,502,708	1	3	–	1	1	3	93
Bihar	56,353,369	3	2	1	1	–	2	51
Delhi	465,698	11	18	6	5	4	5	411
Gujarat	28,697,475	5	6	5	5	2	2	192
Madhya Pradesh	44,654,119	3	1	–	1	–	–	11
Madras	44,199,168	4	2	1	3	1	3	189
Maharashtra	50,412,235	21	20	14	19	5	9	716
Mysore	29,299,014	3	4	3	4	2	1	85
Oriasa	26,944,615	1	–	–	–	–	–	–
Pondicherry	471,707	1	–	–	–	–	–	–
Punjab	15,551,060	3	7	5	6	1	1	80
Rajasthan	25,765,806	1	–	–	–	–	–	–
Uttar Pradesh	88,341,144	8	4	2	3	1	2	158
W. Bengal	44,312,011	8	5	3	5	1	2	181
Kerla	24,347,375	–	1	1	1	–	–	18
Total	528,317,504	73	73	41	54	18	30	2,185

* (I.C.S.W. News Bulletin, March, 1972, Delhi, India.)

community. Educable and trainable children are admitted into the program; it serves children from the ages 6 to 12 years, but to be admitted, a child must have a mental age of at least 3½. The center has a capacity for 25 resident students and could admit an additional 40 as day students. At the present time, the center accommodates 12 residents and 22 day students. A van provides transportation to the day students to and from their homes. The present population is classified as follows:

Christians	2	Vegetarian	14
Hindus	29	Nonvegetarian*	20
Muslims	3		
	34		

* All Muslims and Christians are nonvegetarians. Among Hindus some sects are also nonvegetarians.

The general policy of the institution is to discharge a student after 12 years of age. At present, however, one fifteen year old is among the student population.

Mother Tongue

India has 14 full-fledged constitutional languages. Each State has its own language. However, regardless of State boundaries, Muslims throughout the country speak Urdu, although English is still the official language. In this institution, however, Hindi is understood by all.

Languages		I.Q. Levels		Sexes	
Hindi	2	30–40	8	Boys	25
Kanda	1	41–50	21	Girls	9
Malayalam	1	51–60	2	Total	34
Tamil	3	61–78	3		
Telugu	23	Total	34		
Urdu	3				
Marathi	1				
Total	34				

Types of Services Offered

Psychological Services

A trained psychologist performs the intake evaluation. She interviews the parents, and also administers psychological tests to the students to determine their I.Q.'s and mental ages. She also is the supervisor of the total program, and oversees the day-to-day functioning. The following are some of the tests that are administered:

1. Binet Kamat test (modified version of Stanford-Binet test)
2. Vineland Social Maturity Scale
3. Arnold Gessel Developmental Reading Schedule
4. Seguin Form Board Test
5. Porteus Maze Test
6. Bhatia's Batteries of Intelligence Test (An adaptation of Wechsler's Intelligence Test.) for chronological ages over 12 years.
7. O'Conner Finger Dexterity Test
8. Raven's Progressive Matrices Test
9. Minnesota Rate of Manipulation
10. Children's Apperception Test
11. Controlled projection for children
12. Rosenzwieg Picture-Frustration Study.

Education

There are four Montessori-trained teachers. Each of them is in charge of one class. Arithmetic and languages (reading and writing of English, the official language, Hindi, the proclaimed national language, and Telugu) are taught in the classrooms. The Hindi and Telugu languages, which are understood by most of the residents, are used as the medium of instruction. Classes are arranged according to the mental ages of the children.

Speech Therapy

There is one speech therapist on the staff. There are 15 children attending speech therapy at present. There is a soundproof room with an audiometer for speech therapy.

Music Education

Music is an integral part of Hindu culture, and the institution reflects this cultural trend. One music teacher is available to teach the students to play different Indian instruments, and also to teach them to sing Indian songs.

Occupational Therapy

One trained occupational therapist is part of the staff to work with the students.

Prevocational Instruction

One person is hired to work as prevocational instructor, who teaches drawing, painting, flower work, clay modeling, etc.

Other Staff

Other workers include 13 attendants, who also work at the dormitory, cook food and serve lunch to all students, as well as three meals to the resident students. The food is all vegetarian to avoid any complications. There is a warden and a matron for the dormitory facility. There are no separate office workers for the center. The staff of the Council of Child Welfare performs all additional clerical and administrative services for the center.

Recreation

There is no program for planned and supervised recreation. The children play in the wide open front yard (surrounded by walls) where there are swings, a jungle jim, etc. The attendants merely keep an eye on them to make sure that the children do not leave the premises.

Clothing

Grayish uniforms, composed of shirts and shorts for boys, and blouse and skirts for girls, are provided by the school to all of its students. This preserves uniformity betwen the haves and the have-nots.

Organization (TABLE 2)

The honorary Secretary of the A. P. State Council for Child Welfare is the top executive. He executes the programs for the council. Running the Rehabilitation Center for Mentally Handicapped Children is only one aspect of the Council's work. Other projects of the Council include a kindergarten program and a Teacher's Training School. The Council also is involved in some other events, e.g., celebration of the World Day for the Disabled, and camping for children.

The Honorary Secretary is also the top executive for the center, although the clinical psychologist supervises the daily routine. He also serves as the chief public relations person for the center. He is responsible for the budget, raising funds, contacting government agencies, private organizations, and philanthropic individuals for supporting the programs of the center as well as the Council.

TABLE 2   TABLE OF ORGANIZATION

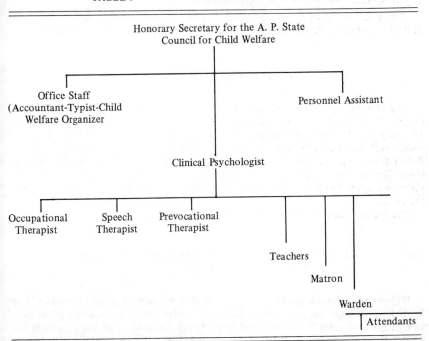

Physical Facilities

The Center is located in one of the better areas of the city, near a lake adjacent to the government guest house called Lake View Guest House. There is a two-story brick building housing the center and the office of the A. P. Council for Child Welfare. Classrooms are located on the first floor, and these are adequately furnished with desk and chairs, except for the music room and the occupational therapy room. Most Indian musical instruments require setting on the floor; therefore the music room has a rug on the floor instead of furniture. The second floor contains the administrative and clerical offices. As the Rehabilitation Center is part of the A. P. State Council for Child Welfare, both agencies are served by the same staff. The Honorary Secretary of the Council also is the chief administrative officer for the center. The residential dorm is not located in the main building, but in one of the out-buildings. A large tin-roofed room is used as the dorm for the children in residence. The furniture in the dorm is very modest by American standards, but adequate by Indian standards. The area has one large front yard and another large backyard. At the other end in the backyard, there is another temporary construction that houses a kindergarten for normal children (and also run by the Council for Child Welfare). The front yard is much wider than the back one. It is composed of a lawn and a playground for children. In the same yard, there is another large temporary construction containing a large room, which is a one-room Teacher's Training College to train teachers for village level primary schools. The best furnished room is the Office of the Honorary Secretary of the Council. Next in rank is the office of the psychologist, who is also responsible for the day-to-day administration and supervision of the Rehabilitation Center for the handicapped children. The furniture in the classrooms is adequate.

The general condition of the building and of the students appears adequate, and the arrangements for sanitation and housekeeping are quite acceptable.

Additional Programmatic Needs

The Center is most interested in developing the following additional programs: (1) A continuing educational program for educables over the age of 12 years; (2) A sheltered workshop for the trainable children over the age of 12, which will enhance the possibility of rehabilitation of the youngsters; and (3) Better transportation arrangements also are urgently needed, as the present van is old and requires frequent repairs. If additional transportation can be provided, there is a great likelihood of having an increased number of students attending the center.

For the sake of contrast, let us take a look at an American facility.

An American State Facility for the Mentally Retarded
(Willowbrook Developmental Center)

Willowbrook Developmental Center, which is located on Staten Island in New York City, houses approximately 3200 mentally retarded residents of all ages and degrees of retardation in 27 different buildings. Most of the residents are drawn from the five boroughs of New York City, and the racial and religious

TABLE 3   TABLE OF ORGANIZATION

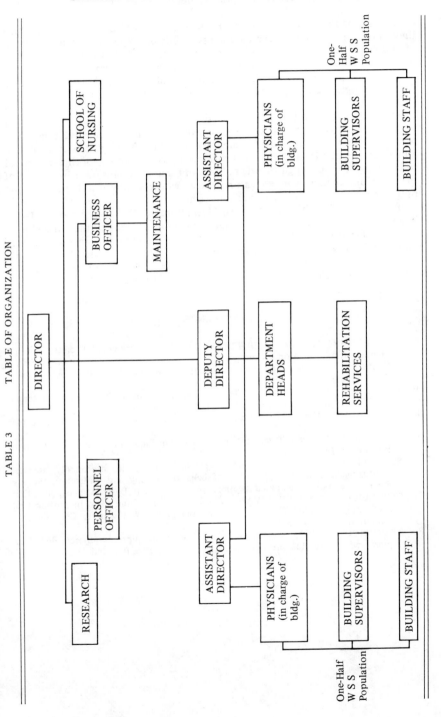

breakdown of the residents mirrors the New York City population from which they have come. To service these residents, Willowbrook has a staff just in excess of 4,000, including a top level management staff of approximately 45. The professional staff consists of: Teachers, 138; recreation therapists, 74; physical therapists, 58; speech therapists, 25; occupational therapists, 73; social workers, 37; psychologists, 20; physicians, 49; and nurses, 180. (see TABLE 3).

Three quarters of this population is profoundly mentally retarded with accompanying physical handicaps. There is a variety of programming that occurs, and the parents are actively involved with their children. Examples of some of these programs are offered by Sternlicht,[5,6,8] and Sternlicht and Sullivan.[7] Emphasis is currently being given to "exodus," or the return of residents to their borough of origin. Staff and training tie-ins occur with staff of the area universities, and educators, social workers, physical therapists, and psychologists find internship opportunities here.

The budget for this facility was 41 million for the fiscal year 1974–75. Willowbrook is currently the defendant in a lawsuit brought by the Willowbrook Benevolent Society and the AHRC, wherein Willowbrook is being asked to provide adequate care, training, and treatment for each of its residents. Should the judge rule in favor of the plaintiffs, almost $90 million more may be required to carry this out fully for each individual resident.

REFERENCES

1. BAUMEISTER, A. A. & E. BUTTERFIELD. 1970. Residential Facilities for the Mentally Retarded. Aldine. Chicago, Ill.
2. CONLEY, R. W. 1974. Economics and mental retardation. Soc. Rehab. Rec. 1 (10): 20–25.
3. KAUR, R. & A. K. SEN. 1974. Training and education of the mentally retarded children: A survey report. Indian J. Ment. Retard. 7 (2): 65–71.
4. NAGARAJA, J. 1967. The mentally retarded – A review. Arch. Chld. Hlth. 8 (4): 128–131.
5. STERNLICHT, M. 1966. Treatment approaches to delinquent retardates. Int. J. Group Psychother. 16: 91–93.
6. STERNLICHT, M. 1972. Reduction of headbanging in profoundly retarded institutionalized boys: Application of behavior therapy and motivation therapy. Paper presented at the annual meeting, Am. Assoc. Ment. Defic., Minneapolis, Minn.
7. STERNLICHT, M. & I. SULLIVAN. 1975. Preparing Deaf and Blind Institutionalized Profoundly Retarded Children for the Community. Willowbrook Developmental Center. Staten Island, N.Y.
8. STERNLICHT, M. 1975. Programming for the severely and profoundly retarded. Paper presented at the annual meeting, Am. Assoc. Ment. Defic., Portland, Ore.

MULTIDISCIPLINARY COLLABORATION IN FIELDWORK: AUSTRALIAN STUDIES

John Cawte

The School of Psychiatry
The University of New South Wales
Sydney, Australia

I am going to discuss the concept of cross-cultural suffering. The two cultures that not long ago came face to face in Australia — "crossed," if you like — were as diametrically adverse as possible. One is the oldest, darkest, least technological, most primeval; the other is the newest, whitest, and most technological and "developed." Australian Aborigines had been cut off from the rest of mankind for about 30,000 years.* When these two diametric streams of mankind finally intermingled, with no preparation on either side there resulted on the part of the Aborigines massive psychophysical trauma, confusion and malfunctioning. In terms of the "emics" of the situation, there was great suffering.

Suffering is emphasized because it is the main raison d'être of the science of cross-cultural psychiatry. At the present time it is also the reason why these people, who are in a painfully sensitive state of mind, even permit research access. On field trips we take care to show that we can relieve some suffering by medical means — even if it is only a case of bedwetting. In Australia, the suffering associated with crossing of cultures is peculiarly intense. This is not simply because, as is sometimes maintained, the bearers of British culture were ruthlessly aggressive.† There were causes on the other side. There are not the social institutions, nor the modal personality patterns in the hunter-gatherer society to achieve even an approximate correspondence with those of industrial society. There is no means of picking up this new culture and using it to advantage.

This much said about suffering in the culture contact, one of our major aims was to discover the extent of the suffering that preceded European contact. We learned this from systematic reconstruction of Aboriginal medicine, made with the help of informants who have experienced the precontact situation. Suffering was pre-existent on an interpersonal, territorial and ecological basis. This historical exercise has affected the yardstick by which we attempt to evaluate

---

* They were cut off for essentially geographic reasons having to do with remoteness, ecology, and ocean currents. Technological development during the exclusive tenure by Australian Aborigines was probably constrained by the ecology. The Australian sub-continent does not possess species adaptable either to agriculture or husbandry. Developments in the rest of the world, such as forms of agriculture that permitted village life and larger-scale social institutions did not diffuse to Australia.

† Hippler[1] writes that concern for people who are marginal to civilization is a comparatively recent phenomenon. In the remoter part of human history marginal peoples were exploited if possible, ignored if unexploitable, and destroyed if troublesome. This was an unquestioned procedure. Only in recent times, and mostly in western-European-derived populations, has there ever been any effective systematic objection to the destruction of peoples, and especially one based not only on simple humanitarianism but also on political theory supported by institutionalized intellectual sanctions.

and measure personality problems in the culture contact. Some of them were there before. This complication highlights the point that one cannot conceive of a science that makes more demands upon more disciplines than does cross-cultural psychiatry. This is because psychiatry itself is an essentially multi-disciplinary science.

Since this conviction may surprise some, it may be useful to elaborate it at the outset. Psychiatry, if it is to be safe, resourceful and effective in the relief of the psychic suffering in its own culture, calls for quite advanced inter-disciplinary thinking on the part of its practitioners. Practitioners who are restricted in the scientific disciplines that they employ are to that extent less safe, less resourceful and less effective. ‡

A case of everyday suffering from my practice will make this clear. A 59-year-old woman who worked in a bonded whiskey warehouse was being treated by her doctor with rauwolfia for raised blood pressure. After her annual vacation she found she could not return to work because of her nervousness and shaky legs. She had many crying spells, slept poorly, and lost weight. Aspirin, which she habitually took for headaches and minor ailments, no longer gave any relief. She thought she might be dying. During the previous year she and her husband had sold their home in the suburbs, where they had lived all their married life, and moved into a new apartment, since he had Parkinson's disease and could no longer handle the garden. It is virtually impossible to understand this humble woman's suffering without some grasp of its interdisciplinary dimensions — biological, psychological, societal and cultural. If one does not understand these aspects, one is less likely to intervene in a safe, resourceful, and effective manner. §

When the contract is made with cross-cultural mental health — once some commitment is accepted to this world of cross-cultural suffering — information relevant to the science becomes vastly expanded. It expands in each of these dimensions: biological, psychological, societal and cultural.

In field work designed to focus adaptational problems of tribal societies, we have engaged specialists help us study the "etics" of these dimensions. From the medical and paramedical disciplines, we have been helped by experts in medicine, paediatrics, social medicine, psychology, sociology, social work, dentistry, and genetics. From the less closely medicine-related disciplines, we have used experts in anthropology, the law, education, theology, town planning, architecture and photography.‖

---

‡ In teaching clinical psychiatry to students, a profitable exercise is to present a series of problems of suffering encountered in everyday practice, particularly those problems that can be satisfactorily resolved only by interdisciplinary thinking. The student is advised to conduct his examination of those problems of suffering along four basic dimensions: biological, psychological, societal and cultural-ecological. He is thus invited to expand his awareness of how other disciplines might approach the problem.

§ Similarly, while books about psychiatry abound, well balanced and sophisticated books are neither common nor popular. Exceptions are Jerome Frank's *Persuasion and Healing*[2] and Leston Havens' *Approaches to the Mind.*[3]

‖ Accounts of these attempts at multidisciplinary collaboration in the field may be found in the literature. The book *Cruel, Poor and Brutal Nations*[4] summarizes the *modus operandi* and findings of a short-stay multidisciplinary team. Another book, *Medicine is the Law*[5] is written from the multidisciplinary viewpoint of physician, anthropologist, and psychiatrist. An account of the stumbling blocks against which we barked our shins in the attempt to achieve multidisciplinary rapport is given in a paper in *Excerpta Medica.*[6]

We learned something from most of them. In return we taught them a little about cross-cultural suffering, or at least we opened their minds to it. We found that other scientific disciplines have stereotypes about psychiatry that, if left unchallenged, might preclude any collaboration at all.

An unexpected bonus of the multidisciplinary approach deserves greater attention. It concerns the contributions arising from the research method, which owes as much to the modal personality of people working in the particular discipline, as to the discipline itself. (One has a strong impression that disciplines have modal personalities).

In a book by Liam Hudson called *Frames of Mind*[7] we are told that there are three types of thinkers: convergent, divergent and art-achievers. Pose a problem to a convergent thinker and he will try to reduce it to a single solution. Pose the same problem to a divergent thinker and he will get involved in related problems. Pose it to the third thinker, and he will make an artistic statement of it. We are indebted to the convergent thinkers of several disciplines for analyses and correlations that would not have been done otherwise. And we are indebted to art-achievers for convincingly human statements of what others only see statistically.

Let me give an illustration of a spontaneously occurring research opportunity, in order to invite you to reflect how these three types of thinkers would utilize it. During our team's expedition to Arnhem Land in early 1974, an epidemic caused by Influenza A virus swept through the population, with some fatal cases. It was accompanied by heightened ceremonial activity.¶

Aboriginal ceremonial (the *corroboree*) has recently been better appreciated by the white man's culture, as theatre, involving music, song, poetry, acting, dancing, and painting. Seen by discerning eyes, these art forms merge into an extravaganza. While appreciation of the etics of the ceremonial is commendable, it still neglects the emics — the purpose to the performers.

Ceremonials reenact myths of the ancestral creators, with the object of releasing their power once more for the benefit of their earthly descendants. The ceremonial is carried out to reduce threats to security. Invoking the power of the ancestors is intended to restore harmony, resolve tensions, and relieve suffering. So the ceremonial may be viewed as contributing to mental health. These anxious people, some depressed and with influenza, whose relatives were dead or dying, enacted it continuously for days and nights in the midst of torrential monsoonal rain and bleak wind. They neglected their rest, their hygiene, and their nutrition. Those of us who were working with the sick in the little aid-post thought that this ceremonial actually added to the risks of disease.

We might consider this example a paradigm of suffering that calls for multidisciplinary sensitivity. Remember that it was the white man's diseases, rather than the white man's guns, that desolated this culture. Here was that same primal action and reaction to disease played out before our eyes. What part of this archetypal situation would our three thinkers use, and which ignore?

The multidisciplinary man does not call in a linguist, ethnomusicologist or mythologist, just to understand the ceremonial. But he will try to read their papers, and he hopes that among their numbers will be some art-achievers who

¶ We were invited by the elders to make a documentary film of these mortuary rites. It is entitled *Aboriginal Mourning* and is available in a 16 mm print, color with sound, from the Australian Institute of Aboriginal Studies, P.O. Box 550, Canberra, A.C.T. Australia 2600. A companion film, *Aboriginal Healing*, is also available.

can offer a convincing human statement of the problem, as well as the usual convergent thinkers, who write articles to each other in a secret language.**

Convergent thinkers dominate research, and they often underestimate the insights of art-achievers. Let me therefore submit an artistic statement about psychiatry. It is the work of Merrill Moore, a psychiatrist-poet who taught me clinical psychiatry twenty years ago in Boston. He also taught me that one could strive to communicate a psychiatric idea through a literary statement of it.†† In this instance Moore reminds us that however much we attempt in psychiatry, it will not be enough.

AND TO THE YOUNG MEN‡‡

And to the young men awaiting their sacrifice
You brought water in an invisible pail
And promised them the plans would surely fail
That were written against them, recorded in the stars.
And you brought straw and padded the cold bars
Of the prison beds whereon the young men lay,
And sung to some at night and fanned by day
Those who were fevering into paradise.

But even then you did not do enough.
For you remember a boy, the silent one?
With a silent eye, who scarcely loved the sun,
And felt too keenly the winter wind's dry sough?
Well, you should have brought him cresses from a far stream
Over which nymphs and under which naiads dream.

Merrill Moore

Cresses from a far stream? — for Aboriginal culture, these rare cresses are the roles, social institutions, aboriginality itself. Now that the two cultures have crossed, these vegetables do not grow so well. But we who work in the area of cross-cultural mental health can bring Aborigines at least this cress, this role. We can help train Aboriginal mental health workers to deliver mental health care to their own people, in their own style. This approach is being attempted among some American Indians.[9] We in Australia are trying to learn it. At this moment in Queensland, we have two consultants: a psychologist who helped create the Papago Psychology Service, and a Papago Indian who is a trained mental health worker in the tribe.

** University departmentalization, which segregates related disciplines and even opposes them to each other, is sometimes held responsible for deficiencies in multidisciplinary thinking in academics. This theme was explored in a previous symposium on interdisciplinary relationships in the social sciences.[8] It is open to question what improvement in departmentalization has taken place since then.

†† As one recalls Merrill Moore, he was a remarkable observer and a capable teacher, especially effective in the area of alcoholism, but perhaps more preoccupied with communicating through his art form. He penned a prodigious number of sonnets expressing ideas from his psychiatric practice, not particularly concerned to retouch them or to shape them into strict sonnet forms. He remains the archpoet of psychiatry.

‡‡ *From*: Moore, Merrill. 1942. *In* The Albatross Book of Living Verse. Louis Untermeyer, Ed. Collins. London, England. Reprinted by permission of Harcourt, Brace & Co. and of the author.

If relief of suffering is our aim, the next discipline we need to involve in cross-cultural research is the discipline represented by the culture that has been crossed.

SUMMARY

The Australian situation offers special insights for cross-cultural psychiatric research. The two cultures that "crossed" in Australia were diametrically opposed in their characteristics. Suffering, which is considered to be the raison d'être of cross-cultural psychiatry, became pandemic among Aborigines, not only because the invading society was ruthlessly aggressive, but also because the invaded society did not have the social institutions and modal personality patterns enabling it to adapt to the introduced culture.

It is suggested that no applied science makes more demands of more scientific disciplines than does cross-cultural psychiatry. Psychiatry itself is a multidisciplinary science. The amount of information needed by the cross-cultural extension of psychiatry is further expanded. Only a multidisciplinary approach can furnish the necessary level of information. An outline is given of multidisciplinary fieldwork in Australia, indicating advantages and difficulties inherent in it. Attention is drawn to literature in which details of the results may be found. The Australian work leads to the conclusion that if the relief of suffering is the aim then greater involvement is needed in cross-cultural psychiatry from the culture that has been "crossed".

REFERENCES

1. HIPPLER, A. 1975. Culture change and the Aboriginal: The ideological problem. Unpublished manuscript in the School of Psychiatry, University of New South Wales, Sydney, Australia.
2. FRANK, J. D. 1961. Persuasion and Healing. A Comparative Study of Psychotherapy. The Johns Hopkins Press. Baltimore, Md.
3. HAVENS, L. L. 1973. Approaches to the Mind. Movement of the Psychiatric Schools from Sects toward Science. Little, Brown and Co. Boston, Mass.
4. CAWTE, J. 1972. Cruel, Poor and Brutal Nations. The Assessment of Mental Health in an Australian Aboriginal Community by Short-Stay Psychiatric Field Team Methods. The University Press of Hawaii. Honolulu, Hawaii.
5. CAWTE, J. 1974. Medicine is the Law. Studies in the Psychiatric Anthropology of Australian Tribal Society. The University Press of Hawaii. Honolulu, Hawaii.
6. CAWTE, J. 1971. Multidisciplinary teamwork in ethnopsychiatry research. Excerpta Medica Congress Series No. 274: 936–940.
7. HUDSON, L. 1968. Frames of Mind. Methuen. London, England.
8. SHERIF, M. & C. W. SHERIF, Eds. 1969. Interdisciplinary Relationships in the Social Sciences. Aldine Publishing Co. Chicago, Ill.
9. KAHN, M. W. & J. L. DELK. 1973. Developing a community mental health clinic on an Indian Reservation. Int. J. Soc. Psychiatry 19: 299–306.

COPING WITH UNWANTED VARIABLES IN CROSS-CULTURAL RESEARCH: EXAMPLES FROM MENTAL HEALTH AND TREATMENT OF THE AGING

S. Stansfeld Sargent*

Oxnard Community Mental Health Center
Oxnard, California 93030

I think of "unwanted variables" as any factors that interfere with meaningful comparisons and conclusions in cross-cultural research. Many researchers interested in methodology have listed factors or variables that need to be controlled: e.g., socioeconomic status; age, sex and ethnic composition; sampling errors; and testing attitudes.[1-7] In this paper I am concerned with the somewhat broader and more subtle variables that are often overlooked.

One such variable may be found in a researcher's motivation, often unconscious, to come up with a specific conclusion, such as finding no mental illness in the Soviet Union or the People's Republic of China. I recall that the psychiatrist, Frankwood Williams, after visiting the USSR wrote a book in 1934 declaring enthusiastically that human nature had become changed, and that the whole theme of Russian life had become one of mental health and security, both economic and psychological. He noted a decline in mental and nervous disease, and saw health and happiness in homes and schools and in the faces of crowds on the street or in the Parks of Culture and Rest.[8] A few years later I visited the Soviet Union, where I observed many examples of the wish to believe or disbelieve. I remember going to see some new apartments on the outskirts of Moscow, and hearing sympathetic tourists exclaim about the beautiful sunny homes that had been built for the workers. One woman, however, was very critical of Soviet policies and practices; she pointed out cracks in the plaster and noted the outside wiring on the buildings. Both observations were correct, but the motives behind them were very different.

Other examples of "premotivated conclusions" might be given: for example, the conservative critic who described the failure of the "welfare state" in Sweden or Denmark, or recent visitors to China whose reports correspond with what they expected to find there.

A related kind of bias might be called "conceptual" — e.g., a strong organic or cultural slant — or a psychoanalytic, behavioristic or humanistic one, for that matter. Some years ago Eric Berne visited Fiji and Tahiti and wrote some articles protesting the overcultural interpretation of mental illness, as compared with the genetic or constitutional. He felt that the rates of mental illness are about the same all over the world, although he admitted the evidence was incomplete, but he proposed that about the same proportion of every large population will suffer from psychosis or neurosis.[9,10] Berne's bias in an organic-constitutional direction could, of course, be matched by an extreme cultural slant on the part of some anthropologists. I am reminded of the two types of criteria or commitment found by Phillips and Draguns in intercultural study of mental illness: the traditional psychiatric one, guided by the categories in the *Diagnostic and Statistical Manual of Mental Disorders*, which seeks constancy in psycho-

* Present address: P.O. Box 1366, Santa Monica, California 90406.

pathology, and the cultural anthropological approach, which seeks diversity, and regards differences in disorders as clues to the culture.[11]

Unwanted variables enter the picture when any investigator becomes a crusader for a particular orientation and discourages attempts to reconcile conflicting views. In the field of aging there is some dispute over the applicability of the "disengagement theory," which explains aging as a kind of generalized withdrawal from activity. Certain studies of aging, both domestic and cross-cultural, have been criticized for using disengagement as a blanket concept or interpretation, supposedly fitting all cases.[12]

Another unwanted variable may be called perceptual; it can operate through ignorance, naïveté, inadequate preparation, inconsistent frames of reference, and the like. Researchers doing comparative studies of mental health or psychotherapy have made great strides in avoiding errors of this kind. For example, they realize that they need to know how mental illness is regarded in a culture and what its causes are assumed to be, as well as knowing something about the tolerance of eccentricity, which varies greatly from one culture to another.[13]

Cross-cultural researchers on aging have improved their methods, not only in regard to comparable samples and interview techniques, but also to be sure that questions used in one culture are meaningful in another.[14] The nature of aging and its role in minority groups is often misperceived, as when norms for white Americans are used in dealing with blacks. The life expectancy of black males in the United States is only 60 years, which means that most black men will not collect social security; of aged blacks, 50 percent are below the poverty level, as compared with 23 percent of whites.[15]

Another perceptual variable centers about the awareness of social change on the part of the investigator. A controversy is now going on as to the role of the aged in Japan. Several observers and researchers find that the traditional honored role of the elderly is being eroded, as is often found with progressing industrialization.[16,17] Palmore, however, presents data showing that the changes in Japan are minimal, and states that the United States could still learn a great deal from Japan in regard to humane treatment of the aging.[18,19]

Perhaps the most obvious unwanted variable involves accuracy of the data themselves. Consider, for example, longevity figures in the Near East, notably Turkey and the Caucasus. A recent article in the *Gerontologist*, written by a Russian investigator, told of meeting and interviewing dozens of centenarians in the Caucasus.[20] He never seemed to question the stated ages or to seek to verify them. He showed a picture of a 138-year-old woman and her 85-year-old son; it probably did not occur to him that she would have been 53 when the son was born, which would have been almost a miracle. Records of births are sketchy or nonexistent in this region (as they were with former slaves in the United States, many of whom were alleged to live to fabulous old age). Apparently a tradition of longevity has grown up in this area and has become almost a cult, encouraged in part by state propaganda, despite efforts by Soviet demographers to track down accurate figures.[21,22]

Even when data are reasonably reliable, different standards for aging, for retirement, granting of pensions, and the like are found (e.g., 60, 62, 65, and 70 years of age), as in a recent comparison between the United States and the USSR.[23] Also other concepts differ: in the USSR "work force" does not include those unemployed who are seeking work; in the United States "work force" does include them.

In this connection, one thinks of the effort of Roger and Louise Barker to find appropriate behavior units that are comparable for cross-cultural study.[24]

The original study of children in Midwest (Kansas) and Yoredale (Yorkshire, England) has been extended so that behavior settings for old people make possible interesting comparisons between the two countries.[25] Whether equivalence of behavior settings can be established between more disparate cultures remains to be seen.

Various problems in cross-cultural communication have been dealt with by many of our conference participants (e.g., Wagatsuma, Brislin, Osgood, and Mehan). Some of the problems are not difficult to identify, such as a noncooperative attitude toward the interviewer or a "yea-saying" or "nay-saying" trend in responding. Others are more subtle such as the nature of a respondent's ideology and role within his or her society.[26]

Sometimes a new approach helps. In a study of social class in an American community 23 years ago, I remember being puzzled about how to get an index of a person's consciousness of class. Direct questioning would not do, since Americans tend to deny thinking in class terms. I finally hit upon a kind of projective technique. I asked the respondent how he divides people up in his mind and what differences among people in his community he notices. This brought forth an interesting variety of categories. Some were class-oriented, like "upper, middle and lower" or "the rich and the poor"; others were not, like "the oldtimers and the newcomers," "the oil people and the navy people" or "the good sports and the killjoys." In this community (Ventura, California) there seemed to be slightly more of the non-class categories mentioned, which agreed with various types of objective data obtained.[27]

I wish to add one more unwanted variable: unwarranted interpretations. Does a researcher say or imply that the size of social security or pension payments to the aging is a measure of their status in the society — or worse still, of their happiness? Or that the figures on mental hospital population are an index to the mental health of the community or the society? As Mensh indicated some years ago, hospital patient-counts are a function not only of new types of treatment (e.g., tranquilizers), but also of changes in admission and discharge policies, which in turn reflect economic and political conditions.[28]

The first step in coping with an unwanted variable is to identify it, which may occur at any stage of the research — but preferably before it is published! One may reasonably ask, can we expect the investigator to discover and estimate the effect of such influences? This is a good question and suggests the importance of having a critic — best of all one with a different background — look over and evaluate the report.

The significance of an unwanted variable often is not clear. It may have to be studied later as an independent variable. If it seems minor, it might be dropped from the report without affecting the results appreciably. If it takes the form of a procedural error, it might be corrected by a methodological change, choice of a different sample, replication using improved techniques, and the like. Some investigators would compensate for unwanted variables such as an unrepresentative sample by the use of statistical techniques. This might be all right if the original data are valid and the error is minor. But in some settings I have seen elaborate and refined statistics used to process and interpret data that were faulty in the first place, which seems the height of futility. Fortunately the growing literature on cross-cultural research discusses extensively ways of handling methodological errors.[1,4,5,29]

More difficult to cope with are motivational and conceptual biases, partly because the researcher may be unaware of them. Brislin and Lonner suggest the "plausible rival hypotheses" approach as a way of correcting for bias (Reference

1, Chapter 1). This is an excellent idea, but how difficult it is for the eager researcher to admit the possible validity and applicability of rival theories! (Think of investigators with a strong cultural orientation struggling to countenance and assay the role of organic, hereditary or constitutional factors; and, of course, vice versa.) Ideally this evaluating and selecting of different hypotheses is done in the planning stages of research, as has been demonstrated recently in several cooperative cross-cultural studies of mental illness and of aging.

Unfortunately, writers and researchers seem to get more attention and reward, generally speaking, for expounding or emphasizing a particular viewpoint rather than for endeavoring to assess the relative value of various approaches or for trying out several supplementary approaches. As a result, the evaluation has to be performed by the reader or auditor, i.e., the consumer who will be making the applications — with little help from the experts!

Let's face it: our field of interest is a thorny one, full of unpleasant variables. Shall a researcher give up if he finds they vitiate his nice quantitative findings, and threaten the validity of that striking cross-cultural contrast he hoped to depict? By no means. Many, and perhaps most, of his data are still valuable. Even if there is real doubt about census figures on centenarians in the Caucasus, the fact is that thousands of vigorous old people live and thrive there, so we can learn a lot about their longevity — even if they are only octogenarians.

Or again, if assorted pesky variables prevent a strict comparison of mental health practices in Russia and the United States, we can still learn a great deal about the operation of each system, as the 1967 NIMH mission to the USSR demonstrated.[30] If the "welfare" or "happiness" of the aged in Japan and the United States cannot yet be compared, we can still collect valuable data on the status, health, living arrangements, employment, income, and social and political participation of the aged in each country, as is being done currently.

Ultimately, of course, it is the "quality of life" in different cultures that we want to compare and evaluate.[31] Each of these is a Gestalt that is difficult to quantify, although we psychological and social researchers work on the assumption that the basic dimensions can be identified, measured, and assessed. Let us accept the challenge highlighted in our meetings by the interchange between Margaret Mead and Charles Osgood as we seek to harmonize quantitative and qualitative data in an imaginative yet realistic synthesis.

REFERENCES

1. BRISLIN, R. W., W. J. LONNER & R. M. THORNDIKE. 1973. Cross-Cultural Research Methods. Wiley. New York, N.Y.
2. DOHRENWEND, B. & B. S. DOHRENWEND. 1969. Social Status and Psychological Disorder. Wiley. New York, N.Y.
3. KIEV, ARI. Transcultural Psychiatry. 1972. Free Press. Glencoe, Ill.
4. MANASTER, G. J. & R. J. HAVIGHURST. 1972. Cross-national Research: Social Psychological Methods and Problems. Houghton, Mifflin. New York, N.Y.
5. PLOG, S. C. & R. B. EDGERTON, Eds. 1969. Changing Perspectives in Mental Illness. Holt. New York, N.Y.
6. WHITING, J. W. M. 1968. Methods and problems in cross-cultural research. *In* Handbook of Social Psychology, 2nd. ed. Vol. 2. G. Lindzey and E. Aronson, Eds. Addison-Wesley. Reading, Mass.
7. WITTKOWER, E. D. & J. FRIED. 1958. Internat. J. Soc. Psychiat. **3**: 245–52. Reprinted *in* Opler, M. K., Ed. Culture and Mental Health. 1959. Macmillan. New York, N.Y.

8. WILLIAMS, F. E. 1934. Russia, Youth and the Present-day World. Farrar and Rinehart. New York, N.Y.

9. BERNE, E. 1959. Difficulties of comparative psychiatry – Fiji Islands. Amer. J. Psychiat. **116**: 104 ff.

10. BERNE, E. 1959. Cultural problems: Psychopathology in Tahiti. Amer. J. Psychiat. **116**: 1076 ff.

11. PHILLIPS, L. & J. G. DRAGUNS. 1971. Some issues in intercultural research on psychopathology. *In* Mental Health Research in Asia and the Pacific. W. Caudill and T. Lin, Eds. University Press of Hawaii. Honolulu, Hawaii.

12. HAVIGHURST, R. J. 1963. Successful aging. *In* Processes of Aging. R. H. Williams, C. Tibbitts and W. Donahue, Eds. Atherton. New York, N.Y.

13. CARSTAIRS, G. M. 1959. The social limits of eccentricity. *In* Culture and Mental Health. Opler, M. K., Ed. Macmillan. New York, N.Y.

14. SHANAS, E. *et al.* 1968. Old People in Three Industrial Societies. Atherton, New York, N.Y.

15. BENITEZ, R. 1973. Aging in regard to social policy and ethnicity. *In* Aging – Prospects and Issues. Davis and Neiswender, Eds. Andrus Center. Los Angeles, Calif.

16. COWGILL, D. O. 1972. Theory of aging in cross-cultural perspective. *In* Aging and Modernization. D. O. Cowgill and Holmes, Eds. Appleton-Century-Crofts. New York, N.Y.

17. AP report from Tokyo, August 10, 1975. Tradition changes: Japan's aged demand share.

18. PALMORE, E. 1975. Status and integration of the aged in Japanese society. J. Gerontology **30**: 199–208.

19. PALMORE, E. 1975. What can the U.S. learn from Japan about aging? The Gerontologist **15**: 64 ff.

20. KYUCHARYANTS, V. 1974. Will the human life-span reach one hundred? The Gerontologist **14**: 377–80.

21. MEDVEDEV, Z. A. 1974. Caucasus and Altay longevity: A biological social problem? The Gerontologist **14**: 381–87.

22. MEDVEDEV, Z. A. 1975. Aging and longevity: New Approaches and new perspectives. The Gerontologist **15**: 196–201.

23. RIMLAND, R. H. 1975. Withdrawal from work force among persons of retirement age in the USSR (1959–70). Industrial Gerontology **2**: 2 ff.

24. BARKER, R. G. & L. S. BARKER. 1961. Behavior units for the comparative study of cultures. *In* Studying Personality Cross-Culturally. B. Kaplan, Ed. Harper and Row. New York, N.Y.

25. BARKER, R. G. & L. S. BARKER. 1963. Sixty-five and over. *In* Processes of Aging. R. H. Williams, C. Tibbitts, and W. Donahue, Eds. Atherton. New York, N.Y.

26. MURPHY, R. J. 1969. Stratification and mental illness: Issues and strategies for research. *In* Changing Perspectives in Mental Illness. S. C. Plog and R. B. Edgerton, Eds.: 312 ff. Holt. New York, N.Y.

27. SARGENT, S. S. 1953. Class and class consciousness in a California town. Social Problems **1**: 22–27.

28. MENSH, I. 1963. Studies of older psychiatric patients. The Gerontologist. **3**: 100–04.

29. DRAGUNS, J. G. & L. PHILLIPS. 1971. Psychiatric Classification and Diagnosis; an Overview and Critique. General Learning Corporation.

30. YOLLES, S. F. *et al.* 1973. The 1967 NIMH mission to assess mental health services in the U.S.S.R. *In* International Collaboration in Mental Health. B. S. Brown and E. F. Torrey, Eds. U.S. Department of Health, Education and Welfare. Rockville, Md.

31. ABRAMS, M. 1974. The quality of life. World Health November 1974: 4–11.

SOCIETAL MORPHOGENESIS AND INTRAFAMILY VIOLENCE IN CROSS-CULTURAL PERSPECTIVE*

Murray A. Straus

Department of Sociology
University of New Hampshire
Durham, New Hampshire 03824

"How do I know that he loves me if he doesn't beat me?"[3][7]

(Statement by a Mangaia wife)

"What makes you think he doesn't love you any more" asks a woman on a BBC program in the spring of 1974. The reply: "He hasn't bashed me in a fortnight."

There is an obvious similarity between what these two inhabitants of such vastly dissimilar islands are saying: namely, that the marital relationship is tinged by physical aggression, to say nothing of other forms of aggression.† The fact that the marital relationship is also often characterized by warmth, affection, or solidarity is not inconsistent with the simultaneous existence of aggression because aggressive acts can be counternormative, or because norms permitting or encouraging aggression between spouses can and do exist simultaneously with norms stressing warmth and solidarity.[64]

I began this paper with these two quotations because they dramatically illustrate the high frequency — or perhaps even the near universality — with which aggression and violence of all types occur within the family. Obviously, I

---

* This paper is part of a research program on intrafamily violence supported by grants from the National Institute of Mental Health; specifically Grant No. MH 15521 for research training in family and deviance and Grant No. MH 27557 for a study of physical violence in American families. A list of the program publications is available on request.

† The concepts of aggression, violence, and war are the subject of considerable controversy and definitional confusion. It is beyond the scope of this paper to resolve even part of this conceptual problem (but see Gelles and Straus[23]). However, I can at least make clear the sense in which I am using these terms:

Aggression: An act carried out with the intent of, or which is perceived as being with the intent of, injuring another person. The injury may be of many kinds, including psychological, material deprivation, or physical injury. It can range from minor noxious acts, such as a disparaging look, to murder.

There are many other dimensions that must be considered and specified in addition to the dimensions of "motivation," "attribution," "type of injury," and "seriousness of injury" just mentioned. Much of the confusion and seemingly contradictory findings in aggression research probably occurs because these dimensions are not specified. Among these other dimensions are the degree of normative legitimacy, and the extent to which the aggression is "instrumental" to some other purpose, versus "expressive" i.e., carried out as an end in itself.

Violence: An act carried out with the intent of, or which is perceived as being with the intent of, *physically* injuring another person. A more specific and less value-laden term is "physical aggression."

War: Formally organized armed combat between groups of people who constitute territorial teams or political communities.[26][45]

need hardly comment to a group such as this on the danger of referring to any phenomenon as a "cross-cultural universal." Not even those social forms to which the term "family" is usually applied are universal, except in the most limited and technical sense suggested by Weigert and Thomas.[69] However, the family in the sense used by Murdock [38] is an example of a social form that is so widespread that it constitutes what might be called a "near universal." A "near universal" obviously does not have the same theoretical importance as a true universal would have — if such existed. But a near universal is none the less extremely important because (by definition) it affects such a large proportion of humanity, and also for theoretical reasons. The theoretical value of attention to near universals stems from the assumption that any social form which occurs that frequently must somehow be related to the most fundamental aspects of human association. Hence the importance of the first objective of this paper: to explore the question of whether intrafamily violence (i.e., physical aggression between family members) is so frequent that it can be considered a near universal. I will also summarize some of the cross-cultural research on the factors that may make intrafamily aggression typical of most societies, and then conclude with a consideration of the wider theoretical import of violence in the family, and specifically, the view that the level of intrafamily violence is related to the ecological conditions in which a society is operating and the society's "technico-economic" adaptation to these ecological realities and to changes in the subsistence basis of the society. I will also suggest that these relationships can be understood best from the perspective of general systems theory because this perspective focuses on morphological changes in society as a model of system maintenance.

THE PREVELANCE OF CONJUGAL VIOLENCE

In previous books and papers, my colleagues and I have presented evidence that in the United States — and probably also in most other Euroamerican societies — the family is the preeminent social setting for all types of aggression and violence, ranging from the cutting remark to slaps, kicks, torture, and murder.[22,58,62,63] The frequency of aggressive acts between children (who will often be siblings) is remarkably constant across the societies of the Six Cultures Study,[32] and probably also including societies such as the !Ko-Bushmen who are renowned for their nonaggressive and peaceful social patterns.[19] In the United States, Straus found that 62 percent of his sample engaged in a nonplayful physical fight with a sibling during their senior year in high school. Parent-child physical violence is truly ubiquitous in the form of physical punishment, not only in the United States and Britain,[58-60] but also in many other societies, again including the !Ko.[19]

Probably the most dramatic cross-cultural evidence on intrafamily violence is found for murder. Because murder is such an extreme and difficult-to-conceal form of violence, it is the subject of official recording in many societies and is more readily researched in all societies than "ordinary" wife (or husband) beating. Thus, Bohannan[9] and his collaborator were able to collect what seems to be reasonably good statistical evidence in four different African societies. As a result, there is evidence covering a number of societies. This evidence clearly indicates that more murders take place between members of the same family than occur with any other murderer-victim relationship. This assertion holds for all 18 societies for which data are summarized in the recent book by Curtis on criminal violence.[16] To this we can add the findings for the Mexican village studied by June Nash.[40] My tabulation of the data given in her Table 1 reveals that a family member or lover was the probable killer in 52 percent of the instances in which a suspect was identified.

In considering these statistics on the high proportion of homicides that occur within families, there are numerous complications. For example, although the largest *proportion* of homicides are between kin, and especially husbands and wives, in absolute terms killing one's husband or wife is rare even in those societies that have a high homicide rate. In fact, the figures are somewhat deceptive because there is some tendency for the proportion of all homicides that are intrafamily to be greatest in the societies with a *low* overall homicide rate. For example, the Danish homicide rate is only 0.2 per 100,000 compared to the United States' rate of about 7 or 8 per 100,000. Thus, the very high proportion of within-family homicides in Denmark (57 percent as compared with the United States' figure of about 25 percent) must be seen as a large slice of a very small pie. But perhaps a more telling interpretation of these relationships is the possibility of their having the following meaning: Even in societies such as Denmark, in which homicide has practically been eliminated, the last remaining locus of this form of aggression is within the family.

Less drastic forms of aggression between family members are of course more prevalent in the absolute sense. This can be seen both within American society, where my colleagues and I have been gathering such data, and in a few cross-cultural studies. In the United States, the evidence we have gathered — although tentative — suggests that perhaps 60 to 70 percent of all couples have used physical violence at least once in their marriage, and that for about one out of four couples, there has been a recurring pattern of physical violence between the couple.[22,58,62,63] These rates are somewhat lower for middle-class couples, but not enough lower to support the widely held view that husband-wife violence is primarily found in the lowest socioeconomic strata.

Turning to other societies, my general impression is that high rates of conjugal violence characterize many other societies, including urban-industrial, agrarian, nonliterate societies; and also including societies that are otherwise low in violence, such as England. But on theoretical grounds which I will come to shortly, we can expect the highest rates of husband-wife violence to be in those societies which have high rates of violence in other institutional spheres. Thus, it is doubtful that many other societies could match the frequency and intensity of assaults by husbands on their wives than is found among "the fierce people" as the Yanomamo call themselves.[8,14] Finally, we can gain some idea of the prevalence of conjugal violence from Schlegel's ratings of 45 societies.[54] Her analysis reveals that 75 percent of these societies permitted husbands to aggress against their wives. On the other hand, I do not know how representative Schlegel's 45 societies are, and only a relatively limited number of more detailed ethnographies are cited at various places in this paper. So, although what evidence there is points to high rates of conjugal violence in a great many societies, the question of the "prevalence," much less of the "near-universality" of intrafamily violence, is far from definitively established.

THE CAUSES OF CONJUGAL VIOLENCE

A full causal explanation of the ubiquity of conjugal violence is a vast undertaking. Richard Gelles and I have made a start in that direction in a long chapter of a forthcoming book.[23] For example, among the factors we examined in that paper are (1) *"Time at risk,"* i.e., the fact that in many societies family members spend considerable amounts of time with each other. Other things being equal, they therefore are more likely to engage in disputes and conflicts with each other than with those whom they spend less time. But of course, other things are not equal, and particularly: (2) Family members are likely to share a wider *range of activities and interests* with each other than with others with whom they may also spend much time. This means that there are more "events" over which a dispute or a failure to meet expectations can occur. (3) Not only is there a greater probability of hurting family members than others because of the greater time exposure and the greater number of spheres of overlapping activity and interests, but in addition, the degree of injury experienced when the problem arises with a family member is greater than when it arises with someone else because of the *intensity of involvement and attachment* that is typical of family relationships. (4) *Sexual inequality* and the typical pattern of ascribed superior position for the husband has a high conflict potential built in because it is inevitable that not all husbands will be able to perform the culturally expected leadership role and/or not all wives will be willing to accept the subordinate role.[1] (5) The *privacy* of the family in many societies insulates it both from assistance in coping with intrafamily disputes and from social control by neighbors and other kin. This factor is, of course, most present in the conjugal family of urban-industrial societies and least present among societies such as the Bushmen, where virtually all of family life is carried within the small circle of the Bushmen camp and is open to immediate intercession by others. (6) Cultural norms legitimizing the use of violence between members of the same family in situations that would make violence a serious normative violation if it occurred outside the family. In Euroamerican societies, to this day, there is a strong, though largely unverbalized, norm that makes the marriage licence also a hitting licence.[64]

Each of the above, together with other factors, merits detailed consideration. However, within the confines of this paper there is only room to consider those causal factors that have been empirically studied in at least two societies. Although this is not adequate theoretical basis for selection, it has the merits of being appropriate for the focus of this conference and of reducing the range of materials to be considered to what can be fitted within the pages of a single paper.

Aggression as a Cultural and Structural Pattern

I have already alluded to what may be the most general causal factor. This is the fact that, as Russell[52] notes on the basis of a factor analysis of 78 variables for the societies in Textor's Cross Cultural Summary,[65] "... all forms of aggression tend to be strongly related to each other." This finding and its theoretical explication stand in sharp contrast to drive theories of aggression. Drive theories assume that aggression expressed in one sphere of activity will — roughly to that extent — not be expressed in other spheres of social interaction. Steinmetz and I[59] have elsewhere called this the "catharsis myth" because of the large number of studies that not only fail to support the idea of catharsis, but that almost always show exactly the opposite: that the more aggression in one sphere, the more in others.

Excellent and devastating reviews of the research on aggression catharsis at the individual level have been published by Bandura,[5] Berkowitz,[7] and

Hokanson[28]; and a study by Straus[62] of within-family "ventilation" of aggression shows clearly that verbal, symbolic, and physical aggression, rather than being substitutes for each other, are highly correlated. Consequently, in this paper I will mention only cross-cultural studies that bear on aggression as a pervasive cultural pattern. An interesting starting place is Sipes'[56] study of the relationship between aggressive sports and warfare. He shows that both cross-culturally and in a time-series analysis for the United States, the higher the level of armed combat, the more common are aggressive sports. Vayda's review of anthropological explanations of primitive warfare and aggression is also critical of the catharsis theory.[68] A study by Archer and Gartner[2] of 110 nations find that, contrary to the catharsis theory, homicide rates increase with the occurrence of war. In respect to the mass media, the nations or periods with the most actual violence are those with the most violent popular literature.[15,29,54] Finally, in respect to husband-wife violence itself, Steinmetz[57] studied the families of university students in an American and a Canadian city using identical instruments. She wanted to compare Canadian and American families because these two societies are alike in so many ways, yet Canadian rates for homicide, assault and rape and only a fraction of the rates in the United States. The Canadian families turned out to have a considerably lower frequency of husband-wife physical aggression. I conclude from these and other studies that each modality of aggression in a society, rather than serving as a means of "draining off hostility," serves as a means to learn aggressive roles and as a kind of cultural and structural "theme,"[44] template, or paradigm for interaction in other spheres of activity.‡

Aggression as a Family Pattern

The same theoretical principle also applies *within* the family. That is, violence in one family role is associated with violence in other family roles. Thus, studies of child-abusing parents in three countries found that such parents had

‡ Concepts such as "theme" and "pattern" have come into disrepute because they are associated with a kind of mystical "cultural determinism" which diverts attention from the issue of *why* a particular cultural pattern came into being and why it continues to exist. However, this needed reaction to such concepts has "thrown the baby out with the bath water." One need not deny the existence of culture as system manifesting themes and interrelated patterns in order to deal with the questions of why such a cultural system exists and how it operates. In fact, I take the view that unless one can identify cultural themes and patterns, the likelihood of understanding the more fundamental causes of the most basic aspects of a society is greatly diminished. An additional reason for not discarding the concept of a cultural pattern is that, in my belief, once in existence, such a pattern has a causal efficacy of its own, exerting influence on other aspects of the culture, personality, and social organization of a society. That assertion has also come into disrepute because it is so often associated with a static "functionalist" view of human society. But that is a particular historical accident of a certain period in the history of social science. My view of the relationships between the biological, cultural, personality and social organizational systems is that each is constantly changing and therefore creating discrepancies or discordancies that are resolved by still further changes. Thus, the assumption of functional integration within and between these spheres directs attention to processes of social change rather than social stasis.

themselves experienced severe physical punishment as children.[47] At the macro level of analysis, although child-abuse statistics can be best considered only as educated guesses, there seems to be some correlation with the frequency with which physical punishment occurs in a society. Goode,[24] for example, suggests that child abuse is rare in Japan because physical punishment is rarely used. Finally, the study by Steinmetz of United States' and Canadian families found that couples who use physical force on each other use physical punishment more often than other couples. Moreover, their children, in turn, use physical aggression against siblings more often than do the children of parents who do not hit each other.

Protest Masculinity

There is an impressive group of studies — both cross-cultural and studies within a number of societies — which suggest that what might be called "psychological father absence" or low saliency of the father during infancy or childhood leads to a pattern of male behavior that has variously been called protest masculinity, hyperaggressive masculinity, compulsive masculinity, etc. It is probably most widely known to social scientists in the United States as the complex of traits characterizing the *machismo* pattern of many Latin American males. The low saliency of the father is most obvious in mother-child households, but it is sometimes possible for the father to be a salient figure in the lives of children even if he is not physically present, as in the *kibbutzim*. Conversely, the father can be physically but not psychologically present, as often happens in the extremely sex-role-differentiated pattern of the urban lower class.

Low father saliency — however it is manifested — has been found to be associated with such traits as a preference for segregated sex roles, subordination of women, aggressive sexuality, and the glorification of physical aggression.[4,10,21,27,36,66,70] Within the family, this manifests itself in a high frequency of wife-beating, and cross-culturally is also associated with probably the most violent marital arrangement of all — true bride-theft as opposed to mock bride-theft.[3] Ayres summarizes the theory accounting for these relationships as follows:

> The widely accepted explanation for these relationships is that such behaviors represent exaggerated attempts to demonstrate masculinity by individuals who have a high level of sex identity conflict and anxiety. This conflict arises when individuals who have formed an initial feminine identification during infancy come into contact with society's demand that adult males show assertive behavior and assume dominant status. The resulting initiation ceremonies, crime and deliquency, are interpreted as resolving the conflict and enhancing the individual's sense of masculinity. §

§ Professor Ayres has also pointed out to me that the causal sequence in respect to societal change (as compared to the causal sequence for individuals at one point in history) can equally plausibly go from aggressive masculinity to sex-role segregation and low father-saliency. Such an interpretation, in fact, is consistent with Harris' theory of male dominance and female infanticide as adaptations to the institutions of warfare.[25,26]

Male Dominance

Since I have elsewhere devoted most of two entire papers to the issue of the linkage between sexual inequality and wife-beating in just one society,[1,64] it is clear that only the briefest summary of the complex links between male dominance and intrafamily violence can be presented here. Probably the best place to begin is with Schlegel's finding that 88 percent of the male-dominant societies in her sample permitted aggression by husbands against wives, as compared to only 33 percent of the non-male-dominant societies.[54]

A number of factors underlie this relationship, starting with the simple fact that men in all societies have superior physical strength as an ultimate resource to enforce a superior position, and they make frequent use of this resource.[1] However, as Harris[25,26] notes, the physical-strength advantage is relatively slight and by itself does not seem to be an adequate explanation since superior strength is unnecessary to make effective use of knives and male infanticide. Very likely, as Harris suggests, the institution of warfare is an important underlying factor and this in turn is related to such things as the antagonism between the sexes engendered by sex role segregation[70] and the inability of women to escape from a violent husband in many societies, including most Euroamerican societies. Such societies throw the full burden of child-rearing on women, deny them equal job opportunities even when they can make alternative child-care arrangements, inculcate a negative self image in roles other than that of wife and mother, and reinforce the dependency of women on their husbands by emphasizing the idea that divorce is bad for children. Finally, in most societies, there is a male-oriented legal and judicial system, which makes it extremely difficult for women to secure legal protection from assault by their husbands except under the most extreme circumstances.

Intrafamily Aggression and Group Survival

Many hunting and gathering societies such as the Eskimo and the !Ko-Bushmen are noted for their peacefulness and lack of physical aggression. A distinctive trait of such societies is their openness and sharing. Yet these same societies also provide an instructive example of intrafamily aggression. First, it is clear from both cross-cultural studies of the correlates of war and aggressiveness and from detailed ethnographies, that a primary basis of their peacefulness is to be found in the cross-cutting group affiliations inherent in the kinship system and in the system of food-sharing. Or, as Eibl-Eibesfeldt puts it in relation to the !Ko, "What is striking when observing the Bushmen is not their lack of aggression, but their efficient way of coping with it."[19] The second instructive feature of this type of society is to be found in their response to famine. When, as in the case of the Eskimo, the normal subsistence base of the society is precarious, the culturally evolved response calls for intrafamily aggression in the form of abandonment of the old and infanticide.¶ In addition, when the

---

¶ Some readers may question categorizing abandonment and infanticide as "aggression" because they are culturally legitimate acts, necessary for group survival. My position is that the normative approval versus disapproval of an injurious act is an important but separate

subsistence base is further reduced, new forms of competitiveness and aggression may appear, as illustrated by Riches'[50] work on the effects of "environmental stress" among the Netsilik Eskimo, and Opler's on Apache witchcraft. Probably the most dramatic example is the Ik, as described by Turnbull.[67] The food-sharing reciprocity that lies at the heart of the nonaggressiveness of such foraging societies became impossible and many social bonds disintegrated with a resultant almost unspeakable cruelty and callousness; for example, watching with amusement as a crawling child puts his hand in a fire, leaving children as young as three years old to fend for themselves, and children and young men pushing over a group of tottering old men as though they were bowling pins, and shrieking with laughter as the old men fell and struggled to stand up.

I disagree with Turnbull's suggestion that the destruction of the Ik economy and the resulting cruelty and inhumanity reveal the basic feature of human nature. Their aggressiveness under these circumstances is no more – and no less – indicative of human nature than was their peacefulness and sharing when food was plentiful. Rather, what the Ik and the Eskimo tell us is that the level of aggression within families is governed by the complex interrelation of the constraints and resources of the particular ecological niche occupied by a society, the social organization of that society that evolved in relation to their particular ecological niche, the position of the family in that social organization, and the behavioral and personality characteristics that are congruent with these life circumstances.

SUMMARY AND CONCLUSIONS

If time permitted, a similar analysis to the one just presented could be developed for parent-child and sibling-sibling violence. Indeed, in pointing out the isomorphism between the level of violence in the husband-wife role and the parent-child role, a start has already been made in that direction. Similarly, just as the level of physical aggression in the conjugal relationship tends to be isomorphic with the level of physical aggression in nonfamily spheres of life, the same principle seems to hold for the parental relationship.[6,33,45,46]

A detailed analysis of parent-child and sibling-sibling violence – and also of aggression and sexuality – along the lines of the suggestive paper by Prescott[49] would strengthen the case for the theoretical conclusions I am about to put forth because they would add processes that are specific to violence in these relationships, yet at the same time are illustrative of the more general theory.

---

dimension that must be separately analyzed. There are numerous other instances of normatively legitimate aggression, ranging from physical punishment by parents to the bombing of Hanoi, the former being legitimized because it is presumably necessary for the welfare of the child, and for the society as a whole, for parents to be able to control and train children; and the latter because it was presumably necessary for national survival in the face of a world communist threat. Obviously, I have picked these examples because they also indicate that the question of normative legitimacy is itself extremely complex, especially when one faces up to the fact that there is seldom unanimity concerning these norms.[23] In addition, the fact that the overwhelming majority of Americans approve of physical punishment, and favored the bombing of North Vietnam, does not place them outside the scope of "aggression" as defined earlier in this paper. Finally, I should point out that Harris[26] also considers infanticide as aggression when he defines it as ". . . homicide and acts of malign and benign aggression and neglect that consciously or unconsciously [affect] . . . survival . . ." of an infant.

For example, this would include analysis of the fact that (1) within-society, the larger the number of children in a household, the greater the use of physical punishment;[20,34,41-43] and (2) of the social class differences in the frequency and purposes of physical punishment.[12,17,18,30,31,34,39,48] But even without this additional evidence, the analysis of conjugal violence presented in this paper suggests the following theoretical conclusions:

I began the paper with the assumption that it is important to study near-universals of human social behavior because any social form that occurs that frequently must somehow be related to the most fundamental aspects of human society. One of the fundamental features that this paper illustrates is the fact that human societies are cybernetic and morphogenic systems operating as part of a larger ecological system.** The materials presented show five aspects of this: the first three illustrating systemic linkages and the last two morphogenic processes: (1) The link between aggression and violence in the society and the level of violence within the family. I suggest that this is in the form of a positive feedback relationship: as societal violence increases, there is a tendency for intrafamily violence to increase; and as intrafamily violence increases, there is a tendency for societal violence to increase. Harris' interpretation of the changes in Yanomamo society over the past 100 or so years[26] seems to illustrate such processes. (2) The link between violence in one family role with violence in other family roles, which is also a positive feedback relationship. There are a number of reasons for this, including the tendency to respond to violence by violence (if the situation permits), role-modeling, and generalization of behavior patterns learned in one role to other roles ("transfer of training").†† (3) The

---

** Readers of this paper who are anthropologists might find the concept "evolution" preferable (or at least more familiar) than the concept of "morphogenesis." I use the latter term because I do not want to confuse processes of cultural and social organizational change (the focus of this paper) with biological change processes, however analogous the two may seem to be. I have also chosen the concept of morphogenesis because it is consistent with a "general systems theory" (as opposed to a functionalist systems theory) framework, and I want these comments and speculations to be understood within the former framework. There are many subtle but extremely important differences between these two seemingly similar theoretical perspectives.[13,61] However, for the present purposes, the difference that is most crucial concerns the morphostatic focus of functionalist theory versus the emphasis on morphogenesis in general systems theory. In the former, the analyst asks how the system can adapt to internal and external influences and retain its basic *goals*, one of the most frequent adaptive mechanisms being a change in structure.

†† Although I have emphasized positive feedback processes, it is equally important to identify "dampening" or negative feedback processes, which sooner or later must enter the picture. For an illustration of such negative feedback loops in relation to intrafamily violence in the United States see Straus.[61] Looked at cross-culturally, the issue becomes one of identifying the factors that make the upper limit of permissible violence vary from society to society, one of which has already been mentioned: Whether the victims of intrafamily violence (more typically women than men) have an alternative to tolerating aggression by their spouse. If the structure of the society provides other marriage opportunities, or the possibility of return to the wife's natal family, it seems likely that this will impose an upper limit on the level of violence that will be tolerated. Another aspect of this is the importance of the domestic group and/or lineage itself. Sahlins, for example, acknowledges that ". . . considering interpersonal relations as such . . . the closer the social bond the greater the hostility [potential]." But paradoxically, he also notes that "The closer the relationship the greater the restraint on belligerence and violence . . ."[53] because the focus of his discussion is societies with a segmentary lineage organization in which the lineage is a property-controlling corporate group on which individual survival depends, and which therefore must be protected from internal disruption.

identification of the system-maintaining contributions of intrafamily violence, as illustrated in the emergence of "protest masculinity" on the part of young men whose sexual identity is made problematic because of household structure or other circumstances of child-rearing; and also as illustrated by the use or threat of physical force to maintain the structure of male dominance. (4) The change from a nonviolent to a violent structure of interaction as an adaption to changes in the critical exogenous variable of the subsistence basis of the society as illustrated by the Ik and the Yanomamo. (5) Changes in personality as actors adapt to the new behaviors required by the changed structure of interaction, which, in turn, brings about changes in other spheres of interaction. Since this last point has only indirectly been hinted at in the paper, I will close by discussing the morphogenic processes that are mediated through changes in the personality of members of a society.

For a variety of reasons the rate of internal or external warfare can increase sharply, or a previously peaceful society can become involved in either external war or internal feuds. If this happens, members of the society must learn to behave more aggressively, as a matter of both individual and group survival. This may be what happened in the case of the Yanomamo and the Ik. But the aggressive behavior patterns learned as a means of carrying out war or internal conflict are not easily turned off when it comes to relationships within the family. That is, such a situation brings about personality characteristics that exert a strain toward isomorphism between patterns of social interaction between and within families. Of course, one must not put the whole burden of change-producing linkages on the mechanism of intraindividual carryover of personality. Other social institutions are also important, as is shown by the studies of the correlation between conceptions of supernatural beings as benevolent or malevolent with indices of warfare and aggression and of punitiveness in child training[33,46]; studies that show that sports (and in literate societies, fiction) are also related to warfare[29,56]; and the integration of the religious, ecological, and warfare systems of the Tsembaga Maring.[51]

In conclusion, this paper has dealt with both the external changes faced by society and the internal conflicts and systematic linkages that are equally a part of social life. In the history of a society (sometimes even over as short a period of time as a generation or two), these external changes and internal conflicts can lead to changes in the structure of the society itself as a result of the cybernetic processes by which events are monitored and controlled in accordance with system goals. The tragic case of the Ik provides a dramatic example of morphogenesis in the structure of interpersonal relationships (the system of reciprocity) to serve more fundamental system goals. Turnbull interprets their behavior as reversion to a primitive aggressive individualism. But the reanalysis of his report by McCall[35] and Wilson[71] suggests that, had *individual* survival been the primary goal, the course of events might have been much different: The Ik could have accepted the government's repeated offers to relocate to a "more favorable" location. Instead, the deep attachment of the Ik to their society and to its sacred territory and way of life led them to the almost unimaginable cruelties against each other (particularly the old and the young), and to drastic changes in the pattern of interaction so that the essential nature of their society, as they saw it, could be maintained.

ACKNOWLEDGMENTS

I would like to thank Professor Barbara Ayres of the University of Massachusetts/Boston, and Professors Rand B. Foster and Stephen Reyna of the University of New Hampshire for comments and criticisms that aided in the revision of this paper.

REFERENCES

1. ALLEN, C. M. & M. A. STRAUS. 1975. Resources, power, and husband-wife violence. Paper presented at the National Council on Family Relations 1975 Annual Meeting.
2. ARCHER, D. & R. GARTNER. 1976. Violent acts and violent times: A comparative approach to postwar homicide rates. American Sociological Review 41(6): 937–963.
3. AYRES, B. 1974. Bride theft and raiding for wives in cross-cultural perspective. Anthropological Quarterly 47(3): 238–252.
4. BACON, M. K., I. L. CHILD & H. BARRY, III. 1963. A cross-cultural study of correlates of crime. Journal of Abnormal and Social Psychology 66(4): 291–300.
5. BANDURA, A. 1973. Aggression: A Social Learning Analysis. Prentice-Hall. Englewood Cliffs, N.J.
6. BELLAK, L. & M. ANTELL. 1974. An intercultural study of aggressive behavior on children's playground. American Journal of Orthopsychiatry 44: 503–511.
7. BERKOWITZ, L. 1973. The case for bottling up rage. Psychology Today 7 (July): 24–31.
8. BIOCCA, E. 1969. Yanoáma: The Story of a Woman Abducted by Brazilian Indians. George Allen and Unwin. London, England.
9. BOHANNAN, P. 1960. African Homicide and Suicide. Atheneum. New York, N.Y.
10. BOHANNAN, P. 1969. Cross-cultural comparison of aggression and violence. In Crimes of Violence. Donald Mulvihull & Melvin M. Tumin, Appendix 25. Vol. 13 of the Staff Reports to the National Commission on the Causes and Prevention of Violence. United States Government Printing Office. Washington, D.C.
11. BRIGGS, J. L. 1970. Never in Anger: Portrait of an Eskimo Family. Harvard University Press. Cambridge, Mass.
12. BRONFENBRENNER, U. 1958. Socialization and social class through time and space. In Readings in Social Psychology. E. E. Maccoby, T. M. Newcomb, and E. L. Hartley, Eds.: 400–425. Holt. New York, N.Y.
13. BUCKLEY, W. 1967. Sociology and Modern Systems Theory. Prentice-Hall. Englewood Cliffs, N.Y.
14. CHAGNON, N. A. 1968. Yanomamo: The Fierce People. Holt, Rinehart and Winston. New York, N.Y.
15. COMSTOCK, G. A. & E. A. RUBINSTEIN. 1972. Television and Social Behavior. Reports and Papers: A Technical Report to the Surgeon General's Scientific Advisory Committee on Television and Social Behavior, Vol. I. United States Government Printing Office. Washington, D.C.
16. CURTIS, L. A. 1974. Criminal Violence: National Patterns and Behavior. (Table 3.3.) Lexington Books. Lexington, Mass.
17. DEVEREUX, E. C. 1970. Socialization in cross-cultural perspective: Comparative study of England, Germany and the United States. In Families in East and West. Reuben Hill and René König, Eds. Paris.
18. DEVEREUX, E. C., U. BRONFENBRENNER & R. R. RODGERS. 1969. Child-rearing in England and the United States: a cross-national comparison. Journal of Marriage and the Family 31(2): 257–270.
19. EIBL-EIBESFELDT, I. 1974. Aggression in the !Ko-Bushmen. In Aggression. Shervert H. Frazier, Ed.: 10–17. Williams & Wilkens. Baltimore, Md.

20. ELDER, G. H. & C. E. BOWERMAN. 1963. Family structure and child rearing patterns: the effect of family size and sex composition. American Sociological Review **28**: 891–905.

21. FERRACUTI, F. & S. DINITZ. 1974. Cross-cultural aspects of delinquent and criminal behavior. *In* Aggression. Shervert H. Frazier, Ed. Williams & Wilkens. Baltimore, Md.

22. GELLES, R. J. 1974. The Violent Home: A Study of Physical Aggression between Husbands and Wives. Sage Publications. Beverly Hills, Calif.

23. GELLES, R. J. & M. A. STRAUS. 1977. Determinants of violence in the family: toward a theoretical integration. *In* Contemporary Theories about the Family. Wesley R. Burr, Reuben Hill, F. Ivan Nye and Ira L. Reiss, Eds. The Free Press. New York, N.Y.

24. GOODE, W. J. 1971. Force and violence in the family. Journal of Marriage and the Family **33** (November: 624–636. (Also reprinted in Steinmetz and Straus, 1974.)

25. HARRIS, M. 1974. "The savage male." *In* Cows, Pigs, Wars, and Witches: The Riddles of Culture. Random House. New York, N.Y.

26. HARRIS, M. 1975. Culture, People, Nature: An Introduction to General Anthropology, second ed.: 258–280, 276–279. New York: Thomas Y. Crowell.

27. HOFFMAN, M. L. 1971. Father absence and conscience development. Developmental Psychology **4** (May): 400–406.

28. HOKANSON, J. E. 1970. Psychophysiological evaluation of the catharsis hypothesis. *In* The Dynamics of Aggression. E. I. Megargee and J. E. Hokanson, Eds. Harper and Row. New York, N.Y.

29. HUGGINS, M. D. & M. A. STRAUS. 1975. Violence and the social structure as reflected in children's books from 1850 to 1970. Paper read at the 1975 annual meeting of the Eastern Sociological Society.

30. KEARNS, B. J. 1970. Childrearing practices among selected culturally deprived minorities. Journal of Genetic Psychology **116**(2): 149–155.

31. KOHN, M. L. 1969. Class and Conformity. Dorsey Press. Homewood, Ill.

32. LAMBERT, W. W. 1974. Promise and problems of cross-cultural exploration of children's aggressive strategies. *In* Determinants and Origins of Aggressive Behavior. Jan De Wit and Willard W. Hartup, Eds.: 444–447. Mouton. The Netherlands.

33. LAMBERT, W. W., L. M. TRIANDIS & M. WOLF. 1959. Some correlates of beliefs in the malevolence and benevolence of supernatural beings: A cross-societal study. Journal of Abnormal and Social Psychology **58** (March): 162–169.

34. LIGHT, R. 1973. Abuse and neglected children in America: a study of alternative policies. Harvard Educational Review **43**: 556–598.

35. McCALL, G. 1975. More thoughts on the Ik and anthropology. Current Anthropology **16** (September): 344–348.

36. McKINLEY, D. G. 1964. Social Class and Family Life. Free Press. New York, N.Y.

37. MARSHALL, D. S. 1971. Sexual behavior on Mangaia. *In* Human Sexual Behavior. Donald S. Marshall and Robert C. Suggs, Eds.: 153. Prentice-Hall. Englewood Cliffs, N.J.

38. MURDOCK, G. P. 1949. Social Structure. Macmillan. New York, N.Y.

39. MUSSEN, PAUL & L. A. BEYTAGH. 1969. Industrialization, child-rearing practices, and children's personality. Journal of Genetic Psychology **115**(2): 195–216.

40. NASH, J. 1967. Death as a way of life: The increasing resort to homicide in a Maya Indian community. American Anthropologist **69** (October): 455–470.

41. NUTTALL, E. V. & R. L. NUTTALL. 1971. The effect of size of family on parent-child relationships. Proceedings of the Annual Convention of the American Psychological Association **6** (part 1): 267–268.

42. NYE, I., J. CARLSON & G. GERRETT. 1970. Family size, interaction, affect and stress. Journal of Marriage and the Family **32**: 216–226.

43. OLSEN, N. J. 1974. Family structure and socialization patterns in Taiwan. American Journal of Sociology **79** (May): 1395–1417.

44. OPLER, M. E. 1946. Themes as dynamic forces in culture. American Journal of Sociology **LI**: 198–206.

45. OTTERBEIN, K. F. 1974. The anthropology of war. *In* Handbook of Social and Cultural Anthropology. John J. Honigmann, Eds. Rand McNally. Chicago, Ill.

46. OTTERBEIN, C. S. & K. F. OTTERBEIN. 1973. Believers and beaters: A case study of supernatural beliefs and child rearing in the Bahama Islands. American Anthropologist 75(5): 1670–1681.

47. PARKE, R. D. & C. W. COLLMAR. 1975. Child abuse: an interdisciplinary review. *In* Review of Child Development Research, Vol. 5. E. Mavis Hetherington, Eds. University of Chicago Press. Chicago, Ill.

48. PEARLIN, L. I. 1970. Class Context and Family Relations: A Cross-National Study. Little, Brown and Co. Boston, Mass.

49. PRESCOTT, J. W. 1975. Body pleasure and the origins of violence. The Futurist April: 64–74.

50. RICHES, D. 1974. The Netsilik Eskimo: A special case of selective female infanticide. Ethnology 13 (Oct.): 351–361.

51. RAPPAPORT, R. A. 1968. Pigs for the Ancestors: Ritual in the Ecology of a New Guinea People. Yale University Press. New Haven, Conn.

52. RUSSELL, E. W. 1972. Factors of human aggression: a cross-cultural factor analysis of characteristics related to warfare and crime. Behavior Science Notes 7(4): 291.

53. SAHLINS, M. D. 1961. The segmentary lineage: An organization of predatory expansion. American Anthropologist 63 (April): 322–337.

54. SCHLEGEL, A. 1972. Male Dominance and Female Autonomy: Domestic Authority in Matrilineal Societies.: 62–103. Hraf Press. New Haven, Conn.

55. SINGER, J. L. 1971. The influence of violence portrayed in television or motion pictures upon overt aggressive behavior. *In* The Control of Aggression and Violence. Jerome L. Singer, Eds.: 19–56. Academic Press. New York, N.Y.

56. SIPES, R. G. 1973. War, sports, and aggression: An empirical test of two rival theories. American Anthropologist 75 (February: 64–68.

57. STEINMETZ, S. K. 1974. Occupational environment in relation to physical punishment and dogmatism. *In* Violence in the Family. Suzanne K. Steinmetz and Murray A. Straus, Eds. Dodd, Mead & Co. New York, N.Y.

58. STEINMETZ, S. K. 1974. Intrafamilial patterns of conflict resolution: United States and Canadian comparisons. Paper presented at the annual meeting of the Society for the Study of Social Problems.

59. STEINMETZ, S. K. & M. A. STRAUS, Eds. 1974. Violence in the Family. Harper & Row. New York. (Originally published by Dodd, Mead).

60. STRAUS, M. A. 1971. Some social antecedents of physical punishment: A linkage theory interpretation. Journal of Marriage and the Family 33 (November): 658–663.

61. STRAUS, M. A. 1973. A general systems theory approach to a theory of violence between family members. Social Science Information 12 (June): 105–125.

62. STRAUS, M. A. 1974. Leveling, civility, and violence in the family. Journal of Marriage and the Family 36 (February): 13–29 (plus addendum in August 1974 issue.)

63. STRAUS, M. A. 1974. Cultural and social organizational influences on violence between family members. *In* Configurations: Biological and Cultural Factors in Sexuality and Family Life. Raymond Price and Dorothy Barrier, Eds. Lexington Books-D. C. Heath. Lexington, Mass.

64. STRAUS, M. A. 1976. Sexual inequality, cultural norms, and wife-beating. Victimology 1(1): 54–76. (Reprinted *in* Victims and Society. Emilio Viano, Ed. Visage Press. Washington, D.C.)

65. TEXTOR, R. B. 1967. A Cross-Cultural Summary. Area Files Press. New Haven, Conn.

66. TOBY, J. 1966. Violence and the masculine ideal: Some qualitative data. *In* Patterns of Violence: The Annals of the American Academy of Political and Social Science. Marvin E. Wolfgang, Ed. Vol. 364: 20–27. American Academy of Political and Social Science. Philadelphia. (Also reprinted in Steinmetz and Straus, 1974.)

67. TURNBULL, C. 1972. The Mountain People. Simon and Schuster. New York, N.Y.

68. VAYDA, A. P. 1961. Expansion and warfare among swidden agriculturalists. Amer. Anthrop. **63**: 346–358.
69. WEIGERT, A. J. & D. L. THOMAS. 1971. Family as a conditional universal. Journal of Marriage and the Family **33** (February): 188–194.
70. WHITING, B. B. 1965. Sex identity conflict and physical violence: a comparative study. American Anthropologist **67**: 123–140.
71. WILSON, P. J. 1975. More thoughts on the Ik and Anthropology. Current Anthropology **16** (September): 343–344.

OH WOULD SOME POWER THE GIFTIE GIE US, TO SEE OURSELVES AS OTHERS SEE US

John Beatty

Department of Anthropology
Brooklyn College
The City University of New York
Brooklyn, New York 11210

The problems that arise when members of one group attempt to do research on a different group probably vary directly as a function of the differences between them. More simply, this implies that the more differences that exist between two groups, the more problems are likely to occur between them.

Anthropology has traditionally been a discipline concerned with non-Western cultures. Recently, of course, anthropologists have become more interested in Western society, and new fields, such as urban anthropology and ethnicity have opened in areas that were previously the domain of sociology.

Even in these "Western" groups, the anthropologist is still an outsider, and the people being studied are insiders. As a result, anthropologists have been particularly concerned with the problems of the perception and interpretation that is made by members of other cultures, and anthropology as a discipline has striven to be more than usually critical of its own perceptions. The concepts of cultural relativism and ethnocentrism were early attempts by anthropologists to see cultures in their own setting and relative to their own values rather than forcing Western standards and values upon those cultures.

The history of the discipline reveals a growing concern for the problems faced by "outsiders" attempting to describe the cultures of others. Kenneth Pike's "emic-etic" theory[1] attempted to show how the same "reality" could be interpreted differently by different peoples. This approach, which was simultaneous with the study of various cultures, proceeded for some time. The fields of cognitive anthropology developed and flourished.

More recently, however, anthropology has returned to the ideas of universals in culture, and the ideas of cultural relativism and "emics-etics" have begun to be questioned. The questioning has taken place on many levels; has ramifications into ideas of universal morals, ethics, and values; and has influenced scientists in terms of activism and social responsibility. In fact, the very possibility of an outsider being able to do research has been questioned by Hsu,[2]* once again raising the question of the validity of research done by outsiders. Although these problems are very great, I do not plan to discuss them fully here. Such an opus would take many volumes. Rather, I plan to discuss the ways in which groups

---

* Hsu's argument basically states that outsiders can never understand an alien culture, and insiders are too close to the culture to see it. This led me to suspect that anthropology could not be done at all, since one must be either an insider or an outsider. Hsu has pointed out, however, that what he really was objecting to is that "whites" claim that they possess objectivity when studying non-white cultures, but do not grant "nonwhites" the same ability to be nonsubjective. I believe Hsu and I are in agreement on this and that we both feel that having both insiders and outsiders work on the same project is a distinct advantage since we then check one another's prejudices and biases.

731

are affected by the discrepancies in perception between the members of the group itself and those outside the group.

It must be made clear at once that members of a group are probably varied in their perception of themselves; this should not come as a great surprise. We are all aware that each of us speaks English somewhat differently from our neighbors, but this does not prohibit us from writing grammars of English or even from discussing "the English language." We simply override certain differences and stress the similarities. Just as some native speakers hold some sentences of English to be ungrammatical, there are other native speakers who hold those very sentences to be in fact grammatical; likewise there will be some disagreement between the members of the groups. This variation is usually minor.

In the following discussion, I plan to look at three different groups and attempt to show the ways in which they have been affected by a "conflict" in the perception of the group by "insiders" and "outsiders." The first group to be discussed is homosexual males, the second, American Indians; and the third, scientists. This is not to imply that the three groups are mutually exclusive!

In my early work with homosexuals, one man said to me "we are not deviant. It is the child molesters, the sado-masochists, the rapists who are deviant." This particular sentence set off some questions in my mind about the nature of deviance. Anthropologists, for whatever reason, rarely deal with deviance; and being an anthropologist myself, I had not really ever considered the question. My first reaction was to try to formulate a definition of deviance that might have some sort of cross-cultural validity (much the way Pospisil[3] attempted a cross-cultural definition of law). While the results of my deliberation are of little interest here (and in fact are not worked through to my satisfaction), my interest was aroused by the lack of questioning of the concept of "deviance" on the part of this particular homosexual. In fact, in the time that followed, it appeared that he was not alone. Many homosexuals have indicated to me that they do not consider themselves deviant, but they are perfectly willing to put others in that category without questioning the term itself.† The introductory issue of *Pro-Me-Thee-Us*, a publication of the Eulenspiegel Society (a masochist liberation group whose SM logo has been altered from sado-masochism to sexual minorities), implies that while "consensual" rape (?) is fine (in fact everything consensual is fine), lack of consent is out. Now while I certainly don't want to argue the pros and cons of such a philosophy, I do want to point out that a distinction is still being made that does not question the underlying principles of the classification. The same paper criticizes *Playboy*, *Screw*, and like publications by saying that while they have done a great deal to secure some freedoms, "they also feel they have the right to draw lines and limits regarding what kind of sex everyone should have. They'll acknowledge the fact that there are sexual variants who dance to a different piper. At the same time they'll make it quite clear that they consider such things as perversions, or sick, and they will not hesitate to put them down at every opportunity."

It should also be clear that the underlying questions that need to be asked are not being asked by scientists either. I have not been able to extract the American Psychiatric Association's definition of "illness," "disease," "pathology," or

---

† Another example of this can be seen at the time of the start of the gay activist movements. There was a great deal of fighting concerning whether or not certain effeminate homosexuals should or should not be tolerated in the movement.

"perversion." I have only been able to learn that the members of that society voted that homosexuality was not in those categories. While it may be that labels may be more damaging to people than the behaviors they exhibit, it is not clear how we decide just when that is. Most people are not ready to admit that rapists are really fine people, nor will they allow that the fact that they are called rapists (a culturally stigmatic term) may be the source of some of their problems.

From this situation we can see that at least some groups are willing to accept a particular category, but are not willing to challenge the defining characteristics of the category. All they ask is that they not be included therein.

With American Indians, another similar problem arises. There seems to be no defining characteristic for this group other than that they are the descendants of the people who lived in the Americas before the arrival of the Europeans. Culturally and linguistically, those people called American Indians (or Native Americans) constitute a widely diversified group of cultures.

The arriving Europeans were generally not very interested in the variety of American Indian cultures and languages. Basically the people who came here from Europe and elsewhere came to regard the aboriginal peoples as being all the same (and often "the enemy"). In time the idea of a culturally and linguistically homogenous population became standard. People ask "Are you Indian?" or "Do you speak Indian?" (roughly the equivalent of "Do you speak a language?"). The society that surrounds the various tribes has ultimately created a stereotype, based on an artifical Plains Indian culture, and has concluded that all members of all tribes must be like that image.

In recent years, for a variety of reasons, which includes lack of access to their own histories, large numbers of American Indians have come to believe the stereotype put forth on television, in the movies, in books and so on. I have collected data from members of American Indian tribes that are virtually verbatim from the productions of M.G.M. and Twentieth-Century Fox. Many of today's Indians have adopted symbols to demonstrate their "Indian-ness" which are those that will be accepted by non-Indians. The beaded headband, which was first used by Indians in Wild West shows, is one such example (the beaded headband was used to secure the wigs which the Indians wore in the shows, since they had short hair). Other Indians have said to me "There aren't any more Indians. No one hunts buffalo on horseback anymore. Those were the real Indians". This is said despite the fact that the horse was introduced by the Spanish and that Indians lived without horses for tens of thousands of years. The Indian mounted on horseback is another part of the stereotype that has found its way into the lives of the Indians.

In these and other instances, the American Indian has "bought" the image of the "Wild West" that the (European) Western culture has projected. The category "Indian" has been accepted like the horse, and in many instances the Indians are attempting to conform to the image in order to maintain a nonwhite identity.

In this instance, American Indians have not responded like the homosexual minorities. The Indians have accepted an identity as Indians, but it is an identity that has no basis in their aboriginal cultures. The homosexuals, who are at least a part of Western culture, do have a category "deviant." The American Indians have never had a category "Indian." As homosexuals struggle to free themselves from the category "deviant," the American Indians seem to be struggling to stay in the category "Indian."

The last group to be considered here are the scientists. They too, like homosexuals and American Indians, constitute a minority and have their own self-image. Like the other two groups, scientists also have to cope with an additional image from the surrounding populations. The question of how scientists see themselves is not an easy one to answer.

Anthropologists, the scientists with whom I have the most association, and who are almost always involved in cross-cultural research seem peculiarly divided on this issue. In the past, many anthropologists felt that they, like other scientists, were out to raise more and more complex questions. This approach unfortunately leads to a kind of "ivory tower" science. It may have little immediate practical application; it tends to raise questions about the discipline rather than to give answers. It tends to be concerned more with theories, methods and the goals of the discipline rather than in producing quick cures for all manner of ills.

This approach, complete with "cultural relativism" and the idea that one should not impose our societal values on others, implies an ethical relativism, which more and more people find not to their liking. The return to cultural universals and the cultural similarity that makes all people *Homo sapiens* has become more important than the study of the differences between the various cultures. Cultural and ethical relativism give way to universals in culture and ethics.

How do these different attitudes affect the anthropologists themselves? In order to abide by the doctrines of "social responsibility" and "political activism" some scientists feel the need to explain their new-found truths (often political and economic) to the groups they study. How then are these scientists perceived by their subjects?

In several interviews with a number of American Indians, the findings were remarkable. The anthropologists were perceived as undertaking the new "white man's burden" or as being "the new missionaries."

These are, of course, rather extreme perceptions of some scientists by the groups being studied, but they are by no means unique. In a recent dispute between some Iroquois and the governments of the United States and Canada, it was argued by some Iroquois that they would like to see the governments forced out of the political systems on the reserves. The idea met with great support from many anthropologists, who were later shocked to learn that those Iroquois wanted to go back to a traditional quasi-inherited and limited-suffrage system of obtaining chiefs. Since the approach was not by democratic election with universal suffrage, the anthropologists who had been involved were rather annoyed. One Iroquois to whom I spoke later was not surprised. "You can do anything you like as long as you do it their way," he said. I could not help but note the parallel between that statement and one from *Pro-Me-Thee-Us*: "The liberation movements will fight tooth and nail for your right to be different, as long as it is their kind of different".

The results of the conflicts between in-group and out-group perception have had more theoretical ramifications when one of the groups involved is "scientists."

At a first level of abstraction, we may regard the recent article by Brown[4] in *Science* which discusses Native Americans and science. Brown argued therein that Native Americans do in fact have science and/or scientific approaches. It is not clear from the article whether Brown simply meant that Native Americans see regularity in the universe and are thus scientists in a pragmatic way, or whether the author was simply reiterating Malinowski's position that all cultures have science.[5] Malinowski was trying to indicate that science had not grown out of magic and religion, but that all three exist simultaneously in all societies. But it seems that Malinowski saw anything that people did as science if he could explain it as science in a Western sense. To irrigate a field was scientific. To plant a stone to ward off evil spirits was not. He tried to distinguish science from the supernatural by employing as a criterion the feelings the people had when they performed certain acts. Magic and religion were done with awe. Of course there would have been some serious flaws in the anthropologist's conclusions had the fields been irrigated with awe (as well as with water!).

If one is to take a psychological-cognitive approach, then it is possible to ask if the people themselves have some word for "science" or a cognitive category "science." and if they do, whether the meaning contain the same things that the English term does.

The crux of the problem rests of course on one's definition of science. To my knowledge, no anthropologist has formulated a clear cross-cultural definition of science the way Pospisil[3] postulated one for law.

Yet the question of the insider-outsider has affected our own theories of anthropology. Cognitive anthropologists may feel that the ultimate goal of their work is to give the reader the knowledge that is "in the native's head" so that the reader could then understand like a native. This is certainly the goal of some schools of linguistics relative to a description of the grammar. On the other hand, many people feel that explanatory power is sufficient. A grammar that produces all and only the sentences of a language need not be the one that is in the head of the speaker, but may be the construct of an outsider.

When a similar approach is brought to anthropology, the question tends to be equally complex. If a cognitive view tries to explain the way in which a native behaves, then one is trying to produce an insider's view. But if one only tries to produce the rules that will allow one to predict or explain native behavior, then an insider's view is not being sought. What happens when a native explanation and an anthropologist's explanation are at variance? Do we draw up sides and hold that either the native or the anthropologist is correct (thus opting for either the insider or outsider view)? There are other options, but basically it is a question of orientation. Do natives know their own cultures better than non-natives and can they explain the culture "scientifically"?

When confronted with the practice of acupuncture, most scientists agreed it worked, but (and it is a very large but) the scientists didn't know why. The Chinese, of course, did. They explain it through a complex relationship between vital forces, five basic elements, some Taoist terms and five organs relating to the five elements. Their explanation was not accepted. But while the underlying scientific theoretical system of the Chinese was rejected, the data were accepted. This is very similar to the problem Hsu[2] cites in anthropological research done by westerners and natives. Even when the natives are anthropologically trained, they do the collecting, and the westerner does the theorizing. Western science, like Western religion, tends to reject alternate theoretical systems and gods (perhaps this is why early evolutionists saw religion as evolving into science).

It might indeed have been far more interesting for Hymes[6] to have asked "What would anthropology be like if it had been invented by the Swazi, the Gururumba or the Iroquois?" rather than "What would anthropology be like if *we* had to reinvent it today?". Indeed, what would anthropology be like if the Chinese or Japanese had invented it? Maybe they did too, but it is so different we don't even recognize it!

On the most practical level, however, the problem of intergroup perception possibly becomes most aggravated in the relationships between scientists and nonscientists. Most laymen tend to believe that scientists are people who learn "the truth". And scientists don't go out of their way to discourage such ideas. Years ago Ashley Montagu pointed out that ". . . all but a few persons take it completely for granted that scientists have established the 'facts' about 'race' and that they have long ago recognized and classified the 'races' of mankind. Scientists do little to discourage this view, and indeed, many of them are quite as deluded as most laymen. . . ."[7]

Lately, however, the idea that scientists deal with cold, hard facts has been replaced by the idea that they deal instead with warm, soft theories. This may have come about from the highly publicized debates between people like Shockley, Jensen, Skinner *et al.*, or from the growing concern over the ecology and the constant debates between the ecological "scientists"and the industry "scientists." Whatever the cause, this sudden disjunct between the idea of what scientists were believed to have been and what scientists are coming to be believed to be is likely to shift the relationship between the general public and the scientist. Just how or what the result of such a shift will be is not yet known, although some of the cutbacks in funding, and some of the political comments made about research may well be the result of such a shift.

In general, we may conclude that various groups of people are going to be perceived by themselves and others in different ways. As long as the two groups must interact, it will be necessary for each group to worry about the ways in which the perceptions of outsiders and insiders differ, since these perceptions will ultimately affect the interaction between them.

REFERENCES

1. PIKE, K. 1967. Language in Relation to a Unified Theory of the Structure of Human Behavior. Mouton. The Hague, The Netherlands.
2. HSU, F. H. K. 1973. Prejudice and its intellectual effect on American anthropology: An ethnographic report. Amer. Anthropologist 75 (1): 1–19.
3. POSPISIL, L. 1972. The Ethnography of Law. Addison-Wesley Publishing Co. Reading, Mass.
4. BROWN, J. 1975. Native American contributions of science, engineering and medicine. Science 189 (4196), July 4, 1975.
5. MALINOWSKI, B. 1948. Magic, Science and Religion. Doubleday (Anchor Books). Garden City, N.Y.
6. HYMES, D. 1969. Reinventing Anthropology. Random House. New York, N.Y. (Reprinted in 1974 by Vintage Books, New York, N.Y.)
7. MONTAGU, A. 1942. Man's Most Dangerous Myth. Harper and Row. New York, N.Y.

REMARKS ON CROSS-CULTURAL PSYCHOTHERAPY RESEARCH

Discussant: Gordon F. Derner

Institute of Advanced Psychological Studies
Adelphi University
Garden City, Long Island, New York 11530

We are all grateful to Leonore Adler and to The New York Academy of Sciences for the excellent conference organized for us. I am delighted to have the opportunity to share some thoughts about the material presented in this volume.

The various authors have directed our attention to cross-cultural research in psychopathology, ethnopsychiatry, and psychotherapy, although psychotherapy was not a central theme of any of the papers. Draguns gave us a framework within which we can view problems of cross-cultural research in psychopathology and mental health. Additional problems were presented by Sargent and by Beatty. Cross-cultural comparison studies of two cultures were presented by Zubin and Gurland, who compared the U.K. and the U.S., by Field, who compared the U.S.S.R. and the U.S., by Sternlicht and Ali, who compared India and the U.S., by Cawte, who made an intracountry comparison in Australia. Our attention was directed toward specific conditions of cross-cultural study of aging and other such cultural facets by Sargent and the psychosocial phenomenon of aggression and violence by Straus.

Cross-cultural study and research become particularly complicated in the mental health areas, since the very essence of the activity in mental health depends upon conceptualization and language, which, of course, vary by culture and subculture. Even within the somewhat consistent framework of culture in the U.S., we frequently find cultural dissimilarity in the incidence of a particular disorder in one area of the country or one hospital as compared with its incidence in another area or another hospital. This discrepancy was also illustrated between the U.S. and the U.K. by Zubin. Taking into consideration that the nomenclature used to describe emotional conditions and personality is faulty, and compounding this with the differences in the subtleties of language and conceptualization that humans have, it is easy to understand that errors and misunderstandings occur in communication.

The problem of deciding what is normal and what is abnormal was pointed out by Draguns' paper. He indicates that computerized procedures can bridge the gap between symptomatic observations and diagnostic judgments, but in his listing of complexities it would appear that the whole issue of how to define the behavior called symptoms is still to be answered. Clearly the use of the American Psychiatric Association nomenclature is an inaccurate way of collecting research data since the diagnostic standards are frequently over-inclusive, as when they include nail-biting as an emotional disorder, or they change on the basis of a vote, as was done in the case of homosexuality. Draguns' call for scientists to establish more meaningful standards for comparison is a highly appropriate request. The particular issue of indigenous culture-bound syndromes, in which the culture produces a unique disorder, is one that has been frequently misused.

Field's chapter gives an illustration of how ideology can enter into the determination of psychopathology. The explanation of the cause of a particular defined pathology or the kinds of behavior that are viewed as pathological are

737

culture-related or culturally defined. Soviet psychopathologists state that mental illness is a consequence of the capitalistic system and use their method of defining pathology to show that the socialist system produces less pathology. They can further decide that persons who are unable to accept the political regime are not political dissenters but are suffering from mental aberrations. The notion that dissent is evidence of some mental problem is not completely alien in the United States either. Curiously, on the other side of the issue, evidence of pathology can be dismissed or not attended to. We can note some top U.S. officials who gave many clinical or behavioral signs that should have caused concern about their mental condition, but the signs were disregarded.

Clearly what Field brings to our attention is the fluidity of cultural differences and the difficulty language and variations in concepts make for cross-cultural study. We are reminded of the fact that the word "democracy" as defined in Soviet language and in English has some remarkable differences in meaning. Field's illustration of how change in the American institutional practice of limiting hospitalization, which paralleled the practice in U.S.S.R., gives the impression of the morbidity rate's becoming more equal since fewer beds are needed in the U.S. for psychiatric conditions. The example demonstrates the care that we must take in interpreting objective factual data, even those as simple as bed counts.

Zubin's report on the U.S.-U.K. joint research points out some of the discrepancies of cross-cultural research, even given the many factors the two countries have in common. In the U.S.-U.K. study there is a common language, which is usually not the case in cross-cultural studies. The two countries have also had a common awareness of mental health problems for a long time. The populations were sharply defined by limiting the subjects to those whose emotional problems required hospitalization. Very detailed behavior samples were collected through observation and interview. Still, cross-cultural issues arose. Zubin stated that the U.K. psychopathologists wished to have more intensive interviewing and added questions for this purpose. That is, these two groups working together did not see eye-to-eye on what were appropriate data to collect, even when sentence by sentence control was used. Further, the criteria were open to individual and cross-cultural interpretation as, for example, in the tabulation of whether speech was slow or rapid. Is it not possible that various people would define what is slow speech or rapid speech somewhat differently?

Another interesting aspect of the research is the continued use of the often-questioned nomenclature of the American Psychiatric Association and letting the research revolve around the characteristics of two major mental disorders, that is, schizophrenic disorder and affective disorder. The U.K. study showed a greater incidence of affective disorder. The conclusion of the joint research, however, is that the differences are in styles of diagnosis rather than in the patients of the two countries, which would suggest that the diagnostic categories are wanting. Maybe in cross-cultural psychopathology research we will have to stop at the descriptive level, even if we grant that the observations themselves are culturally influenced.

Sternlicht's paper on cultural differences in the care of retardation in the U.S. and India not only allows for cross-cultural study but helps us become strikingly aware that the U.S. has a shortage of appropriate facilities and highly inadequate treatment for the care of those of limited intellectual capacity. The deficiencies in the U.S. are evident even when the figures for care for retardation are contrasted with those of India. A very crucial aspect of the problem of the study of retardation is brought about by the confusion of retardation, which requires an educational program with supporting services, and mental disorder, which requires a variety of treatment modalities. Supporting services for retardates and treatment services for mental disorders may include similar facilities such as half-way housing, day and/or night residential settings, medication, psychotherapy, behavioral training, but they generally have a different focus. As long as we confuse the two conditions by using the common term "mental," we will continue to have confusion in diagnosis, treatment, and life planning.

Sternlicht's paper notes that the cultures and subcultures of India may more reasonably use the attributes and capacities of a person that do not demand the "book-learning" type of intelligence. There are also other differences to which he does not allude in his paper, such as the effect of the religious belief that a person's present state of being is the result of behavior from a prior life; it is also true that severely retarded people who have physical disorders are very apt to die from them when they are small infants in India, whereas in the U.S. we frequently maintain people for long periods of time through excellent medical care. One interesting aside is that in mental hospitals and wards, which are also too few for the size of the problem in India, they have a system of treatment that allows the patient's family to move into the hospital with the patient. For example, in the associated hospital facility of the All India Institute of Health in New Delhi, which is the top medical school of India, members of a patient's family can be seen sleeping in the room with the patient. Although the visitors have separate dormitories, they are very apt to bring in a mat and sleep on the floor next to the patient's bed, which is a remarkably different way of treating patients from that followed in the U.S.

Cawte brings experience from Australia, a country in which the exogenous culture has engulfed the indigenous culture. In some ways Australia is not unlike the U.S., and our early history with our indigenous population, the American Indian or native American is somewhat similar. The history of American relationships with the indigenous population has in general been shameful. It is hard to believe, but the U.S. government once paid a head bounty for each dead Indian a person killed. As humanitarian efforts have turned away from such ruthlessness, we have something to learn from Australia. Cawte offers us a blueprint for assisting in the relief of suffering by fuller involvement of the other culture, even though he modestly indicates the idea is from the U.S. In the U.S. these recommendations would seem particularly fruitful as we turn to increasing awareness of the subcultures of our minority groups. Particularly refreshing at a cross-cultural conference on mental health is that Cawte turns our attention away from the abstractions in definitions of psychiatry and psychology to the human attributes and conditions of suffering. This new perspective requires us to draw upon a variety of disciplines to be helpful. The physical health hazard of the prolonged rituals used by the aborigines to ward off influenza supplies a first-rate example of the variety of judgments that can be made about relief of suffering and what must be considered when interventions are planned.

Sargent contributes to precision in dealing with the difficulty of cross-cultural research in mental health by paying attention to what he calls "unwanted variables." After delineating the variables, he presents some of the unresolved complexity of how to cross-define variables that are crucial to the cross-culture investigation. The example of "happiness" is a particularly pertinent one. In the U.S. one of our "inalienable rights" is the "pursuit of happiness." And yet this concept is on Sargent's list of words difficult to define. He has shown how we can improve data collection, when faced with such words, by using methods that do not run counter to people's prejudices against certain types of categories. He illustrated the method by reference to the unwillingness among Americans to use class structure categories. He could have noted how in America, middle-class is so important that we just have variations of middle-class, such as low, middle, and upper and thus avoid labeling persons as lower-class. He offers cautions but also enthusiasm for cross-cultural research. His long involvement, running more than 30 years, shows he has retained his enthusiasm.

Straus' paper is an excellent example of the value of cross-cultural research in the broadening of psychological knowledge. To understand and predict human behavior we need to expand our knowledge of *in vivo* human behavior, not just of behavior manifested in the university psychology laboratory.

Straus uses observable behavior in studying aggression by studying homicides and assaultive behavior of husbands to wives. The ubiquity of conjugal violence permits the development of theoretical models for the cause. The overall generalization that comes out of such cross-cultural study is that all forms of aggression tend to be related to other forms of aggression. This hypothesis leads to the rejection of catharsis of the aggression drive. It is not clear, however, from Straus' discussion how he would deal with the theory that people learn of a way to deal with frustrating or interfering circumstances and use goal-directed behavior when the interference occurs. They learn to use a characteristic response and, therefore, aggression is a specific behavior in a specific circumstance rather than a quantum that can be drained off.

Beatty, through looking at three subcultures, has afforded us a sharp prospective of how the observed as well as the observer may deal with stereotypes. Homosexuals do not see themselves as deviant even if others do. American Indians accept inaccurate stereotypes about themselves and then act like the stereotype. However, it is with anthropological scientists that he makes his most telling points for the topics discussed in this volume. By describing the differences in perception of the insider's view and the outsider's view of a culture, he poses the complex dilemma of distinguishing which view of another culture is the correct one. It would be easy to say that maybe both are correct and when the views are contradictory just to say that they contradict. It does seem useful for study to observe and describe as the insider and predict and explain as the outsider. Cross-cultural studies can attempt to regularize the observations and descriptions from culture to culture although, as Zubin has shown, even such activities can be disparate. Scientists may argue at their meetings and in their books and articles as to the meaning of these observations, but careful and detailed observations will continue to be basic to cross-cultural research.

In this short review some issues have not been covered. A marvelous example of the problems of cross-cultural understanding that could be referred to is the paper by Aaron Canter on how a Navaho girl had hallucinations in order to talk over matters with her dead father, which was a cultural necessity for her but was viewed by many psychologists and psychiatrists as schizophrenia. Another is the work of Paul Ekman, who has done marvelous basic research on facial expressions, which are used to show emotional states. Ekman, from that research, has concluded that all cultures use the same facial expressions for the same emotional states. Still another example is the fact that psychotherapies are very culturally related: there are Morita therapy, which grows out of Zen; the use of medicines with "mystical" powers or "scientific worth;" the work of shamans, witch doctors, psychoanalysts, psychologists, each with a cultural attitude; and the use of biofeedback, which has adapted methods of relaxation and of meditation more typical of Eastern philosophies as part of the treatment procedure.

Those of us interested in cross-cultural psychological research have many interesting questions to ponder. Are human beings alike except for an envelope of insignificant differences? Are these insignificant differences additive or multiplicative so that human beings really are different? The interaction of culture, personality, and personality disturbance continues to be an inviting area of research and offers a lovely set of problems. The articles here presented continue our thrust at the frontiers of knowledge.

Now to close, a cross-cultural anecdote concerning cultural definition. On a Caribbean Island where, as far as one can observe, nearly everyone has black skin, a visitor asked the Prime Minister one day, "What's the racial composition of the Island?" The Prime Minister said, "About 95 percent white." The visitor said, with surprise, "That really astonishes me because when I look I see all those black skins." The Prime Minister answered, "We use the same definition for white on this island that America uses for black. One drop of white blood in a person's veins means the person is white."

PERSPECTIVES ON PSYCHOPATHOLOGY

Discussant: Herbert Krauss*

Department of Psychology
Hunter College
The City University of New York
New York, New York 10021

Instead of attempting to summarize or comment upon each of the papers presented in this session, I shall try to say something reasonable about a theme that is common to all of them. To be sure, I may be forcing the data; in fact, I probably am. My excuse is that Dr. Derner's admirable summation has relieved me of some responsibility for reporting on what has transpired; the very heterogeneity of the papers themselves makes a comprehensive synthesis difficult; and to raise questions about each paper individually would serve more to diffuse rather than focus on the issues of which they treat.

What is that mysterious theme? Let me maintain the suspense by repeating a little story told to me by a Chicago cab driver. There was this man who was getting up in the world, a farmer who wanted to buy another mule to help him work his field. He bought a likely prospect and set it to work, but instead of plowing a straight line, as he was promised it would, the mule meandered to the garden and started eating shoots. Mules being what they are, it was a while before he could budge him. The farmer thought it out and decided the mule was blind. It wasn't only the meandering that convinced him that the mule couldn't see, but also the dreamy stare that crossed that brute's eyes whenever he tried to reason with it. So, he half dragged, half prodded, and half begged (you've heard of overdeterminism) that animal back to the man who sold it to him. "This damn animal's blind; I want my money back," he screamed. The man who had sold him the mule looked at the mule, looked at him, shook his head, much the way you might expect, and picked up a big stick. Without warning, he smacked the mule. Then he waved the stick in front of the mule and raised it again. The animal blinked. "That mule ain't blind," he said, "he jest needs to be convinced." End of story.

What does that story have to do with psychopathology or the theme that I believe is common to each of the papers presented? It is simply that the area of psychopathology, like the silent, erratic, and unbudging mule, more now than ever before, is the target of inferences and arm-waving which attempt to "convince" the data of psychopathology to behave as we know it should. In the story, no mention or investigation is made of probable competing causes of the mule's behavior: hunger, prior training, poor eyesight, age, vitamin-deficiency, or the nature of mulishness, for example — but whatever causes are present are destined to be sold on the block or overwhelmed and beaten away by stick-waving to attain a "proper" outcome in behavior. What constitutes a "proper" outcome in the study of psychopathology largely depends, at this point on the theoretical or ideological stance of the investigator. The three major ideologies, in this regard, are well known to each of us: they are the biological, psychological, and sociological explanations of "abnormal" behavior.

* Present address: Department of Behavioral Sciences, University of Houston, Clear Lake City, Houston, Texas 77058.

In starkest relief, those imbued with biological irredentism believe that psychopathology is the result of organic dysfunction arising out of a primarily organic nexus; those invested in psychology aim to describe the onset of abnormality in terms representative of modern psychology, for example; and those dedicated to sociological explanation tend to view psychopathology as the natural operation of certain social forces, those that manufacture deviancy, or those that enhance anomie. So far as I know, there is no simple way to wave a metaphorical stick in front of someone who is identified as abnormal to determine whether he is physically diseased, morally defective, improperly trained, socially deformed, or what have you. In large measure, we cannot even achieve a consensus that it is justified to talk about abnormality at all, or of individuals instead of social systems for that matter. To be sure, some argue that the solution to our difficulties lies in an interactionist approach. Abnormality is some as yet unspecified combination of social, biological, and psychological variables. Undoubtedly that is a correct view, but until those variables are delineated and the appropriate specification equations elucidated, we shall not know whether we are coming or going. And, the procedure by which we will figure out those complex and varied interactions are far from clear, those witnessing for "Brand X" to the contrary. One can be certain that we are going to have a far rougher time of it than we have had with the issue of nature versus nurture in intelligence.

In many respects, perhaps because of my realism about the present status of the field, I see the current confusion as healthy. It is about time that we took a more complex view of human nature and eschewed pronouncements of good and evil translated into scientism. If we had learned to be a bit more humble about our current beliefs; if we had learned that skepticism is more a product of historical realism than lack of faith; if we had learned that the way to solve a puzzle is not to declare that there is no puzzle, that the best way to unravel a knot is not always to chop at it with a meat ax, we professionals would be less likely to fall into such abominations as rubber-stamping the assumption that dissidents are mentally ill, blacks are retarded paranoid psychopaths, or the better society will be born through the use of the syringe, cattle prod, or the timely administration of "M & Ms" candy. The temptation to act on those "religious" beliefs is indeed mighty, especially when there is so much that we as individuals can gain by so doing — fame, power, money, respect, even full professorships — but that temptation must be resisted and a new behavior may have to be learned. The temptation is further aggravated by the fact that the total society very nearly begs one to act, with whatever tools of knowledge may be at hand, since the problems of "abnormality" are so frequent and so profound (the cost of schizophrenia alone in this country has been estimated at $11.6 – 19.5 billion annually).[1]

To cite but one example, Rose and Rose[2] estimate that in the last two decades between 75 and 90 percent of the annual total "science budgets" of Britain and the United States were expended under two heads: (1) production (e.g., how to increase industrial development) and (2) social control (e.g., developing techniques for defending against potential enemies, internal or external).

To suggest that our clinical practices and our public policies toward psychopathology are in large measure based upon belief instead of knowledge is in many respects to state the obvious. At this stage of our scientific development, it could hardly be otherwise. Self-consciousness about our ideas, values, treatments, and implicit assumptions is just arising, or re-emerging in a more coherent fashion. (Here I am probably being a bit too optimistic by suggesting that we will more meaningfully come to grips with what we have previously sealed over, the "moral treatment" of mental patients being one example.) Clearly if there is anything the cross-cultural perspective or any truly cross-sectional and longitudinal perspective of human behavior can teach us, it is to be hesitant in our rush to judgment. In our search for cultural universals, in which we are only equipped with an as yet undeveloped methodology to differentiate between cultural phenotypes and genotypes or between our projections and what is truly there, we may temporarily (again optimism) blind ourselves to the alternative rival hypotheses that that perspective, by its very nature, ought to help us in generating.

Self-consciousness, ambiguity, and doubt often lead to indecision. And, to be sure, they ought. For example, it is not entirely clear to me and to a great many others, given the present state of the art, that mental health professionals ought to be "treating" many of the patients for whom they have accepted responsibility. To be sure, social control or coercion in some form or another is common to all societies of which I know, but it does not necessarily follow that "mental health" professionals are necessarily the best or most incorruptible policemen available. It is surely no accident, for example, that "behavior modification," an interesting euphemism in its own right, has been practiced most frequently upon the powerless: children, the institutionalized, and so forth. Yet, the political and ideological implications of such "professional activities" are only *now* legally being discussed.

Self-consciousness, ambiguity, and doubt also often lend impetus to a search for information that may reduce self-consciousness, ambiguity, and doubt. This too is as it should be. This search for both new information and new conceptualizations ought to be pursued in a variety of ways. We need a great deal more information of a kind that can only be generated by scientists operating within the normal limits of their disciplines. We also require a great deal more cross-disciplinary work, in both the fish-scale style advocated by Donald T. Campbell[3] and in the macro-system generalist-synthesist tradition, which, relatively speaking, is the most underrepresented of all. We must continually remind ourselves that the divisions among the subdisciplines of science originated more out of accident and convenience than from inspiration.

In the meantime, many of us who are interested in "psychopathology" (at this point the quotation marks ought to seem appropriate) will be asked to act, to help, to modify. If we choose to attempt to do so, it is incumbent upon us to act humanely, self-consciously, and as openly as possible. We must let cant and self-interest interfere as little as possible with decency. We must make as explicit as is practical our actions and their impact (unintended as well as intentional) as well as what we think our actions are and what we think their impact will be. We must make "objective" evaluation of our deeds possible, if not by us, then by the others who should be interested. Scrutiny, analysis, evaluation, and open debate ought to attend our conceptualizations and our treatment. There are no other alternatives for a science of man and a science of "psychopathology."

My optimism about the future of investigations into "psychopathology" is increased by the self-searching and straightforward styles of the papers presented in this session. The questions of values that they explicitly raise are no longer hidden, but are subject to study themselves.

REFERENCES

1. GUNDERSON, J. & L. MOSHER. 1975. The cost of schizophrenia. Amer. J. Psychiat. **132**: 901–906.
2. ROSE, H. A. & S. P. R. ROSE. 1975. The incorporation of science. Ann. N.Y. Acad. Sci. **260**: 7–21.
3. CAMPBELL, D. T. 1969. Ethnocentrism of disciplines and the fish-scale model of omniscience. *In* Interdisciplinary Relationships in the Social Sciences. M. Sherif and C. Sherif, Eds. Aldine Publishing Co. Chicago, Ill.

OPEN DISCUSSION: VI

DR. ENDLEMAN: Dr. Field, do you have data on the proportion of Soviet doctors who are women and of Soviet psychiatrists who are women? How do these figures connect with the doctor-psychiatrist being a public servant under the authority of a (usually male) bureaucrat or party *apparatchik*?

DR. FIELD: Close to three-fourths of all physicians in the USSR are women, although the number has recently started to decline as admissions to medical schools in the last few years have tended to be evenly divided between men and women, and as apparently between two equally well-qualified individuals, one male and the other female, priority would go to the male. With such a proportion of women in medicine at present, it stands to reason that the proportion of psychiatrists who are women should not be too different from the proportion in the medical contingent. (In 1972 the percentage of psychiatrists and neurologists to all physicians was slightly above 5.) As to the implied question about male bureaucrats dictating to (compliant) female psychiatrists or physicians, I cannot give an answer. Most of the top psychiatrists involved in the commitments of dissidents are men, but I do not believe that in this case the sex of either bureaucrat or physician makes much of a difference.

RENA KAPLOWITZ: Dr Field, you made the point that in the USSR "political" dissenters are institutionalized in mental hospitals rather than sent to labor camps. You failed to mention the use of "jail" in this country for the same purpose, e.g., the cases of Angela Davis, Alger Hiss, and the Rosenbergs, all of whom were incarcerated without the psychiatric label of "insanity." Could it be that *all* societies have the means to detain or ostracize individuals because of deviant beliefs?

DR. FIELD: Since we have been using stories to illustrate some of the points made here, I would like to recount one Soviet story having to do with the manner in which the culturally uninitiated can be misclued. It concerns the Soviet citizen who spent two to three weeks in the United States and returned home as an "expert" on American society and culture. Asked to give a report of his observations in the United States he said: "Comrades, as Marx and Lenin had predicted, the situation of the proletariat under advanced capitalism can only deteriorate. This certainly is true of the American proletariat. Just imagine, comrades, that American workers are so poor that they resort to eating dog meat, which is sold openly in sausages called, appropriately enough, *hot dogs*. I went to one of these baseball games," he added, "that the American capitalists organize to keep the unemployed workers off the streets and to distract them from mounting a revolution. I distinctly heard one worker ask his companion whether she wanted to have one of these dog-meat sausages, and do you know, comrades, what she answered; 'Yes, please, John, I am dying of hunger!' So you see how bad it is for the American worker!" It certainly is true that no society can tolerate and absorb an unlimited amount of deviance. It is also true that the Soviet Union has (and has had) a much lower threshold of tolerance for deviance then has the United States, as witness the purges of the Stalin years, before and after the war, and the concentration camp system so graphically described in the *Gulag Archipelago*. The persons you mentioned were tried in open courts of law, and legal procedures were observed. The purpose of a trial is not necessarily to guarantee justness and fairness, but to ensure that procedural matters are observed. None of the persons mentioned was deprived of his basic dignity and humanity by being branded as mentally ill, as crazy, as sick, and as such, irresponsible. None of these was tried *in absentia*. The situation is not comparable – there is a quantum difference. In the Soviet Union the precise difference in the treatment of the dissidents consists in depriving them of a trial, and this for two fairly "good" reasons: (1) the "crimes" with which they would be charged are not violations of legal codes, and (2) a trial would provide the accused with a platform where he or she could make speeches that would be embarrassing to the regime. The failure to appreciate the magnitude of the difference between the two systems never fails to amaze me, though this difference is not lost on Soviet dissidents, as is evidenced by the following appeal by Vassily L. Chernisov, a graduate of the Faculty of Mechanics and Mathematics of Leningrad State University and a former assistant lecturer in the Leningrad Branch of the Moscow Technical Institute:

> It is difficult from within the walls of a lunatic asylum to prove that you are of sound mind. . . . In America Angela Davis is under arrest. The whole world knows about her fate, she has barristers defending her, protests are made on her behalf. But I am deprived of any rights; I was not present at my trial. I have no right to make a complaint. . . . I myself have seen protesting political prisoners in mental hospitals who refuse to take food or "medicine" tied up, given injections of sulfur, after which a person is motionless. . . . [As a result of treatment with aminazine] a person loses his individuality, his mind is dulled, his emotions destroyed, his memory lost . . . it is death for creativeness.*

DR. RICHARD BRISLIN: Dr Straus, you gave evidence that in a society violent sport does *not* have a cathartic effect and thus does *not* lessen, for instance, the probability of war. But what are the possible cathartic effects on an *individual* in that society (or within various societies) who engages in such activities as aggressive sport, thus possibly lessening other violent activity (e.g., abusing family members)?

DR. STRAUS: The reviews of research (cited in a section of my paper) all conclude that the idea of aggression-catharsis is a myth. In fact, the weight of the evidence is in exactly the opposite direction: the more an idividual observes or gives vent to either verbal or physical aggression, the *greater* probability of subsequent aggression. Research on this issue varies greatly in method and quality, but it includes several rigorously designed and executed experiments, such as those by Hokanson, and also the cross-cultural and time-series analysis of Sipes on precisely the issue of aggressive sports. The theoretical arguments against the catharsis view are equally cogent. The instinct theory assumptions that underlie the idea of catharsis have long been discarded in social science. Modern social-psychological theories – including social learning theory, symbolic interaction theory, and labeling theory – would all predict the opposite of catharsis theory. That is, a deduction from any one of these theories predicts that the more frequently an act is performed, the greater the likelihood that it will become a standard part of the behavior repertory of the individual and of the expectations of others for the behavior of that individual.

Now this poses an interesting paradox because, despite the negative empirical evidence and the cogent theoretical arguments against the idea of catharsis, it continues to gain in popularity among the general public and among a vocal and influential minority of therapists. In fact, a sizable industry to supply oppor-tunities for the presumed therapeutic value of "letting it out" has arisen in

---

* U.S. Senate Judiciary Committee, 1972. Abuse of Psychiatry for Political Repression in The United States. U.S. Government Printing Office. Washington, D.C.

recent years. The popular marketing of aggression includes a vast proliferation of encounter groups that encourage participants to shake off their inhibitions and verbally express their aggressive fantasies, and even provide styrofoam clubs to be used in mock fights!

The reasons for the startling hiatus between the scientific facts and the beliefs and practices of the general public and certain professionals who presume to base the professional practice on scientific evidence are very complicated. Some of them have to do with nature of contemporary American society (such as alienation and the implicit sanction the catharsis theory gives for the actual high level of aggression and violence), and some have to do with simple errors of logic and inference (such as a confusing short-term satiation with the long-term reinforcement that comes from the very fact of the short-term satiation). In a previous paper entitled "Leveling, Civility, and Violence in the Family," I identified and discussed twelve such factors that might account for this fascinating example of the nonapplication of social science to a vital area of human concern.

DR. HELEN HACKER: Aggression would appear to be a normal or predictable outcome of complex social factors. (Bandura says it is learned, but the capacity must be part of the human repertory.) Goldberg, writing on the inevitability of patriarchy, argues that testosterone inevitably produces greater aggression in men than in women. Do you rule out this possiblity as a factor in husband-to-wife aggression?

DR. STRAUS: I do not rule out the possibility of hormonal and neurological influences on differences in the level of aggression between men and women or between individuals of the same sex. However, if such effects exist, they exist as complex interactions with other factors, including social factors. I think the situation may be analogous to that of the effects of marijuana. Both field studies by sociologists such as Becker, and laboratory studies by psychologists such as Schacter, show that what is experienced when "high" depends on the social meanings that people have learned through interaction with other marijuana users. In any case, the extensive research on hormones and aggression to date has produced very complicated and often contradictory findings. For example, some animal experiments have shown that prenatal injections of male hormones produce females who act more masculine as adults. But studies by John Money of girls exposed prenatally to high levels of androgen found them to be no more aggressive than other girls. Postnatally, early injections of testosterone have been shown to *accelerate* the development of aggressivness in male animals, but not to make them more aggressive. Other studies show that castration reduces aggression. On the other hand, attempts to increase the aggressiveness of adult primates by injecting hormones have not been successful. Finally, a classic study by Rose found that the dominant monkey in a group had higher testosterone levels, but when the dominant monkey was removed and a new hierarchy established, the testosterone level of the now dominant (but formerly sub-ordinate) monkey went up.

RENA KAPLOWITZ: What is your definition of deviance?

DR. JOHN BEATTY: I wish I were good at making up quick definitions. Dr. Kinsey was once asked "What is a nymphomaniac?" He responded "Anyone who likes sex more than you do." Unfortunately, I am not so skilled as he is. I am afraid that my definition of "deviance" is not well worked through, and the best I can do is to present you with some quick thoughts. I had initially thought to use a statistical definition; something like "that which occurs in a small percent of the population." I immediately realized that that would make

Einstein deviant, and that would never do. So I added the criterion of "and in addition has a negative sanction placed upon it."

This definition still didn't satisfy me. The same problem arose that faced me when I attempted to define "superstition" by saying that it was that which you believe in that I do not. That, however, precluded my saying "I am superstitious," which we all know is a perfectly good English sentence. I then tried something to the effect that superstition is that which the members of the culture believe it is foolish to believe in. Hence the term is culturally relative.

I suspect that the same may be true of deviance. A universal definition will probably not include any specific behavior, but rather will include some statement about the way that the people with whom you are dealing regard certain behavior. I remember reading sometime ago, while I was in Japan, that some American actor was being ridiculed by the press in the United States because he still as an adult lived with his widowed mother. The Japanese regard such behavior as admirable, while the American press seemed to think it was deviant.

EPILOGUE: AN EXALTATION OF CROSS-CULTURAL RESEARCH — THE NATURE AND HABITS OF THE HYPHENATED ELEPHANT

Kurt Salzinger

Biometrics Research Unit
New York State Psychiatric Institute
New York, New York 10032; and
Polytechnic Institute of New York
Brooklyn, New York 11201

When Dr. Adler invited me to present an epilogue for this conference, the time of reckoning was just far enough away for me to agree to do it. Since that time, I have had some second thoughts. I looked up the exact meaning of the word "epilogue" in the dictionary and discovered that it is "a speech, usually in verse, delivered by one of the actors after the conclusion of a play." Right then and there I knew my epilogue couldn't be verse. I took some solace in discovering, while passing other entries in the dictionary, that I was not going to deliver myself of an epidemic either, but solace was not enough.

I therefore turned to examine the program of diverse papers that make up this conference and realized that it would be a long time before such a galaxy of stars in this field would be seen together again. I know that while the cross-cultural research to be presented here was exalted, the problems of integration of the different approaches are truly formidable. Hence my title. Let us look at it in some detail.

First, exaltation — I am using that word as a venereal term. I refer here not to sexual activity or disease, but rather to its meaning as a collective, employed by noblemen early in the seventeenth century to refer to the game they hunted. These terms of venery are collectives that refer to groups of animals. For example, a group of larks is called an "exaltation of larks," which provided the title of a book on the subject of venereal terms, *An Exaltation of Larks*, by James Lipton. So, I thought that, just for a lark, I might use that same term to describe a collection of papers on cross-cultural research. Happily, the term "exaltation" also means an uplifting and so I hope that there will not be too many objections. I am aware that the term "cross-cultural" is perhaps even more in need of definition than the term "exaltation," but clearly my attempt to mediate in that sea of contradictory statements is more than anyone in the audience would care to hear.

That brings us to the term "elephant." Now everybody here is aware of what an elephant is, and many probably much better than I. Nevertheless, I must tell you that my elephant is not to be taken literally, but figuratively. I am referring to the elephant and the blind people who are examining it in an effort to describe it. As most of you know, one of the blind people finds the elephant to be a snake, one a wall, one a pillar, and so on.

My object in portraying the elephant as hyphenated is to call your attention to the fact that the cross-cultural elephant is still more difficult to describe than the simple single-word elephant. And, of course, my blind investigators find the elephant to be a hyphen.

So while all of you, accredited experts in the area of cross-cultural research, have discussed the elephant as pillar, snake, and wall, I intend to describe the cross-cultural elephant as connective tissue. What is this connective tissue? For me it is a body of theory necessary to integrate the interesting but as yet splintered body of research.

I find behavior theory stemming from Skinner's work admirably suited for integration. Most important in this theory is the concept of the reinforcement contingency. This concept states that much of our behavior, if not all (technically we call it operant behavior), is of the nature of being controlled by its consequences. The formula is the following: Behavior occurs on particular occasions with specific consequences. Thus, on an occasion such as this, having been asked to give a talk, I speak into a microphone and my response is strengthened by avoiding the shouts from the audience of "louder" or "speak into the microphone, you dummy," as well as by the positive reinforcers given to me by some members of the audiences (who are not my mother) for previous talks. Essentially I am suggesting that much of people's behavior, like that of other animals, is controlled by the classes of stimuli that precede and the classes of stimuli that follow that behavior. We need to add to this that behavior too is conceived of in terms of classes.

The usual definition of a culture is to describe it as consisting of the behavior patterns of people at a particular time and place that distinguishes their behavior from the behavior of other groups. Furthermore, the behavior in question includes both what people do, and what people say they do or say they ought to do. For all these classes of behavior (verbal and nonverbal) the same triumvirate of concepts relates: the occasion for the response, the response itself, and the consequence of the emission of the response on the particular occasion.

To examine behavioral patterns in different cultures, we must view them in the context of the preceding and the following events. Thus, in our society, while it is considered to be quite normal to get undressed in a bathroom before taking a shower, one is likely to be sent for an extensive psychiatric examination if found getting undressed, in exactly the same way, on Times Square; furthermore, taking a shower with one's clothing on will also make people suspect one's sanity.

Let us look at an example of the cross-cultural problem in a paper that was presented at this conference. Beginning with the interesting observation that hospitals in the United Kingdom admitted twice as many patients with affective psychoses as with schizophrenia, while hospitals in the United States admitted twice as many schizophrenics as patients suffering from affective psychoses, Drs. Zubin and Gurland investigated whether the cause of this difference is ascribable to the behavior of the patients or of the psychiatrists. Their analysis showed that the difference inheres in the psychiatrists' behavior.

A reinforcement-contingency analysis would ask, first of all, about the kinds of behaviors that bring patients into the hospitals, for example, violent behavior committed against persons in the public light as opposed to such behavior against relatively unknown persons. It would ask secondly what kinds of behaviors in the patients would elicit certain diagnoses from different psychiatrists, for example, the patient's inadequacy in terms of problem-solving ability as opposed to feelings expressed. It would ask thirdly about the stimuli that the psychiatric interviewer presents to the patient to respond to, and thus to be classified in a particular way. Furthermore, for each of these behaviors (on the part of the patient as well as on the part of the psychiatrist), it would ask what the varying consequences of the behaviors are. The patient whose aberrant behavior (whether it is depression or hallucinations) is followed by hospitalization and the cessation of further responsibility for having brought about, say, the bankruptcy of a business, would show control by a different kind of contingency than the patient whose bizarre behavior appears to be caused by the ingestion of a drug. One question about differences in diagnosis might then be rephrased in terms of the role that hospitals play in providing safety valves in each culture for "leaving the field," as it were.

The pay-off of different behaviors in the culture at large may not be the same as in the psychiatric culture, or for that matter in the legal-system culture. Thus the reinforcement-contingency analysis would also tell us about the differential pay-off of different behaviors vis-à-vis psychiatrists. Will the psychiatrist most likely keep a patient in the hospital if the patient threatens suicide or if he or she expresses delusions? An interview with a patient is, of course, a situation in which the psychiatrist is collecting data to arrive at a judgment. How that is done will depend on the consequences of that psychiatrist's judgment. In its relatively benign form, the influence of others over the judgment made by an individual psychiatrist takes the form of coinciding with a particular theoretical predilection of one's superior. A more malignant form of influence arises when diagnoses are given for political purposes, as suggested at this conference by Dr. Field. Yet before we smugly state that this could not happen here, we must evaluate the effect on the diagnostic procedure of a state policy that asks that the population of hospitals be markedly reduced within short periods of time and that uses the hospital census as one index for the promotion of those arriving at diagnoses or supervising the process.

The concept of reinforcement contingency has still other advantages in cross-cultural research. As a tool for the analysis of behavior, it calls attention to the fact that the naked count of behaviors is never enough; it calls for the kind of information that good studies of cross-cultural comparison already collect. Coming as it does from learning theory, reinforcement contingency provides a dynamic concept that allows one to analyze for change in a culture as well as for its status at a given time. Thus to the extent that a culture tolerates greater variation in dress and reduces the correlation between dress and socioeconomic class, to that extent such "symptoms" can no longer be considered to be discriminative stimuli or occasions for psychiatric intervention.

It might be of interest to trace such changes in the general reinforcement contingencies as they become translated into hospital-census and prison-census figures.

The reinforcement-contingency analysis would allow us to examine such important questions as the effect of changing environments on the learning behavior of children in schools. In our society, the setting for learning is made everywhere the same irrespective of the nature of the children's cultural background: some backgrounds, for example, might prepare children for sitting still for a long time under some circumstances, and for running around or flitting from subject to subject at other times; other backgrounds, on the other hand, may not prepare children for quiet activity at all. The ill fit between the environment or the school procedures employed and the learner, in any given place or time, might well be the source for the fluctuation in such diagnostic categories as hyperkinesis.

The area of cross-cultural testing is replete with problems that would be solved by taking into account the reinforcement contingencies acting on the children when they are tested by different people and under different circumstances. The result that children may know the right answer under so-called "natural" conditions, but not in a strict test situation, is not a good enough analysis of the testing situations. One must analyze the different situations in terms of the variables specified by the reinforcement contingency, namely, that particular behaviors are reinforced (positively or negatively) on particular occasions, and that these contingencies are learned.

What then can we say about the elephant as hyphen? We can analyze it by using a behavior-theory concept that has elucidated not only the behavior of animals but also the behavior of human beings. I submit that in cross-cultural research, where conceptualization is so important because there is so much data to be looked at, this concept will prove even more useful.